The Microsoft Open Database Standard for
Microsoft Windows® and Windows NT® Operating Systems

Microsoft® ODBC 3.0

Programmer's Reference, Volume 1, and SDK Guide

Programmer's Reference, Volume 1

Microsoft Press

PUBLISHED BY
Microsoft Press
A Division of Microsoft Corporation
One Microsoft Way
Redmond, Washington 98052-6399

Library of Congress Cataloging-in-Publication Data
Microsoft ODBC 3.0 software development kit and programmer's reference
/ Microsoft Corporation.
p. cm.
Includes index.
ISBN 1-57231-516-4
1. Computer software--Development. 2. Microsoft ODBC.
I. Microsoft Corporation.
QA76.76.D47M523 1997
005.74--dc21 96-45660
CIP

Printed and bound in the United States of America.

1 2 3 4 5 6 7 8 9 RTRT 2 1 0 9 8 7

097-0001687

Distributed to the book trade in Canada by Macmillan of Canada, a division of Canada Publishing Corporation.

A CIP catalogue record for this book is available from the British Library.

Microsoft Press books are available through booksellers and distributors worldwide. For further information about international editions, contact your local Microsoft Corporation office. Or contact Microsoft Press International directly at fax (206) 936-7329.

Acquisitions Editor: Casey D. Doyle
Project Editor: Maureen Williams Zimmerman
Technical Editor: Zephan Schroeder

Contents

PART 1

Introduction to ODBC

About This Manual

The Microsoft Open Database Connectivity (ODBC) interface is a C programming language interface for database connectivity. This manual addresses the following questions:

- What is the ODBC interface?
- What features does ODBC offer?
- How do applications use the interface?
- How do drivers implement the interface?

Organization of this Manual

This manual is divided into the following parts:

- Part 1 *Introduction to ODBC,* providing a brief history of Structured Query Language and ODBC and conceptual information about the ODBC interface
- Part 2 *Developing Applications and Drivers,* containing information about developing applications that use the ODBC interface and drivers that implement it
- Part 3 *Installing and Configuring ODBC Software*, providing information about installation and a setup DLL function reference
- Part 4 *API Reference*, containing syntax and semantic information for all ODBC functions
- Appendixes, containing technical details

Audience

The ODBC interface is designed for use with the C programming language. Use of the ODBC interface spans three areas: SQL statements, ODBC function calls, and C programming. This manual assumes:

- A working knowledge of the C programming language.
- General DBMS knowledge and a familiarity with SQL.

Document Conventions

This manual uses the following typographic conventions.

Format	Used for
WIN.INI	Uppercase letters indicate file names, SQL statements, macro names, and terms used at the operating-system command level.
`SQLRETURNCODE` `SQLFetch(hdbc)`	Sans serif font is used for sample command lines and program code.
argument	Italicized words indicate information that the user or the application must provide, or word emphasis.
SQLEndTran	Bold type indicates that syntax must be typed exactly as shown, including function names.
[ ]	Brackets indicate optional items; if in bold text, brackets must be included in the syntax.
|	A vertical bar separates two mutually exclusive choices in a syntax line.
{ }	Braces delimit a set of mutually exclusive choices in a syntax line; if in bold text, braces must be included in the syntax.
...	An ellipsis indicates that arguments can be repeated several times.
. . .	A column of three dots indicates continuation of previous lines of code.
↪	A curved arrow indicates that the next line is a continuation of the previous line and that no carriage return exists at the end of the previous line.

About the Code Examples

The code examples in this book are designed for illustrative purposes only. Because they are written primarily to demonstrate ODBC principles, efficiency has sometimes been set aside in the interest of clarity. In addition, whole sections of code have sometimes been omitted for clarity. These include the definitions of non-ODBC functions (those functions whose names do not start with "SQL") and most error handling.

The code examples all use ANSI strings and use the same database schema, which is shown at the start of Chapter 7, "Catalog Functions."

Recommended Reading

For more information about SQL, the following standards are available:

- Database Language—SQL with Integrity Enhancement, ANSI, 1989 ANSI X3.135-1989.
- Database Language—SQL: ANSI X3H2 and ISO/IEC JTC1/SC21/WG3 9075:1992 (SQL-92).
- X/Open CAE Specification, *Structured Query Language (SQL), C201* (X/Open Company Ltd., U.K., 1992).

In addition to standards and vendor-specific SQL guides, there are many books that describe SQL, including:

- Date, C. J., with Darwen, Hugh: *A Guide to the SQL Standard* (Addison-Wesley, 1993).
- Emerson, Sandra L., Darnovsky, Marcy, and Bowman, Judith S.: *The Practical SQL Handbook* (Addison-Wesley, 1989).
- Groff, James R. and Weinberg, Paul N.: *Using SQL* (Osborne McGraw-Hill, 1990).
- Gruber, Martin: *Understanding SQL* (Sybex, 1990).
- Hursch, Jack L. and Carolyn J.: *SQL, The Structured Query Language* (TAB Books, 1988).
- Melton, Jim, and Simon, Alan R.: *Understanding the New SQL: A Complete Guide* (Morgan Kaufmann Publishers, 1993).
- Pascal, Fabian: *SQL and Relational Basics* (M & T Books, 1990).
- Trimble, J. Harvey, Jr. and Chappell, David: *A Visual Introduction to SQL* (Wiley, 1989).
- Van der Lans, Rick F.: *Introduction to SQL* (Addison-Wesley, 1988).
- Vang, Soren: *SQL and Relational Databases* (Microtrend Books, 1990).
- Viescas, John: *Quick Reference Guide to SQL* (Microsoft Corp., 1989).

For additional information about transaction processing, see:

- Gray, J. N. and Reuter, Andreas: *Transaction Processing: Concepts and Techniques* (Morgan Kaufmann Publishers, 1993).
- Hackathorn, Richard D.: *Enterprise Database Connectivity* (Wiley & Sons, 1993).

For more information about Call-Level Interfaces, the following standards are available:

- X/Open CAE Specification, *Data Management: SQL Call Level Interface (CLI), C451* (X/Open Company Ltd., U.K., 1995).
- ISO/IEC 9075-3:1995, Call-Level Interface (SQL/CLI).

For additional information about ODBC, a number of books are available, including:

- Geiger, Kyle: *Inside ODBC* (Microsoft Press, 1995).
- Gryphon, Robert, Charpentier, Luc, Oelschlager, Jon, Shoemaker, Andrew, Cross, Jim, and Lilley, Albert W.: *Using ODBC 2* (Que, 1994).
- Johnston, Tom and Osborne, Mark: *ODBC Developers Guide* (Howard W. Sams & Company, 1994).
- North, Ken: *Windows Multi-DBMS Programming: Using C++, Visual Basic, ODBC, OLE 2 and Tools for DBMS Projects* (John Wiley & Sons, Inc., 1995).
- Stegman, Michael O., Signore, Robert, and Creamer, John: *The ODBC Solution, Open Database Connectivity in Distributed Environments* (McGraw-Hill, 1995).
- Welch, Keith: *Using ODBC 2* (Que, 1994).
- Whiting, Bill: *Teach Yourself ODBC in Twenty-One Days* (Howard W. Sams & Company, 1994).

Acknowledgments

ODBC 3.0 is a major upgrade to ODBC 2.0 and represents the combined work of numerous individuals working at Microsoft and other companies. The people directly involved with the production of the *ODBC 3.0 Programmer's Reference* have been aided by many others, at Microsoft and elsewhere, who have provided helpful support and feedback. Their contributions have significantly enhanced ODBC and this reference, and are greatly appreciated.

One of the primary goals of ODBC 3.0 was to align of Microsoft ODBC with the X/Open CAE and ISO/IEC Call-Level Interface specifications. Microsoft Program Managers Mike Pizzo and Murali Venkatrao led this effort, and their relentless pursuit of industry-wide acceptance and enhancement of ODBC has not only achieved that goal, but has also produced the *ODBC 3.0 Programmer's Reference* and the Microsoft ODBC 3.0 Driver Manager. Their contributions to the ODBC standards, this *Programmer's Reference*, and the design of the Microsoft ODBC Driver Manager cannot be overstated, representing years of work creating and refining the features of ODBC. They provided a tremendous amount of guidance in the organization, accuracy, and wording of the *Programmer's Reference*.

Margaret Li made great contributions to the standards and to implementing ODBC at Microsoft. Mitchell Hughes and M. Alam Ali not only helped implement ODBC, but also provided excellent feedback on the writing and were responsible for the *ODBC 3.0 Software Development Kit (SDK)*.

The effort to align the *Microsoft ODBC 3.0 Programmer's Reference* with the X/Open and ISO specifications has been successful in large part due to Spike, the editor at X/Open who provided invaluable editorial feedback on the *Programmer's Reference*. John Goodson of Intersolv and Frank Pellow and Paul Cotton of IBM provided significant input to ODBC 3.0 in the course of working on the standards.

The ODBC Development team performed original design work on and made significant contributions to the ODBC 3.0 specification. In the course of producing the Microsoft ODBC 3.0 Driver Manager and implementing the features of ODBC 3.0, they guided the writing of the *ODBC 3.0 Programmer's Reference*. Their reviews were, as always, invaluable. Led by Paul Archer, this team consisted of George Rankin, Lijiang Fang, and Matt Woodward. Also guiding the development of ODBC 3.0 was Kerry Chesbro, whose knowledge of ODBC and work on the SQL Server ODBC driver were exemplary.

ODBC 3.0 has undergone countless review cycles, review meetings, and bug bashes by the ODBC Test team, whose persistence has ensured the quality of the *Programmer's Reference*, the Microsoft ODBC Driver Manager, and the Software Development Kit. Led by manager Kathleen Carey and lead Steve Hale, the team included Doug Bell, Alan Benson, Scott Beste, Sumit Chauhan, Ron Fast, Chris Fisher, Moshe Feuer, Clay Hall, David Hoff, John Koropchak, Joon Lee, Warren Read, and David Zimmerman. John Elion and Chalakanth Reddy of Whitfield Software Services also made significant contributions to the testing and documentation of ODBC 3.0.

The User Education team wrote the *ODBC Programmer's Reference* and the documentation for the software in the *ODBC SDK*. Led by Jim van de Erve, the writing team included Ronald Bourret and Jim Gordon. Ronald Bourret, who has worked on the ODBC documentation and design since ODBC 1.0, not only provided sure-handed guidance for the entire writing effort, but also completely rewrote the first part of the *Programmer's Reference*, greatly improving the narrative explanation of ODBC. Editor Diana Boyle was also instrumental in the writing effort. The User Education manager, Maya Opavska, and lead writer, Mark Bukovec, provided invaluable support for the entire team.

The UE Production staff of Melissa Shaw, Mike McKay, and John Zilly did a tremendous job on the *Programmer's Reference* and *SDK Guide*, not only for the final Microsoft Press product, but also for the many preliminary releases and the Help files in the SDK. The quality of this book is a direct reflection of their long and hard work. Art support came from Patricia Hunter, Steven Fulgham, and Andrea Heuston. Casey Doyle, Maureen Zimmerman, Peter Lundstrom, and Zephon Shroeder did a great job producing the Microsoft Press book.

Dave Cameron and Bill Baker provided management leadership and support to the entire ODBC team. Dave Cameron, Mike Pizzo, Greg Nelson, and Caribe Browne spearheaded marketing efforts for ODBC 3.0. Henry Lau and Joyce Chen of the ODBC Product Support team provided great documentation feedback. Other significant contributors to ODBC 3.0 include Amrish Kumar, Paul Oeuvray, David Jones, Neil Black, and George Snelling.

And none of this would be possible without Kyle Geiger, the ODBC architect who has continued to champion the cause.

CHAPTER 1

Introduction

Open Database Connectivity (ODBC) is a widely accepted application programming interface (API) for database access. It is based on the Call-Level Interface (CLI) specifications from X/Open and ISO/IEC for database APIs and uses Structured Query Language (SQL) as its database access language.

ODBC is designed for maximum *interoperability*—that is, the ability of a single application to access different database management systems (DBMSs) with the same source code. Database applications call functions in the ODBC interface, which are implemented in database-specific modules called *drivers*. The use of drivers isolates applications from database-specific calls in the same way that printer drivers isolate word processing programs from printer-specific commands. Because drivers are loaded at run time, a user only has to add a new driver to access a new DBMS; it is not necessary to recompile or relink the application.

Why was ODBC Created?

Historically, companies used a single DBMS. All database access was done either through the front end of that system or through applications written to work exclusively with that system. However, as the use of computers grew and more computer hardware and software became available, companies started to acquire different DBMSs. The reasons were many: People bought what was cheapest, what was fastest, what they already knew, what was latest on the market, what worked best for a single application. Other reasons were reorganizations and mergers, where departments that previously had a single DBMS now had several.

The issue grew even more complex with the advent of personal computers. These computers brought in a host of tools for querying, analyzing, and displaying data, along with a number of inexpensive, easy-to-use databases. From then on, a single corporation often had data scattered across a myriad of desktops, servers, and minicomputers, stored in a variety of incompatible databases, and accessed by a vast number of different tools, few of which could get at all of the data.

The final challenge came with the advent of client/server computing, which seeks to make the most efficient use of computer resources. Inexpensive personal computers (the clients) sit on the desktop and provide both a graphical front end to the data and a number of inexpensive tools, such as spreadsheets, charting programs, and report builders. Mini-computers and mainframe computers (the servers) host the DBMSs, where they can use their computing power and central location to provide quick, coordinated data access. How then was the front-end software to be connected to the back-end databases?

A similar problem faced independent software vendors (ISVs). Vendors writing database software for mini-computers and mainframes were usually forced to write one version of an application for each DBMS or write DBMS-specific code for each DBMS they wanted to access. Vendors writing software for personal computers had to write data-access routines for each different DBMS with which they wanted to work. This often meant a huge amount of resources were spent writing and maintaining data-access routines, rather than applications, and applications were often sold not on their quality but on whether they could access data in a given DBMS.

What both sets of developers needed was a way to access data in different DBMSs. The former group needed a way to merge data from different DBMSs in a single application, while the latter group needed this ability and a way to write a single application that was independent of any one DBMS. In short, both groups needed an interoperable way to access data; they needed open database connectivity.

What is ODBC?

Many misconceptions about ODBC exist in the computing world. To the end user, it is an icon in the Windows Control Panel. To the application programmer, it is a library containing data-access routines. To many others, it is the answer to all database access problems ever imagined.

First and foremost, ODBC is a specification for a database API. This API is independent of any one DBMS or operating system; although this manual uses C, the ODBC API is language-independent. The ODBC API is based on the CLI specifications from X/Open and ISO/IEC. ODBC 3.0 fully implements both of these specifications—earlier versions of ODBC were based on preliminary versions of these specifications but did not fully implement them—and adds features commonly needed by developers of screen-based database applications, such as scrollable cursors.

The functions in the ODBC API are implemented by developers of DBMS-specific drivers. Applications call the functions in these drivers to access data in a DBMS-independent manner. A Driver Manager manages communication between applications and drivers.

Although Microsoft provides a Driver Manager for computers running Windows NT Server, Windows NT Workstation, and Windows 95; has written several ODBC drivers; and calls ODBC functions from some of its applications; anybody can write ODBC applications and drivers. In fact, the vast majority of ODBC applications and drivers available for computers running Windows NT Server, Windows NT Workstation, and Windows 95 are produced by companies other than Microsoft. Furthermore, ODBC drivers and applications exist on the Macintosh and a variety of UNIX platforms.

To help application and driver developers, Microsoft offers an ODBC Software Development Kit (SDK) for computers running Windows NT Server, Windows NT Workstation, and Windows 95 that provides the Driver Manager, installer DLL, test tools, and sample applications. Microsoft has teamed with Visigenic Software to port these SDKs to the Macintosh and a variety of UNIX platforms.

It is important to understand that ODBC is designed to expose database capabilities, not supplement them. Thus, application writers should not expect that using ODBC will suddenly transform a simple database into fully featured relational database engine. Nor are driver writers expected to implement functionality not found in the underlying database. An exception to this is that developers who write drivers that directly access file data (such as data in an Xbase file) are required to write a database engine that supports at least minimal SQL functionality. Another exception is that the ODBC SDK provides a cursor library that simulates scrollable cursors for drivers that implement a certain level of functionality.

Applications that use ODBC are responsible for any cross-database functionality. For example, ODBC is not a heterogeneous join engine, nor is it a distributed transaction processor. However, because it is DBMS-independent, it can be used to build such cross-database tools.

ODBC and the Standard CLI

ODBC aligns with the following specifications and standards that deal with the Call-Level Interface (CLI). (ODBC's features are a superset of each of these standards.)

- The X/Open CAE Specification "Data Management: SQL Call-Level Interface (CLI)"
- ISO/IEC 9075-3:1995 (E) Call-Level Interface (SQL/CLI)

As a result of this alignment, the following are true:

- An application written to the X/Open and ISO CLI specifications will work with an ODBC 3.0 driver or a standards-compliant driver when it is compiled with the ODBC 3.0 header files and linked with ODBC 3.0 libraries, and when it gains access to the driver through the ODBC 3.0 Driver Manager.
- A driver written to the X/Open and ISO CLI specifications will work with an ODBC 3.0 application or a standards-compliant application when it is compiled with the ODBC 3.0 header files and linked with ODBC 3.0 libraries, and when the application gains access to the driver through the ODBC 3.0 Driver Manager. (For more information, see "Standards-Compliant Applications and Drivers" in Chapter 17, "Programming Considerations.")

The Core interface conformance level encompasses all the features in the ISO CLI and all the non-optional features in the X/Open CLI. Optional features of the X/Open CLI appear in higher interface conformance levels. Because all ODBC 3.0 drivers are required to support the features in the Core interface conformance level, the following are true:

- An ODBC 3.0 driver will support all the features used by a standards-compliant application.
- An ODBC 3.0 application using only the features in ISO CLI and the non-optional features of the X/Open CLI will work with any standards-compliant driver.

In addition to the call-level interface specifications contained in the ISO/IEC and X/Open CLI standards, ODBC implements the following features. Note that some of these features existed in versions of ODBC prior to ODBC 3.0:

- Multirow fetches by a single function call
- Binding to an array of parameters
- Bookmark support including fetching by bookmark, variable-length bookmarks, and bulk update and delete by bookmark operations on discontiguous rows
- Row-wise binding
- Binding offsets
- Support for batches of SQL statements, either in a stored procedure or as a sequence of SQL statements executed through **SQLExecute** or **SQLExecDirect**
- Exact or approximate cursor row counts
- Positioned update and delete operations and batched updates and deletes by function call (**SQLSetPos**)

- Catalog functions that extract information from the information schema without the need for supporting information schema views
- Escape sequences for outer joins, scalar functions, datetime literals, interval literals, and stored procedures
- Code-page translation libraries
- Reporting of a driver's ANSI-conformance level and SQL support
- On-demand automatic population of implementation parameter descriptor
- Enhanced diagnostics and row and parameter status arrays
- Datetime, interval, numeric/decimal, and 64-bit integer application buffer types
- Asynchronous execution
- Stored procedure support, including escape sequences, output parameter binding mechanisms, and catalog functions
- Connection enhancements including support for connection attributes and attribute browsing

CHAPTER 2

An Introduction to SQL and ODBC

ODBC was created to provide a uniform method of access to different, or heterogeneous, database management systems. This chapter discusses some of the concepts and history behind the development of ODBC, including:

- SQL and the various ways that applications use it.
- How network database access is done in the real world and what parts of this process can easily be standardized.
- Strategies used by ODBC and why those strategies were chosen.

Structured Query Language (SQL)

A typical DBMS allows users to store, access, and modify data in an organized, efficient way. Originally, the users of DBMSs were programmers. Accessing the stored data required writing a program in a programming language such as COBOL. While these programs were often written to present a relatively friendly interface to a non-technical user, access to the data itself required the services of a knowledgeable programmer. Casual access to the data was not practical.

Users were not entirely happy with this situation. While they could access data, it often required convincing a DBMS programmer to write special software. For example, if a sales department wanted to see the total sales in the previous month by each of its salespeople, and it wanted this information ranked in order by each salesperson's length of service in the company, it had two choices: Either a program already existed that allowed the information to be accessed in exactly this way, or the department had to ask a programmer to write such a program. In many cases, this was more work than it was worth, and it was always an expensive solution for one-time, or ad-hoc, inquiries. As more and more users wanted easy access, this problem grew larger and larger.

Allowing users to access data on an ad-hoc basis required giving them a language in which to express their requests. A single request to a database is defined as a query; such a language is called a query language. Many query languages were developed for this purpose but one of these became the most popular: Structured Query Language, invented at IBM in the 1970s. It is more commonly known by its acronym, SQL, and is pronounced both as "ess-cue-ell" and "sequel"; this manual uses the former pronunciation. SQL became an ANSI standard in 1986 and an ISO standard in 1987; it is used today in a great many database management systems.

Although SQL solved the ad-hoc needs of users, the need for data access by computer programs did not go away. In fact, most database access still was (and is) programmatic, in the form of regularly scheduled reports and statistical analyses, data entry programs such as those used for order entry, and data manipulation programs, such as those used to reconcile accounts and generate work orders.

These programs also use SQL, using one of the following three techniques:

- **Embedded SQL**, in which SQL statements are embedded in a host language such as C or COBOL.
- **SQL Modules**, in which SQL statements are compiled on the DBMS and called from a host language.
- **Call-Level Interface**, or CLI, which consists of functions called to pass SQL statements to the DBMS and to retrieve results from the DBMS.

  Note It is a historical accident that the term Call-Level Interface is used instead of Application Programming Interface (API), another term for the same thing. In the database world, API is used to describe SQL itself: It is the API to a DBMS.

Of these choices, embedded SQL is the most commonly used, although most major DBMSs support proprietary CLIs.

Processing an SQL Statement

Before discussing the techniques for using SQL programmatically, it is necessary to discuss how an SQL statement is processed. The steps involved are common to all three techniques, although each technique performs them at different times. Figure 2.1 shows the steps involved in processing an SQL statement, which are discussed throughout the rest of this section.

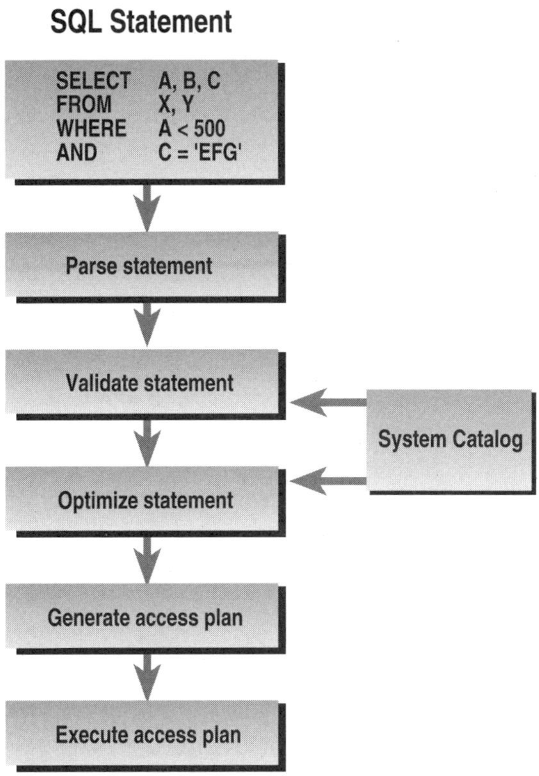

Figure 2.1 Processing an SQL statement

To process an SQL statement, a DBMS performs the following five steps:

1. The DBMS first parses the SQL statement. It breaks the statement up into individual words, called tokens, makes sure that the statement has a valid verb and valid clauses, and so on. Syntax errors and misspellings can be detected in this step.
2. The DBMS validates the statement. It checks the statement against the system catalog. Do all the tables named in the statement exist in the database? Do all of the columns exist and are the column names unambiguous? Does the user have the required privileges to execute the statement? Certain semantic errors can be detected in this step.
3. The DBMS generates an access plan for the statement. The access plan is a binary representation of the steps that are required to carry out the statement; it is the DBMS equivalent of executable code.

4. The DBMS optimizes the access plan. It explores various ways to carry out the access plan. Can an index be used to speed a search? Should the DBMS first apply a search condition to Table A and then join it to Table B, or should it begin with the join and use the search condition afterward? Can a sequential search through a table be avoided or reduced to a subset of the table? After exploring the alternatives, the DBMS chooses one of them.
5. The DBMS executes the statement by running the access plan.

The steps used to process an SQL statement vary in the amount of database access they require and the amount of time they take. Parsing an SQL statement does not require access to the database and typically can be done very quickly. Optimization, on the other hand, is a very CPU-intensive process and requires access to the system catalog. For a complex, multitable query, the optimizer may explore thousands of different ways of carrying out the same query. However, the cost of executing the query inefficiently is usually so high that the time spent in optimization is more than regained in increased query execution speed. This is even more significant if the same optimized access plan can be used over and over to perform repetitive queries.

Embedded SQL

The first technique for sending SQL statements to the DBMS is embedded SQL. Because SQL does not use variables and control-of-flow statements, it is often used as a database sub-language that can be added to a program written in a conventional programming language, such as C or COBOL. This is a central idea of embedded SQL: placing SQL statements in a program written in a host programming language. Briefly, the following techniques are used to embed SQL statements into a host language:

- Embedded SQL statements are processed by a special SQL precompiler. All SQL statements begin with an introducer and end with a terminator, both of which flag the SQL statement for the precompiler. The introducer and terminator vary with the host language. For example, the introducer is "EXEC SQL" in C and "&SQL(" in MUMPS, and the terminator is a semicolon (;) in C and a right parenthesis in MUMPS.
- Variables from the application program, called host variables, can be used in embedded SQL statements wherever constants are allowed. These can be used on input to tailor an SQL statement to a particular situation and on output to receive the results of a query.
- Queries that return a single row of data are handled with a singleton SELECT statement; this statement specifies both the query and the host variables in which to return data.

- Queries that return multiple rows of data are handled with cursors. A cursor keeps track of the current row within a result set. The DECLARE CURSOR statement defines the query, the OPEN statement begins the query processing, the FETCH statement retrieves successive rows of data, and the CLOSE statement ends query processing.
- While a cursor is open, positioned update and positioned delete statements can be used to update or delete the row currently selected by the cursor.

Embedded SQL Example

The following code is a simple embedded SQL program, written in C. The program illustrates many, but not all, of the embedded SQL techniques. The program prompts the user for an order number, retrieves the customer number, salesperson, and status of the order, and displays them on the screen.

```
main()
{
   EXEC SQL INCLUDE SQLCA;
   EXEC SQL BEGIN DECLARE SECTION;
      int   OrderID;          /* Employee ID (from user)     */
      int   CustID;           /* Retrieved customer ID       */
      char  SalesPerson[10]   /* Retrieved salesperson name */
      char  Status[6]         /* Retrieved order status      */
   EXEC SQL END DECLARE SECTION;

   /* Set up error processing */
   EXEC SQL WHENEVER SQLERROR GOTO query_error;
   EXEC SQL WHENEVER NOT FOUND GOTO bad_number;

   /* Prompt the user for order number */
   printf ("Enter order number: ");
   scanf("%d", &OrderID);

   /* Execute the SQL query */
   EXEC SQL SELECT CustID, SalesPerson, Status
            FROM Orders
            WHERE OrderID = :OrderID
            INTO :CustID, :SalesPerson, :Status;

   /* Display the results */
   printf ("Customer number:  %d\n", CustID);
   printf ("Salesperson: %s\n", SalesPerson);
   printf ("Status: %s\n", Status);
   exit();
```

```
query_error:
   printf ("SQL error: %ld\n", SQLCA.SQLCODE);
   exit();

bad_number:
   printf ("Invalid order number.\n");
   exit();
}
```

Note the following about this program:

- **Host Variables**. The host variables are declared in a section enclosed by the **BEGIN DECLARE SECTION** and **END DECLARE SECTION** keywords. Each host variable name is prefixed by a colon (:) when it appears in an embedded SQL statement. The colon allows the precompiler to distinguish between host variables and database objects, such as tables and columns, that have the same name.
- **Data Types**. The data types supported by a DBMS and a host language can be quite different. This affects host variables because they play a dual role. On one hand, host variables are program variables, declared and manipulated by host language statements. On the other hand, they are used in embedded SQL statements to retrieve database data. If there is no host language type that corresponds to a DBMS data type, then the DBMS automatically converts the data. However, because each DBMS has its own rules and idiosyncrasies associated with the conversion process, the host variable types must be chosen carefully.
- **Error Handling**. The DBMS reports run-time errors to the applications program through a SQL Communications Area, or SQLCA. In the code example, the first embedded SQL statement is INCLUDE SQLCA. This tells the precompiler to include the SQLCA structure in the program. This is required whenever the program will process errors returned by the DBMS. The WHENEVER...GOTO statement tells the precompiler to generate error-handling code that branches to a specific label when an error occurs.
- **Singleton SELECT**. The statement used to return the data is a singleton SELECT statement; that is, it returns only a single row of data. Therefore, the code example does not declare or use cursors.

Compiling an Embedded SQL Program

Because an embedded SQL program contains a mix of SQL and host language statements, it cannot be submitted directly to a compiler for the host language. Instead, it is compiled through a multistep process. Although this process differs from product to product, the steps are roughly the same for all products.

Figure 2.2 illustrates the steps necessary to compile an embedded SQL program.

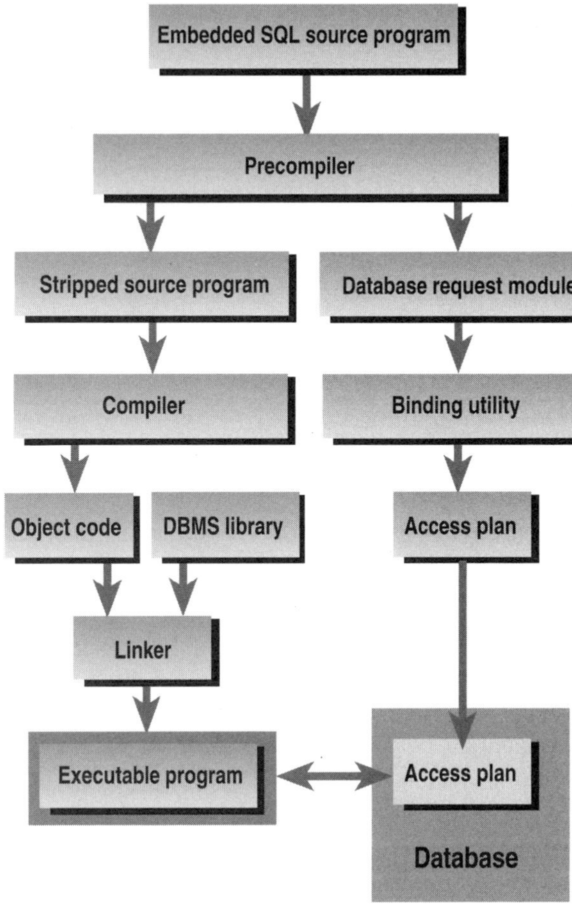

Figure 2.2 Compiling an embedded SQL program

Five steps are involved in compiling an embedded SQL program:

1. The embedded SQL program is submitted to the SQL precompiler, a programming tool. The precompiler scans the program, finds the embedded SQL statements, and processes them. A different precompiler is required for each programming language supported by the DBMS. DBMS products typically offer precompilers for one or more languages, including C, Pascal, COBOL, Fortran, Ada, PL/I, and various assembly languages.
2. The precompiler produces two output files. The first file is the source file, stripped of its embedded SQL statements. In their place, the precompiler substitutes calls to proprietary DBMS routines that provide the run-time link between the program and the DBMS. Typically, the names and the calling sequences of these routines are

known only to the precompiler and the DBMS; they are not a public interface to the DBMS. The second file is a copy of all the embedded SQL statements used in the program. This file is sometimes called a database request module, or DBRM.

3. The source file output from the precompiler is submitted to the standard compiler for the host programming language (such as a C or COBOL compiler). The compiler processes the source code and produces object code as its output. Note that this step has nothing to do with the DBMS or with SQL.
4. The linker accepts the object modules generated by the compiler, links them with various library routines, and produces an executable program. The library routines linked into the executable program include the proprietary DBMS routines described in step 2.
5. The database request module generated by the precompiler is submitted to a special binding utility. This utility examines the SQL statements, parses, validates, and optimizes them, and produces an access plan for each statement. The result is a combined access plan for the entire program, representing an executable version of the embedded SQL statements. The binding utility stores the plan in the database, usually assigning it the name of the application program that will use it. Whether this step takes place at compile time or run time depends on the DBMS.

Notice that the steps use to compile an embedded SQL program correlate very closely with the steps described earlier in "Processing an SQL Statement." In particular, notice that the precompiler separates the SQL statements from the host language code and the binding utility parses and validates the SQL statements and creates the access plans. In DBMSs where step 5 takes place at compile time, the first four steps of processing an SQL statement take place at compile time, while the last step (execution) takes place at run time. This has the effect of making query execution in such DBMSs very fast.

Static SQL

The embedded SQL shown in the "Embedded SQL Example" section is known as static SQL. It is called static SQL because the SQL statements in the program are static; that is, they do not change each time the program is run. As described in the previous section, these statements are compiled when the rest of the program is compiled.

Static SQL works well in many situations. In fact, it can be used in any application for which the data access can be determined at program design time. For example, an order entry program always uses the same statement to insert a new order and an airline reservation system always uses the same statement to change the status of a seat from available to reserved. Each of these statements would be generalized through the use of host variables; different values can be inserted in a sales order and different seats can be reserved. Because such statements can be hard-coded in the program, such programs have the advantage that the statements need to be parsed, validated, and optimized only once, at compile time. This results in relatively fast code.

Dynamic SQL

Although static SQL works well in many situations, there is a class of applications in which the data access cannot be determined in advance. For example, suppose a spreadsheet allows a user to enter a query, which the spreadsheet then sends to the DBMS to retrieve data. The contents of this query obviously cannot be known to the programmer when the spreadsheet program is written.

To solve this problem, the spreadsheet uses a form of embedded SQL called dynamic SQL. Unlike static SQL statements, which are hard-coded in the program, dynamic SQL statements can be built at run time and placed in a string host variable. They are then sent to the DBMS for processing. Because the DBMS must generate an access plan at run time for dynamic SQL statements, dynamic SQL is generally slower than static SQL. When a program containing dynamic SQL statements is compiled, the dynamic SQL statements are not stripped from the program, as in static SQL. Instead, they are replaced by a function call that passes the statement to the DBMS; static SQL statements in the same program are treated normally.

The simplest way to execute a dynamic SQL statement is with an EXECUTE IMMEDIATE statement. This statement passes the SQL statement to the DBMS for compilation and execution.

One disadvantage of the EXECUTE IMMEDIATE statement is that the DBMS must go through each of the five steps of processing an SQL statement each time the statement is executed. The overhead involved in this process can be significant if many statements are executed dynamically, and it is wasteful if those statements are similar. To address this situation, dynamic SQL offers an optimized form of execution called prepared execution, which uses the following steps:

1. The program constructs an SQL statement in a buffer, just as it does for the EXECUTE IMMEDIATE statement. Instead of host variables, a question mark (?) can be substituted for a constant anywhere in the statement text to indicate that a value for the constant will be supplied later. The question mark is called as a parameter marker.
2. The program passes the SQL statement to the DBMS with a PREPARE statement, which requests that the DBMS parse, validate, and optimize the statement and generate an execution plan for it. The program then uses an EXECUTE statement (not an EXECUTE IMMEDIATE statement) to execute the prepare statement at a later time. It passes parameter values for the statement through a special data structure called the SQL Data Area or SQLDA.
3. The program can use the EXECUTE statement repeatedly, supplying different parameter values each time the dynamic statement is executed.

Prepared execution is still not the same as static SQL. In static SQL, the first four steps of processing an SQL statement take place at compile time. In prepared execution, these steps still take place at run time. However, they are performed only once; execution of the plan takes place only when EXECUTE is called. This helps eliminate some of the performance disadvantages inherent in the architecture of dynamic SQL. Figure 2.3 shows the differences between static SQL, dynamic SQL with immediate execution, and dynamic SQL with prepared execution.

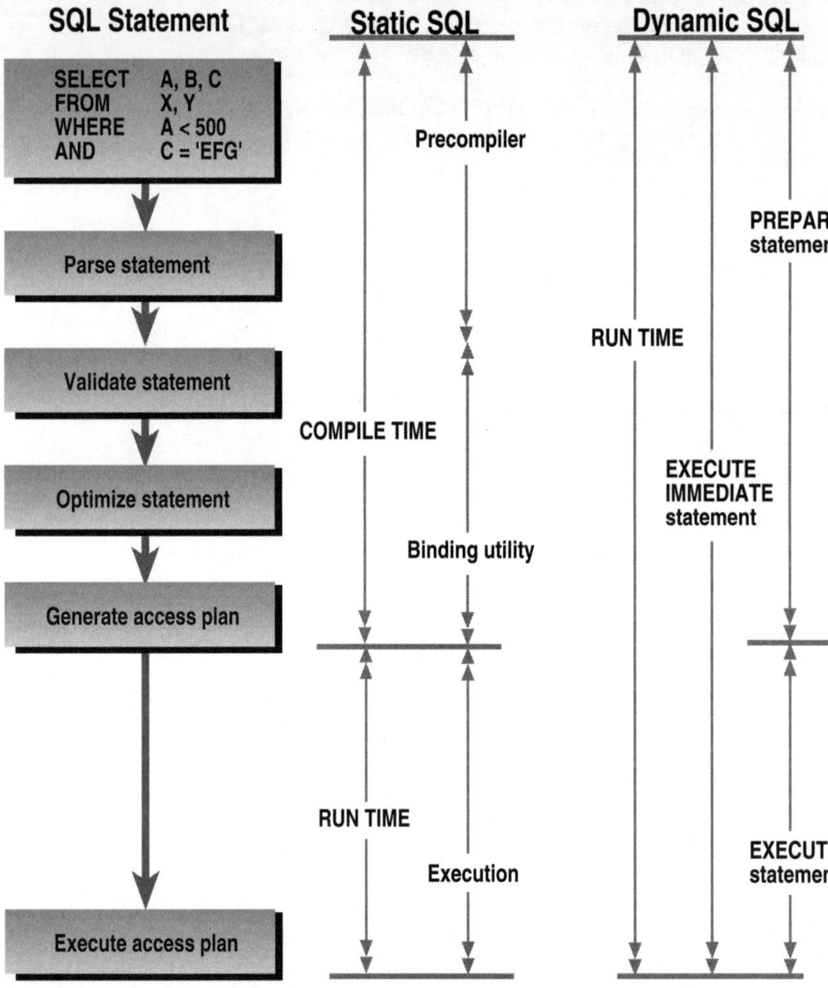

Figure 2.3 Processing static and dynamic SQL statements

SQL Modules

The second technique for sending SQL statements to the DBMS is through modules. Briefly, a module consists of a group of procedures, which are called from the host programming language. Each procedure contains a single SQL statement and data is passed to and from the procedure through parameters.

A module can be thought of as an object library that is linked to the application code. However, exactly how the procedures and the rest of the application are linked is implementation-dependent. For example, the procedures could be compiled into object code and linked directly to the application code, they could be compiled and stored on the DBMS and calls to access plan identifiers placed in the application code, or they could be interpreted at run time.

The main advantage of modules is that they cleanly separate SQL statements from the programming language. In theory, it should be possible to change one without changing the other and simply relink them.

Call-Level Interfaces

The final technique for sending SQL statements to the DBMS is through a call-level interface (CLI). A call-level interface provides a library of DBMS functions that can be called by the application program. Thus, instead of trying to blend SQL with another programming language, a call-level interface is similar to the routine libraries most programmers are accustomed to using, such as the string, I/O, or math libraries in C. Note that DBMSs that support embedded SQL already have a call-level interface, the calls to which are generated by the precompiler. However, these calls are undocumented and subject to change without notice.

Call-level interfaces are commonly used in client/server architectures, in which the application program (the client) resides on one computer and the DBMS (the server) resides on a different computer. The application calls CLI functions on the local system, and those calls are sent across the network to the DBMS for processing.

A call-level interface is similar to dynamic SQL, in that SQL statements are passed to the DBMS for processing at run time, but it differs from embedded SQL as a whole in that there are no embedded SQL statements and no precompiler is required.

Using a call-level interface typically involves the following steps:

1. The application calls a CLI function to connect to the DBMS.
2. The application builds an SQL statement and places it in a buffer. It then calls one or more CLI functions to send the statement to the DBMS for preparation and execution.

3. If the statement is a SELECT statement, the application calls a CLI function to return the results in application buffers. Typically, this function returns one row or one column of data at a time.
4. The application calls a CLI function to disconnect from the DBMS.

Database Access Architecture

One of the questions in the development of ODBC was which part of the database access architecture to standardize. The SQL programming interfaces described in the previous section—embedded SQL, SQL modules, and CLIs—are only one part of this architecture. In fact, because ODBC was primarily intended to connect personal computer–based applications to mini-computer and mainframe DBMSs, there were also a number of network components, some of which could be standardized.

Network Database Access

Accessing a database across a network requires a number of components, each of which is independent of, and resides beneath, the programming interface. These components are shown in Figure 2.4.

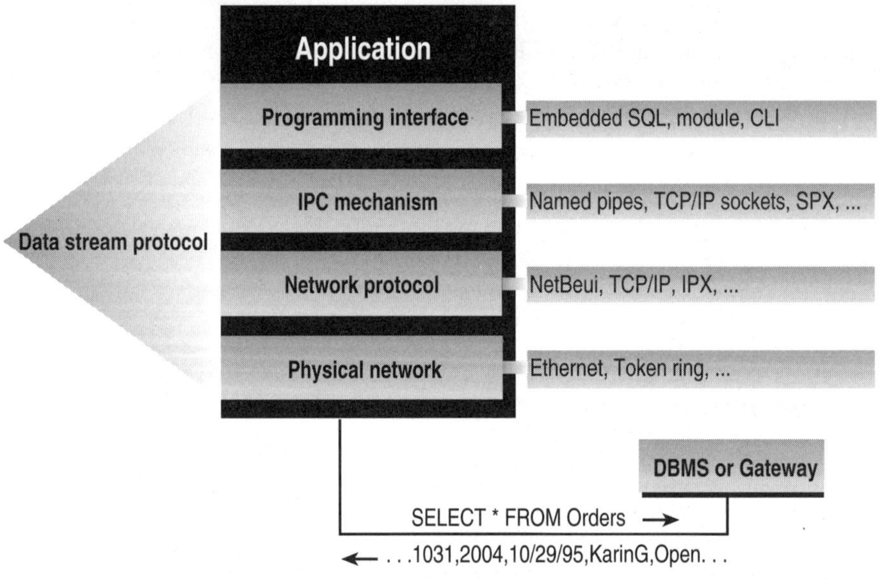

Figure 2.4 Network database access

A further description of each component follows:

- **Programming Interface**. As described earlier in this chapter, the programming interface contains the calls made by the application. These interfaces (embedded SQL, SQL modules, and call-level interfaces) are generally specific to each DBMS, although they are usually based on an ANSI or ISO standard.
- **Data Stream Protocol**. The data stream protocol describes the stream of data transferred between the DBMS and its client. For example, the protocol might require the first byte to describe what the rest of the stream contains: an SQL statement to be executed, a returned error value, or returned data. The format of the rest of the data in the stream would then depend on this flag. For example, an error stream might contain the flag, a 2-byte integer error code, a 2-byte integer error message length, and an error message.

  The data stream protocol is a logical protocol and is independent of the protocols used by the underlying network. Thus, a single data stream protocol can generally be used on a number of different networks. Data stream protocols are typically proprietary and have been optimized to work with a particular DBMS.
- **Interprocess Communication Mechanism**. The interprocess communication (IPC) mechanism is the process by which one process communicates with another. Examples include named pipes, TCP/IP sockets, and DECnet sockets. The choice of IPC mechanism is constrained by the operating system and network being used.
- **Network Protocol**. The network protocol is used to transport the data stream over a network. It can be considered the plumbing that supports the IPC mechanisms used to implement the data stream protocol, as well as supporting basic network operations such as file transfers and print sharing. Network protocols include NetBEUI, TCP/IP, DECnet, and SPX/IPX and are specific to each network.

Standard Database Access Architectures

In looking at the database access components described in the previous section, it turns out that two of them—programming interfaces and data stream protocols—are good candidates for standardization. The other two components—IPC mechanism and network protocols—not only reside at too low a level, they are both highly dependent on the network and operating system. There is also a third approach—gateways—that provides possibilities for standardization.

Standard Programming Interface

The programming interface is perhaps the most obvious candidate for standardization. In fact, when ODBC was being developed, ANSI and ISO already provided standards for embedded SQL and SQL modules. Although no standards existed for a database CLI, the SQL Access Group—an industry consortium of database vendors—was considering whether to create one; parts of ODBC later became the basis for their work.

One of the requirements for ODBC was that a single application binary had to work with multiple DBMSs. It is for this reason that ODBC does not use embedded SQL or module languages. Although the language in embedded SQL and module languages is standardized, each is tied to DBMS-specific precompilers. Thus, applications must be recompiled for each DBMS and the resulting binaries work only with a single DBMS. While this is acceptable for the low-volume applications found in the mini-computer and mainframe worlds, it is unacceptable in the personal computer world. First, it is a logistical nightmare to deliver multiple versions of high-volume, "shrink-wrapped" software to customers; second, personal computer applications often need to access multiple DBMSs simultaneously.

On the other hand, a call-level interface can be implemented through libraries, or database drivers, that reside on each local machine; a different driver is required for each DBMS. Because modern operating systems can load such libraries (such as dynamic-link libraries on the Windows operating system) at run time, a single application can not only access data from different DBMSs without recompilation, but can also access data from multiple databases simultaneously; as new database drivers become available, users can just install these on their computers without having to modify, recompile, or relink their database applications. Furthermore, a call-level interface was a good candidate for ODBC because Windows—the platform for which ODBC was originally developed—already made extensive use of such libraries.

Standard Data Stream Protocol

A standard data stream protocol is one way to access data in heterogenous DBMSs. In fact, standard data stream protocols already exist: the proposed ANSI/ISO Relational Data Access (RDA) standard and the IBM Distributed Relational Database Architecture (DRDA). Although both systems show promise, neither is widely implemented today.

Standard Gateway

A *gateway* is a piece of software that causes one DBMS to look like another. That is, the gateway accepts the programming interface, SQL grammar, and data stream protocol of a single DBMS, and translates it to the programming interface, SQL grammar, and data stream protocol of the hidden DBMS. For example, applications written to use SQL Server can also access DB2 data through the Micro Decisionware DB2 Gateway; this product causes DB2 to look like SQL Server. When gateways are used, a different gateway must be written for each target database.

Although gateways are limited by architectural differences among DBMSs, they are a good candidate for standardization. However, if all DBMSs are to standardize on the programming interface, SQL grammar, and data stream protocol of a single DBMS, whose DBMS is to be chosen as the standard? Certainly no commercial DBMS vendor is likely to agree to standardize on their competitor's product. And if a standard programming interface, SQL grammar, and data stream protocol are developed, no gateway is needed.

The ODBC Solution

Our final question, then, is how does ODBC standardize database access? There are two architectural requirements:

- Applications must be able to access multiple DBMSs using the same source code without recompiling or relinking.
- Applications must be able to access multiple DBMSs simultaneously.

There is one more question, due to marketplace reality:

- Which DBMS features should ODBC expose? Only features that are common to all DBMSs or any feature that is available in any DBMS?

ODBC solves these problems in the following manner:

- **ODBC is a call-level interface.** To solve the problem of how applications access multiple DBMSs using the same source code, ODBC defines a standard call-level interface (CLI). This contains all of the functions in the CLI specifications from X/Open and ISO/IEC and provides additional functions commonly required by applications.

  A different library, or driver, is required for each DBMS that supports ODBC. The driver implements the functions in the ODBC API. To use a different driver, the application does not need to be recompiled or relinked. Instead, the application simply loads the new driver and calls the functions in it. To access multiple DBMSs simultaneously, the application loads multiple drivers. How drivers are supported is operating system – specific. For example, on the Windows operating system, drivers are dynamic-link libraries (DLLs).

- **ODBC defines a standard SQL grammar.** In addition to a standard call-level interface, ODBC defines a standard SQL grammar. This grammar is based on the X/Open SQL CAE specification. Differences between the two grammars are minor and primarily due to the differences between the SQL grammar required by embedded SQL (X/Open) and a CLI (ODBC). There are also some extensions to the grammar to expose commonly available language features not covered by the X/Open grammar.

  Applications can submit statements using ODBC or DBMS-specific grammar. If a statement uses ODBC grammar that is different from DBMS-specific grammar, the driver converts it before sending it to the data source. However, such conversions are rare as most DBMSs already use standard SQL grammar.

- **ODBC provides a Driver Manager to manage simultaneous access to multiple DBMSs.** Although the use of drivers solves the problem of accessing multiple DBMSs simultaneously, the code to do this can be complex. Applications that are designed to work with all drivers cannot be statically linked to any drivers. Instead, they must load drivers at run time and call the functions in them through a table of function pointers. The situation becomes more complex if the application uses multiple drivers simultaneously.

  Rather than forcing each application to do this, ODBC provides a Driver Manager. The Driver Manager implements all of the ODBC functions—mostly as pass-through calls to ODBC functions in drivers—and is statically linked to the application or loaded by the application at run time. Thus, the application calls ODBC functions by name in the Driver Manager, rather than by pointer in each driver.

  When an application needs a particular driver, it first requests a connection handle with which to identify the driver, and then requests that the Driver Manager load the driver. The Driver Manager loads the driver and stores the address of each function in the driver. To call an ODBC function in the driver, the application calls that function in the Driver Manager and passes the connection handle for the driver. The Driver Manager then calls the function using the address it stored earlier.

- **ODBC exposes a significant number of DBMS features but does not require drivers to support all of them.** If ODBC exposed only features that are common to all DBMSs, it would be of little use; after all, the reason so many different DBMSs exist today is that they have different features. If ODBC exposed every feature that is available in any DBMS, it would be impossible for drivers to implement.

  Instead, ODBC exposes a significant number of features—more than are supported by most DBMSs—but requires drivers to implement only a subset of those features. Drivers implement the remaining features only if they are supported by the underlying DBMS or if they choose to emulate them. Thus, applications can be written to exploit the features of a single DBMS as exposed by the driver for that DBMS, to use only those features used by all DBMSs, or to check for support of a particular feature and react accordingly.

  So that an application can determine what features a driver and DBMS support, ODBC provides two functions (**SQLGetInfo** and **SQLGetFunctions**) that return general information about the driver and DBMS capabilities and a list of functions the driver supports. ODBC also defines API and SQL grammar conformance levels, which specify broad ranges of features supported by the driver. For more information, see "Conformance Levels" in Chapter 4, "ODBC Fundamentals."

It is important to remember that ODBC defines a common interface for all of the features it exposes. Because of this, applications contain feature-specific code, not DBMS-specific code, and can use any drivers that expose those features. One advantage of this is that applications do not need to be updated when the features supported by a DBMS are enhanced; instead, when an updated driver is installed, the application automatically uses the features because its code is feature-specific, not driver- or DBMS-specific.

CHAPTER 3

ODBC Architecture

The ODBC architecture has four components:

- **Application**. Performs processing and calls ODBC functions to submit SQL statements and retrieve results.
- **Driver Manager**. Loads and unloads drivers on behalf of an application. Processes ODBC function calls or passes them to a driver.
- **Driver**. Processes ODBC function calls, submits SQL requests to a specific data source, and returns results to the application. If necessary, the driver modifies an application's request so that the request conforms to syntax supported by the associated DBMS.
- **Data source**. Consists of the data the user wants to access and its associated operating system, DBMS, and network platform (if any) used to access the DBMS.

The following figure shows the relationship between these four components.

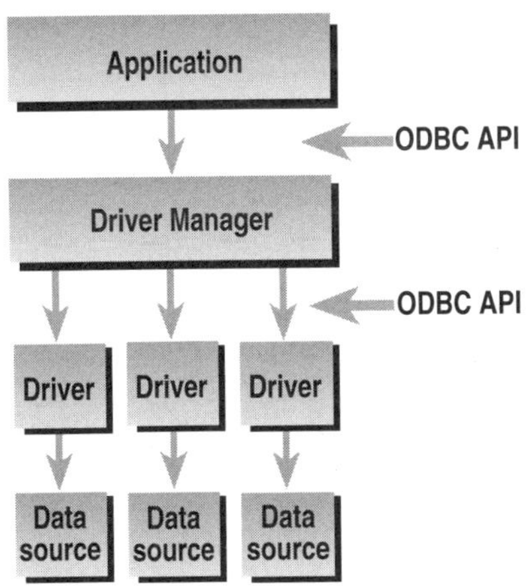

Figure 3.1 ODBC Architecture

Note the following about this diagram. First, multiple drivers and data sources can exist, which allows the application to simultaneously access data from more than one data source. Second, the ODBC API is used in two places: between the application and the Driver Manager, and between the Driver Manager and each driver. The interface between the Driver Manager and the drivers is sometimes referred to as the *service provider interface*, or *SPI*. For ODBC, the application programming interface (API) and the service provider interface (SPI) are the same; that is, the Driver Manager and each driver have the same interface to the same functions.

Applications

An *application* is a program that calls the ODBC API to access data. Although many types of applications are possible, most fall into three categories, which are used as examples throughout this book.

- **Generic Applications**. These are also referred to as shrink-wrapped applications or off-the-shelf applications. Generic applications are designed to work with a variety of different DBMSs. Examples include a spreadsheet or statistics package that uses ODBC to import data for further analysis and a word processor that uses ODBC to get a mailing list from a database.

  An important subcategory of generic applications is application development environments, such as PowerBuilder or Microsoft Visual Basic. Although the applications constructed with these environments will probably work only with a single DBMS, the environment itself needs to work with multiple DBMSs.

  What all generic applications have in common is that they are highly interoperable among DBMSs and they need to use ODBC in a relatively generic manner. For more information about interoperability, see "Choosing a Level of Interoperability" in Chapter 16, "Interoperability."

- **Vertical Applications**. Vertical applications perform a single type of task, such as order entry or tracking manufacturing data, and work with a database schema that is controlled by the developer of the application. For a particular customer, the application works with a single DBMS. For example, a small business might use the application with dBase, while a large business might use it with Oracle.

  The application uses ODBC in such a manner that the application is not tied to any one DBMS, although it might be tied to a limited number of DBMSs that provide similar functionality. Thus, the application developer can sell the application independently from the DBMS. Vertical applications are interoperable when they are developed but are sometimes modified to include noninteroperable code once the customer has chosen a DBMS.

- **Custom Applications**. Custom applications are used to perform a specific task in a single company. For example, an application in a large company might gather sales data from several divisions (each of which uses a different DBMS) and create a single report. ODBC is used because it is a common interface and saves programmers from having to learn multiple interfaces. Such applications are generally not interoperable and are written to specific DBMSs and drivers.

A number of tasks are common to all applications, no matter how they use ODBC. Taken together, they largely define the flow of any ODBC application. The tasks are:

- Selecting a data source and connecting to it.
- Submitting an SQL statement for execution.
- Retrieving results (if any).
- Processing errors.
- Committing or rolling back the transaction enclosing the SQL statement.
- Disconnecting from the data source.

Because the majority of data access work is done with SQL, the primary task for which applications use ODBC is to submit SQL statements and retrieve the results (if any) generated by those statements. Other tasks for which applications use ODBC include determining and adjusting to driver capabilities and browsing the database catalog.

The Driver Manager

The *Driver Manager* is a library that manages communication between applications and drivers. For example, on Windows platforms, the Driver Manager is a dynamic-link library (DLL) that is written by Microsoft and can be redistributed by users of the Microsoft ODBC Software Development Kit (SDK).

The Driver Manager exists mainly as a convenience to application writers and solves a number of problems common to all applications. These include determining which driver to load based on a data source name, loading and unloading drivers, and calling functions in drivers.

To see why the latter is a problem, consider what would happen if the application called functions in the driver directly. Unless the application was linked directly to a particular driver, it would have to build a table of pointers to the functions in that driver and call those functions by pointer. Using the same code for more than one driver at a time would add yet another level of complexity. The application would first have to set a function pointer to point to the correct function in the correct driver, and then call the function through that pointer.

The Driver Manager solves this problem by providing a single place to call each function. The application is linked to the Driver Manager and calls ODBC functions in the Driver Manager, not the driver. The application identifies the target driver and data source with a *connection handle*. When it loads a driver, the Driver Manager builds a table of pointers to the functions in that driver. It uses the connection handle passed by the application to find the address of the function in the target driver and calls that function by address.

For the most part, the Driver Manager just passes function calls from the application to the correct driver. However, it also implements some functions (**SQLDataSources**, **SQLDrivers**, and **SQLGetFunctions**) and performs basic error checking. For example, the Driver Manager checks that handles are not null pointers, that functions are called in the correct order, and that certain function arguments are valid. For a complete description of the errors checked by the Driver Manager, see the reference section for each function and Appendix B, "ODBC State Transition Tables."

The final major role of the Driver Manager is loading and unloading drivers. The application loads and unloads only the Driver Manager. When it wants to use a particular driver, it calls a connection function (**SQLConnect**, **SQLDriverConnect**, or **SQLBrowseConnect**) in the Driver Manager and specifies the name of a particular data source or driver, such as "Accounting" or "SQL Server." Using this name, the Driver Manager searches the data source information for the driver's file name, such as SQLSRVR.DLL. It then loads the driver (assuming it is not already loaded), stores the address of each function in the driver, and calls the connection function in the driver, which then initializes itself and connects to the data source.

When the application is done using the driver, it calls **SQLDisconnect** in the Driver Manager. The Driver Manager calls this function in the driver, which disconnects from the data source. However, the Driver Manager keeps the driver in memory in case the application reconnects to it. It unloads the driver only when the application frees the connection used by the driver or uses the connection for a different driver, and no other connections use the driver. For a complete description of the Driver Manager's role in loading and unloading drivers, see "Driver Manager's Role in the Connection Process" in Chapter 6, "Connecting to a Data Source or Driver."

Drivers

Drivers are libraries that implement the functions in the ODBC API. Each is specific to a particular DBMS; for example, a driver for Oracle cannot directly access data in an Informix DBMS. Drivers expose the capabilities of the underlying DBMSs; they are not required to implement capabilities not supported by the DBMS. For example, if the underlying DBMS does not support outer joins, then neither should the driver. The only major exception to this is that drivers for DBMSs that do not have standalone database engines, such as Xbase, must implement a database engine that at least supports a minimal amount of SQL.

Driver Tasks

Specific tasks performed by drivers include:

- Connecting to and disconnecting from the data source.
- Checking for function errors not checked by the Driver Manager.
- Initiating transactions; this is transparent to the application.

- Submitting SQL statements to the data source for execution. The driver must modify ODBC SQL to DBMS-specific SQL; this is often limited to replacing escape clauses defined by ODBC with DBMS-specific SQL.
- Sending data to and retrieving data from the data source, including converting data types as specified by the application.
- Mapping DBMS-specific errors to ODBC SQLSTATEs.

Driver Architecture

Driver architecture falls into two categories, depending on which software processes SQL statements:

- **File-based drivers**. The driver accesses the physical data directly. In this case, the driver acts as both driver and data source; that is, it processes ODBC calls and SQL statements. For example, dBASE drivers are file-based drivers because dBASE does not provide a standalone database engine the driver can use. It is important to note that developers of file-based drivers must write their own database engines.
- **DBMS-based drivers**. The driver accesses the physical data through a separate database engine. In this case the driver processes only ODBC calls; it passes SQL statements to the database engine for processing. For example, Oracle drivers are DBMS-based drivers because Oracle has a standalone database engine the driver uses. Where the database engine resides is immaterial. It can reside on the same machine as the driver or a different machine on the network; it might even be accessed through a gateway.

Driver architecture is generally interesting only to driver writers; that is, driver architecture generally makes no difference to the application. However, the architecture can affect whether an application can use DBMS-specific SQL. For example, Microsoft Access provides a standalone database engine. If a Microsoft Access driver is DBMS-based—it accesses the data through this engine—the application can pass Microsoft Access–SQL statements to the engine for processing.

However, if the driver is file-based—that is, it contains a proprietary engine that accesses the Microsoft Access .mdb file directly—any attempts to pass Microsoft Access–specific SQL statements to the engine are likely to result in syntax errors. The reason is that the proprietary engine is likely to implement only ODBC SQL.

File-Based Drivers

File-based drivers are used with data sources such as dBASE that do not provide a standalone database engine for the driver to use. These drivers access the physical data directly and must implement a database engine to process SQL statements. Generally, the database engines in file-based drivers implement the subset of ODBC SQL defined by the *Minimum SQL conformance level*; for a list of the SQL statements in this conformance level, see Appendix C, "SQL Grammar."

In comparing file-based and DBMS-based drivers, file-based drivers are harder to write because of the database engine component, less complicated to configure because there are no network pieces, and less powerful because few people have the time to write database engines as powerful as those produced by database companies.

Figure 3.2 shows two different configurations of file-based drivers, one in which the data resides locally and the other in which it resides on a network file server.

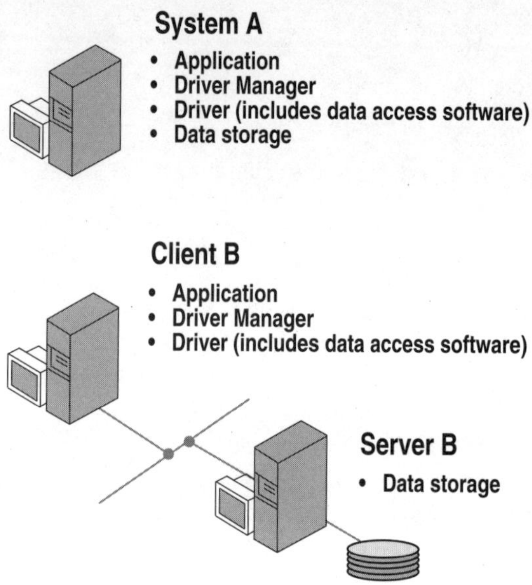

Figure 3.2 Configuration of file-based drivers

DBMS-Based Drivers

DBMS-based drivers are used with data sources such as Oracle or SQL Server that provide a standalone database engine for the driver to use. These drivers access the physical data through the standalone engine; that is, they submit SQL statements to and retrieve results from the engine.

Because DBMS-based drivers use an existing database engine, they are generally easier to write than file-based drivers. Although a DBMS-based driver can be easily implemented by translating ODBC calls to native API calls, this results in a slower driver. A better way to implement a DBMS-based driver is to use the underlying data stream protocol, which is usually what the native API does. For example, a SQL Server driver should use TDS (the data stream protocol for SQL Server) rather than DB Library (the native API for SQL Server). An exception to this rule is when ODBC is the native API. For example, Watcom SQL is a standalone engine that resides on the same machine as the application and is loaded directly as the driver.

DBMS-based drivers act as the client in a client/server configuration where the data source acts as the server. Generally, the client (driver) and server (data source) reside on different machines, although both could reside on the same machine running a multitasking operating system. A third possibility is a *gateway*, which sits between the driver and data source. A gateway is a piece of software that causes one DBMS to look like another. For example, applications written to use SQL Server can also access DB2 data through the Micro Decisionware DB2 Gateway; this product causes DB2 to look like SQL Server.

Figure 3.3 shows three different configurations of DBMS-based drivers. In the first configuration, the driver and data source reside on the same machine. In the second, the driver and data source reside on different machines. In the third, the driver and data source reside on different machines and a gateway sits between them, residing on yet another machine.

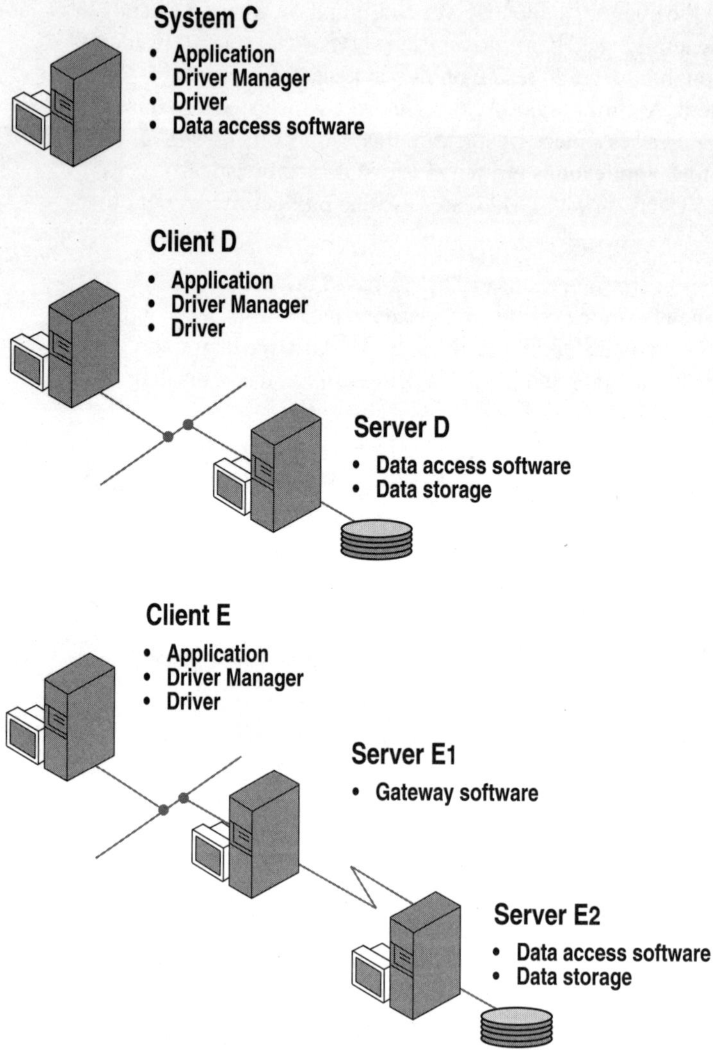

Figure 3.3 Configuration of DBMS-based drivers

Network Example

Figure 3.4 shows how each of the preceding configurations could appear in a single network.

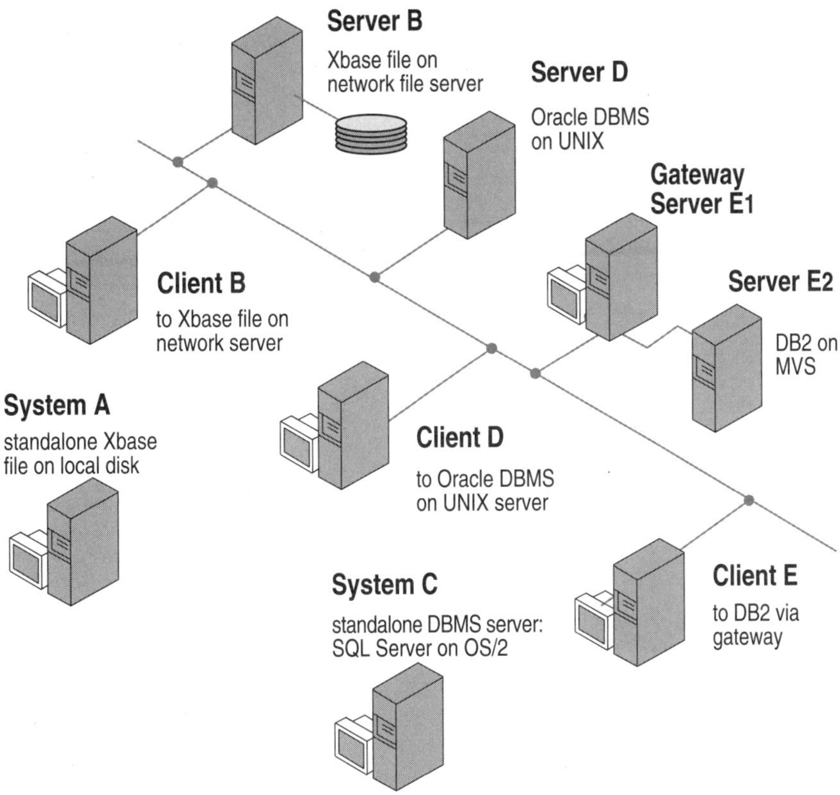

Figure 3.4 Configurations in a single network

Other Driver Architectures

Some ODBC drivers do not strictly conform to the architecture described previously. This may be because the drivers perform duties other than those of a traditional ODBC driver, or are not drivers in the normal sense.

The Driver as a Middle Component

The ODBC driver may reside between the Driver Manager and one or more other ODBC drivers. When the driver in the middle is capable of working with multiple data sources, it acts as a dispatcher of ODBC calls (or appropriately translated calls) to other modules that actually access the data sources. In this architecture, the driver in the middle is taking on some of the role of a Driver Manager.

Another example of this sort of driver is a spy program for ODBC, which intercepts and copies ODBC functions being sent between the Driver Manager and the driver. This layer can be used to emulate either a driver or an application. To the Driver Manager, the layer appears to be the driver; to the driver, the layer appears to be the Driver Manager.

Heterogeneous Join Engines

Some ODBC drivers are built upon a query engine for performing heterogeneous joins. In one architecture of a heterogeneous join engine (see Figure 3.5), the driver appears to the application as a driver, but appears to another instance of the Driver Manager as an application. This driver processes a heterogeneous join from the application by calling separate SQL statements in drivers for each joined database.

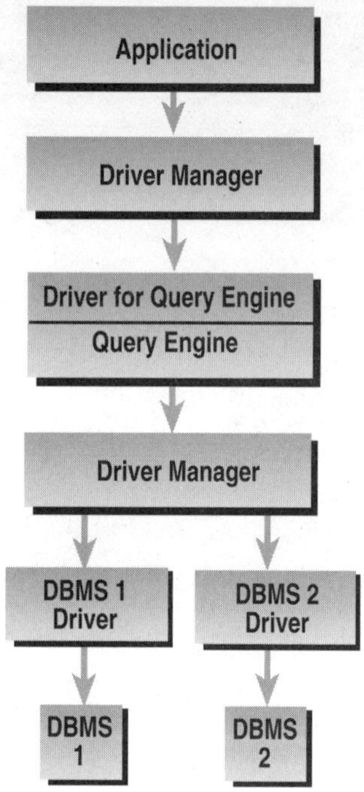

Figure 3.5 Heterogeneous join engine architecture

This architecture provides a common interface for the application to access data from different databases. It can use a common way to retrieve metadata, such as information about special columns (row identifiers), and it can call common catalog functions to retrieve data dictionary information. By calling the ODBC function **SQLStatistics**, for instance, the application can retrieve information about the indexes on the tables to be joined, even if the tables are on two separate databases. The query processor does not have to worry about how the databases store metadata.

The application also has standard access to data types. ODBC defines common SQL data types that DBMS-specific data types are mapped to. An application can call **SQLGetTypeInfo** to retrieve information about data types on different databases.

When the application generates a heterogeneous join statement, the query processor in this architecture parses the SQL statement, then generates separate SQL statements for each database to be joined. By using metadata about each driver, the query processor can determine the most efficient, intelligent join. For example, if the statement joins two tables on one database with one table on another database, the query processor can join the two tables on the one database before joining the result with the table from the other database.

ODBC on the Server

ODBC drivers can be installed on a server so that they can be used by applications on any of a series of client machines. In this architecture (see Figure 3.6), a Driver Manager and a single ODBC driver are installed on each client, and another Driver Manager and a series of ODBC drivers are installed on the server. This allows each client access to a variety of drivers used and maintained on the server.

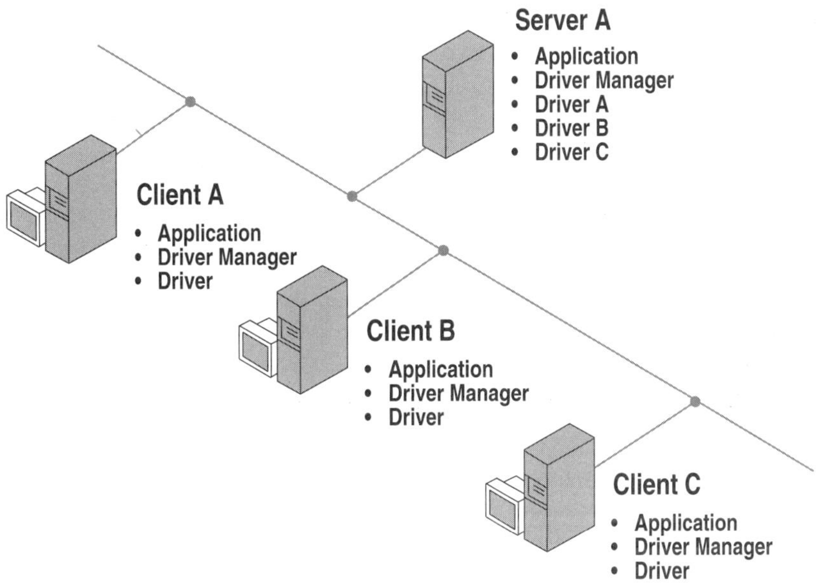

Figure 3.6 ODBC on the server

One advantage of this architecture is efficient software maintenance and configuration. Drivers need only be updated in one place: on the server. By using system data sources, data sources can be defined on the server for use by all clients. The data sources need not be defined on the client. Connection pooling can be used to streamline the process by which clients connect to data sources.

The driver on the client is generally a very small driver that transfers the Driver Manager call to the server. Its footprint can be significantly smaller than the fully functional ODBC drivers on the server. In this architecture, client resources can be freed if the server has more computing power. In addition, the efficiency and security of the entire system can be enhanced by installing backup servers, and performing load balancing to optimize server use.

Data Sources

A *data source* is simply the source of the data. It can be a file, a particular database on a DBMS, or even a live data feed. For example, a data source might be an Oracle DBMS running on an OS/2® operating system, accessed by Novell® Netware; an IBM DB2 DBMS accessed through a gateway; a collection of Xbase files in a server directory; or a local Microsoft Access database file.

The purpose of a data source is to gather all of the technical information needed to access the data—the driver name, network address, network software, and so on—into a single place and hide it from the user. The user should be able to look at a list that includes Payroll, Inventory, and Personnel, choose Payroll from the list, and have the application connect to the payroll data, all without knowing where the payroll data resides or how the application got to it.

The term *data source* should not be confused with similar terms. In this manual, *DBMS* or *database* refers to a database program or engine. A further distinction is made between *desktop databases*, designed to run on personal computers and often lacking in full SQL and transaction support, and *server databases*, designed to run in a client/server situation and characterized by a standalone database engine and rich SQL and transaction support. Database also refers to a particular collection of data, such as a collection of Xbase files in a directory or a database on SQL Server. It is generally equivalent to the term *catalog*, used elsewhere in this manual, or the term *qualifier* in earlier versions of ODBC.

Types of Data Sources

There are two types of data sources: machine data sources and file data sources. Although both contain similar information about the source of the data, they differ in the way this information is stored. Because of these differences, they are used in somewhat different manners.

Machine Data Sources

Machine data sources are stored on the system with a user-defined name. Associated with the data source name is all of the information the Driver Manager and driver need to connect to the data source. For an Xbase data source, this might be the name of the Xbase driver, the full path of the directory containing the Xbase files, and some options that tell the driver how to use those files, such as single-user mode or read-only. For an Oracle data source, this might be the name of the Oracle driver, the server where the Oracle DBMS resides, the SQL*Net connection string which identifies the SQL*Net driver to use, and the system ID of the database on the server.

File Data Sources

File data sources are stored in a file and allow connection information to be used repeatedly by a single user or shared among several users. When a file data source is used, the Driver Manager makes the connection to the data source using the information in a .dsn file. This file can be manipulated like any other file. A file data source does not have a data source name, as does a machine data source, and is not registered to any one user or machine.

A file data source streamlines the connection process, because the .dsn file contains the connection string that would otherwise have to be built for a call to the **SQLDriverConnect** function. Another advantage of the .dsn file is that it can be copied to any machine, so that identical data sources can be used by many machines as long as they have the appropriate driver installed. A file data source can also be shared by applications. A shareable file data source can be placed on a network, and used simultaneously by multiple applications.

A .dsn file can also be unshareable. An unshareable .dsn file resides on a single machine, and points to a machine data source. Unshareable file data sources exist mainly to allow the easy conversion of machine data sources to file data sources so that an application can be designed to work solely with file data sources. When the Driver Manager is sent the information in an unshareable file data source, it connects as necessary to the machine data source that the .dsn file points to.

For more information about file data sources, see "Connecting Using File Data Sources" in Chapter 6, "Connecting to a Data Source or Driver," or the **SQLDriverConnect** function description.

Using Data Sources

Data sources are generally created by the end user or a technician with a program called the *ODBC Administrator*. The ODBC Administrator prompts the user for the driver to use and then calls that driver. The driver displays a dialog box that requests the information it needs to connect to the data source. After the user enters the information, the driver stores it on the system.

At a later point in time, the application calls the Driver Manager and passes it the name of a machine data source or the path of a file containing a file data source. When passed a machine data source name, the Driver Manager searches the system to find the driver used by the data source. It then loads the driver and passes the data source name to it. The driver uses the data source name to find the information it needs to connect to the data source. Finally, it connects to the data source, typically prompting the user for a user ID and password, which are generally not stored.

When passed a file data source, the Driver Manager opens the file and loads the specified driver. If the file also contains a connection string, it passes this to the driver. Using the information in the connection string, the driver connects to the data source. If no connection string was passed, the driver generally prompts the user for the necessary information.

Data Source Example

On computers running Microsoft Windows NT Server, Microsoft Windows NT Workstation, or Microsoft Windows 95, machine data source information is stored in the registry. Depending on which registry key the information is stored under, the data source is known as a *user data source* or a *system data source*. User data sources are stored under the HKEY_CURRENT_USER key and are available only to the current user. System data sources are stored under the HKEY_LOCAL_MACHINE key and can be used by more than one user on one machine. They can also be used by system-wide services, which can then gain access to the data source even if no user is logged onto the machine. For more information about user and system data sources, see **SQLManageDataSources** in Chapter 23, "Installer DLL Function Reference."

Suppose a user has three user data sources: Personnel and Inventory, which use an Oracle DBMS; and Payroll, which uses a Microsoft SQL Server DBMS. The registry values for data sources might be:

```
HKEY_CURRENT_USER
    SOFTWARE
        ODBC
            ODBC.INI

                ODBC Data Sources
                    Personnel : REG_SZ : Oracle
                    Inventory : REG_SZ : Oracle
                    Payroll : REG_SZ : SQL Server
```

and the registry values for the Payroll data source might be:

```
HKEY_CURRENT_USER
    SOFTWARE
        ODBC
            ODBC.INI
                Payroll
                    Driver : REG_SZ : C:\WINDOWS\SYSTEM\SQLSRVR.DLL
                    Description : REG_SZ : Payroll database
                    Server : REG_SZ : PYRLL1
                    FastConnectOption : REG_SZ : No
                    UseProcForPrepare : REG_SZ : Yes
                    OEMTOANSI : REG_SZ : No
                    LastUser : REG_SZ : smithjo
                    Database : REG_SZ : Payroll
                    Language : REG_SZ :
```

PART 2

Developing Applications and Drivers

CHAPTER 4

ODBC Fundamentals

This chapter covers a number of concepts fundamental to writing ODBC applications and drivers:

- Handles
- Buffers
- Data types
- Conformance levels
- Environment, connection, and statement attributes

Handles

Handles are opaque, 32-bit values that identify a particular item; in ODBC, this item can be an environment, connection, statement, or descriptor. When the application calls **SQLAllocHandle**, the Driver Manager or driver creates a new item of the specified type and returns the handle to it to the application. The application later uses the handle to identify that item when calling ODBC functions. The Driver Manager and driver use the handle to locate information about the item.

For example, the following code uses two statement handles (*hstmtOrder* and *hstmtLine*) to identify the statements on which to create result sets of sales orders and sales order line numbers. It later uses these handles to identify which result set to fetch data from.

```
SQLHSTMT    hstmtOrder, hstmtLine;   // Statement handles.
SQLUINTEGER OrderID;
SQLINTEGER  OrderIDInd = 0;
SQLRETURN   rc;

// Prepare the statement that retrieves line number information.
SQLPrepare(hstmtLine, "SELECT * FROM Lines WHERE OrderID = ?", SQL_NTS);

// Bind OrderID to the parameter in the preceding statement.
SQLBindParameter(hstmtLine, 1, SQL_PARAM_INPUT, SQL_C_ULONG, SQL_INTEGER, 5, 0,
                 &OrderID, 0, &OrderIDInd);
```

```
// Bind the result sets for the Order table and the Lines table. Bind OrderID to the
// OrderID column in the Orders table. When each row is fetched, OrderID will contain
// the current order ID, which will then be passed as a parameter to the statement to
// fetch line number information. Code not shown.

// Create a result set of sales orders.
SQLExecDirect(hstmtOrder, "SELECT * FROM Orders", SQL_NTS);

// Fetch and display the sales order data. Code to check if rc equals SQL_ERROR or
// SQL_SUCCESS_WITH_INFO not shown.
while ((rc = SQLFetch(hstmtOrder)) != SQL_NO_DATA) {
   // Display the sales order data.  Code not shown.

   // Create a result set of line numbers for the current sales order.
   SQLExecute(hstmtLine);

   // Fetch and display the sales order line number data. Code to check if rc equals
   // SQL_ERROR or SQL_SUCCESS_WITH_INFO not shown.
   while ((rc = SQLFetch(hstmtLine)) != SQL_NO_DATA) {
      // Display the sales order line number data. Code not shown.
   }

   // Close the sales order line number result set.
   SQLCloseCursor(hstmtLine);
}

// Close the sales order result set.
SQLCloseCursor(hstmtOrder);
```

Handles are meaningful only to the ODBC component that created them; that is, only the Driver Manager can interpret Driver Manager handles and only a driver can interpret its own handles.

For example, suppose the driver in the preceding example allocates a structure to store information about a statement and returns the pointer to this structure as the statement handle. When the application calls **SQLPrepare**, it passes an SQL statement and the handle of the statement used for sales order line numbers. The driver sends the SQL statement to the data source, which prepares it and returns an access plan identifier. The driver uses the handle to find the structure in which to store this identifier.

Later, when the application calls **SQLExecute** to generate the result set of line numbers for a particular sales order, it passes the same handle. The driver uses the handle to retrieve the access plan identifier from the structure. It sends the identifier to the data source to tell it which plan to execute.

ODBC has two levels of handles: Driver Manager handles and driver handles. The application uses Driver Manager handles when calling ODBC functions because it calls those functions in the Driver Manager. The Driver Manager uses this handle to find the corresponding driver handle and uses the driver handle when calling the function in the driver. For an example of how driver and Driver Manager handles are used, see "Driver Manager's Role in the Connection Process" in Chapter 6, "Connecting to a Data Source or Driver."

That there are two levels of handles is an artifact of the ODBC architecture; it is generally not relevant to either the application or driver. Although there is generally no reason to do so, it is possible for the application to determine the driver handles by calling **SQLGetInfo**.

Environment Handles

An *environment* is a global context in which to access data; associated with an environment is any information that is global in nature, such as:

- The environment's state
- The current environment-level diagnostics
- The handles of connections currently allocated on the environment
- The current settings of each environment attribute

Within a piece of code that implements ODBC (the Driver Manager or a driver), an environment handle identifies a structure to contain this information.

Environment handles are not frequently used in ODBC applications. They are always used in calls to **SQLDataSources** and **SQLDrivers** and sometimes used in calls to **SQLAllocHandle**, **SQLEndTran**, **SQLFreeHandle**, **SQLGetDiagField**, and **SQLGetDiagRec**.

Each piece of code that implements ODBC (the Driver Manager or a driver) contains one or more environment handles. For example, the Driver Manager maintains a separate environment handle for each application that is connected to it. Environment handles are allocated with **SQLAllocHandle** and freed with **SQLFreeHandle**.

Connection Handles

A *connection* comprises a driver and a data source. A connection handle identifies each connection. The connection handle defines not only which driver to use, but which data source to use with that driver. Within a piece of code that implements ODBC (the Driver Manager or a driver), the connection handle identifies a structure that contains connection information, such as:

- The connection's state
- The current connection-level diagnostics
- The handles of statements and descriptors currently allocated on the connection
- The current settings of each connection attribute

ODBC does not prevent multiple simultaneous connections, if the driver supports them. Thus, in a particular ODBC environment, multiple connection handles might point to a variety of drivers and data sources, the same driver and a variety of data sources, or even multiple connections to the same driver and data source. Some drivers limit the number of active connections they support; the SQL_MAX_DRIVER_CONNECTIONS option in **SQLGetInfo** specifies how many active connections a particular driver supports.

Connection handles are used primarily when connecting to the data source (**SQLConnect**, **SQLDriverConnect**, or **SQLBrowseConnect**), disconnecting from the data source (**SQLDisconnect**), getting information about the driver and data source (**SQLGetInfo**), retrieving diagnostics (**SQLGetDiagField** and **SQLGetDiagRec**) and performing transactions (**SQLEndTran**). They are also used when setting and getting connection attributes (**SQLSetConnectAttr** and **SQLGetConnectAttr**) and when getting the native format of an SQL statement (**SQLNativeSql**).

Connection handles are allocated with **SQLAllocHandle** and freed with **SQLFreeHandle**.

Statement Handles

A *statement* is most easily thought of as an SQL statement, such as **SELECT * FROM Employee**. However, a statement is more than just an SQL statement—it consists of all of the information associated with that SQL statement, such as any result sets created by the statement and parameters used in the execution of the statement. A statement does not even need to have an application-defined SQL statement. For example, when a catalog function such as **SQLTables** is executed on a statement, it executes a predefined SQL statement that returns a list of table names.

Each statement is identified by a statement handle. A statement is associated with a single connection, and there can be multiple statements on that connection. Some drivers limit the number of active statements they support; the SQL_MAX_CONCURRENT_ACTIVITIES option in **SQLGetInfo** specifies how many active statements a driver supports on a single connection. A statement is defined to be "active" if it has results pending, where results are either a result set or the count of rows affected by an **INSERT**, **UPDATE**, or **DELETE** statement, or data is being sent with multiple calls to **SQLPutData**.

Within a piece of code that implements ODBC (the Driver Manager or a driver), the statement handle identifies a structure that contains statement information, such as:

- The statement's state
- The current statement-level diagnostics
- The addresses of the application variables bound to the statement's parameters and result set columns
- The current settings of each statement attribute.

Statement handles are used in most ODBC functions. Notably, they are used in the functions to bind parameters and result set columns (**SQLBindParameter** and

SQLBindCol), prepare and execute statements (**SQLPrepare**, **SQLExecute**, and **SQLExecDirect**), retrieve metadata (**SQLColAttribute** and **SQLDescribeCol**), fetch results (**SQLFetch**), and retrieve diagnostics (**SQLGetDiagField** and **SQLGetDiagRec**). They are also used in catalog functions (**SQLColumns**, **SQLTables**, and so on) and a number of other functions.

Statement handles are allocated with **SQLAllocHandle** and freed with **SQLFreeHandle**.

Descriptor Handles

A *descriptor* is a collection of metadata that describes the parameters of an SQL statement or the columns of a result set, as seen by the application or driver (also known as the *implementation*). Thus, a descriptor can fill any of four roles:

- **Application Parameter Descriptor (APD)**. Contains information about the application buffers bound to the parameters in an SQL statement, such as their addresses, lengths, and C data types.
- **Implementation Parameter Descriptor (IPD)**. Contains information about the parameters in an SQL statement, such as their SQL data types, lengths, and nullability.
- **Application Row Descriptor (ARD)**. Contains information about the application buffers bound to the columns in a result set, such as their addresses, lengths, and C data types.
- **Implementation Row Descriptor (IRD)**. Contains information about the columns in a result set, such as their SQL data types, lengths, and nullability.

Four descriptors (one filling each role) are allocated automatically when a statement is allocated. These are known as *automatically allocated descriptors* and are always associated with that statement. Applications can also allocate descriptors with **SQLAllocHandle**. These are known as *explicitly allocated descriptors*. They are allocated on a connection and can be associated with one or more statements on that connection to fulfill the role of an APD or ARD on those statements.

Most operations in ODBC can be performed without explicit use of descriptors by the application. However, descriptors provide a convenient shortcut for some operations. For example, suppose an application wants to insert data from two different sets of buffers. To use the first set of buffers, it would repeatedly call **SQLBindParameter** to bind them to the parameters in an **INSERT** statement, and then execute the statement. To use the second set of buffers, it would repeat this process. Alternatively, it could set up bindings to the first set of buffers in one descriptor and to the second set of buffers in another descriptor. To switch between the sets of bindings, it would simply call **SQLSetStmtAttr** and associate the correct descriptor with the statement as the APD.

For more information about descriptors, see "Types of Descriptors" in Chapter 13, "Descriptors."

State Transitions

ODBC defines discrete *states* for each environment, each connection, and each statement. For example, the environment has three possible states: Unallocated (in which no environment is allocated), Allocated (in which an environment is allocated but no connections are allocated), and Connection (in which an environment and one or more connections are allocated). Connections have seven possible states and statements have thirteen possible states.

A particular item, as identified by its handle, moves from one state to another when the application calls a certain function or functions and passes the handle to that item. Such movement is called a *state transition*. For example, allocating an environment handle with **SQLAllocHandle** moves the environment from Unallocated to Allocated and freeing that handle with **SQLFreeHandle** returns it from Allocated to Unallocated. ODBC defines a limited number of legal state transitions, which is another way of saying that functions must be called in a certain order.

Some functions, such as **SQLGetConnectAttr**, do not affect state at all. Other functions affect the state of a single item. For example, **SQLDisconnect** moves a connection from a Connection state to an Allocated state. Finally, some functions affect the state of more than one item. For example, allocating a connection handle with **SQLAllocHandle** moves a connection from an Unallocated to an Allocated state and moves the environment from an Allocated to a Connection state.

If an application calls a function out of order, the function returns a *state transition error*. For example, if an environment is in a Connection state and the application calls **SQLFreeHandle** with that environment handle, **SQLFreeHandle** returns SQLSTATE HY010 (Function sequence error), because it can be called only when the environment is in an Allocated state. By defining this as an invalid state transition, ODBC prevents the application from freeing the environment while there are active connections.

Some state transitions are inherent in the design of ODBC. For example, it is not possible to allocate a connection handle without first allocating an environment handle, because the function that allocates a connection handle requires an environment handle. Other state transitions are enforced by the Driver Manager and the drivers. For example, **SQLExecute** executes a prepared statement. If the statement handle passed to it is not in a Prepared state, **SQLExecute** returns SQLSTATE HY010 (Function sequence error).

From the application's point of view, state transitions are generally straightforward: Legal state transitions tend to go hand-in-hand with the flow of a well-written application. State transitions are more complex for the Driver Manager and the drivers, as they must track the state of the environment, each connection, and each statement. Most of this work is done by the Driver Manager; the majority of the work that must be done by drivers occurs with statements with pending results.

Parts 1 and 2 of this manual ("Introduction to ODBC" and "Developing Applications and Drivers") tend not to explicitly mention state transitions. Instead, they describe the order in which functions must be called. For example, Chapter 9, "Executing SQL Statements," states that a statement must be prepared with **SQLPrepare** before it can be executed with **SQLExecute**. For a complete description of states and state transitions, including which transitions are checked by the Driver Manager and which must be checked by drivers, see Appendix B, "ODBC State Transition Tables."

Buffers

A buffer is any piece of application memory used to pass data between the application and the driver. For example, application buffers can be associated with, or *bound to*, result set columns with **SQLBindCol**. As each row is fetched, the data is returned for each column in these buffers. *Input buffers* are used to pass data from the application to the driver; *output buffers* are used to return data from the driver to the application.

Note If an ODBC function returns SQL_ERROR, the contents of any output arguments to that function are undefined.

This discussion concerns itself primarily with buffers of indeterminate type. The addresses of these buffers appear as arguments of type SQLPOINTER, such as the *TargetValuePtr* argument in **SQLBindCol**. However, some of the items discussed here, such as the arguments used with buffers, also apply to arguments used to pass strings to the driver, such as the *TableName* argument in **SQLTables**.

These buffers generally come in pairs. *Data buffers* are used to pass the data itself, while *length/indicator buffers* are used to pass the length of the data in the data buffer or a special value such as SQL_NULL_DATA, which indicates that the data is NULL. Note that the length of the data in a data buffer is different from the length of the data buffer itself. The following diagram shows the relationship between the data buffer and the length/indicator buffer.

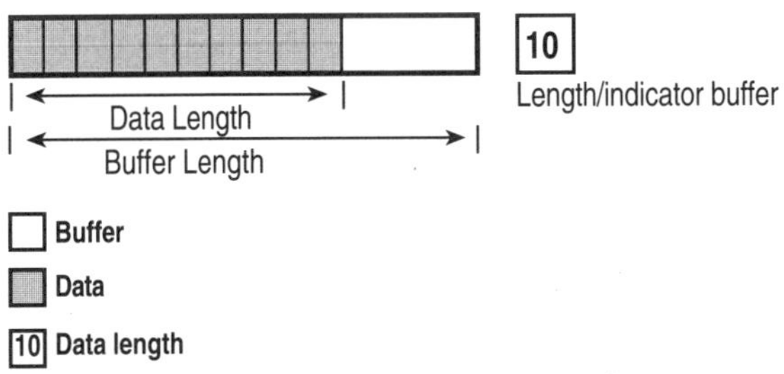

Figure 4.1 Data and Buffer Lengths

A length/indicator buffer is required any time the data buffer contains variable-length data, such as character or binary data. If the data buffer contains fixed-length data, such as an integer or date structure, a length/indicator buffer is needed only to pass indicator values because the length of the data is already known. If an application uses a length/indicator buffer with fixed-length data, the driver ignores any lengths passed in it.

The length of both the data buffer and the data it contains is measured in bytes, as opposed to characters. This distinction is unimportant for programs that use ANSI strings because lengths in bytes and characters are the same.

When the data buffer represents a driver-defined descriptor field, diagnostic field, or attribute, the application should indicate to the Driver Manager the nature of the function argument that indicates the value for the field or attribute. The application does this by setting the length argument in any function call that sets the field or attribute to one of the following values. (The same is true for functions that retrieve the values of the field or attribute, with the exception that the argument points to the values that for the setting function are in the argument itself.)

- If the function argument that indicates the value for the field or attribute is a pointer to a character string, then the *length* argument is the length of the string or SQL_NTS.
- If the function argument that indicates the value for the field or attribute is a pointer to a binary buffer, then the application places the result of the SQL_LEN_BINARY_ATTR(*length*) macro in *length* argument. This places a negative value in the *length* argument.
- If the function argument that indicates the value for the field or attribute is a pointer to a value other than a character string or a binary string, then the *length* argument should have the value SQL_IS_POINTER.
- If the function argument that indicates the value for the field or attribute contains a fixed-length value, then the *length* argument is either SQL_IS_INTEGER, SQL_IS_UINTEGER, SQL_SMALLINT, or SQL_USMALLINT, as appropriate.

Deferred Buffers

A *deferred buffer* is one whose value is used not at the time it is specified in a function call but at a later point in time. For example, **SQLBindParameter** is used to associate, or *bind*, a data buffer with a parameter in an SQL statement. The application specifies the number of the parameter and passes the address, byte length, and type of the buffer. The driver saves this information but does not examine the contents of the buffer. Later, when the application executes the statement, the driver retrieves the information and uses it to retrieve the parameter data and send it to the data source. Thus, the input of data in the buffer is deferred. Because deferred buffers are specified in one function and used in another, it is an application programming error to free a deferred buffer while the driver still expects it to exist; for more information, see "Allocating and Freeing Buffers," later in this chapter.

Both input and output buffers can be deferred. The following table summarizes the uses of deferred buffers. Note that deferred buffers bound to result set columns are specified with **SQLBindCol** and deferred buffers bound to SQL statement parameters are specified with **SQLBindParameter**.

Buffer use	Type	Specified with	Used by
Sending data for input parameters	Deferred input	**SQLBindParameter**	**SQLExecute** **SQLExecDirect**
Sending data to update or insert a row in a result set	Deferred input	**SQLBindCol**	**SQLSetPos**
Returning data for output and input/output parameters	Deferred output	**SQLBindParameter**	**SQLExecute** **SQLExecDirect**
Returning result set data	Deferred output	**SQLBindCol**	**SQLFetch** **SQLFetchScroll** **SQLSetPos**

Allocating and Freeing Buffers

All buffers are allocated and freed by the application. If a buffer is not deferred, it need only exist for the duration of the call to a function. For example, **SQLGetInfo** returns the value associated with a particular option in the buffer pointed to by the *InfoValuePtr* argument. This buffer can be freed immediately after the call to **SQLGetInfo**, as shown in the following code example:

```
SQLSMALLINT InfoValueLen;
SQLCHAR     *InfoValuePtr = malloc(50);  // Allocate InfoValuePtr.

SQLGetInfo(hdbc, SQL_DBMS_NAME, (SQLPOINTER)InfoValuePtr, 50,
           &InfoValueLen);

free(InfoValuePtr);                      // OK to free InfoValuePtr.
```

Because deferred buffers are specified in one function and used in another, it is an application programming error to free a deferred buffer while the driver still expects it to exist. For example, the address of the **ValuePtr* buffer is passed to **SQLBindCol** for later use by **SQLFetch**. This buffer cannot be freed until the column is unbound, such as with a call to **SQLBindCol** or **SQLFreeStmt** as shown in the following code example:

```
SQLRETURN   rc;
SQLINTEGER  ValueLenOrInd;
SQLHSTMT    hstmt;

// Allocate ValuePtr
SQLCHAR    *ValuePtr = malloc(50);

// Bind ValuePtr to column 1. It is an error to free ValuePtr here.
```

```
SQLBindCol(hstmt, 1, SQL_C_CHAR, ValuePtr, 50, &ValueLenOrInd);

// Fetch each row of data and place the value for column 1 in *ValuePtr. Code
// to check if rc equals SQL_ERROR or SQL_SUCCESS_WITH_INFO not shown.
while ((rc = SQLFetch(hstmt)) != SQL_NO_DATA) {
   // It is an error to free ValuePtr here.
}

// Unbind ValuePtr from column 1.  It is now OK to free ValuePtr.
SQLFreeStmt(hstmt, SQL_UNBIND);
free(ValuePtr);
```

Such an error is easily made by declaring the buffer locally in a function; the buffer is freed when the application leaves the function. For example, the following code causes undefined and probably fatal behavior in the driver:

```
SQLRETURN rc;
SQLHSTMT    hstmt;

BindAColumn(hstmt);

// Fetch each row of data and try to place the value for column 1 in *ValuePtr. Because
// ValuePtr has been freed, the behavior is undefined and probably fatal. Code to check
// if rc equals SQL_ERROR or SQL_SUCCESS_WITH_INFO not shown.
while ((rc = SQLFetch(hstmt)) != SQL_NO_DATA) {}

   .
   .
   .

void BindAColumn(SQLHSTMT hstmt)      // WARNING! This function won't work!
{
   // Declare ValuePtr locally.
   SQLCHAR    ValuePtr[50];
   SQLINTEGER ValueLenOrInd;

   // Bind rgbValue to column.
   SQLBindCol(hstmt, 1, SQL_C_CHAR, ValuePtr, sizeof(ValuePtr), &ValueLenOrInd);

   // ValuePtr is freed when BindAColumn exits.
}
```

Using Data Buffers

Data buffers are described by three pieces of information: their type, address, and byte length. Whenever a function needs one of these pieces of information and does not already know it, it has an argument with which the application passes it.

Data Buffer Type

The C data type of a buffer is specified by the application. In the case of a single variable, this occurs when the application allocates the variable. In the case of generic memory—that is, memory pointed to by a pointer of type void *—this occurs when the application casts the memory to a particular type. There are two ways in which the driver discovers this type:

- **Data buffer type argument.** Buffers used to transfer parameter values and result set data, such as the buffer bound with *TargetValuePtr* in **SQLBindCol**, usually have an associated type argument, such as the *TargetType* argument in **SQLBindCol**. In this argument, the application passes the C type identifier corresponding to the type of the buffer. For example, in the following call to **SQLBindCol**, the value SQL_C_TYPE_DATE tells the driver that the *Date* buffer is an SQL_DATE_STRUCT.

  ```
  SQL_DATE_STRUCT Date;
  SQLINTEGER      DateInd;
  SQLBindCol(hstmt, 1, SQL_C_TYPE_DATE, &Date, 0, &DateInd);
  ```

  For more information on type identifiers, see the "Data Types in ODBC" section, later in this chapter.

- **Predefined type.** Buffers used to send and retrieve options or attributes, such as the buffer pointed to by the *InfoValuePtr* argument in **SQLGetInfo**, have a fixed type that depends on the option specified. The driver assumes that the data buffer is of this type; it is the application's responsibility to allocate a buffer of this type. For example, in the following call to **SQLGetInfo**, the driver assumes the buffer is a 32-bit integer because this is what the SQL_STRING_FUNCTIONS option requires:

  ```
  SQLUINTEGER StringFuncs;
  SQLGetInfo(hdbc, SQL_STRING_FUNCTIONS, (SQLPOINTER) &StringFuncs, 0,
             NULL);
  ```

The driver uses the C data type to interpret the data in the buffer.

Data Buffer Address

The application passes the address of the data buffer to the driver in an argument, often named *ValuePtr* or a similar name. For example, in the following call to **SQLBindCol**, the application specifies the address of the *Date* variable.

```
SQL_DATE_STRUCT Date;
SQLINTEGER      DateInd;
SQLBindCol(hstmt, 1, SQL_C_TYPE_DATE, &dsDate, 0, &DateInd);
```

As mentioned in the "Allocating and Freeing Buffers" section in this chapter, the address of a deferred buffer must remain valid until the buffer is unbound.

Unless it is specifically prohibited, the address of a data buffer can be a null pointer. For buffers used to send data to the driver, this causes the driver to ignore the information normally contained in the buffer. For buffers used to retrieve data from the driver, this causes the driver to not return a value. In both cases, the driver ignores the corresponding data buffer length argument.

Data Buffer Length

The application passes the byte length of the data buffer to the driver in an argument, named *BufferLength* or a similar name. For example, in the following call to **SQLBindCol**, the application specifies the length of the *ValuePtr* buffer (**sizeof**(*ValuePtr*)).

```
SQLCHAR    ValuePtr[50];
SQLINTEGER ValueLenOrInd;
SQLBindCol(hstmt, 1, SQL_C_CHAR, ValuePtr, sizeof(ValuePtr), &ValueLenOrInd);
```

A driver will always return the number of bytes, not the number of characters, in the buffer length argument of any function that has an output string argument.

Data buffer lengths are required only for output buffers; the driver uses them to avoid writing past the end of the buffer. However, the driver checks the data buffer length only when the buffer contains variable-length data, such as character or binary data. If the buffer contains fixed-length data, such as an integer or date structure, the driver ignores the data buffer length and assumes the buffer is large enough to hold the data; that is, it never truncates fixed-length data. It is therefore important for the application to allocate a large enough buffer for fixed-length data.

When a truncation of non-data output strings occurs (such as the cursor name returned for **SQLGetCursorName**), the returned length in the buffer length argument is the maximum byte length possible. That means that it is twice the number of characters, because the string could contain DBCS characters. For example, if the cursor name is 10 ANSI characters long (10 bytes), and an application calls **SQLGetCursorName** to try to retrieve the cursor name into a buffer that is 6 bytes long, the value returned in **NameLengthPtr* will be 20.

Data buffer lengths are not required for input buffers because the driver does not write to these buffers.

Using Length/Indicator Values

The length/indicator buffer is used to pass the byte length of the data in the data buffer or a special indicator such as SQL_NULL_DATA, which indicates that the data is NULL. Depending on the function in which it is used, a length/indicator buffer is defined to be an SQLINTEGER or an SQLSMALLINT. Therefore, a single argument is needed to describe it. If the data buffer is a non-deferred input buffer, this argument contains the byte length of the data itself or an indicator value. It is often named *StrLen_or_Ind* or a similar name. For example, the following code calls **SQLPutData** to pass a buffer full of data; the byte length (*ValueLen*) is passed directly because the data buffer (*ValuePtr*) is an input buffer.

```
SQLCHAR    ValuePtr[50];
SQLINTEGER ValueLen;

// Call local function to place data in ValuePtr. In ValueLen, return the number
// of bytes of data placed in ValuePtr. If there is not enough data, this will be
// less than 50.
FillBuffer(ValuePtr, sizeof(ValuePtr), &ValueLen);

// Call SQLPutData to send the data to the driver.
SQLPutData(hstmt, ValuePtr, ValueLen);
```

If the data buffer is a deferred input buffer, a non-deferred output buffer, or an output buffer, the argument contains the address of the length/indicator buffer. It is often named *StrLen_or_IndPtr* or a similar name. For example, the following code calls **SQLGetData** to retrieve a buffer full of data; the byte length is returned to the application in the length/indicator buffer (*ValueLenOrInd*), whose address is passed to **SQLGetData** because the corresponding data buffer (*ValuePtr*) is a non-deferred output buffer.

```
SQLCHAR    ValuePtr[50];
SQLINTEGER ValueLenOrInd;
SQLGetData(hstmt, 1, SQL_C_CHAR, ValuePtr, sizeof(ValuePtr), &ValueLenOrInd);
```

Unless it is specifically prohibited, a length/indicator buffer argument can be 0 (if non-deferred input) or a null pointer (if output or deferred input). For input buffers, this causes the driver to ignore the byte length of the data. This returns an error when passing variable-length data but is common when passing non-null, fixed-length data, as neither a length nor an indicator value is needed. For output buffers, this causes the driver to not return the byte length of the data or an indicator value. This is an error if the data returned by the driver is NULL but is common when retrieving fixed-length, non-nullable data as neither a length nor an indicator value is needed.

As is the case when the address of a deferred data buffer is passed to the driver, the address of a deferred length/indicator buffer must remain valid until the buffer is unbound.

The following lengths are valid as length/indicator values:

- *n*, where *n* > 0.
- 0.
- SQL_NTS. A string sent to the driver in the corresponding data buffer is null-terminated; this is a convenient way for C programmers to pass strings without having to calculate their byte length. This value is legal only when the application sends data to the driver. When the driver returns data to the application, it always returns the actual byte length of the data.

The following values are valid as length/indicator values. SQL_NULL_DATA is stored in the SQL_DESC_INDICATOR_PTR descriptor field; all other values are stored in the SQL_DESC_OCTET_LENGTH_PTR descriptor field.

- SQL_NULL_DATA. The data is a NULL data value and the value in the corresponding data buffer is ignored. This value is legal only for SQL data sent to or retrieved from the driver.
- SQL_DATA_AT_EXEC. The data buffer does not contain any data. Instead, the data will be sent with **SQLPutData** when the statement is executed, or when **SQLBulkOperations** or **SQLSetPos** is called. This value is legal only for SQL data sent to the driver. For more information, see **SQLBindParameter**, **SQLBulkOperations**, and **SQLSetPos**.
- Result of the SQL_LEN_DATA_AT_EXEC(*length*) macro. This value is similar to SQL_DATA_AT_EXEC. For more information, see "Sending Long Data" in Chapter 9, "Executing Statements."
- SQL_NO_TOTAL. The driver cannot determine the number of bytes of long data still available to return in an output buffer. This value is legal only for SQL data retrieved from the driver.
- SQL_DEFAULT_PARAM. A procedure is to use the default value of an input parameter in a procedure instead of the value in the corresponding data buffer.
- SQL_COLUMN_IGNORE. **SQLBulkOperations** or **SQLSetPos** is to ignore the value in the data buffer. When updating a row of data by a call to **SQLBulkOperations** or **SQLSetPos**, the column value is not changed. When inserting a new row of data by a call to **SQLBulkOperations**, the column value is set to its default or, if the column does not have a default, to NULL.

Data Length, Buffer Length, and Truncation

The *data length* is the byte length of the data as it would be stored in the application's data buffer, not as it is stored in the data source. This distinction is important because the data is often stored in different types in the data buffer and in the data source. Thus, for data being sent to the data source, this is the byte length of the data before conversion to the data source's type. For data being retrieved from the data source, this is the byte length of the data after conversion to the data buffer's type and before any truncation is done.

For fixed-length data, such as an integer or a date structure, the byte length of the data is always the size of the data type. In general, applications allocate a data buffer that is the size of the data type. If the application allocates a smaller buffer, the consequences are undefined as the driver assumes the data buffer is the size of the data type and does not truncate the data to fit into a smaller buffer. If the application allocates a larger buffer, the extra space is never used.

For variable-length data, such as character or binary data, it is important to recognize that the byte length of the data is separate from and often different than the byte length of the buffer. The relation of these two lengths is shown in the "Buffers" section, earlier in this chapter. If the byte length of the data is greater than the byte length of the buffer, the driver truncates data being fetched to the byte length of the buffer and returns SQL_SUCCESS_WITH_INFO with SQLSTATE 01004 (Data truncated). However, the returned byte length is the length of the untruncated data.

For example, suppose an application allocates 50 bytes for a binary data buffer. If the driver has 10 bytes of binary data to return, it returns those 10 bytes in the buffer. The byte length of the data is 10, and the byte length of the buffer is 50. If the driver has 60 bytes of binary data to return, it truncates the data to 50 bytes, returns those bytes in the buffer and returns SQL_SUCCESS_WITH_INFO. The byte length of the data is 60 (the length before truncation), and the byte length of the buffer is still 50.

A diagnostic record is created for each column that is truncated. Because it takes time for the driver to create these records and for the application to process them, truncation can degrade performance. Usually, an application can avoid this problem by allocating large enough buffers, although this might not be possible when working with long data. When data truncation occurs, the application can sometimes allocate a larger buffer and refetch the data; this is not true in all cases. If truncation occurs while getting data with calls to **SQLGetData**, the application need not call **SQLGetData** for data that has already been returned; for more information, see "Getting Long Data" in Chapter 10, "Retrieving Results (Basic)."

Character Data and C Strings

Input parameters that refer to variable-length character data (such as column names, dynamic parameters, and string attribute values) have an associated length parameter. If the application terminates strings with the null character, as is typical in C, then it provides as an argument either the length in bytes of the string (not including the null-terminator) or SQL_NTS (Null-Terminated String). A non-negative length argument specifies the actual length of the associated string. The length argument may be 0 to specify a zero-length string, which is distinct from a NULL value. The negative value SQL_NTS directs the driver to determine the length of the string by locating the null-termination character.

When character data is returned from the driver to the application, the driver must always null-terminate it. This gives the application the choice of whether to handle the data as a string or a character array. If the application buffer is not large enough to return all of the character data, the driver truncates it to the byte length of the buffer less the number of bytes required by the null-termination character, null-terminates the truncated data, and stores it in the buffer. Thus, applications must always allocate extra space for the null-termination character in buffers used to retrieve character data. For example, a 51-byte buffer is needed to retrieve 50 characters of data.

Special care must be taken by both the application and driver when sending or retrieving long character data in parts with **SQLPutData** or **SQLGetData**. If the data is passed as a series of null-terminated strings, the null-termination characters on these strings must be stripped before the data can be reassembled.

A number of ODBC programmers have confused character data and C strings. That this has occurred is an artifact of using the C language when defining ODBC functions. If an ODBC driver or application uses another language—remember that ODBC is language independent—this confusion is less likely to arise.

When C strings are used to hold character data, the null-termination character is not considered to be part of the data and is not counted as part of its byte length. For example, the character data "ABC" can be held as the C string "ABC\0" or the character array {'A', 'B', 'C'}. The byte length of the data is three regardless of whether it is treated as a string or a character array.

Although applications and drivers commonly use C strings (null-terminated arrays of characters) to hold character data, there is no requirement to do this. In C, character data can also be treated as an array of characters (without null termination) and its byte length passed separately in the length/indicator buffer.

Because character data can be held in a non-null terminated array and its byte length passed separately, it is possible to embed null characters in character data. However, the behavior of ODBC functions in this case is undefined and it is driver-specific whether a driver handles this correctly. Thus, interoperable applications should always handle character data that can contain embedded null characters as binary data.

Data Types in ODBC

ODBC uses two sets of data types: SQL data types and C data types. SQL data types are used in the data source and C data types are used in C code in the application.

Type Identifiers

To describe SQL and C data types, ODBC defines two sets of *type identifiers*. A type identifier describes the type of an SQL column or a C buffer. It is a **#define** value and is generally passed as a function argument or returned in metadata. For example, the following call to **SQLBindParameter** binds a variable of type SQL_DATE_STRUCT to a date parameter in an SQL statement. The C type identifier SQL_C_TYPE_DATE specifies the type of the *Date* variable and the SQL type identifier SQL_TYPE_DATE specifies the type of the dynamic parameter.

```
SQL_DATE_STRUCT Date;
SQLINTEGER      DateInd = 0;
SQLBindParameter(hstmt, 1, SQL_PARAM_INPUT, SQL_C_TYPE_DATE, SQL_TYPE_DATE, 0, 0,
                 &Date, 0, &DateInd);
```

SQL Data Types in ODBC

SQL data types are the types in which data is stored in the data source.

SQL Type Identifiers

Each data source defines its own SQL data types. ODBC defines type identifiers and describes the general characteristics of the SQL data types that might be mapped to each type identifier. It is driver-specific how each data type in the underlying data source is mapped to an SQL type identifier of ODBC.

For example, SQL_CHAR is the type identifier for a character column with a fixed length, typically between 1 and 254 characters. These characteristics correspond to the CHAR data type found in many SQL data sources. Thus, when an application discovers that the type identifier for a column is SQL_CHAR, it can assume it is probably dealing with a CHAR column. However, it should still check the byte length of the column before assuming it is between 1 and 254 characters; the driver for a non-SQL data source, for example, might map a fixed-length character column of 500 characters to SQL_CHAR or SQL_LONGVARCHAR, since neither is an exact match.

ODBC defines a wide variety of SQL type identifiers. However, the driver is not required to use all of these identifiers. Instead, it only uses those identifiers it needs to expose the SQL data types supported by the underlying data source. If the underlying data source supports SQL data types to which no type identifier corresponds, the driver can define additional type identifiers. For more information, see "Driver-Specific Data Types, Descriptor Types, Information Types, Diagnostic Types, and Attributes," in Chapter 17, "Programming Considerations."

For a complete description of SQL type identifiers, see Appendix D, "Data Types."

Retrieving Data Type Information with SQLGetTypeInfo

Because the mappings from underlying SQL data types to ODBC type identifiers are approximate, ODBC provides a function (**SQLGetTypeInfo**) through which a driver can completely describe each SQL data type in the data source. This function returns a result set, each row of which describes the characteristics of a single data type, such as name, type identifier, precision, scale, and nullability.

This information is generally used by generic applications that allow the user to create and alter tables. Such applications call **SQLGetTypeInfo** to retrieve the data type information and then present some or all of it to the user. Such applications need to be aware of two things:

- More than one SQL data type can map to a single type identifier, which can make it difficult to determine which data type to use. To solve this, the result set is ordered first by type identifier and second by closeness to the type identifier's definition. In addition, data source–defined data types take precedence over user-defined data types. For example, suppose that a data source defines the INTEGER and COUNTER data types to be the same except that COUNTER is auto-incrementing. Suppose also that the user-defined type WHOLENUM is a synonym of INTEGER. Each of these types maps to SQL_INTEGER. In the **SQLGetTypeInfo** result set, INTEGER appears first, followed by WHOLENUM and then COUNTER.

WHOLENUM appears after INTEGER because it is user-defined but before COUNTER because it more closely matches the definition of the SQL_INTEGER type identifier.

- ODBC does not define data type names for use in **CREATE TABLE** and **ALTER TABLE** statements. Instead, the application should use the name returned in the TYPE_NAME column of the result set returned by **SQLGetTypeInfo**. The reason for this is that although most of SQL does not vary much across DBMSs, data type names vary tremendously. Rather than forcing drivers to parse SQL statements and replace standard data type names with DBMS-specific data type names, ODBC requires applications to use the DBMS-specific names in the first place.

Note that **SQLGetTypeInfo** does not necessarily describe all of the data types an application can encounter. In particular, result sets might contain data types not directly supported by the data source. For example, the data types of the columns in result sets returned by catalog functions are defined by ODBC and these data types might not be supported by the data source. To determine the characteristics of the data types in a result set, an application calls **SQLColAttribute**.

C Data Types in ODBC

ODBC defines the C data types that are used by application variables and their corresponding type identifiers. Among other things, these are used by the buffers that are bound to result set columns and statement parameters. For example, suppose an application wants to retrieve data from a result set column in character format. It declares a variable with the SQLCHAR * data type and binds this variable to the result set column with a type identifier of SQL_C_CHAR. For a complete list of C data types and type identifiers, see Appendix D, "Data Types."

ODBC also defines a default mapping from each SQL data type to a C data type. For example, a 2-byte integer in the data source is mapped to a 2-byte integer in the application. To use the default mapping, an application specifies the SQL_C_DEFAULT type identifier. However, use of this identifier is discouraged for interoperability reasons.

All integer C data types defined in ODBC 1.*x* were signed. Unsigned C data types and their corresponding type identifiers were added in ODBC 2.0. Because of this, applications and drivers need to be particularly careful when dealing with 1.*x* versions.

Data Type Conversions

Data can be converted from one type to another at one of four times: when data is transferred from one application variable to another (C to C), when data in an application variable is sent to a statement parameter (C to SQL), when data in a result set column is returned in an application variable (SQL to C), and when data is transferred from one data source column to another (SQL to SQL).

Any conversion that occurs when data is transferred from one application variable to another is outside the scope of this document.

When an application binds a variable to a result set column or statement parameter, it implicitly specifies a data type conversion in its choice of the data type of the application variable. For example, suppose a column contains integer data. If the application binds an integer variable to the column, it specifies that no conversion be done; if it binds a character variable to the column, it specifies that the data be converted from integer to character.

ODBC defines how data is converted between each SQL and C data type. Basically, it supports all reasonable conversions, such as character to integer and integer to float, and does not support ill-defined conversions, such as float to date. Drivers are required to support all conversions for each SQL data type they support. For a complete list of conversions between SQL and C data types, see "Converting Data from SQL to C Data Types" and "Converting Data from C to SQL Data Types" in Appendix D, "Data Types."

ODBC also defines a scalar function for converting data from one SQL data type to another. The **CONVERT** scalar function is mapped by the driver to the underlying scalar function or functions defined to perform conversions in the data source. Because it is mapped to DBMS-specific functions, ODBC does not define how these conversions work or what conversions must be supported. An application discovers what conversions are supported by a particular driver and data source through the SQL_CONVERT options in **SQLGetInfo**. For more information about the **CONVERT** scalar function, see "Escape Sequences in ODBC" in Chapter 8, "SQL Statements" and Appendix E, "Scalar Functions."

Conformance Levels

ODBC drivers give the application access to diverse data sources. Each driver lets the application determine at run time what ODBC capabilities and what SQL grammar the driver and each data source supports. Note that this is not a requirement of applications designed to work with a single driver or a small, known set of drivers, because these applications can simply be written to the capabilities of that driver or drivers. To help applications discover driver and data source capabilities, two areas of conformance are available: the ODBC interface and SQL grammar.

Interface Conformance Levels

The purpose of leveling is to inform the application what features are available to it from the driver. A leveling scheme based on functions does not sufficiently achieve this goal. In ODBC 3.0, drivers are classified based on the features they possess. Supporting the feature may include supporting the function; it may also include supporting a descriptor field, a statement attribute, a "Y" value for an information type returned by **SQLGetInfo**, and so on.

To simplify specification of interface conformance, ODBC defines three conformance levels. To meet a particular conformance level, a driver must satisfy all of the requirements of that conformance level. Conformance with a given level implies complete conformance with all lower levels.

Conformance levels do not always divide neatly into support for a specific list of ODBC functions, but specify supported features as listed in the following sections. To provide support for a feature, a driver must support some or all forms of calls to certain ODBC functions (for more information, see "Function Conformance"), setting certain attributes (for more information, see "Attribute Conformance"), and certain descriptor fields (for more information, see "Descriptor Field Conformance").

The application discovers a driver's interface conformance level by connecting to a data source, and calling **SQLGetInfo** with the SQL_ODBC_INTERFACE_CONFORMANCE option.

Drivers are free to implement features beyond the level to which they claim complete conformance. Applications discover any such additional capabilities by calling **SQLGetFunctions** (to determine which ODBC functions are present) and **SQLGetInfo** (to query various other ODBC capabilities).

There are three ODBC interface conformance levels: Core, Level 1, and Level 2.

Note These conformance levels have different requirements than the ODBC API conformance levels of the same name in ODBC 2.x. In particular, all the features implied by ODBC 2.x API conformance Level 1 are now part of the Core interface conformance level. As a result, many ODBC drivers may report Core-level interface conformance.

Core Interface Conformance

All ODBC drivers must exhibit at least Core-level interface conformance. Since the features in the Core level are chosen such that they are what is required by most generic interoperable applications, this lets the driver work with such applications; it also corresponds to the features defined in the ISO CLI specification and the non-optional features defined in the X/Open CLI specification. A Core-level interface–conformant ODBC driver allows the application to do all of the following:

1. Allocate and free all types of handles, by calling **SQLAllocHandle** and **SQLFreeHandle**.
2. Use all forms of the **SQLFreeStmt** function.
3. Bind result set columns, by calling **SQLBindCol**.
4. Handle dynamic parameters, including arrays of parameters, in the input direction only, by calling **SQLBindParameter** and **SQLNumParams**. (Parameters in the output direction are feature 203 in "Level 2 Interface Conformance.")
5. Specify a bind offset.
6. Use the data-at-execution dialog, involving calls to **SQLParamData** and **SQLPutData**.

7. Manage cursors and cursor names, by calling **SQLCloseCursor**, **SQLGetCursorName**, and **SQLSetCursorName**.
8. Gain access to the description (metadata) of result sets, by calling **SQLColAttribute**, **SQLDescribeCol**, **SQLNumResultCols**, and **SQLRowCount**. (Use of these functions on column number 0 to retrieve bookmark metadata is feature 204 in "Level 2 Interface Conformance.")
9. Query the data dictionary, by calling the catalog functions **SQLColumns**, **SQLGetTypeInfo**, **SQLStatistics**, and **SQLTables**. (The driver is not required to support multipart names of database tables and views. For more information, see feature 101 in "Level 1 Interface Conformance" and feature 201 in "Level 2 Interface Conformance.") However, certain features of the SQL-92 specification, such as column qualification and names of indexes, are syntactically comparable to multipart naming. The present list of ODBC features is not intended to introduce new optionality into these aspects of SQL-92.)
10. Manage data sources and connections, by calling **SQLConnect**, **SQLDataSources**, **SQLDisconnect**, and **SQLDriverConnect**. Obtain information on drivers, no matter which ODBC level they support, by calling **SQLDrivers**.
11. Prepare and execute SQL statements, by calling **SQLExecDirect**, **SQLExecute**, and **SQLPrepare**.
12. Fetch one row of a result set or multiple rows, in the forward direction only, by calling **SQLFetch**, or by calling **SQLFetchScroll** with the *FetchOrientation* argument set to SQL_FETCH_NEXT.
13. Obtain an unbound column in parts, by calling **SQLGetData**.
14. Obtain current values of all attributes, by calling **SQLGetConnectAttr**, **SQLGetEnvAttr**, and **SQLGetStmtAttr**; and set all attributes to their default values and set certain attributes to non-default values by calling **SQLSetConnectAttr**, **SQLSetEnvAttr**, and **SQLSetStmtAttr**.
15. Manipulate certain fields of descriptors, by calling SQLCopyDesc, SQLGetDescField, SQLGetDescRec, SQLSetDescField, and SQLSetDescRec.
16. Obtain diagnostic information, by calling **SQLGetDiagField** and **SQLGetDiagRec**.
17. Detect driver capabilities, by calling **SQLGetFunctions** and **SQLGetInfo**. Also, detect the result of any text substitutions made to an SQL statement before it is sent to the data source, by calling **SQLNativeSql**.
18. Use the syntax of **SQLEndTran** to commit a transaction. A Core-level driver need not support true transactions; therefore, the application cannot specify SQL_ROLLBACK, nor specify SQL_AUTOCOMMIT_OFF for the SQL_ATTR_AUTOCOMMIT connection attribute. (For more information, see feature 109 in "Level 2 Interface Conformance.")

19. Call **SQLCancel** to cancel the data-at-execution dialog and, in multithread environments, to cancel an ODBC function executing in another thread. Core-level interface conformance does not mandate support for asynchronous execution of functions nor the use of **SQLCancel** to cancel an ODBC function executing asynchronously. Neither the platform nor the ODBC driver need be multithread for the driver to conduct independent activities at the same time. However, in multithread environments, the ODBC driver must be thread-safe. Serialization of requests from the application is a conformant way to implement this specification, even though it may create serious performance problems.
20. Obtain the SQL_BEST_ROWID row-identifying column of tables, by calling **SQLSpecialColumns**. (Support for SQL_ROWVER is feature 208 in "Level 2 Interface Conformance.")

Important ODBC Drivers must implement the functions in the Core interface conformance level.

Level 1 Interface Conformance

The Level 1 interface conformance level includes the Core interface conformance level functionality, plus additional features, such as transactions, that are usually available in an OLTP relational DBMS. A Level 1 interface–conformant driver lets the application do the following, in addition to the features in the Core interface conformance level:

101 Specify the schema of database tables and views (using two-part naming). (For more information, see the three-part naming feature 201 in "Level 2 Interface Conformance.")

102 Invoke true asynchronous execution of ODBC functions, where applicable ODBC functions are all synchronous or all asynchronous on a given connection.

103 Use scrollable cursors, and thereby achieve access to a result set in methods other than forward-only, by calling **SQLFetchScroll** with the *FetchOrientation* argument other than SQL_FETCH_NEXT. (The SQL_FETCH_BOOKMARK *FetchOrientation* is in feature 204 in "Level 2 Interface Conformance.")

104 Obtain primary keys of tables, by calling **SQLPrimaryKeys**.

105 Use stored procedures, through the ODBC escape sequence for procedure calls; and query the data dictionary regarding stored procedures, by calling **SQLProcedureColumns** and **SQLProcedures**. (The process by which procedures are created and stored on the data source is outside the scope of this document.)

106 Connect to a data source by interactively browsing the available servers, by calling **SQLBrowseConnect**.

107 Use ODBC functions instead of SQL statements to perform certain database operations: **SQLSetPos** with SQL_POSITION and SQL_REFRESH.

108 Gain access to the contents of multiple result sets generated by batches and stored procedures, by calling **SQLMoreResults**.

109 Delimit transactions spanning several ODBC functions, with true atomicity and the ability to specify SQL_ROLLBACK in **SQLEndTran**.

Level 2 Interface Conformance

The Level 2 interface conformance level includes the Level 1 interface conformance–level functionality, plus the following features:

201 Use three-part names of database tables and views. (For more information, see the two-part naming support feature 101 in "Level 1 Interface Conformance.")

202 Describe dynamic parameters, by calling **SQLDescribeParam**.

203 Use not only input parameters, but also output and input/output parameters, and result values of stored procedures.

204 Use bookmarks, including retrieving bookmarks by calling **SQLDescribeCol** and **SQLColAttribute** on column number 0; fetching based on a bookmark by calling **SQLFetchScroll** with the *FetchOrientation* argument set to SQL_FETCH_BOOKMARK; and update, delete, and fetch by bookmark operations by calling **SQLBulkOperations** with the *Operation* argument set to SQL_UPDATE_BY_BOOKMARK, SQL_DELETE_BY_BOOKMARK, or SQL_FETCH_BY_BOOKMARK.

205 Retrieve advanced information on the data dictionary, by calling **SQLColumnPrivileges**, **SQLForeignKeys**, and **SQLTablePrivileges**.

206 Use ODBC functions instead of SQL statements to perform additional database operations, by calling **SQLBulkOperations** with SQL_ADD, or **SQLSetPos** with SQL_DELETE or SQL_UPDATE. (Support for calls to **SQLSetPos** with the *LockType* argument set to SQL_LOCK_EXCLUSIVE or SQL_LOCK_UNLOCK is not a part of the conformance levels, but is an optional feature.)

207 Enable asynchronous execution of ODBC functions for specified individual statements.

208 Obtain the SQL_ROWVER row-identifying column of tables, by calling **SQLSpecialColumns**. (For more information, see the support for **SQLSpecialColumns** with the *IdentifierType* argument set to SQL_BEST_ROWID as feature 20 in "Core Interface Conformance.")

209 Set the SQL_ATTR_CONCURRENCY statement attribute to at least one value other than SQL_CONCUR_READ_ONLY.

210 The ability to time out login request and SQL queries (SQL_ATTR_LOGIN_TIMEOUT and SQL_ATTR_QUERY_TIMEOUT).

211 The ability to change the default isolation level; the ability to execute transactions with the "serializable" level of isolation.

Function Conformance

The following table indicates the conformance level of each ODBC function, where this is well-defined.

Function	Conformance level
SQLAllocHandle	Core
SQLBindCol	Core
SQLBindParameter	Core [1]
SQLBrowseConnect	Level 1

Function	Conformance level
SQLBulkOperations	Level 1
SQLCancel	Core [1]
SQLCloseCursor	Core
SQLColAttribute	Core [1]
SQLColumnPrivileges	Level 2
SQLColumns	Core
SQLConnect	Core
SQLCopyDesc	Core
SQLDataSources	Core
SQLDescribeCol	Core [1]
SQLDescribeParam	Level 2
SQLDisconnect	Core
SQLDriverConnect	Core
SQLDrivers	Core
SQLEndTran	Core [1]
SQLExecDirect	Core
SQLExecute	Core
SQLFetch	Core
SQLFetchScroll	Core [1]
SQLForeignKeys	Level 2
SQLFreeHandle	Core
SQLFreeStmt	Core
SQLGetConnectAttr	Core
SQLGetCursorName	Core
SQLGetData	Core
SQLGetDescField	Core
SQLGetDescRec	Core
SQLGetDiagField	Core
SQLGetDiagRec	Core
SQLGetEnvAttr	Core
SQLGetFunctions	Core

Function	Conformance level
SQLGetInfo	Core
SQLGetStmtAttr	Core
SQLGetTypeInfo	Core
SQLMoreResults	Level 1
SQLNativeSql	Core
SQLNumParams	Core
SQLNumResultCols	Core
SQLParamData	Core
SQLPrepare	Core
SQLPrimaryKeys	Level 1
SQLProcedureColumns	Level 1
SQLProcedures	Level 1
SQLPutData	Core
SQLRowCount	Core
SQLSetConnectAttr	Core [2]
SQLSetCursorName	Core
SQLSetDescField	Core [1]
SQLSetDescRec	Core
SQLSetEnvAttr	Core [2]
SQLSetPos	Level 1 [1]
SQLSetStmtAttr	Core [2]
SQLSpecialColumns	Core [1]
SQLStatistics	Core
SQLTablePrivileges	Level 2
SQLTables	Core

1 Significant features of this function are available only at higher conformance levels.

2 Setting certain attributes to non-default values depends on the conformance level. For more information, see the next section, "Attribute Conformance."

Attribute Conformance

The following table indicates the conformance level of each ODBC environment attribute, where this is well-defined.

Function	Conformance level
SQL_ATTR_CONNECTION_POOLING	-- [1]
SQL_ATTR_CP_MATCH	-- [1]
SQL_ATTR_ODBC_VER	Core
SQL_ATTR_OUTPUT_NTS	-- [1]

1 This is an optional feature and as such is not part of the conformance levels.

The following table indicates the conformance level of each ODBC connection attribute, where this is well-defined.

Function	Conformance level
SQL_ATTR_ACCESS_MODE	Core
SQL_ATTR_ASYNC_ENABLE	Level 1/Level 2 [1]
SQL_ATTR_AUTO_IPD	Level 2
SQL_ATTR_AUTOCOMMIT	Level 1
SQL_ATTR_CONNECTION_TIMEOUT	Level 2
SQL_ATTR_CURRENT_CATALOG	Level 2
SQL_ATTR_LOGIN_TIMEOUT	Level 2
SQL_ATTR_ODBC_CURSORS	Core
SQL_ATTR_PACKET_SIZE	Level 2
SQL_ATTR_QUIET_MODE	Core
SQL_ATTR_TRACE	Core

Function	Conformance level
SQL_ATTR_TRACEFILE	Core
SQL_ATTR_TRANSLATE_LIB	Core
SQL_ATTR_TRANSLATE_OPTION	Core
SQL_ATTR_TXN_ISOLATION	Level 1/Level 2 [2]

1 Applications that support connection-level asynchrony (required for Level 1) must support setting this attribute to SQL_TRUE by calling **SQLSetConnectAttr**; the attribute need not be settable to a value other than its default value through **SQLSetStmtAttr**. Applications that support statement-level asynchrony (required for Level 2) must support setting this attribute to SQL_TRUE using either function.

2 For Level 1 interface conformance, the driver must support one value in addition to the driver-defined default value (available by calling **SQLGetInfo** with the SQL_DEFAULT_TXN_ISOLATION option). For Level 2 interface conformance, the driver must also support SQL_TXN_SERIALIZABLE.

The following table indicates the conformance level of each ODBC statement attribute, where this is well-defined.

Function	Conformance level
SQL_ATTR_APP_PARAM_DESC	Core
SQL_ATTR_APP_ROW_DESC	Core
SQL_ATTR_ASYNC_ENABLE	Level 1/Level 2 [1]
SQL_ATTR_CONCURRENCY	Level 1/Level 2 [2]
SQL_ATTR_CURSOR_SCROLLABLE	Level 1
SQL_ATTR_CURSOR_SENSITIVITY	Level 2
SQL_ATTR_CURSOR_TYPE	Core/Level 2 [3]
SQL_ATTR_ENABLE_AUTO_IPD	Level 2
SQL_ATTR_FETCH_BOOKMARK_PTR	Level 2
SQL_ATTR_IMP_PARAM_DESC	Core
SQL_ATTR_IMP_ROW_DESC	Core
SQL_ATTR_KEYSET_SIZE	Level 2
SQL_ATTR_MAX_LENGTH	Level 1
SQL_ATTR_MAX_ROWS	Level 1
SQL_ATTR_METADATA_ID	Core
SQL_ATTR_NOSCAN	Core
SQL_ATTR_PARAM_BIND_OFFSET_PTR	Core
SQL_ATTR_PARAM_BIND_TYPE	Core
SQL_ATTR_PARAM_OPERATION_PTR	Core

Function	Conformance level
SQL_ATTR_PARAM_STATUS_PTR	Core
SQL_ATTR_PARAMS_PROCESSED_PTR	Core
SQL_ATTR_PARAMSET_SIZE	Core
SQL_ATTR_QUERY_TIMEOUT	Level 2
SQL_ATTR_RETRIEVE_DATA	Level 1
SQL_ATTR_ROW_ARRAY_SIZE	Core
SQL_ATTR_ROW_BIND_OFFSET_PTR	Core
SQL_ATTR_ROW_BIND_TYPE	Core
SQL_ATTR_ROW_NUMBER	Level 1
SQL_ATTR_ROW_OPERATION_PTR	Level 1
SQL_ATTR_ROW_STATUS_PTR	Core
SQL_ATTR_ROWS_FETCHED_PTR	Core
SQL_ATTR_SIMULATE_CURSOR	Level 2
SQL_ATTR_USE_BOOKMARKS	Level 2

1 Applications that support connection-level asynchrony (required for Level 1) must support setting this attribute to SQL_TRUE by calling **SQLSetConnectAttr**; the attribute need not be settable to a value other than its default value through **SQLSetStmtAttr**. Applications that support statement-level asynchrony (required for Level 2) must support setting this attribute to SQL_TRUE using either function.

2 For Level 2 interface conformance, the driver must support SQL_CONCUR_READ_ONLY and at least one other value.

3 For Level 1 interface conformance, the driver must support SQL_CURSOR_FORWARD_ONLY and at least one other value. For Level 2 interface conformance, the driver must support all values defined in this document.

Descriptor Field Conformance

The following table indicates the conformance level of each ODBC descriptor header field, where this is well-defined.

Function	Conformance level
SQL_DESC_ALLOC_TYPE	Core
SQL_DESC_ARRAY_SIZE	Core
SQL_DESC_ARRAY_STATUS_PTR	Core (for APD, IPR, and IRD); Level 1 (for ARD)
SQL_DESC_BIND_OFFSET_PTR	Core
SQL_DESC_BIND_TYPE	Core
SQL_DESC_COUNT	Core
SQL_DESC_ROWS_PROCESSED_PTR	Core

The following table indicates the conformance level of each ODBC descriptor record field, where this is well-defined.

Function	Conformance level
SQL_DESC_AUTO_UNIQUE_VALUE	Level 2
SQL_DESC_BASE_COLUMN_NAME	Core
SQL_DESC_BASE_TABLE_NAME	Level 1
SQL_DESC_CASE_SENSITIVE	Core
SQL_DESC_CATALOG_NAME	Level 2
SQL_DESC_CONCISE_TYPE	Core
SQL_DESC_DATA_PTR	Core
SQL_DESC_DATETIME_INTERVAL_ CODE	Core [1]
SQL_DESC_DATETIME_INTERVAL_ PRECISION	Core [1]
SQL_DESC_DISPLAY_SIZE	Core
SQL_DESC_FIXED_PREC_SCALE	Core
SQL_DESC_INDICATOR_PTR	Core
SQL_DESC_LABEL	Level 2
SQL_DESC_LENGTH	Core
SQL_DESC_LITERAL_PREFIX	Core
SQL_DESC_LITERAL_SUFFIX	Core
SQL_DESC_LOCAL_TYPE_NAME	Core
SQL_DESC_NAME	Core
SQL_DESC_NULLABLE	Core
SQL_DESC_OCTET_LENGTH	Core
SQL_DESC_OCTET_LENGTH_PTR	Core
SQL_DESC_PARAMETER_TYPE	Core/Level 2 [2]
SQL_DESC_PRECISION	Core
SQL_DESC_SCALE	Core
SQL_DESC_SCHEMA_NAME	Level 1
SQL_DESC_SEARCHABLE	Core
SQL_DESC_TABLE_NAME	Level 1
SQL_DESC_TYPE	Core

Function	Conformance level
SQL_DESC_TYPE_NAME	Core
SQL_DESC_UNNAMED	Core
SQL_DESC_UNSIGNED	Core
SQL_DESC_UPDATABLE	Core

1 Support for these record fields is required only if the driver supports the applicable data types.

2 For Core-level conformance, the driver must support SQL_PARAM_INPUT. For Level 2 interface conformance, the driver must also support SQL_PARAM_INPUT_OUTPUT and SQL_PARAM_OUTPUT.

SQL Conformance Levels

The level of SQL-92 grammar supported by a driver is indicated by the value returned by a call to **SQLGetInfo** with the SQL_SQL_CONFORMANCE information type. This indicates whether the driver conforms to the Entry, FIPS Transitional, Intermediate, or Full levels defined in SQL-92.

All ODBC drivers must support the minimum SQL grammar described in "SQL Minimum Grammar" in Appendix C, "SQL Grammar." This grammar is a subset of the Entry level of SQL-92. Drivers may support additional SQL and, in fact, be conformant to the SQL-92 Entry, Intermediate, or Full level, or to the FIPS 127-2 Transitional level. Drivers that comply to a given level of SQL-92 or FIPS 127-2 can support additional features in any of the higher levels, yet not be fully conformant to that level. To determine whether a feature is supported, an application should call **SQLGetInfo** with the appropriate information type. The conformance level of an SQL feature is described in the corresponding information type (see the **SQLGetInfo** function description).

Environment, Connection, and Statement Attributes

ODBC defines a number of attributes that are associated with environments, connections, or statements.

Environment attributes affect the entire environment, such as whether connection pooling is enabled. Environment attributes are set with **SQLSetEnvAttr** and retrieved with **SQLGetEnvAttr**.

Connection attributes affect each connection individually, such as how long a driver should wait while attempting to connect to a data source before timing out. Connection attributes are set with **SQLSetConnectAttr** and retrieved with **SQLGetConnectAttr**. For more information about connection attributes, see "Connection Attributes" in Chapter 6, "Connecting to a Data Source or Driver."

Statement attributes affect each statement individually, such as whether a statement should be executed asynchronously. Statement attributes are set with **SQLSetStmtAttr** and retrieved with **SQLGetStmtAttr**. A few statement attributes are read-only attributes and cannot be set. For example, the SQL_ATTR_ROW_NUMBER statement attribute, which is used to retrieve the number of the current row in the cursor, is read-only. For more information about statement attributes, see "Statement Attributes" in Chapter 9, "Executing Statements."

In addition to attributes defined by ODBC, a driver can define its own connection and statement attributes. Driver-defined attributes must be registered with X/Open to ensure that two driver vendors do not assign the same integer value to different, proprietary attributes. For more information, see "Driver-Specific Data Types, Descriptor Types, Information Types, Diagnostic Types, and Attributes" in Chapter 17, "Programming Considerations."

For a complete list of attributes, see **SQLSetEnvAttr**, **SQLSetConnectAttr**, and **SQLSetStmtAttr**. Most attributes are also described in the description of the ODBC function that they affect.

Tables and Views

In ODBC functions, tables and views are interchangeable. The term *table* is used for both tables and views, except where the term *view* is used explicitly.

CHAPTER 5

Basic Application Steps

This chapter describes the general flow of ODBC applications. It is unlikely that any application calls all of these functions in exactly this order. However, most applications use some variation of these steps. The basic application steps are shown in Figure 5.1.

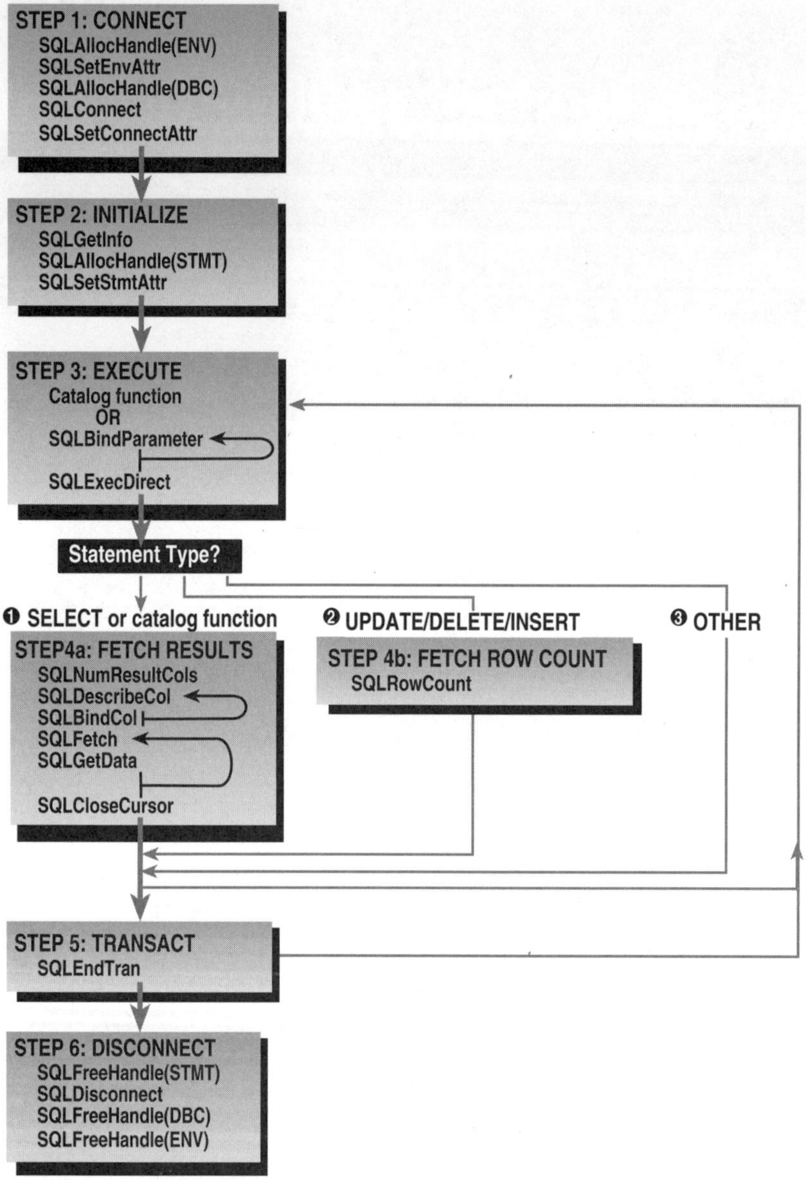

Figure 5.1 Basic application steps

Step 1: Connect to the Data Source

The first step in any application is to connect to the data source. This phase, including the functions it requires, is illustrated in the following figure.

STEP 1: CONNECT
- SQLAllocHandle(ENV)
- SQLSetEnvAttr
- SQLAllocHandle(DBC)
- SQLConnect
- SQLSetConnectAttr

The first step in connecting to the data source is to load the Driver Manager and allocate the environment handle with **SQLAllocHandle**. For more information, see "Allocating the Environment Handle" in Chapter 6, "Connecting to a Data Source or Driver."

The application then registers the version of ODBC to which it conforms by calling **SQLSetEnvAttr** with the SQL_ATTR_APP_ODBC_VER environment attribute. For more information, see the "Declaring the Application's ODBC Version" section in Chapter 6, "Connecting to a Data Source or Driver," and the "Backward Compatibility and Standards Compliance" section in Chapter 17, "Programming Considerations."

Next, the application allocates a connection handle with **SQLAllocHandle** and connects to the data source with **SQLConnect**, **SQLDriverConnect**, or **SQLBrowseConnect**. For more information, see "Allocating a Connection Handle" and "Establishing a Connection" in Chapter 6, "Connecting to a Data Source or Driver."

The application then sets any connection attributes, such as whether to manually commit transactions. For more information, see "Connection Attributes" in Chapter 6, "Connecting to a Data Source or Driver."

Step 2: Initialize the Application

The second step is to initialize the application, as illustrated in the following figure. Exactly what is done here varies with the application.

STEP 2: INITIALIZE
- SQLGetInfo
- SQLAllocHandle(STMT)
- SQLSetStmtAttr

At this point, it is common to use **SQLGetInfo** to discover the capabilities of the driver. For more information, see “Considering Database Features to Use” in Chapter 16, “Interoperability.”

All applications need to allocate a statement handle with **SQLAllocHandle** and many applications set statement attributes, such as the cursor type, with **SQLSetStmtAttr**. For more information, see “Allocating a Statement Handle” and “Statement Attributes” in Chapter 9, “Executing Statements.”

Step 3: Build and Execute an SQL Statement

The third step is to build and execute an SQL statement, as shown in the following figure. How this is done is likely to vary tremendously. The application might prompt the user to enter an SQL statement, build an SQL statement based on user input, or use a hard-coded SQL statement. For more information, see “Constructing SQL Statements” in Chapter 8, “SQL Statements.”

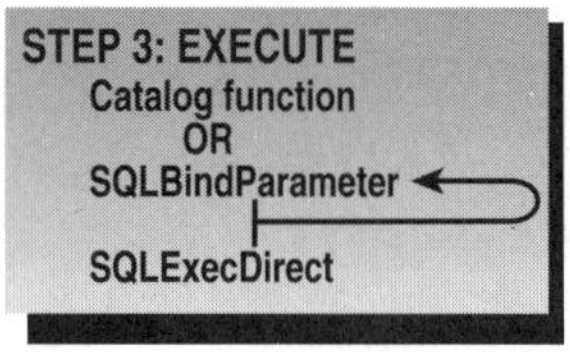

If the SQL statement contains parameters, the application binds them to application variables by calling **SQLBindParameter** for each parameter. For more information, see “Statement Parameters” in Chapter 9, “Executing Statements.”

After the SQL statement is built and any parameters are bound, the statement is executed with **SQLExecDirect**. If the statement will be executed multiple times, it can be prepared with **SQLPrepare** and executed with **SQLExecute**. For more information, see “Executing a Statement” in Chapter 9, “Executing Statements.”

The application might also forgo executing an SQL statement altogether and instead call a function to return a result set containing catalog information, such as the available columns or tables. For more information, see “Uses of Catalog Data” in Chapter 7, “Catalog Functions.”

What the application does next depends on the type of SQL statement executed.

Type of SQL statement	Proceed to
SELECT or catalog function	"Step 4a: Fetch the Results"
UPDATE, **DELETE**, or **INSERT**	"Step 4b: Fetch the Row Count"
All other SQL statements	"Step 3: Build and Execute an SQL Statement" (this topic) or "Step 5: Commit the Transaction"

Step 4a: Fetch the Results

The next step is to fetch the results, as shown in the following figure.

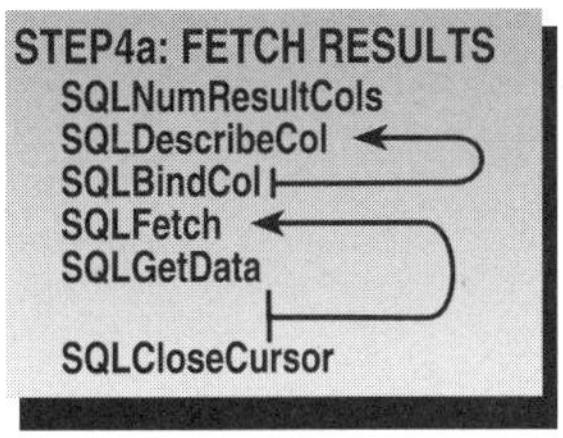

If the statement executed in Step 3, "Build and Execute an SQL Statement" was a **SELECT** statement or a catalog function, the application first calls **SQLNumResultCols** to determine the number of columns in the result set. This step is not necessary if the application already knows the number of result set columns, such as when the SQL statement is hard-coded in a vertical or custom application.

Next, the application retrieves the name, data type, precision, and scale of each result set column with **SQLDescribeCol**. Again, this is not necessary for applications such as vertical and custom applications that already know this information. It passes this information to **SQLBindCol**, which binds an application variable to a column in the result set.

The application now calls **SQLFetch** to retrieve the first row of data and place the data from that row in the variables bound with **SQLBindCol**. If there is any long data in the row, it then calls **SQLGetData** to retrieve that data. The application continues to call **SQLFetch** and **SQLGetData** to retrieve additional data. After it has finished fetching data, it calls **SQLCloseCursor** to close the cursor.

For a complete description of retrieving results, see Chapter 10, "Retrieving Results (Basic)" and Chapter 11, "Retrieving Results (Advanced)."

The application now returns to Step 3, "Build and Execute an SQL Statement," to execute another statement in the same transaction or proceeds to Step 5, "Commit the Transaction," to commit or roll back the transaction.

Step 4b: Fetch the Row Count

STEP 4b: FETCH ROW COUNT
SQLRowCount

If the statement executed in Step 3 was an **UPDATE**, **DELETE**, or **INSERT** statement, the application retrieves the count of affected rows with **SQLRowCount**. For more information, see "Determining the Number of Affected Rows" in Chapter 12, "Updating Data."

The application now returns to Step 3 to execute another statement in the same transaction or proceeds to Step 5 to commit or roll back the transaction.

Step 5: Commit the Transaction

STEP 5: TRANSACT
SQLEndTran

The fifth step is to call **SQLEndTran** to commit or roll back the transaction. The application performs this step only if it set the transaction commit mode to manual commit; if the transaction commit mode is auto-commit, which is the default, the transaction is automatically committed when the statement is executed. For more information, see Chapter 14, "Transactions."

To execute a statement in a new transaction, the application returns to Step 3. To disconnect from the data source, the application proceeds to Step 6.

Step 6: Disconnect from the Data Source

The final step is to disconnect from the data source, as illustrated in the following figure. First, the application frees any statement handles by calling **SQLFreeHandle**. For more information, see "Freeing a Statement Handle" in Chapter 9, "Executing Statements."

STEP 6: DISCONNECT
SQLFreeHandle(STMT)
SQLDisconnect
SQLFreeHandle(DBC)
SQLFreeHandle(ENV)

Next, the application disconnects from the data source with **SQLDisconnect** and frees the connection handle with **SQLFreeHandle**. For more information, see "Disconnecting from a Data Source or Driver" in Chapter 6, "Connecting to a Data Source or Driver."

Finally, the application frees the environment handle with **SQLFreeHandle** and unloads the Driver Manager. For more information, see "Allocating the Environment Handle" in Chapter 6, "Connecting to a Data Source or Driver."

CHAPTER 6

Connecting to a Data Source or Driver

An application can be connected to any number of drivers and data sources. These can be a variety of drivers and data sources, the same driver and a variety of data sources, or even multiple connections to the same driver and data source.

Allocating the Environment Handle

The first task for any ODBC application is to load the Driver Manager; how this is done is operating-system dependent. For example, on a computer running Windows NT Server, Windows NT Workstation, or Windows 95, the application either links to the Driver Manager library or calls LoadLibrary to load the Driver Manager DLL.

The next task, which must be done before an application can call any other ODBC function, is to initialize the ODBC environment and allocate an environment handle. To do this:

1. The application declares a variable of type SQLHENV. It then calls **SQLAllocHandle** and passes the address of this variable and the SQL_HANDLE_ENV option. For example:

   ```
   SQLHENV henv1;

   SQLAllocHandle(SQL_HANDLE_ENV, SQL_NULL_HANDLE, &henv1);
   ```

2. The Driver Manager allocates a structure in which to store information about the environment, and returns the environment handle in the variable.

The Driver Manager does not call **SQLAllocHandle** in the driver at this time, as it does not know which driver to call. It delays calling **SQLAllocHandle** in the driver until the application calls a function to connect to a data source. For more information, see "Driver Manager's Role in the Connection Process," later in this chapter.

When the application has finished using ODBC, it frees the environment handle with **SQLFreeHandle**. After freeing the environment, it is an application programming error to use the environment's handle in a call to an ODBC function; doing so has undefined but probably fatal consequences.

When **SQLFreeHandle** is called, the driver releases the structure used to store information about the environment. Note that **SQLFreeHandle** cannot be called for an environment handle until after all connection handles on that environment handle have been freed.

For more information about the environment handle, see "Environment Handles" in Chapter 4, "ODBC Fundamentals."

Declaring the Application's ODBC Version

Before an application allocates a connection, it must set the SQL_ATTR_ODBC_VERSION environment attribute. This attribute states that the application follows the ODBC 2.*x* or ODBC 3.0 specification when using the following items:

- **SQLSTATEs**. Many SQLSTATE values are different in ODBC 2.*x* and ODBC 3.0.
- **Date, Time, and Timestamp Type Identifiers**. The following table shows the type identifiers for date, time, and timestamp data in ODBC 2.*x* and ODBC 3.0.

ODBC 2.*x*	ODBC 3.0
SQL Type Identifiers	
SQL_DATE	SQL_TYPE_DATE
SQL_TIME	SQL_TYPE_TIME
SQL_TIMESTAMP	SQL_TYPE_TIMESTAMP
C Type Identifiers	
SQL_C_DATE	SQL_C_TYPE_DATE
SQL_C_TIME	SQL_C_TYPE_TIME
SQL_C_TIMESTAMP	SQL_C_TYPE_TIMESTAMP

- ***CatalogName* Argument in SQLTables**. In ODBC 2.*x*, the wild card characters ("%" and "_") in the *CatalogName* argument are treated literally. In ODBC 3.0, they are treated as wild cards. Thus, an application that follows the ODBC 2.*x* specification cannot use these as wild cards and does not escape them when using them as literals. An application that follows the ODBC 3.0 specification can use these as wild cards or escape them and use them as literals. For more information, see "Arguments in Catalog Functions" in Chapter 7, "Catalog Functions."

The ODBC 3.0 Driver Manager and ODBC 3.0 drivers check the version of the ODBC specification to which an application is written and respond accordingly. For example, if the application follows the ODBC 2.*x* specification and calls **SQLExecute** before calling **SQLPrepare**, the ODBC 3.0 Driver Manager returns SQLSTATE S1010 (Function sequence error). If the application follows the ODBC 3.0 specification, the Driver Manager returns SQLSTATE HY010 (Function sequence error). For more information, see "Backward Compatibility and Standards Compliance" in Chapter 17, "Programming Considerations."

Important Applications that follow the ODBC 3.0 specification must use conditional code to avoid using functionality new to ODBC 3.0 when working with ODBC 2.x drivers. ODBC 2.x drivers do not support functionality new to ODBC 3.0 just because the application declares that it follows the ODBC 3.0 specification. Furthermore, ODBC 3.0 drivers do not cease to support functionality new to ODBC 3.0 just because the application declares that it follows the ODBC 2.x specification.

Choosing a Data Source or Driver

The data source or driver used by an application is sometimes hard-coded in the application. For example, a custom application written by an MIS department to transfer data from one data source to another would contain the names of those data sources—the application simply would not work with any other data sources. Another example is a vertical application, such as one to do order entry. Such an application always uses the same data source, which has a predefined schema known by the application.

Other applications choose the data source or driver at run time. Usually, these are generic applications that do ad hoc queries, such as a spreadsheet that uses ODBC to import data. Such applications usually list the available data sources or drivers and let users choose the ones they want to work with. Whether a generic application lists data sources, drivers, or both often depends on whether the application uses DBMS- or file-based drivers.

DBMS-based drivers usually require a fairly complex set of connection information, such as the network address, network protocol, database name, and so on. The purpose of a data source is to hide all of this information. Hence, the data source paradigm lends itself to use with DBMS-based drivers. An application can display a list of data sources to the user in one of two ways. It can call **SQLDriverConnect** with the **DSN** (Data Source Name) keyword and no associated value; the Driver Manager will display a list of data source names. If the application wants control over the appearance of the list, it calls **SQLDataSources** to retrieve a list of available data sources and constructs its own dialog box. This function is implemented by the Driver Manager and can be called before any drivers are loaded. The application then calls a connection function and passes it the name of the chosen data source.

If a data source is not specified, the default data source indicated by the system information is used. (For more information, see "Default Subkey" in Chapter 19, "Configuring Data Sources.") If **SQLConnect** is called with a *ServerName* argument that cannot be found, is a null pointer, or is "DEFAULT", the Driver Manager connects to the default data source. The default data source is also used if the connection string used in a call to **SQLDriverConnect** does not contain the DSN keyword, the DSN keyword is set to "DEFAULT", or the data source is not found, or if the connection string used in a call to **SQLBrowseConnect** contains a DSN keyword set to "DEFAULT", or the data source is not found.

With file-based drivers, it is possible to use a file paradigm. For data stored on the local machine, users often know that their data is in a particular file, such as EMPLOYEE.DBF. Rather than choosing an unknown data source, it is easier for such users to choose the file they know. To implement this, the application first calls **SQLDrivers**. This function is implemented by the Driver Manager and can be called before any drivers are loaded. **SQLDrivers** returns a list of available drivers; it also returns values for the **FileUsage** and **FileExtns** keywords. The **FileUsage** keyword explains whether file-based drivers treat files as tables, such as Xbase, or databases, such as Microsoft Access. The **FileExtns** keyword lists the file extensions the driver recognizes, such as .dbf for an Xbase driver. Using this information, the application constructs a dialog box with which the user chooses a file. Based on the extension of the chosen file, the application then connects directly to the driver by calling **SQLDriverConnect** with the **DRIVER** keyword.

There is nothing to stop an application from using a data source with a file-based driver or calling **SQLDriverConnect** with the **DRIVER** keyword to connect directly to a DBMS-based driver. Several common uses of the **DRIVER** keyword for DBMS-based drivers are:

- **Not creating data sources.** For example, a custom application might use a particular driver and database. If the driver name and all information needed to connect to the database are hard-coded in the application, users do not need to create a data source on their computer to run the application—all they need to do is install the application and driver.

  A disadvantage of this method is that the application must be recompiled and redistributed if the connection information changes. If a data source name is hard-coded in the application instead of complete connection information, then each user only needs to change the information in the data source.

- **Accessing a particular DBMS a single time.** For example, a spreadsheet that retrieves data by calling ODBC functions might contain the **DRIVER** keyword to identify a particular driver. Because the driver name is meaningful to any users that have that driver, the spreadsheet could be passed among those users. If the spreadsheet contained a data source name, each user would have to create the same data source to use the spreadsheet.

- **Browsing the system for all databases accessible to a particular driver.** For more information, see "Connecting with SQLBrowseConnect," later in this chapter.

Allocating a Connection Handle

Before the application can connect to a data source or driver, it must allocate a connection handle. To do this:

1. The application declares a variable of type SQLHDBC. It then calls **SQLAllocHandle** and passes the address of this variable, the handle of the environment in which to allocate the connection, and the SQL_HANDLE_DBC option. For example:

   ```
   SQLHDBC hdbc1;

   SQLAllocHandle(SQL_HANDLE_DBC, henv1, &hdbc1);
   ```

2. The Driver Manager allocates a structure in which to store information about the statement and returns the connection handle in the variable.

The Driver Manager does not call **SQLAllocHandle** in the driver at this time, as it does not know which driver to call. It delays calling **SQLAllocHandle** in the driver until the application calls a function to connect to a data source. For more information, see "Driver Manager's Role in the Connection Process," later in this chapter.

It is important to note that allocating a connection handle is not the same as loading a driver. The driver is not loaded until a connection function is called. Thus, after allocating a connection handle and before connecting to the driver or data source, the only functions the application can call with the connection handle are **SQLSetConnectAttr**, **SQLGetConnectAttr**, or **SQLGetInfo** with the SQL_ODBC_VER option. Calling other functions with the connection handle, such as **SQLEndTran**, returns SQLSTATE 08003 (Connection not open). For complete details, see Appendix B, "ODBC State Transition Tables."

For more information about connection handles, see "Connection Handles" in Chapter 4, "ODBC Fundamentals."

Connection Attributes

Connection attributes are characteristics of the connection. For example, because transactions occur at the connection level, the transaction isolation level is a connection attribute. Similarly, the login timeout, or number of seconds to wait while trying to connect before timing out, is a connection attribute.

Connection attributes are set with **SQLSetConnectAttr** and their current settings retrieved with **SQLGetConnectAttr**. If **SQLSetConnectAttr** is called before the driver is loaded, the Driver Manager stores the attributes in its connection structure and sets them in the driver as part of the connection process. There is no requirement that an application set any connection attributes; all connection attributes have defaults, some of which are driver specific.

A connection attribute can be set before or after connection, or either, depending on the attribute and the driver. The login timeout (SQL_ATTR_LOGIN_TIMEOUT) applies to the connection process and is effective only if set before connecting. The attributes that specify whether to use the ODBC cursor library (SQL_ATTR_ODBC_CURSORS) and the network packet size (SQL_ATTR_PACKET_SIZE) must be set before connecting. The reason for this is that the ODBC cursor library resides between the Driver Manager and the driver and therefore must be loaded before the driver.

The attributes to specify whether a data source is read-only or read-write (SQL_ATTR_ACCESS_MODE) and the current catalog (SQL_ATTR_CURRENT_CATALOG) can be set before or after connecting, depending on the driver. However, interoperable applications set them before connecting because some drivers do not support changing these after connecting.

Some connection attributes have a default before the connection is made, while others do not. Those that do are SQL_ATTR_ACCESS_MODE, SQL_ATTR_AUTOCOMMIT, SQL_ATTR_LOGIN_TIMEOUT, SQL_ATTR_ODBC_CURSORS, SQL_ATTR_TRACE, and SQL_ATTR_TRACEFILE.

The translation connection attributes (SQL_ATTR_TRANSLATE_DLL and SQL_ATTR_TRANSLATE_OPTION) must be set after connecting.

All other connection attributes can be set at any time. For more information, see the **SQLSetConnectAttr** function description. (Connection attributes cannot be set on the environment level by a call to **SQLSetEnvAttr**.)

Establishing a Connection

After allocating environment and connection handles and setting any connection attributes, the application is ready to connect to the data source or driver. There are three different functions the application can use to do this: **SQLConnect** (Core interface conformance level), **SQLDriverConnect** (Core), and **SQLBrowseConnect** (Level 1). Each of the three is designed to be used in a different scenario. Before connecting, the application can determine which of these functions is supported with the **ConnectFunctions** keyword returned by **SQLDrivers**.

Note Some drivers limit the number of active connections they support. An application calls **SQLGetInfo** with the SQL_MAX_DRIVER_CONNECTIONS option to determine how many active connections a particular driver supports.

Default Data Source

The driver may select a data source, called the default data source, in certain cases where the application does not explicitly specify one:

- In a call to **SQLConnect** where the *ServerName* argument is a zero-length string, a null pointer, or DEFAULT.
- In a call to **SQLDriverConnect** where *InConnectionString* either specifies DSN=DEFAULT or specifies with the DSN keyword a data source that is not contained in the system information.

It is driver-defined how the default data source is specified. This may involve administrative action and may depend on the user.

Connecting with SQLConnect

SQLConnect is the simplest connection function. It requires a data source name and accepts an optional user ID and password. It works well for applications that hard-code a data source name and do not require a user ID or password. It also works well for applications that want to control their own "look and feel," or that have no user interface. Such applications can build a list of data sources using **SQLDataSources**; prompt the user for data source, user ID, and password; and then call **SQLConnect**.

Connection Strings

A connection string is a string that contains information used for establishing a connection. A complete connection string contains all the information needed to establish a connection. The connection string is a series of keyword/value pairs separated by semicolons. (For the complete syntax of a connection string, see the **SQLDriverConnect** function description.) The connection string is used by:

- **SQLDriverConnect**, which completes it by interaction with the user.
- **SQLBrowseConnect**, which completes it iteratively with the data source.

SQLConnect does not use a connection string; using **SQLConnect** is analogous to connecting using a connection string with exactly three keyword/value pairs (for data source name, and optionally user ID and password).

Connecting with SQLDriverConnect

SQLDriverConnect is used to connect to a data source using a connection string. **SQLDriverConnect** is used instead of **SQLConnect** for the following reasons:

- To let the application use driver-specific connection information.
- To request that the driver prompt the user for connection information.
- To connect without specifying a data source.

Driver-Specific Connection Information

SQLConnect assumes that a data source name, user ID, and password are sufficient to connect to a data source and that all other connection information can be stored on the system. This is often not the case. For example, a driver might need one user ID and password to log into a server and a different user ID and password to log into a DBMS. Because **SQLConnect** accepts a single user ID and password, this means that the other user ID and password must be stored with the data source information on the system if **SQLConnect** is to be used. This is a potential breach of security and should be avoided unless the password is encrypted.

SQLDriverConnect allows the driver to define an arbitrary amount of connection information in the keyword-value pairs of the connection string. For example, suppose a driver requires a data source name, a user ID and password for the server, and a user ID and password for the DBMS. A custom program that always uses the XYZ Corp data source might prompt the user for IDs and passwords and build the following set of keyword-value pairs, or *connection string*, to pass to **SQLDriverConnect**:

```
DSN=XYZ Corp;UID=Gomez;PWD=Sesame;UIDDBMS=JGomez;PWDDBMS=Shazam;
```

The **DSN** (Data Source Name) keyword names the data source, the **UID** and **PWD** keywords specify the user ID and password for the server, and the **UIDDBMS** and **PWDDBMS** keywords specify the user ID and password for the DBMS. Note that the final semicolon is optional. **SQLDriverConnect** parses this string; uses the XYZ Corp data source name to retrieve additional connection information from the system, such as the server address; and logs in to the server and DBMS using the specified user IDs and passwords.

Keyword-value pairs in **SQLDriverConnect** must follow certain syntax rules. The keywords and their values should not contain the []{}(),;?*=!@ characters. The value of the **DSN** keyword cannot consist only of blanks, and should not contain leading blanks. Because of the registry grammar, keywords and data source names cannot contain the backslash (\) character. Spaces are not allowed around the equal sign in the keyword-value pair.

The **FILEDSN** keyword can be used in a call to **SQLDriverConnect** to specify the name of a file containing data source information (see "Connecting Using File Data Sources" later in this section). The **SAVEFILE** keyword can be used to specify the name of a .dsn file in which the keyword-value pairs of a successful connection made by the call to **SQLDriverConnect** will be saved. For more information on file data sources, see the **SQLDriverConnect** function description.

Prompting the User for Connection Information

If the application uses **SQLConnect** and needs to prompt the user for any connection information, such as a user name and password, it must do so itself. While this allows the application to control its "look and feel," it might force the application to contain driver-specific code. This occurs when the application needs to prompt the user for driver-specific connection information. This presents an impossible situation for generic applications, which are designed to work with any and all drivers, including drivers that do not exist when the application is written.

SQLDriverConnect can prompt the user for connection information. For example, the custom program mentioned earlier could pass the following connection string to **SQLDriverConnect**:

```
DSN=XYZ Corp;
```

The driver might then display a dialog box similar to the following, which prompts for user IDs and passwords.

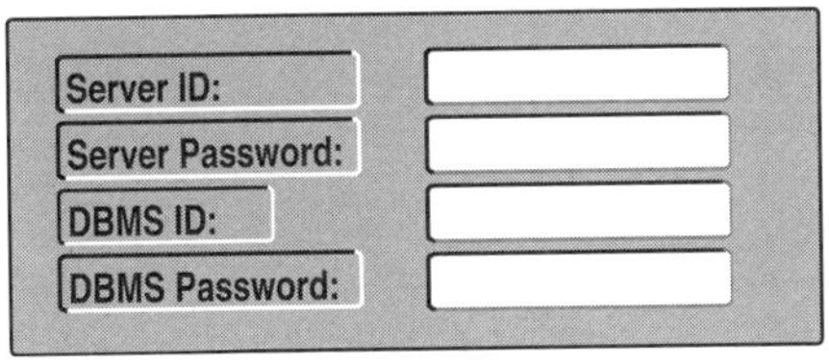

That the driver can prompt for connection information is particularly useful to generic and vertical applications. These applications should not contain driver-specific information, and having the driver prompt for the information it needs keeps that information out of the application. This is shown by the previous two examples. When the application passed only the data source name to the driver, the application did not contain any driver-specific information and was therefore not tied to a particular driver; when the application passed a complete connection string to the driver, it was tied to the driver that could interpret that string.

A generic application might take this one step further and not even specify a data source. When **SQLDriverConnect** receives an empty connection string, the Driver Manager displays the following dialog box.

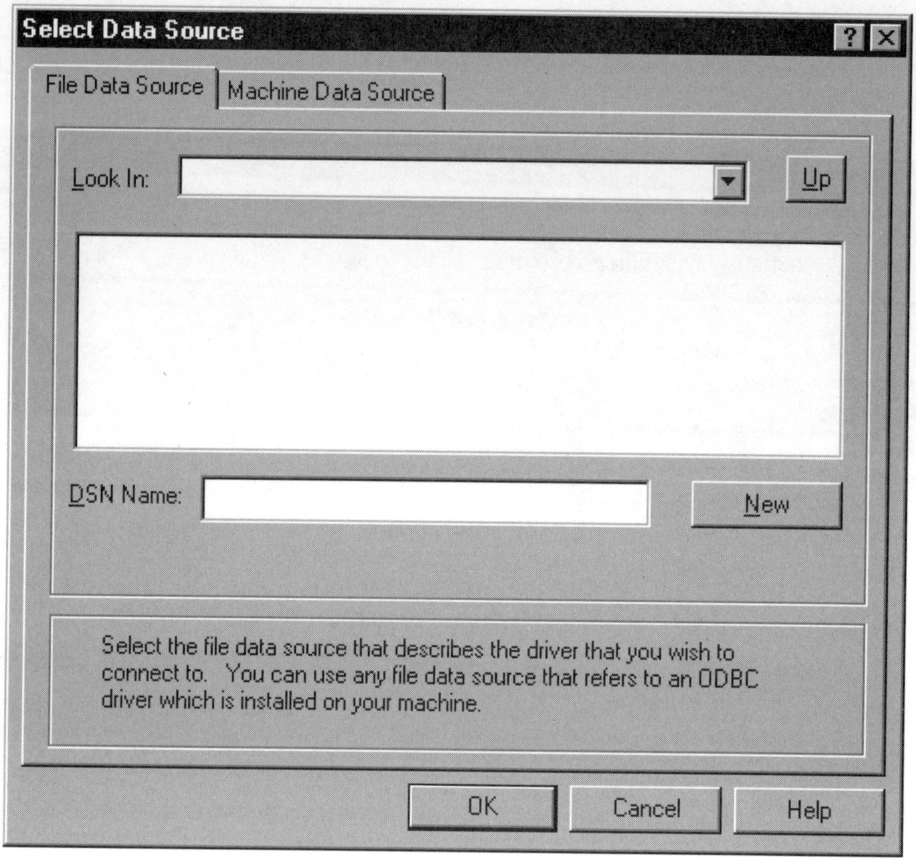

After the user selects a data source, the Driver Manager constructs a connection string specifying that data source and passes it to the driver. The driver can then prompt the user for any additional information it needs.

The conditions under which the driver prompts the user is controlled by the *DriverCompletion* flag; there are options to always prompt, prompt if necessary, or never prompt. For a complete description of this flag, see the **SQLDriverConnect** function description.

Connecting Using File Data Sources

The connection information for a *file data source* is stored in a .dsn file. As a result, the connection string can be used repeatedly by a single user or shared among several users if they have the appropriate driver installed. The file contains a driver name (or another data source name in the case of an unshareable file data source), and optionally, a connection string that can be used by **SQLDriverConnect**. The Driver Manager builds the connection string for the call to **SQLDriverConnect** from the keywords in the .dsn file.

A file data source allows an application to specify connection options without having to build a connection string for use with **SQLDriverConnect**. The file data source is usually created by specifying the **SAVEFILE** keyword, which causes the Driver Manager to save the output connection string created by a call to **SQLDriverConnect** to the .dsn file. That connection string can be used repeatedly by calling **SQLDriverConnect** with the **FILEDSN** keyword. This streamlines the connection process, and provides a persistent source of the connection string.

File data sources can also be created by calling **SQLCreateDataSource** in the installer DLL. Information can be written into the .dsn file by calling **SQLWriteFileDSN**, and read from the .dsn file by calling **SQLReadFileDSN**; both of these functions are also in the installer DLL. For information about the installer DLL, see Chapter 19, "Configuring Data Sources."

The keywords used for connection information are in the [ODBC] section of a .dsn file. The minimum information that a shareable .dsn file would have in the [ODBC] section is the DRIVER keyword:

```
DRIVER = SQL Server
```

The shareable .dsn file usually contains a connection string, as follows:

```
DRIVER = SQL Server
UID = Larry
DATABASE = MyDB
```

When the file data source is unshareable, the .dsn file contains only a **DSN** keyword. When the Driver Manager is sent the information in an unshareable file data source, it connects as necessary to the data source indicated by the **DSN** keyword. An unshareable .dsn file would contain the following keyword:

```
DSN = MyDataSource
```

The connection string used for a file data source is the union of the keywords specified in the .dsn file and the keywords specified in the connection string in the call to **SQLDriverConnect**. If any of the keywords in the .dsn file conflict with keywords in the connection string, the Driver Manager decides which keyword value should be used. For more information, see **SQLDriverConnect**.

Connecting Directly to Drivers

As was discussed in "Choosing a Data Source or Driver," earlier in this chapter, some applications do not want to use a data source at all. Instead, they want to connect directly to a driver. **SQLDriverConnect** provides a way for the application to connect directly to a driver without specifying a data source. Conceptually, a temporary data source is created at run time.

To connect directly to a driver, the application specifies the **DRIVER** keyword in the connection string instead of the **DSN** keyword. The value of the **DRIVER** keyword is the description of the driver as returned by **SQLDrivers**. For example, suppose a driver has the description Paradox Driver and requires the name of a directory containing the data files. To connect to this driver, the application might use either of the following connection strings:

```
DRIVER={Paradox Driver};Directory=C:\PARADOX;
DRIVER={Paradox Driver};
```

With the first string, the driver would not need any additional information. With the second string, the driver would need to prompt for the name of the directory containing the data files.

Connecting with SQLBrowseConnect

SQLBrowseConnect, like **SQLDriverConnect**, uses a connection string. However, by using **SQLBrowseConnect**, an application can construct a complete connection string at run time. This allows the application to do two things:

- Build its own dialog boxes to prompt for this information, thereby retaining control over its "look and feel."
- Browse the system for data sources that can be used by a particular driver, possibly in several steps. For example, the user might first browse the network for servers and, after choosing a server, browse the server for databases accessible by the driver.

The application calls **SQLBrowseConnect** and passes a connection string, known as the *browse request connection string*, that specifies a driver or data source. The driver returns a connection string, known as the *browse result connection string*, that contains keywords, possible values (if the keyword accepts a discrete set of values), and user-friendly names. The application builds a dialog box with the user-friendly names and prompts the user for values. It then builds a new browse request connection string from these values and returns this to the driver with another call to **SQLBrowseConnect**.

Because connection strings are passed back and forth, the driver can provide several levels of browsing by returning a new connection string when the application returns the old one. For example, the first time an application calls **SQLBrowseConnect**, the driver might return keywords to prompt the user for a server name. When the application returns the server name, the driver might return keywords to prompt the user for a database. The browsing process would be complete after the application returned the database name.

Each time **SQLBrowseConnect** returns a new browse result connection string, it returns SQL_NEED_DATA as its return code. This tells the application that the connection process is not complete. Until **SQLBrowseConnect** returns SQL_SUCCESS, the connection is in a Need Data state and cannot be used for other purposes, such as to set a connection attribute. The application can terminate the connection browsing process by calling **SQLDisconnect**.

SQL Server Browsing Example

The following example shows how **SQLBrowseConnect** might be used to browse the connections available with a driver for SQL Server. First, the application requests a connection handle:

```
SQLAllocHandle(SQL_HANDLE_DBC, henv, &hdbc);
```

Next, the application calls **SQLBrowseConnect** and specifies the SQL Server driver, using the driver description returned by **SQLDrivers**:

```
SQLBrowseConnect(hdbc, "DRIVER={SQL Server};", SQL_NTS, BrowseResult,
                 sizeof(BrowseResult), &BrowseResultLen);
```

Because this is the first call to **SQLBrowseConnect**, the Driver Manager loads the SQL Server driver and calls the driver's **SQLBrowseConnect** function with the same arguments it received from the application.

The driver determines that this is the first call to **SQLBrowseConnect** and returns the second level of connection attributes: server, user name, password, application name, and workstation ID. For the server attribute, it returns a list of valid server names. The return code from **SQLBrowseConnect** is SQL_NEED_DATA. The browse result string is:

```
"SERVER:Server={red,blue,green,yellow};UID:Login ID=?;PWD:Password=?;
➥ *APP:AppName=?;*WSID:WorkStation ID=?;"
```

Each keyword in the browse result string is followed by a colon and one or more words before the equal sign. These words are the user-friendly name that an application can use to build a dialog box. The **APP** and **WSID** keywords are prefixed by an asterisk, which means they are optional. The **SERVER**, **UID**, and **PWD** keywords are not prefixed by an asterisk; values must be supplied for them in the next browse request string. The value for the **SERVER** keyword may be one of the servers returned by **SQLBrowseConnect** or a user-supplied name.

The application calls **SQLBrowseConnect** again, specifying the green server and omitting the **APP** and **WSID** keywords and the user-friendly names after each keyword:

```
SQLBrowseConnect(hdbc, "SERVER=green;UID=Smith;PWD=Sesame;", SQL_NTS,
                 BrowseResult, sizeof(BrowseResult), &BrowseResultLen);
```

The driver attempts to connect to the green server. If there are any nonfatal errors, such as a missing keyword-value pair, **SQLBrowseConnect** returns SQL_NEED_DATA and remains in the same state as it was prior to the error. The application can call **SQLGetDiagField** or **SQLGetDiagRec** to determine the error. If the connection is successful, the driver returns SQL_NEED_DATA and returns the browse result string:

```
"*DATABASE:Database={master,model,pubs,tempdb};
➥ *LANGUAGE:Language={us_english,Français};"
```

Because the attributes in this string are optional, the application can omit them. However, the application must call **SQLBrowseConnect** again. If the application chooses to omit the database name and language, it specifies an empty browse request string. In this example, the application chooses the pubs database and calls **SQLBrowseConnect** a final time, omitting the **LANGUAGE** keyword and the asterisk before the **DATABASE** keyword:

```
SQLBrowseConnect(hdbc, "DATABASE=pubs;", SQL_NTS, BrowseResult,
                 sizeof(BrowseResult), &BrowseResultLen);
```

Because the **DATABASE** attribute is the final connection attribute required by the driver, the browsing process is complete, the application is connected to the data source, and **SQLBrowseConnect** returns SQL_SUCCESS. **SQLBrowseConnect** also returns the complete connection string as the browse result string:

```
"DSN=MySQLServer;SERVER=green;UID=Smith;PWD=Sesame;DATABASE=pubs;"
```

The final connection string returned by the driver does not contain the user-friendly names after each keyword, nor does it contain optional keywords not specified by the application. The application can use this string with **SQLDriverConnect** to reconnect to the data source on the current connection handle (after disconnecting) or to connect to the data source on a different connection handle. For example:

```
SQLDriverConnect(hdbc, hwnd, BrowseResult, SQL_NTS, ConnStrOut,
                 sizeof(ConnStrOut), &ConnStrOutLen, SQL_DRIVER_NOPROMPT);
```

Connection Pooling

Connection pooling enables an application to use a connection from a pool of connections that do not need to be reestablished for each use. Once a connection has been created and placed in a pool, an application can reuse that connection without performing the complete connection process.

Using a pooled connection can result in significant performance gains, because applications can save the overhead involved in making a connection. This can be particularly significant for middle-tier applications that connect over a network, or for applications that repeatedly connect and disconnect, such as Internet applications.

In addition to performance gains, the connection pooling architecture enables an environment and its associated connections to be used by multiple components in a single process. This means that standalone components in the same process can interact with each other without being aware of each other. A connection in a connection pool can be used repeatedly by multiple components.

Note Connection pooling can be used by an ODBC application exhibiting ODBC 2.*x* behavior, as long as the application can call **SQLSetEnvAttr**. When using connection pooling, the application must not execute SQL statements that change the database or the context of the database, such as changing the <database name>, which changes the catalog used by a data source.

The connection pool is maintained by the Driver Manager. Connections are drawn from the pool when the application calls **SQLConnect** or **SQLDriverConnect**, and are returned to the pool when the application calls **SQLDisconnect**. The size of the pool grows dynamically based upon the requested resource allocations. It shrinks based on the inactivity timeout: If a connection is inactive for a period of time (it has not been used in a connection), it is removed from the pool. The size of the pool is limited only by memory constraints and limits on the server.

The Driver Manager determines whether a specific connection in a pool should be used according to the arguments passed in **SQLConnect** or **SQLDriverConnect**, and the connection attributes set after the connection was allocated.

To use a connection pool, an application performs the following steps:

1. Enables connection pooling by calling **SQLSetEnvAttr** to set the SQL_ATTR_CONNECTION_POOLING environment attribute to SQL_CP_ONE_PER_DRIVER or SQL_CP_ONE_PER_HENV. This call must be made before the application allocates the shared environment for which connection pooling is to be enabled. The environment handle in the call to **SQLSetEnvAttr** should be set to null, which makes SQL_ATTR_CONNECTION_POOLING a process-level attribute. If the attribute is set to SQL_CP_ONE_PER_DRIVER, a single connection pool is supported for each driver. If an application works with many drivers and few environments, this may be more efficient because fewer comparisons may be required. If set to SQL_CP_ONE_PER_HENV, a single connection pool is supported for each environment. If an application works with many environments and few drivers, this may be more efficient because fewer comparisons may be required. Connection pooling is disabled by setting SQL_ATTR_CONNECTION_POOLING to SQL_CP_OFF.
2. Allocates an environment by calling **SQLAllocHandle** with the *HandleType* argument set to SQL_HANDLE_ENV. The environment allocated by this call will be an implicit shared environment because connection pooling has been enabled. The environment to be used is not determined, however, until **SQLAllocHandle** with a *HandleType* of SQL_HANDLE_DBC is called on this environment.
3. Allocates a connection by calling **SQLAllocHandle** with *InputHandle* set to SQL_HANDLE_DBC, and the *InputHandle* set to the environment handle allocated for connection pooling. The Driver Manager attempts to find an existing environment that matches the environment attributes set by the application. If no such environment exists, one is created, with a reference count (maintained by the Driver Manager) of 1. If a matching shared environment is found, the environment is returned to the application, and its reference count is incremented.

   The actual connection to be used is not determined by the Driver Manager until **SQLConnect** or **SQLDriverConnect** is called.

4. Calls **SQLConnect** or **SQLDriverConnect** to make the connection. The Driver Manager uses the connection options in the call to **SQLConnect** (or the connection keywords in the call to **SQLDriverConnect**) and the connection attributes set after connection allocation to determine which connection in the pool should be used.

   Note How a requested connection is matched to a pooled connection is determined by the SQL_ATTR_CP_MATCH environment attribute. For more information, see **SQLSetEnvAttr**.

5. Calls **SQLDisconnect** when done with the connection. The connection is returned to the connection pool, and is available for reuse.

Disconnecting from a Data Source or Driver

When an application has finished using a data source, it calls **SQLDisconnect**. **SQLDisconnect** frees any statements that are allocated on the connection and disconnects the driver from the data source. It returns an error if a transaction is in process.

After disconnecting, the application can call **SQLFreeHandle** to free the connection. After freeing the connection, it is an application programming error to use the connection's handle in a call to an ODBC function; doing so has undefined but probably fatal consequences. When **SQLFreeHandle** is called, the driver releases the structure used to store information about the connection.

The application can also reuse the connection, either to connect to a different data source or reconnect to the same data source. The decision to remain connected, as opposed to disconnecting and reconnecting later, requires that the application writer consider the relative costs of each option; both connecting to a data source and remaining connected can be relatively costly depending on the connection medium. In making a correct tradeoff, the application must also make assumptions about the likelihood and timing of further operations on the same data source.

Driver Manager's Role in the Connection Process

Remember that applications do not call driver functions directly. Instead, they call Driver Manager functions with the same name and the Driver Manager calls the driver functions. Usually, this happens almost immediately. For example, the application calls **SQLExecute** in the Driver Manager and after a few error checks, the Driver Manager calls **SQLExecute** in the driver.

The connection process is different. When the application calls **SQLAllocHandle** with the SQL_HANDLE_ENV and SQL_HANDLE_DBC options, the function allocates handles only in the Driver Manager. The Driver Manager does not call this function in the driver, because it does not know which driver to call. Similarly, if the application passes the handle of an unconnected connection to **SQLSetConnectAttr** or **SQLGetConnectAttr**, only the Driver Manager executes the function. It stores or gets the attribute value from its connection handle and returns SQLSTATE 08003 (Connection not open) when getting a value for an attribute that has not been set and for which ODBC does not define a default value.

When the application calls **SQLConnect**, **SQLDriverConnect**, or **SQLBrowseConnect**, the Driver Manager first determines which driver to use. It then checks whether a driver is currently loaded on the connection:

- If no driver is loaded on the connection, the Driver Manager checks whether the specified driver is loaded on another connection in the same environment. If not, the Driver Manager loads the driver on the connection and calls **SQLAllocHandle** in the driver with the SQL_HANDLE_ENV option.

  The Driver Manager then calls **SQLAllocHandle** in the driver with the SQL_HANDLE_DBC option, regardless of whether it was just loaded. If the application set any connection attributes, the Driver Manager calls **SQLSetConnectAttr** in the driver; if an error occurs, the Driver Manager's connection function returns SQLSTATE IM006 (Driver's **SQLSetConnectAttr** failed). Finally, the Driver Manager calls the connection function in the driver.
- If the specified driver is loaded on the connection, the Driver Manager only calls the connection function in the driver. In this case, the driver must make sure that all connection attributes on the connection maintain their current settings.
- If a different driver is loaded on the connection, the Driver Manager calls **SQLFreeHandle** in the driver to free the connection. If there are no other connections that use the driver, the Driver Manager calls **SQLFreeHandle** in the driver to free the environment and unloads the driver. The Driver Manager then performs the same operations as when a driver is not loaded on the connection.

When the application calls **SQLDisconnect**, the Driver Manager calls **SQLDisconnect** in the driver. However, it leaves the driver loaded in case the application reconnects to the driver. When the application calls **SQLFreeHandle** with the SQL_HANDLE_DBC option, the Driver Manager calls **SQLFreeHandle** in the driver. If the driver is not used by any other connections, the Driver Manager then calls **SQLFreeHandle** in the driver with the SQL_HANDLE_ENV option and unloads the driver.

C H A P T E R 7

Catalog Functions

All databases have a structure that outlines how data will be stored in the database. For example, a simple sales order database might have the structure shown in Figure 7.1, in which the ID columns are used to link the tables.

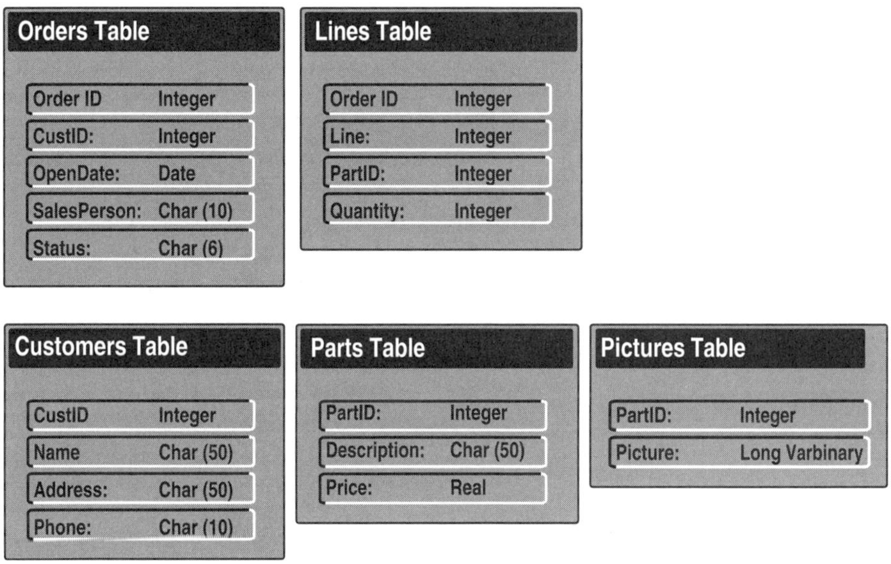

Figure 7.1 Sales order database structure

This structure, along with other information such as privileges, is stored in a set of system tables called the database's *catalog*, which is also known as a *data dictionary*.

An application can discover this structure through calls to the *catalog functions*. The catalog functions return information in result sets and are usually implemented through **SELECT** statements against the tables in the catalog. For example, an application might request a result set containing information about all the tables on the system or all the columns in a particular table.

Uses of Catalog Data

Applications use catalog data in a variety of ways. Some common uses are:

- **Constructing SQL statements at run time.** Vertical applications, such as an order entry application, contain hard-coded SQL statements. The tables and columns that are used by the application are fixed ahead of time, as are the statements that access these tables. For example, an order entry application usually contains a single, parameterized **INSERT** statement for adding new orders to the system.

  Generic applications, such as a spreadsheet program that uses ODBC to retrieve data, often construct SQL statements at run time based on input from the user. Such an application could require the user to type the names of the tables and columns to use. However, it would be easier for the user if the application displayed lists of tables and columns from which the user could make selections. To build these lists, the application would call the **SQLTables** and **SQLColumns** catalog functions.

- **Constructing SQL statements during development.** Application development environments typically allow the programmer to create database queries while developing a program. The queries are then hard-coded in the application being built.

  Such environments could also use **SQLTables** and **SQLColumns** to create lists from which the programmer could make selections. They might also use **SQLPrimaryKeys** and **SQLForeignKeys** to automatically determine and show relationships between selected tables, and use **SQLStatistics** to determine and highlight indexed fields so the programmer can create efficient queries.

- **Constructing cursors.** An application, driver, or middleware that provides a scrollable cursor engine could use **SQLSpecialColumns** to determine which column or columns uniquely identify a row. The program could build a *keyset* containing the values of these columns for each row that has been fetched. When the application scrolls back to the row, it would then use these values to fetch the most recent data for the row. For more information about scrollable cursors and keysets, see "Scrollable Cursors" in Chapter 11, "Retrieving Results (Advanced)."

Catalog Functions in ODBC

ODBC contains the following catalog functions:

Function	Description
SQLTables	Returns a list of catalogs, schemas, tables, or table types in the data source.
SQLColumns	Returns a list of columns in one or more tables.
SQLStatistics	Returns a list of statistics about a single table. Also returns a list of indexes associated with that table.
SQLSpecialColumns	Returns a list of columns that uniquely identifies a row in a single table. Also returns a list of columns in that table that are automatically updated.
SQLPrimaryKeys	Returns a list of columns that compose the primary key of a single table.
SQLForeignKeys	Returns a list of foreign keys in a single table or a list of foreign keys in other tables that refer to a single table.
SQLTablePrivileges	Returns a list of privileges associated with one or more tables.
SQLColumnPrivileges	Returns a list of privileges associated with one or more columns in a single table.
SQLProcedures	Returns a list of procedures in the data source.
SQLProcedureColumns	Returns a list of input and output parameters, the return value, and the columns in the result set of a single procedure.
SQLGetTypeInfo	Returns a list of the SQL data types supported by the data source. These data types are generally used in **CREATE TABLE** and **ALTER TABLE** statements.

Because **SQLTables**, **SQLColumns**, **SQLStatistics**, and **SQLSpecialColumns** conform to the X/Open CLI, and **SQLGetTypeInfo** conforms to the ISO 92 CLI, they are implemented by most drivers. The remaining catalog functions are in the ODBC conformance level.

Data Returned by Catalog Functions

Each catalog function returns data as a result set. This result set is no different from any other result set. It is usually generated by a predefined, parameterized **SELECT** statement that is hard-coded in the driver or stored in a procedure in the data source. For information on how to retrieve data from a result set, see "Was a Result Set Created?" in Chapter 10, "Retrieving Results (Basic)."

The result set for each catalog function is described in the reference entry for that function. In addition to the listed columns, the result set can contain driver-specific columns after the last predefined column. These columns (if any) are described in the driver documentation.

Applications should bind driver-specific columns relative to the end of the result set. That is, they should calculate the number of a driver-specific column as the number of the last column—retrieved with **SQLNumResultCols**—less the number of columns that occur after the required column. This saves having to change the application when new columns are added to the result set in future versions of ODBC or the driver. Note that for this scheme to work, drivers must add new driver-specific columns before old driver-specific columns so that column numbers do not change relative to the end of the result set.

Identifiers that are returned in the result set are not quoted, even if they contain special characters. For example, suppose the identifier quote character (which is driver-specific and returned through **SQLGetInfo**) is a double quotation mark (") and the Accounts Payable table contains a column named Customer Name. In the row returned by **SQLColumns** for this column, the value of the TABLE_NAME column is Accounts Payable, not "Accounts Payable", and the value of the COLUMN_NAME column is Customer Name, not "Customer Name". To retrieve the names of customers in the Accounts Payable table, the application would quote these names:

```
SELECT "Customer Name" FROM "Accounts Payable"
```

For more information, see "Quoted Identifiers" in Chapter 8, "SQL Statements."

The catalog functions are based upon an SQL-like authorization model in which a connection is made based upon a username and password, and only data for which the user has a privilege is returned. Password protection of individual files, which does not fit into this model, is driver-defined.

The result sets returned by the catalog functions are almost never updatable and applications should not expect to be able to change the structure of the database by changing the data in these result sets.

Arguments in Catalog Functions

All catalog functions accept arguments with which an application can restrict the scope of the data returned. For example, the first and second calls to **SQLTables** in the following code return a result set containing information about all tables, while the third call returns information about the Orders table:

```
SQLTables(hstmt1, NULL, 0, NULL, 0, NULL, 0, NULL, 0);
SQLTables(hstmt2, NULL, 0, NULL, 0, "%", SQL_NTS, NULL, 0);
SQLTables(hstmt3, NULL, 0, NULL, 0, "Orders", SQL_NTS, NULL, 0);
```

Catalog function string arguments fall into four different types: ordinary arguments (OA), pattern value arguments (PV), identifier arguments (ID), and value list arguments (VL). Most string arguments can be of one of two different types, depending on the value of the SQL_ATTR_METADATA_ID statement attribute. The following table lists the arguments for each catalog function, and describes the type of the argument for a SQL_TRUE or SQL_FALSE value of SQL_ATTR_METADATA_ID.

Function	Argument	Type when QL_ ATTR_METADATA_ ID = SQL_FALSE	Type when SQL_ ATTR_METADATA_ ID = SQL_TRUE
SQLColumnPrivileges	*CatalogName*	OA	ID
	SchemaName	OA	ID
	TableName	OA	ID
	ColumnName	PV	ID
SQLColumns	*CatalogName*	OA	ID
	SchemaName	PV	ID
	TableName	PV	ID
	ColumnName	PV	ID
SQLForeignKeys	*PKCatalogName*	OA	ID
	PKSchemaName	OA	ID
	PKTableName	OA	ID
	FKCatalogName	OA	ID
	FKSchemaName	OA	ID
	FKTableName	OA	ID
SQLPrimaryKeys	*CatalogName*	OA	ID
	SchemaName	OA	ID
	TableName	OA	ID
SQLProcedureColumns	*CatalogName*	OA	ID
	SchemaName	PV	ID
	ProcName	PV	ID
	ColumnName	PV	ID
SQLProcedures	*CatalogName*	OA	ID
	SchemaName	PV	ID
	ProcName	PV	ID
SQLSpecialColumns	*CatalogName*	OA	ID
	SchemaName	OA	ID
	TableName	OA	ID
SQLStatistics	*CatalogName*	OA	ID
	SchemaName	OA	ID
	TableName	OA	ID
SQLTablePrivileges	*CatalogName*	OA	ID
	SchemaName	PV	ID
	TableName	PV	ID
SQLTables	*CatalogName*	PV	ID
	SchemaName	PV	ID
	TableName	PV	ID
	TableType	VL	VL

Ordinary Arguments

When a catalog function string argument is an ordinary argument, it is treated as a literal string. An ordinary argument accepts neither a string search pattern, nor a list of values. The case of an ordinary argument is significant, and quote characters in the string are taken literally. These arguments are treated as ordinary arguments if the SQL_ATTR_METADATA_ID statement attribute is set to SQL_FALSE; they are treated as identifier arguments instead if this attribute is set to SQL_TRUE.

If an ordinary argument is set to a null pointer and the argument is a required argument, the function returns SQL_ERROR and SQLSTATE HY009 (Invalid use of null pointer). If an ordinary argument is set to a null pointer and the argument is not a required argument, the argument's behavior is driver-dependent. The following arguments are required arguments:

Function	Required arguments
SQLColumnPrivileges	*TableName*
SQLForeignKeys	*PKTableName*, *FKTableName*
SQLPrimaryKeys	*TableName*
SQLSpecialColumns	*TableName*
SQLStatistics	*TableName*

Pattern Value Arguments

Some arguments in the catalog functions, such as the *TableName* argument in **SQLTables**, accept search patterns. These arguments accept search patterns if the SQL_ATTR_METADATA_ID statement attribute is set to SQL_FALSE; they are identifier arguments that do not accept a search pattern if this attribute is set to SQL_TRUE.

The search pattern characters are:

- An underscore (_), which represents any single character.
- A percent sign (%), which represents any sequence of zero or more characters.
- An escape character, which is driver-specific and is used to include underscores, percent signs, and the escape character as literals.

The escape character is retrieved with the SQL_SEARCH_PATTERN_ESCAPE option in **SQLGetInfo**. It must precede any underscore, percent sign, or escape character in an argument that accepts search patterns to include that character as a literal. For example:

Search pattern	Description
%A%	All identifiers containing the letter A
ABC_	All four character identifiers starting with ABC
ABC_	The identifier ABC_, assuming the escape character is a backslash (\)
\\%	All identifiers starting with a backslash (\), assuming the escape character is a backslash

Special care must be taken to escape search pattern characters in arguments that accept search patterns. This is particularly true for the underscore character, which is commonly used in identifiers. A common mistake in applications is to retrieve a value from one catalog function and pass that value to a search pattern argument in another catalog function. For example, suppose an application retrieves the table name MY_TABLE from the result set for **SQLTables** and passes this to **SQLColumns** to retrieve a list of columns in MY_TABLE. Instead of getting the columns for MY_TABLE, the application will get the columns for all the tables that match the search pattern MY_TABLE, such as MY_TABLE, MY1TABLE, MY2TABLE, and so on.

Note ODBC 2.*x* drivers do not support search patterns in the *CatalogName* argument in **SQLTables**. ODBC 3.0 drivers accept search patterns in this argument if the SQL_ATTR_ODBC_VERSION environment attribute is set to SQL_OV_ODBC3; they do not accept search patterns in this argument if it is set to SQL_OV_ODBC2.

Passing a null pointer to a search pattern argument does not constrain the search for that argument; that is, a null pointer and the search pattern % (any characters) are equivalent. However, a zero-length search pattern—that is, a valid pointer to a string of length zero—matches only the empty string ("").

Identifier Arguments

If a string in an identifier argument is quoted, the driver removes leading and trailing blanks, and treats the string within the quotation marks literally. If the string is not quoted, the driver removes trailing blanks, and folds the string to uppercase. Setting an identifier argument to a null pointer returns SQL_ERROR and SQLSTATE HY009 (Invalid use of null pointer), unless the argument is a catalog name and catalogs are not supported.

These arguments are treated as identifier arguments if the SQL_ATTR_METADATA_ID statement attribute is set to SQL_TRUE. In this case, the underscore (_) and the percent sign (%) will be treated as the actual character, not as a search pattern character. These arguments are treated as either an ordinary argument or a pattern argument, depending on the argument, if this attribute is set to SQL_FALSE.

Although identifiers containing special characters must be quoted in SQL statements, they must not be quoted when passed as catalog function arguments, because quote characters passed to catalog functions are interpreted literally. For example, suppose the identifier quote character (which is driver-specific and returned through **SQLGetInfo**) is a double quotation mark ("). The first call to **SQLTables** returns a result set containing information about the Accounts Payable table, while the second call returns information about the "Accounts Payable" table, which is probably not what was intended.

```
SQLTables(hstmt1, NULL, 0, NULL, 0, "Accounts Payable", SQL_NTS, NULL, 0);
SQLTables(hstmt2, NULL, 0, NULL, 0, "\"Accounts Payable\"", SQL_NTS, NULL, 0);
```

Quoted identifiers are used to distinguish a true column name from a pseudo-column of the same name, such as ROWID in Oracle. If "ROWID" is passed in an argument of a catalog function, the function will work with the ROWID pseudo-column if it exists. If the pseudo-column does not exist, the function will work with the "ROWID" column. If ROWID is passed in an argument of a catalog function, the function will work with the ROWID column.

For more information about quoted identifiers, see "Quoted Identifiers" in Chapter 8, "SQL Statements."

Value List Arguments

A value list argument consists of a list of comma-separated values to be used for matching. There is only one value list argument in the ODBC catalog functions: the *TableType* argument in **SQLTables**. Setting *TableType* to a null pointer is the same as if it is set to SQL_ALL_TABLE_TYPES, which enumerates all possible members of the value list. This argument is not affected by the SQL_ATTR_METADATA_ID statement attribute. For more information, see the **SQLTables** function description.

Schema Views

An application can retrieve metadata information from the DBMS either by calling ODBC catalog functions or by using INFORMATION_SCHEMA views. The views are defined by the ANSI SQL-92 standard.

If supported by the DBMS and the driver, the INFORMATION_SCHEMA views provide a more powerful and comprehensive means of retrieving metadata than the ODBC catalog functions provide. An application can execute its own custom **SELECT** statement against one of these views, can join views, or can perform a union on views. While offering greater utility and a wider range of metadata, INFORMATION_SCHEMA views are often not supported by the DBMS. This may change as more DBMSs and drivers achieve compliance with SQL-92.

To determine which views are supported, an application calls **SQLGetInfo** with the SQL_INFO_SCHEMA_VIEWS option. To retrieve metadata from a supported view, the application executes a **SELECT** statement that specifies the schema information required.

CHAPTER 8

SQL Statements

ODBC applications perform almost all of their database access by executing SQL statements. The form of these statements—hard-coded or constructed at run time, interoperable or data source–specific, and so on—depends on the needs of the application.

Constructing SQL Statements

SQL statements can be constructed in one of three ways: hard-coded during development, constructed at run time, or entered directly by the user.

Hard-Coded SQL Statements

Applications that perform a fixed task usually contain hard-coded SQL statements. For example, an order entry system might use the following call to list open sales orders:

```
SQLExecDirect(hstmt, "SELECT OrderID FROM Orders WHERE Status = 'OPEN'", SQL_NTS);
```

There are several advantages to hard-coded SQL statements: they can be tested when the application is written, they are simpler to implement than statements constructed at run time, and they simplify the application.

Using statement parameters and preparing statements provide even better ways to use hard-coded SQL statements. For example, suppose the Parts table contains the PartID, Description, and Price columns. One way to insert a new row into this table would be to construct and execute an **INSERT** statement:

```
#define DESC_LEN 51
#define STATEMENT_LEN 51

SQLUINTEGER PartID;
SQLCHAR     Desc[DESC_LEN], Statement[STATEMENT_LEN];
SQLREAL     Price;
```

```
// Set part ID, description, and price.
GetNewValues(&PartID, Desc, &Price);

// Build INSERT statement.
sprintf(Statement, "INSERT INTO Parts (PartID, Description, Price) "
        "VALUES (%d, '%s', %f)", PartID, Desc, Price);

// Execute the statement.
SQLExecDirect(hstmt, Statement, SQL_NTS);
```

An even better way is to use a hard-coded, parameterized statement. This has two advantages over a statement with hard-coded data values. First, it is easier to construct a parameterized statement because the data values can be sent in their native types, such as integers and floating point numbers, rather than converting them to strings. Second, such a statement can be easily used more than once by just changing the parameter values and reexecuting it; there is no need to rebuild it.

```
#define DESC_LEN 51

SQLCHAR *   Statement = "INSERT INTO Parts (PartID, Description, Price) "
                        "VALUES (?, ?, ?)";
SQLUINTEGER PartID;
SQLCHAR     Desc[DESC_LEN];
SQLREAL     Price;
SQLINTEGER  PartIDInd = 0, DescLenOrInd = SQL_NTS, PriceInd = 0;

// Bind the parameters.
SQLBindParameter(hstmt, 1, SQL_PARAM_INPUT, SQL_C_ULONG, SQL_INTEGER, 5, 0,
                 &PartID, 0, &PartIDInd);
SQLBindParameter(hstmt, 2, SQL_PARAM_INPUT, SQL_C_CHAR, SQL_CHAR, DESC_LEN - 1, 0,
                 Desc, sizeof(Desc), &DescLenOrInd);
SQLBindParameter(hstmt, 3, SQL_PARAM_INPUT, SQL_C_FLOAT, SQL_REAL, 7, 0,
                 &Price, 0, &PriceInd);

// Set part ID, description, and price.
GetNewValues(&PartID, Desc, &Price);

// Execute the statement
SQLExecDirect(hstmt, Statement, SQL_NTS);
```

Assuming this statement is to be executed more than once, it can be prepared for even greater efficiency:

```
#define DESC_LEN 51

SQLCHAR *Statement = "INSERT INTO Parts (PartID, Description, Price) "
                     "VALUES (?, ?, ?)";
SQLUINTEGER PartID;
SQLCHAR     Desc[DESC_LEN];
SQLREAL     Price;
SQLINTEGER  PartIDInd = 0, DescLenOrInd = SQL_NTS, PriceInd = 0;
```

```
// Prepare the INSERT statement.
SQLPrepare(hstmt, Statement, SQL_NTS);

// Bind the parameters.
SQLBindParameter(hstmt, 1, SQL_PARAM_INPUT, SQL_C_ULONG, SQL_INTEGER, 5, 0,
                 &PartID, 0, &PartIDInd);
SQLBindParameter(hstmt, 2, SQL_PARAM_INPUT, SQL_C_CHAR, SQL_CHAR, DESC_LEN - 1, 0,
                 Desc, sizeof(Desc), &DescLenOrInd);
SQLBindParameter(hstmt, 3, SQL_PARAM_INPUT, SQL_C_FLOAT, SQL_REAL, 7, 0,
                 &Price, 0, &PriceInd);

// Loop to continually get new values and insert them.
while (GetNewValues(&PartID, Desc, &Price))
   SQLExecute(hstmt);
```

Perhaps the most efficient way to use the statement is to construct a procedure containing the statement, as shown in the following code example. Because the procedure is constructed at development time and stored on the data source, it does not need to be prepared at run time. A drawback of this method is that the syntax for creating procedures is DBMS-specific and procedures must be constructed separately for each DBMS on which the application is to run.

```
#define DESC_LEN 51

SQLUINTEGER PartID;
SQLCHAR     Desc[DESC_LEN];
SQLREAL     Price;
SQLINTEGER  PartIDInd = 0, DescLenOrInd = SQL_NTS, PriceInd = 0;

// Bind the parameters.
SQLBindParameter(hstmt, 1, SQL_PARAM_INPUT, SQL_C_ULONG, SQL_INTEGER, 5, 0,
                 &PartID, 0, &PartIDInd);
SQLBindParameter(hstmt, 2, SQL_PARAM_INPUT, SQL_C_CHAR, SQL_CHAR, DESC_LEN - 1, 0,
                 Desc, sizeof(Desc), &DescLenOrInd);
SQLBindParameter(hstmt, 3, SQL_PARAM_INPUT, SQL_C_FLOAT, SQL_REAL, 7, 0,
                 &Price, 0, &PriceInd);

// Loop to continually get new values and insert them.
while (GetNewValues(&PartID, Desc, &Price))
   SQLExecDirect(hstmt, "{call InsertPart(?, ?, ?)}", SQL_NTS);
```

For more information on parameters, prepared statements, and procedures, see “Executing a Statement” in Chapter 9, “Executing Statements.”

SQL Statements Constructed at Run Time

Applications that perform ad hoc analysis commonly build SQL statements at run time. For example, a spreadsheet might allow a user to select columns from which to retrieve data:

```
SQLCHAR     *Statement, *TableName;
SQLCHAR     **TableNamesArray, **ColumnNamesArray;
BOOL        *ColumnSelectedArray;
BOOL        CommaNeeded;
SQLSMALLINT i, NumColumns;

// Use SQLTables to build a list of tables (TableNamesArray[]). Let the user select a
// table and store the selected table in TableName.

// Use SQLColumns to build a list of the columns in the selected table
// (ColumnNamesArray). Set NumColumns to the number of columns in the table. Let the
// user select one or more columns and flag these columns in ColumnSelectedArray[].

// Build a SELECT statement from the selected columns.
CommaNeeded = FALSE;
strcpy(Statement, "SELECT ");
for (i = 0; i = NumColumns; i++) {
   if (ColumnSelectedArray[i]) {
      if (CommaNeeded)
        strcat(Statement, ",");
      else
        CommaNeeded = TRUE;
      strcat(Statement, ColumnNamesArray[i]);
   }
}

strcat(Statement, " FROM ");
strcat(Statement, TableName);

// Execute the statement directly. Because it will only be executed once, do not
// prepare it.
SQLExecDirect(hstmt, Statement, SQL_NTS);
```

Another class of applications that commonly constructs SQL statements at run time are application development environments. However, the statements they construct are hard-coded in the application they are building, where they can usually be optimized and tested.

Applications that construct SQL statements at run time can provide tremendous flexibility to the user. As can be seen from the preceding example, which did not even support such common operations as **WHERE** clauses, **ORDER BY** clauses, or joins, constructing SQL statements at run time is vastly more complex than hard-coding statements. Furthermore, testing such applications is problematic, as they can construct an arbitrary number of SQL statements.

A potential disadvantage of constructing SQL statements at run time is that it takes far more time to construct a statement than use a hard-coded statement. Fortunately, this is rarely a concern. Such applications tend to be very user interface intensive and the time the application spends constructing SQL statements is generally small compared to the time the user spends entering criteria.

SQL Statements Entered by the User

Applications that perform ad hoc analysis also commonly allow the user to enter SQL statements directly. For example:

```
SQLCHAR     *Statement, SqlState[6], Msg[SQL_MAX_MESSAGE_LENGTH];
SQLSMALLINT i, MsgLen;
SQLINTEGER NativeError;
SQLRETURN  rc1, rc2;

// Prompt user for SQL statement.
GetSQLStatement(Statement);

// Execute the statement directly. Because it will only be executed once, do not
// prepare it.
rc1 = SQLExecDirect(hstmt, Statement, SQL_NTS);

// Process any errors or returned information.
if ((rc1 == SQL_ERROR) || rc1 == SQL_SUCCESS_WITH_INFO) {
   i = 1;
   while ((rc2 = SQLGetDiagRec(SQL_HANDLE_STMT, hstmt, i, SqlState, &NativeError,
                Msg, sizeof(Msg), &MsgLen)) != SQL_NO_DATA) {
      DisplayError(SqlState, NativeError, Msg, MsgLen);
      i++;
   }
}
```

This approach simplifies application coding; the application relies on the user to build the SQL statement and on the data source to check the statement's validity. Because writing a graphical user interface that adequately exposes the intricacies of SQL is a difficult task, simply asking the user to enter the SQL statement text may be a preferable alternative. However, this requires the user to know not only SQL but also the schema of the data source being queried. Some applications provide a graphical user interface by which the user can create a basic SQL statement, and a text interface with which the user can modify it.

Interoperability of SQL Statements

Like the rest of an application, SQL statements can be interoperable or DBMS-specific. And like the rest of the application, the choice of how interoperable SQL statements need to be depends on the type of application. Custom applications are less likely to use interoperable SQL statements because they are usually designed to exploit the capabilities of one or possibly two DBMSs. Generic applications use interoperable SQL statements because they are designed to work with a variety of DBMSs. And vertical applications usually fall somewhere in between, demanding a certain level of functionality, but otherwise using interoperable SQL statements.

Choosing an SQL Grammar

The first decision to be made when constructing SQL statements is which grammar to use. In addition to the grammars available from the various standards bodies, such as X/Open, ANSI, and ISO, virtually every DBMS vendor defines their own grammar, each of which varies slightly from the standard.

Appendix C, "SQL Grammar," describes the minimum SQL grammar that all ODBC drivers must support. This grammar is a subset of the Entry level of SQL-92. Drivers may support additional grammar to conform to the Intermediate, Full, or FIPS 127-2 Transitional levels defined by SQL-92. For more information, see Appendix C, "SQL Grammar," and SQL-92.

Appendix C also defines *escape sequences* containing standard grammar for commonly available language features, such as outer joins, that are not covered by the SQL-92 grammar. For more information, see Appendix C, "SQL Grammar," and "Escape Sequences," later in this chapter.

The grammar that is chosen affects how the driver processes the statement. Drivers must modify SQL-92 SQL and the ODBC-defined escape sequences to DBMS-specific SQL. Because most SQL grammars are based on one or more of the various standards, most drivers do little or no work to meet this requirement. It often consists only of searching for the escape sequences defined by ODBC and replacing them with DBMS-specific grammar. When a driver encounters grammar it does not recognize, it assumes the grammar is DBMS-specific and passes the SQL statement without modification to the data source for execution.

Thus, there are really two choices of grammar to use: the SQL-92 grammar (and the ODBC escape sequences) and a DBMS-specific grammar. Of the two, only the SQL-92 grammar is interoperable, so all interoperable applications should use it. Applications that are not interoperable can use the SQL-92 grammar or a DBMS-specific grammar. DBMS-specific grammars have two advantages: they can exploit any features not covered by SQL-92 and they are marginally faster because the driver does not have to modify them. The latter feature can be partially enforced by setting the SQL_ATTR_NOSCAN statement attribute, which stops the driver from searching for and replacing escape sequences.

If the SQL-92 grammar is used, the application can discover how it is modified by the driver by calling **SQLNativeSql**. This is often useful when debugging applications. **SQLNativeSql** accepts an SQL statement and returns it after the driver has modified it. Because this function is in the Core interface conformance level, it is supported by all drivers.

Constructing Interoperable SQL Statements

As mentioned in the previous sections, interoperable applications should use the ODBC SQL grammar. Beyond using this grammar, however, there are a number of additional problems faced by interoperable applications. For example, what does an application do if it wants to use a feature, such as outer joins, that is not supported by all data sources?

At this point, the application writer must make some decisions about what language features are required and what features are optional. Generally, if a particular driver does not support a feature required by the application, the application simply refuses to run with that driver. However, if the feature is optional, the application can work around the feature. For example, it might disable those parts of the interface that allow the user to use the feature.

To determine which features are supported, applications start by calling **SQLGetInfo** with the SQL_SQL_CONFORMANCE option. The SQL conformance level gives the application a broad view of what SQL is supported. To refine this view, the application calls **SQLGetInfo** with any of a number of other options. For a complete list of these options, see the **SQLGetInfo** function description. Finally, **SQLGetTypeInfo** returns information about the data types supported by the data source.

The following sections list a number of things that applications should watch for when constructing interoperable SQL statements.

Catalog and Schema Usage

Data sources do not necessarily support catalog and schema names as object name identifiers in all SQL statements. Data sources might support catalog and schema names in one or more of the following classes of SQL statements: Data Manipulation Language (DML) statements, procedure calls, table definition statements, index definition statements, and privilege definition statements. To determine the classes of SQL statements in which catalog and schema names can be used, an application calls **SQLGetInfo** with the SQL_CATALOG_USAGE and SQL_SCHEMA_USAGE options.

Catalog Position

The position of a catalog name in an identifier and how it is separated from the rest of the identifier varies from data source to data source. For example, in an Xbase data source, the catalog name is a directory and, in Windows, is separated from the table name (which is a file name) by a backslash (\). The following figure illustrates this condition.

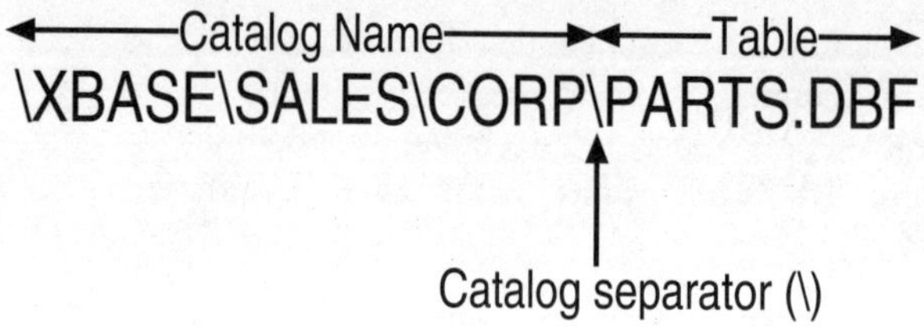

In a SQL Server data source, the catalog is a database and is separated from the schema and table names by a period (.).

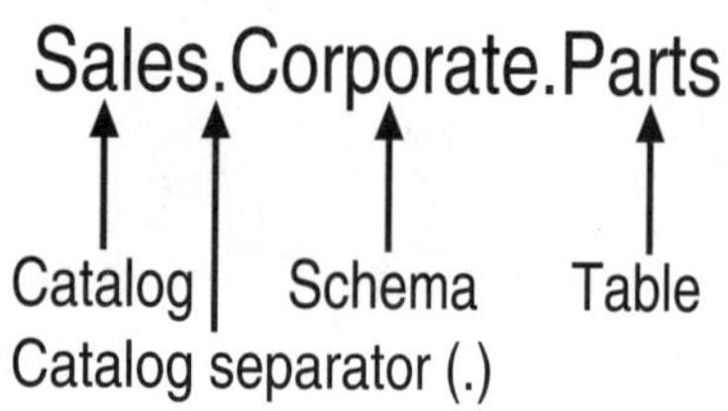

In an Oracle data source, the catalog is also the database, but follows the table name and is separated from the schema and table names by an at sign (@).

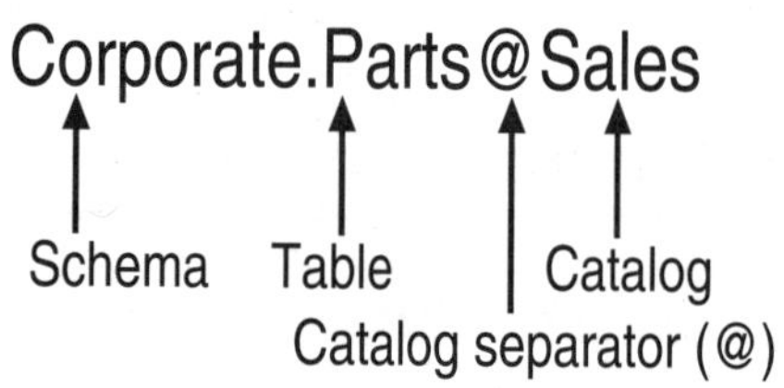

To determine the catalog separator and the location of the catalog name, an application calls **SQLGetInfo** with the SQL_CATALOG_NAME_SEPARATOR and SQL_CATALOG_LOCATION options. Interoperable applications should construct identifiers according to these values.

When quoting identifiers that contain more than one part, applications must be careful to quote each part separately and not quote the character that separates the identifiers. For example, the following statement to select all of the rows and columns of an Xbase table quotes the catalog (\XBASE\SALES\CORP) and table (PARTS.DBF) names, but not the catalog separator (\):

```
SELECT * FROM "\XBASE\SALES\CORP"\"PARTS.DBF"
```

The following statement to select all of the rows and columns of an Oracle table quotes the catalog (Sales), schema (Corporate), and table (Parts) names, but not the catalog (@) or schema (.) separators:

```
SELECT * FROM "Corporate"."Parts"@"Sales"
```

For information about quoting identifiers, see the next section, "Quoted Identifiers."

Quoted Identifiers

In an SQL statement, identifiers containing special characters or match keywords must be enclosed in *identifier quote characters*; identifiers enclosed in such characters are known as *quoted identifiers* (also known as *delimited identifiers* in SQL-92). For example, the Accounts Payable identifier is quoted in the following **SELECT** statement:

```
SELECT * FROM "Accounts Payable"
```

The reason for quoting identifiers is to make the statement parseable. For example, if Accounts Payable was not quoted in the previous statement, the parser would assume there were two tables, Accounts and Payable, and return a syntax error that they were not separated by a comma. The identifier quote character is driver-specific and is retrieved with the SQL_IDENTIFIER_QUOTE_CHAR option in **SQLGetInfo**. The lists of special characters and of keywords are retrieved with the SQL_SPECIAL_CHARACTERS and SQL_KEYWORDS options in **SQLGetInfo**.

To be safe, interoperable applications often quote all identifiers except those for pseudo-columns, such as the ROWID column in Oracle. **SQLSpecialColumns** returns a list of pseudo-columns.

Identifier Case

In SQL statements and catalog function arguments, identifiers and quoted identifiers can be either case sensitive not. An application determines which they are by calling **SQLGetInfo** with the SQL_IDENTIFIER_CASE and SQL_QUOTED_IDENTIFIER_CASE options.

Each of these options has four possible return values: one stating that the identifier or quoted identifier case is sensitive and three stating that it is not sensitive. The three not case sensitive values further describe the case in which identifiers are stored in the system catalog. How identifiers are stored in the system catalog is relevant only for display purposes, such as when an application displays the results of a catalog function; it does not change the case sensitivity of identifiers.

Escape Sequences

ODBC defines escape sequences containing standard grammar for date, time, timestamp, and datetime interval literals, scalar function calls, **LIKE** predicate escape characters, outer joins, and procedure calls. Interoperable applications should use these sequences whenever possible.

To determine if a driver supports the escape sequences for date, time, timestamp, or datetime interval literals, an application calls **SQLGetTypeInfo**. If the data source supports a date, time, timestamp, or datetime interval data type, it must also support the corresponding escape sequence. To determine if the other escape sequences are supported, an application calls **SQLGetInfo**.

For more information, see "Escape Sequences in ODBC," later in this chapter.

Literal Prefixes and Suffixes

In an SQL statement, a *literal* is a character representation of an actual data value. For example, in the following statement, ABC, FFFF, and 10 are literals:

```
SELECT CharCol, BinaryCol, IntegerCol FROM MyTable
   WHERE CharCol = 'ABC' AND BinaryCol = 0xFFFF AND IntegerCol = 10
```

Literals for some data types require special prefixes and suffixes. In the preceding example, the character literal (ABC) requires a single quotation mark (') as both a prefix and a suffix, the binary literal (FFFF) requires the characters 0x as a prefix, and the integer literal (10) does not require a prefix or suffix.

For all data types except date, time, and timestamps, interoperable applications should use the values returned in the LITERAL_PREFIX and LITERAL_SUFFIX columns in the result set created by **SQLGetTypeInfo**. For date, time, timestamp, and datetime interval literals, interoperable applications should use the escape sequences discussed in the previous section.

Parameter Markers in Procedure Calls

When calling procedures that accept parameters, interoperable applications should use parameter markers instead of literal parameter values. Some data sources do not support the use of literal parameter values in procedure calls. For more information about parameters, see "Statement Parameters" in Chapter 9, "Executing Statements." For more information about calling procedures, see "Procedure Calls," later in this chapter.

DDL Statements

Data Definition Language (DDL) statements vary tremendously among DBMSs. ODBC SQL defines statements for the most common data definition operations: creating and dropping tables, indexes, and views, altering tables, and granting and revoking privileges. All other DDL statements are data source–specific. Thus, interoperable applications cannot perform some data definition operations. In general, this is not a problem, as such operations tend to be highly DBMS-specific and are best left to the proprietary database administration software shipped with most DBMSs or the setup program shipped with the driver.

Another problem in data definition is that data type names also vary tremendously among DBMSs. Rather than defining standard data type names and forcing drivers to convert them to DBMS-specific names, **SQLGetTypeInfo** provides a way for applications to discover DBMS-specific data type names. Interoperable applications should use these names in SQL statements to create and alter tables; the names listed in Appendix C, "SQL Grammar," and Appendix D, "Data Types," are examples only.

Escape Sequences in ODBC

A number of language features, such as outer joins and scalar function calls, are commonly implemented by DBMSs. However, the syntaxes for these features tend to be DBMS-specific, even when standard syntaxes are defined by the various standards bodies. Because of this, ODBC defines escape sequences that contain standard syntaxes for the following language features:

- Date, time, timestamp, and datetime interval literals
- Scalar functions such as numeric, string, and data type conversion functions
- LIKE predicate escape character
- Outer joins
- Procedure calls

The escape sequence used by ODBC is as follows:

{*extension*}

The escape sequence is recognized and parsed by drivers, which replace the escape sequences with DBMS-specific grammar. For more information about escape sequence syntax, see Appendix C, "SQL Grammar."

Note In ODBC 2.*x*, the standard syntax of the escape sequence was:

--(*vendor(*vendor-name***), product(***product-name***)** *extension* ***)--**

In addition to this syntax, a shorthand syntax was defined of the form: {*extension*}. In ODBC 3.0, the long form of the escape sequence has been deprecated, and the shorthand form is used exclusively.

Because the escape sequences are mapped by the driver to DBMS-specific syntaxes, an application can use either the escape sequence or DBMS-specific syntax. However, applications that use the DBMS-specific syntax will not be interoperable. When using the escape sequence, applications should make sure that the SQL_ATTR_NOSCAN statement attribute is turned off, which it is by default. Otherwise, the escape sequence will be sent directly to the data source, where it will generally cause a syntax error.

Drivers only support those escape sequences that they can map to underlying language features. For example, if the data source does not support outer joins, neither will the driver. To determine which escape sequences are supported, an application calls **SQLGetTypeInfo** and **SQLGetInfo**. For more information, see the next section, "Date, Time, and Timestamp Literals."

Date, Time, and Timestamp Literals

The escape sequence for date, time, and timestamp literals is:

{*literal-type* '*value*'}

where *literal-type* is one of the following:

literal-type	Meaning	Format of *value*
d	Date	*yyyy-mm-dd*
t	Time	*hh:mm:ss* [1]
ts	Timestamp	*yyyy-mm-dd hh:mm:ss*[*.f...*] [1]

1 The number of digits to the right of the decimal point in a time or timestamp interval literal containing a seconds component is dependent upon the seconds precision, as contained in the SQL_DESC_PRECISION descriptor field (for more information, see **SQLSetDescField**).

For more information on the date, time, and timestamp escape sequences, see "Date, Time, and Timestamp Escape Sequences" in Appendix C, "SQL Grammar."

For example, both of the following SQL statements updates the open date of sales order 1023 in the Orders table. The first statement uses the escape sequence syntax. The second statement uses the native syntax for a DATE column in the Rdb from Digital Equipment Corporation; this statement is not interoperable.

```
UPDATE Orders SET OpenDate={d '1995-01-15'} WHERE OrderID=1023
```

```
UPDATE Orders SET OpenDate='15-Jan-1995' WHERE OrderID=1023
```

The escape sequence for a date, time, or timestamp literal can also be placed in a character variable bound to a date, time, or timestamp parameter. For example, the following code uses a date parameter bound to a character variable to update the open date of sales order 1023 in the Orders table:

```
SQLCHAR    OpenDate[56];   // The size of a date literal is 55.
SQLINTEGER OpenDateLenOrInd = SQL_NTS;
```

```
// Bind the parameter.
SQLBindParameter(hstmt, 1, SQL_PARAM_INPUT, SQL_C_CHAR, SQL_TYPE_DATE, 0, 0,
                 OpenDate, sizeof(OpenDate), &OpenDateLenOrInd);

// Place the date in the OpenDate variable. In addition to the escape sequence shown,
// it would also be possible to use either of the strings "{d '1995-01-15'}" and
// "15-Jan-1995", although the latter is data source-specific.
strcpy(OpenDate, "{d '1995-01-15'}");

// Execute the statement.
SQLExecDirect(hstmt, "UPDATE Orders SET OpenDate=? WHERE OrderID = 1023", SQL_NTS);
```

However, it is usually more efficient to bind the parameter directly to a date structure:

```
SQL_DATE_STRUCT OpenDate;
SQLINTEGER      OpenDateInd = 0;

// Bind the parameter.
SQLBindParameter(hstmt, 1, SQL_PARAM_INPUT, SQL_C_TYPE_DATE, SQL_TYPE_DATE, 0, 0,
                 &OpenDate, 0, &OpenDateLen);

// Place the date in the dsOpenDate structure.
OpenDate.year = 1995;
OpenDate.month = 1;
OpenDate.day = 15;

// Execute the statement.
SQLExecDirect(hstmt, "UPDATE Employee SET OpenDate=? WHERE OrderID = 1023", SQL_NTS);
```

To determine if a driver supports the ODBC escape sequences for date, time, or timestamp literals, an application calls **SQLGetTypeInfo**. If the data source supports a date, time, or timestamp data type, it must also support the corresponding escape sequence.

Data sources can also support the datetime literals defined in the ANSI SQL92 specification, which are different from the ODBC escape sequences for date, time, or timestamp literals. To determine if a data source supports the ANSI literals, an application calls **SQLGetInfo** with the SQL_ANSI_SQL_DATETIME_LITERALS option.

To determine if a driver supports the ODBC escape sequences for interval literals, an application calls **SQLGetTypeInfo**. If the data source supports a datetime interval data type, it must also support the corresponding escape sequence.

Data sources can also support the datetime literals defined in the ANSI SQL92 specification, which are different from the ODBC escape sequences for datetime interval literals. To determine if a data source supports the ANSI literals, an application calls **SQLGetInfo** with the SQL_ANSI_SQL_DATETIME_LITERALS option.

Scalar Function Calls

Scalar functions return a value for each row. For example, the absolute value scalar function takes a numeric column as an argument and returns the absolute value of each value in the column. The escape sequence for calling a scalar function is:

{fn *scalar-function***}**

where *scalar-function* is one of the functions listed in Appendix E, "Scalar Functions." For more information on the scalar function escape sequence, see "Scalar Function Escape Sequence" in Appendix C, "SQL Grammar."

For example, the following SQL statements create the same result set of uppercase customer names. The first statement uses the escape-sequence syntax. The second statement uses the native syntax for Ingres for OS/2 and is not interoperable.

```
SELECT {fn UCASE(Name)} FROM Customers

SELECT uppercase(Name) FROM Customers
```

An application can mix calls to scalar functions that use native syntax and calls to scalar functions that use ODBC syntax. For example, assume that names in the Employee table are stored as a last name, a comma, and a first name. The following SQL statement creates a result set of last names of employees in the Employee table. The statement uses the ODBC scalar function **SUBSTRING** and the SQL Server scalar function **CHARINDEX** and will execute correctly only on SQL Server.

```
SELECT {fn SUBSTRING(Name, 1, CHARINDEX(',', Name) - 1)} FROM Customers
```

For maximum interoperability, applications should use the **CONVERT** scalar function to make sure the output of a scalar function is the required type. The **CONVERT** function converts data from one SQL data type to the specified SQL data type. The syntax of the **CONVERT** function is:

CONVERT(*value_exp***,** *data_type***)**

where *value_exp* is a column name, the result of another scalar function, or a literal value, and *data_type* is a keyword that matches the **#define** name used by an SQL data type identifier as defined in Appendix D, "Data Types." For example, the following SQL statement uses the **CONVERT** function to make sure that the output of the **CURDATE** function is a date, rather than a timestamp or character data:

```
INSERT INTO Orders (OrderID, CustID, OpenDate, SalesPerson, Status)
   VALUES (?, ?, {fn CONVERT({fn CURDATE()}, SQL_DATE)}, ?, ?)
```

To determine which scalar functions are supported by a data source, an application calls **SQLGetInfo** with the SQL_CONVERT_FUNCTIONS, SQL_NUMERIC_FUNCTIONS, SQL_STRING_FUNCTIONS, SQL_SYSTEM_FUNCTIONS, and SQL_TIMEDATE_FUNCTIONS options. To determine which conversion operations are supported by the **CONVERT** function, an application calls **SQLGetInfo** with any of the options that start with SQL_CONVERT.

LIKE Predicate Escape Character

In a **LIKE** predicate, the percent sign (%) matches zero or more of any character and the underscore(_) matches any one character. To match an actual percent sign or underscore in a **LIKE** predicate, an escape character must precede the percent sign or underscore. The escape sequence that defines the **LIKE** predicate escape character is:

{escape '*escape-character*'**}**

where *escape-character* is any character supported by the data source.

For more information on the LIKE escape sequence, see "Like Escape Sequence" in Appendix C, "SQL Grammar."

For example, the following SQL statements create the same result set of customer names that start with the characters "%AAA". The first statement uses the escape-sequence syntax. The second statement uses the native syntax for Microsoft Access and is not interoperable. Note that the second percent character in each **LIKE** predicate is a wild card that matches zero or more of any character.

```
SELECT Name FROM Customers WHERE Name LIKE '\%AAA%' {escape '\'}

SELECT Name FROM Customers WHERE Name LIKE '[%]AAA%'
```

To determine whether the **LIKE** predicate escape character is supported by a data source, an application calls **SQLGetInfo** with the SQL_LIKE_ESCAPE_CLAUSE option.

Outer Joins

ODBC supports the SQL-92 left, right, and full outer join syntax. The escape sequence for outer joins is:

{oj *outer-join***}**

where *outer-join* is:

table-reference **{LEFT | RIGHT | FULL} OUTER JOIN**
{*table-reference* | *outer-join*} **ON** *search-condition*

table-reference specifies a table name, and *search-condition* specifies the join condition between the *table-references*.

An outer join request must appear after the **FROM** keyword and before the **WHERE** clause (if one exists). For complete syntax information, see "Outer Join Escape Sequence" in Appendix C, "SQL Grammar."

For example, the following SQL statements create the same result set that lists all customers and shows which has open orders. The first statement uses the escape-sequence syntax. The second statement uses the native syntax for Oracle and is not interoperable.

```
SELECT Customers.CustID, Customers.Name, Orders.OrderID, Orders.Status
   FROM {oj Customers LEFT OUTER JOIN Orders ON Customers.CustID=Orders.CustID}
   WHERE Orders.Status='OPEN'

SELECT Customers.CustID, Customers.Name, Orders.OrderID, Orders.Status
   FROM Customers, Orders
   WHERE (Orders.Status='OPEN') AND (Customers.CustID= Orders.CustID(+))
```

To determine the types of outer joins that a data source and driver support, an application calls **SQLGetInfo** with the SQL_OJ_CAPABILITIES flag. The types of outer joins that might be supported are left, right, full, or nested outer joins; outer joins in which the column names in the **ON** clause do not have the same order as their respective table names in the **OUTER JOIN** clause; inner joins in conjunction with outer joins; and outer joins using any ODBC comparison operator. If the SQL_OJ_CAPABILITIES information type returns 0, no outer join clause is supported.

Procedure Calls

A *procedure* is an executable object stored on the data source. Generally, it is one or more SQL statements that have been precompiled. The escape sequence for calling a procedure is:

{[?=]call *procedure-name*[([*parameter*][**,**[*parameter*]]...)]**}**

where *procedure-name* specifies the name of a procedure and *parameter* specifies a procedure parameter.

For more information on the procedure call escape sequence, see "Procedure Call Escape Sequence" in Appendix C, "SQL Grammar."

A procedure can have zero or more parameters. It can also return a value, as indicated by the optional parameter marker **?=** at the start of the syntax. If *parameter* is an input or an input/output parameter, it can be a literal or a parameter marker. However, interoperable applications should always use parameter markers, as some data sources do not accept literal parameter values. If *parameter* is an output parameter, it must be a parameter marker. Parameter markers must be bound with **SQLBindParameter** before the procedure call statement is executed.

Input and input/output parameters can be omitted from procedure calls. If a procedure is called with parentheses but without any parameters, such as {call *procedure-name*()}, the driver instructs the data source to use the default value for the first parameter. If the procedure does not have any parameters, this may cause the procedure to fail. If a procedure is called without parentheses, such as {call *procedure-name*}, the driver does not send any parameter values.

Literals can be specified for input and input/output parameters in procedure calls. For example, suppose the procedure InsertOrder has five input parameters. The following call to InsertOrder omits the first parameter, provides a literal for the second parameter, and uses a parameter marker for the third, fourth, and fifth parameters:

```
{call InsertOrder(, 10, ?, ?, ?)}    // Not interoperable!
```

Note that if a parameter is omitted, the comma delimiting it from other parameters must still appear. If an input or input/output parameter is omitted, the procedure uses the default value of the parameter. Another way to specify the default value of an input or input/output parameter is to set the value of the length/indicator buffer bound to the parameter to SQL_DEFAULT_PARAM.

If an input/output parameter is omitted or if a literal is supplied for the parameter, the driver discards the output value. Similarly, if the parameter marker for the return value of a procedure is omitted, the driver discards the return value. Finally, if an application specifies a return value parameter for a procedure that does not return a value, the driver sets the value of the length/indicator buffer bound to the parameter to SQL_NULL_DATA.

Suppose the procedure PARTS_IN_ORDERS creates a result set containing a list of orders which contain a particular part number. The following code calls this procedure for part number 544:

```
SQLUINTEGER PartID;
SQLINTEGER  PartIDInd = 0;

// Bind the parameter.
SQLBindParameter(hstmt, 1, SQL_PARAM_INPUT, SQL_C_SLONG, SQL_INTEGER, 0, 0,
                 &PartID, 0, PartIDInd);

// Place the department number in PartID.
PartID = 544;

// Execute the statement.
SQLExecDirect(hstmt, "{call PARTS_IN_ORDERS(?)}", SQL_NTS);
```

To determine if a data source supports procedures, an application calls **SQLGetInfo** with the SQL_PROCEDURES option.

For more information about procedures, see "Procedures" in Chapter 9, "Executing Statements."

CHAPTER 9

Executing Statements

ODBC applications perform almost all of their database access by executing SQL statements. The general sequence of events is to allocate a statement handle, set any statement attributes, execute the statement, retrieve any results, and free the statement handle.

Allocating a Statement Handle

Before the application can execute a statement, it must allocate a statement handle. To do this:

1. The application declares a variable of type HSTMT. It then calls **SQLAllocHandle** and passes the address of this variable, the handle of the connection in which to allocate the statement, and the SQL_HANDLE_STMT option. For example:

   ```
   SQLHSTMT hstmt1;

   SQLAllocHandle(SQL_HANDLE_STMT, hdbc1, &hstmt1);
   ```

2. The Driver Manager allocates a structure in which to store information about the statement and calls **SQLAllocHandle** in the driver with the SQL_HANDLE_STMT option.
3. The driver allocates its own structure in which to store information about the statement and returns the driver statement handle to the Driver Manager.
4. The Driver Manager returns the Driver Manager statement handle to the application in the application variable.

The statement handle identifies which statement to use when calling ODBC functions. For more information about statement handles, see "Statement Handles" in Chapter 4, "ODBC Fundamentals."

Statement Attributes

Statement attributes are characteristics of the statement. For example, whether to use bookmarks and what kind of cursor to use with the statement's result set are statement attributes.

Statement attributes are set with **SQLSetStmtAttr** and their current settings retrieved with **SQLGetStmtAttr**. There is no requirement that an application set any statement attributes; all statement attributes have defaults, some of which are driver-specific.

When a statement attribute can be set depends on the attribute itself. The SQL_ATTR_CONCURRENCY, SQL_ATTR_CURSOR_TYPE, SQL_ATTR_SIMULATE_CURSOR, and SQL_ATTR_USE_BOOKMARKS statement attributes must be set before the statement is executed. The SQL_ATTR_ASYNC_ENABLE and SQL_ATTR_NOSCAN statement attributes can be set at any time, but are not applied until the statement is used again. SQL_ATTR_MAX_LENGTH, SQL_ATTR_MAX_ROWS, and SQL_ATTR_QUERY_TIMEOUT statement attributes can be set at any time, but it is driver-specific whether they are applied before the statement is used again. The remaining statement attributes can be set at any time.

Note The ability to set statement attributes at the connection level by calling **SQLSetConnectAttr** has been deprecated in ODBC 3.0. ODBC 3.0 applications should never set statement attributes at the connection level. ODBC 3.0 drivers need only support this functionality if they should work with ODBC 2.*x* applications. For more information, see "SQLSetConnectOption Mapping" in Appendix G, "Driver Guidelines for Backward Compatibility."

An exception to this is the SQL_ATTR_METADATA_ID and SQL_ATTR_ASYNC_ENABLE attributes, which are both connection attributes and statement attributes, and can be set either at the connection level or the statement level.

None of the statement attributes introduced in ODBC 3.0 (except for SQL_ATTR_METADATA_ID) can be set at the connection level.

For more information, see the **SQLSetStmtAttr** function description.

Executing a Statement

There are four ways to execute a statement, depending on when they are compiled (prepared) by the database engine and who defines them:

- **Direct execution**. The application defines the SQL statement. It is prepared and executed at run time in a single step.
- **Prepared execution**. The application defines the SQL statement. It is prepared and executed at run time in separate steps. The statement can be prepared once and executed multiple times.
- **Procedures**. The application can define and compile one or more SQL statements at development time and store these statements on the data source as a procedure. The procedure is executed one or more times at run time. The application can enumerate available stored procedures using catalog functions.
- **Catalog functions**. The driver writer creates a function that returns a predefined result set. Usually, this function submits a predefined SQL statement or calls a procedure created for this purpose. The function is executed one or more times at run time.

A particular statement (as identified by its statement handle) can be executed any number of times. The statement can be executed with a variety of different SQL statements or it can be repeatedly executed with the same SQL statement. For example, the following code uses the same statement handle (*hstmt1*) to retrieve and display the tables in the Sales database. It then reuses this handle to retrieve the columns in a table selected by the user.

```
SQLHSTMT hstmt1;
SQLCHAR * Table;

// Create a result set of all tables in the Sales database.
SQLTables(hstmt1, "Sales", SQL_NTS, "sysadmin", SQL_NTS, NULL, 0, NULL, 0);

// Fetch and display the table names, then close the cursor.
// Code not shown.

// Have the user select a particular table.
SelectTable(Table);

// Reuse hstmt1 to create a result set of all columns in Table.
SQLColumns(hstmt1, "Sales", SQL_NTS, "sysadmin", SQL_NTS, Table, SQL_NTS, NULL, 0);

// Fetch and display the column names in Table, then close the cursor.
// Code not shown.
```

And the following code shows how a single handle is used to repeatedly execute the same statement to delete rows from a table.

```
SQLHSTMT    hstmt1;
SQLUINTEGER OrderID;
SQLINTEGER  OrderIDInd = 0;

// Prepare a statement to delete orders from the Orders table.
SQLPrepare(hstmt1, "DELETE FROM Orders WHERE OrderID = ?", SQL_NTS);

// Bind OrderID to the parameter for the OrderID column.
SQLBindParameter(hstmt1, 1, SQL_PARAM_INPUT, SQL_C_ULONG, SQL_INTEGER, 5, 0,
                 &OrderID, 0, &OrderIDInd);

// Repeatedly execute hstmt1 with different values of OrderID.
while ((OrderID = GetOrderID()) != 0) {
   SQLExecute(hstmt1);
}
```

For many drivers, allocating statements is an expensive task, so reusing the same statement in this manner is usually more efficient than freeing existing statements and allocating new ones. Applications that create result sets on a statement must be careful to close the cursor over the result set before reexecuting the statement; for more information, see "Closing the Cursor" in Chapter 10, "Retrieving Results (Basic)."

Reusing statements also forces the application to avoid a limitation in some drivers of the number of statements that can be active at one time. The exact definition of "active" is driver-specific, but it often refers to any statement that has been prepared or executed and still has results available. For example, after an **INSERT** statement has been prepared, it is generally considered to be active; after a **SELECT** statement has been executed and the cursor is still open, it is generally considered to be active; after a **CREATE TABLE** statement has been executed, it is not generally considered to be active.

An application determines how many statements can be active on a single connection at one time by calling **SQLGetInfo** with the SQL_MAX_CONCURRENT_ACTIVITIES option. An application can use more active statements than this limit by opening multiple connections to the data source; because connections can be expensive, however, the effect on performance should be considered.

Applications can limit the amount of time allotted for a statement to execute with the SQL_ATTR_QUERY_TIMEOUT statement attribute. If the timeout period expires before the data source returns the result set, the function executing the SQL statement returns SQLSTATE HYT00 (Timeout expired). By default, there is no timeout.

Direct Execution

Direct execution is the simplest way to execute a statement. When the statement is submitted for execution, the data source compiles it into an access plan and then executes that access plan.

Direct execution is commonly used by generic applications that build and execute statements at run time. For example, the following code builds an SQL statement and executes it a single time:

```
SQLCHAR *SQLStatement;

// Build an SQL statement.
BuildStatement(SQLStatement);

// Execute the statement.
SQLExecDirect(hstmt, SQLStatement, SQL_NTS);
```

Direct execution works best for statements that will be executed a single time. Its major drawback is that the SQL statement is parsed every time it is executed. In addition, the application cannot retrieve information about the result set created by the statement (if any) until after the statement is executed; this is possible if the statement is prepared and executed in two separate steps.

To execute a statement directly, the application:

1. Sets the values of any parameters. For more information, see "Statement Parameters," later in this chapter.
2. Calls **SQLExecDirect** and passes it a string containing the SQL statement.

When **SQLExecDirect** is called, the driver:

1. Modifies the SQL statement to use the data source's SQL grammar without parsing the statement; this includes replacing the escape sequences discussed in "Escape Sequences in ODBC" in Chapter 8, "SQL Statements." The application can retrieve the modified form of an SQL statement by calling **SQLNativeSql**. Note that escape sequences are not replaced if the SQL_ATTR_NOSCAN statement attribute is set.
2. Retrieves the current parameter values and converts them as necessary. For more information, see "Statement Parameters," later in this chapter.
3. Sends the statement and converted parameter values to the data source for execution.
4. Returns any errors. These include sequencing or state diagnostics such as SQLSTATE 24000 (Invalid cursor state), syntactic errors such as SQLSTATE 42000 (Syntax error or access violation), and semantic errors such as SQLSTATE 42S02 (Base table or view not found).

Prepared Execution

Prepared execution is an efficient way to execute a statement more than once. The statement is first compiled, or *prepared*, into an access plan. The access plan is then executed one or more times at a later time. For more information about access plans, see "Processing an SQL Statement" in Chapter 2, "An Introduction to SQL and ODBC."

Prepared execution is commonly used by vertical and custom applications to repeatedly execute the same, parameterized SQL statement. For example, the following code prepares a statement to update the prices of different parts. It then executes the statement multiple times with different parameter values each time.

```
SQLREAL      Price;
SQLUINTEGER PartID;
SQLINTEGER  PartIDInd = 0, PriceInd = 0;

// Prepare a statement to update salaries in the Employees table.
SQLPrepare(hstmt, "UPDATE Parts SET Price = ? WHERE PartID = ?", SQL_NTS);

// Bind Price to the parameter for the Price column and PartID to
// the parameter for the PartID column.
SQLBindParameter(hstmt, 1, SQL_PARAM_INPUT, SQL_C_FLOAT, SQL_REAL, 7, 0,
                 &Price, 0, &PriceInd);
SQLBindParameter(hstmt, 2, SQL_PARAM_INPUT, SQL_C_ULONG, SQL_INTEGER, 10, 0,
                 &PartID, 0, &PartIDInd);

// Repeatedly execute the statement.
while (GetPrice(&PartID, &Price)) {
   SQLExecute(hstmt);
}
```

Prepared execution is faster than direct execution for statements executed more than once, primarily because the statement is compiled only once; statements executed directly are compiled each time they are executed. Prepared execution can also provide a reduction in network traffic because the driver can send an access plan identifier to the data source each time the statement is executed, rather than an entire SQL statement, if the data source supports access plan identifiers.

The application can retrieve the metadata for the result set after the statement is prepared and before it is executed. However, returning metadata for prepared, unexecuted statements is expensive for some drivers and should be avoided by interoperable applications if possible. For more information, see "Result Set Metadata" in Chapter 10, "Retrieving Results (Basic)."

Prepared execution should not be used for statements executed a single time. For such statements, it is slightly slower than direct execution because it requires an additional ODBC function call.

Important Committing or rolling back a transaction, either by explicitly calling **SQLEndTran** or by working in autocommit mode, causes some data sources to delete the access plans for all statements on a connection. For more information, see the SQL_CURSOR_COMMIT_BEHAVIOR and SQL_CURSOR_ROLLBACK_BEHAVIOR options in the **SQLGetInfo** function description.

To prepare and execute a statement, the application:

1. Calls **SQLPrepare** and passes it a string containing the SQL statement.
2. Sets the values of any parameters. Parameters can actually be set before or after preparing the statement. For more information, see "Statement Parameters," later in this chapter.
3. Calls **SQLExecute** and does any additional processing that is necessary, such as fetching data.
4. Repeats steps 2 and 3 as necessary.

When **SQLPrepare** is called, the driver:

1. Modifies the SQL statement to use the data source's SQL grammar without parsing the statement. This includes replacing the escape sequences discussed in "Escape Sequences in ODBC" in Chapter 8, "SQL Statements." The application can retrieve the modified form of an SQL statement by calling **SQLNativeSql**. Note that escape sequences are not replaced if the SQL_ATTR_NOSCAN statement attribute is set.
2. Sends the statement to the data source for preparation.
3. Stores the returned access plan identifier for later execution (if the preparation succeeded) or returns any errors (if the preparation failed). Errors include syntactic errors such as SQLSTATE 42000 (Syntax error or access violation) and semantic errors such as SQLSTATE 42S02 (Base table or view not found).

   Note Some drivers do not return errors at this point, but instead return them when the statement is executed or when catalog functions are called. Thus, **SQLPrepare** might appear to have succeeded when in fact it has failed.

When **SQLExecute** is called, the driver:

1. Retrieves the current parameter values and converts them as necessary. For more information, see "Statement Parameters," later in this chapter.
2. Sends the access plan identifier and converted parameter values to the data source.
3. Returns any errors. These are generally run-time errors such as SQLSTATE 24000 (Invalid cursor state). However, some drivers return syntactic and semantic errors at this point.

If the data source does not support statement preparation, the driver must emulate it to the extent possible. For example, the driver might do nothing when **SQLPrepare** is called, then perform direct execution of the statement when **SQLExecute** is called.

If the data source supports syntax checking without execution, the driver might submit the statement for checking when **SQLPrepare** is called and submit the statement for execution when **SQLExecute** is called.

If the driver cannot emulate statement preparation, it stores the statement when **SQLPrepare** is called and submits it for execution when **SQLExecute** is called.

Because emulated statement preparation is not perfect, **SQLExecute** can return any errors normally returned by **SQLPrepare**.

Procedures

A *procedure* is an executable object stored on the data source. Generally, it is one or more SQL statements that have been precompiled.

When to Use Procedures

There are a number of advantages to using procedures, all based on the fact that using procedures moves SQL statements from the application to the data source. What is left in the application is an interoperable procedure call. These advantages include:

- **Performance**. Procedures are usually the fastest way to execute SQL statements. Like prepared execution, the statement is compiled and executed in two separate steps. Unlike prepared execution, procedures are executed only at run time. They are compiled at a different time.
- **Business rules**. A *business rule* is a rule about the way in which a company does business. For example, only someone with the title Sales Person might be allowed to add new sales orders. Placing these rules in procedures allows individual companies to customize vertical applications by rewriting the procedures called by the application without having to modify the application code. For example, an order entry application might call the procedure InsertOrder with a fixed number of parameters; exactly how InsertOrder is implemented can vary from company to company.
- **Replaceability**. Closely related to placing business rules in procedures is the fact that procedures can be replaced without recompiling the application. If a business rule changes after a company has bought and installed an application, the company can change the procedure containing that rule. From the application's standpoint, nothing has changed; it still calls a particular procedure to accomplish a particular task.
- **DBMS-specific SQL**. Procedures provide a way for applications to exploit DBMS-specific SQL and still remain interoperable. For example, a procedure on a DBMS that supports control-of-flow statements in SQL might trap and recover from errors, while a procedure on a DBMS that does not support control-of-flow statements might simply return an error.

- **Procedures survive transactions**. On some data sources, the access plans for all prepared statements on a connection are deleted when a transaction is committed or rolled back. By placing SQL statements in procedures, which are permanently stored in the data source, the statements survive the transaction. Whether the procedures survive in a prepared, partially prepared, or unprepared state is DBMS-specific.
- **Separate development**. Procedures can be developed separately from the rest of the application. In large corporations, this might provide a way to further exploit the skills of highly specialized programmers. In other words, application programmers can write user interface code and database programmers can write procedures.

Procedures are generally used by vertical and custom applications. These applications tend to perform fixed tasks, and it is possible to hard-code procedure calls in them. For example, an order entry application might call the procedures InsertOrder, DeleteOrder, UpdateOrder, and GetOrders.

There is little reason to call procedures from generic applications. Procedures are generally written to perform a task in the context of a particular application and so have no use to generic applications. For example, a spreadsheet has no reason to call the InsertOrder procedure just mentioned. Furthermore, generic applications should not construct procedures at run time in hopes of providing faster statement execution; not only is this likely to be slower than prepared or direct execution, it also requires DBMS-specific SQL statements.

An exception to this is application development environments, which often provide a way for programmers to build SQL statements that execute procedures and may provide a way for programmers to test procedures. Such environments call **SQLProcedures** to list available procedures and **SQLProcedureColumns** to list the input, input/output, and output parameters, the procedure return value, and the columns of any result sets created by a procedure. However, such procedures must be developed beforehand on each data source; doing so requires DBMS-specific SQL statements.

There are three major disadvantages to using procedures. The first is that procedures must be written and compiled for each DBMS with which the application is to run. While this is not a problem for custom applications, it can significantly increase development and maintenance time for vertical applications designed to run with a number of DBMSs.

The second disadvantage is that many DBMSs do not support procedures. Again, this is most likely to be a problem for vertical applications designed to run with a number of DBMSs. To determine whether procedures are supported, an application calls **SQLGetInfo** with the SQL_PROCEDURES option.

The third disadvantage, which is particularly applicable to application development environments, is that ODBC does not define a standard grammar for creating procedures. Thus, although applications can call procedures interoperably, they cannot create them interoperably.

Executing Procedures

ODBC defines a standard escape sequence for executing procedures. For the syntax of this sequence and a code example that uses it, see "Procedure Calls" in Chapter 8, "SQL Statements."

To execute a procedure, an application:

1. Sets the values of any parameters. For more information, see "Statement Parameters," later in this chapter.
2. Calls **SQLExecDirect** and passes it a string containing the SQL statement that executes the procedure. This statement can use the escape sequence defined by ODBC or DBMS-specific syntax; statements that use DBMS-specific syntax are not interoperable.

When **SQLExecDirect** is called, the driver:

1. Retrieves the current parameter values and converts them as necessary. For more information, see "Statement Parameters," later in this chapter.
2. Calls the procedure in the data source and sends it the converted parameter values. How the driver calls the procedure is driver-specific. For example, it might modify the SQL statement to use the data source's SQL grammar and submit this statement for execution, or it might call the procedure directly using a Remote Procedure Call (RPC) mechanism that is defined in the data stream protocol of the DBMS.
3. Returns the values of any input/output or output parameters or the procedure return value, assuming the procedure succeeds. Note that these values might not be available until after all other results (row counts and result sets) generated by the procedure have been processed. If the procedure fails, the driver returns any errors.

Batches of SQL Statements

A batch of SQL statements is a group of two or more SQL statements or a single SQL statement that has the same effect as a group of two or more SQL statements. In some implementations, the entire batch statement is executed before any results are available. This is often more efficient than submitting statements separately, as network traffic can often be reduced and the data source can sometimes optimize execution of a batch of SQL statements. In other implementations, calling **SQLMoreResults** triggers the execution of the next statement in the batch. ODBC supports the following types of batches:

- **Explicit batches**. An explicit batch is two or more SQL statements separated by semicolons (;). For example, the following batch of SQL statements opens a new sales order. This requires inserting rows into both the Orders and Lines tables. Note that there is no semicolon after the last statement.

```
INSERT INTO Orders (OrderID, CustID, OpenDate, SalesPerson, Status)
   VALUES (2002, 1001, {fn CURDATE()}, 'Garcia', 'OPEN');
INSERT INTO Lines (OrderID, Line, PartID, Quantity)
   VALUES (2002, 1, 1234, 10);
INSERT INTO Lines (OrderID, Line, PartID, Quantity)
   VALUES (2002, 2, 987, 8);
INSERT INTO Lines (OrderID, Line, PartID, Quantity)
   VALUES (2002, 3, 566, 17);
INSERT INTO Lines (OrderID, Line, PartID, Quantity)
   VALUES (2002, 4, 412, 500)
```

- **Procedures**. If a procedure contains more than one SQL statement, it is considered to be a batch of SQL statements. For example, the following SQL Server–specific statement creates a procedure that returns a result set containing information about a customer and a result set listing all the open sales orders for that customer:

```
CREATE PROCEDURE GetCustInfo (@CustomerID INT) AS
   SELECT * FROM Customers WHERE CustID = @CustomerID
   SELECT OrderID FROM Orders
      WHERE CustID = @CustomerID AND Status = 'OPEN'
```

  The **CREATE PROCEDURE** statement itself is not a batch of SQL statements. However, the procedure it creates is a batch of SQL statements. Note that no semicolons separate the two **SELECT** statements because the **CREATE PROCEDURE** statement is specific to SQL Server and SQL Server does not require semicolons to separate multiple statements in a **CREATE PROCEDURE** statement.

- **Arrays of parameters**. Arrays of parameters can be used with a parameterized SQL statement as an effective way to perform bulk operations. For example, arrays of parameters can be used with the following **INSERT** statement to insert multiple rows into the Lines table while only executing a single SQL statement:

```
INSERT INTO Lines (OrderID, Line, PartID, Quantity)
   VALUES (?, ?, ?, ?)
```

  If a data source does not support arrays of parameters, the driver can emulate them by executing the SQL statement once for each set of parameters. For more information, see "Statement Parameters" and "Arrays of Parameter Values," later in this chapter.

The different types of batches cannot be mixed in an interoperable manner. That is, how an application determines the result of executing an explicit batch that includes procedure calls, an explicit batch that uses arrays of parameters, and a procedure call that uses arrays of parameters is driver-specific.

Result-Generating and Result-Free Statements

SQL statements can be loosely divided into the following five categories:

- **Result set–generating statements**. These are SQL statements that generate a result set. For example, a **SELECT** statement.
- **Row count–generating statements**. These are SQL statements that generate a count of affected rows. For example, an **UPDATE** or **DELETE** statement.
- **Data Definition Language (DDL) statements**. These are SQL statements that modify the structure of the database. For example, **CREATE TABLE** or **DROP INDEX**.
- **Context-changing statements**. These are SQL statements that change the context of a database. For example, the **USE** and **SET** statements in SQL Server.
- **Administrative statements**. These are SQL statements used for administrative purposes in a database. For example, **GRANT** and **REVOKE**.

SQL statements in the first two categories are collectively known as *result-generating statements*. SQL statements in the latter three categories are collectively known as *result-free statements*. ODBC defines the semantics of batches that include only result-generating statements. The semantics of batches that include result-free statements vary widely and are therefore data source–specific. For example, the SQL Server driver does not support dropping an object, and then referring to or re-creating the same object, in the same batch. Thus, the term *batch* as used in this manual refers only to batches of result-generating statements.

Executing Batches

Before an application executes a batch of statements, it should first check whether they are supported. To do this, the application calls **SQLGetInfo** with the SQL_BATCH_SUPPORT, SQL_PARAM_ARRAY_ROW_COUNTS, and SQL_PARAM_ARRAY_SELECTS options. The first option returns whether row count–generating and result set–generating statements are supported in explicit batches and procedures, while the latter two options return information about the availability of row counts and result sets in parameterized execution.

Batches of statements are executed through **SQLExecute** or **SQLExecDirect**. For example, the following call executes an explicit batch of statements to open a new sales order.

```
SQLCHAR *BatchStmt =
   "INSERT INTO Orders (OrderID, CustID, OpenDate, SalesPerson, Status)"
      "VALUES (2002, 1001, {fn CURDATE()}, 'Garcia', 'OPEN');"
   "INSERT INTO Lines (OrderID, Line, PartID, Quantity) VALUES (2002, 1, 1234, 10);"
   "INSERT INTO Lines (OrderID, Line, PartID, Quantity) VALUES (2002, 2, 987, 8);"
   "INSERT INTO Lines (OrderID, Line, PartID, Quantity) VALUES (2002, 3, 566, 17);"
   "INSERT INTO Lines (OrderID, Line, PartID, Quantity) VALUES (2002, 4, 412, 500)";

SQLExecDirect(hstmt, BatchStmt, SQL_NTS);
```

When a batch of result-generating statements is executed, it returns one or more row counts or result sets. For information about how to retrieve these, see "Multiple Results" in Chapter 11, "Retrieving Results (Advanced)."

If a batch of statements includes parameter markers, these are numbered in increasing parameter order as they are in any other statement. For example, the following batch of statements has parameters numbered from 1 to 21; those in the first **INSERT** statement are numbered 1 to 5 and those in the last **INSERT** statement are numbered 18 to 21.

```
INSERT INTO Orders (OrderID, CustID, OpenDate, SalesPerson, Status)
   VALUES (?, ?, ?, ?, ?);
INSERT INTO Lines (OrderID, Line, PartID, Quantity) VALUES (?, ?, ?, ?);
INSERT INTO Lines (OrderID, Line, PartID, Quantity) VALUES (?, ?, ?, ?);
INSERT INTO Lines (OrderID, Line, PartID, Quantity) VALUES (?, ?, ?, ?);
INSERT INTO Lines (OrderID, Line, PartID, Quantity) VALUES (?, ?, ?, ?);
```

For more information about parameters, see "Statement Parameters," later in this chapter.

Errors and Batches

When an error occurs while executing a batch of SQL statements, one of four things can happen; which one happens is data source–specific and may even depend on the statements included in the batch.

- No statements in the batch are executed.
- No statements in the batch are executed and the transaction is rolled back.
- All of the statements before the error statement are executed.
- All of the statements except the error statement are executed.

In the first two cases, **SQLExecute** and **SQLExecDirect** return SQL_ERROR. In the latter two cases, they may return SQL_SUCCESS_WITH_INFO or SQL_SUCCESS, depending on the implementation. In all cases, further error information can be retrieved with **SQLGetDiagField**, **SQLGetDiagRec**, or **SQLError**. However, the nature and depth of this information is data source–specific. Furthermore, this information is unlikely to exactly identify the statement in error.

Executing Catalog Functions

Because a catalog function creates a result set, it is equivalent to executing any result set–generating SQL statement. In fact, catalog functions are often implemented by executing predefined SQL statements or calling predefined procedures that are shipped with the driver or DBMS. Almost anything that applies to SQL statements that create result sets also applies to catalog functions. For example, the SQL_ATTR_MAX_ROWS statement attribute limits the number of rows returned by the catalog function, just as it limits the number of rows returned by a **SELECT** statement.

To execute a catalog function, an application just calls the function.

For more information about catalog functions, see Chapter 7, "Catalog Functions."

Statement Parameters

A *parameter* is a variable in an SQL statement. For example, suppose a Parts table has columns named PartID, Description, and Price. To add a part without parameters would require constructing an SQL statement such as:

```
INSERT INTO Parts (PartID, Description, Price) VALUES (2100, 'Drive shaft', 50.00)
```

Although this statement inserts a new order, it is not a good solution for an order entry application because the values to insert cannot be hard-coded in the application. An alternative is to construct the SQL statement at run time, using the values to be inserted. This also is not a good solution, due to the complexity of constructing statements at run time. The best solution is to replace the elements of the **VALUES** clause with question marks (?), or *parameter markers*:

```
INSERT INTO Parts (PartID, Description, Price) VALUES (?, ?, ?)
```

The parameter markers are then bound to application variables. To add a new row, the application has only to set the values of the variables and execute the statement. The driver then retrieves the current values of the variables and sends them to the data source. If the statement will be executed multiple times, the application can make the process even more efficient by preparing the statement.

The statement just shown might be hard-coded in an order entry application to insert a new row. However, parameter markers are not limited to vertical applications. For any application, they ease the difficulty of constructing SQL statements at run time by avoiding conversions to and from text. For example, the part ID just shown is most likely stored in the application as an integer. If the SQL statement is constructed without parameter markers, the application must convert the part ID to text and the data source must convert it back to an integer. By using a parameter marker, the application can send the part ID to the driver as an integer, which usually can send it to the data source as an integer, thereby saving two conversions. For long data values this is critical, as the text forms of such values often exceed the allowable length of an SQL statement.

Parameters are legal only in certain places in SQL statements. For example, they are not allowed in the select list (the list of columns to be returned by a **SELECT** statement), nor are they allowed as both operands of a binary operator such as the equals sign (=), as it would be impossible to determine the parameter type. In general, parameters are legal only in Data Manipulation Language (DML) statements, and not in Data Definition Language (DDL) statements. For details, see "Parameter Markers" in Appendix C, "SQL Grammar."

When the SQL statement invokes a procedure, named parameters can be used. Named parameters are identified by their name, not by their position in the SQL statement. They can be bound by a call to **SQLBindParameter**, but the parameter is identified by the SQL_DESC_NAME field of the IPD (implementation parameter descriptor), not by the *ParameterNumber* argument of **SQLBindParameter**. They can also be bound by calling **SQLSetDescField** or **SQLSetDescRec**. For more information on named parameters, see "Binding Parameters by Name (Named Parameters)" later in this chapter. For more information on descriptors, see Chapter 13, "Descriptors."

Binding Parameters

Each parameter in an SQL statement must be associated, or *bound*, to a variable in the application before the statement is executed. When the application binds a variable to a parameter, it describes that variable—address, C data type, and so on—to the driver. It also describes the parameter itself—SQL data type, precision, and so on. The driver stores this information in the structure it maintains for that statement and uses the information to retrieve the value from the variable when the statement is executed.

Parameters can be bound or rebound at any time before a statement is executed. If a parameter is rebound after a statement is executed, the binding does not apply until the statement is executed again. To bind a parameter to a different variable, an application simply rebinds the parameter with the new variable; the previous binding is automatically released.

A variable remains bound to a parameter until a different variable is bound to the parameter, all parameters are unbound by calling **SQLFreeStmt** with the SQL_RESET_PARAMS option, or the statement is released. For this reason, the application must be sure that variables are not freed until after they are unbound. For more information, see "Allocating and Freeing Buffers" in Chapter 4, "ODBC Fundamentals."

Because parameter bindings are just information stored in the structure maintained by the driver for the statement, they can be set in any order. They are also independent of the SQL statement that is executed. For example, suppose an application binds three parameters and then executes the following SQL statement:

```
INSERT INTO Parts (PartID, Description, Price) VALUES (?, ?, ?)
```

If the application then immediately executes the SQL statement:

```
SELECT * FROM Orders WHERE OrderID = ?, OpenDate = ?, Status = ?
```

on the same statement handle, the parameter bindings for the **INSERT** statement are used because those are the bindings stored in the statement structure. In most cases, this is a poor programming practice and should be avoided. Instead, the application should call **SQLFreeStmt** with the SQL_RESET_PARAMS option to unbind all the old parameters and then bind new ones.

Binding Parameter Markers

The application binds parameters by calling **SQLBindParameter**. **SQLBindParameter** binds one parameter at a time. With it, the application specifies:

- The parameter number. Parameters are numbered in increasing parameter order in the SQL statement, starting with the number 1. While it is legal to specify a parameter number that is higher than there are parameters in the SQL statement, the parameter value will be ignored when the statement is executed.
- The parameter type (input, input/output, or output). Except for parameters in procedure calls, all parameters are input parameters. For more information, see "Procedure Parameters," later in this chapter.
- The C data type, address, and byte length of the variable bound to the parameter. The driver must be able to convert the data from the C data type to the SQL data type or an error is returned. For a list of supported conversions, see Appendix D, "Data Types."
- The SQL data type, precision, and scale of the parameter itself.
- The address of a length/indicator buffer. It provides the byte length of binary or character data, specifies that the data is NULL, or specifies that the data will be sent with **SQLPutData**. For more information, see "Using Length/Indicator Values" in Chapter 4, "ODBC Fundamentals."

For example, the following code binds *SalesPerson* and *CustID* to parameters for the SalesPerson and CustID columns. Because *SalesPerson* contains character data, which is variable length, the code specifies the byte length of *SalesPerson* (11) and binds *SalesPersonLenOrInd* to contain the byte length of the data in *SalesPerson*. This information is not necessary for *CustID* because it contains integer data, which is of fixed length.

```
SQLCHAR     SalesPerson[11];
SQLINTEGER  SalesPersonLenOrInd, CustIDInd;
SQLUINTEGER CustID;

// Bind SalesPerson to the parameter for the SalesPerson column and
// CustID to the parameter for the CustID column.
SQLBindParameter(hstmt1, 1, SQL_PARAM_INPUT, SQL_C_CHAR, SQL_CHAR, 10, 0,
                 SalesPerson, sizeof(SalesPerson), &SalesPersonLenOrInd);
SQLBindParameter(hstmt1, 2, SQL_PARAM_INPUT, SQL_C_ULONG, SQL_INTEGER, 10, 0,
                 &CustID, 0, &CustIDInd);

// Set the values of the salesperson and customer ID variables and length/indicators.
strcpy(SalesPerson, "Garcia");
SalesPersonLenOrInd = SQL_NTS;
CustID = 1331;
CustIDInd = 0;

// Execute a statement to get data for all orders made to the specified
// customer by the specified salesperson.
SQLExecDirect(hstmt1,"SELECT * FROM Orders WHERE SalesPerson=? AND CustID=?",SQL_NTS);
```

When **SQLBindParameter** is called, the driver stores this information in the structure for the statement. When the statement is executed, it uses the information to retrieve the parameter data and send it to the data source.

Note In ODBC 1.0, parameters were bound with **SQLSetParam**. The Driver Manager maps calls between **SQLSetParam** and **SQLBindParameter**, depending on the versions of ODBC used by the application and driver.

Binding Parameters by Name (Named Parameters)

Certain DBMSs allow an application to specify the parameters to a stored procedure by name, instead of by position in the procedure call. Such parameters are called *named parameters*. ODBC supports the use of named parameters. In ODBC, named parameters are only used in calls to stored procedures, and cannot be used in other SQL statements.

The driver checks the value of the SQL_DESC_UNNAMED field of the IPD to determine whether named parameters are used. If SQL_DESC_UNNAMED is not set to SQL_UNNAMED, the driver uses the name in the SQL_DESC_NAME field of the IPD to identify the parameter. To bind the parameter, an application can call **SQLBindParameter** to specify the parameter information, and then call **SQLSetDescField** to set the SQL_DESC_NAME field of the IPD. When named parameters are used, the order of the parameter in the procedure call is not important, and the parameter's record number is ignored.

The difference between unnamed parameters and named parameters is in the relationship between the record number of the descriptor and the parameter number in the procedure. When unnamed parameters are used, the first parameter marker is related to the first record in the parameter descriptor, which in turn is related to the first parameter (in creation order) in the procedure call. When named parameters are used, the first parameter marker is still related to the first record of the parameter descriptor, but the relationship between the record number of the descriptor and the parameter number in the procedure does not exist anymore. Named parameters do not use the mapping of the descriptor record number to the procedure parameter position; it is replaced by the mapping of the descriptor record name to the procedure parameter name.

Note If automatic population of the IPD is enabled, the driver will populate the descriptor such that the order of the descriptor records will match the order of the parameters in the procedure definition, even if named parameters are used.

If a named parameter is used, all parameters must be named parameters. If any parameter is not a named parameter, then all parameters must not be named parameters. If there were a mixture of named parameters and unnamed parameters, the behavior would be driver-dependent.

As an example of named parameters, suppose a SQL Server stored procedure has been defined as follows:

```
CREATE PROCEDURE test @title_id int = 1, @quote char(30) AS <blah>
```

In this procedure, the first parameter, @title_id, has a default value of 1. An application can use the following code to invoke this procedure such that it specifies only one dynamic parameter. This parameter is a named parameter with the name "@quote".

```
// prepare the procedure invocation statement.
SQLPrepare(hstmt, "{call test(?)}", SQL_NTS);

// populate record 1 of ipd.
SQLBindParameter(hstmt, 1, SQL_PARAM_INPUT, SQL_C_CHAR, SQL_CHAR,
                 30, 0, szQuote, 0, &cbValue);

// get ipd handle and set the SQL_DESC_NAMED and SQL_DESC_UNNAMED fields for record #1.
SQLGetStmtAttr(hstmt, SQL_ATTR_IMP_PARAM_DESC, &hIpd, 0, 0);
SQLSetDescField(hIpd, 1, SQL_DESC_NAME, "@quote", SQL_NTS);
SQLSetDescField(hIpd, 1, SQL_DESC_UNNAMED, SQL_NAMED, 0);

// assuming that szQuote has been appropriately initialized,
// execute
SQLExecute(hstmt);
```

Parameter Binding Offsets

An application can specify that an offset is added to bound parameter buffer addresses and the corresponding length/indicator buffer addresses when **SQLExecDirect** or **SQLExecute** is called. The result of these additions determines the addresses used in these operations.

Bind offsets allow an application to change bindings without calling **SQLBindParameter** for previously bound parameters. A call to **SQLBindParameter** to rebind a parameter changes the buffer address and the length/indicator pointer. Rebinding with an offset, on the other hand, simply adds an offset to the existing bound parameter buffer address and length/indicator buffer address. When offsets are used, the bindings are a "template" of how the application buffers are laid out and the application can move this "template" to different areas of memory by changing the offset. A new offset can be specified at any time, and is always added to the originally bound values.

To specify a bind offset, the application sets the SQL_ATTR_PARAM_BIND_OFFSET_PTR statement attribute to the address of an SQLINTEGER buffer. Before the application calls a function that uses the bindings, it places an offset in bytes in this buffer, as long as neither the parameter buffer address nor the length/indicator buffer address is 0, and the bound parameter is in the SQL statement. The sum of the address and the offset must be a valid address. (This means that either or both of the offset and the address to which the offset is added, can be invalid, as long as the sum of them is a valid address.)

Note Binding offsets are not supported by ODBC 2.*x* drivers.

Describing Parameters

SQLBindParameter has arguments that describe the parameter: its SQL type, precision, and scale. The driver uses this information, or *metadata*, to convert the parameter value to the type needed by the data source. At first glance, it might seem that the driver is in a better position to know the parameter metadata than the application; after all, the driver can easily discover the metadata for a result set column. As it turns out, this is not the case. First, most data sources do not provide a way for the driver to discover parameter metadata. Second, most applications already know the metadata.

If an SQL statement is hard-coded in the application, then the application writer already knows the type of each parameter. If an SQL statement is constructed by the application at run time, the application can determine the metadata as it builds the statement. For example, when the application constructs the clause

```
WHERE OrderID = ?
```

it can call **SQLColumns** for the OrderID column.

The only situation in which the application cannot easily determine the parameter metadata is when the user enters a parameterized statement. In this case, the application calls **SQLPrepare** to prepare the statement, **SQLNumParams** to determine the number of parameters, and **SQLDescribeParam** to describe each parameter. However, as was noted earlier, most data sources do not provide a way for the driver to discover parameter metadata, so **SQLDescribeParam** is not widely supported.

Setting Parameter Values

To set the value of a parameter, the application simply sets the value of the variable bound to the parameter. It is not important when this value is set, as long as it is set before the statement is executed. The application can set the value before or after binding the variable and it can change the value as many times as it wants. When the statement is executed, the driver simply retrieves the current value of the variable. This is particularly useful when a prepared statement is executed more than once; the application sets new values for some or all of the variables each time the statement is executed. For an example of this, see "Prepared Execution," earlier in this chapter.

If a length/indicator buffer was bound in the call to **SQLBindParameter**, it must be set to one of the following values before the statement is executed:

- The byte length of the data in the bound variable. The driver checks this length only if the variable is character or binary (*ValueType* is SQL_C_CHAR or SQL_C_BINARY).
- SQL_NTS. The data is a null-terminated string.
- SQL_NULL_DATA. The data value is NULL and the driver ignores the value of the bound variable.
- SQL_DATA_AT_EXEC or the result of the SQL_LEN_DATA_AT_EXEC macro. The value of the parameter is to be sent with **SQLPutData**. For more information, see "Sending Long Data," later in this chapter.

The following table shows the values of the bound variable and the length/indicator buffer that the application sets for a variety of parameter values.

Parameter value	Parameter (SQL) data type	Variable (C) data type	Value in bound variable	Value in length/ indicator buffer [d]
"ABC"	SQL_CHAR	SQL_C_CHAR	ABC\0 [a]	SQL_NTS or 3
10	SQL_INTEGER	SQL_C_SLONG	10	--
10	SQL_INTEGER	SQL_C_CHAR	10\0 [a]	SQL_NTS or 2
1 P.M.	SQL_TYPE_TIME	SQL_C_TYPE_ TIME	13,0,0 [b]	--
1 P.M.	SQL_TYPE_TIME	SQL_C_CHAR	{t '13:00:00'}\0 [a, c]	SQL_NTS or 14
NULL	SQL_SMALLINT	SQL_C_SSHORT	--	SQL_NULL_DATA

[a] "\0" represents a null-termination character. The null-termination character is required only if the value in the length/indicator buffer is SQL_NTS.

[b] The numbers in this list are the numbers stored in the fields of the TIME_STRUCT structure.

[c] The string uses the ODBC date escape clause. For more information, see "Date, Time, and Timestamp Literals" in Chapter 8, "SQL Statements."

[d] Drivers must always check this value to see if it is a special value such as SQL_NULL_DATA.

What a driver does with a parameter value at execution time is driver-dependent. If necessary, the driver converts the value from the C data type and byte length of the bound variable to the SQL data type, precision, and scale of the parameter. In most cases, the driver then sends the value to the data source. In some cases, it formats the value as text and inserts it into the SQL statement before sending the statement to the data source.

Sending Long Data

DBMSs define *long data* as any character or binary data over a certain size, such as 254 characters. It may not be possible to store an entire item of long data in memory, such as when the item represents a long text document or a bitmap. Because such data cannot be stored in a single buffer, the data source sends it to the driver in parts with **SQLPutData** when the statement is executed. Parameters for which data is sent at execution time are known as *data-at-execution parameters*.

Note An application can actually send any type of data at execution time with **SQLPutData**, although only character and binary data can be sent in parts. However, if the data is small enough to fit in a single buffer, there is generally no reason to use **SQLPutData**. It is much easier to bind the buffer and let the driver retrieve the data from the buffer.

To send data at execution time, the application:

1. Passes a 32-bit value that identifies the parameter in the *ParameterValuePtr* argument in **SQLBindParameter** rather than the address of a buffer. This value is not analyzed by the driver. It will be returned to the application later, so it should mean something to the application. For example, it might be the number of the parameter or the handle of a file containing data.
2. Passes the address of a length/indicator buffer in the *StrLen_or_IndPtr* argument of **SQLBindParameter**.
3. Stores SQL_DATA_AT_EXEC or the result of the SQL_LEN_DATA_AT_EXEC(*length*) macro in the length/indicator buffer. Both of these values indicate to the driver that the data for the parameter will be sent with **SQLPutData**. SQL_LEN_DATA_AT_EXEC(*length*) is used when sending long data to a data source that needs to know how many bytes of long data will be sent so that it can preallocate space. To determine if a data source requires this value, the application calls **SQLGetInfo** with the SQL_NEED_LONG_DATA_LEN option. All drivers must support this macro; if the data source does not require the byte length, the driver can ignore it.
4. Calls **SQLExecute** or **SQLExecDirect**. The driver discovers that a length/indicator buffer contains the value SQL_DATA_AT_EXEC or the result of the SQL_LEN_DATA_AT_EXEC(*length*) macro and returns SQL_NEED_DATA as the return value of the function.

5. Calls **SQLParamData** in response to the SQL_NEED_DATA return value. If long data needs to be sent, **SQLParamData** returns SQL_NEED_DATA. In the buffer pointed to by the *ValuePtrPtr* argument, the driver returns the value that identifies the data-at-execution parameter. If there is more than one data-at-execution parameter, the application must use this value to determine which parameter to send data for; the driver is not required to request data for data-at-execution parameters in any particular order.
6. Calls **SQLPutData** to send the parameter data to the driver. If the parameter data does not fit into a single buffer, as is often the case with long data, the application calls **SQLPutData** repeatedly to send the data in parts; it is up to the driver and data source to reassemble the data. If the application passes null-terminated string data, the driver or data source must remove the null-termination character as part of the reassembly process.
7. Calls **SQLParamData** again to indicate that it has sent all of the data for the parameter. If there are any data-at-execution parameters for which data has not been sent, the driver returns SQL_NEED_DATA and the value that identifies the next parameter; the application returns to step 6. If data has been sent for all data-at-execution parameters, the statement is executed. **SQLParamData** returns SQL_SUCCESS or SQL_SUCCESS_WITH_INFO, and can return any return value or diagnostic that **SQLExecute** or **SQLExecDirect** can return.

After **SQLExecute** or **SQLExecDirect** returns SQL_NEED_DATA and before data has been completely sent for the last data-at-execution parameter, the statement is in a Need Data state. While a statement is in a Need Data state, the application can call only **SQLPutData**, **SQLParamData**, **SQLCancel**, **SQLGetDiagField**, or **SQLGetDiagRec**; all other functions return SQLSTATE HY010 (Function sequence error). Calling **SQLCancel** cancels execution of the statement and returns it to its previous state. For more information, see Appendix B, "ODBC State Transition Tables."

For an example of sending data at execution time, see the **SQLPutData** function description.

Retrieving Output Parameters by SQLGetData

An application may retrieve bound output parameters by calling **SQLBindParameter**, in which case output values are present in the application variables to which the respective parameters are bound. If the output parameters are unbound, on the other hand, the application can read argument values by calling **SQLGetData**. The application may use both these techniques if some parameters are bound and some are unbound.

For unbound output parameters following the highest-numbered bound parameter, portable applications obtain the parameter data by calling **SQLGetData** in ascending order of parameter number. It is driver-defined whether an application can obtain parameter data in a different sequence. It is driver-defined whether parameter data for lower-numbered, unbound parameters is available.

The application can achieve type conversion of the parameter data by specifying in the call to **SQLGetData** either the desired target type or the value SQL_APD_TYPE, which means that the APD indicates the desired target type even though the parameter is unbound.

If the length of the unbound output parameter value exceeds the length of the application's buffer, **SQLGetData** may be called multiple times to obtain the value of a single parameter of SQL_CHAR or SQL_VARCHAR type in pieces of manageable size.

Procedure Parameters

Parameters in procedure calls can be input, input/output, or output parameters. This is different from parameters in all other SQL statements, which are always input parameters.

Input parameters are used to send values to the procedure. For example, suppose the Parts table has PartID, Description, and Price columns. The InsertPart procedure might have an input parameter for each column in the table. For example:

```
{call InsertPart(?, ?, ?)}
```

A driver should not modify the contents of an input buffer until **SQLExecDirect** or **SQLExecute** returns SQL_SUCCESS, SQL_SUCCESS_WITH_INFO, SQL_ERROR, SQL_INVALID_HANDLE, or SQL_NO_DATA. The contents of the input buffer should not be modified while **SQLExecDirect** or **SQLExecute** returns SQL_NEED_DATA or SQL_STILL_EXECUTING.

Input/output parameters are used both to send values to procedures and retrieve values from procedures. Using the same parameter as both an input and an output parameter tends to be confusing and should be avoided. For example, suppose a procedure accepts an order ID and returns the ID of the customer. This can be defined with a single input/output parameter:

```
{call GetCustID(?)}
```

It may be better to use two parameters: an input parameter for the order ID and an output or input/output parameter for the customer ID:

```
{call GetCustID(?, ?)}
```

Output parameters are used to retrieve the procedure return value and to retrieve values from procedure arguments; procedures that return values are sometimes known as *functions*. For example, suppose the GetCustID procedure just mentioned returns a value that indicates whether it was able to find the order. In the following call, the first parameter is an output parameter used to retrieve the procedure return value, the second parameter is an input parameter used to specify the order ID, and the third parameter is an output parameter used to retrieve the customer ID:

```
{? = call GetCustID(?, ?)}
```

Drivers handle values for input and input/output parameters in procedures no differently than input parameters in other SQL statements. When the statement is executed, they retrieve the values of the variables bound to these parameters and send them to the data source.

After the statement has been executed, drivers store the returned values of input/output and output parameters in the variables bound to those parameters. Note that these are not guaranteed to be set until after all results returned by the procedure have been fetched and **SQLMoreResults** has returned SQL_NO_DATA. If executing the statement results in an error, the contents of the input/output parameter buffer or output parameter buffer are undefined.

An application calls **SQLProcedure** to determine if a procedure has a return value. It calls **SQLProcedureColumns** to determine the type (return value, input, input/output, or output) of each procedure parameter.

Arrays of Parameter Values

It is often useful for applications to pass arrays of parameters. For example, using arrays of parameters and a parameterized **INSERT** statement, an application can insert a number of rows at once. There are several advantages to using arrays. First, network traffic is reduced, because the data for many statements is sent in a single packet (if the data source supports parameter arrays natively). Second, some data sources can execute SQL statements using arrays faster than executing the same number of separate SQL statements. Finally, when the data is stored in an array, as often the case for screen data, the application can bind all of the rows in a particular column with a single call to **SQLBindParameter** and update them by executing a single statement.

Unfortunately, not many data sources support parameter arrays. However, a driver can emulate parameter arrays by executing an SQL statement once for each set of parameter values. This can lead to increases in speed, since the driver can then prepare the statement that it plans to execute once for each parameter set. It might also lead to simpler application code.

Binding Arrays of Parameters

Applications that use arrays of parameters bind the arrays to the parameters in the SQL statement. There are two binding styles:

- Bind an array to each parameter. Each data structure (array) contains all the data for a single parameter. This is called *column-wise binding* because it binds a column of values for a single parameter.
- Define a structure to hold the parameter data for an entire set of parameters and bind an array of these structures. Each data structure contains the data for a single SQL statement. This is called *row-wise binding* because it binds a row of parameters.

As when the application binds single variables to parameters, it calls **SQLBindParameter** to bind arrays to parameters. The only difference is that the addresses passed are array addresses, not single-variable addresses. The application sets the SQL_ATTR_PARAM_BIND_TYPE statement attribute to specify whether it is using column-wise (the default) or row-wise binding. Whether to use column-wise or row-wise binding is largely a matter of application preference. Depending on how the processor accesses memory, row-wise binding might be faster. However, the difference is likely to be negligible except for very large numbers of rows of parameters.

Column-Wise Binding

When using column-wise binding, an application binds one or two arrays to each parameter for which data is to be provided. The first array holds the data values and the second array holds length/indicator buffers. Each array contains as many elements as there are values for the parameter.

Column-wise binding is the default. The application can also change from row-wise binding to column-wise binding by setting the SQL_ATTR_PARAM_BIND_TYPE statement attribute. The following diagram shows how column-wise binding works.

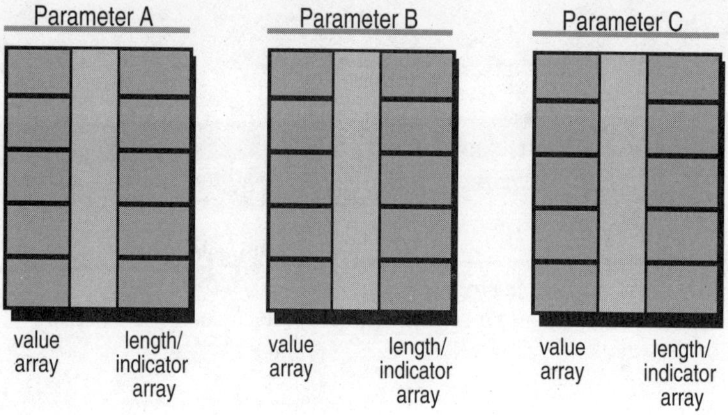

Figure 9.1 Column-wise binding of parameters

For example, the following code binds 10-element arrays to parameters for the PartID, Description, and Price columns and executes a statement to insert ten rows. It uses column-wise binding.

```
#define DESC_LEN 51
#define ARRAY_SIZE 10

SQLCHAR *      Statement = "INSERT INTO Parts (PartID, Description, Price) "
                           "VALUES (?, ?, ?)";
SQLUINTEGER  PartIDArray[ARRAY_SIZE];
SQLCHAR      DescArray[ARRAY_SIZE][DESC_LEN];
SQLREAL      PriceArray[ARRAY_SIZE];
SQLINTEGER   PartIDIndArray[ARRAY_SIZE], DescLenOrIndArray[ARRAY_SIZE],
             PriceIndArray[ARRAY_SIZE];
SQLUSMALLINT i, ParamsProcessed, ParamStatusArray[ARRAY_SIZE];

// Set the SQL_ATTR_PARAM_BIND_TYPE statement attribute to use column-wise binding.
SQLSetStmtAttr(hstmt, SQL_ATTR_PARAM_BIND_TYPE, SQL_PARAMETER_BIND_BY_COLUMN, 0);

// Specify the number of elements in each parameter array.
SQLSetStmtAttr(hstmt, SQL_ATTR_PARAMSET_SIZE, ARRAY_SIZE, 0);

// Specify an array in which to return the status of each set of parameters.
SQLSetStmtAttr(hstmt, SQL_ATTR_PARAM_STATUS_PTR, ParamStatusArray, 0);

// Specify an SQLUINTEGER value in which to return the number of sets of parameters
// processed.
SQLSetStmtAttr(hstmt, SQL_ATTR_PARAMS_PROCESSED_PTR, &ParamsProcessed, 0);
```

```
// Bind the parameters in column-wise fashion.
SQLBindParameter(hstmt, 1, SQL_PARAM_INPUT, SQL_C_ULONG, SQL_INTEGER, 5, 0,
                 PartIDArray, 0, PartIDIndArray);
SQLBindParameter(hstmt, 2, SQL_PARAM_INPUT, SQL_C_CHAR, SQL_CHAR, DESC_LEN - 1, 0,
                 DescArray, DESC_LEN, DescLenOrIndArray);
SQLBindParameter(hstmt, 3, SQL_PARAM_INPUT, SQL_C_FLOAT, SQL_REAL, 7, 0,
                 PriceArray, 0, PriceIndArray);

// Set part ID, description, and price.
for (i = 0; i < ARRAY_SIZE; i++) {
   GetNewValues(&PartIDArray[i], DescArray[i], &PriceArray[i]);
   PartIDIndArray[i] = 0;
   DescLenOrIndArray[i] = SQL_NTS;
   PriceIndArray[i] = 0;
}

// Execute the statement.
SQLExecDirect(hstmt, Statement, SQL_NTS);

// Check to see which sets of parameters were processed successfully.
for (i = 0; i < ParamsProcessed; i++) {
   printf("Parameter Set  Status\n");
   printf("-------------  -------------\n");
   switch (ParamStatusArray[i]) {
      case SQL_PARAM_SUCCESS:
      case SQL_PARAM_SUCCESS_WITH_INFO:
         printf("%13d  Success\n", i);
         break;

      case SQL_PARAM_ERROR:
         printf("%13d  Error\n", i);
         break;

      case SQL_PARAM_UNUSED:
         printf("%13d  Not processed\n", i);
         break;

      case SQL_PARAM_DIAG_UNAVAILABLE:
         printf("%13d  Unknown\n", i);
         break;

   }
}
```

Row-Wise Binding

When using row-wise binding, an application defines a structure for each set of parameters. The structure contains one or two elements for each parameter. The first element holds the parameter value and the second element holds the length/indicator buffer. The application then allocates an array of these structures, which contains as many elements as there are values for each parameter.

The application declares the size of the structure to the driver with the SQL_ATTR_PARAM_BIND_TYPE statement attribute. The application binds the addresses of the parameters in the first structure of the array. Thus, the driver can calculate the address of the data for a particular row and column as:

```
Address = Bound Address + ((Row Number - 1) * Structure Size) + Offset
```

where rows are numbered from 1 to the size of the parameter set, and the offset, if defined, is the value pointed to by the SQL_ATTR_PARAM_BIND_OFFSET_PTR statement attribute. The following diagram shows how row-wise binding works. The parameters can be placed in the structure in any order, but are shown in sequential order for clarity.

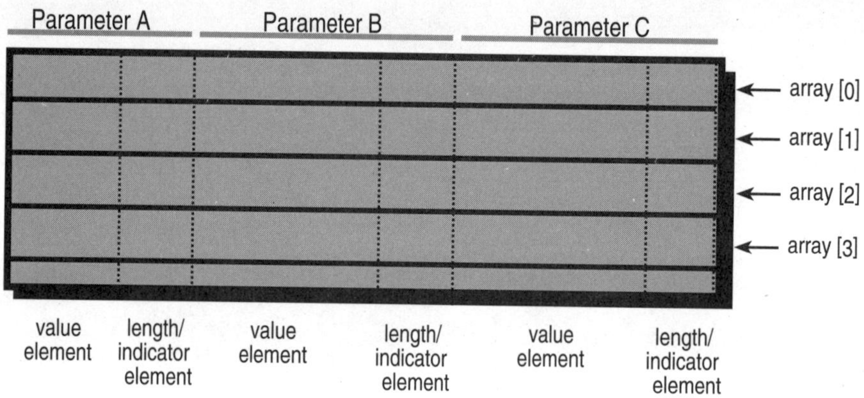

Figure 9.2 Row-wise binding of parameters

For example, the following code creates a structure with elements for the values to store in the PartID, Description, and Price column. It then allocates a 10-element array of these structures and binds it to parameters for the PartID, Description, and Price columns, using row-wise binding. It then executes a statement to insert 10 rows.

```
#define DESC_LEN 51
#define ARRAY_SIZE 10

typedef tagPartStruct {
   SQLREAL      Price;
   SQLUINTEGER PartID;
   SQLCHAR      Desc[DESC_LEN];
   SQLINTEGER  PriceInd;
   SQLINTEGER  PartIDInd;
   SQLINTEGER  DescLenOrInd;
} PartStruct;
```

```
PartStruct PartArray[ARRAY_SIZE];
SQLCHAR *    Statement = "INSERT INTO Parts (PartID, Description, Price) "
                         "VALUES (?, ?, ?)";
SQLUSMALLINT i, ParamsProcessed, ParamStatusArray[ARRAY_SIZE];

// Set the SQL_ATTR_PARAM_BIND_TYPE statement attribute to use column-wise binding.
SQLSetStmtAttr(hstmt, SQL_ATTR_PARAM_BIND_TYPE, sizeof(PartStruct), 0);

// Specify the number of elements in each parameter array.
SQLSetStmtAttr(hstmt, SQL_ATTR_PARAMSET_SIZE, ARRAY_SIZE, 0);

// Specify an array in which to return the status of each set of parameters.
SQLSetStmtAttr(hstmt, SQL_ATTR_PARAM_STATUS_PTR, ParamStatusArray, 0);

// Specify an SQLUINTEGER value in which to return the number of sets of parameters
// processed.
SQLSetStmtAttr(hstmt, SQL_ATTR_PARAMS_PROCESSED_PTR, &ParamsProcessed, 0);

// Bind the parameters in row-wise fashion.
SQLBindParameter(hstmt, 1, SQL_PARAM_INPUT, SQL_C_ULONG, SQL_INTEGER, 5, 0,
                 &PartArray[0].PartID, 0, &PartArray[0].PartIDInd);
SQLBindParameter(hstmt, 2, SQL_PARAM_INPUT, SQL_C_CHAR, SQL_CHAR, DESC_LEN - 1, 0,
                 PartArray[0].Desc, DESC_LEN, &PartArray[0].DescLenOrInd);
SQLBindParameter(hstmt, 3, SQL_PARAM_INPUT, SQL_C_FLOAT, SQL_REAL, 7, 0,
                 &PartArray[0].Price, 0, &PartArray[0].PriceInd);

// Set part ID, description, and price.
for (i = 0; i < ARRAY_SIZE; i++) {
   GetNewValues(&PartArray[i].PartID, PartArray[i].Desc, &PartArray[i].Price);
   PartArray[0].PartIDInd = 0;
   PartArray[0].DescLenOrInd = SQL_NTS;
   PartArray[0].PriceInd = 0;
}

// Execute the statement.
SQLExecDirect(hstmt, Statement, SQL_NTS);

// Check to see which sets of parameters were processed successfully.
for (i = 0; i < ParamsProcessed; i++) {
   printf("Parameter Set  Status\n");
   printf("-------------  -------------\n");
   switch (ParamStatusArray[i]) {
      case SQL_PARAM_SUCCESS:
      case SQL_PARAM_SUCCESS_WITH_INFO:
         printf("%13d  Success\n", i);
         break;

      case SQL_PARAM_ERROR:
         printf("%13d  Error\n", i);
         break;

      case SQL_PARAM_UNUSED:
         printf("%13d  Not processed\n", i);
         break;
```

```
      case SQL_PARAM_DIAG_UNAVAILABLE:
         printf("%13d  Unknown\n", i);
         break;

   }
```

Using Arrays of Parameters

To use arrays of parameters, the application calls **SQLSetStmtAttr** with an *Attribute* argument of SQL_ATTR_PARAMSET_SIZE to specify the number of sets of parameters. It calls **SQLSetStmtAttr** with an *Attribute* argument of SQL_ATTR_PARAMS_PROCESSED_PTR to specify the address of a variable in which the driver can return the number of sets of parameters processed, including error sets. It calls **SQLSetStmtAttr** with an *Attribute* argument of SQL_ATTR_PARAM_STATUS_PTR to point to an array in which to return status information for each row of parameter values. The driver stores these addresses in the structure it maintains for the statement.

Note In ODBC 2.*x*, **SQLParamOptions** was called to specify multiple values for a parameter. In ODBC 3.0, the call to **SQLParamOptions** has been replaced by calls to **SQLSetStmtAttr** to set the SQL_ATTR_PARAMSET_SIZE and SQL_ATTR_PARAMS_PROCESSED_ARRAY attributes.

Before executing the statement, the application sets the value of each element of each bound array. When the statement is executed, the driver uses the information it stored to retrieve the parameter values and send them to the data source; if possible, the driver should send these values as arrays. Although the use of arrays of parameters is best implemented by executing the SQL statement with all of the parameters in the array with a single call to the data source, this capability is not widely available in DBMSs today. Thus, drivers can simulate it by executing an SQL statement multiple times, each with a single set of parameters.

Before an application uses arrays of parameters, it must be sure that they are supported by the drivers used by the application. There are two ways to do this:

- Use only drivers known to support arrays of parameters. The application can hard-code the names of these drivers or the user can be instructed to use only these drivers. Custom applications and vertical applications commonly use a limited set of drivers.
- Check for support of arrays of parameters at run time. A driver supports arrays of parameters if it is possible to set the SQL_ATTR_PARAMSET_SIZE statement attribute to a value greater than 1. Generic applications and vertical applications commonly check for support of arrays of parameters at run time.

The availability of row counts and result sets in parameterized execution can be determined by calling **SQLGetInfo** with the SQL_PARAM_ARRAY_ROW_COUNTS and SQL_PARAM_ARRAY_SELECTS

not if SQL_PARC_NO_BATCH is returned. For **SELECT** statements, the parameter status array is filled in if SQL_PAS_BATCH is returned for SQL_PARAM_ARRAY_SELECT, but not if SQL_PAS_NO_BATCH or SQL_PAS_NO_SELECT is returned.

Data-at-Execution Parameters

If any of the values in the length/indicator array are SQL_DATA_AT_EXEC or the result of the SQL_LEN_DATA_AT_EXEC(*length*) macro, the data for those values is sent with **SQLPutData** in the usual way. Two aspects of this process bear special comment, as they are not readily obvious:

- When the driver returns SQL_NEED_DATA, it must set the address of the row number variable to the row for which it needs data. As in the single-valued case, the application cannot make any assumptions about the order in which the driver will request parameter values within a single set of parameters. If an error occurs in the execution of a data-at-execution parameter, the buffer specified by the SQL_ATTR_PARAMS_PROCESSED_PTR statement attribute is set to the number of the row on which the error occurred, the status for the row in the row status array specified by the SQL_ATTR_PARAM_STATUS_PTR statement attribute is set to SQL_PARAM_ERROR, and the call to **SQLExecute**, **SQLExecDirect**, **SQLParamData**, or **SQLPutData** returns SQL_ERROR. The contents of this buffer are undefined if **SQLExecute**, **SQLExecDirect**, or **SQLParamData** return SQL_STILL_EXECUTING.
- Because the driver does not interpret the value in the *ParameterValuePtr* argument of **SQLBindParameter** for data-at-execution parameters, if the application provides a pointer to an array, **SQLParamData** does not extract and return an element of this array to the application. Instead, it returns the scalar value the application had supplied. This means the value returned by **SQLParamData** is not sufficient to specify the parameter for which the application needs to send data; the application also needs to consider the current row number.

  When only some of the elements of an array of parameters are data-at-execution parameters, the application must pass the address of an array in *ParameterValuePtr* that contains elements for all the parameters. This array is interpreted normally for the parameters that are not data-at-execution parameters. For the data-at-execution parameters, the value that **SQLParamData** provides to the application, which normally could be used to identify the data that the driver is requesting on this occasion, is always the address of the array.

options. For **INSERT**, **UPDATE**, and **DELETE** statements, the SQL_PARAM_ARRAY_ROW_COUNTS option indicates whether individual row counts (one for each parameter set) are available (SQL_PARC_BATCH), or row counts are rolled up into one (SQL_PARC_NO_BATCH). For **SELECT** statements, the SQL_PARAM_ARRAY_SELECTS option indicates whether a result set is available for each set of parameters (SQL_PAS_BATCH), or only one result set is available (SQL_PAS_NO_BATCH). If the driver does not allow result set–generating statements to be executed with an array of parameters, SQL_PARAM_ARRAY_SELECTS returns SQL_PAS_NO_SELECT. It is data source–specific whether arrays of parameters can be used with other types of statements, especially because the use of parameters in these statements would be data source–specific, and would not follow ODBC SQL grammar.

The array pointed to by the SQL_ATTR_PARAM_OPERATION_PTR statement attribute can be used to ignore rows of parameters. If an element of the array is set to SQL_PARAM_IGNORE, the set of parameters corresponding to that element is excluded from the **SQLExecute** or **SQLExecDirect** call. The array pointed to by the SQL_ATTR_PARAM_OPERATION_PTR attribute is allocated and filled in by the application, and read by the driver. If fetched rows are used as input parameters, the values of the row status array can be used in the parameter operation array.

Error Processing

If an error occurs while executing the statement, the execution function returns an error and sets the row number variable to the number of the row containing the error. It is data source–specific whether all rows except the error set are executed, or all rows before (but not after) the error set are executed. Because it processes sets of parameters, the driver sets the buffer specified by the SQL_ATTR_PARAMS_PROCESSED_PTR statement attribute to the number of the row currently being processed. If all sets except the error set are executed, the driver sets this buffer to SQL_ATTR_PARAMSET_SIZE after all rows are processed.

If the SQL_ATTR_PARAM_STATUS_PTR statement attribute has been set, **SQLExecute** or **SQLExecDirect** returns the *parameter status array*, which provides the status of each set of parameters. The parameter status array is allocated by the application and filled in by the driver. Its elements indicate whether the SQL statement was executed successfully for the row of parameters, or whether an error occurred while processing the set of parameters. If an error occurred, the driver sets the corresponding value in the parameter status array to SQL_PARAM_ERROR, and returns SQL_SUCCESS_WITH_INFO. The application can check the status array to determine which rows were processed. Using the row number, the application can often correct the error and resume processing.

How the parameter status array is used is determined by the SQL_PARAM_ARRAY_ROW_COUNTS and SQL_PARAM_ARRAY_SELECTS options returned by a call to **SQLGetInfo**. For **INSERT**, **UPDATE**, and **DELETE** statements, the parameter status array is filled in with status information if SQL_PARC_BATCH is returned for SQL_PARAM_ARRAY_ROW_COUNTS, but

Asynchronous Execution

By default, drivers execute ODBC functions synchronously; that is, the application calls a function and the driver does not return control to the application until it has finished executing the function. However, some functions can be executed asynchronously; that is, the application calls the function and the driver, after minimal processing, returns control to the application. The application can then call other functions while the first function is still executing.

Asynchronous execution is supported for most functions that are largely executed on the data source, such as the functions to prepare and execute SQL statements, retrieve metadata, and fetch data. It is most useful when the task being executed on the data source takes a long time, such as a complex query against a large database.

Note In general, applications should execute functions asynchronously only on single-threaded operating systems. On multithread operating systems, applications should execute functions on separate threads, rather than executing them asynchronously on the same thread. No functionality is lost if drivers that operate only on multithread operating systems do not support asynchronous execution.

Asynchronous execution is controlled on either a per-statement or per-connection basis, depending on the data source. That is, the application specifies not that a particular function is to be executed asynchronously, but that any function executed on a particular statement or a particular connection is to be executed asynchronously. To find out which one is supported, an application calls **SQLGetInfo** with an option of SQL_ASYNC_MODE. SQL_AM_CONNECTION is returned if connection-level asynchronous execution is supported; SQL_AM_STATEMENT if statement-level asynchronous execution is supported.

To specify that functions executed with a particular statement are to be executed asynchronously, the application calls **SQLSetStmtAttr** with the SQL_ATTR_ASYNC_ENABLE attribute and sets it to SQL_ASYNC_ENABLE_ON. If connection-level asynchronous processing is supported, the SQL_ATTR_ASYNC_ENABLE statement attribute is read-only, and its value is the same as the connection attribute of the connection on which the statement was allocated. It is driver-specific whether the value of the statement attribute is set at statement allocation time or later. Attempting to set it will return SQL_ERROR and SQLSTATE HYC00 (Optional feature not implemented).

The maximum number of active concurrent statements in asynchronous mode that the driver can support on a given connection can be determined by calling **SQLGetInfo** with the SQL_MAX_ASYNC_CONCURRENT_STATEMENTS option.

To specify that functions executed with a particular connection are to be executed asynchronously, the application calls **SQLSetConnectAttr** with the SQL_ATTR_ASYNC_ENABLE attribute and sets it to SQL_ASYNC_ENABLE_ON. All future statement handles allocated on the connection will be enabled for asynchronous execution; it is driver-defined whether existing statement handles will be enabled by this action. If SQL_ATTR_ASYNC_ENABLE is set to SQL_ASYNC_ENABLE_OFF, all statements on the connection are in synchronous mode. Note that an error is returned if asynchronous execution is enabled while there is an active statement on the connection.

When the application executes a function with a statement that is enabled for asynchronous processing, the driver performs a minimal amount of processing (such as checking arguments for errors), hands processing to the data source, and returns control to the application with the SQL_STILL_EXECUTING return code. The application then performs other tasks. To determine when the asynchronous function has finished, the application polls the driver at regular intervals by calling the function with the same arguments as it originally used. If the function is still executing, it returns SQL_STILL_EXECUTING; if it has finished executing, it returns the code it would have returned had it executed synchronously, such as SQL_SUCCESS, SQL_ERROR, or SQL_NEED_DATA. For example:

```
SQLHSTMT  hstmt1;
SQLRETURN rc;

// Specify that the statement is to be executed asynchronously.
SQLSetStmtAttr(hstmt1, SQL_ATTR_ASYNC_ENABLE, SQL_ASYNC_ENABLE_ON, 0);

// Execute a SELECT statement asynchronously.
while ((rc=SQLExecDirect(hstmt1,"SELECT * FROM Orders",SQL_NTS))==SQL_STILL_EXECUTING)
{
   // While the statement is still executing, do something else.
   // Do not use hstmt1, as it is being used asynchronously.
}

// When the statement has finished executing, retrieve the results.
```

Whether the driver executes the function synchronously or asynchronously is up to the driver. For example, suppose the result set metadata is cached in the driver. In this case, it takes very little time to execute **SQLDescribeCol** and the driver should simply execute the function, rather than artificially delaying execution. On the other hand, if the driver needs to retrieve the metadata from the data source, it should return control to the application while it is doing this. Thus, the application must be able to handle a return code other than SQL_STILL_EXECUTING when it first executes a function asynchronously.

While the function is being executed asynchronously, the application can call functions on any other statements. It can also call functions on any connection except the one associated with the asynchronous statement. On the asynchronous statement, the application can call only the asynchronously executing function, or **SQLCancel**, **SQLGetDiagField**, or **SQLGetDiagRec**. **SQLGetDiagField** or **SQLGetDiagRec** can be called on an asynchronously executing statement handle to return a header diagnostic field but not a record diagnostic field. On the connection associated with the asynchronous statement, the application can call only **SQLAllocHandle** (to allocate a statement handle), **SQLGetDiagField**, **SQLGetDiagRec**, or **SQLGetFunctions**. If the application calls any other function with the asynchronous statement or with the connection associated with that statement, the function returns SQLSTATE HY010 (Function sequence error). The application can call any function using handles other than the original statement handle or the original connection handle. For example:

```
SQLHDBC      hdbc1, hdbc2;
SQLHSTMT     hstmt1, hstmt2, hstmt3;
SQLCHAR      *SQLStatement = "SELECT * FROM Orders";
SQLUINTEGER InfoValue;
SQLRETURN    rc;

SQLAllocHandle(SQL_HANDLE_STMT, hdbc1, &hstmt1);
SQLAllocHandle(SQL_HANDLE_STMT, hdbc1, &hstmt2);
SQLAllocHandle(SQL_HANDLE_STMT, hdbc2, &hstmt3);

// Specify that hstmt1 is to be executed asynchronously.
SQLSetStmtAttr(hstmt1, SQL_ATTR_ASYNC_ENABLE, SQL_ASYNC_ENABLE_ON, 0);

// Execute hstmt1 asynchronously.
while ((rc = SQLExecDirect(hstmt1, SQLStatement, SQL_NTS)) == SQL_STILL_EXECUTING) {
   // The following calls return HY010 because the previous call to SQLExecDirect is
   // still executing asynchronously on hstmt1. The first call uses hstmt1 and the
   // second call uses hdbc1, on which hstmt1 is allocated.
   SQLExecDirect(hstmt1, SQLStatement, SQL_NTS);                            // Error!
   SQLGetInfo(hdbc1, SQL_UNION, (SQLPOINTER) &InfoValue, 0, NULL);   // Error!

   // The following calls do not return errors. They use a statement handle other than
   // hstmt1 or a connection handle other than hdbc1.
   SQLExecDirect(hstmt2, SQLStatement, SQL_NTS);                       // OK
   SQLTables(hstmt3, NULL, 0, NULL, 0, NULL, 0, NULL, 0);              // OK
   SQLGetInfo(hdbc2, SQL_UNION, (SQLPOINTER) &InfoValue, 0, NULL);  // OK
}
```

When an application calls a function to determine if it is still executing asynchronously, it must use the original statement handle. This is because asynchronous execution is tracked on a per-statement basis. The application must also supply valid values for the other arguments—the original arguments will do—to get past error checking in the Driver Manager. However, after the driver checks the statement handle and determines that the statement is executing asynchronously, it ignores all other arguments.

While a function is executing asynchronously—that is, after it has returned SQL_STILL_EXECUTING and before it returns a different code—the application can cancel it by calling **SQLCancel** with the same statement handle. This is not guaranteed to cancel function execution. For example, the function might have already finished. Furthermore, the code returned by **SQLCancel** indicates whether **SQLCancel** successfully attempted to cancel the function, not whether it actually did cancel the function. To determine if the function was canceled, the application calls the function again. If the function was canceled, it returns SQL_ERROR and SQLSTATE HY008 (Operation canceled). If the function was not canceled, it returns another code, such as SQL_SUCCESS, SQL_STILL_EXECUTING, or SQL_ERROR with a different SQLSTATE.

To disable asynchronous execution of a particular statement when the driver supports statement-level asynchronous processing, the application calls **SQLSetStmtAttr** with the SQL_ATTR_ASYNC_ENABLE attribute and sets it to SQL_ASYNC_ENABLE_OFF. If the driver supports connection-level asynchronous processing, the application calls **SQLSetConnectAttr** to set SQL_ATTR_ASYNC_ENABLE to SQL_ASYNC_ENABLE_OFF, which disables asynchronous execution of all statements on the connection.

When **SQLGetDiagField** is called on a statement handle on which a function is currently executing asynchronously, the following values are returned:

- What the SQL_DIAG_CURSOR_ROW_COUNT, SQL_DIAG_DYNAMIC_FUNCTION, SQL_DIAG_DYNAMIC_FUNCTION_CODE, and SQL_DIAG_ROW_COUNT header fields return are undefined.
- The SQL_DIAG_NUMBER header field returns 0.
- The SQL_DIAG_RETURNCODE header field returns SQL_STILL_EXECUTING.
- All record fields return SQL_NO_DATA.

SQLGetDiagRec always returns SQL_NO_DATA when it is called on a statement handle on which a function is currently executing asynchronously.

For a list of functions that can be executed asynchronously, see the SQL_ATTR_ASYNC_ENABLE attribute in the **SQLSetStmtAttr** function description.

Freeing a Statement Handle

As mentioned earlier, it is more efficient to reuse statements than drop them and allocate new ones. Before executing a new SQL statement on a statement, applications should be sure that the current statement settings are appropriate. These include statement attributes, parameter bindings, and result set bindings. Generally, parameters and result sets for the old SQL statement need to be unbound (by calling **SQLFreeStmt** with the SQL_RESET_PARAMS and SQL_UNBIND options) and rebound for the new SQL statement.

When the application has finished using the statement, it calls **SQLFreeHandle** to free the statement. After freeing the statement, it is an application programming error to use the statement's handle in a call to an ODBC function; doing so has undefined but probably fatal consequences.

When **SQLFreeHandle** is called, the driver releases the structure used to store information about the statement. Note that **SQLDisconnect** automatically frees all statements on a connection.

CHAPTER 10

Retrieving Results (Basic)

A *result set* is a set of rows on the data source that match certain criteria. It is a conceptual table that results from a query and that is available to an application in tabular form. **SELECT** statements, catalog functions, and some procedures create result sets. For example, the first SQL statement creates a result set containing all the rows and all the columns in the Orders table and the second SQL statement creates a result set containing OrderID, SalesPerson, and Status columns for the rows in the Orders table in which the Status is OPEN.

```
SELECT * FROM Orders
SELECT OrderID, SalesPerson, Status FROM Orders WHERE Status = 'OPEN'
```

A result set can be empty, which is different from no result set at all. For example, the following SQL statement creates an empty result set:

```
SELECT * FROM Orders WHERE 1 = 2
```

An empty result set is no different from any other result set except that it has no rows. For example, the application can retrieve metadata for the result set, can attempt to fetch rows, and must close the cursor over the result set.

The process of retrieving rows from the data source and returning them to the application is called *fetching*. This chapter explains the basic parts of that process. For information about more advanced topics, such as block and scrollable cursors, see "Block Cursors" and "Scrollable Cursors" in Chapter 11, "Retrieving Results (Advanced)." For information about updating, deleting, and inserting rows, see Chapter 12, "Updating Data."

Was a Result Set Created?

In most situations, application programmers know whether the statements their application executes will create a result set. This is the case if the application uses hard-coded SQL statements written by the programmer. It is usually the case when the application constructs SQL statements at run time: The programmer can easily include code that flags whether a **SELECT** statement or an **INSERT** statement is being constructed. In a few situations, the programmer cannot possibly know whether a statement will create a result set. This is true if the application provides a way for the user to enter and execute an SQL statement. It is also true when the application constructs a statement at run time to execute a procedure.

In such cases, the application calls **SQLNumResultCols** to determine the number of columns in the result set. If this is 0, the statement did not create a result set; if it is any other number, the statement did create a result set.

The application can call **SQLNumResultCols** at any time after the statement is prepared or executed. However, because some data sources cannot easily describe the result sets that will be created by prepared statements, performance will suffer if **SQLNumResultCols** is called after a statement is prepared, but before it is executed.

Some data sources also support determining the number of rows that an SQL statement returns in a result set. To do so, the application calls **SQLRowCount**. Exactly what the row count represents is indicated by the setting of the SQL_DYNAMIC_CURSOR_ATTRIBUTES2, SQL_FORWARD_ONLY_CURSOR_ATTRIBUTES2, SQL_KEYSET_CURSOR_ATTRIBUTES2, or SQL_STATIC_CURSOR_ATTRIBUTES2 option (depending on the type of the cursor) returned by a call to **SQLGetInfo**. This bitmask indicates for each cursor type whether the row count returned is exact or approximate, or is not available at all. Whether row counts for static or keyset-driven cursors are affected by changes made through **SQLBulkOperations** or **SQLSetPos**, or by positioned update or delete statements, depends upon other bits returned by the same option arguments listed previously. For more information, see the **SQLGetInfo** function description.

Result Set Metadata

Metadata is data that describes other data. For example, result set metadata describes the result set, such as the number of columns in the result set, the data types of those columns, their names, precision, nullability, and so on.

Interoperable applications should always check the metadata of result set columns. The metadata for a column in a result set might differ from the metadata for the column as returned by a catalog function. For example, suppose that an updatable column is included in a result set created by joining two tables. While **SQLColumnPrivileges** might indicate that a user can update the column, the result set metadata might not if the column is on the “many” side of the join; many data sources can update columns on the “one” side of a join but not on the “many” side. Even data types cannot be assumed to be the same, as the data source might promote the data type while creating the result set.

How is Metadata Used?

Applications require metadata for most result set operations. For example, the application uses the data type of a column to determine what kind of variable to bind to that column. It uses the byte length of a character column to determine how much space it needs to display data from that column. How an application determines the metadata for a column depends on the type of the application.

Vertical applications work with predefined tables and perform predefined operations on those tables. Because the result set metadata for such applications is defined before the application is even written and is controlled by the application developer, it can be hard-coded into the application. For example, if an order ID column is defined as a 4-byte integer in the data source, the application can always bind a 4-byte integer to that column. When metadata is hard-coded in the application, a change to the tables used by the application generally implies a change to the application code. This is rarely a problem, as such changes are generally made as part of a new release of the application.

Like vertical applications, custom applications generally work with predefined tables and perform predefined operations on those tables. For example, an application might be written to transfer data among three different data sources; the data to be transferred is generally known when the application is written. Thus, custom applications also tend to have hard-coded metadata.

Generic applications, especially applications that support ad-hoc queries, almost never know the metadata of the result sets they create. Therefore, they must discover the metadata at run time using the functions **SQLNumResultCols**, **SQLDescribeCol**, and **SQLColAttribute**, which are described in the next section, "SQLDescribeCol and SQLColAttribute."

All applications, regardless of their type, can hard-code metadata for the result sets returned by the catalog functions. These result sets are defined in the reference section of this manual.

SQLDescribeCol and SQLColAttribute

SQLDescribeCol and **SQLColAttribute** are used to retrieve result set metadata. The difference between these two functions is that **SQLDescribeCol** always returns the same five pieces of information (a column's name, data type, precision, scale, and nullability), while **SQLColAttribute** returns a single piece of information requested by the application. However, **SQLColAttribute** can return a much richer selection of metadata, including a column's case sensitivity, display size, updatability, and searchability.

Many applications, especially ones that only display data, only require the metadata returned by **SQLDescribeCol**. For these applications, it is faster to use **SQLDescribeCol** than **SQLColAttribute** because the information is returned in a single call. Other applications, especially ones that update data, require the additional metadata returned by **SQLColAttribute** and so use both functions. In addition, **SQLColAttribute** supports driver-specific metadata; for more information, see "Driver-Specific Data Types, Descriptor Types, Information Types, Diagnostic Types, and Attributes" in Chapter 17, "Programming Considerations."

An application can retrieve result set metadata at any time after a statement has been prepared or executed and before the cursor over the result set is closed. Very few applications require result set metadata after the statement is prepared and before it is executed. If possible, applications should wait to retrieve metadata until after the statement is executed. The reason is that some data sources cannot return metadata for prepared statements and emulating this capability in the driver is often a slow process. For example, the driver might generate a zero row result set by replacing the **WHERE** clause of a **SELECT** statement with the clause **WHERE 1 = 2** and executing the resulting statement.

Metadata is often expensive to retrieve from the data source. Because of this, drivers should cache any metadata they retrieve from the server and hold it for as long as the cursor over the result set is open. Also, applications should request only the metadata they absolutely need.

Binding Result Set Columns

Data fetched from the data source is returned to the application in variables that the application has allocated for this purpose. Before this can be done, the application must associate, or *bind,* these variables to the columns of the result set; conceptually, this process is the same as binding application variables to statement parameters. When the application binds a variable to a result set column, it describes that variable—address, data type, and so on—to the driver. The driver stores this information in the structure it maintains for that statement and uses the information to return the value from the column when the row is fetched.

Overview

Applications can bind as many or as few columns of the result set as they choose, including binding no columns at all. When a row of data is fetched, the driver returns the data for the bound columns to the application. Whether the application binds all of the columns in the result set depends on the application. For example, applications that generate reports usually have a fixed format; such applications create a result set containing all of the columns used in the report, then bind and retrieve the data for all of these columns. Applications that display screens full of data sometimes allow the user to decide which columns to display; such applications create a result set containing all columns the user might want, but bind and retrieve the data only for those columns chosen by the user.

Data can be retrieved from unbound columns by calling **SQLGetData**. This is commonly called to retrieve long data, which often exceeds the length of a single buffer and must be retrieved in parts.

Columns can be bound at any time, even after rows have been fetched. However, the new bindings do not take effect until the next time a row is fetched; they are not applied to data from rows already fetched.

A variable remains bound to a column until a different variable is bound to the column; the column is unbound by calling **SQLBindCol** with a null pointer as the variable's address; all columns are unbound by calling **SQLFreeStmt** with the SQL_UNBIND option; or the statement is released. For this reason, the application must be sure that all bound variables remain valid as long as they are bound. For more information, see "Allocating and Freeing Buffers" in Chapter 4, "ODBC Fundamentals."

Because column bindings are just information associated with the statement structure, they can be set in any order. They are also independent of the result set. For example, suppose an application binds the columns of the result set generated by the following SQL statement:

```
SELECT * FROM Orders
```

If the application then executes the SQL statement:

```
SELECT * FROM Lines
```

on the same statement handle, the column bindings for the first result set are still in effect because those are the bindings stored in the statement structure. In most cases, this is a poor programming practice and should be avoided. Instead, the application should call **SQLFreeStmt** with the SQL_UNBIND option to unbind all the old columns and then bind new ones.

Using SQLBindCol

The application binds columns by calling **SQLBindCol**. This function binds one column at a time. With it, the application specifies:

- The column number. Column 0 is the bookmark column; this column is not included in some result sets. All other columns are numbered starting with the number 1. It is an error to bind a higher numbered column than there are columns in the result set; this error cannot be detected until the result set has been created, so it is returned by **SQLFetch**, not **SQLBindCol**.
- The C data type, address, and byte length of the variable bound to the column. It is an error to specify a C data type to which the SQL data type of the column cannot be converted; this error might not be detected until the result set has been created, so it is returned by **SQLFetch**, not **SQLBindCol**. For a list of supported conversions, see Appendix D, "Data Types." For information about the byte length, see "Data Buffer Length" in Chapter 4, "ODBC Fundamentals."

- The address of a length/indicator buffer. The length/indicator buffer is optional. It is used to return the byte length of binary or character data or return SQL_NULL_DATA if the data is NULL. For more information, see "Using Length/Indicator Values" in Chapter 4, "ODBC Fundamentals."

When **SQLBindCol** is called, the driver associates this information with the statement. When each row of data is fetched, it uses the information to place the data for each column in the bound application variables.

For example, the following code binds variables to the SalesPerson and CustID columns. Data for the columns will be returned in *SalesPerson* and *CustID*. Because *SalesPerson* is a character buffer, the application specifies its byte length (11) so the driver can determine whether to truncate the data. The byte length of the returned title, or whether it is NULL, will be returned in *SalesPersonLenOrInd*.

Because *CustID* is an integer variable and has fixed length, there is no need to specify its byte length; the driver assumes it is **sizeof(SQLUINTEGER)**. The byte length of the returned customer ID data, or whether it is NULL, will be returned in *CustIDInd*. Note that the application is only interested in whether the salary is NULL, as the byte length is always **sizeof(SQLUINTEGER)**.

```
SQLCHAR      SalesPerson[11];
SQLUINTEGER CustID;
SQLINTEGER   SalesPersonLenOrInd, CustIDInd;
SQLRETURN    rc;
SQLHSTMT     hstmt;

// Bind SalesPerson to the SalesPerson column and CustID to the CustID column.
SQLBindCol(hstmt, 1, SQL_C_CHAR, SalesPerson, sizeof(SalesPerson),
           &SalesPersonLenOrInd);
SQLBindCol(hstmt, 2, SQL_C_ULONG, &CustID, 0, &CustIDInd);

// Execute a statement to get the sales person/customer of all orders.
SQLExecDirect(hstmt, "SELECT SalesPerson, CustID FROM Orders ORDER BY SalesPerson",
              SQL_NTS);

// Fetch and print the data.  Print "NULL" if the data is NULL.  Code to check if rc
// equals SQL_ERROR or SQL_SUCCESS_WITH_INFO not shown.
while ((rc = SQLFetch(hstmt)) != SQL_NO_DATA) {
   if (SalesPersonLenOrInd == SQL_NULL_DATA)
       printf("NULL       ");
   else
       printf("%10s  ", SalesPerson);
   if (CustIDInd == SQL_NULL_DATA)
       printf("NULL\n");
   else
       printf("%d\n", CustID);
}

// Close the cursor.
SQLCloseCursor(hstmt);
```

The following code executes a **SELECT** statement entered by the user and prints each row of data in the result set. Because the application cannot predict the shape of the result set created by the **SELECT** statement, it cannot bind hard-coded variables to the result set as in the previous example. Instead, the application allocates a buffer that holds the data and a length/indicator buffer for each column in that row. For each column, it calculates the offset to the start of the memory for the column and adjusts this offset so that the data and length/indicator buffers for the column start on alignment boundaries. It then binds the memory starting at the offset to the column. From the driver's point of view, the address of this memory is indistinguishable from the address of a variable bound in the previous example. For more information about alignment, see "Alignment" in Chapter 17, "Programming Considerations."

```
// This application allocates a buffer at run time. For each column, this buffer
// contains memory for the column's data and length/indicator. For example:
//
//    column 1         column 2   column 3   column 4
// <------------><--------------><-----><------------>
//      db1    li1      db2      li2 db3 li3    db4   li4
//       |      |        |        |   |   |      |     |
//  _____V______V________V________V___V___V______V_____V_
// |__________|__|____________|__|__|__|__________|__|
//
// dbn = data buffer for column n
// lin = length/indicator buffer for column n

// Define a macro to increase the size of a buffer so it is a multiple of the alignment
// size. Thus, if a buffer starts on an alignment boundary, it will end just before the
// next alignment boundary. In this example, an alignment size of 4 is used because
// this is the size of the largest data type used in the application's buffer -- the
// size of an SDWORD and of the largest default C data type are both 4. If a larger
// data type (such as _int64) was used, it would be necessary to align for that size.
#define ALIGNSIZE 4
#define ALIGNBUF(Length) Length % ALIGNSIZE ? \
                         Length + ALIGNSIZE - (Length % ALIGNSIZE) : Length

SQLCHAR     SelectStmt[100];
SQLSMALLINT NumCols, *CTypeArray, i;
SQLINTEGER  *ColLenArray, *OffsetArray, SQLType, *DataPtr;
SQLRETURN   rc;
SQLHSTMT    hstmt;

// Get a SELECT statement from the user and execute it.
GetSelectStmt(SelectStmt, 100);
SQLExecDirect(hstmt, SelectStmt, SQL_NTS);

// Determine the number of result set columns.  Allocate arrays to hold the C type,
// byte length, and buffer offset to the data.
SQLNumResultCols(hstmt, &NumCols);
CTypeArray = (SQLSMALLINT *) malloc(NumCols * sizeof(SQLSMALLINT));
ColLenArray = (SQLINTEGER *) malloc(NumCols * sizeof(SQLINTEGER));
OffsetArray = (SQLINTEGER *) malloc(NumCols * sizeof(SQLINTEGER));
```

```
OffsetArray[0] = 0;
for (i = 0; i < NumCols; i++) {
   // Determine the column's SQL type. GetDefaultCType contains a switch statement that
   // returns the default C type for each SQL type.
   SQLColAttribute(hstmt, ((SQLUSMALLINT) i) + 1, SQL_DESC_TYPE, NULL, 0, NULL,
(SQLPOINTER) &SQLType);
   CTypeArray[i] = GetDefaultCType(SQLType);

   // Determine the column's byte length. Calculate the offset in the buffer to the
   // data as the offset to the previous column, plus the byte length of the previous
   // column, plus the byte length of the previous column's length/indicator buffer.
   // Note that the byte length of the column and the length/indicator buffer are
   // increased so that, assuming they start on an alignment boundary, they will end on
   // the byte before the next alignment boundary. Although this might leave some holes
   // in the buffer, it is a relatively inexpensive way to guarantee alignment.
   SQLColAttribute(hstmt, ((SQLUSMALLINT) i)+1, SQL_DESC_OCTET_LENGTH, NULL, 0, NULL,
&ColLenArray[i]);
   ColLenArray[i] = ALIGNBUF(ColLenArray[i]);
   if (i)
      OffsetArray[i] = OffsetArray[i-1]+ColLenArray[i-1]+ALIGNBUF(sizeof(SQLINTEGER));
}

// Allocate the data buffer. The size of the buffer is equal to the offset to the data
// buffer for the final column, plus the byte length of the data buffer and
// length/indicator buffer for the last column.
void *DataPtr = malloc(OffsetArray[NumCols - 1] +
                    ColLenArray[NumCols - 1] + ALIGNBUF(sizeof(SQLINTEGER)));

// For each column, bind the address in the buffer at the start of the memory allocated
// for that column's data and the address at the start of the memory allocated for that
// column's length/indicator buffer.
for (i = 0; i < NumCols; i++)
   SQLBindCol(hstmt,
              ((SQLUSMALLINT) i) + 1,
              CTypeArray[i],
              (SQLPOINTER)((SQLCHAR *)DataPtr + OffsetArray[i]),
              ColLenArray[i],
              (SQLINTEGER *)((SQLCHAR *)DataPtr + OffsetArray[i] + ColLenArray[i]));

// Retrieve and print each row. PrintData accepts a pointer to the data, its C type,
// and its byte length/indicator. It contains a switch statement that casts and prints
// the data according to its type. Code to check if rc equals SQL_ERROR or
// SQL_SUCCESS_WITH_INFO not shown.
while ((rc = SQLFetch(hstmt)) != SQL_NO_DATA) {
   for (i = 0; i < NumCols; i++) {
      PrintData((SQLCHAR *)DataPtr[OffsetArray[i]], CTypeArray[i],
                (SQLINTEGER *)((SQLCHAR *)DataPtr[OffsetArray[i] + ColLenArray[i]]));
   }
}

// Close the cursor.
SQLCloseCursor(hstmt);
```

Fetching Data

The process of retrieving rows from the result set and returning them to the application is called *fetching*. This section describes how to fetch data.

Cursors

An application fetches data with a *cursor*. A cursor is different from a result set: A result set is the set of rows that match a particular search criteria, while a cursor is the software that returns those rows to the application. The name "cursor" as it applies to databases probably originated from the blinking cursor on a computer terminal. Just as that cursor indicates the current position on the screen and where the typed words will appear next, a cursor on a result set indicates the current position in the result set and what row will be returned next.

The cursor model in ODBC is based on the cursor model in embedded SQL. One notable difference between these models is the way cursors are opened. In embedded SQL, a cursor must be explicitly declared and opened before it can be used. In ODBC, a cursor is implicitly opened when a statement that creates a result set is executed. When the cursor is opened, it is positioned before the first row of the result set. In both embedded SQL and ODBC, a cursor must be closed after the application has finished using it.

Different cursors have different characteristics. The most common type of cursor, which is called a *forward-only cursor*, can only move forward through the result set. To return to a previous row, the application must close and reopen the cursor, then read rows from the beginning of the result set until it reaches the required row. Forward-only cursors provide a fast mechanism for making a single pass through a result set.

Forward-only cursors are less useful for screen-based applications, in which the user scrolls backward and forward through the data. Such applications can use a forward-only cursor by reading the result set once, caching the data locally, and performing scrolling themselves. However, this works well only with small amounts of data. A better solution is to use a *scrollable cursor*, which provides random access to the result set. Such applications can also increase performance by fetching more than one row of data at a time, using what is called a *block cursor.* For more information on block cursors, see "Using Block Cursors," in Chapter 11, "Retrieving Results (Advanced)."

The forward-only cursor is the default cursor type in ODBC and is discussed in the following sections. For more information about block cursors and scrollable cursors, see "Block Cursors" and "Scrollable Cursors" in Chapter 11, "Retrieving Results (Advanced)."

Important Committing or rolling back a transaction, either by explicitly calling **SQLEndTran** or by operating in autocommit mode, causes some data sources to close all the cursors on all statements on a connection. For more information, see the SQL_CURSOR_COMMIT_BEHAVIOR and SQL_CURSOR_ROLLBACK_BEHAVIOR attributes in the **SQLGetInfo** function description.

Fetching a Row of Data

To fetch a row of data, an application calls **SQLFetch**. **SQLFetch** can be called with any kind of cursor, but it only moves the rowset cursor in a forward-only direction. **SQLFetch** advances the cursor to the next row and returns the data for any columns that were bound with calls to **SQLBindCol**. When the cursor reaches the end of the result set, **SQLFetch** returns SQL_NO_DATA. For examples of calling **SQLFetch**, see "Using SQLBindCol," earlier in this chapter.

Exactly how **SQLFetch** is implemented is driver-specific, but the general pattern is for the driver to retrieve the data for any bound columns from the data source, convert it according to the types of the bound variables, and place the converted data in those variables. If the driver cannot convert any data, **SQLFetch** returns an error. The application can continue fetching rows, but the data for the current row is lost. What happens to the data for unbound columns depends on the driver, but most drivers either retrieve and discard it or never retrieve it at all.

The driver also sets the values of any length/indicator buffers that have been bound. If the data value for a column is NULL, the driver sets the corresponding length/indicator buffer to SQL_NULL_DATA. If the data value is not NULL, the driver sets the length/indicator buffer to the byte length of the data after conversion. If this length cannot be determined, as is sometimes the case with long data that is retrieved by more than one function call, the driver sets the length/indicator buffer to SQL_NO_TOTAL. Note that for fixed-length data types, such as integers and date structures, the byte length is the size of the data type.

For variable-length data, such as character and binary data, the driver checks the byte length of the converted data against the byte length of the buffer bound to the column; the buffer's length is specified in the *BufferLength* argument in **SQLBindCol**. If the byte length of the converted data is greater than the byte length of the buffer, the driver truncates the data to fit in the buffer, returns the untruncated length in the length/indicator buffer, returns SQL_SUCCESS_WITH_INFO, and places SQLSTATE 01004 (Data truncated) in the diagnostics. The only exception to this is if a variable-length bookmark is truncated when returned by **SQLFetch**, which returns SQLSTATE 22001 (String data, right truncated).

Fixed-length data is never truncated, as the driver assumes that the size of the bound buffer is the size of the data type. Data truncation tends to be rare, as the application usually binds a buffer large enough to hold the entire data value; it determines the necessary size from the metadata. However, the application might explicitly bind a buffer it knows to be too small. For example, it might retrieve and display the first 20 characters of a part description or the first 100 characters of a long text column.

Character data must be null-terminated by the driver before it is returned to the application, even if it has been truncated. The null-termination character is not included in the returned byte length, but does require space in the bound buffer. For example, suppose an application uses strings composed of character data in the ASCII character set, a driver has 50 characters of data to return, and the application's buffer is 25 bytes long. In the application's buffer, the driver returns the first 24 characters followed by a null-termination character. In the length/indicator buffer, it returns a byte length of 50.

The application can restrict the number of rows in the result set by setting the SQL_ATTR_MAX_ROWS statement attribute before executing the statement that creates the result set. For example, the preview mode in an application used to format reports only needs enough data to display the first page of the report. By restricting the size of the result set, such a feature would run faster. This statement attribute is intended to reduce network traffic and might not be supported by all drivers.

Getting Long Data

DBMSs define *long data* as any character or binary data over a certain size, such as 255 characters. This data may be small enough to be stored in a single buffer, such as a part description of several thousand characters. However, it may be too long to store in memory, such as long text documents or bitmaps. Because such data cannot be stored in a single buffer, it is retrieved from the driver in parts with **SQLGetData** after the other data in the row has been fetched.

Note An application can actually retrieve any type of data with **SQLGetData**, not just long data, although only character and binary data can be retrieved in parts. However, if the data is small enough to fit in a single buffer, there is generally no reason to use **SQLGetData**. It is much easier to bind a buffer to the column and let the driver return the data in the buffer.

To retrieve long data from a column, an application first calls **SQLFetchScroll** or **SQLFetch** to move to a row and fetch the data for bound columns. The application then calls **SQLGetData**. **SQLGetData** has the same arguments as **SQLBindCol**: a statement handle, a column number, the C data type, address, and byte length of an application variable, and the address of a length/indicator buffer. Both functions have the same arguments because they perform essentially the same task: They both describe an application variable to the driver and specify that the data for a particular column should be returned in that variable. The major differences are that **SQLGetData** is called after a row is fetched (and is sometimes called *late binding* for this reason), and that the binding specified by **SQLGetData** only lasts for the duration of the call.

With respect to a single column, **SQLGetData** behaves in the same manner as **SQLFetch**: It retrieves the data for the column, converts it to the type of the application variable, and returns it in that variable. It also returns the byte length of the data in the length/indicator buffer. For more information on how **SQLFetch** returns data, see the immediately preceding section, "Fetching a Row of Data."

SQLGetData differs from **SQLFetch** in one important respect. If it is called more than once in succession for the same column, each call returns a successive part of the data. Each call except the last call returns SQL_SUCCESS_WITH_INFO and SQLSTATE 01004 (String data, right truncated); the last call returns SQL_SUCCESS. This is how **SQLGetData** is used to retrieve long data in parts. When there is no more data to return, **SQLGetData** returns SQL_NO_DATA. The application is responsible for putting the long data together, which might mean concatenating the parts of the data. Each part is null-terminated; the application must remove the null-termination character if concatenating the parts. Retrieving data in parts can be done for variable-length bookmarks, as well as other long data. The value returned in the length/indicator buffer decreases in each call by the number of bytes returned in the previous call, although it is common for the driver to be unable to discover the amount of available data and return an byte length of SQL_NO_TOTAL. For example:

```
// Declare a binary buffer to retrieve 5000 bytes of data at a time.
SQLCHAR     BinaryPtr[5000];
SQLUINTEGER PartID;
SQLINTEGER  PartIDInd, BinaryLenOrInd, NumBytes;
SQLRETURN   rc;
SQLHSTMT    hstmt;

// Create a result set containing the ID and picture of each part.
SQLExecDirect(hstmt, "SELECT PartID, Picture FROM Pictures", SQL_NTS);

// Bind PartID to the PartID column.
SQLBindCol(hstmt, 1, SQL_C_ULONG, &PartID, 0, &PartIDInd);

// Retrieve and display each row of data.
while ((rc = SQLFetch(hstmt)) != SQL_NO_DATA) {
   // Display the part ID and initialize the picture.
   DisplayID(PartID, PartIDInd);
   InitPicture();
```

```
   // Retrieve the picture data in parts. Send each part and the number of bytes in
   // each part to a function that displays it. The number of bytes is always 5000 if
   // there were more than 5000 bytes available to return (cbBinaryBuffer > 5000).
   // Code to check if rc equals SQL_ERROR or SQL_SUCCESS_WITH_INFO not shown.
   while ((rc = SQLGetData(hstmt, 2, SQL_C_BINARY, BinaryPtr, sizeof(BinaryPtr),
                           &BinaryLenOrInd)) != SQL_NO_DATA) {
      NumBytes = (BinaryLenOrInd > 5000) || (BinaryLenOrInd == SQL_NO_TOTAL) ?
                 5000 : BinaryLenOrInd;
      DisplayNextPictPart(BinaryPtr, NumBytes);
   }
}

// Close the cursor.
SQLCloseCursor(hstmt);
```

There are a number of restrictions on using **SQLGetData**. In general, columns accessed with **SQLGetData**:

- Must be accessed in order of increasing column number (because of the way the columns of a result set are read from the data source). For example, it is an error to call **SQLGetData** for column 5 and then call it for column 4.
- Cannot be bound.
- Must have a higher column number than the last bound column. For example, if the last bound column is column 3, it is an error to call **SQLGetData** for column 2. For this reason, applications should be careful to place long data columns at the end of the select list.
- Cannot be used if **SQLFetch** or **SQLFetchScroll** was called to retrieve more than one row. For more information, see "Using Block Cursors" in Chapter 11, "Retrieving Results (Advanced)."

Some drivers do not enforce these restrictions. Interoperable applications should either assume they exist or determine which restrictions are not enforced by calling **SQLGetInfo** with the SQL_GETDATA_EXTENSIONS option.

If the application does not need all of the data in a character or binary data column, it can reduce network traffic in DBMS-based drivers by setting the SQL_ATTR_MAX_LENGTH statement attribute before executing the statement. This restricts the number of bytes of data that will be returned for any character or binary column. For example, suppose a column contains long text documents. An application that browses the table containing this column might only need to display the first page of each document. Although this statement attribute can be simulated in the driver, there is no reason to do so. In particular, if an application wants to truncate character or binary data, it should bind a small buffer to the column with **SQLBindCol** and let the driver truncate the data.

Closing the Cursor

When an application has finished using a cursor, it calls **SQLCloseCursor** to close the cursor. For example:

```
SQLCloseCursor(hstmt);
```

Until the application closes the cursor, the statement on which the cursor is opened cannot be used for most other operations, such as executing another SQL statement. For a complete list of functions that can be called while a cursor is open, see Appendix B, "ODBC State Transition Tables."

Note To close a cursor, an application should call **SQLCloseCursor**, not **SQLCancel**.

Cursors remain open until they are explicitly closed, except when a transaction is committed or rolled back, in which case some data sources close the cursor. In particular, reaching the end of the result set, when **SQLFetch** returns SQL_NO_DATA, does not close a cursor. Even cursors on empty result sets (result sets created when a statement executed successfully but which returned no rows) must be explicitly closed.

CHAPTER 11

Retrieving Results (Advanced)

An application can specify that an offset is added to bound data buffer addresses and the corresponding length/indicator buffer addresses when **SQLBulkOperations**, **SQLFetch**, **SQLFetchScroll**, or **SQLSetPos** is called. The results of these additions determine the addresses used in these operations.

Bind offsets allow an application to change bindings without calling **SQLBindCol** for previously bound columns. A call to **SQLBindCol** to rebind data changes the buffer address and the length/indicator pointer. Rebinding with an offset, on the other hand, simply adds an offset to the existing bound data buffer address and length/indicator buffer address. When offsets are used, the bindings are a "template" of how the application buffers are laid out and the application can move this "template" to different areas of memory by changing the offset. A new offset can be specified at any time, and is always added to the originally bound values.

To specify a bind offset, the application sets the SQL_ATTR_ROW_BIND_OFFSET_PTR statement attribute to the address of an SQLINTEGER buffer. Before the application calls a function that uses the bindings, such as **SQLBulkOperations**, **SQLFetch**, **SQLFetchScroll**, or **SQLSetPos**, it places an offset in bytes in this buffer, as long as neither the data buffer address nor the length/indicator buffer address is 0, and the bound column is in the result set. The sum of the address and the offset must be a valid address. (This means that either or both of the offset and the address to which the offset is added can be invalid, as long as the sum of them is a valid address.) The SQL_ATTR_ROW_BIND_OFFSET_PTR statement attribute is a pointer so that the offset value can be applied to more than one set of binding data, all of which can be changed by changing one offset value. An application must make sure that the pointer remains valid until the cursor is closed.

Note Binding offsets are not supported by ODBC 2.*x* drivers.

Block Cursors

Many applications spend a significant amount of time bringing data across the network. Part of this time is spent actually bringing the data across the network and part of it is spent on network overhead, such as the call made by the driver to request a row of data. The latter time can be reduced if the application makes efficient use of *block*, or *fat*, *cursors*, which can return more than one row at a time.

An application always has the option of using a block cursor. On data sources from which only one row at a time can be fetched, block cursors must be simulated in the driver. This can be done by performing multiple single-row fetches. While this is unlikely to provide any performance gains, it opens opportunities for applications. Such applications will then experience performance increases as DBMSs implement block cursors natively and the drivers associated with those DBMSs expose them.

The rows returned in a single fetch with a block cursor are called the *rowset*. It is important not to confuse the rowset with the result set. The result set is maintained at the data source, while the rowset is maintained in application buffers. While the result set is fixed, the rowset is not—it changes position and contents each time a new set of rows is fetched. Just as a single-row cursor such as the traditional SQL forward-only cursor points to a current row, a block cursor points to the rowset, which can be thought of as "current rows."

To perform operations that operate on a single row when multiple rows have been fetched, the application must first indicate which row is the *current row*. The current row is required by calls to **SQLGetData** and positioned update and delete statements. When a block cursor first returns a rowset, the current row is the first row of the rowset. To change the current row, the application calls **SQLSetPos** or **SQLBulkOperations** (to update by bookmark). Figure 11.1 shows the relationship of the result set, rowset, current row, rowset cursor, and block cursor. For more information, see "Using Block Cursors," later in this chapter, and "Positioned Update and Delete Statements" and "Updating Data with SQLSetPos" in Chapter 12, "Updating Data."

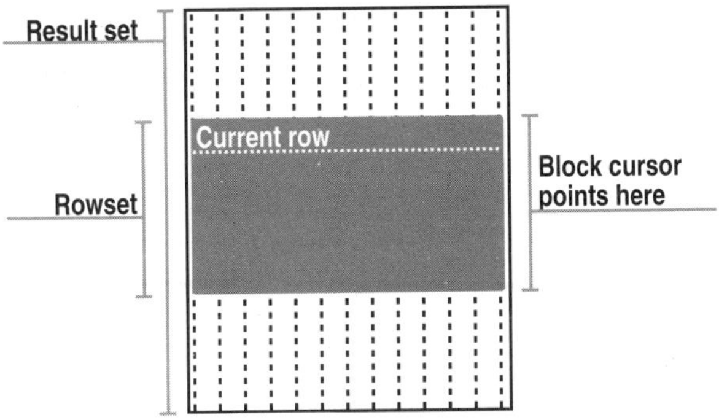

Figure 11.1 Block cursor and rowset cursor

Whether a cursor is a block cursor is independent of whether it is scrollable. For example, most of the work in a report application is spent retrieving and printing rows. Because of this, it will work fastest with a forward-only, block cursor. It uses a forward-only cursor to avoid the expense of a scrollable cursor, and a block cursor to reduce the network traffic.

Binding Columns for Use with Block Cursors

Because block cursors return multiple rows, applications that use them must bind an array of variables to each column instead of a single variable. These arrays are collectively known as the *rowset buffers*. The two styles of binding are to:

- Bind an array to each column. This is called *column-wise binding* because each data structure (array) contains data for a single column.
- Define a structure to hold the data for an entire row and bind an array of these structures. This is called *row-wise binding* because each data structure contains the data for a single row.

As when the application binds single variables to columns, it calls **SQLBindCol** to bind arrays to columns. The only difference is that the addresses passed are array addresses, not single variable addresses. The application sets the SQL_ATTR_ROW_BIND_TYPE statement attribute to specify whether it is using column-wise or row-wise binding. Whether to use column-wise or row-wise binding is largely a matter of application preference. Row-wise binding might correspond more closely to the application's layout of data, in which case it would provide better performance.

Column-Wise Binding

When using column-wise binding, an application binds one or two, or in some cases three, arrays to each column for which data is to be returned. The first array holds the data values and the second array holds length/indicator buffers. Indicators and length values can be stored in separate buffers by setting the

SQL_DESC_INDICATOR_PTR and SQL_DESC_OCTET_LENGTH_PTR descriptor fields to different values; if this is done, a third array is bound. Each array contains as many elements as there are rows in the rowset.

The application declares that it is using column-wise binding with the SQL_ATTR_ROW_BIND_TYPE statement attribute, which determines the bind type for rowset buffers, as opposed to parameter set buffers. The driver returns the data for each row in successive elements of each array. Figure 11.2 shows how column-wise binding works.

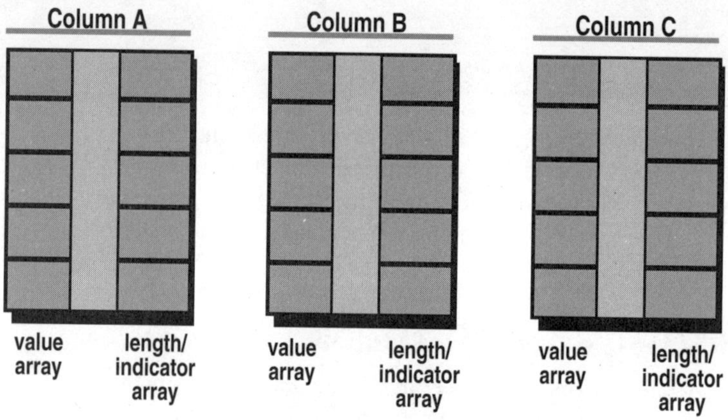

Figure 11.2 Column-wise binding of column data

For example, the following code binds 10-element arrays to the OrderID, SalesPerson, and Status columns.

```
#define ROW_ARRAY_SIZE 10

SQLUINTEGER  OrderIDArray[ROW_ARRAY_SIZE], NumRowsFetched;
SQLCHAR      SalesPersonArray[ROW_ARRAY_SIZE][11], StatusArray[ROW_ARRAY_SIZE][7];
SQLINTEGER   OrderIDIndArray[ROW_ARRAY_SIZE], SalesPersonLenOrIndArray[ROW_ARRAY_SIZE],
             StatusLenOrIndArray[ROW_ARRAY_SIZE];
SQLUSMALLINT RowStatusArray[ROW_ARRAY_SIZE], i;
SQLRETURN    rc;
SQLHSTMT     hstmt;

// Set the SQL_ATTR_ROW_BIND_TYPE statement attribute to use column-wise binding.
// Declare the rowset size with the SQL_ATTR_ROW_ARRAY_SIZE statement attribute. Set
the
// SQL_ATTR_ROW_STATUS_PTR statement attribute to point to the row status array. Set
// the SQL_ATTR_ROWS_FETCHED_PTR statement attribute to point to cRowsFetched.
SQLSetStmtAttr(hstmt, SQL_ATTR_ROW_BIND_TYPE, SQL_BIND_BY_COLUMN, 0);
SQLSetStmtAttr(hstmt, SQL_ATTR_ROW_ARRAY_SIZE, ROW_ARRAY_SIZE, 0);
SQLSetStmtAttr(hstmt, SQL_ATTR_ROW_STATUS_PTR, RowStatusArray, 0);
SQLSetStmtAttr(hstmt, SQL_ATTR_ROWS_FETCHED_PTR, &NumRowsFetched, 0);
```

```
// Bind arrays to the OrderID, SalesPerson, and Status columns.
SQLBindCol(hstmt, 1, SQL_C_ULONG, OrderIDArray, 0, OrderIDIndArray);
SQLBindCol(hstmt, 2, SQL_C_CHAR, SalesPersonArray, sizeof(SalesPersonArray[0]),
           SalesPersonLenOrIndArray);
SQLBindCol(hstmt, 3, SQL_C_CHAR, StatusArray, sizeof(StatusArray[0]),
           StatusLenOrIndArray);

// Execute a statement to retrieve rows from the Orders table.
SQLExecDirect(hstmt, "SELECT OrderID, SalesPerson, Status FROM Orders", SQL_NTS);

// Fetch up to the rowset size number of rows at a time. Print the actual number of
rows fetched; this number
// is returned in NumRowsFetched. Check the row status array to only print those rows
// successfully fetched. Code to check if rc equals SQL_SUCCESS_WITH_INFO or SQL_ERROR
// not shown.
while ((rc = SQLFetchScroll(hstmt,SQL_FETCH_NEXT,0)) != SQL_NO_DATA) {
   for (i = 0; i < NumRowsFetched; i++) {
      if ((RowStatusArray[i] == SQL_ROW_SUCCESS) ||
          (RowStatusArray[i] == SQL_ROW_SUCCESS_WITH_INFO)) {
         if (OrderIDIndArray[i] == SQL_NULL_DATA)
            printf(" NULL      ");
         else
            printf("%d\t", OrderIDArray[i]);
         if (SalesPersonLenOrIndArray[i] == SQL_NULL_DATA)
            printf(" NULL      ");
         else
            printf("%s\t", SalesPersonArray[i]);
         if (StatusLenOrIndArray[i] == SQL_NULL_DATA)
            printf(" NULL\n");
         else
            printf("%s\n", StatusArray[i]);
      }
   }
}

// Close the cursor.
SQLCloseCursor(hstmt);
```

Row-Wise Binding

When using row-wise binding, an application defines a structure containing one or two, or in some cases three, elements for each column for which data is to be returned. The first element holds the data value and the second element holds the length/indicator buffer. Indicators and length values can be stored in separate buffers by setting the SQL_DESC_INDICATOR_PTR and SQL_DESC_OCTET_LENGTH_PTR descriptor fields to different values; if this is done, the structure contains a third element. The application then allocates an array of these structures, which contains as many elements as there are rows in the rowset.

The application declares the size of the structure to the driver with the SQL_ATTR_ROW_BIND_TYPE statement attribute and binds the address of each member in the first element of the array. Thus, the driver can calculate the address of the data for a particular row and column as:

```
Address = Bound Address + ((Row Number - 1) * Structure Size)
```

where rows are numbered from 1 to the size of the rowset. (One is subtracted from the row number because array indexing in C is zero-based.) Figure 11.3 shows how row-wise binding works. Generally, only columns that will be bound are included in the structure. The structure can contain fields that are unrelated to result set columns. The columns can be placed in the structure in any order, but are shown in sequential order for clarity.

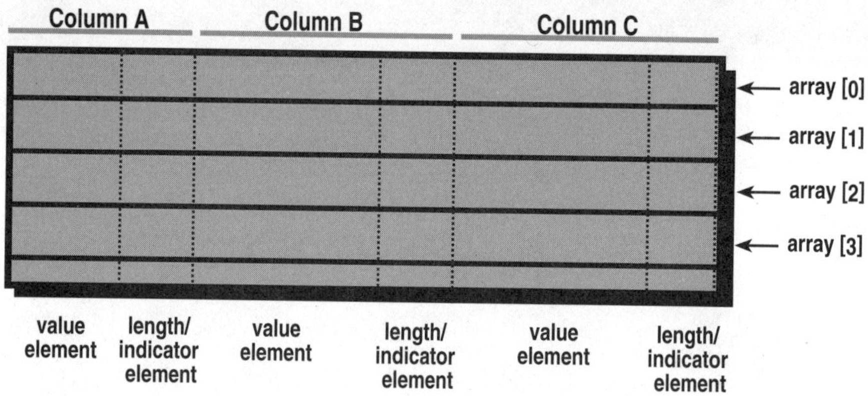

Figure 11.3 Row-wise binding of column data

For example, the following code creates a structure with elements in which to return data for the OrderID, SalesPerson, and Status columns and length/indicators for the SalesPerson and Status columns. It allocates 10 of these structures and binds them to the OrderID, SalesPerson, and Status columns.

```
#define ROW_ARRAY_SIZE 10

// Define the ORDERINFO struct and allocate an array of 10 structs.
typedef struct {
   SQLUINTEGER OrderID;
   SQLINTEGER  OrderIDInd;
   SQLCHAR     SalesPerson[11];
   SQLINTEGER  SalesPersonLenOrInd;
   SQLCHAR     Status[7];
   SQLINTEGER  StatusLenOrInd;
} ORDERINFO;
ORDERINFO OrderInfoArray[ROW_ARRAY_SIZE];

SQLUINTEGER  NumRowsFetched;
SQLUSMALLINT RowStatusArray[ROW_ARRAY_SIZE], i;
SQLRETURN      rc;
SQLHSTMT     hstmt;
```

```
// Specify the size of the structure with the SQL_ATTR_ROW_BIND_TYPE statement
// attribute. This also declares that row-wise binding will be used. Declare the rowset
// size with the SQL_ATTR_ROW_ARRAY_SIZE statement attribute. Set the
// SQL_ATTR_ROW_STATUS_PTR statement attribute to point to the row status array. Set
// the SQL_ATTR_ROWS_FETCHED_PTR statement attribute to point to NumRowsFetched.
SQLSetStmtAttr(hstmt, SQL_ATTR_ROW_BIND_TYPE, sizeof(ORDERINFO), 0);
SQLSetStmtAttr(hstmt, SQL_ATTR_ROW_ARRAY_SIZE, ROW_ARRAY_SIZE, 0);
SQLSetStmtAttr(hstmt, SQL_ATTR_ROW_STATUS_PTR, RowStatusArray, 0);
SQLSetStmtAttr(hstmt, SQL_ATTR_ROWS_FETCHED_PTR, &NumRowsFetched, 0);

// Bind elements of the first structure in the array to the OrderID, SalesPerson, and
// Status columns.
SQLBindCol(hstmt, 1, SQL_C_ULONG, &OrderInfoArray[0].OrderID, 0,
&OrderInfoArray[0].OrderIDInd);
SQLBindCol(hstmt, 2, SQL_C_CHAR, OrderInfoArray[0].SalesPerson,
           sizeof(OrderInfoArray[0].SalesPerson),
           &OrderInfoArray[0].SalesPersonLenOrInd);
SQLBindCol(hstmt, 3, SQL_C_CHAR, OrderInfoArray[0].Status,
           sizeof(OrderInfoArray[0].Status), &OrderInfoArray[0].StatusLenOrInd);

// Execute a statement to retrieve rows from the Orders table.
SQLExecDirect(hstmt, "SELECT OrderID, SalesPerson, Status FROM Orders", SQL_NTS);

// Fetch up to the rowset size number of rows at a time. Print the actual number of
rows fetched; this number
// is returned in NumRowsFetched. Check the row status array to only print those rows
// successfully fetched. Code to check if rc equals SQL_SUCCESS_WITH_INFO or SQL_ERROR
// not shown.
while ((rc = SQLFetchScroll(hstmt,SQL_FETCH_NEXT,0)) != SQL_NO_DATA) {
   for (i = 0; i < NumRowsFetched; i++) {
      if (RowStatusArray[i] == SQL_ROW_SUCCESS|| RowStatusArray[i] ==
         SQL_ROW_SUCCESS_WITH_INFO) {
         if (OrderInfoArray[i].OrderIDInd == SQL_NULL_DATA)
            printf(" NULL      ");
         else
            printf("%d\t", OrderInfoArray[i].OrderID);
         if (OrderInfoArray[i].SalesPersonLenOrInd == SQL_NULL_DATA)
            printf(" NULL       ");
         else
            printf("%s\t", OrderInfoArray[i].SalesPerson);
         if (OrderInfoArray[i].StatusLenOrInd == SQL_NULL_DATA)
            printf(" NULL\n");
         else
            printf("%s\n", OrderInfoArray[i].Status);
      }
   }
}

// Close the cursor.
SQLCloseCursor(hstmt);
```

Using Block Cursors

Support for block cursors is built into ODBC 3.0. **SQLFetch** can only be used for multirow fetches when called in ODBC 3.0; if an ODBC 2.*x* application calls **SQLFetch**, it will only open a single-row, forward-only cursor. When an ODBC 3.0 application calls **SQLFetch** in an ODBC 2.*x* driver, it returns a single row unless the driver supports **SQLExtendedFetch**. For more information, see Appendix G, "Driver Guidelines for Backward Compatibility."

To use block cursors, the application sets the rowset size, binds the rowset buffers (as described in the previous section), optionally sets the SQL_ATTR_ROWS_FETCHED_PTR and SQL_ATTR_ROW_STATUS_PTR statement attributes, and calls **SQLFetch** or **SQLFetchScroll** to fetch a block of rows. Note that the application can change the rowset size and bind new rowset buffers (by calling **SQLBindCol** or specifying a bind offset) even after rows have been fetched.

Rowset Size

Which rowset size to use depends on the application. Screen-based applications commonly follow one of two strategies. The first is to set the rowset size to the number of rows displayed on the screen; if the user resizes the screen, the application changes the rowset size accordingly. The second is to set the rowset size to a larger number, such as 100, which reduces the number of calls to the data source. The application scrolls locally within the rowset when possible and fetches new rows only when it scrolls outside the rowset.

Other applications, such as reports, tend to set the rowset size to the largest number of rows the application can reasonably handle—with a larger rowset, the network overhead per row is sometimes reduced. Exactly how large a rowset can be depends on the size of each row and the amount of memory available.

Rowset size is set by a call to **SQLSetStmtAttr** with an *Attribute* argument of SQL_ATTR_ROW_ARRAY_SIZE. The application can change the rowset size, bind new rowset buffers (by calling **SQLBindCol** or specifying a binding offset) even after rows have been fetched, or both. The implications of changing the rowset size depend on the function:

- **SQLFetch** and **SQLFetchScroll** use the rowset size at the time of the call to determine how many rows to fetch. Note, however, that **SQLFetchScroll** with a *FetchOrientation* of SQL_FETCH_NEXT increments the cursor based on the rowset of the previous fetch, and then fetches a rowset based on the current rowset size.
- **SQLSetPos** uses the rowset size that is in effect as of the preceding call to **SQLFetch** or **SQLFetchScroll**, because **SQLSetPos** operates on a rowset that has already been set. **SQLSetPos** will also pick up the new rowset size if **SQLBulkOperations** has been called after the rowset size was changed.
- **SQLBulkOperations** uses the rowset size in effect at the time of the call, since it performs operations on a table independent of any fetched rowset.

Number of Rows Fetched and Status

If the SQL_ATTR_ROWS_FETCHED_PTR statement attribute has been set, it specifies a buffer that returns the number of rows fetched by the call to **SQLFetch** or **SQLFetchScroll**, and error rows. (This number is a count of all rows that do not have the status SQL_ROW_NO_ROWS.) After a call to **SQLBulkOperations** or **SQLSetPos**, the buffer contains the number of rows that were affected by a bulk operation performed by the function. If the SQL_ATTR_ROW_STATUS_PTR statement attribute has been set, **SQLFetch** or **SQLFetchScroll** returns the *row status array*, which provides the status of each returned row. Both of the buffers pointed to by these fields are allocated by the application and populated by the driver. An application must make sure that these pointers remain valid until the cursor is closed.

Entries in the row status array state whether each row was fetched successfully, whether it was updated, added, or deleted since it was last fetched, and whether an error occurred while fetching the row. Note that if **SQLFetch** or **SQLFetchScroll** encounters an error while retrieving one row of a multirow rowset, or if **SQLBulkOperations** with an *Operation* argument of SQL_FETCH_BY_BOOKMARK encounters an error while performing a bulk fetch, it sets the corresponding value in the row status array to SQL_ROW_ERROR, continues fetching rows, and returns SQL_SUCCESS_WITH_INFO. For more information about error handling and the row status array, see the **SQLFetch** and **SQLFetchScroll** function descriptions.

SQLGetData and Block Cursors

SQLGetData operates on a single column of a single row and cannot fetch an array containing data from multiple rows. The reason for this is that the primary use of **SQLGetData** is to fetch long data in parts and there is little or no reason to do this for more than one row at a time.

To use **SQLGetData** with a block cursor, an application first calls **SQLSetPos** to position the cursor on a single row. It then calls **SQLGetData** for a column in that row. However, this behavior is optional. To determine if a driver supports the use of

SQLGetData with block cursors, an application calls **SQLGetInfo** with the SQL_GETDATA_EXTENSIONS option.

Row Status Array

In addition to data, **SQLFetch** and **SQLFetchScroll** can return an array that gives the status of each row in the rowset. This array is specified through the SQL_ATTR_ROW_STATUS_PTR statement attribute. This array is allocated by the application and must have as many elements as are specified by the SQL_ATTR_ROW_ARRAY_SIZE statement attribute. The values in the array are set by **SQLBulkOperations**, **SQLFetch**, **SQLFetchScroll**, and **SQLSetPos**. The values describe the status of the row and whether that status has changed since it was last fetched:

Row status array value	Description
SQL_ROW_SUCCESS	The row was successfully fetched and has not changed since it was last fetched.
SQL_ROW_SUCCESS_WITH_INFO	The row was successfully fetched and has not changed since it was last fetched. However, a warning was returned about the row.
SQL_ROW_ERROR	An error occurred while fetching the row.
SQL_ROW_UPDATED	The row was successfully fetched and has been updated since it was last fetched. If the row is fetched again, or refreshed by **SQLSetPos**, its status is changed to the new status. Some drivers cannot detect changes to data and therefore, cannot return this value. To determine whether a driver can detect updates to refetched rows, an application calls **SQLGetInfo** with the SQL_ROW_UPDATES option.
SQL_ROW_DELETED	The row has been deleted since it was last fetched.
SQL_ROW_ADDED	The row was inserted by **SQLBulkOperations**. If the row is fetched again, or is refreshed by **SQLSetPos**, its status is SQL_ROW_SUCCESS. This value is not set by **SQLFetch** or **SQLFetchScroll**.
SQL_ROW_NOROW	The rowset overlapped the end of the result set and no row was returned that corresponded to this element of the row status array.

Scrollable Cursors

In modern screen-based applications, the user scrolls backward and forward through the data. For such applications, returning to a previously fetched row is a problem. One possibility is to close and reopen the cursor, then fetch rows until the cursor reaches the required row. Another possibility is to read the result set, cache it locally, and implement scrolling in the application. Both possibilities work well only with small result sets, and the latter possibility is difficult to implement. A better solution is to use a *scrollable cursor*, which can move backward and forward in the result set.

A *scrollable cursor* is commonly used in modern screen-based applications in which the user scrolls back and forth through the data. However, applications should use scrollable cursors only when forward-only cursors will not do the job, as scrollable cursors are generally more expensive than forward-only cursors.

The ability to move backward raises a question not applicable to forward-only cursors: Should a scrollable cursor detect changes made to rows previously fetched? That is, should it detect updated, deleted, and newly inserted rows?

This question arises because the definition of a result set—the set of rows that matches certain criteria—does not state when rows are checked to see if they match that criteria, nor does it state whether rows must contain the same data each time they are fetched. The former omission makes it possible for scrollable cursors to detect whether rows have been inserted or deleted, while the latter makes it possible for them to detect updated data.

The ability to detect changes is sometimes useful, sometimes not. For example, an accounting application needs a cursor that ignores all changes; balancing books is impossible if the cursor shows the latest changes. On the other hand, an airline reservation system needs a cursor that shows the latest changes to the data; without such a cursor, it must continually requery the database to show the most up-to-date flight availability.

To cover the needs of different applications, ODBC defines four different types of scrollable cursors. These cursors vary both in expense and in their ability to detect changes to the result set. Note that if a scrollable cursor can detect changes to rows, it can only detect them when it attempts to refetch those rows; there is no way for the data source to notify the cursor of changes to the currently fetched rows. Note also that visibility of changes is also controlled by the transaction isolation level; for more information, see "Transaction Isolation" in Chapter 14, "Transactions."

Scrollable Cursor Types

The four types of scrollable cursors are: static, dynamic, keyset-driven, and mixed. Static cursors detect few or no changes, but are relatively cheap to implement. Dynamic cursors detect all changes, but are expensive to implement. Keyset-driven and mixed cursors lie in between, detecting most changes but at less expense than dynamic cursors.

The following terms are used to define the characteristics of each type of scrollable cursor:

- **Own updates, deletes, and inserts**. Updates, deletes, and inserts made through the cursor, either with a call to **SQLBulkOperations** or **SQLSetPos** or with a positioned update or delete statement.
- **Other updates, deletes, and inserts**. Updates, deletes, and inserts not made by the cursor, including those made by other operations in the same transaction, those made through other transactions, and those made by other applications.
- **Membership**. The set of rows in the result set.
- **Order**. The order in which rows are returned by the cursor.
- **Values**. The values in each row in the result set.

For information about how to update, delete, and insert data, see Chapter 12, "Updating Data."

Static Cursors

A static cursor is one in which the result set appears to be static. It does not usually detect changes made to the membership, order, or values of the result set after the cursor is opened. For example, suppose a static cursor fetches a row and another application then updates that row. If the static cursor refetches the row, the values it sees are unchanged, despite the changes made by the other application.

Static cursors may detect their own updates, deletes, and inserts, although they are not required to do so. Whether a particular static cursor detects these changes is reported through the SQL_STATIC_SENSITIVITY option in **SQLGetInfo**. Static cursors never detect other updates, deletes, and inserts.

The row status array specified by the SQL_ATTR_ROW_STATUS_PTR statement attribute can contain SQL_ROW_SUCCESS, SQL_ROW_SUCCESS_WITH_INFO, or SQL_ROW_ERROR for any row. It returns SQL_ROW_UPDATED, SQL_ROW_DELETED, or SQL_ROW_ADDED for rows updated, deleted, or inserted by the cursor, assuming that the cursor is capable of detecting such changes.

Static cursors are commonly implemented by locking the rows in the result set or making a copy, or snapshot, of the result set. While locking rows is relatively easy to do, it has the drawback of significantly reducing concurrency. Making a copy allows greater concurrency and allows the cursor to keep track of its own updates, deletes, and inserts by modifying the copy. However, a copy is more expensive to make and can diverge from the underlying data as that data is changed by others.

Dynamic Cursors

A dynamic cursor is just that: dynamic. It can detect any changes made to the membership, order, and values of the result set after the cursor is opened. For example, suppose a dynamic cursor fetches two rows and another application then updates one of those rows and deletes the other. If the dynamic cursor then attempts to refetch those rows, it will not find the deleted row, but will return the new values for the updated row.

Dynamic cursors detect all updates, deletes, and inserts, both their own and those made by others. (This is subject to the isolation level of the transaction, as set by the SQL_ATTR_TXN_ISOLATION connection attribute.) The row status array specified by the SQL_ATTR_ROW_STATUS_PTR statement attribute reflects these changes and can contain SQL_ROW_SUCCESS, SQL_ROW_SUCCESS_WITH_INFO, SQL_ROW_ERROR, SQL_ROW_UPDATED, and SQL_ROW_ADDED. It cannot return SQL_ROW_DELETED because a dynamic cursor does not return deleted rows outside the rowset, so no longer recognizes the existence of the deleted row in the result set or its corresponding element in the row status array. SQL_ROW_ADDED is returned only when a row is updated by a call to **SQLSetPos**, not when it is updated by another cursor.

One way of implementing dynamic cursors in the database is by creating a selective index that defines the membership and ordering of the result set. Because the index is updated when others make changes, a cursor based on such an index is sensitive to all changes. Additional selection within the result set defined by this index is possible by processing along the index.

Dynamic cursors can be simulated by requiring the result set to be ordered by a unique key. With such a restriction, fetches are made by executing a **SELECT** statement each time the cursor fetches rows. For example, suppose the result set is defined by the statement:

```
SELECT * FROM Customers ORDER BY Name, CustID
```

To fetch the next rowset in this result set, the simulated cursor sets the parameters in the following **SELECT** statement to the values in the last row of the current rowset, and then executes it:

```
SELECT * FROM Customers WHERE (Name > ?) AND (CustID > ?)
   ORDER BY Name, CustID
```

This statement creates a second result set, the first rowset of which is the next rowset in the original result set—in this case, the set of rows in the Customers table. The cursor returns this rowset to the application.

It is interesting to note that a dynamic cursor implemented in this manner actually creates many result sets, which allows it to detect changes to the original result set.

The application never learns of the existence of these auxiliary result sets; it simply appears as if the cursor is able to detect changes to the original result set.

Keyset-Driven Cursors

A keyset-driven cursor lies between a static and a dynamic cursor in its ability to detect changes. Like a static cursor, it does not always detect changes to the membership and order of the result set. Like a dynamic cursor, it does detect changes to the values of rows in the result set (subject to the isolation level of the transaction, as set by the SQL_ATTR_TXN_ISOLATION connection attribute).

When a keyset-driven cursor is opened, it saves the keys for the entire result set; this fixes the apparent membership and order of the result set. As the cursor scrolls through the result set, it uses the keys in this *keyset* to retrieve the current data values for each row. For example, suppose a keyset-driven cursor fetches a row and another application then updates that row. If the cursor refetches the row, the values it sees are the new ones, because it refetched the row using its key. Because of this, the keyset-driven cursors always detect changes made by themselves and others.

When the cursor attempts to retrieve a row that has been deleted, this row appears as a "*hole*" in the result set: The key for the row exists in the keyset but the row no longer exists in the result set. If the key values in a row are updated, the row is considered to have been deleted and then inserted, so such rows also appear as holes in the result set. While a keyset-driven cursor can always detect rows deleted by others, it can optionally remove the keys for rows it deletes itself from the keyset. Keyset-driven cursors that do this cannot detect their own deletes. Whether a particular keyset-driven cursor detects its own deletes is reported through the SQL_STATIC_SENSITIVITY option in **SQLGetInfo**.

Rows inserted by others are never visible to a keyset-driven cursor because no keys for these rows exist in the keyset. However, a keyset-driven cursor can optionally add the keys for rows it inserts itself to the keyset. Keyset-driven cursors that do this can detect their own inserts. Whether a particular keyset-driven cursor detects its own inserts is reported through the SQL_STATIC_SENSITIVITY option in **SQLGetInfo**.

The row status array specified by the SQL_ATTR_ROW_STATUS_PTR statement attribute can contain SQL_ROW_SUCCESS, SQL_ROW_SUCCESS_WITH_INFO, or SQL_ROW_ERROR for any row. It returns SQL_ROW_UPDATED, SQL_ROW_DELETED, or SQL_ROW_ADDED for rows it detects as updated, deleted, or inserted.

Keyset-driven cursors are commonly implemented by creating a temporary table that contains the keys for each row in the result set. Because the cursor must also determine if rows have been updated, this table also commonly contains a column with row versioning information.

To scroll over the original result set, the keyset-driven cursor opens a static cursor over the temporary table. To retrieve a row in the original result set, the cursor first retrieves the appropriate key from the temporary table, and then retrieves the current values for the row. If block cursors are used, the cursor must retrieve multiple keys and rows.

Mixed Cursors

A mixed cursor is a combination of a keyset-driven cursor and a dynamic cursor. It is used when the result set is too large to reasonably save keys for the entire result set. Mixed cursors are implemented by creating a keyset that is smaller than the entire result set but larger than the rowset.

As long as the application scrolls within the keyset, the behavior is keyset-driven. When the application scrolls outside the keyset, the behavior is dynamic: The cursor fetches the requested rows and creates a new keyset. Note that after the new keyset is created, the behavior reverts to keyset-driven within that keyset.

For example, suppose a result set has 1,000 rows and uses a mixed cursor with a keyset size of 100 and a rowset size of 10. When the first rowset is fetched, the cursor creates a keyset consisting of the keys for the first 100 rows. It then returns the first 10 rows, as requested.

Now suppose another application deletes rows 11 and 101. If the cursor attempts to retrieve row 11, it will encounter a hole because it has a key for this row but no row exists; this is keyset-driven behavior. If the cursor attempts to retrieve row 101, the cursor will not detect that the row is missing because it does not have a key for the row. Instead, it will retrieve what was previously row 102. This is dynamic cursor behavior.

A mixed cursor is equivalent to a keyset-driven cursor when the keyset size is equal to the result set size. A mixed cursor is equivalent to a dynamic cursor when the keyset size is equal to 1.

Using Scrollable Cursors

Using a scrollable cursor requires these three steps:

1. Determine the cursor capabilities.
2. Set up the cursor.
3. Scroll and fetch rows.

Determining Cursor Capabilities

The following four options in **SQLGetInfo** describe what types of cursors are supported and what their capabilities are:

- SQL_CURSOR_SENSITIVITY. Indicates whether a cursor is sensitive to changes made by another cursor.
- SQL_SCROLL_OPTIONS. Lists the supported cursor types (forward-only, static, keyset-driven, dynamic, or mixed). All data sources must support forward-only cursors.
- SQL_DYNAMIC_CURSOR_ATTRIBUTES1, SQL_FORWARD_ONLY_CURSOR_ATTRIBUTES1, SQL_KEYSET_CURSOR_ATTRIBUTES1, or SQL_STATIC_CURSOR_ATTRIBUTES1 (depending on the type of the cursor). Lists the fetch types supported by scrollable cursors. The bits in the return value correspond to the fetch types in **SQLFetchScroll**.
- SQL_KEYSET_CURSOR_ATTRIBUTES2 or SQL_STATIC_CURSOR_ATTRIBUTES2 (depending on the type of the cursor). Lists whether static and keyset-driven cursors can detect their own updates, deletes, and inserts.

An application can determine cursor capabilities at run time by calling **SQLGetInfo** with these options. This is commonly done by generic applications. Cursor capabilities can also be determined during application development and their use hard-coded into the application. This is commonly done by vertical and custom applications, but can also be done by generic applications that use a client-side cursor implementation such as the ODBC cursor library.

Setting Up the Cursor

The application can specify the cursor type before executing a statement that creates a result set. It does this with the SQL_ATTR_CURSOR_TYPE statement attribute. If the application does not explicitly specify a type, a forward-only cursor will be used. To get a mixed cursor, an application specifies a keyset-driven cursor but declares a keyset size less than the result set size.

For keyset-driven and mixed cursors, the application can also specify the keyset size. It does this with the SQL_ATTR_KEYSET_SIZE statement attribute. If the keyset size is set to 0—which is the default—the keyset size is set to the result set size and a keyset-driven cursor is used. Note that the keyset size can be changed after the cursor has been opened.

The application can also set the rowset size; for more information, see "Using Block Cursors," earlier in this chapter.

Cursor Characteristics and Cursor Type

An application can specify the characteristics of a cursor rather than specifying the cursor type (forward-only, static, keyset-driven, or dynamic). To do so, the application selects the cursor's scrollability (by setting the SQL_ATTR_CURSOR_SCROLLABLE statement attribute) and sensitivity (by setting the SQL_ATTR_CURSOR_SENSITIVITY statement attribute) before opening the cursor on the statement handle. The driver then chooses the cursor type that most efficiently provides the characteristics that the application requested.

Whenever an application sets any of the statement attributes SQL_ATTR_CONCURRENCY, SQL_ATTR_CURSOR_SCROLLABLE, SQL_ATTR_CURSOR_SENSITIVITY, or SQL_ATTR_CURSOR_TYPE, the driver makes any required change to the other statement attributes in this set of four attributes, so that their values remain consistent. As a result, when the application specifies a cursor characteristic, the driver can change the attribute that indicates cursor type based on this implicit selection; when the application specifies a type, the driver can change any of the other attributes to be consistent with the characteristics of the selected type. For more information on these statement attributes, see the **SQLSetStmtAttr** function description.

An application that sets statement attributes to specify both a cursor type and cursor characteristics runs the risk of obtaining a cursor that is not the most efficient method available on that driver of meeting the application's requirements.

The implicit setting of statement attributes is driver-defined except that it must follow these rules:

- Forward-only cursors are never scrollable; see the definition of SQL_ATTR_CURSOR_SCROLLABLE in **SQLSetStmtAttr**.
- Insensitive cursors are never updatable (and thus their concurrency is read-only); this is based on their definition of insensitive cursors in the ISO SQL standard.

Consequently, the implicit setting of statement attributes occurs in the following cases:

Application sets attribute to	Other attributes set implicitly
SQL_ATTR_CONCURRENCY to SQL_CONCUR_READ_ONLY	SQL_ATTR_CURSOR_SENSITIVITY to SQL_INSENSITIVE
SQL_ATTR_CONCURRENCY to SQL_CONCUR_LOCK, SQL_CONCUR_ROWVER, or SQL_CONCUR_VALUES	SQL_ATTR_CURSOR_SENSITIVITY to SQL_UNSPECIFIED or SQL_SENSITIVE, as defined by the driver. It can never be set to SQL_INSENSITIVE, since insensitive cursors are always read-only.
SQL_ATTR_CURSOR_SCROLLABLE to SQL_NONSCROLLABLE	SQL_ATTR_CURSOR_TYPE to SQL_CURSOR_FORWARD_ONLY

Application sets attribute to:	Other attributes set implicitly:
SQL_ATTR_CURSOR_SCROLLABLE to SQL_SCROLLABLE	SQL_ATTR_CURSOR_TYPE to either SQL_CURSOR_STATIC, SQL_CURSOR_KEYSET_DRIVEN, or SQL_CURSOR_DYNAMIC, as specified by the driver. It is never set to SQL_CURSOR_FORWARD_ONLY.
SQL_ATTR_CURSOR_SENSITIVITY to SQL_INSENSITIVE	SQL_ATTR_CONCURRENCY to SQL_CONCUR_READ_ONLY
	SQL_ATTR_CURSOR_TYPE to SQL_CURSOR_STATIC
SQL_ATTR_CURSOR_SENSITIVITY to SQL_SENSITIVE	SQL_ATTR_CONCURRENCY to SQL_CONCUR_LOCK, SQL_CONCUR_ROWVER, or SQL_CONCUR_VALUES, as specified by the driver. It is never set to SQL_CONCUR_READ_ONLY
	SQL_ATTR_CURSOR_TYPE to SQL_CURSOR_FORWARD_ONLY, SQL_CURSOR_STATIC, SQL_CURSOR_KEYSET_DRIVEN, or SQL_CURSOR_DYNAMIC, as specified by the driver
SQL_ATTR_CURSOR_SENSITIVITY to SQL_UNSPECIFIED	SQL_ATTR_CONCURRENCY to SQL_CONCUR_READ_ONLY, SQL_CONCUR_LOCK, SQL_CONCUR_ROWVER, or SQL_CONCUR_VALUES, as specified by the driver
	SQL_ATTR_CURSOR_TYPE to SQL_CURSOR_FORWARD_ONLY, SQL_CURSOR_STATIC, SQL_CURSOR_KEYSET_DRIVEN, or SQL_CURSOR_DYNAMIC, as specified by the driver
SQL_ATTR_CURSOR_TYPE to SQL_CURSOR_DYNAMIC	SQL_ATTR_SCROLLABLE to SQL_SCROLLABLE
	SQL_ATTR_CURSOR_SENSITIVITY to SQL_SENSITIVE (but only if SQL_ATTR_CONCURRENCY is not equal to SQL_CONCUR_READ_ONLY. Updatable dynamic cursors are always sensitive to changes made in their own transaction.)
SQL_ATTR_CURSOR_TYPE to SQL_CURSOR_FORWARD_ONLY	SQL_ATTR_CURSOR_SCROLLABLE to SQL_NONSCROLLABLE

Application sets attribute to:	Other attributes set implicitly:
SQL_ATTR_CURSOR_TYPE to SQL_CURSOR_KEYSET_DRIVEN	SQL_ATTR_SCROLLABLE to SQL_SCROLLABLE SQL_ATTR_SENSITIVITY to SQL_UNSPECIFIED or SQL_SENSITIVE (according to driver-defined criteria, if SQL_ATTR_CONCURRENCY is not SQL_CONCUR_READ_ONLY)
SQL_ATTR_CURSOR_TYPE to SQL_CURSOR_STATIC	SQL_ATTR_SCROLLABLE to SQL_SCROLLABLE SQL_ATTR_SENSITIVITY to SQL_INSENSITIVE (if SQL_ATTR_CONCURRENCY is SQL_CONCUR_READ_ONLY) SQL_ATTR_SENSITIVITY to SQL_UNSPECIFIED or SQL_SENSITIVE (if SQL_ATTR_CONCURRENCY is not SQL_CONCUR_READ_ONLY)

Scrolling and Fetching Rows

When using a scrollable cursor, applications call **SQLFetchScroll** to position the cursor and fetch rows. **SQLFetchScroll** supports relative scrolling (next, prior, and relative *n* rows), absolute scrolling (first, last, and row *n*), and positioning by bookmark. The *FetchOrientation* and *FetchOffset* arguments in **SQLFetchScroll** specify which rowset to fetch, as shown in the following diagrams.

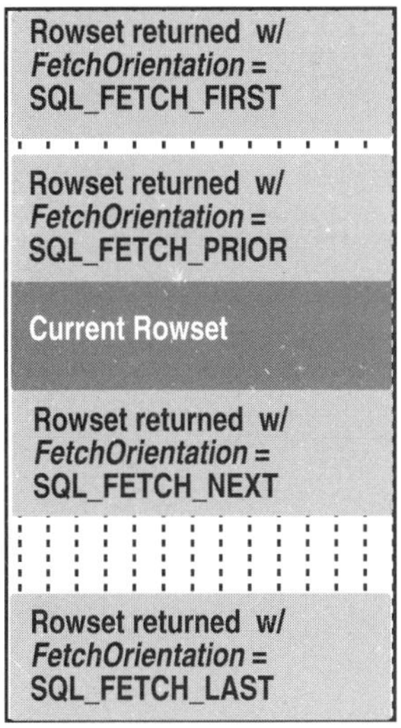

Figure 11.4 Fetching next, prior, first, and last rowsets

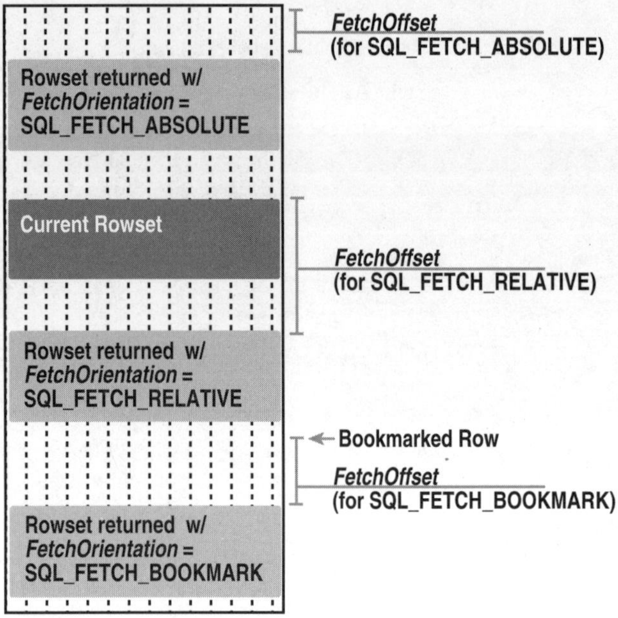

Figure 11.5 Fetching absolute, relative, and bookmarked rowsets

SQLFetchScroll positions the cursor to the specified row and returns the rows in the rowset starting with that row. If the specified rowset overlaps the end of the result set, a partial rowset is returned. If the specified rowset overlaps the start of the result set, the first rowset in the result set is usually returned; for complete details, see the **SQLFetchScroll** function description.

In some cases, the application may want to position the cursor without retrieving any data. For example, it might want to test whether a row exists or just get the bookmark for the row without bringing other data across the network. To do this, it sets the SQL_ATTR_RETRIEVE_DATA statement attribute to SQL_RD_OFF. Note that the variable bound to the bookmark column (if any) is always updated, regardless of the setting of this statement attribute.

After the rowset has been retrieved, the application can call **SQLSetPos** to position to a particular row in the rowset or refresh rows in the rowset. For more information on using **SQLSetPos**, see "Updating Data with SQLSetPos" in Chapter 12, "Updating Data."

Note Scrolling is supported in ODBC 2.*x* drivers by **SQLExtendedFetch**. For more information, see "Block Cursors, Scrollable Cursors, and Backward Compatibility" in Appendix G, "Driver Guidelines for Backward Compatibility."

Relative and Absolute Scrolling

Most of the scrolling options in **SQLFetchScroll** position the cursor relative to the current position or to an absolute position. **SQLFetchScroll** supports fetching the next, prior, first, and last rowsets, as well as relative fetching (fetch the rowset *n* rows from the start of the current rowset) and absolute fetching (fetch the rowset starting at row *n*). If *n* is negative in an absolute fetch, rows are counted from the end of the result set. Thus, an absolute fetch of row–1 means to fetch the rowset that starts with the last row in the result set.

Dynamic cursors detect rows inserted into and deleted from the result set, so there is no easy way for dynamic cursors to retrieve the row at a particular number other than reading from the start of the result set, which is likely to be slow. Furthermore, absolute fetching is not very useful in dynamic cursors because row numbers change as rows are inserted and deleted; thus, successively fetching the same row number can yield different rows.

Applications that use **SQLFetchScroll** only for its block cursor capabilities, such as reports, are likely to pass through the result set a single time, using only the option to fetch the next rowset. Screen-based applications, on the other hand, can take advantage of all of the capabilities of **SQLFetchScroll**. If the application sets the rowset size to the number of rows displayed on the screen and binds the screen buffers to the result set, it can translate scroll bar operations directly to calls to **SQLFetchScroll**:

Scroll bar operation	SQLFetchScroll scrolling option
Page up	SQL_FETCH_PRIOR
Page down	SQL_FETCH_NEXT
Line up	SQL_FETCH_RELATIVE with *FetchOffset* equal to –1
Line down	SQL_FETCH_RELATIVE with *FetchOffset* equal to 1
Scroll box at top	SQL_FETCH_FIRST
Scroll box at bottom	SQL_FETCH_LAST
Random scroll box position	SQL_FETCH_ABSOLUTE

Such applications also need to position the scroll box after a scrolling operation, which requires the current row number and the number of rows. For the current row number, applications can either keep track of the current row number or call **SQLGetStmtAttr** with the SQL_ATTR_ROW_NUMBER attribute to retrieve it.

The number of rows in the cursor, which is the size of the result set, is available as the SQL_DIAG_CURSOR_ROW_COUNT field of the diagnostic header. The value in this field is defined only after **SQLExecute**, **SQLExecDirect**, or **SQLMoreResult** has been called. This count can be either an approximate count or an exact count, depending on the capabilities of the driver. The driver's support can be determined by calling **SQLGetInfo** with the cursor attributes information types, and checking whether the SQL_CA2_CRC_APPROXIMATE or SQL_CA2_CRC_EXACT bit is returned for the type of cursor.

An exact row count is never supported for a dynamic cursor. For other types of cursors, the driver can either support exact or approximate row counts, but not both. If the driver supports neither exact nor approximate row counts for a specific cursor type, then the SQL_DIAG_CURSOR_ROW_COUNT field contains the number of rows that have been fetched so far. Regardless of what the driver supports, **SQLFetchScroll** with an *Operation* of SQL_FETCH_LAST will cause the SQL_DIAG_CURSOR_ROW_COUNT field to contain the exact row count.

Bookmarks

A bookmark is a value used to identify a row of data. The meaning of the bookmark value is known only to the driver or data source. For example, it might be as simple as a row number or as complex as a disk address. Bookmarks in ODBC are a bit different from bookmarks in real books. In a real book, the reader places a bookmark at a specific page, then looks for that bookmark to return to the page. In ODBC, the application requests a bookmark for a particular row, stores it, and passes it back to the cursor to return to the row. Thus, bookmarks in ODBC are similar to a reader writing down a page number, remembering it, and then looking the page up again.

To determine a driver's support of bookmarks, an application calls **SQLGetInfo** with the SQL_BOOKMARK_PERSISTENCE option. The bits in this value describe what operations bookmarks survive, such as whether bookmarks are still valid after the cursor is closed.

Bookmark Types

All bookmarks in ODBC 3.0 are variable-length bookmarks. This allows a primary key or a unique index associated with a table to be used as a bookmark. The bookmark can also be a 32-bit value, as was used in ODBC 2.*x*. To specify that a bookmark is used with a cursor, an ODBC 3.0 application sets the SQL_ATTR_USE_BOOKMARK statement attribute to SQL_UB_VARIABLE. A variable-length bookmark is automatically used.

An application can call **SQLColAttribute** with the *FieldIdentifier* argument set to SQL_DESC_OCTET_LENGTH to obtain the length of the bookmark. Because a variable-length bookmark can be a long value, an application should not bind to column 0 unless it will use the bookmark for many of the rows in the rowset.

Fixed-length bookmarks are supported only for backward compatibility. If an ODBC 2.*x* application working with an ODBC 3.0 driver calls **SQLSetStmtOption** to set SQL_USE_BOOKMARKS to SQL_UB_ON, it is mapped in the Driver Manager to SQL_UB_VARIABLE. A variable-length bookmark is used, even if only 32 bits of it are populated. If a driver supports fixed-length bookmarks, it will support variable-length bookmarks. If an ODBC 3.0 application working with an ODBC 2.*x* driver calls **SQLSetStmtAttr** to set SQL_ATTR_USE_BOOKMARKS to

SQL_UB_VARIABLE, it is mapped in the Driver Manager to SQL_UB_ON, and a 32-bit fixed-length bookmark is used. The SQL_ATTR_FETCH_BOOKMARK_PTR statement attribute must then point to a 32-bit bookmark. If the bookmarks used are longer than 32-bits, such as when primary keys are used as bookmarks, the cursor must map the actual values to 32-bit values. It could, for example, build a hash table of them. When an ODBC 3.0 application working with an ODBC 2.*x* driver binds a bookmark, the buffer length must be 4.

Retrieving Bookmarks

If the application will use bookmarks, it must set the SQL_ATTR_USE_BOOKMARKS statement attribute to SQL_UB_VARIABLE before preparing or executing the statement. This is necessary because building and maintaining bookmarks can be an expensive operation, so bookmarks should be enabled only when an application can make good use of them.

Bookmarks are returned as column 0 of the result set. There are three ways an application can retrieve them:

- Bind column 0 of the result set. **SQLFetch** or **SQLFetchScroll** returns the bookmarks for each row in the rowset along with the data for other bound columns.
- Call **SQLSetPos** to position to a row in the rowset, then call **SQLGetData** for column 0. Note that if a driver supports bookmarks, it must always support the ability to call **SQLGetData** for column 0, even if it does not allow applications to call **SQLGetData** for other columns before the last bound column.
- Call **SQLBulkOperations** with the *Operation* argument set to SQL_ADD, and column 0 bound. The cursor inserts the row and returns the bookmark for the row in the bound buffer.

Scrolling by Bookmark

When fetching rows with **SQLFetchScroll**, an application can use a bookmark as a basis for selecting the starting row. This is a form of absolute addressing because it does not depend on the current cursor position. To scroll to a bookmarked row, the application calls **SQLFetchScroll** with a *FetchOrientation* of SQL_FETCH_BOOKMARK. This operation uses the bookmark pointed to by the SQL_ATTR_FETCH_BOOKMARK_PTR statement attribute. It returns the rowset starting with the row identified by that bookmark. An application can specify an offset for this operation in the *FetchOffset* argument of the call to **SQLFetchScroll**. When an offset is specified, the first row of the returned rowset is determined by adding the number in the *FetchOffset* argument to the number of the row identified by the bookmark. This use of the *FetchOffset* argument is not supported when used with ODBC 2.*x* drivers; when an application calls **SQLFetchScroll** in an ODBC 2.*x* driver with *FetchOrientation* set to SQL_FETCH_BOOKMARK, the *FetchOffset* argument must be set to 0.

Updating, Deleting, or Fetching by Bookmark

Bookmarks can be used to identify data to be updated in the result set, deleted from the result set, or fetched from the result set to the rowset buffers. These operations are performed by a call to **SQLBulkOperations** with an *Option* argument of SQL_UPDATE_BY_BOOKMARK, SQL_DELETE_BY_BOOKMARK, or SQL_FETCH_BY_BOOKMARK. The bookmarks used in these operations are stored in column 0 of the rowset buffers. When updating by bookmark, the data that result set columns are updated to is retrieved from the rowset buffers. For more information, see "Updating Data with SQLBulkOperations" in Chapter 12, "Updating Data."

Comparing Bookmarks

Because bookmarks are byte-comparable, they can be compared for equality or inequality. To do so, an application treats each bookmark as an array of bytes, and compares two bookmarks byte-by-byte. Because bookmarks are guaranteed to be distinct only within a result set, it makes no sense to compare bookmarks that were obtained from different result sets.

The ODBC Cursor Library

Block and scrollable cursors are very useful additions to many applications. However, not all drivers support block and scrollable cursors. The same is true of positioned update and delete statements and **SQLSetPos**, which are discussed in Chapter 12, "Updating Data."

Because of this, the ODBC Software Development Kit (SDK) includes a cursor library. The cursor library implements block, static cursors, positioned update and delete statements, and **SQLSetPos** for any driver that meets the X/Open Standard CLI conformance level. The cursor library may be redistributed with ODBC applications; see the licensing agreement in the ODBC SDK for details.

To use the cursor library, an application sets the SQL_ATTR_ODBC_CURSORS connection attribute before connecting to the data source. For more information about the cursor library, see Appendix F, "ODBC Cursor Library."

Multiple Results

A *result* is something returned by the data source after a statement is executed. ODBC has two types of results: result sets and row counts. Row counts are the number of rows affected by an update, delete, or insert statement. Batches—described in "Batches of SQL Statements" in Chapter 9, "Executing Statements"—can generate multiple results.

The following table lists the **SQLGetInfo** options an application uses to determine whether a data source returns multiple results for each different type of batch. In particular, a data source can return a single row count for the entire batch of statements or individual row counts for each statement in the batch. In the case of a result set–generating statement executed with an array of parameters, the data source can return a single result set for all sets of parameters or individual result sets for each set of parameters.

Batch type	Row counts	Result sets
Explicit batch	SQL_BATCH_ROW_COUNT [a]	-- [b]
Procedure	SQL_BATCH_ROW_COUNT [a]	-- [b]
Arrays of parameters	SQL_PARAM_ARRAYS_ROW_COUNTS	SQL_PARAM_ARRAYS_SELECTS

[a] Row count–generating statements in a batch may be supported, yet the return of the row counts not supported. The SQL_BATCH_SUPPORT option in **SQLGetInfo** indicates whether row count–generating statements are allowed in batches; the SQL_BATCH_ROW_COUNTS option indicates whether these row counts are returned to the application.

[b] Explicit batches and procedures always return multiple result sets when they include multiple result set–generating statements.

Note The SQL_MULT_RESULT_SETS option introduced in ODBC 1.0 provides only general information about whether multiple result sets can be returned. In particular, it is set to "Y" if the SQL_BS_SELECT_EXPLICIT or SQL_BS_SELECT_PROC bits are returned for SQL_BATCH_SUPPORT or if SQL_PAS_BATCH is returned for SQL_PARAM_ARRAYS_SELECT.

To process multiple results, an application calls **SQLMoreResults**. This function discards the current result and makes the next result available. It returns SQL_NO_DATA when no more results are available. For example, suppose the following statements are executed as a batch:

```
SELECT * FROM Parts WHERE Price > 100.00;
UPDATE Parts SET Price = 0.9 * Price WHERE Price > 100.00
```

After these statements are executed, the application fetches rows from the result set created by the **SELECT** statement. When it is done fetching rows, it calls **SQLMoreResults** to make available the number of parts that were repriced. If necessary, **SQLMoreResults** discards unfetched rows and closes the cursor. The application then calls **SQLRowCount** to determine how many parts were repriced by the **UPDATE** statement.

It is driver-specific whether the entire batch statement is executed before any results are available. In some implementations, this is the case; in others, calling **SQLMoreResults** triggers the execution of the next statement in the batch.

If one of the statements in a batch fails, **SQLMoreResults** will return either SQL_ERROR or SQL_SUCCESS_WITH_INFO. If the batch was aborted when the statement failed, or the failed statement was the last statement in the batch, **SQLMoreResults** will return SQL_ERROR. If the batch was not aborted when the statement failed, and the failed statement was not the last statement in the batch, **SQLMoreResults** will return SQL_SUCCESS_WITH_INFO. SQL_SUCCESS_WITH_INFO indicates that at least one result set or count was generated, and that the batch was not aborted.

CHAPTER 12

Updating Data

Applications can update data either by executing SQL statements or by calling **SQLSetPos** or **SQLBulkOperations**. **UPDATE**, **DELETE**, and **INSERT** statements act directly on the data source and are usually supported by drivers. Searched update and delete statements contain a specification of the rows to change. Positioned update and delete statements and **SQLSetPos** act on the data source through a cursor and are less widely supported.

Whether cursors can detect changes made to the result set with the methods described in this chapter depends on the type of the cursor and how it is implemented. Forward-only cursors do not revisit rows and therefore will not detect any changes. For information about whether scrollable cursors can detect changes, see "Scrollable Cursors" in Chapter 11, "Retrieving Results (Advanced)."

UPDATE, DELETE, and INSERT Statements

SQL-based applications make changes to tables by executing the **UPDATE**, **DELETE**, and **INSERT** statements. These statements are part of the Minimum SQL grammar conformance level and must be supported by all drivers and data sources.

The syntax of these statements is:

UPDATE *table-name*
    SET *column-identifier* = {*expression* | **NULL**}
        [**,** *column-identifier* = {*expression* | **NULL**}]...
    [**WHERE** *search-condition*]

DELETE FROM *table-name* [**WHERE** *search-condition*]

INSERT INTO *table-name* [(*column-identifier* [**,** *column-identifier*]...)]
    {*query-specification* | **VALUES** (*insert-value* [**,** *insert-value*]...)}

Note that the *query-specification* element is valid only in the Core and Extended SQL grammars, and that the *expression* and *search-condition* elements become more complex in the Core and Extended SQL grammars.

Like other SQL statements, **UPDATE**, **DELETE**, and **INSERT** statements are often more efficient when they use parameters. For example, the following statement can be prepared and repeatedly executed to insert multiple rows in the Orders table:

```
INSERT INTO Orders (PartID, Description, Price) VALUES (?, ?, ?)
```

This efficiency can be increased by passing arrays of parameter values. For more information about statement parameters and arrays of parameter values, see "Statement Parameters" in Chapter 9, "Executing Statements."

Positioned Update and Delete Statements

Applications can update or delete the current row in a result set with a positioned update or delete statement. Positioned update and delete statements are supported by some data sources, but not all of them. To determine whether a data source supports positioned update and delete statements, an application calls **SQLGetInfo** with the SQL_DYNAMIC_CURSOR_ATTRIBUTES1, SQL_FORWARD_ONLY_CURSOR_ATTRIBUTES1, SQL_KEYSET_CURSOR_ATTRIBUTES1, or SQL_STATIC_CURSOR_ATTRIBUTES1 *InfoType* (depending on the type of the cursor). Note that the ODBC cursor library simulates positioned update and delete statements.

To use a positioned update or delete statement, the application must create a result set with a **SELECT FOR UPDATE** statement. The syntax of this statement is:

SELECT [**ALL** | **DISTINCT**] *select-list*
    FROM *table-reference-list*
    [**WHERE** *search-condition*]
    FOR UPDATE OF [*column-name* [**,** *column-name*]...]

The application then positions the cursor on the row to be updated or deleted. It can do this by calling **SQLFetchScroll** to retrieve a rowset containing the required row and calling **SQLSetPos** to position the rowset cursor on that row. The application then executes the positioned update or delete statement on a different statement than the statement being used by the result set. The syntax of these statements is:

UPDATE *table-name*
    SET *column-identifier* = {*expression* | **NULL**}
        [**,** *column-identifier* = {*expression* | **NULL**}]...
    WHERE CURRENT OF *cursor-name*

DELETE FROM *table-name* **WHERE CURRENT OF** *cursor-name*

Notice that these statements require a cursor name. The application can either specify a cursor name with **SQLSetCursorName** before executing the statement that creates the result set or it can let the data source automatically generate a cursor name when the cursor is created. In the latter case, the application retrieves this cursor name for use in positioned update and delete statements by calling **SQLGetCursorName**.

For example, the following code allows a user to scroll through the Customers table and delete customer records or update their addresses and phone numbers. It calls **SQLSetCursorName** to specify a cursor name before it creates the result set of customers and uses three statement handles: *hstmtCust* for the result set, *hstmtUpdate* for a positioned update statement, and *hstmtDelete* for a positioned delete statement. Although the code could bind separate variables to the parameters in the positioned update statement, it updates the rowset buffers and binds the elements of these buffers. This keeps the rowset buffers synchronized with the updated data.

```
#define POSITIONED_UPDATE 100
#define POSITIONED_DELETE 101

SQLUINTEGER  CustIDArray[10];
SQLCHAR      NameArray[10][51], AddressArray[10][51], PhoneArray[10][11];
SQLINTEGER   CustIDIndArray[10], NameLenOrIndArray[10], AddressLenOrIndArray[10],
             PhoneLenOrIndArray[10];
SQLUSMALLINT RowStatusArray[10], Action, RowNum;
SQLHSTMT     hstmtCust, hstmtUpdate, hstmtDelete;

// Set the SQL_ATTR_BIND_TYPE statement attribute to use column-wise binding. Declare
// the rowset size with the SQL_ATTR_ROW_ARRAY_SIZE statement attribute. Set the
// SQL_ATTR_ROW_STATUS_PTR statement attribute to point to the row status array.
SQLSetStmtAttr(hstmtCust, SQL_ATTR_ROW_BIND_TYPE, SQL_BIND_BY_COLUMN, 0);
SQLSetStmtAttr(hstmtCust, SQL_ATTR_ROW_ARRAY_SIZE, 10, 0);
SQLSetStmtAttr(hstmtCust, SQL_ATTR_ROW_STATUS_PTR, RowStatusArray, 0);

// Bind arrays to the CustID, Name, Address, and Phone columns.
SQLBindCol(hstmtCust, 1, SQL_C_ULONG, CustIDArray, 0, CustIDIndArray);
SQLBindCol(hstmtCust, 2, SQL_C_CHAR, NameArray, sizeof(NameArray[0]),
           NameLenOrIndArray);
SQLBindCol(hstmtCust, 3, SQL_C_CHAR, AddressArray, sizeof(AddressArray[0]),
           AddressLenOrIndArray);
SQLBindCol(hstmtCust, 4, SQL_C_CHAR, PhoneArray, sizeof(PhoneArray[0]),
           PhoneLenOrIndArray);

// Set the cursor name to Cust.
SQLSetCursorName(hstmtCust, "Cust", SQL_NTS);

// Prepare positioned update and delete statements.
SQLPrepare(hstmtUpdate,
   "UPDATE Customers SET Address = ?, Phone = ? WHERE CURRENT OF Cust",
   SQL_NTS);
SQLPrepare(hstmtDelete, "DELETE FROM Customers WHERE CURRENT OF Cust", SQL_NTS);
```

```
// Execute a statement to retrieve rows from the Customers table.
SQLExecDirect(hstmtCust,
   "SELECT CustID, Name, Address, Phone FROM Customers FOR UPDATE OF Address, Phone",
   SQL_NTS);

// Fetch and display the first 10 rows.
SQLFetchScroll(hstmtCust, SQL_FETCH_NEXT, 0);
DisplayData(CustIDArray, CustIDIndArray, NameArray, NameLenOrIndArray, AddressArray,
            AddressLenOrIndArray, PhoneArray, PhoneLenOrIndArray, RowStatusArray);

// Call GetAction to get an action and a row number from the user.
while (GetAction(&Action, &RowNum)) {
   switch (Action) {

      case SQL_FETCH_NEXT:
      case SQL_FETCH_PRIOR:
      case SQL_FETCH_FIRST:
      case SQL_FETCH_LAST:
      case SQL_FETCH_ABSOLUTE:
      case SQL_FETCH_RELATIVE:
         // Fetch and display the requested data.
         SQLFetchScroll(hstmtCust, Action, RowNum);
         DisplayData(CustIDArray, CustIDIndArray, NameArray, NameLenOrIndArray,
                     AddressArray, AddressLenOrIndArray, PhoneArray,
                     PhoneLenOrIndArray, RowStatusArray);
         break;

      case POSITIONED_UPDATE:
         // Get the new data and place it in the rowset buffers.
         GetNewData(AddressArray[RowNum - 1], &AddressLenOrIndArray[RowNum - 1],
                    PhoneArray[RowNum - 1], &PhoneLenOrIndArray[RowNum - 1]);

         // Bind the elements of the arrays at position RowNum-1 to the parameters
         // of the positioned update statement.
         SQLBindParameter(hstmtUpdate, 1, SQL_PARAM_INPUT, SQL_C_CHAR, SQL_CHAR,
                          50, 0, AddressArray[RowNum - 1], sizeof(AddressArray[0]),
                          &AddressLenOrIndArray[RowNum - 1]);
         SQLBindParameter(hstmtUpdate, 2, SQL_PARAM_INPUT, SQL_C_CHAR, SQL_CHAR,
                          10, 0, PhoneArray[RowNum - 1], sizeof(PhoneArray[0]),
                          &PhoneLenOrIndArray[RowNum - 1]);

         // Position the rowset cursor. The rowset is 1-based.
         SQLSetPos(hstmtCust, RowNum, SQL_POSITION, SQL_LOCK_NO_CHANGE);

         // Execute the positioned update statement to update the row.
         SQLExecute(hstmtUpdate);
         break;

      case POSITIONED_DELETE:
         // Position the rowset cursor. The rowset is 1-based.
         SQLSetPos(hstmtCust, RowNum, SQL_POSITION, SQL_LOCK_NO_CHANGE);
```

```
            // Execute the positioned delete statement to delete the row.
            SQLExecute(hstmtDelete);
            break;
      }
   }

   // Close the cursor.
   SQLCloseCursor(hstmtCust);
```

Simulating Positioned Update and Delete Statements

If the data source does not support positioned update and delete statements, the driver can simulate these. For example, the ODBC cursor library simulates positioned update and delete statements. The general strategy for simulating positioned update and delete statements is to convert positioned statements to searched ones. This is done by replacing the **WHERE CURRENT OF** clause with a searched **WHERE** clause that identifies the current row.

For example, because the CustID column uniquely identifies each row in the Customers table, the positioned delete statement:

```
DELETE FROM Customers WHERE CURRENT OF CustCursor
```

might be converted to:

```
DELETE FROM Customers WHERE (CustID = ?)
```

The driver may use one of the following *row identifiers* in the **WHERE** clause:

- Columns whose values serve to identify uniquely every row in the table. For example, calling **SQLSpecialColumns** with SQL_BEST_ROWID returns the optimal column or set of columns that serve this purpose.
- Pseudo-columns, provided by some data sources, for the purpose of uniquely identifying every row. These may also be retrievable by calling **SQLSpecialColumns**.
- A unique index, if available.
- All the columns in the result set.

Exactly which columns a driver should use in the **WHERE** clause it constructs depends on the driver. On some data sources, determining a row identifier can be costly. However, it is faster to execute and guarantees that a simulated statement updates or deletes at most one row. Depending on the capabilities of the underlying DBMS, using a row identifier can be expensive to set up. However, it is faster to execute and guarantees that a simulated statement will update or delete only one row. Using all the columns in the result set is usually much easier to set up. However, it is slower to execute and, if the columns do not uniquely identify a row, can result in rows being unintentionally updated or deleted, especially when the select list for the result set does not contain all the columns that exist in the underlying table.

Depending upon which of these strategies the driver supports, an application can choose which strategy it wants the driver to use with the SQL_ATTR_SIMULATE_CURSOR statement attribute. Although it might seem odd for an application to risk unintentionally updating or deleting a row, the application can remove this risk by ensuring that the columns in the result set uniquely identify each row in the result set. This saves the driver the effort of having to do this.

If the driver chooses to use a row identifier, it intercepts the **SELECT FOR UPDATE** statement that creates the result set. If the columns in the select list do not effectively identify a row, the driver adds the necessary columns to the end of the select list. Some data sources have a single column that always uniquely identifies a row, such as the ROWID column in Oracle; if so, the driver uses this. Otherwise, the driver calls **SQLSpecialColumns** for each table in the **FROM** clause to retrieve a list of the columns that uniquely identify each row. A common restriction that results from this technique is that cursor simulation fails if there is more than one table in the **FROM** clause.

No matter how the driver identifies rows, it usually strips the **FOR UPDATE OF** clause off the **SELECT FOR UPDATE** statement before sending it to the data source. The **FOR UPDATE OF** clause is used only with positioned update and delete statements. Data sources that do not support positioned update and delete statements generally do not support it.

When the application submits a positioned update or delete statement for execution, the driver replaces the **WHERE CURRENT OF** clause with a **WHERE** clause containing the row identifier. The values of these columns are retrieved from a cache maintained by the driver for each column it uses in the **WHERE** clause. After the driver has replaced the **WHERE** clause, it sends the statement to the data source for execution.

For example, suppose that the application submits the following statement to create a result set:

```
SELECT Name, Address, Phone FROM Customers FOR UPDATE OF Phone, Address
```

If the application has set SQL_ATTR_SIMULATE_CURSOR to request a guarantee of uniqueness and if the data source does not provide a pseudo-column that always uniquely identifies a row, the driver calls **SQLSpecialColumns** for the Customers table, discovers that CustID is the key to the Customers table and adds this to the select list, and strips the **FOR UPDATE OF** clause:

```
SELECT Name, Address, Phone, CustID FROM Customers
```

If the application has not requested a guarantee of uniqueness, the driver only strips the **FOR UPDATE OF** clause:

```
SELECT Name, Address, Phone FROM Customers
```

Suppose the application scrolls through the result set and submits the following positioned update statement for execution, where Cust is the name of the cursor over the result set:

```
UPDATE Customers SET Address = ?, Phone = ? WHERE CURRENT OF Cust
```

If the application has not requested a guarantee of uniqueness, the driver replaces the **WHERE** clause and binds the CustID parameter to the variable in its cache:

```
UPDATE Customers SET Address = ?, Phone = ? WHERE (CustID = ?)
```

If the application has not requested a guarantee of uniqueness, the driver replaces the **WHERE** clause and binds the Name, Address, and Phone parameters in this clause to the variables in its cache:

```
UPDATE Customers SET Address = ?, Phone = ?
   WHERE (Name = ?) AND (Address = ?) AND (Phone = ?)
```

Determining the Number of Affected Rows

After an application updates, deletes, or inserts rows, it can call **SQLRowCount** to determine how many rows were affected. **SQLRowCount** returns this value regardless of whether the rows were updated, deleted, or inserted by executing an **UPDATE**, **DELETE**, or **INSERT** statement, by executing a positioned update or delete statement, or by calling **SQLSetPos**.

If a batch of SQL statements is executed, the count of affected rows might be a total count for all statements in the batch or individual counts for each statement in the batch. For more information, see "Batches of SQL Statements" in Chapter 9, "Executing Statements," and "Multiple Results" in Chapter 11, "Retrieving Results (Advanced)."

The number of affected rows is also returned in the SQL_DIAG_ROW_COUNT diagnostic header field in the diagnostic area associated with the statement handle. However, the data in this field is reset after every function call on the same statement handle, whereas the value returned by **SQLRowCount** remains the same until a call to **SQLBulkOperations**, **SQLExecute**, **SQLExecDirect**, **SQLPrepare**, or **SQLSetPos**.

Updating Data with SQLSetPos

Applications can update or delete any row in the rowset with **SQLSetPos**. Calling **SQLSetPos** is a convenient alternative to constructing and executing an SQL statement. It lets an ODBC driver support positioned updates even when the data source does not support positioned SQL statements. It is part of the paradigm of achieving complete database access by means of function calls.

SQLSetPos operates on the current rowset and can be used only after a call to **SQLFetchScroll**. The application specifies the number of the row to update, delete, or insert, and the driver retrieves the new data for that row from the rowset buffers. **SQLSetPos** can also be used to designate a specified row as the current row, or to refresh a particular row in the rowset from the data source.

Rowset size is set by a call to **SQLSetStmtAttr** with an *Attribute* argument of SQL_ATTR_ROW_ARRAY_SIZE. **SQLSetPos** uses a new rowset size, however, only after a call to **SQLFetch** or **SQLFetchScroll**. For example, if the rowset size is changed, then **SQLSetPos** is called, then **SQLFetch** or **SQLFetchScroll** is called, the call to **SQLSetPos** uses the old rowset size, but **SQLFetch** or **SQLFetchScroll** uses the new rowset size.

The first row in the rowset is row number 1. The *RowNumber* argument in **SQLSetPos** must identify a row in the rowset; that is, its value must be in the range between 1 and the number of rows that were most recently fetched (which may be less than the rowset size). If *RowNumber* is 0, the operation applies to every row in the rowset.

Because most interaction with relational databases is done through SQL, **SQLSetPos** is not widely supported. However, a driver can easily emulate it by constructing and executing an **UPDATE** or **DELETE** statement.

To determine what operations **SQLSetPos** supports, an application calls **SQLGetInfo** with the SQL_DYNAMIC_CURSOR_ATTRIBUTES1, SQL_FORWARD_ONLY_CURSOR_ATTRIBUTES1, SQL_KEYSET_CURSOR_ATTRIBUTES1, or SQL_STATIC_CURSOR_ATTRIBUTES1 information option (depending on the type of the cursor).

Updating Rows in the Rowset with SQLSetPos

The update operation of **SQLSetPos** makes the data source update one or more selected rows of a table, using data in the application buffers for each bound column (unless the value in the length/indicator buffer is SQL_COLUMN_IGNORE). Columns that are not bound will not be updated.

To update rows with **SQLSetPos**, the application does the following:

1. Places the new data values in the rowset buffers. For information on how to send long data with **SQLSetPos**, see "Long Data and SQLSetPos and SQLBulkOperations," later in this chapter.
2. Sets the value in the length/indicator buffer of each column as necessary. This is the byte length of the data or SQL_NTS for columns bound to string buffers, the byte length of the data for columns bound to binary buffers, and SQL_NULL_DATA for any columns to be set to NULL.
3. Sets the value in the length/indicator buffer of those columns which are not to be updated to SQL_COLUMN_IGNORE. Although the application can skip this step and resend existing data, this is inefficient and risks sending values to the data source that were truncated when they were read.
4. Calls **SQLSetPos** with *Operation* set to SQL_UPDATE and *RowNumber* set to the number of the row to update. If *RowNumber* is 0, all rows in the rowset are updated.

After **SQLSetPos** returns, the current row is set to the updated row.

When updating all rows of the rowset (*RowNumber* is equal to 0), an application can disable the update of certain rows by setting the corresponding elements of the row operation array (pointed to by the SQL_ATTR_ROW_OPERATION_PTR statement attribute) to SQL_ROW_IGNORE. The row operation array corresponds in size and number of elements to the row status array (pointed to by the SQL_ATTR_ROW_STATUS_PTR statement attribute). To update only those rows in the result set that were successfully fetched and have not been deleted from the rowset, the application uses the row status array from the function that fetched the rowset as the row operation array to **SQLSetPos**.

For every row that is sent to the data source as an update, the application buffers should have valid row data. If the application buffers were filled by fetching and if a row status array has been maintained, its values at each of these row positions should not be SQL_ROW_DELETED, SQL_ROW_ERROR, or SQL_ROW_NOROW.

For example, the following code allows a user to scroll through the Customers table and update, delete, or add new rows. It places the new data in the rowset buffers before calling **SQLSetPos** to update or add new rows. An extra row is allocated at the end of the rowset buffers to hold new rows; this prevents existing data from being overwritten when data for a new row is placed in the buffers.

```
#define UPDATE_ROW 100
#define DELETE_ROW 101
#define ADD_ROW    102
```

```
SQLUINTEGER  CustIDArray[11];
SQLCHAR      NameArray[11][51], AddressArray[11][51], PhoneArray[11][11];
SQLINTEGER   CustIDIndArray[11], NameLenOrIndArray[11], AddressLenOrIndArray[11],
             PhoneLenOrIndArray[11];
SQLUSMALLINT RowStatusArray[10], Action, RowNum;
SQLRETURN    rc;
SQLHSTMT     hstmt;

// Set the SQL_ATTR_ROW_BIND_TYPE statement attribute to use column-wise binding.
// Declare the rowset size with the SQL_ATTR_ROW_ARRAY_SIZE statement attribute.
// Set the SQL_ATTR_ROW_STATUS_PTR statement attribute to point to the row status
// array.
SQLSetStmtAttr(hstmt, SQL_ATTR_CURSOR_TYPE, SQL_CURSOR_KEYSET_DRIVEN, 0);
SQLSetStmtAttr(hstmt, SQL_ATTR_ROW_BIND_TYPE, SQL_BIND_BY_COLUMN, 0);
SQLSetStmtAttr(hstmt, SQL_ATTR_ROW_ARRAY_SIZE, 10, 0);
SQLSetStmtAttr(hstmt, SQL_ATTR_ROW_STATUS_PTR, RowStatusArray, 0);

// Bind arrays to the CustID, Name, Address, and Phone columns.
SQLBindCol(hstmt, 1, SQL_C_ULONG, CustIDArray, 0, CustIDIndArray);
SQLBindCol(hstmt, 2, SQL_C_CHAR, NameArray, sizeof(NameArray[0]), NameLenOrIndArray);
SQLBindCol(hstmt, 3, SQL_C_CHAR, AddressArray, sizeof(AddressArray[0]),
           AddressLenOrIndArray);
SQLBindCol(hstmt, 4, SQL_C_CHAR, PhoneArray, sizeof(PhoneArray[0]),
           PhoneLenOrIndArray);

// Execute a statement to retrieve rows from the Customers table.
SQLExecDirect(hstmt, "SELECT CustID, Name, Address, Phone FROM Customers", SQL_NTS);

// Fetch and display the first 10 rows.
rc = SQLFetchScroll(hstmt, SQL_FETCH_NEXT, 0);
DisplayData(CustIDArray, CustIDIndArray, NameArray, NameLenOrIndArray, AddressArray,
            AddressLenOrIndArray, PhoneArray, PhoneLenOrIndArray, RowStatusArray);

// Call GetAction to get an action and a row number from the user.
while (GetAction(&Action, &RowNum)) {
   switch (Action) {

      case SQL_FETCH_NEXT:
      case SQL_FETCH_PRIOR:
      case SQL_FETCH_FIRST:
      case SQL_FETCH_LAST:
      case SQL_FETCH_ABSOLUTE:
      case SQL_FETCH_RELATIVE:
         // Fetch and display the requested data.
         SQLFetchScroll(hstmt, Action, RowNum);
         DisplayData(CustIDArray, CustIDIndArray,
                     NameArray, NameLenOrIndArray,
                     AddressArray, AddressLenOrIndArray,
                     PhoneArray, PhoneLenOrIndArray, RowStatusArray);
         break;
```

```
      case UPDATE_ROW:
         // Place the new data in the rowset buffers and update the specified row.
         GetNewData(&CustIDArray[RowNum - 1], &CustIDIndArray[RowNum - 1],
                    NameArray[RowNum - 1], &NameLenOrIndArray[RowNum - 1],
                    AddressArray[RowNum - 1], &AddressLenOrIndArray[RowNum - 1],
                    PhoneArray[RowNum - 1], &PhoneLenOrIndArray[RowNum - 1]);
         SQLSetPos(hstmt, RowNum, SQL_UPDATE, SQL_LOCK_NO_CHANGE);
         break;

      case DELETE_ROW:
         // Delete the specified row.
         SQLSetPos(hstmt, RowNum, SQL_DELETE, SQL_LOCK_NO_CHANGE);
         break;

      case ADD_ROW:
         // Place the new data in the rowset buffers at index 10. This is an extra
         // element for new rows so rowset data is not overwritten. Insert the new
         // row. Row 11 corresponds to index 10.
         GetNewData(&CustIDArray[10], &CustIDIndArray[10],
                    NameArray[10], &NameLenOrIndArray[10],
                    AddressArray[10], &AddressLenOrIndArray[10],
                    PhoneArray[10], &PhoneLenOrIndArray[10]);
         SQLSetPos(hstmt, 11, SQL_ADD, SQL_LOCK_NO_CHANGE);
         break;
   }
}

// Close the cursor.
SQLCloseCursor(hstmt);
```

Deleting Rows in the Rowset with SQLSetPos

The delete operation of **SQLSetPos** makes the data source delete one or more selected rows of a table. To delete rows with **SQLSetPos**, the application calls **SQLSetPos** with *Operation* set to SQL_DELETE and *RowNumber* set to the number of the row to delete. If *RowNumber* is 0, all rows in the rowset are deleted.

After **SQLSetPos** returns, the deleted row is the current row, and its status is SQL_ROW_DELETED. The row cannot be used in any further positioned operations, such as calls to **SQLGetData** or **SQLSetPos**.

When deleting all rows of the rows (*RowNumber* is equal to 0), the application can prevent the driver from deleting certain rows by using the row operation array, in the same way as for the update operation of **SQLSetPos** (see "Updating Rows in the Rowset with SQLSetPos" earlier in this chapter).

Every row that is deleted should be a row that exists in the result set. If the application buffers were filled by fetching and if a row status array has been maintained, its values at each of these row positions should not be SQL_ROW_DELETED, SQL_ROW_ERROR, or SQL_ROW_NOROW.

Updating Data with SQLBulkOperations

Applications can perform bulk update, delete, fetch, or insertion operations on the underlying table at the data source with a call to **SQLBulkOperations**. Calling **SQLBulkOperations** is a convenient alternative to constructing and executing an SQL statement. It lets an ODBC driver support positioned updates even when the data source does not support positioned SQL statements. It is part of the paradigm of achieving complete database access by means of function calls.

SQLBulkOperations operates on the current rowset and can be used only after a call to **SQLFetch** or **SQLFetchScroll**. The application specifies the rows to update, delete, or refresh by caching their bookmarks. The driver retrieves the new data for rows to be updated, or the new data to be inserted into the underlying table, from the rowset buffers.

The rowset size to be used by **SQLBulkOperations** is set by a call to **SQLSetStmtAttr** with an *Attribute* argument of SQL_ATTR_ROW_ARRAY_SIZE. Unlike **SQLSetPos**, which uses a new rowset size only after a call to **SQLFetch** or **SQLFetchScroll**, **SQLBulkOperations** uses the new rowset size after the call to **SQLSetStmtAttr**.

Because most interaction with relational databases is done through SQL, **SQLBulkOperations** is not widely supported. However, a driver can easily emulate it by constructing and executing an **UPDATE**, **DELETE**, or **INSERT** statement.

To determine what operations **SQLBulkOperation** supports, an application calls **SQLGetInfo** with the SQL_DYNAMIC_CURSOR_ATTRIBUTES1, SQL_FORWARD_ONLY_CURSOR_ATTRIBUTES1, SQL_KEYSET_CURSOR_ATTRIBUTES1, or SQL_STATIC_CURSOR_ATTRIBUTES1 information option (depending on the type of the cursor).

Updating Rows by Bookmark with SQLBulkOperations

When updating a row by bookmark, **SQLBulkOperations** makes the data source update one or more rows of the table. The rows are identified by the bookmark in a bound bookmark column. The row is updated using data in the application buffers for each bound column (except when the value in the length/indicator buffer for a column is SQL_COLUMN_IGNORE). Unbound columns will not be updated.

To update rows by bookmark with **SQLBulkOperations**, the application:

1. Retrieves and caches the bookmarks of all rows to be updated. If there is more than one bookmark, and column-wise binding is used, the bookmarks are stored in an array; if there is more than one bookmark and row-wise binding is used, the bookmarks are stored in an array of row structures.
2. Sets the SQL_ATTR_ROW_ARRAY_SIZE statement attribute to the number of bookmarks, and binds the buffer containing the bookmark value, or the array of bookmarks, to column 0.
3. Places the new data values in the rowset buffers. For information on how to send long data with **SQLBulkOperations**, see "Long Data and SQLSetPos and SQLBulkOperations" later in this chapter.
4. Sets the value in the length/indicator buffer of each column as necessary. This is the byte length of the data or SQL_NTS for columns bound to string buffers, the byte length of the data for columns bound to binary buffers, and SQL_NULL_DATA for any columns to be set to NULL.
5. Sets the value in the length/indicator buffer of those columns that are not to be updated to SQL_COLUMN_IGNORE. Although the application can skip this step and resend existing data, this is inefficient and risks sending values to the data source that were truncated when they were read.
6. Calls **SQLBulkOperations** with the *Operation* argument set to SQL_UPDATE_BY_BOOKMARK.

For every row that is sent to the data source as an update, the application buffers should have valid row data. If the application buffers were filled by fetching, a row status array has been maintained, and the status value for a row is SQL_ROW_DELETED, SQL_ROW_ERROR, or SQL_ROW_NOROW, invalid data could inadvertently be sent to the data source.

Deleting Rows by Bookmark with SQLBulkOperations

When deleting a row by bookmark, **SQLBulkOperations** makes the data source delete one or more selected rows of the table. The rows are identified by the bookmark in a bound bookmark column.

To delete rows by bookmark with **SQLBulkOperations**, the application:

1. Retrieves and caches the bookmarks of all rows to be deleted. If there is more than one bookmark, and column-wise binding is used, the bookmarks are stored in an array; if there is more than one bookmark and row-wise binding is used, the bookmarks are stored in an array of row structures.
2. Sets the SQL_ATTR_ROW_ARRAY_SIZE statement attribute to the number of bookmarks, and binds the buffer containing the bookmark value, or the array of bookmarks, to column 0.
3. Calls **SQLBulkOperations** with *Operation* set to SQL_DELETE_BY_BOOKMARK.

Inserting Rows with SQLBulkOperations

Inserting data with **SQLBulkOperations** is similar to updating data with **SQLBulkOperations**, as it uses data from the bound application buffers.

So that each column in the new row has a value, all bound columns with a length/indicator value of SQL_COLUMN_IGNORE and all unbound columns must either accept NULL values or have a default.

To insert rows with **SQLBulkOperations**, the application:

1. Sets the SQL_ATTR_ROW_ARRAY_SIZE statement attribute to the number of rows to insert, and places the new data values in the bound application buffers. For information on how to send long data with **SQLBulkOperations**, see "Long Data and SQLSetPos and SQLBulkOperations" later in this chapter.
2. Sets the value in the length/indicator buffer of each column as necessary. This is the byte length of the data or SQL_NTS for columns bound to string buffers, the byte length of the data for columns bound to binary buffers, and SQL_NULL_DATA for any columns to be set to NULL. The application sets the value in the length/indicator buffer of those columns which are to be set to their default (if one exists) or NULL (if one does not) to SQL_COLUMN_IGNORE.
3. Calls **SQLBulkOperations** with the *Operation* argument set to SQL_ADD.

After **SQLBulkOperations** returns, the current row is unchanged. If the bookmark column (column 0) is bound, **SQLBulkOperations** returns the bookmarks of the inserted rows in the rowset buffer bound to that column.

Fetching Rows with SQLBulkOperations

Data can be refetched into a rowset using bookmarks by a call to **SQLBulkOperations**. The rows to be fetched are identified by the bookmarks in a bound bookmark column. Columns with a value of SQL_COLUMN_IGNORE are not fetched.

To perform bulk fetches with **SQLBulkOperations**, the application:

1. Retrieves and caches the bookmarks of all rows to be updated. If there is more than one bookmark, and column-wise binding is used, the bookmarks are stored in an array; if there is more than one bookmark and row-wise binding is used, the bookmarks are stored in an array of row structures.
2. Sets the SQL_ATTR_ROW_ARRAY_SIZE statement attribute to the number of rows to fetch, and binds the buffer containing the bookmark value, or the array of bookmarks, to column 0.
3. Sets the value in the length/indicator buffer of each column as necessary. This is the byte length of the data or SQL_NTS for columns bound to string buffers, the byte length of the data for columns bound to binary buffers, and SQL_NULL_DATA for any columns to be set to NULL. The application sets the value in the length/indicator buffer of those columns which are to be set to their default (if one exists) or NULL (if one does not) to SQL_COLUMN_IGNORE.
4. Calls **SQLBulkOperations** with the *Operation* argument set to SQL_FETCH_BY_BOOKMARK.

There is no need for the application to use the row operation array to prevent the operation to be performed on certain columns. The application selects the rows it wants to fetch by copying only the bookmarks for those rows into the bound bookmark array.

Long Data and SQLSetPos and SQLBulkOperations

As is the case with parameters in SQL statements, long data can be sent when updating rows with **SQLBulkOperations** or **SQLSetPos** or inserting rows with **SQLBulkOperations**. The data is sent in parts with multiple calls to **SQLPutData**. Columns for which data is sent at execution time are known as *data-at-execution columns*.

Note An application can actually send any type of data at execution time with **SQLPutData**, although only character and binary data can be sent in parts. However, if the data is small enough to fit in a single buffer, there is generally no reason to use **SQLPutData**. It is much easier to bind the buffer and let the driver retrieve the data from the buffer.

Because long data columns are typically not bound, the application must bind the column before calling **SQLBulkOperations** or **SQLSetPos**, and unbind it after calling **SQLBulkOperations** or **SQLSetPos**. The column must be bound because **SQLBulkOperations** or **SQLSetPos** operates only on bound columns, and must be unbound so **SQLGetData** can be used to retrieve data from the column.

To send data at execution time, the application:

1. Places a 32-bit value in the rowset buffer instead of a data value. This value will be returned to the application later, so the application should set it to a meaningful value, such as the number of the column or the handle of a file containing data.
2. Sets the value in the length/indicator buffer to the result of the SQL_LEN_DATA_AT_EXEC(*length*) macro. This value indicates to the driver that the data for the parameter will be sent with **SQLPutData**. The *length* value is used when sending long data to a data source that needs to know how many bytes of long data will be sent so that it can preallocate space. To determine if a data source requires this value, the application calls **SQLGetInfo** with the SQL_NEED_LONG_DATA_LEN option. All drivers must support this macro; if the data source does not require the byte length, the driver can ignore it.
3. Calls **SQLBulkOperations** or **SQLSetPos**. The driver discovers that a length/indicator buffer contains the result of the SQL_LEN_DATA_AT_EXEC(*length*) macro and returns SQL_NEED_DATA as the return value of the function.
4. Calls **SQLParamData** in response to the SQL_NEED_DATA return value. If long data needs to be sent, **SQLParamData** returns SQL_NEED_DATA. In the buffer pointed to by the *ValuePtrPtr* argument, the driver returns the unique value that the application placed in the rowset buffer. If there is more than one data-at-execution column, the application uses this value to determine which column to send data for; the driver is not required to request data for data-at-execution columns in any particular order.
5. Calls **SQLPutData** to send the column data to the driver. If the column data does not fit in a single buffer, as is often the case with long data, the application calls **SQLPutData** repeatedly to send the data in parts; it is up to the driver and data source to reassemble the data. If the application passes null-terminated string data, the driver or data source must remove the null-termination character as part of the reassembly process.
6. Calls **SQLParamData** again to indicate that it has sent all of the data for the column. If there are any data-at-execution columns for which data has not been sent, the driver returns SQL_NEED_DATA and the unique value for the next data-at-execution column; the application returns to step 5. If data has been sent for all data-at-execution columns, the data for the row is sent to the data source. **SQLParamData** then returns SQL_SUCCESS or SQL_SUCCESS_WITH_INFO, and can return any SQLSTATE that **SQLBulkOperations** or **SQLSetPos** can return.

After **SQLBulkOperations** or **SQLSetPos** returns SQL_NEED_DATA and before data has been completely sent for the last data-at-execution column, the statement is in a Need Data state. While a statement is in a Need Data state, the application can call only **SQLPutData**, **SQLParamData**, or **SQLCancel**, **SQLGetDiagField**, or **SQLGetDiagRec**; all other functions return SQLSTATE HY010 (Function sequence error). Calling **SQLCancel** cancels execution of the statement and returns it to its previous state. For more information, see Appendix B, "ODBC State Transition Tables."

CHAPTER 13

Descriptors

A descriptor handle refers to a data structure that holds information about either columns or dynamic parameters.

ODBC functions that operate on column and parameter data implicitly set and retrieve descriptor fields. For instance, when **SQLBindCol** is called to bind column data, it sets descriptor fields that completely describe the binding. When **SQLColAttribute** is called to describe column data, it returns data stored in descriptor fields.

An application calling ODBC functions need not concern itself with descriptors. No database operation requires that the application gain direct access to descriptors. However, for some applications, gaining direct access to descriptors streamlines many operations. For example, direct access to descriptors provides a way to rebind column data that may be more efficient than calling **SQLBindCol** again.

Note The physical representation of the descriptor is not defined. Applications gain direct access to a descriptor only by manipulating its fields by calling ODBC functions with the descriptor handle.

Types of Descriptors

A descriptor is used to describe one of the following:

- A set of zero or more parameters. A parameter descriptor can be used to describe:
  - The *application parameter buffer*, which contains either the input dynamic arguments as set by the application or the output dynamic arguments following the execution of a **CALL** statement of SQL.
  - The *implementation parameter buffer*. For input dynamic arguments, this contains the same arguments as the application parameter buffer, after any data conversion the application may specify. For output dynamic arguments, this contains the returned arguments, before any data conversion that the application may specify.

For input dynamic arguments, the application must operate on an application parameter descriptor before executing any SQL statement that contains dynamic parameter markers. For both input and output dynamic arguments, the application may specify different data types from those in the implementation parameter descriptor to achieve data conversion.

- A single row of database data. A row descriptor can be used to describe:
  - The *implementation row buffer*, which contains the row from the database. (These buffers conceptually contain data as written to, or read from, the database. However, the stored form of database data is not specified. A database could perform additional conversion on the data from its form in the implementation buffer.)
  - The *application row buffer*, which contains the row of data as presented to the application, following any data conversion that the application may specify.

  The application operates on the application row descriptor in any case where column data from the database must appear in application variables. The application may specify different data types from those in the implementation row descriptor to achieve data conversion of column data.

The descriptor types are summarized in the following table:

	Rows	Dynamic parameters
Application buffer	Application row descriptor (ARD)	Application parameter descriptor (APD)
Implementation buffer	Implementation row descriptor (IRD)	Implementation parameter descriptor (IPD)

For either the parameter or row buffers, if the application specifies different data types in corresponding records of the implementation and application descriptor, the driver performs data conversion when it uses the descriptors. For example, it may convert numeric and datetime values to character-string format. (For valid conversions, see Appendix D, "Data Types.")

A descriptor may perform different roles. Different statements can share any descriptor that the application explicitly allocates. A row descriptor in one statement can serve as a parameter descriptor in another statement.

It is always known whether a given descriptor is an application descriptor or an implementation descriptor, even if the descriptor has not yet been used in a database operation. For the descriptors that the implementation implicitly allocates, the implementation records the predefined row relative to the statement handle. Any descriptor that the application allocates by calling **SQLAllocHandle** is an application descriptor.

Descriptor Fields

Descriptors contain *header* and *record* fields that completely describe columns or parameters.

A descriptor contains a single copy of the following header fields. Changing a header field affects all columns or parameters.

SQL_DESC_ALLOC_TYPE	SQL_DESC_BIND_TYPE
SQL_DESC_ARRAY_SIZE	SQL_DESC_COUNT
SQL_DESC_ARRAY_STATUS_PTR	SQL_DESC_ROWS_PROCESSED_PTR
SQL_DESC_BIND_OFFSET_PTR	

A descriptor contains zero or more descriptor records. Each record describes a column or parameter, depending on the type of descriptor. When a new column or parameter is bound, a new record is added to the descriptor. When a column or parameter is unbound, a record is removed from the descriptor. Each record contains a single copy of the following fields.

SQL_DESC_AUTO_UNIQUE_VALUE	SQL_DESC_LOCAL_TYPE_NAME
SQL_DESC_BASE_COLUMN_NAME	SQL_DESC_NAME
SQL_DESC_BASE_TABLE_NAME	SQL_DESC_NULLABLE
SQL_DESC_CASE_SENSITIVE	SQL_DESC_OCTET_LENGTH
SQL_DESC_CATALOG_NAME	SQL_DESC_OCTET_LENGTH_PTR
SQL_DESC_CONCISE_TYPE	SQL_DESC_PARAMETER_TYPE
SQL_DESC_DATA_PTR	SQL_DESC_PRECISION
SQL_DESC_DATETIME_INTERVAL_CODE	SQL_DESC_SCALE
SQL_DESC_DATETIME_INTERVAL_PRECISION	SQL_DESC_SCHEMA_NAME
SQL_DESC_DISPLAY_SIZE	SQL_DESC_SEARCHABLE
SQL_DESC_FIXED_PREC_SCALE	SQL_DESC_TABLE_NAME
SQL_DESC_INDICATOR_PTR	SQL_DESC_TYPE
SQL_DESC_LABEL	SQL_DESC_TYPE_NAME
SQL_DESC_LENGTH	SQL_DESC_UNNAMED
SQL_DESC_LITERAL_PREFIX	SQL_DESC_UNSIGNED
SQL_DESC_LITERAL_SUFFIX	SQL_DESC_UPDATABLE

Many statement attributes correspond to the header field of a descriptor. Setting these attributes through a call to **SQLSetStmtAttr** and setting the corresponding descriptor header field by calling **SQLSetDescField** have the same effect. The same is true for **SQLGetStmtAttr** and **SQLGetDescField**, both of which retrieve the same information. Calling the statement functions instead of the descriptor functions has the advantage that a descriptor handle does not have to be retrieved.

The following header fields can be set by setting statement attributes:

SQL_DESC_ARRAY_SIZE
SQL_DESC_ARRAY_STATUS_PTR
SQL_DESC_BIND_OFFSET_PTR
SQL_DESC_BIND_TYPE
SQL_DESC_ROWS_PROCESSED_PTR

Record Count

The SQL_DESC_COUNT header field of a descriptor is the one-based index of the highest-numbered record that contains data. This field is not a count of all columns or parameters that are bound. When a descriptor is allocated, the initial value of SQL_DESC_COUNT is 0.

The driver takes any action necessary to allocate and maintain whatever storage it requires to hold descriptor information. The application does not explicitly specify the size of a descriptor nor allocate new records. When the application provides information for a descriptor record whose number is higher than the value of SQL_DESC_COUNT, the driver automatically increases SQL_DESC_COUNT. When the application unbinds the highest-numbered descriptor record, the driver automatically decreases SQL_DESC_COUNT to contain the number of the highest remaining bound record.

Bound Descriptor Records

When the application sets the SQL_DESC_DATA_PTR field of a descriptor record, so that it no longer contains a null value, the record is said to be *bound*.

If the descriptor is an APD, then each bound record constitutes a bound parameter. For input parameters, the application must bind a parameter for each dynamic parameter marker in the SQL statement before executing the statement. For output parameters, the application need not bind the parameter.

If the descriptor is an ARD, which describes a row of database data, then each bound record constitutes a bound column.

Deferred Fields

The values of *deferred fields* are not used when they are set, but the driver saves the addresses of the variables for a deferred effect. For an application parameter descriptor, the driver uses the contents of the variables at the time of the call to **SQLExecDirect** or **SQLExecute**. For an application row descriptor, the driver uses the contents of the variables at the time of the fetch.

The following are deferred fields:

- The SQL_DESC_DATA_PTR and SQL_DESC_INDICATOR_PTR fields of a descriptor record.
- The SQL_DESC_OCTET_LENGTH_PTR field of an application descriptor record.
- In the case of a multirow fetch, the SQL_DESC_ARRAY_STATUS_PTR, and SQL_DESC_ROWS_PROCESSED_PTR fields of a descriptor header.

When a descriptor is allocated, the deferred fields of each descriptor record initially have a null value. The meaning of the null value is as follows:

- If SQL_DESC_ARRAY_STATUS_PTR has a null value, a multirow fetch fails to return this component of the per-row diagnostic information.
- If SQL_DESC_DATA_PTR has a null value, the record is unbound.
- If the SQL_DESC_OCTET_LENGTH_PTR field of an ARD has a null value, the driver does not return length information for that column.
- If the SQL_DESC_OCTET_LENGTH_PTR field of an APD has a null value, and the parameter is a character string, the driver assumes that string is null-terminated. For output dynamic parameters, a null value in this field prevents the driver from returning length information. (If the SQL_DESC_TYPE field does not indicate a character-string parameter, the SQL_DESC_OCTET_LENGTH_PTR field is ignored.)

The application must not deallocate or discard variables used for deferred fields between the time it associates them with the fields and the time the driver reads or writes them.

Consistency Check

A consistency check is performed by the driver automatically whenever an application sets the SQL_DESC_DATA_PTR field of the APD, ARD, or IPD. Whenever this field is set, the driver checks that the value of the SQL_DESC_TYPE field and the values applicable to the SQL_DESC_TYPE field in the same record are valid and consistent.

The SQL_DESC_DATA_PTR field of an IPD is not normally set; however, an application can do so to force a consistency check of IPD fields. The value that the SQL_DESC_DATA_PTR field of the IPD is set to is not actually stored, and cannot be retrieved by a call to **SQLGetDescField** or **SQLGetDescRec**; the setting is made only to force the consistency check. A consistency check cannot be performed on an IRD.

For more information on the consistency check, see **SQLSetDescRec**.

Allocating and Freeing Descriptors

Descriptors are either implicitly or explicitly allocated, as described in the following sections.

Implicitly Allocated Descriptors

When a statement handle is allocated, the application implicitly allocates one set of four descriptors. The application can obtain the handles of these implicitly allocated descriptors as attributes of the statement handle. When the application frees the statement handle, the driver frees all implicitly allocated descriptors on that handle.

Explicitly Allocated Descriptors

An application can explicitly allocate an application descriptor on a connection at any time it is connected to the database. By specifying that descriptor handle as an attribute of a statement handle using **SQLSetStmtAttr**, the application directs the driver to use that descriptor in place of the corresponding implicitly allocated application descriptors. The application cannot specify alternate implementation descriptors.

An application can associate an explicitly allocated descriptor with more than one statement. Only when an application is actually connected to the database can a descriptor be an explicitly allocated descriptor. The application can free such a descriptor explicitly, or implicitly by freeing its connection.

Initialization of Descriptor Fields

When an application row descriptor is allocated, its fields receive initial values as indicated in **SQLSetDescField**. The initial value of the SQL_DESC_TYPE field is SQL_DEFAULT. This provides for a standard treatment of database data for presentation to the application. The application may specify different treatment of the data by setting fields of the descriptor record.

The initial value of SQL_DESC_ARRAY_SIZE in the descriptor header is 1. The application can modify this field to enable multirow fetch.

The concept of a default value is not valid for the fields of an IRD. The only time an application can gain access to the fields of an IRD is when there is a prepared or executed statement associated with it.

Certain fields of an IPD are defined only after the IPD has been automatically populated by the driver. If not, they are undefined. These fields are SQL_DESC_CASE_SENSITIVE, SQL_DESC_FIXED_PREC_SCALE, SQL_DESC_TYPE_NAME, SQL_DESC_UNSIGNED, and SQL_DESC_LOCAL_TYPE_NAME.

Automatic Population of the IPD

Some drivers are capable of setting the fields of the IPD after a parameterized query has been prepared. The descriptor fields are automatically populated with information about the parameter, including the data type, precision, scale, and other characteristics. This is equivalent to supporting **SQLDescribeParam**. This information can be particularly valuable to an application when it has no other way to discover it, such as when an ad-hoc query is performed with parameters that the application does not know about.

An application determines whether the driver supports automatic population by calling **SQLGetConnectAttr** with an *Attribute* of SQL_ATTR_AUTO_IPD. If SQL_TRUE is returned, the driver supports it, and the application can enable it by setting the SQL_ATTR_ENABLE_AUTO_IPD statement attribute to SQL_TRUE.

When automatic population is supported and enabled, the driver populates the fields of the IPD after an SQL statement containing parameter markers has been prepared by a call to **SQLPrepare**. An application can retrieve this information by calling **SQLGetDescField** or **SQLGetDescRec**, or **SQLDescribeParam**. The application can use the information to bind the most appropriate application buffer for a parameter, or to specify a data conversion for it.

Automatic population of the IPD may produce a performance penalty. An application can turn it off by resetting the SQL_ATTR_ENABLE_AUTO_IPD statement attribute to SQL_FALSE (which is the default value).

Freeing Descriptors

Explicitly allocated descriptors can be freed either explicitly by calling **SQLFreeHandle** with *HandleType* of SQL_HANDLE_DESC, or implicitly when the connection handle is freed. When an explicitly allocated descriptor is freed, all statement handles to which the freed descriptor applied automatically revert to the descriptors implicitly allocated for them.

Implicitly allocated descriptors can only be freed by calling **SQLDisconnect**, which drops any statements or descriptors open on the connection, or by calling **SQLFreeHandle** with a *HandleType* of SQL_HANDLE_STMT to free a statement handle and all the implicitly allocated descriptors associated with the statement. An implicitly allocated descriptor cannot be freed by calling **SQLFreeHandle** with a *HandleType* of SQL_HANDLE_DESC.

Even when freed, an implicitly allocated descriptor remains valid, and **SQLGetDescField** can be called on its fields.

Getting and Setting Descriptor Fields

The following sections describe the methods an application can use to retrieve or set the values in descriptor fields.

Obtaining Descriptor Handles

An application obtains the handle of any explicitly allocated descriptor as an output argument of the call to **SQLAllocHandle**. The handle of an implicitly allocated descriptor is obtained by calling **SQLGetStmtAttr**.

Retrieving the Values in Descriptor Fields

An application can call **SQLGetDescField** to obtain a single field of a descriptor record. **SQLGetDescField** gives the application access to all the descriptor fields defined in ODBC, and to driver-defined fields as well.

SQLGetDescRec can be called to retrieve the settings of multiple descriptor fields that affect the data type and storage of column or parameter data.

Setting Descriptor Fields

To modify the fields of a descriptor, an application can call **SQLSetDescField**. Some fields are read-only and cannot be set (see the **SQLSetDescField** function description).

Descriptor record fields are set with a record number (*RecNumber*) of 1 or higher, while descriptor header fields are set with a record number of 0. A record number of 0 is also used to set bookmark fields, in accordance with the convention that bookmarks are contained in column 0. This may leave the impression that bookmark fields are contained within the descriptor header, but this is not the case. Bookmark fields are distinct from header fields.

When setting fields individually, the application should follow the sequence defined in **SQLSetDescField**. Setting some fields causes the driver to set other fields. This ensures that the descriptor is always ready to use once the application has specified a data type. When the application sets the SQL_DESC_TYPE field, the driver checks that other fields that specify the type are valid and consistent.

If a function call that would set a descriptor field fails, the contents of the descriptor field are undefined after the failed function call.

Copying Descriptors

The **SQLCopyDesc** function is called to copy the fields of one descriptor to another descriptor. Fields can only be copied to an application descriptor or an IPD, but not to an IRD. Fields can be copied from any type of descriptor. Only those fields that are defined for both the source and target descriptors are copied. **SQLCopyDesc** does not copy the SQL_DESC_ALLOC_TYPE field, because a descriptor's allocation type cannot be changed. Copied fields overwrite the existing fields.

An ARD on one statement handle can serve as the APD on another statement handle. This allows an application to copy rows between tables without copying data at the application level. To do this, a row descriptor that describes a fetched row of a table is reused as a parameter descriptor for a parameter in an INSERT statement. The SQL_MAX_CONCURRENT_ACTIVITIES information type must be greater than 1 for this operation to succeed.

Using Concise Functions

Some ODBC functions gain implicit access to descriptors. Application writers may find them more convenient than calling **SQLSetDescField** or **SQLGetDescField**. These functions are called *concise* functions because they perform a number of functions, including setting or getting descriptor fields. Some concise functions let an application set or retrieve several related descriptor fields in a single function call.

Concise functions can be called without first retrieving a descriptor handle for use as an argument. These functions work with the descriptor fields associated with the statement handle that they are called on.

The concise functions **SQLBindCol** and **SQLBindParameter** bind a column or parameter by setting the descriptor fields that correspond to their arguments. Each of these functions performs more tasks than simply setting descriptors. **SQLBindCol** and **SQLBindParameter** provide a complete specification of the binding of a data column or dynamic parameter. An application can, however, change individual details of a binding by calling **SQLSetDescField** or **SQLSetDescRec**, and can completely bind a column or parameter by making a series of suitable calls to these functions.

The concise functions **SQLColAttribute**, **SQLDescribeCol**, **SQLDescribeParam**, **SQLNumParams**, and **SQLNumResultCols** retrieve values in descriptor fields.

SQLSetDescRec and **SQLGetDescRec** are concise functions that with one call set or get multiple descriptor fields that affect the data type and storage of column or parameter data. **SQLSetDescRec** is an effective way to change the binding of column or parameter data in one step.

SQLSetStmtAttr and **SQLGetStmtAttr** serve as concise functions in some cases (see "Descriptor Fields" earlier in this chapter).

CHAPTER 14

Transactions

A *transaction* is a unit of work that is done as a single, atomic operation; that is, the operation succeeds or fails as a whole. For example, consider transferring money from one bank account to another. This involves two steps: withdrawing the money from the first account and depositing it in the second. It is important that both steps succeed; it is not acceptable for one step to succeed and the other to fail. A database that supports transactions is able to guarantee this.

Transactions can be completed by either being *committed* or being *rolled back*. When a transaction is committed, the changes made in that transaction are made permanent. When a transaction is rolled back, the affected rows are returned to the state they were in before the transaction was started. To extend the account transfer example, an application executes one SQL statement to debit the first account and a different SQL statement to credit the second account. If both statements succeed, the application then commits the transaction. But if either statement fails for any reason, the application rolls back the transaction. In either case, the application guarantees a consistent state at the end of the transaction.

A single transaction can encompass multiple database operations that occur at different times. If other transactions had complete access to the intermediate results, the transactions might interfere with one another. For example, suppose one transaction inserts a row, a second transaction reads that row, and the first transaction is rolled back. The second transaction now has data for a row that does not exist.

To solve this problem, there are various schemes to isolate transactions from each other. *Transaction isolation* is generally implemented by locking rows, which precludes more than one transaction from using the same row at the same time. In some databases, locking a row may also lock other rows.

With increased transaction isolation comes reduced *concurrency*, or the ability of two transactions to use the same data at the same time. For more information, see "Setting the Transaction Isolation Level" later in this chapter.

A full discussion of transactions is well beyond the scope of this book. For more information on transactions, see the "Recommended Reading" section of the introduction.

Transactions in ODBC

Transactions in ODBC are completed at the connection level; that is, when an application completes a transaction, it commits or rolls back all work done through all statement handles on that connection.

Transaction Support

The degree of support for transactions is driver-defined. ODBC is designed to be implementable on a single-user or desktop database that has no need to manage multiple updates to its data. Moreover, some databases that support transactions do so only for the Data Manipulation Language (DML) statements of SQL; there are restrictions or special transaction semantics regarding the use of Data Definition Language (DDL) when a transaction is active. That is, there may be transaction support for multiple simultaneous updates to tables, but not for changing the number and definition of tables during a transaction.

An application determines whether transactions are supported, whether DDL can be included in a transaction, and any special effects of including DDL in a transaction, by calling **SQLGetInfo** with the SQL_TXN_CAPABLE option. For more information, see the **SQLGetInfo** function description.

If the driver does not support transactions, but the application has the ability (using an API other than ODBC) to lock and unlock data, applications can achieve transaction support by locking and unlocking records and tables as needed. To implement the account-transfer example, the application would lock the records for both accounts, copy the current values, debit the first account, credit the second account, and unlock the records. If any steps failed, the application would reset the accounts using the copies.

Even data sources that support transactions might not be able to support more than one transaction at a time within a particular environment. Applications call **SQLGetInfo** with the SQL_MULTIPLE_ACTIVE_TXN option to determine whether a data source can support simultaneous active transactions on more than one connection in the same environment. Because there is one transaction per connection, this is only interesting to applications that have multiple connections to the same data source.

Commit Mode

Transactions in ODBC can be in one of two modes: auto-commit mode or manual-commit mode, as described in the following sections.

Auto-Commit Mode

In *auto-commit mode,* every database operation is a transaction that is committed when performed. This mode is suitable for many real-world transactions that consist of a single SQL statement. It is unnecessary to delimit or specify completion of these transactions. In databases without transaction support, auto-commit mode is the only supported mode. In such databases, statements are committed when they are executed and there is no way to roll them back; they are therefore always in auto-commit mode.

If the underlying DBMS does not support auto-commit mode transactions, the driver can emulate them by manually committing each SQL statement as it is executed.

If a batch of SQL statements is executed in auto-commit mode, it is data source–specific when the statements in the batch are committed. They can be committed as they are executed or as a whole after the entire batch has been executed. Some data sources may support both of these behaviors and may provide a way of selecting one or the others. In particular, if an error occurs in the middle of the batch, it is data source–specific whether the already-executed statements are committed or rolled back. Thus, interoperable applications that use batches and require them to be committed or rolled back as a whole should only execute batches in manual-commit mode.

Manual-Commit Mode

In *manual-commit mode,* applications must explicitly complete transactions by calling **SQLEndTran** to commit them or roll them back. This is the normal transaction mode for most relational databases.

Transactions in ODBC do not have to be explicitly initiated. Instead, a transaction begins implicitly whenever the application starts operating on the database. If the data source requires explicit transaction initiation, the driver must provide it whenever the application executes a statement requiring a transaction and there is no current transaction.

Setting the Commit Mode

Applications specify the transaction mode with the SQL_ATTR_AUTOCOMMIT connection attribute. By default, ODBC transactions are in auto-commit mode (unless **SQLSetConnectAttr** and **SQLSetConnectOption** are not supported, which is unlikely). Switching from manual-commit mode to auto-commit mode automatically commits any open transaction on the connection.

Committing and Rolling Back Transactions

To commit or roll back a transaction in manual-commit mode, an application calls **SQLEndTran**. Drivers for DBMSs that support transactions typically implement this function by executing a **COMMIT** or **ROLLBACK** statement. The Driver Manager does not call **SQLEndTran** when the connection is in auto-commit mode; it simply returns SQL_SUCCESS, even if the application attempts to roll back the transaction. Because drivers for DBMSs that do not support transactions are always in auto-commit mode, they can either implement **SQLEndTran** to return SQL_SUCCESS without doing anything or not implement it at all.

Note Applications should not commit or roll back transactions by executing **COMMIT** or **ROLLBACK** statements with **SQLExecute** or **SQLExecDirect**. The effects of doing this are undefined. Possible problems include the driver no longer knowing when a transaction is active and these statements failing against data sources that do not support transactions. These applications should call **SQLEndTran** instead.

If an application passes the environment handle to **SQLEndTran** but does not pass a connection handle, the Driver Manager conceptually calls **SQLEndTran** with the environment handle for each driver that has one or more active connections in the environment. The driver then commits the transactions on each connection in the environment. However, it is important to realize that neither the driver nor the Driver Manager performs a two-phase commit on the connections in the environment; this is merely a programming convenience to simultaneously call **SQLEndTran** for all connections in the environment.

(A *two-phase commit* is generally used to commit transactions that are spread across multiple data sources. In its first phase, the data sources are polled as to whether they can commit their part of the transaction. In the second phase, the transaction is actually committed on all data sources. If any data sources reply in the first phase that they cannot commit the transaction, the second phase does not occur.)

Effect of Transactions on Cursors and Prepared Statements

Committing or rolling back a transaction has the following effect on cursors and access plans:

- All cursors are closed and access plans for prepared statements on that connection are deleted.
- All cursors are closed and access plans for prepared statements on that connection remain intact.
- All cursors remain open and access plans for prepared statements on that connection remain intact.

For example, suppose a data source exhibits the first behavior in this list, the most restrictive of these behaviors. Now suppose an application does the following:

1. Sets the commit mode to manual commit.
2. Creates a result set of sales orders on statement 1.
3. Creates a result set of the lines in a sales order on statement 2 when the user highlights that order.
4. Calls **SQLExecute** to execute a positioned update statement that has been prepared on statement 3 when the user updates a line.
5. Calls **SQLEndTran** to commit the positioned update statement.

Because of the data source's behavior, the call to **SQLEndTran** in step 5 causes it to close the cursors on statements 1 and 2 and to delete the access plan on all statements. The application must reexecute statements 1 and 2 to re-create the result sets and reprepare the statement on statement 3.

In auto-commit mode, functions other than **SQLEndTran** commit transactions:

- **SQLExecute** or **SQLExecDirect**. In the previous example, the call to **SQLExecute** in step 4 commits a transaction. This causes the data source to close the cursors on statements 1 and 2 and delete the access plan on all statements on that connection.
- **SQLBulkOperations** or **SQLSetPos**. In the previous example, suppose that in step 4 the application calls **SQLSetPos** with the SQL_UPDATE option on statement 2 instead of executing a positioned update statement on statement 3. This commits a transaction and causes the data source to close the cursors on statements 1 and 2, and discards all access plans on that connection.
- **SQLCloseCursor**. In the previous example, suppose that, when the user highlights a different sales order, the application calls **SQLCloseCursor** on statement 2 before creating a result of the lines for the new sales order. The call to **SQLCloseCursor** commits the **SELECT** statement that created the result set of lines and causes the data source to close the cursor on statement 1, and discards all access plans on that connection.

Applications, especially screen-based applications in which the user scrolls around the result set and updates or deletes rows, must be careful to code around this behavior.

To determine how a data source behaves when a transaction is committed or rolled back, an application calls **SQLGetInfo** with the SQL_CURSOR_COMMIT_BEHAVIOR and SQL_CURSOR_ROLLBACK_BEHAVIOR options.

Transaction Isolation

Transaction isolation refers to the degree of interaction between multiple concurrent transactions. To see why this is important, you'll need to first look at the idea of serializability.

Serializability

Ideally, transactions should be *serializable*. Transactions are said to be serializable if the results of running transactions simultaneously are the same as the results of running them serially, that is, one after the other. It is not important which transaction executes first, only that the result does not reflect any mixing of the transactions.

For example, suppose transaction A multiplies data values by 2 and transaction B adds 1 to data values. Now suppose that there are two data values: 0 and 10. If these transactions are run one after another, the new values will be 1 and 21 if the transaction A is run first or 2 and 22 if the transaction B is run first. But what if the order in which the two transactions are run is different for each value? If transaction A is run first on the first value and transaction B is run first on the second value, the new values will be 1 and 22. If this order is reversed, the new values are 2 and 21. The transactions are serializable if 1, 21 and 2, 22 are the only possible results. The transactions are not serializable if 1, 22 or 2, 21 is a possible result.

So why is serializability desirable? In other words, why is it important that it appears that one transaction finishes before the next transaction starts? Consider the following problem. A salesman is entering orders at the same time a clerk is sending out bills. Suppose the salesman enters an order from Company X but does not commit it; the salesman is still talking to the representative from Company X. The clerk requests a list of all open orders and discovers the order for Company X and sends them a bill. Now the representative from Company X decides they want to change their order, so the salesman changes it before committing the transaction. Company X gets an incorrect bill.

If the salesman's and clerk's transactions were serializable, this problem would never have occurred. Either the salesman's transaction would have finished before the clerk's transaction started, in which case the clerk would have sent out the correct bill, or the clerk's transaction would have finished before the salesman's transaction started, in which case the clerk would not have sent a bill to Company X at all.

Transaction Isolation Levels

Transaction isolation levels are a measure of the extent to which transaction isolation succeeds. In particular, transaction isolation levels are defined by the presence or absence of the following phenomena:

- **Dirty Reads**. A *dirty read* occurs when a transaction reads data that has not yet been committed. For example, suppose transaction 1 updates a row. Transaction 2 reads the updated row before transaction 1 commits the update. If transaction 1 rolls back the change, transaction 2 will have read data that is considered never to have existed.
- **Nonrepeatable Reads**. A *nonrepeatable read* occurs when a transaction reads the same row twice but gets different data each time. For example, suppose transaction 1 reads a row. Transaction 2 updates or deletes that row and commits the update or delete. If transaction 1 rereads the row, it retrieves different row values or discovers that the row has been deleted.
- **Phantoms**. A *phantom* is a row that matches the search criteria but is not initially seen. For example, suppose transaction 1 reads a set of rows that satisfy some search criteria. Transaction 2 generates a new row (either through an update or insert) that matches the search criteria for transaction 1. If transaction 1 reexecutes the statement that reads the rows, it gets a different set of rows.

The four transaction isolation levels (as defined by SQL-92) are defined in terms of these phenomena. In the following table, an "X" marks each phenomenon that can occur:

Transaction isolation level	Dirty reads	Nonrepeatable reads	Phantoms
Read uncommitted	X	X	X
Read committed	--	X	X
Repeatable read	--	--	X
Serializable	--	--	--

The following table describes simple ways that a DBMS might implement the transaction isolation levels.

Important Most DBMSs use more complex schemes than these to increase concurrency. These examples are provided for illustrative purposes only. In particular, ODBC does not prescribe how particular DBMSs isolate transactions from each other.

Transaction isolation	Possible implementation
Read uncommitted	Transactions are not isolated from each other. If the DBMS supports other transaction isolation levels, it ignores whatever mechanism it uses to implement those levels. So that they do not adversely affect other transactions, transactions running at the Read Uncommitted level are usually read-only.
Read committed	The transaction waits until rows write-locked by other transactions are unlocked; this prevents it from reading any "dirty" data. The transaction holds a read lock (if it only reads the row) or write lock (if it updates or deletes the row) on the current row to prevent other transactions from updating or deleting it. The transaction releases read locks when it moves off the current row. It holds write locks until it is committed or rolled back.
Repeatable read	The transaction waits until rows write-locked by other transactions are unlocked; this prevents it from reading any "dirty" data. The transaction holds read locks on all rows it returns to the application and write locks on all rows it inserts, updates, or deletes. For example, if the transaction includes the SQL statement **SELECT * FROM Orders**, the transaction read-locks rows as the application fetches them. If the transaction includes the SQL statement **DELETE FROM Orders WHERE Status = 'CLOSED'**, the transaction write-locks rows as it deletes them. Because other transactions cannot update or delete these rows, the current transaction avoids any nonrepeatable reads. The transaction releases its locks when it is committed or rolled back.
Serializable	The transaction waits until rows write-locked by other transactions are unlocked; this prevents it from reading any "dirty" data. The transaction holds a read lock (if it only reads rows) or write lock (if it can update or delete rows) on the range of rows it affects. For example, if the transaction includes the SQL statement **SELECT * FROM Orders**, the range is the entire Orders table; the transaction read-locks the table and does not allow any new rows to be inserted into it. If the transaction includes the SQL statement **DELETE FROM Orders WHERE Status = 'CLOSED'**, the range is all rows with a Status of "CLOSED"; the transaction write-locks all rows in the Orders table with a Status of "CLOSED" and does not allow any rows to be inserted or updated such that the resulting row has a Status of "CLOSED". Because other transactions cannot update or delete the rows in the range, the current transaction avoids any nonrepeatable reads. Because other transactions cannot insert any rows in the range, the current transaction avoids any phantoms. The transaction releases its lock when it is committed or rolled back.

It is important to note that the transaction isolation level does not affect a transaction's ability to see its own changes; transactions can always see any changes they make. For example, a transaction might consist of two **UPDATE** statements, the first of which raises the pay of all employees by ten percent and the second of which sets the pay of any employees over some maximum amount to that amount. This succeeds as a single transaction only because the second **UPDATE** statement can see the results of the first.

Setting the Transaction Isolation Level

To set the transaction isolation level, an application uses the SQL_ATTR_TXN_ISOLATION connection attribute. If the data source does not support the requested isolation level, the driver or data source can set a higher level. To determine what transaction isolation levels a data source supports and what the default isolation level is, an application calls **SQLGetInfo** with the SQL_TXN_ISOLATION_OPTION and SQL_DEFAULT_TXN_ISOLATION options, respectively.

Higher levels of transaction isolation offer the most protection for the integrity of database data. Serializable transactions are guaranteed to be unaffected by other transactions and therefore guaranteed to maintain database integrity.

However, a higher level of transaction isolation can cause slower performance because it increases the chances that the application will have to wait for locks on data to be released. An application may specify a lower level of isolation to increase performance in the following cases:

- When it can be guaranteed that no other transactions exist that might interfere with an application's transactions. This situation occurs only in limited circumstances, such as when one person in a small company maintains dBASE files containing personnel data on their computer and does not share these files.
- When speed is more critical than accuracy and any errors are likely to be small. For example, suppose that a company makes many small sales and that large sales are rare. A transaction that estimates the total value of all open sales might safely use the Read Uncommitted isolation level. Although the transaction would include orders in the process of being opened or closed that are subsequently rolled back, these would tend to cancel each other out and the transaction would be much faster because it is not blocked each time it encounters such an order.

For more information, see the "Optimistic Concurrency" section later in this chapter.

Scrollable Cursors and Transaction Isolation

The following table lists the factors governing the visibility of changes.

Changes made by:	Visibility depends on:
Cursor	Cursor type, cursor implementation
Other statements in same transaction	Cursor type
Statements in other transactions	Cursor type, transaction isolation level

These factors are illustrated in the following diagram.

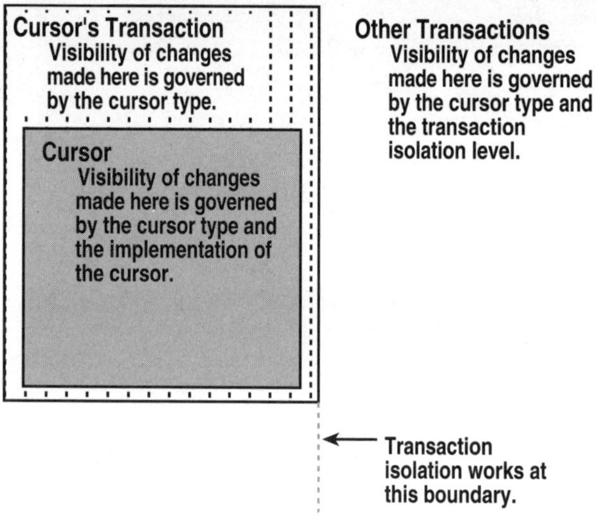

Figure 14.1 Visibility of changes

The following table summarizes the ability of each cursor type to detect changes made by itself, by other operations in its own transaction, and by other transactions. The visibility of the latter changes depends on the cursor type and the isolation level of the transaction containing the cursor.

	Self	Own Txn	Othr Txn (RU [a])	Othr Txn (RC [a])	Othr Txn (RR [a])	Othr Txn (S [a])
Static						
Insert	Maybe [b]	No	No	No	No	No
Update	Maybe [b]	No	No	No	No	No
Delete	Maybe [b]	No	No	No	No	No
Keyset -driven						
Insert	Maybe [b]	No	No	No	No	No
Update	Yes	Yes	Yes	Yes	No	No
Delete	Maybe [b]	Yes	Yes	Yes	No	No
Dynamic						
Insert	Yes	Yes	Yes	Yes	Yes	No
Update	Yes	Yes	Yes	Yes	No	No
Delete	Yes	Yes	Yes	Yes	No	No

a The letters in parentheses indicate the isolation level of the transaction containing the cursor; the isolation level of the other transaction (in which the change was made) is irrelevant.

RU: Read uncommitted
RC: Read committed
RR: Repeatable read
S: Serializable

b Depends on how the cursor is implemented. Whether the cursor can detect such changes is reported through the SQL_STATIC_SENSITIVITY option in **SQLGetInfo**.

Concurrency Control

With increased transaction isolation usually comes reduced *concurrency*, or the ability of two transactions to use the same data at the same time. The reason for this is that transaction isolation is usually implemented by locking rows and, as more rows are locked, fewer transactions can be completed without being blocked at least temporarily by a locked row. While reduced concurrency is generally accepted as a trade-off for the higher transaction isolation levels necessary to maintain database integrity, it can become a problem in interactive applications with high read/write activity that use cursors.

For example, suppose an application executes the SQL statement **SELECT * FROM Orders**. It calls **SQLFetchScroll** to scroll around the result set and allows the user to update, delete, or insert orders. After the user updates, deletes, or inserts an order, the application commits the transaction.

If the isolation level is Repeatable Read, the transaction might—depending on how it is implemented—lock each row returned by **SQLFetchScroll**. If the isolation level is Serializable, the transaction might lock the entire Orders table. In either case, the transaction releases its locks only when it is committed or rolled back. Thus, if the user spends a lot of time reading orders and very little time updating, deleting, or inserting them, the transaction could easily lock a large number of rows, making them unavailable to other users.

Note that this is a problem even if the cursor is read-only and the application only allows the user to read existing orders. In this case, the application commits the transaction—and releases locks—when it calls **SQLCloseCursor** (in auto-commit mode) or **SQLEndTran** (in manual-commit mode).

Concurrency Types

To solve the problem of reduced concurrency in cursors, ODBC exposes four different types of cursor concurrency:

- **Read-only**. The cursor can read data but cannot update or delete data. This is the default concurrency type. Although the DBMS might lock rows to enforce the Repeatable Read and Serializable isolation levels, it can use read locks instead of write locks. This results in higher concurrency because other transactions can at least read the data.
- **Locking**. The cursor uses the lowest level of locking necessary to make sure it can update or delete rows in the result set. This usually results in very low concurrency levels, especially at the Repeatable Read and Serializable transaction isolation levels.
- **Optimistic concurrency using row versions** and **optimistic concurrency using values**. The cursor uses optimistic concurrency: It updates or deletes rows only if they have not changed since they were last read. To detect changes, it compares row versions or values. There is no guarantee that the cursor will be able to update or delete a row, but concurrency is much higher than when locking is used. For more information, see the following section, "Optimistic Concurrency."

An application specifies what type of concurrency it wants the cursor to use with the SQL_ATTR_CONCURRENCY statement attribute. To determine what types are supported, it calls **SQLGetInfo** with the SQL_SCROLL_CONCURRENCY option.

Optimistic Concurrency

Optimistic concurrency derives its name from the optimistic assumption that collisions between transactions will rarely occur; a collision is said to have occurred when another transaction updates or deletes a row of data between the time it is read by the current transaction and it is updated or deleted. It is the opposite of *pessimistic concurrency*, or locking, in which the application developer believes that such collisions are commonplace.

In optimistic concurrency, a row is left unlocked until the time comes to update or delete it. At that point, the row is reread and checked to see if it has been changed since it was last read. If the row has changed, the update or delete fails and must be tried again.

To determine whether a row has been changed, its new version is checked against a cached version of the row. This checking can be based on the row version, such as the timestamp column in SQL Server or the ROWID column in Oracle, or the values of each column in the row. Note that many DBMSs do not support row versions.

Optimistic concurrency can be implemented by the data source or the application. In either case, the application should use a low transaction isolation level such as Read Committed; using a higher level negates the increased concurrency gained by using optimistic concurrency.

If optimistic concurrency is implemented by the data source, the application sets the SQL_ATTR_CONCURRENCY statement attribute to SQL_CONCUR_ROWVER or SQL_CONCUR_VALUES. To update or delete a row, it executes a positioned update or delete statement or calls **SQLSetPos** just as it would with pessimistic concurrency; the driver or data source returns SQLSTATE 01001 (Cursor operation conflict) if the update or delete fails due to a collision.

If the application implements optimistic concurrency itself, then it sets the SQL_ATTR_CONCURRENCY statement attribute to SQL_CONCUR_READ_ONLY to read a row. If it will compare row versions and does not know the row version column, it calls **SQLSpecialColumns** with the SQL_ROWVER option to determine the name of this column.

The application updates or deletes the row by increasing the concurrency to SQL_CONCUR_LOCK (to gain write access to the row) and executing an **UPDATE** or **DELETE** statement with a **WHERE** clause that specifies the version or values the row had when the application read it. If the row has changed since then, the statement will fail. If the **WHERE** clause does not uniquely identify the row, the statement might also update or delete other rows; row versions always uniquely identify rows, but row values uniquely identify rows only if they include the primary key.

CHAPTER 15

Diagnostics

Functions in ODBC return diagnostic information in two ways. The return code indicates the overall success or failure of the function while diagnostic records provide detailed information about the function. At least one diagnostic record—the header record—is returned even if the function succeeds.

Diagnostic information is used at development time to catch programming errors such as invalid handles and syntax errors in hard-coded SQL statements. It is used at run time to catch run-time errors and warnings such as data truncation, access violations, and syntax errors in SQL statements entered by the user.

Return Codes

Each function in ODBC returns a code, known as its *return code*, which indicates the overall success or failure of the function. Program logic is generally based on return codes.

For example, the following code calls **SQLFetch** to retrieve the rows in a result set. It checks the return code of the function to determine if the end of the result set was reached (SQL_NO_DATA), if any warning information was returned (SQL_SUCCESS_WITH_INFO), or if an error occurred (SQL_ERROR).

```
SQLRETURN rc;
SQLHSTMT  hstmt;

while ((rc=SQLFetch(hstmt)) != SQL_NO_DATA) {
   if (rc == SQL_SUCCESS_WITH_INFO) {
      // Call function to display warning information.
   } else if (rc == SQL_ERROR) {
      // Call function to display error information.
      break;
   }
   // Process row.
}
```

The return code SQL_INVALID_HANDLE always indicates a programming error and should never be encountered at run time. All other return codes provide run-time information, although SQL_ERROR may indicate a programming error.

The following table defines the return codes.

Return code	Description
SQL_SUCCESS	Function completed successfully. The application calls **SQLGetDiagField** to retrieve additional information from the header record.
SQL_SUCCESS_WITH_INFO	Function completed successfully, possibly with a nonfatal error (warning). The application calls **SQLGetDiagRec** or **SQLGetDiagField** to retrieve additional information.
SQL_ERROR	Function failed. The application calls **SQLGetDiagRec** or **SQLGetDiagField** to retrieve additional information. The contents of any output arguments to the function are undefined.
SQL_INVALID_HANDLE	Function failed due to an invalid environment, connection, statement, or descriptor handle. This indicates a programming error. No additional information is available from **SQLGetDiagRec** or **SQLGetDiagField**. This code is returned only when the handle is a null pointer or is the wrong type, such as when a statement handle is passed for an argument that requires a connection handle.
SQL_NO_DATA	No more data was available. The application calls **SQLGetDiagRec** or **SQLGetDiagField** to retrieve additional information. One or more driver-defined status records in class 02xxx may be returned. **Note** In ODBC 2.*x*, this return code was named SQL_NO_DATA_FOUND.
SQL_NEED_DATA	More data is needed, such as when parameter data is sent at execution time or additional connection information is required. The application calls **SQLGetDiagRec** or **SQLGetDiagField** to retrieve additional information, if any.
SQL_STILL_EXECUTING	A function that was started asynchronously is still executing. The application calls **SQLGetDiagRec** or **SQLGetDiagField** to retrieve additional information, if any.

Diagnostic Records

Associated with each environment, connection, statement, and descriptor handle are *diagnostic records*. These records contain diagnostic information about the last function called that used a particular handle. The records are replaced only when another function is called using that handle. There is no limit to the number of diagnostic records that can be stored at any one time.

There are two types of diagnostic records: a *header record* and zero or more *status records*. The header record is record 0; the status records are records 1 and above. Diagnostic records are composed of a number of separate fields. These fields are different for the header record and the status records. In addition, ODBC components can define their own diagnostic record fields.

Although diagnostic records can be thought of as structures, there is no requirement for them to actually be structures; how a driver stores the diagnostic information is driver-specific.

Fields in diagnostic records are retrieved with **SQLGetDiagField**. The SQLSTATE, native error number, and diagnostic message fields of status records can be retrieved in a single call with **SQLGetDiagRec**.

Header Record

The fields in the header record contain general information about a function's execution, including the return code, row count, number of status records, and type of statement executed. The header record is always created unless the function returns SQL_INVALID_HANDLE. For a complete list of fields in the header record, see the **SQLGetDiagField** function description.

Status Records

The fields in the status records contain information about specific errors or warnings returned by the Driver Manager, driver, or data source, including the SQLSTATE, native error number, diagnostic message, column number, and row number. Status records can be created only if the function returns SQL_ERROR, SQL_SUCCESS_WITH_INFO, SQL_NO_DATA, SQL_NEED_DATA, or SQL_STILL_EXECUTING. For a complete list of fields in the status records, see the **SQLGetDiagField** function description.

Sequence of Status Records

If two or more status records are returned, the Driver Manager and driver rank them according to the following rules. The record with the highest rank is the first record. The source of a record (Driver Manager, driver, gateway, and so on) is not considered when ranking records.

- **Errors**. Status records that describe errors have the highest rank. Among error records, records that indicate a transaction failure or possible transaction failure outrank all other records. If two or more records describe the same error condition, then SQLSTATEs defined by the X/Open CLI specification (classes 03 through HZ) outrank ODBC- and driver-defined SQLSTATEs.
- **Implementation-defined No Data values**. Status records that describe driver-defined No Data values (class 02) have the second highest rank.
- **Warnings**. Status records that describe warnings (class 01) have the lowest rank. If two or more records describe the same warning condition, then warning SQLSTATEs defined by the X/Open CLI specification outrank ODBC- and driver-defined SQLSTATEs.

If there are two or more records with the highest rank, it is undefined which record is the first record. The order of all other records is undefined. In particular, because warnings may appear before errors, applications should check all status records when a function returns a value other than SQL_SUCCESS.

SQLSTATEs

SQLSTATEs provide detailed information about the cause of a warning or error. The SQLSTATEs in this manual are based on those found in the ISO/IEF CLI specification, although those SQLSTATEs that start with IM are specific to ODBC.

Unlike return codes, the SQLSTATEs in this manual are guidelines and drivers are not required to return them. Thus, while drivers should return the proper SQLSTATE for any error or warning they are capable of detecting, applications should not count on this always occurring. The reasons for this situation are two-fold:

- **Incompleteness**. Although this manual lists a large number of errors and warnings and possible causes for those errors and warnings, it is not complete and probably never will be; driver implementations simply vary too much for this to ever occur. Any given driver probably will not return all of the SQLSTATEs listed in this manual and might return SQLSTATEs not listed in this manual.
- **Complexity**. Some database engines—particularly relational database engines—return literally thousands of errors and warnings. The drivers for such engines are unlikely to map all of these errors and warnings to SQLSTATEs because of the effort involved, the inexactness of the mappings, the large size of the resulting code, and the low value of the resulting code, which often returns programming errors that should never be encountered at run time. Thus, drivers should map as many errors and warnings as seems reasonable and be sure to map those errors and warnings on which application logic might be based, such as SQLSTATE 01004 (Data truncated).

Because SQLSTATEs are not returned reliably, most applications just display them to the user along with their associated diagnostic message, which is often tailored to the specific error or warning that occurred, and native error code. There is rarely any loss of functionality in doing this, as applications cannot base programming logic on most SQLSTATEs anyway. For example, suppose **SQLExecDirect** returns SQLSTATE 42000 (Syntax error or access violation). If the SQL statement that caused this error is hard-coded or built by the application, this is a programming error and the code needs to be fixed. If the SQL statement is entered by the user, this is a user error and the application has done all that is possible by informing the user of the problem.

When applications do base programming logic on SQLSTATEs, they should be prepared for the SQLSTATE not to be returned or for a different SQLSTATE to be returned. Exactly which SQLSTATEs are returned reliably can be based only on experience with numerous drivers. However, a general guideline is that SQLSTATEs for errors that occur in the driver or Driver Manager, as opposed to the data source, are more likely to be returned reliably. For example, most drivers probably return SQLSTATE HYC00 (Optional feature not implemented) while fewer drivers probably return SQLSTATE 42021 (Column already exists).

The following SQLSTATEs indicate run-time errors or warnings and are good candidates on which to base programming logic. However, there is no guarantee that all drivers return them.

- 01004 (Data truncated)
- 01S02 (Option value changed)
- HY008 (Operation canceled)
- HYC00 (Optional feature not implemented)
- HYT00 (Timeout expired)

SQLSTATE HYC00 (Optional feature not implemented) is particularly significant, as it is the only way in which an application can determine whether a driver supports a particular statement or connection attribute.

For a complete list of SQLSTATEs and what functions return them, see Appendix A, "ODBC Error Codes." For a detailed explanation of the conditions under which each function might return a particular SQLSTATE, see that function.

Diagnostic Messages

A diagnostic message is returned with each SQLSTATE. The same SQLSTATE is often returned with a number of different messages. For example, SQLSTATE 42000 (Syntax error or access violation) is returned for most errors in SQL syntax. However, each syntax error is likely to be described by a different message.

Sample diagnostic messages are listed in the Error column in the table of SQLSTATEs in Appendix A and in each function. Although drivers can return these messages, they are more likely to return whatever message is passed to them by the data source.

Applications generally display diagnostic messages to the user, along with the SQLSTATE and native error code. This helps the user and support personnel determine the cause of any problems. The component information embedded in the message is particularly helpful in doing this.

Diagnostic messages come from data sources and components in an ODBC connection, such as drivers, gateways, and the Driver Manager. Typically, data sources do not directly support ODBC. Consequently, if a component in an ODBC connection receives a message from a data source, it must identify the data source as the source of the message. It must also identify itself as the component that received the message.

If the source of an error or warning is a component itself, the diagnostic message must explain this. Therefore, the text of messages has two different formats. For errors and warnings that do not occur in a data source, the diagnostic message must use the format:

[*vendor-identifier*][*ODBC-component-identifier*]*component-supplied-text*

For errors and warnings that occur in a data source, the diagnostic message must use the format:

[*vendor-identifier*][*ODBC-component-identifier*][*data-source-identifier*]*data-source-supplied-text*

The following table shows the meaning of each element.

Element	Meaning
vendor-identifier	Identifies the vendor of the component in which the error or warning occurred or that received the error or warning directly from the data source.
ODBC-component-identifier	Identifies the component in which the error or warning occurred or that received the error or warning directly from the data source.
data-source-identifier	Identifies the data source. For file-based drivers, this is typically a file format, such as Xbase. [1] For DBMS-based drivers, this is the DBMS product.
component-supplied-text	Generated by the ODBC component.
data-source-supplied-text	Generated by the data source.

[1] In this case, the driver is acting as both the driver and the data source.

Brackets ([ ]) must be included in the message and do not indicate optional items.

Using SQLGetDiagRec and SQLGetDiagField

Applications call **SQLGetDiagRec** or **SQLGetDiagField** to retrieve diagnostic information. These functions accept an environment, connection, statement, or descriptor handle and return diagnostics from the function that last used that handle. The diagnostics logged on a particular handle are discarded when a new function is called using that handle. If the function returned multiple diagnostic records, the application calls these functions multiple times; the total number of status records is retrieved by calling **SQLGetDiagField** for the header record (record 0) with the SQL_DIAG_NUMBER option.

Applications retrieve individual diagnostic fields by calling **SQLGetDiagField** and specifying the field to retrieve. Certain diagnostic fields do not have any meaning for certain types of handles. For a list of diagnostic fields and their meaning, see the **SQLGetDiagField** function description.

Applications retrieve the SQLSTATE, native error code, and diagnostic message in a single call by calling **SQLGetDiagRec**; **SQLGetDiagRec** cannot be used to retrieve information from the header record.

For example, the following code prompts the user for an SQL statement and executes it. If any diagnostic information was returned, it calls **SQLGetDiagField** to get the number of status records and **SQLGetDiagRec** to get the SQLSTATE, native error code, and diagnostic message from those records.

```
SQLCHAR     SqlState[6], SQLStmt[100], Msg[SQL_MAX_MESSAGE_LENGTH];
SQLINTEGER NativeError;
SQLSMALLINT i, MsgLen;
SQLRETURN  rc1, rc2;
SQLHSTMT   hstmt;

// Prompt the user for an SQL statement.
GetSQLStmt(SQLStmt);

// Execute the SQL statement and return any errors or warnings.
rc1 = SQLExecDirect(hstmt, SQLStmt, SQL_NTS);
if ((rc1 == SQL_SUCCESS_WITH_INFO) || (rc1 == SQL_ERROR)) {
   // Get the status records.
   i = 1;
   while ((rc2 = SQLGetDiagRec(SQL_HANDLE_STMT, hstmt, i, SqlState, &NativeError,
                Msg, sizeof(Msg), &MsgLen)) != SQL_NO_DATA) {
      DisplayError(SqlState,NativeError,Msg,MsgLen);
      i++;
```

```
    }
}

if ((rc1 == SQL_SUCCESS) || (rc1 == SQL_SUCCESS_WITH_INFO)) {
    // Process statement results, if any.
}
```

Implementing SQLGetDiagRec and SQLGetDiagField

SQLGetDiagRec and **SQLGetDiagField** are implemented by the Driver Manager and each driver. The Driver Manager and each driver maintain diagnostic records for each environment, connection, statement, and descriptor handle and free those records only when another function is called with that handle or the handle is freed.

Although both the Driver Manager and each driver must determine the first status record according to the rankings in "Sequence of Status Records," earlier in this chapter, the Driver Manager determines the final sequence of records.

SQLGetDiagRec and **SQLGetDiagField** do not post diagnostic records about themselves.

Diagnostic Handling Rules

The following rules govern diagnostic handling in **SQLGetDiagRec** and **SQLGetDiagField**.

All ODBC components:

- Must not replace, alter, or mask errors or warnings received from another ODBC component.
- May add an additional status record when they receive a diagnostic message from another ODBC component. The added record must add real information value to the original message.

The ODBC component that directly interfaces a data source:

- Must prefix its vendor identifier, its component identifier, and the data source's identifier to the diagnostic message it receives from the data source.
- Must preserve the data source's native error code.
- Must preserve the data source's diagnostic message.

Any ODBC component that generates an error or warning independent of the data source:

- Must supply the correct SQLSTATE for the error or warning.
- Must generate the text of the diagnostic message.
- Must prefix its vendor identifier and its component identifier to the diagnostic message.
- Must return a native error code, if one is available and meaningful.

The ODBC component that interfaces with the Driver Manager:

- Must initialize the output arguments of **SQLGetDiagRec** and **SQLGetDiagField**.
- Must format and return the diagnostic information as output arguments of **SQLGetDiagRec** and **SQLGetDiagField** when that function is called.

One ODBC component other than the Driver Manager:

- Must set the SQLSTATE based on the native error. For file-based drivers and DBMS-based drivers that do not use a gateway, the driver must set the SQLSTATE. For DBMS-based drivers that use a gateway, either the driver or a gateway that supports ODBC may set the SQLSTATE.

Role of the Driver Manager

The Driver Manager determines the final order in which to return status records that it generates. In particular, it determines which record has the highest rank and is to be returned first. The driver is responsible for ordering status records that it generates. If status records are posted by both the Driver Manager and the driver, the Driver Manager is responsible for ordering them. For more information, see "Sequence of Status Records," earlier in this chapter.

The Driver Manager does as much error checking as it can. This saves every driver from checking for the same errors. For example, if a function argument accepts a discrete number of values, such as *Operation* in **SQLSetPos**, the Driver Manager checks that the specified value is legal.

The following sections describe the types of conditions checked by the Driver Manager. They are not intended to be exhaustive; for a complete list of the SQLSTATEs the Driver Manager returns, see the "Diagnostics" section of each function; the description of each check made by the Driver Manager starts with the letters "(DM)". Also see the state transition tables in Appendix B, "ODBC State Transition Tables"; errors shown in parentheses are detected by the Driver Manager.

Argument Value Checks

The Driver Manager checks the following types of arguments. Unless otherwise noted, the Driver Manager returns SQL_ERROR for errors in argument values.

- Environment, connection, and statement handles usually cannot be null pointers. The Driver Manager returns SQL_INVALID_HANDLE when it finds a null handle.
- Required pointer arguments, such as *OutputHandlePtr* in **SQLAllocHandle** and *CursorName* in **SQLSetCursorName**, cannot be null pointers.
- Option flags that do not support driver-specific values must be a legal value. For example, *Operation* in **SQLSetPos** must be SQL_POSITION, SQL_REFRESH, SQL_UPDATE, SQL_DELETE, or SQL_ADD.
- Option flags must be supported in the version of ODBC supported by the driver. For example, *InfoType* in **SQLGetInfo** cannot be SQL_ASYNC_MODE (introduced in ODBC 3.0) when calling an ODBC 2.0 driver.
- Column and parameter numbers must be greater than 0 or greater than or equal to 0, depending on the function. The driver must check the upper limit of these argument values based on the current result set or SQL statement.
- Length/indicator arguments and data buffer length arguments must contain appropriate values. For example, the argument that specifies the length of a table name in **SQLColumns** (*NameLength3*) must be SQL_NTS or a value greater than 0; *BufferLength* in **SQLDescribeCol** must be greater than or equal to 0. The driver might also need to check these arguments. For example, it might check that *NameLength3* is less than or equal to the maximum length of a table name in the data source.

State Transition Checks

The Driver Manager checks that the state of the environment, connection, or statement is appropriate for the function being called. For example, a connection must be in an allocated state when **SQLConnect** is called and a statement must be in a prepared state when **SQLExecute** is called. The Driver Manager returns SQL_ERROR for state transition errors.

General Error Checks

The Driver Manager checks one general error. It always returns SQL_ERROR when it encounters this error.

- The function must be supported by the driver.

Driver Manager Error and Warning Checks

The Driver Manager completely or partially implements a number of functions and therefore checks for all or some of the errors and warnings in those functions.

- The Driver Manager implements **SQLDataSources** and **SQLDrivers** and checks for all errors and warnings in these functions.
- The Driver Manager checks whether a driver implements **SQLGetFunctions**. If the driver does not implement **SQLGetFunctions**, the Driver Manager implements and checks for all errors and warnings in it.
- The Driver Manager partially implements **SQLAllocHandle**, **SQLConnect**, **SQLDriverConnect**, **SQLBrowseConnect**, **SQLFreeHandle**, **SQLGetDiagRec**, and **SQLGetDiagField** and checks for some errors in these functions. It may return the same errors as the driver for some of these functions, as both perform similar operations. For example, the Driver Manager or driver may return SQLSTATE IM008 (Dialog failed) if they are unable to display a login dialog box for **SQLDriverConnect**.

Role of the Driver

The driver checks for all errors and warnings not checked by the Driver Manager, and orders status records that it generates. (An ODBC 2.*x* driver does not order status records.) This includes errors and warnings in data truncation, data conversion, syntax, and some state transitions. The driver might also check errors and warnings partially checked by the Driver Manager. For example, although the Driver Manager checks whether the value of *Operation* in **SQLSetPos** is legal, the driver must check whether it is supported.

The driver also maps *native errors*, or errors returned by the data source, to SQLSTATEs. For example, the driver might map a number of different native errors for illegal SQL syntax to SQLSTATE 42000 (Syntax error or access violation). The driver returns the native error number in the SQL_DIAG_NATIVE field of the status record. Driver documentation should show how errors and warnings are mapped from the data source to arguments in **SQLGetDiagRec** and **SQLGetDiagField**.

Diagnostic Handling Examples

The following examples show how various components in an ODBC connection might generate diagnostic messages and how various drivers might return diagnostics to the application with **SQLGetDiagRec**.

File-Based Driver Diagnostic Example

A file-based driver acts both as an ODBC driver and as a data source. It can therefore generate errors and warnings both as a component in an ODBC connection and as a data source. Because it also is the component that interfaces with the Driver Manager, it formats and returns arguments for **SQLGetDiagRec**.

For example, if a Microsoft driver for dBASE could not allocate sufficient memory, it might return the following values from **SQLGetDiagRec**:

```
SQLSTATE:        "HY001"
Native Error:    42052
Diagnostic Msg: "[Microsoft][ODBC dBASE Driver]Unable to allocate sufficient memory."
```

Because this error was not related to the data source, the driver only added prefixes to the diagnostic message for the vendor ([Microsoft]) and the driver ([ODBC dBASE Driver]).

If the driver could not find the file EMPLOYEE.DBF, it might return the following values from **SQLGetDiagRec**:

```
SQLSTATE:        "42S02"
Native Error:     -1305
Diagnostic Msg: "[Microsoft][ODBC dBASE Driver][dBASE]No such table or object"
```

Because this error was related to the data source, the driver added the file format of the data source ([dBASE]) as a prefix to the diagnostic message. Because the driver was also the component that interfaced with the data source, it added prefixes for the vendor ([Microsoft]) and the driver ([ODBC dBASE Driver]).

DBMS-Based Driver Diagnostic Example

A DBMS-based driver sends requests to a DBMS and returns information to the application through the Driver Manager. Because it is the component that interfaces with the Driver Manager, it formats and returns arguments for **SQLGetDiagRec**.

For example, if a Microsoft driver for DEC's Rdb using SQL/Services encountered an invalid cursor name, it might return the following values from **SQLGetDiagRec**:

```
SQLSTATE:        "34000"
Native Error:    0
Diagnostic Msg: "[Microsoft][ODBC Rdb Driver]Invalid cursor name: EMPLOYEE_CURSOR."
```

Because the error occurred in the driver, it added prefixes to the diagnostic message for the vendor ([Microsoft]) and the driver ([ODBC Rdb Driver]).

If the DBMS could not find the table EMPLOYEE, the driver might format and return the following values from **SQLGetDiagRec**:

```
SQLSTATE:        "42S02"
Native Error:    -1
Diagnostic Msg: "[Microsoft][ODBC Rdb Driver][Rdb] %SQL-F-RELNOTDEF, Table EMPLOYEE "
                "is not defined in schema."
```

Because the error occurred in the data source, the driver added a prefix for the data source identifier ([Rdb]) to the diagnostic message. Because the driver was the component that interfaced with the data source, it added prefixes for its vendor ([Microsoft]) and identifier ([ODBC Rdb Driver]) to the diagnostic message.

Gateways Diagnostic Example

In a gateway architecture, a driver sends requests to a gateway that supports ODBC. The gateway sends the requests to a DBMS. Because it is the component that interfaces with the Driver Manager, the driver formats and returns arguments for **SQLGetDiagRec**.

For example, if DEC based a gateway to Rdb on Microsoft Open Data Services, and Rdb could not find the table EMPLOYEE, the gateway might generate the diagnostic message:

```
"[42S02][-1][DEC][ODS Gateway][Rdb]%SQL-F-RELNOTDEF, Table EMPLOYEE is not defined "
   "in schema."
```

Because the error occurred in the data source, the gateway added a prefix for the data source identifier ([Rdb]) to the diagnostic message. Because the gateway was the component that interfaced with the data source, it added prefixes for its vendor ([DEC]) and identifier ([ODS Gateway]) to the diagnostic message. Note that it also added the SQLSTATE value and the Rdb error code to the beginning of the diagnostic message. This permitted it to preserve the semantics of its own message structure and still supply the ODBC diagnostic information to the driver. The driver parses the error information attached to the error statement by the gateway.

Because the gateway driver is the component that interfaces with the Driver Manager, it would use the preceding diagnostic message to format and return the following values from **SQLGetDiagRec**:

```
SQLSTATE:        "42S02"
Native Error:    -1
Diagnostic Msg: "[DEC][ODS Gateway][Rdb]%SQL-F-RELNOTDEF, Table EMPLOYEE is not "
                "defined in schema."
```

Driver Manager Diagnostic Example

The Driver Manager can also generate diagnostic messages. For example, if an application passed an invalid direction option to **SQLDataSources**, the Driver Manager might format and return the following values from **SQLGetDiagRec**:

```
SQLSTATE:        "HY103"
Native Error:    0
Diagnostic Msg: "[Microsoft][ODBC Driver Manager]Direction option out of range"
```

Because the error occurred in the Driver Manager, it added prefixes to the diagnostic message for its vendor ([Microsoft]) and its identifier ([ODBC Driver Manager]).

CHAPTER 16

Interoperability

Interoperability is the ability of a single application to operate with many different DBMSs. The need to write generic, interoperable applications was one of the major factors leading to the development of ODBC. However, interoperability is not a simple path followed from not interoperable to completely interoperable. The path has many branches and each requires tradeoffs between features, speed, code complexity, and development time.

The process of writing an interoperable application follows several steps:

- Deciding whether the application will use ODBC at all.
- Choosing a level of interoperability and deciding which tradeoffs are necessary to reach that level.
- Writing interoperable code and testing it as fully as possible.

Before continuing, it should be noted that interoperability is primarily the domain of the application writer. Drivers are designed to work with a single DBMS and, by definition, are not interoperable. They play a role in interoperability by correctly implementing and exposing ODBC over a single DBMS.

Is ODBC the Answer?

Before delving into the question of interoperability, consider the following question: Should the application use ODBC at all? This might seem a strange question to ask in a guide to ODBC, but is in fact a legitimate one. ODBC was not designed to completely replace native database APIs, nor was it designed to provide database access in all circumstances. It was designed to provide a common interface to databases and was intended to free application programmers from having to learn about and maintain links to multiple databases.

Custom applications are prime candidates for native database APIs. The main reason for this is that custom applications often work with a single DBMS and have no need to be interoperable. Native database APIs might do a better job than ODBC of exposing the capabilities of a particular DBMS and might expose capabilities not exposed by ODBC. Furthermore, because the developers of custom applications are usually familiar with the native database API for their DBMS, there is little reason to learn ODBC. However, it is interesting to note that for some DBMSs, ODBC is the native database API.

So which applications are candidates for ODBC? The best candidates are applications that work with more than one DBMS. This includes virtually all generic and vertical applications. It also includes a number of custom applications. For example, custom applications that use several different DBMSs are much easier and cleaner to write with ODBC than with multiple native APIs. And custom applications written with ODBC are much easier to migrate as a company moves from one DBMS to another or deploys the same application against different DBMSs.

Choosing a Level of Interoperability

Assuming the application will use ODBC, the next step is to determine what level of interoperability is required. The basic level of interoperability is generally a function of the application type: Custom applications tend not to be interoperable, vertical applications tend to be interoperable among a limited number of DBMSs, and generic applications tend to be interoperable among all DBMSs.

Custom Applications

Custom applications typically perform a specific task for a few DBMSs. For example, an application might retrieve data from a single DBMS and generate a report, or it might transfer data among several DBMSs. What these applications have in common is that these DBMSs are known before the application is written and are unlikely to change over the life of the application.

The custom application thus requires little or no interoperability. The application developer can choose a single driver for each DBMS and code directly to those drivers. The application can safely contain driver-specific code to exploit the capabilities of those drivers and might even make calls to the native database API to use functionality not supported by ODBC.

The major interoperability concern of most custom applications is whether the target DBMSs will change in the future. If so, this process can be simplified by writing more interoperable code to start with. However, such changing DBMSs is rare and generally entails a large amount of work. Because of this, developers of custom applications rarely choose to increase interoperability at the expense of functionality, as they can recode that functionality when they change DBMSs.

Vertical Applications

Vertical applications typically perform a well-defined task against a single DBMS. For example, an order entry application tracks the orders in a company. What these types of applications have in common is that the database schema is usually designed by the application developer and, while the application might work with a number of different DBMSs, it works with a single DBMS for a single customer.

Because vertical applications usually require certain functionality, such as scrollable cursors or transactions, they rarely support all DBMSs. Instead, they tend to be highly interoperable among a limited set of DBMSs. Typically, vertical application developers choose to support those DBMSs that represent a large fraction of the market and ignore the rest. They might even choose to support specific drivers for those DBMSs to reduce their testing and product support costs.

Because vertical applications can support a known set of DBMSs, they sometimes contain driver- or DBMS-specific code. However, such code is best kept to a minimum, as it requires extra time to maintain.

Generic Applications

Generic applications sometimes perform a hard-coded task, such as when a spreadsheet retrieves data from a database. They might also perform a variety of user-defined tasks, such as when a generic query application lets the user enter and execute an SQL statement. What generic applications have in common is that they must work with a variety of different DBMSs and that the developer does not know beforehand what these DBMSs will be.

Therefore, generic applications need to be highly interoperable. The developer must make many choices trading off interoperability for features and must write code that expects drivers to support a wide range of functionality. While generic applications might be tuned to work with popular DBMSs, they rarely contain driver- or DBMS-specific code.

Determining the Target DBMSs and Drivers

The next question to consider is what are the target DBMSs for the application and what drivers are available that support those DBMSs. Because generic applications tend to be highly interoperable, the question of target DBMSs is most applicable to custom and vertical applications. However, the question of target drivers applies to all applications, as drivers vary widely in speed, quality, feature support, and availability. Also, if drivers are to be redistributed with the application, the cost and availability of licensing plans needs to be considered.

For many custom applications, the target DBMSs are obvious: They are existing DBMSs that the application is designed to access. DBMSs to which future migration is planned should also be considered. However, the major question for these applications is which driver or drivers to use with them. For other custom applications—those which are not designed to access an existing DBMS—the target DBMSs can be chosen based on feature support, concurrent user support, driver availability, and affordability.

For vertical applications, the target DBMSs are usually chosen based on feature support, driver availability, and market. For example, a vertical application designed for small businesses must target DBMSs that are affordable to those businesses; a vertical application designed as an add-on to existing DBMSs must target widely used DBMSs.

When choosing target DBMSs, the differences between desktop and server databases should be considered. Desktop databases such as dBASE, Paradox, and Btrieve are less powerful than server databases. Because they are generally accessed through the less-powerful SQL engines found in most file-based drivers, they often lack full transaction support, support fewer concurrent users, and have limited SQL. However, they are inexpensive and have a large installed base.

Server databases such as Oracle, DB2, and SQL Server provide full transaction support, support many concurrent users, and have rich SQL. They are much more expensive and have a smaller installed base. On the other hand, software prices tend to be higher, somewhat offsetting a smaller potential market.

Thus, target DBMSs can sometimes be chosen based on the features required by the application and the application's target market. For example, an order entry system for large corporations might not target desktop databases, as these lack adequate transaction support. A similar system designed for small businesses might exclude most server databases on the basis of cost. And developers of generic applications might target both, but avoid using the advanced features found in server databases.

Considering Database Features to Use

After the basic level of interoperability is known, the database features used by the application must be considered. For example, what SQL statements will the application execute? Will the application use scrollable cursors? Transactions? Procedures? Long data? For ideas about what features might not be supported by all DBMSs, see the **SQLGetInfo**, **SQLSetConnectAttr**, and **SQLSetStmtAttr** function descriptions, and Appendix C, "SQL Grammar." The features required by an application might eliminate some DBMSs from the list of target DBMSs. They might also show that the application can easily target many DBMSs.

For example, if the required features are simple, they can usually be implemented with a high degree of interoperability. An application that executes a simple **SELECT** statement and retrieves results with a forward-only cursor is likely to be highly interoperable by virtue of its simplicity: Almost all drivers and DBMSs support the functionality it needs.

On the other hand, if the required features are more complex, such as scrollable cursors, positioned update and delete statements, and procedures, tradeoffs must often be made. There are several possibilities:

- **Lower interoperability, more features**. The application includes the features, but works only with DBMSs that support them.
- **Higher interoperability, fewer features**. The application drops the features, but works with more DBMSs.
- **Higher interoperability, optional features**. The application includes the features, but makes them available only with those DBMSs that support them.
- **Higher interoperability, more features**. The application uses the features with DBMSs that support them and emulates them for DBMSs that do not.

The first two cases are relatively simple to implement, as the features are either used with all supported DBMSs or with none. The latter two cases, on the other hand, are more complex. It is necessary in both cases to check whether the DBMS supports the features and in the last case to write a potentially large amount of code to emulate these features. Thus, these schemes are likely to require more development time and may be slower at run time.

Consider a generic query application that can connect to a single data source. The application accepts a query from the user and displays the results in a window. Now suppose that a feature of this application is that users can display the results of multiple queries simultaneously; that is, they can execute a query and look at some of the results, execute a different query and look at some of its results, and then return to the first query. This presents an interoperability problem because some drivers support only a single active statement.

The application has a number of choices, based on what the driver returns for the SQL_MAX_CONCURRENT_ACTIVITIES option in **SQLGetInfo**:

- **Always support multiple queries**. After connecting to a driver, the application checks the number of active statements. If the driver supports only one active statement, the application closes the connection and informs the user that the driver does not support required functionality. The application is easy to implement and has full functionality, but has lower interoperability.
- **Never support multiple queries**. The application drops the feature altogether. It is easy to implement and has high interoperability, but has less functionality.

- **Support multiple queries only if the driver does**. After connecting to a driver, the application checks the number of active statements. The application allows the user to start a new statement when one is already active only if the driver supports multiple active statements. The application has higher functionality and interoperability, but is harder to implement.
- **Always support multiple queries and emulate them when necessary**. After connecting to a driver, the application checks the number of active statements. The application always allows the user to start a new statement when one is already active; if the driver supports only one active statement, the application opens an additional connection to that driver and executes the new statement on that connection. The application has full functionality and high interoperability, but is harder to implement.

Length of the Product Cycle

The final question about interoperability is time. Developing an interoperable application usually takes longer than developing a noninteroperable one. The reason for this is that the application must check DBMS capabilities, perform the same tasks differently for different DBMSs, work around functionality supported by some DBMSs but not others, and so on.

In addition to development time, product lifetime must also be considered. If the application is designed to be used once, such as an application that transfers data when migrating from one DBMS to another, there is no point in making it interoperable. The application will be used once and discarded.

On the other hand, if the application will exist for a long time, it might be easier to maintain as an interoperable application. This is true even for custom applications that have a single DBMS as a target. The reason is that interoperable code uses a limited subset of database features. The driver is required to keep those features available, even in the face of changes to the underlying DBMS. Thus, interoperable code can shift the burden of coping with changes to the DBMS from the application developer to the driver developer.

Writing an Interoperable Application

Whenever an application uses the same code against more than one driver, that code must be interoperable among those drivers. In most cases, this is an easy task. For example, the code to fetch rows with a forward-only cursor is the same for all drivers. In some cases, this can be more difficult. For example, the code to construct identifiers for use in SQL statements needs to consider identifier case, quoting, and one-, two-, and three-part naming conventions.

In general, interoperable code must cope with problems of feature support and feature variability. *Feature support* refers to whether or not a particular feature is supported.

For example, not all DBMSs support transactions, and interoperable code must work correctly regardless of transaction support. *Feature variability* refers to variation in the manner in which a particular feature is supported. For example, catalog names are placed at the start of identifiers in some DBMSs and at the end of identifiers in others.

Applications can deal with feature support and feature variability at design time or at run time. To deal with feature support and variability at design time, a developer looks at the target DBMSs and drivers and makes sure that the same code will be interoperable among them. This is generally the way in which applications with low or limited interoperability deal with these problems.

For example, if the developer guarantees that a vertical application will work only with four particular DBMSs, and each of those DBMSs supports transactions, the application does not need code to check for transaction support at run time. It can always assume transactions are available because of the design-time decision to use only four DBMSs, each of which supports transactions.

To deal with feature support and variability at run time, the application must test for different capabilities at run time and act accordingly. This is generally the way in which highly interoperable applications deal with these problems. For feature support problems, this means writing code that makes the feature optional or writing code that emulates the feature when it is not available. For feature variability problems, this means writing code that supports all possible variations.

Checking Feature Support and Variability

To check feature support and variability, applications generally call **SQLGetInfo**, **SQLGetFunctions**, and **SQLGetTypeInfo**. A good starting place is the driver's API and SQL grammar conformance levels. These describe broad levels of feature support. The application can then call **SQLGetInfo** with other options to determine the support or variability of features it needs, **SQLGetFunctions** to determine whether functions it needs beyond the returned conformance level are supported, and **SQLGetTypeInfo** to determine what SQL data types are supported.

An application can determine whether a statement or connection attribute is supported by calling **SQLSetStmtAttr** or **SQLSetConnectAttr** with that attribute. If the function returns SQL_SUCCESS or SQL_SUCCESS_WITH_INFO, the attribute is supported; if it returns SQL_ERROR and SQLSTATE HYC00 (Optional feature not implemented), the attribute is not supported.

Applications can also determine a limited amount of information before connecting to the driver by calling **SQLDrivers**.

Features to Watch For

This section describes a number of features that application developers often take for granted. In fact, these features vary widely in support and manner of support among DBMSs; failure to code for them is likely to cause problems in interoperable applications.

This section does not list all features that application developers need to consider. For that information, see the **SQLGetInfo**, **SQLSetStmtAttr**, and **SQLSetConnectAttr** function descriptions, Appendix C, "SQL Grammar," and the sections of this manual that discuss each feature.

Version Number

There are three versions of ODBC, each with different features. An application determines which ODBC version the Driver Manager and a particular driver support by calling **SQLGetInfo** with the SQL_ODBC_VER and SQL_DRIVER_ODBC_VER options.

Multiple Active Statements and Connections

Some drivers and DBMSs limit the number of statements and connections that can be active at one time. These numbers can be as small as one. For more information, see the SQL_MAX_CONCURRENT_ACTIVITIES and SQL_MAX_DRIVER_CONNECTIONS options in the **SQLGetInfo** function description and "Statement Handles" and "Connection Handles" in Chapter 4, "ODBC Fundamentals."

Transaction Support in DBMSs

Some databases, especially desktop databases such as dBASE, Paradox, and Btrieve, do not support transactions. Even among databases that support transactions, there is variation in what kinds of SQL statements can be in a transaction. For more information, see the SQL_TXN_CAPABLE option in the **SQLGetInfo** function description.

Commit and Rollback Behavior

A common behavior among server DBMSs is to close cursors and discard prepared statements when a statement is committed or rolled back. Desktop databases are more likely to keep cursors open and keep prepared statements. For more information, see the SQL_CURSOR_COMMIT_BEHAVIOR and SQL_CURSOR_ROLLBACK_BEHAVIOR options in the **SQLGetInfo** function description and "Effect of Transactions on Cursors and Prepared Statements" in Chapter 14, "Transactions."

NOT NULL in CREATE TABLE Statements

Some databases, and especially desktop databases, do not support the **NOT NULL** column constraint in **CREATE TABLE** statements. For more information, see the SQL_NON_NULLABLE_COLUMNS option in the **SQLGetInfo** function description.

Supported Data Types

The data types supported by DBMSs vary considerably. An application can determine the names and characteristics of supported data types by calling **SQLGetTypeInfo**. Because of wide variation in data type names, the application must use the data type names returned by **SQLGetTypeInfo** in **CREATE TABLE** statements. For more information, see "Data Types in ODBC" in Chapter 4, "ODBC Fundamentals."

ODBC SQL Grammar

Interoperable applications should always use the ODBC SQL grammar in SQL statements. However, considerable variation is possible even within this grammar. For more information, see "Interoperability of SQL Statements" in Chapter 8, "SQL Statements."

Batch Processing

Support for batches of SQL statements is not widespread, so interoperable applications should use them conditionally, or not at all. For more information, see "Executing Batches" in Chapter 9, "Executing Statements."

Testing Interoperable Applications

Testing interoperable applications is at best a time-consuming business and at worst impossible because new drivers continually appear on the market. However, a reasonable degree of testing is possible. Applications with limited or low interoperability need only be tested against those drivers they are guaranteed to support. However, they must be fully tested against these drivers.

Highly interoperable applications cannot be practically tested against all drivers. The best most application developers can do is to test them fully against a small number of drivers and cursorily against several more. Tested drivers should include the most popular drivers for the most popular DBMSs in the application's market; if the market covers all DBMSs, then drivers for both desktop and server DBMSs should be tested.

One of the problems in testing ODBC applications is the number of components involved: the application itself, the Driver Manager, the driver, the DBMS, and possibly network software or gateways. Applications can make it easier to track errors by posting the error messages returned by ODBC functions through **SQLGetDiagField** and **SQLGetDiagRec**. These messages identify the manufacturer and component in which errors occur. For more information, see Chapter 15, "Diagnostics."

CHAPTER 17

Programming Considerations

This chapter briefly discusses a number of topics related to writing ODBC applications and drivers.

Multithreading

On multithread operating systems, drivers must be thread safe. That is, it must be possible for applications to use the same handle on more than one thread. How this is achieved is driver-specific, and it is likely that drivers will serialize any attempts to concurrently use the same handle on two different threads.

Applications commonly use multiple threads instead of asynchronous processing. The application creates a separate thread and calls an ODBC function on it, and then continues processing on the main thread. Rather than having to continually poll the asynchronous function, as is the case when the SQL_ATTR_ASYNC_ENABLE statement attribute is used, the application can simply let the newly created thread finish.

Functions that accept a statement handle and are running on one thread can be canceled by calling **SQLCancel** with the same statement handle from another thread. Although drivers should not serialize the use of **SQLCancel** in this manner, there is no guarantee that calling **SQLCancel** will actually cancel the function running on the other thread.

Alignment

The alignment issues in an ODBC application are generally no different than they are in any other application. That is, most ODBC applications have few or no problems with alignment. The penalties for not aligning addresses vary with the hardware and operating system, and may be as minor as a slight performance penalty or as major as a fatal run-time error. Thus, ODBC applications—and portable ODBC applications in particular—should be careful to align data properly.

One place where ODBC applications encounter alignment issues is when they allocate a large block of memory and bind different parts of that memory to the columns in a result set. This is most likely to occur when a generic application must determine the shape of a result set at run time and allocate and bind memory accordingly.

For example, suppose an application executes a **SELECT** statement entered by the user and fetches the results from this statement. Because the shape of this result set is not known when the program is written, the application must determine the type of each column after the result set is created and bind memory accordingly. The easiest way to do this is to allocate a large block of memory and bind different addresses in that block to each column. To access the data in a column, the application casts the memory bound to that column.

The following diagram shows a sample result set and how a block of memory might be bound to it using the default C data type for each SQL data type. Each "X" represents a single byte of memory. Note that this example only shows the data buffers that are bound to the columns. This is done for simplicity. In actual code, the length/indicator buffers must also be aligned.

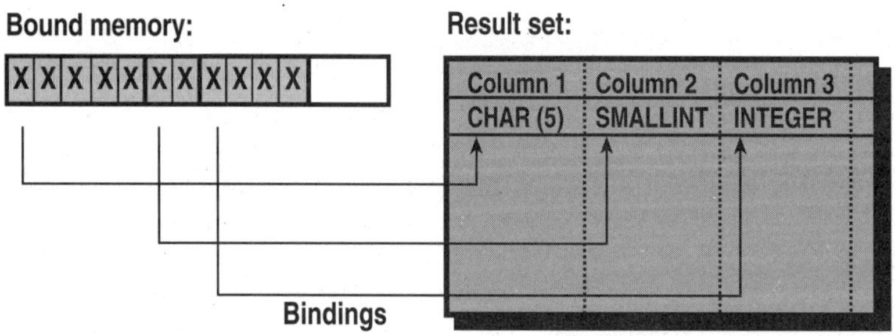

Assuming the bound addresses are stored in the *Address* array, the application uses the following expressions to access the memory bound to each column:

```
(SQLCHAR *)       Address[0]
(SQLSMALLINT *)   Address[1]
(SQLINTEGER *)    Address[2]
```

Notice that the addresses bound to the second and third columns start on odd-numbered bytes and that the address bound to the third column is not divisible by 4, which is the size of an SDWORD. On some machines, this will not be a problem, on others, it will cause a slight performance penalty, on still others, it will cause a fatal run-time error. A better solution would be to align each bound address on its natural alignment boundary. Assuming this is 1 for a UCHAR, 2 for an SWORD, and 4 for an SDWORD, this would give the following, where an "X" represents a byte of memory that is used and an "O" represents a byte of memory that is unused:

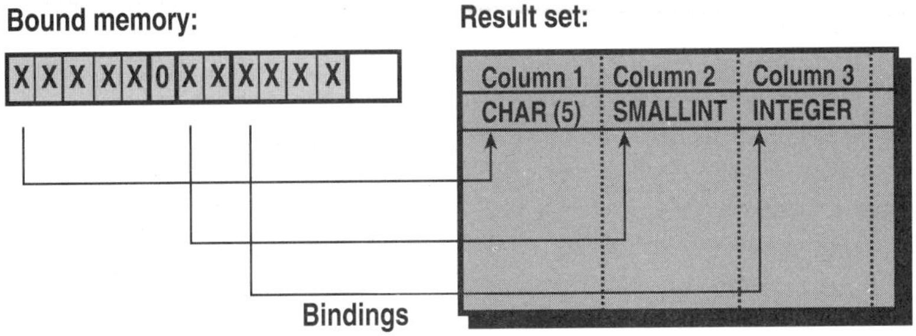

While this solution does not use all of the application's memory, it does not encounter any alignment problems. Unfortunately, it takes a fair amount of code to implement this solution, as each column must be aligned individually according to its type. A simpler solution is to align all columns on the size of the largest alignment boundary, which is 4 in this case:

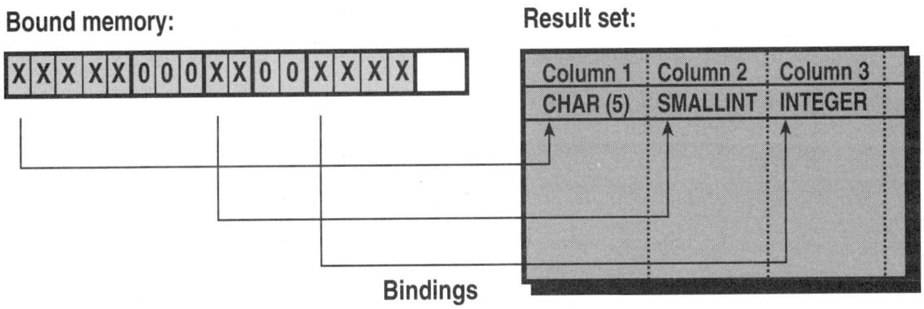

Although this solution leaves larger holes, the code to implement it is relatively simple and fast. In most cases, this offsets the penalty paid in unused memory. For an example that uses this method, see "Using SQLBindCol" in Chapter 10, "Retrieving Results (Basic)."

Translation DLLs

The application and data source often store data in different character sets. ODBC provides a generic mechanism that allows the driver to translate data from one character set to another. It consists of a DLL that implements the translation functions **SQLDriverToDataSource** and **SQLDataSourceToDriver** which is called by the driver to translate all data flowing between the data source and driver. This DLL can be written by the application developer, the driver developer, or a third party.

The translation DLL for a particular data source can be specified in the system information for that data source; for more information, see "Data Source Specification Subkeys" in Chapter 19, "Configuring Data Sources." It can also be set at run time with the SQL_ATTR_TRANSLATE_DLL and SQL_ATTR_TRANSLATE_OPTION connection attributes.

The translation option is a value that can be interpreted only by a particular translation DLL. For example, if the translation DLL translates between different code pages, the option might give the numbers of the code pages used by the application and the data source. There is no requirement for a translation DLL to use a translation option.

After a translation DLL has been specified, the driver loads it and calls it to translate all data flowing between the application and data source. This includes all SQL statements and character parameters being sent to the data source and all character results, character metadata such as column names, and error messages retrieved from the data source. Note that connection data is not translated, as the translation DLL is not loaded until after the application has connected to the data source.

Tracing

The ODBC Driver Manager has a trace facility that allows the sequence of function calls made by an ODBC application to be recorded and transcribed into a log file. Tracing is performed by a trace DLL that captures calls between the application and the Driver Manager, and the Driver Manager and the driver. This method of tracing replaces the tracing performed by the ODBC 2.*x* Driver Manager and the tracing performed in ODBC 2.*x* by ODBC Spy.

Trace DLL

The DLL that performs tracing is one of the ODBC core components. The trace DLL is provided as a sample DLL in the ODBC SDK, so the registry entry, interface, and source code for the trace DLL are available. This DLL can be replaced by a trace DLL produced by either an ODBC user or a third-party vendor. A custom trace DLL should be given a different name than the original sample trace DLL.

The trace DLL traces input arguments, output arguments, deferred arguments, return codes, and SQLSTATEs. When tracing is enabled, the Driver Manager calls the trace DLL at two points: once upon function entry (before argument validation) and again just before the function returns.

When an application calls a function, the Driver Manager calls a trace function in the trace DLL before calling the function in the driver or processing the call itself. Each ODBC function has a corresponding trace function (prefixed with "TRACE") that is identical to the ODBC function with the exception of the name. When the trace function is called, the trace DLL captures the input arguments and returns a return code. Because the trace DLL is called before the Driver Manager validates arguments, invalid function calls are traced, so state transition errors and invalid arguments are logged.

After calling the trace function in the trace DLL, the Driver Manager calls the ODBC function in the driver. It then calls the **TraceAfter** macro in the trace DLL. This macro takes two arguments: the value returned by the trace DLL for the trace function, and the return code returned by the driver to the Driver Manager for the ODBC function (or the value returned by the Driver Manager itself if it processed the function). The macro uses the value returned for the trace function to manipulate captured input argument values. It writes the code returned for the ODBC function to the log file (or displays it dynamically, if that is enabled). It dereferences the output argument pointers, and logs the output argument values.

Trace File

An application specifies the trace file either by setting the **TraceFile** keyword in the ODBC.INI registry entry, or by calling **SQLSetConnectAttr** with the SQL_ATTR_TRACEFILE connection attribute. If the file does not exist when tracing is enabled, the Driver Manager will create the file. Each application should have its own dedicated trace file to avoid contention. An application can use more than one trace file; an application's setup program can provide the user with a choice of trace files. If tracing is enabled dynamically, an application can also display trace results, rather than logging to the trace file.

The trace file provides a log of each ODBC function call with the data types and values of all arguments. It logs all input functions, and all returned functions with return codes and error states.

Caution User names and passwords are logged in ODBC 3.0 tracing. ODBC tracing does not ensure secured access to user names and passwords.

Enabling Tracing

Tracing can be enabled in the following three ways:

- By setting the **Trace** and **TraceFile** keywords in the ODBC.INI registry entry. This enables or disables tracing when **SQLAllocHandle** with a *HandleType* of SQL_HANDLE_ENV is called. These options are set in the **Tracing** tab of the **ODBC Data Source Administrator** dialog box displayed during data source setup. For more information, see "Registry Entries for Data Sources" in Chapter 19, "Configuring Data Sources."
- By calling **SQLSetConnectAttr** to set the SQL_ATTR_TRACE connection attribute to SQL_OPT_TRACE_ON. This enables or disables tracing for the duration of the connection. For more information, see the **SQLSetConnectAttr** function description.
- By using **ODBCSharedTraceFlag** to turn tracing on or off dynamically. (For more information, see the next section, "Dynamic Tracing.")

Dynamic Tracing

Tracing can be enabled or disabled at any point in an application run. This allows an application to trace any number of function calls.

The variable **ODBCSharedTraceFlag** is set to enable tracing dynamically. This variable is shared among all running copies of the Driver Manager. If any application sets this variable, tracing is enabled for all ODBC applications currently running. To turn tracing off when dynamic tracing is enabled, an application calls **SQLSetConnectAttr** to set SQL_ATTR_TRACE to SQL_TRACE_OFF. This call will turn tracing off for that application only. Applications that are linked with ODBC32.LIB can modify use of this variable. Trace data can be displayed in a real-time window, instead of the trace file, which must be opened after the ODBC session. Controls can be added to an application's screen to turn tracing on or off at will.

The trace DLL shipped with the ODBC 3.0 SDK is not thread-safe. It is not guaranteed that the log file is written correctly if global tracing is enabled (the variable **ODBCSharedTraceFlag** is set) and more than one application writes to the trace file at the same time. This condition does not return an error.

Driver-Specific Data Types, Descriptor Types, Information Types, Diagnostic Types, and Attributes

Drivers can allocate driver-specific values for the following:

- **SQL data type indicators**. These are used in *ParameterType* in **SQLBindParameter** and *DataType* in **SQLGetTypeInfo** and returned by **SQLColAttribute**, **SQLColumns**, **SQLDescribeCol**, **SQLGetTypeInfo**, **SQLDescribeParam**, **SQLProcedureColumns**, and **SQLSpecialColumns**.
- **Descriptor fields**. These are used in *FieldIdentifier* in **SQLColAttribute**, **SQLGetDescField**, and **SQLSetDescField**.
- **Diagnostic fields**. These are used in *DiagIdentifier* in **SQLGetDiagField** and **SQLGetDiagRec**.
- **Information types**. These are used in *InfoType* in **SQLGetInfo**.
- **Connection and statement attributes**. These are used in *Attribute* in **SQLGetConnectAttr**, **SQLGetStmtAttr**, **SQLSetConnectAttr**, and **SQLSetStmtAttr**.

For each of these items, there are two sets of values: values reserved for use by ODBC, and values reserved for use by drivers. Before implementing driver-specific values, a driver writer must request a value for each driver-specific type, field, or attribute from X/Open. Driver-specific data types, descriptor fields, diagnostic fields, information types, statement attributes, and connection attributes must be described in the driver documentation.

When any of these values is passed to an ODBC function, the driver must check whether the value is valid. Note that drivers return SQLSTATE HYC00 (Optional feature not implemented) for driver-specific values that apply to other drivers.

Backward Compatibility and Standards Compliance

Backward compatibility is the ability of newer ODBC components to work with old ODBC components. The following sections discuss how these components are affected by the changes in ODBC 3.0. The information contained in them primarily addresses the writing of an ODBC 3.0 application and how backward compatibility issues are handled by ODBC drivers. For specific guidelines on how backward compatibility issues affect the writing of an ODBC 3.0 drivers, see Appendix G, "Driver Guidelines for Backward Compatibility."

Affected ODBC Components

Backward compatibility describes how applications, the Driver Manager, and drivers are affected by the introduction of a new version of the Driver Manager. This affects applications and driver when either or both of them remain in the old version. There are, therefore, three types of backward compatibility to consider:

Type	Version of DM	Version of application	Version of driver
Backward Compatibility of Driver Manager	3.0	2.*x*	2.*x*
Backward Compatibility of Driver [1]	3.0	2.*x*	3.0
Backward Compatibility of Application	3.0	3.0	2.*x*

1 The backward compatibility of drivers is primarily discussed in Appendix G, "Driver Guidelines for Backward Compatibility."

Note A standards-compliant application, for example, an application that has been written in accordance with the X/Open or ISO CLI standards, is guaranteed to work with an ODBC 3.0 driver through the ODBC 3.0 Driver Manager. It is assumed that the functionality that the application is using is available in the driver. It is also assumed that the standards-compliant application has been compiled with the ODBC 3.0 header files.

Types of Changes

Three types of changes are made in ODBC 3.0 (and any version of ODBC). Each of these affects backward compatibility differently and is handled in a different way. These changes are as follows:

Type of change	Description
New features	These are features that are new to ODBC 3.0, such as out-of-line binding or descriptors. These are only implemented when the application and driver, as well as the Driver Manager, are of version 3.0, so there is no attempt to make these backward compatible.
Duplicated features	These are features that exist in both ODBC 2.*x* and ODBC 3.0, but are implemented in different ways in both. The functions **SQLAllocHandle** and **SQLAllocStmt** are an example. Backward compatibility issues for these and other duplicated features are mostly handled by mappings in the Driver Manager.

Type of change	Description
Behavioral changes	These are features that are handled differently in ODBC 2.*x* and ODBC 3.0. A datetime **#define** is an example. These features are handled by the ODBC 3.0 driver based on an environment attribute setting (see the "Behavioral Changes" section later in this chapter).

Application/Driver Compatibility

ODBC applications and driver fall into a number of categories in addition to their version. Some of these applications are incompatible with some drivers; in other cases, the type of the application or driver may have a bearing on the backward compatibility issues between them.

Types of Applications

ODBC applications can be classified as follows:

- **Pure ODBC 2.*x* application**. A 32-bit application that:
  - Calls only ODBC 2.*x* functions (including the ODBC 1.0 function **SQLSetParam**). These include ODBC 1.*x* applications that have been ported to 32-bit.
  - Expects ODBC 2.*x* behavior for features that have had behavioral changes (see "Behavioral Changes" later in this chapter).
  - Has not been recompiled with ODBC 3.0 headers.
- **Pure ODBC 2.*x* Recompiled application**. A pure ODBC 2.*x* application that has been recompiled using the ODBC 3.0 header files, by setting ODBCVER=0x0250.
- **Pure X/Open and ISO–compliant ODBC application**. A 32-bit application that:
  - Calls functions defined in the X/Open or ISO CLI standards. (These functions may include deprecated 3.0 functions.)
  - Does not use the Unicode data types.
  - Expects ODBC 3.0 behavior for features that have had.
- **Pure ODBC 3.0 application**. A 32-bit application that:
  - Calls any ODBC 3.0 function, possibly including those that are deprecated.
  - Expects ODBC 3.0 behavior for features that have had behavioral changes.
- **Replaced application**. A 32-bit application that:
  - Implements ODBC 3.0 behavior for duplicated functionality.
  - Uses any new features in ODBC 3.0 only within conditional code.
  - Has limited conditional code to handle behavioral changes or has registered itself to be an ODBC 2.*x* application.

Types of Drivers

ODBC drivers can be classified as follows:

- **32-bit ODBC 2.*x* driver**. A 32-bit driver that:
  - Exports only ODBC 2.*x* functions.
  - Exhibits ODBC 2.*x* behavior for behavioral changes.
- **ISO and X/Open–compliant driver**. A 32-bit driver that:
  - Exports all functions that are documented in the X/Open or ISO CLI documents. This will include some of functions that are deprecated in ODBC.
  - Exhibits ODBC 3.0 behavior for behavioral changes.
  - Does not necessarily go through the ODBC 3.0 Driver Manager.
- **ODBC 3.0 driver**. A 32-bit driver that:
  - Exports only functions that are in ODBC 3.0 minus deprecated functions.
  - Is capable of exhibiting ODBC 2.*x* behavior or ODBC 3.0 behavior with respect to behavioral changes, based on the SQL_ATTR_APP_ODBC_VERSION environment attribute.

Note 16-bit ODBC drivers will not work with the ODBC 3.0 Driver Manager. Existing 16-bit applications will work only with the ODBC 2.*x* Driver Manager.

Compatibility Matrix

The following table describes the compatibility of the types of applications and drivers defined previously in this chapter.

Application type and version	32-bit ODBC 2.*x* driver	ODBC 3.0 driver	ISO and X/Open–compliant driver
16-bit application, any version	Compatible	Compatible	Compatible
Pure 2.*x* application	Compatible	Compatible	Not compatible [3]
Pure 2.*x* recompiled application	Compatible	Compatible [1]	Not compatible [3]
Pure X/Open and ISO–compliant application	Not compatible	Compatible [2]	Compatible [2]
Pure 3.0 application	Not compatible	Compatible	Not compatible [4]
Replaced application	Compatible	Compatible	Not compatible [3]

1 The application must recompile using ODBC 3.0 headers and must set ODBCVER to 0x0250.

2 The application must compile using ODBC 3.0 headers, and link with the ODBC Driver Manager. It must also set the header flag ODBC_STD.

3 This configuration can potentially fail to work because there are features in ODBC 2.*x* that are not in the standards, such as bookmarks.

4 This configuration can potentially fail to work because there are features in ODBC 3.0 that are not in the standards, such as bookmarks.

New Features

The following new functionality has been introduced in ODBC 3.0. An ODBC 3.0 application working with an ODBC 2.*x* driver will not be able to use this functionality. The ODBC 3.0 Driver Manager does not map these features when working with an ODBC 2.*x* driver.

- Functions that take a descriptor handle as an argument: **SQLSetDescField**, **SQLGetDescField**, **SQLSetDescRec**, **SQLGetDescRec**, and **SQLCopyDesc**.
- The functions **SQLSetEnvAttr** and **SQLGetEnvAttr**.
- The use of **SQLAllocHandle** to allocate a descriptor handle. (The use of **SQLAllocHandle** to allocate environment, connection, and statement handles is duplicated, not new, functionality.)
- The use of **SQLGetConnectAttr** to get the SQL_ATTR_AUTO_IPD connection attributes. (The use of **SQLSetConnectAttr** to set, and **SQLGetConnectAttr** to get, other connection attributes is duplicated, not new, functionality.)
- The use of **SQLSetStmtAttr** to set, and **SQLGetStmtAttr** to get, the following statement attributes. (The use of **SQLSetStmtAttr** to set, and **SQLGetStmtAttr** to get, other statement attributes is duplicated, not new, functionality.):

  SQL_ATTR_APP_ROW_DESC
  SQL_ATTR_APP_PARAM_DESC
  SQL_ATTR_ENABLE_AUTO_IPD
  SQL_ATTR_FETCH_BOOKMARK_PTR
  SQL_ATTR_BIND_OFFSET
  SQL_ATTR_METADATA_ID
  SQL_ATTR_PARAM_BIND_OFFSET_PTR
  SQL_ATTR_PARAM_BIND_TYPE
  SQL_ATTR_PARAM_OPERATION_PTR
  SQL_DESC_PARAM_STATUS_PTR
  SQL_ATTR_PARAMS_PROCESSED_PTR
  SQL_ATTR_PARAMSET_SIZE
  SQL_ATTR_ROW_BIND_OFFSET_PTR
  SQL_ATTR_ROW_OPERATION_PTR
  SQL_ATTR_ROW_ARRAY_SIZE

- The use of **SQLGetStmtAttr** to get the following statement attributes. (The use of **SQLGetStmtAttr** to get other statement attributes is duplicated functionality, not new functionality.):

  SQL_ATTR_IMP_ROW_DESC
  SQL_ATTR_IMP_PARAM_DESC

- Use of the interval C data type, the interval SQL data types, the BIGINT C data types, and the SQL_C_NUMERIC data structure.
- Row-wise binding of parameters.

- Offset-based bookmark fetches, such as calling **SQLFetchScroll** with an *FetchOrientation* of SQL_FETCH_BOOKMARK, and specifying an offset other than 0.
- **SQLFetch** returning the row status array, number of rows fetched, fetching multiple rows, intermixing calls with **SQLFetchScroll**, and intermixing calls with **SQLBulkOperations** or **SQLSetPos**. For more information, see the next section, "Block Cursors, Scrollable Cursors, and Backward Compatibility for ODBC 3.0 Applications."
- Named parameters.
- Any of the ODBC 3.0–specific **SQLGetInfo** options. (If an ODBC 3.0 application working with an ODBC 2.*x* driver calls the SQL_XXX_CURSOR_ATTRIBUTES1 information types, which have replaced several ODBC 2.*x* information types, some of the information may be reliable, but some may be unreliable. For more information, see **SQLGetInfo**.)
- Bind offsets.
- Updating, refreshing, and deleting by bookmarks (through a call to **SQLBulkOperations**).
- Calling **SQLBulkOperations** or **SQLSetPos** in the S5 state.
- The ROW_NUMBER and COLUMN_NUMBER fields in the diagnostic record (which have to be retrieved by the replacement functions **SQLGetDiagField** or **SQLGetDiagRec**).
- Approximate row counts.
- Warning information (SQL_ROW_SUCCESS_WITH_INFO from **SQLFetchScroll**).
- Variable-length bookmarks.
- Extended error information for arrays of parameters.
- All of the new columns in the result sets returned by the catalog functions.
- Use of **SQLDescribeCol** and **SQLColAttribute** on column 0.
- Use of any ODBC 3.0–specific column attributes in a call to **SQLColAttribute**.
- Use of multiple environment handles.

Block Cursors, Scrollable Cursors, and Backward Compatibility for ODBC 3.0 Applications

The existence of both **SQLFetchScroll** and **SQLExtendedFetch** represents the first clear split in ODBC between the Application Programming Interface (API), which is the set of functions the application calls, and the Service Provider Interface (SPI), which is the set of functions the driver implements. This split is required to balance the requirement in ODBC 3.0 to align with the standards, which uses

SQLFetchScroll, and be compatible with ODBC 2.*x*, which uses **SQLExtendedFetch**.

The ODBC 3.0 API, which is the set of functions the application calls, includes **SQLFetchScroll** and related statement attributes. The ODBC 3.0 SPI, which is the set of functions the driver implements, includes **SQLFetchScroll**, **SQLExtendedFetch**, and related statement attributes. Note that because ODBC does not formally enforce this split between the API and the SPI, it is possible for ODBC 3.0 applications to call **SQLExtendedFetch** and related statement attributes. However, there is no reason for ODBC 3.0 application to do this. For more information about APIs and SPIs, see the introduction to Chapter 3, "ODBC Architecture."

For information about how the ODBC 3.0 Driver Manager maps calls to ODBC 2.*x* and ODBC 3.0 drivers, and what functions and statement attributes an ODBC 3.0 driver should implement for block and scrollable cursors, see "What the Driver Does" in Appendix G, "Driver Guidelines for Backward Compatibility."

The following table summarizes what functions and statement attributes an ODBC 3.0 application should use with block and scrollable cursors. It also lists changes between ODBC 2.*x* and ODBC 3.0 in this area that ODBC 3.0 applications should be aware of to be compatible with ODBC 2.*x* drivers.

Function or statement attribute	Comments
SQL_ATTR_FETCH_BOOKMARK_PTR	Points to the bookmark to use with **SQLFetchScroll**. The following are implementation details: • When an application sets this in an ODBC 2.*x* driver, this must point to a fixed-length bookmark.
SQL_ATTR_ROW_STATUS_PTR	Points to the row status array filled by **SQLFetch**, **SQLFetchScroll**, **SQLBulkOperations**, and **SQLSetPos**. The following are implementation details: • If an application sets this in an ODBC 2.*x* driver and calls **SQLBulkOperation** with an *Operation* of SQL_ADD before calling **SQLFetchScroll**, **SQLFetch**, or **SQLExtendedFetch**, **SQLSTATE HY011** (Attribute cannot be set now) is returned. Note that when an application calls **SQLFetch** in an ODBC 2.*x* driver, **SQLFetch** is mapped to **SQLExtendedFetch**, so returns values in this array.
SQL_ATTR_ROWS_FETCHED_PTR	Points to the buffer in which **SQLFetch** and **SQLFetchScroll** return the number of rows fetched. Note that when an application calls **SQLFetch** in an ODBC 2.*x* driver, **SQLFetch** is mapped to **SQLExtendedFetch**, so returns a value in this buffer.

Function or statement attribute	Comments
SQL_ATTR_ ROW_ARRAY_SIZE	Sets the rowset size. If an application calls **SQLBulkOperations** with an *Operation* of SQL_ADD in an ODBC 2.*x* driver, SQL_ROWSET_SIZE will be used for the call, not SQL_ATTR_ROW_ARRAY_SIZE, because the call is mapped to **SQLSetPos** with an *Operation* of SQL_ADD, which uses SQL_ROWSET_SIZE. Calling **SQLSetPos** with an *Operation* of SQL_ADD or **SQLExtendedFetch** in an ODBC 2.*x* driver uses SQL_ROWSET_SIZE. Calling **SQLFetch** or **SQLFetchScroll** in an ODBC 2.*x* driver uses SQL_ATTR_ROW_ARRAY_SIZE.
SQLBulkOperations	Performs insert and bookmark operations. When **SQLBulkOperations** with an *Operation* of SQL_ADD is called in an ODBC 2.*x* driver, it is mapped to **SQLSetPos** with an *Operation* of SQL_ADD. The following are implementation details: • When working with an ODBC 2.x driver, an application must use only the implicitly allocated ARD associated with the *StatementHandle*; it cannot allocate another ARD for adding rows, because explicit descriptor operations are not supported in an ODBC 2.*x* driver. An application must use **SQLBindCol** to bind to the ARD, not **SQLSetDescField** or **SQLSetDescRec**. • When calling an ODBC 3.0 driver, an application can call **SQLBulkOperations** with an *Operation* of SQL_ADD before calling **SQLFetch** or **SQLFetchScroll**. When calling an ODBC 2.*x* driver, an application must call **SQLFetchScroll** before calling **SQLBulkOperations** with an Operation of SQL_ADD.

Function or statement attribute	Comments
SQLFetch	Returns the next rowset. The following are implementation details: • When an application calls **SQLFetch** in an ODBC 2.*x* driver, it is mapped to **SQLExtendedFetch**. • When an application calls **SQLFetch** in an ODBC 3.0 driver, it returns the number of rows specified with the SQL_ATTR_ROW_ARRAY_SIZE statement attribute.
SQLFetchScroll	Returns the specified rowset. The following are implementation details: • When an application calls **SQLFetchScroll** in an ODBC 2.*x* driver, it returns SQLSTATE 01S01 (Error in row) before each error that applies to a single row. It does this only because the ODBC 3.0 Driver Manager maps this to **SQLExtendedFetch** and **SQLExtendedFetch** returns this SQLSTATE. When an application calls **SQLFetchScroll** in an ODBC 3.0 driver, it never returns SQLSTATE 01S01 (Error in row). • When an application calls **SQLFetchScroll** in an ODBC 2.*x* driver with *FetchOrientation* set to SQL_FETCH_BOOKMARK, the *FetchOffset* argument must be set to 0. SQLSTATE HYC00 (Optional feature not implemented) is returned if offset-based bookmark fetching is attempted with an ODBC 2.*x* driver.

Note ODBC 3.0 applications should not use **SQLExtendedFetch** or the SQL_ROWSET_SIZE statement attribute. Instead, they should use **SQLFetchScroll** and the SQL_ATTR_ROW_ARRAY_SIZE statement attribute. ODBC 3.0 applications should not use **SQLSetPos** with an *Operation* of SQL_ADD, but should use **SQLBulkOperations** with an *Operation* of SQL_ADD.

Duplicated Features

The following ODBC 2.*x* functions have been duplicated by ODBC 3.0 functions. As a result, the ODBC 2.*x* functions are deprecated in ODBC 3.0. The ODBC 3.0 functions are referred to as replacement functions.

When an application uses a deprecated ODBC 2.*x* function, and the underlying driver is an ODBC 3.0 driver, the Driver Manager maps the function call to the corresponding replacement function. The only exception to this rule is **SQLExtendedFetch** (see footnote in the following table). For more information on these mappings, see Appendix G, "Driver Guidelines for Backward Compatibility."

When an application uses a replacement function, and the underlying driver is an ODBC 2.*x* driver, the Driver Manager maps the function call to the corresponding deprecated function.

ODBC 2.*x* function	ODBC 3.0 function
SQLAllocConnect	**SQLAllocHandle**
SQLAllocEnv	**SQLAllocHandle**
SQLAllocStmt	**SQLAllocHandle**
SQLColAttributes	**SQLColAttribute**
SQLError	**SQLGetDiagRec**
SQLExtendedFetch [1]	**SQLFetchScroll**
SQLFreeConnect	**SQLFreeHandle**
SQLFreeEnv	**SQLFreeHandle**
SQLGetConnectOption	**SQLGetConnectAttr**
SQLGetStmtOption	**SQLGetStmtAttr**
SQLParamOptions	**SQLSetStmtAttr**, **SQLGetStmtAttr**
SQLSetConnectOption	**SQLSetConnectAttr**
SQLSetParam	**SQLBindParameter**
SQLSetStmtOption	**SQLSetStmtAttr**
SQLTransact	**SQLEndTran**

1 The function **SQLExtendedFetch** is duplicated functionality; **SQLFetchScroll** provides the same functionality in ODBC 3.0. However, the Driver Manager does not map **SQLExtendedFetch** to **SQLFetchScroll** when going against an ODBC 3.0 driver. For more details, see "What the Driver Manager Does" in Appendix G, "Driver Guidelines for Backward Compatibility." The Driver Manager maps **SQLFetchScroll** to **SQLExtendedFetch** when going against an ODBC 2.*x* driver.

Note The function **SQLBindParam** is a special case. **SQLBindParam** is duplicated functionality. This is not an ODBC 2.*x* function, but a function that is present in the X/Open and ISO standards. The functionality provided by this function is completely subsumed by that of **SQLBindParameter**. As a result, the Driver Manager maps a call to **SQLBindParam** to **SQLBindParameter** when the underlying driver is an ODBC 3.0 driver. When the underlying driver is an ODBC 2.*x* driver, however, the Driver Manager does not perform this mapping.

Behavioral Changes

Behavioral changes are those changes for which the *syntax* of the interface remains the same, but the *semantics* have changed. For these changes, functionality used in ODBC 2.*x* behaves differently than the same functionality in ODBC 3.0.

Whether an application exhibits ODBC 2.*x* behavior or ODBC 3.0 behavior is determined by the SQL_ATTR_ODBC_VERSION environment attribute. This 32-bit value is set to SQL_OV_ODBC2 to exhibit ODBC 2.*x* behavior, and SQL_OV_ODBC3 to exhibit ODBC 3.0 behavior.

The SQL_ATTR_ODBC_VERSION environment attribute is set by a call to **SQLSetEnvAttr**. When an application calls **SQLAllocHandle** to allocate an environment handle, then it must call **SQLSetEnvAttr** immediately to set the behavior it exhibits. (As a result, there is a new environment state to describe the environment handle in an allocated, but versionless state.) For more information, see Appendix B, "ODBC State Transition Tables."

An application states what behavior it exhibits with the SQL_ATTR_ODBC_VERSION environment attribute, but the attribute has no effect on the application's connection with an ODBC 2.*x* or ODBC 3.0 driver. An ODBC 3.0 application will be able to connect to either an ODBC 2.*x* or 3.0 driver, no matter what the setting of the environment attribute.

ODBC 3.0 applications should never call **SQLAllocEnv**. As a result, if the Driver Manager receives a call to **SQLAllocEnv**, it recognizes the application as an ODBC 2.*x* application.

The SQL_ATTR_ODBC_VERSION attribute affects three different aspects of an ODBC 3.0 driver's behavior:

- SQLSTATEs
- Data types for date, time, and timestamp
- The *CatalogName* argument in **SQLTables** accepts search patterns in ODBC 3.0, but not in ODBC 2.*x*

The setting of the SQL_ATTR_ODBC_VERSION environment attribute does not affect **SQLSetParam** or **SQLBindParam**. **SQLColAttribute** is also not affected by this bit. Although **SQLColAttribute** returns attributes that are affected by the version of ODBC (date type, precision, scale and length), the intended behavior is determined by the value of the *FieldIdentifier* argument. When *FieldIdentifier* is equal to SQL_DESC_TYPE, **SQLColAttribute** returns the ODBC 3.0 codes for date, time, and timestamp; when *FieldIdentifier* is equal to SQL_COLUMN_TYPE, **SQLColAttribute** returns the ODBC 2.*x* codes for date, time, and timestamp.

SQLSTATE Mappings

In ODBC 3.0, HYxxx SQLSTATEs are returned instead of S1xxx, and 42Sxx SQLSTATEs are returned instead of S00XX. This was done to align with X/Open and ISO standards. In many cases, the mapping is not one-to-one because the standards have redefined the interpretation of several SQLSTATEs.

When an ODBC 2.*x* application is upgraded to an ODBC 3.0 application, the application has to be changed to expect ODBC 3.0 SQLSTATEs instead of ODBC 2.*x* SQLSTATEs. The following table lists the ODBC 3.0 SQLSTATEs that each ODBC 2.*x* SQLSTATE is mapped to.

When the SQL_ATTR_ODBC_VERSION environment attribute is set to SQL_OV_ODBC2, the driver posts ODBC 2.*x* SQLSTATEs instead of ODBC 3.0 SQLSTATEs when **SQLGetDiagField** or **SQLGetDiagRec** is called. A specific mapping can be determined by noting the ODBC 2.*x* SQLSTATE in column 1 of the following table that corresponds to the ODBC 3.0 SQLSTATE in column 2.

ODBC 2.*x* SQLSTATE	ODBC 3.0 SQLSTATE	Comments
01S03	01001	
01S04	01001	
22003	HY019	
22008	22007	
22005	22018	
24000	07005	
37000	42000	
70100	HY018	
S0001	42S01	
S0002	42S02	
S0011	42S11	
S0012	42S12	
S0021	42S21	
S0022	42S22	
S0023	42S23	
S1000	HY000	
S1001	HY001	
S1002	07009	ODBC 2.*x* SQLSTATE S1002 is mapped to ODBC 3.0 SQLSTATE 07009 if the underlying function is **SQLBindCol**, **SQLColAttribute**, **SQLExtendedFetch**, **SQLFetch**, **SQLFetchScroll**, or **SQLGetData**.
S1003	HY003	
S1004	HY004	
S1008	HY008	
S1009	HY009	Returned for an invalid use of a null pointer.
S1009	HY024	Returned for an invalid attribute value.

ODBC 2.*x* SQLSTATE	ODBC 3.0 SQLSTATE	Comments
S1009	HY092	Returned for updating or deleting data by a call to **SQLSetPos**, or adding, updating, or deleting data by a call to **SQLBulkOperations**, when the concurrency is read-only.
S1010	HY007 HY010	SQLSTATE S1010 is mapped to SQLSTATE HY007 when **SQLDescribeCol** is called prior to calling **SQLPrepare**, **SQLExecDirect**, or a catalog function for the *StatementHandle*. Otherwise, SQLSTATE S1010 is mapped to SQLSTATE HY010.
S1011	HY011	
S1012	HY012	
S1090	HY090	
S1091	HY091	
S1092	HY092	
S1093	07009	ODBC 3.0 SQLSTATE 07009 is mapped to ODBC 2.*x* SQLSTATE S1093 if the underlying function is **SQLBindParameter** or **SQLDescribeParam**.
S1096	HY096	
S1097	HY097	
S1098	HY098	
S1099	HY099	
S1100	HY100	
S1101	HY101	
S1103	HY103	
S1104	HY104	

ODBC 2.*x* SQLSTATE	ODBC 3.0 SQLSTATE	Comments
S1105	HY105	
S1106	HY106	
S1107	HY107	
S1108	HY108	
S1109	HY109	
S1110	HY110	
S1111	HY111	
S1C00	HYC00	
S1T00	HYT00	

Note ODBC 3.0 SQLSTATE 07008 is mapped to ODBC 2.*x* SQLSTATE S1000.

Datetime Data Type Changes

In ODBC 3.0, the identifiers for date, time, and timestamp SQL data types have changed from SQL_DATE, SQL_TIME, and SQL_TIMESTAMP (with instances of **#define** in the header file of 9, 10, and 11) to SQL_TYPE_DATE, SQL_TYPE_TIME, and SQL_TYPE_TIMESTAMP (with instances of **#define** in the header file of 91, 92, and 93), respectively. The corresponding C type identifiers have changed from SQL_C_DATE, SQL_C_TIME, and SQL_C_TIMESTAMP to SQL_C_TYPE_DATE, SQL_C_TYPE_TIME, and SQL_C_TYPE_TIMESTAMP, respectively.

The column size and decimal digits returned for the SQL datetime data types in ODBC 3.0 are the same as the precision and scale returned for them in ODBC 2.*x*. These values are different than the values in the SQL_DESC_PRECISION and SQL_DESC_SCALE descriptor fields. (For more information, see Appendix D, "Data Types.")

These changes affect **SQLDescribeCol**, **SQLDescribeParam**, and **SQLColAttribute**; **SQLBindCol**, **SQLBindParameter**, and **SQLGetData**; and **SQLColumns**, **SQLGetTypeInfo**, **SQLProcedureColumns**, **SQLStatistics**, and **SQLSpecialColumns**.

The following table shows how the ODBC 3.0 Driver Manager performs mapping of the date, time, and timestamp C data types entered in the *TargetType* arguments of **SQLBindCol** and **SQLGetData** or the *ValueType* argument of **SQLBindParameter**.

Data type code entered	2.*x* app to 2.*x* driver	2.*x* app to 3.0 driver	3.0 app to 2.*x* driver	3.0 app to 3.0 driver
SQL_C_DATE (9)	No mapping	SQL_C_ TYPE_DATE (91)	No mapping [1]	SQL_C_ TYPE_DATE (91)
SQL_C_ TYPE_DATE (91)	Error (from DM)	Error (from DM)	SQL_C_DATE (9)	No mapping [2]
SQL_C_TIME (10)	No mapping	SQL_C_ TYPE_TIME (92)	No mapping [1]	SQL_C_ TYPE_TIME (92)
SQL_C_ TYPE_TIME (92)	Error (from DM)	Error (from DM)	SQL_C_TIME (10)	No mapping [2]
SQL_C_ TIMESTAMP (11)	No mapping	SQL_C_ TYPE_ TIMESTAMP (93)	No mapping [1]	SQL_C_ TYPE_ TIMESTAMP (93)
SQL_C_ TYPE_ TIMESTAMP (93)	Error (from DM)	Error (from DM)	SQL_C_ TIMESTAMP (11)	No mapping [2]

1 As a result of this, an ODBC 3.0 application working with an ODBC 2.*x* driver can use the date, time, or timestamp codes returned in the result sets that are returned by the catalog functions.

2 As a result of this, an ODBC 3.0 application working with an ODBC 3.0 driver can use the date, time, or timestamp codes returned in the result sets that are returned by the catalog functions.

The following table shows how the ODBC 3.0 Driver Manager performs mapping of the date, time, and timestamp SQL data types entered in the *ParameterType* argument of **SQLBindParameter** or the *DataType* argument of **SQLGetTypeInfo**.

Data type code entered	2.*x* app to 2.*x* driver	2.*x* app to 3.0 driver	3.0 app to 2.*x* driver	3.0 app to 3.0 driver
SQL_DATE (9)	No mapping	SQL_TYPE_ DATE (91)	No mapping [1]	SQL_TYPE_ DATE (91)
SQL_TYPE_ DATE (91)	Error (from DM)	Error (from DM)	SQL_DATE (9)	No mapping [2]
SQL_TIME (10)	No mapping	SQL_TYPE_ TIME (92)	No mapping [1]	SQL_TYPE_ TIME (92)
SQL_TYPE_ TIME (92)	Error (from DM)	Error (from DM)	SQL_TIME (10)	No mapping [2]
SQL_ TIMESTAMP (11)	No mapping	SQL_TYPE_ TIMESTAMP (93)	No mapping [1]	SQL_TYPE_ TIMESTAMP (93)
SQL_TYPE_ TIMESTAMP (93)	Error (from DM)	Error (from DM)	SQL_ TIMESTAMP (11)	No mapping [2]

1 As a result of this, an ODBC 3.0 application working with an ODBC 2.*x* driver can used the date, time, or timestamp codes returned in the result sets that are returned by the catalog functions.

2 As a result of this, an ODBC 3.0 application working with an ODBC 3.0 driver can used the date, time, or timestamp codes returned in the result sets that are returned by the catalog functions.

Writing ODBC 3.0 Applications

When an ODBC 2.*x* application is upgraded to ODBC 3.0, it should be written such that it works with both ODBC 2.*x* and 3.0 drivers. The application should incorporate conditional code to take full advantage of the ODBC 3.0 features.

The SQL_ATTR_ODBC_VERSION environment attribute should be set to SQL_OV_ODBC2. This will ensure that the driver behaves like an ODBC 2.*x* driver with respect to the changes described in the "Behavioral Changes" section earlier in this chapter are concerned.

If the application will use any of the features described in the "New Features" section earlier in this chapter, conditional code should be used to determine whether the driver is an ODBC 3.0 or ODBC 2.*x* driver. The application uses **SQLGetDiagField** and **SQLGetDiagRec** to obtain ODBC 3.0 SQLSTATEs while doing error processing on these conditional code fragments. The following points about the new functionality should be considered:

- An application affected by the change in rowset size behavior should be careful not to call **SQLFetch** when the array size is greater than 1. These applications should replace calls to **SQLExtendedFetch** with calls to **SQLSetStmtAttr** to set the SQL_ATTR_ARRAY_STATUS_PTR statement attribute and **SQLFetchScroll**, so they have common code that works with both ODBC 3.0 and ODBC 2.*x* drivers. Because **SQLSetStmtAttr** with SQL_ATTR_ROW_ARRAY_SIZE will be mapped to **SQLSetStmtAttr** with SQL_ROWSET_SIZE for ODBC 2.*x* drivers, applications can just set SQL_ATTR_ROW_ARRAY_SIZE for their multirow fetch operations.
- Most applications that are upgrading are not actually affected by changes in SQLSTATE codes. For those applications that are affected, they can do a mechanical search and replace in most cases using the error conversion table in the "SQLSTATE Mapping" section to convert ODBC 3.0 error codes to ODBC 2.*x* codes. Since the ODBC 3.0 Driver Manager will perform mapping from ODBC 2.*x* SQLSTATEs to ODBC 3.0 SQLSTATEs, these application writers need only check for the ODBC 3.0 SQLSTATEs and not worry about including ODBC 2.*x* SQLSTATEs in conditional code.
- If an application makes great use of date, time, and timestamp data types, the application can declare itself to be an ODBC 2.*x* application and use its existing code, instead of using conditioning code.

The upgrade should also include the following steps:

- Call **SQLSetEnvAttr** before allocating a connection to set the SQL_ATTR_ODBC_VERSION environment attribute to SQL_OV_ODBC2.
- Replace all calls to **SQLAllocEnv**, **SQLAllocConnect**, or **SQLAllocStmt** with calls to **SQLAllocHandle** with the appropriate *HandleType* argument of SQL_HANDLE_ENV, SQL_HANDLE_DBC, or SQL_HANDLE_STMT.
- Replace all calls to **SQLFreeEnv** or **SQLFreeConnect** with calls to **SQLFreeHandle** with the appropriate *HandleType* argument of SQL_HANDLE_DBC or SQL_HANDLE_STMT.
- Replace all calls to **SQLSetConnectOption** with calls to **SQLSetConnectAttr**. If setting an attribute whose value is a string, set the *StringLength* argument appropriately. Change *Attribute* argument from SQL_XXXX to SQL_ATTR_XXXX.
- Replace all calls to **SQLGetConnectOption** with calls to **SQLGetConnectAttr**. If getting a string or binary attribute, set *BufferLength* to the appropriate value and pass in a *StringLength* argument. Change *Attribute* argument from SQL_XXXX to SQL_ATTR_XXXX.
- Replace all calls to **SQLSetStmtOption** with calls to **SQLSetStmtAttr**. If setting an attribute whose value is a string, set the *StringLength* argument appropriately. Change *Attribute* argument from SQL_XXXX to SQL_ATTR_XXXX.
- Replace all calls to **SQLGetStmtOption** with calls to **SQLGetStmtAttr**. If getting a string or binary attribute, set *BufferLength* to the appropriate value and pass in a *StringLength* argument. Change *Attribute* argument from SQL_XXXX to SQL_ATTR_XXXX.
- Replace all calls to **SQLTransact** with calls to **SQLEndTran**. If the rightmost valid handle in the **SQLTransact** call is an environment handle, then a *HandleType* argument of SQL_HANDLE_ENV should be used in the **SQLEndTran** call with the appropriate *Handle* argument. If the rightmost valid handle in your **SQLTransact** call is a connection handle, then a *HandleType* argument of SQL_HANDLE_DBC should be used in the **SQLEndTran** call with the appropriate *Handle* argument.
- Replace all calls to **SQLColAttributes** with calls to **SQLColAttribute**. If the *FieldIdentifier* argument is either SQL_COLUMN_PRECISION, SQL_COLUMN_SCALE, or SQL_COLUMN_LENGTH, then do not change anything other than the name of the function. If not, change *FieldIdentifier* from SQL_COLUMN_XXXX to SQL_DESC_XXXX. If *FieldIdentifier* is SQL_DESC_CONCISE_TYPE and the data type is a datetime data type, change to the corresponding ODBC 3.0 data type.

- If using block cursors, scrollable cursors, or both then the application:
  - Sets the rowset size, cursor type, and cursor concurrency using **SQLSetStmtAttr**.
  - Calls **SQLSetStmtAttr** to set SQL_ATTR_ROW_STATUS_PTR to point to an array of status records.
  - Calls **SQLSetStmtAttr** to set SQL_ATTR_ROWS_FETCHED_PTR to point to an SQLINTEGER.
  - Performs the required bindings and executes the SQL statement.
  - Calls **SQLFetchScroll** in a loop to fetch rows and move around in the result set.
  - If it wants to fetch by bookmark, then the application calls **SQLSetStmtAttr** to set SQL_ATTR_FETCH_BOOKMARK_PTR to a variable that will contain the bookmark for the row that it wants to fetch, and calls **SQLFetchScroll** with a *FetchOrientation* argument of SQL_FETCH_BOOKMARK.
- If using arrays of parameters, then the application:
  - Calls **SQLSetStmtAttr** to set the SQL_ATTR_PARAMSET_SIZE attribute to the size of the parameter array.
  - Calls **SQLSetStmtAttr** to set SQL_ATTR_ROWS_PROCESSED_PTR to point to an internal UDWORD variable.
  - Performs prepare, bind, and execute operations as appropriate.
  - If execution halts for some reason (such as SQL_NEED_DATA), it can find the "current" row of parameters by inspecting the location pointed to by SQL_ATTR_ROWS_PROCESSED_PTR.

Mapping Replacement Functions for Backward Compatibility of Applications

An ODBC 3.0 application working through the ODBC 3.0 Driver Manager will work against an ODBC 2.*x* driver as long as no new features are used. Both duplicated functionality and behavioral changes do, however, affect the way that the ODBC 3.0 application works on an ODBC 2.*x* driver. When working with an ODBC 2.*x* driver, the Driver Manager maps the following ODBC 3.0 functions, which have replaced one or more ODBC 2.*x* functions, into the corresponding ODBC 2.*x* functions.

ODBC 3.0 function	ODBC 2.*x* function
SQLAllocHandle	**SQLAllocEnv**, **SQLAllocConnect**, or **SQLAllocStmt**
SQLBulkOperations	**SQLSetPos**
SQLColAttribute	**SQLColAttributes**
SQLEndTran	**SQLTransact**
SQLFetch	**SQLExtendedFetch**
SQLFetchScroll	**SQLExtendedFetch**
SQLFreeHandle	**SQLFreeEnv**, **SQLFreeConnect**, or **SQLFreeStmt**
SQLGetConnectAttr	**SQLGetConnectOption**
SQLGetDiagRec	**SQLError**
SQLGetStmtAttr	**SQLGetStmtOption** [1]
SQLSetConnectAttr	**SQLSetConnectOption**
SQLSetStmtAttr	**SQLSetStmtOption** [1]

1 Other actions might also be taken, depending on the attribute being requested.

SQLAllocHandle

The Driver Manager maps this to **SQLAllocEnv**, **SQLAllocConnect**, or **SQLAllocStmt**, as appropriate. The following call to **SQLAllocHandle**:

```
SQLAllocHandle(HandleType, InputHandle, OutputHandlePtr);
```

will result in the Driver Manager performing the following (conceptual, no error checking) mapping:

```
switch (HandleType) {
   case SQL_HANDLE_ENV: return (SQLAllocEnv(OutputHandlePtr));
   case SQL_HANDLE_DBC: return (SQLAllocConnect (InputHandle, OutputHandlePtr));
   case SQL_HANDLE_STMT: return (SQLAllocStmt (InputHandle, OutputHandlePtr));
   default: // return SQL_ERROR, SQLSTATE HY092 ("Invalid attribute/option identifier")
}
```

SQLBulkOperations

The Driver Manager maps this to **SQLSetPos**. The following call to **SQLBulkOperations**:

```
SQLBulkOperations(hstmt, Operation);
```

will result in the following sequence of steps:

1. If the *Operation* argument is SQL_ADD, the Driver Manager calls **SQLSetPos** as follows:

   ```
   SQLSetPos (hstmt, 0, SQL_ADD, SQL_LOCK_NO_CHANGE);
   ```

2. If the *Operation* argument is not SQL_ADD, the driver returns SQLSTATE HY092 (Invalid attribute/option identifier).
3. If the application attempts to change the SQL_ATTR_ROW_STATUS_PTR between calls to **SQLFetch** or **SQLFetchScroll** and **SQLBulkOperations**, the Driver Manager will return SQLSTATE HY011 (Attribute cannot be set now).
4. If the *Operation* argument is SQL_ADD, the application must call **SQLBindCol** to bind the data to be inserted. It cannot call **SQLSetDescField** or **SQLSetDescRec** to bind the data to be inserted.
5. If the *Operation* argument is SQL_ADD, and the number of rows to be inserted is not the same as the current rowset size, then **SQLSetStmtAttr** must be called to set the SQL_ATTR_ROW_ARRAY_SIZE statement attribute to the number of rows to be inserted before calling **SQLBulkOperations**. To revert back to the previous rowset size, the application must set the SQL_ATTR_ROW_ARRAY_SIZE statement attribute before **SQLFetch**, **SQLFetchScroll**, or **SQLSetPos** is called.

SQLColAttribute

The Driver Manager maps this to **SQLColAttributes**. The following call to **SQLColAttribute**:

```
SQLColAttribute(StatementHandle, ColumnNumber, FieldIdentifier, CharacterAttributePtr,
BufferLength, StringLengthPtr, NumericAttributePtr);
```

will result in the following sequence of steps:

1. If *FieldIdentifier* is one of the following:

   SQL_DESC_PRECISION, SQL_DESC_SCALE, SQL_DESC_LENGTH, SQL_DESC_OCTET_LENGTH, SQL_DESC_UNNAMED, SQL_DESC_BASE_COLUMN_NAME, SQL_DESC_LITERAL_PREFIX, SQL_DESC_LITERAL_SUFFIX, or SQL_DESC_LOCAL_TYPE_NAME

   then the Driver Manager returns SQL_ERROR with SQLSTATE HY091 (Invalid descriptor field identifier). No further rules of this section apply.

2. The Driver Manager maps SQL_COLUMN_COUNT, SQL_COLUMN_NAME, or SQL_COLUMN_NULLABLE to SQL_DESC_COUNT, SQL_DESC_NAME, or SQL_DESC_NULLABLE, respectively. (An ODBC 2.*x* driver need only support SQL_COLUMN_COUNT, SQL_COLUMN_NAME, and SQL_COLUMN_NULLABLE, not SQL_DESC_COUNT, SQL_DESC_NAME, and SQL_DESC_NULLABLE.) The call to **SQLColAttribute** is mapped to:

   ```
   SQLColAttributes(StatementHandle, ColumnNumber, FieldIdentifier,
   CharacterAttributePtr, BufferLength, StringLengthPtr,
   NumericAttributePtr);
   ```

3. All other *FieldIdentifier* values are passed through to the driver, with **SQLColAttribute** mapped to **SQLColAttributes** as shown previously.
4. If *BufferLength* is less than 0, then the Driver Manager returns SQL_ERROR with SQLSTATE HY090 (Invalid string or buffer length). No further rules of this section apply.
5. If *FieldIdentifier* is SQL_DESC_CONCISE_TYPE, and the returned type is a concise datetime data type, the Driver Manager maps the return values for date, time, and timestamp codes.
6. The Driver Manager performs necessary checks to see if SQLSTATE HY010 (Function sequence error) needs to be raised. If so, the Driver Manager returns SQL_ERROR and SQLSTATE HY010 (Function sequence error). No further rules of this section apply.

SQLEndTran

The Driver Manager maps this to **SQLTransact**. The following call to **SQLEndTran**:

```
SQLEndTran(HandleType, Handle, CompletionType);
```

will result in the Driver Manager performing the following (conceptual, no error checking) mapping:

```
switch (HandleType) {
   case SQL_HANDLE_ENV:return(SQLTransact(Handle, SQL_NULL_HDBC, CompletionType));
   case SQL_HANDLE_DBC:return(SQLTransact(SQL_NULL_HENV, Handle, CompletionType);
   default: // return SQL_ERROR, SQLSTATE HY092 ("Invalid attribute/option identifier")
}
```

SQLFetch

The Driver Manager maps this to **SQLExtendedFetch** with a *FetchOrientation* of SQL_FETCH_NEXT. The following call to **SQLFetch**:

```
SQLFetch (StatementHandle);
```

will result in the Driver Manager calling **SQLExtendedFetch**, as follows:

```
rc = SQLExtendedFetch(StatementHandle, FetchOrientation, FetchOffset, &RowCount,
RowStatusArray);
```

In this call, the *pcRow* argument is set to the value that the application sets the SQL_ATTR_ROWS_FETCHED_PTR statement attribute to through a call to **SQLSetStmtAttr**.

Recall that when the application calls **SQLSetStmtAttr** to set SQL_ATTR_ROW_STATUS_PTR to point to a status array, the Driver Manager caches the pointer. *RowStatusArray* can be equal to a null pointer.

If the driver does not support **SQLExtendedFetch** and the cursor library is loaded, then the Driver Manager uses the cursor library's **SQLExtendedFetch** to map **SQLFetch** to **SQLExtendedFetch**. If the driver does not support **SQLExtendedFetch** and the cursor library is not loaded, the Driver Manager passes the call to **SQLFetch** through to the driver. If the application calls **SQLSetStmtAttr** to set SQL_ATTR_ROW_STATUS_PTR, then the Driver Manager ensures that the array is populated. If the application calls **SQLSetStmtAttr** to set SQL_ATTR_ROWS_FETCHED_PTR, then the Driver Manager sets this field to 1.

SQLFetchScroll

The Driver Manager maps this to **SQLExtendedFetch**. The following call to **SQLFetchScroll**:

```
SQLFetchScroll(StatementHandle, FetchOrientation, FetchOffset);
```

will result in the following sequence of steps:

1. Recall that when the application calls **SQLSetStmtAttr** to set SQL_ATTR_ROW_STATUS_PTR (which sets the SQL_DESC_ARRAY_STATUS_PTR field in the IRD) to point to a status array, the Driver Manager caches this pointer. Let this pointer be *RowStatusArray*; otherwise, let *RowStatusArray* be equal to a null pointer. If the *RowStatusArray* arguments is set to a null pointer, the Driver Manager generates a row-status array.
2. If *FetchOrientation* is not one of SQL_FETCH_NEXT, SQL_FETCH_PRIOR, SQL_FETCH_ABSOLUTE, SQL_FETCH_RELATIVE, SQL_FETCH_FIRST, SQL_FETCH_LAST, or SQL_FETCH_BOOKMARK, then the Driver Manager returns with SQL_ERROR and SQLSTATE HY106 (Fetch type out of range). No further rules of this section apply.
3. Case:

- If *FetchOrientation* is equal to SQL_FETCH_BOOKMARK, then:
  - If **SQLSetStmtAttr** was called earlier to set the value of SQL_ATTR_FETCH_BOOKMARK_PTR, then let *Bmk* be the value obtained by dereferencing the pointer SQL_DESC_FETCH_BOOKMARK_PTR.
  - Otherwise, return SQL_ERROR with SQLSTATE HY111 (Invalid bookmark value). No further rules of this section apply.

  The Driver Manager now calls **SQLExtendedFetch**, as follows:

  ```
  rc = SQLExtendedFetch(StatementHandle, FetchOrientation, Bmk, pcRow,
  RowStatusArray);
  ```

- Otherwise, the Driver Manager calls **SQLExtendedFetch**, as follows:

  ```
  rc = SQLExtendedFetch(StatementHandle, FetchOrientation, FetchOffset,
  pcRow, RowStatusArray);
  ```

  In these calls, the *pcRow* argument is set to the value that the application sets the SQL_ATTR_ROWS_FETCHED_PTR statement attribute to through a call to **SQLSetStmtAttr**.

4. SQL_ATTR_ROW_ARRAY_SIZE is mapped to SQL_ROWSET_SIZE.
5. If *rc* is equal to SQL_SUCCESS or SQL_SUCCESS_WITH_INFO, and if *FetchOrientation* is equal to SQL_FETCH_BOOKMARK and *FetchOffset* is not equal to 0, then the Driver Manager posts a warning, SQLSTATE 01S10 (Attempt to fetch by a bookmark offset, offset value ignored), and returns SQL_SUCCESS_WITH_INFO.

SQLFreeHandle

The Driver Manager maps this to **SQLFreeEnv**, **SQLFreeConnect**, or **SQLFreeStmt** as appropriate. The following call to **SQLFreeHandle**:

```
SQLFreeHandle(HandleType, Handle);
```

will result in the Driver Manager performing the following (conceptual, no error checking) mapping:

```
switch (HandleType) {
   case SQL_HANDLE_ENV: return (SQLFreeEnv(Handle));
   case SQL_HANDLE_DBC: return (SQLFreeConnect(Handle));
   case SQL_HANDLE_STMT: return (SQLFreeStmt(Handle, SQL_DROP));
   default: // return SQL_ERROR, SQLSTATE HY092 ("Invalid attribute/option identifier")
}
```

SQLGetConnectAttr

The Driver Manager maps this to **SQLGetConnectOption**. The following call to **SQLGetConnectAttr**:

```
SQLGetConnectAttr(ConnectionHandle, Attribute, ValuePtr, BufferLength,
StringLengthPtr);
```

will result in the following sequence of steps:

1. If *Attribute* is not a driver-defined connection or statement attribute, and is not an attribute defined in ODBC 2.*x*, then the Driver Manager returns SQL_ERROR with SQLSTATE HY092 (Invalid attribute/option identifier). No further rules in this section apply.
2. If *Attribute* is equal to SQL_ATTR_AUTO_IPD or SQL_ATTR_METADATA_ID, then the Driver Manager returns SQL_ERROR with SQLSTATE HY092 (Invalid attribute/option identifier).

3. The Driver Manager performs necessary checks to see if SQLSTATE 08003 (Connection not open) or SQLSTATE HY010 (Function sequence error) needs to be raised. If so, the Driver Manager returns SQL_ERROR and posts the appropriate error message. No further rules of this section apply.
4. The Driver Manager calls **SQLGetConnectOption** as follows:

   ```
   SQLGetConnectOption (ConnectionHandle, Attribute, ValuePtr);
   ```

   Note that the *BufferLength* and *StringLengthPtr* are ignored.

SQLGetData

When an ODBC 3.0 application working with an ODBC 2.*x* driver calls **SQLGetData** with the *ColumnNumber* argument equal to 0, the ODBC 3.0 Driver Manager maps this to a call to **SQLGetStmtOption** with the *Option* attribute set to SQL_GET_BOOKMARK.

SQLGetStmtAttr

The Driver Manager maps this to **SQLGetStmtOption**. The following call to **SQLGetStmtAttr**:

```
SQLGetStmtAttr(StatementHandle, Attribute, ValuePtr, BufferLength, StringLengthPtr);
```

will result in the following sequence of steps:

1. If *Attribute* is not a driver-defined connection or statement attribute, and is not an attribute defined in ODBC 2.*x*, then the Driver Manager returns SQL_ERROR with SQLSTATE HY092 (Invalid attribute/option identifier). No further rules in this section apply.
2. If *Attribute* is one of the following:

   SQL_ATTR_APP_ROW_DESC, SQL_ATTR_APP_PARAM_DESC,
   SQL_ATTR_AUTO_IPD, SQL_ATTR_ROW_BIND_TYPE.
   SQL_ATTR_IMP_ROW_DESC, SQL_ATTR_IMP_PARAM_DESC,
   SQL_ATTR_METADATA_ID, SQL_ATTR_PARAM_BIND_TYPE,
   SQL_ATTR_PREDICATE_PTR,
   SQL_ATTR_PREDICATE_OCTET_LENGTH_PTR,
   SQL_ATTR_PARAM_BIND_OFFSET_PTR,
   SQL_ATTR_ROW_BIND_OFFSET_PTR,
   SQL_ATTR_ROW_OPERATION_PTR,
   SQL_ATTR_PARAM_OPERATION_PTR

   Then the Driver Manager returns SQL_ERROR with SQLSTATE HY092 (Invalid attribute/option identifier). No further rules of this section apply.
3. The Driver Manager performs necessary checks to see if SQLSTATE HY010 (Function sequence error) needs to be raised. If so, the Driver Manager returns SQL_ERROR and SQLSTATE HY010 (Function sequence error). No further rules of this section apply.

4. If *Attribute* is equal to SQL_ATTR_ROWS_FETCHED_PTR, the Driver Manager returns a pointer to the internal Driver Manager variable *cRow*, which it has used or will use in a call to **SQLExtendedFetch**. No further rules of this section apply.
5. If *Attribute* is equal to SQL_DESC_FETCH_BOOKMARK_PTR, the Driver Manager returns the appropriate pointer that it had cached during a call to **SQLSetStmtAttr**.
6. If *Attribute* is equal to SQL_ATTR_ROW_STATUS_PTR, the Driver Manager returns the appropriate pointer that it had cached during a call to **SQLSetStmtAttr**.
7. The Driver Manager calls **SQLGetStmtOption** as follows:

   ```
   SQLGetStmtOption (hstmt, fOption, pvParam);
   ```

   where *hstmt*, *fOption*, and *pvParam* will be set to the values of *StatementHandle*, *Attribute*, and *ValuePtr*, respectively. Note that the *BufferLength* and *StringLengthPtr* are ignored.

SQLSetConnectAttr

The Driver Manager maps this to **SQLSetConnectOption**. The following call to **SQLSetConnectAttr**:

```
SQLSetConnectAttr(ConnectionHandle, Attribute, ValuePtr, StringLength);
```

will result in the following sequence of steps:

1. If *Attribute* is not a driver-defined connection or statement attribute, and is not an attribute defined in ODBC 2.*x*, then the Driver Manager returns SQL_ERROR with SQLSTATE HY092 (Invalid attribute/option identifier). No further rules in this section apply.
2. If *Attribute* is equal to SQL_ATTR_AUTO_IPD, then the Driver Manager returns SQL_ERROR with SQLSTATE HY092 (Invalid attribute/option identifier).
3. The Driver Manager performs necessary checks to see if SQLSTATE 08003 (Connection not open) or SQLSTATE HY010 (Function sequence error) need to be raised. If one of these errors needs to be raised, the Driver Manager returns SQL_ERROR and posts the appropriate error message. No further rules of this section apply.
4. The Driver Manager calls **SQLSetConnectOption** as follows:

   ```
   SQLSetConnectOption (hdbc, fOption, vParam);
   ```

   where *hdbc*, *fOption*, and *vParam* will be set to the values of *ConnectionHandle*, *Attribute*, and *ValuePtr*, respectively. Note that *StringLengthPtr* is ignored.

Note The ability to set statement attributes on the connection level has been deprecated. Statement attributes should never be set on the connection level by an ODBC 3.0 application.

SQLSetStmtAttr

The Driver Manager maps this to **SQLSetStmtOption**. The following call to **SQLSetStmtAttr**:

```
SQLSetStmtAttr(StatementHandle, Attribute, ValuePtr, StringLength);
```

will result in the following sequence of steps:

1. If *Attribute* is not a driver-defined connection or statement attribute, and is not an attribute defined in ODBC 2.*x*, then the Driver Manager returns SQL_ERROR with SQLSTATE HY092 (Invalid attribute/option identifier). No further rules in this section apply.
2. If *Attribute* is one of the following:

   SQL_ATTR_APP_ROW_DESC, SQL_ATTR_APP_PARAM_DESC, SQL_ATTR_AUTO_IPD, SQL_ATTR_ROW_BIND_TYPE. SQL_ATTR_IMP_ROW_DESC, SQL_ATTR_IMP_PARAM_DESC, SQL_ATTR_METADATA_ID, SQL_ATTR_PARAM_BIND_TYPE, SQL_ATTR_PREDICATE_PTR, SQL_ATTR_PREDICATE_OCTET_LENGTH_PTR, SQL_ATTR_PARAM_BIND_OFFSET_PTR, SQL_ATTR_ROW_BIND_OFFSET_PTR, SQL_ATTR_ROW_OPERATION_PTR, SQL_ATTR_PARAM_OPERATION_PTR.

   Then the Driver Manager returns SQL_ERROR with SQLSTATE HY092 (Invalid attribute/option identifier). No further rules of this section apply.
3. The Driver Manager performs the necessary checks to see if SQLSTATE HY010 (Function sequence error) need to be raised. If so, the Driver Manager returns SQL_ERROR and SQLSTATE HY010 (Function sequence error). No further rules of this section apply.
4. If *Attribute* is equal to SQL_ATTR_PARAMSET_SIZE or SQL_ATTR_PARAMS_PROCESSED_PTR, then see the section "Mappings for Handling Parameter Arrays" later in this topic. No further rules of this section apply.
5. If *Attribute* is equal to SQL_ATTR_ROWS_FETCHED_PTR, then the Driver Manager caches the pointer value, for later use with **SQLFetchScroll**.
6. If *Attribute* is equal to SQL_ATTR_ROW_STATUS_PTR, then the Driver Manager caches the pointer value, for later use with **SQLFetchScroll** or **SQLSetPos**. No further rules of this section apply.

7. If *Attribute* is equal to SQL_ATTR_FETCH_BOOKMARK_PTR, the Driver Manager caches *ValuePtr* and it will use the cached value later in a call to **SQLFetchScroll**. No further rules of this section apply.
8. The Driver Manager calls **SQLSetStmtOption** as follows:

   ```
   SQLSetStmtOption (hstmt, fOption, vParam);
   ```

   where *hstmt*, *fOption*, and *vParam* will be set to the values of *StatementHandle*, *Attribute*, and *ValuePtr*, respectively. Note that the *StringLength* argument is ignored.

   If an ODBC 2.*x* driver supports character-string, driver-specific statement options, an ODBC 3.0 application should call **SQLSetStmtOption** to set those options.

Mappings For Handling Parameter Arrays

When the application calls:

```
SQLSetStmtAttr (StatementHandle, SQL_ATTR_PARAMSET_SIZE, Size, StringLength);
```

the Driver Manager calls:

```
SQLParamOptions (StatementHandle, Size, &RowCount);
```

The Driver Manager later returns a pointer to this variable when the application calls **SQLGetStmtAttr** to retrieve SQL_ATTR_PARAMS_PROCESSED_PTR. Note that the Driver Manager cannot change this internal variable until the statement handle is returned to the prepared or allocated state.

An ODBC 3.0 application can call **SQLGetStmtAttr** to obtain the value of SQL_ATTR_PARAMS_PROCESSED_PTR even though it has not explicitly set the SQL_DESC_ARRAY_SIZE field in the APD. This situation could arise, for example, if the application has a generic routine that checks for the current "row" of parameters being processed when **SQLExecute** returns SQL_NEED_DATA. This routine is invoked regardless of whether the SQL_DESC_ARRAY_SIZE is 1 or is greater than 1. To account for this, the Driver Manager will need to define this internal variable regardless of whether or not the application has called **SQLSetStmtAttr** to set the SQL_DESC_ARRAY_SIZE field in APD. If SQL_DESC_ARRAY_SIZE has not been set, the Driver Manager has to make sure that this variable contains the value 1 prior to returning from **SQLExecDirect** or **SQLExecute**.

Error Handling

In ODBC 3.0, calling **SQLFetch** or **SQLFetchScroll** populates the SQL_DESC_ARRAY_STATUS_PTR in the IRD, and the SQL_DIAG_ROW_NUMBER field of a given diagnostic record contains the number of the row in the rowset that this record pertains to. Using this, the application can correlate an error message with a given row position.

An ODBC 2.*x* driver will be unable to provide this functionality. However, it will provide error demarcation with SQLSTATE 01S01 (Error in row). An ODBC 3.0 application that is using **SQLFetch** or **SQLFetchScroll** while going against an ODBC

2.*x* driver needs to be aware of this fact. Note also that such an application will be unable to call **SQLGetDiagField** to actually get the SQL_DIAG_ROW_NUMBER field anyway. An ODBC 3.0 application working with an ODBC 2.*x* driver will only be able to call **SQLGetDiagField** with a *DiagIdentifier* argument of SQL_DIAG_MESSAGE_TEXT, SQL_DIAG_NATIVE, SQL_DIAG_RETURNCODE, or SQL_DIAG_SQLSTATE. The ODBC 3.0 Driver Manager maintains the diagnostic data structure when working with an ODBC 2.*x* driver, but the ODBC 2.*x* driver only returns these four fields.

When an ODBC 2.*x* application is working with an ODBC 2.*x* driver, if an operation can cause multiple errors to be returned by the Driver Manager, different errors may be returned by the ODBC 3.0 Driver Manager than by the ODBC 2.*x* Driver Manager.

Mappings For Bookmark Operations

The ODBC 3.0 Driver Manager performs the following mappings when an ODBC 3.0 application working with an ODBC 2.*x* driver performs bookmark operations.

SQLBindCol

When an ODBC 3.0 application working with an ODBC 2.*x* driver calls **SQLBindCol** to bind to column 0 with *fCType* equal to SQL_C_VARBOOKMARK, the ODBC 3.0 Driver Manager checks to see whether the *BufferLength* argument is less than 4, or greater than 4, and if so, returns SQLSTATE HY090 (Invalid string or buffer length). If the *BufferLength* argument is equal to 4, the Driver Manager calls **SQLBindCol** in the driver, after replacing *fCType* with SQL_C_BOOKMARK.

SQLColAttribute

When an ODBC 3.0 application working with an ODBC 2.*x* driver calls **SQLColAttribute** with the *ColumnNumber* argument set to 0, the Driver Manager returns the following *FieldIdentifier* values:

FieldIdentifier	Value
SQL_DESC_AUTO_UNIQUE_VALUE	SQL_FALSE
SQL_DESC_CASE_SENSITIVE	SQL_FALSE
SQL_DESC_CATALOG_NAME	"" (empty string)
SQL_DESC_CONCISE_TYPE	SQL_BINARY
SQL_DESC_COUNT	The same value returned by **SQLNumResultCols**
SQL_DESC_DATETIME_INTERVAL_CODE	0
SQL_DESC_DISPLAY_SIZE	8
SQL_DESC_FIXED_PREC_SCALE	SQL_FALSE

FieldIdentifier	Value
SQL_DESC_LABEL	"" (empty string)
SQL_DESC_LENGTH	0
SQL_DESC_LITERAL_PREFIX	"" (empty string)
SQL_DESC_LITERAL_SUFFIX	"" (empty string)
SQL_DESC_LOCAL_TYPE_NAME	"" (empty string)
SQL_DESC_NAME	"" (empty string)
SQL_DESC_NULLABLE	SQL_NO_NULLS
SQL_DESC_OCTET_LENGTH	4
SQL_DESC_PRECISION	4
SQL_DESC_SCALE	0
SQL_DESC_SCHEMA_NAME	"" (empty string)
SQL_DESC_SEARCHABLE	SQL_PRED_NONE
SQL_DESC_TABLE_NAME	"" (empty string)
SQL_DESC_TYPE	SQL_BINARY
SQL_DESC_TYPE_NAME	"" (empty string)
SQL_DESC_UNNAMED	SQL_UNNAMED
SQL_DESC_UNSIGNED	SQL_FALSE
SQL_DESC_UPDATEABLE	SQL_ATTR_READ_ONLY

SQLDescribeCol

When an ODBC 3.0 application working with an ODBC 2.*x* driver calls **SQLDescribeCol** with the *ColumnNumber* argument set to 0, the Driver Manager returns the following values:

Buffer	Value
ColumnName	"" (empty string)
*NameLengthPtr	0
*DataTypePtr	SQL_BINARY
*ColumnSizePtr	4
*DecimalDigitsPtr	0
*NullablePtr	SQL_NO_NULLS

SQLGetData

When an ODBC 3.0 application working with an ODBC 2.*x* driver makes the following call to **SQLGetData** to retrieve a bookmark:

```
SQLGetData(StatementHandle, 0, SQL_C_VARBOOKMARK, TargetValuePtr, BufferLength,
StrLen_or_IndPtr)
```

the call is mapped to **SQLGetStmtOption** with an *fOption* of SQL_GET_BOOKMARK, as follows:

```
SQLGetStmtOption(hstmt, SQL_GET_BOOKMARK, TargetValuePtr)
```

where *hstmt* and *pvParam* are set to the values in *StatementHandle* and *TargetValuePtr*, respectively. The bookmark is returned in the buffer pointed to by the *pvParam* (*TargetValuePtr*) argument. The value in the buffer pointed to by the *StrLen_or_IndPtr* argument in the call to **SQLGetData** is set to 4.

This mapping is necessary to account for the case in which **SQLFetch** was called prior to the call to **SQLGetData**, and the ODBC 2.*x* driver did not support **SQLExtendedFetch**. In this case, **SQLFetch** would be passed through to the ODBC 2.*x* driver, in which case bookmark retrieval is not supported.

SQLGetData cannot be called multiple times in an ODBC 2.*x* driver to retrieve a bookmark in parts, so calling **SQLGetData** with the *BufferLength* argument set to a value less than 4 and the *ColumnNumber* argument set to 0 will return SQLSTATE HY090 (Invalid string or buffer length). **SQLGetData** can, however, be called multiple times to retrieve the same bookmark.

SQLSetStmtAttr

When an ODBC 3.0 application working with an ODBC 2.*x* driver calls **SQLSetStmtAttr** to set the SQL_ATTR_USE_BOOKMARKS attribute to SQL_UB_VARIABLE, the Driver Manager sets the attribute to SQL_UB_ON in the underlying ODBC 2.*x* driver.

Calling SQLCloseCursor

Because **SQLCloseCursor** is almost the same as **SQLFreeStmt** with SQL_CLOSE, the Driver Manager does not map this function. Replacement functions are mapped so that existing ODBC 2.*x* applications can easily move to ODBC 3.0 by using the new functions. Such a move makes it easier for such applications to begin using new ODBC 3.0 functionality inside of conditional code in a modular fashion. **SQLCloseCursor** does not represent any new functionality. An application does not gain any advantage by moving to **SQLCloseCursor** from **SQLFreeStmt** with SQL_CLOSE.

Calling SQLGetDiagField

When an ODBC 3.0 application calls **SQLGetDiagField** in an ODBC 2.*x* driver, the driver will return SQL_SUCCESS and the appropriate information in **DiagInfoPtr* if the *DiagIdentifier* argument is SQL_DIAG_CLASS_ORIGIN,

SQL_DIAG_CLASS_SUBCLASS_ORIGIN, SQL_DIAG_CONNECTION_NAME, SQL_DIAG_MESSAGE_TEXT, SQL_DIAG_NATIVE, SQL_DIAG_NUMBER, SQL_DIAG_RETURNCODE, SQL_DIAG_SERVER_NAME, or SQL_DIAG_SQLSTATE. All other diagnostic fields will return SQL_ERROR.

Calling SQLSetPos

In ODBC 2.*x*, the pointer to the row status array was an argument to **SQLExtendedFetch**. The row status array was later updated by a call to **SQLSetPos**. Some drivers have relied on the fact that this array does not change between **SQLExtendedFetch** and **SQLSetPos**. In ODBC 3.0, the pointer to the status array is a descriptor field and so the application can easily change it to point to a different array. This can be a problem when an ODBC 3.0 application is working with an ODBC 2.*x* driver, but is calling **SQLSetStmtAttr** to set the array status pointer and is calling **SQLFetchScroll** to fetch data. The Driver Manager maps it as a sequence of calls to **SQLExtendedFetch**. In the following code, an error would normally be raised when the Driver Manager maps the second **SQLSetStmtAttr** call when working with an ODBC 2.*x* driver:

```
SQLSetStmtAttr(hstmt, SQL_ATTR_ROW_STATUS_PTR, rgfRowStatus, 0);
SQLFetchScroll(hstmt, fFetchType, iRow);
SQLSetStmtAttr(hstmt, SQL_ATTR_ROW_STATUS_PTR, rgfRowStat1, 0);
SQLSetPos(hstmt, iRow, fOption, fLock);
```

The error would be raised if there were no way to change the row status pointer in ODBC 2.*x* between calls to **SQLExtendedFetch**. Instead, the Driver Manager performs the following when working with an ODBC 2.*x* driver:

1. Initializes an internal Driver Manager flag *fSetPosError* to TRUE.
2. When an application calls **SQLFetchScroll**, the Driver Manager sets *fSetPosError* to FALSE.
3. When the application calls **SQLSetStmtAttr** to set SQL_ATTR_ROW_STATUS_PTR, the Driver Manager sets *fSetPosError* equal to TRUE.
4. When the application calls **SQLSetPos**, with *fSetPosError* equal to TRUE, the Driver Manager raises SQL_ERROR with SQLSTATE HY011 (Attribute cannot be set now) to indicate that the application attempted to call **SQLSetPos** after changing the row status pointer, but prior to calling **SQLFetchScroll**.

Cursor Library Operations

If an application working with an ODBC 2.*x* driver makes calls to the ODBC 3.0 cursor library, the application may be able to use ODBC 3.0 features that are not supported by the ODBC 2.*x* driver. An application writer should be careful how these features are used, however. Use of the ODBC 3.0 cursor library does not make an ODBC 2.*x* driver into an ODBC 3.0 driver.

Mapping the Cursor Attributes1 Information Types

When an ODBC 3.0 application calls **SQLGetInfo** in an ODBC 2.*x* driver with the SQL_XXXX_CURSOR_ATTRIBUTES1 information type (for dynamic, forward-only, keyset-driver, or static cursors), the setting of the bits returned by Driver Manager depends upon what the ODBC 2.*x* driver returns for the corresponding ODBC 2.*x* information types. The bits are set as follows:

Bit in SQL_XXXX_ CURSOR_ ATTRIBUTES1	Cursor type	ODBC 2.*x* information type
SQL_CA1_NEXT	All	SQL_FETCH_ DIRECTION
SQL_CA1_ ABSOLUTE SQL_CA1_ RELATIVE SQL_CA1_ BOOKMARK	Dynamic, keyset-driver, static	SQL_FETCH_ DIRECTION
SQL_CA1_LOCK_ NO_CHANGE SQL_CA1_LOCK_ UNLOCK SQL_CA1_LOCK_ EXCLUSIVE	Dynamic, keyset-driver, static	SQL_LOCK_TYPES
SQL_CA1_ POSITIONED_ UPDATE SQL_CA1_ POSITIONED_ DELETE SQL_CA1_SELECT_ FOR_UPDATE	All	SQL_POSITIONED_STATE MENTS
SQL_CA1_POS_ POSITION SQL_CA1_POS_ DELETE SQL_CA1_POS_ REFRESH SQL_CA1_POS_ BULK_ADD	Dynamic, keyset-driver, static	SQL_POS_ OPERATIONS

SQL_NO_DATA

When an ODBC 3.0 application calls **SQLExecDirect**, **SQLExecute**, or **SQLParamData** in an ODBC 2.*x* driver to execute a searched update or delete statement that does not affect any rows at the data source, the driver should return SQL_SUCCESS, not SQL_NO_DATA. When an ODBC 2.*x* or ODBC 3.0 application working with an ODBC 3.0 driver calls **SQLExecDirect**, **SQLExecute**, or **SQLParamData** with the same result, the ODBC 3.0 driver should return SQL_NO_DATA.

Writing ODBC 3.0 Drivers

The following table shows function support in an ODBC 3.0 driver and an ODBC application, and the mapping performed by the Driver Manager when the functions are called against an ODBC 3.0 driver.

Function	Supported by an ODBC 3.0 driver?	Supported by an ODBC 3.0 application?	Mapped/supported by the ODBC 3.0 Driver Manager to an ODBC 3.0 driver?
SQLAllocConnect	No	No [1]	Yes
SQLAllocEnv	No	No [1]	Yes
SQLAllocHandle	Yes	Yes	No
SQLAllocStmt	No	No [1]	Yes
SQLBindCol	Yes	Yes	No
SQLBindParam	No	Yes [2]	Yes
SQLBindParameter	Yes	Yes	No
SQLBrowseConnect	Yes	Yes	No
SQLCancel	Yes	Yes	No
SQLCloseCursor	Yes	Yes	No
SQLColAttribute	Yes	Yes	No
SQLColAttributes	No [3]	No	Yes
SQLColumnPrivileges	Yes	Yes	No
SQLColumns	Yes	Yes	No
SQLConnect	Yes	Yes	No
SQLCopyDesc	Yes	Yes	Yes [4]
SQLDataSources	No	Yes	Yes
SQLDescribeCol	Yes	Yes	No
SQLDescribeParam	Yes	Yes	No
SQLDisconnect	Yes	Yes	No

Function	Supported by an ODBC 3.0 driver?	Supported by an ODBC 3.0 application?	Mapped/supported by the ODBC 3.0 Driver Manager to an ODBC 3.0 driver?
SQLDriverConnect	Yes	Yes	No
SQLDrivers	No	Yes	Yes
SQLEndTran	Yes	Yes	No
SQLError	No	No [1]	Yes
SQLExecDirect	Yes	Yes	No
SQLExecute	Yes	Yes	No
SQLExtendedFetch	Yes	No	No
SQLFetch	Yes	Yes	No
SQLFetchScroll	Yes	Yes	No
SQLForeignKeys	Yes	Yes	No
SQLFreeConnect	No	Yes [1]	Yes
SQLFreeEnv	No	Yes [1]	Yes
SQLFreeHandle	Yes	Yes	No
SQLFreeStmt	Yes	Yes	No
SQLGetConnectAttr	Yes	Yes	No
SQLGetConnectOption	No [5]	No [1]	Yes
SQLGetCursorName	Yes	Yes	No
SQLGetData	Yes	Yes	No
SQLGetDescField	Yes	Yes	No
SQLGetDescRec	Yes	Yes	No
SQLGetDiagField	Yes	Yes	No
SQLGetDiagRec	Yes	Yes	No
SQLGetEnvAttr	Yes	Yes	No
SQLGetFunctions	No [6]	Yes	Yes
SQLGetInfo	Yes	Yes	No
SQLGetStmtAttr	Yes	Yes	No
SQLGetStmtOption	No [5]	No [1]	Yes
SQLGetTypeInfo	Yes	Yes	No
SQLMoreResults	Yes	Yes	No
SQLNativeSql	Yes	Yes	No
SQLNumParams	Yes	Yes	No
SQLNumResultCols	Yes	Yes	No
SQLParamData	Yes	Yes	No

Function	Supported by an ODBC 3.0 driver?	Supported by an ODBC 3.0 application?	Mapped/supported by the ODBC 3.0 Driver Manager to an ODBC 3.0 driver?
SQLParamOptions	No	No	Yes
SQLPrepare	Yes	Yes	No
SQLPrimaryKeys	Yes	Yes	No
SQLProcedureColumns	Yes	Yes	No
SQLProcedures	Yes	Yes	No
SQLPutData	Yes	Yes	No
SQLRowCount	Yes	Yes	No
SQLSetConnectAttr	Yes	Yes	No
SQLSetConnectOption	No [5]	No [1]	Yes
SQLSetCursorName	Yes	Yes	No
SQLSetDescField	Yes	Yes	No
SQLSetDescRec	Yes	Yes	No
SQLSetEnvAttr	Yes	Yes	No
SQLSetPos	Yes	Yes	No
SQLSetParam	No	No	Yes
SQLSetScrollOption	Yes	Yes	No
SQLSetStmtAttr	Yes	Yes	No
SQLSetStmtOption	No [5]	No [1]	Yes
SQLSpecialColumns	Yes	Yes	No
SQLStatistics	Yes	Yes	No
SQLTablePrivileges	Yes	Yes	No
SQLTables	Yes	Yes	No
SQLTransact	No	No [1]	Yes

1 This function is deprecated in ODBC 3.0. ODBC 3.0 applications should not use this function. However, an X/Open or ISO CLI–compliant application can call this function.

2 ODBC 3.0 applications should use **SQLBindParameter** instead of **SQLBindParam**. However, an X/Open or ISO CLI–compliant application can call this function.

3 Driver writers note that the ODBC 2.*x* column attributes SQL_COLUMN_PRECISION, SQL_COLUMN_SCALE, and SQL_COLUMN_LENGTH must be supported with **SQLColAttribute**.

4 Note that **SQLCopyDesc** is partially implemented by the Driver Manager when a descriptor is being copied across connections that belong to different drivers. Drivers are required to support **SQLCopyDesc** across two of their own connections. Functions such as **SQLDrivers**, which are implemented solely by the Driver Manager, do not show up on this list.

5 Under certain circumstances, drivers may need to support this function. See the reference manual page for this function for more information.

6 The driver may choose to support **SQLGetFunctions** if the functions that it supports varies from connection to connection.

ODBC in Windows

The following items apply only to ODBC running in Windows NT and Windows 95 operating systems.

Standards-Compliant Applications and Drivers

A standards-compliant application or driver is one that conforms to the X/Open CAE Specification "Data Management: SQL Call-Level Interface (CLI)," and the ISO/IEC 9075-3:1995 (E) Call-Level Interface (SQL/CLI).

ODBC 3.0 guarantees that:

- An application written to the X/Open and ISO CLI specifications will work with an ODBC 3.0 driver or a standards-compliant driver when it is compiled with the ODBC 3.0 header files and linked with ODBC 3.0 libraries, and when it gains access to the driver through the ODBC 3.0 Driver Manager.
- A driver written to the X/Open and ISO CLI specifications will work with an ODBC 3.0 application or a standards-compliant application when it is compiled with the ODBC 3.0 header files and linked with ODBC 3.0 libraries, and when the application gains access to the driver through the ODBC 3.0 Driver Manager.

Standards-compliant applications and drivers are compiled with the ODBC_STD compile flag.

Standards-compliant applications exhibit the following behavior:

- If a standards-compliant application calls **SQLAllocEnv** (which may occur because **SQLAllocEnv** is a valid function in the X/Open and ISO CLI), the call is mapped to **SQLAllocHandleStd** at compile time. As a result, at run time, the application calls **SQLAllocHandleStd**. During the course of processing this call, the Driver Manager sets the SQL_ATTR_ODBC_VERSION environment attribute to SQL_OV_ODBC3. A call to **SQLAllocHandleStd** is equivalent to a call to **SQLAllocHandle** with a *HandleType* of SQL_HANDLE_ENV and a call to **SQLSetEnvAttr** to set SQL_ATTR_ODBC_VERSION to SQL_OV_ODBC3.
- If a standards-compliant application calls **SQLBindParam** (which may occur because **SQLBindParam** is a valid function in the X/Open and ISO CLI), the ODBC 3.0 Driver Manager maps the call to the equivalent call in **SQLBindParameter** (see "SQLBindParam Mapping" in Appendix G, "Driver Guidelines for Backward Compatibility").

- To align with the ISO CLI, the ODBC 3.0 header files contain aliases for information types used in calls to **SQLGetInfo**. A standards-compliant application can used these aliases instead of the ODBC 3.0 information types. For more information, see the next section, "Header Files."
- A standards-compliant application must verify that all features it supports are supported in the driver it will work with. Setting the SQL_ATTR_CURSOR_SCROLLABLE statement attribute to SQL_SCROLLABLE, and setting the SQL_ATTR_CURSOR_SENSITIVITY statement attribute to SQL_INSENSITIVE or SQL_SENSITIVE are capabilities that are available as optional features in the standards, but are not included in the ODBC 3.0 Core level, so may not be supported by all ODBC 3.0 drivers. If a standards-compliant application uses these capabilities, it should verify that the driver that it will work with supports them.

Header Files

The SQL.H header file contains prototypes for the functions and features in the Core ODBC Interface conformance level. The SQLEXT.H header file contains prototypes for the functions and features in the Level 1 and Level 2 API conformance levels. The SQLTYPES.H header file contains type definitions and indicators for the SQL data types.

The header files all contain a **#define**, ODBCVER, that an application or driver can set to be compiled for different versions of ODBC.

To align with the ISO CLI and X/Open CLI, the header files contain aliases for the following information types used in calls to **SQLGetInfo**. In the following table, the column "ODBC name" indicates the ODBC name for the information type in Chapter 21, "ODBC API Reference." The column "Alias in header file" indicates the name that is used in the ISO CLI and the X/Open CLI. The actual numeric value of these manifest names is the same in both ODBC and the standard CLIs. These aliases enable a standards-compliant application or driver to compile with the ODBC 3.0 header files.

These alias include expansions of abbreviations in the ODBC names, so that the names are more understandable. "MAX" is expanded to "MAXIMUM", "LEN" to "LENGTH", "MULT" to "MULTIPLE", "OJ" to "OUTER_JOIN", and "TXN" to "TRANSACTION."

ODBC name	Alias in header file
SQL_MAX_CATALOG_NAME_LEN	SQL_MAXIMUM_CATALOG_NAME_LENGTH
SQL_MAX_COLUMN_NAME_LEN	SQL_MAXIMUM_COLUMN_NAME_LENGTH
SQL_MAX_COLUMNS_IN_GROUP_BY	SQL_MAXIMUM_COLUMNS_IN_GROUP_BY
SQL_MAX_COLUMNS_IN_ORDER_BY	SQL_MAXIMUM_COLUMNS_IN_ORDER_BY
SQL_MAX_COLUMNS_IN_SELECT	SQL_MAXIMUM_COLUMNS_IN_SELECT
SQL_MAX_COLUMNS_IN_TABLE	SQL_MAXIMUM_COLUMNS_IN_TABLE
SQL_MAX_CONCURRENT_ACTIVITIES	SQL_MAXIMUM_CONCURRENT_ACTIVITIES
SQL_MAX_CURSOR_NAME_LEN	SQL_MAXIMUM_CURSOR_NAME_LENGTH
SQL_MAX_DRIVER_CONNECTIONS	SQL_MAXIMUM_DRIVER_CONNECTIONS
SQL_MAX_IDENTIFIER_LEN	SQL_MAXIMUM_IDENTIFIER_LENGTH
SQL_MAX_SCHEMA_NAME_LEN	SQL_MAXIMUM_SCHEMA_NAME_LENGTH
SQL_MAX_STATEMENT_LEN	SQL_MAXIMUM_STATEMENT_LENGTH
SQL_MAX_TABLE_NAME_LEN	SQL_MAXIMUM_TABLE_NAME_LENGTH
SQL_MAX_TABLES_IN_SELECT	SQL_MAXIMUM_TABLES_IN_SELECT
SQL_MAX_USER_NAME_LEN	SQL_MAXIMUM_USER_NAME_LENGTH
SQL_MULT_RESULT_SETS	SQL_MULTIPLE_RESULT_SETS
SQL_OJ_CAPABILITIES	SQL_OUTER_JOIN_CAPABILITIES
SQL_TXN_CAPABLE	SQL_TRANSACTION_CAPABLE
SQL_TXN_ISOLATION_OPTION	SQL_TRANSACTION_ISOLATION_OPTION

CString Class

Because objects of the CString class in Microsoft Visual C++ are signed and string arguments in ODBC functions are unsigned, applications that pass CString objects to ODBC functions without casting them will receive compiler warnings.

Creating and Terminating Threads

Multithread applications that use ODBC should call the Microsoft Visual C++ Run-Time Library functions **_beginthread** and **_endthread** (or **_beginthreadex** and **_endthreadex**) to create and terminate threads that call the ODBC Driver Manager. If applications call the Windows NT functions **CreateThread** and **EndThread** instead, memory leaks will occur because the Driver Manager and some ODBC drivers call C run-time functions that will not work on a thread created by calling **CreateThread**. For more information, see the Microsoft Windows documentation.

PART 3

Installing and Configuring ODBC Software

CHAPTER 18

Installing ODBC Components

This chapter describes how ODBC components are installed and removed. Because driver developers always install an ODBC component (their driver), they need to read this chapter. Application developers need to read this chapter only if they will ship ODBC components with their application. ODBC components are defined to be the Driver Manager, drivers, translators, the installer DLL, the cursor library, and any related files. For the purposes of this chapter, ODBC applications are not considered to be ODBC components.

Note This chapter is specific to Windows platforms. How ODBC components are installed on other platforms is platform-specific.

ODBC components are installed and removed on a component-by-component basis, not a file-by-file basis. For example, if a translator consists of the translator itself and a number of data files, these files are installed and removed as a group; they must not be installed and removed on a file-by-file basis. The reason for this is to make sure that only complete components exist on the system.

For purposes of installing and removing components, the following are defined to be ODBC components:

- **Core components**. The Driver Manager, cursor library, installer DLL, and any other related files make up the core components and must be installed and removed as a group.
- **Drivers**. Each driver is a separate component.
- **Translators**. Each translator is a separate component.

Installation Components

The installation process starts when the user runs the setup program. The setup program works in conjunction with the *installer DLL* and a *driver setup DLL* for each driver. Both the setup program and the installer DLL use the arguments in the **SQLInstallDriverEx** and **SQLInstallTranslatorEx** functions to determine which files to copy or delete for each component. The following diagram shows the relationship between these installation components

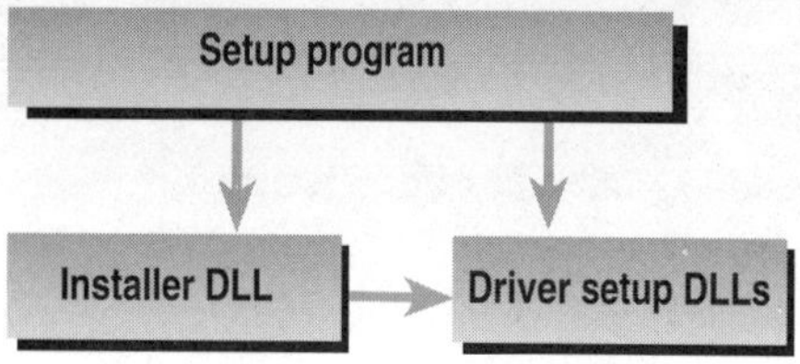

Figure 18.1 Installation components

Important The ODBC.INF file that was used in ODBC 2.*x* to describe the files required by each ODBC component is not used in ODBC 3.0. Drivers that ship ODBC 3.0 components do not need to create an ODBC.INF file. The removal of **SQLInstallDriver** and **SQLInstallODBC**, and the deprecation of **SQLInstallTranslator**, have rendered ODBC.INF unnecessary. The driver information that used to be in the Driver Keyword sections of ODBC.INF is now provided in the *lpszDriver* argument in **SQLInstallDriverEx**. The translator information that used to be in the [ODBC Translator] and Translator Specification sections of ODBC.INF is now provided in the *lpszTranslator* argument of **SQLInstallTranslatorEx**. These changes allow the ODBC Installer to be more portable across platforms.

Setup Program

The setup program is what the user runs to start the setup process. It is written by the application or driver developer. In addition to installing ODBC components, it can install other software. For example, application developers might use the same setup program to install both ODBC components and their application.

Developers can write the setup program from scratch, using the Windows SDK setup utilities or setup software from other vendors. This gives them complete control over the setup program's look and feel. The setup program can be written to install additional software, such as an ODBC application. For more information on the Windows SDK setup utilities, see the Windows SDK documentation.

How much of the installation is actually done by the setup program depends on what functions it calls in the installer DLL. The installer DLL contains functions to install ODBC components in the following ways:

- **Install individual ODBC components**. The setup program calls **SQLInstallDriverManager**, **SQLInstallDriverEx**, or **SQLInstallTranslatorEx** in the installer DLL to retrieve the path of the directory in which the component is to be installed and to add information about the component to the registry. Note that these functions do not actually copy files; the setup program does this using the information in the arguments of these functions.

The installer DLL contains functions to remove ODBC components in the following ways:

- **Remove individual ODBC components**. The setup program calls **SQLRemoveDriverManager**, **SQLRemoveDriver**, or **SQLRemoveTranslator** in the installer DLL to decrement a component's usage count in the registry and, if the component's new usage count falls to 0, remove all information about the component from the registry. Note that these functions do not actually remove the files for the component; the setup program does this if the new usage count falls to 0.

Installer DLL

The installer DLL contains functions to install and remove ODBC components, maintain registry information about those components, and maintain registry information about data sources. It is written by Microsoft and can be redistributed by users of the Microsoft ODBC SDK. For a complete description of the functions in the installer DLL, see Chapter 23, "Installer DLL API Reference."

Driver Setup DLL

The driver setup DLL contains the **ConfigDriver** and **ConfigDSN** functions. **ConfigDriver** performs driver-specific installation tasks, such as entering driver-specific information into the registry. **ConfigDSN** maintains driver-specific information about data sources in the registry. For a complete description of these functions, see Chapter 22, "Setup DLL API Reference."

The driver setup DLL is written by the driver developer. It can be part of the driver DLL or a separate DLL.

Usage Counting

Two types of usage counts are maintained in the registry for each component: a component usage count and one or more optional file usage counts. The component usage count helps the installer DLL maintain registry entries. It is stored in the UsageCount value under the ODBC Core, driver, and translator subkeys. For the format of the UsageCount value and more information about these subkeys, see "Registry Entries for ODBC Components" later in this chapter.

When a component is first installed, the installer DLL creates a subkey for it and sets the data for the UsageCount value in that subkey to 1. When the component is installed again, the installer DLL increments the usage count. When the component is removed, the installer DLL decrements the usage count. If the usage count falls to 0, the installer DLL removes the subkey for the component.

Caution An application should not physically remove Driver Manager files when the component usage count and the file usage count reach zero.

File usage counts help determine when a file must actually be copied or deleted as opposed to incrementing or decrementing the usage count. This is important because ODBC components—and therefore the files in ODBC components—are shared and can be installed or removed by a variety of applications. The application can physically delete driver and translator files if the component usage count and the file usage count reaches zero. Driver Manager files should not, however, be physically deleted when both the component usage count and the file usage count have reached zero, because these files may be used by other applications that have not incremented the file usage count.

Note File usage counts are optional in Windows NT and Windows 95.

File usage counts are maintained by the setup program after it calls **SQLInstallDriverManager**, **SQLInstallDriverEx**, **SQLInstallTranslatorEx**, **SQLRemoveDriverManager**, **SQLRemoveDriver**, or **SQLRemoveTranslator**.

When a component is first installed, the setup program or installer DLL creates a value under the following key for each file in that component that is not already on the system:

```
HKEY_LOCAL_MACHINE
    SOFTWARE
        Microsoft
            Windows
                CurrentVersion
                    SharedDlls
```

It sets the data for those values to 1 and copies the file to the system. When the component is installed again, the setup program or installer DLL increments the usage counts. When the component is removed, the setup program or installer DLL decrements the usage counts. If any usage count falls to 0, the setup program or installer DLL removes the value for the file, and if the component is a driver or a translator, deletes the file. Driver Manager files should not be deleted.

The format of the file usage count value is:

Name	Data type	Data
full-path	REG_DWORD	*count*

For example, suppose a driver for Informix uses the INFRMX32.DLL and INFRMX32.HLP files and that this driver has been installed twice. The values under the SharedDlls subkey for the Informix driver would be:

```
C:\WINDOWS\SYSTEM32\INFRMX32.DLL : REG_DWORD : 0x2
C:\WINDOWS\SYSTEM32\INFRMX32.HLP : REG_DWORD : 0x2
```

Redistributable Files

A number of files that are shipped with the ODBC SDK may be redistributed by application and driver developers. All developers who ship ODBC drivers must redistribute the following files:

ODBC component	File	Core Component?
Administrator	ODBCAD32.EXE	No
Code page	12520437.CPX	No
	12520850.CPX	No
	MSCPXL32.DLL	No
Connection pooling	MTXDM.DLL	No
Driver Manager	DS16GT.DLL	Yes
	DS32GT.DLL	Yes
	ODBC16GT.DLL	Yes
	ODBC32.DLL	Yes
	ODBC32GT.DLL	Yes
	ODBCCP32.CPL	Yes
	ODBCCP32.DLL	Yes
	ODBCCR32.DLL	Yes
	ODBCINT.DLL	Yes
	ODBCTRAC.DLL	Yes
Header files	ODBCINST.H	No
	SQL.H	No
	SQLEXT.H	No
	SQLTYPES.H	No
	SQLUCODE.H	No

ODBC component	File	Core Component?
Help	ODBC.CNT	No
	ODBC.HLP	No
	ODBCINST.CNT	Yes
	ODBCINST.HLP	Yes
	SDKGUIDE.CNT	No
	SDKGUIDE.HLP	No
Support files	MSVCRT40.DLL	No

Registry Entries for ODBC Components

The installer DLL maintains information in the registry about each installed ODBC component. On computers running Windows NT and Windows 95, this information is stored in subkeys under the following key in the registry:

```
HKEY_LOCAL_MACHINE
    SOFTWARE
        ODBC
            ODBCINST.INI
```

Because ODBCINST.INI is a subkey of the HKEY_LOCAL_MACHINE tree, the information about ODBC components is available to all users of the machine. For information on the registry, see the Win32 SDK documentation.

ODBC Core Subkey

The value under the ODBC Core subkey gives the usage count for the core components (Driver Manager, cursor library, installer DLL, and so on). The format of this value is:

Name	Data type	Data
UsageCount	REG_DWORD	*count*

For example, suppose the ODBC Core components have been installed by the setup programs for three different applications and two different drivers. The value under the ODBC Core subkey would be:

```
UsageCount : REG_DWORD : 0x5
```

ODBC Drivers Subkey

The values under the ODBC Drivers subkey list the installed drivers. The format of these values is:

Name	Data type	Data
driver-description	REG_SZ	**Installed**

where *driver-description* is defined by the driver developer. It is usually the name of the DBMS associated with the driver.

For example, suppose drivers have been installed for formatted text files and SQL Server. The values under the ODBC Drivers subkey might be:

```
Text : REG_SZ : Installed
SQL Server : REG_SZ : Installed
```

Driver Specification Subkeys

Each driver listed in the ODBC Drivers subkey has a subkey of its own. This subkey has the same name as the corresponding value under the ODBC Drivers subkey. The values under this subkey list the full paths of the driver and driver setup DLLs, the values of the driver keywords returned by **SQLDrivers**, and the usage count. The formats of the values are:

Name	Data type	Data
APILevel	REG_SZ	**0** | **1** | **2**
ConnectFunctions	REG_SZ	{**Y**|**N**}{**Y**|**N**}{**Y**|**N**}
CreateDSN	REG_SZ	*driver-description*
Driver	REG_SZ	*driver-DLL-path*
DriverODBCVer	REG_SZ	*nn.nn*
FileExtns	REG_SZ	*.*file-extension1*[,*.*file-extension2*]...
FileUsage	REG_SZ	**0** | **1** | **2**
Setup	REG_SZ	*setup-DLL-path*
SQLLevel	REG_SZ	**0** | **1** | **2**
UsageCount	REG_DWORD	*count*

where the use of each keyword is:

Keyword	Usage
APILevel	A number indicating the ODBC interface conformance level supported by the driver: 0 = None 1 = Level 1 supported 2 = Level 2 supported This must be the same as the value returned for the SQL_ODBC_INTERFACE_CONFORMANCE option in **SQLGetInfo**.
CreateDSN	The name of one or more data sources to be created when the driver is installed. The system information must include one data source specification section for each data source listed with the **CreateDSN** keyword. These sections should not include the **Driver** keyword, since this is specified in the driver specification section, but must include enough information for the **ConfigDSN** function in the driver setup DLL to create a data source specification without displaying any dialog boxes. For the format of a data source specification section, see "Data Source Specification Subkeys" in Chapter 19, "Configuring Data Sources."
ConnectFunctions	A three-character string indicating whether the driver supports **SQLConnect**, **SQLDriverConnect**, and **SQLBrowseConnect**. If the driver supports **SQLConnect**, the first character is "Y"; otherwise, it is "N". If the driver supports **SQLDriverConnect**, the second character is "Y"; otherwise, it is "N". If the driver supports **SQLBrowseConnect**, the third character is "Y"; otherwise, it is "N". For example, if a driver supports **SQLConnect** and **SQLDriverConnect**, but not **SQLBrowseConnect**, the three-character string is "YYN".
DriverODBCVer	A character string with the version of ODBC that the driver supports. The version is of the form *nn.nn*, where the first two digits are the major version and the next two digits are the minor version. For the version of ODBC described in this manual, the driver must return "03.00". This must be the same as the value returned for the SQL_DRIVER_ODBC_VER option in **SQLGetInfo**.
FileExtns	For file-based drivers, a comma-separated list of extensions of the files the driver can use. For example, a dBASE driver might specify *.dbf and a formatted text file driver might specify *.txt,*.csv. For an example of how an application might use this information, see the **FileUsage** keyword.

Keyword	Usage
FileUsage	A number indicating how a file-based driver directly treats files in a data source. 0 = The driver is not a file-based driver. For example, an ORACLE driver is a DBMS-based driver. 1 = A file-based driver treats files in a data source as tables. For example, an Xbase driver treats each Xbase file as a table. 2 = A file-based driver treats files in a data source as a catalog. For example, a Microsoft Access driver treats each Microsoft Access file as a complete database. An application might use this to determine how users will select data. For example, Xbase and Paradox users often think of data as stored in files, while ORACLE and Microsoft Access users generally think of data as stored in tables. When a user selects **Open Data File** from the **File** menu, an application could display the **Windows File Open** common dialog box. The list of file types would use the file extensions specified with the **FileExtns** keyword for drivers that specify a **FileUsage** value of 1 and "Y" as the second character of the value of the **ConnectFunctions** keyword. After the user selects a file, the application would call **SQLDriverConnect** with the **DRIVER** keyword, then execute a **SELECT * FROM** ***table-name*** statement. When the user selects **Import Data** from the **File** menu, an application could display a list of descriptions for drivers that specify a **FileUsage** value of 0 or 2 and "Y" as the second character of the value of the **ConnectFunctions** keyword. After the user selects a driver, the application would call **SQLDriverConnect** with the **DRIVER** keyword, then display a custom **Select Table** dialog box.
SQLLevel	A number indicating the SQL-92 grammar supported by the driver: 0 = SQL-92 Entry 1 = FIPS127-2 Transitional 2 = SQL-92 Intermediate 3 = SQL-92 Full This must be the same as the value returned for the SQL_SQL_CONFORMANCE option in **SQLGetInfo**.

For information on usage counts, see "Usage Counting" earlier in this chapter.

For example, suppose a driver for formatted text files has a driver DLL named TEXT.DLL, a separate driver setup DLL named TXTSETUP.DLL, and has been installed three times. If the driver supports the Level 1 API conformance level, supports the Minimum SQL grammar conformance level, treats files as tables, and can use files with the .txt and .csv extensions, the values under the Text subkey might be:

```
APILevel : REG_SZ : 1
ConnectFunctions : REG_SZ : YYN
Driver : REG_SZ : C:\WINDOWS\SYSTEM32\TEXT.DLL
DriverODBCVer : REG_SZ : 03.00.00
FileExtns : REG_SZ : *.txt,*.csv
FileUsage : REG_SZ : 1
Setup : REG_SZ : C:\WINDOWS\SYSTEM32\TXTSETUP.DLL
SQLLevel : REG_SZ : 0
UsageCount : REG_DWORD : 0x3
```

Default Driver Subkey

The Default subkey contains a single value that describes the driver used by the default data source. The format of this value is:

Name	Data type	Data
Driver	REG_SZ	*default-driver-description*

where *default-driver-description* is the same as the name of the value under the ODBC Drivers subkey that describes the driver.

For example, if the default data source uses the SQL Server driver, the value under the Default subkey might be:

```
Driver : REG_SZ : SQL Server
```

Note The default driver contained in the Default subkey can refer to either a default user DSN or a default system DSN. If both a default user DSN and a default system DSN have been created, the default driver is determined by the DSN that was created last, so might not be a valid entry for the DSN that was created first.

ODBC Translators Subkey

The values under the ODBC Translators subkey list the installed translators. The format of these values is:

Name	Data type	Data
translator-desc	REG_SZ	**Installed**

where *translator-desc* is defined by the translator developer.

For example, suppose a user has installed the Microsoft Code Page Translator and a custom ASCII to EBCDIC translator. The values under the ODBC Translators subkey might be:

```
MS Code Page Translator: REG_SZ : Installed
ASCII to EBCDIC: REG_SZ : Installed.
```

Translator Specification Subkeys

Each translator listed in the ODBC Translators subkey has a subkey of its own. This subkey has the same name as the corresponding value under the ODBC Translators subkey. The values under this subkey list the full paths of the translator and translator setup DLLs and the usage count. The formats of the values are:

Name	Data type	Data
Translator	REG_SZ	*translator-DLL-path*
Setup	REG_SZ	*setup-DLL-path*
UsageCount	REG_DWORD	*count*

For example, suppose the Microsoft Code Page Translator has a translation DLL named MSCPXL32.DLL, that the translator setup functions are in the same DLL, and that the translator has been installed three times. The values under the Microsoft Code Page Translator subkey might be:

```
Translator : REG_SZ : C:\WINDOWS\SYSTEM32\MSCPXL32.DLL
Setup : REG_SZ : C:\WINDOWS\SYSTEM32\MSCPXL32.DLL
UsageCount : REG_DWORD : 0x3
```

CHAPTER 19

Configuring Data Sources

Information about data sources is stored in the system registry. Users modify data source information through an administration program. This can be the ODBC Administrator shipped with the Microsoft ODBC SDK, the ODBC Control Panel device, or an administration program written by an application or driver developer.

Note This chapter is specific to Windows platforms. How data sources are configured on other platforms is platform-specific.

Configuration Components

Data sources are configured by the installer DLL, which in turn calls driver setup DLLs and translator setup DLLs as needed. The installer DLL is either invoked directly from the Control Panel or loaded and called by another program, known as the *administration program*. The following diagram shows the relationship between the configuration components.

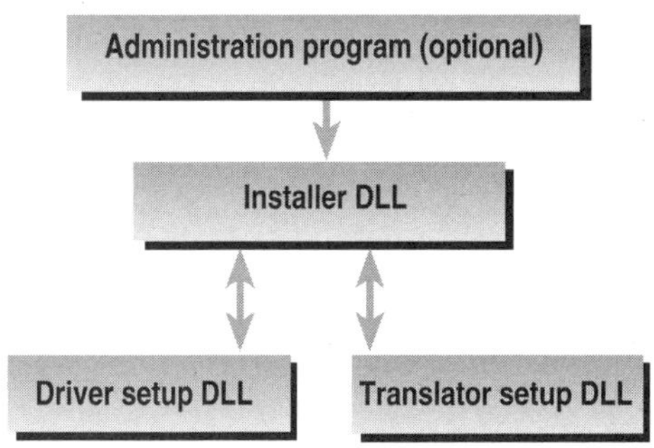

Figure 19.1 Configuration components

Administration Program

An administration program, the ODBC Administrator, is shipped with the ODBC SDK and can be redistributed by users of the ODBC SDK. In addition, developers can write their own administration program. Generally, developers write their own administration program only if they want to retain complete control over data source configuration, or if they are configuring data sources directly from their application, which is acting as an administration program. For example, a spreadsheet program might allow users to add and then use data sources at run time.

The administration program first loads the installer DLL. It then calls functions in the installer DLL to perform the following tasks:

- **Add, modify, or delete data sources interactively**. The administration program can call **SQLManageDataSources**, **SQLCreateDataSource**, or **SQLConfigDataSource**.

  SQLManageDataSources displays a dialog box with which the user can add, modify, or delete data sources and specify tracing options; this is the function that is called when the installer DLL is invoked directly from the Control Panel. **SQLCreateDataSource** displays a dialog box with which the user can only add data sources. **SQLConfigDataSource** passes the call directly to the driver setup DLL.

  In all cases, the installer DLL calls **ConfigDSN** in the driver setup DLL to actually add, modify, or delete the data source. The driver setup DLL may prompt the user for additional information.

- **Add, modify, or delete data sources silently**. The administration program calls **SQLConfigDataSource** in the installer DLL and passes it a null window handle, the name of a data source to add, modify, or delete, and a list of values for the registry. The installer DLL calls **ConfigDSN** in the driver setup DLL to actually add, modify, or delete the data source.

- **Add, modify, or delete a default data source**. The default data source is the same as any other data source, except that its name is Default. It is added, modified, or deleted in the same fashion as any other data source.

The Installer DLL

The installer DLL contains functions to maintain registry information about data sources, install and remove ODBC components, and maintain registry information about those components. It is written by Microsoft and can be redistributed by users of the Microsoft ODBC SDK. For a complete description of the functions in the installer DLL, see Chapter 23, "Installer DLL API Reference."

Driver Setup DLL

The driver setup DLL contains the **ConfigDriver** and **ConfigDSN** functions. **ConfigDSN** maintains driver-specific information about data sources in the registry. **ConfigDriver** performs driver-specific installation tasks, such as entering driver-specific information into the registry. For a complete description of these functions, see Chapter 22, "Setup DLL API Reference."

ConfigDSN calls the following functions in the installer DLL to maintain data source information in the registry:

- **SQLWriteDSNToIni**. Add a data source.
- **SQLRemoveDSNFromIni**. Delete a data source.
- **SQLWritePrivateProfileString**. Write a driver-specific value under a data source specification subkey.
- **SQLGetPrivateProfileString**. Read a driver-specific value from a data source specification subkey.
- **SQLGetTranslator**. Prompt the user for a translator name and option. This function calls **ConfigTranslator** in the translator setup DLL.

The driver setup DLL is written by the driver developer. It can be part of the driver DLL or a separate DLL.

Translator Setup DLLs

The translator setup DLL contains the **ConfigTranslator** function, which returns the default option for a translator. If necessary, it prompts the user for this information. For a complete description of this function, see Chapter 22, "Setup DLL API Reference."

The translator setup DLL is written by the translator developer. It can be part of the translator DLL or a separate DLL.

Registry Entries for Data Sources

The installer DLL maintains information in the registry about each data source. On Windows NT and Windows 95, this information is stored in subkeys under one of the following two keys in the registry:

HKEY_LOCAL_MACHINE
        SOFTWARE
                ODBC
                        ODBC.INI

HKEY_CURRENT_USER
        SOFTWARE
                ODBC
                        ODBC.INI

Which key is used depends on whether the data source is a *system data source*, which is available to all users, or a *user data source*, which is available only to the current user. System data sources are stored on the HKEY_LOCAL_MACHINE tree and user data sources are stored on the HKEY_CURRENT_USER tree. In all other respects, system data sources and user data sources are identical. For information on the registry, see the Win32 SDK documentation.

ODBC Data Sources Subkey

The values under the ODBC Data Sources subkey list the data sources. The format of these values is:

Name	Data type	Data
data-source-name	REG_SZ	*driver-description*

where *data-source-name* is defined by the administration program (which usually prompts the user for it) and *driver-description* is defined by the driver developer (it is usually the name of the DBMS associated with the driver).

For example, suppose three data sources have been defined: Inventory, which uses SQL Server; Payroll, which uses dBASE; and Personnel, which uses formatted text files. The values under the ODBC Data Sources subkey might be:

```
Inventory : REG_SZ : SQL Server
Payroll : REG_SZ : dBASE
Personnel : REG_SZ : Text
```

Data Source Specification Subkeys

Each data source listed in the ODBC Data Sources subkey has a subkey of its own. This subkey has the same name as the corresponding value under the ODBC Data Sources subkey. The values under this subkey must list the driver DLL and may list a description of the data source. If the driver supports translators, the values may list the name of a default translator, the default translation DLL, and the default translation option. The values may also list other information required by the driver to connect to the data source. For example, the driver might require a server name, database name, or schema name.

The formats of the values are as follows. Only the Driver value is required.

Name	Data type	Data
Description	REG_SZ	*description*
Driver	REG_SZ	*driver-DLL-path*
TranslationDLL	REG_SZ	*translator-DLL-path*
TranslationName	REG_SZ	*translator-name*
TranslationOption	REG_SZ	*translation-option*
opt-value-name	*opt-value-type*	*opt-value-data*

For example, suppose the SQL Server driver requires the server name and a flag for OEM to ANSI conversion and defines the Server and OEMTOANSI values for these. Suppose also that the Inventory data source uses the Microsoft Code Page Translator to translate between the Windows Latin 1 (1250) and Multilingual (850) code pages. The values under the Inventory subkey might be:

```
Description : REG_SZ : Inventory database on server InvServ
Driver : REG_SZ : C:\WINDOWS\SYSTEM32\SQLSRV32.DLL
OEMTOANSI : REG_SZ : Yes
Server : REG_SZ : InvServ
TranslationDLL : REG_SZ : C:\WINDOWS\SYSTEM32\MSCPXL32.DLL
TranslationName : REG_SZ : MS Code Page Translator
TranslationOption : REG_SZ : 12500850
```

Default Subkey

The registry may specify a default data source with the Default subkey. This subkey is a special case of a data source specification subkey and has the same values as any other data source specification subkey. The only difference is that it is not listed as a value under the ODBC Data Sources subkey.

ODBC Subkey

The values under the ODBC subkey specify ODBC tracing options. These options are set through the Tracing tab of the ODBC Data Source Administrator dialog box displayed by **SQLManageDataSources**. The ODBC subkey itself is optional. The format of these values is:

Name	Data type	Data
Trace	REG_SZ	**0 | 1**
TraceAutoStop	REG_SZ	**0 | 1**
TraceFile	REG_SZ	*tracefile-path*

where the values have the following meanings:

Value	Meaning
Trace	If the Trace value is set to 1 when an application calls **SQLAllocHandle** with the SQL_HANDLE_ENV option, then tracing is enabled for the calling application. If the Trace keyword is set to 0 when an application calls **SQLAllocHandle** with the SQL_HANDLE_ENV option, then tracing is disabled for the calling application. This is the default value. An application can enable or disable tracing with the SQL_ATTR_TRACE connection attribute. However, doing so does not change the data for this value.
TraceFile	If tracing is enabled, the Driver Manager writes to the trace file specified by the TraceFile value. If no trace file is specified, the Driver Manager writes to the \SQL.LOG file on the current drive. This is the default value. Tracing should only be used for a single application or each application should specify a different trace file. Otherwise, two or more applications will attempt to open the same trace file at the same time, causing an error. An application can specify a new trace file with the SQL_ATTR_TRACEFILE connection attribute. However, doing so does not change the data for this value.
TraceAutoStop	If the TraceAutoStop value is set to 1 when an application calls **SQLFreeHandle** with the SQL_HANDLE_ENV option, then tracing is disabled for all applications and the Trace value is set to 0. This is the default value. If the TraceAutoStop value is set to 0, then tracing must be disabled through the Tracing tab of the ODBC Data Source Administrator dialog box displayed by the **SQLManageDataSources** function.

For example, suppose that tracing is enabled, the trace file is C:\ODBC.LOG, and that tracing is to stop automatically. The values under the ODBC subkey would be:

```
Trace : REG_SZ : 1
TraceAutoStop : REG_SZ : 1
TraceFile : REG_SZ : C:\ODBC.LOG
```

The controls in the **Tracing** tab of the **Administrator** dialog box are "Don't Trace", "All the time", and "One-time only". These controls are related to the ODBC Subkey options as follows:

- "All the time" is set if **Trace** is equal to 1, and **TraceAutoStop** is equal to 0.
- "Trace one-time only" is set if **Trace** is equal to 1, and **TraceAutoStop** is equal to 1.
- "Don't trace" is set if **Trace** is not equal to 1.

Glossary

A

Access plan A plan generated by the database engine to execute an SQL statement. Equivalent to executable code compiled from a third-generation language such as C.

Aggregate function A function that generates a single value from a group of values, often used with GROUP BY and HAVING clauses. Aggregate functions include AVG, COUNT, MAX, MIN, and SUM. Also known as *set functions*. *See also* scalar function.

ANSI American National Standards Institute. The ODBC API is based on the ANSI Call-Level Interface.

APD Application parameter descriptor

API Application Programming Interface. A set of routines that an application uses to request and carry out lower-level services. The ODBC API is composed of the ODBC functions.

Application An executable program that calls functions in the ODBC API.

Application parameter descriptor (APD) A descriptor that describes the dynamic parameters used in an SQL statement before any conversion specified by the application.

Application row descriptor (ARD) A descriptor that represents the column metadata and data in the application's buffers, describing a row of data following any data conversion specified by the application.

ARD Application row descriptor.

Auto-commit mode A transaction commit mode in which transactions are committed immediately after they are executed.

B

Behavioral change A change in certain functionality from ODBC 3.0 behavior to ODBC 2.*x* behavior, or vice versa. Caused by changing the SQL_ATTR_ODBC_VERSION environment attribute.

Binary large object (BLOB) Any binary data over a certain number of bytes, such as 255. Typically much longer. Such data is generally sent to and retrieved from the data source in parts. Also known as *long data*.

Binding As a verb, the act of associating a column in a result set or a parameter in an SQL statement with an application variable. As a noun, the association.

Binding offset A value added to the data buffer addresses and length/indicator buffer addresses for all bound column or parameter data, producing new addresses.

Block cursor A cursor capable of fetching more than one row of data at a time.

Buffer A piece of application memory used to pass data between the application and driver. Buffers often come in pairs: a *data buffer* and a *data length buffer*.

Byte Eight bits or one octet. *See also* octet.

C

C data type The data type of a variable in a C program, in this case the application.

Catalog The set of system tables in a database that describe the shape of the database. Also known as a *schema* or *data dictionary*.

Catalog function An ODBC function used to retrieve information from the database's catalog.

CLI *See* API.

Client/server A database access strategy in which one or more clients access data through a server. The clients generally implement the user interface while the server controls database access.

Column The container for a single item of information in a row. Also known as *field*.

Commit To make the changes in a transaction permanent.

Concurrency The ability of more than one transaction to access the same data at the same time.

Conformance level A discrete set of functionality supported by a driver or data source. ODBC defines API conformance levels and SQL conformance levels.

Connection A particular instance of a driver and data source.

Connection browsing Searching the network for data sources to connect to. Connection browsing might involve several steps. For example, the user might first browse the network for servers, then browse a particular server for a database.

Connection handle A handle to a data structure that contains information about a connection.

Current row The row currently pointed to by the cursor. Positioned operations act on the current row.

Cursor A piece of software that returns rows of data to the application. Probably named after the blinking cursor on a computer terminal; just as that cursor indicates the current position on the screen, a cursor on a result set indicates the current position in the result set.

D

Data buffer A buffer used to pass data. Often associated with a data buffer is a *data length buffer*.

Data dictionary *See* catalog.

Data length buffer A buffer used to pass the length of the value in a corresponding *data buffer*. The data length buffer is also used to store indicators, such as whether the data value is null-terminated.

Data source The data that the user wants to access and its associated operating system, DBMS, and network platform (if any).

Data type The type of a piece of data. ODBC defines C and SQL data types. *See also* type indicator.

Data-at-execution column A column for which data is sent after **SQLSetPos** is called. So named because the data is sent at execution time rather than being placed in a rowset buffer. Long data is generally sent in parts at execution time.

Data-at-execution parameter A parameter for which data is sent after **SQLExecute** or **SQLExecDirect** is called. So named because the data is sent when the SQL statement is executed rather than being placed in a parameter buffer. Long data is generally sent in parts at execution time.

Database A discrete collection of data in a DBMS. Also a DBMS.

Database engine The software in a DBMS that parses and executes SQL statements and accesses the physical data.

DBMS Database Management System. A layer of software between the physical database and the user. The DBMS manages all access to the database.

DBMS-based driver A driver that accesses physical data through a standalone database engine.

DDL Data Definition Language. Those statements in SQL that define, as opposed to manipulate, data. For example, **CREATE TABLE**, **CREATE INDEX**, **GRANT**, and **REVOKE**.

Delimited Identifier An identifier that is enclosed in identifier quote characters so it can contain special characters or match keywords (also known as a quoted identifier).

Descriptor A data structure that holds information about either column data or dynamic parameters. The physical representation of the descriptor is not defined; applications gain direct access to a descriptor only by manipulating its fields by calling ODBC functions with the descriptor handle.

Desktop database A DBMS designed to run on a personal computer. Generally, these DBMSs do not provide a standalone database engine and must be accessed through a file-based driver. The engines in these drivers generally have reduced support for SQL and transactions. For example, dBASE, Paradox, Btrieve, or FoxPro.

Diagnostic A record containing diagnostic information about the last function called that used a particular handle. Diagnostic records are associated with environment, connection, statement, and descriptor handles.

DML Data Manipulation Language. Those statements in SQL that manipulate, as opposed to define, data. For example, **INSERT**, **UPDATE**, **DELETE**, and **SELECT**.

Driver A routine library that exposes the functions in the ODBC API. Drivers are specific to a single DBMS.

Driver Manager A routine library that manages access to drivers for the application. The Driver Manager loads and unloads drivers and passes calls to ODBC functions to the correct driver.

Driver setup DLL A DLL that contains driver-specific installation and configuration functions.

Dynamic cursor A scrollable cursor capable of detecting rows updated, deleted, or inserted in the result set.

Dynamic SQL A type of embedded SQL in which SQL statements are created and compiled at run time. *See also* static SQL.

E

Embedded SQL SQL statements that are included directly in a program written in another language, such as COBOL or C. ODBC does not use embedded SQL. *See also* static SQL *and* dynamic SQL.

Environment A global context in which to access data; associated with the environment is any information that is global in nature, such as a list of all connections in that environment.

Environment handle A handle to a data structure that contains information about the environment.

Escape clause A clause in an SQL statement

Execute To run an SQL statement.

F

Fat cursor *See* block cursor.

Fetch To retrieve one or more rows from a result set.

Field *See* column.

File-based driver A driver that accesses physical data directly. In this case, the driver contains a database engine and acts as both driver and data source.

File data source A data source for which connection information is stored in a .DSN file.

Foreign key A column or columns in a table that match the primary key in another table.

Forward-only cursor A cursor that can only move forward through the result set and generally fetching one row at a time. Most relational databases support only forward-only cursors.

H

Handle A value that uniquely identifies something such as a file or data structure. Handles are meaningful only to the software that creates and uses them, but are passed by other software to identify things. ODBC defines handles for environments, connections, statements, and descriptors.

I

Implementation parameter descriptor (IPD) A descriptor that describes the dynamic parameters used in an SQL statement after any conversion specified by the application.

Implementation row descriptor (IRD) A descriptor that describes a row of data before any conversion specified by the application.

Installer DLL A DLL that installs ODBC components and configures data sources.

Integrity Enhancement Facility A subset of SQL designed to maintain the integrity of a database.

Interface conformance level The level of the ODBC 3.0 interface supported by a driver; can be Core, Level 1, or Level 2.

Interoperability The ability of one application to use the same code when accessing data in different DBMSs.

IPD Implementation parameter descriptor.

IRD Implementation row descriptor.

ISO/IEC International Standards Organization/International Electrotechnical Commission. The ODBC API is based on the ISO/IEC Call-Level Interface.

J

Join An operation in a relational database that links the rows in two or more tables by matching values in specified columns.

K

Key A column or columns whose values identify a row. *See also* primary key *and* foreign key.

Keyset A set of keys used by a mixed or keyset-driven cursor to refetch rows.

Keyset-driven cursor A scrollable cursor that detects updated and deleted rows by using a keyset.

L

Literal A character representation of an actual data value in an SQL statement.

Locking The process by which a DBMS restricts access to a row in a multiuser environment. The DBMS usually sets a bit on a row or the physical page containing a row that indicates the row or page is locked.

Long data Any binary or character data over a certain length, such as 255 bytes or characters. Typically much longer. Such data is generally sent to and retrieved from the data source in parts. Also known as *BLOBs* or *CLOBs*.

M

Machine data source A data source for which connection information is stored on the system (for example, the registry).

Manual-commit mode A transaction commit mode in which transactions must be explicitly committed by calling **SQLTransact**.

Metadata Data that describes a parameter in an SQL statement or a column in a result set. For example, the data type, byte length, and precision of a parameter.

Multiple-tier driver *See* DBMS-based driver.

N

NULL value Having no explicitly assigned value. In particular, a NULL value is different from a zero or a blank.

O

Octet Eight bits or one byte. *See also* byte.

Octet length The length in octets of a buffer or the data it contains.

ODBC Open Database Connectivity. A specification for an API that defines a standard set of routines with which an application can access data in a data source.

ODBC Administrator An executable program that calls the installer DLL to configure data sources.

ODBC SDK ODBC Software Development Kit. A product used to help develop ODBC applications and drivers.

Optimistic concurrency A strategy to increase concurrency in which rows are not locked. Instead, before they are updated or deleted, a cursor checks to see if they have been changed since they were last read. If so, the update or delete fails. *See also* pessimistic concurrency.

Outer join A join in which both matching and nonmatching rows are returned. The values of all columns from the unmatched table in nonmatching rows are set to NULL.

Owner The owner of a table.

P

Parameter A variable in an SQL statement, marked with a parameter marker or question mark (?). Parameters are bound to application variables and their values retrieved when the statement is executed.

Parameter descriptor A descriptor that describes the run-time parameters used in an SQL statement, either before any conversion specified by the application (an application parameter descriptor, or APD) or after any conversion specified by the application (an implementation parameter descriptor, or APD).

Parameter operation array An array containing values that an application can set to indicate that the corresponding parameter should be ignored in an **SQLExecDirect** or **SQLExecute** operation.

Parameter status array An array containing the status of a parameter after a call to **SQLExecDirect** or **SQLExecute**.

Pessimistic concurrency A strategy for implementing serializability in which rows are locked so that other transactions cannot change them. *See also* optimistic concurrency.

Positioned operation Any operation that acts on the current row. For example, positioned update and delete statements, **SQLGetData**, and **SQLSetPos**.

Positioned update statement An SQL statement used to update the values in the current row.

Positioned delete statement An SQL statement used to delete the current row.

Prepare To compile an SQL statement. An access plan is created by preparing an SQL statement.

Primary key A column or columns that uniquely identifies a row in a table.

Procedure A group of one or more precompiled SQL statements that are stored as a named object in a database.

Procedure column An argument in a procedure call, the value returned by a procedure, or a column in a result set created by a procedure.

Q

Qualifier A database that contains one or more tables.

Query An SQL statement. Sometimes used to mean a **SELECT** statement.

Quoted Identifier An identifier that is enclosed in identifier quote characters so it can contain special characters or match keywords (also known in SQL-92 as a delimited identifier).

R

Radix The base of a number system. Usually 2 or 10.

Record *See* row.

Result set The set of rows created by executing a **SELECT** statement.

Return code The value returned by an ODBC function.

Roll back To return the values changed by a transaction to their original state.

Row A set of related columns that describe a specific entity. Also known as a *record*.

Row descriptor A descriptor that describes the columns of a result set, either before any conversion specified by the application (an implementation row descriptor, or IRD) or after any conversion specified by the application (an application row descriptor, or ARD).

Row operation array An array containing values that an application can set to indicate that the corresponding row should be ignored in a **SQLSetPos** operation.

Row status array An array containing the status of a row after a call to **SQLFetch**, **SQLFetchScroll**, or **SQLSetPos**.

Rowset The set of rows returned in a single fetch by a block cursor.

Rowset buffers The buffers bound to the columns of a result set and in which the data for an entire rowset is returned.

S

SAG SQL Access Group. An industry consortium of companies concerned with SQL DBMSs. The X/Open Call-Level Interface is based on work originally done by the SQL Access Group.

Scalar function A function that generates a single value from a single value. For example, a function that changes the case of character data.

Schema *See* catalog.

Scrollable cursor A cursor that can move forward or backward through the result set.

Serializability Whether two transactions executing simultaneously produce a result that is the same as the serial (or sequential) execution of those transactions. Serializable transactions are required to maintain database integrity.

Server database A DBMS designed to be run in a client/server environment. These DBMSs provide a standalone database engine that provides rich support for SQL and transactions. They are accessed through DBMS-based drivers. For example, Oracle, Informix, DB/2, or Microsoft SQL Server.

Set function *See* aggregate function.

Setup DLL *See* driver setup DLL *and* translator setup DLL.

Single-tier driver *See* file-based driver.

SQL Structured Query Language. A language used by relational databases to query, update, and manage data.

SQL conformance level The level of SQL-92 grammar supported by a driver; can be Entry, FIPS Transitional, Intermediate, or Full.

SQL data type The data type of a column or parameter as it is stored in the data source.

SQLSTATE A five-character value that indicates a particular error.

SQL statement A complete phrase in SQL that begins with a keyword and completely describes an action to be taken. For example, **SELECT * FROM Orders**. SQL statements should not be confused with statements.

State A well-defined condition of an item. For example, a connection has seven states, including unallocated, allocated, connected, and needing data. Certain operations can only be done when an item is in a particular state. For example, a connection can be freed only when it is in an allocated state and not, for example, when it is in a connected state.

State transition The movement of an item from one state to another. ODBC defines rigorous state transitions for environments, connections, and statements.

Statement A container for all the information related to an SQL statement. Statements should not be confused with SQL statements.

Statement handle A handle to a data structure that contains information about a statement.

Static cursor A scrollable cursor that cannot detect updates, deletes, or inserts in the result set. Usually implemented by making a copy of the result set.

Static SQL A type of embedded SQL in which SQL statements are hard-coded and compiled when the rest of the program is compiled. *See also* dynamic SQL.

Stored procedure *See* procedure.

T

Table A collection of rows.

Transaction An atomic unit of work. The work in a transaction must be completed as a whole; if any part of the transaction fails, the entire transaction fails.

Transaction isolation The act of isolating one transaction from the effects of all other transactions.

Transaction isolation level A measure of how well a transaction is isolated. There are five transaction isolation levels: Read Uncommitted, Read Committed, Repeatable Read, Serializable, and Versioning.

Translator DLL A DLL used to translate data from one character set to another.

Translator setup DLL A DLL that contains translator-specific installation and configuration functions.

Two-phase commit The process of committing a distributed transaction in two phases. In the first phase, the transaction processor checks that all parts of the transaction can be committed. In the second phase, all parts of the transaction are committed. If any part of the transaction indicates in the first phase that it cannot be committed, the second phase does not occur. ODBC does not support two-phase commits.

Type indicator An integer value passed to or returned from an ODBC function to indicate the data type of an application variable, a parameter, or a column. ODBC defines type indicators for both C and SQL data types.

V

View An alternative way of looking at the data in one or more tables. A view is usually created as a subset of the columns from one or more tables. In ODBC, views are generally equivalent to tables.

X

X/Open A company that publishes standards. In particular, it publishes SAG standards.

Index

Symbols

A

B

D

E

F

G

H

I

J

K

L

M

N

O

P

Q

R

U

V

W

X

Y

The Microsoft Open Database Standard for
Microsoft Windows® and Windows NT® Operating Systems

Microsoft® ODBC 3.0

Programmer's Reference, Volume 1, and SDK Guide

SDK Guide

Microsoft Press

PUBLISHED BY
Microsoft Press
A Division of Microsoft Corporation
One Microsoft Way
Redmond, Washington 98052-6399

Library of Congress Cataloging-in-Publication Data
Microsoft ODBC 3.0 software development kit and programmer's reference
/ Microsoft Corporation.
p. cm.
Includes index.
ISBN 1-57231-516-4
1. Computer software--Development. 2. Microsoft ODBC.
I. Microsoft Corporation.
QA76.76.D47M523 1997
005.74--dc21 96-45660
CIP

Printed and bound in the United States of America.

1 2 3 4 5 6 7 8 9 RTRT 2 1 0 9 8 7

097-0001687

Distributed to the book trade in Canada by Macmillan of Canada, a division of Canada Publishing Corporation.

A CIP catalogue record for this book is available from the British Library.

Microsoft Press books are available through booksellers and distributors worldwide. For further information about international editions, contact your local Microsoft Corporation office. Or contact Microsoft Press International directly at fax (206) 936-7329.

Acquisitions Editor: Casey D. Doyle
Project Editor: Maureen Williams Zimmerman
Technical Editor: Zephan Schroeder

Contents

CHAPTER 1

Overview of the ODBC SDK

The Microsoft® Open Database Connectivity™ (ODBC) interface is an industry standard and a component of the Microsoft Windows Open Services Architecture (WOSA).

The ODBC interface makes it possible for applications to access data from a variety of database management systems (DBMSs). The ODBC interface permits maximum interoperability—an application can access data in diverse DBMSs through a single interface. Furthermore, that application will be independent of any DBMS from which it accesses data. Users of the application can add software components called *drivers*, which interface between an application and a specific DBMS. For more information on drivers, see the *Microsoft ODBC SDK 3.0 Programmer's Reference*.

The Microsoft Open Database Connectivity Software Development Kit (ODBC SDK) 3.0 is a set of software components, tools, and documentation designed to help you in developing ODBC drivers and ODBC-enabled applications for the Windows® 95 and Windows NT® operating systems.

Note The Driver Manager and Installer for the ODBC SDK 3.0 do not support Windows 3.1 or earlier, or Windows NT 3.5 or earlier. Drivers developed with the ODBC SDK 3.0 will not work with Windows 3.1 or earlier, and may not work with Windows NT 3.5 or earlier.

Product Contents

The ODBC SDK contains setup, installation, administration, and ODBC program files. In addition, a set of libraries, include files, Help files, utilities, the SQL Server driver, and sample programs are included.

In addition to the software, the ODBC SDK includes the following Help files:

- The *Microsoft ODBC SDK Guide* (this file), which explains how to install the SDK software.
- The *ODBC SDK Programmer's Reference*, which introduces the ODBC architecture and explains how to write ODBC drivers and applications that use ODBC. It also explains how to use the ODBC setup, installation, and administration programs in conjunction with your drivers or applications. And, it contains the *ODBC API Reference*, in which each of the functions in the ODBC API is listed in alphabetic order and described in detail.
- Help files for the samples included in the SDK, and for the ODBC Test application.
- A Help file for the SQL Server Demonstration driver.

Samples, ODBC Test, and Sample Driver

The ODBC SDK includes several samples, utilities, and drivers you can use to begin implementing open database connectivity as quickly as possible.

Samples

The ODBC SDK Setup program copies the source code files and makefiles for each of the samples listed in this section into subdirectories of the \ODBCSDK\SAMPLES directory. Executable sample files are copied to the \ODBCSDK\BIN32 directory. For more information on each sample, see the Samples Help file.

Sample Auto-Test DLLs for ODBC Test

The Quick Test is a C-language DLL written for ODBC Test. It contains a set of test cases which cover basic areas of ODBC driver conformance. Driver writers can use it as a basis for writing automated acceptance tests for ensuring their drivers conform to the ODBC standard. A source code template (CUSTOM.C) is also provided to help you write an autotest DLL that will work with ODBC Test. For more information on automated test DLLs, see the ODBC Test Help file (ODBCTEST.HLP).

Cursor Sample Application

The Cursor Sample Application is a C-language program written to show how to take advantage of the block cursor, scrolling, and positioned update and delete capabilities of the ODBC cursor library. For information about the ODBC cursor library, see the *Microsoft ODBC SDK Programmer's Reference*.

ODBC Table Administration Sample

The ODBC Table Administration Sample is a C-language program that uses the ODBC API to execute common administrative requests for a DBMS.

Query Sample Application

The SQL Query program is a simple C-language program that demonstrates multiple simultaneous connections using ODBC. It enables you to type any SQL query and browse the results.

Sample SQL Server Driver

The ODBC SDK includes a sample SQL Server Driver is a sample Microsoft SQL Server 3.0 driver for use in developing SQL Server 7.0 applications.

Caution The sample SQL Server 3.0 driver has been provided for development purposes only. This driver should not be used for production purposes.

ODBC Test

ODBC Test is an interactive utility you can use to perform ad hoc and standardized testing on drivers. ODBC Test is covered in detail in Chapter 4, "Using ODBC Test," and the ODBC Test Help file (ODBCTEST.HLP).

Hardware and Software Requirements

To use the ODBC SDK, you will need the following minimum hardware configuration:

- A personal computer using the Intel® 80386 (386 DX or 386 SX) or newer processor and a VGA or higher-resolution graphics card.
- At least 16 MB of random-access memory (RAM).
- CD-ROM drive (if installing from the ODBC 3.0 SDK CD).
- Approximately 10 MB of hard disk space for the complete installation (including samples) of the SDK (additional disk space for developing ODBC drivers or applications is also required).

Before installing the SDK, make sure that the following software is already installed on your system or available for use:

- Microsoft Windows 95 or Microsoft Windows NT 3.51 or 4.0
- Microsoft Win32® Software Development Kit
- A C compiler compatible with Windows dynamic link libraries and Microsoft C libraries (such as the Microsoft® C compiler version 7.0 or later)

Refer to your Microsoft Windows SDK documentation for additional hardware or software requirements.

Documentation

The print and online documentation has been extensively reworked for ODBC SDK version 3.0. Many user-suggested corrections and changes have been implemented. Most technical questions can be answered by reading the appropriate sections of the *Microsoft ODBC SDK Programmer's Reference*. For information on specific Help documentation, refer to the following table.

For help on	See
ODBC SDK Installation	"Installing the ODBC SDK" in this book
ODBC	*Microsoft ODBC SDK Programmer's Reference* (\ODBCSDK\DOC\ODBC.HLP).
Sample Programs	ODBC Sample Programs Help (\ODBCSDK\DOC\ODBCSMPL.HLP)
ODBC Test	ODBC Test Help (\ODBCSDK\DOC\ODBCTEST.HLP)
ODBC Drivers	ODBC Administrator Help (\ODBCSDK\DOC\ODBCINST.HLP)
ODBC Administrator	ODBC Administrator Help (\ODBCSDK\REDIST32\ODBCINST.HLP)

All documents use the following typographic conventions:

Format	Used for
WIN.INI	Uppercase letters indicate file names, SQL statements, macro names, and terms used at the operating-system–command level.
`RETCODE SQLFetch(hdbc)`	This font is used for sample command lines and program code.
argument	Italicized words indicate information that the user or the application must provide, or word emphasis.

Format	Used for
SQLEndTran	Bold type indicates that syntax must be typed exactly as shown, including function names.
[ ]	Brackets indicate optional items; if in bold text, brackets must be included in the syntax.
|	A vertical bar separates two mutually exclusive choices in a syntax line.
{ }	Braces delimit a set of mutually exclusive choices in a syntax line; if in bold text, braces must be included in the syntax.
...	An ellipsis indicates that arguments can be repeated several times.
. . .	A column of three dots indicates continuation of previous lines of code.

Getting Help

Additional assistance on using the ODBC SDK is provided through Microsoft Internet Web sites and various support plans available from Microsoft.

ODBC Web Sites

Information on using the ODBC SDK is provided through the following Microsoft Internet Web sites:

- Microsoft ODBC Web site: http://www.microsoft.com/odbc
- Microsoft ODBC newsgroup: http://www.microsoft.public.odbc

Support Plans

Microsoft offers a range of comprehensive support plans. For information about Microsoft support offerings, call Microsoft Answerpoint Support Sales at (800) 936-3500, Monday through Friday, 6:00 A.M. to 6:00 P.M., Pacific time, excluding holidays, or call your local Microsoft subsidiary outside of the U.S.

CHAPTER 2

Installing the ODBC SDK

The ODBC SDK Setup program (SETUP.EXE) is a straightforward installation program. It installs the ODBC SDK in several steps, depending on the operating system with which you plan to use it (Windows 95 or Windows NT). Setup automatically detects which operating system is running. During setup, you are prompted for the directory name in which you want the ODBC SDK to reside, as well as for the SDK options you want installed.

Installation Overview

When Setup runs, it identifies the running operating system and then installs the required ODBC SDK files, as well as the libraries, include files, tools, ODBC Help files, and sample programs that you choose to install. You can select either a Complete installation of all ODBC components, or a Custom installation of any or all of the following:

- SQL Server 3.0 driver
- ODBC system components
- ODBC SDK

The ODBC SDK Setup program continues installation as follows:

- Installs and configures the SQL Server ODBC drivers.
- Installs the ODBC Administrator control panel device.
- Creates the ODBC SDK 3.0 program group.
- Adds icons for SDK components to the ODBC SDK 3.0 program group.
- Adds icons for the ODBC Administrator to the ODBC SDK 3.0 program group.
- Adds icons for the sample applications.

Once the ODBC SDK 3.0 program group and ODBC Administrator are installed, Setup invokes the ODBC Administrator for your system to enable you to configure the sample SQL Server driver supplied with the ODBC SDK. For information on using the ODBC Administrator, see the ODBC Installer Help file (ODBCINST.HLP).

Running ODBC SDK Setup

▶ To install the Microsoft ODBC SDK

1. If Windows 95 or Windows NT is not already running, boot your workstation and log in.
2. Once your Windows operating system is running, close all open applications.
3. From the **Start-Run** dialog box, run SETUP.EXE.
4. Follow the instructions displayed in the Setup program's dialog boxes.
5. After it has copied files to your system, Setup displays the **User DSN** tab in the **ODBC Administrator** dialog box. Select a data source you want to modify, or choose **Add** to add a data source. To modify or add a system DSN or a file DSN, choose one of those tabs. (For more information, see Chapter 3, "Managing Data Sources and Drivers.")

   Note The Driver Manager is copied to the \ODBCSDK\REDIST32 directory during setup. To install ODBC drivers, perform the driver setup procedure that comes with the driver. Drivers cannot be added from the ODBC Administrator.

6. The setup process is now complete. To exit the Setup program, choose **OK** or press ENTER.

CHAPTER 3

Managing Data Sources

This chapter explains how to use the ODBC Administrator to manage database drivers and data sources. The ODBC SDK Setup program invokes the ODBC Administrator after it has finished copying the essential SDK program files.

The ODBC Administrator is a Control Panel device on workstations running the Windows NT or Windows 95 operating system. The ODBC Administrator is both a Control Panel device and a program item.

About Drivers and Data Sources

Drivers are the components that process ODBC requests and return data to the application. If necessary, drivers modify an application's request into a form that is understood by the data source. You must use the driver's setup program to add or delete a driver from your system.

Data sources are the databases or files accessed by a driver. You use the ODBC Administrator to add, configure, and delete data sources from your system. The following types of data sources can be used:

- User data sources   These data sources are local to a computer, and may only be used by the current user. User DSNs are registered in the HKEY_LOCAL_MACHINE registry key.
- System data sources   These data sources are local to a computer, rather than dedicated to a user. The system, or any user having privileges, can use a data source set up with a system data source. System DSNs are registered in the HKEY_CURRENT_USER registry key.
- File data sources   These data sources are file-based sources that may be shared between all users that have the same drivers installed, and so have access to the database. These data sources need not be dedicated to a user or local to a computer. File data sources do not have a data source name, as user or system data sources do; they are identified by a file name with a DSN extension.

User and system data sources are collectively known as *machine* data sources, since they are local to a computer.

Each of these data sources has a tab in the ODBC Administrator that is dedicated to that type. For more information on data sources, see “Data Sources” in Chapter 3, “ODBC Architecture,” in the *ODBC 3.0 Programmer’s Reference*.

Running the ODBC Administrator

You can open the ODBC Administrator in two ways: from the Control Panel, or from the ODBC SDK 3.0 program group.

▶ To open the ODBC Administrator from the Control Panel

1. Click the **Start** button, then choose the **Settings** icon.
2. Choose the **Control Panel** icon. The Control Panel window will open.
3. Double-click the 32-bit ODBC icon in the Control Panel window. The ODBC Administrator will run.

▶ To open the ODBC Administrator from the ODBC SDK program group

1. Click the **Start** button, then choose the **Programs** icon.
2. Choose the ODBC SDK 3.0 icon.
3. Click the 32-bit Administrator icon. The ODBC Administrator will run.

Once the ODBC Administrator is running, the ODBC Data Source Administrator dialog box appears. (See Figure 3.1.)

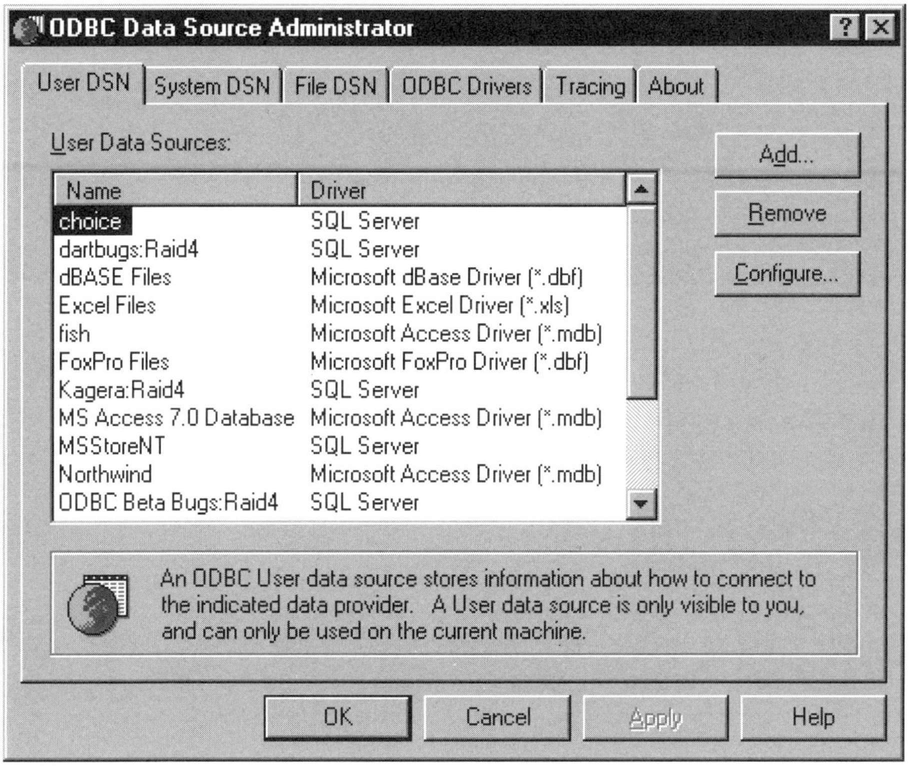

Figure 3.1 ODBC Data Source Administrator dialog box (User tab)

Managing Data Sources

After you have installed an ODBC driver from the driver's setup program, you can define one or more data sources for it. The data source name should provide a unique description of the data; for example, Payroll or Accounts Payable. The user and system data sources that are defined for all the currently installed drivers are listed in the **User DSN** or **System DSN** tabs of the **Administrator** dialog box. The file data sources in a given directory are listed in the **File DSN** tab; the directory to be shown is entered in the **Look In** text box in the **File DSN** tab.

A data source associates a particular ODBC driver with the data you want to access through that driver. For example, you might create a data source to use the ODBC dBASE driver to access one or more dBASE files found in a specific directory on your hard disk or a network drive. With the ODBC Administrator, you can add, delete, and configure the data sources you require.

Note Data sources for 32-bit drivers can be used by both 16-bit and 32-bit applications. The Driver Manager provides thunking layers to allow 16-bit applications to use 32-bit drivers.

Adding Data Sources

You can add multiple data sources, each one associating a driver with some data you want to access using that driver. You need to give each data source a name that uniquely identifies that data source. For example, if you create a data source for a set of dBASE files that contain customer information, you might name the data source "Customers." Applications typically display data source names for users to choose from.

▶ To add a user or system data source

1 Make sure the ODBC Administrator is running. (See "Running the ODBC Administrator" in the previous section.)

2 Choose the **User DSN** or **System DSN** tab, then choose the **Add** button. The **Create New Data Source** dialog box appears.

   The list box displays the names of installed drivers. If the data source you want to add requires a driver that has not been installed, you will have to install the driver first using the driver's setup program.

3 From the ODBC drivers list, select the driver for the data source to use.

4 Choose the **Finish** button.

A driver-specific **Setup** dialog box for the data source appears.

Since each driver is different, each data source requires a slightly different configuration. Because of this, each data source has a unique **Setup** dialog box. For detailed information on the options in a data source **Setup** dialog box, choose the **Help** button in the dialog box.

5 Type the required information about the data source, such as its name and file version (for example, dBASE III or dBASE IV).

6 When you have finished configuring the data source, choose the **OK** button. The driver-specific **Setup** dialog box disappears.

7 You can repeat steps 2 through 6 if you want to add more user data sources.

8 Choose the **Cancel** button to close the ODBC Administrator.

▶ To add a file data source

1 Make sure the ODBC Administrator is running. (See "Running the ODBC Administrator" in the previous section.)

2 Choose the **File DSN** tab.

3 In the **Look In** text box, enter the directory in which the file data source should be saved.

4 Choose the **Add** button. The **Create New Data Source** dialog box appears.

The list box displays the names of installed drivers. If the data source you want to add requires a driver that has not been installed, you will have to install the driver first using the driver's setup program.

5 From the drivers list, select the driver for the data source to use.

6 To enter driver-specific information, choose the **Advanced** button.

   a. Enter keyword value pairs in the text box. (For more information on driver-specific keywords, see the driver's documentation.)

   b. Choose **Verify This Connection** to verify that the connection is valid before creating the file data source.

   c. Choose **OK**.

7 Choose the **Next** button.

8 Type the name of the file data source, or click **Browse**, find the name you want in the directory structure, then click **Save**.

9 Click the **Next** button.

10 Verify that the information displayed is as you want, then click **Finish**.

A driver-specific Setup dialog box for the data source appears. Since each driver is different, each data source requires a slightly different configuration. Because of this, each data source has a unique Setup dialog box. For detailed information on the options in a data source Setup dialog box, choose the **Help** button in the dialog box.

When creating a file data source, entering a name is not necessary. When **OK** is chosen, a file data source with the name entered in step 8 and a DSN extension is created in the selected directory.

For more information on file data sources, see "Connecting Using File Data Sources" in Chapter 6, "Connecting to a Data Source or Driver," or the **SQLDriverConnect** function reference, in the *ODBC 3.0 Programmer's Reference*.

Modifying Data Sources

Depending on your requirements, you may find it necessary to reconfigure your data sources. The ODBC Administrator makes it easy.

▶ To modify a data source

1 Make sure the ODBC Administrator is running. (See "Running the ODBC Administrator" earlier in this chapter.)

2 Select the data source you want to modify from the **User DSN**, **System DSN**, or **File DSN** tab. (See Figure 3.1.)

3 Choose the **Configure** button.

A driver-specific Setup dialog box appears.

Since each driver is different, each data source requires a slightly different configuration. Because of this, each data source has a unique Setup dialog box. For detailed information on the options in a data source Setup dialog box, choose the **Help** button in the dialog box.

4 Modify the data source information, such as its name and file version (for example, dBASE III or dBASE IV).

5 When you have finished configuring the data source, choose the **OK** button. The driver-specific Setup dialog box disappears.

6 You can repeat steps 2 through 5 if you want to modify more data sources.

7 Choose the **Cancel** button to close the ODBC Administrator.

Deleting Data Sources

▶ To delete a data source

1. Make sure the ODBC Administrator is running. (See “Running the ODBC Administrator” earlier in this chapter.)
2. Select the data source you want to delete from the **User DSN**, **System DSN**, or **File DSN** tab. (See Figure 3.1.)
3. Choose the **Remove** button.
4. A message box appears asking you to confirm removing the data source you have selected:
   - Choose the **Yes** button to delete the data source.
   - Choose the **No** button to return to the **Data Sources** dialog box without deleting the data source.
5. Repeat steps 2 through 4 until you have finished deleting data sources.
6. Choose the **Cancel** button to close the ODBC Administrator.

Setting Tracing Options

The **Tracing** tab of the **Administrator** dialog box enables you to configure the way ODBC functions calls are traced. (See Figure 3.2.)

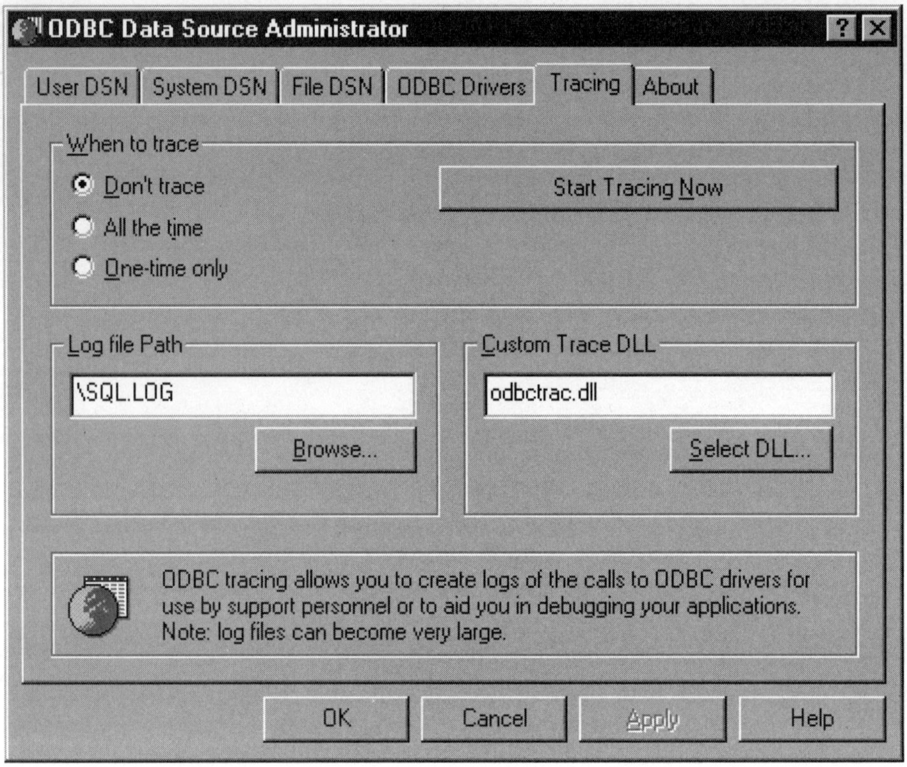

Figure 3.2 Tracing options

Note The **Trace ODBC Calls** box in the **Tracing** tab does not take precedence over the **ODBC Test Tools** menu **Trace** command. For more information, see Chapter 4, "Using ODBC Test."

How Tracing Works

When you activate tracing from the **Tracing** tab, the Driver Manager will log all ODBC function calls for all subsequently run applications. ODBC function calls from applications running before tracing is activated are not logged. Logging is done by writing all ODBC function calls to a log file you specify.

By default, tracing will stop as soon as any application being traced closes. You can choose to have tracing continue after an ODBC application closes. However, keep in mind that while tracing is on, the log file will continue to increase in size, and that the performance of your ODBC applications will be affected.

For more information about tracing, see "Tracing" in Chapter 17, "Programming Considerations," in the *ODBC 3.0 Programmer's Reference*.

Enabling and Disabling Tracing

▶ To enable tracing

1 Make sure the ODBC Administrator is running. (See "Running the ODBC Administrator" earlier in this chapter.)

2 Choose the **Tracing** tab.

3 To enable tracing to be performed automatically at all times, for all connections on the machine, click **All The Time**. To enable tracing to be performed only for the next connection, click **One-Time Only**; tracing will be disabled after the next connection is disconnected. (These settings can only be set when there is no active connection.)

4 To enable tracing to be performed as long as the **ODBC Administrator** dialog box is displayed, choose Start Tracing Now. This is called *dynamic tracing*. Dynamic tracing can be enabled whether a connection has been made or not. After it is chosen, the **Start Tracing Now** button is replaced by a **Stop Tracing Now** button, which can be used to disable the tracing.

5 To change the path and file name of the log file, enter text into the **Log File Path** text box. This box displays the path and file name for the file that the tracing information will be stored in. The default path and file name (sql.log) are taken from the system information, but a new file can be specified by either entering a new path and file name, or choosing the **Browse** button and selecting a directory and file.

6 To select a trace DLL other than odbctrac.dll to perform tracing, enter a path and file name in the **Custom Trace DLL** text box. The odbctrac.dll file that is shipped with the ODBC SDK can be replaced by a custom DLL of your choice. Enter the path and file name of the custom DLL, or choose the **Select DLL** button to browse the directories for the custom DLL.

7 Choose the **OK** button. The **Administrator** dialog box closes. If tracing was enabled in the **When To Trace** control of the **Tracing** tab, all ODBC applications that you run after you close the **Data Sources** dialog box will have all ODBC function calls appended to the file you selected. If tracing was enabled with the **Start Tracing Now** button, tracing ends when the **Administrator** dialog box is closed.

▶ To disable tracing

1 Make sure the ODBC Administrator is running. (See "Running the ODBC Administrator" earlier in this chapter.)

2 Choose the **Tracing** tab.

3 To disable tracing that was enabled by choosing the **All The Time** or **One-Time Only** button, choose **Don't trace**.

4 To disable tracing that was enabled dynamically by choosing the **Start Tracing Now** button, choose the **Stop Tracing Now** button, or close the ODBC Administrator dialog box. (When the Administrator dialog box is closed, dynamic tracing is automatically disabled.)

Viewing Drivers

To configure data sources, you must have installed at least one driver onto your system. The **ODBC Drivers** tab in the Administrator displays a list of the drivers installed on your computer, including the name, version, company, file name, and file creation date of each driver. You must use the driver's setup program to add or delete a driver from your system.

▶ To view installed drivers and driver details

1 Make sure the ODBC Administrator is running. (See "Running the ODBC Administrator" earlier in this chapter.)

2 Choose the **Drivers** tab. A list of the drivers installed on your system, and information about the drivers, are displayed. The date displayed is the creation date of the driver. (See Figure 3.3.)

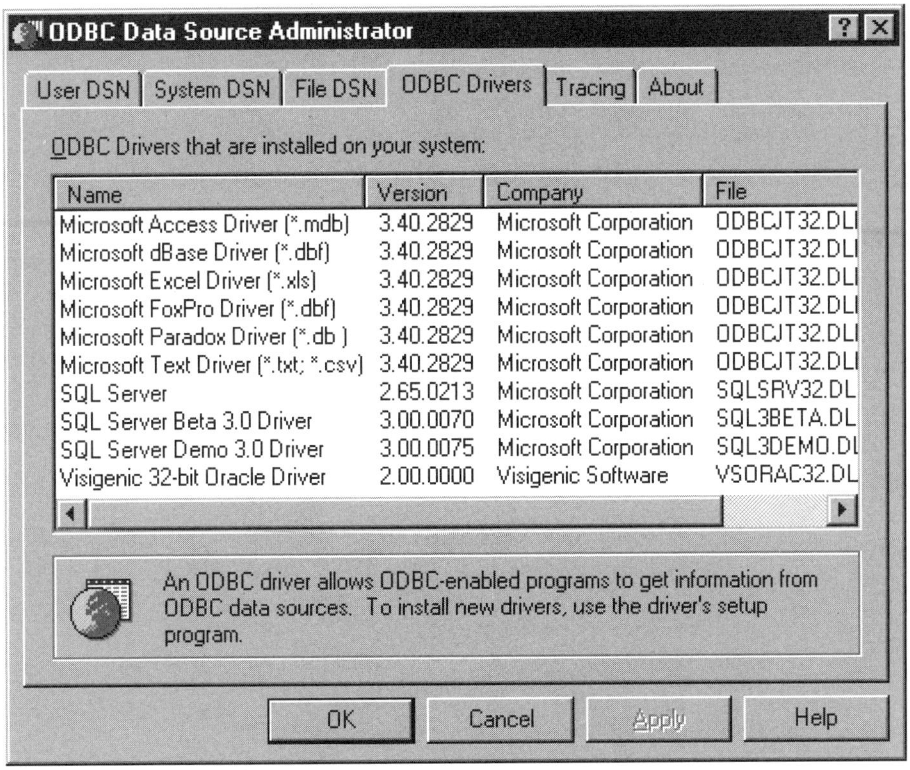

Figure 3.3 ODBC drivers installed

CHAPTER 4

Using ODBC Test

Microsoft ODBC Test is an ODBC-enabled application that you can use to test ODBC drivers. ODBC Test has four distinct types of menu items that you can use to execute ODBC functions:

- **Functions** *Functions* are menu items that call ODBC functions. When you select a function from an ODBC Test menu, ODBC Test displays a dialog box that has one control for each argument in the function. When you select the **OK** button in the dialog box, ODBC Test executes the function using the values specified for each argument.

  ODBC Test allows you to determine which functions are included in the menus. If the **ODBC Menu Version** control in the **User Options** dialog box is set to 3.0, the ODBC Test menus include only ODBC 3.0 functions. If the version is set to 2.*x*, the menus include only ODBC 2.*x* functions. If the version control is set to both 2.x and 3.0, the menus include both ODBC 3.0 and ODBC 2.*x* functions.

  The menus themselves are titled differently depending upon the version of the functions they contain.

- **Function Tools** *Function tools* are menu items that call a group of related ODBC functions or help you use an ODBC function. For example, **Full Disconnect** calls **SQLDisconnect**, **SQLFreeHandle** with a *HandleType* of SQL_HANDLE_DBC, and **SQLFreeHandle** with a *HandleType* of SQL_HANDLE_ENV; **Fill Param** displays a dialog box in which you enter parameter values. Function tools are listed at the bottom of the **Diag**, **Env**, **Conn**, **Desc**, **Stmt**, and **Results** menus beneath a separator line.

  If the **ODBC Menu Version** control in the **User Options** dialog box is set to 3.0 or Both, the Function Tools use ODBC 3.0 functions. If the version is set to 2.*x*, the Function Tools use ODBC 2.*x* functions.

- **Tools** *Tools* are menu items that help you configure ODBC Test, such as the level of errors to report or whether menu items for functions the driver does not support are disabled.
- **Auto Tests** Automated tests, or *auto tests*, are dynamic-link libraries (DLLs) that you have written. Each auto test DLL contains one or more test cases. For example, an auto test for **SQLAllocHandle** might contain test cases to call **SQLAllocHandle** with valid and invalid arguments and to call **SQLAllocHandle** with a *HandleType* of SQL_HANDLE_STMT until the driver runs out of statement handles. The source code for a sample auto test that tests basic driver functionality (the Quick Test) is shipped with the ODBC SDK in the \ODBCSDK\SAMPLES\QUIKTEST directory.

To use ODBC Test, you must understand the ODBC API, the C language, and SQL. For more information on the ODBC API, see the *Microsoft ODBC SDK Programmer's Reference*.

Using the ODBC Test Interface

The ODBC Test interface contains elements that are familiar to programmers. The short tutorial in the next section acquaints you with the interface. If you want to skip the tutorial, the following section discusses only the parts of the interface you may be unfamiliar with: output windows, connection windows, and function dialog boxes.

Tutorial

This tutorial illustrates how to connect to a data source, create a table and insert values into it, retrieve those values, and disconnect from the data source. In so doing, it acquaints you with most of the ODBC Test user interface.

▶ To connect to a data source

1. Create a dBASE data source called Test Data using the ODBC Administrator. (For information on creating data sources with the ODBC Administrator, see Chapter 3, "Managing Data Sources and Drivers.")
2. Start ODBC Test. Either select **ODBC Test** from the **ODBC SDK 3.0** folder from the **Start-Programs** menu or choose **Run** from the **Start** menu and type \ODBCSDK\BIN32\ODBCTE32.EXE.
3. From the **Conn** menu, choose **Full Connect**. ODBC Test displays the Full Connect dialog box.
4. Select **Test Data** from the list of data sources and click the **OK** button. ODBC Test connects to the Test Data data source and allocates a statement handle. It displays the connection window and the allocated statement handle in the statement handle list.

▶ To create a table and insert values into it

1 Using the connection window from the previous procedure, type the following SQL statement in the input window:

```
CREATE TABLE NewTable (City CHAR(10), State CHAR(2))
```

2 From the **Stmt** menu, choose **SQLExecDirect**. ODBC Test displays the **SQLExecDirect** dialog box. The value of <input window> in the *StatementText* argument indicates that ODBC Test will retrieve the SQL statement from the input window.

3 Choose the **OK** button to execute **SQLExecDirect**. ODBC Test calls **SQLExecDirect** with the specified arguments and displays the function name, input argument values, and return code in the output window.

4 Type the following SQL statements in the input window. You do not need to delete the CREATE TABLE statement.

```
INSERT INTO NewTable VALUES ('Erie', 'PA')
INSERT INTO NewTable VALUES ('Atlanta', 'GA')
INSERT INTO NewTable VALUES ('Cheyenne', 'WY')
```

5 Using the mouse, select the first **INSERT** statement.

6 From the **Stmt** menu, choose **SQLExecDirect** again, then choose the **OK** button to execute **SQLExecDirect** with the new arguments. ODBC Test calls the driver to insert the values in the table and displays information about the function call in the output window.

Note If you don't select the line you want to execute, ODBC Test passes all the statements in the input window to the driver. Although some drivers can process multiple statements, the dBASE driver used in this example cannot.

7 Repeat steps 5 and 6 for the other two **INSERT** statements.

▶ To retrieve data from a table

1 Using the connection window and the table from the previous procedure, type the following SQL statement in the input window and select it with the mouse:

```
SELECT * FROM NewTable
```

2 From the **Stmt** menu, choose **SQLExecDirect** again, then choose the **OK** button to execute **SQLExecDirect** with the new arguments. ODBC Test calls the driver to select the data from the table and displays information about the function call in the output window.

3 From the **Results** menu, select the **Get Data All** function tool. The **Get Data All** function tool retrieves all of the data in the result set created by the **SELECT** statement. It displays the column count, the column names, the data, and the number of rows fetched in the output window:

```
"CITY", "STATE"
"Erie      ", "PA"
"Atlanta   ", "GA"
"Cheyenne  ", "WY"
3 rows fetched from 2 columns.
```

▶ To disconnect from a data source

For the connection window used in the previous procedure, select **Full Disconnect** from the **Conn** menu. ODBC Test disconnects from the data source and removes the connection window.

Using Windows

ODBC Test has three types of windows: a general output window, zero or more connection windows, and zero or more rowset windows. These are illustrated in Figure 4.1.

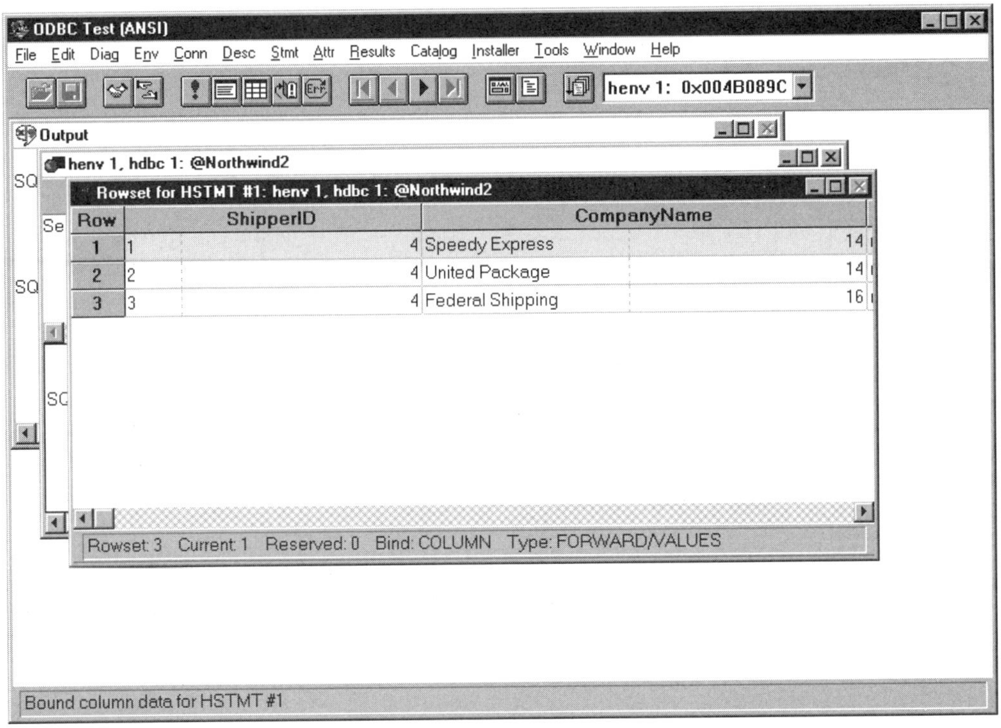

Figure 4.1 ODBC Test windows

General Output Window

ODBC Test has a single general output window. It uses this window to display information that is not directly related to a connection. For example, ODBC Test displays the output of **SQLAllocHandle** with a *HandleType* of SQL_HANDLE_ENV function in the general output window.

Connection Windows

ODBC Test creates a connection window each time **SQLAllocHandle** with a *HandleType* of SQL_HANDLE_DBC (or **SQLAllocConnect**) is successfully executed; it closes the specified connection window each time **SQLFreeHandle** with a *HandleType* of SQL_HANDLE_DBC (or **SQLFreeConnect**) is successfully executed. To use a specific connection, select the window for that connection.

Each connection window has three parts:

1. **Statement Handle List** At the top of the connection window is a list of allocated statement handles and their values. The value is a 32-bit address. Each time **SQLAllocHandle** with a *HandleType* of SQL_HANDLE_STMT (or **SQLAllocStmt**) is called, the new statement handle is added to this list; each time **SQLFreeHandle** with a *HandleType* of SQL_HANDLE_STMT (or **SQLFreeStmt** with the SQL_DROP option) is called, the specified statement handle is removed from the list.

   To select a statement handle to use when calling an ODBC function, select the handle from this list. You can also select a null handle (SQL_NULL_HSTMT).

2. **Input Window** The top half of each connection window is used to enter SQL statements for the **SQLExecDirect**, **SQLNativeSql**, and **SQLPrepare** functions, and data for the **SQLPutData** function. ODBC Test passes the highlighted statements or data to the function. If no statements or data are highlighted, ODBC Test uses all the statements or data in the input window.

   To load a text file into the input window, choose **Open** from the **File** menu. To save the statements in the input window, choose **Save As** from the **File** menu.

3. **Output Window** The bottom half of each connection window is used by ODBC Test to display information about each function that it executes, such as the return code and the input and output argument values. To control what information is displayed, choose **User Options** from the **Tools** menu and select the level you want from the Logging Level list. To control whether the output wraps from line to line, choose **Word Wrap** from the **Edit** menu.

The input and output windows can each contain up to 60,000 characters. When the number of characters in one of these windows reaches this limit, ODBC Test deletes the first 2,000 characters in the window. To clear the input or output window, choose **Clear** from the **Edit** menu and specify whether to clear one or both windows.

Rowset Windows

ODBC Test creates a rowset window when **SQLFetch**, **SQLFetchScroll**, or **SQLExtendedFetch** is called for the first time on a statement handle. It closes the rowset window when the cursor associated with the statement handle is closed. The rowset window displays the contents of the *ParameterValuePtr* and *StrLen_or_IndPtr* buffers bound to the result set with **SQLBindCol** and the contents of the *RowStatusArray* buffer specified in **SQLSetStmtAttr**, **SQLSetDescRec**, **SQLSetDescField**, or **SQLExtendedFetch**. You can use the **Rowset Options** item on the **Tools** menu to control whether the status values, length values array, and column names are displayed.

Note Rowset windows do not display the results of calls to **SQLGetData**; these are displayed in the output window of the connection window.

To update the value of a cell in a rowset window, double-click the cell. Enter the appropriate value, then call **SQLSetPos** with *Operation* set to SQL_UPDATE. The SQL_ATTR_CURSOR_TYPE statement attribute must not be SQL_CURSOR_FORWARD_ONLY and the SQL_ATTR_CONCURRENCY statement attribute must not be SQL_CONCUR_READ_ONLY.

Using Function Dialog Boxes

When you choose an ODBC function from a menu, ODBC Test displays a dialog box in which you can specify argument values. The dialog box contains one control for each argument; it may contain additional controls for supplemental information. For example, the **SQLSetStmtAttr** dialog box contains a list from which you can select the C data type of the *Attribute* argument for a driver-specific statement option. For information about the dialog box for a specific function, see that function in "Function Reference" later in this chapter.

ODBC Test uses text boxes, drop-down combo boxes, and check boxes in function dialog boxes. These are illustrated in Figure 4.2, the dialog box for the **SQLDriverConnect** function.

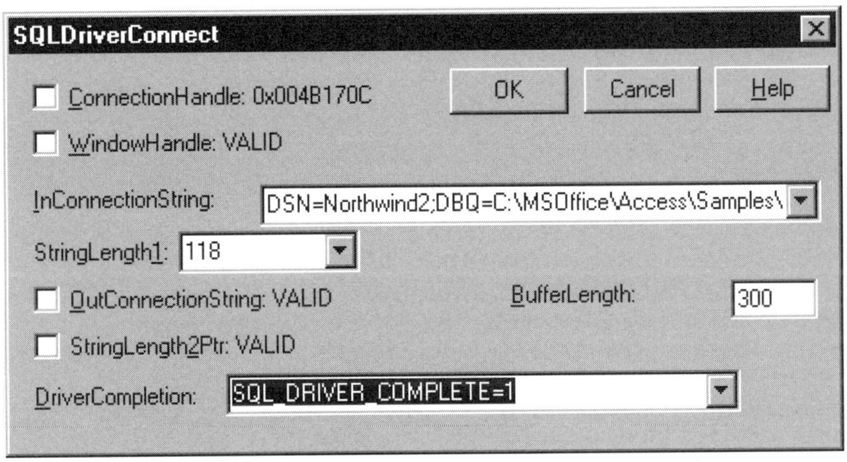

Figure 4.2 SQLDriverConnect dialog box

Text Boxes

Text boxes are used to specify values for numeric arguments for which no **#define** values (such as SQL_NTS or SQL_NULL_DATA) apply. For example, text boxes are used to specify values for the *BufferLength* argument in **SQLDriverConnect** (shown in Figure 4.2) and the *TargetValuePtr* argument in **SQLBindCol**.

Drop-Down Combo Boxes

Drop-down combo boxes are used to specify values for most arguments. For example, drop-down combo boxes are used to specify values for the *InConnectionString*, *StringLength1*, and *DriverCompletion* arguments in **SQLDriverConnect** (shown in Figure 4.2).

For numeric arguments, such as the *Attribute* argument in **SQLSetStmtAttr**, the list consists of all applicable **#define** names and the numeric value associated with each **#define** name. If **Version Numbers** in the **User Options** dialog box is selected, the version of ODBC in which each **#define** name was introduced is also displayed.

For character arguments, such as the *InConnectionString* argument in **SQLDriverConnect**, the list always contains <empty string> and <null pointer>. It may contain <input window> or <input window selection> (to use the currently selected text in the input window or, if no text is selected, all text in the input window), and it may contain any known text values, such as data source names. For character arguments, ODBC Test automatically places the length of the character argument in the corresponding length argument when you move the focus to a different control.

For some arguments, such as the *ParameterValuePtr* argument in **SQLBindParameter**, the list may contain <rowset values>. This activates the Rowset hdbc and Rowset hstmt list boxes, which enable you to specify the connection handle and statement handle of the bound rowset. The **Row** and **Column** text boxes allow you to specify the row number and column number, respectively.

For pointer arguments, the list includes <valid pointer> and <null pointer>. If <valid pointer> is chosen, ODBC Test frees the existing pointer, and creates a new pointer. If <null pointer> is chosen, ODBC Test passes a null pointer. This is true for the *ParameterValuePtr* argument in **SQLSetDescRec**, the *ParameterValuePtr* argument in **SQLSetDescField** for a field that is a pointer, or the *ParameterValuePtr* argument in **SQLSetStmtAttr** when the statement attribute is a pointer.

You can either select a value from the list or type a value in the text box. If the argument accepts values for which **#define** names apply, you can type the **#define** name (or any unambiguous portion of it) in the text box. For example, to specify that the driver prompt the user for connection information, select SQL_DRIVER_COMPLETE from the list of values for *DriverCompletion* in the **SQLDriverConnect** dialog box, or type 1, 0x01, or SQL_DRIVER_COMPLETE (COM would be sufficient). The entered text will automatically change to the appropriate value when you move the focus to a different control.

Check Boxes

Check boxes are used to specify values for input arguments that accept environment, connection, or statement handles; input arguments that accept window handles; and output arguments that accept pointers to handles or pointers to output buffers. For example, check boxes are used to specify values for the *ConnectionHandle*, *WindowHandle*, *OutConnectionString*, and *StringLength2Ptr* arguments in **SQLDriverConnect** (shown in Figure 4.2).

After each check box is the name of the argument and its value:

- For input arguments that accept handles, the value is either the handle value or a null handle (such as SQL_NULL_HDBC or SQL_NULL_HANDLE). ODBC Test retrieves this value from the current environment handle, the connection handle of the current connection window, or the statement handle of the current statement in the current connection window.
- For input arguments that accept window handles and output arguments that accept pointers to handles or pointers to output buffers, the value is either VALID or NULL (such as SQL_NULL_HANDLE).

A handle value or VALID indicates that ODBC Test will pass a valid, non-null pointer or handle; NULL indicates that ODBC Test will pass a null pointer or handle. To switch between the two, check or clear the check box.

Data Formats

ODBC Test accepts data in the following formats:

Data type	Valid formats
Binary	Hexadecimal. The value must contain an even number of hexadecimal characters. For example, 0x0100 is legal; 0xF is not.
Bit	Decimal (0 to 255).
	Hexadecimal (0x00 to 0xFF).
Character	Character. For example, abc.
	Hexadecimal. The value must contain an even number of hexadecimal characters. For example, 0x 61 62 63 is legal; 0x616 is not.
Date	YYYY-MM-DD. For example, 1993-10-25.
	Hexadecimal. The hexadecimal characters match the SQL_DATE_STRUCT structure. You must enter exactly 12 hexadecimal characters. For example, 0x 07C9 000A 0019.

Data type	Valid formats
Floating Point	Decimal. For example, 1234.46. Scientific notation. For example, 1.23446E3. Hexadecimal. The value must contain the exact number of hexadecimal characters required by the floating-point data type. For example, type 0xA64E9A44 for the SFLOAT 1234.46 and type 0x1D5A643BDFD98E40 for the SDOUBLE 987.234.
Integer	Decimal. For example, 255. Hexadecimal. The value can contain any number of hexadecimal characters up to the length of the integer. For example, 0xFF or 0xF.
Interval	Interval data is entered in one of the 13 interval formats: year, month, day, hour, minute, second, year to month, day to hour, day to minute, day to second, hour to minute, hour to second, or minute to second. The length of the data depends upon the interval leading precision (for a single-field interval or the first field of a two-field interval) or the seconds precision (for the second field of a two-field interval when that field includes a seconds components). The interval leading precision is defined in the SQL_DESC_DATETIME_INTERVAL_PRECISION descriptor field; the seconds precision is determined by the SQL_DESC_PRECISION descriptor field. The number of digits in the month, day, or hour component of the second field of a two-field interval is determined by the constraints of the Gregorian calendar. Interval data is entered as follows: Year, month, day, hour, minute, second: NNN (with the number of digits determined by the interval leading precision) Year to month: YYY-MM (with the number of year digits determined by the interval leading precision; and two month digits) Day to hour: DDD HH (with the number of day digits determined by the interval leading precision; and two hour digits) Day to minute: DDD HH:MM (with the number of day digits determined by the interval leading precision; two hour digits and two minute digits) Day to second: DDD HH:MM:SS.FFF (with the number of day digits determined by the interval leading precision; two hour digits, two minute digits, two second digits; and the number of fractional seconds digits determined by the seconds precision) Hour to minute: HHH:MM (with the number of hour digits determined by the interval leading precision; and two minute digits) Hour to second: HHH:MM:SS.FFF (with the number of hour digits determined by the interval leading precision; two minute digits, two second digits; and the number of fractional seconds digits determined by the seconds precision)

Data type	Valid formats
Interval (*continued*)	Minute to second: MMM:SS.FFF (with the number of minute digits determined by the interval leading precision; two second digits; and the number of fractional seconds digits determined by the seconds precision) For more information about interval literals, see "Interval Literals" in Appendix D, "Data Types," of the *ODBC 3.0 Programmer's Reference*.
Time	HH:MM:SS. For example, 12:34:56. Hexadecimal. The hexadecimal characters match the SQL_TIME_STRUCT structure. You must enter exactly 12 hexadecimal characters. For example, 0x 000C 0022 0038.
Timestamp	YYYY-MM-DD (time is set to 0). For example, 1993-10-25. HH:MM:SS (date is set to current date). For example, 12:34:56. YYYY-MM-DD HH:MM:SS[.F...]. For example, 1993-10-25 12:34:56. Hexadecimal. The hexadecimal characters match the SQL_TIMESTAMP_STRUCT structure. If you specify the fractional part of a timestamp, you must enter exactly 32 hexadecimal characters. If you do not specify the fractional part of a timestamp, you must enter exactly 24 hexadecimal characters. For example, 0x 07C9 000A 0019 000C 0022 0038 0000 0000 (with the fractional part) or 0x 07C9 000A 0019 000C 0022 0038 (without the fractional part).

Hexadecimal values are subject to the following constraints:

- Values must be in order of most-significant byte to least-significant byte. ODBC Test will convert these values to the byte order of the machine it is running on.
- Letters in hexadecimal values can be uppercase or lowercase. For example, 0xFF, 0xfF, 0xFf, and 0xff are the same.
- Hexadecimal values can contain spaces at any point after the 0x characters; ODBC Test ignores these spaces. For example, 0xFF and 0x FF are the same.

Using Auto Tests

Auto tests are DLLs that you have written to test your driver. An auto test is a self-contained ODBC application, except that it must be run by ODBC Test. It allocates and frees handles, connects and disconnects from data sources, and accesses data in those data sources.

Creating Auto Tests

The following sections describe how to write auto tests, use the Quick Test sample, and build auto tests.

Writing an Auto Test

Writing an auto test is like writing any other ODBC application. You must write code to allocate and free handles, connect to and disconnect from data sources, and access data. As a starting point, you can use CUSTOM.C or QUIKTEST.C in the \ODBCSDK\SAMPLES\QUIKTEST directory.

Note An auto test does not have to manage handles or connections if it uses the ODBC Test Handles test source. For more information, see the **AutoTestFunc** function description in "Auto Test Function Reference," later in this chapter.

An auto test contains one or more *test cases*, each of which tests some specific functionality. For example, an auto test for **SQLAllocStmt** might contain two test cases, one to call **SQLAllocStmt** with all combinations of valid and invalid arguments and one to call **SQLAllocStmt** repeatedly until the driver runs out of statement handles.

The BUILD program shipped with the ODBC SDK requires specified names for the source files for an auto test DLL. For more information, see "Required Files," later in this section.

The auto test must export the following functions, which are called by ODBC Test:

- **AutoTestName** This function returns the name of the auto test and the number of test cases it includes. ODBC Test displays the auto test name in the **Manage Auto Tests**, **Manage Test Groups**, and **Run Auto Test** dialog boxes.
- **AutoTestDesc** This function returns the name and description of a specific test case. ODBC Test displays the test case name and description in the **Run Auto Tests** dialog box.
- **AutoTestFunc** This function invokes the auto test for a specific test source. Information about the test source and a bit array of the test cases to execute are passed to the auto test in a structure created by ODBC Test.

An auto test can call the following two functions in GTRTST32.DLL:

- **szLogPrintf** An auto test calls this function to log test results and other information to the screen and the log file.
- **szMessageBox** An auto test calls this function to display a message box. This function encapsulates the **MessageBox** function in the Windows API. Unlike the **MessageBox** function, it accepts a format string and a list of arguments with which it constructs a string to pass to **MessageBox**.

For more information about these functions, see "Auto Test Function Reference" and "ODBC Test Function Reference," later in this chapter.

The Quick Test Sample

You can use the Quick Test (\ODBCSDK\SAMPLES\QUIKTEST\QUIKTEST.C) as a starting point for both writing your own auto tests and testing your driver. The Quick Test calls each ODBC function and verifies that it returns the expected code. Next, it calls **SQLGetDiagRec** until that function returns SQL_NO_DATA, verifying that the expected SQLSTATEs are returned. Finally, for some functions, it checks whether the function returns the expected data.

Note The Quick Test is *not* an ODBC acceptance or compliance test. It is a starting point for your testing.

Building an Auto Test

To build an auto test DLL from code you have written, change your directory to \ODBCSDK\SAMPLES\QUIKTEST. You can use the BUILD.BAT file to set the proper environment and invoke the appropriate compiler and linker.

```
BUILD tstname [options]
```

where *tstname* is the base name of your .C file and *options* are one or more of the following:

Option	Meaning
-CLEAN	Build all targets, even if the targets are not out-of-date with respect to their dependencies.
-DEBUG32	Build the 32-bit debug version in the \ODBCSDK\SAMPLES\QUIKTEST\DEBUG32 directory.
-NDEBUG32	Build the 32-bit non-debug version in the \ODBCSDK\SAMPLES\QUIKTEST\NDEBUG32 directory.
-?	Display usage information.

BUILD.BAT calls NMAKE, the Microsoft Program Maintenance Utility provided with Microsoft C, version 7.0 or later, to process MAKEFILE to build the auto test DLL. If MAKEFILE is not modified, BUILD.BAT rebuilds the original QUIKTEST.DLL.

Required Files

To build an auto test, BUILD.BAT needs the following files:

File name	Description
AUTOTEST.H	Include file containing the constants and prototypes required to build an auto test DLL. All auto tests must include this file.
DLLSTUB.C	Source file containing the library entry points for 16-bit and 32-bit DLLs.
MAKEFILE	Makefile for auto test DLLs.

File name	Description
TSTNAME.C *TSTNAME*1.C *TSTNAME*2.C	Source files. Only *TSTNAME*.C is required. However, if your auto test requires additional source files, the MAKEFILE makefile requires that they are named *TSTNAME*1.C and *TSTNAME*2.C.
TSTNAME.H	Optional include file.
TSTNAME.RC	Optional resource file.

Running an Auto Test

To run an auto test, you must:

- Create test sources to run the auto test against or plan to run the auto test against the ODBC Test Handles test source, which uses the current connection.
- Install the auto test in ODBC Test.
- Optionally, add the auto test to a test group.

Managing Test Sources

A test source is an ODBC data source and, optionally, all the information necessary to connect silently to that data source. Generally, auto tests are run as a background task—either overnight or on a separate machine—so they should be able to connect to a data source without prompting you for connection information. The ODBC Test Handles test source, which uses the connection and statement handles from the current connection, is always available.

▶ To create a test source

1. In ODBC Test, choose **Manage Test Sources** from the Tools menu. ODBC Test displays the **Manage Test Sources** dialog box.
2. Choose the **New** button, type the name of your test source in the **Test Source** box, and choose the **OK** button.
3. Select the data source you want to access from the DSN list. If there are no data sources in the list, you can create them with the ODBC Administrator. For more information, see Chapter 3, "Using the ODBC Administrator."
4. If your data source requires a user and password, type the user ID in the **UID** box and the password in the **PWD** box.

Caution The password is stored in the \WINDOWS\GATOR32.INI file in unencrypted form. Because of this, you may want to create special data sources and passwords for use with ODBC Test or use only the ODBC Test Handles test source.

5 If your auto tests require any other keywords or attribute values, type these as a string in the **Keywords** box. Your test will be passed the keywords by ODBC Test. For example, to specify the Employee database and the DBNMP3.DLL network library, you might type the keywords:

```
DATABASE=Employee;NetLib=DBNMP3
```

6 Click the **Close** button.

You can also modify or delete test sources with the **Manage Test Sources** dialog box.

Managing Auto Tests

ODBC Test cannot automatically recognize which DLLs on your system are auto tests. For this reason, you must install an auto test before you can include it in a test group or run it.

▶ To install an auto test

1. In ODBC Test, choose **Manage Auto Tests** from the **Tools** menu. ODBC Test displays the **Manage Auto Tests** dialog box.
2. The **Available** list shows all DLLs in the \ODBCSDK\BIN32 directory. To install auto tests from a different directory, choose the **From** button and select that directory.
3. Select the auto test to install from the **Available** list and choose the **Add** button. ODBC Test displays the name of the auto test.
4. Click the **Close** button.

Note If you rebuild an auto test, you do not need to reinstall it. Replace the old auto test DLL with the new auto test DLL while ODBC Test is not running.

You can also remove auto tests with the **Manage Auto Tests** dialog box.

Managing Test Groups

To easily run related auto tests, you can group auto tests together. For example, you might want to create a test group of auto tests for **SQLBindCol**, **SQLGetData**, and **SQLFetch**. An auto test can be included in any number of test groups.

You are not required to create any test groups; all auto tests are automatically included in the All test group.

▶ To create a test group

1. In ODBC Test, choose **Manage Test Groups** from the **Tools** menu. ODBC Test displays the **Manage Test Groups** dialog box.
2. Choose the **New** button, type the name of the test group in the **Group** box, and choose the **OK** button.

3 Select an auto test to add to the test group from the **Installed Auto Tests** list and choose the **Add** button. (The **Installed Auto Tests** list lists all installed auto tests by name. For information about how to install auto tests, see "Managing Auto Tests.") ODBC Test moves the auto test from the **Installed Auto Tests** list to the **Selected Auto Tests** list. Continue to add auto tests to the group until the group contains all of the auto tests that you want.

4 Click the **Close** button.

You can also use the Manage Auto Tests dialog box to add or remove auto tests from an existing test group and delete test groups. Removing an auto test from a test group or deleting a test group that contains an auto test does not affect the auto test; it remains installed in ODBC Test.

Running Auto Tests

After you have created and installed auto tests and created test sources, you can select the test cases you want to run and the test sources you want to run them against.

▶ To run one or more auto tests

1 In ODBC Test, choose **Run Auto Tests** from the **Tools** menu. ODBC Test displays the **Run Auto Tests** dialog box.

2 Select the test cases you want to run from the **Auto Tests** list.

The Auto Tests list shows the test cases in an hierarchical structure: groups contain auto tests and auto tests contain test cases. To expand or collapse how much of the structure is shown, click on the plus or minus sign beside each group or auto test name. You can select test cases in the following ways:

- **By Test Group**   Choose the test group name to select all test cases in all auto tests in a group. For example, to select all test cases in all installed auto tests, choose the **All** group name.
- **By Auto Test**   Choose the auto test name to select all test cases in an auto test.
- **By Test Case**   Choose the test case name to select an individual test case.

To select or unselect a test case or cases, click on the highlighted test group name, auto test name, or test case name with the mouse or press SPACEBAR.

You can save the list of test cases, or *run list*, you have selected by clicking the **Run Lists** button and clicking the **Save As** button. Later, you can select the same test cases by selecting the run list.

3 Select the test sources from the **Test Sources** dialog box that you want to run the test cases against. When ODBC Test runs the auto tests, it will run each selected test case against each selected test source.

4 Select where you want the auto tests to log output:

- **Log File** The default log file is AUTO.LOG in the current directory. To use a different log file, choose the **Log File** button. In the Log File dialog box, you can also specify whether to append to or replace the log file.
- **Screen** Log output to the **Output** window in ODBC Test.

If neither **Log File** nor **Screen** is selected, the tests will not log any information. ODBC Test always displays a list in the **Output** window of which tests were run and how many errors occurred.

5 Select the run-time options you want to use:

- **Debug** Determines whether the *fDebug* flag in the SERVERINFO structure is set to TRUE or FALSE. What a test does when *fDebug* is TRUE depends on how the test was written.
- **Isolate Tests** Determines whether **AutoTestFunc** is called once for each selected test case in an auto test (the tests are isolated) or once for the auto test. If **AutoTestFunc** is called once for each test case, only one bit in the *rglMask* bit mask in the SERVERINFO structure is set each time it is called; if it is called once for the auto test, a bit is set in *rglMask* for each selected test case.
- **Cursor Library** Determines the value of the *vCursorLib* variable in the SERVERINFO structure:

Check box	*vCursorLib* Value
Cleared	SQL_CUR_USE_DRIVER
Filled	SQL_CUR_USE_IF_NEEDED
Selected	SQL_CUR_USE_ODBC

How *vCursorLib* is used depends on how the test was written; it was intended to be used with the SQL_ATTR_ODBC_CURSORS attribute in **SQLSetConnectAttr**.

6 Click **OK**. ODBC Test runs each selected test case against each selected test source.

Auto Test Function Reference

This section describes the three functions that each auto test DLL must contain:

AutoTestName
AutoTestDesc
AutoTestFunc

AutoTestName

Description

AutoTestName returns the name of the auto test and the number of test cases it contains.

Syntax

BOOL EXTFUN AutoTestName(
    LPTSTR *szName*,
    UINT FAR * *piTestCases*);

Arguments

szName

The name of the auto test, such as "SQLAllocStmt Tests," is returned in the *szName* argument. This name must not exceed AUTO_MAX_TEST_NAME characters.

piTestCases

The number of test cases in the auto test is returned in the *piTestCases* argument.

Returns

TRUE if the auto test name is copied (with or without truncation) to *szName* and the number of test cases in the auto test is copied to *piTestCases*. Otherwise, FALSE.

Comments

ODBC Test calls this function to determine the name of the auto test and the number of test cases it contains.

Code Example

The following code example shows a simple **AutoTestName** function:

```
BOOL EXTFUN AutoTestName(LPSTR szName, UINT FAR * iTestCases);
{
   /* The returned name is shorter than AUTO_MAX_TEST_NAME. */
   lstrcpy(szName, "SQLAllocStmt Tests");
   *iTestCases = 10;
   return TRUE;
}
```

AutoTestDesc

Description

AutoTestDesc returns the name and description of the specified test case.

C Prototype

```
BOOL EXTFUN AutoTestDesc(
    UWORD      iTest,      /* Input:  Test case number        */
    LPTSTR     szName,     /* Output: Test case name          */
    LPTSTR     szDesc);    /* Output: Test case description   */
```

Arguments

iTest

The number of the test case. Test cases are numbered sequentially from 1 to the number of test cases in the auto test.

szName

The name of the test case is returned in the *szName* argument. This name must not exceed AUTO_MAX_TESTCASE_NAME characters.

szDesc

The description of the test case is returned in the *szDesc* argument. This description must not exceed AUTO_MAX_TESTDESC_NAME characters.

Return Values

TRUE if the test number was valid, the test case name is copied to *szName*, and the test case description is copied to *szDesc*. Otherwise, FALSE.

Comments

ODBC Test calls this function to determine the name and description of a test case. It displays this information when the user is selecting the test cases to run.

Code Example

The following code example shows a simple **AutoTestDesc** function:

```
#define NumCases(s) (sizeof(s) / sizeof(s[0]))

struct {
   LPSTR szName;   /* Test case name        */
   LPSTR szDesc;   /* Test case description */
} TestInfo[] = {
/* szName                   szDesc                                     */
/* ------------------       --------------------------------------- */
   "Valid connection",       "Call SQLConnect normally.",
   "IM002: No DSN",          "Call SQLConnect with no DSN or default.",
   "IM004: Bad SQLAllocEnv", "Make driver's SQLAllocEnv fail."
};

BOOL EXTFUN AutoTestDesc(UWORD iTest, LPSTR szName, LPSTR szDesc);
{
   if (iTest > NumCases(TestInfo))
      return FALSE;
   lstrcpy(szName, TestInfo[iTest-1].szName);
   lstrcpy(szDesc, TestInfo[iTest-1].szDesc);
   return TRUE;
}
```

AutoTestFunc

Description

AutoTestFunc runs one or more test cases in an auto test.

C Prototype

void EXTFUN AutoTestFunc(
lpSERVERINFO *lpServer*); /* Input: Test information */

Arguments

lpServer

The *lpServer* argument is a SERVERINFO structure containing information that includes the test cases to run, the test source to run them against, and how to run them. The SERVERINFO structure is defined in the AUTOTEST.H file. It has the following members:

hwnd

The handle of the window to which **szLogPrintf** and **szMessageBox** write screen output. *hwnd* is passed by **AutoTestFunc** to calls to **szMessageBox**.

szLogFile

The name of the log file to which **szLogPrintf** writes file output. *szLogFile* is not used by **AutoTestFunc**.

henv, hdbc, hstmt

If the test source is not "ODBC Test Handles," these are null and the auto test must allocate its own handles. If the test source is "ODBC Test Handles," these are the currently selected environment, connection, and statement handles; if there are no currently selected environment, connection, and statement handles, these are SQL_NULL_HANDLE.

szSource

The name of the test source.

szValidServer0

The name of the data source associated with the test source. The auto test connects to this data source. *szValidServer0* is a null pointer if the test source is "ODBC Test Handles."

szValidLogin0

The user ID associated with the test source. The auto test uses this to connect to the data source. *szValidLogin0* is a null pointer if the test source is "ODBC Test Handles."

szValidPassword0

The password associated with the test source. The auto test uses this to connect to the data source. *szValidPassword0* is a null pointer if the test source is "ODBC Test Handles."

Caution The password is stored in the \WINDOWS\GATOR32.INI file in unencrypted form. Because of this, you may want to create special data sources and passwords for use with ODBC Test or use only the ODBC Test Handles test source.

---

szKeywords

The keyword-value pairs associated with the test source. The auto test uses these to connect to the data source. *szKeywords* is a null pointer if the test source is "ODBC Test Handles."

rglMask

A bit mask in which each bit represents a test case to be run. The auto test uses the GETBIT macro from the AUTOTEST.H file to determine which bits are set.

failed

Included for backward compatibility with ODBC Test 1.0.

cErrors

The number of errors that occurred in all test cases run by **AutoTestFunc**. ODBC Test displays this number after it has called **AutoTestFunc**.

fDebug

TRUE if debugging was specified in the **Run Auto Tests** dialog box; otherwise, FALSE. What **AutoTestFunc** does when *fDebug* is TRUE depends on how it was written.

fScreen

TRUE if the **Screen** box was selected in the **Run Auto Tests** dialog box; otherwise, FALSE. *fScreen* is used by the **szLogPrintf** function in ODBC Test to determine whether to log output to the screen; it is not used by **AutoTestFunc**.

fLog

TRUE if the **Log File** box was selected in the **Run Auto Tests** dialog box; otherwise, FALSE. *fLog* is used by the **szLogPrintf** function in ODBC Test to determine whether to log output to the log file; it is not used by **AutoTestFunc**.

fIsolate

If the **Isolate Tests** box was selected in the **Run Auto Tests** dialog box, this will be TRUE and a single bit will be set in the *rglMask* member. Otherwise, FALSE.

vCursorLib

SQL_CUR_USE_IF_NEEDED, SQL_CUR_USE_ODBC, or SQL_CUR_USE_DRIVER, depending on the setting of the **Cursor Library** box in the **Run Auto Tests** dialog box. The auto test can pass this value to **SQLSetConnectAttr** for the SQL_ATTR_ODBC_CURSORS attribute.

hLoadedInst
The auto test DLL instance handle.

szBuff
Used by **szLogPrintf** to buffer output until it receives the string "\r\n". *szBuff* is not used by **AutoTestFunc**.

cBuff
Used by **szLogPrintf** to count the output in *szBuff*. *cBuff* is not used by **AutoTestFunc**.

Return Values

None.

Comments

ODBC Test calls this function to run one or more test cases in the auto test. If the *szSource* member of the SERVERINFO structure specified in the *lpServer* argument is ODBC Test Handles, **AutoTestFunc** uses the handles specified in the *henv*, *hdbc*, and *hstmt* members. Otherwise, it connects to the data source specified in the *szValidServer0* member using the information in the *szValidLogin0*, *szValidPassword0*, and *szKeywords* members.

AutoTestFunc runs the test cases specified in the *rglMask* member, using the GETBIT macro to determine which bits are set. It calls **szLogPrintf** to send output to the screen or log file and stores the total number of errors encountered in the *cErrors* member.

Code Example

The following code example shows a simple **AutoTestFunc** function and supporting function:

```
void EXTFUN AutoTestFunc(lpSERVERINFO lpServer)
{
   UINT iCase;

   InitTest(lpServer);

   /* Loop through the rglMask bitmask with the GETBIT macro to      */
   /* determine the test cases to run. NumTests is the count of test */
   /* cases returned by AutoTestName.                                */

   for (iCase = 1; iCase < NumTests; iCase++)
      if (GETBIT(lpServer->rglMask, iCase))
         RunTestCase(lpServer, iCase);

   EndTest(lpServer);
}

void INTFUN RunTestCase(lpSERVERINFO lpServer, UINT iCase);
{
   szLogPrintf(lpServer, FALSE, "Running test case %u.\r\n", iCase);
```

```
    /* Run the test case specified by iCase. */

    szLogPrintf(lpServer, FALSE, "Test case %u finished.\r\n", iCase);
}
```

ODBC Test Function Reference

This section describes the functions in ODBC Test (in GTRTST32.DLL) that an auto test calls to log output and display screen messages:

szLogPrintf
szMessageBox

szLogPrintf

Description

szLogPrintf prints output from an auto test on the screen, in a log file, or both.

C Prototype

BOOL szLogPrintf(

lpSERVERINFO	*lpServer*,	/* Input: Test information */
BOOL	*fForce*,	/* Input: Force screen output */
LPSTR	*szFmt*,	/* Input: Format string */
...);		/* Input: Arguments for format string */

Arguments

lpServer

The *lpServer* argument is a SERVERINFO structure containing information that includes the output window handle, the log file name, and where to send output. The SERVERINFO structure is defined in the AUTOTEST.H file. For information about the members of the structure, see the *lpServer* argument in **AutoTestFunc**.

When **AutoTestFunc** calls **szLogPrintf**, it should pass the value of *lpServer* that was passed to it by ODBC Test.

fForce

If TRUE, **szLogPrintf** writes the output to the screen regardless of the *fScreen* member of the *lpServer* argument. If FALSE, **szLogPrintf** writes the output to the screen only if the *fScreen* member of the *lpServer* argument is TRUE.

szFmt

A null-terminated format string compatible with the **wsprintf** function.

...

Arguments for the format string specified in the *szFmt* argument.

Return Values

TRUE if the function successfully logged the output; otherwise, FALSE. If FALSE is returned, a message box appears that allows the user to turn off logging.

Comments

Auto tests should call this function to log all output from tests.

Code Example

See **AutoTestFunc**.

szMessageBox

Description

szMessageBox formats a string and displays it using the **MessageBox** function in the Windows API.

C Prototype

```
int szMessageBox(
    HWND        hwnd,       /* Input:  Parent window handle */
    UINT        style,      /* Input:  Style of message box */
    LPSTR       szTitle,    /* Input:  Title of message box */
    LPSTR       szFmt,      /* Input:  Format string */
    ...);                   /* Input:  Arguments for format string */
```

Arguments

hwnd

The parent window handle to be passed to **MessageBox**. This should be the *hwnd* member of the *lpServer* structure passed to **AutoTestFunc**.

style

The style of the message box. For more information, see the *fuStyle* argument of the **MessageBox** function in the Windows API.

szTitle

The title of the message box. For more information, see the *lpszTitle* argument of the **MessageBox** function in the Windows API.

szFmt

A null-terminated format string compatible with the **wsprintf** function.

...

Arguments for the format string specified in the *szFmt* argument.

Return Values

szMessageBox returns the value returned by **MessageBox**.

Comments

Auto tests can call this function to display a message box. Because most auto tests are designed to be run without user interaction, this function should only be called when user interaction is required. To routinely log output, an auto test should call **szLogPrintf**.

Code Example

The following code example shows how **AutoTestFunc** might use **szMessageBox** to tell the user how to use a dialog box displayed by **SQLDriverConnect**:

```
#define CONN_STR_LEN 100
UCHAR InConnectString[CONN_STR_LEN], OutConnectString[CONN_STR_LEN];
SWORD StringLength2;

/* szTestName is the test name returned by AutoTestName */
szMessageBox(lpServer->WindowHandle,
             MB_ICONINFORMATION | MB_OK,
             szTestName,
             "Click the Cancel button in the next dialog box.");

lstrcpy(InConnectString, "DSN=");
lstrcat(InConnectString, lpServer->szValidServer0);
lstrcat(InConnectString, "\0");
SQLDriverConnect(ConnectionHandle, lpServer->WindowHandle,
                 InConnectString, lstrlen(InConnectString),
                 OutConnectString, CONN_STR_LEN, &StringLength2,
                 SQL_DRIVER_PROMPT);
```

Tool Reference

Tools are menu items that help you configure ODBC Test, such as the level of errors to report or whether menu items for functions the driver does not support are disabled.

User Options

The **User Options** item on the **Tools** menu displays the **User Options** dialog box, which controls the ODBC Test user interface. It also controls how ODBC Test checks the result of function calls. The options in this dialog box do not affect auto tests.

Automated Options Tab:

Driver Dependent Menus

If selected, ODBC Test disables those menu items not supported by the driver. For example, if the driver does not support **SQLDescribeParam**, ODBC Test disables the **SQLDescribeParam** menu item.

Automatic Error Checking

If selected, ODBC Test calls the Errors All function tool after each ODBC function is called. For more information, see "Errors All" in the "Function Tool Reference."

Null Terminator Checking

If selected, ODBC Test checks to see that the driver null-terminates all returned character values.

Buffer Overwrite Checking

If selected, ODBC Test fills output buffers with the pattern 0xCA before calling a function. After calling the function, it performs the following tests:

- Checks that the driver writes in the buffer when the function returns SQL_SUCCESS or SQL_SUCCESS_WITH_INFO. For example, if **SQLGetInfo** returns SQL_SUCCESS, ODBC Test checks that the driver wrote in the *InfoValuePtr* buffer.
- Checks that the driver does not write in the buffer when the function returns SQL_NO_DATA, SQL_ERROR, SQL_INVALID_HANDLE, SQL_STILL_EXECUTING, or SQL_NEED_DATA. For example, if **SQLGetInfo** is called with an invalid *InfoType*, ODBC Test checks that no data was written in the *ParameterValuePtr* buffer.
- Checks that the driver does not write past the end of the buffer. ODBC Test allocates an extra byte at the end of the buffer before calling the function. After calling the function, it checks whether the byte was overwritten. For example, if the *BufferLength* argument in **SQLGetInfo** is 10 and the data to be returned is 15 bytes long, ODBC Test checks that only 10 bytes were written in the *InfoValuePtr* buffer.

Note ODBC Test cannot check if the driver writes past the end of an output buffer if that buffer is an array or structure.

Version Numbers

If selected, ODBC Test displays the version number of option values in dialog boxes, such as the values for the *InfoType* argument in **SQLGetInfo**.

Bind Bookmark Column

If selected, ODBC Test automatically binds the bookmark column when binding all columns and the SQL_ATTR_USE_BOOKMARKS statement attribute is turned on.

ODBC Menu Version Tab:

Specifies the function menus to be displayed in the menu bar of ODBC Test, based on the version of ODBC selected. When the version is ODBC 3.0, the menus contain only ODBC 3.0 functions. When the version is ODBC 2.*x*, the menus contain only ODBC 2.*x* functions. When the version selected is Both 2.*x* and 3.0, the menus contain both ODBC 3.0 and ODBC 2.*x* functions.

Buffer Lengths Tab:

Default Buffer Length

Specifies the default length of output buffers, such as *OutConnectionString* in **SQLDriverConnect** or *ValuePtr* in **SQLGetStmtAttr**.

Argument Display Length

Specifies the default length of arguments displayed as output by the W2 logging level.

Max Bind Col All Length

Specifies the maximum length of the *ParameterValuePtr* buffer when the **Bind Col All** function tool is used.

Miscellaneous Tab:

Logging Level

Specifies the level of error output ODBC Test generates. For more information about ODBC Test errors and warnings, see "Error and Warning Messages," later in this chapter.

Error logging level	Error output
W0	Return codes and ODBC Test error messages (TST0*xxx*)
W1	W0 output and ODBC Test warning messages (TST1*xxx*)
W2	W1 output and function name and argument values

Font Button

Displays the Font dialog box in which you can specify the font and point size to be used by all text in the general output, connection, and rowset windows.

Rowset Options Tab:

The **Rowset Options** item in the **User Options** tab of the **Tools** menu displays the **Rowset Options** dialog box, which controls the values displayed in rowset windows and how rowset buffers are allocated.

Status Values

If selected, ODBC Test displays the value of the *RowStatusArray* specified in **SQLFetchScroll** at the start of each row in the rowset window.

Length Values

If selected, ODBC Test displays the value of the *StrLen_or_IndPtr* buffer bound with **SQLBindCol** at the end of each column in the rowset window.

Column Names

If selected, ODBC Test displays the name of each column in the rowset window.

Reserved Rows

Specifies the number of extra rows to allocate in the rowset buffers used with **SQLFetchScroll** and **SQLSetPos**. These rows are generally used for add buffers.

Display Rowset Automatically

If this check box is checked, ODBC Test automatically displays a rowset window when **SQLFetch**, **SQLFetchScroll**, or **SQLExtendedFetch** is called for the first time. This display requires hidden calls to several ODBC functions, which may mask or obscure driver problems. If this check box is unchecked, ODBC Test does not automatically display the rowset window, and so does not make the hidden ODBC function calls. The user may display the rowset window manually by using the **Display Rowset Function** tool in the **Results** menu. This check box controls the default setting of the **Display Rowset** check box in the dialog box displayed when **SQLFetch**, **SQLFetchScroll**, or **SQLExtendedFetch** is called.

Trace

The **Trace** item on the **Tools** menu turns tracing on and off. If tracing is currently disabled, choosing this menu item enables tracing. ODBC Test displays a dialog box in which you can specify a trace file and whether the Driver Manager overwrites or appends to that trace file. It is equivalent to calling **SQLSetConnectAttr** with the SQL_ATTR_TRACE and SQL_ATTR_TRACE_FILE attributes to enable tracing and specify a trace file. While tracing is enabled, ODBC Test places a check mark beside the **Trace** menu item.

If tracing is currently enabled, this menu item disables tracing. It is equivalent to calling **SQLSetConnectAttr** with the SQL_ATTR_TRACE attribute to disable tracing.

Function Tool Reference

Function tools are menu items that call a group of related ODBC functions or help you use an ODBC function. For example, **Full Disconnect** calls **SQLDisconnect**, **SQLFreeHandle** with a *HandleType* of SQL_HANDLE_DBC, and **SQLFreeHandle** with a *HandleType* of SQL_HANDLE_ENV; **Fill Param** displays a dialog box in which you enter parameter values. Function tools are listed at the bottom of the **Diag**, **Env**, **Conn**, **Desc**, **Stmt**, and **Results** menus beneath a separator line.

Note To abort those function tools that run in a loop, press the ESC key.

Bind Col All (Results Menu)

The **Bind Col All** function tool binds all the columns in a result set. If the **Bind Bookmark Column** control in the **User Options** dialog box is checked, and the SQL_ATTR_USE_BOOKMARKS statement attribute is set, **Bind Col All** will bind bookmark columns as well. The **Bind Col All** function tool:

1. Calls **SQLFreeStmt** with *Option* set to SQL_UNBIND to unbind any previously bound columns.
2. Calls **SQLNumResultCols** to determine the number of columns in the result set.
3. Calls **SQLDescribeCol** for each column in the result set to determine the data type and column size of the column. Based on the column size, it allocates a character buffer of up to the number of bytes specified with the **Max Bind Col All Length** box in the **User Options** dialog box.
4. Calls **SQLBindCol** for each column in the result set to bind the column to the default data type.

Data Sources All (Env/Connect Menu)

The **Data Sources All** function tool displays a list of all available data sources. This function tool:

1. Calls **SQLDataSources** with *Direction* set to SQL_FETCH_FIRST.
2. Calls **SQLDataSources** with *Direction* set to SQL_FETCH_NEXT until it returns SQL_NO_DATA.

Describe Col All (Results Menu)

The **Describe Col All** function tool displays the column name, type, column size, decimal digits, and nullability of each column in the result set on the current statement handle. This function tool:

1. Calls **SQLNumResultCols** to determine the number of columns in the result set.
2. Calls **SQLDescribeCol** for each column in the result set.

Display Rowset (Results Menu)

The **Display Rowset** function tool displays the **Rowset** window after **SQLFetch**, **SQLFetchScroll**, or **SQLExtendedFetch** is called for the first time. This tool is valid only if the **Display Rowset Automatically** check box in the Rowset Options dialog box is unchecked, and if columns were bound before the fetch operation.

Drivers All (Env/Connect Menu)

The **Drivers All** function tool displays a list of all available drivers and their attributes. This function tool:

1. Calls **SQLDrivers** with *Direction* set to SQL_FETCH_FIRST.
2. Calls **SQLDrivers** with *Direction* set to SQL_FETCH_NEXT until it returns SQL_NO_DATA.

Errors All (Diag/Misc Menu)

The **Errors All** function tool displays all pending errors.

1. If the **ODBC Menu Version** is set to ODBC 3.0 or Both, **Errors All** calls **SQLGetDiagRec** with a *HandleType* of SQL_HANDLE_STMT and *Handle* set to the current statement handle until **SQLGetDiagRec** returns SQL_NO_DATA. If the **ODBC Menu Version** is set to ODBC 2.*x*, it calls **SQLError** with the current *hstmt* until **SQLError** returns SQL_NO_DATA.
2. If the **ODBC Menu Version** is set to ODBC 3.0 or Both, **Errors All** calls **SQLGetDiagRec** with a *HandleType* of SQL_HANDLE_DBC and *Handle* set to the current connection handle until **SQLGetDiagRec** returns SQL_NO_DATA. If the **ODBC Menu Version** is set to ODBC 2.*x*, it calls **SQLError** with the current *hdbc* until **SQLError** returns SQL_NO_DATA.
3. If the **ODBC Menu Version** is set to ODBC 3.0 or Both, **Errors All** calls **SQLGetDiagRec** with a *HandleType* of SQL_HANDLE_ENV and *Handle* set to the current environment handle until **SQLGetDiagRec** returns SQL_NO_DATA. If the **ODBC Menu Version** is set to ODBC 2.*x*, it calls **SQLError** with the current *henv* until **SQLError** returns SQL_NO_DATA.
4. If the **ODBC Menu Version** is set to ODBC 3.0 or Both, **Errors All** calls **SQLGetDiagRec** with a *HandleType* of SQL_HANDLE_DESC and *Handle* set to the current descriptor handle until **SQLGetDiagRec** returns SQL_NO_DATA.

Fetch All (Results Menu)

The **Fetch All** function tool fetches all remaining rows in all pending result sets on the current statement handle. If any columns were bound, after **Fetch All** has completed these will contain the values from the last row of the last result set. The **Fetch All** function tool:

1. Calls **SQLGetFunctions** to determine if the driver supports **SQLMoreResults**.
2. Calls **SQLFetch** until it returns SQL_NO_DATA.
3. If the driver supports it, calls **SQLMoreResults**. If **SQLMoreResults** returns SQL_SUCCESS or SQL_SUCCESS_WITH_INFO, the **Fetch All** function tool returns to step 2. Otherwise, it stops.

Fill Param (Stmt/Statement Menu)

The **Fill Param** function tool displays a dialog box in which you can enter the values of the *ParameterValuePtr* and *StrLen_or_IndPtr* buffers for a parameter specified with **SQLBindParameter**.

If the parameter is a data-at-execution parameter, you can choose the SQL_LEN_DATA_AT_EXEC check box; if this check box is selected, the value of *StrLen_or_IndPtr* is used as the *length* parameter of the SQL_LEN_DATA_AT_EXEC macro.

If you have called **SQLSetStmtAttr** to set the SQL_ATTR_PARAMSET_SIZE statement attribute to a value greater than 1 (in ODBC 3.0), or if you have called **SQLParamOptions** with *crow* greater than 1 (in ODBC 2.*x*), you can enter parameter values into an array of parameters. Use the **Row** box to specify which element of the parameter array you are entering a value for. The **Row** box is disabled unless the SQL_ATTR_PARAMSET_SIZE statement attribute has been set to a value greater than 1, or **SQLParamOptions** has been called to set *crow* to a value greater than 1. When you change the value in the **Row** box, ODBC Test stores the current values of *ParameterValuePtr* and *StrLen_or_IndPtr* boxes in the previously specified element of the parameter arrays.

Full Connect (Conn/Connect Menu)

The **Full Connect** function tool completely connects to a data source.

1. If the **ODBC Menu Version** is set to ODBC 3.0 or Both, **Full Connect** calls **SQLAllocHandle** with a *HandleType* of SQL_HANDLE_ENV (if necessary). If the **ODBC Menu Version** is set to ODBC 2.*x*, it calls **SQLAllocEnv** (if necessary). If an environment has already been allocated, **Full Connect** will allocate a new environment if the New henv box has been selected in the **Full Connect** dialog box. Both environment handles will be listed in the environment handle list boxes in the tool bar; selecting a different environment in the list box will switch the displayed windows from one environment to the other.
2. **Full Connect** calls **SQLSetEnvAttr** to set the SQL_ATTR_ODBC_VERSION environment attribute to SQL_OV_ODBC3 if the ODBC 3.0 box is selected in the **ODBC Behavior** control of the **Full Connect** dialog box, or to SQL_OV_ODBC2 if the **ODBC 2.x** box is selected. If **Default** is selected, **SQLSetEnvAttr** will not be called.
3. If the **ODBC Menu Version** is set to ODBC 3.0 or Both, **Full Connect** calls **SQLAllocHandle** with a *HandleType* of SQL_HANDLE_DBC. If the **ODBC Menu Version** is set to ODBC 2.*x*, it calls **SQLAllocConnect**.

4. **Full Connect** calls **SQLSetConnectAttr** (ODBC 3.0) or **SQLSetConnectOption** (ODBC 2.*x*) with the SQL_ATTR_ODBC_CURSORS attribute (or SQL_ODBC_CURSORS option) and and the value SQL_CUR_USE_IF_NEEDED (if the **Use If Needed** box is selected in the **Cursor Library** control of the **Full Connect** dialog box), SQL_CUR_USE_ODBC (if **Use ODBC** is selected), or SQL_CUR_USE_DRIVER (if Use Driver is selected). If **Default** is selected, **SQLSetConnectAttr** or **SQLSetConnectOption** will not be called.
5. **Full Connect** calls **SQLDriverConnect** with the *InConnectionString* argument set to a null pointer and the *DriverCompletion* argument set to SQL_DRIVER_COMPLETE. If **SQLDriverConnect** is not supported, it invokes **SQLConnect** with the given connection information.
6. If the **ODBC Menu Version** is set to **ODBC 3.0** or **Both**, calls **SQLAllocHandle** with a *HandleType* of SQL_HANDLE_STMT. If the **ODBC Menu Version** is set to **ODBC 2.x**, calls **SQLAllocStmt**.

Full Disconnect (Conn/Connect Menu)

The **Full Disconnect** function tool completely disconnects from the data source on the current connection handle. This function tool:

1. Calls SQLDisconnect.
2. If the **ODBC Menu Version** is set to **ODBC 3.0** or **Both**, calls **SQLFreeHandle** with a *HandleType* of SQL_HANDLE_DBC. If the **ODBC Menu Version** is set to **ODBC 2.x**, calls SQLFreeConnect.
3. If there are no more connection handles on the current environment handle, calls **SQLFreeHandle** with a *HandleType* of SQL_HANDLE_ENV or **SQLFreeEnv**.

Get Data All (Results Menu)

The **Get Data All** function tool attempts to retrieve and display the data in every row and column in the result set on the current statement handle. The **Get Data All** function tool may not be able to display data for bound columns or columns that occur before the last bound column. This function tool:

1. Calls **SQLGetFunctions** to determine if the driver supports **SQLMoreResults**.
2. Calls **SQLNumResultCols**.
3. If the statement does not return a result set (the number of rows returned by **SQLNumResultCol** is 0), it calls **SQLRowCount**, and displays the number of rows affected by the insert, update, delete, or other statement. Skip to step 8.
4. If the statement returns a result set, it calls **SQLDescribeCol** to retrieve the name and column size of each column in the result set. Based on the column size, it allocates an output buffer of up to 65,535 bytes for each column.

5. Calls **SQLFetch**.
6. Calls **SQLGetData** for each column in the result set with a *TargetType* argument of SQL_C_CHAR. The Get Data All function tool only calls **SQLGetData** once for each column. If the data is longer than 65,535 bytes, <trunc> is displayed before the first byte of data in the buffer.
7. If SQL_ATTR_ROW_ARRAY_SIZE is greater than 1, calls **SQLSetPos** to position to the next row in the rowset.
8. Repeats steps 5 through 7 until **SQLFetch** returns SQL_NO_DATA.
9. If the driver supports it, calls **SQLMoreResults**. If **SQLMoreResults** returns SQL_SUCCESS or SQL_SUCCESS_WITH_INFO, the Get Data All function tool returns to step 2. Otherwise, it calls **SQLFreeHandle** with a *HandleType* of SQL_HANDLE_STMT to clear the result set.

Get Data Row (Results Menu)

The **Get Data Row** function tool retrieves and displays the data for every column in the current row of the result set on the current statement handle. You must call **SQLFetch**, **SQLFetchScroll** (ODBC 3.0), or **SQLExtendedFetch** (ODBC 2.*x*) before calling the **Get Data Row** function tool. The **Get Data Row** function tool:

1. Calls SQLNumResultCols.
2. Calls SQLDescribeCol to retrieve the name and column size of each column in the result set. Based on the column size, it allocates an output buffer of up to 65,535 bytes for each column.
3. Calls SQLGetData for each column in the result set with a *TargetType* argument of SQL_C_CHAR. The **Get Data Row** function tool only calls SQLGetData once for each column. If the data is longer than 65,535 bytes, <trunc> is displayed before the first byte of data in the buffer.

Get Descriptor All (Desc Menu)

The **Get Descriptor All** function tool displays the values for the descriptor fields of all descriptor handles on the connection. Values are displayed for all descriptor fields that either have defaults or have been set. This function tool:

- Calls **SQLGetDescField** for each field of each descriptor handle associated with the connection handle.

Get Functions All (Conn/Misc Menu)

The **Get Functions** All function tool displays whether each ODBC function is supported. This function tool:

- Calls **SQLGetFunctions** for each ODBC function.

Get Info All (Conn/Connect Menu)

The **Get Info All** function tool displays the return value of each information type defined for **SQLGetInfo** in ODBC 2.0. Which information types are returned depends upon the **ODBC Menu Version** selected in the **User Options** dialog box. The function tool:

- Calls **SQLGetInfo** for each value of *InfoType*.

Make Table (Conn Menu)

The **Make Table** function tool creates a table in the data source connected to. This tool is valid only after a data source has been connected to. The table created contains columns for data types supported by the data source; these columns contain random data. This function tool:

- Calls **SQLExecDirect** with a *StatementText* containing a CREATE TABLE statement.
- Calls **SQLExecDirect** with a *StatementText* containing a CREATE INDEX statement to create a unique index.
- Calls **SQLExecDirect** with a *StatementText* containing a SELECT statement selecting data from each column in the table.
- Calls **SQLBindParameter** to bind parameters for each column in the table.
- Calls **SQLExecDirect** with a *StatementText* containing an INSERT statement inserting data into each column of the table.

Set Driver Dependent Menus (Conn Menu)

The **Set Driver Dependent Menus** function tool disables all menu function commands that the driver associated with the connection does not support. This function tool:

- Calls **Get Functions All** to determine whether each ODBC function is supported or not supported by a driver.

Show Bound Cols (Results Menu)

The **Show Bound Cols** function tool displays the binding information and the value of each buffer bound to a column with **SQLBindCol**. If the rowset size (specified with the SQL_ATTR_ROWSET_SIZE statement attribute in ODBC 3.0, or the SQL_ROWSET_SIZE statement option in ODBC 2.*x*) is greater than 1, you must call **SQLFetchScroll** (ODBC 3.0) or **SQLExtendedFetch** (ODBC 2.*x*) to view the rest of the rowset. The **Show Bound Cols** function tool does not call any ODBC functions.

Show Cursor Settings (Stmt Menu)

The **Show Cursor Settings** function tool displays the value of all cursor parameters for the current cursor, including the cursor type, the cursor's concurrency, the rowset size set for calls to **SQLExtendedFetch**, and the rowset size set for calls to **SQLFetch** or **SQLFetchScroll**. This function tool:

1. Calls **SQLGetStmtAttr** with *Attribute* set to SQL_ATTR_CURSOR_TYPE.
2. Calls **SQLGetStmtAttr** with *Attribute* set to SQL_ATTR_CURSOR_CONCURRENCY.
3. Calls **SQLGetStmtAttr** with *Attribute* set to SQL_ATTR_ROW_ARRAY_SIZE.
4. Calls **SQLGetStmtAttr** with *Attribute* set to SQL_ATTR_ROWSET_SIZE.

Show Params (Stmt/Statement Menu)

The **Show Params** function tool displays the value of each buffer bound to a parameter marker with **SQLBindParameter**. It does not call any ODBC functions.

Function Reference

Functions are menu items that call ODBC functions. When you select a function from an ODBC Test menu, ODBC Test displays a dialog box that has one control for each argument in the function. When you choose the **OK** button in the dialog box, ODBC Test executes the function using the values specified for each argument.

Which functions are displayed in ODBC Test is determined by the **ODBC Menu Version** setting displayed by choosing the **Tools-Option** command. The choices are ODBC 2.x functions only, ODBC 3.0 functions only, or both.

This section describes any special characteristics of the dialog boxes that ODBC Test displays for the ODBC functions. The dialog boxes for many functions are straightforward and do not require further explanation. For general information about function dialog boxes, see "Using Function Dialog Boxes," earlier in this chapter. For information about each ODBC function, see the *Microsoft ODBC SDK Programmer's Reference*.

SQLAllocHandle (EnvConnect Menu)

You must allocate an environment handle before you can execute any other ODBC functions through the ODBC Test menu. You can allocate an environment handle by executing **SQLAllocHandle** with a *HandleType* of SQL_HANDLE_ENV or choosing Full Connect on the Connect menu. You do not need to allocate an environment handle before running any auto tests.

After ODBC Test successfully calls **SQLAllocHandle** with a *HandleType* of SQL_HANDLE_STMT, it adds the statement handle to the statement handle list of the current connection window.

SQLBindCol (Results Menu)

If the SQL_ATTR_BIND_TYPE statement attribute specifies row-wise binding, **SQLBindCol** builds a structure containing elements for the *TargetValuePtr* and *StrLen_or_IndPtr* buffers. If you make multiple calls to **SQLBindCol**, each additional pair of elements is added to the end of the structure.

SQLBindParam (Stmt Menu)

SQLBindParam binds a buffer to a parameter marker in an SQL statement. **SQLBindParam** was added to the ODBC API functions for compliance to the X/Open Call-Level Interface for ODBC 3.0, but has since been deprecated. **SQLBindParam** and **SQLBindParameter** both bind parameters. For a single set of input parameters, there is no difference between the two functions. To use input/output parameters, output parameters, or arrays of parameters with **SQLBindParam**, the application must set additional descriptor fields, because **SQLBindParam** does not include parameter type and buffer length arguments.

For more information, see the X/Open CAE Specification: SQL Call-Level Interface (CLI).

SQLBindParameter (Stmt/Statement Menu)

Unless you want to specify a null pointer for the *ParameterValuePtr* argument, you must enter a value for it. You can change this value later with the **Fill Param** function tool. If you have data-at-execution parameters, you must enter a valid value for *ParameterValuePtr* based on the *ValueType* specified. (This is a limitation of ODBC Test, not ODBC.)

To bind the parameter to the address of a specific row and column in a bound rowset on another statement handle, set the parameter to <rowset values> in the *ParameterValuePtr* and *StrLen_or_IndPtr* arguments. This activates the **Rowset hdbc** and **Rowset hstmt** list boxes, which enable you to specify the connection handle and statement handle of the bound rowset. The **Row** and **Column** text boxes allow you specify the row and column number, respectively.

If you have called **SQLSetStmtAttr** to set the SQL_ATTR_PARAMSET_SIZE statement attribute to a value greater than 1, to specify that you will pass an array of parameters, ODBC Test places the values you enter for the *ParameterValuePtr* and *StrLen_or_IndPtr* arguments in the first element of the parameter arrays. You can enter values for the other elements of the parameter arrays with the **Fill Param** function tool.

SQLColAttribute (Results Menu)

If you enter a *FieldIdentifier* that is not recognized by ODBC Test, it is assumed to be a driver-specific descriptor type. So that ODBC Test can correctly display the value returned for this option, you must specify the value's C data type in the *fFieldIdentifier Type* box. If the description type is SQL_C_ULONG, ODBC Test assumes the value is returned in the *NumericAttributePtr* argument; otherwise, it assumes the value is returned in the *CharacterAttributePtr* argument.

SQLFetch, SQLFetchScroll, SQLExtendedFetch (Results Menu)

After ODBC Test successfully calls **SQLFetch**, **SQLFetchScroll**, or **SQLExtendedFetch** on bound data, it creates a rowset window.

SQLFreeHandle (Env Menu)

After ODBC Test successfully calls **SQLFreeHandle** with a *HandleType* of SQL_HANDLE_STMT, it removes the statement handle from the statement handle list of the current connection window.

SQLGetConnectAttr (Attr Menu)

The word "Conn:" prefixes the values in the *Attribute* list to signify these are connection attributes (as opposed to statement attributes).

If you enter an *Attribute* value that is not recognized by ODBC Test, it is assumed to be a driver-specific connection or statement attribute. So that ODBC Test can correctly display the value returned for this attribute, you must specify the value's C data type in the **Parameter Type** box.

SQLGetInfo (Conn/Connect Menu)

If you enter an *InfoType* value that is not recognized by ODBC Test, it is assumed to be a driver-specific information type. So that ODBC Test can correctly display the value returned for this information type, you must specify the value's C data type in the **Information Value Type** box.

SQLGetStmtAttr (Attr Menu)

If you enter an *Attribute* value that is not recognized by ODBC Test, it is assumed to be a driver-specific statement attribute. So that ODBC Test can correctly display the value entered for this attribute, you must specify the value's C data type in the **Parameter Type** box.

SQLInstallODBC (Installer Menu)

SQLInstallODBC has been deprecated for ODBC 3.0. For information on **SQLInstallODBC**, see the *ODBC 2.0 Programmer's Reference*.

SQLSetConnectAttr (Attr Menu)

The word "Conn:" prefixes values in the *Attribute* list that are connection attributes; the word "Stmt:" prefixes values that are statement attributes.

If you enter an *Attribute* value that is not recognized by ODBC Test, it is assumed to be a driver-specific connection or statement attribute. So that ODBC Test can correctly display the value entered for this attribute, you must specify the value's C data type in the **Parameter Type** box.

SQLSetStmtAttr (Attr Menu)

If you enter an *Attribute* value that is not recognized by ODBC Test, it is assumed to be a driver-specific statement attribute. So that ODBC Test can correctly display the value entered for this attribute, you must specify the value's C data type in the **fAttribute Type** box.

Error and Warning Messages

This section lists error and warning messages generated by ODBC Test. All error and warning messages have the following form:

TSTyxxx : message

where

> "y" indicates the message level. Zero indicates an error message and 1 indicates a warning message.
>
> "xxx" is the message number.

For example:

```
TST0001: The value of cbConnStrLen is less than 0 and not SQL_NTS=
- 3
```

The following table lists the messages generated by ODBC Test. The values in *italics* are replaced by ODBC Test when it prints the error message. The value *codes* represents a list of return codes.

Message	Level	Description
TST0001	W0	The value of *%s* is less than 0 and not SQL_NTS=-3.
TST0002	W0	The value returned in *%s* does not match the length of string returned in *%s*.
TST0003	W0	The driver returned SQL_SUCCESS or SQL_SUCCESS_WITH_INFO but did not update *%s*.
TST0004	W0	Invalid return code '*%s*'. Valid return codes are *codes*.
TST0005	W0	Truncation implied but SQL_SUCCESS_WITH_INFO not returned, *%s=%d*. The value returned by the specified *pcb* parameter indicates that truncation occurred. However, SQL_SUCCESS_WITH_INFO was not returned from the driver.
TST0006	W0	The value *%ld* was not a valid named constant for *%s*. The value returned for the function named is not one of the legal values as documented in the *Microsoft ODBC SDK Programmer's Reference*. For example, **SQLGetInfo** should return either 0 or 1 for SQL_ODBC_SAG_CLI_COMPLIANCE.
TST0007	W0	The following set bits do not have a corresponding named constant: *0x%08lX* A bit in the bitmask returned for the function named is not one of the legal values as documented in the *Microsoft ODBC SDK Programmer's Reference*. For example, **SQLGetInfo** should only set bits for SQL_LCK_NO_CHANGE, SQL_LCK_EXCLUSIVE, and SQL_LCK_UNLOCK for the information type SQL_LOCK_TYPES.
TST0008	W0	Cannot allocate more than *%ld* bytes of memory.
TST0009	W0	Buffer %s contained an invalid count byte value.
TST1001	W1	Buffer *%s* was not updated. Buffer checking has been enabled, but after the function call the named buffer was not updated.
TST1002	W1	Truncation implied by SQL_SUCCESS_WITH_INFO, *%s=%d*. The value returned by the specified *pcb* parameter indicates that a truncation occurred, and SQL_SUCCESS_WITH_INFO was returned from the driver.

Message	Level	Description
TST1003	W1	The message for SQLState "*%s*" is longer than SQL_MAX_MESSAGE_LENGTH – 1. The description of *cbErrorMsgMax* indicates that you should allocate no more than SQL_MAX_MESSAGE_LENGTH for an error returned from **SQLError**. This message indicates that the driver has returned a message which exceeds this limit. Since you should not expect this long of a message, this is a warning to the driver writer that the size of the message should be decreased.
TST1004	W1	Data needed for Parameter *#%u* Indicates the parameter that ODBC Test has identified as the next SQL_DATA_AT_EXEC parameter. ODBC Test bases this identification on the value of the *rgbValue* buffer specified in **SQLBindParameter** (or **SQLBindCol** when **SQLSetPos** is used) and returned by **SQLParamData**.
TST1005	W1	Highest bound column is *%u*. Returned by the Get Data All and Get Data Row function tools when columns are bound. Some drivers cannot return data before this column.
TST1006	W1	A zero was received for *%s* indicating the driver does not support this function. In ODBC 2.0, **SQLGetInfo** returns 0 for integer-valued information types that do not apply to the driver or data source. ODBC Test displays this message when **SQLGetInfo** returns 0 for an information type for which there is no #define with a value of 0.
TST1007	W1	Since prgbValue was NULL, ODBC Test was unable to resolve the data type of the parameter. The data type will be set to SQL_C_CHAR by default.
TST1008	W1	Buffer %s was modified beyond indicated length.
TST1009	W1	Buffer %s was modified and should not have been.
TST1010	W1	Buffer %s contained an invalid count byte value.
TST1011	W1	Buffer %s is not properly null-terminated.
TST1012	W1	Buffer %s contains an embedded NULL.

APPENDIX A

Using 16-Bit and 32-Bit Applications with 32-Bit Drivers

16- and 32-bit applications and 32-bit drivers can be used together with the ODBC SDK. Windows 95 and Windows NT support the following combinations of applications and drivers:

- 16-bit applications with 32-bit drivers
- 32-bit applications with 32-bit drivers

Using a 32-bit application with a 16-bit driver is not supported.

Note This release of version 3.0 of the ODBC SDK supports Windows NT 3.51 and 4.0 for Intel, Alpha, and MIPS platforms.

The ODBC SDK includes the ODBC components necessary to support the configurations listed in the previous table: "thunking" dynamic-link libraries (DLLs) to convert 16-bit addresses to 32-bit addresses and vice versa. During the setup process, the Setup program determines which operating system you are using and installs ODBC components required by that system. Optionally, you can choose to install the ODBC components used by all systems.

Generally speaking, porting an application or driver from 16 bits to 32 bits involves five types of changes:

- Changes to message-handling code
- Changes due to integers and handles being 32 bits
- Changes in calls to Windows application programming interfaces (APIs)
- Changes to make the driver thread-safe
- Changes to ODBC components

For information about the first four items, see the Microsoft Win32 SDK documentation.

This appendix discusses the differences between 16-bit and 32-bit ODBC components. From an application or driver programming standpoint, the major difference between 16-bit and 32-bit ODBC components is that they have different file names. From a system standpoint, the architecture of each application-driver connection is different and the tools used to manage data sources are different.

Using 16-Bit Applications with 32-Bit Drivers

You can run 16-bit applications with 32-bit drivers on Windows 95 and Windows NT. The Windows on Windows (WOW) subsystem runs the applications in 16-bit mode and resolves 16-bit calls to the operating system. ODBC thunking DLLs resolve 16-bit calls from the application to 32-bit drivers. 16-bit applications use the Windows API and 32-bit drivers use the Win32 API.

Architecture

Figure A.1 shows how 16-bit applications communicate with 32-bit drivers. Between the 16-bit Driver Manager and the 32-bit drivers are generic thunking DLLs that convert 16-bit ODBC calls to 32-bit ODBC calls.

Note Anytime a 16-bit application interacts with a 32-bit driver, the 32-bit Driver Manager always returns "2.0" as the version of ODBC supported by the driver.

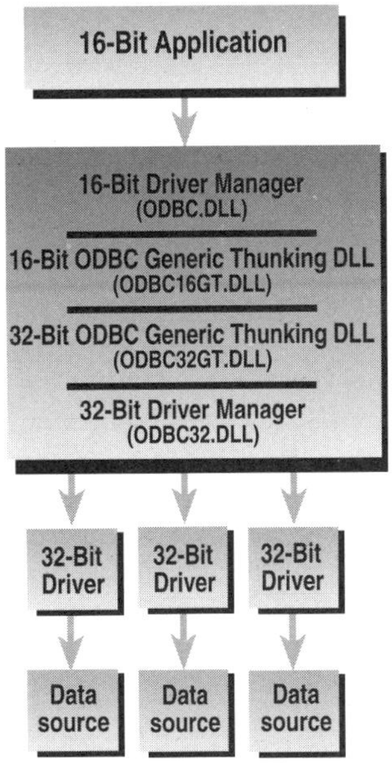

Figure A.1 Using 16-bit applications with 32-bit drivers

Administration

You can manage data sources for 32-bit drivers through the ODBC Control Panel device, the ODBC Administrator program, or the 32-bit ODBC Administrator program.

Figure A.2 shows how a 16-bit application calls a 32-bit driver setup DLL. Between the 16-bit installer DLL and the 32-bit driver setup DLL is a generic thunking DLL that converts 16-bit installer DLL calls to 32-bit installer DLL calls.

In Windows on Windows (16-bit to 32-bit thunking), an additional thunking DLL named DS32GT.DLL converts 16-bit argument values passed through a 32-bit setup DLL back to 16 bit.

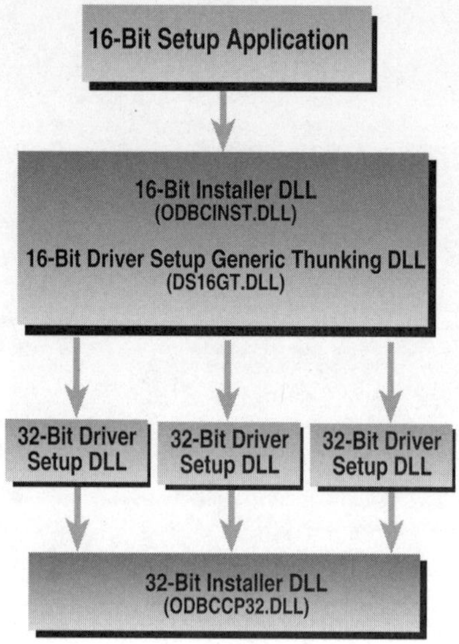

Figure A.2 Using 16-bit applications with 32-bit driver setup DLLs

Components

The ODBC SDK includes the following components for running 16-bit applications with 32-bit drivers. These components are found in the \ODBCSDK\REDIST32 directory.

File	Name
ODBC16GT.DLL	16-bit ODBC generic thunking DLL
ODBC32GT.DLL	32-bit ODBC generic thunking DLL
ODBCCP32.DLL	32-bit installer DLL
ODBCAD32.EXE	32-bit Administrator program
ODBCINST.HLP	Installer Help file
DS16GT.DLL	16-bit driver setup generic thunking DLL
CTL3D32.DLL	32-bit three-dimensional window style library

In addition, the following files, which are not part of the ODBC SDK 3.0, are required by and should be installed with the 16-bit application.

File	Name
ODBC.DLL	16-bit Driver Manager
ODBCINST.DLL	16-bit installer DLL
ODBCADM.EXE	16-bit Administrator program

Using 32-Bit Applications with 32-Bit Drivers

You can run 32-bit applications with 32-bit drivers on Windows 95 and Windows NT. The 32-bit applications and the 32-bit drivers use the Win32 API.

Architecture

Figure A.3 shows how 32-bit applications communicate with 32-bit drivers. The application calls the 32-bit Driver Manager, which in turn calls 32-bit drivers.

Important Do not use the 32-bit thunking installer DLL on Windows NT. Although it has the same file name as the 32-bit installer DLL, it is a different DLL.

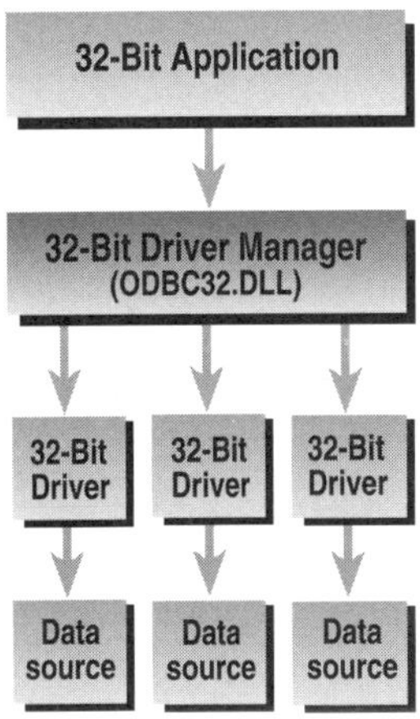

Figure A.3 Using 32-bit applications with 32-bit drivers

Administration

You can manage data sources for 32-bit drivers through the ODBC Control Panel device or the 32-Bit ODBC Administrator program. The icon for the 32-Bit ODBC Administrator program is in the ODBC SDK 3.0 program group.

Components

The ODBC SDK includes the following components for running 32-bit applications with 32-bit drivers. They are in the \ODBCSDK\REDIST32 directory.

File	Name
ODBC32.DLL	32-bit Driver Manager
ODBCCP32.DLL	32-bit installer DLL
ODBCAD32.EXE	32-bit Administrator program
ODBCINST.HLP	Installer Help file
CTL3D32.DLL	32-bit three-dimensional window style library
MSVCRT40.DLL	C run-time library

Index

D

E

F

G

H

I

L

M

N

O

P

Q

R

S

T

U

V

W

The Microsoft Open Database Standard for Microsoft Windows® and Windows NT® Operating Systems

Microsoft® ODBC 3.0

Programmer's Reference, Volume 2

Microsoft Press

PUBLISHED BY
Microsoft Press
A Division of Microsoft Corporation
One Microsoft Way
Redmond, Washington 98052-6399

Library of Congress Cataloging-in-Publication Data
Microsoft ODBC 3.0 software development kit and programmer's reference
/ Microsoft Corporation.
p. cm.
Includes index.
ISBN 1-57231-516-4
1. Computer software--Development. 2. Microsoft ODBC.
I. Microsoft Corporation.
QA76.76.D47M523 1997
005.74--dc21 96-45660
CIP

Printed and bound in the United States of America.

1 2 3 4 5 6 7 8 9 RTRT 2 1 0 9 8 7

097-0001688

Distributed to the book trade in Canada by Macmillan of Canada, a division of Canada Publishing Corporation.

A CIP catalogue record for this book is available from the British Library.

Microsoft Press books are available through booksellers and distributors worldwide. For further information about international editions, contact your local Microsoft Corporation office. Or contact Microsoft Press International directly at fax (206) 936-7329.

Acquisitions Editor: Casey D. Doyle
Project Editor: Maureen Williams Zimmerman
Technical Editor: Zephan Schroeder

Contents

PART 4

API Reference

CHAPTER 20

Function Summary

This chapter summarizes the functions used by ODBC-enabled applications and related software:

- ODBC functions
- Setup DLL functions
- Installer DLL functions
- Translation DLL functions

ODBC Function Summary

The following table lists ODBC functions, grouped by type of task, and includes the conformance designation and a brief description of the purpose of each function. For more information about conformance designations, see "ODBC and the Standard CLI" in Chapter 1, "Introduction." For more information about the syntax and semantics for each function, see Chapter 21, "ODBC API Reference."

An application can call the **SQLGetInfo** function to obtain conformance information about a driver. To obtain information about support for a specific function in a driver, an application can call **SQLGetFunctions**.

Task	Function name	Conformance	Purpose
Connecting to a data source	**SQLAllocHandle**	ISO 92	Obtains an environment, connection, statement, or descriptor handle.
	SQLConnect	ISO 92	Connects to a specific driver by data source name, user ID, and password.
	SQLDriverConnect	ODBC	Connects to a specific driver by connection string or requests that the Driver Manager and driver display connection dialog boxes for the user.
	SQLBrowseConnect	ODBC	Returns successive levels of connection attributes and valid attribute values. When a value has been specified for each connection attribute, connects to the data source.
Obtaining information about a driver and data source	**SQLDataSources**	ISO 92	Returns the list of available data sources.
	SQLDrivers	ODBC	Returns the list of installed drivers and their attributes.
	SQLGetInfo	ISO 92	Returns information about a specific driver and data source.
	SQLGetFunctions	ISO 92	Returns supported driver functions.
	SQLGetTypeInfo	ISO 92	Returns information about supported data types.
Setting and retrieving driver attributes	**SQLSetConnectAttr**	ISO 92	Sets a connection attribute.
	SQLGetConnectAttr	ISO 92	Returns the value of a connection attribute.
	SQLSetEnvAttr	ISO 92	Sets an environment attribute.
	SQLGetEnvAttr	ISO 92	Returns the value of an environment attribute.
	SQLSetStmtAttr	ISO 92	Sets a statement attribute.
	SQLGetStmtAttr	ISO 92	Returns the value of a statement attribute.

Task	Function name	Conformance	Purpose
Setting and retrieving descriptor fields	**SQLGetDescField**	ISO 92	Returns the value of a single descriptor field.
	SQLGetDescRec	ISO 92	Returns the values of multiple descriptor fields.
	SQLSetDescField	ISO 92	Sets a single descriptor field.
	SQLSetDescRec	ISO 92	Sets multiple descriptor fields.
Preparing SQL requests	**SQLPrepare**	ISO 92	Prepares an SQL statement for later execution.
	SQLBindParameter	ODBC	Assigns storage for a parameter in an SQL statement.
	SQLGetCursorName	ISO 92	Returns the cursor name associated with a statement handle.
	SQLSetCursorName	ISO 92	Specifies a cursor name.
	SQLSetScrollOptions	ODBC	Sets options that control cursor behavior.
Submitting requests	**SQLExecute**	ISO 92	Executes a prepared statement.
	SQLExecDirect	ISO 92	Executes a statement.
	SQLNativeSql	ODBC	Returns the text of an SQL statement as translated by the driver.
	SQLDescribeParam	ODBC	Returns the description for a specific parameter in a statement.
	SQLNumParams	ISO 92	Returns the number of parameters in a statement.
	SQLParamData	ISO 92	Used in conjunction with **SQLPutData** to supply parameter data at execution time. (Useful for long data values.)
	SQLPutData	ISO 92	Sends part or all of a data value for a parameter. (Useful for long data values.)

Task	Function name	Conformance	Purpose
Retrieving results and information about results	**SQLRowCount**	ISO 92	Returns the number of rows affected by an insert, update, or delete request.
	SQLNumResultCols	ISO 92	Returns the number of columns in the result set.
	SQLDescribeCol	ISO 92	Describes a column in the result set.
	SQLColAttribute	ISO 92	Describes attributes of a column in the result set.
	SQLBindCol	ISO 92	Assigns storage for a result column and specifies the data type.
	SQLFetch	ISO 92	Returns multiple result rows.
	SQLFetchScroll	ISO 92	Returns scrollable result rows.
	SQLGetData	ISO 92	Returns part or all of one column of one row of a result set (useful for long data values).
	SQLSetPos	ODBC	Positions a cursor within a fetched block of data, and allows an application to refresh data in the rowset, or update or delete data in the result set.
	SQLBulkOperations	ODBC	Performs bulk insertions and bulk bookmark operations, including update, delete, and fetch by bookmark.
	SQLMoreResults	ODBC	Determines whether there are more result sets available and, if so, initializes processing for the next result set.
	SQLGetDiagField	ISO 92	Returns additional diagnostic information (a single field of the diagnostic data structure).
	SQLGetDiagRec	ISO 92	Returns additional diagnostic information (multiple fields of the diagnostic data structure).

Task	Function name	Conformance	Purpose
Obtaining information about the data source's system tables (catalog functions)	**SQLColumnPrivileges**	ODBC	Returns a list of columns and associated privileges for one or more tables.
	SQLColumns	X/Open	Returns the list of column names in specified tables.
	SQLForeignKeys	ODBC	Returns a list of column names that make up foreign keys, if they exist for a specified table.
	SQLPrimaryKeys	ODBC	Returns the list of column names that make up the primary key for a table.
	SQLProcedureColumns	ODBC	Returns the list of input and output parameters, as well as the columns that make up the result set for the specified procedures.
	SQLProcedures	ODBC	Returns the list of procedure names stored in a specific data source.
	SQLSpecialColumns	X/Open	Returns information about the optimal set of columns that uniquely identifies a row in a specified table, or the columns that are automatically updated when any value in the row is updated by a transaction.
	SQLStatistics	ISO 92	Returns statistics about a single table and the list of indexes associated with the table.
	SQLTablePrivileges	ODBC	Returns a list of tables and the privileges associated with each table.
	SQLTables	X/Open	Returns the list of table names stored in a specific data source.
Terminating a statement	**SQLFreeStmt**	ISO 92	Ends statement processing, discards pending results, and, optionally, frees all resources associated with the statement handle.
	SQLCloseCursor	ISO 92	Closes a cursor that has been opened on a statement handle.
	SQLCancel	ISO 92	Cancels an SQL statement.
	SQLEndTran	ISO 92	Commits or rolls back a transaction.
Terminating a connection	**SQLDisconnect**	ISO 92	Closes the connection.
	SQLFreeHandle	ISO 92	Releases an environment, connection, statement, or descriptor handle.

Setup DLL Function Summary

The following table describes setup DLL functions. For more information about the syntax and semantics for each function, see Chapter 22, “Setup DLL API Reference.”

Task	Function name	Purpose
Setting up data sources and translators	**ConfigDriver**	Installs or uninstalls a driver.
	ConfigDSN	Adds, modifies, or deletes a data source.
	ConfigTranslator	Returns a default translation option.

Installer DLL Function Summary

The following table describes the functions in the installer DLL. For more information about the syntax and semantics for each function, see Chapter 23, “Installer DLL API Reference.”

Task	Function name	Purpose
Installing ODBC	**SQLConfigDriver**	Loads the driver-specific setup DLL.
	SQLGetInstalledDrivers	Returns a list of installed drivers.
	SQLInstallDriverEx	Adds a driver to the system information.
	SQLInstallDriverManager	Returns the target directory for the Driver Manager.
	SQLInstallerError	Returns error or status information for the installer functions.
	SQLInstallTranslatorEx	Adds a translator to the system information.
	SQLPostInstallerError	Allows a driver or translator setup library to report errors.
	SQLRemoveDriver	Removes a driver from the system information.
	SQLRemoveDriverManager	Removes ODBC core components from the system information.
	SQLRemoveTranslator	Removes the translator from the system information.

Task	Function name	Purpose
Configuring data sources	**SQLConfigDataSource**	Calls the driver-specific setup DLL.
	SQLCreateDataSource	Displays a dialog box to add a data source.
	SQLGetConfigMode	Retrieves the configuration mode that indicates where the ODBC.ini entry listing DSN values is in the system information.
	SQLGetPrivateProfileString	Writes a value to the system information.
	SQLGetTranslator	Displays a dialog box to select a translator.
	SQLManageDataSources	Displays a dialog box to configure data sources and drivers.
	SQLReadFileDSN	Reads information from file DSNs.
	SQLRemoveDefaultDataSource	Removes the default data source.
	SQLRemoveDSNFromIni	Removes a data source.
	SQLSetConfigMode	Sets the configuration mode that indicates where the ODBC.ini entry listing DSN values is in the system information.
	SQLValidDSN	Checks the length and validity of the data source name.
	SQLWriteDSNToIni	Adds a data source.
	SQLWriteFileDSN	Writes information to file DSNs.
	SQLWritePrivateProfileString	Gets a value from the system information.

Translation DLL Function Summary

The following table describes translation DLL functions. For more information about the syntax and semantics for each function, see Chapter 24, "Translation DLL Function Reference."

Task	Function name	Purpose
Translating data	**SQLDataSourceToDriver**	Translates all data flowing from the data source to the driver.
	SQLDriverToDataSource	Translates all data flowing from the driver to the data source.

CHAPTER 21

ODBC API Reference

The following pages describe each ODBC function in alphabetical order. Each function is defined as a C programming language function. Descriptions include the following:

- Purpose
- ODBC version
- Standard CLI conformance level
- Syntax
- Arguments
- Return values
- Diagnostics
- Comments about usage and implementation
- Code example
- References to related functions

The standard CLI conformance level can be one of the following: ISO 92, X/Open, ODBC, or Deprecated. A function tagged as ISO 92–conformant also appears in X/Open version 1, because X/Open is a pure superset of ISO 92. A function tagged as X/Open-compliant also appears in ODBC 3.0, because ODBC 3.0 is a pure superset of X/Open version 1. A function tagged as ODBC-compliant appears in neither standard. A function tagged as deprecated has been deprecated in ODBC 3.0.

Handling of diagnostic information is described in the **SQLGetDiagField** function description. The text associated with SQLSTATE values is included to provide a description of the condition, but is not intended to prescribe specific text.

SQLAllocConnect

Conformance

Version Introduced: ODBC 1.0
Standards Compliance: Deprecated

Summary

In ODBC 3.0, the ODBC 2.*x* function **SQLAllocConnect** has been replaced by **SQLAllocHandle**. For more information, see **SQLAllocHandle**.

Note For more information about what the Driver Manager maps this function to when an ODBC 2.*x* application is working with an ODBC 3.0 driver, see "Mapping Deprecated Functions" in Appendix G, "Driver Guidelines for Backward Compatibility."

SQLAllocEnv

Conformance

Version Introduced: ODBC 1.0
Standards Compliance: Deprecated

Summary

In ODBC 3.0, the ODBC 2.*x* function **SQLAllocEnv** has been replaced by **SQLAllocHandle**. For more information, see **SQLAllocHandle**.

Note For more information about what the Driver Manager maps this function to when an ODBC 2.*x* application is working with an ODBC 3.0 driver, see "Mapping Deprecated Functions" in Appendix G, "Driver Guidelines for Backward Compatibility."

SQLAllocHandle

Conformance

Version Introduced: ODBC 3.0
Standards Compliance: ISO 92

Summary

SQLAllocHandle allocates an environment, connection, statement, or descriptor handles.

Note This function is a generic function for allocating handles that replaces the ODBC 2.0 functions **SQLAllocConnect**, **SQLAllocEnv**, and **SQLAllocStmt**. To allow applications calling **SQLAllocHandle** to work with ODBC 2.*x* drivers, a call to **SQLAllocHandle** is mapped in the Driver Manager to **SQLAllocConnect**, **SQLAllocEnv**, or **SQLAllocStmt**, as appropriate. For more information, see "Comments." For more information about what the Driver Manager maps this function to when an ODBC 3.0 application is working with an ODBC 2.*x* driver, see "Mapping Replacement Functions for Backward Compatibility of Applications" in Chapter 17, "Programming Considerations."

Syntax

SQLRETURN **SQLAllocHandle**(
    SQLSMALLINT *HandleType*,
    SQLHANDLE *InputHandle*,
    SQLHANDLE * *OutputHandlePtr*);

Arguments

HandleType [Input]
The type of handle to be allocated by **SQLAllocHandle**. Must be one of the following values:

SQL_HANDLE_ENV
SQL_HANDLE_DBC
SQL_HANDLE_STMT
SQL_HANDLE_DESC

InputHandle [Input]
The input handle in whose context the new handle is to be allocated. If *HandleType* is SQL_HANDLE_ENV, this is SQL_NULL_HANDLE. If *HandleType* is SQL_HANDLE_DBC, this must be an environment handle, and if it is SQL_HANDLE_STMT or SQL_HANDLE_DESC, it must be a connection handle.

OutputHandlePtr [Output]
Pointer to a buffer in which to return the handle to the newly allocated data structure.

Returns

SQL_SUCCESS, SQL_SUCCESS_WITH_INFO, SQL_INVALID_HANDLE, or SQL_ERROR.

When allocating a handle other than an environment handle, if **SQLAllocHandle** returns SQL_ERROR, it sets *OutputHandlePtr* to SQL_NULL_HDBC, SQL_NULL_HSTMT, or SQL_NULL_HDESC, depending on the value of *HandleType*, unless the output argument is a null pointer. The application can then obtain additional information from the diagnostic data structure associated with the handle in the *InputHandle* argument.

Environment Handle Allocation Errors

Environment allocation occurs both within the Driver Manager and within each driver. The error returned by **SQLAllocHandle** with a *HandleType* of SQL_HANDLE_ENV depends on the level in which the error occurred.

If the Driver Manager cannot allocate memory for **OutputHandlePtr* when **SQLAllocHandle** with a *HandleType* of SQL_HANDLE_ENV is called, or the application provides a null pointer for *OutputHandlePtr*, **SQLAllocHandle** returns SQL_ERROR. The Driver Manager sets **OutputHandlePtr* to SQL_NULL_HENV (unless the application provided a null pointer, which returns SQL_ERROR). There is no handle with which to associate additional diagnostic information. (If the driver has additional diagnostic information, it will put the information on a skeletal handle that it allocates; the Driver Manager will read the information from the diagnostic structure associated with this handle.)

The Driver Manager does not call the driver-level environment handle allocation function until the application calls **SQLConnect**, **SQLBrowseConnect**, or **SQLDriverConnect**. If an error occurs in the driver-level **SQLAllocHandle** function, then the Driver Manager–level **SQLConnect**, **SQLBrowseConnect**, or **SQLDriverConnect** function returns SQL_ERROR. The diagnostic data structure contains SQLSTATE IM004 (Driver's **SQLAllocHandle** failed), followed by a driver-specific SQLSTATE value from the driver. For example, SQLSTATE HY001 (Memory allocation error) indicates that the Driver Manager's call to the driver-level **SQLAllocHandle** returned SQL_ERROR. The error is returned on a connection handle.

For additional information about the flow of function calls between the Driver Manager and a driver, see **SQLConnect**.

Diagnostics

When **SQLAllocHandle** returns SQL_ERROR or SQL_SUCCESS_WITH_INFO, an associated SQLSTATE value may be obtained by calling **SQLGetDiagRec** with the appropriate *HandleType* and *Handle* set to the value of *InputHandle*. SQL_SUCCESS_WITH_INFO (but not SQL_ERROR) can be returned for the *OutputHandle* argument. The following table lists the SQLSTATE values commonly returned by **SQLAllocHandle** and explains each one in the context of this function; the notation "(DM)" precedes the descriptions of SQLSTATEs returned by the Driver Manager. The return code associated with each SQLSTATE value is SQL_ERROR, unless noted otherwise.

SQLSTATE	Error	Description
01000	General warning	Driver-specific informational message. (Function returns SQL_SUCCESS_WITH_INFO.)
08003	Connection does not exist	(DM) The *HandleType* argument was SQL_HANDLE_STMT or SQL_HANDLE_DESC, but the connection specified by the *InputHandle* argument was not open. The connection process must be completed successfully (and the connection must be open) for the driver to allocate a statement or descriptor handle.
HY000	General error	An error occurred for which there was no specific SQLSTATE and for which no implementation-specific SQLSTATE was defined. The error message returned by **SQLGetDiagRec** in the **MessageText* buffer describes the error and its cause.
HY001	Memory allocation error	(DM) The Driver Manager was unable to allocate memory for the specified handle. The driver was unable to allocate memory for the specified handle.
HY009	Invalid use of null pointer	(DM) The *OutputHandlePtr* argument was a null pointer.
HY010	Function sequence error	(DM) The *HandleType* argument was SQL_HANDLE_DBC, and **SQLSetEnvAttr** has not been called to set the SQL_ODBC_VERSION environment attribute.

SQLSTATE	Error	Description
HY013	Memory management error	The *HandleType* argument was SQL_HANDLE_DBC, SQL_HANDLE_STMT, or SQL_HANDLE_DESC; and the function call could not be processed because the underlying memory objects could not be accessed, possibly because of low memory conditions.
HY014	Limit on the number of handles exceeded	The driver-defined limit for the number of handles that can be allocated for the type of handle indicated by the *HandleType* argument has been reached.
HY092	Invalid attribute/option identifier	(DM) The *HandleType* argument was not: SQL_HANDLE_ENV, SQL_HANDLE_DBC, SQL_HANDLE_STMT, or SQL_HANDLE_DESC.
HYC00	Optional feature not implemented	The *HandleType* argument was SQL_HANDLE_DESC and the driver was an ODBC 2.*x* driver.
HYT01	Connection timeout expired	The connection timeout period expired before the data source responded to the request. The connection timeout period is set through **SQLSetConnectAttr**, SQL_ATTR_CONNECTION_TIMEOUT.
IM001	Driver does not support this function	(DM) The *HandleType* argument was SQL_HANDLE_STMT, and the driver was not a valid ODBC driver. (DM) The *HandleType* argument was SQL_HANDLE_DESC, and the driver does not support allocating a descriptor handle.

Comments

SQLAllocHandle is used to allocate handles for environments, connections, statements, and descriptors, as described in the following sections. For general information about handles, see “Handles” in Chapter 4, “ODBC Fundamentals.”

More than one environment, connection, or statement handle can be allocated by an application at a time if multiple allocations are supported by the driver. There is no limit defined in ODBC on the number of environment, connection, statement, or descriptor handles that can be allocated at any one time. Drivers may impose a limit on the number of a certain type of handle that can be allocated at a time; for more information, see the driver documentation.

If the application calls **SQLAllocHandle** with **OutputHandlePtr* set to an environment, connection, statement, or descriptor handle that already exists, the driver overwrites the information associated with the *handle,* unless the application is using connection pooling (see "Allocating an Environment Attribute for Connection Pooling" later in this section). The Driver Manager does not check to see whether the *handle* entered in **OutputHandlePtr* is already in use, nor does it check the previous contents of a handle before overwriting them.

Note It is incorrect ODBC application programming to call **SQLAllocHandle** twice with the same application variable defined for **OutputHandlePtr* without calling **SQLFreeHandle** to free the handle before reallocating it. Overwriting ODBC handles in such a manner may lead to inconsistent behavior or errors on the part of ODBC drivers.

On operating systems that support multiple threads, applications can use the same environment, connection, statement, or descriptor handle on different threads. Drivers must therefore support safe, multithread access to this information; one way of achieving this, for example, is through the use of a critical section or a semaphore. For more information about threading, see "Multithreading" in Chapter 17, "Programming Considerations."

SQLAllocHandle does not set the SQL_ATTR_ODBC_VERSION environment attribute when it is called to allocate an environment handle; the environment attribute must be set by the application, or SQLSTATE HY010 (Function sequence error) will be returned when **SQLAllocHandle** is called to allocate a connection handle.

For standards-compliant applications, **SQLAllocHandle** is mapped to **SQLAllocHandleStd** at compile time. The difference between these two functions is that **SQLAllocHandleStd** sets the SQL_ATTR_ODBC_VERSION environment attribute to SQL_OV_ODBC3 when it is called with the *HandleType* argument set to SQL_HANDLE_ENV. This is done because standards-compliant applications are always ODBC 3.0 applications. Moreover, the standards do not require that the application version be registered. This is the only difference between these two functions; otherwise, they are identical.

Allocating an Environment Handle

An environment handle provides access to global information such as valid connection handles and active connection handles. For general information about environment handles, see "Environment Handles" in Chapter 4, "ODBC Fundamentals."

To request an environment handle, an application calls **SQLAllocHandle** with a *HandleType* of SQL_HANDLE_ENV and an *InputHandle* of SQL_NULL_HANDLE. The driver allocates memory for the environment information, and passes the value of the associated handle back in the **OutputHandlePtr* argument. The application passes the **OutputHandle* value in all subsequent calls that require an environment handle argument. For more information, see "Allocating the Environment Handle" in Chapter 6, "Connecting to a Data Source or Driver."

Under a Driver Manager's environment handle, if there already exists a driver's environment handle, then **SQLAllocHandle** with a *HandleType* of SQL_HANDLE_ENV is not called in that driver when a connection is made, only **SQLAllocHandle** with a *HandleType* of SQL_HANDLE_DBC. If a driver's environment handle does not exist under the Driver Manager's environment handle, then both **SQLAllocHandle** with a *HandleType* of SQL_HANDLE_ENV and **SQLAllocHandle** with a *HandleType* of SQL_HANDLE_DBC are called in the driver when the first connection handle of the environment is connected to the driver.

When the Driver Manager processes the **SQLAllocHandle** function with a *HandleType* of SQL_HANDLE_ENV, it checks the **Trace** keyword in the [ODBC] section of the system information. If it is set to 1, the Driver Manager enables tracing for the current application on a computer running Windows 95, Windows NT Server, or Windows NT Workstation. If the trace flag is set, tracing starts when the first environment handle is allocated, and ends when the last environment handle is freed. For more information, see Chapter 19, "Configuring Data Sources."

After allocating an environment handle, an application must call **SQLSetEnvAttr** on the environment handle to set the SQL_ATTR_ODBC_VERSION environment attribute. If this attribute is not set before **SQLAllocHandle** is called to allocate a connection handle on the environment, the call to allocate the connection will return SQLSTATE HY010 (Function sequence error). For more information, see "Declaring the Application's ODBC Version" in Chapter 6, "Connecting to a Data Source or Driver."

Allocating Shared Environments for Connection Pooling

Environments can be shared between multiple components on a single process. A shared environment can be used by more than one component simultaneously. When a component uses a shared environment, it can use pooled connections, which allow it to allocate and use an existing connection without re-creating that connection.

Before allocating a shared environment to be used for connection pooling, an application must first call **SQLSetEnvAttr** to set the SQL_ATTR_CONNECTION_POOLING environment attribute to SQL_CP_ONE_PER_DRIVER or SQL_CP_ONE_PER_HENV. **SQLSetEnvAttr** in this case is called with *EnvironmentHandle* set to null, which makes the attribute a process-level attribute.

After connection pooling has been enabled, an application then calls **SQLAllocHandle** with the *HandleType* argument set to SQL_HANDLE_ENV. The environment allocated by this call will be an implicit shared environment because connection pooling has been enabled. (For more information on connection pooling, see **SQLConnect**.)

When a shared environment is allocated, the environment to be used is not determined until **SQLAllocHandle** with a *HandleType* of SQL_HANDLE_DBC is called. At that point, the Driver Manager attempts to find an existing environment that matches the environment attributes requested by the application. If no such environment exists, one is created as a shared environment. The Driver Manager maintains a reference count for each shared environment; the count is set to 1 when the environment is first created. If a matching environment is found, the handle of that environment is returned to the application, and the reference count is incremented. An environment handle allocated this way can be used in any ODBC function that accepts an environment handle as an input argument.

Allocating a Connection Handle

A connection handle provides access to information such as the valid statement and descriptor handles on the connection and whether a transaction is currently open. For general information about connection handles, see "Connection Handles" in Chapter 4, "ODBC Fundamentals."

To request a connection handle, an application calls **SQLAllocHandle** with a *HandleType* of SQL_HANDLE_DBC. The *InputHandle* argument is set to the environment handle that was returned by the call to **SQLAllocHandle** that allocated that handle. The driver allocates memory for the connection information, and passes the value of the associated handle back in **OutputHandlePtr*. The application passes the **OutputHandlePtr* value in all subsequent calls that require a connection handle. For more information, see "Allocating a Connection Handle" in Chapter 6, "Connecting to a Data Source or Driver."

The Driver Manager processes the **SQLAllocHandle** function and calls the driver's **SQLAllocHandle** function when the application calls **SQLConnect**, **SQLBrowseConnect**, or **SQLDriverConnect**. (For more information, see **SQLConnect**.)

If the SQL_ATTR_ODBC_VERSION environment attribute is not set before **SQLAllocHandle** is called to allocate a connection handle on the environment, the call to allocate the connection will return SQLSTATE HY010 (Function sequence error).

When an application calls **SQLAllocHandle** with the *InputHandle* argument set to SQL_HANDLE_DBC, and the *InputHandle* argument set to a shared environment handle, the Driver Manager attempts to find an existing shared environment that matches the environment attributes set by the application. If no such environment exists, one is created, with a reference count (maintained by the Driver Manager) of 1. If a matching shared environment is found, that handle is returned to the application, and its reference count is incremented.

The actual connection to be used is not determined by the Driver Manager until **SQLConnect** or **SQLDriverConnect** is called. The Driver Manager uses the connection options in the call to **SQLConnect** (or the connection keywords in the call to **SQLDriverConnect**) and the connection attributes set after connection allocation to determine which connection in the pool should be used. For more information, see SQLConnect.

Allocating a Statement Handle

A statement handle provides access to statement information, such as error messages, the cursor name, and status information for SQL statement processing. For general information about statement handles, see "Statement Handles" in Chapter 4, "ODBC Fundamentals."

To request a statement handle, an application connects to a data source, and then calls **SQLAllocHandle** prior to submitting SQL statements. In this call, *HandleType* should be set to SQL_HANDLE_STMT and *InputHandle* should be set to the connection handle that was returned by the call to **SQLAllocHandle** that allocated that handle. The driver allocates memory for the statement information, associates the statement handle with the connection specified, and passes the value of the associated handle back in **OutputHandlePtr*. The application passes the **OutputHandlePtr* value in all subsequent calls that require a statement handle. For more information, see "Allocating a Statement Handle" in Chapter 9, "Executing Statements."

When the statement handle is allocated, the driver automatically allocates a set of four descriptors, and assigns the handles for these descriptors to the SQL_ATTR_APP_ROW_DESC, SQL_ATTR_APP_PARAM_DESC, SQL_ATTR_IMP_ROW_DESC, and SQL_ATTR_IMP_PARAM_DESC statement attributes. These are called *implicitly* allocated descriptors. To allocate an application descriptor explicitly, see the following section, "Allocating a Descriptor Handle."

Allocating a Descriptor Handle

When an application calls **SQLAllocHandle** with a *HandleType* of SQL_HANDLE_DESC, the driver allocates an application descriptor. These are called *explicitly* allocated descriptors. The application directs a driver to use an explicitly allocated application descriptor in place of an automatically allocated one for a given statement handle by calling the **SQLSetStmtAttr** function with the SQL_ATTR_APP_ROW_DESC or SQL_ATTR_APP_PARAM_DESC *Attribute*. An implementation descriptor cannot be allocated explicitly, nor can an implementation descriptor be specified in an **SQLSetStmtAttr** function call.

Explicitly allocated descriptors are associated with a connection handle rather than a statement handle (as automatically allocated descriptors are). Descriptors remain allocated only when an application is actually connected to the database. Because explicitly allocated descriptors are associated with a connection handle, an application can associate an explicitly allocated descriptor with more than one statement within a connection. An implicitly allocated application descriptor, on the other hand, cannot be associated with more than one statement handle. (It cannot be associated with any statement handle other than the one that it was allocated for.) Explicitly allocated descriptor handles can either be freed explicitly by the application, by calling **SQLFreeHandle** with a *HandleType* of SQL_HANDLE_DESC, or freed implicitly when the connection is closed.

When the explicitly allocated descriptor is freed, the implicitly allocated descriptor is once again associated with the statement (the SQL_ATTR_APP_ROW_DESC or SQL_ATTR_APP_PARAM_DESC *Attribute* for that statement is once again set to the implicitly allocated descriptor handle). This is true for all statements that were associated with the explicitly allocated descriptor on the connection.

For more information about descriptors, see Chapter 13, "Descriptors."

Code Example

See **SQLBrowseConnect**, **SQLConnect**, and **SQLSetCursorName**.

Related Functions

For information about	See
Executing an SQL statement	**SQLExecDirect**
Executing a prepared SQL statement	**SQLExecute**
Freeing an environment, connection, statement, or descriptor handle	**SQLFreeHandle**
Preparing a statement for execution	**SQLPrepare**
Setting a connection attribute	**SQLSetConnectAttr**
Setting a descriptor field	**SQLSetDescField**
Setting an environment attribute	**SQLSetEnvAttr**
Setting a statement attribute	**SQLSetStmtAttr**

SQLAllocStmt

Conformance

Version Introduced:	ODBC 1.0
Standards Compliance:	Deprecated

Summary

In ODBC 3.0, the ODBC 2.*x* function **SQLAllocStmt** has been replaced by **SQLAllocHandle**. For more information, see **SQLAllocHandle**.

Note For more information about what the Driver Manager maps this function to when an ODBC 2.*x* application is working with an ODBC 3.0 driver, see "Mapping Deprecated Functions" in Appendix G, "Driver Guidelines for Backward Compatibility."

SQLBindCol

Conformance

Version Introduced: ODBC 1.0
Standards Compliance: ISO 92

Summary

SQLBindCol binds application data buffers to columns in the result set.

Syntax

SQLRETURN **SQLBindCol**(
SQLHSTMT *StatementHandle*,
SQLUSMALLINT *ColumnNumber*,
SQLSMALLINT *TargetType*,
SQLPOINTER *TargetValuePtr*,
SQLINTEGER *BufferLength*,
SQLINTEGER * *StrLen_or_IndPtr*);

Arguments

StatementHandle [Input]
Statement handle.

ColumnNumber [Input]
Number of the result set column to bind. Columns are numbered in increasing column order starting at 0, where column 0 is the bookmark column. If bookmarks are not used—that is, the SQL_ATTR_USE_BOOKMARKS statement attribute is set to SQL_UB_OFF—then column numbers start at 1.

TargetType [Input]
The identifier of the C data type of the **TargetValuePtr* buffer. When retrieving data from the data source with **SQLFetch**, **SQLFetchScroll**, **SQLBulkOperations**, or **SQLSetPos**, the driver converts the data to this type; when sending data to the data source with **SQLBulkOperations** or **SQLSetPos**, the driver converts the data from this type. For a list of valid C data types and type identifiers, see the "C Data Types" section in Appendix D, "Data Types."

If the *TargetType* argument is an interval data type, the default interval leading precision (2) and the default interval seconds precision (6), as set in the SQL_DESC_DATETIME_INTERVAL_PRECISION and SQL_DESC_PRECISION fields of the ARD, respectively, are used for the data. If the *TargetType* argument is SQL_C_NUMERIC, the default precision (driver-defined) and default scale (0), as set in the SQL_DESC_PRECISION and SQL_DESC_SCALE fields of the ARD, are used for the data. If any default precision or scale is not appropriate, the application should explicitly set the appropriate descriptor field by a call to **SQLSetDescField** or **SQLSetDescRec**.

TargetValuePtr [Deferred Input/Output]

Pointer to the data buffer to bind to the column. **SQLFetch** and **SQLFetchScroll** return data in this buffer. **SQLBulkOperations** returns data in this buffer when *Operation* is SQL_FETCH_BY_BOOKMARK; it retrieves data from this buffer when *Operation* is SQL_ADD or SQL_UPDATE_BY_BOOKMARK. **SQLSetPos** returns data in this buffer when *Operation* is SQL_REFRESH; it retrieves data from this buffer when *Operation* is SQL_UPDATE.

If *TargetValuePtr* is a null pointer, the driver unbinds the data buffer for the column. An application can unbind all columns by calling **SQLFreeStmt** with the SQL_UNBIND option. An application can unbind the data buffer for a column, but still have a length/indicator buffer bound for the column, if the *TargetValuePtr* argument in the call to **SQLBindCol** is a null pointer, but the *StrLen_or_IndPtr* argument is a valid value.

BufferLength [Input]

Length of the **TargetValuePtr* buffer in bytes.

The driver uses *BufferLength* to avoid writing past the end of the **TargetValuePtr* buffer when returning variable-length data, such as character or binary data. Note that the driver counts the null-termination character when returning character data to **TargetValuePtr*. **TargetValuePtr* must therefore contain space for the null-termination character or the driver will truncate the data.

When the driver returns fixed-length data, such as an integer or a date structure, the driver ignores *BufferLength* and assumes the buffer is large enough to hold the data. It is therefore important for the application to allocate a large enough buffer for fixed-length data or the driver will write past the end of the buffer.

SQLBindCol returns SQLSTATE HY090 (Invalid string or buffer length) when *BufferLength* is less than 0 but not when *BufferLength* is 0. However, if *TargetType* specifies a character type, an application should not set *BufferLength* to 0, because ISO CLI–compliant drivers return SQLSTATE HY090 (Invalid string or buffer length) in that case.

StrLen_or_IndPtr [Deferred Input/Output]

Pointer to the length/indicator buffer to bind to the column. **SQLFetch** and **SQLFetchScroll** return a value in this buffer. **SQLBulkOperations** retrieves a value from this buffer when *Operation* is SQL_ADD, SQL_UPDATE_BY_BOOKMARK, or SQL_DELETE_BY_BOOKMARK. **SQLBulkOperations** returns a value in this buffer when *Operation* is SQL_FETCH_BY_BOOKMARK. **SQLSetPos** returns a value in this buffer when *Operation* is SQL_REFRESH; it retrieves a value from this buffer when *Operation* is SQL_UPDATE.

SQLFetch, **SQLFetchScroll**, **SQLBulkOperations**, and **SQLSetPos** can return the following values in the length/indicator buffer:

- The length of the data available to return
- SQL_NO_TOTAL
- SQL_NULL_DATA

The application can place the following values in the length/indicator buffer for use with **SQLBulkOperations** or **SQLSetPos**:

- The length of the data being sent
- SQL_NTS
- SQL_NULL_DATA
- SQL_DATA_AT_EXEC
- The result of the SQL_LEN_DATA_AT_EXEC macro
- SQL_COLUMN_IGNORE

If the indicator buffer and the length buffer are separate buffers, the indicator buffer can only return SQL_NULL_DATA, while the length buffer can return all others values.

For more information, see **SQLBulkOperations**, **SQLFetch**, **SQLSetPos**, and the "Using Length/Indicator Values" section in Chapter 4, "ODBC Fundamentals."

If *StrLen_or_IndPtr* is a null pointer, no length or indicator value is used. This is an error when fetching data and the data is NULL.

Returns

SQL_SUCCESS, SQL_SUCCESS_WITH_INFO, SQL_ERROR, or SQL_INVALID_HANDLE.

Diagnostics

When **SQLBindCol** returns SQL_ERROR or SQL_SUCCESS_WITH_INFO, an associated SQLSTATE value may be obtained by calling **SQLGetDiagRec** with a *HandleType* of SQL_HANDLE_STMT and a *Handle* of *StatementHandle*. The following table lists the SQLSTATE values commonly returned by **SQLBindCol** and explains each one in the context of this function; the notation "(DM)" precedes the descriptions of SQLSTATEs returned by the Driver Manager. The return code associated with each SQLSTATE value is SQL_ERROR, unless noted otherwise.

SQLSTATE	Error	Description
01000	General warning	Driver-specific informational message. (Function returns SQL_SUCCESS_WITH_INFO.)
07006	Restricted data type attribute violation	(DM) The *ColumnNumber* argument was 0, and the *TargetType* argument was not SQL_C_BOOKMARK or SQL_C_VARBOOKMARK.
07009	Invalid descriptor index	The value specified for the argument *ColumnNumber* exceeded the maximum number of columns in the result set.
HY000	General error	An error occurred for which there was no specific SQLSTATE and for which no implementation-specific SQLSTATE was defined. The error message returned by **SQLGetDiagRec** in the **MessageText* buffer describes the error and its cause.
HY001	Memory allocation error	The driver was unable to allocate memory required to support execution or completion of the function.
HY003	Invalid application buffer type	The argument *TargetType* was neither a valid data type nor SQL_C_DEFAULT.
HY010	Function sequence error	(DM) An asynchronously executing function was called for the *StatementHandle* and was still executing when this function was called. (DM) **SQLExecute**, **SQLExecDirect**, **SQLBulkOperations**, or **SQLSetPos** was called for the *StatementHandle* and returned SQL_NEED_DATA. This function was called before data was sent for all data-at-execution parameters or columns.
HY013	Memory management error	The function call could not be processed because the underlying memory objects could not be accessed, possibly because of low memory conditions.
HY090	Invalid string or buffer length	(DM) The value specified for the argument *BufferLength* was less than 0. (DM) The driver was an ODBC 2.*x* driver, the *ColumnNumber* argument was set to 0, and the value specified for the argument *BufferLength* was not equal to 4.

SQLSTATE	Error	Description
HYC00	Optional feature not implemented	The driver or data source does not support the conversion specified by the combination of the *TargetType* argument and the driver-specific SQL data type of the corresponding column. The argument *ColumnNumber* was 0 and the driver does not support bookmarks. The driver only supports ODBC 2.*x* and the argument *TargetType* was one of the following: SQL_C_NUMERIC SQL_C_SBIGINT SQL_C_UBIGINT and any of the interval C data types listed in "C Data Types" in Appendix D, "Data Types."
HYT01	Connection timeout expired	The connection timeout period expired before the data source responded to the request. The connection timeout period is set through **SQLSetConnectAttr**, SQL_ATTR_CONNECTION_TIMEOUT.
IM001	Driver does not support this function	(DM) The driver associated with the *StatementHandle* does not support the function.

Comments

SQLBindCol is used to associate, or *bind*, columns in the result set to data buffers and length/indicator buffers in the application. When the application calls **SQLFetch**, **SQLFetchScroll**, or **SQLSetPos** to fetch data, the driver returns the data for the bound columns in the specified buffers; for more information, see **SQLFetch**. When the application calls **SQLBulkOperations** to update or insert a row or **SQLSetPos** to update a row, the driver retrieves the data for the bound columns from the specified buffers; for more information, see **SQLBulkOperations** or **SQLSetPos**. For more information about binding, see "Overview" in Chapter 10, "Retrieving Results (Basic)."

Note that columns do not have to be bound to retrieve data from them. An application can also call **SQLGetData** to retrieve data from columns. Although it is possible to bind some columns in a row and call **SQLGetData** for others, this is subject to some restrictions. For more information, see **SQLGetData**.

Binding, Unbinding, and Rebinding Columns

A column can be bound, unbound, or rebound at any time, even after data has been fetched from the result set. The new binding takes effect the next time a function that uses bindings is called. For example, suppose an application binds the columns in a result set and calls **SQLFetch**. The driver returns the data in the bound buffers. Now suppose the application binds the columns to a different set of buffers. The driver does not place the data for the just-fetched row in the newly bound buffers. Instead, it waits until **SQLFetch** is called again and then places the data for the next row in the newly bound buffers.

Note The statement attribute SQL_ATTR_USE_BOOKMARKS should always be set before binding a column to column 0. This is not required, but is strongly recommended.

Binding Columns

To bind a column, an application calls **SQLBindCol** and passes the column number, type, address, and length of a data buffer, and the address of a length/indicator buffer. For information on how these addresses are used, see "Buffer Addresses," later in this section. For more information about binding columns, see "Using SQLBindCol" in Chapter 10, "Retrieving Results (Basic)."

The use of these buffers is deferred; that is, the application binds them in **SQLBindCol** but the driver accesses them from other functions—namely **SQLBulkOperations**, **SQLFetch**, **SQLFetchScroll**, or **SQLSetPos**. It is the application's responsibility to make sure that the pointers specified in **SQLBindCol** remain valid as long as the binding remains in effect. If the application allows these pointers to become invalid—for example, it frees a buffer—and then calls a function that expects them to be valid, the consequences are undefined. For more information, see "Deferred Buffers" in Chapter 4, "ODBC Fundamentals."

The binding remains in effect until it is replaced by a new binding, the column is unbound, or the statement is freed.

Unbinding Columns

To unbind a single column, an application calls **SQLBindCol** with *ColumnNumber* set to the number of that column and *TargetValuePtr* set to a null pointer. If *ColumnNumber* refers to an unbound column, **SQLBindCol** still returns SQL_SUCCESS.

To unbind all columns, an application calls **SQLFreeStmt** with *fOption* set to SQL_UNBIND. This can also be accomplished by setting the SQL_DESC_COUNT field of the ARD to zero.

Rebinding Columns

An application can perform either of two operations to change a binding:

- Call **SQLBindCol** to specify a new binding for a column that is already bound. The driver overwrites the old binding with the new one.
- Specify an offset to be added to the buffer address that was specified by the binding call to **SQLBindCol**. For more information, see the next section, "Binding Offsets."

Binding Offsets

A binding offset is a value that is added to the addresses of the data and length/indicator buffers (as specified in the *TargetValuePtr* and *StrLen_or_IndPtr* arguments) before they are dereferenced. When offsets are used, the bindings are a "template" of how the application's buffers are laid out and the application can move this "template" to different areas of memory by changing the offset. Because the same offset is added to each address in each binding, the relative offsets between buffers for different columns must be the same within each set of buffers. This is always true when row-wise binding is used; the application must carefully lay out its buffers for this to be true when column-wise binding is used.

Using a binding offset has much the same effect as rebinding a column by calling **SQLBindCol**. The difference is that a new call to **SQLBindCol** specifies new addresses for the data buffer and length/indicator buffer, while use of a binding offset does not change the addresses, but merely adds an offset to them. The application can specify a new offset whenever it wants and this offset is always added to the originally bound addresses. In particular, if the offset is set to 0 or if the statement attribute is set to a null pointer, the driver uses the originally bound addresses.

To specify a binding offset, the application sets the SQL_ATTR_ROW_BIND_OFFSET_PTR statement attribute to the address of an SQLINTEGER buffer. Before the application calls a function that uses bindings, it places an offset in bytes in this buffer. To determine the address of the buffer to use, the driver adds the offset to the address in the binding. Note that the sum of the address and the offset must be a valid address, but that the address to which the offset is added need not be a valid address. For more information on how binding offsets are used, see "Buffer Addresses," later in this section.

Binding Arrays

If the rowset size (the value of the SQL_ATTR_ROW_ARRAY_SIZE statement attribute) is greater than 1, the application binds arrays of buffers rather than single buffers. For more information, see "Block Cursors" in Chapter 11, "Retrieving Results (Advanced)."

The application can bind arrays in two ways:

- Bind an array to each column. This is called *column-wise binding* because each data structure (array) contains data for a single column.
- Define a structure to hold the data for an entire row and bind an array of these structures. This is called *row-wise binding* because each data structure contains the data for a single row.

Each array of buffers must have at least as many elements as the size of the rowset.

Note An application must verify that alignment is valid. For more information about alignment considerations, see "Alignment" in Chapter 17, "Programming Considerations."

Column-Wise Binding

In column-wise binding, the application binds separate data and length/indicator arrays to each column.

To use column-wise binding, the application first sets the SQL_ATTR_ROW_BIND_TYPE statement attribute to SQL_BIND_BY_COLUMN (this is the default). For each column to be bound, the application performs the following steps:

1. Allocates a data buffer array.
2. Allocates an array of length/indicator buffers.

   Note If the application writes directly to descriptors when column-wise binding is used, then separate arrays can be used for length and indicator data.

3. Calls **SQLBindCol** with the following arguments:
   - *TargetType* is the type of a single element in the data buffer array.
   - *TargetValuePtr* is the address of the data buffer array.
   - *BufferLength* is the size of a single element in the data buffer array. The *BufferLength* argument is ignored when the data is fixed-length data.
   - *StrLen_or_IndPtr* is the address of the length/indicator array.

For more information on how this information used, see "Buffer Addresses," later in this section. For more information about column-wise binding, see "Column-Wise Binding" in Chapter 11, "Retrieving Results (Advanced)."

Row-Wise Binding

In row-wise binding, the application defines a structure containing data and length/indicator buffers for each column to be bound.

To use row-wise binding, the application performs the following steps:

1. Defines a structure to hold a single row of data (including both data and length/indicator buffers) and allocates an array of these structures.

   Note If the application writes directly to descriptors when row-wise binding is used, then separate fields can be used for length and indicator data.

2. Sets the SQL_ATTR_ROW_BIND_TYPE statement attribute to the size of the structure containing a single row of data, or to the size of an instance of a buffer into which the results columns will be bound. The length must include space for all of the bound columns, and any padding of the structure or buffer to make sure that when the address of a bound column is incremented with the specified length, the result will point to the beginning of the same column in the next row. When using the *sizeof* operator in ANSI C, this behavior is guaranteed.

3. Calls **SQLBindCol** with the following arguments for each column to be bound:
   - *TargetType* is the type of the data buffer member to be bound to the column.
   - *TargetValuePtr* is the address of the data buffer member in the first array element.
   - *BufferLength* is the size of the data buffer member.
   - *StrLen_or_IndPtr* is the address of the length/indicator member to be bound.

For more information on how this information used, see "Buffer Addresses," later in this section. For more information about column-wise binding, see "Row-Wise Binding" in Chapter 11, "Retrieving Results (Advanced)."

Buffer Addresses

The *buffer address* is the actual address of the data or length/indicator buffer. The driver calculates the buffer address just prior to writing to the buffers (such as during fetch time). It is calculated from the following formula, which uses the addresses specified in the *TargetValuePtr* and *StrLen_or_IndPtr* arguments, the binding offset, and the row number:

Bound Address + *Binding Offset* + ((*Row Number* – 1) x *Element Size*)

where:

Variable	Description
Bound Address	For data buffers, the address specified with the *TargetValuePtr* argument in **SQLBindCol**. For length/indicator buffers, the address specified with the *StrLen_or_IndPtr* argument in **SQLBindCol**. For more information, see "Additional Comments" in the "Descriptors and SQLBindCol" section. If the bound address is 0, no data value is returned, even if the address as calculated by the previous formula is non-zero.
Binding Offset	If row-wise binding is used, the value stored at the address specified with the SQL_ATTR_ROW_BIND_OFFSET_PTR statement attribute. If column-wise binding is used or if the value of the SQL_ATTR_ROW_BIND_OFFSET_PTR statement attribute is a null pointer, *Binding Offset* is 0.
Row Number	The 1-based number of the row in the rowset. For single-row fetches, which are the default, this is 1.
Element Size	The size of an element in the bound array. If column-wise binding is used, this is **sizeof(SQLINTEGER)** for length/indicator buffers. For data buffers, it is the value of the *BufferLength* argument in **SQLBindCol** if the data type is variable length and the size of the data type if the data type is fixed length. If row-wise binding is used, this is the value of the SQL_ATTR_ROW_BIND_TYPE statement attribute for both data and length/indicator buffers.

Descriptors and SQLBindCol

The following sections describe how **SQLBindCol** interacts with descriptors.

Caution Calling **SQLBindCol** for one statement can affect other statements. This occurs when the ARD associated with the statement is explicitly allocated and is also associated with other statements. Because **SQLBindCol** modifies the descriptor, the modifications apply to all statements with which this descriptor is associated. If this is not the required behavior, the application should dissociate this descriptor from the other statements before calling **SQLBindCol**.

Argument Mappings

Conceptually, **SQLBindCol** performs the following steps in sequence:

1. Calls **SQLGetStmtAttr** to obtain the ARD handle.
2. Calls **SQLGetDescField** to get this descriptor's SQL_DESC_COUNT field, and if the value in the *ColumnNumber* argument exceeds the value of SQL_DESC_COUNT, calls **SQLSetDescField** to increase the value of SQL_DESC_COUNT to *ColumnNumber*.
3. Calls **SQLSetDescField** multiple times to assign values to the following fields of the ARD:
   - Sets SQL_DESC_TYPE and SQL_DESC_CONCISE_TYPE to the value of *TargetType*, except that if *TargetType* is one of the concise identifiers of a datetime or interval subtype, it sets SQL_DESC_TYPE to SQL_DATETIME or SQL_INTERVAL, respectively, sets SQL_DESC_CONCISE_TYPE to the concise identifier, and sets SQL_DESC_DATETIME_INTERVAL_CODE to the corresponding datetime or interval subcode.
   - Sets one or more of SQL_DESC_LENGTH, SQL_DESC_PRECISION, SQL_DESC_SCALE, and SQL_DESC_DATETIME_INTERVAL_PRECISION, as appropriate for *TargetType*.
   - Sets the SQL_DESC_OCTET_LENGTH field to the value of *BufferLength*.
   - Sets the SQL_DESC_DATA_PTR field to the value of *TargetValue*.
   - Sets the SQL_DESC_INDICATOR_PTR field to the value of *StrLen_or_Ind* (see the following paragraph).
   - Sets the SQL_DESC_OCTET_LENGTH_PTR field to the value of *StrLen_or_Ind* (see the following paragraph).

The variable that the *StrLen_or_Ind* argument refers to is used for both indicator and length information. If a fetch encounters a null value for the column, it stores SQL_NULL_DATA in this variable; otherwise, it stores the data length in this variable. Passing a null pointer as *StrLen_or_Ind* keeps the fetch operation from returning the data length, but makes the fetch fail if it encounters a null value and has no way to return SQL_NULL_DATA.

If the call to **SQLBindCol** fails, the content of the descriptor fields it would have set in the ARD are undefined, and the value of the SQL_DESC_COUNT field of the ARD is unchanged.

Implicit Resetting of COUNT Field

SQLBindCol sets SQL_DESC_COUNT to the value of the *ColumnNumber* argument only when this would increase the value of SQL_DESC_COUNT. If the value in the *TargetValuePtr* argument is a null pointer and the value in the *ColumnNumber* argument is equal to SQL_DESC_COUNT (that is, when unbinding the highest bound column), then SQL_DESC_COUNT is set to the number of the highest remaining bound column.

Cautions Regarding SQL_DEFAULT

To retrieve column data successfully, the application must determine correctly the length and starting point of the data in the application buffer. When the application specifies an explicit *TargetType*, application misconceptions are readily detected. However, when the application specifies a *TargetType* of SQL_DEFAULT, **SQLBindCol** can be applied to a column of a different data type from the one intended by the application, either from changes to the metadata or by applying the code to a different column. In this case, the application may fail to determine the start or length of the fetched column data. This can lead to unreported data errors or memory violations.

Code Example

In the following example, an application executes a **SELECT** statement on the Customers table to return a result set of the customer IDs, names, and phone numbers, sorted by name. It then calls **SQLBindCol** to bind the columns of data to local buffers. Finally, the application fetches each row of data with **SQLFetch** and prints each customer's name, ID, and phone number.

For more code examples, see **SQLBulkOperations**, **SQLColumns**, **SQLFetchScroll**, and **SQLSetPos**.

```
#define NAME_LEN 50
#define PHONE_LEN 10

SQLCHAR      szName[NAME_LEN], szPhone[PHONE_LEN];
SQLINTEGER   sCustID, cbName, cbCustID, cbPhone;
SQLHSTMT     hstmt;
SQLRETURN    retcode;
```

```
retcode = SQLExecDirect(hstmt,
            "SELECT CUSTID, NAME, PHONE FROM CUSTOMERS ORDER BY 2, 1, 3",
            SQL_NTS);

if (retcode == SQL_SUCCESS || retcode == SQL_SUCCESS_WITH_INFO) {

   /* Bind columns 1, 2, and 3 */

   SQLBindCol(hstmt, 1, SQL_C_ULONG, &sCustID, 0, &cbCustID);
   SQLBindCol(hstmt, 2, SQL_C_CHAR, szName, NAME_LEN, &cbName);
   SQLBindCol(hstmt, 3, SQL_C_CHAR, szPhone, PHONE_LEN, &cbPhone);

   /* Fetch and print each row of data.  On */
   /* an error, display a message and exit. */

   while (TRUE) {
      retcode = SQLFetch(hstmt);
      if (retcode == SQL_ERROR || retcode == SQL_SUCCESS_WITH_INFO) {
         show_error();
      }
      if (retcode == SQL_SUCCESS || retcode == SQL_SUCCESS_WITH_INFO){
         fprintf(out, "%-*s %-5d %*s", NAME_LEN-1, szName,
                 sCustID, PHONE_LEN-1, szPhone);
      } else {
         break;
      }
   }
}
```

Related Functions

For information about	See
Returning information about a column in a result set	**SQLDescribeCol**
Fetching a block of data or scrolling through a result set	**SQLFetchScroll**
Fetching multiple rows of data	**SQLFetch**
Releasing column buffers on the statement	**SQLFreeStmt**
Fetching part or all of a column of data	**SQLGetData**
Returning the number of result set columns	**SQLNumResultCols**

SQLBindParameter

Conformance

Version Introduced: ODBC 2.0
Standards Compliance: ODBC

Summary

SQLBindParameter binds a buffer to a parameter marker in an SQL statement.

Note This function replaces the ODBC 1.0 function **SQLSetParam**. For more information, see "Comments."

Syntax

```
SQLRETURN SQLBindParameter(
    SQLHSTMT        StatementHandle,
    SQLUSMALLINT    ParameterNumber,
    SQLSMALLINT     InputOutputType,
    SQLSMALLINT     ValueType,
    SQLSMALLINT     ParameterType,
    SQLUINTEGER     ColumnSize,
    SQLSMALLINT     DecimalDigits,
    SQLPOINTER      ParameterValuePtr,
    SQLINTEGER      BufferLength,
    SQLINTEGER *    StrLen_or_IndPtr);
```

Arguments

StatementHandle [Input]
Statement handle.

ParameterNumber [Input]
Parameter number, ordered sequentially in increasing parameter order, starting at 1.

InputOutputType [Input]
The type of the parameter. For more information, see "*InputOutputType* Argument" in "Comments."

ValueType [Input]
The C data type of the parameter. For more information, see "*ValueType* Argument" in "Comments."

ParameterType [Input]
The SQL data type of the parameter. For more information, see "*ParameterType* Argument" in "Comments."

ColumnSize [Input]
The size of the column or expression of the corresponding parameter marker. For more information, see "*ColumnSize* Argument" in "Comments."

DecimalDigits [Input]
The decimal digits of the column or expression of the corresponding parameter marker. For further information concerning column size, see "Column Size, Decimal Digits, Transfer Octet Length, and Display Size," in Appendix D, "Data Types."

ParameterValuePtr [Deferred Input]
A pointer to a buffer for the parameter's data. For more information, see "*ParameterValuePtr* Argument" in "Comments."

BufferLength [Input/Output]
Length of the *ParameterValuePtr* buffer in bytes. For more information, see "*BufferLength* Argument" in "Comments."

StrLen_or_IndPtr [Deferred Input]
A pointer to a buffer for the parameter's length. For more information, see "*StrLen_or_IndPtr* Argument" in "Comments."

Returns

SQL_SUCCESS, SQL_SUCCESS_WITH_INFO, SQL_ERROR, or SQL_INVALID_HANDLE.

Diagnostics

When **SQLBindParameter** returns SQL_ERROR or SQL_SUCCESS_WITH_INFO, an associated SQLSTATE value may be obtained by calling **SQLGetDiagRec** with a *HandleType* of SQL_HANDLE_STMT and a *Handle* of *StatementHandle*. The following table lists the SQLSTATE values commonly returned by **SQLBindParameter** and explains each one in the context of this function; the notation "(DM)" precedes the descriptions of SQLSTATEs returned by the Driver Manager. The return code associated with each SQLSTATE value is SQL_ERROR, unless noted otherwise.

SQLSTATE	Error	Description
01000	General warning	Driver-specific informational message. (Function returns SQL_SUCCESS_WITH_INFO.)
07006	Restricted data type attribute violation	The data type identified by the *ValueType* argument cannot be converted to the data type identified by the *ParameterType* argument. Note that this error may be returned by **SQLExecDirect**, **SQLExecute**, or **SQLPutData** at execution time, instead of by **SQLBindParameter**.
07009	Invalid descriptor index	(DM) The value specified for the argument *ParameterNumber* was less than 1.

SQLSTATE	Error	Description
HY000	General error	An error occurred for which there was no specific SQLSTATE and for which no implementation-specific SQLSTATE was defined. The error message returned by **SQLGetDiagRec** in the **MessageText* buffer describes the error and its cause.
HY001	Memory allocation error	The driver was unable to allocate memory required to support execution or completion of the function.
HY003	Invalid application buffer type	The value specified by the argument *ValueType* was not a valid C data type or SQL_C_DEFAULT.
HY004	Invalid SQL data type	The value specified for the argument *ParameterType* was neither a valid ODBC SQL data type identifier nor a driver-specific SQL data type identifier supported by the driver.
HY009	Invalid use of null pointer	(DM) The argument *ParameterValuePtr* was a null pointer, the argument *StrLen_or_IndPtr* was a null pointer, and the argument *InputOutputType* was not SQL_PARAM_OUTPUT.
HY010	Function sequence error	(DM) An asynchronously executing function was called for the *StatementHandle* and was still executing when this function was called. (DM) **SQLExecute**, **SQLExecDirect**, **SQLBulkOperations**, or **SQLSetPos** was called for the *StatementHandle* and returned SQL_NEED_DATA. This function was called before data was sent for all data-at-execution parameters or columns.
HY013	Memory management error	The function call could not be processed because the underlying memory objects could not be accessed, possibly because of low memory conditions.
HY021	Inconsistent descriptor information	The descriptor information checked during a consistency check was not consistent. (See the "Consistency Checks" section in **SQLSetDescField**.) The value specified for the argument *DecimalDigits* was outside the range of values supported by the data source for a column of the SQL data type specified by the *ParameterType* argument.

SQLSTATE	Error	Description
HY090	Invalid string or buffer length	(DM) The value in *BufferLength* was less than 0. (See the description of the SQL_DESC_DATA_PTR field in **SQLSetDescField**.) A parameter value, set with **SQLBindParameter**, was a null pointer, and the parameter length was not 0, SQL_NULL_DATA, SQL_DATA_AT_EXEC, SQL_DEFAULT_PARAM, or less than or equal to SQL_LEN_DATA_AT_EXEC_OFFSET.
HY104	Invalid precision or scale value	The value specified for the argument *ColumnSize* or *DecimalDigits* was outside the range of values supported by the data source for a column of the SQL data type specified by the *ParameterType* argument.
HY105	Invalid parameter type	(DM) The value specified for the argument *InputOutputType* was invalid (see "Comments").
HYC00	Optional feature not implemented	The driver or data source does not support the conversion specified by the combination of the value specified for the argument *ValueType* and the driver-specific value specified for the argument *ParameterType*. The value specified for the argument *ParameterType* was a valid ODBC SQL data type identifier for the version of ODBC supported by the driver, but was not supported by the driver or data source. The driver only supports ODBC 2.*x* and the argument *ValueType* was one of the following: SQL_C_NUMERIC SQL_C_SBIGINT SQL_C_UBIGINT and all of the interval C data types listed in "C Data Types" in Appendix D, "Data Types."
HYT01	Connection timeout expired	The connection timeout period expired before the data source responded to the request. The connection timeout period is set through **SQLSetConnectAttr**, SQL_ATTR_CONNECTION_TIMEOUT.
IM001	Driver does not support this function	(DM) The driver associated with the *StatementHandle* does not support the function.

Comments

An application calls **SQLBindParameter** to bind each parameter marker in an SQL statement. Bindings remain in effect until the application calls **SQLBindParameter** again, calls **SQLFreeStmt** with the SQL_RESET_PARAMS option, or calls **SQLSetDescField** to set the SQL_DESC_COUNT header field of the APD to 0.

For more information about parameters, see "Statement Parameters" in Chapter 9, "Executing Statements." For more information concerning parameter data types and parameter markers, see "Parameter Data Types" and "Parameter Markers" in Appendix C, "SQL Grammar."

ParameterNumber Argument

If *ParameterNumber* in the call to **SQLBindParameter** is greater than the value of SQL_DESC_COUNT, **SQLSetDescField** is called to increase the value of SQL_DESC_COUNT to *ParameterNumber*.

InputOutputType Argument

The *InputOutputType* argument specifies the type of the parameter. This argument sets the SQL_DESC_PARAMETER_TYPE field of the IPD. All parameters in SQL statements that do not call procedures, such as **INSERT** statements, are input parameters. Parameters in procedure calls can be input, input/output, or output parameters. (An application calls **SQLProcedureColumns** to determine the type of a parameter in a procedure call; parameters in procedure calls whose type cannot be determined are assumed to be input parameters.)

The *InputOutputType* argument is one of the following values:

- SQL_PARAM_INPUT. The parameter marks a parameter in an SQL statement that does not call a procedure, such as an **INSERT** statement, or it marks an input parameter in a procedure; these are collectively known as *input parameters*. For example, the parameters in **INSERT INTO Employee VALUES (?, ?, ?)** are input parameters, while the parameters in **{call AddEmp(?, ?, ?)}** can be, but are not necessarily, input parameters.

  When the statement is executed, the driver sends data for the parameter to the data source; the **ParameterValuePtr* buffer must contain a valid input value or the **StrLen_or_IndPtr* buffer must contain SQL_NULL_DATA, SQL_DATA_AT_EXEC, or the result of the SQL_LEN_DATA_AT_EXEC macro.

  If an application cannot determine the type of a parameter in a procedure call, it sets *InputOutputType* to SQL_PARAM_INPUT; if the data source returns a value for the parameter, the driver discards it.

- SQL_PARAM_INPUT_OUTPUT. The parameter marks an input/output parameter in a procedure. For example, the parameter in **{call GetEmpDept(?)}** is an input/output parameter that accepts an employee's name and returns the name of the employee's department.

When the statement is executed, the driver sends data for the parameter to the data source; the **ParameterValuePtr* buffer must contain a valid input value or the **StrLen_or_IndPtr* buffer must contain SQL_NULL_DATA, SQL_DATA_AT_EXEC, or the result of the SQL_LEN_DATA_AT_EXEC macro. After the statement is executed, the driver returns data for the parameter to the application; if the data source does not return a value for an input/output parameter, the driver sets the **StrLen_or_IndPtr* buffer to SQL_NULL_DATA.

Note When an ODBC 1.0 application calls **SQLSetParam** in an ODBC 2.0 driver, the Driver Manager converts this to a call to **SQLBindParameter** in which the *InputOutputType* argument is set to SQL_PARAM_INPUT_OUTPUT.

- SQL_PARAM_OUTPUT. The parameter marks the return value of a procedure or an output parameter in a procedure; these are collectively known as *output parameters*. For example, the parameter in **{?=call GetNextEmpID}** is an output parameter that returns the next employee ID.

  After the statement is executed, the driver returns data for the parameter to the application, unless the *ParameterValuePtr* and *StrLen_or_IndPtr* arguments are both null pointers, in which case the driver discards the output value. If the data source does not return a value for an output parameter, the driver sets the **StrLen_or_IndPtr* buffer to SQL_NULL_DATA.

ValueType Argument

The C data type of the parameter. This argument sets the SQL_DESC_TYPE, SQL_DESC_CONCISE_TYPE, and SQL_DESC_DATETIME_INTERVAL_CODE fields of the APD. This must be one of the values in the "C Data Types" section of Appendix D, "Data Types."

If the *ValueType* argument is one of the interval data types, the SQL_DESC_TYPE field of the *ParameterNumber* record of the APD is set to SQL_INTERVAL, the SQL_DESC_CONCISE_TYPE field of the APD is set to the concise interval data type, and the SQL_DESC_DATETIME_INTERVAL_CODE field of the *ParameterNumber* record is set to a subcode for the specific interval data type (see Appendix D, "Data Types"). The default interval leading precision (2) and default interval seconds precision (6), as set in the SQL_DESC_DATETIME_INTERVAL_PRECISION and SQL_DESC_PRECISION fields of the APD, respectively, are used for the data. If either default precision is not appropriate, the application should explicitly set the descriptor field by a call to **SQLSetDescField** or **SQLSetDescRec**.

If the *ValueType* argument is one of the datetime data types, the SQL_DESC_TYPE field of the *ParameterNumber* record of the APD is set to SQL_DATETIME, the SQL_DESC_CONCISE_TYPE field of the *ParameterNumber* record of the APD is set to the concise datetime C data type, and the SQL_DESC_DATETIME_INTERVAL_CODE field of the *ParameterNumber* record is set to a subcode for the specific datetime data type (see Appendix D, "Data Types").

If the *ValueType* argument is a SQL_C_NUMERIC data type, the default precision (which is driver-defined) and the default scale (0), as set in the SQL_DESC_PRECISION and SQL_DESC_SCALE fields of the APD, are used for the data. If the default precision or scale is not appropriate, the application should explicitly set the descriptor field by a call to **SQLSetDescField** or **SQLSetDescRec**.

SQL_C_DEFAULT specifies that the parameter value be transferred from the default C data type for the SQL data type specified with *ParameterType*.

For more information, see "Default C Data Types," "Converting Data from C to SQL Data Types," and "Converting Data from SQL to C Data Types" in Appendix D, "Data Types."

ParameterType Argument

This must be one of the values in the "SQL Data Types" section of Appendix D, "Data Types," or a driver-specific value. This argument sets the SQL_DESC_TYPE, SQL_DESC_CONCISE_TYPE, and SQL_DESC_DATETIME_INTERVAL_CODE fields of the IPD.

If the *ParameterType* argument is one of the datetime identifiers, the SQL_DESC_TYPE field of the IPD is set to SQL_DATETIME, the SQL_DESC_CONCISE_TYPE field of the IPD is set to the concise datetime SQL data type, and the SQL_DESC_DATETIME_INTERVAL_CODE field is set to the appropriate datetime subcode value.

If *ParameterType* is one of the interval identifiers, the SQL_DESC_TYPE field of the IPD is set to SQL_INTERVAL, the SQL_DESC_CONCISE_TYPE field of the IPD is set to the concise SQL interval data type, and the SQL_DESC_DATETIME_INTERVAL_CODE field of the IPD is set to the appropriate interval subcode. The SQL_DESC_DATETIME_INTERVAL_PRECISION field of the IPD is set to the interval leading precision, and the SQL_DESC_PRECISION field is set to the interval seconds precision, if applicable. If the default value of SQL_DESC_DATETIME_INTERVAL_PRECISION or SQL_DESC_PRECISION is not appropriate, the application should explicitly set it by calling **SQLSetDescField**. For more information on any of these fields, see **SQLSetDescField**.

If the *ValueType* argument is a SQL_NUMERIC data type, the default precision (which is driver-defined) and the default scale (0), as set in the SQL_DESC_PRECISION and SQL_DESC_SCALE fields of the IPD, are used for the data. If the default precision or scale is not appropriate, the application should explicitly set the descriptor field by a call to **SQLSetDescField** or **SQLSetDescRec**.

For information about how data is converted, see "Converting Data from C to SQL Data Types" and "Converting Data from SQL to C Data Types" in Appendix D, "Data Types."

ColumnSize Argument

The *ColumnSize* argument specifies the size of the column or expression corresponding to the parameter marker, or the length of that data, or both. This argument sets different fields of the IPD, depending on the SQL data type (the *ParameterType* argument). The following rules apply to this mapping:

- If *ParameterType* is SQL_CHAR, SQL_VARCHAR, SQL_LONGVARCHAR, SQL_BINARY, SQL_VARBINARY, SQL_LONGVARBINARY, or one of the concise SQL datetime or interval data types, the SQL_DESC_LENGTH field of the IPD is set to the value of *ColumnSize*. (For more information, see the "Column Size, Decimal Digits, Transfer Octet Length, and Display Size" section in Appendix D, "Data Types.")
- If *ParameterType* is SQL_DECIMAL, SQL_NUMERIC, SQL_FLOAT, SQL_REAL, or SQL_DOUBLE, the SQL_DESC_PRECISION field of the IPD is set to the value of *ColumnSize*.
- For other data types, the *ColumnSize* argument is ignored.

For more information, see "Passing Parameter Values" and SQL_DATA_AT_EXEC in "*StrLen_or_IndPtr* Argument."

DecimalDigits Argument

If *ParameterType* is SQL_TYPE_TIME, SQL_TYPE_TIMESTAMP, SQL_INTERVAL_SECOND, SQL_INTERVAL_DAY_TO_SECOND, SQL_INTERVAL_HOUR_TO_SECOND, or SQL_INTERVAL_MINUTE_TO_SECOND, the SQL_DESC_PRECISION field of the IPD is set to *DecimalDigits*. If *ParameterType* is SQL_NUMERIC or SQL_DECIMAL, the SQL_DESC_SCALE field of the IPD is set to *DecimalDigits*. For all other data types, the *DecimalDigits* argument is ignored.

ParameterValuePtr Argument

The *ParameterValuePtr* argument points to a buffer that, when **SQLExecute** or **SQLExecDirect** is called, contains the actual data for the parameter. The data must be in the form specified by the *ValueType* argument. This argument sets the SQL_DESC_DATA_PTR field of the APD. An application can set the *ParameterValuePtr* argument to a null pointer, as long as **StrLen_or_IndPtr* is SQL_NULL_DATA or SQL_DATA_AT_EXEC. (This applies only to input or input/output parameters.)

If **StrLen_or_IndPtr* is the result of the SQL_LEN_DATA_AT_EXEC(*length*) macro or SQL_DATA_AT_EXEC, then *ParameterValuePtr* is an application-defined, 32-bit value that is associated with the parameter. It is returned to the application through **SQLParamData**. For example, *ParameterValuePtr* might be a token such as a parameter number, a pointer to data, or a pointer to a structure that the application used to bind input parameters. Note, however, that if the parameter is an input/output parameter, *ParameterValuePtr* must be a pointer to a buffer where the output value will be stored. If the value in the SQL_ATTR_PARAMSET_SIZE statement attribute is greater than 1, the application can use the value pointed to by the SQL_ATTR_PARAMS_PROCESSED_PTR statement attribute in conjunction with the *ParameterValuePtr* argument. For example, *ParameterValuePtr* might point to an array of values and the application might use the value pointed to by SQL_ATTR_PARAMS_PROCESSED_PTR to retrieve the correct value from the array. For more information, see "Passing Parameter Values" later in this section.

If the *InputOutputType* argument is SQL_PARAM_INPUT_OUTPUT or SQL_PARAM_OUTPUT, *ParameterValuePtr* points to a buffer in which the driver returns the output value. If the procedure returns one or more result sets, the **ParameterValuePtr* buffer is not guaranteed to be set until all result sets/row counts have been processed. If the buffer is not set until processing is complete, the output parameters and return values are unavailable until **SQLMoreResults** returns SQL_NO_DATA. Calling **SQLCloseCursor** or **SQLFreeStmt** with an Option of SQL_CLOSE will cause these values to be discarded.

If the value in the SQL_ATTR_PARAMSET_SIZE statement attribute is greater than 1, *ParameterValuePtr* points to an array. A single SQL statement processes the entire array of input values for an input or input/output parameter and returns an array of output values for an input/output or output parameter.

A driver will return SQLSTATE HY090 (Invalid string or buffer length), if *ParameterValuePtr* is not a null pointer and **StrLen_or_IndPtr* is not SQL_NTS, SQL_NULL_DATA, SQL_DATA_AT_EXEC, SQL_DEFAULT_PARAM, greater than or equal to 0, or less than or equal to the value of SQL_LEN_DATA_AT_EXEC_OFFSET.

BufferLength Argument

For character and binary C data, the *BufferLength* argument specifies the length of the **ParameterValuePtr* buffer (if it is a single element) or the length of an element in the **ParameterValuePtr* array (if the value in the SQL_ATTR_PARAMSET_SIZE statement attribute is greater than 1). This argument sets the

SQL_DESC_OCTET_LENGTH record field of the APD. If the application specifies multiple values, *BufferLength* is used to determine the location of values in the **ParameterValuePtr* array, both on input and on output. For input/output and output parameters, it is used to determine whether to truncate character and binary C data on output:

- For character C data, if the number of bytes available to return is greater than or equal to *BufferLength*, the data in **ParameterValuePtr* is truncated to *BufferLength* less the length of a null-termination character and is null-terminated by the driver.
- For binary C data, if the number of bytes available to return is greater than *BufferLength*, the data in **ParameterValuePtr* is truncated to *BufferLength* bytes.

For all other types of C data, the *BufferLength* argument is ignored. The length of the **ParameterValuePtr* buffer (if it is a single element) or the length of an element in the **ParameterValuePtr* array (if the application calls **SQLSetStmtAttr** with an *Attribute* argument of SQL_ATTR_PARAMSET_SIZE to specify multiple values for each parameter) is assumed to be the length of the C data type.

Note When an ODBC 1.0 application calls **SQLSetParam** in an ODBC 3.0 driver, the Driver Manager converts this to a call to **SQLBindParameter** in which the *BufferLength* argument is always SQL_SETPARAM_VALUE_MAX. Because the Driver Manager returns an error if an ODBC 3.0 application sets *BufferLength* to SQL_SETPARAM_VALUE_MAX, an ODBC 3.0 driver can use this to determine when it is called by an ODBC 1.0 application.

In **SQLSetParam**, the way in which an application specifies the length of the **ParameterValuePtr* buffer so that the driver can return character or binary data and the way in which an application sends an array of character or binary parameter values to the driver are driver-defined.

StrLen_or_IndPtr Argument

The *StrLen_or_IndPtr* argument points to a buffer that, when **SQLExecute** or **SQLExecDirect** is called, contains one of the following. This argument sets the SQL_DESC_OCTET_LENGTH_PTR and SQL_DESC_INDICATOR_PTR record fields of the application parameter pointers.

- The length of the parameter value stored in **ParameterValuePtr*. This is ignored except for character or binary C data.
- SQL_NTS. The parameter value is a null-terminated string.
- SQL_NULL_DATA. The parameter value is NULL.

- SQL_DEFAULT_PARAM. A procedure is to use the default value of a parameter, rather than a value retrieved from the application. This value is valid only in a procedure called in ODBC canonical syntax, and then only if the *InputOutputType* argument is SQL_PARAM_INPUT or SQL_PARAM_INPUT_OUTPUT. When **StrLen_or_IndPtr* is SQL_DEFAULT_PARAM, the *ValueType*, *ParameterType*, *ColumnSize*, *DecimalDigits*, *BufferLength,* and *ParameterValuePtr* arguments are ignored for input parameters and are used only to define the output parameter value for input/output parameters.
- The result of the SQL_LEN_DATA_AT_EXEC(*length*) macro. The data for the parameter will be sent with **SQLPutData**. If the *ParameterType* argument is SQL_LONGVARBINARY, SQL_LONGVARCHAR, or a long, data source–specific data type and the driver returns "Y" for the SQL_NEED_LONG_DATA_LEN information type in **SQLGetInfo**, *length* is the number of bytes of data to be sent for the parameter; otherwise, *length* must be a nonnegative value and is ignored. For more information, see "Passing Parameter Values" later in this section.

  For example, to specify that 10,000 bytes of data will be sent with **SQLPutData** for an SQL_LONGVARCHAR parameter, an application sets **StrLen_or_IndPtr* to SQL_LEN_DATA_AT_EXEC(10000).
- SQL_DATA_AT_EXEC. The data for the parameter will be sent with **SQLPutData**. This value is used by ODBC 1.0 applications when calling ODBC 3.0 drivers. For more information, see "Passing Parameter Values" later in this section.

If *StrLen_or_IndPtr* is a null pointer, the driver assumes that all input parameter values are non-NULL and that character and binary data are null-terminated. If *InputOutputType* is SQL_PARAM_OUTPUT and *ParameterValuePtr* and *StrLen_or_IndPtr* are both null pointers, the driver discards the output value.

Note Application developers are strongly discouraged from specifying a null pointer for *StrLen_or_IndPtr* when the data type of the parameter is SQL_C_BINARY. To ensure that a driver does not unexpectedly truncate SQL_C_BINARY data, *StrLen_or_IndPtr* should contain a pointer to a valid length value.

If the *InputOutputType* argument is SQL_PARAM_INPUT_OUTPUT or SQL_PARAM_OUTPUT, *StrLen_or_IndPtr* points to a buffer in which the driver returns SQL_NULL_DATA, the number of bytes available to return in **ParameterValuePtr* (excluding the null-termination byte of character data), or SQL_NO_TOTAL if the number of bytes available to return cannot be determined. If the procedure returns one or more result sets, the **StrLen_or_IndPtr* buffer is not guaranteed to be set until all results have been fetched.

If the value in the SQL_ATTR_PARAMSET_SIZE statement attribute is greater than 1, *StrLen_or_IndPtr* points to an array of SQLINTEGER values. These can be any of the values listed earlier in this section and are processed with a single SQL statement.

Passing Parameter Values

An application can pass the value for a parameter either in the **ParameterValuePtr* buffer or with one or more calls to **SQLPutData**. Parameters whose data is passed with **SQLPutData** are known as *data-at-execution* parameters. These are commonly used to send data for SQL_LONGVARBINARY and SQL_LONGVARCHAR parameters and can be mixed with other parameters.

To pass parameter values, an application performs the following sequence of steps:

1. Calls **SQLBindParameter** for each parameter to bind buffers for the parameter's value (*ParameterValuePtr* argument) and length/indicator (*StrLen_or_IndPtr* argument). For data-at-execution parameters, *ParameterValuePtr* is an application-defined, 32-bit value such as a parameter number or a pointer to data. The value will be returned later and can be used to identify the parameter.
2. Places values for input and input/output parameters in the **ParameterValuePtr* and **StrLen_or_IndPtr* buffers:
   - For normal parameters, the application places the parameter value in the **ParameterValuePtr* buffer and the length of that value in the **StrLen_or_IndPtr* buffer. For more information, see "Setting Parameter Values" in Chapter 9, "Executing Statements."
   - For data-at-execution parameters, the application places the result of the SQL_LEN_DATA_AT_EXEC(*length*) macro (when calling an ODBC 2.0 driver) in the **StrLen_or_IndPtr* buffer.
3. Calls **SQLExecute** or **SQLExecDirect** to execute the SQL statement.
   - If there are no data-at-execution parameters, the process is complete.
   - If there are any data-at-execution parameters, the function returns SQL_NEED_DATA.
4. Calls **SQLParamData** to retrieve the application-defined value specified in the *ParameterValuePtr* argument of **SQLBindParameter** for the first data-at-execution parameter to be processed. **SQLParamData** returns SQL_NEED_DATA.

   Note Although data-at-execution parameters are similar to data-at-execution columns, the value returned by **SQLParamData** is different for each.

   Data-at-execution parameters are parameters in an SQL statement for which data will be sent with **SQLPutData** when the statement is executed with **SQLExecDirect** or **SQLExecute**. They are bound with **SQLBindParameter**. The value returned by **SQLParamData** is a 32-bit value passed to **SQLBindParameter** in the *ParameterValuePtr* argument.

Data-at-execution columns are columns in a rowset for which data will be sent with **SQLPutData** when a row is updated or added with **SQLBulkOperations** or updated with **SQLSetPos**. They are bound with **SQLBindCol**. The value returned by **SQLParamData** is the address of the row in the **TargetValuePtr* buffer (set by a call to **SQLBindCol**) that is being processed.

Calls **SQLPutData** one or more times to send data for the parameter. More than one call is needed if the data value is larger than the **ParameterValuePtr* buffer specified in **SQLPutData**; note that multiple calls to **SQLPutData** for the same parameter are allowed only when sending character C data to a column with a character, binary, or data source–specific data type or when sending binary C data to a column with a character, binary, or data source–specific data type.

5. Calls **SQLParamData** again to signal that all data has been sent for the parameter.
   - If there are more data-at-execution parameters, **SQLParamData** returns SQL_NEED_DATA and the application-defined value for the next data-at-execution parameter to be processed. The application repeats steps 4 and 5.
   - If there are no more data-at-execution parameters, the process is complete. If the statement was successfully executed, **SQLParamData** returns SQL_SUCCESS or SQL_SUCCESS_WITH_INFO; if the execution failed, it returns SQL_ERROR. At this point, **SQLParamData** can return any SQLSTATE that can be returned by the function used to execute the statement (**SQLExecDirect** or **SQLExecute**).

     Output values for any input/output or output parameters are available in the **ParameterValuePtr* and **StrLen_or_IndPtr* buffers after the application retrieves all result sets generated by the statement.

Calling **SQLExecute** or **SQLExecDirect** puts the statement in an SQL_NEED_DATA state. At this point, the application can only call **SQLCancel**, **SQLGetDiagField**, **SQLGetDiagRec**, **SQLGetFunctions**, **SQLParamData**, or **SQLPutData** with the statement or the connection handle associated with the statement. If it calls any other function with the statement or the connection associated with the statement, the function returns SQLSTATE HY010 (Function sequence error). The statement leaves the SQL_NEED_DATA state when **SQLParamData** or **SQLPutData** returns an error, **SQLParamData** returns SQL_SUCCESS or SQL_SUCCESS_WITH_INFO, or the statement is canceled.

If the application calls **SQLCancel** while the driver still needs data for data-at-execution parameters, the driver cancels statement execution; the application can then call **SQLExecute** or **SQLExecDirect** again.

Using Arrays of Parameters

When an application prepares a statement with parameter markers and passes in an array of parameters, there are two different ways this can be executed. One way is for the driver to rely on the array-processing capabilities of the back end, in which case the entire statement with the array of parameters is treated as one atomic unit. An example of a data source that supports array processing capabilities is Oracle. Another way to implement this feature is for the driver to generate a batch of SQL statements, one SQL statement for each set of parameters in the parameter array, and execute the batch. Arrays of parameters cannot be used with an **UPDATE WHERE CURRENT OF** statement.

When an array of parameters is processed, individual result sets/row counts (one for each parameter set) can be available, or result sets/rows counts can be rolled up into one. The SQL_PARAM_ARRAY_ROW_COUNTS option in **SQLGetInfo** indicates whether row counts are available for each set of parameters (SQL_PARC_BATCH), or only one row count is available (SQL_PARC_NO_BATCH).

The SQL_PARAM_ARRAY_SELECTS option in **SQLGetInfo** indicates whether a result set is available for each set of parameters (SQL_PAS_BATCH), or only one result set is available (SQL_PAS_NO_BATCH). If the driver does not allow a result set-generating statement to be executed with an array of parameters, SQL_PARAM_ARRAY_SELECTS returns SQL_PAS_NO_SELECT.

For more information, see **SQLGetInfo**.

To support arrays of parameters, the SQL_ATTR_PARAMSET_SIZE statement attribute is set to specify the number of values for each parameter. If the field is greater than 1, the SQL_DESC_DATA_PTR, SQL_DESC_INDICATOR_PTR, and SQL_DESC_OCTET_LENGTH_PTR fields of the APD must point to arrays. The cardinality of each array is equal to the value of SQL_ATTR_PARAMSET_SIZE.

The SQL_DESC_ROWS_PROCESSED_PTR field of the APD points to a buffer that contains the number of sets of parameters that have been processed, including error sets. As each set of parameters is processed, the driver stores a new value in the buffer. No number will be returned if this is a null pointer. When arrays of parameters are used, the value pointed to by the SQL_DESC_ROWS_PROCESSED_PTR field of the APD is populated even if SQL_ERROR is returned by the setting function. If SQL_NEED_DATA is returned, the value pointed to by the SQL_DESC_ROWS_PROCESSED_PTR field of the APD is set to the set of parameters that is being processed.

It is driver-defined what occurs when an array of parameters is bound and an **UPDATE WHERE CURRENT OF** statement is executed.

Column-Wise Parameter Binding

In column-wise binding, the application binds separate parameter and length/indicator arrays to each parameter.

To use column-wise binding, the application first sets the SQL_ATTR_PARAM_BIND_TYPE statement attribute to SQL_PARAM_BIND_BY_COLUMN (this is the default). For each column to be bound, the application performs the following steps:

1. Allocates a parameter buffer array.
2. Allocates an array of length/indicator buffers.

   Note If the application writes directly to descriptors when column-wise binding is used, then separate arrays can be used for length and indicator data.

3. Calls **SQLBindParameter** with the following arguments:
   - *ValueType* is the C type of a single element in the parameter buffer array.
   - *ParameterType* is the SQL type of the parameter.
   - *ParameterValuePtr* is the address of the parameter buffer array.
   - *BufferLength* is the size of a single element in the parameter buffer array. The *BufferLength* argument is ignored when the data is fixed-length data.
   - *StrLen_or_IndPtr* is the address of the length/indicator array.

For more information on how this information used, see "ParameterValuePtr Argument" in "Comments" later in this section. For more information on column-wise binding of parameters, see the "Binding Arrays of Parameters" section in Chapter 9, "Executing Statements."

Row-Wise Parameter Binding

In row-wise binding, the application defines a structure containing parameter and length/indicator buffers for each parameter to be bound.

To use row-wise binding, the application performs the following steps:

1. Defines a structure to hold a single set of parameters (including both parameter and length/indicator buffers) and allocates an array of these structures.

   Note If the application writes directly to descriptors when row-wise binding is used, then separate fields can be used for length and indicator data.

2. Sets the SQL_ATTR_PARAM_BIND_TYPE statement attribute to the size of the structure containing a single set of parameters, or to the size of an instance of a buffer into which the parameters will be bound. The length must include space for all of the bound parameters, and any padding of the structure or buffer to make sure that when the address of a bound parameter is incremented with the specified length, the result will point to the beginning of the same parameter in the next row. When using the *sizeof* operator in ANSI C, this behavior is guaranteed.

3. Calls **SQLBindParameter** with the following arguments for each parameter to be bound:
   - *ValueType* is the type of the parameter buffer member to be bound to the column.
   - *ParameterType* is the SQL type of the parameter.
   - *ParameterValuePtr* is the address of the parameter buffer member in the first array element.
   - *BufferLength* is the size of the parameter buffer member.
   - *StrLen_or_IndPtr* is the address of the length/indicator member to be bound.

For more information on how this information used, see "*ParameterValuePtr* Argument," later in this section. For more information on row-wise binding of parameters, see the "Binding Arrays of Parameters" section in Chapter 9, "Executing Statements."

Error Information

If a driver does not implement parameter arrays as batches (the SQL_PARAM_ARRAY_ROW_COUNTS option is equal to SQL_PARC_NO_BATCH), error situations are handled as if one statement was executed. If the driver does implement parameter arrays as batches, an application can use the SQL_DESC_ARRAY_STATUS_PTR header field of the IPD to determine which parameter of an SQL statement, or which parameter in an array of parameters, caused **SQLExecDirect** or **SQLExecute** to return an error. This field contains status information for each row of parameter values. If the field indicates that an error has occurred, fields in the diagnostic data structure will indicate the row and parameter number of the parameter that failed. The number of elements in the array will be defined by the SQL_DESC_ARRAY_SIZE header field in the APD, which can be set by the SQL_ATTR_PARAMSET_SIZE statement attribute.

Note The SQL_DESC_ARRAY_STATUS_PTR header field in the APD is used to ignore parameters. For more information on ignoring parameters, see the next section, "Ignoring a Set of Parameters."

When **SQLExecute** or **SQLExecDirect** returns SQL_ERROR, the elements in the array pointed to by the SQL_DESC_ARRAY_STATUS_PTR field in the IPD will contain SQL_PARAM_ERROR, SQL_PARAM_SUCCESS, SQL_PARAM_SUCCESS_WITH_INFO, SQL_PARAM_UNUSED, or SQL_PARAM_DIAG_UNAVAILABLE.

For each in this array, the diagnostic data structure contains one or more status records. The SQL_DIAG_ROW_NUMBER field of the structure indicates the row number of the parameter values that caused the error. If it is possible to determine the particular parameter in a row of parameters that caused the error, then the parameter number will be entered in the SQL_DIAG_COLUMN_NUMBER field.

SQL_PARAM_UNUSED is entered when a parameter has not been used because an error occurred in an earlier parameter that forced **SQLExecute** or **SQLExecDirect** to abort. For example, if there are 50 parameters, and an error occurred while executing the fortieth set of parameters that caused **SQLExecute** or **SQLExecDirect** to abort, then SQL_PARAM_UNUSED is entered in the status array for parameters 41 through 50.

SQL_PARAM_DIAG_UNAVAILABLE is entered when the driver treats arrays of parameters as a monolithic unit, so does not generate this level of error information.

Some errors in the processing of a single set of parameters cause processing of the subsequent sets of parameters in the array to stop. Other errors do not affect the processing of subsequent parameters. It is driver-defined which errors will stop processing. If processing is not stopped, all parameters in the array are processed, SQL_SUCCESS_WITH_INFO is returned as a result of the error, and the buffer defined by SQL_ATTR_PARAMS_PROCESSED_PTR is set to the total number of sets of parameters processed (as defined by the SQL_ATTR_PARAMSET_SIZE statement attribute), which includes error sets.

Caution ODBC behavior when an error occurs in the processing of an array of parameters is different in ODBC 3.0 than it was in ODBC 2.*x*. In ODBC 2.*x*, the function returned SQL_ERROR and processing ceased. The buffer pointed to by the *pirow* argument of **SQLParamOptions** contained the number of the error row. In ODBC 3.0, the function returns SQL_SUCCESS_WITH_INFO and processing may either cease or continue. If it continues, the buffer specified by SQL_ATTR_PARAMS_PROCESSED_PTR will be set to the value of all parameters processed, including those that resulted in an error. This change in behavior may cause problems for existing applications.

When **SQLExecute** or **SQLExecDirect** returns before completing the processing of all parameter sets in a parameter array, such as when SQL_ERROR or SQL_NEED_DATA is returned, the status array contains statuses for those parameters that have already been processed. The location pointed to by the SQL_DESC_ROWS_PROCESSED_PTR field in the IPD contains the row number in the parameter array that caused the SQL_ERROR or SQL_NEED_DATA error code. When an array of parameters is sent to a SELECT statement, the availability of status array values is driver-defined; they may be available after the statement has been executed, or as result sets are fetched.

Ignoring a Set of Parameters

The SQL_DESC_ARRAY_STATUS_PTR field of the APD (as set by the SQL_ATTR_PARAM_STATUS_PTR statement attribute) can be used to indicate that a set of bound parameters in an SQL statement should be ignored. To direct the driver to ignore one or more sets of parameters during execution, an application should perform the following steps:

1. Call **SQLSetDescField** to set the SQL_DESC_ARRAY_STATUS_PTR header field of the APD to point to an array of SQLUSMALLINT values to contain status information. This field can also be set by calling **SQLSetStmtAttr** with an *Attribute* of SQL_ATTR_PARAM_OPERATION_PTR, which allows an application to set the field without obtaining a descriptor handle.
2. Set each element of the array defined by the SQL_DESC_ARRAY_STATUS_PTR field of the APD to one of two values:
   - SQL_PARAM_IGNORE, to indicate that the row is excluded from statement execution.
   - SQL_PARAM_PROCEED, to indicate that the row is included in statement execution.
3. Call **SQLExecDirect** or **SQLExecute** to execute the prepared statement.

The following rules apply to the array defined by the SQL_DESC_ARRAY_STATUS_PTR field of the APD:

- The pointer is set to null by default.
- If the pointer is null, then all sets of parameters are used, as if all elements were set to SQL_ROW_PROCEED.
- Setting an element to SQL_PARAM_PROCEED does not guarantee that the operation will used that particular set of parameters.
- SQL_PARAM_PROCEED is defined as 0 in the header file.

An application can set the SQL_DESC_ARRAY_STATUS_PTR field in the APD to point to the same array as that pointed to by the SQL_DESC_ARRAY_STATUS_PTR field in the IRD. This is useful when binding parameters to row data. Parameters can then be ignored according to the status of the row data. The following codes cause a parameter in a SQL statement to be ignored, in addition to SQL_PARAM_IGNORE: SQL_ROW_DELETED, SQL_ROW_UPDATED, and SQL_ROW_ERROR. The following codes cause a SQL statement to proceed, in addition to SQL_PARAM_PROCEED: SQL_ROW_SUCCESS, SQL_ROW_SUCCESS_WITH_INFO, and SQL_ROW_ADDED.

Rebinding Parameters

An application can perform either of two operations to change a binding:

- Call **SQLBindParameter** to specify a new binding for a column that is already bound. The driver overwrites the old binding with the new one.
- Specify an offset to be added to the buffer address that was specified by the binding call to **SQLBindParameter**. For more information, see the next section, "Rebinding with Offsets."

Rebinding with Offsets

Rebinding of parameters is especially useful when an application has a buffer area setup that is capable of containing many parameters, but a call to **SQLExecDirect** or **SQLExecute** uses only a few of the parameters. The remaining space in the buffer area can be used for the next set of parameters by modifying the existing binding by an offset.

The SQL_DESC_BIND_OFFSET_PTR header field in the APD points to the binding offset. If the field is non-null, the driver dereferences the pointer and if none of the values in the SQL_DESC_DATA_PTR, SQL_DESC_INDICATOR_PTR, and SQL_DESC_OCTET_LENGTH_PTR fields is a null pointer, adds the dereferenced value to those fields in the descriptor records at execution time. The new pointer values are used when the SQL statements are executed. The offset remains valid after rebinding. Because SQL_DESC_BIND_OFFSET_PTR is a pointer to the offset, rather than the offset itself, an application can change the offset directly, without having to call **SQLSetDescField** or **SQLSetDescRec** to change the descriptor field. The pointer is set to null by default. The SQL_DESC_BIND_OFFSET_PTR field of the ARD can be set by a call to **SQLSetDescField** or by a call to **SQLSetStmtAttr** with an *fAttribute* of SQL_ATTR_PARAM_BIND_OFFSET_PTR.

The binding offset is always added directly to the values in the SQL_DESC_DATA_PTR, SQL_DESC_INDICATOR_PTR, and SQL_DESC_OCTET_LENGTH_PTR fields. If the offset is changed to a different value, the new value is still added directly to the value in each descriptor field. The new offset is not added to the sum of the field value and any earlier offsets.

Descriptors

How a parameter is bound is determined by fields of the APDs and IPDs. The arguments in **SQLBindParameter** are used to set those descriptor fields. The fields can also be set by the **SQLSetDescField** functions, although **SQLBindParameter** is more efficient to use because the application does not have to obtain a descriptor handle to call **SQLBindParameter**.

Caution Calling **SQLBindParameter** for one statement can affect other statements. This occurs when the ARD associated with the statement is explicitly allocated and is also associated with other statements. Because **SQLBindParameter** modifies the fields of the APD, the modifications apply to all statements with which this descriptor is associated. If this is not the required behavior, the application should dissociate this descriptor from the other statements before calling **SQLBindParameter**.

Conceptually, **SQLBindParameter** performs the following steps in sequence:

1. Calls **SQLGetStmtAttr** to obtain the APD handle.
2. Calls **SQLGetDescField** to get the APD's SQL_DESC_COUNT field, and if the value of the *ColumnNumber* argument exceeds the value of SQL_DESC_COUNT, calls **SQLSetDescField** to increase the value of SQL_DESC_COUNT to *ColumnNumber*.
3. Calls **SQLSetDescField** multiple times to assign values to the following fields of the APD:
   - Sets SQL_DESC_TYPE and SQL_DESC_CONCISE_TYPE to the value of *ValueType*, except that if *ValueType* is one of the concise identifiers of a datetime or interval subtype, it sets SQL_DESC_TYPE to SQL_DATETIME or SQL_INTERVAL respectively, sets SQL_DESC_CONCISE_TYPE to the concise identifier, and sets SQL_DESC_DATETIME_INTERVAL_CODE to the corresponding datetime or interval subcode.
   - Sets the SQL_DESC_OCTET_LENGTH field to the value of *BufferLength*.
   - Sets the SQL_DESC_DATA_PTR field to the value of *ParameterValue*.
   - Sets the SQL_DESC_OCTET_LENGTH_PTR field to the value of *StrLen_or_Ind*.
   - Sets the SQL_DESC_INDICATOR_PTR field also to the value of *StrLen_or_Ind*.

   The *StrLen_or_Ind* parameter specifies both the indicator information and the length for the parameter value.
4. Calls **SQLGetStmtAttr** to obtain the IPD handle.

5. Calls **SQLGetDescField** to get the IPD's SQL_DESC_COUNT field, and if the value of the *ColumnNumber* argument exceeds the value of SQL_DESC_COUNT, calls **SQLSetDescField** to increase the value of SQL_DESC_COUNT to *ColumnNumber*.
6. Calls **SQLSetDescField** multiple times to assign values to the following fields of the IPD:
   - Sets SQL_DESC_TYPE and SQL_DESC_CONCISE_TYPE to the value of *ParameterType*, except that if *ParameterType* is one of the concise identifiers of a datetime or interval subtype, it sets SQL_DESC_TYPE to SQL_DATETIME or SQL_INTERVAL respectively, sets SQL_DESC_CONCISE_TYPE to the concise identifier, and sets SQL_DESC_DATETIME_INTERVAL_CODE to the corresponding datetime or interval subcode.
   - Sets one or more of SQL_DESC_LENGTH, SQL_DESC_PRECISION, and SQL_DESC_DATETIME_INTERVAL_PRECISION, as appropriate for *ParameterType*.
   - Sets SQL_DESC_SCALE to the value of *DecimalDigits*.

If the call to **SQLBindParameter** fails, the content of the descriptor fields that it would have set in the APD are undefined, and the SQL_DESC_COUNT field of the APD is unchanged. In addition, the SQL_DESC_LENGTH, SQL_DESC_PRECISION, SQL_DESC_SCALE, and SQL_DESC_TYPE fields of the appropriate record in the IPD are undefined and the SQL_DESC_COUNT field of the IPD is unchanged.

Conversion of Calls to and from SQLSetParam

When an ODBC 1.0 application calls **SQLSetParam** in an ODBC 3.0 driver, the ODBC 3.0 Driver Manager maps the call as follows.

Call by ODBC 1.0 application	Call to ODBC 3.0 driver
SQLSetParam(StatementHandle, ParameterNumber, ValueType, ParameterType, LengthPrecision, ParameterScale, ParameterValuePtr, StrLen_or_IndPtr);	SQLBindParameter(StatementHandle, ParameterNumber, SQL_PARAM_INPUT_OUTPUT, ValueType, ParameterType, *ColumnSize*, *DecimalDigits*, ParameterValuePtr, SQL_SETPARAM_VALUE_MAX, StrLen_or_IndPtr);

Code Example

In the following example, an application prepares an SQL statement to insert data into the ORDERS table. The SQL statement contains parameters for the ORDERID, CUSTID, OPENDATE, SALESPERSON, and STATUS columns. For each parameter in the statement, the application calls **SQLBindParameter** to specify the ODBC C data type and the SQL data type of the parameter and to bind a buffer to each parameter. For each row of data, the application assigns data values to each parameter and calls **SQLExecute** to execute the statement.

For more code examples, see **SQLBulkOperations**, **SQLProcedures**, **SQLPutData**, and **SQLSetPos**.

```
#define SALES_PERSON_LEN 10
#define STATUS_LEN 6

SQLSMALLINT      sOrderID;
SQLSMALLINT      sCustID;
DATE_STRUCT dsOpenDate;
SQLCHAR       szSalesPerson[SALES_PERSON_LEN];
SQLCHAR       szStatus[STATUS_LEN);
SQLINTEGER      cbOrderID = 0, cbCustID = 0, cbOpenDate = 0, cbSalesPerson = SQL_NTS,
            cbStatus = SQL_NTS;
SQLRETURN   retcode;
SQLHSTMT    hstmt;

/* Prepare the SQL statement with parameter markers. */
retcode = SQLPrepare(hstmt,
          "INSERT INTO ORDERS (ORDERID, CUSTID, OPENDATE, SALESPERSON,
          STATUS) VALUES (?, ?, ?, ?, ?)", SQL_NTS);

if (retcode == SQL_SUCCESS || retcode == SQL_SUCCESS_WITH_INFO) {

   /* Specify data types and buffers for OrderID, CustID, OpenDate, SalesPerson, */
   /* Status  parameter data. */

   SQLBindParameter(hstmt, 1, SQL_PARAM_INPUT, SQL_C_SSHORT,
                    SQL_INTEGER, 0, 0, &sOrderID, 0, &cbOrderID);
   SQLBindParameter(hstmt, 2, SQL_PARAM_INPUT, SQL_C_SSHORT,
                    SQL_INTEGER, 0, 0, &sCustID, 0, &cbCustID);
   SQLBindParameter(hstmt, 3, SQL_PARAM_INPUT, SQL_C_TYPE_DATE,
                    SQL_TYPE_DATE, 0, 0, &dsOpenDate, 0, &cbOpenDate);
   SQLBindParameter(hstmt, 4, SQL_PARAM_INPUT, SQL_C_CHAR,
                    SQL_CHAR, SALES_PERSON_LEN, 0, szSalesPerson, 0, &cbSalesPerson);
   SQLBindParameter(hstmt, 5, SQL_PARAM_INPUT, SQL_C_CHAR,
                    SQL_CHAR, STATUS_LEN, 0, szStatus, 0, &cbStatus);
```

```
   /* Specify first row of parameter data. */
   sOrderID = 1001;
   sCustID = 298;
   dsOpenDate.year = 1996;
   dsOpenDate.month = 3;
   dsOpenDate.day = 8;
   strcpy(szSalesPerson, "Johnson");
   strcpy(szStatus, "Closed");

/* Execute statement with first row. */
   retcode = SQLExecute(hstmt);

/* Specify second row of parameter data. */
   sOrderID = 1002;
   sCustID = 501;
   dsOpenDate.year = 1996;
   dsOpenDate.month = 3;
   dsOpenDate.day = 9;
   strcpy(szSalesPerson, "Bailey");
   strcpy(szStatus, "Open");

/* Execute statement with second row. */
   retcode = SQLExecute(hstmt);
}
```

Code Example

In the following example, an application executes a SQL Server stored procedure using a named parameter. Note that the named parameter (@quote) is bound with a *ParameterNumber* of 1, while it is the second parameter in the procedure definition. Because the first parameter (@title_id) has a default value of 1, the named parameter is the only dynamic parameter.

```
/* Define the stored procedure "test" */
CREATE PROCEDURE test @title_id int = 1, @quote char(30)
AS <blah>

/* Prepare the procedure invocation statement */
SQLPrepare(hstmt, "{call test(?)}", SQL_NTS);

/* Populate record 1 of IPD */
SQLBindParameter(hstmt, 1, SQL_PARAM_INPUT, SQL_C_CHAR, SQL_CHAR,
                 30, 0, szQuote, 0, &cbValue);

/* Get IPD handle and set the NAMED and UNNAMED fields for record # 1 */
SQLGetStmtAttr(hstmt, SQL_ATTR_IMP_PARAM_DESC, &hIpd, 0, 0);
SQLSetDescField(hIpd, 1, SQL_DESC_NAME, "@quote", SQL_NTS);

/* Assuming that szQuote has been appropriately initialized, execute the statement */
SQLExecute(hstmt);
```

Related Functions

For information about	See
Returning information about a parameter in a statement	**SQLDescribeParam**
Executing an SQL statement	**SQLExecDirect**
Executing a prepared SQL statement	**SQLExecute**
Releasing parameter buffers on the statement	**SQLFreeStmt**
Returning the number of statement parameters	**SQLNumParams**
Returning the next parameter to send data for	**SQLParamData**
Specifying multiple parameter values	**SQLParamOptions**
Sending parameter data at execution time	**SQLPutData**

SQLBrowseConnect

Conformance

Version Introduced: ODBC 1.0
Standards Compliance: ODBC

Summary

SQLBrowseConnect supports an iterative method of discovering and enumerating the attributes and attribute values required to connect to a data source. Each call to **SQLBrowseConnect** returns successive levels of attributes and attribute values. When all levels have been enumerated, a connection to the data source is completed and a complete connection string is returned by **SQLBrowseConnect**. A return code of SQL_SUCCESS or SQL_SUCCESS_WITH_INFO indicates that all connection information has been specified and the application is now connected to the data source.

Syntax

SQLRETURN **SQLBrowseConnect**(
    SQLHDBC *ConnectionHandle*,
    SQLCHAR * *InConnectionString*,
    SQLSMALLINT *StringLength1*,
    SQLCHAR * *OutConnectionString*,
    SQLSMALLINT *BufferLength*,
    SQLSMALLINT * *StringLength2Ptr*);

Arguments

ConnectionHandle [Input]
Connection handle.

InConnectionString [Input]
Browse request connection string (see "*InConnectionString* Argument" in "Comments").

StringLength1 [Input]
Length of **InConnectionString*.

OutConnectionString [Output]
Pointer to a buffer in which to return the browse result connection string (see "*OutConnectionString* Argument" in "Comments").

BufferLength [Input]
Length of the **OutConnectionString* buffer.

StringLength2Ptr [Output]
The total number of bytes (excluding the null-termination byte) available to return in **OutConnectionString*. If the number of bytes available to return is greater than or equal to *BufferLength*, the connection string in **OutConnectionString* is truncated to *BufferLength* minus the length of a null-termination character.

Returns

SQL_SUCCESS, SQL_SUCCESS_WITH_INFO, SQL_NEED_DATA, SQL_ERROR, or SQL_INVALID_HANDLE.

Diagnostics

When **SQLBrowseConnect** returns SQL_ERROR, SQL_SUCCESS_WITH_INFO, or SQL_NEED_DATA, an associated SQLSTATE value may be obtained by calling **SQLGetDiagRec** with a *HandleType* of SQL_HANDLE_STMT and a *Handle* of *ConnectionHandle*. The following table lists the SQLSTATE values commonly returned by **SQLBrowseConnect** and explains each one in the context of this function; the notation "(DM)" precedes the descriptions of SQLSTATEs returned by the Driver Manager. The return code associated with each SQLSTATE value is SQL_ERROR, unless noted otherwise.

SQLSTATE	Error	Description
01000	General warning	Driver-specific informational message. (Function returns SQL_SUCCESS_WITH_INFO.)
01004	String data, right truncated	The buffer **OutConnectionString* was not large enough to return entire browse result connection string, so the string was truncated. The buffer **StringLength2Ptr* contains the length of the untruncated browse result connection string. (Function returns SQL_SUCCESS_WITH_INFO.)
01S00	Invalid connection string attribute	An invalid attribute keyword was specified in the browse request connection string (*InConnectionString*). (Function returns SQL_NEED_DATA.) An attribute keyword was specified in the browse request connection string (*InConnectionString*) that does not apply to the current connection level. (Function returns SQL_NEED_DATA.)
01S02	Value changed	The driver did not support the specified value of the *ValuePtr* argument in **SQLSetConnectAttr** and substituted a similar value. (Function returns SQL_SUCCESS_WITH_INFO.)
08001	Client unable to establish connection	The driver was unable to establish a connection with the data source.

SQLSTATE	Error	Description
08002	Connection name in use	(DM) The specified connection had already been used to establish a connection with a data source and the connection was open.
08004	Server rejected the connection	The data source rejected the establishment of the connection for implementation-defined reasons.
08S01	Communication link failure	The communication link between the driver and the data source to which the driver was attempting to connect failed before the function completed processing.
28000	Invalid authorization specification	Either the user identifier or the authorization string or both as specified in the browse request connection string (*InConnectionString*) violated restrictions defined by the data source.
HY000	General error	An error occurred for which there was no specific SQLSTATE and for which no implementation-specific SQLSTATE was defined. The error message returned by **SQLGetDiagRec** in the **MessageText* buffer describes the error and its cause.
HY001	Memory allocation error	(DM) The Driver Manager was unable to allocate memory required to support execution or completion of the function. The driver was unable to allocate memory required to support execution or completion of the function.
HY013	Memory management error	The function call could not be processed because the underlying memory objects could not be accessed, possibly because of low memory conditions.
HY090	Invalid string or buffer length	(DM) The value specified for argument *StringLength1* was less than 0 and was not equal to SQL_NTS. (DM) The value specified for argument *BufferLength* was less than 0.

SQLSTATE	Error	Description
HYT00	Timeout expired	The login timeout period expired before the connection to the data source completed. The timeout period is set through **SQLSetConnectAttr**, SQL_ATTR_LOGIN_TIMEOUT.
HYT01	Connection timeout expired	The connection timeout period expired before the data source responded to the request. The connection timeout period is set through **SQLSetConnectAttr**, SQL_ATTR_CONNECTION_TIMEOUT.
IM001	Driver does not support this function	(DM) The driver corresponding to the specified data source name does not support the function.
IM002	Data source not found and no default driver specified	(DM) The data source name specified in the browse request connection string (*InConnectionString*) was not found in the system information nor was there a default driver specification. (DM) ODBC data source and default driver information could not be found in the system information
IM003	Specified driver could not be loaded	(DM) The driver listed in the data source specification in the system information, or specified by the **DRIVER** keyword was not found or could not be loaded for some other reason.
IM004	Driver's SQLAllocHandle on SQL_HANDLE _ENV failed	(DM) During **SQLBrowseConnect**, the Driver Manager called the driver's **SQLAllocHandle** function with a *HandleType* of SQL_HANDLE_ENV and the driver returned an error.
IM005	Driver's SQLAllocHandle on SQL_HANDLE _DBC failed	(DM) During **SQLBrowseConnect**, the Driver Manager called the driver's **SQLAllocHandle** function with a *HandleType* of SQL_HANDLE_DBC and the driver returned an error.
IM006	Driver's SQLSetConnectAttr failed	(DM) During **SQLBrowseConnect**, the Driver Manager called the driver's **SQLSetConnectAttr** function and the driver returned an error.

SQLSTATE	Error	Description
IM009	Unable to load translation DLL	The driver was unable to load the translation DLL that was specified for the data source or for the connection.
IM010	Data source name too long	(DM) The attribute value for the DSN keyword was longer than SQL_MAX_DSN_LENGTH characters.
IM011	Driver name too long	(DM) The attribute value for the DRIVER keyword was longer than 255 characters.
IM012	DRIVER keyword syntax error	(DM) The keyword-value pair for the DRIVER keyword contained a syntax error.

Comments

InConnectionString Argument

A browse request connection string has the following syntax:

connection-string ::= *attribute*[;] | *attribute*; *connection-string*
attribute ::= *attribute-keyword*=*attribute-value* | DRIVER=[{]*attribute-value*[}]
attribute-keyword ::= DSN | UID | PWD
| *driver-defined-attribute-keyword*
attribute-value ::= *character-string*
driver-defined-attribute-keyword ::= *identifier*

where *character-string* has zero or more characters; *identifier* has one or more characters; *attribute-keyword* is not case-sensitive; *attribute-value* may be case-sensitive; and the value of the **DSN** keyword does not consist solely of blanks. Because of connection string and initialization file grammar, keywords and attribute values that contain the characters **[]{}(),;?*=!@** should be avoided. Because of the grammar in the system information, keywords and data source names cannot contain the backslash (\) character. For an ODBC 2.*x* driver, braces are required around the attribute value for the DRIVER keyword.

If any keywords are repeated in the browse request connection string, the driver uses the value associated with the first occurrence of the keyword. If the **DSN** and **DRIVER** keywords are included in the same browse request connection string, the Driver Manager and driver use whichever keyword appears first.

For information about how an application chooses a data source or driver, see "Choosing a Data Source or Driver" in Chapter 6, "Connecting to a Data Source or Driver."

OutConnectionString Argument

The browse result connection string is a list of connection attributes. A connection attribute consists of an attribute keyword and a corresponding attribute value. The browse result connection string has the following syntax:

connection-string ::= *attribute*[;] | *attribute*; *connection-string*
attribute ::= [*]*attribute-keyword*=*attribute-value*
attribute-keyword ::= *ODBC-attribute-keyword*
| *driver-defined-attribute-keyword*
ODBC-attribute-keyword = {UID | PWD}[:*localized-identifier*]
driver-defined-attribute-keyword ::= *identifier*[:*localized-identifier*]
attribute-value ::= {*attribute-value-list*} | ?
(The braces are literal; they are returned by the driver.)
attribute-value-list ::= *character-string* [:*localized-character string*] | *character-string* [:*localized-character string*], *attribute-value-list*

where *character-string* and *localized-character string* have zero or more characters; *identifier* and *localized-identifier* have one or more characters; *attribute-keyword* is not case-sensitive; and *attribute-value* may be case-sensitive. Because of connection string and initialization file grammar, keywords, localized identifiers, and attribute values that contain the characters **[]{}(),;?*=!@** should be avoided. Because of the grammar in the system information, keywords and data source names cannot contain the backslash (\) character.

The browse result connection string syntax is used according to the following semantic rules:

- If an asterisk (*) precedes an *attribute-keyword*, the *attribute* is optional, and may be omitted in the next call to **SQLBrowseConnect**.
- The attribute keywords **UID** and **PWD** have the same meaning as defined in **SQLDriverConnect**.
- A *driver-defined-attribute-keyword* names the kind of attribute for which an attribute value may be supplied. For example, it might be **SERVER**, **DATABASE**, **HOST**, or **DBMS**.
- *ODBC-attribute-keywords* and *driver-defined-attribute-keywords* include a localized or user-friendly version of the keyword. This might be used by applications as a label in a dialog box. However, **UID**, **PWD**, or the *identifier* alone must be used when passing a browse request string to the driver.

- The {*attribute-value-list*} is an enumeration of actual values valid for the corresponding *attribute-keyword*. Note that the braces ({}) do not indicate a list of choices; they are returned by the driver. For example, it might be a list of server names or a list of database names.
- If the *attribute-value* is a single question mark (?), a single value corresponds to the *attribute-keyword*. For example, UID=JohnS; PWD=Sesame.
- Each call to **SQLBrowseConnect** returns only the information required to satisfy the next level of the connection process. The driver associates state information with the connection handle so that the context can always be determined on each call.

Using SQLBrowseConnect

SQLBrowseConnect requires an allocated connection. The Driver Manager loads the driver that was specified in or that corresponds to the data source name specified in the initial browse request connection string; for information on when this occurs, see the "Comments" section in **SQLConnect**. It may establish a connection with the data source during the browsing process. If **SQLBrowseConnect** returns SQL_ERROR, outstanding connections are terminated and the connection is returned to an unconnected state.

Note **SQLBrowseConnect** does not support connection pooling. If **SQLBrowseConnect** is called while connection pooling is enabled, SQLSTATE HY000 (General error) will be returned.

When **SQLBrowseConnect** is called for the first time on a connection, the browse request connection string must contain the **DSN** keyword or the **DRIVER** keyword. If the browse request connection string contains the **DSN** keyword, the Driver Manager locates a corresponding data source specification in the system information:

- If the Driver Manager finds the corresponding data source specification, it loads the associated driver DLL; the driver can retrieve information about the data source from the system information.
- If the Driver Manager cannot find the corresponding data source specification, it locates the default data source specification and loads the associated driver DLL; the driver can retrieve information about the default data source from the system information. "DEFAULT" is passed to the driver for the DSN.
- If the Driver Manager cannot find the corresponding data source specification and there is no default data source specification, it returns SQL_ERROR with SQLSTATE IM002 (Data source not found and no default driver specified).

If the browse request connection string contains the **DRIVER** keyword, the Driver Manager loads the specified driver; it does not attempt to locate a data source in the system information. Because the **DRIVER** keyword does not use information from the system information, the driver must define enough keywords so that a driver can connect to a data source using only the information in the browse request connection strings.

On each call to **SQLBrowseConnect**, the application specifies the connection attribute values in the browse request connection string. The driver returns successive levels of attributes and attribute values in the browse result connection string; it returns SQL_NEED_DATA as long as there are connection attributes that have not yet been enumerated in the browse request connection string. The application uses the contents of the browse result connection string to build the browse request connection string for the next call to **SQLBrowseConnect**. All mandatory attributes (those not preceded by an asterisk in the *OutConnectionString* argument) must be included in the next call to **SQLBrowseConnect**. Note that the application cannot use the contents of previous browse result connection strings when building the current browse request connection string; that is, it cannot specify different values for attributes set in previous levels.

When all levels of connection and their associated attributes have been enumerated, the driver returns SQL_SUCCESS, the connection to the data source is complete, and a complete connection string is returned to the application. The connection string is suitable to use in conjunction with **SQLDriverConnect** with the SQL_DRIVER_NOPROMPT option to establish another connection. The complete connection string cannot be used in another call to **SQLBrowseConnect**, however; if **SQLBrowseConnect** were called again, the entire sequence of calls would have to be repeated.

SQLBrowseConnect also returns SQL_NEED_DATA if there are recoverable, nonfatal errors during the browse process; for example, an invalid password or attribute keyword supplied by the application. When SQL_NEED_DATA is returned and the browse result connection string is unchanged, an error has occurred and the application can call **SQLGetDiagRec** to return the SQLSTATE for browse-time errors. This permits the application to correct the attribute and continue the browse.

An application can terminate the browse process at any time by calling **SQLDisconnect**. The driver will terminate any outstanding connections and return the connection to an unconnected state.

For more information, see "Connecting With SQLBrowseConnect" in Chapter 6, "Connecting to a Data Source or Driver."

If a driver supports **SQLBrowseConnect**, the driver keyword section in the system information for the driver must contain the **ConnectFunctions** keyword with the third character set to "Y."

Code Example

In the following example, an application calls **SQLBrowseConnect** repeatedly. Each time **SQLBrowseConnect** returns SQL_NEED_DATA, it passes back information about the data it needs in **OutConnectionString*. The application passes *OutConnectionString* to its routine **GetUserInput** (not shown). **GetUserInput** parses the information, builds and displays a dialog box, and returns the information entered by the user in **InConnectionString*. The application passes the user's information to the driver in the next call to **SQLBrowseConnect**. After the application has provided all necessary information for the driver to connect to the data source, **SQLBrowseConnect** returns SQL_SUCCESS and the application proceeds.

For a more detailed example of connecting to a SQL Server driver by calling **SQLBrowseConnect**, see "SQL Server Browsing Example" in Chapter 6, "Connecting to a Data Source or Driver."

For example, to connect to the data source Sales, the following actions might occur. First, the application passes the following string to **SQLBrowseConnect**:

```
"DSN=Sales"
```

The Driver Manager loads the driver associated with the data source Sales. It then calls the driver's **SQLBrowseConnect** function with the same arguments it received from the application. The driver returns the following string in **OutConnectionString*:

```
"HOST:Server={red,blue,green};UID:ID=?;PWD:Password=?"
```

The application passes this string to its **GetUserInput** routine, which builds a dialog box that asks the user to select the red, blue, or green server, and to enter a user ID and password. The routine passes the following user-specified information back in **InConnectionString*, which the application passes to **SQLBrowseConnect**:

```
"HOST=red;UID=Smith;PWD=Sesame"
```

SQLBrowseConnect uses this information to connect to the red server as Smith with the password Sesame, and then returns the following string in **OutConnectionString*:

```
"*DATABASE:Database={SalesEmployees,SalesGoals,SalesOrders}"
```

The application passes this string to its **GetUserInput** routine, which builds a dialog box that asks the user to select a database. The user selects empdata and the application calls **SQLBrowseConnect** a final time with the string:

```
"DATABASE=SalesOrders"
```

This is the final piece of information the driver needs to connect to the data source; **SQLBrowseConnect** returns SQL_SUCCESS and **OutConnectionString* contains the completed connection string:

```
"DSN=Sales;HOST=red;UID=Smith;PWD=Sesame;DATABASE=SalesOrders"

#define BRWS_LEN 100
SQLHENV      henv;
SQLHDBC      hdbc;
SQLHSTMT     hstmt;
SQLRETURN    retcode;
SQLCHAR      szConnStrIn[BRWS_LEN], szConnStrOut[BRWS_LEN];
SQLSMALLINT  cbConnStrOut;

/* Allocate the environment handle. */
retcode = SQLAllocHandle(SQL_HANDLE_ENV, SQL_NULL_HANDLE, &henv);

if (retcode == SQL_SUCCESS || retcode == SQL_SUCCESS_WITH_INFO) {
   /* Set the version environment attribute. */
   retcode = SQLSetEnvAttr(henv, SQL_ATTR_ODBC_VERSION, SQL_OV_ODBC3, 0);

   if (retcode == SQL_SUCCESS || retcode == SQL_SUCCESS_WITH_INFO) {
      /* Allocate the connection handle. */
      retcode = SQLAllocHandle(SQL_HANDLE_DBC, henv, &hdbc);

      if (retcode == SQL_SUCCESS || retcode == SQL_SUCCESS_WITH_INFO) {

      /* Call SQLBrowseConnect until it returns a value other than */
      /* SQL_NEED_DATA (pass the data source name the first time). */
      /* If SQL_NEED_DATA is returned, call GetUserInput (not      */
      /* shown) to build a dialog from the values in szConnStrOut. */
      /* The user-supplied values are returned in szConnStrIn,     */
      /* which is passed in the next call to SQLBrowseConnect.     */

         lstrcpy(szConnStrIn, "DSN=Sales");
         do {
            retcode = SQLBrowseConnect(hdbc, szConnStrIn, SQL_NTS,
                                       szConnStrOut, BRWS_LEN, &cbConnStrOut);
            if (retcode == SQL_NEED_DATA)
               GetUserInput(szConnStrOut, szConnStrIn);
         } while (retcode == SQL_NEED_DATA);

         if (retcode == SQL_SUCCESS || retcode == SQL_SUCCESS_WITH_INFO){

            /* Allocate the statement handle. */
            retcode = SQLAllocHandle(SQL_HANDLE_STMT, hdbc, &hstmt);
```

```
            if (retcode == SQL_SUCCESS || retcode == SQL_SUCCESS_WITH_INFO) {
            /* Process data after successful connection */
               ...;
               ...;
               ...;
               SQLFreeHandle(SQL_HANDLE_STMT, hstmt);
            }
            SQLDisconnect(hdbc);
         }
      }
      SQLFreeHandle(SQL_HANDLE_DBC, hdbc);
   }
}
SQLFreeHandle(SQL_HANDLE_ENV, henv);
```

Related Functions

For information about	See
Allocating a connection handle	**SQLAllocHandle**
Connecting to a data source	**SQLConnect**
Disconnecting from a data source	**SQLDisconnect**
Connecting to a data source using a connection string or dialog box	**SQLDriverConnect**
Returning driver descriptions and attributes	**SQLDrivers**
Freeing a connection handle	**SQLFreeHandle**

SQLBulkOperations

Conformance

Version Introduced: ODBC 3.0
Standards Compliance: ODBC

Summary

SQLBulkOperations performs bulk insertions and bulk bookmark operations, including update, delete, and fetch by bookmark.

Syntax

SQLRETURN **SQLBulkOperations**(
    SQLHSTMT *StatementHandle*,
    SQLUSMALLINT *Operation*);

Arguments

StatementHandle [Input]
Statement handle.

Operation [Input]
Operation to perform:

SQL_ADD
SQL_UPDATE_BY_BOOKMARK
SQL_DELETE_BY_BOOKMARK
SQL_FETCH_BY_BOOKMARK

For more information, see "Comments."

Returns

SQL_SUCCESS, SQL_SUCCESS_WITH_INFO, SQL_NEED_DATA, SQL_STILL_EXECUTING, SQL_ERROR, or SQL_INVALID_HANDLE.

Diagnostics

When **SQLBulkOperations** returns SQL_ERROR or SQL_SUCCESS_WITH_INFO, an associated SQLSTATE value can be obtained by calling **SQLGetDiagRec** with a *HandleType* of SQL_HANDLE_STMT and a *Handle* of *StatementHandle*. The following table lists the SQLSTATE values commonly returned by **SQLBulkOperations** and explains each one in the context of this function; the notation "(DM)" precedes the descriptions of SQLSTATEs returned by the Driver Manager. The return code associated with each SQLSTATE value is SQL_ERROR, unless noted otherwise.

For all those SQLSTATEs that can return SQL_SUCCESS_WITH_INFO or SQL_ERROR (except 01xxx SQLSTATEs), SQL_SUCCESS_WITH_INFO is returned if an error occurs on one or more, but not all, rows of a multirow operation, and SQL_ERROR is returned if an error occurs on a single-row operation.

SQLSTATE	Error	Description
01000	General warning	Driver-specific informational message. (Function returns SQL_SUCCESS_WITH_INFO.)
01004	String data right truncation	The *Operation* argument was SQL_FETCH_BY_BOOKMARK, and string or binary data returned for a column or columns with a data type of SQL_C_CHAR or SQL_C_BINARY resulted in the truncation of non-blank character or non-NULL binary data.
01S01	Error in row	The *Operation* argument was SQL_ADD, and an error occurred in one or more rows while performing the operation, but at least one row was successfully added. (Function returns SQL_SUCCESS_WITH_INFO.) (This error is raised only when an application is working with an ODBC 2.*x* driver.)
01S07	Fractional truncation	The *Operation* argument was SQL_FETCH_BY_BOOKMARK, the data type of the application buffer was not SQL_C_CHAR or SQL_C_BINARY, and the data returned to application buffers for one or more columns was truncated. (For numeric C data types, the fractional part of the number was truncated. For time, timestamp, and interval C data types containing a time component, the fractional portion of the time was truncated.) (Function returns SQL_SUCCESS_WITH_INFO.)
07006	Restricted data type attribute violation	The *Operation* argument was SQL_FETCH_BY_BOOKMARK, and the data value of a column in the result set could not be converted to the data type specified by the *TargetType* argument in the call to **SQLBindCol**. The *Operation* argument was SQL_UPDATE_BY_BOOKMARK or SQL_ADD, and the data value in the application buffers could not be converted to the data type of a column in the result set.

SQLSTATE	Error	Description
07009	Invalid descriptor index	The argument *Operation* was SQL_ADD and a column was bound with a column number greater than the number of columns in the result set.
21S02	Degree of derived table does not match column list	The argument *Operation* was SQL_UPDATE_BY_BOOKMARK; and no columns were updatable because all columns were either unbound, read-only, or the value in the bound length/indicator buffer was SQL_COLUMN_IGNORE.
22001	String data right truncation	The assignment of a character or binary value to a column in the result set resulted in the truncation of non-blank (for characters) or non-null (for binary) characters or bytes.
22003	Numeric value out of range	The *Operation* argument was SQL_ADD or SQL_UPDATE_BY_BOOKMARK, and the assignment of a numeric value to a column in the result set caused the whole (as opposed to fractional) part of the number to be truncated. The argument *Operation* was SQL_FETCH_BY_BOOKMARK, and returning the numeric value for one or more bound columns would have caused a loss of significant digits.
22007	Invalid datetime format	The *Operation* argument was SQL_ADD or SQL_UPDATE_BY_BOOKMARK, and the assignment of a date or timestamp value to a column in the result set caused the year, month, or day field to be out of range. The argument *Operation* was SQL_FETCH_BY_BOOKMARK, and returning the date or timestamp value for one or more bound columns would have caused the year, month, or day field to be out of range.

SQLSTATE	Error	Description
22008	Date/time field overflow	The *Operation* argument was SQL_ADD or SQL_UPDATE_BY_BOOKMARK, and the performance of datetime arithmetic on data being sent to a column in the result set resulted in a datetime field (the year, month, day, hour, minute, or second field) of the result being outside the permissible range of values for the field, or being invalid based on the natural rules for datetimes based on the Gregorian calendar. The *Operation* argument was SQL_FETCH_BY_BOOKMARK, and the performance of datetime arithmetic on data being retrieved from the result set resulted in a datetime field (the year, month, day, hour, minute, or second field) of the result being outside the permissible range of values for the field, or being invalid based on the natural rules for datetimes based on the Gregorian calendar.
22015	Interval field overflow	The *Operation* argument was SQL_ADD or SQL_UPDATE_BY_BOOKMARK, and the assignment of an exact numeric or interval C type to an interval SQL data type caused a loss of significant digits. The *Operation* argument was SQL_ADD or SQL_UPDATE_BY_BOOKMARK; when assigning to an interval SQL type, there was no representation of the value of the C type in the interval SQL type. The *Operation* argument was SQL_FETCH_BY_BOOKMARK, and assigning from an exact numeric or interval SQL type to an interval C type caused a loss of significant digits in the leading field. The *Operation* argument was SQL_FETCH_BY_BOOKMARK; when assigning to an interval C type, there was no representation of the value of the SQL type in the interval C type.

SQLSTATE	Error	Description
22018	Invalid character value for cast specification	The *Operation* argument was SQL_FETCH_BY_BOOKMARK; the C type was an exact or approximate numeric, a datetime, or an interval data type; the SQL type of the column was a character data type; and the value in the column was not a valid literal of the bound C type. The argument *Operation* was SQL_ADD or SQL_UPDATE_BY_BOOKMARK; the SQL type was an exact or approximate numeric, a datetime, or an interval data type; the C type was SQL_C_CHAR; and the value in the column was not a valid literal of the bound SQL type.
23000	Integrity constraint violation	The *Operation* argument was SQL_ADD, SQL_DELETE_BY_BOOKMARK, or SQL_UPDATE_BY_BOOKMARK, and an integrity constraint was violated. The *Operation* argument was SQL_ADD and a column that was not bound is defined as NOT NULL and has no default. The *Operation* argument was SQL_ADD, the length specified in the bound *StrLen_or_IndPtr* buffer was SQL_COLUMN_IGNORE, and the column did not have a default value.
24000	Invalid cursor state	The *StatementHandle* was in an executed state but no result set was associated with the *StatementHandle*.
40001	Serialization failure	The transaction was rolled back due to a resource deadlock with another transaction.
40003	Statement completion unknown	The associated connection failed during the execution of this function and the state of the transaction cannot be determined.
42000	Syntax error or access violation	The driver was unable to lock the row as needed to perform the operation requested in the *Operation* argument.
44000	WITH CHECK OPTION violation	The *Operation* argument was SQL_ADD or SQL_UPDATE_BY_BOOKMARK, and the insert or update was performed on a viewed table or a table derived from the viewed table which was created by specifying **WITH CHECK OPTION**, such that one or more rows affected by the insert or update will no longer be present in the viewed table.

SQLSTATE	Error	Description
HY000	General error	An error occurred for which there was no specific SQLSTATE and for which no implementation-specific SQLSTATE was defined. The error message returned by **SQLGetDiagRec** in the **MessageText* buffer describes the error and its cause.
HY001	Memory allocation error	The driver was unable to allocate memory required to support execution or completion of the function.
HY008	Operation canceled	Asynchronous processing was enabled for the *StatementHandle*. The function was called and before it completed execution, **SQLCancel** was called on the *StatementHandle*. Then the function was called again on the *StatementHandle*. The function was called and, before it completed execution, **SQLCancel** was called on the *StatementHandle* from a different thread in a multithread application.
HY010	Function sequence error	(DM) The specified *StatementHandle* was not in an executed state. The function was called without first calling **SQLExecDirect**, **SQLExecute**, or a catalog function. (DM) An asynchronously executing function (not this one) was called for the *StatementHandle* and was still executing when this function was called. (DM) **SQLExecute**, **SQLExecDirect**, or **SQLSetPos** was called for the *StatementHandle* and returned SQL_NEED_DATA. This function was called before data was sent for all data-at-execution parameters or columns. (DM) The driver was an ODBC 2.*x* driver and **SQLBulkOperations** was called for a *StatementHandle* before **SQLFetchScroll** or **SQLFetch** was called. (DM) **SQLBulkOperations** was called after **SQLExtendedFetch** was called on the *StatementHandle*.

SQLSTATE	Error	Description
HY011	Attribute cannot be set now	(DM) The driver was an ODBC 2.*x* driver, and the SQL_ATTR_ROW_STATUS_PTR statement attribute was set between calls to **SQLFetch** or **SQLFetchScroll** and **SQLBulkOperations**.
HY013	Memory management error	The function call could not be processed because the underlying memory objects could not be accessed, possibly because of low memory conditions.
HY090	Invalid string or buffer length	The *Operation* argument was SQL_ADD or SQL_UPDATE_BY_BOOKMARK, a data value was a null pointer, and the column length value was not 0, SQL_DATA_AT_EXEC, SQL_COLUMN_IGNORE, SQL_NULL_DATA, or less than or equal to SQL_LEN_DATA_AT_EXEC_OFFSET.
		The *Operation* argument was SQL_ADD or SQL_UPDATE_BY_BOOKMARK, a data value was not a null pointer; the C data type was SQL_C_BINARY or SQL_C_CHAR; and the column length value was less than 0, but not equal to SQL_DATA_AT_EXEC, SQL_COLUMN_IGNORE, SQL_NTS, or SQL_NULL_DATA, or less than or equal to SQL_LEN_DATA_AT_EXEC_OFFSET.
		The value in a length/indicator buffer was SQL_DATA_AT_EXEC; the SQL type was either SQL_LONGVARCHAR, SQL_LONGVARBINARY, or a long, data source–specific data type; and the SQL_NEED_LONG_DATA_LEN information type in **SQLGetInfo** was "Y".
		The *Operation* argument was SQL_ADD, the SQL_ATTR_USE_BOOKMARK statement attribute was set to SQL_UB_VARIABLE, and column 0 was bound to a buffer whose length was not equal to the maximum length for the bookmark for this result set. (This length is available in the SQL_DESC_OCTET_LENGTH field of the IRD, and can be obtained by calling **SQLDescribeCol**, **SQLColAttribute**, or **SQLGetDescField**.)

SQLSTATE	Error	Description
HY092	Invalid attribute identifier	(DM) The value specified for the *Operation* argument was invalid. The *Operation* argument was SQL_ADD, SQL_UPDATE_BY_BOOKMARK, or SQL_DELETE_BY_BOOKMARK, and the SQL_ATTR_CONCURRENCY statement attribute was set to SQL_CONCUR_READ_ONLY. The *Operation* argument was SQL_DELETE_BY_BOOKMARK, SQL_FETCH_BY_BOOKMARK, or SQL_UPDATE_BY_BOOKMARK, and the bookmark column was not bound or the SQL_ATTR_USE_BOOKMARKS statement attribute was set to SQL_UB_OFF.
HYC00	Optional feature not implemented	The driver or data source does not support the operation requested in the *Operation* argument.
HYT00	Timeout expired	The query timeout period expired before the data source returned the result set. The timeout period is set through **SQLSetStmtAttr** with an *Attribute* argument of SQL_ATTR_QUERY_TIMEOUT.
HYT01	Connection timeout expired	The connection timeout period expired before the data source responded to the request. The connection timeout period is set through **SQLSetConnectAttr**, SQL_ATTR_CONNECTION_TIMEOUT.
IM001	Driver does not support this function	(DM) The driver associated with the *StatementHandle* does not support the function.

Comments

Caution For information on what statement states **SQLBulkOperations** can be called in and what it needs to do for compatibility with ODBC 2.*x* applications, see the "Block Cursors, Scrollable Cursors, and Backward Compatibility" section in Appendix G, "Driver Guidelines for Backward Compatibility."

An application uses **SQLBulkOperations** to perform the following operations on the base table or view that corresponds to the current query:

- Add new rows.
- Update a set of rows where each row is identified by a bookmark.

- Delete a set of rows where each row is identified by a bookmark.
- Fetch a set of rows where each row is identified by a bookmark.

After a call to **SQLBulkOperations**, the block cursor position is undefined. The application has to call **SQLFetchScroll** to set the cursor position. An application should only call **SQLFetchScroll** with a *FetchOrientation* argument of SQL_FETCH_FIRST, SQL_FETCH_LAST, SQL_FETCH_ABSOLUTE, or SQL_FETCH_BOOKMARK. The cursor position is undefined if the application calls **SQLFetch**, or **SQLFetchScroll** with a *FetchOrientation* argument of SQL_FETCH_PRIOR, SQL_FETCH_NEXT, or SQL_FETCH_RELATIVE.

A column can be ignored in bulk operations performed by a call to **SQLBulkOperations** by setting the column length/indicator buffer specified in the call to **SQLBindCol**, to SQL_COLUMN_IGNORE.

It is not necessary for the application to set the SQL_ATTR_ROW_OPERATION_PTR statement attribute when calling **SQLBulkOperations** because rows cannot be ignored when performing bulk operations with this function.

The buffer pointed to by the SQL_ATTR_ROWS_FETCHED_PTR statement attribute contains the number of rows affected by a call to **SQLBulkOperations**.

When the *Operation* argument is SQL_ADD or SQL_UPDATE_BY_BOOKMARK, and the select-list of the query specification associated with the cursor contains more than one reference to the same column, it is driver-defined whether:

- An error is generated, or
- The driver ignores the duplicated references and performs the requested operations.

For more information about using **SQLBulkOperations**, see "Updating Data with SQLBulkOperations" in Chapter 12, "Updating Data."

Performing Bulk Inserts

To insert data with **SQLBulkOperations**, an application performs the following sequence of steps:

1. Executes a query that returns a result set.
2. Sets the SQL_ATTR_ROW_ARRAY_SIZE statement attribute to the number of rows that it wants to insert.
3. Calls **SQLBindCol** to bind the data that it wants to insert. The data is bound to an array with a size equal to the value of SQL_ATTR_ROW_ARRAY_SIZE.

   Note The size of the array pointed to by the SQL_ATTR_ROW_STATUS_PTR statement attribute should either be equal to SQL_ATTR_ROW_ARRAY_SIZE or SQL_ATTR_ROW_STATUS_PTR should be a null pointer.

4. Calls **SQLBulkOperations**(*StatementHandle,* SQL_ADD*)* to perform the insertion.
5. If the application has set the SQL_ATTR_ARRAY_STATUS_PTR statement attribute, then it can inspect this array to see the result of the operation.

If an application binds column 0 before calling **SQLBulkOperations** with an *Operation* argument of SQL_ADD, the driver will update the bound column 0 buffers with the bookmark values for the newly inserted row. For this to occur, the application must have set SQL_ATTR_USE_BOOKMARKS statement attribute to SQL_UB_VARIABLE before executing the statement. (This does not work with an ODBC 2.*x* driver.)

Long data can be added in parts by **SQLBulkOperations** using calls to **SQLParamData** and **SQLPutData**. For more information, see "Providing Long Data for Bulk Inserts and Updates" later in this function reference.

It is not necessary for the application to call **SQLFetch** or **SQLFetchScroll** before calling **SQLBulkOperations** (except when going against an ODBC 2.*x* driver; see "Backward Compatibility and Standards Compliance" in Chapter 17, "Programming Considerations").

It is driver-defined what the behavior is if **SQLBulkOperations** with an *Operation* argument of SQL_ADD is called on a cursor that contains duplicate columns. The driver can return a driver-defined SQLSTATE, can add the data to the first column that appears in the result set, or other driver-defined behavior.

Performing Bulk Updates Using Bookmarks

To perform bulk updates using bookmarks with **SQLBulkOperations**, an application performs the following steps in sequence:

1. Sets the SQL_ATTR_USE_BOOKMARKS statement attribute to SQL_UB_VARIABLE.
2. Executes a query that returns a result set.
3. Sets the SQL_ATTR_ROW_ARRAY_SIZE statement attribute to the number of rows that it wants to update.

   Calls **SQLBindCol** to bind the data that it wants to update. The data is bound to an array with a size equal to the value of SQL_ATTR_ROW_ARRAY_SIZE. It also calls **SQLBindCol** to bind column 0 (the bookmark column).

4. Copies the bookmarks for rows that it is interested in updating into the array bound to column 0.
5. Updates the data in the bound buffers.

   Note The size of the array pointed to by the SQL_ATTR_ROW_STATUS_PTR statement attribute should either be equal to SQL_ATTR_ROW_ARRAY_SIZE or SQL_ATTR_ROW_STATUS_PTR should be a null pointer.

6. Calls **SQLBulkOperations**(*StatementHandle,* SQL_UPDATE_BY_BOOKMARK).

Note If the application has set the SQL_ATTR_ARRAY_STATUS_PTR statement attribute, then it can inspect this array to see the result of the operation.

Optionally calls **SQLBulkOperations**(StatementHandle, SQL_FETCH_BY_BOOKMARK) to fetch data into the bound application buffers to verify that the update has occurred.

If data has been updated, the driver changes the value in the row status array for the appropriate rows to SQL_ROW_UPDATED.

Bulk updates performed by **SQLBulkOperations** can include long data by using calls to **SQLParamData** and **SQLPutData**. For more information, see "Providing Long Data for Bulk Inserts and Updates" later in this function reference.

If bookmarks persist across cursors, then there is no need for the application to call **SQLFetch** or **SQLFetchScroll** before updating by bookmarks. It can use bookmarks that it has stored from a previous cursor. If bookmarks do not persist across cursors, then the application has to call **SQLFetch** or **SQLFetchScroll** to retrieve the bookmarks.

It is driver-defined what the behavior is if **SQLBulkOperations** with an *Operation* argument of SQL_UPDATE_BY_BOOKMARK is called on a cursor that contains duplicate columns. The driver can return a driver-defined SQLSTATE, can update the first column that appears in the result set, or other driver-defined behavior.

Performing Bulk Fetches Using Bookmarks

To perform bulk fetches using bookmarks with **SQLBulkOperations**, an application performs the following steps in sequence:

1. Sets the SQL_ATTR_USE_BOOKMARKS statement attribute to SQL_UB_VARIABLE.
2. Executes a query that returns a result set.
3. Sets the SQL_ATTR_ROW_ARRAY_SIZE statement attribute to the number of rows that it wants to fetch.

4. Calls **SQLBindCol** to bind the data that it wants to fetch. The data is bound to an array with a size equal to the value of SQL_ATTR_ROW_ARRAY_SIZE. It also calls **SQLBindCol** to bind column 0 (the bookmark column).
5. Copies the bookmarks for rows that it is interested in fetching into the array bound to column 0. (This assumes that the application has already obtained the bookmarks separately.)

   Note The size of the array pointed to by the SQL_ATTR_ROW_STATUS_PTR statement attribute should either be equal to SQL_ATTR_ROW_ARRAY_SIZE or SQL_ATTR_ROW_STATUS_PTR should be a null pointer.

6. Calls **SQLBulkOperations**(*StatementHandle,* SQL_FETCH_BY_BOOKMARK).
7. If the application has set the SQL_ATTR_ARRAY_STATUS_PTR statement attribute, then it can inspect this array to see the result of the operation.

If bookmarks persist across cursors, then there is no need for the application to call **SQLFetch** or **SQLFetchScroll** before fetching by bookmarks. It can use bookmarks that it has stored from a previous cursor. If bookmarks do not persist across cursors, then the application has to call **SQLFetch** or **SQLFetchScroll** once to retrieve the bookmarks.

Performing Bulk Deletes Using Bookmarks

To perform bulk deletes using bookmarks with **SQLBulkOperations**, an application performs the following steps in sequence:

1. Sets the SQL_ATTR_USE_BOOKMARKS statement attribute to SQL_UB_VARIABLE.
2. Executes a query that returns a result set.
3. Sets the SQL_ATTR_ROW_ARRAY_SIZE statement attribute to the number of rows that it wants to delete.
4. Calls **SQLBindCol** to bind column 0 (the bookmark column).
5. Copies the bookmarks for rows that it is interested in deleting into the array bound to column 0.

   Note The size of the array pointed to by the SQL_ATTR_ROW_STATUS_PTR statement attribute should either be equal to SQL_ATTR_ROW_ARRAY_SIZE or SQL_ATTR_ROW_STATUS_PTR should be a null pointer.

6. Calls **SQLBulkOperations**(*StatementHandle,* SQL_DELETE_BY_BOOKMARK).
7. If the application has set the SQL_ATTR_ARRAY_STATUS_PTR statement attribute, then it can inspect this array to see the result of the operation.

If bookmarks persist across cursors, then there is no need for the application to call **SQLFetch** or **SQLFetchScroll** before deleting by bookmarks. It can use bookmarks that it has stored from a previous cursor. If bookmarks do not persist across cursors, then the application has to call **SQLFetch** or **SQLFetchScroll** once to retrieve the bookmarks.

Providing Long Data for Bulk Inserts and Updates

Long data can be provided for bulk inserts and updates performed by calls to **SQLBulkOperations**. To insert or update long data, an application performs the following steps in addition to the steps described in the "Performing Bulk Inserts" and "Performing Bulk Updates Using Bookmarks" sections earlier in this section.

1. When it binds the data using **SQLBindCol**, the application places an application-defined value, such as the column number, in the **TargetValuePtr* buffer for data-at-execution columns. The value can be used later to identify the column.

   The application places the result of the SQL_LEN_DATA_AT_EXEC(*length*) macro in the **StrLen_or_IndPtr* buffer. If the SQL data type of the column is SQL_LONGVARBINARY, SQL_LONGVARCHAR, or a long, data source–specific data type and the driver returns "Y" for the SQL_NEED_LONG_DATA_LEN information type in **SQLGetInfo**, *length* is the number of bytes of data to be sent for the parameter; otherwise, it must be a nonnegative value and is ignored.

2. When **SQLBulkOperations** is called, if there are data-at-execution columns, the function returns SQL_NEED_DATA, and proceeds to step 3 below. (If there are no data-at-execution columns, the process is complete.)

3. The application calls **SQLParamData** to retrieve the address of the **TargetValuePtr* buffer for the first data-at-execution column to be processed. **SQLParamData** returns SQL_NEED_DATA. The application retrieves the application-defined value from the **TargetValuePtr* buffer.

   Note Although data-at-execution parameters are similar to data-at-execution columns, the value returned by **SQLParamData** is different for each.

   Data-at-execution columns are columns in a rowset for which data will be sent with **SQLPutData** when a row is updated or inserted with **SQLBulkOperations**. They are bound with **SQLBindCol**. The value returned by **SQLParamData** is the address of the row in the **TargetValuePtr* buffer that is being processed.

4. The application calls **SQLPutData** one or more times to send data for the column. More than one call is needed if all the data value cannot be returned in the **TargetValuePtr* buffer specified in **SQLPutData**; note that multiple calls to **SQLPutData** for the same column are allowed only when sending character C data to a column with a character, binary, or data source–specific data type or when sending binary C data to a column with a character, binary, or data source–specific data type.
5. The application calls **SQLParamData** again to signal that all data has been sent for the column.
   - If there are more data-at-execution columns, **SQLParamData** returns SQL_NEED_DATA and the address of the *TargetValuePtr* buffer for the next data-at-execution column to be processed. The application repeats steps 4 and 5 above.
   - If there are no more data-at-execution columns, the process is complete. If the statement was executed successfully, **SQLParamData** returns SQL_SUCCESS or SQL_SUCCESS_WITH_INFO; if the execution failed, it returns SQL_ERROR. At this point, **SQLParamData** can return any SQLSTATE that can be returned by **SQLBulkOperations**.

If the operation is canceled, or an error occurs in **SQLParamData** or **SQLPutData**, after **SQLBulkOperations** returns SQL_NEED_DATA, and before data is sent for all data-at-execution columns, the application can only call **SQLCancel**, **SQLGetDiagField**, **SQLGetDiagRec**, **SQLGetFunctions**, **SQLParamData**, or **SQLPutData** for the statement or the connection associated with the statement. If it calls any other function for the statement or the connection associated with the statement, the function returns SQL_ERROR and SQLSTATE HY010 (Function sequence error).

If the application calls **SQLCancel** while the driver still needs data for data-at-execution columns, the driver cancels the operation. The application can then call **SQLBulkOperations** again; canceling does not affect the cursor state or the current cursor position.

Row Status Array

The row status array contains status values for each row of data in the rowset after a call to **SQLBulkOperations**. The driver sets the status values in this array after a call to **SQLFetch**, **SQLFetchScroll**, **SQLSetPos**, or **SQLBulkOperations**. This array is initially populated by a call to **SQLBulkOperations** if **SQLFetch** or **SQLFetchScroll** has not been called prior to **SQLBulkOperations**. This array is pointed to by the SQL_ATTR_ROW_STATUS_PTR statement attribute. The number of elements in the row status arrays must equal the number of rows in the rowset (as defined by the SQL_ATTR_ROW_ARRAY_SIZE statement attribute). For information about this row status array, see **SQLFetch**.

Code Example

The following example fetches 10 rows of data at a time from the Customers table. It then prompts the user for an action to take. To reduce network traffic, the example buffer updates, deletes, and inserts locally in the bound arrays, but at offsets past the rowset data. When the user chooses to send updates, deletes, and inserts to the data source, the code sets the binding offset appropriately and calls **SQLBulkOperations**. For simplicity, the user cannot buffer more than 10 updates, deletes, or inserts.

```
#define UPDATE_ROW          100
#define DELETE_ROW          101
#define ADD_ROW             102
#define SEND_TO_DATA_SOURCE 103

#define UPDATE_OFFSET 10
#define INSERT_OFFSET 20
#define DELETE_OFFSET 30

// Define a structure to hold the customer data.  Assume we know the maximum bookmark
// size to be 10 bytes.
typedef tagCustStruct {
   SQLCHAR     Bookmark[10];
   SQLINTEGER  BookmarkLen;
   SQLUINTEGER CustID;
   SQLINTEGER  CustIDInd;
   SQLCHAR     Name[51];
   SQLINTEGER  NameLenOrInd;
   SQLCHAR     Address[51];
   SQLINTEGER  AddressLenOrInd;
   SQLCHAR     Phone[11];
   SQLINTEGER  PhoneLenOrInd;
} CustStruct;

// Allocate 40 of these structures. Elements 0-9 are for the current rowset,
// elements 10-19 are for the buffered updates, elements 20-29 are for
// the buffered inserts, and elements 30-39 are for the buffered deletes.
CustStruct CustArray[40];

SQLUSMALLINT RowStatusArray[10], Action, RowNum, NumUpdates = 0, NumInserts = 0,
             NumDeletes = 0;
SQLINTEGER   BindOffset = 0;
SQLRETURN    rc;
SQLHSTMT     hstmt;
```

```
// Set the following statement attributes:
//    SQL_ATTR_CURSOR_TYPE:         Keyset-driven
//    SQL_ATTR_ROW_BIND_TYPE:       Row-wise
//    SQL_ATTR_ROW_ARRAY_SIZE:      10
//    SQL_ATTR_USE_BOOKMARKS:       Use variable-length bookmarks
//    SQL_ATTR_ROW_STATUS_PTR:      Points to RowStatusArray
//    SQL_ATTR_ROW_BIND_OFFSET_PTR: Points to BindOffset
SQLSetStmtAttr(hstmt, SQL_ATTR_CURSOR_TYPE, SQL_CURSOR_KEYSET_DRIVEN, 0);
SQLSetStmtAttr(hstmt, SQL_ATTR_ROW_BIND_TYPE, sizeof(CustStruct), 0);
SQLSetStmtAttr(hstmt, SQL_ATTR_ROW_ARRAY_SIZE, 10, 0);
SQLSetStmtAttr(hstmt, SQL_ATTR_USE_BOOKMARKS, SQL_UB_VARIABLE, 0);
SQLSetStmtAttr(hstmt, SQL_ATTR_ROW_STATUS_PTR, RowStatusArray, 0);
SQLSetStmtAttr(hstmt, SQL_ATTR_ROW_BIND_OFFSET_PTR, &BindOffset, 0);

// Bind arrays to the bookmark, CustID, Name, Address, and Phone columns.
SQLBindCol(hstmt, 0, SQL_C_VARBOOKMARK, CustArray[0].Bookmark,
           sizeof(CustArray[0].Bookmark), &CustArray[0].BookmarkLen);
SQLBindCol(hstmt, 1, SQL_C_ULONG, &CustArray[0].CustID, 0, &CustArray[0].CustIDInd);
SQLBindCol(hstmt, 2, SQL_C_CHAR, CustArray[0].Name, sizeof(CustArray[0].Name),
           &CustArray[0].NameLenOrInd);
SQLBindCol(hstmt, 3, SQL_C_CHAR, CustArray[0].Address, sizeof(CustArray[0].Address),
           &CustArray[0].AddressLenOrInd);
SQLBindCol(hstmt, 4, SQL_C_CHAR, CustArray[0].Phone, sizeof(CustArray[0].Phone),
           &CustArray[0].PhoneLenOrInd);

// Execute a statement to retrieve rows from the Customers table.
SQLExecDirect(hstmt, "SELECT CustID, Name, Address, Phone FROM Customers", SQL_NTS);

// Fetch and display the first 10 rows.
rc = SQLFetchScroll(hstmt, SQL_FETCH_NEXT, 0);
DisplayCustData(CustArray, 10);

// Call GetAction to get an action and a row number from the user.
while (GetAction(&Action, &RowNum)) {
   switch (Action) {

      case SQL_FETCH_NEXT:
      case SQL_FETCH_PRIOR:
      case SQL_FETCH_FIRST:
      case SQL_FETCH_LAST:
      case SQL_FETCH_ABSOLUTE:
      case SQL_FETCH_RELATIVE:
         // Fetch and display the requested data.
         SQLFetchScroll(hstmt, Action, RowNum);
         DisplayCustData(CustArray, 10);
         break;
```

```
case UPDATE_ROW:
   // Check if we have reached the maximum number of buffered updates.
   if (NumUpdates < 10) {
      // Get the new customer data and place it in the next available element of
      // the buffered updates section of CustArray, copy the bookmark of the row
      // being updated to the same element, and increment the update counter.
      // Checking to see we have not already buffered an update for this
      // row not shown.
      GetNewCustData(CustArray, UPDATE_OFFSET + NumUpdates);
      memcopy(CustArray[UPDATE_OFFSET + NumUpdates].Bookmark,
              CustArray[RowNum - 1].Bookmark,
              CustArray[RowNum - 1].BookmarkLen);
      CustArray[UPDATE_OFFSET + NumUpdates].BookmarkLen =
                                              CustArray[RowNum - 1].BookmarkLen;
      NumUpdates++;
   } else {
      DisplayError("Buffers full. Send buffered changes to the data source.");
   }
   break;

case DELETE_ROW:
   // Check if we have reached the maximum number of buffered deletes.
   if (NumDeletes < 10) {
      // Copy the bookmark of the row being deleted to the next available element
      // of the buffered deletes section of CustArray and increment the delete
      // counter. Checking to see we have not already buffered an update for
      // this row not shown.
      memcopy(CustArray[DELETE_OFFSET + NumDeletes].Bookmark,
              CustArray[RowNum - 1].Bookmark,
              CustArray[RowNum - 1].BookmarkLen);
      CustArray[DELETE_OFFSET + NumDeletes].BookmarkLen =
                                              CustArray[RowNum - 1].BookmarkLen;
      NumDeletes++;
   } else {
      DisplayError("Buffers full. Send buffered changes to the data source.");
   }
   break;
case ADD_ROW:
   // Check if we have reached the maximum number of buffered inserts.
   if (NumInserts < 10) {
      // Get the new customer data and place it in the next available element of
      // the buffered inserts section of CustArray and increment the insert
      // counter.
      GetNewCustData(CustArray, INSERT_OFFSET + NumInserts);
      NumInserts++;
   } else {
      DisplayError("Buffers full. Send buffered changes to the data source.");
   }
   break;
```

```
      case SEND_TO_DATA_SOURCE:
         // If there are any buffered updates, inserts, or deletes, set the array size
         // to that number, set the binding offset to use the data in the buffered
         // update, insert, or delete part of CustArray, and call SQLBulkOperations to
         // do the updates, inserts, or deletes. Because we will never have more than
         // ten updates, inserts, or deletes, we can use the same row status array.
         if (NumUpdates) {
            SQLSetStmtAttr(hstmt, SQL_ATTR_ROW_ARRAY_SIZE, NumUpdates, 0);
            BindOffset = UPDATE_OFFSET * sizeof(CustStruct);
            SQLBulkOperations(hstmt, SQL_UPDATE_BY_BOOKMARK);
            NumUpdates = 0;
         }

         if (NumInserts) {
            SQLSetStmtAttr(hstmt, SQL_ATTR_ROW_ARRAY_SIZE, NumInserts, 0);
            BindOffset = INSERT_OFFSET * sizeof(CustStruct);
            SQLBulkOperations(hstmt, SQL_ADD);
            NumInserts = 0;
         }

         if (NumDeletes) {
            SQLSetStmtAttr(hstmt, SQL_ATTR_ROW_ARRAY_SIZE, NumDeletes, 0);
            BindOffset = DELETE_OFFSET * sizeof(CustStruct);
            SQLBulkOperations(hstmt, SQL_DELETE_BY_BOOKMARK);
            NumDeletes = 0;
         }

         // If there were any updates, inserts, or deletes, reset the binding offset
         // and array size to their original values.
         if (NumUpdates || NumInserts || NumDeletes) {
            SQLSetStmtAttr(hstmt, SQL_ATTR_ROW_ARRAY_SIZE, 10, 0);
            BindOffset = 0;
         }
         break;
   }
}

// Close the cursor.
SQLFreeStmt(hstmt, SQL_CLOSE);
```

Related Functions

For information about	See
Binding a buffer to a column in a result set	**SQLBindCol**
Canceling statement processing	**SQLCancel**
Fetching a block of data or scrolling through a result set	**SQLFetchScroll**
Getting a single field of a descriptor	**SQLGetDescField**
Getting multiple fields of a descriptor	**SQLGetDescRec**
Setting a single field of a descriptor	**SQLSetDescField**
Setting multiple fields of a descriptor	**SQLSetDescRec**
Positioning the cursor, refreshing data in the rowset, or updating or deleting data in the rowset	**SQLSetPos**
Setting a statement attribute	**SQLSetStmtAttr**

SQLCancel

Conformance

Version Introduced: ODBC 1.0
Standards Compliance: ISO 92

Summary

SQLCancel cancels the processing on a statement.

Syntax

SQLRETURN **SQLCancel**(
SQLHSTMT *StatementHandle*);

Arguments

StatementHandle [Input]
Statement handle.

Returns

SQL_SUCCESS, SQL_SUCCESS_WITH_INFO, SQL_ERROR, or SQL_INVALID_HANDLE.

Diagnostics

When **SQLCancel** returns SQL_ERROR or SQL_SUCCESS_WITH_INFO, an associated SQLSTATE value can be obtained by calling **SQLGetDiagRec** with a *HandleType* of SQL_HANDLE_STMT and a *Handle* of *StatementHandle*. The following table lists the SQLSTATE values commonly returned by **SQLCancel** and explains each one in the context of this function; the notation "(DM)" precedes the descriptions of SQLSTATEs returned by the Driver Manager. The return code associated with each SQLSTATE value is SQL_ERROR, unless noted otherwise.

SQLSTATE	Error	Description
01000	General warning	Driver-specific informational message. (Function returns SQL_SUCCESS_WITH_INFO.)
HY000	General error	An error occurred for which there was no specific SQLSTATE and for which no implementation-specific SQLSTATE was defined. The error message returned by **SQLGetDiagRec** in the argument **MessageText* buffer describes the error and its cause.
HY001	Memory allocation error	The driver was unable to allocate memory required to support execution or completion of the function.

SQLSTATE	Error	Description
HY013	Memory management error	The function call could not be processed because the underlying memory objects could not be accessed, possibly because of low memory conditions.
HY018	Server declined cancel request	The server declined the cancel request.
HYT01	Connection timeout expired	The connection timeout period expired before the data source responded to the request. The connection timeout period is set through **SQLSetConnectAttr**, SQL_ATTR_CONNECTION_TIMEOUT.
IM001	Driver does not support this function	(DM) The driver associated with the *StatementHandle* does not support the function.

Comments

SQLCancel can cancel the following types of processing on a statement:

- A function running asynchronously on the statement.
- A function on a statement that needs data.
- A function running on the statement on another thread.

In ODBC 2.*x*, if an application calls **SQLCancel** when no processing is being done on the statement, **SQLCancel** has the same effect as **SQLFreeStmt** with the SQL_CLOSE option; this behavior is defined only for completeness and applications should call **SQLFreeStmt** or **SQLCloseCursor** to close cursors. In ODBC 3.0, this is not the case; a call to **SQLCancel** when no processing is being done on the statement is not treated as **SQLFreeStmt** with the SQL_CLOSE option, but has no effect at all. To close a cursor, an application should call **SQLCloseCursor**, not **SQLCancel**.

When **SQLCancel** is called, diagnostic records are returned for a function running asynchronously in a statement, or for a function on a statement that needs data; diagnostic records are not returned, however, for a function running on a statement on another thread.

Canceling Asynchronous Processing

After an application calls a function asynchronously, it calls the function repeatedly to determine whether it has finished processing. If the function is still processing, it returns SQL_STILL_EXECUTING. If the function has finished processing, it returns a different code.

After any call to the function that returns SQL_STILL_EXECUTING, an application can call **SQLCancel** to cancel the function. If the cancel request is successful, the driver returns SQL_SUCCESS. This message does not indicate that the function was actually canceled; it indicates that the cancel request was processed. When or if the function is actually canceled is driver-dependent and data source–dependent. The application must continue to call the original function until the return code is not SQL_STILL_EXECUTING. If the function was successfully canceled, the return code is SQL_ERROR and SQLSTATE HY008 (Operation canceled). If the function completed its normal processing, the return code is SQL_SUCCESS or SQL_SUCCESS_WITH_INFO if the function succeeded or SQL_ERROR and a SQLSTATE other than HY008 (Operation canceled) if the function failed.

For more information about asynchronous processing, see "Asynchronous Execution" in Chapter 9, "Executing Statements."

Canceling Functions that Need Data

After **SQLExecute** or **SQLExecDirect** returns SQL_NEED_DATA and before data has been sent for all data-at-execution parameters, an application can call **SQLCancel** to cancel the statement execution. After the statement has been canceled, the application can call **SQLExecute** or **SQLExecDirect** again. For more information, see **SQLBindParameter**.

After **SQLBulkOperations** or **SQLSetPos** returns SQL_NEED_DATA and before data has been sent for all data-at-execution columns, an application can call **SQLCancel** to cancel the operation. After the operation has been canceled, the application can call **SQLBulkOperations** or **SQLSetPos** again; canceling does not affect the cursor state or the current cursor position. For more information, see **SQLBulkOperations** or **SQLSetPos**.

Canceling Functions in Multithread Applications

In a multithread application, the application can cancel a function that is running synchronously on a statement. To cancel the function, the application calls **SQLCancel** with the same statement handle as that used by the target function, but on a different thread. How the function is canceled depends upon the driver and the operating system. As in canceling a function running asynchronously, the return code of the **SQLCancel** indicates only whether the driver processed the request successfully. Only SQL_SUCCESS or SQL_ERROR can be returned; no SQLSTATEs are returned. If the original function is canceled, it returns SQL_ERROR and SQLSTATE HY008 (Operation canceled).

If an SQL statement is being executed when **SQLCancel** is called on another thread to cancel the statement execution, it is possible that the execution succeeds and returns SQL_SUCCESS, while the cancel is also successful. In this case, the Driver Manager assumes that the cursor opened by the statement execution is closed by the cancel, so the application will not be able to use the cursor.

For more information about threading, see “Multithreading” in Chapter 17, “Programming Considerations.”

Related Functions

For information about	See
Binding a buffer to a parameter	**SQLBindParameter**
Performing bulk insert or update operations	**SQLBulkOperations**
Executing an SQL statement	**SQLExecDirect**
Executing a prepared SQL statement	**SQLExecute**
Freeing a statement handle	**SQLFreeStmt**
Obtaining a field of a diagnostic record or a field of the diagnostic header	**SQLGetDiagField**
Obtaining multiple fields of a diagnostic data structure	**SQLGetDiagRec**
Returning the next parameter to send data for	**SQLParamData**
Sending parameter data at execution time	**SQLPutData**
Positioning the cursor in a rowset, refreshing data in the rowset, or updating or deleting data in the result set	**SQLSetPos**

SQLCloseCursor

Conformance

Version Introduced: ODBC 3.0
Standards Compliance: ISO 92

Summary

SQLCloseCursor closes a cursor that has been opened on a statement, and discards pending results.

Syntax

SQLRETURN **SQLCloseCursor**(
    SQLHSTMT *StatementHandle*);

Arguments

StatementHandle [Input]
Statement handle.

Returns

SQL_SUCCESS, SQL_SUCCESS_WITH_INFO, SQL_ERROR, or SQL_INVALID_HANDLE.

Diagnostics

When **SQLCloseCursor** returns SQL_ERROR or SQL_SUCCESS_WITH_INFO, an associated SQLSTATE value may be obtained by calling **SQLGetDiagRec** with a *HandleType* of SQL_HANDLE_STMT and a *Handle* of *StatementHandle*. The following table lists the SQLSTATE values commonly returned by **SQLCloseCursor** and explains each one in the context of this function; the notation "(DM)" precedes the descriptions of SQLSTATEs returned by the Driver Manager. The return code associated with each SQLSTATE value is SQL_ERROR, unless noted otherwise.

SQLSTATE	Error	Description
01000	General warning	Driver-specific informational message. (Function returns SQL_SUCCESS_WITH_INFO.)
24000	Invalid cursor state	No cursor was open on the *StatementHandle*. (This is returned only by an ODBC 3.0 driver.)
HY000	General error	An error occurred for which there was no specific SQLSTATE and for which no implementation-specific SQLSTATE was defined. The error message returned by **SQLGetDiagRec** in the **MessageText* buffer describes the error and its cause.
HY001	Memory allocation error	The driver was unable to allocate memory required to support execution or completion of the function.

SQLSTATE	Error	Description
HY010	Function sequence error	(DM) An asynchronously executing function was called for the *StatementHandle* and was still executing when this function was called. (DM) **SQLExecute**, **SQLExecDirect**, **SQLBulkOperations**, or **SQLSetPos** was called for the *StatementHandle* and returned SQL_NEED_DATA. This function was called before data was sent for all data-at-execution parameters or columns.
HY013	Memory management error	The function call could not be processed because the underlying memory objects could not be accessed, possibly because of low memory conditions.
HYT01	Connection timeout expired	The connection timeout period expired before the data source responded to the request. The connection timeout period is set through **SQLSetConnectAttr**, SQL_ATTR_CONNECTION_TIMEOUT.
IM001	Driver does not support this function	(DM) The driver associated with the *StatementHandle* does not support the function.

Comments

SQLCloseCursor returns SQLSTATE 24000 (Invalid cursor state) if no cursor is open. Calling **SQLCloseCursor** is equivalent to calling **SQLFreeStmt** with the SQL_CLOSE option, with the exception that **SQLFreeStmt** with SQL_CLOSE has no effect on the application if no cursor is open on the statement, while **SQLCloseCursor** returns SQLSTATE 24000 (Invalid cursor state).

Note If an ODBC 3.0 application working with an ODBC 2.*x* driver calls **SQLCloseCursor** when no cursor is open, SQLSTATE 24000 (Invalid cursor state) is not returned, because the Driver Manager maps **SQLCloseCursor** to **SQLFreeStmt** with SQL_CLOSE.

For more information, see "Closing the Cursor" in Chapter 10, "Retrieving Results (Basic)."

Code Example

See **SQLBrowseConnect** and **SQLConnect**.

Related Functions

For information about	See
Canceling statement processing	**SQLCancel**
Freeing a handle	**SQLFreeHandle**
Processing multiple result sets	**SQLMoreResults**

SQLColAttribute

Conformance

Version Introduced: ODBC 3.0
Standards Compliance: ISO 92

Summary

SQLColAttribute returns descriptor information for a column in a result set. Descriptor information is returned as a character string, a 32-bit descriptor-dependent value, or an integer value.

Note For more information about what the Driver Manager maps this function to when an ODBC 3.0 application is working with an ODBC 2.*x* driver, see "Mapping Replacement Functions for Backward Compatibility of Applications" in Chapter 17, "Programming Considerations."

Syntax

SQLRETURN **SQLColAttribute** (
    SQLHSTMT *StatementHandle*,
    SQLUSMALLINT *ColumnNumber*,
    SQLUSMALLINT *FieldIdentifier*,
    SQLPOINTER *CharacterAttributePtr*,
    SQLSMALLINT *BufferLength*,
    SQLSMALLINT * *StringLengthPtr*,
    SQLPOINTER *NumericAttributePtr*);

Arguments

StatementHandle [Input]
Statement handle.

ColumnNumber [Input]
The number of the record in the IRD from which the field value is to be retrieved. This argument corresponds to the column number of result data, ordered sequentially in increasing column order, starting at 1. Columns can be described in any order.

Column 0 can be specified in this argument, but all values except SQL_DESC_TYPE and SQL_DESC_OCTET_LENGTH will return undefined values.

FieldIdentifier [Input]
The field in row *ColumnNumber* of the IRD that is to be returned (see "Comments").

CharacterAttributePtr [Output]
Pointer to a buffer in which to return the value in the *FieldIdentifier* field of the *ColumnNumber* row of the IRD, if the field is a character string. Otherwise, the field is unused.

BufferLength [Input]

If *FieldIdentifier* is an ODBC-defined field and *CharacterAttributePtr* points to a character string or binary buffer, this argument should be the length of **CharacterAttributePtr*. If *FieldIdentifier* is an ODBC-defined field and **CharacterAttributePtr* is an integer, this field is ignored.

If *FieldIdentifier* is a driver-defined field, the application indicates the nature of the field to the Driver Manager by setting the *BufferLength* argument. *BufferLength* can have the following values:

- If *CharacterAttributePtr* is a pointer to a pointer, then *BufferLength* should have the value SQL_IS_POINTER.
- If *CharacterAttributePtr* is a pointer to a character string, then *BufferLength* is the length of the string or SQL_NTS.
- If *CharacterAttributePtr* is a pointer to a binary buffer, then the application places the result of the SQL_LEN_BINARY_ATTR(*length*) macro in *BufferLength*. This places a negative value in *BufferLength*.
- If *CharacterAttributePtr* is a pointer to a fixed-length data type, then *BufferLength* is either SQL_IS_INTEGER, SQL_IS_UNINTEGER, SQL_SMALLINT, or SQLUSMALLINT.

StringLengthPtr [Output]

Pointer to a buffer in which to return the total number of bytes (excluding the null-termination byte for character data) available to return in **CharacterAttributePtr*.

For character data, if the number of bytes available to return is greater than or equal to *BufferLength*, the descriptor information in **CharacterAttributePtr* is truncated to *BufferLength* minus the length of a null-termination character and is null-terminated by the driver.

For all other types of data, the value of *BufferLength* is ignored and the driver assumes the size of **CharacterAttributePtr* is 32 bits.

NumericAttributePtr [Output]

Pointer to an integer buffer in which to return the value in the *FieldIdentifier* field of the *ColumnNumber* row of the IRD, if the field is a numeric descriptor type, such as SQL_DESC_COLUMN_LENGTH. Otherwise, the field is unused.

Returns

SQL_SUCCESS, SQL_SUCCESS_WITH_INFO, SQL_STILL_EXECUTING, SQL_ERROR, or SQL_INVALID_HANDLE.

Diagnostics

When **SQLColAttribute** returns either SQL_ERROR or SQL_SUCCESS_WITH_INFO, an associated SQLSTATE value may be obtained by calling **SQLGetDiagRec** with a *HandleType* of SQL_HANDLE_STMT and a *Handle* of *StatementHandle*. The following table lists the SQLSTATE values commonly returned by **SQLColAttribute** and explains each one in the context of this function; the notation "(DM)" precedes the descriptions of SQLSTATEs returned by the Driver Manager. The return code associated with each SQLSTATE value is SQL_ERROR, unless noted otherwise.

SQLSTATE	Error	Description
01000	General warning	Driver-specific informational message. (Function returns SQL_SUCCESS_WITH_INFO.)
01004	String data, right truncated	The buffer **CharacterAttributePtr* was not large enough to return the entire string value, so the string value was truncated. The length of the untruncated string value is returned in **StringLengthPtr*. (Function returns SQL_SUCCESS_WITH_INFO.)
07005	Prepared statement not a *cursor-specification*	The statement associated with the *StatementHandle* did not return a result set and *FieldIdentifier* was not SQL_DESC_COUNT. There were no columns to describe.
07009	Invalid descriptor index	(DM) The value specified for *ColumnNumber* was equal to 0, and the SQL_ATTR_USE_BOOKMARKS statement attribute was SQL_UB_OFF. The value specified for the argument *ColumnNumber* was greater than the number of columns in the result set.
HY000	General error	An error occurred for which there was no specific SQLSTATE and for which no implementation-specific SQLSTATE was defined. The error message returned by **SQLGetDiagField** from the diagnostic data structure describes the error and its cause.
HY001	Memory allocation error	The driver was unable to allocate memory required to support execution or completion of the function.

SQLSTATE	Error	Description
HY008	Operation canceled	Asynchronous processing was enabled for the *StatementHandle*. The function was called and before it completed execution, **SQLCancel** was called on the *StatementHandle*. Then the function was called again on the *StatementHandle*. The function was called and, before it completed execution, **SQLCancel** was called on the *StatementHandle* from a different thread in a multithread application.
HY010	Function sequence error	(DM) The function was called prior to calling **SQLPrepare**, **SQLExecDirect**, or a catalog function for the *StatementHandle*. (DM) An asynchronously executing function (not this one) was called for the *StatementHandle* and was still executing when this function was called. (DM) **SQLExecute**, **SQLExecDirect**, **SQLBulkOperations**, or **SQLSetPos** was called for the *StatementHandle* and returned SQL_NEED_DATA. This function was called before data was sent for all data-at-execution parameters or columns.
HY013	Memory management error	The function call could not be processed because the underlying memory objects could not be accessed, possibly because of low memory conditions.
HY090	Invalid string or buffer length	(DM) **CharacterAttributePtr* is a character string, and *BufferLength* was less than 0, but not equal to SQL_NTS.
HY091	Invalid descriptor field identifier	The value specified for the argument *FieldIdentifier* was not one of the defined values, and was not an implementation-defined value.
HYC00	Driver not capable	The value specified for the argument *FieldIdentifier* was not supported by the driver.
HYT01	Connection timeout expired	The connection timeout period expired before the data source responded to the request. The connection timeout period is set through **SQLSetConnectAttr**, SQL_ATTR_CONNECTION_TIMEOUT.
IM001	Driver does not support this function	(DM) The driver associated with the *StatementHandle* does not support the function.

SQLColAttribute can return any SQLSTATE that can be returned by **SQLPrepare** or **SQLExecute** when called after **SQLPrepare** and before **SQLExecute** depending on when the data source evaluates the SQL statement associated with the *StatementHandle*.

For performance reasons, an application should not call **SQLColAttribute** before executing a statement.

Comments

For information about how applications use the information returned by **SQLColAttribute**, see "Result Set Metadata" in Chapter 10, "Retrieving Results (Basic)."

SQLColAttribute returns information either in **NumericAttributePtr* or in **CharacterAttributePtr*. Integer information is returned in **NumericAttributePtr* as a 32-bit, signed value; all other formats of information are returned in **CharacterAttributePtr*. When information is returned in **NumericAttributePtr*, the driver ignores *CharacterAttributePtr*, *BufferLength*, and *StringLengthPtr.* When information is returned in **CharacterAttributePtr*, the driver ignores *NumericAttributePtr*.

SQLColAttribute returns values from the descriptor fields of the IRD. The function is called with a statement handle, rather than a descriptor handle. The values returned by **SQLColAttribute** for the *FieldIdentifier* values listed later in this section can also be retrieved by calling **SQLGetDescField** with the appropriate IRD handle.

The currently defined descriptor fields, the version of ODBC in which they were introduced, and the arguments in which information is returned for them are shown later in this section; more descriptor types may be defined by drivers to take advantage of different data sources.

An ODBC 3.0 driver must return a value for each of the descriptor fields. If a descriptor field does not apply to a driver or data source, then, unless otherwise stated, the driver returns 0 in **StringLengthPtr* or an empty string in **CharacterAttributePtr*.

Backward Compatibility

The ODBC 3.0 function **SQLColAttribute** replaces the deprecated ODBC 2.*x* function **SQLColAttributes**. When mapping **SQLColAttributes** to **SQLColAttribute** (when an ODBC 2.*x* application is working with an ODBC 3.0 driver), or mapping **SQLColAttribute** to **SQLColAttributes** (when an ODBC 3.0

application is working with an ODBC 2.*x* driver), the Driver Manager either passes the value of *FieldIdentifier* through, maps it to a new value, or returns an error, as follows:

Note The prefix used in *FieldIdentifier* values in ODBC 3.0 has been changed from that used in ODBC 2.*x*. The new prefix is "SQL_DESC"; the old prefix was "SQL_COLUMN".

- If the **#define** value of the ODBC 2.*x* *FieldIdentifier* is the same as the **#define** value of the ODBC 3.0 *FieldIdentifier*, the value in the function call is just passed through.
- The **#define** values of the ODBC 2.*x* *FieldIdentifiers* SQL_COLUMN_LENGTH, SQL_COLUMN_PRECISION, and SQL_COLUMN_SCALE are different than the **#define** values of the ODBC 3.0 *FieldIdentifiers* SQL_DESC_PRECISION, SQL_DESC_SCALE, and SQL_DESC_LENGTH. An ODBC 2.*x* driver need only support the ODBC 2.*x* values. An ODBC 3.0 driver must support both "SQL_COLUMN" and "SQL_DESC" values for these three *FieldIdentifiers*. These values are different because precision, scale, and length are defined differently in ODBC 3.0 than they were in ODBC 2.*x*. For more information, see "Column Size, Decimal Digits, Transfer Octet Length, and Display Size" in Appendix D, "Data Types."
- If the **#define** value of the ODBC 2.*x* *FieldIdentifier* is different from the **#define** value of the ODBC 3.0 *FieldIdentifier*, as occurs with the COUNT, NAME, and NULLABLE values, the value in the function call is mapped to the corresponding value. For example, SQL_COLUMN_COUNT is mapped to SQL_DESC_COUNT, and SQL_DESC_COUNT is mapped to SQL_COLUMN_COUNT, depending on the direction of the mapping.
- If *FieldIdentifier* is a new value in ODBC 3.0, for which there was no corresponding value in ODBC 2.*x*, it will not be mapped when an ODBC 3.0 application uses it in a call to **SQLColAttribute** in an ODBC 2.*x* driver, and the call will return SQLSTATE HY091 (Invalid descriptor field identifier).

The following table lists the descriptor types returned by **SQLColAttribute**.

FieldIdentifier	Information returned in	Description
SQL_DESC_AUTO_ UNIQUE_VALUE (ODBC 1.0)	*NumericAttributePtr*	SQL_TRUE if the column is an autoincrementing column. SQL_FALSE if the column is not an autoincrementing column or is not numeric. This field is valid for numeric data type columns only. An application can insert values into a row containing an autoincrement column, but typically cannot update values in the column. When an insert is made into an auto-increment column, a unique value is inserted into the column at insert time. The increment is not defined, but is data-source–specific. An application should not assume that an auto-increment column starts at any particular point or increments by any particular value.
SQL_DESC_BASE_COLUMN_ NAME (ODBC 3.0)	*CharacterAttributePtr*	The base column name for the result set column. If a base column name does not exist (as in the case of columns that are expressions), then this variable contains an empty string. This information is returned from the SQL_DESC_BASE_COLUMN_NAME record field of the IRD, which is a read-only field.
SQL_DESC_BASE_TABLE_ NAME (ODBC 3.0)	*CharacterAttributePtr*	The name of the base table that contains the column. If the base table name cannot be defined or is not applicable, then this variable contains an empty string. This information is returned from the SQL_DESC_BASE_TABLE_NAME record field of the IRD, which is a read-only field.
SQL_DESC_CASE_SENSITIVE (ODBC 1.0)	*NumericAttributePtr*	SQL_TRUE if the column is treated as case-sensitive for collations and comparisons. SQL_FALSE if the column is not treated as case-sensitive for collations and comparisons or is noncharacter.

FieldIdentifier	Information returned in	Description
SQL_DESC_CATALOG_NAME (ODBC 2.0)	*CharacterAttributePtr*	The catalog of the table that contains the column. The returned value is implementation-defined if the column is an expression or if the column is part of a view. If the data source does not support catalogs or the catalog name cannot be determined, an empty string is returned. This VARCHAR record field is not limited to 128 characters.
SQL_DESC_CONCISE_TYPE (ODBC 3.0)	*NumericAttributePtr*	The concise data type. For the datetime and interval data types, this field returns the concise data type; for examples, SQL_TYPE_TIME or SQL_INTERVAL_YEAR. (For more information, see "Data Type Identifiers and Descriptors" in Appendix D, "Data Types.") This information is returned from the SQL_DESC_CONCISE_TYPE record field of the IRD.
SQL_DESC_COUNT (ODBC 1.0)	*NumericAttributePtr*	The number of columns available in the result set. This returns 0 if there are no columns in the result set. The value in the *ColumnNumber* argument is ignored. This information is returned from the SQL_DESC_COUNT header field of the IRD.
SQL_DESC_DISPLAY_SIZE (ODBC 1.0)	*NumericAttributePtr*	Maximum number of characters required to display data from the column. For more information on display size, see "Column Size, Decimal Digits, Transfer Octet Length, and Display Size" in Appendix D, "Data Types."
SQL_DESC_FIXED_ PREC_SCALE (ODBC 1.0)	*NumericAttributePtr*	SQL_TRUE if the column has a fixed precision and non-zero scale that are data-source–specific. SQL_FALSE if the column does not have a fixed precision and non-zero scale that are data-source–specific.

FieldIdentifier	Information returned in	Description
SQL_DESC_LABEL (ODBC 2.0)	*CharacterAttributePtr*	The column label or title. For example, a column named EmpName might be labeled Employee Name, or might be labeled with an alias. If a column does not have a label, the column name is returned. If the column is unlabeled and unnamed, an empty string is returned.
SQL_DESC_LENGTH (ODBC 3.0)	*NumericAttributePtr*	A numeric value that is either the maximum or actual character length of a character string or binary data type. It is the maximum character length for a fixed-length data type, or the actual character length for a variable-length data type. Its value always excludes the null-termination byte that ends the character string. This information is returned from the SQL_DESC_LENGTH record field of the IRD. For more information on length, see "Column Size, Decimal Digits, Transfer Octet Length, and Display Size" in Appendix D, "Data Types."
SQL_DESC_LITERAL_PREFIX (ODBC 3.0)	*CharacterAttributePtr*	This VARCHAR(128) record field contains the character or characters that the driver recognizes as a prefix for a literal of this data type. This field contains an empty string for a data type for which a literal prefix is not applicable. For more information, see "Literal Prefixes and Suffixes" in Chapter 8, "SQL Statements."
SQL_DESC_LITERAL_SUFFIX (ODBC 3.0)	*CharacterAttributePtr*	This VARCHAR(128) record field contains the character or characters that the driver recognizes as a suffix for a literal of this data type. This field contains an empty string for a data type for which a literal suffix is not applicable. For more information, see "Literal Prefixes and Suffixes" in Chapter 8, "SQL Statements."

FieldIdentifier	Information returned in	Description
SQL_DESC_LOCAL_ TYPE_NAME (ODBC 3.0)	*CharacterAttributePtr*	This VARCHAR(128) record field contains any localized (native language) name for the data type that may be different from the regular name of the data type. If there is no localized name, then an empty string is returned. This field is for display purposes only. The character set of the string is locale-dependent and is typically the default character set of the server.
SQL_DESC_NAME (ODBC 3.0)	*CharacterAttributePtr*	The column alias, if it applies. If the column alias does not apply, the column name is returned. In either case, SQL_DESC_UNNAMED is set to SQL_NAMED. If there is no column name or a column alias, an empty string is returned and SQL_DESC_UNNAMED is set to SQL_UNNAMED. This information is returned from the SQL_DESC_NAME record field of the IRD.
SQL_DESC_NULLABLE (ODBC 3.0)	*NumericAttributePtr*	SQL_ NULLABLE if the column can have NULL values; SQL_NO_NULLS if the column does not have NULL values; or SQL_NULLABLE_UNKNOWN if it is not known whether the column accepts NULL values. This information is returned from the SQL_DESC_NULLABLE record field of the IRD.
SQL_DESC_NUM_PREX_ RADIX (ODBC 3.0)	*NumericAttributePtr*	If the data type in the SQL_DESC_TYPE field is an approximate numeric data type, this SQLINTEGER field contains a value of 2 because the SQL_DESC_PRECISION field contains the number of bits. If the data type in the SQL_DESC_TYPE field is an exact numeric data type, this field contains a value of 10 because the SQL_DESC_PRECISION field contains the number of decimal digits. This field is set to 0 for all non-numeric data types.

FieldIdentifier	Information returned in	Description
SQL_DESC_OCTET_LENGTH (ODBC 3.0)	*NumericAttributePtr*	The length, in bytes, of a character string or binary data type. For fixed-length character or binary types, this is the actual length in bytes. For variable-length character or binary types, this is the maximum length in bytes. This value includes the null terminator. This information is returned from the SQL_DESC_OCTET_LENGTH record field of the IRD. For more information on length, see "Column Size, Decimal Digits, Transfer Octet Length, and Display Size" in Appendix D, "Data Types."
SQL_DESC_PRECISION (ODBC 3.0)	*NumericAttributePtr*	A numeric value that for a numeric data type denotes the applicable precision. For data types SQL_TYPE_TIME, SQL_TYPE_TIMESTAMP, and all the interval data types that represent a time interval, its value is the applicable precision of the fractional seconds component. This information is returned from the SQL_DESC_PRECISION record field of the IRD.
SQL_DESC_SCALE (ODBC 3.0)	*NumericAttributePtr*	A numeric value that is the applicable scale for a numeric data type. For DECIMAL and NUMERIC data types, this is the defined scale. It is undefined for all other data types. This information is returned from the SCALE record field of the IRD.
SQL_DESC_SCHEMA_NAME (ODBC 2.0)	*CharacterAttributePtr*	The schema of the table that contains the column. The returned value is implementation-defined if the column is an expression or if the column is part of a view. If the data source does not support schemas or the schema name cannot be determined, an empty string is returned. This VARCHAR record field is not limited to 128 characters.

FieldIdentifier	Information returned in	Description
SQL_DESC_SEARCHABLE (ODBC 1.0)	*NumericAttributePtr*	SQL_PRED_NONE if the column cannot be used in a WHERE clause. (This is the same as the SQL_UNSEARCHEABLE value in ODBC 2.*x*.) SQL_PRED_CHAR if the column can be used in a WHERE clause, but only with the LIKE predicate. (This is the same as the SQL_LIKE_ONLY value in ODBC 2.*x*.) SQL_PRED_BASIC if the column can be used in a WHERE clause with all the comparison operators except LIKE. (This is the same as the SQL_EXCEPT_LIKE value in ODBC 2.*x*.) SQL_PRED_SEARCHABLE if the column can be used in a WHERE clause with any comparison operator. Columns of type SQL_LONGVARCHAR and SQL_LONGVARBINARY usually return SQL_PRED_CHAR.
SQL_DESC_TABLE_NAME (ODBC 2.0)	*CharacterAttributePtr*	The name of the table that contains the column. The returned value is implementation-defined if the column is an expression or if the column is part of a view. If the table name cannot be determined, an empty string is returned.
SQL_DESC_TYPE (ODBC 1.0)	*NumericAttributePtr*	A numeric value that specifies the SQL data type. When *ColumnNumber* is equal to 0, SQL_BINARY is returned for variable-length bookmarks, and SQL_INTEGER is returned for fixed-length bookmarks. For the datetime and interval data types, this field returns the verbose data type: SQL_DATETIME or SQL_INTERVAL. (For more information, see "Data Type Identifiers and Descriptors" in Appendix D, "Data Types.") This information is returned from the SQL_DESC_TYPE record field of the IRD.

FieldIdentifier	Information returned in	Description
SQL_DESC_TYPE_NAME (ODBC 1.0)	*Character AttributePtr*	Data source–dependent data type name; for example, "CHAR", "VARCHAR", "MONEY", "LONG VARBINARY", or "CHAR ( ) FOR BIT DATA". If the type is unknown, an empty string is returned.
SQL_DESC_UNNAMED (ODBC 3.0)	*Numeric AttributePtr*	SQL_NAMED or SQL_UNNAMED. If the SQL_DESC_NAME field of the IRD contains a column alias or a column name, SQL_NAMED is returned. If there is no column name or column alias, SQL_UNNAMED is returned. This information is returned from the SQL_DESC_UNNAMED record field of the IRD.
SQL_DESC_UNSIGNED (ODBC 1.0)	*Numeric AttributePtr*	SQL_TRUE if the column is unsigned (or not numeric). SQL_FALSE if the column is signed.
SQL_DESC_UPDATABLE (ODBC 1.0)	*Numeric AttributePtr*	Column is described by the values for the defined constants: SQL_ATTR_READONLY SQL_ATTR_WRITE SQL_ATTR_READWRITE_UNKNOWN SQL_DESC_UPDATABLE describes the updatability of the column in the result set, not the column in the base table. The updatability of the base column on which the result set column is based may be different than the value in this field. Whether a column is updatable can be based on the data type, user privileges, and the definition of the result set itself. If it is unclear whether a column is updatable, SQL_ATTR_READWRITE_UNKNOWN should be returned.

This function is an extensible alternative to **SQLDescribeCol**. **SQLDescribeCol** returns a fixed set of descriptor information based on ANSI-89 SQL. **SQLColAttribute** allows access to the more extensive set of descriptor information available in ANSI SQL-92 and DBMS vendor extensions.

Related Functions

For information about	See
Binding a buffer to a column in a result set	**SQLBindCol**
Canceling statement processing	**SQLCancel**
Returning information about a column in a result set	**SQLDescribeCol**
Fetching a block of data or scrolling through a result set	**SQLFetchScroll**
Fetching multiple rows of data	**SQLFetch**

SQLColAttributes

Conformance

Version Introduced: ODBC 1.0
Standards Compliance: Deprecated

Summary

In ODBC 3.0, the ODBC 2.0 function **SQLColAttributes** has been replaced by **SQLColAttribute**. For more information, see **SQLColAttribute**.

Note For more information about what the Driver Manager maps this function to when an ODBC 2.*x* application is working with an ODBC 3.0 driver, see "Mapping Deprecated Functions" in Appendix G, "Driver Guidelines for Backward Compatibility."

SQLColumnPrivileges

Conformance

Version Introduced: ODBC 1.0
Standards Compliance: ODBC

Summary

SQLColumnPrivileges returns a list of columns and associated privileges for the specified table. The driver returns the information as a result set on the specified *StatementHandle*.

Syntax

SQLRETURN **SQLColumnPrivileges**(
    SQLHSTMT *StatementHandle*,
    SQLCHAR * *CatalogName*,
    SQLSMALLINT *NameLength1*,
    SQLCHAR * *SchemaName*,
    SQLSMALLINT *NameLength2*,
    SQLCHAR * *TableName*,
    SQLSMALLINT *NameLength3*,
    SQLCHAR * *ColumnName*,
    SQLSMALLINT *NameLength4*);

Arguments

StatementHandle [Input]
Statement handle.

CatalogName [Input]
Catalog name. If a driver supports names for some catalogs but not for others, such as when the driver retrieves data from different DBMSs, an empty string ("") denotes those catalogs that do not have names. *CatalogName* cannot contain a string search pattern.

If the SQL_ATTR_METADATA_ID statement attribute is set to SQL_TRUE, *CatalogName* is treated as an identifier, and its case is not significant. If it is SQL_FALSE, *CatalogName* is an ordinary argument; it is treated literally, and its case is significant. For more information, see "Arguments in Catalog Functions" in Chapter 7, "Catalog Functions."

NameLength1 [Input]
Length of **CatalogName*.

SchemaName [Input]
Schema name. If a driver supports schemas for some tables but not for others, such as when the driver retrieves data from different DBMSs, an empty string ("") denotes those tables that do not have schemas. *SchemaName* cannot contain a string search pattern.

If the SQL_ATTR_METADATA_ID statement attribute is set to SQL_TRUE, *SchemaName* is treated as an identifier. If it is SQL_FALSE, *SchemaName* is an ordinary argument; it is treated literally, and its case is significant.

NameLength2 [Input]
Length of **SchemaName*.

TableName [Input]
Table name. This argument cannot be a null pointer. *TableName* cannot contain a string search pattern.

If the SQL_ATTR_METADATA_ID statement attribute is set to SQL_TRUE, *TableName* is treated as an identifier, and its case is not significant. If it is SQL_FALSE, *TableName* is an ordinary argument; it is treated literally, and its case is significant.

NameLength3 [Input]
Length of **TableName*.

ColumnName [Input]
String search pattern for column names.

If the SQL_ATTR_METADATA_ID statement attribute is set to SQL_TRUE, *ColumnName* is treated as an identifier, and its case is not significant. If it is SQL_FALSE, *ColumnName* is a pattern value argument; it is treated literally, and its case is significant.

NameLength4 [Input]
Length of **ColumnName*.

Returns

SQL_SUCCESS, SQL_SUCCESS_WITH_INFO, SQL_STILL_EXECUTING, SQL_ERROR, or SQL_INVALID_HANDLE.

Diagnostics

When **SQLColumnPrivileges** returns SQL_ERROR or SQL_SUCCESS_WITH_INFO, an associated SQLSTATE value may be obtained by calling **SQLGetDiagRec** with a *HandleType* of SQL_HANDLE_STMT and a *Handle* of *StatementHandle*. The following table lists the SQLSTATE values commonly returned by **SQLColumnPrivileges** and explains each one in the context of this function; the notation "(DM)" precedes the descriptions of SQLSTATEs returned by the Driver Manager. The return code associated with each SQLSTATE value is SQL_ERROR, unless noted otherwise.

SQLSTATE	Error	Description
01000	General warning	Driver-specific informational message. (Function returns SQL_SUCCESS_WITH_INFO.)
08S01	Communication link failure	The communication link between the driver and the data source to which the driver was connected failed before the function completed processing.
24000	Invalid cursor state	A cursor was open on the *StatementHandle* and **SQLFetch** or **SQLFetchScroll** had been called. This error is returned by the Driver Manager if **SQLFetch** or **SQLFetchScroll** has not returned SQL_NO_DATA, and is returned by the driver if **SQLFetch** or **SQLFetchScroll** has returned SQL_NO_DATA. A cursor was open on the *StatementHandle* but **SQLFetch** or **SQLFetchScroll** had not been called.
40001	Serialization failure	The transaction was rolled back due to a resource deadlock with another transaction.
40003	Statement completion unknown	The associated connection failed during the execution of this function and the state of the transaction cannot be determined.
HY000	General error	An error occurred for which there was no specific SQLSTATE and for which no implementation-specific SQLSTATE was defined. The error message returned by **SQLGetDiagRec** in the **MessageText* buffer describes the error and its cause.
HY001	Memory allocation error	The driver was unable to allocate memory required to support execution or completion of the function.
HY008	Operation canceled	Asynchronous processing was enabled for the *StatementHandle*. The function was called and before it completed execution, **SQLCancel** was called on the *StatementHandle*. Then the function was called again on the *StatementHandle*. The function was called and, before it completed execution, **SQLCancel** was called on the *StatementHandle* from a different thread in a multithread application.

SQLSTATE	Error	Description
HY009	Invalid use of null pointer	The *TableName* argument was a null pointer. (DM) The SQL_ATTR_METADATA_ID statement attribute was set to SQL_TRUE, the *CatalogName* argument was a null pointer, and the SQL_CATALOG_NAME *InfoType* returns that catalog names are supported. (DM) The SQL_ATTR_METADATA_ID statement attribute was set to SQL_TRUE, and the *SchemaName* or *ColumnName* argument was a null pointer.
HY010	Function sequence error	(DM) An asynchronously executing function (not this one) was called for the *StatementHandle* and was still executing when this function was called. (DM) **SQLExecute**, **SQLExecDirect**, **SQLBulkOperations**, or **SQLSetPos** was called for the *StatementHandle* and returned SQL_NEED_DATA. This function was called before data was sent for all data-at-execution parameters or columns.
HY013	Memory management error	The function call could not be processed because the underlying memory objects could not be accessed, possibly because of low memory conditions.
HY090	Invalid string or buffer length	(DM) The value of one of the name length arguments was less than 0, but not equal to SQL_NTS. The value of one of the name length arguments exceeded the maximum length value for the corresponding name (see “Comments”).

SQLSTATE	Error	Description
HYC00	Optional feature not implemented	A catalog name was specified and the driver or data source does not support catalogs. A schema name was specified and the driver or data source does not support schemas. A string search pattern was specified for the column name and the data source does not support search patterns for that argument. The combination of the current settings of the SQL_CONCURRENCY and SQL_CURSOR_TYPE statement attributes was not supported by the driver or data source. The SQL_ATTR_USE_BOOKMARKS statement attribute was set to SQL_UB_VARIABLE, and the SQL_ATTR_CURSOR_TYPE statement attribute was set to a cursor type for which the driver does not support bookmarks.
HYT00	Timeout expired	The query timeout period expired before the data source returned the result set. The timeout period is set through **SQLSetStmtAttr**, SQL_ATTR_QUERY_TIMEOUT.
HYT01	Connection timeout expired	The connection timeout period expired before the data source responded to the request. The connection timeout period is set through **SQLSetConnectAttr**, SQL_ATTR_CONNECTION_TIMEOUT.
IM001	Driver does not support this function	(DM) The driver associated with the *StatementHandle* does not support the function.

Comments

SQLColumnPrivileges returns the results as a standard result set, ordered by TABLE_CAT, TABLE_SCHEM, TABLE_NAME, COLUMN_NAME, and PRIVILEGE.

Note **SQLColumnPrivileges** might not return privileges for all columns. For example, a driver might not return information about privileges for pseudo-columns, such as Oracle ROWID. Applications can use any valid column, regardless of whether it is returned by **SQLColumnPrivileges**.

The lengths of VARCHAR columns are not shown in the table; the actual lengths depend on the data source. To determine the actual lengths of the CATALOG_NAME, SCHEMA_NAME, TABLE_NAME, and COLUMN_NAME columns, an application can call **SQLGetInfo** with the SQL_MAX_CATALOG_NAME_LEN, SQL_MAX_SCHEMA_NAME_LEN, SQL_MAX_TABLE_NAME_LEN, and SQL_MAX_COLUMN_NAME_LEN options.

Note For more information about the general use, arguments, and returned data of ODBC catalog functions, see Chapter 7, "Catalog Functions."

The following columns have been renamed for ODBC 3.0. The column name changes do not affect backward compatibility because applications bind by column number.

ODBC 2.0 column	ODBC 3.0 column
TABLE_QUALIFIER	TABLE_CAT
TABLE_OWNER	TABLE_SCHEM

The following table lists the columns in the result set. Additional columns beyond column 8 (IS_GRANTABLE) can be defined by the driver. An application should gain access to driver-specific columns by counting down from the end of the result set rather than specifying an explicit ordinal position. For more information, see "Data Returned by Catalog Functions" in Chapter 7, "Catalog Functions."

Column name	Column number	Data type	Comments
TABLE_CAT (ODBC 1.0)	1	Varchar	Catalog identifier; NULL if not applicable to the data source. If a driver supports catalogs for some tables but not for others, such as when the driver retrieves data from different DBMSs, it returns an empty string ("") for those tables that do not have catalogs.
TABLE_SCHEM (ODBC 1.0)	2	Varchar	Schema identifier; NULL if not applicable to the data source. If a driver supports schemas for some tables but not for others, such as when the driver retrieves data from different DBMSs, it returns an empty string ("") for those tables that do not have schemas.
TABLE_NAME (ODBC 1.0)	3	Varchar not NULL	Table identifier.
COLUMN_NAME (ODBC 1.0)	4	Varchar not NULL	Column name. The driver returns an empty string for a column that does not have a name.

Column name	Column number	Data type	Comments
GRANTOR (ODBC 1.0)	5	Varchar	Name of the user who granted the privilege; NULL if not applicable to the data source. For all rows in which the value in the GRANTEE column is the owner of the object, the GRANTOR column will be "_SYSTEM".
GRANTEE (ODBC 1.0)	6	Varchar not NULL	Name of the user to whom the privilege was granted.
PRIVILEGE (ODBC 1.0)	7	Varchar not NULL	Identifies the column privilege. May be one of the following or others supported by the data source when implementation-defined: SELECT: The grantee is permitted to retrieve data for the column. INSERT: The grantee is permitted to provide data for the column in new rows that are inserted into the associated table. UPDATE: The grantee is permitted to update data in the column. REFERENCES: The grantee is permitted to refer to the column within a constraint (for example, a unique, referential, or table check constraint).
IS_GRANTABLE (ODBC 1.0)	8	Varchar	Indicates whether the grantee is permitted to grant the privilege to other users; "YES," "NO," or NULL if unknown or not applicable to the data source. A privilege is either grantable or not grantable, but not both. The result set returned by **SQLColumnPrivileges** will never contain two rows for which all columns except the IS_GRANTABLE column contain the same value.

Code Example

For a code example of a similar function, see **SQLColumns**.

Related Functions

For information about	See
Binding a buffer to a column in a result set	**SQLBindCol**
Canceling statement processing	**SQLCancel**
Returning the columns in a table or tables	**SQLColumns**
Fetching a block of data or scrolling through a result set	**SQLFetchScroll**
Fetching multiple rows of data	**SQLFetch**
Returning privileges for a table or tables	**SQLTablePrivileges**
Returning a list of tables in a data source	**SQLTables**

SQLColumns

Conformance

Version Introduced: ODBC 1.0
Standards Compliance: X/Open

Summary

SQLColumns returns the list of column names in specified tables. The driver returns this information as a result set on the specified *StatementHandle*.

Syntax

```
SQLRETURN SQLColumns(
      SQLHSTMT      StatementHandle,
      SQLCHAR *     CatalogName,
      SQLSMALLINT   NameLength1,
      SQLCHAR *     SchemaName,
      SQLSMALLINT   NameLength2,
      SQLCHAR *     TableName,
      SQLSMALLINT   NameLength3,
      SQLCHAR *     ColumnName,
      SQLSMALLINT   NameLength4);
```

Arguments

StatementHandle [Input]
Statement handle.

CatalogName [Input]
Catalog name. If a driver supports catalogs for some tables but not for others, such as when the driver retrieves data from different DBMSs, an empty string ("") denotes those tables that do not have catalogs. *CatalogName* cannot contain a string search pattern.

If the SQL_ATTR_METADATA_ID statement attribute is set to SQL_TRUE, *CatalogName* is treated as an identifier, and its case is not significant. If it is SQL_FALSE, *CatalogName* is an ordinary argument; it is treated literally, and its case is significant. For more information, see “Arguments in Catalog Functions” in Chapter 7, “Catalog Functions.”

NameLength1 [Input]
Length of **CatalogName*.

SchemaName [Input]
String search pattern for schema names. If a driver supports schemas for some tables but not for others, such as when the driver retrieves data from different DBMSs, an empty string ("") denotes those tables that do not have schemas.

If the SQL_ATTR_METADATA_ID statement attribute is set to SQL_TRUE, *SchemaName* is treated as an identifier, and its case is not significant. If it is SQL_FALSE, *SchemaName* is a pattern value argument; it is treated literally, and its case is significant.

NameLength2 [Input]
Length of **SchemaName*.

TableName [Input]
String search pattern for table names.

If the SQL_ATTR_METADATA_ID statement attribute is set to SQL_TRUE, *TableName* is treated as an identifier, and its case is not significant. If it is SQL_FALSE, *TableName* is a pattern value argument; it is treated literally, and its case is significant.

NameLength3 [Input]
Length of **TableName*.

ColumnName [Input]
String search pattern for column names.

If the SQL_ATTR_METADATA_ID statement attribute is set to SQL_TRUE, *ColumnName* is treated as an identifier, and its case is not significant. If it is SQL_FALSE, *ColumnName* is a pattern value argument; it is treated literally, and its case is significant.

NameLength4 [Input]
Length of **ColumnName*.

Returns

SQL_SUCCESS, SQL_SUCCESS_WITH_INFO, SQL_STILL_EXECUTING, SQL_ERROR, or SQL_INVALID_HANDLE.

Diagnostics

When **SQLColumns** returns SQL_ERROR or SQL_SUCCESS_WITH_INFO, an associated SQLSTATE value may be obtained by calling **SQLGetDiagRec** with a *HandleType* of SQL_HANDLE_STMT and a *Handle* of *StatementHandle*. The following table lists the SQLSTATE values commonly returned by **SQLColumns** and explains each one in the context of this function; the notation "(DM)" precedes the descriptions of SQLSTATEs returned by the Driver Manager. The return code associated with each SQLSTATE value is SQL_ERROR, unless noted otherwise.

SQLSTATE	Error	Description
01000	General warning	Driver-specific informational message. (Function returns SQL_SUCCESS_WITH_INFO.)
08S01	Communication link failure	The communication link between the driver and the data source to which the driver was connected failed before the function completed processing.
24000	Invalid cursor state	A cursor was open on the *StatementHandle* and **SQLFetch** or **SQLFetchScroll** had been called. This error is returned by the Driver Manager if **SQLFetch** or **SQLFetchScroll** has not returned SQL_NO_DATA, and is returned by the driver if **SQLFetch** or **SQLFetchScroll** has returned SQL_NO_DATA. A cursor was open on the *StatementHandle* but **SQLFetch** or **SQLFetchScroll** had not been called.
40001	Serialization failure	The transaction was rolled back due to a resource deadlock with another transaction.
40003	Statement completion unknown	The associated connection failed during the execution of this function and the state of the transaction cannot be determined.
HY000	General error	An error occurred for which there was no specific SQLSTATE and for which no implementation-specific SQLSTATE was defined. The error message returned by **SQLGetDiagRec** in the **MessageText* buffer describes the error and its cause.
HY001	Memory allocation error	The driver was unable to allocate memory required to support execution or completion of the function.
HY008	Operation canceled	Asynchronous processing was enabled for the *StatementHandle*. The function was called and before it completed execution, **SQLCancel** was called on the *StatementHandle*. Then the function was called again on the *StatementHandle*. The function was called and, before it completed execution, **SQLCancel** was called on the *StatementHandle* from a different thread in a multithread application.

SQLSTATE	Error	Description
HY009	Invalid use of null pointer	(DM) The SQL_ATTR_METADATA_ID statement attribute was set to SQL_TRUE, the *CatalogName* argument was a null pointer, and the SQL_CATALOG_NAME *InfoType* returns that catalog names are supported. (DM) The SQL_ATTR_METADATA_ID statement attribute was set to SQL_TRUE, and the *SchemaName*, *TableName*, or *ColumnName* argument was a null pointer.
HY010	Function sequence error	(DM) An asynchronously executing function (not this one) was called for the *StatementHandle* and was still executing when this function was called. (DM) **SQLExecute**, **SQLExecDirect**, **SQLBulkOperations**, or **SQLSetPos** was called for the *StatementHandle* and returned SQL_NEED_DATA. This function was called before data was sent for all data-at-execution parameters or columns.
HY013	Memory management error	The function call could not be processed because the underlying memory objects could not be accessed, possibly because of low memory conditions.
HY090	Invalid string or buffer length	(DM) The value of one of the name length arguments was less than 0, but not equal to SQL_NTS. The value of one of the name length arguments exceeded the maximum length value for the corresponding catalog or name. The maximum length of each catalog or name may be obtained by calling **SQLGetInfo** with the *InfoType* values (see "Comments").

SQLSTATE	Error	Description
HYC00	Optional feature not implemented	A catalog name was specified and the driver or data source does not support catalogs. A schema name was specified and the driver or data source does not support schemas. A string search pattern was specified for the schema name, table name, or column name and the data source does not support search patterns for one or more of those arguments. The combination of the current settings of the SQL_ATTR_CONCURRENCY and SQL_ATTR_CURSOR_TYPE statement attributes was not supported by the driver or data source. The SQL_ATTR_USE_BOOKMARKS statement attribute was set to SQL_UB_VARIABLE, and the SQL_ATTR_CURSOR_TYPE statement attribute was set to a cursor type for which the driver does not support bookmarks.
HYT00	Timeout expired	The query timeout period expired before the data source returned the result set. The timeout period is set through **SQLSetStmtAttr**, SQL_ATTR_QUERY_TIMEOUT.
HYT01	Connection timeout expired	The connection timeout period expired before the data source responded to the request. The connection timeout period is set through **SQLSetConnectAttr**, SQL_ATTR_CONNECTION_TIMEOUT.
IM001	Driver does not support this function	(DM) The driver associated with the *StatementHandle* does not support the function.

Comments

This function is typically used before statement execution to retrieve information about columns for a table or tables from the data source's catalog. **SQLColumns** can be used to retrieve data for all types of items returned by **SQLTables**. In addition to base tables, this may include (but is not limited to) views, synonyms, system tables, and so on. Note by contrast, that the functions **SQLColAttribute** and **SQLDescribeCol** describe the columns in a result set and that the function **SQLNumResultCols** returns the number of columns in a result set. For more information, see "Uses of Catalog Data" in Chapter 7, "Catalog Functions."

Note For more information about the general use, arguments, and returned data of ODBC catalog functions, see Chapter 7, "Catalog Functions."

SQLColumns returns the results as a standard result set, ordered by TABLE_CAT, TABLE_SCHEM, TABLE_NAME, and ORDINAL_POSITION.

Note When an application works with an ODBC 2.*x* driver, no ORDINAL_POSITION column is returned in the result set. As a result, when working with ODBC 2.*x* drivers, the order of the columns in the column list returned by **SQLColumns** is not necessarily the same as the order of the columns returned when the application performs a SELECT statement on all columns in that table.

Note **SQLColumns** might not return all columns. For example, a driver might not return information about pseudo-columns, such as Oracle ROWID. Applications can use any valid column, regardless of whether it is returned by **SQLColumns**.

Some columns that can be returned by **SQLStatistics** are not returned by **SQLColumns**. For example, **SQLColumns** does not return the columns in an index created over an expression or filter, such as SALARY + BENEFITS or DEPT = 0012.

The lengths of VARCHAR columns are not shown in the table; the actual lengths depend on the data source. To determine the actual lengths of the TABLE_CAT, TABLE_SCHEM, TABLE_NAME, and COLUMN_NAME columns, an application can call **SQLGetInfo** with the SQL_MAX_CATALOG_NAME_LEN, SQL_MAX_SCHEMA_NAME_LEN, SQL_MAX_TABLE_NAME_LEN, and SQL_MAX_COLUMN_NAME_LEN options.

The following columns have been renamed for ODBC 3.0. The column name changes do not affect backward compatibility because applications bind by column number.

ODBC 2.0 column	ODBC 3.0 column
TABLE_QUALIFIER	TABLE_CAT
TABLE_OWNER	TABLE_SCHEM
PRECISION	COLUMN_SIZE
LENGTH	BUFFER_LENGTH
SCALE	DECIMAL_DIGITS
RADIX	NUM_PREC_RADIX

The following columns have been added to the results set returned by **SQLColumns** for ODBC 3.0:

CHAR_OCTET_LENGTH	ORDINAL_POSITION
COLUMN_DEF	SQL_DATA_TYPE
IS_NULLABLE	SQL_DATETIME_SUB

The following table lists the columns in the result set. Additional columns beyond column 18 (IS_NULLABLE) can be defined by the driver. An application should gain access to driver-specific columns by counting down from the end of the result set rather than specifying an explicit ordinal position. For more information, see "Data Returned by Catalog Functions" in Chapter 7, "Catalog Functions."

Column name	Column number	Data type	Comments
TABLE_CAT (ODBC 1.0)	1	Varchar	Catalog name; NULL if not applicable to the data source. If a driver supports catalogs for some tables but not for others, such as when the driver retrieves data from different DBMSs, it returns an empty string ("") for those tables that do not have catalogs.
TABLE_SCHEM (ODBC 1.0)	2	Varchar	Schema name; NULL if not applicable to the data source. If a driver supports schemas for some tables but not for others, such as when the driver retrieves data from different DBMSs, it returns an empty string ("") for those tables that do not have schemas.
TABLE_NAME (ODBC 1.0)	3	Varchar not NULL	Table name.
COLUMN_NAME (ODBC 1.0)	4	Varchar not NULL	Column name. The driver returns an empty string for a column that does not have a name.
DATA_TYPE (ODBC 1.0)	5	Smallint not NULL	SQL data type. This can be an ODBC SQL data type or a driver-specific SQL data type. For datetime and interval data types, this column returns the concise data type (such as SQL_TYPE_DATE or SQL_INTERVAL_YEAR_TO_ MONTH, rather than the non-concise data type such as SQL_DATETIME or SQL_INTERVAL). For a list of valid ODBC SQL data types, see "SQL Data Types" in Appendix D, "Data Types." For information about driver-specific SQL data types, see the driver's documentation.

Column name	Column number	Data type	Comments
DATA_TYPE (ODBC 1.0) (*continued*)	5	Smallint not NULL	The data types returned for ODBC 3.0 and ODBC 2.*x* applications may be different. For more information, see "Backward Compatibility and Standards Compliance" in Chapter 17, "Programming Considerations."
TYPE_NAME (ODBC 1.0)	6	Varchar not NULL	Data source–dependent data type name; for example, "CHAR", "VARCHAR", "MONEY", "LONG VARBINAR", or "CHAR ( ) FOR BIT DATA".
COLUMN_SIZE (ODBC 1.0)	7	Integer	If DATA_TYPE is SQL_CHAR or SQL_VARCHAR, then this column contains the maximum length in characters of the column. For datetime data types, this is the total number of characters required to display the value when converted to characters. For numeric data types, this is either the total number of digits or the total number of bits allowed in the column, according to the NUM_PREC_RADIX column. For interval data types, this is the number of characters in the character representation of the interval literal (as defined by the interval leading precision, see "Interval Data Type Length" in Appendix D, "Data Types"). For more information, see "Column Size, Decimal Digits, Transfer Octet Length, and Display Size" in Appendix D, "Data Types."

Column name	Column number	Data type	Comments
BUFFER_LENGTH (ODBC 1.0)	8	Integer	The length in bytes of data transferred on an **SQLGetData**, **SQLFetch**, or **SQLFetchScroll** operation if SQL_C_DEFAULT is specified. For numeric data, this size may be different than the size of the data stored on the data source. This value is the same as the COLUMN_SIZE column for character or binary data. For more information about length, see "Column Size, Decimal Digits, Transfer Octet Length, and Display Size" in Appendix D, "Data Types."
DECIMAL_DIGITS (ODBC 1.0)	9	Smallint	The total number of significant digits to the right of the decimal point. For SQL_TYPE_TIME and SQL_TYPE_TIMESTAMP, this column contains the number of digits in the fractional seconds component. For the other data types this is the decimal digits of the column on the data source. For interval data types that contain a time component, this column contains the number of digits to the right of the decimal point (fractional seconds). For interval data types that do not contain a time component, this column is 0. For more information on decimal digits, see "Column Size, Decimal Digits, Transfer Octet Length, and Display Size" in Appendix D, "Data Types." NULL is returned for data types where decimal digits is not applicable.

Column name	Column number	Data type	Comments
NUM_PREC_RADIX (ODBC 1.0)	10	Smallint	For numeric data types, either 10 or 2. If it is 10, the values in COLUMN_SIZE and DECIMAL_DIGITS give the number of decimal digits allowed for the column. For example, a DECIMAL(12,5) column would return a NUM_PREC_RADIX of 10, a COLUMN_SIZE of 12, and a DECIMAL_DIGITS of 5; a FLOAT column could return a NUM_PREC_RADIX of 10, a COLUMN_SIZE of 15 and a DECIMAL_DIGITS of NULL. If it is 2, the values in COLUMN_SIZE and DECIMAL_DIGITS give the number of bits allowed in the column. For example, a FLOAT column could return a RADIX of 2, a COLUMN_SIZE of 53, and a DECIMAL_DIGITS of NULL. NULL is returned for data types where NUM_PREC_RADIX is not applicable.
NULLABLE (ODBC 1.0)	11	Smallint not NULL	SQL_NO_NULLS if the column could not include NULL values. SQL_NULLABLE if the column accepts NULL values. SQL_NULLABLE_UNKNOWN if it is not known whether the column accepts NULL values. The value returned for this column is different than the value returned for the IS_NULLABLE column. The NULLABLE column indicates with certainty that a column can accept NULLs, but cannot indicate with certainty that a column does not accept NULLs. The IS_NULLABLE column indicates with certainty that a column cannot accept NULLs, but cannot indicate with certainty that a column accepts NULLs.

Column name	Column number	Data type	Comments
REMARKS (ODBC 1.0)	12	Varchar	A description of the column.
COLUMN_DEF (ODBC 3.0)	13	Varchar	The default value of the column. The value in this column should be interpreted as a string if it is enclosed in quotation marks. If NULL was specified as the default value, then this column is the word NULL, not enclosed in quotation marks. If the default value cannot be represented without truncation, then this column contains TRUNCATED, with no enclosing single quotation marks. If no default value was specified, then this column is NULL. The value of COLUMN_DEF can be used in generating a new column definition, except when it contains the value TRUNCATED.
SQL_DATA_TYPE (ODBC 3.0)	14	Smallint not NULL	SQL data type, as it appears in the SQL_DESC_TYPE record field in the IRD. This can be an ODBC SQL data type or a driver-specific SQL data type. This column is the same as the DATA_TYPE column, with the exception of datetime and interval data types. This column returns the non-concise data type (such as SQL_DATETIME or SQL_INTERVAL), rather than the concise data type (such as SQL_TYPE_DATE or SQL_INTERVAL_YEAR_TO_MONTH) for datetime and interval data types. If this column returns SQL_DATETIME or SQL_INTERVAL, the specific data type can be determined from the SQL_DATETIME_SUB column. For a list of valid ODBC SQL data types, see "SQL Data Types" in Appendix D, "Data Types." For information about driver-specific SQL data types, see the driver's documentation.

Column name	Column number	Data type	Comments
SQL_DATA_TYPE (ODBC 3.0) (*continued*)	14	Smallint not NULL	The data types returned for ODBC 3.0 and ODBC 2.*x* applications may be different. For more information, see "Backward Compatibility and Standards Compliance" in Chapter 17, "Programming Considerations."
SQL_DATETIME_ SUB (ODBC 3.0)	15	Smallint	The subtype code for datetime and interval data types. For other data types, this column returns a NULL. For more information about datetime and interval subcodes, see "SQL_DESC_DATETIME_ INTERVAL_CODE" in **SQLSetDescField**.
CHAR_OCTET_ LENGTH (ODBC 3.0)	16	Integer	The maximum length in bytes of a character or binary data type column. For all other data types, this column returns a NULL.
ORDINAL_ POSITION (ODBC 3.0)	17	Integer not NULL	The ordinal position of the column in the table. The first column in the table is number 1.
IS_NULLABLE (ODBC 3.0)	18	Varchar	"NO" if the column does not include NULLs. "YES" if the column could include NULLs. This column returns a zero-length string if nullability is unknown. ISO rules are followed to determine nullability. An ISO SQL–compliant DBMS cannot return an empty string. The value returned for this column is different than the value returned for the NULLABLE column. (See the description of the NULLABLE column.)

Code Example

In the following example, an application declares buffers for the result set returned by **SQLColumns**. It calls **SQLColumns** to return a result set that describes each column in the EMPLOYEE table. It then calls **SQLBindCol** to bind the columns in the result set to the buffers. Finally, the application fetches each row of data with **SQLFetch** and processes it.

```
#define STR_LEN 128+1
#define REM_LEN 254+1

/* Declare buffers for result set data */

SQLCHAR      szCatalog[STR_LEN], szSchema[STR_LEN];
SQLCHAR      szTableName[STR_LEN], szColumnName[STR_LEN];
SQLCHAR      szTypeName[STR_LEN], szRemarks[REM_LEN];
SQLCHAR      szColumnDefault[STR_LEN], szIsNullable[STR_LEN];
SQLINTEGER   ColumnSize, BufferLength, CharOctetLength, OrdinalPosition;
SQLSMALLINT  DataType, DecimalDigits, NumPrecRadix, Nullable;
SQLSMALLINT  SQLDataType, DatetimeSubtypeCode;
SQLRETURN    retcode;
SQLHSTMT     hstmt;

/* Declare buffers for bytes available to return */

SQLINTEGER cbCatalog, cbSchema, cbTableName, cbColumnName;
SQLINTEGER cbDataType, cbTypeName, cbColumnSize, cbBufferLength;
SQLINTEGER cbDecimalDigits, cbNumPrecRadix, cbNullable, cbRemarks;
SQLINTEGER cbColumnDefault, cbSQLDataType, cbDatetimeSubtypeCode, cbCharOctetLength;
SQLINTEGER cbOrdinalPosition, cbIsNullable;

retcode = SQLColumns(hstmt,
                     NULL, 0,               /* All catalogs */
                     NULL, 0,               /* All schemas     */
                     "CUSTOMERS", SQL_NTS, /* CUSTOMERS table */
                     NULL, 0);             /* All columns    */

if (retcode == SQL_SUCCESS || retcode == SQL_SUCCESS_WITH_INFO) {

   /* Bind columns in result set to buffers */

   SQLBindCol(hstmt, 1, SQL_C_CHAR, szCatalog, STR_LEN,&cbCatalog);
   SQLBindCol(hstmt, 2, SQL_C_CHAR, szSchema, STR_LEN, &cbSchema);
   SQLBindCol(hstmt, 3, SQL_C_CHAR, szTableName, STR_LEN,&cbTableName);
   SQLBindCol(hstmt, 4, SQL_C_CHAR, szColumnName, STR_LEN, &cbColumnName);
   SQLBindCol(hstmt, 5, SQL_C_SSHORT, &DataType, 0, &cbDataType);
   SQLBindCol(hstmt, 6, SQL_C_CHAR, szTypeName, STR_LEN, &cbTypeName);
   SQLBindCol(hstmt, 7, SQL_C_SLONG, &ColumnSize, 0, &cbColumnSize);
   SQLBindCol(hstmt, 8, SQL_C_SLONG, &BufferLength, 0, &cbBufferLength);
   SQLBindCol(hstmt, 9, SQL_C_SSHORT, &DecimalDigits, 0, &cbDecimalDigits);
   SQLBindCol(hstmt, 10, SQL_C_SSHORT, &NumPrecRadix, 0, &cbNumPrecRadix);
   SQLBindCol(hstmt, 11, SQL_C_SSHORT, &Nullable, 0, &cbNullable);
   SQLBindCol(hstmt, 12, SQL_C_CHAR, szRemarks, REM_LEN, &cbRemarks);
   SQLBindCol(hstmt, 13, SQL_C_CHAR, szColumnDefault, STR_LEN, &cbColumnDefault);
```

```
SQLBindCol(hstmt, 14, SQL_C_SSHORT, &SQLDataType, 0, &cbSQLDataType);
   SQLBindCol(hstmt, 15, SQL_C_SSHORT, &DatetimeSubtypeCode, 0,
              &cbDatetimeSubtypeCode);
   SQLBindCol(hstmt, 16, SQL_C_SLONG, &CharOctetLength, 0, &cbCharOctetLength);
   SQLBindCol(hstmt, 17, SQL_C_SLONG, &OrdinalPosition, 0, &cbOrdinalPosition);
   SQLBindCol(hstmt, 18, SQL_C_CHAR, szIsNullable, STR_LEN, &cbIsNullable);
   while(TRUE) {
      retcode = SQLFetch(hstmt);
      if (retcode == SQL_ERROR || retcode == SQL_SUCCESS_WITH_INFO) {
         show_error( );
      }
      if (retcode == SQL_SUCCESS || retcode == SQL_SUCCESS_WITH_INFO){
         ...;  /* Process fetched data */
      } else {
         break;
      }
   }
}
```

Related Functions

For information about	See
Binding a buffer to a column in a result set	**SQLBindCol**
Canceling statement processing	**SQLCancel**
Returning privileges for a column or columns	**SQLColumnPrivileges**
Fetching a block of data or scrolling through a result set	**SQLFetchScroll**
Fetching multiple rows of data	**SQLFetch**
Returning columns that uniquely identify a row, or columns automatically updated by a transaction	**SQLSpecialColumns**
Returning table statistics and indexes	**SQLStatistics**
Returning a list of tables in a data source	**SQLTables**
Returning privileges for a table or tables	**SQLTablePrivileges**

SQLConnect

Conformance

Version Introduced: ODBC 1.0
Standards Compliance: ISO 92

Summary

SQLConnect establishes connections to a driver and a data source. The connection handle references storage of all information about the connection to the data source, including status, transaction state, and error information.

Syntax

```
SQLRETURN SQLConnect(
     SQLHDBC       ConnectionHandle,
     SQLCHAR *     ServerName,
     SQLSMALLINT   NameLength1,
     SQLCHAR *     UserName,
     SQLSMALLINT   NameLength2,
     SQLCHAR *     Authentication,
     SQLSMALLINT   NameLength3);
```

Arguments

ConnectionHandle [Input]
Connection handle.

ServerName [Input]
Data source name. For information about how an application chooses a data source, see "Choosing a Data Source or Driver" in Chapter 6, "Connecting to a Data Source or Driver."

NameLength1 [Input]
Length of **ServerName*.

UserName [Input]
User identifier.

NameLength2 [Input]
Length of **UserName*.

Authentication [Input]
Authentication string (typically the password).

NameLength3 [Input]
Length of **Authentication*.

Returns

SQL_SUCCESS, SQL_SUCCESS_WITH_INFO, SQL_ERROR, or SQL_INVALID_HANDLE.

Diagnostics

When **SQLConnect** returns SQL_ERROR or SQL_SUCCESS_WITH_INFO, an associated SQLSTATE value can be obtained by calling **SQLGetDiagRec** with a *HandleType* of SQL_HANDLE_DBC and a *Handle* of *ConnectionHandle*. The following table lists the SQLSTATE values commonly returned by **SQLConnect** and explains each one in the context of this function; the notation "(DM)" precedes the descriptions of SQLSTATEs returned by the Driver Manager. The return code associated with each SQLSTATE value is SQL_ERROR, unless noted otherwise.

SQLSTATE	Error	Description
01000	General warning	Driver-specific informational message. (Function returns SQL_SUCCESS_WITH_INFO.)
01S02	Option value changed	The driver did not support the specified value of the *ValuePtr* argument in **SQLSetConnectAttr** and substituted a similar value. (Function returns SQL_SUCCESS_WITH_INFO.)
08001	Client unable to establish connection	The driver was unable to establish a connection with the data source.
08002	Connection name in use	(DM) The specified *ConnectionHandle* had already been used to establish a connection with a data source and the connection was still open or the user was browsing for a connection.
08004	Server rejected the connection	The data source rejected the establishment of the connection for implementation-defined reasons.
08S01	Communication link failure	The communication link between the driver and the data source to which the driver was attempting to connect failed before the function completed processing.
28000	Invalid authorization specification	The value specified for the argument *UserName* or the value specified for the argument *Authentication* violated restrictions defined by the data source.
HY000	General error	An error occurred for which there was no specific SQLSTATE and for which no implementation-specific SQLSTATE was defined. The error message returned by **SQLGetDiagRec** in the **MessageText* buffer describes the error and its cause.
HY001	Memory allocation error	(DM) The Driver Manager was unable to allocate memory required to support execution or completion of the function. The driver was unable to allocate memory required to support execution or completion of the function.

SQLSTATE	Error	Description
HY013	Memory management error	The function call could not be processed because the underlying memory objects could not be accessed, possibly because of low memory conditions.
HY090	Invalid string or buffer length	(DM) The value specified for argument *NameLength1, NameLength2*, or *NameLength3* was less than 0, but not equal to SQL_NTS. (DM) The value specified for argument *NameLength1* exceeded the maximum length for a data source name.
HYT00	Timeout expired	The query timeout period expired before the connection to the data source completed. The timeout period is set through **SQLSetConnectAttr**, SQL_ATTR_LOGIN_TIMEOUT.
HYT01	Connection timeout expired	The connection timeout period expired before the data source responded to the request. The connection timeout period is set through **SQLSetConnectAttr**, SQL_ATTR_CONNECTION_TIMEOUT.
IM001	Driver does not support this function	(DM) The driver specified by the data source name does not support the function.
IM002	Data source not found and no default driver specified	(DM) The data source name specified in the argument *ServerName* was not found in the system information, nor was there a default driver specification.
IM003	Specified driver could not be connected to	(DM) The driver listed in the data source specification in system information was not found or could not be connected to for some other reason.
IM004	Driver's SQLAllocHandle on SQL_HANDLE_ ENV failed	(DM) During **SQLConnect**, the Driver Manager called the driver's **SQLAllocHandle** function with a *HandleType* of SQL_HANDLE_ENV and the driver returned an error.
IM005	Driver's SQLAllocHandle on SQL_HANDLE_ DBC failed	(DM) During **SQLConnect**, the Driver Manager called the driver's **SQLAllocHandle** function with a *HandleType* of SQL_HANDLE_DBC and the driver returned an error.

SQLSTATE	Error	Description
IM006	Driver's SQLSetConnectAttr failed	During **SQLConnect**, the Driver Manager called the driver's **SQLSetConnectAttr** function and the driver returned an error. (Function returns SQL_SUCCESS_WITH_INFO).
IM009	Unable to connect to translation DLL	The driver was unable to connect to the translation DLL that was specified for the data source.
IM010	Data source name too long	(DM) **ServerName* was longer than SQL_MAX_DSN_LENGTH characters.

Comments

For information about why an application uses **SQLConnect**, see "Connecting with SQLConnect" in Chapter 6, "Connecting to a Data Source or Driver."

The Driver Manager does not connect to a driver until the application calls a function (**SQLConnect**, **SQLDriverConnect**, or **SQLBrowseConnect**) to connect to the driver. Until that point, the Driver Manager works with its own handles and manages connection information. When the application calls a connection function, the Driver Manager checks whether a driver is currently connected to for the specified *ConnectionHandle*:

- If a driver is not connected to, the Driver Manager connects to the driver and calls **SQLAllocHandle** with a *HandleType* of SQL_HANDLE_ENV, **SQLAllocHandle** with a *HandleType* of SQL_HANDLE_DBC, **SQLSetConnectAttr** (if the application specified any connection attributes), and the connection function in the driver. The Driver Manager returns SQLSTATE IM006 (Driver's **SQLSetConnectOption** failed) and SQL_SUCCESS_WITH_INFO for the connection function if the driver returned an error for **SQLSetConnectAttr**. For more information, see Chapter 6, "Connecting to a Data Source or Driver."
- If the specified driver is already connected to on the *ConnectionHandle*, the Driver Manager only calls the connection function in the driver. In this case, the driver must make sure that all connection attributes for the *ConnectionHandle* maintain their current settings.
- If a different driver is connected to, the Driver Manager calls **SQLFreeHandle** with a *HandleType* of SQL_HANDLE_DBC, and then, if no other driver is connected to in that environment, it calls **SQLFreeHandle** with a *HandleType* of SQL_HANDLE_ENV in the connected driver and then disconnects that driver. It then performs the same operations as when a driver is not connected to.

The driver then allocates handles and initializes itself.

When the application calls **SQLDisconnect**, the Driver Manager calls **SQLDisconnect** in the driver. However, it does not disconnect the driver. This keeps the driver in memory for applications that repeatedly connect to and disconnect from a data source. When the application calls **SQLFreeHandle** with a *HandleType* of SQL_HANDLE_DBC, the Driver Manager calls **SQLFreeHandle** with a *HandleType* of SQL_HANDLE_DBC and then **SQLFreeHandle** with a *HandleType* of SQL_HANDLE_ENV in the driver, and then disconnects the driver.

An ODBC application can establish more than one connection.

Driver Manager Guidelines

The contents of **ServerName* affect how the Driver Manager and a driver work together to establish a connection to a data source.

- If **ServerName* contains a valid data source name, the Driver Manager locates the corresponding data source specification in the system information and connects to the associated driver. The Driver Manager passes each **SQLConnect** argument to the driver.
- If the data source name cannot be found or *ServerName* is a null pointer, the Driver Manager locates the default data source specification and connects to the associated driver. The Driver Manager passes to the driver the *UserName* and *Authentication* arguments unmodified, and "DEFAULT" for the *ServerName* argument.
- If the *ServerName* argument is "DEFAULT," the Driver Manager locates the default data source specification and connects to the associated driver. The Driver Manager passes each **SQLConnect** argument to the driver.
- If the data source name cannot be found or *ServerName* is a null pointer, and the default data source specification does not exist, the Driver Manager returns SQL_ERROR with SQLSTATE IM002 (Data source name not found and no default driver specified).

After being connected to by the Driver Manager, a driver can locate its corresponding data source specification in the system information and use driver-specific information from the specification to complete its set of required connection information.

If a default translation library is specified in the system information for the data source, the driver connects to it. A different translation library can be connected to by calling **SQLSetConnectAttr** with the SQL_ATTR_TRANSLATE_LIB attribute. A translation option can be specified by calling **SQLSetConnectAttr** with the SQL_ATTR_TRANSLATE_OPTION attribute.

If a driver supports **SQLConnect**, the driver keyword section of the system information for the driver must contain the **ConnectFunctions** keyword with the first character set to "Y."

Connection Pooling

Connection pooling allows an application to reuse a connection that has already been created. When connection pooling is enabled and **SQLConnect** is called, the Driver Manager attempts to make the connection using a connection that is part of a pool of connections in an environment that has been designated for connection pooling. This environment is a shared environment that is used by all applications that use the connections in the pool.

Connection pooling is enabled before the environment is allocated by calling **SQLSetEnvAttr** to set SQL_ATTR_CONNECTION_POOLING to SQL_CP_ONE_PER_DRIVER (which specifies a maximum of one pool per driver) or SQL_CP_ONE_PER_HENV (which specifies a maximum of one pool per environment). **SQLSetEnvAttr** in this case is called with *EnvironmentHandle* set to null, which makes the attribute a process-level attribute. If SQL_ATTR_CONNECTION_POOLING is set to SQL_CP_OFF, connection pooling is disabled.

Once connection pooling has been enabled, **SQLAllocHandle** with a *HandleType* of SQL_HANDLE_ENV is called to allocate an environment. The environment allocated by this call is a shared environment because connection pooling has been enabled. The environment to be used is not determined, however, until **SQLAllocHandle** with a *HandleType* of SQL_HANDLE_DBC is called.

SQLAllocHandle with a *HandleType* of SQL_HANDLE_DBC is called to allocate a connection. The Driver Manager attempts to find an existing shared environment that matches the environment attributes set by the application. If no such environment exists, one is created as an implicit *shared environment*. If a matching shared environment is found, the environment handle is returned to the application, and its reference count is incremented.

The connection to be used is not determined, however, until **SQLConnect** is called. At that point, the Driver Manager attempts to find an existing connection in the connection pool that matches the criteria requested by the application. This criteria includes the connection options requested in the call to **SQLConnect** (the values of the *ServerName*, *UserName*, and *Authentication* keywords) and any connection attributes set since **SQLAllocHandle** with a *HandleType* of SQL_HANDLE_DBC was called. The Driver Manager checks this criteria against the corresponding connection keywords and attributes in connections in the pool. If a match is found, the connection in the pool is used. If no match is found, a new connection is created.

If the SQL_ATTR_CP_MATCH environment attribute is set to SQL_CP_STRICT_MATCH, the match must be exact for a connection in the pool to be used. If the SQL_ATTR_CP_MATCH environment attribute is set to SQL_CP_RELAXED_MATCH, the connection options in the call to **SQLConnect** must match, but not all of the connection attributes must match.

The following rules are applied when a connection attribute, as set by the application before **SQLConnect** is called, does not match the connection attribute of the connection in the pool:

- If the connection attribute must be set before the connection is made:

  If SQL_ATTR_CP_MATCH is SQL_CP_STRICT_MATCH, SQL_ATTR_PACKET_SIZE in the pooled connection must be identical to the attribute set by the application. If SQL_CP_RELAXED_MATCH, the values of SQL_ATTR_PACKET_SIZE can be different.

  The value of SQL_ATTR_LOGIN_VALUE does not affect the match.

- If the connection attribute can be set either before or after the connection is made:

  If the connection attribute has not been set by the application, but has been set on the connection in the pool, and there is a default, the connection attribute in the pooled connection is set back to the default, and a match is declared. If there is no default, the pooled connection is not considered a match.

  If the connection attribute has been set by the application, but has not been set on the connection in the pool, the connection attribute on the pool is changed to that set by the application, and a match is declared.

  If the connection attribute has been set by the application, and has also been set on the connection in the pool, but the values are different, the value of the application's connection attribute is used, and a match is declared.

- If the values of driver-specific connection attributes are not identical and SQL_ATTR_CP_MATCH is set to SQL_CP_STRICT_MATCH, the connection in the pool is not used.

When the application calls **SQLDisconnect** to disconnect, the connection is returned to the connection pool, and is available for reuse.

Code Example

In the following example, an application allocates environment and connection handles. It then connects to the SalesOrders data source with the user ID JohnS and the password Sesame and processes data. When it has finished processing data, it disconnects from the data source and frees the handles.

```
SQLHENV     henv;
SQLHDBC     hdbc;
SQLHSTMT    hstmt;
SQLRETURN   retcode;

      /*Allocate environment handle */
retcode = SQLAllocHandle(SQL_HANDLE_ENV, SQL_NULL_HANDLE, &henv);

if (retcode == SQL_SUCCESS || retcode == SQL_SUCCESS_WITH_INFO) {
   /* Set the ODBC version environment attribute */
   retcode = SQLSetEnvAttr(henv, SQL_ATTR_ODBC_VERSION, (void*)SQL_OV_ODBC3, 0);
```

```
if (retcode == SQL_SUCCESS || retcode == SQL_SUCCESS_WITH_INFO) {
   /* Allocate connection handle */
   retcode = SQLAllocHandle(SQL_HANDLE_DBC, henv, &hdbc);

   if (retcode == SQL_SUCCESS || retcode == SQL_SUCCESS_WITH_INFO) {
      /* Set login timeout to 5 seconds. */
      SQLSetConnectAttr(hdbc, (void*)SQL_LOGIN_TIMEOUT, 5, 0);

      /* Connect to data source */
      retcode = SQLConnect(hdbc, (SQLCHAR*) "Sales", SQL_NTS,
                                 (SQLCHAR*) "JohnS", SQL_NTS,
                                 (SQLCHAR*) "Sesame", SQL_NTS);

      if (retcode == SQL_SUCCESS || retcode == SQL_SUCCESS_WITH_INFO){
         /* Allocate statement handle */
         retcode = SQLAllocHandle(SQL_HANDLE_STMT, hdbc, &hstmt);

         if (retcode == SQL_SUCCESS || retcode == SQL_SUCCESS_WITH_INFO) {
         /* Process data */
            ...;
            ...;
            ...;

            SQLFreeHandle(SQL_HANDLE_STMT, hstmt);
         }
         SQLDisconnect(hdbc);
      }
      SQLFreeHandle(SQL_HANDLE_DBC, hdbc);
   }
}
SQLFreeHandle(SQL_HANDLE_ENV, henv);
```

Related Functions

For information about	See
Allocating a handle	**SQLAllocHandle**
Discovering and enumerating values required to connect to a data source	**SQLBrowseConnect**
Disconnecting from a data source	**SQLDisconnect**
Connecting to a data source using a connection string or dialog box	**SQLDriverConnect**
Returning the setting of a connection attribute	**SQLGetConnectAttr**
Setting a connection attribute	**SQLSetConnectAttr**

SQLCopyDesc

Conformance

Version Introduced: ODBC 3.0
Standards Compliance: ISO 92

Summary

SQLCopyDesc copies descriptor information from one descriptor handle to another.

Syntax

SQLRETURN **SQLCopyDesc**(
    SQLHDESC *SourceDescHandle*,
    SQLHDESC *TargetDescHandle*);

Arguments

SourceDescHandle [Input]
Source descriptor handle.

TargetDescHandle [Input]
Target descriptor handle. The *TargetDescHandle* argument can be a handle to an application descriptor or an IPD. *TargetDescHandle* cannot be set to a handle to an IRD, or **SQLCopyDesc** will return SQLSTATE HY016 (Cannot modify an implementation row descriptor).

Returns

SQL_SUCCESS, SQL_SUCCESS_WITH_INFO, SQL_ERROR, or SQL_INVALID_HANDLE.

Diagnostics

When **SQLCopyDesc** returns SQL_ERROR or SQL_SUCCESS_WITH_INFO, an associated SQLSTATE value can be obtained by calling **SQLGetDiagRec** with a *HandleType* of SQL_HANDLE_DESC and a *Handle* of *TargetDescHandle*. If an invalid *SourceDescHandle* was passed in the call, SQL_INVALID_HANDLE will be returned, but no SQLSTATE will be returned. The following table lists the SQLSTATE values commonly returned by **SQLCopyDesc** and explains each one in the context of this function; the notation "(DM)" precedes the descriptions of SQLSTATEs returned by the Driver Manager. The return code associated with each SQLSTATE value is SQL_ERROR, unless noted otherwise.

When an error is returned, the call to **SQLCopyDesc** is immediately aborted, and the contents of the fields in the *TargetDescHandle* descriptor are undefined.

Because **SQLCopyDesc** may be implemented by calling **SQLGetDescField** and **SQLSetDescField**, **SQLCopyDesc** may return SQLSTATEs returned by **SQLGetDescField** or **SQLSetDescField**.

SQLSTATE	Error	Description
01000	General warning	Driver-specific informational message. (Function returns SQL_SUCCESS_WITH_INFO.)
08S01	Communication link failure	The communication link between the driver and the data source to which the driver was connected failed before the function completed processing.
HY000	General error	An error occurred for which there was no specific SQLSTATE and for which no implementation-specific SQLSTATE was defined. The error message returned by **SQLGetDiagRec** in the **MessageText* buffer describes the error and its cause.
HY001	Memory allocation error	The driver was unable to allocate the memory required to support execution or completion of the function.
HY007	Associated statement is not prepared	*SourceDescHandle* was associated with an IRD, and the associated statement handle was not in the prepared or executed state.
HY010	Function sequence error	(DM) The descriptor handle in *SourceDescHandle* or *TargetDescHandle* was associated with a *StatementHandle* for which an asynchronously executing function (not this one) was called and was still executing when this function was called. (DM) The descriptor handle in *SourceDescHandle* or *TargetDescHandle* was associated with a *StatementHandle* for which **SQLExecute**, **SQLExecDirect**, **SQLBulkOperations**, or **SQLSetPos** was called and returned SQL_NEED_DATA. This function was called before data was sent for all data-at-execution parameters or columns.
HY013	Memory management error	The function call could not be processed because the underlying memory objects could not be accessed, possibly because of low memory conditions.
HY016	Cannot modify an implementation row descriptor	*TargetDescHandle* was associated with an IRD.
HY021	Inconsistent descriptor information	The descriptor information checked during a consistency check was not consistent. For more information, see "Consistency Checks" in **SQLSetDescField**.

SQLSTATE	Error	Description
HY092	Invalid attribute/option identifier	The call to **SQLCopyDesc** prompted a call to **SQLSetDescField**, but **ValuePtr* was not valid for the *FieldIdentifier* argument on *TargetDescHandle*.
HYT01	Connection timeout expired	The connection timeout period expired before the data source responded to the request. The connection timeout period is set through **SQLSetConnectAttr**, SQL_ATTR_CONNECTION_TIMEOUT.
IM001	Driver does not support this function	(DM) The driver associated with the *SourceDescHandle* or *TargetDescHandle* does not support the function.

Comments

A call to **SQLCopyDesc** copies the fields of the source descriptor handle to the target descriptor handle. Fields can be copied only to an application descriptor or an IPD, but not to an IRD. Fields can be copied from either an application or an implementation descriptor.

Fields can be copied from an IRD only if the statement handle is in the prepared or executed state; otherwise, the function returns SQLSTATE HY007 (Associated statement is not prepared).

Fields can be copied from an IPD whether a statement has been prepared or not. If an SQL statement with dynamic parameters has been prepared, and automatic population of the IPD is supported and enabled, then the IPD is populated by the driver. When **SQLCopyDesc** is called with the IPD as the *SourceDescHandle*, the populated fields are copied. If the IPD is not populated by the driver, the contents of the fields originally in the IPD are copied.

All fields of the descriptor, except SQL_DESC_ALLOC_TYPE (which specifies whether the descriptor handle was automatically or explicitly allocated) are copied, whether or not the field is defined for the destination descriptor. Copied fields overwrite the existing fields.

The driver copies all descriptor fields if the *SourceDescHandle* and *TargetDescHandle* arguments are associated with the same driver, even if the drivers are on two different connections or environments. If the *SourceDescHandle* and *TargetDescHandle* arguments are associated with different drivers, the Driver Manager copies ODBC-defined fields, but does not copy driver-defined fields or fields that are not defined by ODBC for the type of descriptor.

The call to **SQLCopyDesc** is immediately aborted if an error occurs.

When the SQL_DESC_DATA_PTR field is copied, a consistency check is performed on the target descriptor. If the consistency check fails, SQLSTATE HY021 (Inconsistent descriptor information) is returned and the call to **SQLCopyDesc** is immediately aborted. For more information on consistency checks, see "Consistency Checks" in **SQLSetDescRec**.

Descriptor handles can be copied across connections even if the connections are under different environments. If the Driver Manager detects that the source and the destination descriptor handles do not belong to the same connection and the two connections belong to separate drivers, it implements **SQLCopyDesc** by performing a field-by-field copy using **SQLGetDescField** and **SQLSetDescField**.

When **SQLCopyDesc** is called with a *SourceDescHandle* on one driver, and a *TargetDescHandle* on another driver, the error queue of the *SourceDescHandle* is cleared. This occurs because **SQLCopyDesc** in this case is implemented by calls to **SQLGetDescField** and **SQLSetDescField**.

Note An application may be able to associate an explicitly allocated descriptor handle with a *StatementHandle*, rather than calling **SQLCopyDesc** to copy fields from one descriptor to another. An explicitly allocated descriptor can be associated with another *StatementHandle* on the same *ConnectionHandle* by setting the SQL_ATTR_APP_ROW_DESC or SQL_ATTR_APP_PARAM_DESC statement attribute to the handle of the explicitly allocated descriptor. When this is done, **SQLCopyDesc** does not have to be called to copy descriptor field values from one descriptor to another. A descriptor handle cannot be associated with a *StatementHandle* on another *ConnectionHandle*, however; to use the same descriptor field values on *StatementHandles* on different *ConnectionHandles*, **SQLCopyDesc** has to be called.

For a description of the fields in a descriptor header or record, see **SQLSetDescField**. For more information on descriptors, see Chapter 13, "Descriptors."

Copying Rows between Tables

An application may copy data from one table to another without copying the data at the application level. To do this, the application binds the same data buffers and descriptor information to a statement that fetches the data and another statement that inserts the data into a copy. This can be accomplished either by sharing an application descriptor (binding an explicitly allocated descriptor as both the ARD to one statement and the APD in another), or by using **SQLCopyDesc** to copy the bindings between the ARD and the APD of the two statements. If the statements are on different connections, **SQLCopyDesc** must be used. In addition, **SQLCopyDesc** has to be called to copy the bindings between the IRD and the IPD of the two statements. When copying across statements on the same connection, the SQL_ACTIVE_STATEMENTS information type returned by the driver for a call to **SQLGetInfo** must be greater than 1 for this operation to succeed (this is not the case when copying across connections).

Code Example

In the following example, descriptor operations are used to copy the fields of the PartsSource table into the PartsCopy table. The contents of the PartsSource table are fetched into rowset buffers in *hstmt0*. These values are used as parameters of an INSERT statement on *hstmt1* to populate the columns of the PartsCopy table. To do so, the fields of the IRD of *hstmt0* are copied to the fields of the IPD of *hstmt1*, and the fields of the ARD of *hstmt0* are copied to the fields of the APD of *hstmt1*.

```
#define ROWS 100
#define DESC_LEN 50
#define SQL_SUCCEEDED(rc) (rc == SQL_SUCCESS || rc == SQL_SUCCESS_WITH_INFO)

// Template for a row
typedef struct {
   SQLINTEGER    sPartID;
   SQLINTEGER    cbPartID;
   SQLUCHAR      szDescription[DESC_LENGTH];
   SQLINTEGER    cbDescription;
   REAL          sPrice;
   SQLINTEGER    cbPrice;
}  PartsSource;

PartsSource    rget[ROWS]; // rowset buffer
SQLUSMALLINT   sts_ptr[ROWS];        //status pointer
SQLHSTMT       hstmt0, hstmt1;
SQLHDESC       hArd0, hIrd0, hApd1, hIpd1;

// ARD and IRD of hstmt0
SQLGetStmtAttr(hstmt0, SQL_ATTR_APP_ROW_DESC, &hArd0, 0, NULL);
SQLGetStmtAttr(hstmt0, SQL_ATTR_IMP_ROW_DESC, &hIrd0, 0, NULL);

// APD and IPD of hstmt1
SQLGetStmtAttr(hstmt1, SQL_ATTR_APP_PARAM_DESC, &hApd1, 0, NULL);
SQLGetStmtAttr(hstmt1, SQL_ATTR_IMP_PARAM_DESC, &hIpd1, 0, NULL);

// Use row-wise binding on hstmt0 to fetch rows
SQLSetStmtAttr(hstmt0, SQL_ATTR_ROW_BIND_TYPE, (SQLPOINTER) sizeof(PartsSource), 0);

// Set rowset size for hstmt0
SQLSetStmtAttr(hstmt0, SQL_ATTR_ROW_ARRAY_SIZE, (SQLPOINTER) ROWS, 0);

// Execute a select statement
SQLExecDirect(hstmt0, "SELECT PARTID, DESCRIPTION, PRICE FROM PARTS ORDER BY 3, 1, 2",
              SQL_NTS);

// Bind
SQLBindCol(hstmt0, 1, SQL_C_SLONG, rget[0].sPartID, 0,
           &rget[0].cbPartID);
SQLBindCol(hstmt0, 2, SQL_C_CHAR, &rget[0].szDescription, DESC_LEN,
           &rget[0].cbDescription);
SQLBindCol(hstmt0, 3, SQL_C_FLOAT, rget[0].sPrice,
           0, &rget[0].cbPrice);
```

```
// Perform parameter bindings on hstmt1.
SQLCopyDesc(hArd0, hApd1);
SQLCopyDesc(hIrd0, hIpd1);

// Set the array status pointer of IRD
SQLSetStmtAttr(hstmt0, SQL_ATTR_ROW_STATUS_PTR, sts_ptr, SQL_IS_POINTER);

// Set the ARRAY_STATUS_PTR field of APD to be the same
// as that in IRD.
SQLSetStmtAttr(hstmt1, SQL_ATTR_PARAM_OPERATION_PTR, sts_ptr, SQL_IS_POINTER);

// Prepare an insert statement on hstmt1. PartsCopy is a copy of
// PartsSource
SQLPrepare(hstmt1, "INSERT INTO PARTS_COPY VALUES (?, ?, ?)", SQL_NTS);

// In a loop, fetch a rowset, and copy the fetched rowset to PARTS_COPY

rc = SQLFetchScroll(hstmt0, SQL_FETCH_NEXT, 0);
while (SQL_SUCCEEDED(rc)) {

   // After the call to SQLFetchScroll, the status array has row
   // statuses. This array is used as input status in the APD
   // and hence determines which elements of the rowset buffer
   // are inserted.
   SQLExecute(hstmt1);

   rc = SQLFetchScroll(hstmt0, SQL_FETCH_NEXT, 0);
} // while
```

Related Functions

For information about	See
Getting multiple descriptor fields	**SQLGetDescRec**
Setting a single descriptor field	**SQLSetDescField**
Setting multiple descriptor fields	**SQLSetDescRec**

SQLDataSources

Conformance

Version Introduced:	ODBC 1.0
Standards Compliance:	ISO 92

Summary

SQLDataSources returns information about a data source. This function is implemented solely by the Driver Manager.

Syntax

```
SQLRETURN SQLDataSources(
   SQLHENV          EnvironmentHandle,
   SQLUSMALLINT     Direction,
   SQLCHAR *        ServerName,
   SQLSMALLINT      BufferLength1,
   SQLSMALLINT *    NameLength1Ptr,
   SQLCHAR *        Description,
   SQLSMALLINT      BufferLength2,
   SQLSMALLINT *    NameLength2Ptr);
```

Arguments

EnvironmentHandle [Input]
Environment handle.

Direction [Input]
Determines which data source the Driver Manager returns information on. Can be:

SQL_FETCH_NEXT (to fetch the next data source name in the list),
SQL_FETCH_FIRST (to fetch from the beginning of the list),
SQL_FETCH_FIRST_USER (to fetch the first user DSN), or
SQL_FETCH_FIRST_SYSTEM (to fetch the first system DSN).

When *Direction* is set to SQL_FETCH_FIRST, subsequent calls to **SQLDataSources** with *Direction* set to SQL_FETCH_NEXT return both user and system DSNs. When *Direction* is set to SQL_FETCH_FIRST_USER, all subsequent calls to **SQLDataSources** with *Direction* set to SQL_FETCH_NEXT return only user DSNs. When *Direction* is set to SQL_FETCH_FIRST_SYSTEM, all subsequent calls to **SQLDataSources** with *Direction* set to SQL_FETCH_NEXT return only system DSNs.

ServerName [Output]
Pointer to a buffer in which to return the data source name.

BufferLength1 [Input]
Length of the **ServerName* buffer, in bytes; this does not need to be longer than SQL_MAX_DSN_LENGTH plus the null-termination character.

NameLength1Ptr [Output]

Pointer to a buffer in which to return the total number of bytes (excluding the null-termination byte) available to return in **ServerName*. If the number of bytes available to return is greater than or equal to *BufferLength1*, the data source name in **ServerName* is truncated to *BufferLength1* minus the length of a null-termination character.

Description [Output]

Pointer to a buffer in which to return the description of the driver associated with the data source. For example, dBASE or SQL Server.

BufferLength2 [Input]

Length of the **Description* buffer.

NameLength2Ptr [Output]

Pointer to a buffer in which to return the total number of bytes (excluding the null-termination byte) available to return in **Description*. If the number of bytes available to return is greater than or equal to *BufferLength2*, the driver description in **Description* is truncated to *BufferLength2* minus the length of a null-termination character.

Returns

SQL_SUCCESS, SQL_SUCCESS_WITH_INFO, SQL_NO_DATA, SQL_ERROR, or SQL_INVALID_HANDLE.

Diagnostics

When **SQLDataSources** returns either SQL_ERROR or SQL_SUCCESS_WITH_INFO, an associated SQLSTATE value may be obtained by calling **SQLGetDiagRec** with a *HandleType* of SQL_HANDLE_ENV and a *Handle* of *EnvironmentHandle*. The following table lists the SQLSTATE values commonly returned by **SQLDataSources** and explains each one in the context of this function; the notation "(DM)" precedes the descriptions of SQLSTATEs returned by the Driver Manager. The return code associated with each SQLSTATE value is SQL_ERROR, unless noted otherwise.

SQLSTATE	Error	Description
01000	General warning	(DM) Driver Manager–specific informational message. (Function returns SQL_SUCCESS_WITH_INFO.)
01004	String data, right truncated	(DM) The buffer **ServerName* was not large enough to return the entire data source name, so the name was truncated. The length of the entire data source name is returned in **NameLength1Ptr*. (Function returns SQL_SUCCESS_WITH_INFO.) (DM) The buffer **Description* was not large enough to return the entire driver description, so the description was truncated. The length of the untruncated data source description is returned in **NameLength2Ptr*. (Function returns SQL_SUCCESS_WITH_INFO.)
HY000	General error	(DM) An error occurred for which there was no specific SQLSTATE and for which no implementation-specific SQLSTATE was defined. The error message returned by **SQLGetDiagRec** in the **MessageText* buffer describes the error and its cause.
HY001	Memory allocation error	(DM) The Driver Manager was unable to allocate memory required to support execution or completion of the function.
HY013	Memory management error	The function call could not be processed because the underlying memory objects could not be accessed, possibly because of low memory conditions.
HY090	Invalid string or buffer length	(DM) The value specified for argument *BufferLength1* was less than 0. (DM) The value specified for argument *BufferLength2* was less than 0.
HY103	Invalid retrieval code	(DM) The value specified for the argument *Direction* was not equal to SQL_FETCH_FIRST, SQL_FETCH_FIRST_USER, SQL_FETCH_FIRST_SYSTEM, or SQL_FETCH_NEXT.

Comments

Because **SQLDataSources** is implemented in the Driver Manager, it is supported for all drivers regardless of a particular driver's standards compliance.

An application can call **SQLDataSources** multiple times to retrieve all data source names. The Driver Manager retrieves this information from the system information. When there are no more data source names, the Driver Manager returns SQL_NO_DATA. If **SQLDataSources** is called with SQL_FETCH_NEXT immediately after it returns SQL_NO_DATA, it will return the first data source name. For information about how an application uses the information returned by **SQLDataSources**, see "Choosing a Data Source or Driver" in Chapter 6, "Connecting to a Data Source or Driver."

If SQL_FETCH_NEXT is passed to **SQLDataSources** the very first time it is called, it will return the first data source name.

The driver determines how data source names are mapped to actual data sources.

Related Functions

For information about	See
Discovering and listing values required to connect to a data source	**SQLBrowseConnect**
Connecting to a data source	**SQLConnect**
Connecting to a data source using a connection string or dialog box	**SQLDriverConnect**
Returning driver descriptions and attributes	**SQLDrivers**

SQLDescribeCol

Conformance

Version Introduced:	ODBC 1.0
Standards Compliance:	ISO 92

Summary

SQLDescribeCol returns the result descriptor—column name, type, column size, decimal digits, and nullability—for one column in the result set. This information is also available in the fields of the IRD.

Syntax

```
SQLRETURN SQLDescribeCol(
    SQLHSTMT          StatementHandle,
    SQLSMALLINT       ColumnNumber,
    SQLCHAR *         ColumnName,
    SQLSMALLINT       BufferLength,
    SQLSMALLINT *     NameLengthPtr,
    SQLSMALLINT *     DataTypePtr,
    SQLUINTEGER *     ColumnSizePtr,
    SQLSMALLINT *     DecimalDigitsPtr,
    SQLSMALLINT *     NullablePtr);
```

Arguments

StatementHandle [Input]
Statement handle.

ColumnNumber [Input]
Column number of result data, ordered sequentially in increasing column order, starting at 1. The *ColumnNumber* argument can also be set to 0 to describe the bookmark column.

ColumnName [Output]
Pointer to a buffer in which to return the column name. This value is read from the SQL_DESC_NAME field of the IRD. If the column is unnamed or the column name cannot be determined, the driver returns an empty string.

BufferLength [Input]
Length of the **ColumnName* buffer, in bytes.

NameLengthPtr [Output]
Pointer to a buffer in which to return the total number of bytes (excluding the null-termination byte) available to return in **ColumnName*. If the number of bytes available to return is greater than or equal to *BufferLength*, the column name in **ColumnName* is truncated to *BufferLength* minus the length of a null-termination character.

DataTypePtr [Output]

Pointer to a buffer in which to return the SQL data type of the column. This value is read from the SQL_DESC_CONCISE_TYPE field of the IRD. This will be one of the values in the "SQL Data Types" section of Appendix D, "Data Types," or a driver-specific SQL data type. If the data type cannot be determined, the driver returns SQL_UNKNOWN_TYPE.

In ODBC 3.0, SQL_TYPE_DATE, SQL_TYPE_TIME, or SQL_TYPE_TIMESTAMP is returned in **DataTypePtr* for date, time, or timestamp data, respectively; in ODBC 2.*x*, SQL_DATE, SQL_TIME, or SQL_TIMESTAMP is returned. The Driver Manager performs the required mappings when an ODBC 2.*x* application is working with an ODBC 3.0 driver, or an ODBC 3.0 application is working with an ODBC 2.*x* driver.

When *ColumnNumber* is equal to 0 (for a bookmark column), SQL_BINARY is returned in **DataTypePtr* for variable-length bookmarks. (SQL_INTEGER is returned if bookmarks are used by an ODBC 3.0 application working with an ODBC 2.*x* driver, or an ODBC 2.*x* application working with an ODBC 3.0 driver.)

For more information on these data types, see "SQL Data Types" in Appendix D, "Data Types." For information about driver-specific SQL data types, see the driver's documentation.

ColumnSizePtr [Output]

Pointer to a buffer in which to return the size of the column on the data source. If the column size cannot be determined, the driver returns 0. For more information on column size, see "Column Size, Decimal Digits, Transfer Octet Length, and Display Size" in Appendix D, "Data Types."

DecimalDigitsPtr [Output]

Pointer to a buffer in which to return the number of decimal digits of the column on the data source. If the number of decimal digits cannot be determined or is not applicable, the driver returns 0. For more information on decimal digits, see "Column Size, Decimal Digits, Transfer Octet Length, and Display Size" in Appendix D, "Data Types."

NullablePtr [Output]

Pointer to a buffer in which to return a value that indicates whether the column allows NULL values. This value is read from the SQL_DESC_NULLABLE field of the IRD. The value is one of the following:

SQL_NO_NULLS: The column does not allow NULL values.

SQL_NULLABLE: The column allows NULL values.

SQL_NULLABLE_UNKNOWN: The driver cannot determine if the column allows NULL values.

Returns

SQL_SUCCESS, SQL_SUCCESS_WITH_INFO, SQL_STILL_EXECUTING, SQL_ERROR, or SQL_INVALID_HANDLE.

Diagnostics

When **SQLDescribeCol** returns either SQL_ERROR or SQL_SUCCESS_WITH_INFO, an associated SQLSTATE value can be obtained by calling **SQLGetDiagRec** with a *HandleType* of SQL_HANDLE_STMT and a *Handle* of *StatementHandle*. The following table lists the SQLSTATE values commonly returned by **SQLDescribeCol** and explains each one in the context of this function; the notation "(DM)" precedes the descriptions of SQLSTATEs returned by the Driver Manager. The return code associated with each SQLSTATE value is SQL_ERROR, unless noted otherwise.

SQLSTATE	Error	Description
01000	General warning	Driver-specific informational message. (Function returns SQL_SUCCESS_WITH_INFO.)
01004	String data, right truncated	The buffer **ColumnName* was not large enough to return the entire column name, so the column name was truncated. The length of the untruncated column name is returned in **NameLengthPtr*. (Function returns SQL_SUCCESS_WITH_INFO.)
07005	Prepared statement not a *cursor-specification*	The statement associated with the *StatementHandle* did not return a result set. There were no columns to describe.
07009	Invalid descriptor index	(DM) The value specified for the argument *ColumnNumber* was equal to 0, and the SQL_ATTR_USE_BOOKMARKS statement option was SQL_UB_OFF. (DM) The value specified for the argument *ColumnNumber* was less than 0. The value specified for the argument *ColumnNumber* was greater than the number of columns in the result set.
08S01	Communication link failure	The communication link between the driver and the data source to which the driver was connected failed before the function completed processing.
HY000	General error	An error occurred for which there was no specific SQLSTATE and for which no implementation-specific SQLSTATE was defined. The error message returned by **SQLGetDiagRec** in the **MessageText* buffer describes the error and its cause.

SQLSTATE	Error	Description
HY001	Memory allocation failure	The driver was unable to allocate memory required to support execution or completion of the function.
HY008	Operation canceled	Asynchronous processing was enabled for the *StatementHandle*. The function was called and before it completed execution, **SQLCancel** was called on the *StatementHandle*. Then the function was called again on the *StatementHandle*. The function was called and, before it completed execution, **SQLCancel** was called on the *StatementHandle* from a different thread in a multithread application.
HY010	Function sequence error	(DM) An asynchronously executing function (not this one) was called for the *StatementHandle* and was still executing when this function was called. (DM) The function was called prior to calling **SQLPrepare**, **SQLExecute**, or a catalog function on the statement handle. (DM) **SQLExecute**, **SQLExecDirect**, **SQLBulkOperations**, or **SQLSetPos** was called for the *StatementHandle* and returned SQL_NEED_DATA. This function was called before data was sent for all data-at-execution parameters or columns.
HY013	Memory management error	The function call could not be processed because the underlying memory objects could not be accessed, possibly because of low memory conditions.
HY090	Invalid string or buffer length	(DM) The value specified for argument *BufferLength* was less than 0.
HYT01	Connection timeout expired	The connection timeout period expired before the data source responded to the request. The connection timeout period is set through **SQLSetConnectAttr**, SQL_ATTR_CONNECTION_TIMEOUT.
IM001	Driver does not support this function	(DM) The driver associated with the *StatementHandle* does not support the function.

SQLDescribeCol can return any SQLSTATE that can be returned by **SQLPrepare** or **SQLExecute** when called after **SQLPrepare** and before **SQLExecute** depending on when the data source evaluates the SQL statement associated with the statement handle.

For performance reasons, an application should not call **SQLDescribeCol** before executing a statement.

Comments

An application typically calls **SQLDescribeCol** after a call to **SQLPrepare** and before or after the associated call to **SQLExecute**. An application can also call **SQLDescribeCol** after a call to **SQLExecDirect**. For more information, see "Result Set Metadata" in Chapter 10, "Retrieving Results (Basic)."

SQLDescribeCol retrieves the column name, type, and length generated by a **SELECT** statement. If the column is an expression, **ColumnName* is either an empty string or a driver-defined name.

Note ODBC supports SQL_NULLABLE_UNKNOWN as an extension, even though the X/Open and SQL Access Group Call Level Interface specification does not specify the option for **SQLDescribeCol**.

Related Functions

For information about	See
Binding a buffer to a column in a result set	**SQLBindCol**
Canceling statement processing	**SQLCancel**
Returning information about a column in a result set	**SQLColAttribute**
Fetching multiple rows of data	**SQLFetch**
Returning the number of result set columns	**SQLNumResultCols**
Preparing a statement for execution	**SQLPrepare**

SQLDescribeParam

Conformance

Version Introduced: ODBC 1.0
Standards Compliance: ODBC

Summary

SQLDescribeParam returns the description of a parameter marker associated with a prepared SQL statement. This information is also available in the fields of the IPD.

Syntax

```
SQLRETURN SQLDescribeParam(
     SQLHSTMT         StatementHandle,
     SQLUSMALLINT     ParameterNumber,
     SQLSMALLINT *    DataTypePtr,
     SQLUINTEGER *    ParameterSizePtr,
     SQLSMALLINT *    DecimalDigitsPtr,
     SQLSMALLINT *    NullablePtr);
```

Argument

StatementHandle [Input]
Statement handle.

ParameterNumber [Input]
Parameter marker number ordered sequentially in increasing parameter order, starting at 1.

DataTypePtr [Output]
Pointer to a buffer in which to return the SQL data type of the parameter. This value is read from the SQL_DESC_CONCISE_TYPE record field of the IPD. This will be one of the values in the "SQL Data Types" section of Appendix D, "Data Types," or a driver-specific SQL data type.

In ODBC 3.0, SQL_TYPE_DATE, SQL_TYPE_TIME, or SQL_TYPE_TIMESTAMP will be returned in **DataTypePtr* for date, time, or timestamp data, respectively; in ODBC 2.*x*, SQL_DATE, SQL_TIME, or SQL_TIMESTAMP will be returned. The Driver Manager performs the required mappings when an ODBC 2.*x* application is working with an ODBC 3.0 driver, or an ODBC 3.0 application is working with an ODBC 2.*x* driver.

When *ColumnNumber* is equal to 0 (for a bookmark column), SQL_BINARY is returned in **DataTypePtr* for variable-length bookmarks. (SQL_INTEGER is returned if bookmarks are used by an ODBC 3.0 application working with an ODBC 2.*x* driver, or an ODBC 2.*x* application working with an ODBC 3.0 driver.)

For more information, see "SQL Data Types" in Appendix D, "Data Types." For information about driver-specific SQL data types, see the driver's documentation.

ParameterSizePtr [Output]
Pointer to a buffer in which to return the size of the column or expression of the corresponding parameter marker as defined by the data source. For further information concerning column size, see "Column Size, Decimal Digits, Transfer Octet Length, and Display Size," in Appendix D, "Data Types."

DecimalDigitsPtr [Output]
Pointer to a buffer in which to return the number of decimal digits of the column or expression of the corresponding parameter as defined by the data source. For more information on decimal digits, see "Column Size, Decimal Digits, Transfer Octet Length, and Display Size," in Appendix D, "Data Types."

NullablePtr [Output]
Pointer to a buffer in which to return a value that indicates whether the parameter allows NULL values. This value is read from the SQL_DESC_NULLABLE field of the IPD. One of the following:

- SQL_NO_NULLS: The parameter does not allow NULL values (this is the default value).
- SQL_NULLABLE: The parameter allows NULL values.
- SQL_NULLABLE_UNKNOWN: The driver cannot determine if the parameter allows NULL values.

Returns

SQL_SUCCESS, SQL_SUCCESS_WITH_INFO, SQL_STILL_EXECUTING, SQL_ERROR, or SQL_INVALID_HANDLE.

Diagnostics

When **SQLDescribeParam** returns SQL_ERROR or SQL_SUCCESS_WITH_INFO, an associated SQLSTATE value may be obtained by calling **SQLGetDiagRec** with a *HandleType* of SQL_HANDLE_STMT and a *Handle* of *StatementHandle*. The following table lists the SQLSTATE values commonly returned by **SQLDescribeParam** and explains each one in the context of this function; the notation "(DM)" precedes the descriptions of SQLSTATEs returned by the Driver Manager. The return code associated with each SQLSTATE value is SQL_ERROR, unless noted otherwise.

SQLSTATE	Error	Description
01000	General warning	Driver-specific informational message. (Function returns SQL_SUCCESS_WITH_INFO.)
07009	Invalid descriptor index	(DM) The value specified for the argument *ParameterNumber* less than 1. The value specified for the argument *ParameterNumber* was greater than the number of parameters in the associated SQL statement. The parameter marker was part of a non-DML statement. The parameter marker was part of a **SELECT** list.
08S01	Communication link failure	The communication link between the driver and the data source to which the driver was connected failed before the function completed processing.
21S01	Insert value list does not match column list	The number of parameters in the **INSERT** statement did not match the number of columns in the table named in the statement.
HY000	General error	An error occurred for which there was no specific SQLSTATE and for which no implementation-specific SQLSTATE was defined. The error message returned by **SQLGetDiagRec** in the **MessageText* buffer describes the error and its cause.
HY001	Memory allocation error	The driver was unable to allocate memory required to support execution or completion of the function.
HY008	Operation canceled	Asynchronous processing was enabled for the *StatementHandle*. The function was called and, before it completed execution, **SQLCancel** was called on the *StatementHandle*. Then the function was called again on the *StatementHandle*. The function was called and, before it completed execution, **SQLCancel** was called on the *StatementHandle* from a different thread in a multithread application.

SQLSTATE	Error	Description
HY010	Function sequence error	(DM) The function was called prior to calling **SQLPrepare** or **SQLExecDirect** for the *StatementHandle*. (DM) An asynchronously executing function (not this one) was called for the *StatementHandle* and was still executing when this function was called. (DM) **SQLExecute**, **SQLExecDirect**, **SQLBulkOperations**, or **SQLSetPos** was called for the *StatementHandle* and returned SQL_NEED_DATA. This function was called before data was sent for all data-at-execution parameters or columns.
HY013	Memory management error	The function call could not be processed because the underlying memory objects could not be accessed, possibly because of low memory conditions.
HYT01	Connection timeout expired	The connection timeout period expired before the data source responded to the request. The connection timeout period is set through **SQLSetConnectAttr**, SQL_ATTR_CONNECTION_TIMEOUT.
IM001	Driver does not support this function	(DM) The driver associated with the *StatementHandle* does not support the function.

Comments

Parameter markers are numbered in increasing parameter order, starting with 1, in the order they appear in the SQL statement.

SQLDescribeParam does not return the type (input, input/output, or output) of a parameter in an SQL statement. Except in calls to procedures, all parameters in SQL statements are input parameters. To determine the type of each parameter in a call to a procedure, an application calls **SQLProcedureColumns**.

For more information, see "Describing Parameters" in Chapter 9, "Executing Statements."

Code Example

The following example prompts the user for an SQL statement and then prepares that statement. Next, it calls **SQLNumParams** to determine if the statement contains any parameters. If so, it calls **SQLDescribeParam** to describe those parameters and **SQLBindParameter** to bind them. Finally, it prompts the user for the values of any parameters and then executes the statement.

```
SQLCHAR     Statement[100];
SQLSMALLINT NumParams, i, DataType, DecimalDigits, Nullable;
SQLUINTEGER ParamSize;
SQLHSTMT    hstmt;

// Prompt the user for an SQL statement and prepare it.
GetSQLStatement(Statement);
SQLPrepare(hstmt, Statement, SQL_NTS);

// Check to see if there are any parameters. If so, process them.
SQLNumParams(hstmt, &NumParams);
if (NumParams) {
   // Allocate memory for three arrays. The first holds pointers to buffers in which
   // each parameter value will be stored in character form. The second contains the
   // length of each buffer. The third contains the length/indicator value for each
   // parameter.
   SQLPOINTER * PtrArray = (SQLPOINTER *) malloc(NumParams * sizeof(SQLPOINTER));
   SQLINTEGER * BufferLenArray (SQLINTEGER *) malloc(NumParams * sizeof(SQLINTEGER));
   SQLINTEGER * LenOrIndArray = (SQLINTEGER *) malloc(NumParams * sizeof(SQLINTEGER));

   for (i = 0; i < NumParams; i++) {
      // Describe the parameter.
      SQLDescribeParam(hstmt, i + 1, &DataType, &ParamSize, &DecimalDigits, &Nullable);

      // Call a helper function to allocate a buffer in which to store the parameter
      // value in character form. The function determines the size of the buffer from
      // the SQL data type and parameter size returned by SQLDescribeParam and returns
      // a pointer to the buffer and the length of the buffer.
      AllocParamBuffer(DataType, ParamSize, &PtrArray[i], &BufferLenArray[i]);

      // Bind the memory to the parameter. Assume that we only have input parameters.
      SQLBindParameter(hstmt, i + 1, SQL_PARAM_INPUT, SQL_C_CHAR, DataType, ParamSize,
                       DecimalDigits, PtrArray[i], BufferLenArray[i],
                       &LenOrIndArray[i]);

      // Prompt the user for the value of the parameter and store it in the memory
      // allocated earlier. For simplicity, this function does not check the value
      // against the information returned by SQLDescribeParam. Instead, the driver does
      // this when the statement is executed.
      GetParamValue(PtrArray[i], BufferLenArray[i], &LenOrIndArray[i]);
   }
}

// Execute the statement.
SQLExecute(hstmt);
```

```
// Process the statement further, such as retrieving results (if any) and closing the
// cursor (if any). Code not shown.

// Free the memory allocated for each parameter and the memory allocated for the arrays
// of pointers, buffer lengths, and length/indicator values.
for (i = 0; i < NumParams; i++) free(PtrArray[i]);
free(PtrArray);
free(BufferLenArray);
free(LenOrIndArray);
```

Related Functions

For information about	See
Binding a buffer to a parameter	**SQLBindParameter**
Canceling statement processing	**SQLCancel**
Executing a prepared SQL statement	**SQLExecute**
Preparing a statement for execution	**SQLPrepare**

SQLDisconnect

Conformance

Version Introduced: ODBC 1.0
Standards Compliance: ISO 92

Summary

SQLDisconnect closes the connection associated with a specific connection handle.

Syntax

SQLRETURN **SQLDisconnect**(
    SQLHDBC *ConnectionHandle*);

Arguments

ConnectionHandle [Input]
Connection handle.

Returns

SQL_SUCCESS, SQL_SUCCESS_WITH_INFO, SQL_ERROR, or SQL_INVALID_HANDLE.

Diagnostics

When **SQLDisconnect** returns SQL_ERROR or SQL_SUCCESS_WITH_INFO, an associated SQLSTATE value may be obtained by calling **SQLGetDiagRec** with a *HandleType* of SQL_HANDLE_DBC and a *Handle* of *ConnectionHandle*. The following table lists the SQLSTATE values commonly returned by **SQLDisconnect** and explains each one in the context of this function; the notation "(DM)" precedes the descriptions of SQLSTATEs returned by the Driver Manager. The return code associated with each SQLSTATE value is SQL_ERROR, unless noted otherwise.

SQLSTATE	Error	Description
01000	General warning	Driver-specific informational message. (Function returns SQL_SUCCESS_WITH_INFO.)
01002	Disconnect error	An error occurred during the disconnect. However, the disconnect succeeded. (Function returns SQL_SUCCESS_WITH_INFO.)
08003	Connection does not exist	(DM) The connection specified in the argument *ConnectionHandle* was not open.
25000	Invalid transaction state	There was a transaction in process on the connection specified by the argument *ConnectionHandle*. The transaction remains active.

SQLSTATE	Error	Description
HY000	General error	An error occurred for which there was no specific SQLSTATE and for which no implementation-specific SQLSTATE was defined. The error message returned by **SQLGetDiagRec** in the **MessageText* buffer describes the error and its cause.
HY001	Memory allocation error	The driver was unable to allocate memory required to support execution or completion of the function.
HY010	Function sequence error	(DM) An asynchronously executing function was called for a *StatementHandle* associated with the *ConnectionHandle* and was still executing when **SQLDisconnect** was called. (DM) **SQLExecute**, **SQLExecDirect**, **SQLBulkOperations**, or **SQLSetPos** was called for a *StatementHandle* associated with the *ConnectionHandle* and returned SQL_NEED_DATA. This function was called before data was sent for all data-at-execution parameters or columns.
HY013	Memory management error	The function call could not be processed because the underlying memory objects could not be accessed, possibly because of low memory conditions.
HYT01	Connection timeout expired	The connection timeout period expired before the data source responded to the request, and the connection is still active. The connection timeout period is set through **SQLSetConnectAttr**, SQL_ATTR_CONNECTION_TIMEOUT.
IM001	Driver does not support this function	(DM) The driver associated with the *ConnectionHandle* does not support the function.

Comments

If an application calls **SQLDisconnect** after **SQLBrowseConnect** returns SQL_NEED_DATA and before it returns a different return code, the driver cancels the connection browsing process and returns the connection to an unconnected state.

If an application calls **SQLDisconnect** while there is an incomplete transaction associated with the connection handle, the driver returns SQLSTATE 25000 (Invalid transaction state), indicating that the transaction is unchanged and the connection is open. An incomplete transaction is one that has not been committed or rolled back with **SQLEndTran**.

If an application calls **SQLDisconnect** before it has freed all statements associated with the connection, the driver frees those statements, and all descriptors that have been explicitly allocated on the connection, after it successfully disconnects from the data source. However, if one or more of the statements associated with the connection are still executing asynchronously, **SQLDisconnect** returns SQL_ERROR with a SQLSTATE value of HY010 (Function sequence error).

For information about how an application uses **SQLDisconnect**, see "Disconnecting from a Data Source or Driver" in Chapter 6, "Connecting to a Data Source or Driver."

Disconnecting From a Pooled Connection

If connection pooling is enabled for a shared environment, and an application calls **SQLDisconnect** on a connection in that environment, the connection is returned to the connection pool, and is still available to other components using the same shared environment.

Code Example

See **SQLBrowseConnect** and **SQLConnect**.

Related Functions

For information about	See
Allocating a handle	**SQLAllocHandle**
Connecting to a data source	**SQLConnect**
Connecting to a data source using a connection string or dialog box	**SQLDriverConnect**
Executing a commit or rollback operation	**SQLEndTran**
Freeing a connection handle	**SQLFreeConnect**

SQLDriverConnect

Conformance

Version Introduced:	ODBC 1.0
Standards Compliance:	ODBC

Summary

SQLDriverConnect is an alternative to **SQLConnect**. It supports data sources that require more connection information than the three arguments in **SQLConnect**, dialog boxes to prompt the user for all connection information, and data sources that are not defined in the system information.

SQLDriverConnect provides the following connection attributes:

- Establish a connection using a connection string that contains the data source name, one or more user IDs, one or more passwords, and other information required by the data source.
- Establish a connection using a partial connection string or no additional information; in this case, the Driver Manager and the driver can each prompt the user for connection information.
- Establish a connection to a data source that is not defined in the system information. If the application supplies a partial connection string, the driver can prompt the user for connection information.
- Establish a connection to a data source using a connection string constructed from the information in a .dsn file.

After a connection is established, **SQLDriverConnect** returns the completed connection string. The application can use this string for subsequent connection requests. For more information, see "Connecting with SQLDriverConnect" in Chapter 6, "Connecting to a Data Source or Driver."

Syntax

SQLRETURN **SQLDriverConnect**(

SQLHDBC	*ConnectionHandle*,
SQLHWND	*WindowHandle*,
SQLCHAR *	*InConnectionString*,
SQLSMALLINT	*StringLength1*,
SQLCHAR *	*OutConnectionString*,
SQLSMALLINT	*BufferLength*,
SQLSMALLINT *	*StringLength2Ptr*,
SQLUSMALLINT	*DriverCompletion*);

Arguments

ConnectionHandle [Input]
Connection handle.

WindowHandle [Input]
Window handle. The application can pass the handle of the parent window, if applicable, or a null pointer if either the window handle is not applicable or if **SQLDriverConnect** will not present any dialog boxes.

InConnectionString [Input]
A full connection string (see the syntax in "Comments"), a partial connection string, or an empty string.

StringLength1 [Input]
Length of **InConnectionString*, in bytes.

OutConnectionString [Output]
Pointer to a buffer for the completed connection string. Upon successful connection to the target data source, this buffer contains the completed connection string. Applications should allocate at least 1,024 bytes for this buffer.

BufferLength [Input]
Length of the **OutConnectionString* buffer.

StringLength2Ptr [Output]
Pointer to a buffer in which to return the total number of bytes (excluding the null-termination byte) available to return in **OutConnectionString*. If the number of bytes available to return is greater than or equal to *BufferLength*, the completed connection string in **OutConnectionString* is truncated to *BufferLength* minus the length of a null-termination character.

DriverCompletion [Input]
Flag that indicates whether the Driver Manager or driver must prompt for more connection information:

SQL_DRIVER_PROMPT,
SQL_DRIVER_COMPLETE,
SQL_DRIVER_COMPLETE_REQUIRED, or
SQL_DRIVER_NOPROMPT.

(See "Comments," for additional information.)

Returns

SQL_SUCCESS, SQL_SUCCESS_WITH_INFO, SQL_NO_DATA, SQL_ERROR, or SQL_INVALID_HANDLE.

Diagnostics

When **SQLDriverConnect** returns either SQL_ERROR or SQL_SUCCESS_WITH_INFO, an associated SQLSTATE value may be obtained by calling **SQLGetDiagRec** with an *fHandleType* of SQL_HANDLE_DBC and an *hHandle* of *ConnectionHandle*. The following table lists the SQLSTATE values commonly returned by **SQLDriverConnect** and explains each one in the context of this function; the notation "(DM)" precedes the descriptions of SQLSTATEs returned by the Driver Manager. The return code associated with each SQLSTATE value is SQL_ERROR, unless noted otherwise.

SQLSTATE	Error	Description
01000	General warning	Driver-specific informational message. (Function returns SQL_SUCCESS_WITH_INFO.)
01004	String data, right truncated	The buffer **OutConnectionString* was not large enough to return the entire connection string, so the connection string was truncated. The length of the untruncated connection string is returned in **StringLength2Ptr*. (Function returns SQL_SUCCESS_WITH_INFO.)
01S00	Invalid connection string attribute	An invalid attribute keyword was specified in the connection string (*InConnectionString*), but the driver was able to connect to the data source anyway. (Function returns SQL_SUCCESS_WITH_INFO.)
01S02	Option value changed	The driver did not support the specified value pointed to by the *ValuePtr* argument in **SQLSetConnectAttr** and substituted a similar value. (Function returns SQL_SUCCESS_WITH_INFO.)
01S08	Error saving file DSN	The string in **InConnectionString* contained a **FILEDSN** keyword, but the .dsn file was not saved. (Function returns SQL_SUCCESS_WITH_INFO.)
01S09	Invalid keyword	(DM) The string in **InConnectionString* contained a **SAVEFILE** keyword, but not a **DRIVER** or a **FILEDSN** keyword. (Function returns SQL_SUCCESS_WITH_INFO.)
08001	Client unable to establish connection	The driver was unable to establish a connection with the data source.

SQLSTATE	Error	Description
08002	Connection name in use	(DM) The specified *ConnectionHandle* had already been used to establish a connection with a data source and the connection was still open.
08004	Server rejected the connection	The data source rejected the establishment of the connection for implementation-defined reasons.
08S01	Communication link failure	The communication link between the driver and the data source to which the driver was attempting to connect failed before the function completed processing.
28000	Invalid authorization specification	Either the user identifier or the authorization string or both as specified in the connection string (*InConnectionString*) violated restrictions defined by the data source.
HY000	General error	An error occurred for which there was no specific SQLSTATE and for which no implementation-specific SQLSTATE was defined. The error message returned by **SQLGetDiagRec** in the **szMessageText* buffer describes the error and its cause.
HY001	Memory allocation error	The Driver Manager was unable to allocate memory required to support execution or completion of the function. The driver was unable to allocate memory required to support execution or completion of the function.
HY013	Memory management error	The function call could not be processed because the underlying memory objects could not be accessed, possibly because of low memory conditions.
HY090	Invalid string or buffer length	(DM) The value specified for argument *StringLength1* was less than 0 and was not equal to SQL_NTS. (DM) The value specified for argument *BufferLength* was less than 0.

SQLSTATE	Error	Description
HY092	Invalid attribute/option identifier	(DM) The *DriverCompletion* argument was SQL_DRIVER_PROMPT, and the *WindowHandle* argument was a null pointer.
HY110	Invalid driver completion	(DM) The value specified for the argument *DriverCompletion* was not equal to SQL_DRIVER_PROMPT, SQL_DRIVER_COMPLETE, SQL_DRIVER_COMPLETE_REQUIRED, or SQL_DRIVER_NOPROMPT. (DM) Connection pooling was enabled, and the value specified for the argument *DriverCompletion* was not equal to SQL_DRIVER_NOPROMPT.
HYC00	Optional feature not implemented	The driver does not support the version of ODBC behavior that the application requested.
HYT00	Timeout expired	The login timeout period expired before the connection to the data source completed. The timeout period is set through **SQLSetConnectAttr**, SQL_ATTR_LOGIN_TIMEOUT.
HYT01	Connection timeout expired	The connection timeout period expired before the data source responded to the request. The connection timeout period is set through **SQLSetConnectAttr**, SQL_ATTR_CONNECTION_TIMEOUT.
IM001	Driver does not support this function	(DM) The driver corresponding to the specified data source name does not support the function.
IM002	Data source not found and no default driver specified	(DM) The data source name specified in the connection string (*InConnectionString*) was not found in the system information and there was no default driver specification. (DM) ODBC data source and default driver information could not be found in the system information.
IM003	Specified driver could not be loaded	(DM) The driver listed in the data source specification in the system information, or specified by the **DRIVER** keyword, was not found or could not be loaded for some other reason.
IM004	Driver's SQLAllocHandle on SQL_HANDLE_ ENV failed	(DM) During **SQLDriverConnect**, the Driver Manager called the driver's **SQLAllocHandle** function with an *fHandleType* of SQL_HANDLE_ENV and the driver returned an error.

SQLSTATE	Error	Description
IM005	Driver's SQLAllocHandle on SQL_HANDLE_ DBC failed.	(DM) During **SQLDriverConnect**, the Driver Manager called the driver's **SQLAllocHandle** function with an *fHandleType* of SQL_HANDLE_DBC and the driver returned an error.
IM006	Driver's SQLSetConnectAttr failed	(DM) During **SQLDriverConnect**, the Driver Manager called the driver's **SQLSetConnectAttr** function and the driver returned an error.
IM007	No data source or driver specified; dialog prohibited	No data source name or driver was specified in the connection string and *DriverCompletion* was SQL_DRIVER_NOPROMPT.
IM008	Dialog failed	The driver attempted to display its login dialog box and failed. *WindowHandle* was a null pointer, and *DriverCompletion* was not SQL_DRIVER_NO_PROMPT.
IM009	Unable to load translation DLL	The driver was unable to load the translation DLL that was specified for the data source or for the connection.
IM010	Data source name too long	(DM) The attribute value for the DSN keyword was longer than SQL_MAX_DSN_LENGTH characters.
IM011	Driver name too long	(DM) The attribute value for the **DRIVER** keyword was longer than 255 characters.
IM012	DRIVER keyword syntax error	(DM) The keyword-value pair for the **DRIVER** keyword contained a syntax error. (DM) The string in **InConnectionString* contained a **FILEDSN** keyword, but the .dsn file did not contain a **DRIVER** keyword or a **DSN** keyword.
IM014	Invalid name of file DSN	(DM) The string in **InConnectionString* contained a **FILEDSN** keyword, but the name of the .dsn file was invalid.
IM015	Corrupt file data source	(DM) The string in **InConnectionString* contained a **FILEDSN** keyword, but the .dsn file was unreadable.

Comments

Connection Strings

A connection string has the following syntax:

connection-string ::= *empty-string*[;] | *attribute*[;] | *attribute*; *connection-string*
empty-string ::=
attribute ::= *attribute-keyword*=*attribute-value* | DRIVER=[{]*attribute-value*[}]
attribute-keyword ::= DSN | UID | PWD
| *driver-defined-attribute-keyword*
attribute-value ::= *character-string*
driver-defined-attribute-keyword ::= *identifier*

where *character-string* has zero or more characters; *identifier* has one or more characters; *attribute-keyword* is not case-sensitive; *attribute-value* may be case-sensitive; and the value of the **DSN** keyword does not consist solely of blanks. Because of connection string and initialization file grammar, keywords and attribute values that contain the characters []{}(),;?*=!@ should be avoided. The value of the **DSN** keyword cannot consist only of blanks, and should not contain leading blanks. Because of the grammar of the system information, keywords and data source names cannot contain the backslash (\) character. Applications do not have to add braces around the attribute value after the **DRIVER** keyword unless the attribute contains a semicolon (;), in which case the braces are required. If the attribute value that the driver receives includes braces, the driver should not remove them, but they should be part of the returned connection string.

Keyword-Value Pairs

The connection string may include any number of driver-defined keywords. Because the **DRIVER** keyword does not use information from the system information, the driver must define enough keywords so that a driver can connect to a data source using only the information in the connection string. (For more information, see "Driver Guidelines," later in this section.) The driver defines which keywords are required to connect to the data source.

The following table describes the attribute values of the **DSN**, **FILEDSN**, **DRIVER**, **UID**, **PWD**, and **SAVEFILE** keywords.

Keyword	Attribute value description
DSN	Name of a data source as returned by **SQLDataSources** or the data sources dialog box of **SQLDriverConnect**.
FILEDSN	Name of a .dsn file from which a connection string will be built for the data source. These data sources are called file data sources.
DRIVER	Description of the driver as returned by the **SQLDrivers** function. For example, Rdb or SQL Server.

Keyword	Attribute value description
UID	A user ID.
PWD	The password corresponding to the user ID, or an empty string if there is no password for the user ID (PWD=;).
SAVEFILE	The file name of a .dsn file in which the attribute values of keywords used in making the present, successful connection should be saved.

For information about how an application chooses a data source or driver, see "Choosing a Data Source or Driver" in Chapter 6, "Connecting to a Data Source or Driver."

If any keywords are repeated in the connection string, the driver uses the value associated with the first occurrence of the keyword. If the **DSN** and **DRIVER** keywords are included in the same connection string, the Driver Manager and the driver use whichever keyword appears first.

The **FILEDSN** and **DSN** keywords are mutually exclusive: whichever keyword appears first is used, and the one that appears second is ignored. The **FILEDSN** and **DRIVER** keywords, on the other hand, are not mutually exclusive. If any keyword appears in a connection string with **FILEDSN**, then the attribute value of the keyword in the connection string is used rather than the attribute value of the same keyword in the .dsn file.

If the **FILEDSN** keyword is used, the keywords specified in a .dsn file are used to create a connection string. (For more information, see "File Data Sources" later in this section.) The **UID** keyword is optional; a .dsn file may be created with only the **DRIVER** keyword. The **PWD** keyword is not stored in a .dsn file. The default directory for saving and loading a .dsn file will be a combination of the path specified by **CommonFileDir** in HKEY_LOCAL_MACHINE\SOFTWARE\Microsoft\Windows\CurrentVersion and "ODBC\DataSources". (If CommonFileDir were "C:\Program Files\Common Files", the default directory would be "C:\Program Files\Common Files\ODBC\Data Sources".)

Note A .dsn file can be manipulated directly by calling the **SQLReadFileDSN** and **SQLWriteFileDSN** functions in the installer DLL.

If the **SAVEFILE** keyword is used, the attribute values of keywords used in making the present, successful connection will be saved as a .dsn file with the name of the attribute value of the **SAVEFILE** keyword. The **SAVEFILE** keyword must be used in conjunction with the **DRIVER** keyword, the **FILEDSN** keyword, or both, or the function returns SQL_SUCCESS_WITH_INFO with SQLSTATE 01S09 (Invalid keyword). The **SAVEFILE** keyword must appear before the **DRIVER** keyword in the connection string, or the results will be undefined.

Driver Manager Guidelines

The Driver Manager constructs a connection string to pass to the driver in the *InConnectionString* argument of the driver's **SQLDriverConnect** function. Note that the Driver Manager does not modify the *InConnectionString* argument passed to it by the application.

The action of the Driver Manager is based on the value of the *DriverCompletion* argument:

- SQL_DRIVER_PROMPT: If the connection string does not contain either the **DRIVER**, **DSN**, or **FILEDSN** keyword, the Driver Manager displays the Data Sources dialog box. It constructs a connection string from the data source name returned by the dialog box and any other keywords passed to it by the application. If the data source name returned by the dialog box is empty, the Driver Manager specifies the keyword-value pair DSN=Default. (This dialog box will not display a data source with the name "Default".)
- SQL_DRIVER_COMPLETE or SQL_DRIVER_COMPLETE_REQUIRED: If the connection string specified by the application includes the **DSN** keyword, the Driver Manager copies the connection string specified by the application. Otherwise, it takes the same actions as it does when *DriverCompletion* is SQL_DRIVER_PROMPT.
- SQL_DRIVER_NOPROMPT: The Driver Manager copies the connection string specified by the application.

If the connection string specified by the application contains the **DRIVER** keyword, the Driver Manager copies the connection string specified by the application.

Using the connection string it has constructed, the Driver Manager determines which driver to use, connects to that driver, and passes the connection string it has constructed to the driver; for more information about the interaction of the Driver Manager and the driver, see the "Comments" section in **SQLConnect**. If the connection string does not contain the **DRIVER** keyword, the Driver Manager determines which driver to use as follows:

1. If the connection string contains the **DSN** keyword, the Driver Manager retrieves the driver associated with the data source from the system information.
2. If the connection string does not contain the **DSN** keyword or the data source is not found, the Driver Manager retrieves the driver associated with the Default data source from the system information. (For more information, see "Default Subkey" in Chapter 19, "Configuring Data Sources.") The Driver Manager changes the value of the **DSN** keyword in the connection string to "DEFAULT."

3. If the **DSN** keyword in the connection string is set to "DEFAULT," the Driver Manager retrieves the driver associated with the Default data source from the system information.
4. If the data source is not found and the Default data source is not found, the Driver Manager returns SQL_ERROR with SQLSTATE IM002 (Data source not found and no default driver specified).

File Data Sources

If the connection string specified by the application in the call to **SQLDriverConnect** contains the **FILEDSN** keyword, and this keyword is not superseded by either the **DSN** or **DRIVER** keyword, then the Driver Manager creates a connection string using the information in the .dsn file and the *InConnectionString* argument. The Driver Manager proceeds as follows:

1. Checks whether the file name of the .dsn file is valid. If not, it returns SQL_ERROR with SQLSTATE IM014 (Invalid name of file DSN). If the file name is an empty string (""), and SQL_DRIVER_NOPROMPT is not specified, then the File-Open dialog box is displayed. If the file name contains a valid path but no file name or an invalid file name, and SQL_DRIVER_NOPROMPT is not specified, then the File-Open dialog box is displayed with the current directory set to the one specified in the file name. If the file name is an empty string ("") or the file name contains a valid path but no file name or an invalid file name, and SQL_DRIVER_NOPROMPT is specified, then SQL_ERROR is returned with SQLSTATE IM014 (Invalid name of file DSN).
2. Reads all of the keywords in the [ODBC] section of the .dsn file. If the **DRIVER** keyword is not present, it returns SQL_ERROR with SQLSTATE IM012 (Driver keyword syntax error), except where the .dsn file is unshareable, and so contains only the **DSN** keyword.

   If the file data source is unshareable, the Driver Manager reads the value of the **DSN** keyword, and connects as necessary to the user or system data source pointed to by the unshareable file data source. Steps 3 through 5 are not performed.
3. Constructs a connection string for the driver. The driver connection string is the union of the keywords specified in the .dsn file and those specified in the original application connection string. Rules for the construction of the driver connection string where keywords overlap are as follows:
   - If the **DRIVER** keyword exists in the application connection string, and the drivers specified by the **DRIVER** keywords are not the same in the .dsn file and the application connection string, then the driver information in the .dsn file is ignored and the driver information in the application connection string is used. If the drivers specified by the **DRIVER** keyword are the same in the .dsn file and the application's connection string, then where all keywords overlap, those specified in the application connection string have precedence over those specified in the .dsn file.
   - In the new connection string, the **FILEDSN** keyword is eliminated.

4. Loads the driver by looking in the registry entry HKEY_LOCAL_MACHINE\SOFTWARE\ODBC\ODBCINST.INI\<Driver Name>\Driver where <Driver Name> is specified by the **DRIVER** keyword.
5. Passes the driver the new connections string.

For examples of .dsn files, see "Connecting Using File Data Sources" in Chapter 6, "Connecting to a Data Source or Driver."

SAVEFILE Keyword

If the connection string specified by the application contains the **SAVEFILE** keyword, then the Driver Manager saves the connection string in a .dsn file. The Driver Manager proceeds as follows:

1. Checks whether the file name of the .dsn file included as the attribute value of the **SAVEFILE** keyword is valid. If not, it returns SQL_ERROR with SQLSTATE IM014 (Invalid name of file DSN). The validity of the file name is determined by standard system naming rules. If the file name is an empty string (""), and the *DriverCompletion* argument is not SQL_DRIVER_NOPROMPT, then the file name is valid. If the file name already exists, then if *DriverCompletion* is SQL_DRIVER_NOPROMPT, the file is overwritten. If *DriverCompletion* is SQL_DRIVER_PROMPT, SQL_DRIVER_COMPLETE, or SQL_DRIVER_COMPLETE_REQUIRED, a dialog box is displayed prompting the user to specify whether the file should be overwritten. If No is entered, then the **File-Save** dialog box is displayed.
2. If the driver returns SQL_SUCCESS, and the file name was not an empty string, then the Driver Manager writes the connection information returned in the *OutConnectionString* argument to the specified file with the format specified in the "Connection Strings" section earlier in this chapter.
3. If the driver returns SQL_SUCCESS, and the file name was an empty string (""), then the Driver Manager calls the File-Save common dialog box with the *hwnd* specified, and writes the connection information returned in *OutConnectionString* to the file specified in the File-Save common dialog box with the format specified in the "Connection Strings" section earlier in this chapter.
4. If the driver returns SQL_SUCCESS, it returns the *OutConnectionString* argument containing the connection string to the application.
5. If the driver returns SQL_SUCCESS_WITH_INFO or SQL_ERROR, then the Driver Manager returns the SQLSTATE to the application.

Driver Guidelines

The driver checks whether the connection string passed to it by the Driver Manager contains the **DSN** or **DRIVER** keyword. If the connection string contains the **DRIVER** keyword, the driver cannot retrieve information about the data source from the system information. If the connection string contains the **DSN** keyword or does not contain either the **DSN** or the **DRIVER** keyword, the driver can retrieve information about the data source from the system information as follows:

1. If the connection string contains the **DSN** keyword, the driver retrieves the information for the specified data source.
2. If the connection string does not contain the **DSN** keyword, the specified data source is not found, or the **DSN** keyword is set to "DEFAULT," the driver retrieves the information for the Default data source.

The driver uses any information it retrieves from the system information to augment the information passed to it in the connection string. If the information in the system information duplicates information in the connection string, the driver uses the information in the connection string.

Based on the value of *DriverCompletion*, the driver prompts the user for connection information, such as the user ID and password, and connects to the data source:

- SQL_DRIVER_PROMPT: The driver displays a dialog box, using the values from the connection string and system information (if any) as initial values. When the user exits the dialog box, the driver connects to the data source. It also constructs a connection string from the value of the **DSN** or **DRIVER** keyword in **InConnectionString* and the information returned from the dialog box. It places this connection string in the **OutConnectionString* buffer.
- SQL_DRIVER_COMPLETE or SQL_DRIVER_COMPLETE_REQUIRED: If the connection string contains enough information, and that information is correct, the driver connects to the data source and copies **InConnectionString* to **OutConnectionString*. If any information is missing or incorrect, the driver takes the same actions as it does when *DriverCompletion* is SQL_DRIVER_PROMPT, except that if *DriverCompletion* is SQL_DRIVER_COMPLETE_REQUIRED, the driver disables the controls for any information not required to connect to the data source.
- SQL_DRIVER_NOPROMPT: If the connection string contains enough information, the driver connects to the data source and copies **InConnectionString* to **OutConnectionString*. Otherwise, the driver returns SQL_ERROR for **SQLDriverConnect**.

On successful connection to the data source, the driver also sets **StringLength2Ptr* to the length of the output connection string that is available to return in **OutConnectionString*.

If the user cancels a dialog box presented by the Driver Manager or the driver, **SQLDriverConnect** returns SQL_NO_DATA.

For information about how the Driver Manager and the driver interact during the connection process, see **SQLConnect**.

If a driver supports **SQLDriverConnect**, the driver keyword section of the system information for the driver must contain the **ConnectFunctions** keyword with the second character set to "Y".

Connecting when Connection Pooling is Enabled

Connection pooling allows an application to reuse a connection that has already been created. When **SQLDriverConnect** is called, the Driver Manager attempts to make the connection using a connection that is part of a pool of connections in an environment that has been designated for connection pooling. For more information on connection pooling, see **SQLConnect**.

The following restrictions apply when an application calls **SQLDriverConnect** to connect to a pooled connection:

- No connection pooling processing is performed when the **SAVEFILE** keyword is specified in the connection string.
- If connection pooling is enabled, **SQLDriverConnect** can only be called with a *DriverCompletion* argument of SQL_DRIVER_NOPROMPT; if **SQLDriverConnect** is called with any other *DriverCompletion*, SQLSTATE HY110 (Invalid driver completion) will be returned.

Connection Attributes

The SQL_ATTR_LOGIN_TIMEOUT connection attribute, set using **SQLSetConnectAttr**, defines the number of seconds to wait for a login request to complete with a successful connection by the driver before returning to the application. If the user is prompted to complete the connection string, a waiting period for each login request begins when the driver starts the connection process.

The driver opens the connection in SQL_MODE_READ_WRITE access mode by default. To set the access mode to SQL_MODE_READ_ONLY, the application must call **SQLSetConnectAttr** with the SQL_ATTR_ACCESS_MODE attribute prior to calling **SQLDriverConnect**.

If a default translation library is specified in the system information for the data source, the driver loads it. A different translation library can be loaded by calling **SQLSetConnectAttr** with the SQL_ATTR_TRANSLATE_LIB attribute. A translation option can be specified by calling **SQLSetConnectAttr** with the SQL_ATTR_TRANSLATE_OPTION option.

Code Example

See the "Connecting with SQLDriverConnect" section of Chapter 6, "Connecting to a Data Source or Driver."

Related Functions

For information about	See
Allocating a handle	**SQLAllocHandle**
Discovering and enumerating values required to connect to a data source	**SQLBrowseConnect**
Connecting to a data source	**SQLConnect**
Disconnecting from a data source	**SQLDisconnect**
Returning driver descriptions and attributes	**SQLDrivers**
Freeing a handle	**SQLFreeHandle**
Setting a connection attribute	**SQLSetConnectAttr**

SQLDrivers

Conformance

Version Introduced: ODBC 2.0
Standards Compliance: ODBC

Summary

SQLDrivers lists driver descriptions and driver attribute keywords. This function is implemented solely by the Driver Manager.

Syntax

SQLRETURN **SQLDrivers**(
    SQLHENV *EnvironmentHandle*,
    SQLUSMALLINT *Direction*,
    SQLCHAR * *DriverDescription*,
    SQLSMALLINT *BufferLength1*,
    SQLSMALLINT * *DescriptionLengthPtr*,
    SQLCHAR * *DriverAttributes*,
    SQLSMALLINT *BufferLength2*,
    SQLSMALLINT * *AttributesLengthPtr*);

Arguments

EnvironmentHandle [Input]
Environment handle.

Direction [Input]
Determines whether the Driver Manager fetches the next driver description in the list (SQL_FETCH_NEXT) or whether the search starts from the beginning of the list (SQL_FETCH_FIRST).

DriverDescription [Output]
Pointer to a buffer in which to return the driver description.

BufferLength1 [Input]
Length of the **DriverDescription* buffer, in bytes.

DescriptionLengthPtr [Output]
Pointer to a buffer in which to return the total number of bytes (excluding the null-termination byte) available to return in **DriverDescription*. If the number of bytes available to return is greater than or equal to *BufferLength1*, the driver description in **DriverDescription* is truncated to *BufferLength1* minus the length of a null-termination character.

DriverAttributes [Output]

Pointer to a buffer in which to return the list of driver attribute value pairs (see "Comments").

BufferLength2 [Input]

Length of the **DriverAttributes* buffer, in bytes.

AttributesLengthPtr [Output]

Pointer to a buffer in which to return the total number of bytes (excluding the null-termination byte) available to return in **DriverAttributes*. If the number of bytes available to return is greater than or equal to *BufferLength2*, the list of attribute value pairs in **DriverAttributes* is truncated to *BufferLength2* minus the length of the null-termination character.

Returns

SQL_SUCCESS, SQL_SUCCESS_WITH_INFO, SQL_NO_DATA, SQL_ERROR, or SQL_INVALID_HANDLE.

Diagnostics

When **SQLDrivers** returns either SQL_ERROR or SQL_SUCCESS_WITH_INFO, an associated SQLSTATE value may be obtained by calling **SQLGetDiagRec** with a *HandleType* of SQL_HANDLE_ENV and a *Handle* of *EnvironmentHandle*. The following table lists the SQLSTATE values commonly returned by **SQLDrivers** and explains each one in the context of this function; the notation "(DM)" precedes the descriptions of SQLSTATEs returned by the Driver Manager. The return code associated with each SQLSTATE value is SQL_ERROR, unless noted otherwise.

SQLSTATE	Error	Description
01000	General warning	(DM) Driver Manager–specific informational message. (Function returns SQL_SUCCESS_WITH_INFO.)
01004	String data, right truncated	(DM) The buffer **DriverDescription* was not large enough to return the entire driver description, so the description was truncated. The length of the entire driver description is returned in **DescriptionLengthPtr*. (Function returns SQL_SUCCESS_WITH_INFO.) (DM) The buffer **DriverAttributes* was not large enough to return the entire list of attribute value pairs, so the list was truncated. The length of the untruncated list of attribute value pairs is returned in **AttributesLengthPtr*. (Function returns SQL_SUCCESS_WITH_INFO.)

SQLSTATE	Error	Description
HY000	General error	An error occurred for which there was no specific SQLSTATE and for which no implementation-specific SQLSTATE was defined. The error message returned by **SQLGetDiagRec** in the **MessageText* buffer describes the error and its cause.
HY001	Memory allocation error	(DM) The Driver Manager was unable to allocate memory required to support execution or completion of the function.
HY013	Memory management error	The function call could not be processed because the underlying memory objects could not be accessed, possibly because of low memory conditions.
HY090	Invalid string or buffer length	(DM) The value specified for argument *BufferLength1* was less than 0. (DM) The value specified for argument *BufferLength2* was less than 0 or equal to 1.
HY103	Invalid retrieval code	(DM) The value specified for the argument *Direction* was not equal to SQL_FETCH_FIRST or SQL_FETCH_NEXT.

Comments

SQLDrivers returns the driver description in the **DriverDescription* buffer. It returns additional information about the driver in the **DriverAttributes* buffer as a list of keyword-value pairs. All keywords listed in the system information for drivers will be returned for all drivers, except for **CreateDSN**, which is used to prompt creation of data sources, and therefore is optional. Each pair is terminated with a null byte, and the entire list is terminated with a null byte (that is, two null bytes mark the end of the list). For example, a file-based driver using C syntax might return the following list of attributes ("\0" represents a null character):

```
FileUsage=1\0FileExtns=*.dbf\0\0
```

If **DriverAttributes* is not large enough to hold the entire list, the list is truncated, **SQLDrivers** returns SQLSTATE 01004 (Data truncated), and the length of the list (excluding the final null-termination byte) is returned in **AttributesLengthPtr*.

Driver attribute keywords are added from the system information when the driver is installed. For more information, see Chapter 18, "Installing ODBC Components."

An application can call **SQLDrivers** multiple times to retrieve all driver descriptions. The Driver Manager retrieves this information from the system information. When there are no more driver descriptions, **SQLDrivers** returns SQL_NO_DATA. If **SQLDrivers** is called with SQL_FETCH_NEXT immediately after it returns SQL_NO_DATA, it returns the first driver description. For information about how an application uses the information returned by **SQLDrivers**, see "Choosing a Data Source or Driver" in Chapter 6, "Connecting to a Data Source or Driver."

If SQL_FETCH_NEXT is passed to **SQLDrivers** the very first time it is called, **SQLDrivers** returns the first data source name.

Because **SQLDrivers** is implemented in the Driver Manager, it is supported for all drivers regardless of a particular driver's standards compliance.

Related Functions

For information about	See
Discovering and listing values required to connect to a data source	**SQLBrowseConnect**
Connecting to a data source	**SQLConnect**
Returning data source names	**SQLDataSources**
Connecting to a data source using a connection string or dialog box	**SQLDriverConnect**

SQLEndTran

Conformance

Version Introduced: ODBC 3.0
Standards Compliance: ISO 92

Summary

SQLEndTran requests a commit or rollback operation for all active operations on all statements associated with a connection. **SQLEndTran** can also request that a commit or rollback operation be performed for all connections associated with an environment.

Note For more information about what the Driver Manager maps this function to when an ODBC 3.0 application is working with an ODBC 2.*x* driver, see "Mapping Replacement Functions for Backward Compatibility of Applications" in Chapter 17, "Programming Considerations."

Syntax

SQLRETURN **SQLEndTran**(
    SQLSMALLINT *HandleType*,
    SQLHANDLE *Handle*,
    SQLSMALLINT *CompletionType*);

Arguments

HandleType [Input]
Handle type identifier. Contains either SQL_HANDLE_ENV if *Handle* is an environment handle, or SQL_HANDLE_DBC if *Handle* is a connection handle.

Handle [Input]
The handle, of the type indicated by *HandleType*, indicating the scope of the transaction. See "Comments" for more information.

CompletionType [Input]
One of the following two values:

SQL_COMMIT
SQL_ROLLBACK

Returns

SQL_SUCCESS, SQL_SUCCESS_WITH_INFO, SQL_ERROR, or SQL_INVALID_HANDLE.

Diagnostics

When **SQLEndTran** returns SQL_ERROR or SQL_SUCCESS_WITH_INFO, an associated SQLSTATE value may be obtained by calling **SQLGetDiagRec** with the appropriate *HandleType* and *Handle*. The following table lists the SQLSTATE values commonly returned by **SQLEndTran** and explains each one in the context of this function; the notation "(DM)" precedes the descriptions of SQLSTATEs returned by the Driver Manager. The return code associated with each SQLSTATE value is SQL_ERROR, unless noted otherwise.

SQLSTATE	Error	Description
01000	General warning	Driver-specific informational message. (Function returns SQL_SUCCESS_WITH_INFO.)
08003	Connection not open	(DM) The *HandleType* was SQL_HANDLE_DBC, and the *Handle* was not in a connected state.
08007	Connection failure during transaction	The *HandleType* was SQL_HANDLE_DBC, and the connection associated with the *Handle* failed during the execution of the function and it cannot be determined whether the requested **COMMIT** or **ROLLBACK** occurred before the failure.
25S01	Transaction state unknown	One or more of the connections in *Handle* failed to complete the transaction with the outcome specified, and the outcome is unknown.
25S02	Transaction is still active	The driver was not able to guarantee that all work in the global transaction could be completed atomically, and the transaction is still active.
25S03	Transaction is rolled back	The driver was not able to guarantee that all work in the global transaction could be completed atomically, and all work in the transaction active in *Handle* was rolled back.
40001	Serialization failure	The transaction was rolled back due to a resource deadlock with another transaction.
HY000	General error	An error occurred for which there was no specific SQLSTATE and for which no implementation-specific SQLSTATE was defined. The error message returned by **SQLGetDiagRec** in the **szMessageText* buffer describes the error and its cause.
HY001	Memory allocation error	The driver was unable to allocate memory required to support execution or completion of the function.

SQLSTATE	Error	Description
HY010	Function sequence error	(DM) An asynchronously executing function was called for a *StatementHandle* associated with the *ConnectionHandle* and was still executing when **SQLEndTran** was called. (DM) **SQLExecute**, **SQLExecDirect**, **SQLBulkOperations**, or **SQLSetPos** was called for a *StatementHandle* associated with the *ConnectionHandle* and returned SQL_NEED_DATA. This function was called before data was sent for all data-at-execution parameters or columns.
HY012	Invalid transaction operation code	(DM) The value specified for the argument *CompletionType* was neither SQL_COMMIT nor SQL_ROLLBACK.
HY013	Memory management error	The function call could not be processed because the underlying memory objects could not be accessed, possibly because of low memory conditions.
HY092	Invalid attribute/option identifier	(DM) The value specified for the argument *HandleType* was neither SQL_HANDLE_ENV nor SQL_HANDLE_DBC.
HYC00	Optional feature not implemented	The driver or data source does not support the **ROLLBACK** operation.
HYT01	Connection timeout expired	The connection timeout period expired before the data source responded to the request. The connection timeout period is set through **SQLSetConnectAttr**, SQL_ATTR_CONNECTION_TIMEOUT.
IM001	Driver does not support this function	(DM) The driver associated with the *ConnectionHandle* does not support the function.

Comments

For an ODBC 3.0 driver, if *HandleType* is SQL_HANDLE_ENV and *Handle* is a valid environment handle, then the Driver Manager will calls **SQLEndTran** in each driver associated with the environment. The *Handle* argument for the call to a driver will be the driver's environment handle. For an ODBC 2.*x* driver, if *HandleType* is SQL_HANDLE_ENV and *Handle* is a valid environment handle, and there are multiple connections in a connected state in that environment, then the Driver Manager will call **SQLTransact** in the driver once for each connection in a connected state in that environment. The *Handle* argument in each call will be the connection's handle. In either case, the driver will attempt to commit or roll back transactions, depending on the value of *CompletionType*, on all connections that are in a connected state on that environment. Connections that are not active do not affect the transaction.

Note **SQLEndTran** cannot be used to commit or roll back transactions on a shared environment. SQLSTATE HY092 (Invalid attribute/option identifier) will be returned if **SQLEndTran** is called with *Handle* set to either the handle of a shared environment, or the handle of a connection on a shared environment.

The Driver Manager will return SQL_SUCCESS only if it receives SQL_SUCCESS for each connection. If the Driver Manager receives SQL_ERROR on one or more connections, it returns SQL_ERROR to the application, and the diagnostic information is placed in the diagnostic data structure of the environment. To determine which connection or connections failed during the commit or rollback operation, the application can call **SQLGetDiagRec** for each connection.

Note The Driver Manager does not simulate a global transaction across all connections and therefore does not use two-phase commit protocols.

If *CompletionType* is SQL_COMMIT, **SQLEndTran** issues a commit request for all active operations on any statement associated with an affected connection. If *CompletionType* is SQL_ROLLBACK, **SQLEndTran** issues a rollback request for all active operations on any statement associated with an affected connection. If no transactions are active, **SQLEndTran** returns SQL_SUCCESS with no effect on any data sources. For more information, see "Committing and Rolling Back Transactions" in Chapter 14, "Transactions."

If the driver is in manual-commit mode (by calling **SQLSetConnectAttr** with the SQL_ATTR_AUTOCOMMIT attribute set to SQL_AUTOCOMMIT_OFF), a new transaction is implicitly started when an SQL statement that can be contained within a transaction is executed against the current data source. For more information, see "Commit Mode" in Chapter 14, "Transactions."

To determine how transaction operations affect cursors, an application calls **SQLGetInfo** with the SQL_CURSOR_ROLLBACK_BEHAVIOR and SQL_CURSOR_COMMIT_BEHAVIOR options. For more information, see the following paragraphs and "Effect of Transactions on Cursors and Prepared Statements" in Chapter 14, "Transactions."

If the SQL_CURSOR_ROLLBACK_BEHAVIOR or SQL_CURSOR_COMMIT_BEHAVIOR value equals SQL_CB_DELETE, **SQLEndTran** closes and deletes all open cursors on all statements associated with the connection and discards all pending results. **SQLEndTran** leaves any statement present in an allocated (unprepared) state; the application can reuse them for subsequent SQL requests or can call **SQLFreeStmt** or **SQLFreeHandle** with a *HandleType* of SQL_HANDLE_STMT to deallocate them.

If the SQL_CURSOR_ROLLBACK_BEHAVIOR or SQL_CURSOR_COMMIT_BEHAVIOR value equals SQL_CB_CLOSE, **SQLEndTran** closes all open cursors on all statements associated with the connection. **SQLEndTran** leaves any statement present in a prepared state; the application can call **SQLExecute** for a statement associated with the connection without first calling **SQLPrepare**.

If the SQL_CURSOR_ROLLBACK_BEHAVIOR or SQL_CURSOR_COMMIT_BEHAVIOR value equals SQL_CB_PRESERVE, **SQLEndTran** does not affect open cursors associated with the connection. Cursors remain at the row they pointed to prior to the call to **SQLEndTran**.

For drivers and data sources that support transactions, calling **SQLEndTran** with either SQL_COMMIT or SQL_ROLLBACK when no transaction is active returns SQL_SUCCESS (indicating that there is no work to be committed or rolled back) and has no effect on the data source.

When a driver is in autocommit mode, the Driver Manager does not call **SQLEndTran** in the driver. **SQLEndTran** always returns SQL_SUCCESS regardless of whether it is called with a *CompletionType* of SQL_COMMIT or SQL_ROLLBACK.

Drivers or data sources that do not support transactions (**SQLGetInfo** *option* SQL_TXN_CAPABLE is SQL_TC_NONE) are effectively always in autocommit mode, and therefore, always return SQL_SUCCESS for **SQLEndTran** regardless of whether they are called with a *CompletionType* of SQL_COMMIT or SQL_ROLLBACK. Such drivers and data sources do not actually roll back transactions when requested to do so.

Related Functions

For information about	See
Returning information about a driver or data source	**SQLGetInfo**
Freeing a handle	**SQLFreeHandle**
Freeing a statement handle	**SQLFreeStmt**

SQLError

Conformance

Version Introduced:	ODBC 1.0
Standards Compliance:	Deprecated

Summary

SQLError returns error or status information.

For more information about what the Driver Manager maps this function to when an ODBC 2.*x* application is working with an ODBC 3.0 driver, see “Mapping Deprecated Functions” in Appendix G, “Driver Guidelines for Backward Compatibility.”

SQLExecDirect

Conformance

Version Introduced:	ODBC 1.0
Standards Compliance:	ISO 92

Summary

SQLExecDirect executes a preparable statement, using the current values of the parameter marker variables if any parameters exist in the statement. **SQLExecDirect** is the fastest way to submit an SQL statement for one-time execution.

Syntax

```
SQLRETURN SQLExecDirect(
      SQLHSTMT      StatementHandle,
      SQLCHAR *     StatementText,
      SQLINTEGER    TextLength);
```

Arguments

StatementHandle [Input]
Statement handle.

StatementText [Input]
SQL statement to be executed.

TextLength [Input]
Length of **StatementText*.

Returns

SQL_SUCCESS, SQL_SUCCESS_WITH_INFO, SQL_NEED_DATA, SQL_STILL_EXECUTING, SQL_ERROR, SQL_NO_DATA, or SQL_INVALID_HANDLE.

Diagnostics

When **SQLExecDirect** returns either SQL_ERROR or SQL_SUCCESS_WITH_INFO, an associated SQLSTATE value can be obtained by calling **SQLGetDiagRec** with a *HandleType* of SQL_HANDLE_STMT and a *Handle* of *StatementHandle*. The following table lists the SQLSTATE values commonly returned by **SQLExecDirect** and explains each one in the context of this function; the notation "(DM)" precedes the descriptions of SQLSTATEs returned by the Driver Manager. The return code associated with each SQLSTATE value is SQL_ERROR, unless noted otherwise.

SQLSTATE	Error	Description
01000	General warning	Driver-specific informational message. (Function returns SQL_SUCCESS_WITH_INFO.)
01001	Cursor operation conflict	**StatementText* contained a positioned update or delete statement and no rows or more than one row were updated or deleted. (For more information about updates to more than one row, see the description of the SQL_ATTR_SIMULATE_CURSOR *Attribute* in **SQLSetStmtAttr**.) (Function returns SQL_SUCCESS_WITH_INFO.)
01003	NULL value eliminated in set function	The argument *StatementText* contained a set function (such as **AVG**, **MAX**, **MIN**, and so on), but not the **COUNT** set function, and NULL argument values were eliminated before the function was applied. (Function returns SQL_SUCCESS_WITH_INFO.)
01004	String data, right truncated	String or binary data returned for an input/output or output parameter resulted in the truncation of non-blank character or non-NULL binary data. If it was a string value, it was right-truncated. (Function returns SQL_SUCCESS_WITH_INFO.)
01006	Privilege not revoked	**StatementText* contained a **REVOKE** statement and the user did not have the specified privilege. (Function returns SQL_SUCCESS_WITH_INFO.)
01007	Privilege not granted	**StatementText* was a **GRANT** statement and the user could not be granted the specified privilege.

SQLSTATE	Error	Description
01S02	Option value changed	A specified statement attribute was invalid because of implementation working conditions, so a similar value was temporarily substituted. (**SQLGetStmtAttr** can be called to determine what the temporarily substituted value is.) The substitute value is valid for the *StatementHandle* until the cursor is closed, at which point the statement attribute reverts to its previous value. The statement attributes that can be changed are: SQL_ ATTR_CONCURRENCY SQL_ ATTR_CURSOR_TYPE SQL_ ATTR_KEYSET_SIZE SQL_ ATTR_MAX_LENGTH SQL_ ATTR_MAX_ROWS SQL_ ATTR_QUERY_TIMEOUT SQL_ ATTR_SIMULATE_CURSOR (Function returns SQL_SUCCESS_WITH_INFO.)
01S07	Fractional truncation	The data returned for an input/output or output parameter was truncated such that the fractional part of a numeric data type was truncated or the fractional portion of the time component of a time, timestamp, or interval data type was truncated. (Function returns SQL_SUCCESS_WITH_INFO.)
07002	COUNT field incorrect	The number of parameters specified in **SQLBindParameter** was less than the number of parameters in the SQL statement contained in **StatementText*. **SQLBindParameter** was called with *ParameterValuePtr* set to a null pointer, *StrLen_or_IndPtr* not set to SQL_NULL_DATA or SQL_DATA_AT_EXEC, and *InputOutputType* not set to SQL_PARAM_OUTPUT, so that the number of parameters specified in **SQLBindParameter** was greater than the number of parameters in the SQL statement contained in **StatementText*.

SQLSTATE	Error	Description
07006	Restricted data type attribute violation	The data value identified by the *ValueType* argument in **SQLBindParameter** for the bound parameter could not be converted to the data type identified by the *ParameterType* argument in **SQLBindParameter**. The data value returned for a parameter bound as SQL_PARAM_INPUT_OUTPUT or SQL_PARAM_OUTPUT could not be converted to the data type identified by the *ValueType* argument in **SQLBindParameter**. (If the data values for one or more rows could not be converted, but one or more rows were successfully returned, this function returns SQL_SUCCESS_WITH_INFO.)
07S01	Invalid use of default parameter	A parameter value, set with **SQLBindParameter**, was SQL_DEFAULT_PARAM, and the corresponding parameter did not have a default value.
08S01	Communication link failure	The communication link between the driver and the data source to which the driver was connected failed before the function completed processing.
21S01	Insert value list does not match column list	**StatementText* contained an **INSERT** statement and the number of values to be inserted did not match the degree of the derived table.
21S02	Degree of derived table does not match column list	**StatementText* contained a **CREATE VIEW** statement and the unqualified column list (the number of columns specified for the view in the *column-identifier* arguments of the SQL statement) contained more names than the number of columns in the derived table defined by the *query-specification* argument of the SQL statement.
22001	String data, right truncation	The assignment of a character or binary value to a column resulted in the truncation of non-blank character data or non-null binary data.
22002	Indicator variable required but not supplied	NULL data was bound to an output parameter whose *StrLen_or_IndPtr* set by **SQLBindParameter** was a null pointer.

SQLSTATE	Error	Description
22003	Numeric value out of range	**StatementText* contained an SQL statement that contained a bound numeric parameter or literal and the value caused the whole (as opposed to fractional) part of the number to be truncated when assigned to the associated table column. Returning a numeric value (as numeric or string) for one or more input/output or output parameters would have caused the whole (as opposed to fractional) part of the number to be truncated.
22007	Invalid datetime format	**StatementText* contained an SQL statement that contained a date, time, or timestamp structure as a bound parameter and the parameter was, respectively, an invalid date, time, or timestamp. An input/output or output parameter was bound to a date, time, or timestamp C structure, and a value in the returned parameter was, respectively, an invalid date, time, or timestamp. (Function returns SQL_SUCCESS_WITH_INFO.)
22008	Datetime field overflow	**StatementText* contained an SQL statement that contained a datetime expression that when computed resulted in a date, time, or timestamp structure that was invalid. A datetime expression computed for an input/output or output parameter resulted in a date, time, or timestamp C structure that was invalid.
22012	Division by zero	**StatementText* contained an SQL statement which contained an arithmetic expression which caused division by zero. An arithmetic expression calculated for an input/output or output parameter resulted in division by zero.

SQLSTATE	Error	Description
22015	Interval field overflow	**StatementText* contained an exact numeric or interval parameter that when converted to an interval SQL data type caused a loss of significant digits. **StatementText* contained an interval parameter with more than one field that when converted to a numeric data type in a column had no representation in the numeric data type. **StatementText* contained parameter data that was assigned to an interval SQL type, and there was no representation of the value of the C type in the interval SQL type. Assigning an input/output or output parameter that was an exact numeric or interval SQL type to an interval C type caused a loss of significant digits. When an input/output or output parameter was assigned to an interval C structure, there was no representation of the data in the interval data structure.
22018	Invalid character value for cast specification	**StatementText* contained a C type was an exact or approximate numeric, a datetime, or an interval data type; the SQL type of the column was a character data type; and the value in the column was not a valid literal of the bound C type. When an input/output or output parameter was returned, the SQL type was an exact or approximate numeric, a datetime, or an interval data type; the C type was SQL_C_CHAR; and the value in the column was not a valid literal of the bound SQL type.
22019	Invalid escape character	**StatementText* contained an SQL statement that contained a **LIKE** predicate with an **ESCAPE** in the **WHERE** clause, and the length of the escape character following **ESCAPE** was not equal to 1.
22025	Invalid escape sequence	**StatementText* contained an SQL statement that contained "**LIKE** *pattern value* **ESCAPE** *escape character*" in the **WHERE** clause, and the character following the escape character in the pattern value was not one of "%" or "_".

SQLSTATE	Error	Description
23000	Integrity constraint violation	**StatementText* contained an SQL statement that contained a parameter or literal. The parameter value was NULL for a column defined as NOT NULL in the associated table column, a duplicate value was supplied for a column constrained to contain only unique values, or some other integrity constraint was violated.
24000	Invalid cursor state	A cursor was positioned on the *StatementHandle* by **SQLFetch** or **SQLFetchScroll**. This error is returned by the Driver Manager if **SQLFetch** or **SQLFetchScroll** has not returned SQL_NO_DATA, and is returned by the driver if **SQLFetch** or **SQLFetchScroll** has returned SQL_NO_DATA. A cursor was open, but not positioned on the *StatementHandle*. **StatementText* contained a positioned update or delete statement and the cursor was positioned before the start of the result set or after the end of the result set.
34000	Invalid cursor name	**StatementText* contained a positioned update or delete statement and the cursor referenced by the statement being executed was not open.
3D000	Invalid catalog name	The catalog name specified in *StatementText* was invalid.
3F000	Invalid schema name	The schema name specified in *StatementText* was invalid.
40001	Serialization failure	The transaction was rolled back due to a resource deadlock with another transaction.
40003	Statement completion unknown	The associated connection failed during the execution of this function and the state of the transaction cannot be determined.
42000	Syntax error or access violation	**StatementText* contained an SQL statement that was not preparable or contained a syntax error. The user did not have permission to execute the SQL statement contained in **StatementText*.

SQLSTATE	Error	Description
42S01	Base table or view already exists	**StatementText* contained a **CREATE TABLE** or **CREATE VIEW** statement and the table name or view name specified already exists.
42S02	Base table or view not found	**StatementText* contained a **DROP TABLE** or a **DROP VIEW** statement and the specified table name or view name did not exist. **StatementText* contained an **ALTER TABLE** statement and the specified table name did not exist. **StatementText* contained a **CREATE VIEW** statement and a table name or view name defined by the query specification did not exist. **StatementText* contained a **CREATE INDEX** statement and the specified table name did not exist. **StatementText* contained a **GRANT** or **REVOKE** statement and the specified table name or view name did not exist. **StatementText* contained a **SELECT** statement and a specified table name or view name did not exist. **StatementText* contained a **DELETE**, **INSERT**, or **UPDATE** statement and the specified table name did not exist. **StatementText* contained a **CREATE TABLE** statement and a table specified in a constraint (referencing a table other than the one being created) did not exist. **StatementText* contained a **CREATE SCHEMA** statement and a specified table name or view name did not exist.
42S11	Index already exists	**StatementText* contained a **CREATE INDEX** statement and the specified index name already existed. **StatementText* contained a **CREATE SCHEMA** statement and the specified index name already existed.
42S12	Index not found	**StatementText* contained a **DROP INDEX** statement and the specified index name did not exist.

SQLSTATE	Error	Description
42S21	Column already exists	**StatementText* contained an **ALTER TABLE** statement and the column specified in the **ADD** clause is not unique or identifies an existing column in the base table.
42S22	Column not found	**StatementText* contained a **CREATE INDEX** statement and one or more of the column names specified in the column list did not exist. **StatementText* contained a **GRANT** or **REVOKE** statement and a specified column name did not exist. **StatementText* contained a **SELECT**, **DELETE**, **INSERT**, or **UPDATE** statement and a specified column name did not exist. **StatementText* contained a **CREATE TABLE** statement and a column specified in a constraint (referencing a table other than the one being created) did not exist. **StatementText* contained a **CREATE SCHEMA** statement and a specified column name did not exist.
44000	WITH CHECK OPTION violation	The argument *StatementText* contained an **INSERT** statement performed on a viewed table or a table derived from the viewed table which was created by specifying **WITH CHECK OPTION**, such that one or more rows affected by the **INSERT** statement will no longer be present in the viewed table. The argument *StatementText* contained an **UPDATE** statement performed on a viewed table or a table derived from the viewed table which was created by specifying **WITH CHECK OPTION**, such that one or more rows affected by the **UPDATE** statement will no longer be present in the viewed table.
HY000	General error	An error occurred for which there was no specific SQLSTATE and for which no implementation-specific SQLSTATE was defined. The error message returned by **SQLGetDiagRec** in the **MessageText* buffer describes the error and its cause.
HY001	Memory allocation error	The driver was unable to allocate memory required to support execution or completion of the function.

SQLSTATE	Error	Description
HY008	Operation canceled	Asynchronous processing was enabled for the *StatementHandle*. The function was called and before it completed execution, **SQLCancel** was called on the *StatementHandle*. Then the function was called again on the *StatementHandle*. The function was called and, before it completed execution, **SQLCancel** was called on the *StatementHandle* from a different thread in a multithread application.
HY009	Invalid use of null pointer	(DM) **StatementText* was a null pointer.
HY010	Function sequence error	(DM) An asynchronously executing function (not this one) was called for the *StatementHandle* and was still executing when this function was called. (DM) **SQLExecute**, **SQLExecDirect**, **SQLBulkOperations**, or **SQLSetPos** was called for the *StatementHandle* and returned SQL_NEED_DATA. This function was called before data was sent for all data-at-execution parameters or columns.
HY013	Memory management error	The function call could not be processed because the underlying memory objects could not be accessed, possibly because of low memory conditions.

SQLSTATE	Error	Description
HY090	Invalid string or buffer length	(DM) The argument *TextLength* was less than or equal to 0, but not equal to SQL_NTS. A parameter value, set with **SQLBindParameter**, was a null pointer and the parameter length value was not 0, SQL_NULL_DATA, SQL_DATA_AT_EXEC, SQL_DEFAULT_PARAM, or less than or equal to SQL_LEN_DATA_AT_EXEC_OFFSET. A parameter value, set with **SQLBindParameter**, was not a null pointer; the C data type was SQL_C_BINARY or SQL_C_CHAR; and the parameter length value was less than 0, but was not SQL_NTS, SQL_NULL_DATA, SQL_DATA_AT_EXEC, SQL_DEFAULT_PARAM, or less than or equal to SQL_LEN_DATA_AT_EXEC_OFFSET. A parameter length value bound by **SQLBindParameter** was set to SQL_DATA_AT_EXEC; the SQL type was either SQL_LONGVARCHAR, SQL_LONGVARBINARY, or a long, data source–specific data type; and the SQL_NEED_LONG_DATA_LEN information type in **SQLGetInfo** was "Y".
HY105	Invalid parameter type	The value specified for the argument *InputOutputType* in **SQLBindParameter** was SQL_PARAM_OUTPUT, and the parameter was an input parameter.
HY109	Invalid cursor position	**StatementText* contained a positioned update or delete statement and the cursor was positioned (by **SQLSetPos** or **SQLFetchScroll**) on a row that had been deleted or could not be fetched.

SQLSTATE	Error	Description
HYC00	Optional feature not implemented	The combination of the current settings of the SQL_ATTR_CONCURRENCY and SQL_ATTR_CURSOR_TYPE statement attributes was not supported by the driver or data source. The SQL_ATTR_USE_BOOKMARKS statement attribute was set to SQL_UB_VARIABLE, and the SQL_ATTR_CURSOR_TYPE statement attribute was set to a cursor type for which the driver does not support bookmarks.
HYT00	Timeout expired	The query timeout period expired before the data source returned the result set. The timeout period is set through **SQLSetStmtAttr**, SQL_ATTR_QUERY_TIMEOUT.
HYT01	Connection timeout expired	The connection timeout period expired before the data source responded to the request. The connection timeout period is set through **SQLSetConnectAttr**, SQL_ATTR_CONNECTION_TIMEOUT.
IM001	Driver does not support this function	(DM) The driver associated with the *StatementHandle* does not support the function.

Comments

The application calls **SQLExecDirect** to send an SQL statement to the data source. For more information about direct execution, see "Direct Execution" in Chapter 9, "Executing Statements." The driver modifies the statement to use the form of SQL used by the data source, and then submits it to the data source. In particular, the driver modifies the escape sequences used to define certain features in SQL. For the syntax of escape sequences, see "Escape Sequences in ODBC" in Chapter 8, "SQL Statements."

The application can include one or more parameter markers in the SQL statement. To include a parameter marker, the application embeds a question mark (?) into the SQL statement at the appropriate position. For information about parameters, see "Statement Parameters" in Chapter 9, "Executing Statements."

If the SQL statement is a **SELECT** statement, and if the application called **SQLSetCursorName** to associate a cursor with a statement, then the driver uses the specified cursor. Otherwise, the driver generates a cursor name.

If the data source is in manual-commit mode (requiring explicit transaction initiation), and a transaction has not already been initiated, the driver initiates a transaction before it sends the SQL statement. For more information, see "Manual-Commit Mode" in Chapter 14, "Transactions."

If an application uses **SQLExecDirect** to submit a **COMMIT** or **ROLLBACK** statement, it will not be interoperable between DBMS products. To commit or roll back a transaction, an application calls **SQLEndTran**.

If **SQLExecDirect** encounters a data-at-execution parameter, it returns SQL_NEED_DATA. The application sends the data using **SQLParamData** and **SQLPutData**. See **SQLBindParameter**, **SQLParamData**, **SQLPutData**, and "Sending Long Data" in Chapter 9, "Executing Statements" for more information.

If **SQLExecDirect** executes a searched update or delete statement that does not affect any rows at the data source, the call to **SQLExecDirect** returns SQL_NO_DATA.

If the value of the SQL_ATTR_PARAMSET_SIZE statement attribute is greater than 1, and the SQL statement contains at least one parameter marker, **SQLExecDirect** will execute the SQL statement once for each set of parameter values from the arrays pointed to by the *ParameterValuePointer* argument in the call to **SQLBindParameter**. For more information, see "Arrays of Parameter Values" in Chapter 9, "Executing Statements."

If bookmarks are turned on, and a query is executed that cannot support bookmarks, then the driver should attempt to coerce the environment to one that supports bookmarks by changing an attribute value and returning SQLSTATE 01S02 (Option value changed). If the attribute cannot be changed, the driver should return SQLSTATE HY024 (Invalid attribute value).

Note When using connection pooling, an application must not execute SQL statements that change the database or the context of the database, such as the **USE** *database* statement in SQL Server, which changes the catalog used by a data source.

Code Example

See **SQLBindCol** and **SQLGetData**.

Related Functions

For information about	See
Binding a buffer to a column in a result set	**SQLBindCol**
Canceling statement processing	**SQLCancel**
Executing a commit or rollback operation	**SQLEndTran**
Executing a prepared SQL statement	**SQLExecute**
Fetching multiple rows of data	**SQLFetch**
Fetching a block of data or scrolling through a result set	**SQLFetchScroll**
Returning a cursor name	**SQLGetCursorName**
Fetching part or all of a column of data	**SQLGetData**
Returning the next parameter to send data for	**SQLParamData**
Preparing a statement for execution	**SQLPrepare**
Sending parameter data at execution time	**SQLPutData**
Setting a cursor name	**SQLSetCursorName**
Setting a statement attribute	**SQLSetStmtAttr**

SQLExecute

Conformance

Version Introduced: ODBC 1.0
Standards Compliance: ISO 92

Summary

SQLExecute executes a prepared statement, using the current values of the parameter marker variables if any parameter markers exist in the statement.

Syntax

SQLRETURN **SQLExecute**(
    SQLHSTMT *StatementHandle*);

Arguments

StatementHandle [Input]
Statement handle.

Returns

SQL_SUCCESS, SQL_SUCCESS_WITH_INFO, SQL_NEED_DATA, SQL_STILL_EXECUTING, SQL_ERROR, SQL_NO_DATA, or SQL_INVALID_HANDLE.

Diagnostics

When **SQLExecute** returns either SQL_ERROR or SQL_SUCCESS_WITH_INFO, an associated SQLSTATE value can be obtained by calling **SQLGetDiagRec** with a *HandleType* of SQL_HANDLE_STMT and a *Handle* of *StatementHandle*. The following table lists the SQLSTATE values commonly returned by **SQLExecute** and explains each one in the context of this function; the notation "(DM)" precedes the descriptions of SQLSTATEs returned by the Driver Manager. The return code associated with each SQLSTATE value is SQL_ERROR, unless noted otherwise.

SQLSTATE	Error	Description
01000	General warning	Driver-specific informational message. (Function returns SQL_SUCCESS_WITH_INFO.)
01001	Cursor operation conflict	The prepared statement associated with the *StatementHandle* contained a positioned update or delete statement and no rows or more than one row were updated or deleted. (For more information about updates to more than one row, see the description of the SQL_ATTR_SIMULATE_CURSOR *Attribute* in **SQLSetStmtAttr**.) (Function returns SQL_SUCCESS_WITH_INFO.)

SQLSTATE	Error	Description
01003	NULL value eliminated in set function	The prepared statement associated with *StatementHandle* contained a set function (such as **AVG**, **MAX**, **MIN**, and so on), but not the **COUNT** set function, and NULL argument values were eliminated before the function was applied. (Function returns SQL_SUCCESS_WITH_INFO.)
01004	String data, right truncated	String or binary data returned for an output parameter resulted in the truncation of non-blank character or non-NULL binary data. If it was a string value, it was right-truncated. (Function returns SQL_SUCCESS_WITH_INFO.)
01006	Privilege not revoked	The prepared statement associated with the *StatementHandle* was a **REVOKE** statement and the user did not have the specified privilege. (Function returns SQL_SUCCESS_WITH_INFO.)
01007	Privilege not granted	The prepared statement associated with the *StatementHandle* was a **GRANT** statement and the user could not be granted the specified privilege.
01S02	Option value changed	A specified statement attribute was invalid because of implementation working conditions, so a similar value was temporarily substituted. (**SQLGetStmtAttr** can be called to determine what the temporarily substituted value is.) The substitute value is valid for the *StatementHandle* until the cursor is closed, at which point the statement attribute reverts to its previous value. The statement attributes that can be changed are: SQL_ATTR_CONCURRENCY, SQL_ATTR_CURSOR_TYPE, SQL_ATTR_KEYSET_SIZE, SQL_ATTR_MAX_LENGTH, SQL_ATTR_MAX_ROWS, SQL_ATTR_QUERY_TIMEOUT, and SQL_ATTR_SIMULATE_CURSOR. (Function returns SQL_SUCCESS_WITH_INFO.)

SQLSTATE	Error	Description
01S07	Fractional truncation	The data returned for an input/output or output parameter was truncated such that the fractional part of a numeric data type was truncated or the fractional portion of the time component of a time, timestamp, or interval data type was truncated. (Function returns SQL_SUCCESS_WITH_INFO.)
07002	COUNT field incorrect	The number of parameters specified in **SQLBindParameter** was less than the number of parameters in the SQL statement contained in **StatementText*. **SQLBindParameter** was called with *ParameterValuePtr* set to a null pointer, *StrLen_or_IndPtr* not set to SQL_NULL_DATA or SQL_DATA_AT_EXEC, and *InputOutputType* not set to SQL_PARAM_OUTPUT, so that the number of parameters specified in **SQLBindParameter** was greater than the number of parameters in the SQL statement contained in **StatementText*.
07006	Restricted data type attribute violation	The data value identified by the *ValueType* argument in **SQLBindParameter** for the bound parameter could not be converted to the data type identified by the *ParameterType* argument in **SQLBindParameter**. The data value returned for a parameter bound as SQL_PARAM_INPUT_OUTPUT or SQL_PARAM_OUTPUT could not be converted to the data type identified by the *ValueType* argument in **SQLBindParameter**. (If the data values for one or more rows could not be converted, but one or more rows were successfully returned, this function returns SQL_SUCCESS_WITH_INFO.)
07S01	Invalid use of default parameter	A parameter value, set with **SQLBindParameter**, was SQL_DEFAULT_PARAM, and the corresponding parameter was not a parameter for an ODBC canonical procedure invocation.
08S01	Communication link failure	The communication link between the driver and the data source to which the driver was connected failed before the function completed processing.

SQLSTATE	Error	Description
21S02	Degree of derived table does not match column list	The prepared statement associated with the *StatementHandle* contained a **CREATE VIEW** statement and the unqualified column list (the number of columns specified for the view in the *column-identifier* arguments of the SQL statement) contained more names than the number of columns in the derived table defined by the *query-specification* argument of the SQL statement.
22001	String data, right truncation	The assignment of a character or binary value to a column resulted in the truncation of non-blank (character) or non-null (binary) characters or bytes.
22002	Indicator variable required but not supplied	NULL data was bound to an output parameter whose *StrLen_or_IndPtr* set by **SQLBindParameter** was a null pointer.
22003	Numeric value out of range	The prepared statement associated with the *StatementHandle* contained a bound numeric parameter and the parameter value caused the whole (as opposed to fractional) part of the number to be truncated when assigned to the associated table column. Returning a numeric value (as numeric or string) for one or more input/output or output parameters would have caused the whole (as opposed to fractional) part of the number to be truncated.
22007	Invalid datetime format	The prepared statement associated with the *StatementHandle* contained an SQL statement that contained a date, time, or timestamp structure as a bound parameter and the parameter was, respectively, an invalid date, time, or timestamp. An input/output or output parameter was bound to a date, time, or timestamp C structure, and a value in the returned parameter was, respectively, an invalid date, time, or timestamp. (Function returns SQL_SUCCESS_WITH_INFO.)

SQLSTATE	Error	Description
22008	Datetime field overflow	The prepared statement associated with the *StatementHandle* contained an SQL statement that contained a datetime expression that when computed resulted in a date, time, or timestamp structure that was invalid. A datetime expression computed for an input/output or output parameter resulted in a date, time, or timestamp C structure that was invalid.
22012	Division by zero	The prepared statement associated with the *StatementHandle* contained an arithmetic expression which caused division by zero. An arithmetic expression calculated for an input/output or output parameter resulted in division by zero.
22015	Interval field overflow	**StatementText* contained an exact numeric or interval parameter that when converted to an interval SQL data type caused a loss of significant digits. **StatementText* contained an interval parameter with more than one field that when converted to a numeric data type in a column had no representation in the numeric data type. **StatementText* contained parameter data that was assigned to an interval SQL type, and there was no representation of the value of the C type in the interval SQL type. Assigning an input/output or output parameter that was an exact numeric or interval SQL type to an interval C type caused a loss of significant digits. When an input/output or output parameter was assigned to an interval C structure, there was no representation of the data in the interval data structure.

SQLSTATE	Error	Description
22018	Invalid character value for cast specification	**StatementText* contained a C type was an exact or approximate numeric, a datetime, or an interval data type; the SQL type of the column was a character data type; and the value in the column was not a valid literal of the bound C type. When an input/output or output parameter was returned, the SQL type was an exact or approximate numeric, a datetime, or an interval data type; the C type was SQL_C_CHAR; and the value in the column was not a valid literal of the bound SQL type.
22019	Invalid escape character	The prepared statement associated with *StatementHandle* contained a **LIKE** predicate with an **ESCAPE** in the **WHERE** clause, and the length of the escape character following **ESCAPE** was not equal to 1.
22025	Invalid escape sequence	The prepared statement associated with *StatementHandle* contained "**LIKE** *pattern value* **ESCAPE** *escape character*" in the **WHERE** clause, and the character following the escape character in the pattern value was not one of "%" or "_".
23000	Integrity constraint violation	The prepared statement associated with the *StatementHandle* contained a parameter. The parameter value was NULL for a column defined as NOT NULL in the associated table column, a duplicate value was supplied for a column constrained to contain only unique values, or some other integrity constraint was violated.
24000	Invalid cursor state	A cursor was positioned on the *StatementHandle* by **SQLFetch** or **SQLFetchScroll**. This error is returned by the Driver Manager if **SQLFetch** or **SQLFetchScroll** has not returned SQL_NO_DATA, and is returned by the driver if **SQLFetch** or **SQLFetchScroll** has returned SQL_NO_DATA. A cursor was open on the *StatementHandle*. The prepared statement associated with the *StatementHandle* contained a positioned update or delete statement and the cursor was positioned before the start of the result set or after the end of the result set.

SQLSTATE	Error	Description
40001	Serialization failure	The transaction was rolled back due to a resource deadlock with another transaction.
40003	Statement completion unknown	The associated connection failed during the execution of this function and the state of the transaction cannot be determined.
42000	Syntax error or access violation	The user did not have permission to execute the prepared statement associated with the *StatementHandle*.
44000	WITH CHECK OPTION violation	The prepared statement associated with *StatementHandle* contained an **INSERT** statement performed on a viewed table or a table derived from the viewed table which was created by specifying **WITH CHECK OPTION**, such that one or more rows affected by the **INSERT** statement will no longer be present in the viewed table. The prepared statement associated with the *StatementHandle* contained an **UPDATE** statement performed on a viewed table or a table derived from the viewed table which was created by specifying **WITH CHECK OPTION**, such that one or more rows affected by the **UPDATE** statement will no longer be present in the viewed table.
HY000	General error	An error occurred for which there was no specific SQLSTATE and for which no implementation-specific SQLSTATE was defined. The error message returned by **SQLGetDiagRec** in the **MessageText* buffer describes the error and its cause.
HY001	Memory allocation error	The driver was unable to allocate memory required to support execution or completion of the function.
HY008	Operation canceled	Asynchronous processing was enabled for the *StatementHandle*. The function was called and before it completed execution, **SQLCancel** was called on the *StatementHandle*. Then the function was called again on the *StatementHandle*. The function was called and, before it completed execution, **SQLCancel** was called on the *StatementHandle* from a different thread in a multithread application.

SQLSTATE	Error	Description
HY010	Function sequence error	(DM) An asynchronously executing function (not this one) was called for the *StatementHandle* and was still executing when this function was called. (DM) **SQLExecute**, **SQLExecDirect**, **SQLBulkOperations**, or **SQLSetPos** was called for the *StatementHandle* and returned SQL_NEED_DATA. This function was called before data was sent for all data-at-execution parameters or columns. (DM) The *StatementHandle* was not prepared.
HY013	Memory management error	The function call could not be processed because the underlying memory objects could not be accessed, possibly because of low memory conditions.
HY090	Invalid string or buffer length	A parameter value, set with **SQLBindParameter**, was a null pointer and the parameter length value was not 0, SQL_NULL_DATA, SQL_DATA_AT_EXEC, SQL_DEFAULT_PARAM, or less than or equal to SQL_LEN_DATA_AT_EXEC_OFFSET. A parameter value, set with **SQLBindParameter**, was not a null pointer; the C data type was SQL_C_BINARY or SQL_C_CHAR; and the parameter length value was less than 0, but was not SQL_NTS, SQL_NULL_DATA, SQL_DEFAULT_PARAM, or SQL_DATA_AT_EXEC, or less than or equal to SQL_LEN_DATA_AT_EXEC_OFFSET. A parameter length value bound by **SQLBindParameter** was set to SQL_DATA_AT_EXEC; the SQL type was either SQL_LONGVARCHAR, SQL_LONGVARBINARY, or a long, data source–specific data type; and the SQL_NEED_LONG_DATA_LEN information type in **SQLGetInfo** was "Y".
HY105	Invalid parameter type	The value specified for the argument *InputOutputType* in **SQLBindParameter** was SQL_PARAM_OUTPUT, and the parameter was an input parameter.

SQLSTATE	Error	Description
HY109	Invalid cursor position	The prepared statement was a positioned update or delete statement and the cursor was positioned (by **SQLSetPos** or **SQLFetchScroll**) on a row that had been deleted or could not be fetched.
HYC00	Optional feature not implemented	The combination of the current settings of the SQL_ATTR_CONCURRENCY and SQL_ATTR_CURSOR_TYPE statement attributes was not supported by the driver or data source. The SQL_ATTR_USE_BOOKMARKS statement attribute was set to SQL_UB_VARIABLE, and the SQL_ATTR_CURSOR_TYPE statement attribute was set to a cursor type for which the driver does not support bookmarks.
HYT00	Timeout expired	The query timeout period expired before the data source returned the result set. The timeout period is set through **SQLSetStmtAttr**, SQL_ATTR_QUERY_TIMEOUT.
HYT01	Connection timeout expired	The connection timeout period expired before the data source responded to the request. The connection timeout period is set through **SQLSetConnectAttr**, SQL_ATTR_CONNECTION_TIMEOUT.
IM001	Driver does not support this function	(DM) The driver associated with the *StatementHandle* does not support the function.

SQLExecute can return any SQLSTATE that can be returned by **SQLPrepare** based on when the data source evaluates the SQL statement associated with the statement.

Comments

SQLExecute executes a statement prepared by **SQLPrepare**. After the application processes or discards the results from a call to **SQLExecute**, the application can call **SQLExecute** again with new parameter values. For more information about prepared execution, see "Prepared Execution" in Chapter 9, "Executing Statements."

To execute a **SELECT** statement more than once, the application must call **SQLCloseCursor** before reexecuting the **SELECT** statement.

If the data source is in manual-commit mode (requiring explicit transaction initiation), and a transaction has not already been initiated, the driver initiates a transaction before it sends the SQL statement. For more information, see "Manual-Commit Mode" in Chapter 14, "Transactions."

If an application uses **SQLPrepare** to prepare and **SQLExecute** to submit a **COMMIT** or **ROLLBACK** statement, it will not be interoperable between DBMS products. To commit or roll back a transaction, call **SQLEndTran**.

If **SQLExecute** encounters a data-at-execution parameter, it returns SQL_NEED_DATA. The application sends the data using **SQLParamData** and **SQLPutData**. See **SQLBindParameter**, **SQLParamData**, **SQLPutData**, and "Sending Long Data" in Chapter 9, "Executing Statements" for more information.

If **SQLExecute** executes a searched update or delete statement that does not affect any rows at the data source, the call to **SQLExecute** returns SQL_NO_DATA.

If the value of the SQL_ATTR_PARAMSET_SIZE statement attribute is greater than 1, and the SQL statement contains at least one parameter marker, **SQLExecute** executes the SQL statement once for each set of parameter values in the arrays pointed to by the **ParameterValuePtr* argument in the calls to **SQLBindParameter**. For more information, see "Arrays of Parameter Values" in Chapter 9, "Executing Statements."

If bookmarks are enabled, and a query is executed that cannot support bookmarks, then the driver should attempt to coerce the environment to one that supports bookmarks by changing an attribute value and returning SQLSTATE 01S02 (Option value changed). If the attribute cannot be changed, the driver should return SQLSTATE HY024 (Invalid attribute value).

Note When using connection pooling, an application must not execute SQL statements that change the database or the context of the database, such as the **USE** *database* statement in SQL Server, which changes the catalog used by a data source.

Code Example

See **SQLBindParameter**, **SQLBulkOperations**, **SQLPutData**, and **SQLSetPos**.

Related Functions

For information about	See
Binding a buffer to a column in a result set	**SQLBindCol**
Canceling statement processing	**SQLCancel**
Closing the cursor	**SQLCloseCursor**
Executing a commit or rollback operation	**SQLEndTran**
Executing an SQL statement	**SQLExecDirect**
Fetching multiple rows of data	**SQLFetch**
Fetching a block of data or scrolling through a result set	**SQLFetchScroll**

For information about	See
Freeing a statement handle	**SQLFreeStmt**
Returning a cursor name	**SQLGetCursorName**
Fetching part or all of a column of data	**SQLGetData**
Returning the next parameter to send data for	**SQLParamData**
Preparing a statement for execution	**SQLPrepare**
Sending parameter data at execution time	**SQLPutData**
Setting a cursor name	**SQLSetCursorName**
Setting a statement attribute	**SQLSetStmtAttr**

SQLExtendedFetch

Conformance

Version Introduced: ODBC 1.0
Standards Compliance: Deprecated

Summary

SQLExtendedFetch fetches the specified rowset of data from the result set and returns data for all bound columns. Rowsets can be specified at an absolute or relative position or by bookmark.

Note In ODBC 3.0, **SQLExtendedFetch** has been replaced by **SQLFetchScroll**. ODBC 3.0 applications should not call **SQLExtendedFetch**; instead they should call **SQLFetchScroll**. The Driver Manager maps **SQLFetchScroll** to **SQLExtendedFetch** when working with an ODBC 2.*x* driver. ODBC 3.0 drivers should support **SQLExtendedFetch** if they want to work with ODBC 2.*x* applications that call it. For more information, see "Comments" and "Block Cursors, Scrollable Cursors, and Backward Compatibility" in Appendix G, "Driver Guidelines for Backward Compatibility."

Syntax

```
SQLRETURN SQLExtendedFetch(
      SQLHSTMT          StatementHandle,
      SQLUSMALLINT      FetchOrientation,
      SQLINTEGER        FetchOffset,
      SQLUINTEGER *     RowCountPtr,
      SQLUSMALLINT *    RowStatusArray);
```

Arguments

StatementHandle [Input]
Statement handle.

FetchOrientation [Input]
Type of fetch. This is the same as *FetchOrientation* in **SQLFetchScroll**.

FetchOffset [Input]
Number of the row to fetch. This is the same as *FetchOffset* in **SQLFetchScroll** with one exception. When *FetchOrientation* is SQL_FETCH_BOOKMARK, *FetchOffset* is a fixed-length bookmark, not an offset from a bookmark. In other words, **SQLExtendedFetch** retrieves the bookmark from this argument, not the SQL_ATTR_FETCH_BOOKMARK_PTR statement attribute. It does not support variable-length bookmarks and does not support fetching a rowset at an offset (other than 0) from a bookmark.

RowCountPtr [Output]
Pointer to a buffer in which to return the number of rows actually fetched. This buffer is used in the same manner as the buffer specified by the SQL_ATTR_ROWS_FETCHED_PTR statement attribute. This buffer is used only by **SQLExtendedFetch**. It is not used by **SQLFetch** or **SQLFetchScroll**.

RowStatusArray [Output]

Pointer to an array in which to return the status of each row. This array is used in the same manner as the array specified by the SQL_ATTR_ROW_STATUS_PTR statement attribute.

However, the address of this array is not stored in the SQL_DESC_STATUS_ARRAY_PTR field in the IRD. Furthermore, this array is used only by **SQLExtendedFetch** and by **SQLBulkOperations** with an *Operation* of SQL_ADD or **SQLSetPos** when it is called after **SQLExtendedFetch**. It is not used by **SQLFetch** or **SQLFetchScroll** and it is not used by **SQLBulkOperations** or **SQLSetPos** when they are called after **SQLFetch** or **SQLFetchScroll**. It is also not used when **SQLBulkOperations** with an *Operation* of SQL_ADD is called before any fetch function is called. In other words, it is used only in statement state S7. It is not used in statement states S5 or S6. For more information, see "Statement Transitions" in Appendix B, "ODBC State Transition Tables."

Applications should provide a valid pointer in the *RowStatusArray* argument; if not, the behavior of **SQLExtendedFetch** and the behavior of calls to **SQLBulkOperations** or **SQLSetPos** after a cursor has been positioned by **SQLExtendedFetch** are undefined.

Returns

SQL_SUCCESS, SQL_SUCCESS_WITH_INFO, SQL_NO_DATA, SQL_STILL_EXECUTING, SQL_ERROR, or SQL_INVALID_HANDLE.

Diagnostics

When **SQLExtendedFetch** returns either SQL_ERROR or SQL_SUCCESS_WITH_INFO, an associated SQLSTATE value can be obtained by calling **SQLError**. The following table lists the SQLSTATE values commonly returned by **SQLExtendedFetch** and explains each one in the context of this function; the notation "(DM)" precedes the descriptions of SQLSTATEs returned by the Driver Manager. The return code associated with each SQLSTATE value is SQL_ERROR, unless noted otherwise. If an error occurs on a single column, **SQLGetDiagField** can be called with a *DiagIdentifier* of SQL_DIAG_COLUMN_NUMBER to determine the column the error occurred on; and **SQLGetDiagField** can be called with a *DiagIdentifier* of SQL_DIAG_ROW_NUMBER to determine the row containing that column.

SQLSTATE	Error	Description
01000	General warning	Driver-specific informational message. (Function returns SQL_SUCCESS_WITH_INFO.)
01004	String data, right truncated	String or binary data returned for a column resulted in the truncation of non-blank character or non-NULL binary data. If it was a string value, it was right truncated. If it was a numeric value, the fractional part of the number was truncated. (Function returns SQL_SUCCESS_WITH_INFO.)
01S01	Error in row	An error occurred while fetching one or more rows. (Function returns SQL_SUCCESS_WITH_INFO.)
01S06	Attempt to fetch before the result set returned the first rowset	The requested rowset overlapped the start of the result set when the current position was beyond the first row, and either *FetchOrientation* was SQL_PRIOR, or *FetchOrientation* was SQL_RELATIVE with a negative *FetchOffset* whose absolute value was less than or equal to the current SQL_ROWSET_SIZE. (Function returns SQL_SUCCESS_WITH_INFO.)
01S07	Fractional truncation	The data returned for a column was truncated. For numeric data types, the fractional part of the number was truncated. For time, timestamp, and interval data types containing a time component, the fractional portion of the time was truncated. (Function returns SQL_SUCCESS_WITH_INFO.)
07006	Restricted data type attribute violation	A data value could not be converted to the C data type specified by *TargetType* in **SQLBindCol**.
07009	Invalid descriptor index	Column 0 was bound with **SQLBindCol** and the SQL_ATTR_USE_BOOKMARKS statement attribute was set to SQL_UB_OFF.
08S01	Communication link failure	The communication link between the driver and the data source to which the driver was connected failed before the function completed processing.
22002	Indicator variable required but not supplied	NULL data was fetched into a column whose *StrLen_or_IndPtr* set by **SQLBindCol** was a null pointer. (Function returns SQL_SUCCESS_WITH_INFO.)

SQLSTATE	Error	Description
22003	Numeric value out of range	Returning the numeric value (as numeric or string) for one or more columns would have caused the whole (as opposed to fractional) part of the number to be truncated. (Function returns SQL_SUCCESS_WITH_INFO.) For more information, see Appendix D, "Data Types."
22007	Invalid datetime format	A character column in the result set was bound to a date, time, or timestamp C structure, and a value in the column was, respectively, an invalid date, time, or timestamp. (Function returns SQL_SUCCESS_WITH_INFO.)
22012	Division by zero	A value from an arithmetic expression was returned which resulted in division by zero. (Function returns SQL_SUCCESS_WITH_INFO.)
22015	Interval field overflow	Assigning from an exact numeric or interval SQL type to an interval C type caused a loss of significant digits in the leading field. When fetching data to an interval C type, there was no representation of the value of the SQL type in the interval C type. (Function returns SQL_SUCCESS_WITH_INFO.)
22018	Invalid character value for cast specification	The C type was an exact or approximate numeric, a datetime, or an interval data type; the SQL type of the column was a character data type; and the value in the column was not a valid literal of the bound C type. (Function returns SQL_SUCCESS_WITH_INFO.)
24000	Invalid cursor state	The *StatementHandle* was in an executed state but no result set was associated with the *StatementHandle*.
HY000	General error	An error occurred for which there was no specific SQLSTATE and for which no implementation-specific SQLSTATE was defined. The error message returned by **SQLError** in the **MessageText* buffer describes the error and its cause.

SQLSTATE	Error	Description
HY001	Memory allocation error	The driver was unable to allocate memory required to support execution or completion of the function.
HY008	Operation canceled	Asynchronous processing was enabled for the *StatementHandle*. The function was called and before it completed execution, **SQLCancel** was called on the *StatementHandle*, and then the function was called again on the *StatementHandle*. The function was called and, before it completed execution, **SQLCancel** was called on the *StatementHandle* from a different thread in a multithread application.
HY010	Function sequence error	(DM) The specified *StatementHandle* was not in an executed state. The function was called without first calling **SQLExecDirect**, **SQLExecute**, or a catalog function. (DM) An asynchronously executing function (not this one) was called for the *StatementHandle* and was still executing when this function was called. (DM) **SQLExecute**, **SQLExecDirect**, **SQLBulkOperations**, or **SQLSetPos** was called for the *StatementHandle* and returned SQL_NEED_DATA. This function was called before data was sent for all data-at-execution parameters or columns. (DM) **SQLExtendedFetch** was called for the *StatementHandle* after **SQLFetch** or **SQLFetchScroll** was called and before **SQLFreeStmt** was called with the SQL_CLOSE option. (DM) **SQLBulkOperations** was called for a statement before **SQLFetch**, **SQLFetchScroll**, or **SQLExtendedFetch** was called, and then **SQLExtendedFetch** was called before **SQLFreeStmt** was called with the SQL_CLOSE option.
HY013	Memory management error	The function call could not be processed because the underlying memory objects could not be accessed, possibly because of low memory conditions.

SQLSTATE	Error	Description
HY106	Fetch type out of range	(DM) The value specified for the argument *FetchOrientation* was invalid (see "Comments"). The argument *FetchOrientation* was SQL_FETCH_BOOKMARK, and the SQL_ATTR_USE_BOOKMARKS statement attribute was set to SQL_UB_OFF. The value of the SQL_CURSOR_TYPE statement option was SQL_CURSOR_FORWARD_ONLY and the value of argument *FetchOrientation* was not SQL_FETCH_NEXT. The argument *FetchOrientation* was SQL_FETCH_RESUME.
HY107	Row value out of range	The value specified with the SQL_CURSOR_TYPE statement option was SQL_CURSOR_KEYSET_DRIVEN, but the value specified with the SQL_KEYSET_SIZE statement attribute was greater than 0 and less than the value specified with the SQL_ROWSET_SIZE statement attribute.
HY111	Invalid bookmark value	The argument *FetchOrientation* was SQL_FETCH_BOOKMARK and the bookmark specified in the *FetchOffset* argument was not valid.
HYC00	Optional feature not implemented	Driver or data source does not support the specified fetch type. The driver or data source does not support the conversion specified by the combination of the *TargetType* in **SQLBindCol** and the SQL data type of the corresponding column. This error applies only when the SQL data type of the column was mapped to a driver-specific SQL data type.
HYT00	Timeout expired	The query timeout period expired before the data source returned the result set. The timeout period is set through **SQLSetStmtOption**, SQL_QUERY_TIMEOUT.
HYT01	Connection timeout expired	The connection timeout period expired before the data source responded to the request. The connection timeout period is set through **SQLSetConnectAttr**, SQL_ATTR_CONNECTION_TIMEOUT.
IM001	Driver does not support this function	(DM) The driver associated with the *StatementHandle* does not support the function.

Comments

The behavior of **SQLExtendedFetch** is identical to that of **SQLFetchScroll** with the following exceptions:

- **SQLExtendedFetch** and **SQLFetchScroll** use different methods to return the number of rows fetched. **SQLExtendedFetch** returns the number of rows fetched in **RowCountPtr*; **SQLFetchScroll** returns the number of rows fetched directly to the buffer pointed to by SQL_ATTR_ROWS_FETCHED_PTR. For more information, see the *RowCountPtr* argument.
- **SQLExtendedFetch** and **SQLFetchScroll** return the status of each row in different arrays. For more information, see the *RowStatusArray* argument.
- **SQLExtendedFetch** and **SQLFetchScroll** use different methods to retrieve the bookmark when *FetchOrientation* is SQL_FETCH_BOOKMARK. **SQLExtendedFetch** does not support variable-length bookmarks or fetching rowsets at an offset other than 0 from a bookmark. For more information, see the *FetchOffset* argument.
- **SQLExtendedFetch** and **SQLFetchScroll** use different rowset sizes. **SQLExtendedFetch** uses the value of the SQL_ROWSET_SIZE statement attribute and **SQLFetchScroll** uses the value of the SQL_ATTR_ROW_ARRAY_SIZE statement attribute.
- **SQLExtendedFetch** has slightly different error handling semantics than **SQLFetchScroll**. For more information, see "Error Handling" in the "Comments" section of **SQLFetchScroll**.
- **SQLExtendedFetch** does not support binding offsets (the SQL_ATTR_ROW_BIND_OFFSET_PTR statement attribute).
- Calls to **SQLExtendedFetch** cannot be mixed with calls to **SQLFetch** or **SQLFetchScroll** and, if **SQLBulkOperations** is called before any fetch function is called, **SQLExtendedFetch** cannot be called until the cursor is closed and reopened. That is, **SQLExtendedFetch** can only be called in statement state S7. For more information, see "Statement Transitions" in Appendix B, "ODBC State Transition Tables."

When an application calls **SQLFetchScroll** while using an ODBC 2.*x* driver, the Driver Manager maps this call to **SQLExtendedFetch**. For more information, see "SQLFetchScroll and ODBC 2.*x* Drivers" in **SQLFetchScroll**.

In ODBC 2.*x*, **SQLExtendedFetch** was called to fetch multiple rows, and **SQLFetch** was called to fetch a single row. In ODBC 3.0, on the other hand, **SQLFetch** can be called to fetch multiple rows.

Related Functions

For information about	See
Binding a buffer to a column in a result set	**SQLBindCol**
Performing bulk insert, update, or delete operations	**SQLBulkOperations**
Canceling statement processing	**SQLCancel**
Returning information about a column in a result set	**SQLDescribeCol**
Executing an SQL statement	**SQLExecDirect**
Executing a prepared SQL statement	**SQLExecute**
Returning the number of result set columns	**SQLNumResultCols**
Positioning the cursor, refreshing data in the rowset, or updating or deleting data in the result set.	**SQLSetPos**
Setting a statement attribute	**SQLSetStmtAttr**

SQLFetch

Conformance

Version Introduced:	ODBC 1.0
Standards Compliance:	ISO 92

Summary

SQLFetch fetches the next rowset of data from the result set and returns data for all bound columns.

Syntax

SQLRETURN **SQLFetch**(
    SQLHSTMT *StatementHandle*);

Arguments

StatementHandle [Input]
Statement handle.

Returns

SQL_SUCCESS, SQL_SUCCESS_WITH_INFO, SQL_NO_DATA, SQL_STILL_EXECUTING, SQL_ERROR, or SQL_INVALID_HANDLE.

Diagnostics

When **SQLFetch** returns either SQL_ERROR or SQL_SUCCESS_WITH_INFO, an associated SQLSTATE value can be obtained by calling **SQLGetDiagRec** with a *HandleType* of SQL_HANDLE_STMT and a *Handle* of *StatementHandle*. The following table lists the SQLSTATE values commonly returned by **SQLFetch** and explains each one in the context of this function; the notation "(DM)" precedes the descriptions of SQLSTATEs returned by the Driver Manager. The return code associated with each SQLSTATE value is SQL_ERROR, unless noted otherwise. If an error occurs on a single column, **SQLGetDiagField** can be called with a *DiagIdentifier* of SQL_DIAG_COLUMN_NUMBER to determine the column the error occurred on; and **SQLGetDiagField** can be called with a *DiagIdentifier* of SQL_DIAG_ROW_NUMBER to determine the row containing that column.

For all those SQLSTATEs that can return SQL_SUCCESS_WITH_INFO or SQL_ERROR (except 01xxx SQLSTATEs), SQL_SUCCESS_WITH_INFO is returned if an error occurs on one or more, but not all, rows of a multirow operation, and SQL_ERROR is returned if an error occurs on a single-row operation.

SQLSTATE	Error	Description
01000	General warning	Driver-specific informational message. (Function returns SQL_SUCCESS_WITH_INFO.)
01004	String data, right truncated	String or binary data returned for a column resulted in the truncation of non-blank character or non-NULL binary data. If it was a string value, it was right truncated.
01S01	Error in row	An error occurred while fetching one or more rows. (If this SQLSTATE is returned when an ODBC 3.0 application is working with an ODBC 2.*x* driver, it can be ignored.)
01S07	Fractional truncation	The data returned for a column was truncated. For numeric data types, the fractional part of the number was truncated. For time, timestamp, and interval data types containing a time component, the fractional portion of the time was truncated. (Function returns SQL_SUCCESS_WITH_INFO.)
07006	Restricted data type attribute violation	The data value of a column in the result set could not be converted to the data type specified by *TargetType* in **SQLBindCol**. Column 0 was bound with a data type of SQL_C_BOOKMARK and the SQL_ATTR_USE_BOOKMARKS statement attribute was set to SQL_UB_VARIABLE. Column 0 was bound with a data type of SQL_C_VARBOOKMARK and the SQL_ATTR_USE_BOOKMARKS statement attribute was not set to SQL_UB_VARIABLE.
07009	Invalid descriptor index	The driver was an ODBC 2.*x* driver that does not support **SQLExtendedFetch**, and a column number specified in the binding for a column was 0. Column 0 was bound and the SQL_ATTR_USE_BOOKMARKS statement attribute was set to SQL_UB_OFF.
08S01	Communication link failure	The communication link between the driver and the data source to which the driver was connected failed before the function completed processing.
22001	String data, right truncated	A variable-length bookmark returned for a column was truncated.

SQLSTATE	Error	Description
22002	Indicator variable required but not supplied	NULL data was fetched into a column whose *StrLen_or_IndPtr* set by **SQLBindCol** (or SQL_DESC_INDICATOR_PTR set by **SQLSetDescField** or **SQLSetDescRec**) was a null pointer.
22003	Numeric value out of range	Returning the numeric value (as numeric or string) for one or more bound columns would have caused the whole (as opposed to fractional) part of the number to be truncated. For more information, see "Converting Data from SQL to C Data Types" in Appendix D, "Data Types."
22007	Invalid datetime format	A character column in the result set was bound to a date, time, or timestamp C structure, and a value in the column was, respectively, an invalid date, time, or timestamp.
22012	Division by zero	A value from an arithmetic expression was returned which resulted in division by zero.
22015	Interval field overflow	Assigning from an exact numeric or interval SQL type to an interval C type caused a loss of significant digits in the leading field. When fetching data to an interval C type, there was no representation of the value of the SQL type in the interval C type.
22018	Invalid character value for cast specification	A character column in the result set was bound to a character C buffer and the column contained a character for which there was no representation in the character set of the buffer. The C type was an exact or approximate numeric, a datetime, or an interval data type; the SQL type of the column was a character data type; and the value in the column was not a valid literal of the bound C type.
24000	Invalid cursor state	The *StatementHandle* was in an executed state but no result set was associated with the *StatementHandle*.
40001	Serialization failure	The transaction in which the fetch was executed was terminated to prevent deadlock.
40003	Statement completion unknown	The associated connection failed during the execution of this function and the state of the transaction cannot be determined.

SQLSTATE	Error	Description
HY000	General error	An error occurred for which there was no specific SQLSTATE and for which no implementation-specific SQLSTATE was defined. The error message returned by **SQLGetDiagRec** in the **MessageText* buffer describes the error and its cause.
HY001	Memory allocation error	The driver was unable to allocate memory required to support execution or completion of the function.
HY008	Operation canceled	Asynchronous processing was enabled for the *StatementHandle*. The function was called and before it completed execution, **SQLCancel** was called on the *StatementHandle*. Then the function was called again on the *StatementHandle*. The function was called and, before it completed execution, **SQLCancel** was called on the *StatementHandle* from a different thread in a multithread application.
HY010	Function sequence error	(DM) The specified *StatementHandle* was not in an executed state. The function was called without first calling **SQLExecDirect**, **SQLExecute**, or a catalog function. (DM) An asynchronously executing function (not this one) was called for the *StatementHandle* and was still executing when this function was called. (DM) **SQLExecute**, **SQLExecDirect**, **SQLBulkOperations**, or **SQLSetPos** was called for the *StatementHandle* and returned SQL_NEED_DATA. This function was called before data was sent for all data-at-execution parameters or columns. (DM) **SQLFetch** was called for the *StatementHandle* after **SQLExtendedFetch** was called and before **SQLFreeStmt** with the SQL_CLOSE option was called.
HY013	Memory management error	The function call could not be processed because the underlying memory objects could not be accessed, possibly because of low memory conditions.

SQLSTATE	Error	Description
HY090	Invalid string or buffer length	The SQL_ATTR_USE_BOOKMARK statement attribute was set to SQL_UB_VARIABLE, and column 0 was bound to a buffer whose length was not equal to the maximum length for the bookmark for this result set. (This length is available in the SQL_DESC_OCTET_LENGTH field of the IRD, and can be obtained by calling **SQLDescribeCol**, **SQLColAttribute**, or **SQLGetDescField**.)
HY107	Row value out of range	The value specified with the SQL_ATTR_CURSOR_TYPE statement attribute was SQL_CURSOR_KEYSET_DRIVEN, but the value specified with the SQL_ATTR_KEYSET_SIZE statement attribute was greater than 0 and less than the value specified with the SQL_ATTR_ROW_ARRAY_SIZE statement attribute.
HYC00	Optional feature not implemented	The driver or data source does not support the conversion specified by the combination of the *TargetType* in **SQLBindCol** and the SQL data type of the corresponding column.
HYT01	Connection timeout expired	The connection timeout period expired before the data source responded to the request. The connection timeout period is set through **SQLSetConnectAttr**, SQL_ATTR_CONNECTION_TIMEOUT.
IM001	Driver does not support this function	(DM) The driver associated with the *StatementHandle* does not support the function.

Comments

SQLFetch returns the next rowset in the result set. It can be called only while a result set exists—that is, after a call that creates a result set and before the cursor over that result set is closed. If any columns are bound, it returns the data in those columns. If the application has specified a pointer to a row status array or a buffer in which to return the number of rows fetched, **SQLFetch** returns this information as well. Calls to **SQLFetch** can be mixed with calls to **SQLFetchScroll** but cannot be mixed with calls to **SQLExtendedFetch**. For more information, see “Fetching a Row of Data” in Chapter 10, “Retrieving Results (Basic).”

If an ODBC 3.0 application works with an ODBC 2.*x* driver, the Driver Manager maps **SQLFetch** calls to **SQLExtendedFetch** for an ODBC 2.*x* driver that supports **SQLExtendedFetch**. If the ODBC 2.*x* driver does not support **SQLExtendedFetch**, the Driver Manager maps **SQLFetch** calls to **SQLFetch** in the ODBC 2.*x* driver, which can only fetch a single row.

For more information, see "Block Cursors, Scrollable Cursors, and Backward Compatibility" in Appendix G, "Driver Guidelines for Backward Compatibility."

Positioning the Cursor

When the result set is created, the cursor is positioned before the start of the result set. **SQLFetch** fetches the next rowset. It is equivalent to calling **SQLFetchScroll** with *FetchOrientation* set to SQL_FETCH_NEXT. For more information about cursors, see "Cursors" in Chapter 10, "Retrieving Results (Basic)" and "Block Cursors" in Chapter 11, "Retrieving Results (Advanced)."

The SQL_ATTR_ROW_ARRAY_SIZE statement attribute specifies the number of rows in the rowset. If the rowset being fetched by **SQLFetch** overlaps the end of the result set, **SQLFetch** returns a partial rowset. That is, if S + R–1 is greater than L, where S is the starting row of the rowset being fetched, R is the rowset size, and L is the last row in the result set, then only the first L–S+1 rows of the rowset are valid. The remaining rows are empty and have a status of SQL_ROW_NOROW.

After **SQLFetch** returns, the current row is the first row of the rowset.

The following rules describe cursor positioning after a call to **SQLFetch**:

Condition	First row of new rowset
Before start	1
CurrRowsetStart ≤ *LastResultRow* – *RowsetSize* [1]	*CurrRowsetStart* + *RowsetSize* [2]
CurrRowsetStart > *LastResultRow* – *RowsetSize* [1]	After end
After end	After end

1 If the rowset size is changed between fetches, this is the rowset size that was used with the previous fetch.

2 If the rowset size is changed between fetches, this is the rowset size that was used with the new fetch.

where:

Notation	Meaning
Before start	The block cursor is positioned before the start of the result set. If the first row of the new rowset is before the start of the result set, **SQLFetch** returns SQL_NO_DATA.
After end	The block cursor is positioned after the end of the result set. If the first row of the new rowset is after the end of the result set, **SQLFetch** returns SQL_NO_DATA.
CurrRowsetStart	The number of the first row in the current rowset.
LastResultRow	The number of the last row in the result set.
RowsetSize	The rowset size.

For example, suppose a result set has 100 rows and the rowset size is 5. The following table shows the rowset and return code returned by **SQLFetch** for different starting positions.

Current rowset	Return code	New rowset	# of rows fetched
Before start	SQL_SUCCESS	1 to 5	5
1 to 5	SQL_SUCCESS	6 to 10	5
52 to 56	SQL_SUCCESS	57 to 61	5
91 to 95	SQL_SUCCESS	96 to 100	5
93 to 97	SQL_SUCCESS	98 to 100. Rows 4 and 5 of the row status array are set to SQL_ROW_NOROW.	3
96 to 100	SQL_NO_DATA	None.	0
99 to 100	SQL_NO_DATA	None.	0
After end	SQL_NO_DATA	None.	0

Returning Data in Bound Columns

As **SQLFetch** returns each row, it places the data for each bound column in the buffer bound to that column. If no columns are bound, **SQLFetch** does not return any data but does move the block cursor forward. The data can still be retrieved with **SQLGetData**. If the cursor is a multirow cursor (that is, the SQL_ATTR_ROW_ARRAY_SIZE is greater than 1), **SQLGetData** can be called only if SQL_GD_BLOCK is returned when **SQLGetInfo** is called with an *InfoType* of SQL_GETDATA_EXTENSIONS. (For more information, see **SQLGetData**.)

For each bound column in a row, **SQLFetch** does the following:

1. Sets the length/indicator buffer to SQL_NULL_DATA and proceeds to the next column if the data is NULL. If the data is NULL and no length/indicator buffer was bound, **SQLFetch** returns SQLSTATE 22002 (Indicator variable required but not supplied) for the row and proceeds to the next row. For information about how to determine the address of the length/indicator buffer, see "Buffer Addresses" in **SQLBindCol**.

   If the data for the column is not NULL, **SQLFetch** proceeds to step 2.

2. If the SQL_ATTR_MAX_LENGTH statement attribute is set to a nonzero value and the column contains character or binary data, the data is truncated to SQL_ATTR_MAX_LENGTH bytes.

   Note The SQL_ATTR_MAX_LENGTH statement attribute is intended to reduce network traffic. It is generally implemented by the data source, which truncates the data before returning it across the network. Drivers and data sources are not required to support it. Therefore, to guarantee that data is truncated to a particular size, an application should allocate a buffer of that size and specify the size in the *cbValueMax* argument in **SQLBindCol**.

3. Converts the data to the type specified by *TargetType* in **SQLBindCol**.

4. If the data was converted to a variable-length data type, such as character or binary, **SQLFetch** checks whether the length of the data exceeds the length of the data buffer. If the length of character data (including the null-termination character) exceeds the length of the data buffer, **SQLFetch** truncates the data to the length of the data buffer less the length of a null-termination character. It then null-terminates the data. If the length of binary data exceeds the length of the data buffer, **SQLFetch** truncates it to the length of the data buffer. The length of the data buffer is specified with *BufferLength* in **SQLBindCol**.

   SQLFetch never truncates data converted to fixed-length data types; it always assumes that the length of the data buffer is the size of the data type.

5. Places the converted (and possibly truncated) data in the data buffer. For information about how to determine the address of the data buffer, see "Buffer Addresses" in **SQLBindCol**.

6. Places the length of the data in the length/indicator buffer. If the indicator pointer and the length pointer were both set to the same buffer (as a call to **SQLBindCol** does), the length is written in the buffer for valid data and SQL_NULL_DATA is written in the buffer for NULL data. If no length/indicator buffer was bound, **SQLFetch** does not return the length.

- For character or binary data, this is the length of the data after conversion and before truncation due to the data buffer being too small. If the driver cannot determine the length of the data after conversion, as is sometimes the case with long data, it sets the length to SQL_NO_TOTAL. If data was truncated due to the SQL_ATTR_MAX_LENGTH statement attribute, the value of this attribute—as opposed to the actual length—is placed in the length/indicator buffer. This is because this attribute is designed to truncate data on the server before conversion, so the driver has no way of figuring out what the actual length is.
- For all other data types, this is the length of the data after conversion; that is, it is the size of the type to which the data was converted.

For information about how to determine the address of the length/indicator buffer, see "Buffer Addresses" in **SQLBindCol**.

7. If the data is truncated during conversion without a loss of significant digits (for example, the real number 1.234 is truncated when converted to the integer 1) and **SQLFetch** returns SQLSTATE 01S07 (Fractional truncation) and SQL_SUCCESS_WITH_INFO. If the data is truncated because the length of the data buffer is too small (for example, the string "abcdef" is placed in a 4-byte buffer), **SQLFetch** returns SQLSTATE 01004 (Data truncated) and SQL_SUCCESS_WITH_INFO. If data is truncated due to the SQL_ATTR_MAX_LENGTH statement attribute, **SQLFetch** returns SQL_SUCCESS and does not return SQLSTATE 01S07 (Fractional truncation) or SQLSTATE 01004 (Data truncated). If data is truncated during conversion with a loss of significant digits (for example, if an SQL_INTEGER value greater than 100,000 were converted to an SQL_C_TINYINT), **SQLFetch** returns SQLSTATE 22003 (Numeric value out of range) and SQL_ERROR (if the rowset size is 1) or SQL_SUCCESS_WITH_INFO (if the rowset size is greater than 1).

The contents of the bound data buffer and the length/indicator buffer are undefined if **SQLFetch** or **SQLFetchScroll** does not return SQL_SUCCESS or SQL_SUCCESS_WITH_INFO.

Row Status Array

The row status array is used to return the status of each row in the rowset. The address of this array is specified with the SQL_ATTR_ROW_STATUS_PTR statement attribute. The array is allocated by the application and must have as many elements as are specified by the SQL_ATTR_ROW_ARRAY_SIZE statement attribute. Its values are set by **SQLFetch**, **SQLFetchScroll**, and **SQLBulkOperations** or **SQLSetPos** (except when they have been called after the cursor has been positioned by **SQLExtendedFetch**). If the value of the SQL_ATTR_ROW_STATUS_PTR statement attribute is a null pointer, these functions do not return the row status.

The contents of the row status array buffer are undefined if **SQLFetch** or **SQLFetchScroll** does not return SQL_SUCCESS or SQL_SUCCESS_WITH_INFO.

The following values are returned in the row status array.

Row status array value	Description
SQL_ROW_SUCCESS	The row was successfully fetched and has not changed since it was last fetched from this result set.
SQL_ROW_SUCCESS_WITH_INFO	The row was successfully fetched and has not changed since it was last fetched from this result set. However, a warning was returned about the row.
SQL_ROW_ERROR	An error occurred while fetching the row.
SQL_ROW_UPDATED [1,2, and 3]	The row was successfully fetched and has changed since it was last fetched from this result set. If the row is fetched again from this result set, or is refreshed by **SQLSetPos**, the status changed to the row's new status.
SQL_ROW_DELETED [3]	The row has been deleted since it was last fetched from this result set.
SQL_ROW_ADDED [4]	The row was inserted by **SQLBulkOperations**. If the row is fetched again from this result set, or is refreshed by **SQLSetPos**, its status is SQL_ROW_SUCCESS.
SQL_ROW_NOROW	The rowset overlapped the end of the result set and no row was returned that corresponded to this element of the row status array.

1 For keyset, mixed, and dynamic cursors, if a key value is updated, the row of data is considered to have been deleted and a new row added.

2 Some drivers cannot detect updates to data and therefore cannot return this value. To determine whether a driver can detect updates to refetched rows, an application calls **SQLGetInfo** with the SQL_ROW_UPDATES option.

3 **SQLFetch** can return this value only when it is intermixed with calls to **SQLFetchScroll**. The reason for this is that **SQLFetch** moves forward through the result set and, when used exclusively, does not refetch any rows. Because no rows are refetched, **SQLFetch** does not detect changes made to previously fetched rows. However, if **SQLFetchScroll** positions the cursor before any previously fetched rows and **SQLFetch** is used to fetch those rows, **SQLFetch** can detect any changes to those rows.

4 Returned by **SQLBulkOperations** only. Not set by **SQLFetch** or **SQLFetchScroll**.

Rows Fetched Buffer

The rows fetched buffer is used to return the number of rows fetched, including those rows for which no data was returned because an error occurred while they were being fetched. In other words, it is the number of rows for which the value in the row status array is not SQL_ROW_NOROW. The address of this buffer is specified with the SQL_ATTR_ROWS_FETCHED_PTR statement attribute. The buffer is allocated by the application. It is set by **SQLFetch** and **SQLFetchScroll**. If the value of the SQL_ATTR_ROWS_FETCHED_PTR statement attribute is a null pointer, these functions do not return the number of rows fetched. To determine the number of the current row in the result set, an application can call **SQLGetStmtAttr** with the SQL_ATTR_ROW_NUMBER attribute.

The contents of the rows fetched buffer are undefined if **SQLFetch** or **SQLFetchScroll** does not return SQL_SUCCESS or SQL_SUCCESS_WITH_INFO, except when SQL_NO_DATA is returned, in which case the value in the rows fetched buffer is set to 0.

Error Handling

Errors and warnings can apply to individual rows or to the entire function. For more information about diagnostic records, see Chapter 15, "Diagnostics," and **SQLGetDiagField**.

Errors and Warnings on the Entire Function

If an error applies to the entire function, such as SQLSTATE HYT00 (Timeout expired) or SQLSTATE 24000 (Invalid cursor state), **SQLFetch** returns SQL_ERROR and the applicable SQLSTATE. The contents of the rowset buffers are undefined and the cursor position is unchanged.

If a warning applies to the entire function, **SQLFetch** returns SQL_SUCCESS_WITH_INFO and the applicable SQLSTATE. The status records for warnings that apply to the entire function are returned before the status records that apply to individual rows.

Errors and Warnings in Individual Rows

If an error (such as SQLSTATE 22012 (Division by zero)) or a warning (such as SQLSTATE 01004 (Data truncated)) applies to a single row, **SQLFetch**:

- Sets the corresponding element of the row status array to SQL_ROW_ERROR for errors or SQL_ROW_SUCCESS_WITH_INFO for warnings.
- Adds zero or more status records containing SQLSTATEs for the error or warning.
- Sets the row and column number fields in the status records. If **SQLFetch** cannot determine a row or column number, it sets that number to SQL_ROW_NUMBER_UNKNOWN or SQL_COLUMN_NUMBER_UNKNOWN respectively. If the status record does not apply to a particular column, **SQLFetch** sets the column number to SQL_NO_COLUMN_NUMBER.

SQLFetch continues fetching rows until it has fetched all of the rows in the rowset. It returns SQL_SUCCESS_WITH_INFO unless an error occurs in every row of the rowset (not counting rows with status SQL_ROW_NOROW), in which case it returns SQL_ERROR. In particular, if the rowset size is 1 and an error occurs in that row, **SQLFetch** returns SQL_ERROR.

SQLFetch returns the status records in row number order. That is, it returns all status records for unknown rows (if any), then all status records for the first row (if any), then all status records for the second row (if any), and so on. The status records for each individual row are ordered according to the normal rules for ordering status records; for more information, see "Sequence of Status Records" in **SQLGetDiagField**.

Descriptors and SQLFetch

The following sections describe how **SQLFetch** interacts with descriptors.

Argument Mappings

The driver does not set any descriptor fields based on the arguments of **SQLFetch**.

Other Descriptor Fields

The following descriptor fields are used by **SQLFetch**.

Descriptor field	Desc.	Field in	Set through
SQL_DESC_ARRAY_SIZE	ARD	header	SQL_ATTR_ROW_ARRAY_SIZE statement attribute
SQL_DESC_ARRAY_STATUS_PTR	IRD	header	SQL_ATTR_ROW_STATUS_PTR statement attribute
SQL_DESC_BIND_OFFSET_PTR	ARD	header	SQL_ATTR_ROW_BIND_OFFSET_PTR statement attribute
SQL_DESC_BIND_TYPE	ARD	header	SQL_ATTR_ROW_BIND_TYPE statement attribute
SQL_DESC_COUNT	ARD	header	*ColumnNumber* argument of **SQLBindCol**
SQL_DESC_DATA_PTR	ARD	records	*TargetValuePtr* argument of **SQLBindCol**
SQL_DESC_INDICATOR_PTR	ARD	records	*StrLen_or_IndPtr* argument in **SQLBindCol**
SQL_DESC_OCTET_LENGTH	ARD	records	*BufferLength* argument in **SQLBindCol**
SQL_DESC_OCTET_LENGTH_PTR	ARD	records	*StrLen_or_IndPtr* argument in **SQLBindCol**
SQL_DESC_ROWS_PROCESSED_PTR	IRD	header	SQL_ATTR_ROWS_FETCHED_PTR statement attribute
SQL_DESC_TYPE	ARD	records	*TargetType* argument in **SQLBindCol**

All descriptor fields can also be set through **SQLSetDescField**.

Separate Length and Indicator Buffers

Applications can bind a single buffer or two separate buffers to be used to hold length and indicator values. When an application calls **SQLBindCol**, the driver sets the SQL_DESC_OCTET_LENGTH_PTR and SQL_DESC_INDICATOR_PTR fields of the ARD to the same address, which is passed in the *StrLen_or_IndPtr* argument. When an application calls **SQLSetDescField** or **SQLSetDescRec**, it can set these two fields to different addresses.

SQLFetch determines whether the application has specified separate length and indicator buffers. In this case, when the data is not NULL, **SQLFetch** sets the indicator buffer to 0 and returns the length in the length buffer. When the data is NULL, **SQLFetch** sets the indicator buffer to SQL_NULL_DATA and does not modify the length buffer.

Code Example

See **SQLBindCol**, **SQLColumns**, **SQLGetData**, and **SQLProcedures**.

Related Functions

For information about	See
Binding a buffer to a column in a result set	**SQLBindCol**
Canceling statement processing	**SQLCancel**
Returning information about a column in a result set	**SQLDescribeCol**
Executing an SQL statement	**SQLExecDirect**
Executing a prepared SQL statement	**SQLExecute**
Fetching a block of data or scrolling through a result set	**SQLFetchScroll**
Closing the cursor on the statement	**SQLFreeStmt**
Fetching part or all of a column of data	**SQLGetData**
Returning the number of result set columns	**SQLNumResultCols**
Preparing a statement for execution	**SQLPrepare**

SQLFetchScroll

Conformance

Version Introduced: ODBC 3.0
Standards Compliance: ISO 92

Summary

SQLFetchScroll fetches the specified rowset of data from the result set and returns data for all bound columns. Rowsets can be specified at an absolute or relative position or by bookmark.

When working with an ODBC 2.*x* driver, the Driver Manager maps this function to **SQLExtendedFetch**. For more information, see "Mapping Replacement Functions for Backward Compatibility of Applications" in Chapter 17, "Programming Considerations."

Syntax

SQLRETURN **SQLFetchScroll**(
    SQLHSTMT *StatementHandle*,
    SQLSMALLINT *FetchOrientation*,
    SQLINTEGER *FetchOffset*);

Arguments

StatementHandle [Input]
Statement handle.

FetchOrientation [Input]
Type of fetch:

SQL_FETCH_NEXT
SQL_FETCH_PRIOR
SQL_FETCH_FIRST
SQL_FETCH_LAST
SQL_FETCH_ABSOLUTE
SQL_FETCH_RELATIVE
SQL_FETCH_BOOKMARK

For more information, see "Positioning the Cursor" in the "Comments" section.

FetchOffset [Input]
Number of the row to fetch. The interpretation of this argument depends on the value of the *FetchOrientation* argument. For more information, see "Positioning the Cursor" in the "Comments" section.

Returns

SQL_SUCCESS, SQL_SUCCESS_WITH_INFO, SQL_NO_DATA, SQL_STILL_EXECUTING, SQL_ERROR, or SQL_INVALID_HANDLE.

Diagnostics

When **SQLFetchScroll** returns either SQL_ERROR or SQL_SUCCESS_WITH_INFO, an associated SQLSTATE value can be obtained by calling **SQLGetDiagRec** with a *HandleType* of SQL_HANDLE_STMT and a *Handle* of *StatementHandle*. The following table lists the SQLSTATE values commonly returned by **SQLFetchScroll** and explains each one in the context of this function; the notation "(DM)" precedes the descriptions of SQLSTATEs returned by the Driver Manager. The return code associated with each SQLSTATE value is SQL_ERROR, unless noted otherwise. If an error occurs on a single column, **SQLGetDiagField** can be called with a *DiagIdentifier* of SQL_DIAG_COLUMN_NUMBER to determine the column the error occurred on; and **SQLGetDiagField** can be called with a *DiagIdentifier* of SQL_DIAG_ROW_NUMBER to determine the row containing that column.

For all those SQLSTATEs that can return SQL_SUCCESS_WITH_INFO or SQL_ERROR (except 01xxx SQLSTATEs), SQL_SUCCESS_WITH_INFO is returned if an error occurs on one or more, but not all, rows of a multirow operation, and SQL_ERROR is returned if an error occurs on a single-row operation.

SQLSTATE	Error	Description
01000	General warning	Driver-specific informational message. (Function returns SQL_SUCCESS_WITH_INFO.)
01004	String data, right truncated	String or binary data returned for a column resulted in the truncation of non-blank character or non-NULL binary data. String values are right truncated.
01S01	Error in row	An error occurred while fetching one or more rows. (This SQLSTATE is returned only by ODBC 2.*x* drivers.)

SQLSTATE	Error	Description
01S06	Attempt to fetch before the result set returned the first rowset	The requested rowset overlapped the start of the result set when *FetchOrientation* was SQL_FETCH_PRIOR, the current position was beyond the first row, and the number of the current row is less than or equal to the rowset size. The requested rowset overlapped the start of the result set when *FetchOrientation* was SQL_FETCH_PRIOR, the current position was beyond the end of the result set, and the rowset size was greater than the result set size. The requested rowset overlapped the start of the result set when *FetchOrientation* was SQL_FETCH_RELATIVE, *FetchOffset* was negative, and the absolute value of *FetchOffset* was less than or equal to the rowset size. The requested rowset overlapped the start of the result set when *FetchOrientation* was SQL_FETCH_ABSOLUTE, *FetchOffset* was negative, and the absolute value of *FetchOffset* was greater than the result set size but less than or equal to the rowset size. (Function returns SQL_SUCCESS_WITH_INFO.)
01S07	Fractional truncation	The data returned for a column was truncated. For numeric data types, the fractional part of the number was truncated. For time, timestamp, and interval data types containing a time component, the fractional portion of the time was truncated. (Function returns SQL_SUCCESS_WITH_INFO.)
07006	Restricted data type attribute violation	A data value of a column in the result set could not be converted to the C data type specified by *TargetType* in **SQLBindCol**. Column 0 was bound with a data type of SQL_C_BOOKMARK and the SQL_ATTR_USE_BOOKMARKS statement attribute was set to SQL_UB_VARIABLE. Column 0 was bound with a data type of SQL_C_VARBOOKMARK and the SQL_ATTR_USE_BOOKMARKS statement attribute was not set to SQL_UB_VARIABLE.

SQLSTATE	Error	Description
07009	Invalid descriptor index	Column 0 was bound and the SQL_ATTR_USE_BOOKMARKS statement attribute was set to SQL_UB_OFF.
08S01	Communication link failure	The communication link between the driver and the data source to which the driver was connected failed before the function completed processing
22001	String data, right truncation	A variable-length bookmark returned for a row was truncated.
22002	Indicator variable required but not supplied	NULL data was fetched into a column whose *StrLen_or_IndPtr* set by **SQLBindCol** (or SQL_DESC_INDICATOR_PTR set by **SQLSetDescField** or **SQLSetDescRec**) was a null pointer.
22003	Numeric value out of range	Returning the numeric value (as numeric or string) for one or more bound columns would have caused the whole (as opposed to fractional) part of the number to be truncated. For more information, see Appendix D, "Data Types."
22007	Invalid datetime format	A character column in the result set was bound to a date, time, or timestamp C structure, and a value in the column was, respectively, an invalid date, time, or timestamp.
22012	Division by zero	A value from an arithmetic expression was returned which resulted in division by zero.
22015	Interval field overflow	Assigning from an exact numeric or interval SQL type to an interval C type caused a loss of significant digits in the leading field. When fetching data to an interval C type, there was no representation of the value of the SQL type in the interval C type.
22018	Invalid character value for cast specification	A character column in the result set was bound to a character C buffer and the column contained a character for which there was no representation in the character set of the buffer. The C type was an exact or approximate numeric, a datetime, or an interval data type; the SQL type of the column was a character data type; and the value in the column was not a valid literal of the bound C type.

SQLSTATE	Error	Description
24000	Invalid cursor state	The *StatementHandle* was in an executed state but no result set was associated with the *StatementHandle*.
40001	Serialization failure	The transaction in which the fetch was executed was terminated to prevent deadlock.
40003	Statement completion unknown	The associated connection failed during the execution of this function and the state of the transaction cannot be determined.
HY000	General error	An error occurred for which there was no specific SQLSTATE and for which no implementation-specific SQLSTATE was defined. The error message returned by **SQLGetDiagRec** in the **MessageText* buffer describes the error and its cause.
HY001	Memory allocation error	The driver was unable to allocate memory required to support execution or completion of the function.
HY008	Operation canceled	Asynchronous processing was enabled for the *StatementHandle*. The function was called and before it completed execution, **SQLCancel** was called on the *StatementHandle*. Then the function was called again on the *StatementHandle*. The function was called and, before it completed execution, **SQLCancel** was called on the *StatementHandle* from a different thread in a multithread application.
HY010	Function sequence error	(DM) The specified *StatementHandle* was not in an executed state. The function was called without first calling **SQLExecDirect**, **SQLExecute**, or a catalog function. (DM) An asynchronously executing function (not this one) was called for the *StatementHandle* and was still executing when this function was called. (DM) **SQLExecute**, **SQLExecDirect**, **SQLBulkOperations**, or **SQLSetPos** was called for the *StatementHandle* and returned SQL_NEED_DATA. This function was called before data was sent for all data-at-execution parameters or columns. (DM) **SQLFetchScroll** was called for a *StatementHandle* after **SQLExtendedFetch** was called and before **SQLFreeStmt** with SQL_CLOSE was called.

SQLSTATE	Error	Description
HY013	Memory management error	The function call could not be processed because the underlying memory objects could not be accessed, possibly because of low memory conditions.
HY090	Invalid string or buffer length	The SQL_ATTR_USE_BOOKMARK statement attribute was set to SQL_UB_VARIABLE, and column 0 was bound to a buffer whose length was not equal to the maximum length for the bookmark for this result set. (This length is available in the SQL_DESC_OCTET_LENGTH field of the IRD, and can be obtained by calling **SQLDescribeCol**, **SQLColAttribute**, or **SQLGetDescField**.)
HY106	Fetch type out of range	(DM) The value specified for the argument *FetchOrientation* was invalid. (DM) The argument *FetchOrientation* was SQL_FETCH_BOOKMARK, and the SQL_ATTR_USE_BOOKMARKS statement attribute was set to SQL_UB_OFF. The value of the SQL_ATTR_CURSOR_TYPE statement attribute was SQL_CURSOR_FORWARD_ONLY and the value of argument *FetchOrientation* was not SQL_FETCH_NEXT. The value of the SQL_ATTR_CURSOR_SCROLLABLE statement attribute was SQL_NONSCROLLABLE and the value of argument *FetchOrientation* was not SQL_FETCH_NEXT.
HY107	Row value out of range	The value specified with the SQL_ATTR_CURSOR_TYPE statement attribute was SQL_CURSOR_KEYSET_DRIVEN, but the value specified with the SQL_ATTR_KEYSET_SIZE statement attribute was greater than 0 and less than the value specified with the SQL_ATTR_ROW_ARRAY_SIZE statement attribute.

SQLSTATE	Error	Description
HY111	Invalid bookmark value	The argument *FetchOrientation* was SQL_FETCH_BOOKMARK and the bookmark pointed to by the value in the SQL_ATTR_FETCH_BOOKMARK_PTR statement attribute was not valid or was a null pointer.
HYC00	Optional feature not implemented	Driver or data source does not support the specified fetch type. The driver or data source does not support the conversion specified by the combination of the *TargetType* in **SQLBindCol** and the SQL data type of the corresponding column. *FetchOrientation* was SQL_FETCH_BOOKMARK, *FetchOffset* was not equal to 0, and the underlying driver is an ODBC 2.*x* driver.
HYT01	Connection timeout expired	The connection timeout period expired before the data source responded to the request. The connection timeout period is set through **SQLSetConnectAttr**, SQL_ATTR_CONNECTION_TIMEOUT.
IM001	Driver does not support this function	(DM) The driver associated with the *StatementHandle* does not support the function.

Comments

SQLFetchScroll returns a specified rowset from the result set. Rowsets can be specified by absolute or relative position or by bookmark. **SQLFetchScroll** can be called only while a result set exists—that is, after a call that creates a result set and before the cursor over that result set is closed. If any columns are bound, it returns the data in those columns. If the application has specified a pointer to a row status array or a buffer in which to return the number of rows fetched, **SQLFetchScroll** returns this information as well. Calls to **SQLFetchScroll** can be mixed with calls to **SQLFetch** but cannot be mixed with calls to **SQLExtendedFetch**.

For more information, see "Using Block Cursors" and "Using Scrollable Cursors" in Chapter 11, "Retrieving Results (Advanced)."

Positioning the Cursor

When the result set is created, the cursor is positioned before the start of the result set. **SQLFetchScroll** positions the block cursor based on the values of the *FetchOrientation* and *FetchOffset* arguments as shown in the following table. The exact rules for determining the start of the new rowset are shown in the next section.

FetchOrientation	Meaning
SQL_FETCH_NEXT	Return the next rowset. This is equivalent to calling **SQLFetch**. **SQLFetchScroll** ignores the value of *FetchOffset*.
SQL_FETCH_PRIOR	Return the prior rowset. **SQLFetchScroll** ignores the value of *FetchOffset*.
SQL_FETCH_RELATIVE	Return the rowset *FetchOffset* from the start of the current rowset.
SQL_FETCH_ABSOLUTE	Return the rowset starting at row *FetchOffset*.
SQL_FETCH_FIRST	Return the first rowset in the result set. **SQLFetchScroll** ignores the value of *FetchOffset*.
SQL_FETCH_LAST	Return the last complete rowset in the result set. **SQLFetchScroll** ignores the value of *FetchOffset*.
SQL_FETCH_BOOKMARK	Return the rowset *FetchOffset* rows from the bookmark specified by the SQL_ATTR_FETCH_BOOKMARK_PTR statement attribute.

Drivers are not required to support all fetch orientations; an application calls **SQLGetInfo** with an information type of SQL_DYNAMIC_CURSOR_ATTRIBUTES1, SQL_KEYSET_CURSOR_ATTRIBUTES1, or SQL_STATIC_CURSOR_ATTRIBUTES1 (depending on the type of the cursor) to determine which fetch orientations are supported by the driver. The application should look at the SQL_CA1_NEXT, SQL_CA1_RELATIVE, SQL_CA1_ABSOLUTE, and WQL_CA1_BOOKMARK bitmasks in these information types. Furthermore, if the cursor is forward-only and *FetchOrientation* is not SQL_FETCH_NEXT, **SQLFetchScroll** returns SQLSTATE HY106 (Fetch type out of range).

The SQL_ATTR_ROW_ARRAY_SIZE statement attribute specifies the number of rows in the rowset. If the rowset being fetched by **SQLFetchScroll** overlaps the end of the result set, **SQLFetchScroll** returns a partial rowset. That is, if S + R–1 is greater than L, where S is the starting row of the rowset being fetched, R is the rowset size, and L is the last row in the result set, then only the first L–S+1 rows of the rowset are valid. The remaining rows are empty and have a status of SQL_ROW_NOROW.

After **SQLFetchScroll** returns, the current row is the first row of the rowset.

Cursor Positioning Rules

The following sections describe the exact rules for each value of *FetchOrientation*. These rules use the following notation.

Notation	Meaning
Before start	The block cursor is positioned before the start of the result set. If the first row of the new rowset is before the start of the result set, **SQLFetchScroll** returns SQL_NO_DATA.
After end	The block cursor is positioned after the end of the result set. If the first row of the new rowset is after the end of the result set, **SQLFetchScroll** returns SQL_NO_DATA.
CurrRowsetStart	The number of the first row in the current rowset.
LastResultRow	The number of the last row in the result set.
RowsetSize	The rowset size.
FetchOffset	The value of the *FetchOffset* argument.
BookmarkRow	The row corresponding to the bookmark specified by the SQL_ATTR_FETCH_BOOKMARK_PTR statement attribute.

SQL_FETCH_NEXT

The following rules apply.

Condition	First row of new rowset
Before start	1
CurrRowsetStart + *RowsetSize* [1] ≤ *LastResultRow*	*CurrRowsetStart* + *RowsetSize* [1]
CurrRowsetStart + *RowsetSize* [1] > *LastResultRow*	*After end*
After end	*After end*

1 If the rowset size has been changed since the previous call to fetch rows, this is the rowset size that was used with the previous call.

SQL_FETCH_PRIOR

The following rules apply.

Condition	First row of new rowset
Before start	*Before start*
CurrRowsetStart = 1	*Before start*
1 < *CurrRowsetStart* ≤ *RowsetSize* [2]	1 [1]
CurrRowsetStart > *RowsetSize* [2]	*CurrRowsetStart* – *RowsetSize* [2]
After end AND *LastResultRow* < *RowsetSize* [2]	1 [1]
After end AND *LastResultRow* ≥ *RowsetSize* [2]	*LastResultRow* – *RowsetSize* + 1 [2]

1 **SQLFetchScroll** returns SQLSTATE 01S06 (Attempt to fetch before the result set returned the first rowset) and SQL_SUCCESS_WITH_INFO.

2 If the rowset size has been changed since the previous call to fetch rows, this is the new rowset size.

SQL_FETCH_RELATIVE

The following rules apply.

Condition	First row of new rowset
(*Before start* AND *FetchOffset* > 0) OR (*After end AND FetchOffset < 0)*	-- [1]
BeforeStart AND *FetchOffset* ≤ 0	*Before start*
CurrRowsetStart = 1 AND *FetchOffset < 0*	*Before start*
CurrRowsetStart > 1 AND *CurrRowsetStart* + *FetchOffset* < 1 AND | *FetchOffset* | > *RowsetSize* [3]	*Before start*
CurrRowsetStart > 1 AND *CurrRowsetStart* + *FetchOffset* < 1 AND | *FetchOffset* | ≤ *RowsetSize* [3]	1 [2]
1 ≤ *CurrRowsetStart* + *FetchOffset* ≤ *LastResultRow*	*CurrRowsetStart* + *FetchOffset*
CurrRowsetStart + *FetchOffset* > *LastResultRow*	*After end*
After end AND FetchOffset ≥ *0*	*After end*

1 **SQLFetchScroll** returns the same rowset as if it was called with *FetchOrientation* set to SQL_FETCH_ABSOLUTE. For more information, see the "SQL_FETCH_ABSOLUTE" section.

2 **SQLFetchScroll** returns SQLSTATE 01S06 (Attempt to fetch before the result set returned the first rowset) and SQL_SUCCESS_WITH_INFO.

3 If the rowset size has been changed since the previous call to fetch rows, this is the new rowset size.

SQL_FETCH_ABSOLUTE

The following rules apply.

Condition	First row of new rowset
FetchOffset < 0 AND | *FetchOffset* | ≤ *LastResultRow*	*LastResultRow* + *FetchOffset* + 1
FetchOffset < 0 AND | *FetchOffset* | > *LastResultRow* AND | *FetchOffset* | > *RowsetSize* [2]	*Before start*
FetchOffset < 0 AND | *FetchOffset* | > *LastResultRow* AND | *FetchOffset* | ≤ *RowsetSize* [2]	1 [1]
FetchOffset = 0	*Before start*
1 ≤ *FetchOffset* ≤ *LastResultRow*	*FetchOffset*
FetchOffset > *LastResultRow*	*After end*

1 **SQLFetchScroll** returns SQLSTATE 01S06 (Attempt to fetch before the result set returned the first rowset) and SQL_SUCCESS_WITH_INFO.

2 If the rowset size has been changed since the previous call to fetch rows, this is the new rowset size.

An absolute fetch performed against a dynamic cursor cannot provide the required result because row positions in a dynamic cursor are undetermined. Such an operation is equivalent to a fetch first followed by a fetch relative; it is not an atomic operation, as an absolute fetch on a static cursor is.

SQL_FETCH_FIRST
The following rules apply.

Condition	First row of new rowset
Any	1

SQL_FETCH_LAST
The following rules apply.

Condition	First row of new rowset
RowsetSize [1] ≤ *LastResultRow*	*LastResultRow* – *RowsetSize* + 1 [1]
RowsetSize [1] > *LastResultRow*	1

[1] If the rowset size has been changed since the previous call to fetch rows, this is the new rowset size.

SQL_FETCH_BOOKMARK
The following rules apply.

Condition	First row of new rowset
BookmarkRow + *FetchOffset* < 1	*Before start*
1 ≤ *BookmarkRow* + *FetchOffset* ≤ *LastResultRow*	*BookmarkRow* + *FetchOffset*
BookmarkRow + *FetchOffset* > *LastResultRow*	*After end*

For information about bookmarks, see the "Bookmarks" section in Chapter 11, "Retrieving Results (Advanced)."

Effect of Deleted, Added, and Error Rows on Cursor Movement

Static and keyset-driven cursors sometimes detect rows added to the result set and remove rows deleted from the result set. An application determines whether the cursors implemented by a particular driver do this by calling **SQLGetInfo** with the SQL_STATIC_CURSOR_ATTRIBUTES2 and SQL_KEYSET_CURSOR_ATTRIBUTES2 options, and looking at the SQL_CA2_SENSITIVITY_ADDITIONS, SQL_CA2_SENSITIVITY_DELETIONS, and SQL_CA2_SENSITIVITY_UPDATES bitmasks. For drivers that can detect deleted rows and remove them, the following paragraphs describe the effects of this behavior. For drivers that can detect deleted rows but cannot remove them, deletions have no effect on cursor movements, and the following paragraphs do not apply.

If the cursor detects rows added to the result set or removes rows deleted from the result set, it appears as if it detects these changes only when it fetches data. This includes the case when **SQLFetchScroll** is called with *FetchOrientation* set to SQL_FETCH_RELATIVE and *FetchOffset* set to 0 to refetch the same rowset but does not include the case when **SQLSetPos** is called with *fOption* set to SQL_REFRESH. In the latter case, the data in the rowset buffers is refreshed, but not refetched, and deleted rows are not removed from the result set. Thus, when a row is deleted from or inserted into the current rowset, the cursor does not modify the rowset buffers. Instead, it detects the change when it fetches any rowset that previously included the deleted row or now includes the inserted row.

For example:

```
// Fetch the next rowset.
SQLFetchScroll(hstmt, SQL_FETCH_NEXT, 0);

// Delete third row of the rowset. Does not modify the rowset buffers.
SQLSetPos(hstmt, 3, SQL_DELETE, SQL_LOCK_NO_CHANGE);

// The third row has a status of SQL_ROW_DELETED after this call.
SQLSetPos(hstmt, 3, SQL_REFRESH, SQL_LOCK_NO_CHANGE);

// Refetch the same rowset. The third row is removed, replaced by what
// was previously the fourth row.
SQLFetchScroll(hstmt, SQL_FETCH_RELATIVE, 0);
```

When **SQLFetchScroll** returns a new rowset that has a position relative to the current rowset—that is, *FetchOrientation* is SQL_FETCH_NEXT, SQL_FETCH_PRIOR, or SQL_FETCH_RELATIVE—it does not include changes to the current rowset when calculating the starting position of the new rowset. However, it does include changes outside the current rowset if it is capable of detecting them. Furthermore, when **SQLFetchScroll** returns a new rowset that has a position independent of the current rowset—that is, *FetchOrientation* is SQL_FETCH_FIRST, SQL_FETCH_LAST, SQL_FETCH_ABSOLUTE, or SQL_FETCH_BOOKMARK—it includes all changes it is capable of detecting, even if they are in the current rowset.

When determining whether newly added rows are inside or outside the current rowset, a partial rowset is considered to end at the last valid row; that is, the last row for which the row status is not SQL_ROW_NOROW. For example, suppose the cursor is capable of detecting newly added rows, the current rowset is a partial rowset, the application adds new rows, and the cursor adds these rows to the end of the result set. If the application calls **SQLFetchScroll** with *FetchOrientation* set to SQL_FETCH_NEXT, **SQLFetchScroll** returns the rowset starting with the first newly added row.

For example, suppose the current rowset comprises rows 21 to 30, the rowset size is 10, the cursor removes rows deleted from the result set, and the cursor detects rows added to the result set. The following table shows the rows **SQLFetchScroll** returns in various situations.

Change	Fetch type	FetchOffset	New rowset [1]
Delete row 21	NEXT	0	31 to 40
Delete row 31	NEXT	0	32 to 41
Insert row between rows 21 and 22	NEXT	0	31 to 40
Insert row between rows 30 and 31	NEXT	0	Inserted row, 31 to 39
Delete row 21	PRIOR	0	11 to 20
Delete row 20	PRIOR	0	10 to 19
Insert row between rows 21 and 22	PRIOR	0	11 to 20
Insert row between rows 20 and 21	PRIOR	0	12 to 20, inserted row
Delete row 21	RELATIVE	0	22 to 31 [2]
Delete row 21	RELATIVE	1	22 to 31
Insert row between rows 21 and 22	RELATIVE	0	21, inserted row, 22 to 29
Insert row between rows 21 and 22	RELATIVE	1	22 to 31
Delete row 21	ABSOLUTE	21	22 to 31 [2]
Delete row 22	ABSOLUTE	21	21, 23 to 31
Insert row between rows 21 and 22	ABSOLUTE	22	Inserted row, 22 to 29

1 This column uses the row numbers before any rows were inserted or deleted.

2 In this case, the cursor attempts to return rows starting with row 21. Because row 21 has been deleted, the first row it returns is row 22.

Error rows (that is, rows with a status of SQL_ROW_ERROR) do not affect cursor movement. For example, if the current rowset starts with row 11 and the status of row 11 is SQL_ROW_ERROR, calling **SQLFetchScroll** with *FetchOrientation* set to SQL_FETCH_RELATIVE and *FetchOffset* set to 5 returns the rowset starting with row 16, just as it would if the status for row 11 was SQL_SUCCESS.

Returning Data in Bound Columns

SQLFetchScroll returns data in bound columns in the same way as **SQLFetch**. For more information, see "Returning Data in Bound Columns" in **SQLFetch**.

If no columns are bound, **SQLFetchScroll** does not return data but does move the block cursor to the specified position. Whether data can be retrieved from unbound columns of a block cursor with **SQLGetData** depends on the driver. This capability is supported if a call to **SQLGetInfo** returns the SQL_GD_BLOCK bit for the SQL_GETDATA_EXTENSIONS information type.

Buffer Addresses

SQLFetchScroll uses the same formula to determine the address of data and length/indicator buffers as **SQLFetch**. For more information, see "Buffer Addresses" in **SQLBindCol**.

Row Status Array

SQLFetchScroll sets values in the row status array in the same manner as **SQLFetch**. For more information, see "Row Status Array" in **SQLFetch**.

Rows Fetched Buffer

SQLFetchScroll returns the number of rows fetched in the rows fetched buffer in the same manner as **SQLFetch**. For more information, see "Rows Fetched Buffer" in **SQLFetch**.

Error Handling

When an application calls **SQLFetchScroll** in an ODBC 3.0 driver, the Driver Manager calls **SQLFetchScroll** in the driver. When an application calls **SQLFetchScroll** in an ODBC 2.*x* driver, the Driver Manager calls **SQLExtendedFetch** in the driver. Because **SQLFetchScroll** and **SQLExtendedFetch** handle errors in a slightly different manner, the application sees slightly different error behavior when it calls **SQLFetchScroll** in ODBC 2.*x* and ODBC 3.0 drivers.

SQLFetchScroll returns errors and warnings in the same manner as **SQLFetch**; for more information, see "Error Handling" in **SQLFetch**. **SQLExtendedFetch** returns errors in the same manner as **SQLFetch** with the following exceptions:

- When a warning occurs that applies to a particular row in the rowset, **SQLExtendedFetch** sets the corresponding entry in the row status array to SQL_ROW_SUCCESS, not SQL_ROW_SUCCESS_WITH_INFO.
- If errors occur in every row in the rowset, **SQLExtendedFetch** returns SQL_SUCCESS_WITH_INFO, not SQL_ERROR.
- In each group of status records that applies to an individual row, the first status record returned by **SQLExtendedFetch** must contain SQLSTATE 01S01 (Error in row); **SQLFetchScroll** does not return this SQLSTATE. Note that if **SQLExtendedFetch** is unable to return additional SQLSTATEs, it still must return this SQLSTATE.

SQLFetchScroll and Optimistic Concurrency

If a cursor uses optimistic concurrency—that is, the SQL_ATTR_CONCURRENCY statement attribute has a value of SQL_CONCUR_VALUES or SQL_CONCUR_ROWVER—**SQLFetchScroll** updates the optimistic concurrency values used by the data source to detect whether a row has changed. This happens whenever **SQLFetchScroll** fetches a new rowset, including when it refetches the current rowset (it is called with *FetchOrientation* set to SQL_FETCH_RELATIVE and *FetchOffset* set to 0).

SQLFetchScroll and ODBC 2.*x* Drivers

When an application calls **SQLFetchScroll** in an ODBC 2.*x* driver, the Driver Manager maps this call to **SQLExtendedFetch**. It passes the following values for the arguments of **SQLExtendedFetch**.

SQLExtendedFetch Argument	Value
StatementHandle	*StatementHandle* in **SQLFetchScroll**.
FetchOrientation	*FetchOrientation* in **SQLFetchScroll**.
FetchOffset	If *FetchOrientation* is not SQL_FETCH_BOOKMARK, the value of the *FetchOffset* argument in **SQLFetchScroll** is used. If *FetchOrientation* is SQL_FETCH_BOOKMARK, the value stored at the address specified by the SQL_ATTR_FETCH_BOOKMARK_PTR statement attribute is used.
RowCountPtr	The address specified by the SQL_ATTR_ROWS_FETCHED_PTR statement attribute.
RowStatusArray	The address specified by the SQL_ATTR_ROW_STATUS_PTR statement attribute.

For more information, see "Block Cursors, Scrollable Cursors, and Backward Compatibility" in Appendix G, "Driver Guidelines for Backward Compatibility."

Descriptors and SQLFetchScroll

SQLFetchScroll interacts with descriptors in the same manner as **SQLFetch**. For more information, see the "Descriptors and SQLFetchScroll" section in **SQLFetch**.

Code Example

See "Column-Wise Binding" and "Row-Wise Binding" in Chapter 11, "Retrieving Results (Advanced)", and "Positioned Update and Delete Statements" and "Updating Rows in the Rowset with SQLSetPos" in Chapter 12, "Updating Data."

Related Functions

For information about	See
Binding a buffer to a column in a result set	**SQLBindCol**
Performing bulk insert, update, or delete operations	**SQLBulkOperations**
Canceling statement processing	**SQLCancel**
Returning information about a column in a result set	**SQLDescribeCol**
Executing an SQL statement	**SQLExecDirect**
Executing a prepared SQL statement	**SQLExecute**

For information about	See
Fetching a single row or a block of data in a forward-only direction	**SQLFetch**
Closing the cursor on the statement	**SQLFreeStmt**
Returning the number of result set columns	**SQLNumResultCols**
Positioning the cursor, refreshing data in the rowset, or updating or deleting data in the result set	**SQLSetPos**
Setting a statement attribute	**SQLSetStmtAttr**

SQLForeignKeys

Conformance

Version Introduced: ODBC 1.0
Standards Compliance: ODBC

Summary

SQLForeignKeys can return:

- A list of foreign keys in the specified table (columns in the specified table that refer to primary keys in other tables).
- A list of foreign keys in other tables that refer to the primary key in the specified table.

The driver returns each list as a result set on the specified statement.

Syntax

```
SQLRETURN SQLForeignKeys(
      SQLHSTMT       StatementHandle,
      SQLCHAR *      PKCatalogName,
      SQLSMALLINT NameLength1,
      SQLCHAR *      PKSchemaName,
      SQLSMALLINT NameLength2,
      SQLCHAR *      PKTableName,
      SQLSMALLINT NameLength3,
      SQLCHAR *      FKCatalogName,
      SQLSMALLINT NameLength4,
      SQLCHAR *      FKSchemaName,
      SQLSMALLINT NameLength5,
      SQLCHAR *      FKTableName,
      SQLSMALLINT NameLength6);
```

Arguments

StatementHandle [Input]
Statement handle.

PKCatalogName [Input]
Primary key table catalog name. If a driver supports catalogs for some tables but not for others, such as when the driver retrieves data from different DBMSs, an empty string ("") denotes those tables that do not have catalogs. *PKCatalogName* cannot contain a string search pattern.

If the SQL_ATTR_METADATA_ID statement attribute is set to SQL_TRUE, *PKCatalogName* is treated as an identifier, and its case is not significant. If it is SQL_FALSE, *PKCatalogName* is an ordinary argument; it is treated literally, and its case is significant. For more information, see "Arguments in Catalog Functions" in Chapter 7, "Catalog Functions."

NameLength1 [Input]
Length of **PKCatalogName*, in bytes.

PKSchemaName [Input]
Primary key table schema name. If a driver supports schemas for some tables but not for others, such as when the driver retrieves data from different DBMSs, an empty string ("") denotes those tables that do not have schemas. *PKSchemaName* cannot contain a string search pattern.

If the SQL_ATTR_METADATA_ID statement attribute is set to SQL_TRUE, *PKSchemaName* is treated as an identifier, and its case is not significant. If it is SQL_FALSE, *PKSchemaName* is an ordinary argument; it is treated literally, and its case is significant.

NameLength2 [Input]
Length of **PKSchemaName*, in bytes.

PKTableName [Input]
Primary key table name. *PKTableName* cannot contain a string search pattern.

If the SQL_ATTR_METADATA_ID statement attribute is set to SQL_TRUE, *PKTableName* is treated as an identifier, and its case is not significant. If it is SQL_FALSE, *PKTableName* is an ordinary argument; it is treated literally, and its case is significant.

NameLength3 [Input]
Length of **PKTableName*.

FKCatalogName [Input]
Foreign key table catalog name. If a driver supports catalogs for some tables but not for others, such as when the driver retrieves data from different DBMSs, an empty string ("") denotes those tables that do not have catalogs. *FKCatalogName* cannot contain a string search pattern.

If the SQL_ATTR_METADATA_ID statement attribute is set to SQL_TRUE, *FKCatalogName* is treated as an identifier, and its case is not significant. If it is SQL_FALSE, *FKCatalogName* is an ordinary argument; is treated literally, and its case is significant.

NameLength4 [Input]
Length of **FKCatalogName*.

FKSchemaName [Input]
Foreign key table schema name. If a driver supports schemas for some tables but not for others, such as when the driver retrieves data from different DBMSs, an empty string ("") denotes those tables that do not have schemas. *FKSchemaName* cannot contain a string search pattern.

If the SQL_ATTR_METADATA_ID statement attribute is set to SQL_TRUE, *FKSchemaName* is treated as an identifier, and its case is not significant. If it is SQL_FALSE, *FKSchemaName* is an ordinary argument; it is treated literally, and its case is significant.

NameLength5 [Input]
Length of **FKSchemaName*.

FKTableName [Input]
Foreign key table name. *FKTableName* cannot contain a string search pattern.

If the SQL_ATTR_METADATA_ID statement attribute is set to SQL_TRUE, *FKTableName* is treated as an identifier, and its case is not significant. If it is SQL_FALSE, *FKTableName* is an ordinary argument; it is treated literally, and its case is significant.

NameLength6 [Input]
Length of **FKTableName*.

Returns

SQL_SUCCESS, SQL_SUCCESS_WITH_INFO, SQL_STILL_EXECUTING, SQL_ERROR, or SQL_INVALID_HANDLE.

Diagnostics

When **SQLForeignKeys** returns SQL_ERROR or SQL_SUCCESS_WITH_INFO, an associated SQLSTATE value may be obtained by calling **SQLGetDiagRec** with a *HandleType* of SQL_HANDLE_STMT and a *Handle* of *StatementHandle*. The following table lists the SQLSTATE values commonly returned by **SQLForeignKeys** and explains each one in the context of this function; the notation "(DM)" precedes the descriptions of SQLSTATEs returned by the Driver Manager. The return code associated with each SQLSTATE value is SQL_ERROR, unless noted otherwise.

SQLSTATE	Error	Description
01000	General warning	Driver-specific informational message. (Function returns SQL_SUCCESS_WITH_INFO.)
08S01	Communication link failure	The communication link between the driver and the data source to which the driver was connected failed before the function completed processing.
24000	Invalid cursor state	A cursor was open on the *StatementHandle* and **SQLFetch** or **SQLFetchScroll** had been called. This error is returned by the Driver Manager if **SQLFetch** or **SQLFetchScroll** has not returned SQL_NO_DATA, and is returned by the driver if **SQLFetch** or **SQLFetchScroll** has returned SQL_NO_DATA. A cursor was open on the *StatementHandle* but **SQLFetch** or **SQLFetchScroll** had not been called.
40001	Serialization failure	The transaction was rolled back due to a resource deadlock with another transaction.

SQLSTATE	Error	Description
40003	Statement completion unknown	The associated connection failed during the execution of this function and the state of the transaction cannot be determined.
HY000	General error	An error occurred for which there was no specific SQLSTATE and for which no implementation-specific SQLSTATE was defined. The error message returned by **SQLGetDiagRec** in the **MessageText* buffer describes the error and its cause.
HY001	Memory allocation error	The driver was unable to allocate memory required to support execution or completion of the function.
HY008	Operation canceled	Asynchronous processing was enabled for the *StatementHandle*. The function was called and before it completed execution, **SQLCancel** was called on the *StatementHandle*, and then the function was called again on the *StatementHandle*. The function was called and, before it completed execution, **SQLCancel** was called on the *StatementHandle* from a different thread in a multithread application.
HY009	Invalid use of null pointer	(DM) The arguments *PKTableName* and *FKTableName* were both null pointers. (DM) The SQL_ATTR_METADATA_ID statement attribute was set to SQL_TRUE, the *FKCatalogName* or *PKCatalogName* argument was a null pointer, and the SQL_CATALOG_NAME *InfoType* returns that catalog names are supported. (DM) The SQL_ATTR_METADATA_ID statement attribute was set to SQL_TRUE, and the *FKSchemaName*, *PKSchemaName*, *FKTableName*, or *PKTableName* argument was a null pointer.
HY010	Function sequence error	(DM) An asynchronously executing function (not this one) was called for the *StatementHandle* and was still executing when this function was called. (DM) **SQLExecute**, **SQLExecDirect**, **SQLBulkOperations**, or **SQLSetPos** was called for the *StatementHandle* and returned SQL_NEED_DATA. This function was called before data was sent for all data-at-execution parameters or columns.

SQLSTATE	Error	Description
HY013	Memory management error	The function call could not be processed because the underlying memory objects could not be accessed, possibly because of low memory conditions.
HY090	Invalid string or buffer length	(DM) The value of one of the name length arguments was less than 0, but not equal to SQL_NTS. The value of one of the name length arguments exceeded the maximum length value for the corresponding name (see "Comments").
HYC00	Optional feature not implemented	A catalog name was specified and the driver or data source does not support catalogs. A schema name was specified and the driver or data source does not support schemas. The combination of the current settings of the SQL_ATTR_CONCURRENCY and SQL_ATTR_CURSOR_TYPE statement attributes was not supported by the driver or data source. The SQL_ATTR_USE_BOOKMARKS statement attribute was set to SQL_UB_VARIABLE, and the SQL_ATTR_CURSOR_TYPE statement attribute was set to a cursor type for which the driver does not support bookmarks.
HYT00	Timeout expired	The query timeout period expired before the data source returned the result set. The timeout period is set through **SQLSetStmtAttr**, SQL_ATTR_QUERY_TIMEOUT.
HYT01	Connection timeout expired	The connection timeout period expired before the data source responded to the request. The connection timeout period is set through **SQLSetConnectAttr**, SQL_ATTR_CONNECTION_TIMEOUT.
IM001	Driver does not support this function	(DM) The driver associated with the *StatementHandle* does not support the function.

Comments

For information how about the information returned by this function might be used, see "Uses of Catalog Data" in Chapter 7, "Catalog Functions."

If **PKTableName* contains a table name, **SQLForeignKeys** returns a result set containing the primary key of the specified table and all of the foreign keys that refer to it. The list of foreign keys in other tables does not include foreign keys that point to unique constraints in the specified table.

If **FKTableName* contains a table name, **SQLForeignKeys** returns a result set containing all of the foreign keys in the specified table that point to primary keys in others tables, and the primary keys in the other tables to which they refer. The list of foreign keys in the specified table does not contain foreign keys that refer to unique constraints in other tables.

If both **PKTableName* and **FKTableName* contain table names, **SQLForeignKeys** returns the foreign keys in the table specified in **FKTableName* that refer to the primary key of the table specified in **PKTableName*. This should be one key at most.

Note For more information about the general use, arguments, and returned data of ODBC catalog functions, see Chapter 7, "Catalog Functions."

SQLForeignKeys returns results as a standard result set. If the foreign keys associated with a primary key are requested, the result set is ordered by FKTABLE_CAT, FKTABLE_SCHEM, FKTABLE_NAME, and KEY_SEQ. If the primary keys associated with a foreign key are requested, the result set is ordered by PKTABLE_CAT, PKTABLE_SCHEM, PKTABLE_NAME, and KEY_SEQ. The following table lists the columns in the result set.

The lengths of VARCHAR columns are not shown in the table; the actual lengths depend on the data source. To determine the actual lengths of the PKTABLE_CAT or FKTABLE_CAT, PKTABLE_SCHEM or FKTABLE_SCHEM, PKTABLE_NAME or FKTABLE_NAME, and PKCOLUMN_NAME or FKCOLUMN_NAME columns, an application can call **SQLGetInfo** with the SQL_MAX_CATALOG_NAME_LEN, SQL_MAX_SCHEMA_NAME_LEN, SQL_MAX_TABLE_NAME_LEN, and SQL_MAX_COLUMN_NAME_LEN options.

The following columns have been renamed for ODBC 3.0. The column name changes do not affect backward compatibility because applications bind by column number.

ODBC 2.0 column	ODBC 3.0 column
PKTABLE_QUALIFIER	PKTABLE_CAT
PKTABLE_OWNER	PKTABLE_SCHEM
FKTABLE_QUALIFIER	FK_TABLE_CAT
FKTABLE_OWNER	FKTABLE_SCHEM

The following table lists the columns in the result set. Additional columns beyond column 17 (REMARKS) can be defined by the driver. An application should gain access to driver-specific columns by counting down from the end of the result set rather than specifying an explicit ordinal position. For more information, see "Data Returned by Catalog Functions" in Chapter 7, "Catalog Functions."

Column name	Column Number	Data type	Comments
PKTABLE_CAT (ODBC 1.0)	1	Varchar	Primary key table catalog name; NULL if not applicable to the data source. If a driver supports catalogs for some tables but not for others, such as when the driver retrieves data from different DBMSs, it returns an empty string ("") for those tables that do not have catalogs.
PKTABLE_SCHEM (ODBC 1.0)	2	Varchar	Primary key table schema name; NULL if not applicable to the data source. If a driver supports schemas for some tables but not for others, such as when the driver retrieves data from different DBMSs, it returns an empty string ("") for those tables that do not have schemas.
PKTABLE_NAME (ODBC 1.0)	3	Varchar not NULL	Primary key table name.
PKCOLUMN_NAME (ODBC 1.0)	4	Varchar not NULL	Primary key column name. The driver returns an empty string for a column that does not have a name.
FKTABLE_CAT (ODBC 1.0)	5	Varchar	Foreign key table catalog name; NULL if not applicable to the data source. If a driver supports catalogs for some tables but not for others, such as when the driver retrieves data from different DBMSs, it returns an empty string ("") for those tables that do not have catalogs.
FKTABLE_SCHEM (ODBC 1.0)	6	Varchar	Foreign key table schema name; NULL if not applicable to the data source. If a driver supports schemas for some tables but not for others, such as when the driver retrieves data from different DBMSs, it returns an empty string ("") for those tables that do not have schemas.
FKTABLE_NAME (ODBC 1.0)	7	Varchar not NULL	Foreign key table name.

Column name	Column Number	Data type	Comments
FKCOLUMN_NAME (ODBC 1.0)	8	Varchar not NULL	Foreign key column name. The driver returns an empty string for a column that does not have a name.
KEY_SEQ (ODBC 1.0)	9	Smallint not NULL	Column sequence number in key (starting with 1).
UPDATE_RULE (ODBC 1.0)	10	Smallint	Action to be applied to the foreign key when the SQL operation is **UPDATE**. Can have one of the following values. (The referenced table is the table that has the primary key; the referencing table is the table that has the foreign key): SQL_CASCADE: When the primary key of the referenced table is updated, the foreign key of the referencing table is also updated. SQL_NO_ACTION: If an update of the primary key of the referenced table would cause a "dangling reference" in the referencing table (that is, rows in the referencing table would have no counterparts in the referenced table), then the update is rejected. If an update of the foreign key of the referencing table would introduce a value that does not exist as a value of the primary key of the referenced table, then the update is rejected. (This action is the same as the SQL_RESTRICT action in ODBC 2.*x*.) SQL_SET_NULL: When one or more rows in the referenced table are updated such that one or more components of the primary key are changed, the components of the foreign key in the referencing table that correspond to the changed components of the primary key are set to NULL in all matching rows of the referencing table.

Column name	Column Number	Data type	Comments
UPDATE_RULE (ODBC 1.0) (*continued*)	10	Smallint	SQL_SET_DEFAULT: When one or more rows in the referenced table are updated such that one or more components of the primary key are changed, the components of the foreign key in the referencing table that correspond to the changed components of the primary key are set to the applicable default values in all matching rows of the referencing table. NULL if not applicable to the data source.
DELETE_RULE (ODBC 1.0)	11	Smallint	Action to be applied to the foreign key when the SQL operation is **DELETE**. Can have one of the following values (The referenced table is the table that has the primary key; the referencing table is the table that has the foreign key): SQL_CASCADE: When a row in the referenced table is deleted, all the matching rows in the referencing tables are also deleted. SQL_NO_ACTION: If a delete of a row in the referenced table would cause a "dangling reference" in the referencing table (that is, rows in the referencing table would have no counterparts in the referenced table), then the update is rejected. (This action is the same as the SQL_RESTRICT action in ODBC 2.*x*.)

DELETE_RULE (ODBC 1.0) (*continued*)	11	Smallint	SQL_SET_NULL: When one or more rows in the referenced table are deleted, each component of the foreign key of the referencing table is set to NULL in all matching rows of the referencing table. SQL_SET_DEFAULT: When one or more rows in the referenced table are deleted, each component of the foreign key of the referencing table is set to the applicable default in all matching rows of the referencing table. NULL if not applicable to the data source.
FK_NAME (ODBC 2.0)	12	Varchar	Foreign key name. NULL if not applicable to the data source.
PK_NAME (ODBC 2.0)	13	Varchar	Primary key name. NULL if not applicable to the data source.
DEFERRABILITY (ODBC 3.0)	14	Smallint	SQL_INITIALLY_DEFERRED: SQL_INITIALLY_IMMEDIATE: SQL_NOT_DEFERRABLE:

Code Example

This example uses three tables:

ORDERS	LINES	CUSTOMERS
ORDERID	ORDERID	CUSTID
CUSTID	LINES	NAME
OPENDATE	PARTID	ADDRESS
SALESPERSON	QUANTITY	PHONE
STATUS		

In the ORDERS table, CUSTID identifies the customer to whom the sale has been made. It is a foreign key that refers to CUSTID in the CUSTOMERS table.

In the LINES table, ORDERID identifies the sales order with which the line item is associated. It is a foreign key that refers to ORDERID in the ORDERS table.

This example calls **SQLPrimaryKeys** to get the primary key of the ORDERS table. The result set will have one row and the significant columns are:

TABLE_NAME	COLUMN_NAME	KEY_SEQ
ORDERS	ORDERID	1

Next, the example calls **SQLForeignKeys** to get the foreign keys in other tables that reference the primary key of the ORDERS table. The result set will have one row and the significant columns are:

PKTABLE_ NAME	PKCOLUMN_ NAME	FKTABLE_ NAME	FKCOLUMN_ NAME	KEY_SEQ
ORDERS	CUSTID	LINES	CUSTID	1

Finally, the example calls **SQLForeignKeys** to get the foreign keys in the ORDERS table that refer to the primary keys of other tables. The result set will have one row and the significant columns are:

PKTABLE_ NAME	PKCOLUMN_ NAME	FKTABLE_ NAME	FKCOLUMN_ NAME	KEY_SEQ
CUSTOMERS	CUSTID	ORDERS	CUSTID	1

```
#define TAB_LEN SQL_MAX_TABLE_NAME_LEN + 1
#define COL_LEN SQL_MAX_COLUMN_NAME_LEN + 1

LPSTR szTable;              /* Table to display      */

UCHAR szPkTable[TAB_LEN];   /* Primary key table name */
UCHAR szFkTable[TAB_LEN];   /* Foreign key table name */
UCHAR szPkCol[COL_LEN];     /* Primary key column     */
UCHAR szFkCol[COL_LEN];     /* Foreign key column     */

SQLHSTMT       hstmt;
SQLINTEGER     cbPkTable, cbPkCol, cbFkTable, cbFkCol, cbKeySeq;
SQLSMALLINT    iKeySeq;
SQLRETURN      retcode;

/* Bind the columns that describe the primary and foreign keys.  */
/* Ignore the table schema, name, and catalog for this example. */

SQLBindCol(hstmt, 3, SQL_C_CHAR, szPkTable, TAB_LEN, &cbPkTable);
SQLBindCol(hstmt, 4, SQL_C_CHAR, szPkCol, COL_LEN, &cbPkCol);
SQLBindCol(hstmt, 5, SQL_C_SSHORT, &iKeySeq, TAB_LEN, &cbKeySeq);
SQLBindCol(hstmt, 7, SQL_C_CHAR, szFkTable, TAB_LEN, &cbFkTable);
SQLBindCol(hstmt, 8, SQL_C_CHAR, szFkCol, COL_LEN, &cbFkCol);

strcpy(szTable, "ORDERS");

/* Get the names of the columns in the primary key.             */

retcode = SQLPrimaryKeys(hstmt,
                      NULL, 0,           /* Catalog name   */
                      NULL, 0,           /* Schema name       */
                      szTable, SQL_NTS); /* Table name        */
```

```
while ((retcode == SQL_SUCCESS) || (retcode == SQL SUCCESS_WITH_INFO)) {

   /* Fetch and display the result set. This will be a list of the */
   /* columns in the primary key of the ORDERS table.         */

   retcode = SQLFetch(hstmt);
   if (retcode == SQL_SUCCESS || retcode == SQL_SUCCESS_WITH_INFO)
      fprintf(out, "Table: %s    Column: %s    Key Seq: %hd \n", szPkTable, szPkCol,
              iKeySeq);
}

/* Close the cursor (the hstmt is still allocated).                */

SQLFreeStmt(hstmt, SQL_CLOSE);

/* Get all the foreign keys that refer to ORDERS primary key.*/

retcode = SQLForeignKeys(hstmt,
                         NULL, 0,            /* Primary catalog    */
                         NULL, 0,            /* Primary schema     */
                         szTable, SQL_NTS,   /* Primary table      */
                         NULL, 0,            /* Foreign catalog    */
                         NULL, 0,            /* Foreign schema     */
                         NULL, 0);           /* Foreign table      */

while ((retcode == SQL_SUCCESS) || (retcode == SQL_SUCCESS_WITH_INFO)) {

/* Fetch and display the result set. This will be all of the */
/* foreign keys in other tables that refer to the ORDERS   */
/* primary key.                                            */

   retcode = SQLFetch(hstmt);
   if (retcode == SQL_SUCCESS || retcode == SQL_SUCCESS_WITH_INFO)
      fprintf(out, "%-s ( %-s ) <-- %-s ( %-s )\n", szPkTable,
              szPkCol, szFkTable, szFkCol);
}

/* Close the cursor (the hstmt is still allocated). */

SQLFreeStmt(hstmt, SQL_CLOSE);

/* Get all the foreign keys in the ORDERS table. */

retcode = SQLForeignKeys(hstmt,
                         NULL, 0,            /* Primary catalog    */
                         NULL, 0,            /* Primary schema     */
                         NULL, 0,            /* Primary table      */
                         NULL, 0,            /* Foreign catalog    */
                         NULL, 0,            /* Foreign schema     */
                         szTable, SQL_NTS);  /* Foreign table      */
```

```
while ((retcode == SQL_SUCCESS) || (retcode == SQL_SUCCESS_WITH_INFO)) {

/* Fetch and display the result set. This will be all of the */
/* primary keys in other tables that are referred to by foreign */
/* keys in the ORDERS table.                                    */

   retcode = SQLFetch(hstmt);
   if (retcode == SQL_SUCCESS || retcode == SQL_SUCCESS_WITH_INFO)
      fprintf(out, "%-s ( %-s )--> %-s ( %-s )\n", szFkTable,
      szFkCol, szPkTable, szPkCol);
}

/* Free the hstmt. */

SQLFreeStmt(hstmt, SQL_DROP);
```

Related Functions

For information about	See
Binding a buffer to a column in a result set	**SQLBindCol**
Canceling statement processing	**SQLCancel**
Fetching a single row or a block of data in a forward-only direction	**SQLFetch**
Fetching a block of data or scrolling through a result set	**SQLFetchScroll**
Returning the columns of a primary key	**SQLPrimaryKeys**
Returning table statistics and indexes	**SQLStatistics**

SQLFreeConnect

Conformance

Version Introduced: ODBC 1.0
Standards Compliance: Deprecated

Summary

In ODBC 3.0, the ODBC 2.0 function **SQLFreeConnect** has been replaced by **SQLFreeHandle**. For more information, see **SQLFreeHandle**.

Note For more information about what the Driver Manager maps this function to when an ODBC 2.*x* application is working with an ODBC 3.0 driver, see "Mapping Deprecated Functions" in Appendix G, "Driver Guidelines for Backward Compatibility."

SQLFreeEnv

Conformance

Version Introduced: ODBC 1.0
Standards Compliance: Deprecated

Summary

In ODBC 3.0, the ODBC 2.0 function **SQLFreeEnv** has been replaced by **SQLFreeHandle**. For more information, see **SQLFreeHandle**.

Note For more information about what the Driver Manager maps this function to when an ODBC 2.*x* application is working with an ODBC 3.0 driver, see "Mapping Deprecated Functions" in Appendix G, "Driver Guidelines for Backward Compatibility."

SQLFreeHandle

Conformance

Version Introduced: ODBC 3.0
Standards Compliance: ISO 92

Summary

SQLFreeHandle frees resources associated with a specific environment, connection, statement, or descriptor handle.

Note This function is a generic function for freeing handles. It replaces the ODBC 2.0 functions **SQLFreeConnect** (for freeing a connection handle), and **SQLFreeEnv** (for freeing an environment handle). **SQLFreeConnect** and **SQLFreeEnv** are both deprecated in ODBC 3.0. **SQLFreeHandle** also replaces the ODBC 2.0 function **SQLFreeStmt** (with the SQL_DROP *Option*) for freeing a statement handle. For more information, see "Comments." For more information about what the Driver Manager maps this function to when an ODBC 3.0 application is working with an ODBC 2.*x* driver, see "Mapping Replacement Functions for Backward Compatibility of Applications" in Chapter 17, "Programming Considerations."

Syntax

SQLRETURN **SQLFreeHandle**(
    SQLSMALLINT *HandleType*,
    SQLHANDLE *Handle*);

Arguments

HandleType [Input]
The type of handle to be freed by **SQLFreeHandle**. Must be one of the following values:
SQL_HANDLE_ENV
SQL_HANDLE_DBC
SQL_HANDLE_STMT
SQL_HANDLE_DESC

If *HandleType* is not one of these values, **SQLFreeHandle** returns SQL_INVALID_HANDLE.

Handle [Input]
The handle to be freed.

Returns

SQL_SUCCESS, SQL_ERROR, or SQL_INVALID_HANDLE.

If **SQLFreeHandle** returns SQL_ERROR, the handle is still valid.

Diagnostics

When **SQLFreeHandle** returns SQL_ERROR, an associated SQLSTATE value may be obtained from the diagnostic data structure for the handle that **SQLFreeHandle** attempted to free, but could not. The following table lists the SQLSTATE values commonly returned by **SQLFreeHandle** and explains each one in the context of this function; the notation "(DM)" precedes the descriptions of SQLSTATEs returned by the Driver Manager. The return code associated with each SQLSTATE value is SQL_ERROR, unless noted otherwise.

SQLSTATE	Error	Description
HY000	General error	An error occurred for which there was no specific SQLSTATE and for which no implementation-specific SQLSTATE was defined. The error message returned by **SQLGetDiagRec** in the **MessageText* buffer describes the error and its cause.
HY001	Memory allocation error	The driver was unable to allocate memory required to support execution or completion of the function.
HY010	Function sequence error	(DM) The *HandleType* argument was SQL_HANDLE_ENV, and at least one connection was in an allocated or connected state. **SQLDisconnect** and **SQLFreeHandle** with a *HandleType* of SQL_HANDLE_DBC must be called for each connection before calling **SQLFreeHandle** with a *HandleType* of SQL_HANDLE_ENV.
		(DM) The *HandleType* argument was SQL_HANDLE_DBC, and the function was called before calling **SQLDisconnect** for the connection.
		(DM) The *HandleType* argument was SQL_HANDLE_STMT; an asynchronously executing function was called on the statement handle; and the function was still executing when this function was called.
		(DM) The *HandleType* argument was SQL_HANDLE_STMT; **SQLExecute**, **SQLExecDirect**, **SQLBulkOperations**, or **SQLSetPos** was called with the statement handle, and returned SQL_NEED_DATA. This function was called before data was sent for all data-at-execution parameters or columns.
		(DM) All subsidiary handles and other resources were not released before **SQLFreeHandle** was called.

SQLSTATE	Error	Description
HY013	Memory management error	The *HandleType* argument was SQL_HANDLE_STMT or SQL_HANDLE_DESC, and the function call could not be processed because the underlying memory objects could not be accessed, possibly because of low memory conditions.
HY017	Invalid use of an automatically allocated descriptor handle.	(DM) The *Handle* argument was set to the handle for an automatically allocated descriptor.
HYT01	Connection timeout expired	The connection timeout period expired before the data source responded to the request. The connection timeout period is set through **SQLSetConnectAttr**, SQL_ATTR_CONNECTION_TIMEOUT.
IM001	Driver does not support this function	(DM) The *HandleType* argument was SQL_HANDLE_DESC, and the driver was an ODBC 2.*x* driver. (DM) The *HandleType* argument was SQL_HANDLE_STMT, and the driver was not a valid ODBC driver.

Comments

SQLFreeHandle is used to free handles for environments, connections, statements, and descriptors, as described in the following sections. For general information about handles, see "Handles" in Chapter 4, "ODBC Fundamentals."

An application should not use a handle after it has been freed; the Driver Manager does not check the validity of a handle in a function call.

Freeing an Environment Handle

Prior to calling **SQLFreeHandle** with a *HandleType* of SQL_HANDLE_ENV, an application must call **SQLFreeHandle** with a *HandleType* of SQL_HANDLE_DBC for all connections allocated under the environment. Otherwise, the call to **SQLFreeHandle** returns SQL_ERROR and the environment and any active connection remains valid. For more information, see "Environment Handles" in Chapter 4, "ODBC Fundamentals" and "Allocating the Environment Handle" in Chapter 6, "Connecting to a Data Source or Driver."

When the Driver Manager processes the call to **SQLFreeHandle** with a *HandleType* of SQL_HANDLE_ENV, it checks the **TraceAutoStop** keyword in the [ODBC] section of the ODBC subkey of the system information. If it is set to 1, the Driver Manager disables tracing for all applications and sets the **Trace** keyword in the [ODBC] section of the ODBC subkey of the system information to 0. For information on what happens to tracing when **SQLFreeHandle** is called, see "ODBC Subkey" in Chapter 19, "Configuring Data Sources."

If the environment is a shared environment, the application that calls **SQLFreeHandle** with a *HandleType* of SQL_HANDLE_ENV no longer has access to the environment after the call, but the environment's resources are not necessarily freed. The call to **SQLFreeHandle** decrements the environment's reference count, which is maintained by the Driver Manager. If the reference count does not reach zero, the shared environment is not freed, because it is still being used by another component. If the reference count reaches zero, the shared environment's resources are freed.

Freeing a Connection Handle

Prior to calling **SQLFreeHandle** with a *HandleType* of SQL_HANDLE_DBC, an application must call **SQLDisconnect** for the connection if there is a connection on this handle. Otherwise, the call to **SQLFreeHandle** returns SQL_ERROR and the connection remains valid.

For more information, see "Connection Handles" in Chapter 4, "ODBC Fundamentals" and "Disconnecting from a Data Source or Driver" in Chapter 6, "Connecting to a Data Source or Driver."

Freeing a Statement Handle

A call to **SQLFreeHandle** with a *HandleType* of SQL_HANDLE_STMT frees all resources that were allocated by a call to **SQLAllocHandle** with a *HandleType* of SQL_HANDLE_STMT. When an application calls **SQLFreeHandle** to free a statement that has pending results, the pending results are deleted. When an application frees a statement handle, the driver frees the four automatically allocated descriptors associated with that handle. For more information, see "Statement Handles" in Chapter 4, "ODBC Fundamentals" and "Freeing a Statement Handle" in Chapter 9, "Executing Statements."

Note that **SQLDisconnect** automatically drops any statements and descriptors open on the connection.

Freeing a Descriptor Handle

A call to **SQLFreeHandle** with a *HandleType* of SQL_HANDLE_DESC frees the descriptor handle in *Handle*. The call to **SQLFreeHandle** does not release any memory allocated by the application that may be referenced by a pointer field (including SQL_DESC_DATA_PTR, SQL_DESC_INDICATOR_PTR, and SQL_DESC_OCTET_LENGTH_PTR) of any descriptor record of *Handle*. The memory allocated by the driver for fields that are not pointer fields is freed when the handle is freed. When a user-allocated descriptor handle is freed, all statements that the freed handle had been associated with revert to their respective automatically allocated descriptor handle.

Note ODBC 2.*x* drivers do not support freeing descriptor handles, just as they do not support allocating descriptor handles.

Note that **SQLDisconnect** automatically drops any statements and descriptors open on the connection. When an application frees a statement handle, the driver frees all the automatically generated descriptors associated with that handle.

For more information about descriptors, see Chapter 13, "Descriptors."

Code Example

See **SQLBrowseConnect** and **SQLConnect**.

Related Functions

For information about	See
Allocating a handle	**SQLAllocHandle**
Canceling statement processing	**SQLCancel**
Setting a cursor name	**SQLSetCursorName**

SQLFreeStmt

Conformance

Version Introduced:	ODBC 1.0
Standards Compliance:	ISO 92

Summary

SQLFreeStmt stops processing associated with a specific statement, closes any open cursors associated with the statement, discards pending results, or, optionally, frees all resources associated with the statement handle.

Syntax

```
SQLRETURN SQLFreeStmt(
      SQLHSTMT          StatementHandle,
      SQLUSMALLINT      Option);
```

Arguments

StatementHandle [Input]
Statement handle

Option [Input]
One of the following options:

SQL_ CLOSE: Closes the cursor associated with *StatementHandle* (if one was defined) and discards all pending results. The application can reopen this cursor later by executing a **SELECT** statement again with the same or different parameter values. If no cursor is open, this option has no effect for the application. **SQLCloseCursor** can also be called to close a cursor. For more information, see "Closing the Cursor" in Chapter 10, "Retrieving Results (Basic)."

SQL_DROP: This option is deprecated. A call to **SQLFreeStmt** with an *Option* of SQL_DROP is mapped in the Driver Manager to **SQLFreeHandle**.

SQL_UNBIND: Sets the SQL_DESC_COUNT field of the ARD to 0, releasing all column buffers bound by **SQLBindCol** for the given *StatementHandle*. This does not unbind the bookmark column; to do that, the SQL_DESC_DATA_PTR field of the ARD for the bookmark column is set to NULL. Note that if this operation is performed on an explicitly allocated descriptor that is shared by more than one statement, the operation will affect the bindings of all statements that share the descriptor. For more information, see "Overview" in Chapter 10, "Retrieving Results (Basic)."

SQL_RESET_PARAMS: Sets the SQL_DESC_COUNT field of the APD to 0, releasing all parameter buffers set by **SQLBindParameter** for the given *StatementHandle*. Note that if this operation is performed on an explicitly allocated descriptor that is shared by more than one statement, this operation will affect the bindings of all the statements that share the descriptor. For more information, see "Binding Parameters" in Chapter 9, "Executing Statements."

Returns

SQL_SUCCESS, SQL_SUCCESS_WITH_INFO, SQL_ERROR, or SQL_INVALID_HANDLE.

Diagnostics

When **SQLFreeStmt** returns SQL_ERROR or SQL_SUCCESS_WITH_INFO, an associated SQLSTATE value may be obtained by calling **SQLGetDiagRec** with a *HandleType* of SQL_HANDLE_STMT and a *Handle* of *StatementHandle*. The following table lists the SQLSTATE values commonly returned by **SQLFreeStmt** and explains each one in the context of this function; the notation "(DM)" precedes the descriptions of SQLSTATEs returned by the Driver Manager. The return code associated with each SQLSTATE value is SQL_ERROR, unless noted otherwise.

SQLSTATE	Error	Description
01000	General warning	Driver-specific informational message. (Function returns SQL_SUCCESS_WITH_INFO.)
HY000	General error	An error occurred for which there was no specific SQLSTATE and for which no implementation-specific SQLSTATE was defined. The error message returned by **SQLGetDiagRec** in the **MessageText* buffer describes the error and its cause.
HY001	Memory allocation error	The driver was unable to allocate memory required to support execution or completion of the function.
HY010	Function sequence error	(DM) An asynchronously executing function was called for the *StatementHandle* and was still executing when this function was called. (DM) **SQLExecute**, **SQLExecDirect**, **SQLBulkOperations**, or **SQLSetPos** was called for the *StatementHandle* and returned SQL_NEED_DATA. This function was called before data was sent for all data-at-execution parameters or columns.
HY013	Memory management error	The function call could not be processed because the underlying memory objects could not be accessed, possibly because of low memory conditions.
HY092	Option type out of range	(DM) The value specified for the argument *Option* was not: SQL_CLOSE SQL_DROP SQL_UNBIND SQL_RESET_PARAMS

SQLSTATE	Error	Description
HYT01	Connection timeout expired	The connection timeout period expired before the data source responded to the request. The connection timeout period is set through **SQLSetConnectAttr**, SQL_ATTR_CONNECTION_TIMEOUT.
IM001	Driver does not support this function	(DM) The driver associated with the *StatementHandle* does not support the function.

Comments

Calling **SQLFreeStmt** with the SQL_CLOSE option is equivalent to calling **SQLCloseCursor**, with the exception that **SQLFreeStmt** with SQL_CLOSE has no effect on the application if no cursor is open on the statement. If no cursor is open, a call to **SQLCloseCursor** returns SQLSTATE 24000 (Invalid cursor state).

An application should not use a statement handle after it has been freed; the Driver Manager does not check the validity of a handle in a function call.

Code Example

See **SQLBrowseConnect** and **SQLConnect**.

Related Functions

For information about	See
Allocating a handle	**SQLAllocHandle**
Canceling statement processing	**SQLCancel**
Closing a cursor	**SQLCloseCursor**
Freeing a handle	**SQLFreeHandle**
Setting a cursor name	**SQLSetCursorName**

SQLGetConnectAttr

Conformance

Version Introduced: ODBC 3.0
Standards Compliance: ISO 92

Summary

SQLGetConnectAttr returns the current setting of a connection attribute.

Note For more information about what the Driver Manager maps this function to when an ODBC 3.0 application is working with an ODBC 2.*x* driver, see "Mapping Replacement Functions for Backward Compatibility of Applications" in Chapter 17, "Programming Considerations."

Syntax

```
SQLRETURN SQLGetConnectAttr(
     SQLHDBC       ConnectionHandle,
     SQLINTEGER    Attribute,
     SQLPOINTER    ValuePtr,
     SQLINTEGER    BufferLength,
     SQLINTEGER *  StringLengthPtr);
```

Arguments

ConnectionHandle [Input]
Connection handle.

Attribute [Input]
Attribute to retrieve.

ValuePtr [Output]
A pointer to memory in which to return the current value of the attribute specified by *Attribute*.

BufferLength [Input]
If *Attribute* is an ODBC-defined attribute and *ValuePtr* points to a character string or a binary buffer, this argument should be the length of **ValuePtr*. If *Attribute* is an ODBC-defined attribute and **ValuePtr* is an integer, *BufferLength* is ignored.

If *Attribute* is a driver-defined attribute, the application indicates the nature of the attribute to the Driver Manager by setting the *BufferLength* argument. *BufferLength* can have the following values:

- If **ValuePtr* is a pointer to a character string, then *BufferLength* is the length of the string or SQL_NTS.
- If **ValuePtr* is a pointer to a binary buffer, then the application places the result of the SQL_LEN_BINARY_ATTR(*length*) macro in *BufferLength*. This places a negative value in *BufferLength*.
- If **ValuePtr* is a pointer to a value other than a character string or binary string, then *BufferLength* should have the value SQL_IS_POINTER.
- If **ValuePtr* contains a fixed-length data type, then *BufferLength* is either SQL_IS_INTEGER or SQL_IS_UINTEGER, as appropriate.

StringLengthPtr [Output]
A pointer to a buffer in which to return the total number of bytes (excluding the null-termination character) available to return in **ValuePtr*. If *ValuePtr* is a null pointer, no length is returned. If the attribute value is a character string, and the number of bytes available to return is greater than *BufferLength* minus the length of the null-termination character, the data in **ValuePtr* is truncated to *BufferLength* minus the length of the null-termination character and is null-terminated by the driver.

Returns

SQL_SUCCESS, SQL_SUCCESS_WITH_INFO, SQL_NO_DATA, SQL_ERROR, or SQL_INVALID_HANDLE.

Diagnostics

When **SQLGetConnectAttr** returns SQL_ERROR or SQL_SUCCESS_WITH_INFO, an associated SQLSTATE value may be obtained from the diagnostic data structure by calling **SQLGetDiagRec** with a *HandleType* of SQL_HANDLE_DBC and a *Handle* of *ConnectionHandle*. The following table lists the SQLSTATE values commonly returned by **SQLGetConnectAttr** and explains each one in the context of this function; the notation "(DM)" precedes the descriptions of SQLSTATEs returned by the Driver Manager. The return code associated with each SQLSTATE value is SQL_ERROR, unless noted otherwise.

SQLSTATE	Error	Description
01000	General warning	Driver-specific informational message. (Function returns SQL_SUCCESS_WITH_INFO.)
01004	String data, right truncated	The data returned in **ValuePtr* was truncated to be *BufferLength* minus the length of a null-termination character. The length of the untruncated string value is returned in **StringLengthPtr*. (Function returns SQL_SUCCESS_WITH_INFO.)
08003	Connection does not exist	(DM) An *Attribute* value was specified that required an open connection.
08S01	Communication link failure	The communication link between the driver and the data source to which the driver was connected failed before the function completed processing.
HY000	General error	An error occurred for which there was no specific SQLSTATE and for which no implementation-specific SQLSTATE was defined. The error message returned from the diagnostic data structure by the argument *MessageText* in **SQLGetDiagField** describes the error and its cause.
HY001	Memory allocation error	The driver was unable to allocate memory required to support execution or completion of the function.
HY010	Function sequence error	(DM) **SQLBrowseConnect** was called for the *ConnectionHandle* and returned SQL_NEED_DATA. This function was called before **SQLBrowseConnect** returned SQL_SUCCESS_WITH_INFO or SQL_SUCCESS.
HY013	Memory management error	The function call could not be processed because the underlying memory objects could not be accessed, possibly because of low memory conditions.
HY090	Invalid string or buffer length	*(DM) *ValuePtr* is a character string, and BufferLength was less than zero, but not equal to SQL_NTS.
HY092	Invalid attribute/option identifier	The value specified for the argument *Attribute* was not valid for the version of ODBC supported by the driver.
HYC00	Optional feature not implemented	The value specified for the argument *Attribute* was a valid ODBC connection attribute for the version of ODBC supported by the driver, but was not supported by the driver.

SQLSTATE	Error	Description
HYT01	Connection timeout expired	The connection timeout period expired before the data source responded to the request. The connection timeout period is set through **SQLSetConnectAttr**, SQL_ATTR_CONNECTION_TIMEOUT.
IM001	Driver does not support this function	(DM) The driver corresponding to the *ConnectionHandle* does not support the function.

Comments

For general information about connection attributes, see "Connection Attributes" in Chapter 6, "Connecting to a Data Source or Driver."

For a list of attributes that can be set, see SQLSetConnectAttr. Note that if *Attribute* specifies an attribute that returns a string, *ValuePtr* must be a pointer to a buffer for the string. The maximum length of the returned string, including the null-termination character, will be *BufferLength* bytes.

Depending on the attribute, an application does not need to establish a connection prior to calling **SQLGetConnectAttr**. However, if **SQLGetConnectAttr** is called and the specified attribute does not have a default and has not been set by a prior call to **SQLSetConnectAttr**, **SQLGetConnectAttr** will return SQL_NO_DATA.

If *Attribute* is SQL_ATTR_ TRACE or SQL_ATTR_ TRACEFILE, *ConnectionHandle* does not have to be valid, and **SQLGetConnectAttr** will not return SQL_ERROR or SQL_INVALID_HANDLE if *ConnectionHandle* is invalid. These attributes apply to all connections. **SQLGetConnectAttr** will return SQL_ERROR or SQL_INVALID_HANDLE if another argument is invalid.

While an application can set statement attributes using **SQLSetConnectAttr**, an application cannot use **SQLGetConnectAttr** to retrieve statement attribute values; it must call **SQLGetStmtAttr** to retrieve the setting of statement attributes.

The SQL_ATTR_AUTO_IPD connection attribute can be returned by a call to **SQLGetConnectAttr**, but cannot be set by a call to **SQLSetConnectAttr**.

Related Functions

For information about	See
Returning the setting of a statement attribute	**SQLGetStmtAttr**
Setting a connection attribute	**SQLSetConnectAttr**
Setting an environment attribute	**SQLSetEnvAttr**
Setting a statement attribute	**SQLSetStmtAttr**

SQLGetConnectOption

Conformance

Version Introduced: ODBC 1.0
Standards Compliance: Deprecated

Summary

In ODBC 3.0, the ODBC 2.*x* function **SQLGetConnectOption** has been replaced by **SQLGetConnectAttr**. For more information, see **SQLGetConnectAttr**.

Note For more information about what the Driver Manager maps this function to when an ODBC 2.*x* application is working with an ODBC 3.0 driver, see "Mapping Deprecated Functions" in Appendix G, "Driver Guidelines for Backward Compatibility."

SQLGetCursorName

Conformance

Version Introduced:	ODBC 1.0
Standards Compliance:	ISO 92

Summary

SQLGetCursorName returns the cursor name associated with a specified statement.

Syntax

SQLRETURN **SQLGetCursorName**(
SQLHSTMT *StatementHandle*,
SQLCHAR * *CursorName*,
SQLSMALLINT *BufferLength*,
SQLSMALLINT * *NameLengthPtr*);

Arguments

StatementHandle [Input]
Statement handle.

CursorName [Output]
Pointer to a buffer in which to return the cursor name.

BufferLength [Input]
Length of **CursorName*, in bytes.

NameLengthPtr [Output]
Pointer to memory in which to return the total number of bytes (excluding the null-termination character) available to return in **CursorName*. If the number of bytes available to return is greater than or equal to *BufferLength*, the cursor name in **CursorName* is truncated to *BufferLength* minus the length of a null-termination character.

Returns

SQL_SUCCESS, SQL_SUCCESS_WITH_INFO, SQL_ERROR, or SQL_INVALID_HANDLE.

Diagnostics

When **SQLGetCursorName** returns either SQL_ERROR or SQL_SUCCESS_WITH_INFO, an associated SQLSTATE value may be obtained by calling **SQLGetDiagRec** with a *HandleType* of SQL_HANDLE_STMT and a *Handle* of *StatementHandle*. The following table lists the SQLSTATE values commonly returned by **SQLGetCursorName** and explains each one in the context of this function; the notation "(DM)" precedes the descriptions of SQLSTATEs returned by the Driver Manager. The return code associated with each SQLSTATE value is SQL_ERROR, unless noted otherwise.

SQLSTATE	Error	Description
01000	General warning	Driver-specific informational message. (Function returns SQL_SUCCESS_WITH_INFO.)
01004	String data, right truncated	The buffer **CursorName* was not large enough to return the entire cursor name, so the cursor name was truncated. The length of the untruncated cursor name is returned in **NameLengthPtr*. (Function returns SQL_SUCCESS_WITH_INFO.)
HY000	General error	An error occurred for which there was no specific SQLSTATE and for which no implementation-specific SQLSTATE was defined. The error message returned by **SQLGetDiagRec** in the **MessageText* buffer describes the error and its cause.
HY001	Memory allocation error	The driver was unable to allocate memory required to support execution or completion of the function.
HY010	Function sequence error	(DM) An asynchronously executing function was called for the *StatementHandle* and was still executing when this function was called. (DM) **SQLExecute**, **SQLExecDirect**, **SQLBulkOperations**, or **SQLSetPos** was called for the *StatementHandle* and returned SQL_NEED_DATA. This function was called before data was sent for all data-at-execution parameters or columns.
HY013	Memory management error	The function call could not be processed because the underlying memory objects could not be accessed, possibly because of low memory conditions.
HY015	No cursor name available	(DM) The driver was an ODBC 2.*x* driver, there was no open cursor on the statement, and no cursor name had been set with **SQLSetCursorName**.
HY090	Invalid string or buffer length	(DM) The value specified in the argument *BufferLength* was less than 0.
HYT01	Connection timeout expired	The connection timeout period expired before the data source responded to the request. The connection timeout period is set through **SQLSetConnectAttr**, SQL_ATTR_CONNECTION_TIMEOUT.
IM001	Driver does not support this function	(DM) The driver associated with the *StatementHandle* does not support the function.

Comments

Cursor names are used only in positioned update and delete statements (for example, **UPDATE** *table-name* ...**WHERE CURRENT OF** *cursor-name*). For more information, see "Positioned Update and Delete Statements" in Chapter 12, "Updating Data." If the application does not call **SQLSetCursorName** to define a cursor name, the driver generates a name. This name begins with the letters SQL_CUR.

Note In ODBC 2.*x*, when there was no open cursor, and no name had been set by a call to **SQLSetCursorName**, a call to **SQLGetCursorName** returned SQLSTATE HY015 (No cursor name available). In ODBC 3.0, this is no longer true; regardless of when **SQLGetCursorName** is called, the driver returns the cursor name.

SQLGetCursorName returns the name of a cursor regardless of whether the name was created explicitly or implicitly. A cursor name is implicitly generated if **SQLSetCursorName** is not called. **SQLSetCursorName** can be called to rename a cursor on a statement as long as the cursor is in an allocated or prepared state.

A cursor name that is set either explicitly or implicitly remains set until the *StatementHandle* with which it is associated is dropped, using **SQLFreeHandle** with a *HandleType* of SQL_HANDLE_STMT.

Related Functions

For information about	See
Executing an SQL statement	**SQLExecDirect**
Executing a prepared SQL statement	**SQLExecute**
Preparing a statement for execution	**SQLPrepare**
Setting a cursor name	**SQLSetCursorName**

SQLGetData

Conformance

Version Introduced: ODBC 1.0
Standards Compliance: ISO 92

Summary

SQLGetData retrieves data for a single column in the result set. It can be called multiple times to retrieve variable-length data in parts.

Syntax

SQLRETURN **SQLGetData**(
SQLHSTMT *StatementHandle*,
SQLUSMALLINT *ColumnNumber*,
SQLSMALLINT *TargetType*,
SQLPOINTER *TargetValuePtr*,
SQLINTEGER *BufferLength*,
SQLINTEGER * *StrLen_or_IndPtr*);

Arguments

StatementHandle [Input]
Statement handle.

ColumnNumber [Input]
Number of the column for which to return data. Result set columns are numbered in increasing column order starting at 1. The bookmark column is column number 0; this can be specified only if bookmarks are enabled.

TargetType [Input]
The type identifier of the C data type of the **TargetValuePtr* buffer. For a list of valid C data types and type identifiers, see the "C Data Types" section in Appendix D, "Data Types." If *TargetType* is SQL_ARD_TYPE, the driver uses the type identifier specified in the SQL_DESC_CONCISE_TYPE field of the ARD. If it is SQL_C_DEFAULT, the driver selects the default C data type based upon the SQL data type of the source.

TargetValuePtr [Output]
Pointer to the buffer in which to return the data.

BufferLength [Input]
Length of the **TargetValuePtr* buffer in bytes.

The driver uses *BufferLength* to avoid writing past the end of the **TargetValuePtr* buffer when returning variable-length data, such as character or binary data. Note that the driver counts the null-termination character when returning character data to **TargetValuePtr*. **TargetValuePtr* must therefore contain space for the null-termination character or the driver will truncate the data.

When the driver returns fixed-length data, such as an integer or a date structure, the driver ignores *BufferLength* and assumes the buffer is large enough to hold the data. It is therefore important for the application to allocate a large enough buffer for fixed-length data or the driver will write past the end of the buffer.

SQLGetData returns SQLSTATE HY090 (Invalid string or buffer length) when *BufferLength* is less than 0 but not when *BufferLength* is 0. However, if *TargetType* specifies a character type, an application should not set *BufferLength* to 0, because ISO CLI–compliant drivers return SQLSTATE HY090 (Invalid string or buffer length) in that case.

If *TargetValuePtr* is set to a null pointer, *BufferLength* is ignored by the driver.

StrLen_or_IndPtr [Output]
Pointer to the buffer in which to return the length or indicator value. If this is a null pointer, no length or indicator value is returned. This returns an error when the data being fetched is NULL.

SQLGetData can return the following values in the length/indicator buffer:

- The length of the data available to return
- SQL_NO_TOTAL
- SQL_NULL_DATA

For more information, see the "Using Length/Indicator Values" section in Chapter 4, "ODBC Fundamentals" and "Comments" in this section.

Returns

SQL_SUCCESS, SQL_SUCCESS_WITH_INFO, SQL_NO_DATA, SQL_STILL_EXECUTING, SQL_ERROR, or SQL_INVALID_HANDLE.

Diagnostics

When **SQLGetData** returns either SQL_ERROR or SQL_SUCCESS_WITH_INFO, an associated SQLSTATE value can be obtained by calling **SQLGetDiagRec** with a *HandleType* of SQL_HANDLE_STMT and a *Handle* of *StatementHandle*. The following table lists the SQLSTATE values commonly returned by **SQLGetData** and explains each one in the context of this function; the notation "(DM)" precedes the descriptions of SQLSTATEs returned by the Driver Manager. The return code associated with each SQLSTATE value is SQL_ERROR, unless noted otherwise.

SQLSTATE	Error	Description
01000	General warning	Driver-specific informational message. (Function returns SQL_SUCCESS_WITH_INFO.)
01004	String data, right truncated	Not all of the data for the specified column, *ColumnNumber*, could be retrieved in a single call to the function. The length of the data remaining in the specified column prior to the current call to **SQLGetData** is returned in **StrLen_or_IndPtr*. (Function returns SQL_SUCCESS_WITH_INFO.) The *TargetValuePtr* argument was a null pointer and more data was available to return. (Function returns SQL_SUCCESS_WITH_INFO.) For more information on using multiple calls to **SQLGetData** for a single column, see "Comments."
01S07	Fractional truncation	The data returned for one or more columns was truncated. For numeric data types, the fractional part of the number was truncated. For time, timestamp, and interval data types containing a time component, the fractional portion of the time was truncated. (Function returns SQL_SUCCESS_WITH_INFO.)
07006	Restricted data type attribute violation	The data value of a column in the result set cannot be converted to the C data type specified by the argument *TargetType*.
07009	Invalid descriptor index	The value specified for the argument *ColumnNumber* was 0 and the SQL_ATTR_USE_BOOKMARKS statement attribute was set to SQL_UB_OFF. The value specified for the argument *ColumnNumber* was greater than the number of columns in the result set. (DM) The specified column was bound. This description does not apply to drivers that return the SQL_GD_BOUND bitmask for the SQL_GETDATA_EXTENSIONS option in **SQLGetInfo**. (DM) The number of the specified column was less than or equal to the number of the highest bound column. This description does not apply to drivers that return the SQL_GD_ANY_COLUMN bitmask for the SQL_GETDATA_EXTENSIONS option in **SQLGetInfo**.

SQLSTATE	Error	Description
07009 (*continued*)	Invalid descriptor index	(DM) The application has already called **SQLGetData** for the current row; the number of the column specified in the current call was less than the number of the column specified in the preceding call; and the driver does not return the SQL_GD_ANY_ORDER bitmask for the SQL_GETDATA_EXTENSIONS option in **SQLGetInfo**. (DM) The *TargetType* argument was SQL_ARD_TYPE and the *ColumnNumber* descriptor record in the ARD failed the consistency check. (DM) The *TargetType* argument was SQL_ARD_TYPE and the value in the SQL_DESC_COUNT field of the ARD was less than the *ColumnNumber* argument.
08S01	Communication link failure	The communication link between the driver and the data source to which the driver was connected failed before the function completed processing.
22002	Indicator variable required but not supplied	*StrLen_or_IndPtr* was a null pointer and NULL data was retrieved.
22003	Numeric value out of range	Returning the numeric value (as numeric or string) for the column would have caused the whole (as opposed to fractional) part of the number to be truncated. For more information, see Appendix D, "Data Types."
22007	Invalid datetime format	The character column in the result set was bound to a C date, time, or timestamp structure, and the value in the column was an invalid date, time, or timestamp, respectively. For more information, see Appendix D, "Data Types."
22012	Division by zero	A value from an arithmetic expression that resulted in division by zero was returned.
22015	Interval field overflow	Assigning from an exact numeric or interval SQL type to an interval C type caused a loss of significant digits in the leading field. When returning data to an interval C type, there was no representation of the value of the SQL type in the interval C type.

SQLSTATE	Error	Description
22018	Invalid character value for cast specification	A character column in the result set was returned to a character C buffer and the column contained a character for which there was no representation in the character set of the buffer. The C type was an exact or approximate numeric, a datetime, or an interval data type; the SQL type of the column was a character data type; and the value in the column was not a valid literal of the bound C type.
24000	Invalid cursor state	(DM) The *StatementHandle* was in an executed state but no result set was associated with the *StatementHandle*. A cursor was open on the *StatementHandle* and **SQLFetch** or **SQLFetchScroll** had been called, but the cursor was positioned before the start of the result set or after the end of the result set.
HY000	General error	An error occurred for which there was no specific SQLSTATE and for which no implementation-specific SQLSTATE was defined. The error message returned by **SQLGetDiagRec** in the *MessageText* buffer describes the error and its cause.
HY001	Memory allocation error	The driver was unable to allocate memory required to support execution or completion of the function.
HY003	Invalid application buffer type	(DM) The argument *TargetType* was neither a valid data type, SQL_C_DEFAULT, nor SQL_ARD_TYPE. (DM) The argument *ColumnNumber* was 0 and the argument *TargetType* was not SQL_C_BOOKMARK for a fixed-length bookmark or SQL_C_VARBOOKMARK for a variable-length bookmark.
HY008	Operation canceled	Asynchronous processing was enabled for the *StatementHandle*. The function was called and before it completed execution, **SQLCancel** was called on the *StatementHandle*, and then the function was called again on the *StatementHandle*. The function was called and, before it completed execution, **SQLCancel** was called on the *StatementHandle* from a different thread in a multithread application, and then the function was called again on the *StatementHandle*.

SQLSTATE	Error	Description
HY010	Function sequence error	(DM) The specified *StatementHandle* was not in an executed state. The function was called without first calling **SQLExecDirect**, **SQLExecute**, or a catalog function. (DM) An asynchronously executing function (not this one) was called for the *StatementHandle* and was still executing when this function was called. (DM) **SQLExecute**, **SQLExecDirect**, **SQLBulkOperations**, or **SQLSetPos** was called for the *StatementHandle* and returned SQL_NEED_DATA. This function was called before data was sent for all data-at-execution parameters or columns. (DM) The function was called without first calling **SQLFetch** or **SQLFetchScroll** to position the cursor on the row of data required. (DM) The *StatementHandle* was in an executed state but no result set was associated with the *StatementHandle*.
HY013	Memory management error	The function call could not be processed because the underlying memory objects could not be accessed, possibly because of low memory conditions.
HY090	Invalid string or buffer length	(DM) The value specified for argument *BufferLength* was less than 0. The value specified for argument *BufferLength* was less than 4, the *ColumnNumber* argument was set to 0, and the driver was an ODBC 2.*x* driver.
HY109	Invalid cursor position	The cursor was positioned (by **SQLSetPos**, **SQLFetch**, **SQLFetchScroll**, or **SQLBulkOperations**) on a row that had been deleted or could not be fetched. The cursor was a forward-only cursor and the rowset size was greater than one.

SQLSTATE	Error	Description
HYC00	Optional feature not implemented	The driver or data source does not support use of **SQLGetData** with multiple rows in **SQLFetchScroll**. This description does not apply to drivers that return the SQL_GD_BLOCK bitmask for the SQL_GETDATA_EXTENSIONS option in **SQLGetInfo**. The driver or data source does not support the conversion specified by the combination of the *TargetType* argument and the SQL data type of the corresponding column. This error applies only when the SQL data type of the column was mapped to a driver-specific SQL data type. The driver only supports ODBC 2.*x* and the argument *TargetType* was one of the following: SQL_C_NUMERIC SQL_C_SBIGINT SQL_C_UBIGINT and any of the interval C data types listed in "C Data Types" in Appendix D, "Data Types."
HYT01	Connection timeout expired	The connection timeout period expired before the data source responded to the request. The connection timeout period is set through **SQLSetConnectAttr**, SQL_ATTR_CONNECTION_TIMEOUT.
IM001	Driver does not support this function	(DM) The driver corresponding to the *StatementHandle* does not support the function.

Comments

SQLGetData returns the data in a specified column. **SQLGetData** can only be called after one or more rows have been fetched from the result set by **SQLFetch**, **SQLFetchScroll**, or **SQLExtendedFetch**. If variable-length data is too large to be returned in a single call to **SQLGetData** (due to a limitation in the application), **SQLGetData** can retrieve it in parts. It is possible to bind some columns in a row and call **SQLGetData** for others, although this is subject to some restrictions. For more information, see "Getting Long Data" in Chapter 10, "Retrieving Results (Basic)."

Using SQLGetData

If the driver does not support extensions to **SQLGetData**, the function can only return data for unbound columns with a number greater than that of the last bound column. Furthermore, within a row of data, the value of the *ColumnNumber* argument in each call to **SQLGetData** must be greater than or equal to the value of *ColumnNumber* in the previous call; that is, data must be retrieved in increasing column number order. Finally, if no extensions are supported, **SQLGetData** cannot be called if the rowset size is greater than 1.

Drivers can relax any of these restrictions. To determine what restrictions a driver relaxes, an application calls **SQLGetInfo** with any of the following SQL_GETDATA_EXTENSIONS options:

- SQL_GD_ANY_COLUMN. If this option is returned, **SQLGetData** can be called for any unbound column, including those before the last bound column.
- SQL_GD_ANY_ORDER. If this option is returned, **SQLGetData** can be called for unbound columns in any order.
- SQL_GD_BLOCK. If this option is returned by **SQLGetInfo** for the SQL_GETDATA_EXTENSIONS InfoType, the driver supports calls to **SQLGetData** when the rowset size is greater than 1, and the application can call **SQLSetPos** with the SQL_POSITION option to position the cursor on the correct row before calling **SQLGetData**.
- SQL_GD_BOUND. If this option is returned, **SQLGetData** can be called for bound columns as well as unbound columns.

There are two exceptions to these restrictions and a driver's ability to relax them. First, **SQLGetData** should never be called for a forward-only cursor when the rowset size is greater than 1. Second, if a driver supports bookmarks, it must always support the ability to call **SQLGetData** for column 0, even if it does not allow applications to call **SQLGetData** for other columns before the last bound column. (When an application is working with an ODBC 2.*x* driver, **SQLGetData** will successfully return a bookmark when called with *ColumnNumber* equal to 0 after a call to **SQLFetch**, because **SQLFetch** is mapped by the ODBC 3.0 Driver Manager to **SQLExtendedFetch** with a *FetchOrientation* of SQL_FETCH_NEXT, and **SQLGetData** with a *ColumnNumber* of 0 is mapped by the ODBC 3.0 Driver Manager to **SQLGetStmtOption** with an *fOption* of SQL_GET_BOOKMARK.)

Note that **SQLGetData** cannot be used to retrieve the bookmark for a row just inserted by calling **SQLBulkOperations** with the SQL_ADD option, because the cursor is not positioned on the row. An application can retrieve the bookmark for such a row by binding column 0 before calling **SQLBulkOperations** with SQL_ADD, in which case **SQLBulkOperations** returns the bookmark in the bound buffer. **SQLFetchScroll** can then be called with SQL_FETCH_BOOKMARK to reposition the cursor on that row.

If the *TargetType* argument is an interval data type, the default interval leading precision (2) and the default interval seconds precision (6), as set in the SQL_DESC_DATETIME_INTERVAL_PRECISION and SQL_DESC_PRECISION fields of the ARD, respectively, are used for the data. If the *TargetType* argument is an SQL_C_NUMERIC data type, the default precision (driver-defined) and default scale (0), as set in the SQL_DESC_PRECISION and SQL_DESC_SCALE fields of the ARD, are used for the data. If any default precision or scale is not appropriate, the application should explicitly set the appropriate descriptor field by a call to **SQLSetDescField** or **SQLSetDescRec**. It can set the SQL_DESC_CONCISE_TYPE field to SQL_C_NUMERIC, and call **SQLGetData** with a *TargetType* argument of SQL_ARD_TYPE, which will cause the precision and scale values in the descriptor fields to be used.

Note In ODBC 2.*x*, applications set *TargetType* to SQL_C_DATE, SQL_C_TIME, or SQL_C_TIMESTAMP to indicate that **TargetValuePtr* is a date, time, or timestamp structure. In ODBC 3.0, applications set *TargetType* to SQL_C_TYPE_DATE, SQL_C_TYPE_TIME, or SQL_C_TYPE_TIMESTAMP. The Driver Manager makes appropriate mappings, if necessary, based on the application and driver version.

Retrieving Variable-Length Data in Parts

SQLGetData can be used to retrieve data from a column that contains variable-length data in parts—that is, when the identifier of the SQL data type of the column is SQL_CHAR, SQL_VARCHAR, SQL_LONGVARCHAR, SQL_BINARY, SQL_VARBINARY, SQL_LONGVARBINARY, or a driver-specific identifier for a variable-length type.

To retrieve data from a column in parts, the application calls **SQLGetData** multiple times in succession for the same column. On each call, **SQLGetData** returns the next part of the data. It is up to the application to reassemble the parts, taking care to remove the null-termination character from intermediate parts of character data. If there is more data to return, **SQLGetData** returns SQL_SUCCESS_WITH_INFO and SQLSTATE 01004 (Data truncated). When it returns the last part of the data, **SQLGetData** returns SQL_SUCCESS. Neither SQL_NO_TOTAL nor zero can be returned on the last valid call to retrieve data from a column, because the application would then have no way of knowing how much of the data in the application buffer is valid. If **SQLGetData** is called after this, it returns SQL_NO_DATA. For more information, see the next section, "Retrieving Data with SQLGetData."

Variable-length bookmarks can be returned in parts by **SQLGetData**. As with other data, a call to **SQLGetData** to return variable-length bookmarks in parts will return SQLSTATE 01004 (String data, right truncated) and SQL_SUCCESS_WITH_INFO when there is more data to be returned. This is different than the case when a variable-length bookmark is truncated by a call to **SQLFetch** or **SQLFetchScroll**, which returns SQL_ERROR and SQLSTATE 22001 (String data, right truncated).

SQLGetData cannot be used to return fixed-length data in parts. If **SQLGetData** is called more than one time in a row for a column containing fixed-length data, it returns SQL_NO_DATA for all calls after the first.

Retrieving Data with SQLGetData

To return data for the specified column, **SQLGetData** performs the following sequence of steps:

1. Returns SQL_NO_DATA if it has already returned all of the data for the column.
2. Sets **StrLen_or_IndPtr* to SQL_NULL_DATA if the data is NULL. If the data is NULL and *StrLen_or_IndPtr* was a null pointer, **SQLGetData** returns SQLSTATE 22002 (Indicator variable required but not supplied).

   If the data for the column is not NULL, **SQLGetData** proceeds to step 3.
3. If the SQL_ATTR_MAX_LENGTH statement attribute is set to a nonzero value, the column contains character or binary data, and **SQLGetData** has not previously been called for the column, the data is truncated to SQL_ATTR_MAX_LENGTH bytes.

   Note The SQL_ATTR_MAX_LENGTH statement attribute is intended to reduce network traffic. It is generally implemented by the data source, which truncates the data before returning it across the network. Drivers and data sources are not required to support it. Therefore, to guarantee that data is truncated to a particular size, an application should allocate a buffer of that size and specify the size in the *BufferLength* argument.
4. Converts the data to the type specified in *TargetType*. The data is given the default precision and scale for that data type. If *TargetType* is SQL_ARD_TYPE, the data type in the SQL_DESC_CONCISE_TYPE field of the ARD is used. If *TargetType* is SQL_ARD_TYPE, the data is given the precision and scale in the SQL_DESC_DATETIME_INTERVAL_PRECISION, SQL_DESC_PRECISION, and SQL_DESC_SCALE fields of the ARD, depending on the data type in the SQL_DESC_CONCISE_TYPE field. If any default precision or scale is not appropriate, the application should explicitly set the appropriate descriptor field by a call to **SQLSetDescField** or **SQLSetDescRec**.
5. If the data was converted to a variable-length data type, such as character or binary, **SQLGetData** checks whether the length of the data exceeds *BufferLength*. If the length of character data (including the null-termination character) exceeds *BufferLength*, **SQLGetData** truncates the data to *BufferLength* less the length of a null-termination character. It then null-terminates the data. If the length of binary data exceeds the length of the data buffer, **SQLGetData** truncates it to *BufferLength* bytes.

   SQLGetData never truncates data converted to fixed-length data types; it always assumes that the length of **TargetValuePtr* is the size of the data type.
6. Places the converted (and possibly truncated) data in **TargetValuePtr*. Note that **SQLGetData** cannot return data out of line.

7. Places the length of the data in **StrLen_or_IndPtr*. If *StrLen_or_IndPtr* was a null pointer, **SQLGetData** does not return the length.
   - For character or binary data, this is the length of the data after conversion and before truncation due to *BufferLength*. If the driver cannot determine the length of the data after conversion, as is sometimes the case with long data, it returns SQL_SUCCESS_WITH_INFO and sets the length to SQL_NO_TOTAL. (The last call to **SQLGetData** must always return the length of the data, not zero or SQL_NO_TOTAL.) If data was truncated due to the SQL_ATTR_MAX_LENGTH statement attribute, the value of this attribute—as opposed to the actual length—is placed in **StrLen_or_IndPtr*. This is because this attribute is designed to truncate data on the server before conversion, so the driver has no way of figuring out what the actual length is. When **SQLGetData** is called multiple times in succession for the same column, this is the length of the data available at the start of the current call; that is, the length decreases with each subsequent call.
   - For all other data types, this is the length of the data after conversion; that is, it is the size of the type to which the data was converted.
8. If the data is truncated without loss of significance during conversion (for example, the real number 1.234 is truncated when converted to the integer 1) or because *BufferLength* is too small (for example, the string "abcdef" is placed in a 4-byte buffer), **SQLGetData** returns SQLSTATE 01004 (Data truncated) and SQL_SUCCESS_WITH_INFO. If data is truncated without loss of significance due to the SQL_ATTR_MAX_LENGTH statement attribute, **SQLGetData** returns SQL_SUCCESS and does not return SQLSTATE 01004 (Data truncated).

The contents of the bound data buffer (if **SQLGetData** is called on a bound column) and the length/indicator buffer are undefined if **SQLGetData** does not return SQL_SUCCESS or SQL_SUCCESS_WITH_INFO.

Descriptors and SQLGetData

SQLGetData does not interact directly with any descriptor fields.

If *TargetType* is SQL_ARD_TYPE, the data type in the SQL_DESC_CONCISE_TYPE field of the ARD is used. If *TargetType* is either SQL_ARD_TYPE or SQL_C_DEFAULT, the data is given the precision and scale in the SQL_DESC_DATETIME_INTERVAL_PRECISION, SQL_DESC_PRECISION, and SQL_DESC_SCALE fields of the ARD, depending on the data type in the SQL_DESC_CONCISE_TYPE field.

Code Example

In the following example, an application executes a **SELECT** statement to return a result set of the customer IDs, names, and phone numbers sorted by name, ID, and phone number. For each row of data, it calls **SQLFetch** to position the cursor to the next row. It calls **SQLGetData** to retrieve the fetched data; the buffers for the data and the returned number of bytes are specified in the call to **SQLGetData**. Finally, it prints each employee's name, ID, and phone number.

```
#define NAME_LEN 50
#define PHONE_LEN 50

SQLCHAR     szName[NAME_LEN], szPhone[PHONE_LEN];
SQLINTEGER  sCustID, cbName, cbAge, cbBirthday;
SQLRETURN   retcode;
SQLHSTMT    hstmt;

retcode = SQLExecDirect(hstmt,
            "SELECT CUSTID, NAME, PHONE FROM CUSTOMERS ORDER BY 2, 1, 3",
            SQL_NTS);

if (retcode == SQL_SUCCESS) {
   while (TRUE) {
      retcode = SQLFetch(hstmt);
      if (retcode == SQL_ERROR || retcode == SQL_SUCCESS_WITH_INFO) {
         show_error();
      }
      if (retcode == SQL_SUCCESS || retcode == SQL_SUCCESS_WITH_INFO){

         /* Get data for columns 1, 2, and 3 */

         SQLGetData(hstmt, 1, SQL_C_ULONG, &sCustID, 0, &cbCustID);
         SQLGetData(hstmt, 2, SQL_C_CHAR, szName, NAME_LEN, &cbName);
         SQLGetData(hstmt, 3, SQL_C_CHAR, szPhone, PHONE_LEN,
                    &cbPhone);

         /* Print the row of data            */

         fprintf(out, "%-5d %-*s %*s", sCustID, NAME_LEN-1, szName,
                 PHONE_LEN-1, szPhone);
      } else {
         break;
      }
   }
}
```

Related Functions

For information about	See
Assigning storage for a column in a result set	**SQLBindCol**
Performing bulk operations that do not relate to the block cursor position	**SQLBulkOperations**
Canceling statement processing	**SQLCancel**
Executing an SQL statement	**SQLExecDirect**
Executing a prepared SQL statement	**SQLExecute**
Fetching a block of data or scrolling through a result set	**SQLFetchScroll**
Fetching a single row of data or a block of data in a forward-only direction	**SQLFetch**
Sending parameter data at execution time	**SQLPutData**
Positioning the cursor, refreshing data in the rowset, or updating or deleting data in the rowset	**SQLSetPos**

SQLGetDescField

Conformance

Version Introduced: ODBC 3.0
Standards Compliance: ISO 92

Summary

SQLGetDescField returns the current setting or value of a single field of a descriptor record.

Syntax

```
SQLRETURN SQLGetDescField(
     SQLHDESC      DescriptorHandle,
     SQLSMALLINT RecNumber,
     SQLSMALLINT FieldIdentifier,
     SQLPOINTER    ValuePtr,
     SQLINTEGER    BufferLength,
     SQLINTEGER * StringLengthPtr);
```

Arguments

DescriptorHandle [Input]
Descriptor handle.

RecNumber [Input]
Indicates the descriptor record from which the application seeks information. Descriptor records are numbered from 0, with record number 0 being the bookmark record. If the *FieldIdentifier* argument indicates a header field, *RecNumber* is ignored. If *RecNumber* is less than or equal to SQL_DESC_COUNT, but the row does not contain data for a column or parameter, a call to **SQLGetDescField** will return the default values of the fields (for more information, see "Initialization of Descriptor Fields" in SQLSetDescField).

FieldIdentifier [Input]
Indicates the field of the descriptor whose value is to be returned. For more information, see the "*FieldIdentifier* Argument" section in **SQLSetDescField**.

ValuePtr [Output]
Pointer to a buffer in which to return the descriptor information. The data type depends on the value of *FieldIdentifier*.

BufferLength [Input]
If *FieldIdentifier* is an ODBC-defined field and *ValuePtr* points to a character string or a binary buffer, this argument should be the length of **ValuePtr*. If *FieldIdentifier* is an ODBC-defined field and **ValuePtr* is an integer, *BufferLength* is ignored.

If *FieldIdentifier* is a driver-defined field, the application indicates the nature of the field to the Driver Manager by setting the *BufferLength* argument. *BufferLength* can have the following values:

- If **ValuePtr* is a pointer to a character string, then *BufferLength* is the length of the string or SQL_NTS.
- If **ValuePtr* is a pointer to a binary buffer, then the application places the result of the SQL_LEN_BINARY_ATTR(*length*) macro in *BufferLength*. This places a negative value in *BufferLength*.
- If **ValuePtr* is a pointer to a value other than a character string or binary string, then *BufferLength* should have the value SQL_IS_POINTER.
- If **ValuePtr* is contains a fixed-length data type, then *BufferLength* is either SQL_IS_INTEGER, SQL_IS_UINTEGER, SQL_IS_SMALLINT, or SQL_IS_USMALLINT, as appropriate.

StringLengthPtr [Output]
Pointer to the buffer in which to return the total number of bytes (excluding the number of bytes required for the null-termination character) available to return in **ValuePtr*.

Returns

SQL_SUCCESS, SQL_SUCCESS_WITH_INFO, SQL_ERROR, SQL_NO_DATA, or SQL_INVALID_HANDLE.

SQL_NO_DATA is returned if *RecNumber* is greater than the current number of descriptor records.

SQL_NO_DATA is returned if *DescriptorHandle* is an IRD handle and the statement is in the prepared or executed state, but there was no open cursor associated with it.

Diagnostics

When **SQLGetDescField** returns SQL_ERROR or SQL_SUCCESS_WITH_INFO, an associated SQLSTATE value can be obtained by calling **SQLGetDiagRec** with a *HandleType* of SQL_HANDLE_STMT and a *Handle* of *StatementHandle*. The following table lists the SQLSTATE values commonly returned by **SQLGetDescField** and explains each one in the context of this function; the notation "(DM)" precedes the descriptions of SQLSTATEs returned by the Driver Manager. The return code associated with each SQLSTATE value is SQL_ERROR, unless noted otherwise.

SQLSTATE	Error	Description
01000	General warning	Driver-specific informational message. (Function returns SQL_SUCCESS_WITH_INFO.)
01004	String data, right truncated	The buffer **ValuePtr* was not large enough to return the entire descriptor field, so the field was truncated. The length of the untruncated descriptor field is returned in **StringLengthPtr*. (Function returns SQL_SUCCESS_WITH_INFO.)
07009	Invalid descriptor index	(DM) The *RecNumber* argument was equal to 0, the SQL_ATTR_USE_BOOKMARK statement attribute was SQL_UB_OFF, and the *DescriptorHandle* argument was an IRD handle. (This error can be returned for an explicitly allocated descriptor only if the descriptor is associated with a statement handle.) The *FieldIdentifier* argument was a record field, the *RecNumber* argument was 0, and the *DescriptorHandle* argument was an IPD handle. The *RecNumber* argument was less than 0.
08S01	Communication link failure	The communication link between the driver and the data source to which the driver was connected failed before the function completed processing.
HY000	General error	An error occurred for which there was no specific SQLSTATE and for which no implementation-specific SQLSTATE was defined. The error message returned by **SQLGetDiagRec** in the **MessageText* buffer describes the error and its cause.
HY001	Memory allocation error	The driver was unable to allocate the memory required to support execution or completion of the function.
HY007	Associated statement is not prepared	*DescriptorHandle* was associated with a *StatementHandle* as an IRD, and the associated statement handle had not been prepared or executed.

SQLSTATE	Error	Description
HY010	Function sequence error	(DM) *DescriptorHandle* was associated with a *StatementHandle* for which an asynchronously executing function (not this one) was called and was still executing when this function was called. (DM) *DescriptorHandle* was associated with a *StatementHandle* for which **SQLExecute**, **SQLExecDirect**, **SQLBulkOperations**, or **SQLSetPos** was called and returned SQL_NEED_DATA. This function was called before data was sent for all data-at-execution parameters or columns.
HY013	Memory management error	The function call could not be processed because the underlying memory objects could not be accessed, possibly because of low memory conditions.
HY021	Inconsistent descriptor information	The SQL_DESC_TYPE and SQL_DESC_DATETIME_INTERVAL_CODE fields do not form a valid ODBC SQL type, a valid driver-specific SQL type (for IPDs), or a valid ODBC C type (for APDs or ARDs).
HY090	Invalid string or buffer length	(DM) **ValuePtr* was a character string, and *BufferLength* was less than zero.
HY091	Invalid descriptor field identifier	*FieldIdentifier* was not an ODBC-defined field, and was not an implementation-defined value. *FieldIdentifier* was undefined for the *DescriptorHandle*.
HYT01	Connection timeout expired	The connection timeout period expired before the data source responded to the request. The connection timeout period is set through **SQLSetConnectAttr**, SQL_ATTR_CONNECTION_TIMEOUT.
IM001	Driver does not support this function	(DM) The driver associated with the *DescriptorHandle* does not support the function.

Comments

An application can call **SQLGetDescField** to return the value of a single field of a descriptor record. A call to **SQLGetDescField** can return the setting of any field in any descriptor type, including header fields, record fields, and bookmark fields. An application can obtain the settings of multiple fields in the same or different descriptors, in arbitrary order, by making repeated calls to **SQLGetDescField**. **SQLGetDescField** can also be called to return driver-defined descriptor fields.

For performance reasons, an application should not call **SQLGetDescField** for an IRD before executing a statement.

The settings of multiple fields that describe the name, data type, and storage of column or parameter data can also be retrieved in a single call to **SQLGetDescRec**. **SQLGetStmtAttr** can be called to return the setting of a single field in the descriptor header that is also a statement attribute. **SQLColAttribute**, **SQLDescribeCol**, and **SQLDescribeParam** return record or bookmark fields.

When an application calls **SQLGetDescField** to retrieve the value of a field that is undefined for a particular descriptor type, the function returns SQL_SUCCESS but the value returned for the field is undefined. For example, calling **SQLGetDescField** for the SQL_DESC_NAME or SQL_DESC_NULLABLE field of an APD or ARD will return SQL_SUCCESS but an undefined value for the field.

When an application calls **SQLGetDescField** to retrieve the value of a field that is defined for a particular descriptor type, but has no default value and has not been set yet, the function returns SQL_SUCCESS but the value returned for the field is undefined. For more information on the initialization of descriptor fields, and descriptions of the fields, see "Initialization of Descriptor Fields" in **SQLSetDescField**. For more information on descriptors, see Chapter 13, "Descriptors."

Related Functions

For information about	See
Getting multiple descriptor fields	**SQLGetDescRec**
Setting a single descriptor field	**SQLSetDescField**
Setting multiple descriptor fields	**SQLSetDescRec**

SQLGetDescRec

Conformance

Version Introduced: ODBC 3.0
Standards Compliance: ISO 92

Summary

SQLGetDescRec returns the current settings or values of multiple fields of a descriptor record. The fields returned describe the name, data type, and storage of column or parameter data.

Syntax

```
SQLRETURN SQLGetDescRec(
      SQLHDESC          DescriptorHandle,
      SQLSMALLINT       RecNumber,
      SQLCHAR *         Name,
      SQLSMALLINT       BufferLength,
      SQLSMALLINT *     StringLengthPtr,
      SQLSMALLINT *     TypePtr,
      SQLSMALLINT *     SubTypePtr,
      SQLINTEGER *      LengthPtr,
      SQLSMALLINT *     PrecisionPtr,
      SQLSMALLINT *     ScalePtr,
      SQLSMALLINT *     NullablePtr);
```

Arguments

DescriptorHandle [Input]
Descriptor handle.

RecNumber [Input]
Indicates the descriptor record from which the application seeks information. Descriptor records are numbered from 1, with record number 0 being the bookmark record. The *RecNumber* argument must be less than or equal to the value of SQL_DESC_COUNT. If *RecNumber* is less than or equal to SQL_DESC_COUNT, but the row does not contain data for a column or parameter, a call to **SQLGetDescRec** will return the default values of the fields (for more information, see "Initialization of Descriptor Fields" in **SQLSetDescField**).

Name [Output]
A pointer to a buffer in which to return the SQL_DESC_NAME field for the descriptor record.

BufferLength [Input]
Length of the *Name* buffer, in bytes.

StringLengthPtr [Output]
A pointer to a buffer in which to return the number of bytes of data available to return in the **Name* buffer, excluding the null-termination character. If the number of bytes was greater than or equal to *BufferLength*, the data in **Name* is truncated to *BufferLength* minus the length of a null-termination character, and is null-terminated by the driver.

TypePtr [Output]
A pointer to a buffer in which to return the value of the SQL_DESC_TYPE field for the descriptor record.

SubTypePtr [Output]
For records whose type is SQL_DATETIME or SQL_INTERVAL, this is a pointer to a buffer in which to return the value of the SQL_DESC_DATETIME_INTERVAL_CODE field.

LengthPtr [Output]
A pointer to a buffer in which to return the value of the SQL_DESC_OCTET_LENGTH field for the descriptor record.

PrecisionPtr [Output]
A pointer to a buffer in which to return the value of the SQL_DESC_PRECISION field for the descriptor record.

ScalePtr [Output]
A pointer to a buffer in which to return the value of the SQL_DESC_SCALE field for the descriptor record.

NullablePtr [Output]
A pointer to a buffer in which to return the value of the SQL_DESC_NULLABLE field for the descriptor record.

Returns

SQL_SUCCESS, SQL_SUCCESS_WITH_INFO, SQL_ERROR, SQL_NO_DATA, or SQL_INVALID_HANDLE.

SQL_NO_DATA is returned if *RecNumber* is greater than the current number of descriptor records.

SQL_NO_DATA is returned if *DescriptorHandle* is an IRD handle and the statement is in the prepared or executed state, but there was no open cursor associated with it.

Diagnostics

When **SQLGetDescRec** returns SQL_ERROR or SQL_SUCCESS_WITH_INFO, an associated SQLSTATE value can be obtained by calling **SQLGetDiagRec** with a *HandleType* of SQL_HANDLE_DESC and a *Handle* of *DescriptorHandle*. The following table lists the SQLSTATE values commonly returned by **SQLGetDescRec** and explains each one in the context of this function; the notation "(DM)" precedes the descriptions of SQLSTATEs returned by the Driver Manager. The return code associated with each SQLSTATE value is SQL_ERROR, unless noted otherwise.

SQLSTATE	Error	Description
01000	General warning	Driver-specific informational message. (Function returns SQL_SUCCESS_WITH_INFO.)
01004	String data, right truncated	The buffer **Name* was not large enough to return the entire descriptor field, so the field was truncated. The length of the untruncated descriptor field is returned in **StringLengthPtr*. (Function returns SQL_SUCCESS_WITH_INFO.)
07009	Invalid descriptor index	The *FieldIdentifier* argument was a record field, the *RecNumber* argument was set to 0, and the *DescriptorHandle* argument was an IPD handle. (DM) The *RecNumber* argument was set to 0, and the SQL_ATTR_USE_BOOKMARKS statement attribute was set to SQL_UB_OFF, and the *DescriptorHandle* argument was an IRD handle. The *RecNumber* argument was less than 0.
08S01	Communication link failure	The communication link between the driver and the data source to which the driver was connected failed before the function completed processing.
HY000	General error	An error occurred for which there was no specific SQLSTATE and for which no implementation-specific SQLSTATE was defined. The error message returned by **SQLGetDiagRec** in the **MessageText* buffer describes the error and its cause.
HY001	Memory allocation error	The driver was unable to allocate the memory required to support execution or completion of the function.
HY007	Associated statement is not prepared	*DescriptorHandle* was associated with an IRD, and the associated statement handle was not in the prepared or executed state.

SQLSTATE	Error	Description
HY010	Function sequence error	(DM) *DescriptorHandle* was associated with a *StatementHandle* for which an asynchronously executing function (not this one) was called and was still executing when this function was called. (DM) *DescriptorHandle* was associated with a *StatementHandle* for which **SQLExecute**, **SQLExecDirect**, **SQLBulkOperations**, or **SQLSetPos** was called and returned SQL_NEED_DATA. This function was called before data was sent for all data-at-execution parameters or columns.
HY013	Memory management error	The function call could not be processed because the underlying memory objects could not be accessed, possibly because of low memory conditions.
HYT01	Connection timeout expired	The connection timeout period expired before the data source responded to the request. The connection timeout period is set through **SQLSetConnectAttr**, SQL_ATTR_CONNECTION_TIMEOUT.
IM001	Driver does not support this function	(DM) The driver associated with *DescriptorHandle* does not support the function.

Comments

An application can call **SQLGetDescRec** to retrieve the values of the following descriptor fields for a single column or parameter:

- SQL_DESC_NAME
- SQL_DESC_TYPE
- SQL_DESC_DATETIME_INTERVAL_CODE (for records whose type is SQL_DATETIME or SQL_INTERVAL)
- SQL_DESC_OCTET_LENGTH
- SQL_DESC_PRECISION
- SQL_DESC_SCALE
- SQL_DESC_NULLABLE

SQLGetDescRec does not retrieve the values for header fields.

An application can inhibit the return of a field's setting by setting the argument corresponding to the field to a null pointer.

When an application calls **SQLGetDescRec** to retrieve the value of a field that is undefined for a particular descriptor type, the function returns SQL_SUCCESS but the value returned for the field is undefined. For example, calling **SQLGetDescRec** for the SQL_DESC_NAME or SQL_DESC_NULLABLE field of an APD or ARD will return SQL_SUCCESS but an undefined value for the field.

When an application calls **SQLGetDescRec** to retrieve the value of a field that is defined for a particular descriptor type, but has no default value and has not been set yet, the function returns SQL_SUCCESS but the value returned for the field is undefined. For more information, see "Initialization of Descriptor Fields" in SQLSetDescField.

The values of fields can also be retrieved individually by a call to **SQLGetDescField**. For a description of the fields in a descriptor header or record, see **SQLSetDescField**. For more information on descriptors, see Chapter 13, "Descriptors."

Related Functions

For information about	See
Binding a column	**SQLBindCol**
Binding a parameter	**SQLBindParameter**
Getting a descriptor field	**SQLGetDescField**
Setting multiple descriptor fields	**SQLSetDescRec**

SQLGetDiagField

Conformance

Version Introduced: ODBC 3.0
Standards Compliance: ISO 92

Summary

SQLGetDiagField returns the current value of a field of a record of the diagnostic data structure (associated with a specified handle) that contains error, warning, and status information.

Syntax

```
SQLRETURN SQLGetDiagField(
     SQLSMALLINT    HandleType,
     SQLHANDLE      Handle,
     SQLSMALLINT    RecNumber,
     SQLSMALLINT    DiagIdentifier,
     SQLPOINTER     DiagInfoPtr,
     SQLSMALLINT    BufferLength,
     SQLSMALLINT *  StringLengthPtr);
```

Arguments

HandleType [Input]
A handle type identifier that describes the type of handle for which diagnostics are required. Must be one of the following:

SQL_HANDLE_ENV
SQL_HANDLE_DBC
SQL_HANDLE_STMT
SQL_HANDLE_DESC

Handle [Input]
A handle for the diagnostic data structure, of the type indicated by *HandleType*. If *HandleType* is SQL_HANDLE_ENV, *Handle* can be either a shared or unshared environment handle.

RecNumber [Input]
Indicates the status record from which the application seeks information. Status records are numbered from 1. If the *DiagIdentifier* argument indicates any field of the diagnostics header, *RecNumber* is ignored. If not, it should be greater than 0.

DiagIdentifier [Input]
Indicates the field of the diagnostic whose value is to be returned. For more information, see the "*DiagIdentifier* Argument" section in "Comments."

DiagInfoPtr [Output]
Pointer to a buffer in which to return the diagnostic information. The data type depends on the value of *DiagIdentifier*.

BufferLength [Input]

If *DiagIdentifier* is an ODBC-defined diagnostic and *DiagInfoPtr* points to a character string or a binary buffer, this argument should be the length of **DiagInfoPtr*. If *DiagIdentifier* is an ODBC-defined field and **DiagInfoPtr* is an integer, *BufferLength* is ignored.

If *DiagIdentifier* is a driver-defined field, the application indicates the nature of the field to the Driver Manager by setting the *BufferLength* argument. *BufferLength* can have the following values:

- If **ValuePtr* is a pointer to a character string, then *BufferLength* is the length of the string or SQL_NTS.
- If **ValuePtr* is a pointer to a binary buffer, then the application places the result of the SQL_LEN_BINARY_ATTR(*length*) macro in *BufferLength*. This places a negative value in *BufferLength*.
- If **ValuePtr* is a pointer to a value other than a character string or binary string, then *BufferLength* should have the value SQL_IS_POINTER.
- If **ValuePtr* is contains a fixed-length data type, then *BufferLength* is either SQL_IS_INTEGER, SQL_IS_UINTEGER, SQL_IS_SMALLINT, or SQL_IS_USMALLINT, as appropriate.

StringLengthPtr [Output]

Pointer to a buffer in which to return the total number of bytes (excluding the number of bytes required for the null-termination character) available to return in **DiagInfoPtr*, for character data. If the number of bytes available to return is greater than *BufferLength*, then the text in **DiagInfoPtr* is truncated to *BufferLength* minus the length of a null-termination character.

Returns

SQL_SUCCESS, SQL_SUCCESS_WITH_INFO, SQL_ERROR, SQL_INVALID_HANDLE, or SQL_NO_DATA.

Diagnostics

SQLGetDiagField does not post diagnostic records for itself. It uses the following return values to report the outcome of its own execution:

- SQL_SUCCESS: The function successfully returned diagnostic information.
- SQL_SUCCESS_WITH_INFO: **DiagInfoPtr* was too small to hold the requested diagnostic field, so the data in the diagnostic field was truncated. To determine that a truncation occurred, the application must compare *BufferLength* to the actual number of bytes available, which is written to **StringLengthPtr*.
- SQL_INVALID_HANDLE: The handle indicated by *HandleType* and *Handle* was not a valid handle.

- SQL_ERROR: One of the following occurred:
  - *The DiagIdentifier* argument was not one of the valid values.
  - *The DiagIdentifier* argument was SQL_DIAG_CURSOR_ROW_COUNT, SQL_DIAG_DYNAMIC_FUNCTION, SQL_DIAG_DYNAMIC_FUNCTION_CODE, or SQL_DIAG_ROW_COUNT, but *Handle* was not a statement handle. (The Driver Manager returns this diagnostic.)
  - *The RecNumber* argument was negative or 0 when *DiagIdentifier* indicated a field from a diagnostic record. *RecNumber* is ignored for header fields.
  - The value requested was a character string and *BufferLength* was less than zero.
- SQL_NO_DATA: *RecNumber* was greater than the number of diagnostic records that existed for the handle specified in *Handle.* The function also returns SQL_NO_DATA for any positive *RecNumber* if there are no diagnostic records for *Handle*.

Comments

An application typically calls **SQLGetDiagField** to accomplish one of three goals:

1. To obtain specific error or warning information when a function call has returned SQL_ERROR or SQL_SUCCESS_WITH_INFO (or SQL_NEED_DATA for the **SQLBrowseConnect** function).
2. To find out the number of rows in the data source that were affected when insert, delete, or update operations were performed with a call to **SQLExecute**, **SQLExecDirect**, **SQLBulkOperations**, or **SQLSetPos** (from the SQL_DIAG_ROW_COUNT header field), or to find out the number of rows that exist in the current open cursor, if the driver is able to provide this information (from the SQL_DIAG_CURSOR_ROW_COUNT header field).
3. To determine which function was executed by a call to **SQLExecDirect** or **SQLExecute** (from the SQL_DIAG_DYNAMIC_FUNCTION and SQL_DIAG_DYNAMIC_FUNCTION_CODE header fields).

Any ODBC function can post zero or more diagnostic records each time it is called, so an application can call **SQLGetDiagField** after any ODBC function call. There is no limit to the number of diagnostic records that can be stored at any one time. **SQLGetDiagField** retrieves only the diagnostic information most recently associated with the diagnostic data structure specified in the *Handle* argument. If the application calls an ODBC function other than **SQLGetDiagField** or **SQLGetDiagRec**, any diagnostic information from a previous call with the same handle is lost.

An application can scan all diagnostic records by incrementing *RecNumber*, as long as **SQLGetDiagField** returns SQL_SUCCESS. The number of status records is indicated in the SQL_DIAG_NUMBER header field. Calls to **SQLGetDiagField** are non-destructive to the header and record fields. The application can call **SQLGetDiagField** again at a later time to retrieve a field from a record, as long as a function other than the diagnostic functions has not been called in the interim, which would post records on the same handle.

An application can call **SQLGetDiagField** to return any diagnostic field at any time, with the exception of SQL_DIAG_CURSOR_ROW_COUNT or SQL_DIAG_ROW_COUNT, which will return SQL_ERROR if *Handle* is not a statement handle. If any other diagnostic field is undefined, the call to **SQLGetDiagField** will return SQL_SUCCESS (provided no other diagnostic is encountered), and an undefined value is returned for the field.

For more information, see "Using SQLGetDiagRec and SQLGetDiagField" and "Implementing SQLGetDiagRec and SQLGetDiagField" in Chapter 15, "Diagnostics."

HandleType Argument

Each handle type can have diagnostic information associated with it. The *HandleType* argument denotes the handle type of *Handle*.

Some header and record fields cannot be returned for all types of handles: environment, connection, statement, and descriptor. Those handles for which a field is not applicable are indicated in the "Header Field" and "Record Fields" sections following.

If *HandleType* is SQL_HANDLE_ENV, *Handle* can be either a shared or unshared environment handle.

No driver-specific header diagnostic fields should be associated with an environment handle.

The only diagnostic header fields that are defined for a descriptor handle are SQL_DIAG_NUMBER and SQL_DIAG_RETURNCODE.

DiagIdentifier Argument

This argument indicates the identifier of the field required from the diagnostic data structure. If *RecNumber* is greater than or equal to 1, the data in the field describes the diagnostic information returned by a function. If *RecNumber* is 0, the field is in the header of the diagnostic data structure, and therefore contains data pertaining to the function call that returned the diagnostic information, not the specific information.

Drivers can define driver-specific header and record fields in the diagnostic data structure.

An ODBC 3.0 application working with an ODBC 2.*x* driver will only be able to call **SQLGetDiagField** with a *DiagIdentifier* argument of SQL_DIAG_CLASS_ORIGIN, SQL_DIAG_CLASS_SUBCLASS_ORIGIN, SQL_DIAG_CONNECTION_NAME, SQL_DIAG_MESSAGE_TEXT, SQL_DIAG_NATIVE, SQL_DIAG_NUMBER, SQL_DIAG_RETURNCODE, SQL_DIAG_SERVER_NAME, or SQL_DIAG_SQLSTATE. All other diagnostic fields will return SQL_ERROR.

Header Fields

The following header fields can be included in the *DiagIdentifier* argument.

DiagIdentifier	Return type	Returns
SQL_DIAG_CURSOR_ROW_COUNT	SQLINTEGER	This field contains the count of rows in the cursor. Its semantics depend upon the **SQLGetInfo** information types SQL_DYNAMIC_CURSOR_ATTRIBUTES2, SQL_FORWARD_ONLY_CURSOR_ATTRIBUTES2, SQL_KEYSET_CURSOR_ATTRIBUTES2, and SQL_STATIC_CURSOR_ATTRIBUTES2, which indicate which row counts are available for each cursor type (in the SQL_CA2_CRC_EXACT and SQL_CA2_CRC_APPROXIMATE bits). The contents of this field are defined only for statement handles and only after **SQLExecute**, **SQLExecDirect**, or **SQLMoreResults** has been called. Calling **SQLGetDiagField** with a *DiagIdentifier* of SQL_DIAG_CURSOR_ROW_COUNT on other than a statement handle will return SQL_ERROR.

DiagIdentifier	Return type	Returns
SQL_DIAG_DYNAMIC_ FUNCTION	SQLCHAR *	This is a string that describes the SQL statement that the underlying function executed (see "Values of the Dynamic Function fields" later in this section for specific values). The contents of this field are defined only for statement handles, and only after a call to **SQLExecute**, **SQLExecDirect**, or **SQLMoreResults**. Calling **SQLGetDiagField** with a *DiagIdentifier* of SQL_DIAG_DYNAMIC_FUNCTION on other than a statement handle will return SQL_ERROR. The value of this field is undefined before a call to **SQLExecute** or **SQLExecDirect**.
SQL_DIAG_DYNAMIC_ FUNCTION_CODE	SQLINTEGER	This is a numeric code that describes the SQL statement that was executed by the underlying function (see "Values of the Dynamic Function Fields" later in this section for specific values). The contents of this field are defined only for statement handles, and only after a call to **SQLExecute**, **SQLExecDirect**, or **SQLMoreResults**. Calling **SQLGetDiagField** with a *DiagIdentifier* of SQL_DIAG_DYNAMIC_FUNCTION_ CODE on other than a statement handle will return SQL_ERROR. The value of this field is undefined before a call to **SQLExecute** or **SQLExecDirect**.
SQL_DIAG_NUMBER	SQLINTEGER	The number of status records that are available for the specified handle.
SQL_DIAG_ RETURNCODE	SQLRETURN	Return code returned by the function. For a list of return codes, see "Return Codes" in Chapter 15, "Diagnostics." The driver does not have to implement SQL_DIAG_RETURNCODE; it is always implemented by the Driver Manager. If no function has yet been called on the *Handle*, SQL_SUCCESS will be returned for SQL_DIAG_RETURNCODE.

DiagIdentifier	Return type	Returns
SQL_DIAG_ ROW_COUNT	SQLINTEGER	The number of rows affected by an insert, delete, or update performed by **SQLExecute**, **SQLExecDirect**, **SQLBulkOperations**, or **SQLSetPos**. It is driver-defined after a *cursor specification* has been executed. The contents of this field are defined only for statement handles. Calling **SQLGetDiagField** with a *DiagIdentifier* of SQL_DIAG_ROW_COUNT on other than a statement handle will return SQL_ERROR. The data in this field is also returned in the *RowCountPtr* argument of **SQLRowCount**. The data in this field is reset after every non-diagnostic function call, whereas the row count returned by **SQLRowCount** remains the same until the statement is set back to the prepared or allocated state.

Record Fields

The following record fields can be included in the *DiagIdentifier* argument:

DiagIdentifier	Return type	Returns
SQL_DIAG_ CLASS_ORIGIN	SQLCHAR *	A string that indicates the document that defines the class portion of the SQLSTATE value in this record. Its value is "ISO 9075" for all SQLSTATEs defined by X/Open and ISO call-level interface. For ODBC-specific SQLSTATEs (all those whose SQLSTATE class is "IM"), its value is "ODBC 3.0".

DiagIdentifier	Return type	Returns
SQL_DIAG_COLUMN_NUMBER	SQLINTEGER	If the SQL_DIAG_ROW_NUMBER field is a valid row number in a rowset or a set of parameters, then this field contains the value that represents the column number in the result set or the parameter number in the set of parameters. Result set column numbers always start at 1; if this status record pertains to a bookmark column, then the field can be zero. Parameter numbers start at 1. It has the value SQL_NO_COLUMN_NUMBER if the status record is not associated with a column number or parameter number. If the driver cannot determine the column number or parameter number that this record is associated with, this field has the value SQL_COLUMN_NUMBER_UNKNOWN. The contents of this field are defined only for statement handles.
SQL_DIAG_CONNECTION_NAME	SQLCHAR *	A string that indicates the name of the connection that the diagnostic record relates to. This field is driver-defined. For diagnostic data structures associated with the environment handle and for diagnostics that do not relate to any connection, this field is a zero-length string.
SQL_DIAG_MESSAGE_TEXT	SQLCHAR *	An informational message on the error or warning. This field is formatted as described in the "Diagnostic Messages" section of Chapter 15, "Diagnostics." There is no maximum length to the diagnostic message text.
SQL_DIAG_NATIVE	SQLINTEGER	A driver/data source–specific native error code. If there is no native error code, the driver returns 0.

DiagIdentifier	Return type	Returns
SQL_DIAG_ROW_NUMBER	SQLINTEGER	This field contains the row number in the rowset, or the parameter number in the set of parameters, with which the status record is associated. Row numbers and parameter numbers start with 1. This field has the value SQL_NO_ROW_NUMBER if this status record is not associated with a row number or parameter number. If the driver cannot determine the row number or parameter number that this record is associated with, this field has the value SQL_ROW_NUMBER_UNKNOWN. The contents of this field are defined only for statement handles.
SQL_DIAG_SERVER_NAME	SQLCHAR *	A string that indicates the server name that the diagnostic record relates to. It is the same as the value returned for a call to **SQLGetInfo** with the SQL_DATA_SOURCE_NAME *option*. For diagnostic data structures associated with the environment handle and for diagnostics that do not relate to any server, this field is a zero-length string.
SQL_DIAG_SQLSTATE	SQLCHAR *	A five-character SQLSTATE diagnostic code. For more information, see "SQLSTATEs" in Chapter 15, "Diagnostics."
SQL_DIAG_SUBCLASS_ORIGIN	SQLCHAR *	A string with the same format and valid values as SQL_DIAG_CLASS_ORIGIN, that identifies the defining portion of the subclass portion of the SQLSTATE code. The ODBC-specific SQLSTATES for which "ODBC 3.0" is returned include the following: 01S00, 01S01, 01S02, 01S06, 01S07, 07S01, 08S01, 21S01, 21S02, 25S01, 25S02, 25S03, 42S01, 42S02, 42S11, 42S12, 42S21, 42S22, HY095, HY097, HY098, HY099, HY100, HY101, HY105, HY107, HY109, HY110, HY111, HYT00, HYT01, IM001, IM002, IM003, IM004, IM005, IM006, IM007, IM008, IM010, IM011, IM012.

Values of the Dynamic Function Fields

The following table describes the values of SQL_DIAG_DYNAMIC_FUNCTION and SQL_DIAG_DYNAMIC_FUNCTION_CODE that apply to each type of SQL statement executed by a call to **SQLExecute** or **SQLExecDirect**. The driver can add driver-defined values to those listed.

SQL statement executed	Value of SQL_DIAG_ DYNAMIC_FUNCTION	Value of SQL_DIAG_DYNAMIC_ FUNCTION_CODE
alter-domain-statement	"ALTER DOMAIN"	SQL_DIAG_ALTER_DOMAIN
alter-table-statement	"ALTER TABLE"	SQL_DIAG_ALTER_TABLE
assertion-definition	"CREATE ASSERTION"	SQL_DIAG_CREATE_ ASSERTION
character-set-definition	"CREATE CHARACTER SET"	SQL_DIAG_CREATE_ CHARACTER_SET
collation-definition	"CREATE COLLATION"	SQL_DIAG_CREATE_ COLLATION
create-index-statement	"CREATE INDEX"	SQL_DIAG_CREATE_ INDEX
create-table-statement	"CREATE TABLE"	SQL_DIAG_CREATE_ TABLE
create-view-statement	"CREATE VIEW"	SQL_DIAG_CREATE_VIEW
cursor-specification	"SELECT CURSOR"	SQL_DIAG_SELECT_ CURSOR
delete-statement-positioned	"DYNAMIC DELETE CURSOR"	SQL_DIAG_DYNAMIC_ DELETE_CURSOR
delete-statement-searched	"DELETE WHERE"	SQL_DIAG_DELETE_ WHERE
domain-definition	"CREATE DOMAIN"	SQL_DIAG_CREATE_ DOMAIN
drop-assertion-statement	"DROP ASSERTION"	SQL_DIAG_DROP_ ASSERTION
drop-character-set-stmt	"DROP CHARACTER SET"	SQL_DIAG_DROP_ CHARACTER_SET
drop-collation-statement	"DROP COLLATION"	SQL_DIAG_DROP_ COLLATION
drop-domain-statement	"DROP DOMAIN"	SQL_DIAG_DROP_DOMAIN

SQL statement executed	Value of SQL_DIAG_ DYNAMIC_FUNCTION	Value of SQL_DIAG_DYNAMIC_ FUNCTION_CODE
drop-index-statement	"DROP INDEX"	SQL_DIAG_DROP_INDEX
drop-schema-statement	"DROP SCHEMA"	SQL_DIAG_DROP_SCHEMA
drop-table-statement	"DROP TABLE"	SQL_DIAG_DROP_TABLE
drop-translation-statement	"DROP TRANSLATION"	SQL_DIAG_DROP_ TRANSLATION
drop-view-statement	"DROP VIEW"	SQL_DIAG_DROP_VIEW
grant-statement	"GRANT"	SQL_DIAG_GRANT
insert-statement	"INSERT"	SQL_DIAG_INSERT
ODBC-procedure-extension	"CALL"	SQL_DIAG_ CALL
revoke-statement	"REVOKE"	SQL_DIAG_REVOKE
schema-definition	"CREATE SCHEMA"	SQL_DIAG_CREATE_ SCHEMA
translation-definition	"CREATE TRANSLATION"	SQL_DIAG_CREATE_ TRANSLATION
update-statement-positioned	"DYNAMIC UPDATE CURSOR"	SQL_DIAG_DYNAMIC_ UPDATE_CURSOR
update-statement-searched	"UPDATE WHERE"	SQL_DIAG_UPDATE_ WHERE
Unknown	*empty string*	SQL_DIAG_UNKNOWN_ STATEMENT

Sequence of Status Records

Status records are placed in a sequence based upon row number and the type of the diagnostic. The Driver Manager determines the final order in which to return status records that it generates. The driver determines the final order in which to return status records that it generates.

If diagnostic records are posted by both the Driver Manager and the driver, the Driver Manager is responsible for ordering them.

If there are two or more status records, the sequence of the records is determined first by row number. The following rules apply to determining the sequence of diagnostic record by row:

- Records that do not correspond to any row appear in front of records that correspond to a particular row, because SQL_NO_ROW_NUMBER is defined to be –1.
- Records for which the row number is unknown appear in front of all other records, because SQL_ROW_NUMBER_UNKNOWN is defined to be –2.
- For all records that pertain to specific rows, records are sorted by the value in the SQL_DIAG_ROW_NUMBER field. All errors and warnings of the first row affected are listed, then all errors and warnings of the next row affected, and so on.

Note The ODBC 3.0 Driver Manager does not order status records in the diagnostic queue if SQLSTATE 01S01 (Error in row) is returned by an ODBC 2.*x* driver, or SQLSTATE 01S01 (Error in row) is returned by an ODBC 3.0 driver when **SQLExtendedFetch** is called or **SQLSetPos** is called on a cursor that has been positioned with **SQLExtendedFetch**.

Within each row, or for all those records that do not correspond to a row or for which the row number is unknown, or for all those records with a row number equal to SQL_NO_ROW_NUMBER, the first record listed is determined using a set of sorting rules. After the first record, the order of the other records affecting a row is undefined. An application cannot assume that errors precede warnings after the first record. Applications should scan the entire diagnostic data structure to obtain complete information on an unsuccessful call to a function.

The following rules are followed to determine the first record within a row. The record with the highest rank is the first record. The source of a record (Driver Manager, driver, gateway, and so on) is not considered when ranking records.

- **Errors**. Status records that describe errors have the highest rank. The following rules are followed to sort errors:
  - Records that indicate a transaction failure or possible transaction failure outrank all other records.
  - If two or more records describe the same error condition, then SQLSTATEs defined by the X/Open CLI specification (classes 03 through HZ) outrank ODBC- and driver-defined SQLSTATEs.
- **Implementation-defined No Data values**. Status records that describe driver-defined No Data values (class 02) have the second highest rank.
- **Warnings**. Status records that describe warnings (class 01) have the lowest rank. If two or more records describe the same warning condition, then warning SQLSTATEs defined by the X/Open CLI specification outrank ODBC- and driver-defined SQLSTATEs.

Related Functions

For information about	See
Obtaining multiple fields of a diagnostic data structure	**SQLGetDiagRec**

SQLGetDiagRec

Conformance

Version Introduced: ODBC 3.0
Standards Compliance: ISO 92

Summary

SQLGetDiagRec returns the current values of multiple fields of a diagnostic record that contains error, warning, and status information. Unlike **SQLGetDiagField**, which returns one diagnostic field per call, **SQLGetDiagRec** returns several commonly used fields of a diagnostic record, including the SQLSTATE, the native error code, and the diagnostic message text.

Syntax

```
SQLRETURN SQLGetDiagRec(
     SQLSMALLINT     HandleType,
     SQLHANDLE       Handle,
     SQLSMALLINT     RecNumber,
     SQLCHAR *       Sqlstate,
     SQLINTEGER *    NativeErrorPtr,
     SQLCHAR *       MessageText,
     SQLSMALLINT     BufferLength,
     SQLSMALLINT *   TextLengthPtr);
```

Arguments

HandleType [Input]

A handle type identifier that describes the type of handle for which diagnostics are required. Must be one of the following:

SQL_HANDLE_ENV
SQL_HANDLE_DBC
SQL_HANDLE_STMT
SQL_HANDLE_DESC

Handle [Input]

A handle for the diagnostic data structure, of the type indicated by *HandleType*. If *HandleType* is SQL_HANDLE_ENV, *Handle* can be either a shared or unshared environment handle.

RecNumber [Input]

Indicates the status record from which the application seeks information. Status records are numbered from 1.

SQLState [Output]
Pointer to a buffer in which to return a five-character SQLSTATE code pertaining to the diagnostic record *RecNumber*. The first two characters indicate the class; the next three indicate the subclass. This information is contained in the SQL_DIAG_SQLSTATE diagnostic field. For more information, see "SQLSTATEs" in Chapter 15, "Diagnostics."

NativeErrorPtr [Output]
Pointer to a buffer in which to return the native error code, specific to the data source. This information is contained in the SQL_DIAG_NATIVE diagnostic field.

MessageText [Output]
Pointer to a buffer in which to return the diagnostic message text string. This information is contained in the SQL_DIAG_MESSAGE_TEXT diagnostic field. For the format of the string, see the "Diagnostic Messages" section of Chapter 15, "Diagnostics."

BufferLength [Input]
Length (in bytes) of the **MessageText* buffer. There is no maximum length of the diagnostic message text.

TextLengthPtr [Output]
Pointer to a buffer in which to return the total number of bytes (excluding the number of bytes required for the null-termination character) available to return in **MessageText*. If the number of bytes available to return is greater than *BufferLength*, then the diagnostic message text in **MessageText* is truncated to *BufferLength* minus the length of a null-termination character.

Returns

SQL_SUCCESS, SQL_SUCCESS_WITH_INFO, SQL_ERROR, or SQL_INVALID_HANDLE.

Diagnostics

SQLGetDiagRec does not post diagnostic records for itself. It uses the following return values to report the outcome of its own execution:

- SQL_SUCCESS: The function successfully returned diagnostic information.
- SQL_SUCCESS_WITH_INFO: The **MessageText* buffer was too small to hold the requested diagnostic message. No diagnostic records were generated. To determine that a truncation occurred, the application must compare *BufferLength* to the actual number of bytes available, which is written to **StringLengthPtr*.

- SQL_INVALID_HANDLE: The handle indicated by *HandleType* and *Handle* was not a valid handle.
- SQL_ERROR: One of the following occurred:
  - *RecNumber* was negative or 0.
  - *BufferLength* was less than zero.
- SQL_NO_DATA: *RecNumber* was greater than the number of diagnostic records that existed for the handle specified in *Handle.* The function also returns SQL_NO_DATA for any positive *RecNumber* if there are no diagnostic records for *Handle*.

Comments

An application typically calls **SQLGetDiagRec** when a previous call to an ODBC function has returned SQL_SUCCESS or SQL_SUCCESS_WITH_INFO. However, because any ODBC function can post zero or more diagnostic records each time it is called, an application can call **SQLGetDiagRec** after any ODBC function call. An application can call **SQLGetDiagRec** multiple times to return some or all of the records in the diagnostic data structure. ODBC imposes no limit to the number of diagnostic records that can be stored at any one time.

SQLGetDiagRec cannot be used to return fields from the header of the diagnostic data structure (the *RecNumber* argument must be greater than 0). The application should call **SQLGetDiagField** for this purpose.

SQLGetDiagRec retrieves only the diagnostic information most recently associated with the handle specified in the *Handle* argument. If the application calls another ODBC function, except **SQLGetDiagRec**, **SQLGetDiagField**, or **SQLError**, any diagnostic information from the previous calls on the same handle is lost.

An application can scan all diagnostic records by looping, incrementing *RecNumber*, as long as **SQLGetDiagRec** returns SQL_SUCCESS. Calls to **SQLGetDiagRec** are non-destructive to the header and record fields. The application can call **SQLGetDiagRec** again at a later time to retrieve a field from a record, as long as no other function, except **SQLGetDiagRec**, **SQLGetDiagField**, or **SQLError**, has been called in the interim. The application can also retrieve a count of the total number of diagnostic records available by calling **SQLGetDiagField** to retrieve the value of the SQL_DIAG_NUMBER field, and then call **SQLGetDiagRec** that many times.

For a description of the fields of the diagnostic data structure, see **SQLGetDiagField**. For more information, see "Using SQLGetDiagRec and SQLGetDiagField" and "Implementing SQLGetDiagRec and SQLGetDiagField" in Chapter 15, "Diagnostics."

HandleType Argument

Each handle type can have diagnostic information associated with it. The *HandleType* argument denotes the handle type of the *Handle argument.*

Some header and record fields cannot be returned for all types of handles: environment, connection, statement, and descriptor. Those handles for which a field is not applicable are indicated in the "Header Field" and "Record Fields" sections in SQLGetDiagField.

A call to **SQLGetDiagRec** will return SQL_INVALID_HANDLE if *HandleType* is SQL_HANDLE_SENV, which denotes a shared environment handle. However, if *HandleType* is SQL_HANDLE_ENV, *Handle* can be either a shared or unshared environment handle.

Related Functions

For information about	See
Obtaining a field of a diagnostic record or a field of the diagnostic header	**SQLGetDiagField**

SQLGetEnvAttr

Conformance

Version Introduced: ODBC 3.0
Standards Compliance: ISO 92

Summary

SQLGetEnvAttr returns the current setting of an environment attribute.

Syntax

SQLRETURN **SQLGetEnvAttr**(
    SQLHENV *EnvironmentHandle*,
    SQLINTEGER *Attribute*,
    SQLPOINTER *ValuePtr*,
    SQLINTEGER *BufferLength*,
    SQLINTEGER * *StringLengthPtr*);

Arguments

EnvironmentHandle [Input]
Environment handle.

Attribute [Input]
Attribute to retrieve.

ValuePtr [Output]
Pointer to a buffer in which to return the current value of the attribute specified by *Attribute*.

BufferLength [Input]
If *ValuePtr* points to a character string, this argument should be the length of **ValuePtr*. If **ValuePtr* is an integer, *BufferLength* is ignored.

StringLengthPtr [Output]
A pointer to a buffer in which to return the total number of bytes (excluding the null-termination character) available to return in **ValuePtr*. If *ValuePtr* is a null pointer, no length is returned. If the attribute value is a character string, and the number of bytes available to return is greater than or equal to *BufferLength*, the data in **ValuePtr* is truncated to *BufferLength* minus the length of a null-termination character and is null-terminated by the driver.

Returns

SQL_SUCCESS, SQL_SUCCESS_WITH_INFO, SQL_NO_DATA, SQL_ERROR, or SQL_INVALID_HANDLE.

Diagnostics

When **SQLGetEnvAttr** returns SQL_ERROR or SQL_SUCCESS_WITH_INFO, an associated SQLSTATE value can be obtained by calling **SQLGetDiagRec** with a *HandleType* of SQL_HANDLE_ENV and a *Handle* of *EnvironmentHandle*. The following table lists the SQLSTATE values commonly returned by **SQLGetEnvAttr** and explains each one in the context of this function; the notation "(DM)" precedes the descriptions of SQLSTATEs returned by the Driver Manager. The return code associated with each SQLSTATE value is SQL_ERROR, unless noted otherwise.

SQLSTATE	Error	Description
01000	General warning	Driver-specific informational message. (Function returns SQL_SUCCESS_WITH_INFO.)
01004	String data, right truncated	The data returned in **ValuePtr* was truncated to be *BufferLength* minus the null-termination character. The length of the untruncated string value is returned in **StringLengthPtr*. (Function returns SQL_SUCCESS_WITH_INFO.)
HY000	General error	An error occurred for which there was no specific SQLSTATE and for which no implementation-specific SQLSTATE was defined. The error message returned by **SQLGetDiagRec** in the **MessageText* buffer describes the error and its cause.
HY001	Memory allocation error	The driver was unable to allocate memory required to support execution or completion of the function.
HY013	Memory management error	The function call could not be processed because the underlying memory objects could not be accessed, possibly because of low memory conditions.
HY092	Invalid attribute/option identifier	The value specified for the argument *Attribute* was not valid for the version of ODBC supported by the driver.
HYC00	Optional feature not implemented	The value specified for the argument *Attribute* was a valid ODBC environment attribute for the version of ODBC supported by the driver, but was not supported by the driver.
IM001	Driver does not support this function	(DM) The driver corresponding to the *EnvironmentHandle* does not support the function.

Comments

For a list of attributes, see **SQLSetEnvAttr**. There are no driver-specific environment attributes. Note that if *Attribute* specifies an attribute that returns a string, *ValuePtr* must be a pointer to a buffer in which to return the string. The maximum length of the string, including the null-termination byte, will be *BufferLength* bytes.

SQLGetEnvAttr can be called at any time between the allocation and the freeing of an environment handle. All environment attributes successfully set by the application for the environment persist until **SQLFreeHandle** is called on the *EnvironmentHandle* with a *HandleType* of SQL_HANDLE_ENV. More than one environment handle can be allocated simultaneously in ODBC 3.0. An environment attribute on one environment is not affected when another environment has been allocated.

Note The SQL_ATTR_OUTPUT_NTS environment attribute is supported by standards-compliant applications. When **SQLGetEnvAttr** is called, the ODBC 3.0 Driver Manager always returns SQL_TRUE for this attribute. SQL_ATTR_OUTPUT_NTS can only be set to SQL_TRUE by a call to **SQLSetEnvAttr**.

Related Functions

For information about	See
Returning the setting of a connection attribute	**SQLGetConnectAttr**
Returning the setting of a statement attribute	**SQLGetStmtAttr**
Setting a connection attribute	**SQLSetConnectAttr**
Setting an environment attribute	**SQLSetEnvAttr**
Setting a statement attribute	**SQLSetStmtAttr**

SQLGetFunctions

Conformance

Version Introduced:	ODBC 1.0
Standards Compliance:	ISO 92

Summary

SQLGetFunctions returns information about whether a driver supports a specific ODBC function. This function is implemented in the Driver Manager; it can also be implemented in drivers. If a driver implements **SQLGetFunctions**, the Driver Manager calls the function in the driver. Otherwise, it executes the function itself.

Syntax

```
SQLRETURN SQLGetFunctions(
     SQLHDBC           ConnectionHandle,
     SQLUSMALLINT      FunctionId,
     SQLUSMALLINT *    SupportedPtr);
```

Arguments

ConnectionHandle [Input]
Connection handle.

FunctionId [Input]
A **#define** value that identifies the ODBC function of interest; SQL_API_ODBC3_ALL_FUNCTIONS or SQL_API_ALL_FUNCTIONS. SQL_API_ODBC3_ALL_FUNCTIONS is used by an ODBC 3.0 application to determine support of ODBC 3.0 and earlier functions. SQL_API_ALL_FUNCTIONS is used by an ODBC 2.*x* application to determine support of ODBC 2.*x* and earlier functions.

For a list of **#define** values that identify ODBC functions, see the tables in "Comments."

SupportedPtr [Output]
If *FunctionId* identifies a single ODBC function, *SupportedPtr* points to a single SQLUSMALLINT value that is SQL_TRUE if the specified function is supported by the driver, and SQL_FALSE if it is not supported.

If *FunctionId* is SQL_API_ODBC3_ALL_FUNCTIONS, *SupportedPtr* points to a SQLSMALLINT array with a number of elements equal to SQL_API_ODBC3_ALL_FUNCTIONS_SIZE. This array is treated by the Driver Manager as a 4,000-bit bitmap that can be used to determine whether an ODBC 3.0 or earlier function is supported. The SQL_FUNC_EXISTS macro is called to determine function support (see "Comments"). An ODBC 3.0 application can call **SQLGetFunctions** with SQL_API_ODBC3_ALL_FUNCTIONS against either an ODBC 3.0 or ODBC 2.*x* driver.

If *FunctionId* is SQL_API_ALL_FUNCTIONS, *SupportedPtr* points to an SQLUSMALLINT array of 100 elements. The array is indexed by **#define** values used by *FunctionId* to identify each ODBC function; some elements of the array are unused and reserved for future use. An element is SQL_TRUE if it identifies an ODBC 2.*x* or earlier function supported by the driver. It is SQL_FALSE if it identifies an ODBC function not supported by the driver or does not identify an ODBC function.

The arrays returned in **SupportedPtr* use zero-based indexing.

Returns

SQL_SUCCESS, SQL_SUCCESS_WITH_INFO, SQL_ERROR, or SQL_INVALID_HANDLE.

Diagnostics

When **SQLGetFunctions** returns SQL_ERROR or SQL_SUCCESS_WITH_INFO, an associated SQLSTATE value can be obtained by calling **SQLGetDiagRec** with a *HandleType* of SQL_HANDLE_DBC and a *Handle* of *ConnectionHandle*. The following table lists the SQLSTATE values commonly returned by **SQLGetFunctions** and explains each one in the context of this function; the notation "(DM)" precedes the descriptions of SQLSTATEs returned by the Driver Manager. The return code associated with each SQLSTATE value is SQL_ERROR, unless noted otherwise.

SQLSTATE	Error	Description
01000	General warning	Driver-specific informational message. (Function returns SQL_SUCCESS_WITH_INFO.)
08S01	Communication link failure	The communication link between the driver and the data source to which the driver was connected failed before the function completed processing.
HY000	General error	An error occurred for which there was no specific SQLSTATE and for which no implementation-specific SQLSTATE was defined. The error message returned by **SQLGetDiagRec** in the **MessageText* buffer describes the error and its cause.
HY001	Memory allocation error	The driver was unable to allocate memory required to support execution or completion of the function.

SQLSTATE	Error	Description
HY010	Function sequence error	(DM) **SQLGetFunctions** was called before **SQLConnect**, **SQLBrowseConnect**, or **SQLDriverConnect**. (DM) **SQLBrowseConnect** was called for the *ConnectionHandle* and returned SQL_NEED_DATA. This function was called before **SQLBrowseConnect** returned SQL_SUCCESS_WITH_INFO or SQL_SUCCESS.
HY013	Memory management error	The function call could not be processed because the underlying memory objects could not be accessed, possibly because of low memory conditions.
HY095	Function type out of range	(DM) An invalid *FunctionId* value was specified.
HYT01	Connection timeout expired	The connection timeout period expired before the data source responded to the request. The connection timeout period is set through **SQLSetConnectAttr**, SQL_ATTR_CONNECTION_TIMEOUT.

Comments

SQLGetFunctions always returns that **SQLGetFunctions**, **SQLDataSources**, and **SQLDrivers** are supported. It does this because these functions are implemented in the Driver Manager. For information about how applications use **SQLGetFunctions**, see "Interface Conformance Levels" in Chapter 4, "ODBC Fundamentals."

The following is a list of valid values for *FunctionId* for functions that conform to the ISO 92 standards–compliance level:

SQL_API_SQLALLOCHANDLE
SQL_API_SQLBINDCOL
SQL_API_SQLCANCEL
SQL_API_SQLCLOSECURSOR
SQL_API_SQLCOLATTRIBUTE
SQL_API_SQLCONNECT
SQL_API_SQLCOPYDESC
SQL_API_SQLDATASOURCES
SQL_API_SQLDESCRIBECOL
SQL_API_SQLDISCONNECT
SQL_API_SQLDRIVERS
SQL_API_SQLENDTRAN
SQL_API_SQLGETDESCFIELD
SQL_API_SQLGETDESCREC
SQL_API_SQLGETDIAGFIELD
SQL_API_SQLGETDIAGREC
SQL_API_SQLGETENVATTR
SQL_API_SQLGETFUNCTIONS
SQL_API_SQLGETINFO
SQL_API_SQLGETSTMTATTR
SQL_API_SQLGETTYPEINFO
SQL_API_SQLNUMRESULTCOLS
SQL_API_SQLPARAMDATA
SQL_API_SQLPREPARE

SQL_API_SQLEXECDIRECT
SQL_API_SQLEXECUTE
SQL_API_SQLFETCH
SQL_API_SQLFETCHSCROLL
SQL_API_SQLFREEHANDLE
SQL_API_SQLFREESTMT
SQL_API_SQLGETCONNECTATTR
SQL_API_SQLGETCURSORNAME
SQL_API_SQLGETDATA
SQL_API_SQLPUTDATA
SQL_API_SQLROWCOUNT
SQL_API_SQLSETCONNECTATTR
SQL_API_SQLSETCURSORNAME
SQL_API_SQLSETDESCFIELD
SQL_API_SQLSETDESCREC
SQL_API_SQLSETENVATTR
SQL_API_SQLSETSTMTATTR

The following is a list of valid values for *FunctionId* for functions conforming to the X/Open standards–compliance level:

SQL_API_SQLCOLUMNS
SQL_API_SQLSPECIALCOLUMNS
SQL_API_SQLSTATISTICS
SQL_API_SQLTABLES

The following is a list of valid values for *FunctionId* for functions conforming to the ODBC standards–compliance level:

SQL_API_SQLBINDPARAMETER
SQL_API_SQLBROWSECONNECT
SQL_API_SQLBULKOPERATIONS [1]
SQL_API_SQLCOLUMNPRIVILEGES
SQL_API_SQLDESCRIBEPARAM
SQL_API_SQLDRIVERCONNECT
SQL_API_SQLFOREIGNKEYS
SQL_API_SQLMORERESULTS
SQL_API_SQLNATIVESQL
SQL_API_SQLNUMPARAMS
SQL_API_SQLPRIMARYKEYS
SQL_API_SQLPROCEDURECOLUMNS
SQL_API_SQLPROCEDURES
SQL_API_SQLSETPOS
SQL_API_SQLTABLEPRIVILEGES

1 When working with an ODBC 2.*x* driver, **SQLBulkOperations** will be returned as supported only if both of the following are true: the ODBC 2.*x* driver supports **SQLSetPos**, and the information type SQL_POS_OPERATIONS returns the SQL_POS_ADD bit as set.

SQL_FUNC_EXISTS Macro

The SQL_FUNC_EXISTS(*SupportedPtr*, *FunctionID*) macro is used to determine support of ODBC 3.0 or earlier functions after **SQLGetFunctions** has been called with an *FunctionId* argument of SQL_API_ODBC3_ALL_FUNCTIONS. The application calls SQL_FUNC_EXISTS with the *SupportedPtr* argument set to the *SupportedPtr passed in SQLGetFunctions*, and with the *FunctionID* argument set to the **#define** for the function. SQL_FUNC_EXISTS returns SQL_TRUE if the function is supported, and SQL_FALSE otherwise.

Note When working with an ODBC 2.*x* driver, the ODBC 3.0 Driver Manager will return SQL_TRUE for **SQLAllocHandle** and **SQLFreeHandle**, because **SQLAllocHandle** is mapped to **SQLAllocEnv**, **SQLAllocConnect**, or **SQLAllocStmt**, and **SQLFreeHandle** is mapped to **SQLFreeEnv**, **SQLFreeConnect**, or **SQLFreeStmt**. **SQLAllocHandle** or **SQLFreeHandle** with a *HandleType* argument of SQL_HANDLE_DESC is not supported, however, even though SQL_TRUE is returned for the functions, because there is no ODBC 2.*x* function to map to in this case.

Code Example

The following two examples show how an application uses **SQLGetFunctions** to determine if a driver supports **SQLTables**, **SQLColumns**, and **SQLStatistics**. If the driver does not support these functions, the application disconnects from the driver. The first example calls **SQLGetFunctions** once for each function.

```
SQLUSMALLINT TablesExists, ColumnsExists, StatisticsExists;

SQLGetFunctions(hdbc, SQL_API_SQLTABLES, &TablesExists);
SQLGetFunctions(hdbc, SQL_API_SQLCOLUMNS, &ColumnsExists);
SQLGetFunctions(hdbc, SQL_API_SQLSTATISTICS, &StatisticsExists);

if (TablesExists && ColumnsExists && StatisticsExists) {

   /* Continue with application */

}

SQLDisconnect(hdbc);
```

The second example calls **SQLGetFunctions** a single time and passes it an array in which **SQLGetFunctions** returns information about all ODBC functions.

```
#define FUNCTIONS 100

SQLUSMALLINT fExists[FUNCTIONS];

SQLGetFunctions(hdbc, SQL_API_ALL_FUNCTIONS, fExists);

if (fExists[SQL_API_SQLTABLES] &&
    fExists[SQL_API_SQLCOLUMNS] &&
    fExists[SQL_API_SQLSTATISTICS]) {

   /* Continue with application */

}

SQLDisconnect(hdbc);
```

Related Functions

For information about	See
Returning the setting of a connection attribute	**SQLGetConnectAttr**
Returning information about a driver or data source	**SQLGetInfo**
Returning the setting of a statement attribute	**SQLGetStmtAttr**

SQLGetInfo

Conformance

Version Introduced: ODBC 1.0
Standards Compliance: ISO 92

Summary

SQLGetInfo returns general information about the driver and data source associated with a connection.

Syntax

SQLRETURN **SQLGetInfo**(
    SQLHDBC *ConnectionHandle*,
    SQLUSMALLINT *InfoType*,
    SQLPOINTER *InfoValuePtr*,
    SQLSMALLINT *BufferLength*,
    SQLSMALLINT * *StringLengthPtr*);

Arguments

ConnectionHandle [Input]
Connection handle.

InfoType [Input]
Type of information.

InfoValuePtr [Output]
Pointer to a buffer in which to return the information. Depending on the *InfoType* requested, the information returned will be one of the following: a null-terminated character string, an SQLUSMALLINT value, an SQLUINTEGER bitmask, an SQLUINTEGER flag, or a SQLUINTEGER binary value.

If the *InfoType* argument is SQL_DRIVER_HDESC or SQL_DRIVER_HSTMT, the *InfoValuePtr* argument is both input and output. (See the SQL_DRIVER_HDESC or SQL_DRIVER_HSTMT descriptors later in this function description for more information.)

BufferLength [Input]
Length of the **InfoValuePtr* buffer. If the value in **InfoValuePtr* is not a character string, or if *InfoValuePtr* is a null pointer, the *BufferLength* argument is ignored. The driver assumes that the size of **InfoValuePtr* is SQLUSMALLINT or SQLUINTEGER, based on the *InfoType*.

StringLengthPtr [Output]

Pointer to a buffer in which to return the total number of bytes (excluding the null-termination character for character data) available to return in **InfoValuePtr*.

For character data, if the number of bytes available to return is greater than or equal to *BufferLength*, the information in **InfoValuePtr* is truncated to *BufferLength* bytes minus the length of a null-termination character and is null-terminated by the driver.

For all other types of data, the value of *BufferLength* is ignored and the driver assumes the size of **InfoValuePtr* is SQLUSMALLINT or SQLUINTEGER, depending on the *InfoType*.

Returns

SQL_SUCCESS, SQL_SUCCESS_WITH_INFO, SQL_ERROR, or SQL_INVALID_HANDLE.

Diagnostics

When **SQLGetInfo** returns either SQL_ERROR or SQL_SUCCESS_WITH_INFO, an associated SQLSTATE value can be obtained by calling **SQLGetDiagRec** with a *HandleType* of SQL_HANDLE_DBC and a *Handle* of *ConnectionHandle*. The following table lists the SQLSTATE values commonly returned by **SQLGetInfo** and explains each one in the context of this function; the notation "(DM)" precedes the descriptions of SQLSTATEs returned by the Driver Manager. The return code associated with each SQLSTATE value is SQL_ERROR, unless noted otherwise.

SQLSTATE	Error	Description
01000	General warning	Driver-specific informational message. (Function returns SQL_SUCCESS_WITH_INFO.)
01004	String data, right truncated	The buffer **InfoValuePtr* was not large enough to return all of the requested information, so the information was truncated. The length of the requested information in its untruncated form is returned in **StringLengthPtr*. (Function returns SQL_SUCCESS_WITH_INFO.)
08003	Connection does not exist	(DM) The type of information requested in *InfoType* requires an open connection. Of the information types reserved by ODBC, only SQL_ODBC_VER can be returned without an open connection.
08S01	Communication link failure	The communication link between the driver and the data source to which the driver was connected failed before the function completed processing.

SQLSTATE	Error	Description
HY000	General error	An error occurred for which there was no specific SQLSTATE and for which no implementation-specific SQLSTATE was defined. The error message returned by **SQLGetDiagRec** in the **MessageText* buffer describes the error and its cause.
HY001	Memory allocation error	The driver was unable to allocate memory required to support execution or completion of the function.
HY013	Memory management error	The function call could not be processed because the underlying memory objects could not be accessed, possibly because of low memory conditions.
HY024	Invalid attribute value	(DM) The *InfoType* argument was SQL_DRIVER_HSTMT, and the value pointed to by *InfoValuePtr* was not a valid statement handle. (DM) The *InfoType* argument was SQL_DRIVER_HDESC, and the value pointed to by *InfoValuePtr* was not a valid descriptor handle.
HY090	Invalid string or buffer length	(DM) The value specified for argument *BufferLength* was less than 0.
HY096	Information type out of range	The value specified for the argument *InfoType* was not valid for the version of ODBC supported by the driver.
HYC00	Optional field not implemented	The value specified for the argument *InfoType* was a driver-specific value that is not supported by the driver.
HYT01	Connection timeout expired	The connection timeout period expired before the data source responded to the request. The connection timeout period is set through **SQLSetConnectAttr**, SQL_ATTR_CONNECTION_TIMEOUT.
IM001	Driver does not support this function	(DM) The driver corresponding to the *ConnectionHandle* does not support the function.

Comments

The currently defined information types are shown in "Information Types" later in this section; it is expected that more will be defined to take advantage of different data sources. A range of information types is reserved by ODBC; driver developers must reserve values for their own driver-specific use from X/Open. For more information, see "Driver-Specific Data Types, Descriptor Types, Information Types, Diagnostic Types, and Attributes" in Chapter 17, "Programming Considerations."

The format of the information returned in **InfoValuePtr* depends on the *InfoType* requested. **SQLGetInfo** will return information in one of five different formats:

- A null-terminated character string
- An SQLUSMALLINT value
- An SQLUINTEGER bitmask
- An SQLUINTEGER value
- A SQLUINTEGER binary value

The format of each of the following information types is noted in the type's description. The application must cast the value returned in **InfoValuePtr* accordingly. For an example of how an application could retrieve data from a SQLUINTEGER bitmask, see "Code Example."

A driver must return a value for each of the information types defined in the following tables. If an information type does not apply to the driver or data source, then the driver returns one of the following values:

Format of **InfoValuePtr*	Returned value
Character string ("Y" or "N")	"N"
Character string (not "Y" or "N")	Empty string
SQLUSMALLINT	0
SQLUINTEGER bitmask or SQLUINTEGER binary value	0L

For example, if a data source does not support procedures, **SQLGetInfo** returns the following values for the values of *InfoType* that are related to procedures:

InfoType	Returned value
SQL_PROCEDURES	"N"
SQL_ACCESSIBLE_PROCEDURES	"N"
SQL_MAX_PROCEDURE_NAME_LEN	0
SQL_PROCEDURE_TERM	Empty string

SQLGetInfo returns SQLSTATE HY096 (Invalid argument value) for values of *InfoType* that are in the range of information types reserved for use by ODBC but are not defined by the version of ODBC supported by the driver. To determine what version of ODBC a driver conforms to, an application calls **SQLGetInfo** with the SQL_DRIVER_ODBC_VER information type. **SQLGetInfo** returns SQLSTATE HYC00 (Optional feature not implemented) for values of *InfoType* that are in the range of information types reserved for driver-specific use but are not supported by the driver.

All calls to **SQLGetInfo** require an open connection, except when the *InfoType* is SQL_ODBC_VER, which returns the version of the Driver Manager.

Information Types

This section lists the information types supported by **SQLGetInfo**. Information types are grouped categorically and listed alphabetically. Information types that were added or renamed for ODBC 3.0 are also listed.

Driver Information

The following values of the *InfoType* argument return information about the ODBC driver, such as the number of active statements, the data source name, and the interface standards compliance level.

SQL_ACTIVE_ENVIRONMENTS	SQL_GETDATA_EXTENSIONS
SQL_ASYNC_MODE	SQL_INFO_SCHEMA_VIEWS
SQL_BATCH_ROW_COUNT	SQL_KEYSET_CURSOR_ATTRIBUTES1
SQL_BATCH_SUPPORT	SQL_KEYSET_CURSOR_ATTRIBUTES2
SQL_DATA_SOURCE_NAME	SQL_MAX_ASYNC_CONCURRENT_STATEMENTS
SQL_DRIVER_HDBC	SQL_MAX_CONCURRENT_ACTIVITIES
SQL_DRIVER_HDESC	SQL_MAX_DRIVER_CONNECTIONS
SQL_DRIVER_HENV	SQL_ODBC_INTERFACE_CONFORMANCE
SQL_DRIVER_HLIB	SQL_ODBC_STANDARD_CLI_CONFORMANCE
SQL_DRIVER_HSTMT	SQL_ODBC_VER
SQL_DRIVER_NAME	SQL_PARAM_ARRAY_ROW_COUNTS
SQL_DRIVER_ODBC_VER	SQL_PARAM_ARRAY_SELECTS
SQL_DRIVER_VER	SQL_ROW_UPDATES
SQL_DYNAMIC_CURSOR_ATTRIBUTES1	SQL_SEARCH_PATTERN_ESCAPE
SQL_DYNAMIC_CURSOR_ATTRIBUTES2	SQL_SERVER_NAME
SQL_FORWARD_ONLY_CURSOR_ATTRIBUTES1	SQL_STATIC_CURSOR_ATTRIBUTES1
SQL_FORWARD_ONLY_CURSOR_ATTRIBUTES2	SQL_STATIC_CURSOR_ATTRIBUTES2
SQL_FILE_USAGE	

DBMS Product Information

The following values of the *InfoType* argument return information about the DBMS product, such as the DBMS name and version.

SQL_DATABASE_NAME	SQL_DBMS_VER
SQL_DBMS_NAME	

Data Source Information

The following values of the *InfoType* argument return information about the data source, such as cursor characteristics and transaction capabilities.

SQL_ACCESSIBLE_PROCEDURES
SQL_ACCESSIBLE_TABLES
SQL_BOOKMARK_PERSISTENCE
SQL_CATALOG_TERM
SQL_COLLATION_SEQ
SQL_CONCAT_NULL_BEHAVIOR
SQL_CURSOR_COMMIT_BEHAVIOR
SQL_CURSOR_ROLLBACK_BEHAVIOR
SQL_CURSOR_SENSITIVITY
SQL_DATA_SOURCE_READ_ONLY
SQL_DEFAULT_TXN_ISOLATION
SQL_DESCRIBE_PARAMETER
SQL_MULT_RESULT_SETS
SQL_MULTIPLE_ACTIVE_TXN
SQL_NEED_LONG_DATA_LEN
SQL_NULL_COLLATION
SQL_PROCEDURE_TERM
SQL_SCHEMA_TERM
SQL_SCROLL_OPTIONS
SQL_TABLE_TERM
SQL_TXN_CAPABLE
SQL_TXN_ISOLATION_OPTION
SQL_USER_NAME

Supported SQL

The following values of the *InfoType* argument return information about the SQL statements supported by the data source. The SQL syntax of each feature described by these information types is the SQL-92 syntax. These information types do not exhaustively describe the entire SQL-92 grammar. Instead, they describe those parts of the grammar for which data sources commonly offer different levels of support. Specifically, most of the DDL statements in SQL-92 are covered.

Applications should determine the general level of supported grammar from the SQL_SQL_CONFORMANCE information type and use the other information types to determine variations from the stated standards compliance level.

SQL_AGGREGATE_FUNCTIONS
SQL_ALTER_DOMAIN
SQL_ALTER_SCHEMA
SQL_ALTER_TABLE
SQL_ANSI_SQL_DATETIME_LITERALS
SQL_CATALOG_LOCATION
SQL_CATALOG_NAME
SQL_CATALOG_NAME_SEPARATOR
SQL_CATALOG_USAGE
SQL_COLUMN_ALIAS
SQL_CORRELATION_NAME
SQL_DROP_TABLE
SQL_DROP_TRANSLATION
SQL_DROP_VIEW
SQL_EXPRESSIONS_IN_ORDERBY
SQL_GROUP_BY
SQL_IDENTIFIER_CASE
SQL_IDENTIFIER_QUOTE_CHAR
SQL_INDEX_KEYWORDS
SQL_INSERT_STATEMENT
SQL_INTEGRITY
SQL_KEYWORDS

SQL_CREATE_ASSERTION
SQL_CREATE_CHARACTER_SET
SQL_CREATE_COLLATION
SQL_CREATE_DOMAIN
SQL_CREATE_SCHEMA
SQL_CREATE_TABLE
SQL_CREATE_TRANSLATION
SQL_DDL_INDEX
SQL_DROP_ASSERTION
SQL_DROP_CHARACTER_SET
SQL_DROP_COLLATION
SQL_DROP_DOMAIN
SQL_DROP_SCHEMA
SQL_LIKE_ESCAPE_CLAUSE
SQL_NON_NULLABLE_COLUMNS
SQL_SQL_CONFORMANCE
SQL_OJ_CAPABILITIES
SQL_ORDER_BY_COLUMNS_IN_SELECT
SQL_OUTER_JOINS
SQL_PROCEDURES
SQL_QUOTED_IDENTIFIER_CASE
SQL_SCHEMA_USAGE
SQL_SPECIAL_CHARACTERS
SQL_SUBQUERIES
SQL_UNION

SQL Limits

The following values of the *InfoType* argument return information about the limits applied to identifiers and clauses in SQL statements, such as the maximum lengths of identifiers and the maximum number of columns in a select list. Limitations can be imposed by either the driver or the data source.

SQL_MAX_BINARY_LITERAL_LEN
SQL_MAX_CATALOG_NAME_LEN
SQL_MAX_CHAR_LITERAL_LEN
SQL_MAX_COLUMN_NAME_LEN
SQL_MAX_COLUMNS_IN_GROUP_BY
SQL_MAX_COLUMNS_IN_INDEX
SQL_MAX_COLUMNS_IN_ORDER_BY
SQL_MAX_COLUMNS_IN_SELECT
SQL_MAX_COLUMNS_IN_TABLE
SQL_MAX_CURSOR_NAME_LEN
SQL_MAX_IDENTIFIER_LEN
SQL_MAX_INDEX_SIZE
SQL_MAX_PROCEDURE_NAME_LEN
SQL_MAX_ROW_SIZE
SQL_MAX_ROW_SIZE_INCLUDES_LONG
SQL_MAX_SCHEMA_NAME_LEN
SQL_MAX_STATEMENT_LEN
SQL_MAX_TABLE_NAME_LEN
SQL_MAX_TABLES_IN_SELECT
SQL_MAX_USER_NAME_LEN

Scalar Function Information

The following values of the *InfoType* argument return information about the scalar functions supported by the data source and the driver. For more information about scalar functions, see Appendix E, "Scalar Functions."

SQL_CONVERT_FUNCTIONS
SQL_NUMERIC_FUNCTIONS
SQL_STRING_FUNCTIONS
SQL_SYSTEM_FUNCTIONS
SQL_TIMEDATE_ADD_INTERVALS
SQL_TIMEDATE_DIFF_INTERVALS
SQL_TIMEDATE_FUNCTIONS

Conversion Information

The following values of the *InfoType* argument return a list of the SQL data types to which the data source can convert the specified SQL data type with the **CONVERT** scalar function.

SQL_CONVERT_BIGINT
SQL_CONVERT_BINARY
SQL_CONVERT_BIT
SQL_CONVERT_CHAR
SQL_CONVERT_DATE
SQL_CONVERT_DECIMAL
SQL_CONVERT_DOUBLE
SQL_CONVERT_FLOAT
SQL_CONVERT_INTEGER
SQL_CONVERT_INTERVAL_YEAR_MONTH
SQL_CONVERT_INTERVAL_DAY_TIME
SQL_CONVERT_LONGVARBINARY
SQL_CONVERT_LONGVARCHAR
SQL_CONVERT_NUMERIC
SQL_CONVERT_REAL
SQL_CONVERT_SMALLINT
SQL_CONVERT_TIME
SQL_CONVERT_TIMESTAMP
SQL_CONVERT_TINYINT
SQL_CONVERT_VARBINARY
SQL_CONVERT_VARCHAR

Information Types Added for ODBC 3.0

The following values of the *InfoType* argument have been added for ODBC 3.0.

SQL_ACTIVE_ENVIRONMENTS
SQL_AGGREGATE_FUNCTIONS
SQL_ALTER_DOMAIN
SQL_ALTER_SCHEMA
SQL_ANSI_SQL_DATETIME_LITERALS
SQL_ASYNC_MODE
SQL_BATCH_ROW_COUNT
SQL_BATCH_SUPPORT
SQL_DROP_ASSERTION
SQL_DROP_CHARACTER_SET
SQL_DROP_COLLATION
SQL_DROP_DOMAIN
SQL_DROP_SCHEMA
SQL_DROP_TABLE
SQL_DROP_TRANSLATION
SQL_DROP_VIEW

SQL_CATALOG_NAME	SQL_DYNAMIC_CURSOR_ATTRIBUTES1
SQL_COLLATION_SEQ	SQL_DYNAMIC_CURSOR_ATTRIBUTES2
SQL_CONVERT_INTERVAL_YEAR_MONTH	SQL_FORWARD_ONLY_CURSOR_ATTRIBUTES1
SQL_CONVERT_INTERVAL_DAY_TIME	SQL_FORWARD_ONLY_CURSOR_ATTRIBUTES2
SQL_CREATE_ASSERTION	SQL_INFO_SCHEMA_VIEWS
SQL_CREATE_CHARACTER_SET	SQL_INSERT_STATEMENT
SQL_CREATE_COLLATION	SQL_KEYSET_CURSOR_ATTRIBUTES1
SQL_CREATE_DOMAIN	SQL_KEYSET_CURSOR_ATTRIBUTES2
SQL_CREATE_SCHEMA	SQL_MAX_ASYNC_CONCURRENT_STATEMENTS
SQL_CREATE_TABLE	SQL_MAX_IDENTIFIER_LEN
SQL_CREATE_TRANSLATION	SQL_PARAM_ARRAY_ROW_COUNTS
SQL_CURSOR_SENSITIVITY	SQL_PARAM_ARRAY_SELECTS
SQL_DDL_INDEX	SQL_STATIC_CURSOR_ATTRIBUTES1
SQL_DESCRIBE_PARAMETER	SQL_STATIC_CURSOR_ATTRIBUTES2
SQL_DM_VER	SQL_XOPEN_CLI_YEAR
SQL_DRIVER_HDESC	

Information Types Renamed for ODBC 3.0

The following values of the *InfoType* argument have been renamed for ODBC 3.0.

ODBC 2.0 *InfoType*	ODBC 3.0 *InfoType*
SQL_ACTIVE_CONNECTIONS	SQL_MAX_DRIVER_CONNECTIONS
SQL_ACTIVE_STATEMENTS	SQL_MAX_CONCURRENT_ACTIVITIES
SQL_MAX_OWNER_NAME_LEN	SQL_MAX_SCHEMA_NAME_LEN
SQL_MAX_QUALIFIER_NAME_LEN	SQL_MAX_CATALOG_NAME_LEN
SQL_ODBC_SQL_OPT_IEF	SQL_INTEGRITY
SQL_OWNER_TERM	SQL_SCHEMA_TERM
SQL_OWNER_USAGE	SQL_SCHEMA_USAGE
SQL_QUALIFIER_LOCATION	SQL_CATALOG_LOCATION
SQL_QUALIFIER_NAME_SEPARATOR	SQL_CATALOG_NAME_SEPARATOR
SQL_QUALIFIER_TERM	SQL_CATALOG_TERM
SQL_QUALIFIER_USAGE	SQL_CATALOG_USAGE

Information Types Deprecated ODBC 3.0

The following values of the *InfoType* argument have been deprecated in ODBC 3.0. ODBC 3.0 drivers must continue to support these information types for backward compatibility with ODBC 2.*x* applications. (For more information on these types, see "SQLGetInfo Support" in Appendix G, "Driver Guidelines for Backward Compatibility.")

SQL_FETCH_DIRECTION	SQL_POS_OPERATIONS
SQL_LOCK_TYPES	SQL_POSITIONED_STATEMENTS
SQL_ODBC_API_CONFORMANCE	SQL_SCROLL_CONCURRENCY
SQL_ODBC_SQL_CONFORMANCE	SQL_STATIC_SENSITIVITY

Information Type Descriptions

The following table alphabetically lists each information type, the version of ODBC in which it was introduced, and its description.

InfoType	Returns
SQL_ACCESSIBLE_ PROCEDURES (ODBC 1.0)	A character string: "Y" if the user can execute all procedures returned by **SQLProcedures**, "N" if there may be procedures returned that the user cannot execute.
SQL_ACCESSIBLE_TABLES (ODBC 1.0)	A character string: "Y" if the user is guaranteed **SELECT** privileges to all tables returned by **SQLTables**, "N" if there may be tables returned that the user cannot access.
SQL_ACTIVE_ENVIRONMENTS (ODBC 3.0)	An SQLUSMALLINT value specifying the maximum number of active environments that the driver can support. If there is no specified limit or the limit is unknown, this value is set to zero.
SQL_AGGREGATE_FUNCTIONS (ODBC 3.0)	An SQLUINTEGER bitmask enumerating support for aggregation functions: SQL_AF_ALL SQL_AF_AVG SQL_AF_COUNT SQL_AF_DISTINCT SQL_AF_MAX SQL_AF_MIN SQL_AF_SUM An SQL-92 Entry level–conformant driver will always return all of these options as supported.

InfoType	Returns
SQL_ALTER_DOMAIN (ODBC 3.0)	An SQLUINTEGER bitmask enumerating the clauses in the **ALTER DOMAIN** statement, as defined in SQL-92, supported by the data source. An SQL-92 Full level–compliant driver will always return all of the bitmasks. A return value of "0" means that the **ALTER DOMAIN** statement is not supported. The SQL-92 or FIPS conformance level at which this feature needs to be supported is shown in parentheses next to each bitmask. The following bitmasks are used to determine which clauses are supported: SQL_AD_ADD_DOMAIN_CONSTRAINT = Adding a domain constraint is supported (Full level) SQL_AD_ADD_DOMAIN_DEFAULT = <alter domain> <set domain default clause> is supported (Full level) SQL_AD_CONSTRAINT_NAME_DEFINITION = <constraint name definition clause> is supported for naming domain constraint (Intermediate level) SQL_AD_DROP_DOMAIN_CONSTRAINT = <drop domain constraint clause> is supported (Full level) SQL_AD_DROP_DOMAIN_DEFAULT = <alter domain> <drop domain default clause> is supported (Full level) The following bits specify the supported <constraint attributes> if <add domain constraint> is supported (the SQL_AD_ADD_DOMAIN_CONSTRAINT bit is set): SQL_AD_ADD_CONSTRAINT_DEFERRABLE (Full level) SQL_AD_ADD_CONSTRAINT_NON_DEFERRABLE (Full level) SQL_AD_ADD_CONSTRAINT_INITIALLY_DEFERRED (Full level) SQL_AD_ADD_CONSTRAINT_INITIALLY_IMMEDIATE (Full level)
SQL_ALTER_TABLE (ODBC 2.0)	An SQLUINTEGER bitmask enumerating the clauses in the **ALTER TABLE** statement supported by the data source. The SQL-92 or FIPS conformance level at which this feature needs to be supported is shown in parentheses next to each bitmask. The following bitmasks are used to determine which clauses are supported: SQL_AT_ADD_COLUMN_COLLATION = <add column> clause is supported, with facility to specify column collation (Full level) (ODBC 3.0) SQL_AT_ADD_COLUMN_DEFAULT = <add column> clause is supported, with facility to specify column defaults (FIPS Transitional level) (ODBC 3.0)

InfoType	Returns
SQL_ALTER_TABLE (ODBC 2.0) (*continued*)	SQL_AT_ADD_COLUMN_SINGLE = <add column> is supported (FIPS Transitional level) (ODBC 3.0) SQL_AT_ADD_CONSTRAINT = <add column> clause is supported, with facility to specify column constraints (FIPS Transitional level) (ODBC 3.0) SQL_AT_ADD_TABLE_CONSTRAINT = <add table constraint> clause is supported (FIPS Transitional level) (ODBC 3.0) SQL_AT_CONSTRAINT_NAME_DEFINITION = <constraint name definition> is supported for naming column and table constraints (Intermediate level) (ODBC 3.0) SQL_AT_DROP_COLUMN_CASCADE = <drop column> CASCADE is supported (FIPS Transitional level) (ODBC 3.0) SQL_AT_DROP_COLUMN_DEFAULT = <alter column> <drop column default clause> is supported (Intermediate level) (ODBC 3.0) SQL_AT_DROP_COLUMN_RESTRICT = <drop column> RESTRICT is supported (FIPS Transitional level) (ODBC 3.0) SQL_AT_DROP_TABLE_CONSTRAINT_CASCADE (ODBC 3.0) SQL_AT_DROP_TABLE_CONSTRAINT_RESTRICT = <drop column> RESTRICT is supported (FIPS Transitional level) (ODBC 3.0) SQL_AT_SET_COLUMN_DEFAULT = <alter column> <set column default clause> is supported (Intermediate level) (ODBC 3.0) The following bits specify the support <constraint attributes> if specifying column or table constraints is supported (the SQL_AT_ADD_CONSTRAINT bit is set): SQL_AT_CONSTRAINT_INITIALLY_DEFERRED (Full level) (ODBC 3.0) SQL_AT_CONSTRAINT_INITIALLY_IMMEDIATE (Full level) (ODBC 3.0) SQL_AT_CONSTRAINT_DEFERRABLE (Full level) (ODBC 3.0) SQL_AT_CONSTRAINT_NON_DEFERRABLE (Full level) (ODBC 3.0)

InfoType	Returns
SQL_ASYNC_MODE (ODBC 3.0)	An SQLUINTEGER value indicating the level of asynchronous support in the driver: SQL_AM_CONNECTION = Connection level asynchronous execution is supported. Either all statement handles associated with a given connection handle are in asynchronous mode, or all are in synchronous mode. A statement handle on a connection cannot be in asynchronous mode while another statement handle on the same connection is in synchronous mode, and vice versa. SQL_AM_STATEMENT = Statement level asynchronous execution is supported. Some statement handles associated with a connection handle can be in asynchronous mode, while other statement handles on the same connection are in synchronous mode. SQL_AM_NONE = Asynchronous mode is not supported.
SQL_BATCH_ROW_COUNT (ODBC 3.0)	An SQLUINTEGER bitmask enumerating the behavior of the driver with respect to the availability of row counts. The following bit masks are used in conjunction with the information type: SQL_BRC_ROLLED_UP = Row counts for consecutive INSERT, DELETE, or UPDATE statements are rolled up into one. If this bit is not set, then row counts are available for each individual statement. SQL_BRC_PROCEDURES = Row counts, if any, are available when a batch is executed in a stored procedure. If row counts are available, they may be rolled up or individually available, depending on the SQL_BRC_ROLLED_UP bit. SQL_BRC_EXPLICIT = Row counts, if any, are available when a batch is executed directly by calling **SQLExecute** or **SQLExecDirect**. If row counts are available, they may be rolled up or individually available, depending on the SQL_BRC_ROLLED_UP bit.
SQL_BATCH_SUPPORT (ODBC 3.0)	An SQLUINTEGER bitmask enumerating the driver's support for batches. The following bitmasks are used to determine which level is supported: SQL_BS_SELECT_EXPLICIT = The driver supports explicit batches that can have result-set generating statements. SQL_BS_ROW_COUNT_EXPLICIT = The driver supports explicit batches that can have row-count generating statements. SQL_BS_SELECT_PROC = The driver supports explicit procedures that can have result-set generating statements. SQL_BS_ROW_COUNT_PROC = The driver supports explicit procedures that can have row-count generating statements.

InfoType	**Returns**
SQL_BOOKMARK_ PERSISTENCE (ODBC 2.0)	An SQLUINTEGER bitmask enumerating the operations through which bookmarks persist. The following bitmasks are used in conjunction with the flag to determine through which options bookmarks persist: SQL_BP_CLOSE = Bookmarks are valid after an application calls **SQLFreeStmt** with the SQL_CLOSE option, or **SQLCloseCursor** to close the cursor associated with a statement. SQL_BP_DELETE = The bookmark for a row is valid after that row has been deleted. SQL_BP_DROP = Bookmarks are valid after an application calls **SQLFreeHandle** with a *HandleType* of SQL_HANDLE_STMT to drop a statement. SQL_BP_TRANSACTION = Bookmarks are valid after an application commits or rolls back a transaction. SQL_BP_UPDATE = The bookmark for a row is valid after any column in that row has been updated, including key columns. SQL_BP_OTHER_HSTMT = A bookmark associated with one statement can be used with another statement. Unless SQL_BP_CLOSE or SQL_BP_DROP is specified, the cursor on the first statement must be open.
SQL_CATALOG_LOCATION (ODBC 2.0)	An SQLUSMALLINT value indicating the position of the catalog in a qualified table name: SQL_CL_START SQL_CL_END For example, an Xbase driver returns SQL_CL_START because the directory (catalog) name is at the start of the table name, as in \EMPDATA\EMP.DBF. An ORACLE Server driver returns SQL_CL_END, because the catalog is at the end of the table name, as in ADMIN.EMP@EMPDATA. An SQL-92 Full level–conformant driver will always return SQL_CL_START. A value of 0 is returned if catalogs are not supported by the data source. To find out whether catalogs are supported, an application calls **SQLGetInfo** with the SQL_CATALOG_NAME information type. This *InfoType* has been renamed for ODBC 3.0 from the ODBC 2.0 *InfoType* SQL_QUALIFIER_LOCATION.
SQL_CATALOG_NAME (ODBC 3.0)	A character string: “Y” if the server supports catalog names, or “N” if it does not. An SQL-92 Full level–conformant driver will always return “Y”.

InfoType	Returns
SQL_CATALOG_NAME_ SEPARATOR (ODBC 1.0)	A character string: the character or characters that the data source defines as the separator between a catalog name and the qualified name element that follows or precedes it. An empty string is returned if catalogs are not supported by the data source. To find out whether catalogs are supported, an application calls **SQLGetInfo** with the SQL_CATALOG_NAME information type. An SQL-92 Full level–conformant driver will always return ".". This *InfoType* has been renamed for ODBC 3.0 from the ODBC 2.0 *InfoType* SQL_QUALIFIER_NAME_SEPARATOR.
SQL_CATALOG_TERM (ODBC 1.0)	A character string with the data source vendor's name for a catalog; for example, "database" or "directory." This string can be in upper, lower, or mixed case. An empty string is returned if catalogs are not supported by the data source. To find out whether catalogs are supported, an application calls **SQLGetInfo** with the SQL_CATALOG_NAME information type. An SQL-92 Full level–conformant driver will always return "catalog". This *InfoType* has been renamed for ODBC 3.0 from the ODBC 2.0 *InfoType* SQL_QUALIFIER_TERM.
SQL_CATALOG_USAGE (ODBC 2.0)	An SQLUINTEGER bitmask enumerating the statements in which catalogs can be used. The following bitmasks are used to determine where catalogs can be used: SQL_CU_DML_STATEMENTS = Catalogs are supported in all Data Manipulation Language statements: **SELECT**, **INSERT**, **UPDATE**, **DELETE**, and, if supported, **SELECT FOR UPDATE** and positioned update and delete statements. SQL_CU_PROCEDURE_INVOCATION = Catalogs are supported in the ODBC procedure invocation statement. SQL_CU_TABLE_DEFINITION = Catalogs are supported in all table definition statements: **CREATE TABLE**, **CREATE VIEW**, **ALTER TABLE**, **DROP TABLE**, and **DROP VIEW**. SQL_CU_INDEX_DEFINITION = Catalogs are supported in all index definition statements: **CREATE INDEX** and **DROP INDEX**. SQL_CU_PRIVILEGE_DEFINITION = Catalogs are supported in all privilege definition statements: **GRANT** and **REVOKE**.

InfoType	Returns
SQL_CATALOG_USAGE (ODBC 2.0) (*continued*)	A value of 0 is returned if catalogs are not supported by the data source. To find out whether catalogs are supported, an application calls **SQLGetInfo** with the SQL_CATALOG_NAME information type. An SQL-92 Full level–conformant driver will always return a bitmask with all of these bits set. This *InfoType* has been renamed for ODBC 3.0 from the ODBC 2.0 *InfoType* SQL_QUALIFIER_USAGE.
SQL_COLLATION_SEQ (ODBC 3.0)	The name of the collation sequence. This is a character string that indicates the name of the default collation for the default character set for this server (for example 'ISO 8859-1' or EBCDIC). If this is unknown, an empty string will be returned. An SQL-92 Full level–conformant driver will always return a non-empty string.
SQL_COLUMN_ALIAS (ODBC 2.0)	A character string: "Y" if the data source supports column aliases; otherwise, "N". A column alias is an alternate name that can be specified for a column in the select list by using an AS clause. An SQL-92 Entry level–conformant driver will always return "Y".
SQL_CONCAT_NULL_ BEHAVIOR (ODBC 1.0)	An SQLUSMALLINT value indicating how the data source handles the concatenation of NULL valued character data type columns with non-NULL valued character data type columns: SQL_CB_NULL = Result is NULL valued. SQL_CB_NON_NULL = Result is concatenation of non-NULL valued column or columns. An SQL-92 Entry level–conformant driver will always return SQL_CB_NULL.

InfoType	Returns
SQL_CONVERT_BIGINT SQL_CONVERT_BINARY SQL_CONVERT_BIT SQL_CONVERT_CHAR SQL_CONVERT_DATE SQL_CONVERT_DECIMAL SQL_CONVERT_DOUBLE SQL_CONVERT_FLOAT SQL_CONVERT_INTEGER SQL_CONVERT_INTERVAL_YEAR_MONTH SQL_CONVERT_INTERVAL_DAY_TIME SQL_CONVERT_LONGVARBINARY SQL_CONVERT_LONGVARCHAR SQL_CONVERT_NUMERIC SQL_CONVERT_REAL SQL_CONVERT_SMALLINT SQL_CONVERT_TIME SQL_CONVERT_TIMESTAMP SQL_CONVERT_TINYINT SQL_CONVERT_VARBINARY SQL_CONVERT_VARCHAR (ODBC 1.0)	An SQLUINTEGER bitmask. The bitmask indicates the conversions supported by the data source with the **CONVERT** scalar function for data of the type named in the *InfoType*. If the bitmask equals zero, the data source does not support any conversions from data of the named type, including conversion to the same data type. For example, to find out if a data source supports the conversion of SQL_INTEGER data to the SQL_BIGINT data type, an application calls **SQLGetInfo** with the *InfoType* of SQL_CONVERT_INTEGER. The application performs an **AND** operation with the returned bitmask and SQL_CVT_BIGINT. If the resulting value is nonzero, the conversion is supported. The following bitmasks are used to determine which conversions are supported: SQL_CVT_BIGINT (ODBC 1.0) SQL_CVT_BINARY (ODBC 1.0) SQL_CVT_BIT (ODBC 1.0) SQL_CVT_CHAR (ODBC 1.0) SQL_CVT_DATE (ODBC 1.0) SQL_CVT_DECIMAL (ODBC 1.0) SQL_CVT_DOUBLE (ODBC 1.0) SQL_CVT_FLOAT (ODBC 1.0) SQL_CVT_INTEGER (ODBC 1.0) SQL_CVT_INTERVAL_YEAR_MONTH (ODBC 3.0) SQL_CVT_INTERVAL_DAY_TIME (ODBC 3.0) SQL_CVT_LONGVARBINARY (ODBC 1.0) SQL_CVT_LONGVARCHAR (ODBC 1.0) SQL_CVT_NUMERIC (ODBC 1.0) SQL_CVT_REAL ODBC 1.0) SQL_CVT_SMALLINT (ODBC 1.0) SQL_CVT_TIME (ODBC 1.0) SQL_CVT_TIMESTAMP (ODBC 1.0) SQL_CVT_TINYINT (ODBC 1.0) SQL_CVT_VARBINARY (ODBC 1.0) SQL_CVT_VARCHAR (ODBC 1.0)
SQL_CONVERT_FUNCTIONS (ODBC 1.0)	An SQLUINTEGER bitmask enumerating the scalar conversion functions supported by the driver and associated data source. The following bitmask is used to determine which conversion functions are supported: SQL_FN_CVT_CAST SQL_FN_CVT_CONVERT

InfoType	Returns
SQL_CORRELATION_NAME (ODBC 1.0)	An SQLUSMALLINT value indicating whether table correlation names are supported: SQL_CN_NONE = Correlation names are not supported. SQL_CN_DIFFERENT = Correlation names are supported, but must differ from the names of the tables they represent. SQL_CN_ANY = Correlation names are supported and can be any valid user-defined name. An SQL-92 Entry level–conformant driver will always return SQL_CN_ANY.
SQL_CREATE_ASSERTION (ODBC 3.0)	An SQLUINTEGER bitmask enumerating the clauses in the **CREATE ASSERTION** statement, as defined in SQL-92, supported by the data source. The following bitmasks are used to determine which clauses are supported: SQL_CA_CREATE_ASSERTION The following bits specify the supported constraint attribute if the ability to specify constraint attributes explicitly is supported (see the SQL_ALTER_TABLE and SQL_CREATE_TABLE information types): SQL_CA_CONSTRAINT_INITIALLY_DEFERRED SQL_CA_CONSTRAINT_INITIALLY_IMMEDIATE SQL_CA_CONSTRAINT_DEFERRABLE SQL_CA_CONSTRAINT_NON_DEFERRABLE An SQL-92 Full level–conformant driver will always return all of these options as supported. A return value of 0 means that the **CREATE ASSERTION** statement is not supported.
SQL_CREATE_CHARACTER_SET (ODBC 3.0)	An SQLUINTEGER bitmask enumerating the clauses in the **CREATE CHARACTER SET** statement, as defined in SQL-92, supported by the data source. The following bitmasks are used to determine which clauses are supported: SQL_CCS_CREATE_CHARACTER_SET SQL_CCS_COLLATE_CLAUSE SQL_CCS_LIMITED_COLLATION An SQL-92 Full level–conformant driver will always return all of these options as supported. A return value of 0 means that the **CREATE CHARACTER SET** statement is not supported.

InfoType	Returns
SQL_CREATE_COLLATION (ODBC 3.0)	An SQLUINTEGER bitmask enumerating the clauses in the **CREATE COLLATION** statement, as defined in SQL-92, supported by the data source. The following bitmask is used to determine which clauses are supported: SQL_CCOL_CREATE_COLLATION An SQL-92 Full level–conformant driver will always return this option as supported. A return value of 0 means that the **CREATE COLLATION** statement is not supported.
SQL_CREATE_DOMAIN (ODBC 3.0)	An SQLUINTEGER bitmask enumerating the clauses in the **CREATE DOMAIN** statement, as defined in SQL-92, supported by the data source. The following bitmasks are used to determine which clauses are supported: SQL_CDO_CREATE_DOMAIN = The CREATE DOMAIN statement is supported. (Intermediate level) SQL_CDO_CONSTRAINT_NAME_DEFINITION = <constraint name definition> is supported for naming domain constraints (Intermediate level). The following bits specify the ability to create column constraints: SQL_CDO_DEFAULT = Specifying domain constraints is supported (Intermediate level) SQL_CDO_CONSTRAINT = Specifying domain defaults is supported (Intermediate level) SQL_CDO_COLLATION = Specifying domain collation is supported (Full level) The following bits specify the supported constraint attributes if specifying domain constraints is supported (SQL_CDO_DEFAULT is set): SQL_CDO_CONSTRAINT_INITIALLY_DEFERRED (Full level) SQL_CDO_CONSTRAINT_INITIALLY_IMMEDIATE (Full level) SQL_CDO_CONSTRAINT_DEFERRABLE (Full level) SQL_CDO_CONSTRAINT_NON_DEFERRABLE (Full level) A return value of 0 means that the **CREATE DOMAIN** statement is not supported.

InfoType	Returns
SQL_CREATE_SCHEMA (ODBC 3.0)	An SQLUINTEGER bitmask enumerating the clauses in the **CREATE SCHEMA** statement, as defined in SQL-92, supported by the data source. The following bitmasks are used to determine which clauses are supported: SQL_CS_CREATE_SCHEMA SQL_CS_AUTHORIZATION SQL_CS_DEFAULT_CHARACTER_SET An SQL-92 Intermediate level–conformant driver will always return the SQL_CS_CREATE_SCHEMA and SQL_CS_AUTHORIZATION options as supported. These must also be supported at the SQL-92 Entry level, but not necessarily as SQL statements. An SQL-92 Full level–conformant driver will always return all of these options as supported.
SQL_CREATE_TABLE (ODBC 3.0)	An SQLUINTEGER bitmask enumerating the clauses in the **CREATE TABLE** statement, as defined in SQL-92, supported by the data source. The SQL-92 or FIPS conformance level at which this features needs to be supported is shown in parentheses next to each bitmask. The following bitmasks are used to determine which clauses are supported: SQL_CT_CREATE_TABLE = The CREATE TABLE statement is supported. (Entry level) SQL_CT_TABLE_CONSTRAINT = Specifying table constraints is supported (FIPS Transitional level) SQL_CT_CONSTRAINT_NAME_DEFINITION = The <constraint name definition> clause is supported for naming column and table constraints (Intermediate level) The following bits specify the ability to create temporary tables: SQL_CT_COMMIT_PRESERVE = Deleted rows are preserved on commit. (Full level) SQL_CT_COMMIT_DELETE = Deleted rows are deleted on commit. (Full level) SQL_CT_GLOBAL_TEMPORARY = Global temporary tables can be created. (Full level) SQL_CT_LOCAL_TEMPORARY = Local temporary tables can be created. (Full level)

InfoType	**Returns**
SQL_CREATE_TABLE (ODBC 3.0) (*continued*)	The following bits specify the ability to create column constraints: SQL_CT_COLUMN_CONSTRAINT = Specifying column constraints is supported (FIPS Transitional level) SQL_CT_COLUMN_DEFAULT = Specifying column defaults is supported (FIPS Transitional level) SQL_CT_COLUMN_COLLATION = Specifying column collation is supported (Full level) The following bits specify the supported constraint attributes if specifying column or table constraints is supported: SQL_CT_CONSTRAINT_INITIALLY_DEFERRED (Full level) SQL_CT_CONSTRAINT_INITIALLY_IMMEDIATE (Full level) SQL_CT_CONSTRAINT_DEFERRABLE (Full level) SQL_CT_CONSTRAINT_NON_DEFERRABLE (Full level)
SQL_CREATE_TRANSLATION (ODBC 3.0)	An SQLUINTEGER bitmask enumerating the clauses in the **CREATE TRANSLATION** statement, as defined in SQL-92, supported by the data source. The following bitmask is used to determine which clauses are supported: SQL_CTR_CREATE_TRANSLATION An SQL-92 Full level–conformant driver will always return these options as supported. A return value of 0 means that the **CREATE TRANSLATION** statement is not supported.
SQL_CREATE_VIEW (ODBC 3.0)	An SQLUINTEGER bitmask enumerating the clauses in the **CREATE VIEW** statement, as defined in SQL-92, supported by the data source. The following bitmasks are used to determine which clauses are supported: SQL_CV_CREATE_VIEW SQL_CV_CHECK_OPTION SQL_CV_CASCADED SQL_CV_LOCAL A return value of 0 means that the **CREATE VIEW** statement is not supported. An SQL-92 Entry level–conformant driver will always return the SQL_CV_CREATE_VIEW and SQL_CV_CHECK_OPTION options as supported. An SQL-92 Full level–conformant driver will always return all of these options as supported.

InfoType	**Returns**
SQL_CURSOR_COMMIT_ BEHAVIOR (ODBC 1.0)	An SQLUSMALLINT value indicating how a **COMMIT** operation affects cursors and prepared statements in the data source: SQL_CB_DELETE = Close cursors and delete prepared statements. To use the cursor again, the application must reprepare and reexecute the statement. SQL_CB_CLOSE = Close cursors. For prepared statements, the application can call **SQLExecute** on the statement without calling **SQLPrepare** again. SQL_CB_PRESERVE = Preserve cursors in the same position as before the **COMMIT** operation. The application can continue to fetch data or it can close the cursor and reexecute the statement without repreparing it.
SQL_CURSOR_ROLLBACK_ BEHAVIOR (ODBC 1.0)	An SQLUSMALLINT value indicating how a **ROLLBACK** operation affects cursors and prepared statements in the data source: SQL_CB_DELETE = Close cursors and delete prepared statements. To use the cursor again, the application must reprepare and reexecute the statement. SQL_CB_CLOSE = Close cursors. For prepared statements, the application can call **SQLExecute** on the statement without calling **SQLPrepare** again. SQL_CB_PRESERVE = Preserve cursors in the same position as before the **ROLLBACK** operation. The application can continue to fetch data or it can close the cursor and reexecute the statement without repreparing it.
SQL_CURSOR_SENSITIVITY (ODBC 3.0)	An SQLUINTEGER value indicating the support for cursor sensitivity: SQL_INSENSITIVE = All cursors on the statement handle show the result set without reflecting any changes made to it by any other cursor within the same transaction. SQL_UNSPECIFIED = It is unspecified whether cursors on the statement handle make visible the changes made to a result set by another cursor within the same transaction. Cursors on the statement handle may make visible none, some, or all such changes. SQL_SENSITIVE = Cursors are sensitive to changes made by other cursors within the same transaction. An SQL-92 Entry level–conformant driver will always return the SQL_UNSPECIFIED option as supported. An SQL-92 Full level–conformant driver will always return the SQL_INSENSITIVE option as supported.

InfoType	Returns
SQL_DATA_SOURCE_NAME (ODBC 1.0)	A character string with the data source name used during connection. If the application called **SQLConnect**, this is the value of the *szDSN* argument. If the application called **SQLDriverConnect** or **SQLBrowseConnect**, this is the value of the DSN keyword in the connection string passed to the driver. If the connection string did not contain the **DSN** keyword (such as when it contains the **DRIVER** keyword), this is an empty string.
SQL_DATA_SOURCE_READ_ ONLY (ODBC 1.0)	A character string. "Y" if the data source is set to READ ONLY mode, "N" if it is otherwise. This characteristic pertains only to the data source itself; it is not a characteristic of the driver that enables access to the data source. A driver that is read/write can be used with a data source that is read-only. If a driver is read-only, all of its data sources must be read-only, and must return SQL_DATA_SOURCE_READ_ONLY.
SQL_DATABASE_NAME (ODBC 1.0)	A character string with the name of the current database in use, if the data source defines a named object called "database." **Note** In ODBC 3.0, the value returned for this *InfoType* can also be returned by calling **SQLGetConnectAttr** with an *Attribute* argument of SQL_ATTR_CURRENT_CATALOG.
SQL_DATETIME_LITERALS (ODBC 3.0)	An SQLUINTEGER bitmask enumerating the SQL-92 datetime literals supported by the data source. Note that these are the datetime literals listed in the SQL-92 specification and are separate from the datetime literal escape clauses defined by ODBC. For more information about the ODBC datetime literal escape clauses, see "Date, Time, Timestamp, and Datetime Interval Literals" in Chapter 8, "SQL Statements." A FIPS Transitional level–conformant driver will always return the "1" value in the bitmask for the bits listed below. A value of 0 means that SQL-92 datetime literals are not supported. The following bitmasks are used to determine which literals are supported: SQL_DL_SQL92_DATE SQL_DL_SQL92_TIME SQL_DL_SQL92_TIMESTAMP SQL_DL_SQL92_INTERVAL_YEAR SQL_DL_SQL92_INTERVAL_MONTH SQL_DL_SQL92_INTERVAL_DAY SQL_DL_SQL92_INTERVAL_HOUR SQL_DL_SQL92_INTERVAL_MINUTE SQL_DL_SQL92_INTERVAL_SECOND SQL_DL_SQL92_INTERVAL_YEAR_TO_MONTH SQL_DL_SQL92_INTERVAL_DAY_TO_HOUR

InfoType	Returns
SQL_DATETIME_LITERALS (ODBC 3.0) (*continued*)	SQL_DL_SQL92_INTERVAL_DAY_TO_MINUTE SQL_DL_SQL92_INTERVAL_DAY_TO_SECOND SQL_DL_SQL92_INTERVAL_HOUR_TO_MINUTE SQL_DL_SQL92_INTERVAL_HOUR_TO_SECOND SQL_DL_SQL92_INTERVAL_MINUTE_TO_SECOND
SQL_DBMS_NAME (ODBC 1.0)	A character string with the name of the DBMS product accessed by the driver.
SQL_DBMS_VER (ODBC 1.0)	A character string indicating the version of the DBMS product accessed by the driver. The version is of the form ##.##.####, where the first two digits are the major version, the next two digits are the minor version, and the last four digits are the release version. The driver must render the DBMS product version in this form, but can also append the DBMS product-specific version as well. For example, "04.01.0000 Rdb 4.1".
SQL_DDL_INDEX (ODBC 3.0)	An SQLUINTEGER value that indicates support for creation and dropping of indexes: SQL_DI_CREATE_INDEX SQL_DI_DROP_INDEX
SQL_DEFAULT_TXN_ ISOLATION (ODBC 1.0)	An SQLUINTEGER value that indicates the default transaction isolation level supported by the driver or data source, or zero if the data source does not support transactions. The following terms are used to define transaction isolation levels: **Dirty Read** Transaction 1 changes a row. Transaction 2 reads the changed row before transaction 1 commits the change. If transaction 1 rolls back the change, transaction 2 will have read a row that is considered to have never existed. **Nonrepeatable Read** Transaction 1 reads a row. Transaction 2 updates or deletes that row and commits this change. If transaction 1 attempts to reread the row, it will receive different row values or discover that the row has been deleted. **Phantom** Transaction 1 reads a set of rows that satisfy some search criteria. Transaction 2 generates one or more rows (either through inserts or updates) that match the search criteria. If transaction 1 reexecutes the statement that reads the rows, it receives a different set of rows. If the data source supports transactions, the driver returns one of the following bitmasks: SQL_TXN_READ_UNCOMMITTED = Dirty reads, nonrepeatable reads, and phantoms are possible. SQL_TXN_READ_COMMITTED = Dirty reads are not possible. Nonrepeatable reads and phantoms are possible.

InfoType	Returns
SQL_DEFAULT_TXN_ ISOLATION (ODBC 1.0) (*continued*)	SQL_TXN_REPEATABLE_READ = Dirty reads and nonrepeatable reads are not possible. Phantoms are possible. SQL_TXN_SERIALIZABLE = Transactions are serializable. Serializable transactions do not allow dirty reads, nonrepeatable reads, or phantoms.
SQL_DESCRIBE_PARAMETER (ODBC 3.0)	A character string: "Y" if parameters can be described; "N", if not. An SQL-92 Full level–conformant driver will usually return "Y" because it will support the **DESCRIBE INPUT** statement. Since this does not directly specify the underlying SQL support, however, describing parameters may not be supported, even in a SQL-92 Full level–conformant driver.
SQL_DM_VER (ODBC 3.0)	A character string with the version of the Driver Manager. The version is of the form ##.##.####.####, where: The first set of two digits is the major ODBC version, as given by the constant SQL_SPEC_MAJOR. The second set of two digits is the minor ODBC version, as given by the constant SQL_SPEC_MINOR. The third set of four digits is the Driver Manager major build number. The last set of four digits is the Driver Manager minor build number.
SQL_DRIVER_HDBC SQL_DRIVER_HENV (ODBC 1.0)	An SQLUINTEGER value, the driver's environment handle or connection handle, determined by the argument *InfoType*. These information types are implemented by the Driver Manager alone.
SQL_DRIVER_HDESC (ODBC 3.0)	An SQLUINTEGER value, the driver's descriptor handle determined by the Driver Manager's descriptor handle, which must be passed on input in **InfoValuePtr* from the application. Note that in this case, *InfoValuePtr* is both an input and output argument. The input descriptor handle passed in **InfoValuePtr* must have been either explicitly or implicitly allocated on the *ConnectionHandle*. The application should make a copy of the Driver Manager's descriptor handle before calling **SQLGetInfo** with this information type, to ensure that the handle is not overwritten on output. This information type is implemented by the Driver Manager alone.

InfoType	Returns
SQL_DRIVER_HLIB (ODBC 2.0)	An SQLUINTEGER value, the *hinst* from the load library returned to the Driver Manager when it loaded the driver DLL (on a Windows platform) or equivalent on a non-Windows platform. The handle is only valid for the connection handle specified in the call to **SQLGetInfo**. This information type is implemented by the Driver Manager alone.
SQL_DRIVER_HSTMT (ODBC 1.0)	An SQLUINTEGER value, the driver's statement handle determined by the Driver Manager statement handle, which must be passed on input in **InfoValuePtr* from the application. Note that in this case, *InfoValuePtr* is both an input and an output argument. The input statement handle passed in **InfoValuePtr* must have been allocated on the argument *ConnectionHandle*. The application should make a copy of the Driver Manager's statement handle before calling **SQLGetInfo** with this information type, to ensure that the handle is not overwritten on output. This information type is implemented by the Driver Manager alone.
SQL_DRIVER_NAME (ODBC 1.0)	A character string with the file name of the driver used to access the data source.
SQL_DRIVER_ODBC_VER (ODBC 2.0)	A character string with the version of ODBC that the driver supports. The version is of the form ##.##, where the first two digits are the major version and the next two digits are the minor version. SQL_SPEC_MAJOR and SQL_SPEC_MINOR define the major and minor version numbers. For the version of ODBC described in this manual, these are 3 and 0, and the driver should return "03.00".
SQL_DRIVER_VER (ODBC 1.0)	A character string with the version of the driver and, optionally a description of the driver. At a minimum, the version is of the form ##.##.####, where the first two digits are the major version, the next two digits are the minor version, and the last four digits are the release version.
SQL_DROP_ASSERTION (ODBC 3.0)	An SQLUINTEGER bitmask enumerating the clauses in the **DROP ASSERTION** statement, as defined in SQL-92, supported by the data source. The following bitmask is used to determine which clauses are supported: SQL_DA_DROP_ASSERTION An SQL-92 Full level–conformant driver will always return this option as supported.

InfoType	Returns
SQL_DROP_CHARACTER_SET (ODBC 3.0)	An SQLUINTEGER bitmask enumerating the clauses in the **DROP CHARACTER SET** statement, as defined in SQL-92, supported by the data source. The following bitmask is used to determine which clauses are supported: SQL_DCS_DROP_CHARACTER_SET An SQL-92 Full level–conformant driver will always return this option as supported.
SQL_DROP_COLLATION (ODBC 3.0)	An SQLUINTEGER bitmask enumerating the clauses in the **DROP COLLATION** statement, as defined in SQL-92, supported by the data source. The following bitmask is used to determine which clauses are supported: SQL_DC_DROP_COLLATION An SQL-92 Full level–conformant driver will always return this option as supported.
SQL_DROP_DOMAIN (ODBC 3.0)	An SQLUINTEGER bitmask enumerating the clauses in the **DROP DOMAIN** statement, as defined in SQL-92, supported by the data source. The following bitmasks are used to determine which clauses are supported: SQL_DD_DROP_DOMAIN SQL_DD_CASCADE SQL_DD_RESTRICT An SQL-92 Intermediate level–conformant driver will always return all of these options as supported.
SQL_DROP_SCHEMA (ODBC 3.0)	An SQLUINTEGER bitmask enumerating the clauses in the **DROP SCHEMA** statement, as defined in SQL-92, supported by the data source. The following bitmasks are used to determine which clauses are supported: SQL_DS_DROP_SCHEMA SQL_DS_CASCADE SQL_DS_RESTRICT An SQL-92 Intermediate level–conformant driver will always return all of these options as supported.

InfoType	Returns
SQL_DROP_TABLE (ODBC 3.0)	An SQLUINTEGER bitmask enumerating the clauses in the **DROP TABLE** statement, as defined in SQL-92, supported by the data source. The following bitmasks are used to determine which clauses are supported: SQL_DT_DROP_TABLE SQL_DT_CASCADE SQL_DT_RESTRICT An FIPS Transitional level–conformant driver will always return all of these options as supported.
SQL_DROP_TRANSLATION (ODBC 3.0)	An SQLUINTEGER bitmask enumerating the clauses in the **DROP TRANSLATION** statement, as defined in SQL-92, supported by the data source. The following bitmask is used to determine which clauses are supported: SQL_DTR_DROP_TRANSLATION An SQL-92 Full level–conformant driver will always return this option as supported.
SQL_DROP_VIEW (ODBC 3.0)	An SQLUINTEGER bitmask enumerating the clauses in the **DROP VIEW** statement, as defined in SQL-92, supported by the data source. The following bitmasks are used to determine which clauses are supported: SQL_DV_DROP_VIEW SQL_DV_CASCADE SQL_DV_RESTRICT An FIPS Transitional level–conformant driver will always return all of these options as supported.
SQL_DYNAMIC_CURSOR_ ATTRIBUTES1 (ODBC 3.0)	An SQLUINTEGER bitmask that describes the attributes of a dynamic cursor that are supported by the driver. This bitmask contains the first subset of attributes; for the second subset, see SQL_DYNAMIC_CURSOR_ATTRIBUTES2. The following bitmasks are used to determine which attributes are supported: SQL_CA1_NEXT = A *FetchOrientation* argument of SQL_FETCH_NEXT is supported in a call to **SQLFetchScroll** when the cursor is a dynamic cursor.

InfoType	Returns
SQL_DYNAMIC_CURSOR_ATTRIBUTES1 (ODBC 3.0) (*continued*)	SQL_CA1_ABSOLUTE = *FetchOrientation* arguments of SQL_FETCH_FIRST, SQL_FETCH_LAST, and SQL_FETCH_ABSOLUTE are supported in a call to **SQLFetchScroll** when the cursor is a dynamic cursor. (The rowset that will be fetched is independent of the current cursor position.) SQL_CA1_RELATIVE = *FetchOrientation* arguments of SQL_FETCH_PRIOR and SQL_FETCH_RELATIVE are supported in a call to **SQLFetchScroll** when the cursor is a dynamic cursor. (The rowset that will be fetched is dependent of the current cursor position. Note that this is separated from SQL_FETCH_NEXT because in a forward-only cursor, only SQL_FETCH_NEXT is supported.) SQL_CA1_BOOKMARK = A *FetchOrientation* argument of SQL_FETCH_BOOKMARK is supported in a call to **SQLFetchScroll** when the cursor is a dynamic cursor. SQL_CA1_LOCK_EXCLUSIVE = A *LockType* argument of SQL_LOCK_EXCLUSIVE is supported in a call to **SQLSetPos** when the cursor is a dynamic cursor. SQL_CA1_LOCK_NO_CHANGE = A *LockType* argument of SQL_LOCK_NO_CHANGE is supported in a call to **SQLSetPos** when the cursor is a dynamic cursor. SQL_CA1_LOCK_UNLOCK = A *LockType* argument of SQL_LOCK_UNLOCK is supported in a call to **SQLSetPos** when the cursor is a dynamic cursor. SQL_CA1_POS_POSITION = An *Operation* argument of SQL_POSITION is supported in a call to **SQLSetPos** when the cursor is a dynamic cursor. SQL_CA1_POS_UPDATE = An *Operation* argument of SQL_UPDATE is supported in a call to **SQLSetPos** when the cursor is a dynamic cursor. SQL_CA1_POS_DELETE = An *Operation* argument of SQL_DELETE is supported in a call to **SQLSetPos** when the cursor is a dynamic cursor. SQL_CA1_POS_REFRESH = An *Operation* argument of SQL_REFRESH is supported in a call to **SQLSetPos** when the cursor is a dynamic cursor. SQL_CA1_POSITIONED_UPDATE = An UPDATE WHERE CURRENT OF SQL statement is supported when the cursor is a dynamic cursor. (An SQL-92 Entry level–conformant driver will always return this option as supported.)

InfoType	**Returns**
SQL_DYNAMIC_CURSOR_ ATTRIBUTES1 (ODBC 3.0) (*continued*)	SQL_CA1_POSITIONED_DELETE = A DELETE WHERE CURRENT OF SQL statement is supported when the cursor is a dynamic cursor. (An SQL-92 Entry level–conformant driver will always return this option as supported.) SQL_CA1_SELECT_FOR_UPDATE = A SELECT FOR UPDATE SQL statement is supported when the cursor is a dynamic cursor. (An SQL-92 Entry level–conformant driver will always return this option as supported.) SQL_CA1_BULK_ADD = An *Operation* argument of SQL_ADD is supported in a call to **SQLBulkOperations** when the cursor is a dynamic cursor. SQL_CA1_BULK_UPDATE_BY_BOOKMARK = An *Operation* argument of SQL_UPDATE_BY_BOOKMARK is supported in a call to **SQLBulkOperations** when the cursor is a dynamic cursor. SQL_CA1_BULK_DELETE_BY_BOOKMARK = An *Operation* argument of SQL_DELETE_BY_BOOKMARK is supported in a call to **SQLBulkOperations** when the cursor is a dynamic cursor. SQL_CA1_BULK_FETCH_BY_BOOKMARK = An *Operation* argument of SQL_FETCH_BY_BOOKMARK is supported in a call to **SQLBulkOperations** when the cursor is a dynamic cursor. An SQL-92 Intermediate level–conformant driver will usually return the SQL_CA1_NEXT, SQL_CA1_ABSOLUTE, and SQL_CA1_RELATIVE options as supported, because it supports scrollable cursors through the embedded SQL FETCH statement. Since this does not directly determine the underlying SQL support, however, scrollable cursors may not be supported, even for an SQL-92 Intermediate level–conformant driver.
SQL_DYNAMIC_CURSOR_ ATTRIBUTES2 (ODBC 3.0)	An SQLUINTEGER bitmask that describes the attributes of a dynamic cursor that are supported by the driver. This bitmask contains the second subset of attributes; for the first subset, see SQL_DYNAMIC_CURSOR_ATTRIBUTES1. The following bitmasks are used to determine which attributes are supported: SQL_CA2_READ_ONLY_CONCURRENCY = A read-only dynamic cursor, in which no updates are allowed, is supported. (The SQL_ATTR_CONCURRENCY statement attribute can be SQL_CONCUR_READ_ONLY for a dynamic cursor). SQL_CA2_LOCK_CONCURRENCY = A dynamic cursor that uses the lowest level of locking sufficient to ensure that the row can be updated is supported. (The SQL_ATTR_CONCURRENCY statement attribute can be SQL_CONCUR_LOCK for a dynamic cursor). These locks must be consistent with the transaction isolation level set by the SQL_ATTR_TXN_ISOLATION connection attribute.

InfoType	Returns
SQL_DYNAMIC_CURSOR_ ATTRIBUTES2 (ODBC 3.0) (*continued*)	SQL_CA2_OPT_ROWVER_CONCURRENCY = A dynamic cursor that uses the optimistic concurrency control comparing row versions is supported. (The SQL_ATTR_CONCURRENCY statement attribute can be SQL_CONCUR_ROWVER for a dynamic cursor). SQL_CA2_OPT_VALUES_CONCURRENCY = A dynamic cursor that uses the optimistic concurrency control comparing values is supported. (The SQL_ATTR_CONCURRENCY statement attribute can be SQL_CONCUR_VALUES for a dynamic cursor). SQL_CA2_SENSITIVITY_ADDITIONS = Added rows are visible to a dynamic cursor; the cursor can scroll to those rows. (Where these rows are added to the cursor is driver-dependent.) SQL_CA2_SENSITIVITY_DELETIONS = Deleted rows are no longer available to a dynamic cursor, and do not leave a "hole" in the result set; after the dynamic cursor scrolls from a deleted row, it cannot return to that row. SQL_CA2_SENSITIVITY_UPDATES = Updates to rows are visible to a dynamic cursor; if the dynamic cursor scrolls from and returns to an updated row, the data returned by the cursor is the updated data, not the original data. SQL_CA2_MAX_ROWS_SELECT = The SQL_ATTR_MAX_ROWS statement attribute affects **SELECT** statements when the cursor is a dynamic cursor. SQL_CA2_MAX_ROWS_INSERT = The SQL_ATTR_MAX_ROWS statement attribute affects **INSERT** statements when the cursor is a dynamic cursor. SQL_CA2_MAX_ROWS_DELETE = The SQL_ATTR_MAX_ROWS statement attribute affects **DELETE** statements when the cursor is a dynamic cursor. SQL_CA2_MAX_ROWS_UPDATE = The SQL_ATTR_MAX_ROWS statement attribute affects **UPDATE** statements when the cursor is a dynamic cursor. SQL_CA2_MAX_ROWS_CATALOG = The SQL_ATTR_MAX_ROWS statement attribute affects **CATALOG** result sets when the cursor is a dynamic cursor. SQL_CA2_MAX_ROWS_AFFECTS_ALL = The SQL_ATTR_MAX_ROWS statement attribute affects **SELECT**, **INSERT**, **DELETE**, and **UPDATE** statements, and **CATALOG** result sets, when the cursor is a dynamic cursor. SQL_CA2_CRC_EXACT = The exact row count is available in the SQL_DIAG_CURSOR_ROW_COUNT diagnostic field when the cursor is a dynamic cursor.

InfoType	Returns
SQL_DYNAMIC_CURSOR_ ATTRIBUTES2 (ODBC 3.0) (*continued*)	SQL_CA2_CRC_APPROXIMATE = An approximate row count is available in the SQL_DIAG_CURSOR_ROW_COUNT diagnostic field when the cursor is a dynamic cursor. SQL_CA2_SIMULATE_NON_UNIQUE = The driver does not guarantee that simulated positioned update or delete statements will affect only one row when the cursor is a dynamic cursor; it is the application's responsibility to guarantee this. (If a statement affects more than one row, **SQLExecute** or **SQLExecDirect** returns SQLSTATE 01001 (Cursor operation conflict).) To set this behavior, the application calls **SQLSetStmtAttr** with the SQL_ATTR_SIMULATE_CURSOR attribute set to SQL_SC_NON_UNIQUE. SQL_CA2_SIMULATE_TRY_UNIQUE = The driver attempts to guarantee that simulated positioned update or delete statements will affect only one row when the cursor is a dynamic cursor. The driver always executes such statements, even if they might affect more than one row, such as when there is no unique key. (If a statement affects more than one row, **SQLExecute** or **SQLExecDirect** returns SQLSTATE 01001 (Cursor operation conflict).) To set this behavior, the application calls **SQLSetStmtAttr** with the SQL_ATTR_SIMULATE_CURSOR attribute set to SQL_SC_TRY_UNIQUE. SQL_CA2_SIMULATE_UNIQUE = The driver guarantees that simulated positioned update or delete statements will affect only one row when the cursor is a dynamic cursor. If the driver cannot guarantee this for a given statement, **SQLExecDirect** or **SQLPrepare** return SQLSTATE 01001 (Cursor operation conflict). To set this behavior, the application calls **SQLSetStmtAttr** with the SQL_ATTR_SIMULATE_CURSOR attribute set to SQL_SC_UNIQUE
SQL_EXPRESSIONS_IN_ ORDERBY (ODBC 1.0)	A character string: "Y" if the data source supports expressions in the **ORDER BY** list; "N" if it does not.

InfoType	Returns
SQL_FILE_USAGE (ODBC 2.0)	An SQLUSMALLINT value indicating how a single-tier driver directly treats files in a data source: SQL_FILE_NOT_SUPPORTED = The driver is not a single-tier driver. For example, an ORACLE driver is a two-tier driver. SQL_FILE_TABLE = A single-tier driver treats files in a data source as tables. For example, an Xbase driver treats each Xbase file as a table. SQL_FILE_CATALOG = A single-tier driver treats files in a data source as a catalog. For example, a Microsoft Access driver treats each Microsoft Access file as a complete database. An application might use this to determine how users will select data. For example, Xbase users often think of data as stored in files, while ORACLE and Microsoft Access users generally think of data as stored in tables. When a user selects an Xbase data source, the application could display the Windows File Open common dialog box; when the user selects a Microsoft Access or ORACLE data source, the application could display a custom Select Table dialog box.
SQL_FORWARD_ONLY_CURSOR_ATTRIBUTES1 (ODBC 3.0)	An SQLUINTEGER bitmask that describes the attributes of a forward-only cursor that are supported by the driver. This bitmask contains the first subset of attributes; for the second subset, see SQL_FORWARD_ONLY_CURSOR_ATTRIBUTES2. The following bitmasks are used to determine which attributes are supported: SQL_CA1_NEXT SQL_CA1_LOCK_EXCLUSIVE SQL_CA1_LOCK_NO_CHANGE SQL_CA1_LOCK_UNLOCK SQL_CA1_POS_POSITION SQL_CA1_POS_UPDATE SQL_CA1_POS_DELETE SQL_CA1_POS_REFRESH SQL_CA1_POSITIONED_UPDATE SQL_CA1_POSITIONED_DELETE SQL_CA1_SELECT_FOR_UPDATE SQL_CA1_BULK_ADD SQL_CA1_BULK_UPDATE_BY_BOOKMARK SQL_CA1_BULK_DELETE_BY_BOOKMARK SQL_CA1_BULK_FETCH_BY_BOOKMARK For descriptions of these bitmasks, see SQL_DYNAMIC_CURSOR_ATTRIBUTES1 (and substitute "forward-only cursor" for "dynamic cursor" in the descriptions).

InfoType	Returns
SQL_FORWARD_ONLY_ CURSOR_ ATTRIBUTES2 (ODBC 3.0)	An SQLUINTEGER bitmask that describes the attributes of a forward-only cursor that are supported by the driver. This bitmask contains the second subset of attributes; for the first subset, see SQL_FORWARD_ONLY_CURSOR_ATTRIBUTES1. The following bitmasks are used to determine which attributes are supported: SQL_CA2_READ_ONLY_CONCURRENCY SQL_CA2_LOCK_CONCURRENCY SQL_CA2_OPT_ROWVER_CONCURRENCY SQL_CA2_OPT_VALUES_CONCURRENCY SQL_CA2_SENSITIVITY_ADDITIONS SQL_CA2_SENSITIVITY_DELETIONS SQL_CA2_SENSITIVITY_UPDATES SQL_CA2_MAX_ROWS_SELECT SQL_CA2_MAX_ROWS_INSERT SQL_CA2_MAX_ROWS_DELETE SQL_CA2_MAX_ROWS_UPDATE SQL_CA2_MAX_ROWS_CATALOG SQL_CA2_MAX_ROWS_AFFECTS_ALL SQL_CA2_CRC_EXACT SQL_CA2_CRC_APPROXIMATE SQL_CA2_SIMULATE_NON_UNIQUE SQL_CA2_SIMULATE_TRY_UNIQUE SQL_CA2_SIMULATE_UNIQUE For descriptions of these bitmasks, see SQL_DYNAMIC_CURSOR_ATTRIBUTES2 (and substitute "forward-only cursor" for "dynamic cursor" in the descriptions).
SQL_GETDATA_EXTENSIONS (ODBC 2.0)	An SQLUINTEGER bitmask enumerating extensions to **SQLGetData**. The following bitmasks are used in conjunction with the flag to determine what common extensions the driver supports for **SQLGetData**: SQL_GD_ANY_COLUMN = **SQLGetData** can be called for any unbound column, including those before the last bound column. Note that the columns must be called in order of ascending column number unless SQL_GD_ANY_ORDER is also returned. SQL_GD_ANY_ORDER = **SQLGetData** can be called for unbound columns in any order. Note that **SQLGetData** can only be called for columns after the last bound column unless SQL_GD_ANY_COLUMN is also returned.

InfoType	Returns
SQL_GETDATA_EXTENSIONS (ODBC 2.0) (*continued*)	SQL_GD_BLOCK = **SQLGetData** can be called for an unbound column in any row in a block (where the rowset size is greater than 1) of data after positioning to that row with **SQLSetPos**. SQL_GD_BOUND = **SQLGetData** can be called for bound columns as well as unbound columns. A driver cannot return this value unless it also returns SQL_GD_ANY_COLUMN. **SQLGetData** is only required to return data from unbound columns that occur after the last bound column, are called in order of increasing column number, and are not in a row in a block of rows. If a driver supports bookmarks (either fixed- or variable-length), it must support calling **SQLGetData** on column 0. This support is required regardless of what the driver returns for a call to **SQLGetInfo** with the SQL_GETDATA_EXTENSIONS *InfoType*.
SQL_GROUP_BY (ODBC 2.0)	An SQLUSMALLINT value specifying the relationship between the columns in the **GROUP BY** clause and the non-aggregated columns in the select list: SQL_GB_COLLATE = A COLLATE clause can be specified at the end of each grouping column. (ODBC 3.0) SQL_GB_NOT_SUPPORTED = **GROUP BY** clauses are not supported. (ODBC 2.0) SQL_GB_GROUP_BY_EQUALS_SELECT = The **GROUP BY** clause must contain all non-aggregated columns in the select list. It cannot contain any other columns. For example, **SELECT DEPT, MAX(SALARY) FROM EMPLOYEE GROUP BY DEPT**. (ODBC 2.0) SQL_GB_GROUP_BY_CONTAINS_SELECT = The **GROUP BY** clause must contain all non-aggregated columns in the select list. It can contain columns that are not in the select list. For example, **SELECT DEPT, MAX(SALARY) FROM EMPLOYEE GROUP BY DEPT, AGE**. (ODBC 2.0) SQL_GB_NO_RELATION = The columns in the **GROUP BY** clause and the select list are not related. The meaning of non-grouped, non-aggregated columns in the select list is data source–dependent. For example, **SELECT DEPT, SALARY FROM EMPLOYEE GROUP BY DEPT, AGE**. (ODBC 2.0) An SQL-92 Entry level–conformant driver will always return the SQL_GB_GROUP_BY_EQUALS_SELECT option as supported. An SQL-92 Full level–conformant driver will always return the SQL_GB_COLLATE option as supported. If none of the options is supported, the **GROUP BY** clause is not supported by the data source.

InfoType	Returns
SQL_IDENTIFIER_CASE (ODBC 1.0)	An SQLUSMALLINT value as follows: SQL_IC_UPPER = Identifiers in SQL are not case-sensitive and are stored in uppercase in system catalog. SQL_IC_LOWER = Identifiers in SQL are not case-sensitive and are stored in lowercase in system catalog. SQL_IC_SENSITIVE = Identifiers in SQL are case-sensitive and are stored in mixed case in system catalog. SQL_IC_MIXED = Identifiers in SQL are not case-sensitive and are stored in mixed case in system catalog. Since identifiers in SQL-92 are never case-sensitive, a driver that conforms strictly to SQL-92 (any level) will never return the SQL_IC_SENSITIVE option as supported.
SQL_IDENTIFIER_QUOTE_CHAR (ODBC 1.0)	The character string used as the starting and ending delimiter of a quoted (delimited) identifiers in SQL statements. (Identifiers passed as arguments to ODBC functions do not need to be quoted.) If the data source does not support quoted identifiers, a blank is returned. This character string can also be used for quoting catalog function arguments when the connection attribute SQL_ATTR_METADATA_ID is set to SQL_TRUE. Since the identifier quote character in SQL-92 is the double quotation mark ("), a driver that conforms strictly to SQL-92 will always return the double quotation mark character.
SQL_INDEX_KEYWORDS (ODBC 3.0)	An SQLUINTEGER bitmask that enumerates keywords in the CREATE INDEX statement that are supported by the driver. SQL_IK_NONE = None of the keywords are supported. SQL_IK_ASC = ASC keyword is supported. SQL_IK_DESC = DESC keyword is supported. SQL_IK_ALL = All keywords are supported. To see if the CREATE INDEX statement is supported, an application calls **SQLGetInfo** with the SQL_DLL_INDEX information type.

InfoType	Returns
SQL_INFO_SCHEMA_VIEWS (ODBC 3.0)	An SQLUINTEGER bitmask enumerating the views in the INFORMATION_SCHEMA that are supported by the driver. The views in, and the contents of, INFORMATION_SCHEMA are as defined in SQL-92. The SQL-92 or FIPS conformance level at which this feature needs to be supported is shown in parentheses next to each bitmask. The following bitmasks are used to determine which views are supported: SQL_ISV_ASSERTIONS = Identifies the catalog's assertions that are owned by a given user. (Full level) SQL_ISV_CHARACTER_SETS = Identifies the catalog's character sets that are accessible to a given user. (Intermediate level) SQL_ISV_CHECK_CONSTRAINTS = Identifies the CHECK constraints that are owned by a given user. (Intermediate level) SQL_ISV_COLLATIONS = Identifies the character collations for the catalog that are accessible to a given user. (Full level) SQL_ISV_COLUMN_DOMAIN_USAGE = Identifies columns for the catalog that are dependent on domains defined in the catalog and are owned by a given user. (Intermediate level) SQL_ISV_COLUMN_PRIVILEGES = Identifies the privileges on columns of persistent tables that are available to or granted by a given user. (FIPS Transitional level) SQL_ISV_COLUMNS = Identifies the columns of persistent tables that are accessible to a given user. (FIPS Transitional level) SQL_ISV_CONSTRAINT_COLUMN_USAGE = Similar to CONSTRAINT_TABLE_USAGE view, columns are identified for the various constraints that are owned by a given user. (Intermediate level) SQL_ISV_CONSTRAINT_TABLE_USAGE = Identifies the tables that are used by constraints (referential, unique, and assertions), and are owned by a given user. (Intermediate level) SQL_ISV_DOMAIN_CONSTRAINTS = Identifies the domain constraints (of the domains in the catalog) that are accessible to a given user. (Intermediate level) SQL_ISV_DOMAINS = Identifies the domains defined in a catalog that are accessible to the user. (Intermediate level)

InfoType	Returns
SQL_INFO_SCHEMA_VIEWS (ODBC 3.0) (*continued*)	SQL_ISV_KEY_COLUMN_USAGE = Identifies columns defined in the catalog that are constrained as keys by a given user. (Intermediate level) SQL_ISV_REFERENTIAL_CONSTRAINTS = Identifies the referential constraints that are owned by a given user. (Intermediate level) SQL_ISV_SCHEMATA = Identifies the schemas that are owned by a given user. (Intermediate level) SQL_ISV_SQL_LANGUAGES = Identifies the SQL conformance levels, options, and dialects supported by the SQL implementation. (Intermediate level) SQL_ISV_TABLE_CONSTRAINTS = Identifies the table constraints that are owned by a given user. (Intermediate level) SQL_ISV_TABLE_PRIVILEGES = Identifies the privileges on persistent tables that are available to or granted by a given user. (FIPS Transitional level) SQL_ISV_TABLES = Identifies the persistent tables defined in a catalog that are accessible to a given user. (FIPS Transitional level) SQL_ISV_TRANSLATIONS = Identifies character translations for the catalog that are accessible to a given user. (Full level) SQL_ISV_USAGE_PRIVILEGES = Identifies the USAGE privileges on catalog objects that are available to or owned by a given user. (FIPS Transitional level) SQL_ISV_VIEW_COLUMN_USAGE = Identifies the columns on which the catalog's views that are owned by a given user are dependent. (Intermediate level) SQL_ISV_VIEW_TABLE_USAGE = Identifies the tables on which the catalog's views that are owned by a given user are dependent. (Intermediate level) SQL_ISV_VIEWS = Identifies the viewed tables defined in this catalog that are accessible to a given user. (FIPS Transitional level)
SQL_INSERT_STATEMENT (ODBC 3.0)	An SQLUINTEGER bitmask that indicates support for **INSERT** statements: SQL_IS_INSERT_LITERALS SQL_IS_INSERT_SEARCHED SQL_IS_SELECT_INTO An SQL-92 Entry level–conformant driver will always return all of these options as supported.

InfoType	Returns
SQL_INTEGRITY (ODBC 1.0)	A character string: "Y" if the data source supports the Integrity Enhancement Facility; "N" if it does not. This *InfoType* has been renamed for ODBC 3.0 from the ODBC 2.0 *InfoType* SQL_ODBC_SQL_OPT_IEF.
SQL_KEYSET_ CURSOR_ ATTRIBUTES1 (ODBC 3.0)	An SQLUINTEGER bitmask that describes the attributes of a keyset cursor that are supported by the driver. This bitmask contains the first subset of attributes; for the second subset, see SQL_KEYSET_CURSOR_ATTRIBUTES2. The following bitmasks are used to determine which attributes are supported: SQL_CA1_NEXT SQL_CA1_ABSOLUTE SQL_CA1_RELATIVE SQL_CA1_BOOKMARK SQL_CA1_LOCK_EXCLUSIVE SQL_CA1_LOCK_NO_CHANGE SQL_CA1_LOCK_UNLOCK SQL_CA1_POS_POSITION SQL_CA1_POS_UPDATE SQL_CA1_POS_DELETE SQL_CA1_POS_REFRESH SQL_CA1_POSITIONED_UPDATE SQL_CA1_POSITIONED_DELETE SQL_CA1_SELECT_FOR_UPDATE SQL_CA1_BULK_ADD SQL_CA1_BULK_UPDATE_BY_BOOKMARK SQL_CA1_BULK_DELETE_BY_BOOKMARK SQL_CA1_BULK_FETCH_BY_BOOKMARK For descriptions of these bitmasks, see SQL_DYNAMIC_CURSOR_ATTRIBUTES1 (and substitute "keyset-driven cursor" for "dynamic cursor" in the descriptions). An SQL-92 Intermediate level–conformant driver will usually return the SQL_CA1_NEXT, SQL_CA1_ABSOLUTE, and SQL_CA1_RELATIVE options as supported, because it supports scrollable cursors through the embedded SQL FETCH statement. Since this does not directly determine the underlying SQL support, however, scrollable cursors may not be supported, even for an SQL-92 Intermediate level–conformant driver.

InfoType	**Returns**
SQL_KEYSET_CURSOR_ATTRIBUTES2 (ODBC 3.0)	An SQLUINTEGER bitmask that describes the attributes of a keyset cursor that are supported by the driver. This bitmask contains the second subset of attributes; for the first subset, see SQL_KEYSET_CURSOR_ATTRIBUTES1. The following bitmasks are used to determine which attributes are supported: SQL_CA2_READ_ONLY_CONCURRENCY SQL_CA2_LOCK_CONCURRENCY SQL_CA2_OPT_ROWVER_CONCURRENCY SQL_CA2_OPT_VALUES_CONCURRENCY SQL_CA2_SENSITIVITY_ADDITIONS SQL_CA2_SENSITIVITY_DELETIONS SQL_CA2_SENSITIVITY_UPDATES SQL_CA2_MAX_ROWS_SELECT SQL_CA2_MAX_ROWS_INSERT SQL_CA2_MAX_ROWS_DELETE SQL_CA2_MAX_ROWS_UPDATE SQL_CA2_MAX_ROWS_CATALOG SQL_CA2_MAX_ROWS_AFFECTS_ALL SQL_CA2_CRC_EXACT SQL_CA2_CRC_APPROXIMATE SQL_CA2_SIMULATE_NON_UNIQUE SQL_CA2_SIMULATE_TRY_UNIQUE SQL_CA2_SIMULATE_UNIQUE For descriptions of these bitmasks, see SQL_DYNAMIC_CURSOR_ATTRIBUTES1 (and substitute "keyset-driven cursor" for "dynamic cursor" in the descriptions).
SQL_KEYWORDS (ODBC 2.0)	A character string containing a comma-separated list of all data source–specific keywords. This list does not contain keywords specific to ODBC or keywords used by both the data source and ODBC. This list represents all the reserved keywords; interoperable applications should not use these words in object names. For a list of ODBC keywords, see "List of Reserved Keywords" in Appendix C, "SQL Grammar." The **#define** value SQL_ODBC_KEYWORDS contains a comma-separated list of ODBC keywords.
SQL_LIKE_ESCAPE_CLAUSE (ODBC 2.0)	A character string: "Y" if the data source supports an escape character for the percent character (%) and underscore character (_) in a **LIKE** predicate and the driver supports the ODBC syntax for defining a **LIKE** predicate escape character; "N" otherwise.

InfoType	Returns
SQL_MAX_ASYNC_ CONCURRENT_ STATEMENTS (ODBC 3.0)	An SQLUINTEGER value specifying the maximum number of active concurrent statements in asynchronous mode that the driver can support on a given connection. If there is no specific limit or the limit is unknown, this value is zero.
SQL_MAX_BINARY_ LITERAL_LEN (ODBC 2.0)	An SQLUINTEGER value specifying the maximum length (number of hexadecimal characters, excluding the literal prefix and suffix returned by **SQLGetTypeInfo**) of a binary literal in an SQL statement. For example, the binary literal 0xFFAA has a length of 4. If there is no maximum length or the length is unknown, this value is set to zero.
SQL_MAX_CATALOG_ NAME_LEN (ODBC 1.0)	An SQLUSMALLINT value specifying the maximum length of a catalog name in the data source. If there is no maximum length or the length is unknown, this value is set to zero. An FIPS Full level–conformant driver will return at least 128. This *InfoType* has been renamed for ODBC 3.0 from the ODBC 2.0 *InfoType* SQL_MAX_QUALIFIER_NAME_LEN.
SQL_MAX_CHAR_LITERAL_LEN (ODBC 2.0)	An SQLUINTEGER value specifying the maximum length (number of characters, excluding the literal prefix and suffix returned by **SQLGetTypeInfo**) of a character literal in an SQL statement. If there is no maximum length or the length is unknown, this value is set to zero.
SQL_MAX_COLUMN_ NAME_LEN (ODBC 1.0)	An SQLUSMALLINT value specifying the maximum length of a column name in the data source. If there is no maximum length or the length is unknown, this value is set to zero. An FIPS Entry level–conformant driver will return at least 18. An FIPS Intermediate level–conformant driver will return at least 128.
SQL_MAX_COLUMNS_ IN_GROUP_BY (ODBC 2.0)	An SQLUSMALLINT value specifying the maximum number of columns allowed in a **GROUP BY** clause. If there is no specified limit or the limit is unknown, this value is set to zero. An FIPS Entry level–conformant driver will return at least 6. An FIPS Intermediate level–conformant driver will return at least 15.
SQL_MAX_COLUMNS_ IN_INDEX (ODBC 2.0)	An SQLUSMALLINT value specifying the maximum number of columns allowed in an index. If there is no specified limit or the limit is unknown, this value is set to zero.
SQL_MAX_COLUMNS_ IN_ORDER_BY (ODBC 2.0)	An SQLUSMALLINT value specifying the maximum number of columns allowed in an **ORDER BY** clause. If there is no specified limit or the limit is unknown, this value is set to zero. An FIPS Entry level–conformant driver will return at least 6. An FIPS Intermediate level–conformant driver will return at least 15.

InfoType	Returns
SQL_MAX_COLUMNS_ IN_SELECT (ODBC 2.0)	An SQLUSMALLINT value specifying the maximum number of columns allowed in a select list. If there is no specified limit or the limit is unknown, this value is set to zero. An FIPS Entry level–conformant driver will return at least 100. An FIPS Intermediate level–conformant driver will return at least 250.
SQL_MAX_COLUMNS_ IN_TABLE (ODBC 2.0)	An SQLUSMALLINT value specifying the maximum number of columns allowed in a table. If there is no specified limit or the limit is unknown, this value is set to zero. An FIPS Entry level–conformant driver will return at least 100. An FIPS Intermediate level–conformant driver will return at least 250.
SQL_MAX_CONCURRENT_ ACTIVITIES (ODBC 1.0)	An SQLUSMALLINT value specifying the maximum number of active statements that the driver can support for a connection. A statement is defined as active if it has results pending, with the term "results" meaning rows from a **SELECT** operation or rows affected by an **INSERT**, **UPDATE**, or **DELETE** operation (such as a row count), or if it is in a NEED_DATA state. This value can reflect a limitation imposed by either the driver or the data source. If there is no specified limit or the limit is unknown, this value is set to zero. This *InfoType* has been renamed for ODBC 3.0 from the ODBC 2.0 *InfoType* SQL_ACTIVE_STATEMENTS.
SQL_MAX_CURSOR_ NAME_LEN (ODBC 1.0)	An SQLUSMALLINT value specifying the maximum length of a cursor name in the data source. If there is no maximum length or the length is unknown, this value is set to zero. An FIPS Entry level–conformant driver will return at least 18. An FIPS Intermediate level–conformant driver will return at least 128.
SQL_MAX_ DRIVER_CONNECTIONS (ODBC 1.0)	An SQLUSMALLINT value specifying the maximum number of active connections that the driver can support for an environment. This value can reflect a limitation imposed by either the driver or the data source. If there is no specified limit or the limit is unknown, this value is set to zero. This *InfoType* has been renamed for ODBC 3.0 from the ODBC 2.0 *InfoType* SQL_ACTIVE_CONNECTIONS.
SQL_MAX_IDENTIFIER_LEN (ODBC 3.0)	An SQLUSMALLINT that indicates the maximum size in characters that the data source supports for user-defined names. An FIPS Entry level–conformant driver will return at least 18. An FIPS Intermediate level–conformant driver will return at least 128.
SQL_MAX_INDEX_SIZE (ODBC 2.0)	An SQLUINTEGER value specifying the maximum number of bytes allowed in the combined fields of an index. If there is no specified limit or the limit is unknown, this value is set to zero.

InfoType	Returns
SQL_MAX_PROCEDURE_NAME_LEN (ODBC 1.0)	An SQLUSMALLINT value specifying the maximum length of a procedure name in the data source. If there is no maximum length or the length is unknown, this value is set to zero.
SQL_MAX_ROW_SIZE (ODBC 2.0)	An SQLUINTEGER value specifying the maximum length of a single row in a table. If there is no specified limit or the limit is unknown, this value is set to zero. An FIPS Entry level–conformant driver will return at least 2,000. An FIPS Intermediate level–conformant driver will return at least 8,000.
SQL_MAX_ROW_SIZE_INCLUDES_LONG (ODBC 3.0)	A character string: "Y" if the maximum row size returned for the SQL_MAX_ROW_SIZE information type includes the length of all SQL_LONGVARCHAR and SQL_LONGVARBINARY columns in the row; "N" otherwise.
SQL_MAX_SCHEMA_NAME_LEN (ODBC 1.0)	An SQLUSMALLINT value specifying the maximum length of a schema name in the data source. If there is no maximum length or the length is unknown, this value is set to zero. An FIPS Entry level–conformant driver will return at least 18. An FIPS Intermediate level–conformant driver will return at least 128. This *InfoType* has been renamed for ODBC 3.0 from the ODBC 2.0 *InfoType* SQL_MAX_OWNER_NAME_LEN.
SQL_MAX_STATEMENT_LEN (ODBC 2.0)	An SQLUINTEGER value specifying the maximum length (number of characters, including white space) of an SQL statement. If there is no maximum length or the length is unknown, this value is set to zero.
SQL_MAX_TABLE_NAME_LEN (ODBC 1.0)	An SQLUSMALLINT value specifying the maximum length of a table name in the data source. If there is no maximum length or the length is unknown, this value is set to zero. An FIPS Entry level–conformant driver will return at least 18. An FIPS Intermediate level–conformant driver will return at least 128.
SQL_MAX_TABLES_IN_SELECT (ODBC 2.0)	An SQLUSMALLINT value specifying the maximum number of tables allowed in the **FROM** clause of a **SELECT** statement. If there is no specified limit or the limit is unknown, this value is set to zero. An FIPS Entry level–conformant driver will return at least 15. An FIPS Intermediate level–conformant driver will return at least 50.
SQL_MAX_USER_NAME_LEN (ODBC 2.0)	An SQLUSMALLINT value specifying the maximum length of a user name in the data source. If there is no maximum length or the length is unknown, this value is set to zero.

InfoType	Returns
SQL_MULT_RESULT_SETS (ODBC 1.0)	A character string: "Y" if the data source supports multiple result sets, "N" if it does not. For more information on multiple result sets, see "Multiple Results" in Chapter 11, "Retrieving Results (Advanced)."
SQL_MULTIPLE_ACTIVE_TXN (ODBC 1.0)	A character string: "Y" if the driver supports more than one active transaction at the same time, "N" if only one transaction can be active at any time. The information returned for this information type does not apply in the case of distributed transactions.
SQL_NEED_LONG_DATA_LEN (ODBC 2.0)	A character string: "Y" if the data source needs the length of a long data value (the data type is SQL_LONGVARCHAR, SQL_LONGVARBINARY, or a long, data source–specific data type) before that value is sent to the data source, "N" if it does not. For more information, see **SQLBindParameter** and **SQLSetPos**.
SQL_NON_ NULLABLE_COLUMNS (ODBC 1.0)	An SQLUSMALLINT value specifying whether the data source supports NOT NULL in columns: SQL_NNC_NULL = All columns must be nullable. SQL_NNC_NON_NULL = Columns cannot be nullable (the data source supports the **NOT NULL** column constraint in **CREATE TABLE** statements). An SQL-92 Entry level–conformant driver will return SQL_NNC_NON_NULL.
SQL_NULL_COLLATION (ODBC 2.0)	An SQLUSMALLINT value specifying where NULLs are sorted in a result set: SQL_NC_END = NULLs are sorted at the end of the result set, regardless of the ASC or DESC keywords. SQL_NC_HIGH = NULLs are sorted at the high end of the result set, depending on the ASC or DESC keywords. SQL_NC_LOW = NULLs are sorted at the low end of the result set, depending on the ASC or DESC keywords. SQL_NC_START = NULLs are sorted at the start of the result set, regardless of the ASC or DESC keywords.

InfoType	Returns
SQL_NUMERIC_FUNCTIONS (ODBC 1.0) The information type was introduced in ODBC 1.0; each bitmask is labeled with the version in which it was introduced.	An SQLUINTEGER bitmask enumerating the scalar numeric functions supported by the driver and associated data source. The following bitmasks are used to determine which numeric functions are supported: SQL_FN_NUM_ABS (ODBC 1.0) SQL_FN_NUM_ACOS (ODBC 1.0) SQL_FN_NUM_ASIN (ODBC 1.0) SQL_FN_NUM_ATAN (ODBC 1.0) SQL_FN_NUM_ATAN2 (ODBC 1.0) SQL_FN_NUM_CEILING (ODBC 1.0) SQL_FN_NUM_COS (ODBC 1.0) SQL_FN_NUM_COT (ODBC 1.0) SQL_FN_NUM_DEGREES (ODBC 2.0) SQL_FN_NUM_EXP (ODBC 1.0) SQL_FN_NUM_FLOOR (ODBC 1.0) SQL_FN_NUM_LOG (ODBC 1.0) SQL_FN_NUM_LOG10 (ODBC 2.0) SQL_FN_NUM_MOD (ODBC 1.0) SQL_FN_NUM_PI (ODBC 1.0) SQL_FN_NUM_POWER (ODBC 2.0) SQL_FN_NUM_RADIANS (ODBC 2.0) SQL_FN_NUM_RAND (ODBC 1.0) SQL_FN_NUM_ROUND (ODBC 2.0) SQL_FN_NUM_SIGN (ODBC 1.0) SQL_FN_NUM_SIN (ODBC 1.0) SQL_FN_NUM_SQRT (ODBC 1.0) SQL_FN_NUM_TAN (ODBC 1.0) SQL_FN_NUM_TRUNCATE (ODBC 2.0)
SQL_ODBC_INTERFACE_ CONFORMANCE (ODBC 3.0)	An SQLUINTEGER value indicating the level of the ODBC 3.0 interface that the driver conforms to. SQL_OIC_CORE: The minimum level that all ODBC drivers are expected to conform to. This level includes basic interface elements such as connection functions; functions for preparing and executing an SQL statement; basic result set metadata functions; basic catalog functions; and so on. SQL_OIC_LEVEL1: A level including the core standards compliance level functionality, plus scrollable cursors, bookmarks, positioned updates and deletes, and so on.

InfoType	**Returns**
SQL_ODBC_INTERFACE_ CONFORMANCE (ODBC 3.0) (*continued*)	SQL_OIC_LEVEL2: A level including level 1 standards compliance level functionality, plus advanced features such as sensitive cursors; update, delete, and refresh by bookmarks; stored procedure support; catalog functions for primary and foreign keys; multi-catalog support; and so on. For more information, see "Interface Conformance Levels" in Chapter 4, "ODBC Fundamentals."
SQL_ODBC_VER (ODBC 1.0)	A character string with the version of ODBC to which the Driver Manager conforms. The version is of the form ##.##.0000, where the first two digits are the major version and the next two digits are the minor version. This is implemented solely in the Driver Manager.
SQL_OJ_CAPABILITIES (ODBC 2.01)	An SQLUINTEGER bitmask enumerating the types of outer joins supported by the driver and data source. The following bitmasks are used to determine which types are supported: SQL_OJ_LEFT = Left outer joins are supported. SQL_OJ_RIGHT = Right outer joins are supported. SQL_OJ_FULL = Full outer joins are supported. SQL_OJ_NESTED = Nested outer joins are supported. SQL_OJ_NOT_ORDERED = The column names in the ON clause of the outer join do not have to be in the same order as their respective table names in the **OUTER JOIN** clause. SQL_OJ_INNER = The inner table (the right table in a left outer join or the left table in a right outer join) can also be used in an inner join. This does not apply to full outer joins, which do not have an inner table. SQL_OJ_ALL_COMPARISON_OPS = The comparison operator in the ON clause can be any of the ODBC comparison operators. If this bit is not set, only the equals (=) comparison operator can be used in outer joins. If none of these options is returned as supported, no outer join clause is supported. For information on the support of relational join operators in a SELECT statement, as defined by SQL-92, see SQL_SQL92_RELATIONAL_JOIN_OPERATORS.
SQL_ORDER_BY_ COLUMNS_IN_ SELECT (ODBC 2.0)	A character string: "Y" if the columns in the **ORDER BY** clause must be in the select list; otherwise, "N".

InfoType	Returns
SQL_PARAM_ARRAY_ ROW_COUNTS (ODBC 3.0)	An SQLUINTEGER enumerating the driver's properties regarding the availability of row counts in a parameterized execution. Has the following values: SQL_PARC_BATCH = Individual row counts are available for each set of parameters. This is conceptually equivalent to the driver generating a batch of SQL statements, one for each parameter set in the array. Extended error information can be retrieved by using the SQL_PARAM_STATUS_PTR descriptor field. SQL_PARC_NO_BATCH = There is only one row count available, which is the cumulative row count resulting from the execution of the statement for the entire array of parameters. This is conceptually equivalent to treating the statement along with the entire parameter array as one atomic unit. Errors are handled the same as if one statement were executed.
SQL_PARAM_ARRAY_SELECTS (ODBC 3.0)	An SQLUINTEGER enumerating the driver's properties regarding the availability of result sets in a parameterized execution. Has the following values: SQL_PAS_BATCH = There is one result set available per set of parameters. This is conceptually equivalent to the driver generating a batch of SQL statements, one for each parameter set in the array. SQL_PAS_NO_BATCH = There is only one result set available, which represents the cumulative result set resulting from the execution of the statement for the entire array of parameters. This is conceptually equivalent to treating the statement along with the entire parameter array as one atomic unit. SQL_PAS_NO_SELECT = A driver does not allow a result-set generating statement to be executed with an array of parameters.
SQL_PROCEDURE_TERM (ODBC 1.0)	A character string with the data source vendor's name for a procedure; for example, "database procedure," "stored procedure," "procedure," "package," or "stored query."
SQL_PROCEDURES (ODBC 1.0)	A character string: "Y" if the data source supports procedures and the driver supports the ODBC procedure invocation syntax; "N" otherwise.

InfoType	Returns
SQL_QUOTED_ IDENTIFIER_CASE (ODBC 2.0)	An SQLUSMALLINT value as follows: SQL_IC_UPPER = Quoted identifiers in SQL are not case-sensitive and are stored in uppercase in the system catalog. SQL_IC_LOWER = Quoted identifiers in SQL are not case-sensitive and are stored in lowercase in the system catalog. SQL_IC_SENSITIVE = Quoted identifiers in SQL are case-sensitive and are stored in mixed case in the system catalog. (Note that in an SQL-92-compliant database, quoted identifiers are always case-sensitive.) SQL_IC_MIXED = Quoted identifiers in SQL are not case-sensitive and are stored in mixed case in the system catalog. An SQL-92 Entry level–conformant driver will always return SQL_IC_SENSITIVE.
SQL_ROW_UPDATES (ODBC 1.0)	A character string: "Y" if a keyset-driven or mixed cursor maintains row versions or values for all fetched rows and therefore can detect any updates made to a row by any user since the row was last fetched. (This only applies to updates, not to deletions or insertions.) The driver can return the SQL_ROW_UPDATED flag to the row status array when **SQLFetchScroll** is called. Otherwise, "N".
SQL_SCHEMA_TERM (ODBC 1.0)	A character string with the data source vendor's name for an schema; for example, "owner," "Authorization ID," or "Schema." The character string can be returned in upper, lower, or mixed case. An SQL-92 Entry level–conformant driver will always return "schema". This *InfoType* has been renamed for ODBC 3.0 from the ODBC 2.0 *InfoType* SQL_OWNER_TERM.
SQL_SCHEMA_USAGE (ODBC 2.0)	An SQLUINTEGER bitmask enumerating the statements in which schemas can be used: SQL_SU_DML_STATEMENTS = Schemas are supported in all Data Manipulation Language statements: **SELECT**, **INSERT**, **UPDATE**, **DELETE**, and, if supported, **SELECT FOR UPDATE** and positioned update and delete statements. SQL_SU_PROCEDURE_INVOCATION = Schemas are supported in the ODBC procedure invocation statement. SQL_SU_TABLE_DEFINITION = Schemas are supported in all table definition statements: **CREATE TABLE**, **CREATE VIEW**, **ALTER TABLE**, **DROP TABLE**, and **DROP VIEW**. SQL_SU_INDEX_DEFINITION = Schemas are supported in all index definition statements: **CREATE INDEX** and **DROP INDEX**.

InfoType	Returns
SQL_SCHEMA_USAGE (ODBC 2.0) (*continued*)	SQL_SU_PRIVILEGE_DEFINITION = Schemas are supported in all privilege definition statements: **GRANT** and **REVOKE**. An SQL-92 Entry level–conformant driver will always return the SQL_SU_DML_STATEMENTS, SQL_SU_TABLE_DEFINITION, and SQL_SU_PRIVILEGE_DEFINITION options as supported. This *InfoType* has been renamed for ODBC 3.0 from the ODBC 2.0 *InfoType* SQL_OWNER_USAGE.
SQL_SCROLL_OPTIONS (ODBC 1.0) The information type was introduced in ODBC 1.0; each bitmask is labeled with the version in which it was introduced.	An SQLUINTEGER bitmask enumerating the scroll options supported for scrollable cursors. The following bitmasks are used to determine which options are supported: SQL_SO_FORWARD_ONLY = The cursor only scrolls forward. (ODBC 1.0) SQL_SO_STATIC = The data in the result set is static. (ODBC 2.0) SQL_SO_KEYSET_DRIVEN = The driver saves and uses the keys for every row in the result set. (ODBC 1.0) SQL_SO_DYNAMIC = The driver keeps the keys for every row in the rowset (the keyset size is the same as the rowset size). (ODBC 1.0) SQL_SO_MIXED = The driver keeps the keys for every row in the keyset, and the keyset size is greater than the rowset size. The cursor is keyset-driven inside the keyset and dynamic outside the keyset. (ODBC 1.0) For information about scrollable cursors, see "Scrollable Cursors" in Chapter 11, "Retrieving Results (Advanced)"
SQL_SEARCH_ PATTERN_ESCAPE (ODBC 1.0)	A character string specifying what the driver supports as an escape character that permits the use of the pattern match metacharacters underscore (_) and percent sign (%) as valid characters in search patterns. This escape character applies only for those catalog function arguments that support search strings. If this string is empty, the driver does not support a search-pattern escape character. Since this information type does not indicate general support of the escape character in the **LIKE** predicate, SQL-92 does not include requirements for this character string. This *InfoType* is limited to catalog functions. For a description of the use of the escape character in search pattern strings, see "Pattern Value Arguments" in Chapter 7, "Catalog Functions."

InfoType	**Returns**
SQL_SERVER_NAME (ODBC 1.0)	A character string with the actual data source–specific server name; useful when a data source name is used during **SQLConnect**, **SQLDriverConnect**, and **SQLBrowseConnect**.
SQL_SPECIAL_CHARACTERS (ODBC 2.0)	A character string containing all special characters (that is, all characters except a through z, A through Z, 0 through 9, and underscore) that can be used in an identifier name, such as a table, column, or index name, on the data source. For example, "#$^". If an identifier contains one or more of these characters, the identifier must be a delimited identifier.
SQL_SQL_CONFORMANCE (ODBC 3.0)	An SQLUINTEGER value indicating the level of SQL-92 supported by the driver: SQL_SC_SQL92_ENTRY = Entry level SQL-92 compliant SQL_SC_FIPS127_2_TRANSITIONAL = FIPS 127-2 transitional level compliant SQL_SC_SQL92_FULL = Full level SQL-92 compliant SQL_SC_ SQL92_INTERMEDIATE = Intermediate level SQL-92 compliant
SQL_SQL92_DATETIME_ FUNCTIONS (ODBC 3.0)	An SQLUINTEGER bitmask enumerating the datetime scalar functions that are supported by the driver and the associated data source, as defined in SQL-92. The following bitmasks are used to determine which datetime functions are supported: SQL_SDF_CURRENT_DATE SQL_SDF_CURRENT_TIME SQL_SDF_CURRENT_TIMESTAMP
SQL_SQL92_FOREIGN_ KEY_DELETE_RULE (ODBC 3.0)	An SQLUINTEGER bitmask enumerating the rules supported for a foreign key in a **DELETE** statement, as defined in SQL-92. The following bitmasks are used to determine which clauses are supported by the data source: SQL_SFKD_CASCADE SQL_SFKD_NO_ACTION SQL_SFKD_SET_DEFAULT SQL_SFKD_SET_NULL An FIPS Transitional level–conformant driver will always return all of these options as supported.

InfoType	Returns
SQL_SQL92_FOREIGN_ KEY_UPDATE_RULE (ODBC 3.0)	An SQLUINTEGER bitmask enumerating the rules supported for a foreign key in an **UPDATE** statement, as defined in SQL-92. The following bitmasks are used to determine which clauses are supported by the data source: SQL_SFKU_CASCADE SQL_SFKU_NO_ACTION SQL_SFKU_SET_DEFAULT SQL_SFKU_SET_NULL An SQL-92 Full level–conformant driver will always return all of these options as supported.
SQL_SQL92_GRANT (ODBC 3.0)	An SQLUINTEGER bitmask enumerating the clauses supported in the **GRANT** statement, as defined in SQL-92. The SQL-92 or FIPS conformance level at which this features needs to be supported is shown in parentheses next to each bitmask. The following bitmasks are used to determine which clauses are supported by the data source: SQL_SG_DELETE_TABLE (Entry level) SQL_SG_INSERT_COLUMN (Intermediate level) SQL_SG_INSERT_TABLE (Entry level) SQL_SG_REFERENCES_TABLE (Entry level) SQL_SG_REFERENCES_COLUMN (Entry level) SQL_SG_SELECT_TABLE (Entry level) SQL_SG_UPDATE_COLUMN (Entry level) SQL_SG_UPDATE_TABLE (Entry level) SQL_SG_USAGE_ON_DOMAIN (FIPS Transitional level) SQL_SG_USAGE_ON_CHARACTER_SET (FIPS Transitional level) SQL_SG_USAGE_ON_COLLATION (FIPS Transitional level) SQL_SG_USAGE_ON_TRANSLATION (FIPS Transitional level) SQL_SG_WITH_GRANT_OPTION (Entry level)
SQL_SQL92_NUMERIC_VALUE_ FUNCTIONS (ODBC 3.0)	An SQLUINTEGER bitmask enumerating the numeric value scalar functions that are supported by the driver and the associated data source, as defined in SQL-92. The following bitmasks are used to determine which numeric functions are supported: SQL_SNVF_BIT_LENGTH SQL_SNVF_CHAR_LENGTH SQL_SNVF_CHARACTER_LENGTH SQL_SNVF_EXTRACT SQL_SNVF_OCTET_LENGTH SQL_SNVF_POSITION

InfoType	Returns
SQL_SQL92_PREDICATES (ODBC 3.0)	An SQLUINTEGER bitmask enumerating the predicates supported in a **SELECT** statement, as defined in SQL-92. The SQL-92 or FIPS conformance level at which this features needs to be supported is shown in parentheses next to each bitmask. The following bitmasks are used to determine which options are supported by the data source: SQL_SP_BETWEEN (Entry level) SQL_SP_COMPARISON (Entry level) SQL_SP_EXISTS (Entry level) SQL_SP_IN (Entry level) SQL_SP_ISNOTNULL (Entry level) SQL_SP_ISNULL (Entry level) SQL_SP_LIKE (Entry level) SQL_SP_MATCH_FULL (Full level) SQL_SP_MATCH_PARTIAL(Full level) SQL_SP_MATCH_UNIQUE_FULL (Full level) SQL_SP_MATCH_UNIQUE_PARTIAL (Full level) SQL_SP_OVERLAPS (FIPS Transitional level) SQL_SP_QUANTIFIED_COMPARISON (Entry level) SQL_SP_UNIQUE (Entry level)
SQL_SQL92_RELATIONAL_ JOIN_OPERATORS (ODBC 3.0)	An SQLUINTEGER bitmask enumerating the relational join operators supported in a **SELECT** statement, as defined in SQL-92. The SQL-92 or FIPS conformance level at which this features needs to be supported is shown in parentheses next to each bitmask. The following bitmasks are used to determine which options are supported by the data source: SQL_SRJO_CORRESPONDING_CLAUSE (Intermediate level) SQL_SRJO_CROSS_JOIN (Full level) SQL_SRJO_EXCEPT_JOIN (Intermediate level) SQL_SRJO_FULL_OUTER_JOIN (Intermediate level) SQL_SRJO_INNER_JOIN (FIPS Transitional level) SQL_SRJO_INTERSECT_JOIN (Intermediate level) SQL_SRJO_LEFT_OUTER_JOIN (FIPS Transitional level) SQL_SRJO_NATURAL_JOIN (FIPS Transitional level) SQL_SRJO_RIGHT_OUTER_JOIN (FIPS Transitional level) SQL_SRJO_UNION_JOIN (Full level) SQL_SRJO_INNER_JOIN indicates support for the **INNER JOIN** syntax, not for the inner join capability. Support for the **INNER JOIN** syntax is FIPS TRANSITIONAL, while support for the inner join capability is **ENTRY**.

InfoType	Returns
SQL_SQL92_REVOKE (ODBC 3.0)	An SQLUINTEGER bitmask enumerating the clauses supported in the **REVOKE** statement, as defined in SQL-92, supported by the data source. The SQL-92 or FIPS conformance level at which this features needs to be supported is shown in parentheses next to each bitmask. The following bitmasks are used to determine which clauses are supported by the data source: SQL_SR_CASCADE (FIPS Transitional level) SQL_SR_DELETE_TABLE (Entry level) SQL_SR_GRANT_OPTION_FOR (Intermediate level) SQL_SR_INSERT_COLUMN (Intermediate level) SQL_SR_INSERT_TABLE (Entry level) SQL_SR_REFERENCES_COLUMN (Entry level) SQL_SR_REFERENCES_TABLE (Entry level) SQL_SR_RESTRICT (FIPS Transitional level) SQL_SR_SELECT_TABLE (Entry level) SQL_SR_UPDATE_COLUMN (Entry level) SQL_SR_UPDATE_TABLE (Entry level) SQL_SR_USAGE_ON_DOMAIN (FIPS Transitional level) SQL_SR_USAGE_ON_CHARACTER_SET (FIPS Transitional level) SQL_SR_USAGE_ON_COLLATION (FIPS Transitional level) SQL_SR_USAGE_ON_TRANSLATION (FIPS Transitional level)
SQL_SQL92_ROW_VALUE_ CONSTRUCTOR (ODBC 3.0)	An SQLUINTEGER bitmask enumerating the row value constructor expressions supported in a **SELECT** statement, as defined in SQL-92. The following bitmasks are used to determine which options are supported by the data source: SQL_SRVC_VALUE_EXPRESSION SQL_SRVC_NULL SQL_SRVC_DEFAULT SQL_SRVC_ROW_SUBQUERY

<table>
<tr><th>InfoType</th><th>Returns</th></tr>
<tr><td>SQL_SQL92_STRING_
FUNCTIONS
(ODBC 3.0)</td><td>An SQLUINTEGER bitmask enumerating the string scalar functions that are supported by the driver and the associated data source, as defined in SQL-92.

The following bitmasks are used to determine which string functions are supported:

SQL_SSF_CONVERT
SQL_SSF_LOWER
SQL_SSF_UPPER
SQL_SSF_SUBSTRING
SQL_SSF_TRANSLATE
SQL_SSF_TRIM_BOTH
SQL_SSF_TRIM_LEADING
SQL_SSF_TRIM_TRAILING</td></tr>
<tr><td>SQL_SQL92_
VALUE_EXPRESSIONS
(ODBC 3.0)</td><td>An SQLUINTEGER bitmask enumerating the value expressions supported, as defined in SQL-92.

The SQL-92 or FIPS conformance level at which this features needs to be supported is shown in parentheses next to each bitmask.

The following bitmasks are used to determine which options are supported by the data source:

SQL_SVE_CASE (Intermediate level)
SQL_SVE_CAST (FIPS Transitional level)
SQL_SVE_COALESCE (Intermediate level)
SQL_SVE_NULLIF (Intermediate level)</td></tr>
<tr><td>SQL_STANDARD_CLI_
CONFORMANCE
(ODBC 3.0)</td><td>An SQLUINTEGER bitmask enumerating the CLI standard or standards to which the driver conforms. The following bitmasks are used to determine which levels the driver conforms to:

SQL_SCC_XOPEN_CLI_VERSION1: The driver conforms to the X/Open CLI version 1.

SQL_SCC_ISO92_CLI: The driver conforms to the ISO 92 CLI.</td></tr>
</table>

InfoType	Returns
SQL_STATIC_CURSOR_ATTRIBUTES1 (ODBC 3.0)	An SQLUINTEGER bitmask that describes the attributes of a static cursor that are supported by the driver. This bitmask contains the first subset of attributes; for the second subset, see SQL_STATIC_CURSOR_ATTRIBUTES2. The following bitmasks are used to determine which attributes are supported: SQL_CA1_NEXT SQL_CA1_ABSOLUTE SQL_CA1_RELATIVE SQL_CA1_BOOKMARK SQL_CA1_LOCK_NO_CHANGE SQL_CA1_LOCK_EXCLUSIVE SQL_CA1_LOCK_UNLOCK SQL_CA1_POS_POSITION SQL_CA1_POS_UPDATE SQL_CA1_POS_DELETE SQL_CA1_POS_REFRESH SQL_CA1_POSITIONED_UPDATE SQL_CA1_POSITIONED_DELETE SQL_CA1_SELECT_FOR_UPDATE SQL_CA1_BULK_ADD SQL_CA1_BULK_UPDATE_BY_BOOKMARK SQL_CA1_BULK_DELETE_BY_BOOKMARK SQL_CA1_BULK_FETCH_BY_BOOKMARK For descriptions of these bitmasks, see SQL_DYNAMIC_CURSOR_ATTRIBUTES1 (and substitute "static cursor" for "dynamic cursor" in the descriptions). An SQL-92 Intermediate level–conformant driver will usually return the SQL_CA1_NEXT, SQL_CA1_ABSOLUTE, and SQL_CA1_RELATIVE options as supported, because it supports scrollable cursors through the embedded SQL FETCH statement. Since this does not directly determine the underlying SQL support, however, scrollable cursors may not be supported, even for an SQL-92 Intermediate level–conformant driver.

InfoType	Returns
SQL_STATIC_ CURSOR_ ATTRIBUTES2 (ODBC 3.0)	An SQLUINTEGER bitmask that describes the attributes of a static cursor that are supported by the driver. This bitmask contains the second subset of attributes; for the first subset, see SQL_STATIC_CURSOR_ATTRIBUTES1. The following bitmasks are used to determine which attributes are supported: SQL_CA2_READ_ONLY_CONCURRENCY SQL_CA2_LOCK_CONCURRENCY SQL_CA2_OPT_ROWVER_CONCURRENCY SQL_CA2_OPT_VALUES_CONCURRENCY SQL_CA2_SENSITIVITY_ADDITIONS SQL_CA2_SENSITIVITY_DELETIONS SQL_CA2_SENSITIVITY_UPDATES SQL_CA2_MAX_ROWS_SELECT SQL_CA2_MAX_ROWS_INSERT SQL_CA2_MAX_ROWS_DELETE SQL_CA2_MAX_ROWS_UPDATE SQL_CA2_MAX_ROWS_CATALOG SQL_CA2_MAX_ROWS_AFFECTS_ALL SQL_CA2_CRC_EXACT SQL_CA2_CRC_APPROXIMATE SQL_CA2_SIMULATE_NON_UNIQUE SQL_CA2_SIMULATE_TRY_UNIQUE SQL_CA2_SIMULATE_UNIQUE For descriptions of these bitmasks, see SQL_DYNAMIC_CURSOR_ATTRIBUTES2 (and substitute "static cursor" for "dynamic cursor" in the descriptions).
SQL_STRING_FUNCTIONS (ODBC 1.0) The information type was introduced in ODBC 1.0; each bitmask is labeled with the version in which it was introduced.	An SQLUINTEGER bitmask enumerating the scalar string functions supported by the driver and associated data source. The following bitmasks are used to determine which string functions are supported: SQL_FN_STR_ASCII (ODBC 1.0) SQL_FN_STR_BIT_LENGTH (ODBC 3.0) SQL_FN_STR_CHAR (ODBC 1.0) SQL_FN_STR_CHAR_ LENGTH (ODBC 3.0) SQL_FN_STR_CHARACTER_ LENGTH (ODBC 3.0) SQL_FN_STR_CONCAT (ODBC 1.0) SQL_FN_STR_DIFFERENCE (ODBC 2.0) SQL_FN_STR_INSERT (ODBC 1.0) SQL_FN_STR_LCASE (ODBC 1.0) SQL_FN_STR_LEFT (ODBC 1.0) SQL_FN_STR_LENGTH (ODBC 1.0)

InfoType	Returns
SQL_STRING_FUNCTIONS (ODBC 1.0) (*continued*) The information type was introduced in ODBC 1.0; each bitmask is labeled with the version in which it was introduced.	SQL_FN_STR_LOCATE (ODBC 1.0) SQL_FN_STR_LTRIM (ODBC 1.0) SQL_FN_STR_OCTET_ LENGTH (ODBC 3.0) SQL_FN_STR_POSITION (ODBC 3.0) SQL_FN_STR_REPEAT (ODBC 1.0) SQL_FN_STR_REPLACE (ODBC 1.0) SQL_FN_STR_RIGHT (ODBC 1.0) SQL_FN_STR_RTRIM (ODBC 1.0) SQL_FN_STR_SOUNDEX (ODBC 2.0) SQL_FN_STR_SPACE (ODBC 2.0) SQL_FN_STR_SUBSTRING (ODBC 1.0) SQL_FN_STR_UCASE (ODBC 1.0) If an application can call the **LOCATE** scalar function with the *string_exp1*, *string_exp2*, and *start* arguments, the driver returns the SQL_FN_STR_LOCATE bitmask. If an application can call the LOCATE scalar function with only the *string_exp1* and *string_exp2* arguments, the driver returns the SQL_FN_STR_LOCATE_2 bitmask. Drivers that fully support the **LOCATE** scalar function return both bitmasks. (For more information, see Appendix E, "Scalar Functions.")
SQL_SUBQUERIES (ODBC 2.0)	An SQLUINTEGER bitmask enumerating the predicates that support subqueries: SQL_SQ_CORRELATED_SUBQUERIES SQL_SQ_COMPARISON SQL_SQ_EXISTS SQL_SQ_IN SQL_SQ_QUANTIFIED The SQL_SQ_CORRELATED_SUBQUERIES bitmask indicates that all predicates that support subqueries support correlated subqueries. An SQL-92 Entry level–conformant driver will always return a bitmask in which all of these bits are set.
SQL_SYSTEM_FUNCTIONS (ODBC 1.0)	An SQLUINTEGER bitmask enumerating the scalar system functions supported by the driver and associated data source. The following bitmasks are used to determine which system functions are supported: SQL_FN_SYS_DBNAME SQL_FN_SYS_IFNULL SQL_FN_SYS_USERNAME

InfoType	Returns
SQL_TABLE_TERM (ODBC 1.0)	A character string with the data source vendor's name for a table; for example, "table" or "file". This character string can be in upper, lower, or mixed case. An SQL-92 Entry level–conformant driver will always return "table".
SQL_TIMEDATE_ ADD_INTERVALS (ODBC 2.0)	An SQLUINTEGER bitmask enumerating the timestamp intervals supported by the driver and associated data source for the TIMESTAMPADD scalar function. The following bitmasks are used to determine which intervals are supported: SQL_FN_TSI_FRAC_SECOND SQL_FN_TSI_SECOND SQL_FN_TSI_MINUTE SQL_FN_TSI_HOUR SQL_FN_TSI_DAY SQL_FN_TSI_WEEK SQL_FN_TSI_MONTH SQL_FN_TSI_QUARTER SQL_FN_TSI_YEAR An FIPS Transitional level–conformant driver will always return a bitmask in which all of these bits are set.
SQL_TIMEDATE_ DIFF_INTERVALS (ODBC 2.0)	An SQLUINTEGER bitmask enumerating the timestamp intervals supported by the driver and associated data source for the TIMESTAMPDIFF scalar function. The following bitmasks are used to determine which intervals are supported: SQL_FN_TSI_FRAC_SECOND SQL_FN_TSI_SECOND SQL_FN_TSI_MINUTE SQL_FN_TSI_HOUR SQL_FN_TSI_DAY SQL_FN_TSI_WEEK SQL_FN_TSI_MONTH SQL_FN_TSI_QUARTER SQL_FN_TSI_YEAR An FIPS Transitional level–conformant driver will always return a bitmask in which all of these bits are set.

InfoType	**Returns**
SQL_TIMEDATE_FUNCTIONS (ODBC 1.0) The information type was introduced in ODBC 1.0; each bitmask is labeled with the version in which it was introduced.	An SQLUINTEGER bitmask enumerating the scalar date and time functions supported by the driver and associated data source. The following bitmasks are used to determine which date and time functions are supported: SQL_FN_TD_CURRENT_DATE ODBC 3.0) SQL_FN_TD_CURRENT_TIME (ODBC 3.0) SQL_FN_TD_CURRENT_TIMESTAMP (ODBC 3.0) SQL_FN_TD_CURDATE (ODBC 1.0) SQL_FN_TD_CURTIME (ODBC 1.0) SQL_FN_TD_DAYNAME (ODBC 2.0) SQL_FN_TD_DAYOFMONTH (ODBC 1.0) SQL_FN_TD_DAYOFWEEK (ODBC 1.0) SQL_FN_TD_DAYOFYEAR (ODBC 1.0) SQL_FN_TD_EXTRACT (ODBC 3.0) SQL_FN_TD_HOUR (ODBC 1.0) SQL_FN_TD_MINUTE (ODBC 1.0) SQL_FN_TD_MONTH (ODBC 1.0) SQL_FN_TD_MONTHNAME (ODBC 2.0) SQL_FN_TD_NOW (ODBC 1.0) SQL_FN_TD_QUARTER (ODBC 1.0) SQL_FN_TD_SECOND (ODBC 1.0) SQL_FN_TD_TIMESTAMPADD (ODBC 2.0) SQL_FN_TD_TIMESTAMPDIFF (ODBC 2.0) SQL_FN_TD_WEEK (ODBC 1.0) SQL_FN_TD_YEAR (ODBC 1.0)
SQL_TXN_CAPABLE (ODBC 1.0) The information type was introduced in ODBC 1.0; each return value is labeled with the version in which it was introduced.	An SQLUSMALLINT value describing the transaction support in the driver or data source: SQL_TC_NONE = Transactions not supported. (ODBC 1.0) SQL_TC_DML = Transactions can only contain Data Manipulation Language (DML) statements (**SELECT**, **INSERT**, **UPDATE**, **DELETE**). Data Definition Language (DDL) statements encountered in a transaction cause an error. (ODBC 1.0) SQL_TC_DDL_COMMIT = Transactions can only contain DML statements. DDL statements (**CREATE TABLE**, **DROP INDEX**, and so on) encountered in a transaction cause the transaction to be committed. (ODBC 2.0) SQL_TC_DDL_IGNORE = Transactions can only contain DML statements. DDL statements encountered in a transaction are ignored. (ODBC 2.0) SQL_TC_ALL = Transactions can contain DDL statements and DML statements in any order. (ODBC 1.0) (Since support of transactions is mandatory in SQL-92, a SQL-92 conformant driver (any level) will never return SQL_TC_NONE.)

InfoType	Returns
SQL_TXN_ISOLATION_OPTION (ODBC 1.0)	An SQLUINTEGER bitmask enumerating the transaction isolation levels available from the driver or data source. The following bitmasks are used in conjunction with the flag to determine which options are supported: SQL_TXN_READ_UNCOMMITTED SQL_TXN_READ_COMMITTED SQL_TXN_REPEATABLE_READ SQL_TXN_SERIALIZABLE For descriptions of these isolation levels, see the description of SQL_DEFAULT_TXN_ISOLATION. To set the transaction isolation level, an application calls **SQLSetConnectAttr** to set the SQL_ATTR_TXN_ISOLATION attribute. For more information, see **SQLSetConnectAttr**. An SQL-92 Entry level–conformant driver will always return SQL_TXN_SERIALIZABLE as supported. A FIPS Transitional level–conformant driver will always return all of these options as supported.
SQL_UNION (ODBC 2.0)	An SQLUINTEGER bitmask enumerating the support for the **UNION** clause: SQL_U_UNION = The data source supports the **UNION** clause. SQL_U_UNION_ALL = The data source supports the **ALL** keyword in the **UNION** clause. (**SQLGetInfo** returns both SQL_U_UNION and SQL_U_UNION_ALL in this case.) An SQL-92 Entry level–conformant driver will always return both of these options as supported.
SQL_USER_NAME (ODBC 1.0)	A character string with the name used in a particular database, which can be different from the login name.
SQL_XOPEN_CLI_YEAR (ODBC 3.0)	A character string that indicates the year of publication of the X/Open specification with which the version of the ODBC Driver Manager fully complies.

Code Example

SQLGetInfo returns lists of supported options as an SQLUINTEGER bitmask in **InfoValuePtr*. The bitmask for each option is used in conjunction with the flag to determine whether the option is supported.

For example, an application could use the following code to determine whether the SUBSTRING scalar function is supported by the driver associated with the connection:

```
SQLUINTEGER  fFuncs;

SQLGetInfo(hdbc,
           SQL_STRING_FUNCTIONS,
           (SQLPOINTER)&fFuncs,
           sizeof(fFuncs),
           NULL);

if (fFuncs & SQL_FN_STR_SUBSTRING) /* SUBSTRING supported */
   ...;
else                               /* SUBSTRING not supported */
   ...;
```

Related Functions

For information about	See
Returning the setting of a connection attribute	**SQLGetConnectAttr**
Determining if a driver supports a function	**SQLGetFunctions**
Returning the setting of a statement attribute	**SQLGetStmtAttr**
Returning information about a data source's data types	**SQLGetTypeInfo**

SQLGetStmtAttr

Conformance

Version Introduced: ODBC 3.0
Standards Compliance: ISO 92

Summary

SQLGetStmtAttr returns the current setting of a statement attribute.

Note For more information about what the Driver Manager maps this function to when an ODBC 3.0 application is working with an ODBC 2.*x* driver, see "Mapping Replacement Functions for Backward Compatibility of Applications" in Chapter 17, "Programming Considerations."

Syntax

SQLRETURN **SQLGetStmtAttr**(
    SQLHSTMT *StatementHandle*,
    SQLINTEGER *Attribute*,
    SQLPOINTER *ValuePtr*,
    SQLINTEGER *BufferLength*,
    SQLINTEGER * *StringLengthPtr*);

Arguments

StatementHandle [Input]
Statement handle.

Attribute [Input]
Attribute to retrieve.

ValuePtr [Output]
Pointer to a buffer in which to return the value of the attribute specified in *Attribute*.

BufferLength [Input]
If *Attribute* is an ODBC-defined attribute and *ValuePtr* points to a character string or a binary buffer, this argument should be the length of **ValuePtr*. If *Attribute* is an ODBC-defined attribute and **ValuePtr* is an integer, *BufferLength* is ignored.

If *Attribute* is a driver-defined attribute, the application indicates the nature of the attribute to the Driver Manager by setting the *BufferLength* argument. *BufferLength* can have the following values:

- If **ValuePtr* is a pointer to a character string, then *BufferLength* is the length of the string or SQL_NTS.
- If **ValuePtr* is a pointer to a binary buffer, then the application places the result of the SQL_LEN_BINARY_ATTR(*length*) macro in *BufferLength*. This places a negative value in *BufferLength*.
- If **ValuePtr* is a pointer to a value other than a character string or binary string, then *BufferLength* should have the value SQL_IS_POINTER.
- If **ValuePtr* is contains a fixed-length data type, then *BufferLength* is either SQL_IS_INTEGER or SQL_IS_UINTEGER, as appropriate.

StringLengthPtr [Output]

A pointer to a buffer in which to return the total number of bytes (excluding the null-termination character) available to return in **ValuePtr*. If *ValuePtr* is a null pointer, no length is returned. If the attribute value is a character string, and the number of bytes available to return is greater than or equal to *BufferLength*, the data in **ValuePtr* is truncated to *BufferLength* minus the length of a null-termination character and is null-terminated by the driver.

Returns

SQL_SUCCESS, SQL_SUCCESS_WITH_INFO, SQL_ERROR, or SQL_INVALID_HANDLE.

Diagnostics

When **SQLGetStmtAttr** returns SQL_ERROR or SQL_SUCCESS_WITH_INFO, an associated SQLSTATE value may be obtained by calling **SQLGetDiagRec** with a *HandleType* of SQL_HANDLE_STMT and a *Handle* of *StatementHandle*. The following table lists the SQLSTATE values commonly returned by **SQLGetStmtAttr** and explains each one in the context of this function; the notation "(DM)" precedes the descriptions of SQLSTATEs returned by the Driver Manager. The return code associated with each SQLSTATE value is SQL_ERROR, unless noted otherwise.

SQLSTATE	Error	Description
01000	General warning	Driver-specific informational message. (Function returns SQL_SUCCESS_WITH_INFO.)
01004	String data, right truncated	The data returned in **ValuePtr* was truncated to be *BufferLength* minus the length of a null-termination character. The length of the untruncated string value is returned in **StringLengthPtr*. (Function returns SQL_SUCCESS_WITH_INFO.)
24000	Invalid cursor state	The argument *Attribute* was SQL_ATTR_ROW_NUMBER and the cursor was not open, or the cursor was positioned before the start of the result set or after the end of the result set.
HY000	General error	An error occurred for which there was no specific SQLSTATE and for which no implementation-specific SQLSTATE was defined. The error message returned by **SQLGetDiagRec** in the argument *MessageText* describes the error and its cause.
HY001	Memory allocation error	The driver was unable to allocate memory required to support execution or completion of the function.
HY010	Function sequence error	(DM) An asynchronously executing function was called for the *StatementHandle* and was still executing when this function was called. (DM) **SQLExecute**, **SQLExecDirect**, **SQLBulkOperations**, or **SQLSetPos** was called for the *StatementHandle* and returned SQL_NEED_DATA. This function was called before data was sent for all data-at-execution parameters or columns.
HY013	Memory management error	The function call could not be processed because the underlying memory objects could not be accessed, possibly because of low memory conditions.
HY090	Invalid string or buffer length	*(DM) *ValuePtr* is a character string, and BufferLength was less than zero, but not equal to SQL_NTS.
HY092	Invalid attribute/option identifier	The value specified for the argument *Attribute* was not valid for the version of ODBC supported by the driver.
HY109	Invalid cursor position	The *Attribute* argument was SQL_ATTR_ROW_NUMBER and the row had been deleted or could not be fetched.

SQLSTATE	Error	Description
HYC00	Optional feature not implemented	The value specified for the argument *Attribute* was a valid ODBC statement attribute for the version of ODBC supported by the driver, but was not supported by the driver.
HYT01	Connection timeout expired	The connection timeout period expired before the data source responded to the request. The connection timeout period is set through **SQLSetConnectAttr**, SQL_ATTR_CONNECTION_TIMEOUT.
IM001	Driver does not support this function	(DM) The driver corresponding to the *StatementHandle* does not support the function.

Comments

For general information about statement attributes, see "Statement Attributes" in Chapter 9, "Executing Statements."

A call to **SQLGetStmtAttr** returns in **ValuePtr* the value of the statement attribute specified in *Attribute*. That value can either be a 32-bit value or a null-terminated character string. If the value is a null-terminated string, the application specifies the maximum length of that string in the *BufferLength* argument, and the driver returns the length of that string in the **StringLengthPtr* buffer. If the value is a 32-bit value, the *BufferLength* and *StringLengthPtr* arguments are not used.

To allow applications calling **SQLGetStmtAttr** to work with ODBC 2.*x* drivers, a call to **SQLGetStmtAttr** is mapped in the Driver Manager to **SQLGetStmtOption**.

The following statement attributes are read-only, so can be retrieved by **SQLGetStmtAttr**, but not set by **SQLSetStmtAttr**. For a list of attributes that can be set and retrieved, see **SQLSetStmtAttr**.

SQL_ATTR_IMP_PARAM_DESC

SQL_ATTR_IMP_ROW_DESC

SQL_ATTR_ROW_NUMBER

Related Functions

For information about	See
Returning the setting of a connection attribute	**SQLGetConnectAttr**
Setting a connection attribute	**SQLSetConnectAttr**
Setting a statement attribute	**SQLSetStmtAttr**

SQLGetStmtOption

Conformance

Version Introduced: ODBC 1.0
Standards Compliance: Deprecated

Summary

In ODBC 3.0, the ODBC 2.0 function **SQLGetStmtOption** has been replaced by **SQLGetStmtAttr**. For more information, see **SQLGetStmtAttr**.

Note For more information about what the Driver Manager maps this function to when an ODBC 2.*x* application is working with an ODBC 3.0 driver, see "Mapping Deprecated Functions" in Appendix G, "Driver Guidelines for Backward Compatibility."

SQLGetTypeInfo

Conformance

Version Introduced: ODBC 1.0
Standards Compliance: ISO 92

Summary

SQLGetTypeInfo returns information about data types supported by the data source. The driver returns the information in the form of an SQL result set. The data types are intended for use in Data Definition Language (DDL) statements.

Important Applications must use the type names returned in the TYPE_NAME column of the **SQLGetTypeInfo** result set in **ALTER TABLE** and **CREATE TABLE** statements. **SQLGetTypeInfo** may return more than one row with the same value in the DATA_TYPE column.

Syntax

```
SQLRETURN SQLGetTypeInfo(
     SQLHSTMT     StatementHandle,
     SQLSMALLINT DataType);
```

Arguments

StatementHandle [Input]
Statement handle for the result set.

DataType [Input]
The SQL data type. This must be one of the values in the "SQL Data Types" section of Appendix D, "Data Types," or a driver-specific SQL data type. SQL_ALL_TYPES specifies that information about all data types should be returned.

Returns

SQL_SUCCESS, SQL_SUCCESS_WITH_INFO, SQL_STILL_EXECUTING, SQL_ERROR, or SQL_INVALID_HANDLE.

Diagnostics

When **SQLGetTypeInfo** returns SQL_ERROR or SQL_SUCCESS_WITH_INFO, an associated SQLSTATE value may be obtained by calling **SQLGetDiagRec** with a *HandleType* of SQL_HANDLE_STMT and a *Handle* of *StatementHandle*. The following table lists the SQLSTATE values commonly returned by **SQLGetTypeInfo** and explains each one in the context of this function; the notation "(DM)" precedes the descriptions of SQLSTATEs returned by the Driver Manager. The return code associated with each SQLSTATE value is SQL_ERROR, unless noted otherwise.

SQLSTATE	Error	Description
01000	General warning	Driver specific informational message. (Function returns SQL_SUCCESS_WITH_INFO.)
01S02	Option value changed	A specified statement attribute was invalid because of implementation working conditions, so a similar value was temporarily substituted. (**SQLGetStmtAttr** can be called to determine what the temporarily substituted value is.) The substitute value is valid for the *StatementHandle* until the cursor is closed. The statement attributes that can be changed are: SQL_ATTR_CONCURRENCY, SQL_ATTR_CURSOR_TYPE, SQL_ATTR_KEYSET_SIZE, SQL_ATTR_MAX_LENGTH, SQL_ATTR_MAX_ROWS, SQL_ATTR_QUERY_TIMEOUT, and SQL_ATTR_SIMULATE_CURSOR. (Function returns SQL_SUCCESS_WITH_INFO.)
08S01	Communication link failure	The communication link between the driver and the data source to which the driver was connected failed before the function completed processing.
24000	Invalid cursor state	A cursor was open on the *StatementHandle* and **SQLFetch** or **SQLFetchScroll** had been called. This error is returned by the Driver Manager if **SQLFetch** or **SQLFetchScroll** has not returned SQL_NO_DATA, and is returned by the driver if **SQLFetch** or **SQLFetchScroll** has returned SQL_NO_DATA. A result set was open on the *StatementHandle* but **SQLFetch** or **SQLFetchScroll** had not been called.
40001	Serialization failure	The transaction was rolled back due to a resource deadlock with another transaction.
40003	Statement completion unknown	The associated connection failed during the execution of this function and the state of the transaction cannot be determined.
HY000	General error	An error occurred for which there was no specific SQLSTATE and for which no implementation-specific SQLSTATE was defined. The error message returned by **SQLGetDiagRec** in the **MessageText* buffer describes the error and its cause.

SQLSTATE	Error	Description
HY001	Memory allocation error	The driver was unable to allocate memory required to support execution or completion of the function.
HY004	Invalid SQL data type	The value specified for the argument *DataType* was neither a valid ODBC SQL data type identifier nor a driver-specific data type identifier supported by the driver.
HY008	Operation canceled	Asynchronous processing was enabled for the *StatementHandle*, then the function was called and, before it completed execution, **SQLCancel** was called on the *StatementHandle*. Then the function was called again on the *StatementHandle*. The function was called and, before it completed execution, **SQLCancel** was called on the *StatementHandle* from a different thread in a multithread application.
HY010	Function sequence error	(DM) An asynchronously executing function (not this one) was called for the *StatementHandle* and was still executing when this function was called. (DM) **SQLExecute**, **SQLExecDirect**, **SQLBulkOperations**, or **SQLSetPos** was called for the *StatementHandle* and returned SQL_NEED_DATA. This function was called before data was sent for all data-at-execution parameters or columns.
HY013	Memory management error	The function call could not be processed because the underlying memory objects could not be accessed, possibly because of low memory conditions.

SQLSTATE	Error	Description
HYC00	Optional feature not implemented	The value specified for the argument *DataType* was a valid ODBC SQL data type identifier for the version of ODBC supported by the driver, but was not supported by the driver or data source. The combination of the current settings of the SQL_ATTR_CONCURRENCY and SQL_ATTR_CURSOR_TYPE statement attributes was not supported by the driver or data source. The SQL_ATTR_USE_BOOKMARKS statement attribute was set to SQL_UB_VARIABLE, and the SQL_ATTR_CURSOR_TYPE statement attribute was set to a cursor type for which the driver does not support bookmarks.
HYT00	Timeout expired	The query timeout period expired before the data source returned the result set. The timeout period is set through **SQLSetStmtAttr**, SQL_ATTR_QUERY_TIMEOUT.
HYT01	Connection timeout expired	The connection timeout period expired before the data source responded to the request. The connection timeout period is set through **SQLSetConnectAttr**, SQL_ATTR_CONNECTION_TIMEOUT.
IM001	Driver does not support this function	(DM) The driver corresponding to the *StatementHandle* does not support the function.

Comments

SQLGetTypeInfo returns the results as a standard result set, ordered by DATA_TYPE and then by how closely the data type maps to the corresponding ODBC SQL data type. Data types defined by the data source take precedence over user-defined data types. For example, suppose that a data source defined INTEGER and COUNTER data types, where COUNTER is auto-incrementing, and that a user-defined data type WHOLENUM has also been defined. These would be returned in the order INTEGER, WHOLENUM, and COUNTER, because WHOLENUM maps closely to the ODBC SQL data type SQL_INTEGER, while the auto-incrementing data type, even though supported by the data source, does not map closely to an ODBC SQL data type. For information about how this information might be used, see "DDL Statements" in Chapter 8, "SQL Statements."

Note For more information about the general use, arguments, and returned data of ODBC catalog functions, see Chapter 7, "Catalog Functions."

The following columns have been renamed for ODBC 3.0. The column name changes do not affect backward compatibility because applications bind by column number.

ODBC 2.0 column	ODBC 3.0 column
PRECISION	COLUMN_SIZE
MONEY	FIXED_PREC_SCALE
AUTO_INCREMENT	AUTO_UNIQUE_VALUE

The following columns have been added to the results set returned by **SQLGetTypeInfo** for ODBC 3.0:

SQL_DATA_TYPE	INTERVAL_PRECISION
SQL_DATETIME_SUB	NUM_PREC_RADIX

The following table lists the columns in the result set. Additional columns beyond column 19 (INTERVAL_PRECISION) can be defined by the driver. An application should gain access to driver-specific columns by counting down from the end of the result set rather than specifying an explicit ordinal position. For more information, see "Data Returned by Catalog Functions" in Chapter 7, "Catalog Functions."

Note **SQLGetTypeInfo** might not return all data types. For example, a driver might not return user-defined data types. Applications can use any valid data type, regardless of whether it is returned by **SQLGetTypeInfo**.

The data types returned by **SQLGetTypeInfo** are those supported by the data source. They are intended for use in Data Definition Language (DDL) statements. Drivers can return result set data using data types other than the types returned by **SQLGetTypeInfo**. In creating the result set for a catalog function, the driver might use a data type that is not supported by the data source.

Column name	Column number	Data type	Comments
TYPE_NAME (ODBC 2.0)	1	Varchar not NULL	Data source–dependent data type name; for example, "CHAR()", "VARCHAR()", "MONEY", "LONG VARBINARY", or "CHAR ( ) FOR BIT DATA". Applications must use this name in **CREATE TABLE** and **ALTER TABLE** statements.
DATA_TYPE (ODBC 2.0)	2	Smallint not NULL	SQL data type. This can be an ODBC SQL data type or a driver-specific SQL data type. For datetime or interval data types, this column returns the concise data type (such as SQL_TYPE_TIME or SQL_INTERVAL_YEAR_TO_MONTH). For a list of valid ODBC SQL data types, see "SQL Data Types" in Appendix D, "Data Types." For information about driver-specific SQL data types, see the driver's documentation.
COLUMN_SIZE (ODBC 2.0)	3	Integer	The maximum column size that the server supports for this data type. For numeric data, this is the maximum precision. For string data, this is the length in characters. For datetime data types, this is the length in characters of the string representation (assuming the maximum allowed precision of the fractional seconds component.) NULL is returned for data types where column size is not applicable. For interval data types, this is the number of characters in the character representation of the interval literal (as defined by the interval leading precision, see "Interval Data Type Length" in Appendix D, "Data Types"). For more information on column size, see "Column Size, Decimal Digits, Transfer Octet Length, and Display Size" in Appendix D, "Data Types."

Column name	Column number	Data type	Comments
LITERAL_PREFIX (ODBC 2.0)	4	Varchar	Character or characters used to prefix a literal; for example, a single quotation mark (') for character data types or 0x for binary data types; NULL is returned for data types where a literal prefix is not applicable.
LITERAL_SUFFIX (ODBC 2.0)	5	Varchar	Character or characters used to terminate a literal; for example, a single quotation mark (') for character data types; NULL is returned for data types where a literal suffix is not applicable.
CREATE_PARAMS (ODBC 2.0)	6	Varchar	A list of keywords, separated by commas, corresponding to each parameter that the application may specify in parentheses when using the name that is returned in the TYPE_NAME field. The keywords in the list can be any of the following: length, precision, scale. They appear in the order that the syntax requires that they be used. For example, CREATE_PARAMS for DECIMAL would be "precision,scale"; CREATE_PARAMS for VARCHAR would equal "length." NULL is returned if there are no parameters for the data type definition, for example INTEGER. The driver supplies the CREATE_PARAMS text in the language of the country where it is used.
NULLABLE (ODBC 2.0)	7	Smallint not NULL	Whether the data type accepts a NULL value: SQL_NO_NULLS if the data type does not accept NULL values. SQL_NULLABLE if the data type accepts NULL values. SQL_NULLABLE_UNKNOWN if it is not known whether the column accepts NULL values.

Column name	Column number	Data type	Comments
CASE_SENSITIVE (ODBC 2.0)	8	Smallint not NULL	Whether a character data type is case-sensitive in collations and comparisons: SQL_TRUE if the data type is a character data type and is case-sensitive. SQL_FALSE if the data type is not a character data type or is not case-sensitive.
SEARCHABLE (ODBC 2.0)	9	Smallint not NULL	How the data type is used in a **WHERE** clause: SQL_PRED_NONE if the column cannot be used in a **WHERE** clause. (This is the same as the SQL_UNSEARCHABLE value in ODBC 2.*x*.) SQL_PRED_CHAR if the column can be used in a **WHERE** clause, but only with the **LIKE** predicate. (This is the same as the SQL_LIKE_ONLY value in ODBC 2.*x*.) SQL_PRED_BASIC if the column can be used in a **WHERE** clause with all the comparison operators except **LIKE** (comparison, quantified comparison, **BETWEEN**, **DISTINCT**, **IN**, **MATCH**, and **UNIQUE**). (This is the same as the SQL_ALL_EXCEPT_LIKE value in ODBC 2.*x*.) SQL_SEARCHABLE if the column can be used in a **WHERE** clause with any comparison operator.
UNSIGNED_ ATTRIBUTE (ODBC 2.0)	10	Smallint	Whether the data type is unsigned: SQL_TRUE if the data type is unsigned. SQL_FALSE if the data type is signed. NULL is returned if the attribute is not applicable to the data type or the data type is not numeric.

Column name	Column number	Data type	Comments
FIXED_PREC_SCALE (ODBC 2.0)	11	Smallint not NULL	Whether the data type has predefined fixed precision and scale (which are data source–specific), like a money data type: SQL_TRUE if it has predefined fixed precision and scale. SQL_FALSE if it does not have predefined fixed precision and scale.
AUTO_UNIQUE_ VALUE (ODBC 2.0)	12	Smallint	Whether the data type is autoincrementing: SQL_TRUE if the data type is autoincrementing. SQL_FALSE if the data type is not autoincrementing. NULL is returned if the attribute is not applicable to the data type or the data type is not numeric. An application can insert values into a column having this attribute, but typically cannot update the values in the column. When an insert is made into an auto-increment column, a unique value is inserted into the column at insert time. The increment is not defined, but is data source–specific. An application should not assume that an auto-increment column starts at any particular point or increments by any particular value.
LOCAL_TYPE_NAME (ODBC 2.0)	13	Varchar	Localized version of the data source–dependent name of the data type. NULL is returned if a localized name is not supported by the data source. This name is intended for display only, such as in dialog boxes.

Column name	Column number	Data type	Comments
MINIMUM_SCALE (ODBC 2.0)	14	Smallint	The minimum scale of the data type on the data source. If a data type has a fixed scale, the MINIMUM_SCALE and MAXIMUM_SCALE columns both contain this value. For example, an SQL_TYPE_TIMESTAMP column might have a fixed scale for fractional seconds. NULL is returned where scale is not applicable. For more information, see "Column Size, Decimal Digits, Transfer Octet Length, and Display Size" in Appendix D, "Data Types."
MAXIMUM_SCALE (ODBC 2.0)	15	Smallint	The maximum scale of the data type on the data source. NULL is returned where scale is not applicable. If the maximum scale is not defined separately on the data source, but is instead defined to be the same as the maximum precision, this column contains the same value as the COLUMN_SIZE column. For more information, see "Column Size, Decimal Digits, Transfer Octet Length, and Display Size" in Appendix D, "Data Types."
SQL_DATA_TYPE (ODBC 3.0)	16	Smallint NOT NULL	The value of the SQL data type as it appears in the SQL_DESC_TYPE field of the descriptor. This column is the same as the DATA_TYPE column, except for interval and datetime data types. For interval and datetime data types, the SQL_DATA_TYPE field in the result set will return SQL_INTERVAL or SQL_DATETIME, and the SQL_DATETIME_SUB field will return the subcode for the specific interval or datetime data type (see Appendix D, "Data Types").

Column name	Column number	Data type	Comments
SQL_DATETIME_SUB (ODBC 3.0)	17	Smallint	When the value of SQL_DATA_TYPE is SQL_DATETIME or SQL_INTERVAL, this column contains the datetime/interval subcode. For data types other than datetime and interval, this field is NULL. For interval or datetime data types, the SQL_DATA_TYPE field in the result set will return SQL_INTERVAL or SQL_DATETIME, and the SQL_DATETIME_SUB field will return the subcode for the specific interval or datetime data type (see Appendix D, "Data Types").
NUM_PREC_RADIX (ODBC 3.0)	18	Integer	If the data type is an approximate numeric type, this column contains the value 2 to indicate that COLUMN_SIZE specifies a number of bits. For exact numeric types, this column contains the value 10 to indicate that COLUMN_SIZE specifies a number of decimal digits. Otherwise, this column is NULL.
INTERVAL_PRECISION (ODBC 3.0)	19	Smallint	If the data type is an interval data type, then this column contains the value of the interval leading precision (see "Interval Data Type Precision" in Appendix D, "Data Types." Otherwise, this column is NULL.

Attribute information can apply to data types or to specific columns in a result set. **SQLGetTypeInfo** returns information about attributes associated with data types; **SQLColAttribute** returns information about attributes associated with columns in a result set.

Related Functions

For information about	See
Binding a buffer to a column in a result set	**SQLBindCol**
Canceling statement processing	**SQLCancel**
Returning information about a column in a result set	**SQLColAttribute**
Fetching a block of data or scrolling through a result set	**SQLFetchScroll**
Fetching a single row or a block of data in a forward-only direction	**SQLFetch**
Returning information about a driver or data source	**SQLGetInfo**

SQLMoreResults

Conformance

Version Introduced: ODBC 1.0
Standards Compliance: ODBC

Summary

SQLMoreResults determines whether there are more results available on a statement containing **SELECT**, **UPDATE**, **INSERT**, or **DELETE** statements and, if so, initializes processing for those results.

Syntax

```
SQLRETURN SQLMoreResults(
    SQLHSTMT   StatementHandle);
```

Arguments

StatementHandle [Input]
Statement handle.

Returns

SQL_SUCCESS, SQL_SUCCESS_WITH_INFO, SQL_STILL_EXECUTING, SQL_NO_DATA, SQL_ERROR, or SQL_INVALID_HANDLE.

Diagnostics

When **SQLMoreResults** returns SQL_ERROR or SQL_SUCCESS_WITH_INFO, an associated SQLSTATE value may be obtained by calling **SQLGetDiagRec** with a *HandleType* of SQL_HANDLE_STMT and a *Handle* of *StatementHandle*. The following table lists the SQLSTATE values commonly returned by **SQLMoreResults** and explains each one in the context of this function; the notation "(DM)" precedes the descriptions of SQLSTATEs returned by the Driver Manager. The return code associated with each SQLSTATE value is SQL_ERROR, unless noted otherwise.

SQLSTATE	Error	Description
01000	General warning	Driver-specific informational message. (Function returns SQL_SUCCESS_WITH_INFO.)
01S02	Option value has changed	The value of a statement attribute changed as the batch was being processed. (Function returns SQL_SUCCESS_WITH_INFO.)
08S01	Communication link failure	The communication link between the driver and the data source to which the driver was connected failed before the function completed processing.
40001	Serialization failure	The transaction was rolled back due to a resource deadlock with another transaction.

SQLSTATE	Error	Description
40003	Statement completion unknown	The associated connection failed during the execution of this function and the state of the transaction cannot be determined.
HY000	General error	An error occurred for which there was no specific SQLSTATE and for which no implementation-specific SQLSTATE was defined. The error message returned by **SQLGetDiagRec** in the **MessageText* buffer describes the error and its cause.
HY001	Memory allocation error	The driver was unable to allocate memory required to support execution or completion of the function.
HY008	Operation canceled	Asynchronous processing was enabled for the *StatementHandle*. The function was called and before it completed execution, **SQLCancel** was called on the *StatementHandle*. Then the function was called again on the *StatementHandle*. The function was called and, before it completed execution, **SQLCancel** was called on the *StatementHandle* from a different thread in a multithread application.
HY010	Function sequence error	(DM) An asynchronously executing function (not this one) was called for the *StatementHandle* and was still executing when this function was called. (DM) **SQLExecute**, **SQLExecDirect**, **SQLBulkOperations**, or **SQLSetPos** was called for the *StatementHandle* and returned SQL_NEED_DATA. This function was called before data was sent for all data-at-execution parameters or columns.
HY013	Memory management error	The function call could not be processed because the underlying memory objects could not be accessed, possibly because of low memory conditions.
HYT01	Connection timeout expired	The connection timeout period expired before the data source responded to the request. The connection timeout period is set through **SQLSetConnectAttr**, SQL_ATTR_CONNECTION_TIMEOUT.
IM001	Driver does not support this function	(DM) The driver associated with the *StatementHandle* does not support the function.

Comments

SELECT statements return result sets. **UPDATE**, **INSERT**, and **DELETE** statements return a count of affected rows. If any of these statements are batched, submitted with arrays of parameters (numbered in increasing parameter order, in the order that they appear in the batch), or in procedures, they can return multiple result sets or row counts. For information about batches of statements and arrays of parameters, see "Batches of SQL Statements" and "Arrays of Parameter Values" in Chapter 9, "Executing Statements."

After executing the batch, the application is positioned on the first result set. The application can call **SQLBindCol**, **SQLBulkOperations**, **SQLFetch**, **SQLGetData**, **SQLFetchScroll**, **SQLSetPos**, and all the metadata functions, on the first or any subsequent result sets, just as it would if there were just a single result set. Once it is done with the first result set, the application calls **SQLMoreResults** to move to the next result set. If another result set or count is available, **SQLMoreResults** returns SQL_SUCCESS and initializes the result set or count for additional processing. If any row count–generating statements appear in between result set–generating statements, they can be stepped over by calling **SQLMoreResults**. After calling **SQLMoreResults** for **UPDATE**, **INSERT**, or **DELETE** statements, an application can call **SQLRowCount**.

If there was a current result set with unfetched rows, **SQLMoreResults** discards that result set and makes the next result set or count available. If all results have been processed, **SQLMoreResults** returns SQL_NO_DATA. For some drivers, output parameters and return values are not available until all result sets and row counts have been processed. For such drivers, output parameters and return values become available when **SQLMoreResults** returns SQL_NO_DATA.

Any bindings that were established for the previous result set still remain valid. If the column structures are different for this result set, then calling **SQLFetch** or **SQLFetchScroll** may result in an error or truncation. To prevent this, the application has to call **SQLBindCol** to explicitly rebind as appropriate (or do so by setting descriptor fields). Alternatively, the application can call **SQLFreeStmt** with an *Option* of SQL_UNBIND to unbind all the column buffers.

The values of statement attributes such as cursor type, cursor concurrency, keyset size, or maximum length, may change as the application navigates through the batch by calls to **SQLMoreResults**. If this happens, **SQLMoreResults** will return SQL_SUCCESS_WITH_INFO and SQLSTATE 01S02 (Option value has changed).

Calling **SQLCloseCursor**, or **SQLFreeStmt** with an *Option* of SQL_CLOSE, discards all the result sets and row counts that were available as a result of the execution of the batch. The statement handle returns to either the allocated or prepared state. Calling **SQLCancel** to cancel an asynchronously executing function when a batch has been executed and the statement handle is in the executed, cursor-positioned, or asynchronous state results in all the results sets and row counts generated by the batch being discarded if the cancel call was successful. The statement then returns to the prepared or allocated state.

If a batch of statements or a procedure mixes other SQL statements with **SELECT**, **UPDATE**, **INSERT**, and **DELETE** statements, these other statements do not affect **SQLMoreResults**.

For more information, see "Multiple Results" in Chapter 11, "Retrieving Results (Advanced)."

If a searched update or delete statement in a batch of statements does not affect any rows at the data source, **SQLMoreResults** returns SQL_SUCCESS. This is different than the case of a searched update or delete statement that is executed through **SQLExecDirect**, **SQLExecute**, or **SQLParamData**, which returns SQL_NO_DATA if it does not affect any rows at the data source. If an application calls **SQLRowCount** to retrieve the row count after a call to **SQLMoreResults** has not affected any rows, **SQLRowCount** will return SQL_NO_DATA.

For additional information about the valid sequencing of result-processing functions, see Appendix B, "ODBC State Transition Tables."

Availability of Row Counts

When a batch contains multiple consecutive row count–generating statements, it is possible that these row counts are rolled up into just one row count. For example, if a batch has five insert statements, then certain data sources are capable of returning five individual row counts. Certain other data sources return only one row count that represents the sum of the five individual row counts.

When a batch contains a combination of result set–generating and row count–generating statements, row counts may or may not be available at all. The behavior of the driver with respect to the availability of row counts is enumerated in the SQL_BATCH_ROW_COUNT information type available through a call to **SQLGetInfo**. For example, suppose that the batch contains a select, followed by two inserts and another select. Then the following cases are possible:

- The row counts corresponding to the two insert statements are not available at all. The first call to **SQLMoreResults** will position you on the result set of the second select statement.
- The row counts corresponding to the two insert statements are available individually. (A call to **SQLGetInfo** does not return the SQL_BRC_ROLLED_UP bit for the SQL_BATCH_ROW_COUNT information type). The first call to **SQLMoreResults** will position you on the row count of the first insert and the second call will position you on the row count of the second insert. The third call to **SQLMoreResults** will position you on the result set of the second SELECT statement.

- The row counts corresponding to the two inserts are rolled up into one single row count that is available. (A call to **SQLGetInfo** returns the SQL_BRC_ROLLED_UP bit for the SQL_BATCH_ROW_COUNT information type). The first call to **SQLMoreResults** will position on the rolled-up row count, and the second call to **SQLMoreResults** will position on the result set of the second select.

Certain drivers make row counts available only for explicit batches and not for stored procedures.

Related Functions

For information about	See
Canceling statement processing	**SQLCancel**
Fetching a block of data or scrolling through a result set	**SQLFetchScroll**
Fetching a single row or a block of data in a forward-only direction	**SQLFetch**
Fetching part or all of a column of data	**SQLGetData**

SQLNativeSql

Conformance

Version Introduced: ODBC 1.0
Standards Compliance: ODBC

Summary

SQLNativeSql returns the SQL string as modified by the driver. **SQLNativeSql** does not execute the SQL statement.

Syntax

```
SQLRETURN SQLNativeSql(
     SQLHDBC         ConnectionHandle,
     SQLCHAR *       InStatementText,
     SQLINTEGER      TextLength1,
     SQLCHAR *       OutStatementText,
     SQLINTEGER      BufferLength,
     SQLINTEGER *    TextLength2Ptr);
```

Arguments

ConnectionHandle [Input]
Connection handle.

InStatementText [Input]
SQL text string to be translated.

TextLength1 [Input]
Length of **InStatementText* text string.

OutStatementText [Output]
Pointer to a buffer in which to return the translated SQL string.

BufferLength [Input]
Length of the **OutStatementText* buffer.

TextLength2Ptr [Output]
Pointer to a buffer in which to return the total number of bytes (excluding the null-termination byte) available to return in **OutStatementText*. If the number of bytes available to return is greater than or equal to *BufferLength*, the translated SQL string in **OutStatementText* is truncated to *BufferLength* minus the length of a null-termination character.

Returns

SQL_SUCCESS, SQL_SUCCESS_WITH_INFO, SQL_ERROR, or SQL_INVALID_HANDLE.

Diagnostics

When **SQLNativeSql** returns either SQL_ERROR or SQL_SUCCESS_WITH_INFO, an associated SQLSTATE value may be obtained by calling **SQLGetDiagRec** with a *HandleType* of SQL_HANDLE_DBC and a *Handle* of *ConnectionHandle*. The following table lists the SQLSTATE values commonly returned by **SQLNativeSql** and explains each one in the context of this function; the notation "(DM)" precedes the descriptions of SQLSTATEs returned by the Driver Manager. The return code associated with each SQLSTATE value is SQL_ERROR, unless noted otherwise.

SQLSTATE	Error	Description
01000	General warning	Driver-specific informational message. (Function returns SQL_SUCCESS_WITH_INFO.)
01004	String data, right truncated	The buffer **OutStatementText* was not large enough to return the entire SQL string, so the SQL string was truncated. The length of the untruncated SQL string is returned in **TextLength2Ptr*. (Function returns SQL_SUCCESS_WITH_INFO.)
08003	Connection does not exist	The *ConnectionHandle* was not in a connected state.
08S01	Communication link failure	The communication link between the driver and the data source to which the driver was connected failed before the function completed processing.
22007	Invalid datetime format	**InStatementText* contained an escape clause with an invalid date, time, or timestamp value.
24000	Invalid cursor state	The cursor referred to in the statement was positioned before the start of the result set or after the end of the result set. This error may not be returned by a driver having a native DBMS cursor implementation.
HY000	General error	An error occurred for which there was no specific SQLSTATE and for which no implementation-specific SQLSTATE was defined. The error message returned by **SQLGetDiagRec** in the **MessageText* buffer describes the error and its cause.
HY001	Memory allocation error	The driver was unable to allocate memory required to support execution or completion of the function.
HY009	Invalid use of null pointer	(DM) **InStatementText* was a null pointer.

SQLSTATE	Error	Description
HY013	Memory management error	The function call could not be processed because the underlying memory objects could not be accessed, possibly because of low memory conditions.
HY090	Invalid string or buffer length	(DM) The argument *TextLength1* was less than 0, but not equal to SQL_NTS. (DM) The argument *BufferLength* was less than 0 and the argument *OutStatementText* was not a null pointer.
HY109	Invalid cursor position	The current row of the cursor had been deleted or had not been fetched. This error may not be returned by a driver having a native DBMS cursor implementation.
HYT01	Connection timeout expired	The connection timeout period expired before the data source responded to the request. The connection timeout period is set through **SQLSetConnectAttr**, SQL_ATTR_CONNECTION_TIMEOUT.
IM001	Driver does not support this function	(DM) The driver associated with the *ConnectionHandle* does not support the function.

Comments

The following are examples of what **SQLNativeSql** might return for the following input SQL string containing the scalar function CONVERT. Assume that the column empid is of type INTEGER in the data source:

```
SELECT { fn CONVERT (empid, SQL_SMALLINT) } FROM employee
```

A driver for Microsoft SQL Server might return the following translated SQL string:

```
SELECT convert (smallint, empid) FROM employee
```

A driver for ORACLE Server might return the following translated SQL string:

```
SELECT to_number (empid) FROM employee
```

A driver for Ingres might return the following translated SQL string:

```
SELECT int2 (empid) FROM employee
```

For more information, see "Direct Execution" and "Prepared Execution" in Chapter 9, "Executing Statements."

Related Functions

None.

SQLNumParams

Conformance

Version Introduced:	ODBC 1.0
Standards Compliance:	ISO 92

Summary

SQLNumParams returns the number of parameters in an SQL statement.

Syntax

SQLRETURN **SQLNumParams**(
    SQLHSTMT *StatementHandle*,
    SQLSMALLINT * *ParameterCountPtr*);

Arguments

StatementHandle [Input]
Statement handle.

ParameterCountPtr [Output]
Pointer to a buffer in which to return the number of parameters in the statement.

Returns

SQL_SUCCESS, SQL_SUCCESS_WITH_INFO, SQL_STILL_EXECUTING, SQL_ERROR, or SQL_INVALID_HANDLE.

Diagnostics

When **SQLNumParams** returns SQL_ERROR or SQL_SUCCESS_WITH_INFO, an associated SQLSTATE value may be obtained by calling **SQLGetDiagRec** with a *HandleType* of SQL_HANDLE_STMT and a *Handle* of *StatementHandle*. The following table lists the SQLSTATE values commonly returned by **SQLNumParams** and explains each one in the context of this function; the notation "(DM)" precedes the descriptions of SQLSTATEs returned by the Driver Manager. The return code associated with each SQLSTATE value is SQL_ERROR, unless noted otherwise.

SQLSTATE	Error	Description
01000	General warning	Driver-specific informational message. (Function returns SQL_SUCCESS_WITH_INFO.)
08S01	Communication link failure	The communication link between the driver and the data source to which the driver was connected failed before the function completed processing.
HY000	General error	An error occurred for which there was no specific SQLSTATE and for which no implementation-specific SQLSTATE was defined. The error message returned by **SQLGetDiagRec** in the **MessageText* buffer describes the error and its cause.
HY001	Memory allocation error	The driver was unable to allocate memory required to support execution or completion of the function.
HY008	Operation canceled	Asynchronous processing was enabled for the *StatementHandle*. The function was called and before it completed execution, **SQLCancel** was called on the *StatementHandle*; the function was then called again on the *StatementHandle*. The function was called and, before it completed execution, **SQLCancel** was called on the *StatementHandle* from a different thread in a multithread application.
HY010	Function sequence error	(DM) The function was called prior to calling **SQLPrepare** or **SQLExecDirect** for the *StatementHandle*. (DM) An asynchronously executing function (not this one) was called for the *StatementHandle* and was still executing when this function was called. (DM) **SQLExecute**, **SQLExecDirect**, **SQLBulkOperations**, or **SQLSetPos** was called for the *StatementHandle* and returned SQL_NEED_DATA. This function was called before data was sent for all data-at-execution parameters or columns.

SQLSTATE	Error	Description
HY013	Memory management error	The function call could not be processed because the underlying memory objects could not be accessed, possibly because of low memory conditions.
HYT01	Connection timeout expired	The connection timeout period expired before the data source responded to the request. The connection timeout period is set through **SQLSetConnectAttr**, SQL_ATTR_CONNECTION_TIMEOUT.
IM001	Driver does not support this function	(DM) The driver associated with the *StatementHandle* does not support the function.

Comments

SQLNumParams can be called only after **SQLPrepare** has been called.

If the statement associated with *StatementHandle* does not contain parameters, **SQLNumParams** sets **ParameterCountPtr* to 0.

The number of parameters returned by **SQLNumParams** is the same value as the SQL_DESC_COUNT field of the IPD.

For more information, see "Describing Parameters" in Chapter 9, "Executing Statements."

Related Functions

For information about	See
Binding a buffer to a parameter	**SQLBindParameter**
Returning information about a parameter in a statement	**SQLDescribeParam**

SQLNumResultCols

Conformance

Version Introduced: ODBC 1.0
Standards Compliance: ISO 92

Summary

SQLNumResultCols returns the number of columns in a result set.

Syntax

SQLRETURN **SQLNumResultCols**(
  SQLHSTMT *StatementHandle*,
  SQLSMALLINT * *ColumnCountPtr*);

Arguments

StatementHandle [Input]
Statement handle.

ColumnCountPtr [Output]
Pointer to a buffer in which to return the number of columns in the result set. This count does not include a bound bookmark column.

Returns

SQL_SUCCESS, SQL_SUCCESS_WITH_INFO, SQL_STILL_EXECUTING, SQL_ERROR, or SQL_INVALID_HANDLE.

Diagnostics

When **SQLNumResultCols** returns SQL_ERROR or SQL_SUCCESS_WITH_INFO, an associated SQLSTATE value can be obtained by calling **SQLGetDiagRec** with a *HandleType* of SQL_HANDLE_STMT and a *Handle* of *StatementHandle*. The following table lists the SQLSTATE values commonly returned by **SQLNumResultCols** and explains each one in the context of this function; the notation "(DM)" precedes the descriptions of SQLSTATEs returned by the Driver Manager. The return code associated with each SQLSTATE value is SQL_ERROR, unless noted otherwise.

SQLSTATE	Error	Description
01000	General warning	Driver-specific informational message. (Function returns SQL_SUCCESS_WITH_INFO.)
08S01	Communication link failure	The communication link between the driver and the data source to which the driver was connected failed before the function completed processing.
HY000	General error	An error occurred for which there was no specific SQLSTATE and for which no implementation-specific SQLSTATE was defined. The error message returned by **SQLGetDiagRec** in the **MessageText* buffer describes the error and its cause.
HY001	Memory allocation error	The driver was unable to allocate memory required to support execution or completion of the function.
HY008	Operation canceled	Asynchronous processing was enabled for the *StatementHandle*. The function was called and before it completed execution, **SQLCancel** was called on the *StatementHandle*; the function was then called again on the *StatementHandle*. The function was called and, before it completed execution, **SQLCancel** was called on the *StatementHandle* from a different thread in a multithread application.
HY010	Function sequence error	(DM) The function was called prior to calling **SQLPrepare** or **SQLExecDirect** for the *StatementHandle*. (DM) An asynchronously executing function (not this one) was called for the *StatementHandle* and was still executing when this function was called. (DM) **SQLExecute**, **SQLExecDirect**, **SQLBulkOperations**, or **SQLSetPos** was called for the *StatementHandle* and returned SQL_NEED_DATA. This function was called before data was sent for all data-at-execution parameters or columns.
HY013	Memory management error	The function call could not be processed because the underlying memory objects could not be accessed, possibly because of low memory conditions.

SQLSTATE	Error	Description
HYT01	Connection timeout expired	The connection timeout period expired before the data source responded to the request. The connection timeout period is set through **SQLSetConnectAttr**, SQL_ATTR_CONNECTION_TIMEOUT.
IM001	Driver does not support this function	(DM) The driver associated with the *StatementHandle* does not support the function.

SQLNumResultCols can return any SQLSTATE that can be returned by **SQLPrepare** or **SQLExecute** when called after **SQLPrepare** and before **SQLExecute** depending on when the data source evaluates the SQL statement associated with the statement.

Comments

SQLNumResultCols can be called successfully only when the statement is in the prepared, executed, or positioned state.

If the statement associated with *StatementHandle* does not return columns, **SQLNumResultCols** sets **ColumnCountPtr* to 0.

The number of columns returned by **SQLNumResultCols** is the same value as the SQL_DESC_COUNT field of the IRD.

For more information, see "Was a Result Set Created?" and "How is Metadata Used?" in Chapter 10, "Retrieving Results (Basic)."

Related Functions

For information about	See
Binding a buffer to a column in a result set	**SQLBindCol**
Canceling statement processing	**SQLCancel**
Returning information about a column in a result set	**SQLColAttribute**
Returning information about a column in a result set	**SQLDescribeCol**
Executing an SQL statement	**SQLExecDirect**
Executing a prepared SQL statement	**SQLExecute**
Fetching a block of data or scrolling through a result set	**SQLFetchScroll**
Fetching a single row or a block of data in a forward-only direction	**SQLFetch**
Fetching part or all of a column of data	**SQLGetData**
Preparing an SQL statement for execution	**SQLPrepare**
Setting cursor scrolling options	**SQLSetStmtAttr**

SQLParamData

Conformance

Version Introduced: ODBC 1.0
Standards Compliance: ISO 92

Summary

SQLParamData is used in conjunction with **SQLPutData** to supply parameter data at statement execution time.

Syntax

SQLRETURN **SQLParamData**(
    SQLHSTMT *StatementHandle*,
    SQLPOINTER * *ValuePtrPtr*);

Arguments

StatementHandle [Input]
Statement handle.

ValuePtrPtr [Output]
Pointer to a buffer in which to return the address of the *ParameterValuePtr* buffer specified in **SQLBindParameter** (for parameter data) or the address of the *TargetValuePtr* buffer specified in **SQLBindCol** (for column data), as contained in the SQL_DESC_DATA_PTR descriptor record field.

Returns

SQL_SUCCESS, SQL_SUCCESS_WITH_INFO, SQL_NEED_DATA, SQL_NO_DATA, SQL_STILL_EXECUTING, SQL_ERROR, or SQL_INVALID_HANDLE.

Diagnostics

When **SQLParamData** returns SQL_ERROR or SQL_SUCCESS_WITH_INFO, an associated SQLSTATE value can be obtained by calling **SQLGetDiagRec** with a *HandleType* of SQL_HANDLE_STMT and a *Handle* of *StatementHandle*. The following table lists the SQLSTATE values commonly returned by **SQLParamData** and explains each one in the context of this function; the notation "(DM)" precedes the descriptions of SQLSTATEs returned by the Driver Manager. The return code associated with each SQLSTATE value is SQL_ERROR, unless noted otherwise.

SQLSTATE	Error	Description
01000	General warning	Driver-specific informational message. (Function returns SQL_SUCCESS_WITH_INFO.)
07006	Restricted data type attribute violation	The data value identified by the *ValueType* argument in **SQLBindParameter** for the bound parameter could not be converted to the data type identified by the *ParameterType* argument in **SQLBindParameter**. The data value returned for a parameter bound as SQL_PARAM_INPUT_OUTPUT or SQL_PARAM_OUTPUT could not be converted to the data type identified by the *ValueType* argument in **SQLBindParameter**. (If the data values for one or more rows could not be converted, but one or more rows were successfully returned, this function returns SQL_SUCCESS_WITH_INFO.)
08S01	Communication link failure	The communication link between the driver and the data source to which the driver was connected failed before the function completed processing.
22026	String data, length mismatch	The SQL_NEED_LONG_DATA_LEN information type in **SQLGetInfo** was "Y" and less data was sent for a long parameter (the data type was SQL_LONGVARCHAR, SQL_LONGVARBINARY, or a long, data source–specific data type) than was specified with the *StrLen_or_IndPtr* argument in **SQLBindParameter**. The SQL_NEED_LONG_DATA_LEN information type in **SQLGetInfo** was "Y" and less data was sent for a long column (the data type was SQL_LONGVARCHAR, SQL_LONGVARBINARY, or a long, data source–specific data type) than was specified in the length buffer corresponding to a column in a row of data that was added or updated with **SQLBulkOperations**, or updated with **SQLSetPos**.
40001	Serialization failure	The transaction was rolled back due to a resource deadlock with another transaction.
40003	Statement completion unknown	The associated connection failed during the execution of this function and the state of the transaction cannot be determined.

SQLSTATE	Error	Description
HY000	General error	An error occurred for which there was no specific SQLSTATE and for which no implementation-specific SQLSTATE was defined. The error message returned by **SQLGetDiagRec** in the **MessageText* buffer describes the error and its cause.
HY001	Memory allocation error	The driver was unable to allocate memory required to support execution or completion of the function.
HY008	Operation canceled	Asynchronous processing was enabled for the *StatementHandle*. The function was called and before it completed execution, **SQLCancel** was called on the *StatementHandle*; the function was then called again on the *StatementHandle*. The function was called and, before it completed execution, **SQLCancel** was called on the *StatementHandle* from a different thread in a multithread application.
HY010	Function sequence error	(DM) The previous function call was not a call to **SQLExecDirect**, **SQLExecute**, **SQLBulkOperations**, or **SQLSetPos** where the return code was SQL_NEED_DATA, or the previous function call was a call to **SQLPutData**. The previous function call was a call to **SQLParamData**. (DM) An asynchronously executing function (not this one) was called for the *StatementHandle* and was still executing when this function was called. **SQLExecute**, **SQLExecDirect**, **SQLBulkOperations**, or **SQLSetPos** was called for the *StatementHandle* and returned SQL_NEED_DATA. **SQLCancel** was called before data was sent for all data-at-execution parameters or columns.
HY013	Memory management error	The function call could not be processed because the underlying memory objects could not be accessed, possibly because of low memory conditions.

SQLSTATE	Error	Description
HYT01	Connection timeout expired	The connection timeout period expired before the data source responded to the request. The connection timeout period is set through **SQLSetConnectAttr**, SQL_ATTR_CONNECTION_TIMEOUT.
IM001	Driver does not support this function	(DM) The driver that corresponds to the *StatementHandle* does not support the function.

If **SQLParamData** is called while sending data for a parameter in an SQL statement, it can return any SQLSTATE that can be returned by the function called to execute the statement (**SQLExecute** or **SQLExecDirect**). If it is called while sending data for a column being updated or added with **SQLBulkOperations**, or updated with **SQLSetPos**, it can return any SQLSTATE that can be returned by **SQLBulkOperations** or **SQLSetPos**.

Comments

SQLParamData can be called to supply data-at-execution data for two uses: parameter data to be used in a call to **SQLExecute** or **SQLExecDirect**, or column data to be used when a row is updated or added by a call to **SQLBulkOperations** or updated by a call to **SQLSetPos**. At execution time, **SQLParamData** returns to the application an indicator of which data the driver requires.

When an application calls **SQLExecute**, **SQLExecDirect**, **SQLBulkOperations**, or **SQLSetPos**, the driver returns SQL_NEED_DATA if it needs data-at-execution data. An application then calls **SQLParamData** to determine which data it should send. If the driver requires parameter data, the driver returns in the **ValuePtrPtr* output buffer the value that the application placed in the rowset buffer. The application can use this value to determine which parameter data the driver is requesting. If the driver requires column data, the driver returns in the **ValuePtrPtr* buffer the address of the row where the data can be found. It also returns SQL_NEED_DATA, which is an indicator to the application that it should call **SQLPutData** to send the data.

The application calls **SQLPutData** as many times as necessary to send the data-at-execution data for the column or parameter. After all of the data has been sent for the column or parameter, the application calls **SQLParamData** again. If **SQLParamData** again returns SQL_NEED_DATA, data needs to be sent for another parameter or column, so the application again calls **SQLPutData**. If all data-at-execution data has been sent for all parameters or columns, then **SQLParamData** returns SQL_SUCCESS or SQL_SUCCESS_WITH_INFO, the value in **ValuePtrPtr* is undefined, and the SQL statement can be executed or the **SQLBulkOperations** or **SQLSetPos** call can be processed.

If **SQLParamData** supplies parameter data for a searched update or delete statement that does not affect any rows at the data source, the call to **SQLParamData** returns SQL_NO_DATA.

For more information on how data-at-execution parameter data is passed at statement execution time, see "Passing Parameter Values" in **SQLBindParameter** and "Sending Long Data" in Chapter 9, "Executing Statements." For more information on how data-at-execution column data is updated or added, see "Using SQLSetPos" in **SQLSetPos**, "Performing Bulk Updates Using Bookmarks" in **SQLBulkOperations**, and "Long Data and SQLSetPos and SQLBulkOperations" in Chapter 12, "Updating Data."

Code Example

See **SQLPutData**.

Related Functions

For information about	See
Binding a buffer to a parameter	**SQLBindParameter**
Canceling statement processing	**SQLCancel**
Returning information about a parameter in a statement	**SQLDescribeParam**
Executing an SQL statement	**SQLExecDirect**
Executing a prepared SQL statement	**SQLExecute**
Sending parameter data at execution time	**SQLPutData**

SQLParamOptions

Conformance

Version Introduced: ODBC 1.0
Standards Compliance: Deprecated

Summary

The ODBC 2.0 function **SQLParamOptions** has been replaced in ODBC 3.0 by calls to **SQLSetStmtAttr**.

Note For more information about what the Driver Manager maps this function to when an ODBC 2.*x* application is working with an ODBC 3.0 driver, see "Mapping Deprecated Functions" in Appendix G, "Driver Guidelines for Backward Compatibility."

SQLPrepare

Conformance

Version Introduced: ODBC 1.0
Standards Compliance: ISO 92

Summary

SQLPrepare prepares an SQL string for execution.

Syntax

SQLRETURN **SQLPrepare**(
    SQLHSTMT *StatementHandle*,
    SQLCHAR * *StatementText*,
    SQLINTEGER *TextLength*);

Arguments

StatementHandle [Input]
Statement handle.

StatementText [Input]
SQL text string.

TextLength [Input]
Length of **StatementText*.

Returns

SQL_SUCCESS, SQL_SUCCESS_WITH_INFO, SQL_STILL_EXECUTING, SQL_ERROR, or SQL_INVALID_HANDLE.

Diagnostics

When **SQLPrepare** returns SQL_ERROR or SQL_SUCCESS_WITH_INFO, an associated SQLSTATE value can be obtained by calling **SQLGetDiagRec** with a *HandleType* of SQL_HANDLE_STMT and a *Handle* of *StatementHandle*. The following table lists the SQLSTATE values commonly returned by **SQLPrepare** and explains each one in the context of this function; the notation "(DM)" precedes the descriptions of SQLSTATEs returned by the Driver Manager. The return code associated with each SQLSTATE value is SQL_ERROR, unless noted otherwise.

SQLSTATE	Error	Description
01000	General warning	Driver-specific informational message. (Function returns SQL_SUCCESS_WITH_INFO.)
01S02	Option value changed	A specified statement attribute was invalid because of implementation working conditions, so a similar value was temporarily substituted. (**SQLGetStmtAttr** can be called to determine what the temporarily substituted value is.) The substitute value is valid for the *StatementHandle* until the cursor is closed. The statement attributes that can be changed are: SQL_ATTR_CONCURRENCY SQL_ATTR_CURSOR_TYPE SQL_ATTR_KEYSET_SIZE SQL_ATTR_MAX_LENGTH SQL_ATTR_MAX_ROWS SQL_ATTR_QUERY_TIMEOUT SQL_ATTR_SIMULATE_CURSOR (Function returns SQL_SUCCESS_WITH_INFO.)
08S01	Communication link failure	The communication link between the driver and the data source to which the driver was connected failed before the function completed processing.
21S01	Insert value list does not match column list	**StatementText* contained an **INSERT** statement and the number of values to be inserted did not match the degree of the derived table.
21S02	Degree of derived table does not match column list	**StatementText* contained a **CREATE VIEW** statement and the number of names specified is not the same degree as the derived table defined by the query specification.
22018	Invalid character value for cast specification	**StatementText* contained an SQL statement that contained a literal or parameter and the value was incompatible with the data type of the associated table column.
22019	Invalid escape character	The argument *StatementText* contained a **LIKE** predicate with an **ESCAPE** in the **WHERE** clause, and the length of the escape character following **ESCAPE** was not equal to 1.
22025	Invalid escape sequence	The argument *StatementText* contained "**LIKE** *pattern value* **ESCAPE** *escape character*" in the **WHERE** clause, and the character following the escape character in the pattern value was not one of "%" or "_".

SQLSTATE	Error	Description
24000	Invalid cursor state	(DM) A cursor was open on the *StatementHandle* and **SQLFetch** or **SQLFetchScroll** had been called. A cursor was open on the *StatementHandle* but **SQLFetch** or **SQLFetchScroll** had not been called.
34000	Invalid cursor name	**StatementText* contained a positioned **DELETE** or a positioned **UPDATE** and the cursor referenced by the statement being prepared was not open.
3D000	Invalid catalog name	The catalog name specified in *StatementText* was invalid.
3F000	Invalid schema name	The schema name specified in *StatementText* was invalid.
42000	Syntax error or access violation	**StatementText* contained an SQL statement that was not preparable or contained a syntax error. **StatementText* contained a statement for which the user did not have the required privileges.
42S01	Base table or view already exists	**StatementText* contained a **CREATE TABLE** or **CREATE VIEW** statement and the table name or view name specified already exists.
42S02	Base table or view not found	**StatementText* contained a **DROP TABLE** or a **DROP VIEW** statement and the specified table name or view name did not exist. **StatementText* contained an **ALTER TABLE** statement and the specified table name did not exist. **StatementText* contained a **CREATE VIEW** statement and a table name or view name defined by the query specification did not exist. **StatementText* contained a **CREATE INDEX** statement and the specified table name did not exist. **StatementText* contained a **GRANT** or **REVOKE** statement and the specified table name or view name did not exist. **StatementText* contained a **SELECT** statement and a specified table name or view name did not exist.

SQLSTATE	Error	Description
42S02 (*continued*)	Base table or view not found	**StatementText* contained a **DELETE**, **INSERT**, or **UPDATE** statement and the specified table name did not exist. **StatementText* contained a **CREATE TABLE** statement and a table specified in a constraint (referencing a table other than the one being created) did not exist.
42S11	Index already exists	**StatementText* contained a **CREATE INDEX** statement and the specified index name already existed.
42S12	Index not found	**StatementText* contained a **DROP INDEX** statement and the specified index name did not exist.
42S21	Column already exists	**StatementText* contained an **ALTER TABLE** statement and the column specified in the **ADD** clause is not unique or identifies an existing column in the base table.
42S22	Column not found	**StatementText* contained a **CREATE INDEX** statement and one or more of the column names specified in the column list did not exist. **StatementText* contained a **GRANT** or **REVOKE** statement and a specified column name did not exist. **StatementText* contained a **SELECT**, **DELETE**, **INSERT**, or **UPDATE** statement and a specified column name did not exist. **StatementText* contained a **CREATE TABLE** statement and a column specified in a constraint (referencing a table other than the one being created) did not exist.
HY000	General error	An error occurred for which there was no specific SQLSTATE and for which no implementation-specific SQLSTATE was defined. The error message returned by **SQLGetDiagRec** in the **MessageText* buffer describes the error and its cause.
HY001	Memory allocation error	The driver was unable to allocate memory required to support execution or completion of the function.

SQLSTATE	Error	Description
HY008	Operation canceled	Asynchronous processing was enabled for the *StatementHandle*. The function was called and before it completed execution, **SQLCancel** was called on the *StatementHandle*, and then the function was called again on the *StatementHandle*. The function was called and, before it completed execution, **SQLCancel** was called on the *StatementHandle* from a different thread in a multithread application.
HY009	Invalid use of null pointer	(DM) *StatementText* was a null pointer.
HY010	Function sequence error	(DM) An asynchronously executing function (not this one) was called for the *StatementHandle* and was still executing when this function was called. (DM) **SQLExecute**, **SQLExecDirect**, **SQLBulkOperations**, or **SQLSetPos** was called for the *StatementHandle* and returned SQL_NEED_DATA. This function was called before data was sent for all data-at-execution parameters or columns.
HY013	Memory management error	The function call could not be processed because the underlying memory objects could not be accessed, possibly because of low memory conditions.
HY090	Invalid string or buffer length	(DM) The argument *TextLength* was less than or equal to 0, but not equal to SQL_NTS.
HYC00	Optional feature not implemented	The concurrency setting was invalid for the type of cursor defined. The SQL_ATTR_USE_BOOKMARKS statement attribute was set to SQL_UB_VARIABLE, and the SQL_ATTR_CURSOR_TYPE statement attribute was set to a cursor type for which the driver does not support bookmarks.
HYT00	Timeout expired	The timeout period expired before the data source returned the result set. The timeout period is set through **SQLSetStmtAttr**, SQL_ATTR_QUERY_TIMEOUT.

SQLSTATE	Error	Description
HYT01	Connection timeout expired	The connection timeout period expired before the data source responded to the request. The connection timeout period is set through **SQLSetConnectAttr**, SQL_ATTR_CONNECTION_TIMEOUT.
IM001	Driver does not support this function	(DM) The driver associated with the *StatementHandle* does not support the function.

Comments

The application calls **SQLPrepare** to send an SQL statement to the data source for preparation. For more information about prepared execution, see "Prepared Execution" in Chapter 9, "Executing Statements." The application can include one or more parameter markers in the SQL statement. To include a parameter marker, the application embeds a question mark (?) into the SQL string at the appropriate position. For information about parameters, see "Statement Parameters" in Chapter 9, "Executing Statements."

Note If an application uses **SQLPrepare** to prepare and **SQLExecute** to submit a **COMMIT** or **ROLLBACK** statement, it will not be interoperable between DBMS products. To commit or roll back a transaction, call **SQLEndTran**.

The driver can modify the statement to use the form of SQL used by the data source, and then submit it to the data source for preparation. In particular, the driver modifies the escape sequences used to define SQL syntax for certain features. (For a description of SQL statement grammar, see "Escape Sequences in ODBC" in Chapter 8, "SQL Statements," and Appendix C, "SQL Grammar.") For the driver, a statement handle is similar to a statement identifier in embedded SQL code. If the data source supports statement identifiers, the driver can send a statement identifier and parameter values to the data source.

Once a statement is prepared, the application uses the statement handle to refer to the statement in later function calls. The prepared statement associated with the statement handle can be reexecuted by calling **SQLExecute** until the application frees the statement with a call to **SQLFreeStmt** with the SQL_DROP option or until the statement handle is used in a call to **SQLPrepare**, **SQLExecDirect**, or one of the catalog functions (**SQLColumns**, **SQLTables**, and so on). Once the application prepares a statement, it can request information about the format of the result set. For some implementations, calling **SQLDescribeCol** or **SQLDescribeParam** after **SQLPrepare** may not be as efficient as calling the function after **SQLExecute** or **SQLExecDirect**.

Some drivers cannot return syntax errors or access violations when the application calls **SQLPrepare**. A driver can handle syntax errors and access violations, only syntax errors, or neither syntax errors nor access violations. Therefore, an application must be able to handle these conditions when calling subsequent related functions such as **SQLNumResultCols**, **SQLDescribeCol**, **SQLColAttribute**, and **SQLExecute**.

Depending on the capabilities of the driver and data source, parameter information (such as data types) might be checked when the statement is prepared (if all parameters have been bound), or when it is executed (if all parameters have not been bound). For maximum interoperability, an application should unbind all parameters that applied to an old SQL statement before preparing a new SQL statement on the same statement. This prevents errors that are due to old parameter information being applied to the new statement.

Important Committing a transaction, either by explicitly calling **SQLEndTran** or by working in autocommit mode, can cause the data source to delete the access plans for all statements on a connection. For more information, see the SQL_CURSOR_COMMIT_BEHAVIOR and SQL_CURSOR_ROLLBACK_BEHAVIOR information types in **SQLGetInfo** and "Effect of Transactions on Cursors and Prepared Statements" in Chapter 14, "Transactions."

Code Example

See **SQLBindParameter**, **SQLPutData**, and **SQLSetPos**.

Related Functions

For information about	See
Allocating a statement handle	**SQLAllocHandle**
Binding a buffer to a column in a result set	**SQLBindCol**
Binding a buffer to a parameter	**SQLBindParameter**
Canceling statement processing	**SQLCancel**
Executing a commit or rollback operation	**SQLEndTran**
Executing an SQL statement	**SQLExecDirect**
Executing a prepared SQL statement	**SQLExecute**
Returning the number of rows affected by a statement	**SQLRowCount**
Setting a cursor name	**SQLSetCursorName**

SQLPrimaryKeys

Conformance

Version Introduced: ODBC 1.0
Standards Compliance: ODBC

Summary

SQLPrimaryKeys returns the column names that make up the primary key for a table. The driver returns the information as a result set. This function does not support returning primary keys from multiple tables in a single call.

Syntax

```
SQLRETURN SQLPrimaryKeys(
     SQLHSTMT       StatementHandle,
     SQLCHAR *      CatalogName,
     SQLSMALLINT NameLength1,
     SQLCHAR *      SchemaName,
     SQLSMALLINT NameLength2,
     SQLCHAR *      TableName,
     SQLSMALLINT NameLength3);
```

Arguments

StatementHandle [Input]
Statement handle.

CatalogName [Input]
Catalog name. If a driver supports catalogs for some tables but not for others, such as when the driver retrieves data from different DBMSs, an empty string ("") denotes those tables that do not have catalogs. *CatalogName* cannot contain a string search pattern.

If the SQL_ATTR_METADATA_ID statement attribute is set to SQL_TRUE, *CatalogName* is treated as an identifier, and its case is not significant. If it is SQL_FALSE, *CatalogName* is an ordinary argument; it is treated literally, and its case is significant. For more information, see "Arguments in Catalog Functions" in Chapter 7, "Catalog Functions."

NameLength1 [Input]
Length in bytes of **CatalogName*.

SchemaName [Input]
Schema name. If a driver supports schemas for some tables but not for others, such as when the driver retrieves data from different DBMSs, an empty string ("") denotes those tables that do not have schemas. *SchemaName* cannot contain a string search pattern.

If the SQL_ATTR_METADATA_ID statement attribute is set to SQL_TRUE, *SchemaName* is treated as an identifier, and its case is not significant. If it is SQL_FALSE, *SchemaName* is an ordinary argument; it is treated literally, and its case is not significant.

NameLength2 [Input]
Length in bytes of **SchemaName*.

TableName [Input]
Table name. This argument cannot be a null pointer. *TableName* cannot contain a string search pattern.

If the SQL_ATTR_METADATA_ID statement attribute is set to SQL_TRUE, *TableName* is treated as an identifier, and its case is not significant. If it is SQL_FALSE, *TableName* is an ordinary argument; it is treated literally, and its case is not significant.

NameLength3 [Input]
Length in bytes of **TableName*.

Returns

SQL_SUCCESS, SQL_SUCCESS_WITH_INFO, SQL_STILL_EXECUTING, SQL_ERROR, or SQL_INVALID_HANDLE.

Diagnostics

When **SQLPrimaryKeys** returns SQL_ERROR or SQL_SUCCESS_WITH_INFO, an associated SQLSTATE value can be obtained by calling **SQLGetDiagRec** with a *HandleType* of SQL_HANDLE_STMT and a *Handle* of *StatementHandle*. The following table lists the SQLSTATE values commonly returned by **SQLPrimaryKeys** and explains each one in the context of this function; the notation "(DM)" precedes the descriptions of SQLSTATEs returned by the Driver Manager. The return code associated with each SQLSTATE value is SQL_ERROR, unless noted otherwise.

SQLSTATE	Error	Description
01000	General warning	Driver-specific informational message. (Function returns SQL_SUCCESS_WITH_INFO.)
08S01	Communication link failure	The communication link between the driver and the data source to which the driver was connected failed before the function completed processing.
24000	Invalid cursor state	(DM) A cursor was open on the *StatementHandle* and **SQLFetch** or **SQLFetchScroll** had been called. A cursor was open on the *StatementHandle* but **SQLFetch** or **SQLFetchScroll** had not been called.
40001	Serialization failure	The transaction was rolled back due to a resource deadlock with another transaction.
40003	Statement completion unknown	The associated connection failed during the execution of this function and the state of the transaction cannot be determined.
HY000	General error	An error occurred for which there was no specific SQLSTATE and for which no implementation-specific SQLSTATE was defined. The error message returned by **SQLGetDiagRec** in the **MessageText* buffer describes the error and its cause.
HY001	Memory allocation error	The driver was unable to allocate memory required to support execution or completion of the function.
HY008	Operation canceled	Asynchronous processing was enabled for the *StatementHandle*. The function was called and before it completed execution, **SQLCancel** was called on the *StatementHandle*. Then the function was called again on the *StatementHandle*. The function was called and, before it completed execution, **SQLCancel** was called on the *StatementHandle* from a different thread in a multithread application.

SQLSTATE	Error	Description
HY009	Invalid use of null pointer	(DM) The *TableName* argument was a null pointer. (DM) The SQL_ATTR_METADATA_ID statement attribute was set to SQL_TRUE, the *CatalogName* argument was a null pointer, and **SQLGetInfo** with the SQL_CATALOG_NAME information type returns that catalog names are supported. (DM) The SQL_ATTR_METADATA_ID statement attribute was set to SQL_TRUE, and the *SchemaName* argument was a null pointer.
HY010	Function sequence error	(DM) An asynchronously executing function (not this one) was called for the *StatementHandle* and was still executing when this function was called. (DM) **SQLExecute**, **SQLExecDirect**, **SQLBulkOperations**, or **SQLSetPos** was called for the *StatementHandle* and returned SQL_NEED_DATA. This function was called before data was sent for all data-at-execution parameters or columns.
HY013	Memory management error	The function call could not be processed because the underlying memory objects could not be accessed, possibly because of low memory conditions.
HY090	Invalid string or buffer length	(DM) The value of one of the name length arguments was less than 0, but not equal to SQL_NTS, and the associated name argument is not a null pointer. The value of one of the name length arguments exceeded the maximum length value for the corresponding name.
HYC00	Optional feature not implemented	A catalog was specified and the driver or data source does not support catalogs. A schema was specified and the driver or data source does not support schemas.

SQLSTATE	Error	Description
HYC00 (*continued*)	Optional feature not implemented	The combination of the current settings of the SQL_ATTR_CONCURRENCY and SQL_ATTR_CURSOR_TYPE statement attributes was not supported by the driver or data source. The SQL_ATTR_USE_BOOKMARKS statement attribute was set to SQL_UB_VARIABLE, and the SQL_ATTR_CURSOR_TYPE statement attribute was set to a cursor type for which the driver does not support bookmarks.
HYT00	Timeout expired	The timeout period expired before the data source returned the requested result set. The timeout period is set through **SQLSetStmtAttr**, SQL_ATTR_QUERY_TIMEOUT.
HYT01	Connection timeout expired	The connection timeout period expired before the data source responded to the request. The connection timeout period is set through **SQLSetConnectAttr**, SQL_ATTR_CONNECTION_TIMEOUT.
IM001	Driver does not support this function	(DM) The driver associated with the *StatementHandle* does not support the function.

Comments

SQLPrimaryKeys returns the results as a standard result set, ordered by TABLE_CAT, TABLE_SCHEM, TABLE_NAME, and KEY_SEQ. For information about how this information might be used, see "Uses of Catalog Data" in Chapter 7, "Catalog Functions."

The following columns have been renamed for ODBC 3.0. The column name changes do not affect backward compatibility because applications bind by column number.

ODBC 2.0 column	ODBC 3.0 column
TABLE_QUALIFIER	TABLE_CAT
TABLE_OWNER	TABLE_SCHEM

To determine the actual lengths of the TABLE_CAT, TABLE_SCHEM, TABLE_NAME, and COLUMN_NAME columns, call **SQLGetInfo** with the SQL_MAX_CATALOG_NAME_LEN, SQL_MAX_SCHEMA_NAME_LEN, SQL_MAX_TABLE_NAME_LEN, and SQL_MAX_COLUMN_NAME_LEN options.

Note For more information about the general use, arguments, and returned data of ODBC catalog functions, see Chapter 7, "Catalog Functions."

The following table lists the columns in the result set. Additional columns beyond column 6 (PK_NAME) can be defined by the driver. An application should gain access to driver-specific columns by counting down from the end of the result set rather than specifying an explicit ordinal position. For more information, see "Data Returned by Catalog Functions" in Chapter 7, "Catalog Functions."

Column name	Column number	Data type	Comments
TABLE_CAT (ODBC 1.0)	1	Varchar	Primary key table catalog name; NULL if not applicable to the data source. If a driver supports catalogs for some tables but not for others, such as when the driver retrieves data from different DBMSs, it returns an empty string ("") for those tables that do not have catalogs.
TABLE_SCHEM (ODBC 1.0)	2	Varchar	Primary key table schema name; NULL if not applicable to the data source. If a driver supports schemas for some tables but not for others, such as when the driver retrieves data from different DBMSs, it returns an empty string ("") for those tables that do not have schemas.
TABLE_NAME (ODBC 1.0)	3	Varchar not NULL	Primary key table name.
COLUMN_NAME (ODBC 1.0)	4	Varchar not NULL	Primary key column name. The driver returns an empty string for a column that does not have a name.
KEY_SEQ (ODBC 1.0)	5	Smallint not NULL	Column sequence number in key (starting with 1).
PK_NAME (ODBC 2.0)	6	Varchar	Primary key name. NULL if not applicable to the data source.

Code Example

See **SQLForeignKeys**.

Related Functions

For information about	See
Binding a buffer to a column in a result set	**SQLBindCol**
Canceling statement processing	**SQLCancel**
Fetching a block of data or scrolling through a result set	**SQLFetchScroll**
Fetching a single row or a block of data in a forward-only direction	**SQLFetch**
Returning the columns of foreign keys	**SQLForeignKeys**
Returning table statistics and indexes	**SQLStatistics**

SQLProcedureColumns

Conformance

Version Introduced: ODBC 1.0
Standards Compliance: ODBC

Summary

SQLProcedureColumns returns the list of input and output parameters, as well as the columns that make up the result set for the specified procedures. The driver returns the information as a result set on the specified statement.

Syntax

```
SQLRETURN SQLProcedureColumns(
     SQLHSTMT      StatementHandle,
     SQLCHAR *     CatalogName,
     SQLSMALLINT   NameLength1,
     SQLCHAR *     SchemaName,
     SQLSMALLINT   NameLength2,
     SQLCHAR *     ProcName,
     SQLSMALLINT   NameLength3,
     SQLCHAR *     ColumnName,
     SQLSMALLINT   NameLength4);
```

Arguments

StatementHandle [Input]
Statement handle.

CatalogName [Input]
Procedure catalog name. If a driver supports catalogs for some procedures but not for others, such as when the driver retrieves data from different DBMSs, an empty string ("") denotes those procedures that do not have catalogs. *CatalogName* cannot contain a string search pattern.

If the SQL_ATTR_METADATA_ID statement attribute is set to SQL_TRUE, *CatalogName* is treated as an identifier, and its case is not significant. If it is SQL_FALSE, *CatalogName* is an ordinary argument; it is treated literally, and its case is significant. For more information, see "Arguments in Catalog Functions" in Chapter 7, "Catalog Functions."

NameLength1 [Input]
Length of **CatalogName*.

SchemaName [Input]
String search pattern for procedure schema names. If a driver supports schemas for some procedures but not for others, such as when the driver retrieves data from different DBMSs, an empty string ("") denotes those procedures that do not have schemas.

If the SQL_ATTR_METADATA_ID statement attribute is set to SQL_TRUE, *SchemaName* is treated as an identifier, and its case is not significant. If it is SQL_FALSE, *SchemaName* is a pattern value argument; it is treated literally, and its case is significant.

NameLength2 [Input]
Length of **SchemaName*.

ProcName [Input]
String search pattern for procedure names.

If the SQL_ATTR_METADATA_ID statement attribute is set to SQL_TRUE, *ProcName* is treated as an identifier, and its case is not significant. If it is SQL_FALSE, *ProcName* is a pattern value argument; it is treated literally, and its case is significant.

NameLength3 [Input]
Length of **ProcName*.

ColumnName [Input]
String search pattern for column names.

If the SQL_ATTR_METADATA_ID statement attribute is set to SQL_TRUE, *ColumnName* is treated as an identifier, and its case is not significant. If it is SQL_FALSE, *ColumnName* is a pattern value argument; it is treated literally, and its case is significant.

NameLength4 [Input]
Length of **ColumnName*.

Returns

SQL_SUCCESS, SQL_SUCCESS_WITH_INFO, SQL_STILL_EXECUTING, SQL_ERROR, or SQL_INVALID_HANDLE.

Diagnostics

When **SQLProcedureColumns** returns SQL_ERROR or SQL_SUCCESS_WITH_INFO, an associated SQLSTATE value can be obtained by calling **SQLGetDiagRec** with a *HandleType* of SQL_HANDLE_STMT and a *Handle* of *StatementHandle*. The following table lists the SQLSTATE values commonly returned by **SQLProcedureColumns** and explains each one in the context of this function; the notation "(DM)" precedes the descriptions of SQLSTATEs returned by the Driver Manager. The return code associated with each SQLSTATE value is SQL_ERROR, unless noted otherwise.

SQLSTATE	Error	Description
01000	General warning	Driver-specific informational message. (Function returns SQL_SUCCESS_WITH_INFO.)
08S01	Communication link failure	The communication link between the driver and the data source to which the driver was connected failed before the function completed processing.
24000	Invalid cursor state	A cursor was open on the *StatementHandle* and **SQLFetch** or **SQLFetchScroll** had been called. This error is returned by the Driver Manager if **SQLFetch** or **SQLFetchScroll** has not returned SQL_NO_DATA, and is returned by the driver if **SQLFetch** or **SQLFetchScroll** has returned SQL_NO_DATA. A cursor was open on the *StatementHandle* but **SQLFetch** or **SQLFetchScroll** had not been called.
40001	Serialization failure	The transaction was rolled back due to a resource deadlock with another transaction.
40003	Statement completion unknown	The associated connection failed during the execution of this function and the state of the transaction cannot be determined.
HY000	General error	An error occurred for which there was no specific SQLSTATE and for which no implementation-specific SQLSTATE was defined. The error message returned by **SQLError** in the **MessageText* buffer describes the error and its cause.
HY001	Memory allocation error	The driver was unable to allocate memory required to support execution or completion of the function.
HY008	Operation canceled	Asynchronous processing was enabled for the *StatementHandle*. The function was called and before it completed execution, **SQLCancel** was called on the *StatementHandle*. Then the function was called again on the *StatementHandle*. The function was called and, before it completed execution, **SQLCancel** was called on the *StatementHandle* from a different thread in a multithread application.

SQLSTATE	Error	Description
HY009	Invalid use of null pointer	(DM) The SQL_ATTR_METADATA_ID statement attribute was set to SQL_TRUE, the *CatalogName* argument was a null pointer, and the SQL_CATALOG_NAME *InfoType* returns that catalog names are supported. (DM) The SQL_ATTR_METADATA_ID statement attribute was set to SQL_TRUE, and the *SchemaName*, *ProcName*, or *ColumnName* argument was a null pointer.
HY010	Function sequence error	(DM) An asynchronously executing function (not this one) was called for the *StatementHandle* and was still executing when this function was called. (DM) **SQLExecute**, **SQLExecDirect**, **SQLBulkOperations**, or **SQLSetPos** was called for the *StatementHandle* and returned SQL_NEED_DATA. This function was called before data was sent for all data-at-execution parameters or columns.
HY090	Invalid string or buffer length	(DM) The value of one of the name length arguments was less than 0, but not equal to SQL_NTS. The value of one of the name length arguments exceeded the maximum length value for the corresponding catalog, schema, procedure, or column name.
HYC00	Optional feature not implemented	A procedure catalog was specified and the driver or data source does not support catalogs. A procedure schema was specified and the driver or data source does not support schemas. A string search pattern was specified for the procedure schema, procedure name, or column name and the data source does not support search patterns for one or more of those arguments. The combination of the current settings of the SQL_ATTR_CONCURRENCY and SQL_ATTR_CURSOR_TYPE statement attributes was not supported by the driver or data source. The SQL_ATTR_USE_BOOKMARKS statement attribute was set to SQL_UB_VARIABLE, and the SQL_ATTR_CURSOR_TYPE statement attribute was set to a cursor type for which the driver does not support bookmarks.

SQLSTATE	Error	Description
HYT00	Timeout expired	The timeout period expired before the data source returned the result set. The timeout period is set through **SQLSetStmtAttr**, SQL_ATTR_QUERY_TIMEOUT.
HYT01	Connection timeout expired	The connection timeout period expired before the data source responded to the request. The connection timeout period is set through **SQLSetConnectAttr**, SQL_ATTR_CONNECTION_TIMEOUT.
IM001	Driver does not support this function	(DM) The driver associated with the *StatementHandle* does not support the function.

Comments

This function is typically used before statement execution to retrieve information about procedure parameters and the columns that make up the result set or sets returned by the procedure, if any. For more information, see "Procedures" in Chapter 9, "Executing Statements."

Note **SQLProcedureColumns** might not return all columns used by a procedure. For example, a driver might only return information about the parameters used by a procedure and not the columns in a result set it generates.

The *SchemaName*, *ProcName*, and *ColumnName* arguments accept search patterns. For more information about valid search patterns, see "Pattern Value Arguments" in Chapter 7, "Catalog Functions."

Note For more information about the general use, arguments, and returned data of ODBC catalog functions, see Chapter 7, "Catalog Functions."

SQLProcedureColumns returns the results as a standard result set, ordered by PROCEDURE_CAT, PROCEDURE_SCHEM, PROCEDURE_NAME, and COLUMN_TYPE. Column names are returned for each procedure in the following order: the name of the return value, the names of each parameter in the procedure invocation (in call order), and then the names of each column in the result set returned by the procedure (in column order).

Applications should bind driver-specific columns relative to the end of the result set. For more information, see "Data Returned by Catalog Functions" in Chapter 7, "Catalog Functions."

To determine the actual lengths of the PROCEDURE_CAT, PROCEDURE_SCHEM, PROCEDURE_NAME, and COLUMN_NAME columns, an application can call **SQLGetInfo** with the SQL_MAX_CATALOG_NAME_LEN, SQL_MAX_SCHEMA_NAME_LEN, SQL_MAX_PROCEDURE_NAME_LEN, and SQL_MAX_COLUMN_NAME_LEN options.

The following columns have been renamed for ODBC 3.0. The column name changes do not affect backward compatibility because applications bind by column number.

ODBC 2.0 column	ODBC 3.0 column
PROCEDURE_QUALIFIER	PROCEDURE_CAT
PROCEDURE _OWNER	PROCEDURE_SCHEM
PRECISION	COLUMN_SIZE
LENGTH	BUFFER_LENGTH
SCALE	DECIMAL_DIGITS
RADIX	NUM_PREC_RADIX

The following columns have been added to the results set returned by **SQLProcedureColumns** for ODBC 3.0:

COLUMN_DEF

DATETIME_CODE

CHAR_OCTET_LENGTH

ORDINAL_POSITION

IS_NULLABLE

The following table lists the columns in the result set. Additional columns beyond column 19 (IS_NULLABLE) can be defined by the driver. An application should gain access to driver-specific columns by counting down from the end of the result set rather than specifying an explicit ordinal position. For more information, see "Data Returned by Catalog Functions" in Chapter 7, "Catalog Functions."

Column name	Column number	Data type	Comments
PROCEDURE_CAT (ODBC 2.0)	1	Varchar	Procedure catalog name; NULL if not applicable to the data source. If a driver supports catalogs for some procedures but not for others, such as when the driver retrieves data from different DBMSs, it returns an empty string ("") for those procedures that do not have catalogs.
PROCEDURE_SCHEM (ODBC 2.0)	2	Varchar	Procedure schema name; NULL if not applicable to the data source. If a driver supports schemas for some procedures but not for others, such as when the driver retrieves data from different DBMSs, it returns an empty string ("") for those procedures that do not have schemas.

Column name	Column number	Data type	Comments
PROCEDURE_NAME (ODBC 2.0)	3	Varchar not NULL	Procedure name. An empty string is returned for a procedure that does not have a name.
COLUMN_NAME (ODBC 2.0)	4	Varchar not NULL	Procedure column name. The driver returns an empty string for a procedure column that does not have a name.
COLUMN_TYPE (ODBC 2.0)	5	Smallint not NULL	Defines the procedure column as parameter or a result set column: SQL_PARAM_TYPE_UNKNOWN: The procedure column is a parameter whose type is unknown. (ODBC 1.0) SQL_PARAM_INPUT: The procedure column is an input parameter. (ODBC 1.0) SQL_PARAM_INPUT_OUTPUT: the procedure column is an input/output parameter. (ODBC 1.0) SQL_PARAM_OUTPUT: The procedure column is an output parameter. (ODBC 2.0) SQL_RETURN_VALUE: The procedure column is the return value of the procedure. (ODBC 2.0) SQL_RESULT_COL: The procedure column is a result set column. (ODBC 1.0)
DATA_TYPE (ODBC 2.0)	6	Smallint not NULL	SQL data type. This can be an ODBC SQL data type or a driver-specific SQL data type. For datetime and interval data types, this column returns the concise data types (for example, SQL_TYPE_TIME or SQL_INTERVAL_YEAR_TO_MONTH). For a list of valid ODBC SQL data types, see "SQL Data Types" in Appendix D, "Data Types." For information about driver-specific SQL data types, see the driver's documentation.

Column name	Column number	Data type	Comments
TYPE_NAME (ODBC 2.0)	7	Varchar not NULL	Data source–dependent data type name; for example, "CHAR", "VARCHAR", "MONEY", "LONG VARBINARY", or "CHAR ( ) FOR BIT DATA".
COLUMN_SIZE (ODBC 2.0)	8	Integer	The column size of the procedure column on the data source. NULL is returned for data types where column size is not applicable. For more information concerning precision, see "Column Size, Decimal Digits, Transfer Octet Length, and Display Size," in Appendix D, "Data Types."
BUFFER_LENGTH (ODBC 2.0)	9	Integer	The length in bytes of data transferred on an **SQLGetData** or **SQLFetch** operation if SQL_C_DEFAULT is specified. For numeric data, this size may be different than the size of the data stored on the data source. For more information, see "Column Size, Decimal Digits, Transfer Octet Length, and Display Size," in Appendix D, "Data Types."
DECIMAL_DIGITS (ODBC 2.0)	10	Smallint	The decimal digits of the procedure column on the data source. NULL is returned for data types where decimal digits is not applicable. For more information concerning decimal digits, see "Column Size, Decimal Digits, Transfer Octet Length, and Display Size," in Appendix D, "Data Types."

Column name	Column number	Data type	Comments
NUM_PREC_RADIX (ODBC 2.0)	11	Smallint	For numeric data types, either 10 or 2. If it is 10, the values in COLUMN_SIZE and DECIMAL_DIGITS give the number of decimal digits allowed for the column. For example, a DECIMAL(12,5) column would return a NUM_PREC_RADIX of 10, a COLUMN_SIZE of 12, and a DECIMAL_DIGITS of 5; a FLOAT column could return a NUM_PREC_RADIX of 10, a COLUMN_SIZE of 15 and a DECIMAL_DIGITS of NULL. If it is 2, the values in COLUMN_SIZE and DECIMAL_DIGITS give the number of bits allowed in the column. For example, a FLOAT column could return a NUM_PREC_RADIX of 2, a COLUMN_SIZE of 53, and a DECIMAL_DIGITS of NULL. NULL is returned for data types where NUM_PREC_RADIX is not applicable.
NULLABLE (ODBC 2.0)	12	Smallint not NULL	Whether the procedure column accepts a NULL value: SQL_NO_NULLS: The procedure column does not accept NULL values. SQL_NULLABLE: The procedure column accepts NULL values. SQL_NULLABLE_UNKNOWN: It is not known if the procedure column accepts NULL values.
REMARKS (ODBC 2.0)	13	Varchar	A description of the procedure column.

Column name	Column number	Data type	Comments
COLUMN_DEF (ODBC 3.0)	14	Varchar	The default value of the column. If NULL was specified as the default value, then this column is the word NULL, not enclosed in quotation marks. If the default value cannot be represented without truncation, then this column contains TRUNCATED, with no enclosing single quotation marks. If no default value was specified, then this column is NULL. The value of COLUMN_DEF can be used in generating a new column definition, except when it contains the value TRUNCATED.
SQL_DATA_TYPE (ODBC 3.0)	15	Smallint not NULL	The value of the SQL data type as it appears in the SQL_DESC_TYPE field of the descriptor. This column is the same as the DATA_TYPE column, except for datetime and interval data types. For datetime and interval data types, the SQL_DATA_TYPE field in the result set will return SQL_INTERVAL or SQL_DATETIME, and the SQL_DATETIME_SUB field will return the subcode for the specific interval or datetime data type (see Appendix D, "Data Types").
SQL_DATETIME_SUB (ODBC 3.0)	16	Smallint	The subtype code for datetime and interval data types. For other data types, this column returns a NULL.
CHAR_OCTET_ LENGTH (ODBC 3.0)	17	Integer	The maximum length in bytes of a character data type column. For all other data types, this column returns a NULL.

Column name	Column number	Data type	Comments
ORDINAL_POSITION (ODBC 3.0)	18	Integer not NULL	For input and output parameters, the ordinal position of the parameter in the procedure definition (in increasing parameter order, starting at 1). For a return value (if any), 0 is returned. For result-set columns, the ordinal position of the column in the result set, with the first column in the result set being number 1. If there are multiple result sets, column ordinal positions are returned in a driver-specific manner.
IS_NULLABLE (ODBC 3.0)	19	Varchar	"NO" if the column does not include NULLs. "YES" if the column can include NULLs. This column returns a zero-length string if nullability is unknown. ISO rules are followed to determine nullability. An ISO SQL–compliant DBMS cannot return an empty string. The value returned for this column is different than the value returned for the NULLABLE column. (See the description of the NULLABLE column.)

Code Example

See "Procedure Calls" in Chapter 8, "SQL Statements."

Related Functions

For information about	See
Binding a buffer to a column in a result set	**SQLBindCol**
Canceling statement processing	**SQLCancel**
Fetching a single row or a block of data in a forward-only direction	**SQLFetch**
Fetching a block of data or scrolling through a result set	**SQLFetchScroll**
Returning a list of procedures in a data source	**SQLProcedures**

SQLProcedures

Conformance

Version Introduced: ODBC 1.0
Standards Compliance: ODBC

Summary

SQLProcedures returns the list of procedure names stored in a specific data source. *Procedure* is a generic term used to describe an *executable object,* or a named entity that can be invoked using input and output parameters. For more information on procedures, see the "Procedures" section in Chapter 9, "Executing Statements."

Syntax

SQLRETURN **SQLProcedures**(
SQLHSTMT *StatementHandle*,
SQLCHAR * *CatalogName*,
SQLSMALLINT *NameLength1*,
SQLCHAR * *SchemaName*,
SQLSMALLINT *NameLength2*,
SQLCHAR * *ProcName*,
SQLSMALLINT *NameLength3*);

Arguments

StatementHandle [Input]
Statement handle.

CatalogName [Input]
Procedure catalog. If a driver supports catalogs for some tables but not for others, such as when the driver retrieves data from different DBMSs, an empty string ("") denotes those tables that do not have catalogs. *CatalogName* cannot contain a string search pattern.

If the SQL_ATTR_METADATA_ID statement attribute is set to SQL_TRUE, *CatalogName* is treated as an identifier, and its case is not significant. If it is SQL_FALSE, *CatalogName* is an ordinary argument; it is treated literally, and its case is significant. For more information, see "Arguments in Catalog Functions" in Chapter 7, "Catalog Functions."

NameLength1 [Input]
Length in bytes of **CatalogName*.

SchemaName [Input]
String search pattern for procedure schema names. If a driver supports schemas for some procedures but not for others, such as when the driver retrieves data from different DBMSs, an empty string ("") denotes those procedures that do not have schemas.

If the SQL_ATTR_METADATA_ID statement attribute is set to SQL_TRUE, *SchemaName* is treated as an identifier, and its case is not significant. If it is SQL_FALSE, *SchemaName* is a pattern value argument; it is treated literally, and its case is significant.

NameLength2 [Input]
Length in bytes of **SchemaName*.

ProcName [Input]
String search pattern for procedure names.

If the SQL_ATTR_METADATA_ID statement attribute is set to SQL_TRUE, *ProcName* is treated as an identifier, and its case is not significant. If it is SQL_FALSE, *ProcName* is a pattern value argument; it is treated literally, and its case is significant.

NameLength3 [Input]
Length in bytes of **ProcName*.

Returns

SQL_SUCCESS, SQL_SUCCESS_WITH_INFO, SQL_STILL_EXECUTING, SQL_ERROR, or SQL_INVALID_HANDLE.

Diagnostics

When **SQLProcedures** returns SQL_ERROR or SQL_SUCCESS_WITH_INFO, an associated SQLSTATE value can be obtained by calling **SQLGetDiagRec** with a *HandleType* of SQL_HANDLE_STMT and a *Handle* of *StatementHandle*. The following table lists the SQLSTATE values commonly returned by **SQLProcedures** and explains each one in the context of this function; the notation "(DM)" precedes the descriptions of SQLSTATEs returned by the Driver Manager. The return code associated with each SQLSTATE value is SQL_ERROR, unless noted otherwise.

SQLSTATE	Error	Description
01000	General warning	Driver-specific informational message. (Function returns SQL_SUCCESS_WITH_INFO.)
08S01	Communication link failure	The communication link between the driver and the data source to which the driver was connected failed before the function completed processing.
24000	Invalid cursor state	A cursor was open on the *StatementHandle* and **SQLFetch** or **SQLFetchScroll** had been called. This error is returned by the Driver Manager if **SQLFetch** or **SQLFetchScroll** has not returned SQL_NO_DATA, and is returned by the driver if **SQLFetch** or **SQLFetchScroll** has returned SQL_NO_DATA. A cursor was open on the *StatementHandle* but **SQLFetch** or **SQLFetchScroll** had not been called.
40001	Serialization failure	The transaction was rolled back due to a resource deadlock with another transaction.
40003	Statement completion unknown	The associated connection failed during the execution of this function and the state of the transaction cannot be determined.
HY000	General error	An error occurred for which there was no specific SQLSTATE and for which no implementation-specific SQLSTATE was defined. The error message returned by **SQLGetDiagRec** in the **MessageText* buffer describes the error and its cause.
HY001	Memory allocation error	The driver was unable to allocate memory required to support execution or completion of the function.
HY008	Operation canceled	Asynchronous processing was enabled for the *StatementHandle*. The function was called and before it completed execution, **SQLCancel** was called on the *StatementHandle*. Then the function was called again on the *StatementHandle*. The function was called and, before it completed execution, **SQLCancel** was called on the *StatementHandle* from a different thread in a multithread application.

SQLSTATE	Error	Description
HY009	Invalid use of null pointer	(DM) The SQL_ATTR_METADATA_ID statement attribute was set to SQL_TRUE, the *CatalogName* argument was a null pointer, and the SQL_CATALOG_NAME *InfoType* returns that catalog names are supported. (DM) The SQL_ATTR_METADATA_ID statement attribute was set to SQL_TRUE, and the *SchemaName* or *ProcName* argument was a null pointer.
HY010	Function sequence error	(DM) An asynchronously executing function (not this one) was called for the *StatementHandle* and was still executing when this function was called. (DM) **SQLExecute**, **SQLExecDirect**, **SQLBulkOperations**, or **SQLSetPos** was called for the *StatementHandle* and returned SQL_NEED_DATA. This function was called before data was sent for all data-at-execution parameters or columns.
HY013	Memory management error	The function call could not be processed because the underlying memory objects could not be accessed, possibly because of low memory conditions.
HY090	Invalid string or buffer length	(DM) The value of one of the name length arguments was less than 0, but not equal to SQL_NTS. The value of one of the name length arguments exceeded the maximum length value for the corresponding name.

SQLSTATE	Error	Description
HYC00	Optional feature not implemented	A procedure catalog was specified and the driver or data source does not support catalogs. A procedure schema was specified and the driver or data source does not support schemas. A string search pattern was specified for the procedure schema or procedure name and the data source does not support search patterns for one or more of those arguments. The combination of the current settings of the SQL_ATTR_CONCURRENCY and SQL_ATTR_CURSOR_TYPE statement attributes was not supported by the driver or data source. The SQL_ATTR_USE_BOOKMARKS statement attribute was set to SQL_UB_VARIABLE and the SQL_ATTR_CURSOR_TYPE statement attribute was set to a cursor type for which the driver does not support bookmarks.
HYT00	Timeout expired	The query timeout period expired before the data source returned the requested result set. The timeout period is set through **SQLSetStmtAttr**, SQL_ATTR_QUERY_TIMEOUT.
HYT01	Connection timeout expired	The connection timeout period expired before the data source responded to the request. The connection timeout period is set through **SQLSetConnectAttr**, SQL_ATTR_CONNECTION_TIMEOUT.
IM001	Driver does not support this function	(DM) The driver associated with the *StatementHandle* does not support this function.

Comments

SQLProcedures lists all procedures in the requested range. A user may or may not have permission to execute any of these procedures. To check accessibility, an application can call **SQLGetInfo** and check the SQL_ACCESSIBLE_PROCEDURES information value. Otherwise, the application must be able to handle a situation where the user selects a procedure that it cannot execute. For information about how this information might be used, see "Procedures" in Chapter 9, "Executing Statements."

Note For more information about the general use, arguments, and returned data of ODBC catalog functions, see Chapter 7, "Catalog Functions."

SQLProcedures returns the results as a standard result set, ordered by PROCEDURE_CAT, PROCEDURE_SCHEMA, and PROCEDURE_NAME.

Note **SQLProcedures** might not return all procedures. Applications can use any valid procedure, regardless of whether it is returned by **SQLProcedures**.

The following columns have been renamed for ODBC 3.0. The column name changes do not affect backward compatibility because applications bind by column number.

ODBC 2.0 column	ODBC 3.0 column
PROCEDURE_QUALIFIER	PROCEDURE_CAT
PROCEDURE _OWNER	PROCEDURE _SCHEM

To determine the actual lengths of the PROCEDURE_CAT, PROCEDURE_SCHEM, and PROCEDURE_NAME columns, an application can call **SQLGetInfo** with the SQL_MAX_CATALOG_NAME_LEN, SQL_MAX_SCHEMA_NAME_LEN, and SQL_MAX_PROCEDURE_NAME_LEN options.

The following table lists the columns in the result set. Additional columns beyond column 8 (PROCEDURE_TYPE) can be defined by the driver. An application should gain access to driver-specific columns by counting down from the end of the result set rather than specifying an explicit ordinal position. For more information, see "Data Returned by Catalog Functions" in Chapter 7, "Catalog Functions."

Column name	Column number	Data type	Comments
PROCEDURE_CAT (ODBC 2.0)	1	Varchar	Procedure catalog identifier; NULL if not applicable to the data source. If a driver supports catalogs for some procedures but not for others, such as when the driver retrieves data from different DBMSs, it returns an empty string ("") for those procedures that do not have catalogs.
PROCEDURE_SCHEM (ODBC 2.0)	2	Varchar	Procedure schema identifier; NULL if not applicable to the data source. If a driver supports schemas for some procedures but not for others, such as when the driver retrieves data from different DBMSs, it returns an empty string ("") for those procedures that do not have schemas.
PROCEDURE_NAME (ODBC 2.0)	3	Varchar not NULL	Procedure identifier.
NUM_INPUT_ PARAMS (ODBC 2.0)	4	N/A	Reserved for future use. Applications should not rely on the data returned in these result columns.

Column name	Column number	Data type	Comments
NUM_OUTPUT_ PARAMS (ODBC 2.0)	5	N/A	Reserved for future use. Applications should not rely on the data returned in these result columns.
NUM_RESULT_SETS (ODBC 2.0)	6	N/A	Reserved for future use. Applications should not rely on the data returned in these result columns.
REMARKS (ODBC 2.0)	7	Varchar	A description of the procedure.
PROCEDURE_TYPE (ODBC 2.0)	8	Smallint	Defines the procedure type: SQL_PT_UNKNOWN: It cannot be determined whether the procedure returns a value. SQL_PT_PROCEDURE: The returned object is a procedure; that is, it does not have a return value. SQL_PT_FUNCTION: The returned object is a function; that is, it has a return value.

The *SchemaName* and *ProcName* arguments accept search patterns. For more information about valid search patterns, see "Pattern Value Arguments" in Chapter 7, "Catalog Functions."

Code Example

See "Procedure Calls" in Chapter 8, "SQL Statements."

Related Functions

For information about	See
Binding a buffer to a column in a result set	**SQLBindCol**
Canceling statement processing	**SQLCancel**
Fetching a single row or a block of data in a forward-only direction	**SQLFetch**
Fetching a block of data or scrolling through a result set	**SQLFetchScroll**
Returning information about a driver or data source	**SQLGetInfo**
Returning the parameters and result set columns of a procedure	**SQLProcedureColumns**
Syntax for invoking stored procedures	Chapter 8, "Executing Statements"

SQLPutData

Conformance

Version Introduced: ODBC 1.0
Standards Compliance: ISO 92

Summary

SQLPutData allows an application to send data for a parameter or column to the driver at statement execution time. This function can be used to send character or binary data values in parts to a column with a character, binary, or data source–specific data type (for example, parameters of the SQL_LONGVARBINARY or SQL_LONGVARCHAR types).

Syntax

SQLRETURN **SQLPutData**(
    SQLHSTMT *StatementHandle*,
    SQLPOINTER *DataPtr*,
    SQLINTEGER *StrLen_or_Ind*);

Arguments

StatementHandle [Input]
Statement handle.

DataPtr [Input]
Pointer to a buffer containing the actual data for the parameter or column. The data must be in the C data type specified in the *ValueType* argument of **SQLBindParameter** (for parameter data) or the *TargetType* argument of **SQLBindCol** (for column data).

StrLen_or_Ind [Input]
Length of **DataPtr*. Specifies the amount of data sent in a call to **SQLPutData**. The amount of data can vary with each call for a given parameter or column. *StrLen_or_Ind* is ignored unless it is one of the following:

- SQL_NTS, SQL_NULL_DATA, or SQL_DEFAULT_PARAM
- The C data type specified in **SQLBindParameter** or **SQLBindCol** is SQL_C_CHAR or SQL_C_BINARY.
- The C data type is SQL_C_DEFAULT and the default C data type for the specified SQL data type is SQL_C_CHAR or SQL_C_BINARY.

For all other types of C data, if *StrLen_or_Ind* is not SQL_NULL_DATA or SQL_DEFAULT_PARAM, the driver assumes that the size of the **DataPtr* buffer is the size of the C data type specified with *ValueType* or *TargetType* and sends the entire data value. For more information, see "Converting Data from C to SQL Data Types" in Appendix D, "Data Types."

Returns

SQL_SUCCESS, SQL_SUCCESS_WITH_INFO, SQL_STILL_EXECUTING, SQL_ERROR, or SQL_INVALID_HANDLE.

Diagnostics

When **SQLPutData** returns SQL_ERROR or SQL_SUCCESS_WITH_INFO, an associated SQLSTATE value can be obtained by calling **SQLGetDiagRec** with a *HandleType* of SQL_HANDLE_STMT and a *Handle* of *StatementHandle*. The following table lists the SQLSTATE values commonly returned by **SQLPutData** and explains each one in the context of this function; the notation "(DM)" precedes the descriptions of SQLSTATEs returned by the Driver Manager. The return code associated with each SQLSTATE value is SQL_ERROR, unless noted otherwise.

SQLSTATE	Error	Description
01000	General warning	Driver-specific informational message. (Function returns SQL_SUCCESS_WITH_INFO.)
01004	String data, right truncated	String or binary data returned for an output parameter resulted in the truncation of non-blank character or non-NULL binary data. If it was a string value, it was right-truncated. (Function returns SQL_SUCCESS_WITH_INFO.)
07006	Restricted data type attribute violation	The data value identified by the *ValueType* argument in **SQLBindParameter** for the bound parameter could not be converted to the data type identified by the *ParameterType* argument in **SQLBindParameter**.
07S01	Invalid use of default parameter	A parameter value, set with **SQLBindParameter**, was SQL_DEFAULT_PARAM, and the corresponding parameter did not have a default value.
08S01	Communication link failure	The communication link between the driver and the data source to which the driver was connected failed before the function completed processing.

SQLSTATE	Error	Description
22001	String data, right truncation	The assignment of a character or binary value to a column resulted in the truncation of non-blank (character) or non-null (binary) characters or bytes. The SQL_NEED_LONG_DATA_LEN information type in **SQLGetInfo** was "Y" and more data was sent for a long parameter (the data type was SQL_LONGVARCHAR, SQL_LONGVARBINARY, or a long, data source–specific data type) than was specified with the *StrLen_or_IndPtr* argument in **SQLBindParameter**. The SQL_NEED_LONG_DATA_LEN information type in **SQLGetInfo** was "Y" and more data was sent for a long column (the data type was SQL_LONGVARCHAR, SQL_LONGVARBINARY, or a long, data source–specific data type) than was specified in the length buffer corresponding to a column in a row of data that was added or updated with **SQLBulkOperations**, or updated with **SQLSetPos**.
22003	Numeric value out of range	The data sent for a bound numeric parameter or column caused the whole (as opposed to fractional) part of the number to be truncated when assigned to the associated table column. Returning a numeric value (as numeric or string) for one or more input/output or output parameters would have caused the whole (as opposed to fractional) part of the number to be truncated.
22007	Invalid datetime format	The data sent for a parameter or column that was bound to a date, time, or timestamp structure was, respectively, an invalid date, time, or timestamp. An input/output or output parameter was bound to a date, time, or timestamp C structure, and a value in the returned parameter was, respectively, an invalid date, time, or timestamp. (Function returns SQL_SUCCESS_WITH_INFO.)
22008	Datetime field overflow	A datetime expression computed for an input/output or output parameter resulted in a date, time, or timestamp C structure that was invalid.
22012	Division by zero	An arithmetic expression calculated for an input/output or output parameter resulted in division by zero.

SQLSTATE	Error	Description
22015	Interval field overflow	The data sent for an exact numeric or interval column or parameter to an interval SQL data type caused a loss of significant digits. Data was sent for an interval column or parameter with more than one field, and was converted to a numeric data type, and had no representation in the numeric data type. The data sent for column or parameter data was assigned to an interval SQL type, and there was no representation of the value of the C type in the interval SQL type. The data sent for an exact numeric or interval C column or parameter to an interval C type caused a loss of significant digits. The data sent for column or parameter data was assigned to an interval C structure, and there was no representation of the data in the interval data structure.
22018	Invalid character value for cast specification	The C type was an exact or approximate numeric, a datetime, or an interval data type; the SQL type of the column was a character data type; and the value in the column or parameter was not a valid literal of the bound C type. The SQL type was an exact or approximate numeric, a datetime, or an interval data type; the C type was SQL_C_CHAR; and the value in the column or parameter was not a valid literal of the bound SQL type.
HY000	General error	An error occurred for which there was no specific SQLSTATE and for which no implementation-specific SQLSTATE was defined. The error message returned by **SQLGetDiagRec** in the **MessageText* buffer describes the error and its cause.
HY001	Memory allocation error	The driver was unable to allocate memory required to support execution or completion of the function.

SQLSTATE	Error	Description
HY008	Operation canceled	Asynchronous processing was enabled for the *StatementHandle*. The function was called and before it completed execution, **SQLCancel** was called on the *StatementHandle*. Then the function was called again on the *StatementHandle*. The function was called and, before it completed execution, **SQLCancel** was called on the *StatementHandle* from a different thread in a multithread application.
HY009	Invalid use of null pointer	(DM) The argument *DataPtr* was a null pointer and the argument *StrLen_or_Ind* was not 0, SQL_DEFAULT_PARAM, or SQL_NULL_DATA.
HY010	Function sequence error	(DM) The previous function call was not a call to **SQLPutData** or **SQLParamData**. (DM) An asynchronously executing function (not this one) was called for the *StatementHandle* and was still executing when this function was called.
HY013	Memory management error	The function call could not be processed because the underlying memory objects could not be accessed, possibly because of low memory conditions.
HY019	Non-character and non-binary data sent in pieces	**SQLPutData** was called more than once for a parameter or column and it was not being used to send character C data to a column with a character, binary, or data source–specific data type or to send binary C data to a column with a character, binary, or data source–specific data type.
HY020	Attempt to concatenate a null value	**SQLPutData** was called more than once since the call that returned SQL_NEED_DATA, and in one of those calls, the *StrLen_or_Ind* argument contained SQL_NULL_DATA or SQL_DEFAULT_PARAM.
HY090	Invalid string or buffer length	The argument *DataPtr* was not a null pointer and the argument *StrLen_or_Ind* was less than 0, but not equal to SQL_NTS or SQL_NULL_DATA.
HYT01	Connection timeout expired	The connection timeout period expired before the data source responded to the request. The connection timeout period is set through **SQLSetConnectAttr**, SQL_ATTR_CONNECTION_TIMEOUT.
IM001	Driver does not support this function	(DM) The driver associated with the *StatementHandle* does not support the function.

If **SQLPutData** is called while sending data for a parameter in an SQL statement, it can return any SQLSTATE that can be returned by the function called to execute the statement (**SQLExecute** or **SQLExecDirect**). If it is called while sending data for a column being updated or added with **SQLBulkOperations**, or updated with **SQLSetPos**, it can return any SQLSTATE that can be returned by **SQLBulkOperations** or **SQLSetPos**.

Comments

SQLPutData can be called to supply data-at-execution data for two uses: parameter data to be used in a call to **SQLExecute** or **SQLExecDirect**, or column data to be used when a row is updated or added by a call to **SQLBulkOperations**, or updated by a call to **SQLSetPos**.

When an application calls **SQLParamData** to determine which data it should send, the driver returns an indicator that the application can use to determine which parameter data to send, or where column data can be found. It also returns SQL_NEED_DATA, which is an indicator to the application that it should call **SQLPutData** to send the data. In the *DataPtr* argument to **SQLPutData**, the application passes a pointer to the buffer containing the actual data for the parameter or column.

When the driver returns SQL_SUCCESS for **SQLPutData**, the application calls **SQLParamData** again. **SQLParamData** returns SQL_NEED_DATA if more data needs to be sent, in which case the application calls **SQLPutData** again. It returns SQL_SUCCESS if all data-at-execution data has been sent. The application then calls **SQLParamData** again. If the driver returns SQL_NEED_DATA, and another indicator in **ValuePtrPtr*, it requires data for another parameter or column, and **SQLPutData** is called again. If the driver returns SQL_SUCCESS, then all data-at-execution data has been sent, and the SQL statement can be executed or the **SQLBulkOperations** or **SQLSetPos** call can be processed.

For more information on how data-at-execution parameter data is passed at statement execution time, see "Passing Parameter Values" in **SQLBindParameter** and "Sending Long Data" in Chapter 9, "Executing Statements." For more information on how data-at-execution column data is updated or added, see "Using SQLSetPos" in **SQLSetPos**, "Performing Bulk Updates Using Bookmarks" in **SQLBulkOperations**, and "Long Data and SQLSetPos and SQLBulkOperations" in Chapter 12, "Updating Data."

Note An application can use **SQLPutData** to send data in parts only when sending character C data to a column with a character, binary, or data source–specific data type or when sending binary C data to a column with a character, binary, or data source–specific data type. If **SQLPutData** is called more than once under any other conditions, it returns SQL_ERROR and SQLSTATE HY019 (Non-character and non-binary data sent in pieces).

Code Example

In the following example, an application prepares an SQL statement to insert data into the PICTURES table. The statement contains parameters for the PARTID and PICTURE columns. For each parameter, the application calls **SQLBindParameter** to specify the C and SQL data types of the parameter. It also specifies that the data for the second parameter will be passed at execution time, and passes the value 2 for later retrieval by **SQLParamData**. This value will identify the parameter that is being processed.

The application calls **GetNextID** to get the next available part ID number. It then calls **SQLExecute** to execute the statement. **SQLExecute** returns SQL_NEED_DATA when it needs data for the second parameter. The application calls **SQLParamData** to retrieve the value it stored with **SQLBindParameter**; it uses this value to determine which parameter to send data for. For each parameter, the application calls **InitUserData** to initialize the data routine. It repeatedly calls **GetUserData** and **SQLPutData** to get and send the parameter data. Finally, it calls **SQLParamData** to indicate it has sent all the data for the parameter, at which point it returns SQL_SUCCESS.

For the second parameter, **InitUserData** calls a routine to prompt the user for the name of a file containing a bitmap photo of the part and opens the file. **GetUserData** retrieves the next MAX_DATA_LEN bytes of photo data from the file. After it has retrieved all the photo data, it closes the photo file.

Note that some application routines are omitted for clarity.

```
#define     MAX_DATA_LEN 1024
SQLINTEGER   cbPartID = 0, cbPhotoParam, cbData;
SQLUINTEGER  sPartID;
             szPhotoFile;
SQLPOINTER   pToken, InitValue;
SQLCHAR      Data[MAX_DATA_LEN];
SQLRETURN    retcode;
SQLHSTMT     hstmt;

retcode = SQLPrepare(hstmt,
          "INSERT INTO PICTURES (PARTID, PICTURE) VALUES
         (?, ?)", SQL_NTS);
if (retcode == SQL_SUCCESS || retcode == SQL_SUCCESS_WITH_INFO) {

   /* Bind the parameters. For parameter 2, pass */
   /* the parameter number in ParameterValuePtr instead of a buffer */
   /* address.   */

   SQLBindParameter(hstmt, 1, SQL_PARAM_INPUT, SQL_C_ULONG,
                    SQL_INTEGER, 0, 0, &sPartID, 0, &cbPartID);
   SQLBindParameter(hstmt, 2, SQL_PARAM_INPUT,
                    SQL_C_BINARY, SQL_LONGVARBINARY,
                    0, 0, (SQLPOINTER) 2, 0, &cbPhotoParam);
```

```
   /* Set values so data for parameter 2 will be */
   /* passed at execution. Note that the length parameter in */
   /* the macro SQL_LEN_DATA_AT_EXEC is 0. This assumes that */
   /* the driver returns "N" for the SQL_NEED_LONG_DATA_LEN */
   /* information type in SQLGetInfo.                         */

   cbPhotoParam = SQL_LEN_DATA_AT_EXEC(0);

   sPartID = GetNextID();  /* Get next available employee ID */
                  /* number. */

   retcode = SQLExecute(hstmt);

   /* For data-at-execution parameters, call SQLParamData to */
   /* get the parameter number set by SQLBindParameter. */
   /* Call InitUserData. Call GetUserData and SQLPutData */
   /* repeatedly to get and put all data for the parameter. */
   /* Call SQLParamData to finish processing this parameter */

   while (retcode == SQL_NEED_DATA) {
      retcode = SQLParamData(hstmt, &pToken);
      if (retcode == SQL_NEED_DATA) {
         InitUserData((SQLSMALLINT)pToken, InitValue);
         while (GetUserData(InitValue, (SQLSMALLINT)pToken, Data,
                            &cbData))
            SQLPutData(hstmt, Data, cbData);
      }
   }
}

VOID InitUserData(sParam, InitValue)
SQLPOINTER   InitValue;
{
   SQLCHAR  szPhotoFile[MAX_FILE_NAME_LEN];

   /* Prompt user for bitmap file containing employee */
   /* photo. OpenPhotoFile opens the file and returns the */
   /* file handle. */

   PromptPhotoFileName(szPhotoFile);
   OpenPhotoFile(szPhotoFile, (FILE *)InitValue);
   break;
   }

BOOL GetUserData(InitValue, sParam, Data, cbData)
SQLPOINTER   InitValue;
SQLCHAR      *Data;
SQLINTEGER   *cbData;
BOOL         Done;

{
```

```
/* GetNextPhotoData returns the next piece of photo */
/* data and the number of bytes of data returned */
/* (up to MAX_DATA_LEN). */

Done = GetNextPhotoData((FILE *)InitValue, Data,
                        MAX_DATA_LEN, &cbData);
if (Done) {
   ClosePhotoFile((FILE *)InitValue);
return (TRUE);
}
return (FALSE);
}
```

Related Functions

For information about	See
Binding a buffer to a parameter	**SQLBindParameter**
Canceling statement processing	**SQLCancel**
Executing an SQL statement	**SQLExecDirect**
Executing a prepared SQL statement	**SQLExecute**
Returning the next parameter to send data for	**SQLParamData**

SQLRowCount

Conformance

Version Introduced: ODBC 1.0
Standards Compliance: ISO 92

Summary

SQLRowCount returns the number of rows affected by an **UPDATE**, **INSERT**, or **DELETE** statement, an SQL_ADD, SQL_UPDATE_BY_BOOKMARK, or SQL_DELETE_BY_BOOKMARK operation in **SQLBulkOperations**, or an SQL_UPDATE or SQL_DELETE operation in **SQLSetPos**.

Syntax

SQLRETURN **SQLRowCount**(
    SQLHSTMT *StatementHandle*,
    SQLINTEGER * *RowCountPtr*);

Arguments

StatementHandle [Input]
Statement handle.

RowCountPtr [Output]
Points to a buffer in which to return a row count. For **UPDATE**, **INSERT**, and **DELETE** statements, for the SQL_ADD, SQL_UPDATE_BY_BOOKMARK, and SQL_DELETE_BY_BOOKMARK operations in **SQLBulkOperations**, and for the SQL_UPDATE or SQL_DELETE operations in **SQLSetPos**, the value returned in **RowCountPtr* is the number of rows affected by the request or –1 if the number of affected rows is not available.

When **SQLExecute**, **SQLExecDirect**, **SQLBulkOperations**, **SQLSetPos**, or **SQLMoreResults** is called, the SQL_DIAG_ROW_COUNT field of the diagnostic data structure is set to the row count, and the row count is cached in an implementation-dependent way. **SQLRowCount** returns the cached row count value. The cached row count value is valid until the statement handle is set back to the prepared or allocated state, the statement is reexecuted, or **SQLCloseCursor** is called. Note that if a function has been called since the SQL_DIAG_ROW_COUNT field was set, the value returned by **SQLRowCount** might be different from the value in the SQL_DIAG_ROW_COUNT field, because the SQL_DIAG_ROW_COUNT field is reset to 0 by any function call.

For other statements and functions, the driver may define the value returned in **RowCountPtr*. For example, some data sources may be able to return the number of rows returned by a **SELECT** statement or a catalog function before fetching the rows

Note Many data sources cannot return the number of rows in a result set before fetching them; for maximum interoperability, applications should not rely on this behavior.

Returns

SQL_SUCCESS, SQL_SUCCESS_WITH_INFO, SQL_ERROR, or SQL_INVALID_HANDLE.

Diagnostics

When **SQLRowCount** returns SQL_ERROR or SQL_SUCCESS_WITH_INFO, an associated SQLSTATE value can be obtained by calling **SQLGetDiagRec** with a *HandleType* of SQL_HANDLE_STMT and a *Handle* of *StatementHandle*. The following table lists the SQLSTATE values commonly returned by **SQLRowCount** and explains each one in the context of this function; the notation "(DM)" precedes the descriptions of SQLSTATEs returned by the Driver Manager. The return code associated with each SQLSTATE value is SQL_ERROR, unless noted otherwise.

SQLSTATE	Error	Description
01000	General warning	Driver-specific informational message. (Function returns SQL_SUCCESS_WITH_INFO.)
HY000	General error	An error occurred for which there was no specific SQLSTATE and for which no implementation-specific SQLSTATE was defined. The error message returned by **SQLGetDiagRec** in the **MessageText* buffer describes the error and its cause.
HY001	Memory allocation error	The driver was unable to allocate memory required to support execution or completion of the function.
HY010	Function sequence error	(DM) The function was called prior to calling **SQLExecute**, **SQLExecDirect**, **SQLBulkOperations**, or **SQLSetPos** for the *StatementHandle*. (DM) An asynchronously executing function was called for the *StatementHandle* and was still executing when this function was called. (DM) **SQLExecute**, **SQLExecDirect**, **SQLBulkOperations**, or **SQLSetPos** was called for the *StatementHandle* and returned SQL_NEED_DATA. This function was called before data was sent for all data-at-execution parameters or columns.
HY013	Memory management error	The function call could not be processed because the underlying memory objects could not be accessed, possibly because of low memory conditions.

SQLSTATE	Error	Description
HYT01	Connection timeout expired	The connection timeout period expired before the data source responded to the request. The connection timeout period is set through **SQLSetConnectAttr**, SQL_ATTR_CONNECTION_TIMEOUT.
IM001	Driver does not support this function	(DM) The driver associated with the *StatementHandle* does not support the function.

Comments

If the last SQL statement executed on the statement handle was not an **UPDATE**, **INSERT**, or **DELETE** statement, or the *Operation* argument in the previous call to **SQLBulkOperations** was not SQL_ADD, SQL_UPDATE_BY_BOOKMARK, or SQL_DELETE_BY_BOOKMARK,or the *Operation* argument in the previous call to **SQLSetPos** was not SQL_UPDATE or SQL_DELETE, the value of **RowCountPtr* is driver-defined. For more information, see "Determining the Number of Affected Rows" in Chapter 12, "Updating Data."

Related Functions

For information about	See
Executing an SQL statement	**SQLExecDirect**
Executing a prepared SQL statement	**SQLExecute**

SQLSetConnectAttr

Conformance

Version Introduced: ODBC 3.0
Standards Compliance: ISO 92

Summary

SQLSetConnectAttr sets attributes that govern aspects of connections.

Note For more information about what the Driver Manager maps this function to when an ODBC 3.0 application is working with an ODBC 2.*x* driver, see "Mapping Replacement Functions for Backward Compatibility of Applications" in Chapter 17, "Programming Considerations."

Syntax

SQLRETURN **SQLSetConnectAttr**(
SQLHDBC *ConnectionHandle*,
SQLINTEGER *Attribute*,
SQLPOINTER *ValuePtr*,
SQLINTEGER *StringLength*);

Arguments

ConnectionHandle [Input]
Connection handle.

Attribute [Input]
Attribute to set, listed in "Comments."

ValuePtr [Input]
Pointer to the value to be associated with *Attribute*. Depending on the value of *Attribute*, *ValuePtr* will be a 32-bit unsigned integer value or will point to a null-terminated character string. Note that if the *Attribute* argument is a driver-specific value, the value in *ValuePtr* may be a signed integer.

StringLength [Input]
If *Attribute* is an ODBC-defined attribute and *ValuePtr* points to a character string or a binary buffer, this argument should be the length of **ValuePtr*. If *Attribute* is an ODBC-defined attribute and *ValuePtr* is an integer, *StringLength* is ignored.

If *Attribute* is a driver-defined attribute, the application indicates the nature of the attribute to the Driver Manager by setting the *StringLength* argument. *StringLength* can have the following values:

- If *ValuePtr* is a pointer to a character string, then *StringLength* is the length of the string or SQL_NTS.
- If *ValuePtr* is a pointer to a binary buffer, then the application places the result of the SQL_LEN_BINARY_ATTR(*length*) macro in *StringLength*. This places a negative value in *StringLength*.
- If *ValuePtr* is a pointer to a value other than a character string or a binary string, then *StringLength* should have the value SQL_IS_POINTER.
- If *ValuePtr* contains a fixed-length value, then *StringLength* is either SQL_IS_INTEGER or SQL_IS_UINTEGER, as appropriate.

Returns

SQL_SUCCESS, SQL_SUCCESS_WITH_INFO, SQL_ERROR, or SQL_INVALID_HANDLE.

Diagnostics

When **SQLSetConnectAttr** returns SQL_ERROR or SQL_SUCCESS_WITH_INFO, an associated SQLSTATE value can be obtained by calling **SQLGetDiagRec** with a *HandleType* of SQL_HANDLE_DBC and a *Handle* of *ConnectionHandle*. The following table lists the SQLSTATE values commonly returned by **SQLSetConnectAttr** and explains each one in the context of this function; the notation "(DM)" precedes the descriptions of SQLSTATEs returned by the Driver Manager. The return code associated with each SQLSTATE value is SQL_ERROR, unless noted otherwise.

The driver can return SQL_SUCCESS_WITH_INFO to provide information about the result of setting an option.

SQLSTATE	Error	Description
01000	General warning	Driver-specific informational message. (Function returns SQL_SUCCESS_WITH_INFO.)
01S02	Option value changed	The driver did not support the value specified in *ValuePtr* and substituted a similar value. (Function returns SQL_SUCCESS_WITH_INFO.)
08002	Connection name in use	The *Attribute* argument was SQL_ATTR_ODBC_CURSORS and the driver was already connected to the data source.
08003	Connection does not exist	(DM) An *Attribute* value was specified that required an open connection, but the *ConnectionHandle* was not in a connected state.

SQLSTATE	Error	Description
08S01	Communication link failure	The communication link between the driver and the data source to which the driver was connected failed before the function completed processing.
24000	Invalid cursor state	The *Attribute* argument was SQL_ATTR_CURRENT_CATALOG and a result set was pending.
3D000	Invalid catalog name	The *Attribute* argument was SQL_CURRENT_CATALOG, and the specified catalog name was invalid.
HY000	General error	An error occurred for which there was no specific SQLSTATE and for which no implementation-specific SQLSTATE was defined. The error message returned by **SQLGetDiagRec** in the **MessageText* buffer describes the error and its cause.
HY001	Memory allocation error	The driver was unable to allocate memory required to support execution or completion of the function.
HY009	Invalid use of null pointer	The *Attribute* argument identified a connection attribute that required a string value, and the *ValuePtr argument was a null pointer.*
HY010	Function sequence error	(DM) An asynchronously executing function was called for a *StatementHandle* associated with the *ConnectionHandle* and was still executing when **SQLSetConnectAttr** was called. (DM) **SQLExecute**, **SQLExecDirect**, **SQLBulkOperations**, or **SQLSetPos** was called for a *StatementHandle* associated with the *ConnectionHandle* and returned SQL_NEED_DATA. This function was called before data was sent for all data-at-execution parameters or columns. (DM) **SQLBrowseConnect** was called for the *ConnectionHandle* and returned SQL_NEED_DATA. This function was called before **SQLBrowseConnect** returned SQL_SUCCESS_WITH_INFO or SQL_SUCCESS.
HY011	Attribute cannot be set now	The *Attribute* argument was SQL_ATTR_TXN_ISOLATION and a transaction was open.

SQLSTATE	Error	Description
HY013	Memory management error	The function call could not be processed because the underlying memory objects could not be accessed, possibly because of low memory conditions.
HY024	Invalid attribute value	Given the specified *Attribute* value, an invalid value was specified in *ValuePtr*. (The Driver Manager returns this SQLSTATE only for connection and statement attributes that accept a discrete set of values, such as SQL_ATTR_ACCESS_MODE or SQL_ATTR_ASYNC_ENABLE. For all other connection and statement attributes, the driver must verify the value specified in *ValuePtr*.) The *Attribute* argument was SQL_ATTR_TRACEFILE or SQL_ATTR_TRANSLATE_LIB, and *ValuePtr* was an empty string.
HY090	Invalid string or buffer length	*(DM) *ValuePtr is a character string, and t*he *StringLength* argument was less than 0, but was not SQL_NTS.
HY092	Invalid attribute/option identifier	(DM) The value specified for the argument *Attribute* was not valid for the version of ODBC supported by the driver. (DM) The value specified for the argument *Attribute* was a read-only attribute.
HYC00	Optional feature not implemented	The value specified for the argument *Attribute* was a valid ODBC connection or statement attribute for the version of ODBC supported by the driver, but was not supported by the driver.
HYT01	Connection timeout expired	The connection timeout period expired before the data source responded to the request. The connection timeout period is set through **SQLSetConnectAttr**, SQL_ATTR_CONNECTION_TIMEOUT.
IM001	Driver does not support this function	(DM) The driver associated with the *ConnectionHandle* does not support the function.
IM009	Unable to load translation DLL	The driver was unable to load the translation DLL that was specified for the connection. This error can only be returned when *Attribute* is SQL_ATTR_TRANSLATE_LIB.

When *Attribute* is a statement attribute, **SQLSetConnectAttr** can return any SQLSTATEs returned by **SQLSetStmtAttr**.

Comments

For general information about connection attributes, see "Connection Attributes" in Chapter 6, "Connecting to a Data Source or Driver."

The currently defined attributes and the version of ODBC in which they were introduced are shown in the table later in this section; it is expected that more will be defined to take advantage of different data sources. A range of attributes is reserved by ODBC; driver developers must reserve values for their own driver-specific use from X/Open.

Note The ability to set statement attributes at the connection level by calling **SQLSetConnectAttr** has been deprecated in ODBC 3.0. ODBC 3.0 applications should never set statement attributes at the connection level. ODBC 3.0 statement attributes cannot be set at the connection level, with the exception of the SQL_ATTR_METADATA_ID and SQL_ATTR_ASYNC_ENABLE attributes, which are both connection attributes and statement attributes, and can be set either at the connection level or the statement level.

ODBC 3.0 drivers need only support this functionality if they should work with ODBC 2.*x* applications that set ODBC 2.*x* statement options at the connection level. For more information, see "SQLSetConnectOption Mapping" in Appendix G, "Driver Guidelines for Backward Compatibility."

An application can call **SQLSetConnectAttr** at any time between the time the connection is allocated and freed. All connection and statement attributes successfully set by the application for the connection persist until **SQLFreeHandle** is called on the connection. For example, if an application calls **SQLSetConnectAttr** before connecting to a data source, the attribute persists even if **SQLSetConnectAttr** fails in the driver when the application connects to the data source; if an application sets a driver-specific attribute, the attribute persists even if the application connects to a different driver on the connection.

Some connection attributes can be set only before a connection has been made; others can be set only after a connection has been made. The following table indicates those connection attributes that must be set either before or after a connection has been made. "Either" indicates that the attribute can be set either before or after connection.

Attribute	Set before or after connection?
SQL_ATTR_ACCESS_MODE	Either [1]
SQL_ATTR_ASYNC_ENABLE	Either [2]
SQL_ATTR_AUTO_IPD	Either
SQL_ATTR_AUTOCOMMIT	Either
SQL_ATTR_CONNECTION_TIMEOUT	Either
SQL_ATTR_CURRENT_CATALOG	Either [1]
SQL_ATTR_LOGIN_TIMEOUT	Before

Attribute	Set before or after connection?
SQL_ATTR_METADATA_ID	Either
SQL_ATTR_ODBC_CURSORS	Before
SQL_ATTR_PACKET_SIZE	Before
SQL_ATTR_QUIET_MODE	Either
SQL_ATTR_TRACE	Either
SQL_ATTR_TRACEFILE	Either
SQL_ATTR_TRANSLATE_LIB	After
SQL_ATTR_TRANSLATE_ OPTION	After
SQL_ATTR_TXN_ISOLATION	Either [3]

1 SQL_ATTR_ACCESS_MODE and SQL_ATTR_CURRENT_CATALOG can be set before or after connecting, depending on the driver. However, interoperable applications set them before connecting because some drivers do not support changing these after connecting.

2 SQL_ATTR_ASYNC_ENABLE must be set before there is an active statement.

3 SQL_ATTR_TXN_ISOLATION can be set only if there are no open transactions on the connection.

Some connection attributes support substitution of a similar value if the data source does not support the value specified in **ValuePtr*. In such cases, the driver returns SQL_SUCCESS_WITH_INFO and SQLSTATE 01S02 (Option value changed). For example, if *Attribute* is SQL_ATTR_PACKET_SIZE and **ValuePtr* exceeds the maximum packet size, the driver substitutes the maximum size. To determine the substituted value, an application calls **SQLGetConnectAttr**.

The format of information set in the **ValuePtr* buffer depends on the specified *Attribute*. **SQLSetConnectAttr** will accept attribute information in one of two different formats: a null-terminated character string or a 32-bit integer value. The format of each is noted in the attribute's description. Character strings pointed to by the *ValuePtr* argument of **SQLSetConnectAttr** have a length of *StringLength* bytes.

The *StringLength* argument is ignored if the length is defined by the attribute, as is the case for all attributes introduced in ODBC 2.*x* or earlier.

Attribute	***ValuePtr* contents**
SQL_ATTR_ACCESS_MODE (ODBC 1.0)	An SQLUINTEGER value. SQL_MODE_READ_ONLY is used by the driver or data source as an indicator that the connection is not required to support SQL statements that cause updates to occur. This mode can be used to optimize locking strategies, transaction management, or other areas as appropriate to the driver or data source. The driver is not required to prevent such statements from being submitted to the data source. The behavior of the driver and data source when asked to process SQL statements that are not read-only during a read-only connection is implementation-defined. SQL_MODE_READ_WRITE is the default.
SQL_ATTR_ASYNC_ENABLE (ODBC 3.0)	An SQLUINTEGER value that specifies whether a function called with a statement on the specified connection is executed asynchronously: SQL_ASYNC_ENABLE_OFF = Off (the default) SQL_ASYNC_ENABLE_ON = On Setting SQL_ASYNC_ENABLE_ON enables asynchronous execution for all future statement handles allocated on this connection. It is driver-defined whether this enables asynchronous execution for existing statement handles associated with this connection. An error is returned if asynchronous execution is enabled while there is an active statement on the connection. This attribute can be set whether **SQLGetInfo** with the SQL_ASYNC_MODE information type returns SQL_AM_CONNECTION or SQL_AM_STATEMENT. After a function has been called asynchronously, only the original function, **SQLAllocHandle**, **SQLCancel**, **SQLGetDiagField**, or **SQLGetDiagRec** can be called on the statement or the connection associated with *StatementHandle*, until the original function returns a code other than SQL_STILL_EXECUTING. Any other function called on *StatementHandle* or the connection associated with *StatementHandle* returns SQL_ERROR with an SQLSTATE of HY010 (Function sequence error). Functions can be called on other statements. For more information, see "Asynchronous Execution" in Chapter 9, "Executing Statements." In general, applications should execute functions asynchronously only on single-thread operating systems. On multithread operating systems, applications should execute functions on separate threads, rather than executing them asynchronously on the same thread. Drivers that operate only on multithread operating systems do not need to support asynchronous execution.

Attribute	***ValuePtr*** **contents**
SQL_ATTR_ASYNC_ENABLE (ODBC 3.0) (*continued*)	The following functions can be executed asynchronously: **SQLBulkOperations** **SQLColAttribute** **SQLColumnPrivileges** **SQLColumns** **SQLCopyDesc** **SQLDescribeCol** **SQLDescribeParam** **SQLExecDirect** **SQLExecute** **SQLFetch** **SQLFetchScroll** **SQLForeignKeys** **SQLGetData** **SQLGetDescField** [1] **SQLGetDescRec** [1] **SQLGetDiagField** **SQLGetDiagRec** **SQLGetTypeInfo** **SQLMoreResults** **SQLNumParams** **SQLNumResultCols** **SQLParamData** **SQLPrepare** **SQLPrimaryKeys** **SQLProcedureColumns** **SQLProcedures** **SQLPutData** **SQLSetPos** **SQLSpecialColumns** **SQLStatistics** **SQLTablePrivileges** **SQLTables** 1 These functions can be called asynchronously only if the descriptor is an implementation descriptor, not an application descriptor.
SQL_ATTR_AUTO_IPD (ODBC 3.0)	A read-only SQLUINTEGER value that specifies whether automatic population of the IPD after a call to **SQLPrepare** is supported: SQL_TRUE = Automatic population of the IPD after a call to **SQLPrepare** is supported by the driver. SQL_FALSE = Automatic population of the IPD after a call to **SQLPrepare** is not supported by the driver. Servers that do not support prepared statements will not be able to populate the IPD automatically. If SQL_TRUE is returned for the SQL_ATTR_AUTO_IPD connection attribute, the statement attribute SQL_ATTR_ENABLE_AUTO_IPD can be set to turn automatic population of the IPD on or off. If SQL_ATTR_AUTO_IPD is SQL_FALSE, SQL_ATTR_ENABLE_AUTO_IPD cannot be set to SQL_TRUE. The default value of SQL_ATTR_ENABLE_AUTO_IPD is equal to the value of SQL_ATTR_AUTO_IPD. This connection attribute can be returned by **SQLGetConnectAttr**, but cannot be set by **SQLSetConnectAttr**.

Attribute	***ValuePtr* contents**
SQL_ATTR_AUTOCOMMIT (ODBC 1.0)	An SQLUINTEGER value that specifies whether to use auto-commit or manual-commit mode: SQL_AUTOCOMMIT_OFF = The driver uses manual-commit mode, and the application must explicitly commit or roll back transactions with **SQLEndTran**. SQL_AUTOCOMMIT_ON = The driver uses auto-commit mode. Each statement is committed immediately after it is executed. This is the default. Any open transactions on the connection are committed when SQL_ATTR_AUTOCOMMIT is set to SQL_AUTOCOMMIT_ON to change from manual-commit mode to auto-commit mode. For more information, see "Commit Mode" in Chapter 14, "Transactions." **Important** Some data sources delete the access plans and close the cursors for all statements on a connection each time a statement is committed; autocommit mode can cause this to happen after each non-query statement is executed, or when the cursor is closed for a query. For more information, see the SQL_CURSOR_COMMIT_BEHAVIOR and SQL_CURSOR_ROLLBACK_BEHAVIOR information types in SQLGetInfo and "Effect of Transactions on Cursors and Prepared Statements" in Chapter 14, "Transactions." When a batch is executed in autocommit mode, two things are possible. The entire batch can be treated as an autocommitable unit, or each statement in a batch is treated as an autocommitable unit. Certain data sources may support both these behaviors and may provide a way of choosing one or the other. It is driver-defined whether a batch is treated as an autocommitable unit, or whether each individual statement within the batch is autocommitable.
SQL_ATTR_CONNECTION_TIMEOUT (ODBC 3.0)	An SQLUINTEGER value corresponding to the number of seconds to wait for any request on the connection to complete before returning to the application. The driver should return SQLSTATE HYT00 (Timeout expired) anytime that it is possible to timeout in a situation not associated with query execution or login. If *ValuePtr* is equal to 0 (the default), then there is no time out.
SQL_ATTR_CURRENT_CATALOG (ODBC 2.0)	A character string containing the name of the catalog to be used by the data source. For example, in SQL Server, the catalog is a database, so the driver sends a **USE** *database* statement to the data source, where *database* is the database specified in **ValuePtr*. For a single-tier driver, the catalog might be a directory, so the driver changes its current directory to the directory specified in **ValuePtr*.

Attribute	***ValuePtr* contents**
SQL_ATTR_LOGIN_TIMEOUT (ODBC 1.0)	An SQLUINTEGER value corresponding to the number of seconds to wait for a login request to complete before returning to the application. The default is driver-dependent. If *ValuePtr* is 0, the timeout is disabled and a connection attempt will wait indefinitely. If the specified timeout exceeds the maximum login timeout in the data source, the driver substitutes that value and returns SQLSTATE 01S02 (Option value changed).
SQL_ATTR_METADATA_ID (ODBC 3.0)	An SQLUINTEGER value that determines how the string arguments of catalog functions are treated. If SQL_TRUE, the string argument of catalog functions are treated as identifiers. The case is not significant. For non-delimited strings, the driver removes any trailing spaces, and the string is folded to uppercase. For delimited strings, the driver removes any leading or trailing spaces, and takes whatever is between the delimiters literally. If one of these arguments is set to a null pointer, the function returns SQL_ERROR and SQLSTATE HY009 (Invalid use of null pointer). If SQL_FALSE, the string arguments of catalog functions are not treated as identifiers. The case is significant. They can either contain a string search pattern or not, depending on the argument. The default value is SQL_FALSE. The *TableType* argument of **SQLTables**, which takes a list of values, is not affected by this attribute. SQL_ATTR_METADATA_ID can also be set on the statement level. (It is the only connection attribute that is also a statement attribute.) For more information, see "Arguments in Catalog Functions" in Chapter 7, "Catalog Functions."
SQL_ATTR_ODBC_CURSORS (ODBC 2.0)	An SQUINTEGER value specifying how the Driver Manager uses the ODBC cursor library: SQL_CUR_USE_IF_NEEDED = The Driver Manager uses the ODBC cursor library only if it is needed. If the driver supports the SQL_FETCH_PRIOR option in **SQLFetchScroll**, the Driver Manager uses the scrolling capabilities of the driver. Otherwise, it uses the ODBC cursor library. SQL_CUR_USE_ODBC = The Driver Manager uses the ODBC cursor library. SQL_CUR_USE_DRIVER = The Driver Manager uses the scrolling capabilities of the driver. This is the default setting. For more information about the ODBC cursor library, see Appendix F, "ODBC Cursor Library."

Attribute	***ValuePtr* contents**
SQL_ATTR_PACKET_SIZE (ODBC 2.0)	An SQLUINTEGER value specifying the network packet size in bytes. **Note** Many data sources either do not support this option or can only return the network packet size. If the specified size exceeds the maximum packet size or is smaller than the minimum packet size, the driver substitutes that value and returns SQLSTATE 01S02 (Option value changed). If the application sets packet size after a connection has already been made, the driver will return SQLSTATE HY011 (Attribute cannot be set now).
SQL_ATTR_QUIET_MODE (ODBC 2.0)	A 32-bit window handle (*hwnd*). If the window handle is a null pointer, the driver does not display any dialog boxes. If the window handle is not a null pointer, it should be the parent window handle of the application. This is the default. The driver uses this handle to display dialog boxes. **Note** The SQL_ATTR_QUIET_MODE connection attribute does not apply to dialog boxes displayed by **SQLDriverConnect**.

Attribute	***ValuePtr* contents**
SQL_ATTR_TRACE (ODBC 1.0)	An SQLUINTEGER value telling the Driver Manager whether to perform tracing: SQL_OPT_TRACE_OFF = Tracing off (the default) SQL_OPT_TRACE_ON = Tracing on When tracing is on, the Driver Manager writes each ODBC function call to the trace file. **Note** When tracing is on, the Driver Manager can return SQLSTATE IM013 (Trace file error) from any function. An application specifies a trace file with the SQL_ATTR_TRACEFILE option. If the file already exists, the Driver Manager appends to the file. Otherwise, it creates the file. If tracing is on and no trace file has been specified, the Driver Manager writes to the file SQL.LOG in the root directory. An application can set the variable **ODBCSharedTraceFlag** to enable tracing dynamically. Tracing is then enabled for all ODBC applications currently running. If an application turns tracing off, it is turned off only for that application. If the **Trace** keyword in the system information is set to 1 when an application calls **SQLAllocHandle** with a HandleType of SQL_HANDLE_ENV, tracing is enabled for all handles. It is enabled only for the application that called **SQLAllocHandle**. Calling **SQLSetConnectAttr** with an *Attribute* of SQL_ATTR_TRACE does not require that the *ConnectionHandle* argument be valid, and will not return SQL_ERROR if *ConnectionHandle* is NULL. This attribute applies to all connections.
SQL_ATTR_TRACEFILE (ODBC 1.0)	A null-terminated character string containing the name of the trace file. The default value of the SQL_ATTR_TRACEFILE attribute is specified with the **TraceFile** keyword in the system information. For more information, see "ODBC Subkey" in Chapter 19, "Configuring Data Sources." Calling **SQLSetConnectAttr** with an *Attribute* of SQL_ATTR_TRACEFILE does not require that the *ConnectionHandle* argument be valid, and will not return SQL_ERROR if *ConnectionHandle* is invalid. This attribute applies to all connections.

Attribute	***ValuePtr* contents**
SQL_ATTR_TRANSLATE_LIB (ODBC 1.0)	A null-terminated character string containing the name of a library containing the functions **SQLDriverToDataSource** and **SQLDataSourceToDriver** that the driver accesses to perform tasks such as character set translation. This option may be specified only if the driver has connected to the data source. The setting of this attribute will persist across connections. For more information about translating data, see "Translation DLLs" in Chapter 17, "Programming Considerations," and Chapter 24, "Translation DLL Function Reference."
SQL_ATTR_TRANSLATE_ OPTION (ODBC 1.0)	A 32-bit flag value that is passed to the translation DLL. This attribute can only be specified if the driver has connected to the data source. For information about translating data, see "Translation DLLs" in Chapter 17, "Programming Considerations."
SQL_ATTR_TXN_ISOLATION (ODBC 1.0)	A 32-bit bitmask that sets the transaction isolation level for the current connection. An application must call **SQLEndTran** to commit or roll back all open transactions on a connection, before calling **SQLSetConnectAttr** with this option. The valid values for *ValuePtr* can be determined by calling **SQLGetInfo** with *InfoType* equal to SQL_TXN_ISOLATION_OPTIONS. For a description of transaction isolation levels, see the description of the SQL_DEFAULT_TXN_ISOLATION *information type* in **SQLGetInfo** and "Transaction Isolation Levels" in Chapter 14, "Transactions."

Code Example

See **SQLConnect**.

Related Functions

For information about	See
Allocating a handle	**SQLAllocHandle**
Returning the setting of a connection attribute	**SQLGetConnectAttr**

SQLSetConnectOption

Conformance

Version Introduced: ODBC 1.0
Standards Compliance: Deprecated

Summary

In ODBC 3.0, the ODBC 2.0 function **SQLSetConnectOption** has been replaced by **SQLSetConnectAttr**. For more information, see **SQLSetConnectAttr**.

Note For more information about what the Driver Manager maps this function to when an ODBC 2.*x* application is working with an ODBC 3.0 driver, see "Mapping Deprecated Functions" in Appendix G, "Driver Guidelines for Backward Compatibility."

SQLSetCursorName

Conformance

Version Introduced: ODBC 1.0
Standards Compliance: ISO 92

Summary

SQLSetCursorName associates a cursor name with an active statement. If an application does not call **SQLSetCursorName**, the driver generates cursor names as needed for SQL statement processing.

Syntax

```
SQLRETURN SQLSetCursorName(
      SQLHSTMT      StatementHandle,
      SQLCHAR *     CursorName,
      SQLSMALLINT NameLength);
```

Arguments

StatementHandle [Input]
Statement handle.

CursorName [Input]
Cursor name. For efficient processing, the cursor name should not include any leading or trailing spaces in the cursor name, and if the cursor name includes a delimited identifier, the delimiter should be positioned as the first character in the cursor name.

NameLength [Input]
Length of **CursorName*.

Returns

SQL_SUCCESS, SQL_SUCCESS_WITH_INFO, SQL_ERROR, or SQL_INVALID_HANDLE.

Diagnostics

When **SQLSetCursorName** returns SQL_ERROR or SQL_SUCCESS_WITH_INFO, an associated SQLSTATE value can be obtained by calling **SQLGetDiagRec** with a *HandleType* of SQL_HANDLE_STMT and a *Handle* of *StatementHandle*. The following table lists the SQLSTATE values commonly returned by **SQLSetCursorName** and explains each one in the context of this function; the notation "(DM)" precedes the descriptions of SQLSTATEs returned by the Driver Manager. The return code associated with each SQLSTATE value is SQL_ERROR, unless noted otherwise.

SQLSTATE	Error	Description
01000	General warning	Driver-specific informational message. (Function returns SQL_SUCCESS_WITH_INFO.)
01004	String data, right truncated	The cursor name exceeded the maximum limit, so only the maximum allowable number of characters was used.
24000	Invalid cursor state	The statement corresponding to *StatementHandle* was already in an executed or cursor-positioned state.
34000	Invalid cursor name	The cursor name specified in **CursorName* was invalid, because it exceeded the maximum length as defined by the driver, or it started with "SQLCUR" or "SQL_CUR."
3C000	Duplicate cursor name	The cursor name specified in **CursorName* already exists.
HY000	General error	An error occurred for which there was no specific SQLSTATE and for which no implementation-specific SQLSTATE was defined. The error message returned by **SQLGetDiagRec** in the **MessageText* buffer describes the error and its cause.
HY001	Memory allocation error	The driver was unable to allocate memory required to support execution or completion of the function.
HY009	Invalid use of null pointer	(DM) The argument *CursorName* was a null pointer.
HY010	Function sequence error	(DM) An asynchronously executing function was called for the *StatementHandle* and was still executing when this function was called. (DM) **SQLExecute**, **SQLExecDirect**, **SQLBulkOperations**, or **SQLSetPos** was called for the *StatementHandle* and returned SQL_NEED_DATA. This function was called before data was sent for all data-at-execution parameters or columns.
HY013	Memory management error	The function call could not be processed because the underlying memory objects could not be accessed, possibly because of low memory conditions.

SQLSTATE	Error	Description
HY090	Invalid string or buffer length	(DM) The argument *NameLength* was less than 0, but not equal to SQL_NTS.
HYT01	Connection timeout expired	The connection timeout period expired before the data source responded to the request. The connection timeout period is set through **SQLSetConnectAttr**, SQL_ATTR_CONNECTION_TIMEOUT.
IM001	Driver does not support this function	(DM) The driver associated with the *StatementHandle* does not support the function.

Comments

Cursor names are used only in positioned update and delete statements (for example, **UPDATE** *table-name* ...**WHERE CURRENT OF** *cursor-name*). For more information, see "Positioned Update and Delete Statements" in Chapter 12, "Updating Data." If the application does not call **SQLSetCursorName** to define a cursor name, on execution of a query statement the driver generates a name that begins with the letters SQL_CUR and does not exceed 18 characters in length.

All cursor names within the connection must be unique. The maximum length of a cursor name is defined by the driver. For maximum interoperability, it is recommended that applications limit cursor names to no more than 18 characters. In ODBC 3.0, if a cursor name is a quoted identifier, it is treated in a case-sensitive manner, and it can contain characters that the syntax of SQL would not permit or would treat specially, such as blanks or reserved keywords. If a cursor name must be treated in a case-sensitive manner, it must be passed as a quoted identifier.

A cursor name that is set either explicitly or implicitly remains set until the statement with which it is associated is dropped, using **SQLFreeHandle**. **SQLSetCursorName** can be called to rename a cursor on a statement as long as the cursor is in an allocated or prepared state.

Code Example

In the following example, an application uses **SQLSetCursorName** to set a cursor name for a statement. It then uses that statement to retrieve results from the CUSTOMERS table. Finally, it performs a positioned update to change the phone number of John Smith. Note that the application uses different statement handles for the **SELECT** and **UPDATE** statements.

For another code example, see **SQLSetPos**.

```
#define NAME_LEN 50
#define PHONE_LEN 10

SQLHSTMT   hstmtSelect,
SQLHSTMT   hstmtUpdate;
SQLRETURN  retcode;
SQLHDBC    hdbc;
SQLCHAR    szName[NAME_LEN], szPhone[PHONE_LEN];
SQLINTEGER cbName, cbPhone;

/* Allocate the statements and set the cursor name. */

SQLAllocHandle(SQL_HANDLE_STMT, hdbc, &hstmtSelect);
SQLAllocHandle(SQL_HANDLE_STMT, hdbc, &hstmtUpdate);
SQLSetCursorName(hstmtSelect, "C1", SQL_NTS);

/* SELECT the result set and bind its columns to local buffers. */

SQLExecDirect(hstmtSelect,
              "SELECT NAME, PHONE FROM CUSTOMERS",
              SQL_NTS);
SQLBindCol(hstmtSelect, 1, SQL_C_CHAR, szName, NAME_LEN, &cbName);
SQLBindCol(hstmtSelect, 2, SQL_C_CHAR, szPhone, PHONE_LEN, &cbPhone);

/* Read through the result set until the cursor is      */
/* positioned on the row for the John Smith. */

do
   retcode = SQLFetch(hstmtSelect);
while ((retcode == SQL_SUCCESS || retcode == SQL_SUCCESS_WITH_INFO) &&
       (strcmp(szName, "Smith, John") != 0));

/* Perform a positioned update of John Smith's name. */

if (retcode == SQL_SUCCESS || retcode == SQL_SUCCESS_WITH_INFO) {
   SQLExecDirect(hstmtUpdate,
      "UPDATE EMPLOYEE SET PHONE=\"2064890154\" WHERE CURRENT OF C1",
      SQL_NTS);
}
```

Related Functions

For information about	See
Executing an SQL statement	**SQLExecDirect**
Executing a prepared SQL statement	**SQLExecute**
Returning a cursor name	**SQLGetCursorName**
Setting cursor scrolling options	**SQLSetScrollOptions**

SQLSetDescField

Conformance

Version Introduced: ODBC 3.0
Standards Compliance: ISO 92

Summary

SQLSetDescField sets the value of a single field of a descriptor record.

Syntax

```
SQLRETURN SQLSetDescField(
     SQLHDESC     DescriptorHandle,
     SQLSMALLINT  RecNumber,
     SQLSMALLINT  FieldIdentifier,
     SQLPOINTER   ValuePtr,
     SQLINTEGER   BufferLength);
```

Arguments

DescriptorHandle [Input]
Descriptor handle.

RecNumber [Input]
Indicates the descriptor record containing the field that the application seeks to set. Descriptor records are numbered from 0, with record number 0 being the bookmark record. The *RecNumber* argument is ignored for header fields.

FieldIdentifier [Input]
Indicates the field of the descriptor whose value is to be set. For more information, see "*FieldIdentifier* Argument" in the "Comments" section.

ValuePtr [Input]
Pointer to a buffer containing the descriptor information, or a 4-byte value. The data type depends on the value of *FieldIdentifier*. If *ValuePtr* is a 4-byte value, either all four of the bytes are used, or just two of the four are used, depending on the value of the *FieldIdentifier* argument.

BufferLength [Input]
If *FieldIdentifier* is an ODBC-defined field and *ValuePtr* points to a character string or a binary buffer, this argument should be the length of **ValuePtr*. If *FieldIdentifier* is an ODBC-defined field and *ValuePtr* is an integer, *BufferLength* is ignored.

If *FieldIdentifier* is a driver-defined field, the application indicates the nature of the field to the Driver Manager by setting the *BufferLength* argument. *BufferLength* can have the following values:

- If *ValuePtr* is a pointer to a character string, then *BufferLength* is the length of the string or SQL_NTS.
- If *ValuePtr* is a pointer to a binary buffer, then the application places the result of the SQL_LEN_BINARY_ATTR(*length*) macro in *BufferLength*. This places a negative value in *BufferLength*.
- If *ValuePtr* is a pointer to a value other than a character string or a binary string, then *BufferLength* should have the value SQL_IS_POINTER.
- If *ValuePtr* contains a fixed-length value, then *BufferLength* is either SQL_IS_INTEGER, SQL_IS_UINTEGER, SQL_IS_SMALLINT, or SQL_IS_USMALLINT, as appropriate.

Returns

SQL_SUCCESS, SQL_SUCCESS_WITH_INFO, SQL_ERROR, or SQL_INVALID_HANDLE.

Diagnostics

When **SQLSetDescField** returns SQL_ERROR or SQL_SUCCESS_WITH_INFO, an associated SQLSTATE value can be obtained by calling **SQLGetDiagRec** with a *HandleType* of SQL_HANDLE_DESC and a *Handle* of *DescriptorHandle*. The following table lists the SQLSTATE values commonly returned by **SQLSetDescField** and explains each one in the context of this function; the notation "(DM)" precedes the descriptions of SQLSTATEs returned by the Driver Manager. The return code associated with each SQLSTATE value is SQL_ERROR, unless noted otherwise.

SQLSTATE	Error	Description
01000	General warning	Driver-specific informational message. (Function returns SQL_SUCCESS_WITH_INFO.)
01S02	Option value changed	The driver did not support the value specified in **ValuePtr* (if *ValuePtr* was a pointer) or the value in *ValuePtr* (if *ValuePtr* was a 4-byte value), or **ValuePtr* was invalid because of implementation working conditions, so the driver substituted a similar value. (Function returns SQL_SUCCESS_WITH_INFO.)

SQLSTATE	Error	Description
07009	Invalid descriptor index	The *FieldIdentifier* argument was a record field, the *RecNumber* argument was 0, and the *DescriptorHandle* argument referred to an IPD handle. The *RecNumber* argument was less than 0, and the *DescriptorHandle* argument referred to an ARD or an APD. The *RecNumber* argument was greater than the maximum number of columns or parameters that the data source can support, and the *DescriptorHandle* argument referred to an APD or ARD. (DM) The *FieldIdentifier* argument was SQL_DESC_COUNT, and **ValuePtr* argument was less than 0. The *RecNumber* argument was equal to 0, and the *DescriptorHandle* argument referred to an implicitly allocated APD. (This error does not occur with an explicitly allocated application descriptor, because it is not known whether an explicitly allocated application descriptor is an APD or ARD until execute time.)
08S01	Communication link failure	The communication link between the driver and the data source to which the driver was connected failed before the function completed processing.
22001	String data, right truncated	The *FieldIdentifier* argument was SQL_DESC_NAME, and the *BufferLength* argument was a value larger than SQL_MAX_IDENTIFIER_LEN.
HY000	General error	An error occurred for which there was no specific SQLSTATE and for which no implementation-specific SQLSTATE was defined. The error message returned by **SQLGetDiagRec** in the **MessageText* buffer describes the error and its cause.
HY001	Memory allocation error	The driver was unable to allocate memory required to support execution or completion of the function.

SQLSTATE	Error	Description
HY010	Function sequence error	(DM) The *DescriptorHandle* was associated with a *StatementHandle* for which an asynchronously executing function (not this one) was called and was still executing when this function was called. (DM) **SQLExecute**, **SQLExecDirect**, **SQLBulkOperations**, or **SQLSetPos** was called for the *StatementHandle* with which the *DescriptorHandle* was associated and returned SQL_NEED_DATA. This function was called before data was sent for all data-at-execution parameters or columns.
HY013	Memory management error	The function call could not be processed because the underlying memory objects could not be accessed, possibly because of low memory conditions.
HY016	Cannot modify an implementation row descriptor	The *DescriptorHandle* argument was associated with an IRD, and the *FieldIdentifier* argument was not SQL_DESC_ARRAY_STATUS_PTR or SQL_DESC_ROWS_PROCESSED_PTR.
HY021	Inconsistent descriptor information	The SQL_DESC_TYPE and SQL_DESC_DATETIME_INTERVAL_CODE fields do not form a valid ODBC SQL type or a valid driver-specific SQL type (for IPDs) or a valid ODBC C type (for APDs or ARDs). Descriptor information checked during a consistency check was not consistent. (See "Consistency Check" in **SQLSetDescRec**.)
HY090	Invalid string or buffer length	(DM) **ValuePtr* is a character string, and BufferLength was less than zero, but was not equal to SQL_NTS. (DM) The driver was an ODBC 2.*x* driver, the descriptor was an ARD, the *ColumnNumber* argument was set to 0, and the value specified for the argument *BufferLength* was not equal to 4.
HY091	Invalid descriptor field identifier	The value specified for the *FieldIdentifier* argument was not an ODBC-defined field and was not an implementation-defined value. The *FieldIdentifier* argument was invalid for the *DescriptorHandle* argument. The *FieldIdentifier* argument was a read-only, ODBC-defined field.

SQLSTATE	Error	Description
HY092	Invalid attribute/option identifier	The value in **ValuePtr* was not valid for the *FieldIdentifier* argument. The *FieldIdentifier* argument was SQL_DESC_UNNAMED, and *ValuePtr* was SQL_NAMED.
HY105	Invalid parameter type	(DM) The value specified for the SQL_DESC_PARAMETER_TYPE field was invalid. (For more information, see the "*InputOutputType* Argument" section in **SQLBindParameter**.)
HYT01	Connection timeout expired	The connection timeout period expired before the data source responded to the request. The connection timeout period is set through **SQLSetConnectAttr**, SQL_ATTR_CONNECTION_TIMEOUT.
IM001	Driver does not support this function	(DM) The driver associated with the *DescriptorHandle* does not support the function.

Comments

An application can call **SQLSetDescField** to set any descriptor field one at a time. One call to **SQLSetDescField** sets a single field in a single descriptor. This function can be called to set any field in any descriptor type, provided the field can be set (see the table later in this section).

Note If a call to **SQLSetDescField** fails, the contents of the descriptor record identified by the *RecNumber* argument are undefined.

Other functions can be called to set multiple descriptor fields with a single call of the function. The **SQLSetDescRec** function sets a variety of fields that affect the data type and buffer bound to a column or parameter (the SQL_DESC_TYPE, SQL_DESC_DATETIME_INTERVAL_CODE, SQL_DESC_OCTET_LENGTH, SQL_DESC_PRECISION, SQL_DESC_SCALE, SQL_DESC_DATA_PTR, SQL_DESC_OCTET_LENGTH_PTR, and SQL_DESC_INDICATOR_PTR fields). **SQLBindCol** or **SQLBindParameter** can be used to make a complete specification for the binding of a column or parameter. These functions set a specific group of descriptor fields with one function call.

SQLSetDescField can be called to change the binding buffers by adding an offset to the binding pointers (SQL_DESC_DATA_PTR, SQL_DESC_INDICATOR_PTR, or SQL_DESC_OCTET_LENGTH_PTR). This changes the binding buffers without calling **SQLBindCol** or **SQLBindParameter**, which allows an application to change SQL_DESC_DATA_PTR without changing other fields, such as SQL_DESC_DATA_TYPE.

If an application calls **SQLSetDescField** to set any field other than SQL_DESC_COUNT or the deferred fields SQL_DESC_DATA_PTR, SQL_DESC_OCTET_LENGTH_PTR, or SQL_DESC_INDICATOR_PTR, the record becomes unbound.

Descriptor header fields are set by calling **SQLSetDescField** with the appropriate *FieldIdentifier*. Many header fields are also statement attributes, so can also be set by a call to **SQLSetStmtAttr**. This allows applications to set a descriptor field without first obtaining a descriptor handle. When **SQLSetDescField** is called to set a header field, the *RecNumber* argument is ignored.

A *RecNumber* of 0 is used to set bookmark fields.

Note The statement attribute SQL_ATTR_USE_BOOKMARKS should always be set before calling **SQLSetDescField** to set bookmark fields. While this is not mandatory, it is strongly recommended.

Sequence of Setting Descriptor Fields

When setting descriptor fields by calling **SQLSetDescField**, the application must follow a specific sequence:

1. The application must first set the SQL_DESC_TYPE, SQL_DESC_CONCISE_TYPE, or SQL_DESC_DATETIME_INTERVAL_CODE field.
2. After one of these fields has been set, the application can set an attribute of a data type, and the driver sets data type attribute fields to the appropriate default values for the data type. Automatic defaulting of type attribute fields ensures that the descriptor is always ready to use once the application has specified a data type. If the application explicitly sets a data type attribute, it is overriding the default attribute.
3. After one of the fields listed in Step 1 has been set, and data type attributes have been set, the application can set SQL_DESC_DATA_PTR. This prompts a consistency check of descriptor fields. If the application changes the data type or attributes after setting the SQL_DESC_DATA_PTR field, then the driver sets SQL_DESC_DATA_PTR to a null pointer, unbinding the record. This forces the application to complete the proper steps in sequence, before the descriptor record is usable.

Initialization of Descriptor Fields

When a descriptor is allocated, the fields in the descriptor can be initialized to a default value, be initialized without a default value, or be undefined for the type of descriptor. The following tables indicate the initialization of each field for each type of descriptor, with "D" indicating that the field is initialized with a default, and "ND" indicating that the field is initialized without a default. If a number is shown, the default value of the field is that number. The tables also indicate whether a field is read/write (R/W) or read-only (R).

The fields of an IRD have a default value only after the statement has been prepared or executed and the IRD has been populated, not when the statement handle or descriptor has been allocated. Until the IRD has been populated, any attempt to gain access to a field of an IRD will return an error.

Some descriptor fields are defined for one or more, but not all, of the descriptor types (ARDs and IRDs, and APDs and IPDs). When a field is undefined for a type of descriptor, it is not needed by any of the functions that use that descriptor.

The fields that can be accessed by **SQLGetDescField** cannot necessarily be set by **SQLSetDescField**. Fields that can be set by **SQLSetDescField** are listed in the following tables.

The initialization of header fields is as follows:

Header field name	Type	R/W	Default
SQL_DESC_ALLOC_ TYPE	SQLSMALLINT	ARD: R APD: R IRD: R IPD: R	ARD: SQL_DESC_ ALLOC_AUTO for implicit or SQL_DESC_ ALLOC_USER for explicit APD: SQL_DESC_ ALLOC_AUTO for implicit or SQL_DESC_ ALLOC_USER for explicit IRD: SQL_DESC_ ALLOC_AUTO IPD: SQL_DESC_ ALLOC_AUTO
SQL_DESC_ARRAY_ SIZE	SQLUINTEGER	ARD: R/W APD: R/W IRD: Unused IPD: Unused	ARD: [1] APD: [1] IRD: Unused IPD: Unused
SQL_DESC_ARRAY_ STATUS_PTR	SQLUSMALLINT*	ARD: R/W APD: R/W IRD: R/W IPD: R/W	ARD: Null ptr APD: Null ptr IRD: Null ptr IPD: Null ptr
SQL_DESC_BIND_ OFFSET_PTR	SQLINTEGER*	ARD: R/W APD: R/W IRD: Unused IPD: Unused	ARD: Null ptr APD: Null ptr IRD: Unused IPD: Unused
SQL_DESC_BIND_ TYPE	SQLINTEGER	ARD: R/W APD: R/W IRD: Unused IPD: Unused	ARD: SQL_BIND_BY_ COLUMN APD: SQL_BIND_BY_ COLUMN IRD: Unused IPD: Unused

Header field name	Type	R/W	Default
SQL_DESC_COUNT	SQLSMALLINT	ARD: R/W APD: R/W IRD: R IPD: R/W	ARD: 0 APD: 0 IRD: D IPD: 0
SQL_DESC_ROWS_ PROCESSED_PTR	SQLUINTEGER*	ARD: Unused APD: Unused IRD: R/W IPD: R/W	ARD: Unused APD: Unused IRD: Null ptr IPD: Null ptr

1 These fields are defined only when the IPD is automatically populated by the driver. If not, they are undefined. If an application attempts to set these fields, SQLSTATE HY091 (Invalid descriptor field identifier) will be returned.

The initialization of record fields is as follows:

Record field name	Type	R/W	Default
SQL_DESC_ AUTO_UNIQUE_ VALUE	SQLINTEGER	ARD: Unused APD: Unused IRD: R IPD: Unused	ARD: Unused APD: Unused IRD: D IPD: Unused
SQL_DESC_ BASE_COLUMN_ NAME	SQLCHAR *	ARD: Unused APD: Unused IRD: R IPD: Unused	ARD: Unused APD: Unused IRD: D IPD: Unused
SQL_DESC_ BASE_TABLE_ NAME	SQLCHAR *	ARD: Unused APD: Unused IRD: R IPD: Unused	ARD: Unused APD: Unused IRD: D IPD: Unused
SQL_DESC_ CASE_ SENSITIVE	SQLINTEGER	ARD: Unused APD: Unused IRD: R IPD: R	ARD: Unused APD: Unused IRD: D IPD: D [1]
SQL_DESC_CATALOG_ NAME	SQLCHAR *	ARD: Unused APD: Unused IRD: R IPD: Unused	ARD: Unused APD: Unused IRD: D IPD: Unused
SQL_DESC_CONCISE_ TYPE	SQLSMALLINT	ARD: R/W APD: R/W IRD: R IPD: R/W	ARD: SQL_C_ DEFAULT APD: SQL_C_ DEFAULT IRD: D IPD: ND

Record field name	Type	R/W	Default
SQL_DESC_DATA_PTR	SQLPOINTER	ARD: R/W APD: R/W IRD: Unused IPD: Unused	ARD: Null ptr APD: Null ptr IRD: Unused IPD: Unused [2]
SQL_DESC_ DATETIME_ INTERVAL_CODE	SQLSMALLINT	ARD: R/W APD: R/W IRD: R IPD: R/W	ARD: ND APD: ND IRD: D IPD: ND
SQL_DESC_ DATETIME_ INTERVAL_PRECISION	SQLINTEGER	ARD: R/W APD: R/W IRD: R IPD: R/W	ARD: ND APD: ND IRD: D IPD: ND
SQL_DESC_DISPLAY_ SIZE	SQLINTEGER	ARD: Unused APD: Unused IRD: R IPD: Unused	ARD: Unused APD: Unused IRD: D IPD: Unused
SQL_DESC_FIXED_ PREC_SCALE	SQLSMALLINT	ARD: Unused APD: Unused IRD: R IPD: R	ARD: Unused APD: Unused IRD: D IPD: D [1]
SQL_DESC_ INDICATOR_PTR	SQLINTEGER *	ARD: R/W APD: R/W IRD: Unused IPD: Unused	ARD: Null ptr APD: Null ptr IRD: Unused IPD: Unused
SQL_DESC_LABEL	SQLCHAR *	ARD: Unused APD: Unused IRD: R IPD: Unused	ARD: Unused APD: Unused IRD: D IPD: Unused
SQL_DESC_LENGTH	SQLUINTEGER	ARD: R/W APD: R/W IRD: R IPD: R/W	ARD: ND APD: ND IRD: D IPD: ND
SQL_DESC_LITERAL_ PREFIX	SQLCHAR *	ARD: Unused APD: Unused IRD: R IPD: Unused	ARD: Unused APD: Unused IRD: D IPD: Unused
SQL_DESC_LITERAL_ SUFFIX	SQLCHAR *	ARD: Unused APD: Unused IRD: R IPD: Unused	ARD: Unused APD: Unused IRD: D IPD: Unused
SQL_DESC_LOCAL_ TYPE_NAME	SQLCHAR *	ARD: Unused APD: Unused IRD: R IPD: R	ARD: Unused APD: Unused IRD: D IPD: D [1]

Record field name	Type	R/W	Default
SQL_DESC_NAME	SQLCHAR *	ARD: Unused APD: Unused IRD: R IPD: R/W	ARD: ND APD: ND IRD: D IPD: ND
SQL_DESC_NULLABLE	SQLSMALLINT	ARD: Unused APD: Unused IRD: R IPD: R	ARD: ND APD: ND IRD: D IPD: ND
SQL_DESC_NUM_ PREC_RADIX	SQLINTEGER	ARD: R/W APD: R/W IRD: R IPD: R/W	ARD: ND APD: ND IRD: D IPD: ND
SQL_DESC_OCTET_ LENGTH	SQLINTEGER	ARD: R/W APD: R/W IRD: R IPD: R/W	ARD: ND APD: ND IRD: D IPD: ND
SQL_DESC_OCTET_ LENGTH_PTR	SQLINTEGER *	ARD: R/W APD: R/W IRD: Unused IPD: Unused	ARD: Null ptr APD: Null ptr IRD: Unused IPD: Unused
SQL_DESC_ PARAMETER_TYPE	SQLSMALLINT	ARD: Unused APD: Unused IRD: Unused IPD: R/W	ARD: Unused APD: Unused IRD: Unused IPD: D=SQL_PARAM_INPUT
SQL_DESC_PRECISION	SQLSMALLINT	ARD: R/W APD: R/W IRD: R IPD: R/W	ARD: ND APD: ND IRD: D IPD: ND
SQL_DESC_SCALE	SQLSMALLINT	ARD: R/W APD: R/W IRD: R IPD: R/W	ARD: ND APD: ND IRD: D IPD: ND
SQL_DESC_SCHEMA_ NAME	SQLCHAR *	ARD: Unused APD: Unused IRD: R IPD: Unused	ARD: Unused APD: Unused IRD: D IPD: Unused
SQL_DESC_ SEARCHABLE	SQLSMALLINT	ARD: Unused APD: Unused IRD: R IPD: Unused	ARD: Unused APD: Unused IRD: D IPD: Unused
SQL_DESC_TABLE_ NAME	SQLCHAR *	ARD: Unused APD: Unused IRD: R IPD: Unused	ARD: Unused APD: Unused IRD: D IPD: Unused

Record field name	Type	R/W	Default
SQL_DESC_TYPE	SQLSMALLINT	ARD: R/W APD: R/W IRD: R IPD: R/W	ARD: SQL_C_DEFAULT APD: SQL_C_DEFAULT IRD: D IPD: ND
SQL_DESC_TYPE_ NAME	SQLCHAR *	ARD: Unused APD: Unused IRD: R IPD: R	ARD: Unused APD: Unused IRD: D IPD: D [1]
SQL_DESC_UNNAMED	SQLSMALLINT	ARD: Unused APD: Unused IRD: R IPD: R/W	ARD: ND APD: ND IRD: D IPD: ND
SQL_DESC_UNSIGNED	SQLSMALLINT	ARD: Unused APD: Unused IRD: R IPD: R	ARD: Unused APD: Unused IRD: D IPD: D [1]
SQL_DESC_ UPDATABLE	SQLSMALLINT	ARD: Unused APD: Unused IRD: R IPD: Unused	ARD: Unused APD: Unused IRD: D IPD: Unused

1 These fields are defined only when the IPD is automatically populated by the driver. If not, they are undefined. If an application attempts to set these fields, SQLSTATE HY091 (Invalid descriptor field identifier) will be returned.

2 The SQL_DESC_DATA_PTR field in the IPD can be set to force a consistency check. In a subsequent call to **SQLGetDescField** or **SQLGetDescRec**, the driver is not required to return the value that SQL_DESC_DATA_PTR was set to.

FieldIdentifier Argument

The *FieldIdentifier* argument indicates the descriptor field to be set. A descriptor contains the *descriptor header*, consisting of the header fields described in the next section, "Header Fields," and zero or more *descriptor records*, consisting of the record fields described in the section following the "Header Fields" section.

Header Fields

Each descriptor has a header consisting of the following fields.

SQL_DESC_ALLOC_TYPE [All]

This read-only SQLSMALLINT header field specifies whether the descriptor was allocated automatically by the driver or explicitly by the application. The application can obtain, but not modify, this field. The field is set to SQL_DESC_ALLOC_AUTO by the driver if the descriptor was automatically allocated by the driver. It is set to SQL_DESC_ALLOC_USER by the driver if the descriptor was explicitly allocated by the application.

SQL_DESC_ARRAY_SIZE [Application descriptors]

In ARDs, this SQLUINTEGER header field specifies the number of rows in the rowset. This is the number of rows to be returned by a call to **SQLFetch** or **SQLFetchScroll**, or operated on by a call to **SQLBulkOperations** or **SQLSetPos**.

In APDs, this SQLUINTEGER header field specifies the number of values for each parameter.

The default value of this field is 1. If SQL_DESC_ARRAY_SIZE is greater than 1, SQL_DESC_DATA_PTR, SQL_DESC_INDICATOR_PTR, and SQL_DESC_OCTET_LENGTH_PTR of the APD or ARD point to arrays. The cardinality of each array is equal to the value of this field.

This field in the ARD can also be set by calling **SQLSetStmtAttr** with the SQL_ATTR_ROW_ARRAY_SIZE attribute. This field in the APD can also be set by calling **SQLSetStmtAttr** with the SQL_ATTR_PARAMSET_SIZE attribute.

SQL_DESC_ARRAY_STATUS_PTR [All]

For each descriptor type, this SQLUSMALLINT * header field points to an array of SQLUSMALLINT values. These arrays are named as follows: row status array (IRD), parameter status array (IPD), row operation array (ARD), and parameter operation array (APD).

In the IRD, this header field points to a row status array containing status values after a call to **SQLBulkOperations**, **SQLFetch**, **SQLFetchScroll**, or **SQLSetPos**. The array has as many elements as there are rows in the rowset. The application must allocate an array of SQLUSMALLINTs and set this field to point to the array. The field is set to a null pointer by default. The driver will populate the array, unless the SQL_DESC_ARRAY_STATUS_PTR field is set to a null pointer, in which case no status values are generated and the array is not populated.

Caution Driver behavior is undefined if the application sets the elements of the row status array pointed to by the SQL_DESC_ARRAY_STATUS_PTR field of the IRD.

The array is initially populated by a call to **SQLBulkOperations**, **SQLFetch**, **SQLFetchScroll**, or **SQLSetPos**. If the call did not return SQL_SUCCESS or SQL_SUCCESS_WITH_INFO, the contents of the array pointed to by this field are undefined. The elements in the array can contain the following values:

- SQL_ROW_SUCCESS: The row was successfully fetched and has not changed since it was last fetched.
- SQL_ROW_SUCCESS_WITH_INFO: The row was successfully fetched and has not changed since it was last fetched. However, a warning was returned about the row.
- SQL_ROW_ERROR: An error occurred while fetching the row.
- SQL_ROW_UPDATED: The row was successfully fetched and has been updated since it was last fetched. If the row is fetched again, its status is SQL_ROW_SUCCESS.

- SQL_ROW_DELETED: The row has been deleted since it was last fetched.
- SQL_ROW_ADDED: The row was inserted by **SQLBulkOperations**. If the row is fetched again, its status is SQL_ROW_SUCCESS.
- SQL_ROW_NOROW: The rowset overlapped the end of the result set and no row was returned that corresponded to this element of the row status array.

This field in the IRD can also be set by calling **SQLSetStmtAttr** with the SQL_ATTR_ROW_STATUS_PTR attribute.

In the IPD, this header field points to a parameter status array containing status information for each set of parameter values after a call to **SQLExecute** or **SQLExecDirect**. If the call to **SQLExecute** or **SQLExecDirect** did not return SQL_SUCCESS or SQL_SUCCESS_WITH_INFO, the contents of the array pointed to by this field are undefined. The application must allocate an array of SQLUSMALLINTs and set this field to point to the array. The driver will populate the array, unless the SQL_DESC_ARRAY_STATUS_PTR field is set to a null pointer, in which case no status values are generated and the array is not populated. The elements in the array can contain the following values:

- SQL_PARAM_SUCCESS: The SQL statement was successfully executed for this set of parameters.
- SQL_PARAM_SUCCESS_WITH_INFO: The SQL statement was successfully executed for this set of parameters; however, warning information is available in the diagnostics data structure.
- SQL_PARAM_ERROR: An error occurred in processing this set of parameters. Additional error information is available in the diagnostics data structure.
- SQL_PARAM_UNUSED: This parameter set was unused, possibly due to the fact that some previous parameter set caused an error that aborted further processing, or because SQL_PARAM_IGNORE was set for that set of parameters in the array specified by the SQL_DESC_ARRAY_STATUS_PTR field of the APD.
- SQL_PARAM_DIAG_UNAVAILABLE: Diagnostic information is not available. An example of this is when the driver treats arrays of parameters as a monolithic unit and so does not generate this level of error information.

This field in the IPD can also be set by calling **SQLSetStmtAttr** with the SQL_ATTR_PARAM_STATUS_PTR attribute.

In the ARD, this header field points to a row operation array of values that can be set by the application to indicate whether this row is to be ignored for **SQLSetPos** operations. The elements in the array can contain the following values:

- SQL_ROW_PROCEED: The row is included in the bulk operation using **SQLSetPos**. (This setting does not guarantee that the operation will occur on the row. If the row has the status SQL_ROW_ERROR in the IRD row status array, the driver may not be able to perform the operation in the row.)
- SQL_ROW_IGNORE: The row is excluded from the bulk operation using **SQLSetPos**.

If no elements of the array are set, all rows are included in the bulk operation. If the value in the SQL_DESC_ARRAY_STATUS_PTR field of the ARD is a null pointer, all rows are included in the bulk operation; the interpretation is the same as if the pointer pointed to a valid array and all elements of the array were SQL_ROW_PROCEED. If an element in the array is set to SQL_ROW_IGNORE, the value in the row status array for the ignored row is not changed.

This field in the ARD can also be set by calling **SQLSetStmtAttr** with the SQL_ATTR_ROW_OPERATION_PTR attribute.

In the APD, this header field points to a parameter operation array of values that can be set by the application to indicate whether this set of parameters is to be ignored when **SQLExecute** or **SQLExecDirect** is called. The elements in the array can contain the following values:

- SQL_PARAM_PROCEED: The set of parameters is included in the **SQLExecute** or **SQLExecDirect** call.
- SQL_PARAM_IGNORE: The set of parameters is excluded from the **SQLExecute** or **SQLExecDirect** call.

If no elements of the array are set, all sets of parameters in the array are used in the **SQLExecute** or **SQLExecDirect** calls. If the value in the SQL_DESC_ARRAY_STATUS_PTR field of the APD is a null pointer, all sets of parameters are used; the interpretation is the same as if the pointer pointed to a valid array and all elements of the array were SQL_PARAM_PROCEED.

This field in the APD can also be set by calling **SQLSetStmtAttr** with the SQL_ATTR_PARAM_OPERATION_PTR attribute.

SQL_DESC_BIND_OFFSET_PTR [Application descriptors]

This SQLINTEGER * header field points to the binding offset. It is set to a null pointer by default. If this field is not a null pointer, the driver dereferences the pointer and adds the dereferenced value to each of the deferred fields that has a non-null value in the descriptor record (SQL_DESC_DATA_PTR, SQL_DESC_INDICATOR_PTR, and SQL_DESC_OCTET_LENGTH_PTR) at fetch time, and uses the new pointer values when binding.

The binding offset is always added directly to the values in the SQL_DESC_DATA_PTR, SQL_DESC_INDICATOR_PTR, and SQL_DESC_OCTET_LENGTH_PTR fields. If the offset is changed to a different value, the new value is still added directly to the value in each descriptor field. The new offset is not added to the field value plus any earlier offset.

This field is a *deferred field*: It is not used at the time it is set, but is used at a later time by the driver when it needs to determine addresses for data buffers.

This field in the ARD can also be set by calling **SQLSetStmtAttr** with the SQL_ATTR_ROW_BIND_OFFSET_PTR attribute. This field in the ARD can also be set by calling **SQLSetStmtAttr** with the SQL_ATTR_PARAM_BIND_OFFSET_PTR attribute.

For more information, see the description of row-wise binding in **SQLFetchScroll** and **SQLBindParameter**.

SQL_DESC_BIND_TYPE [Application descriptors]

This SQLUINTEGER header field sets the binding orientation to be used for binding either columns or parameters.

In ARDs, this field specifies the binding orientation when **SQLFetchScroll** or **SQLFetch** is called on the associated statement handle.

To select column-wise binding for columns, this field is set to SQL_BIND_BY_COLUMN (the default).

This field in the ARD can also be set by calling **SQLSetStmtAttr** with the SQL_ATTR_ROW_BIND_TYPE *Attribute*.

In APDs, this field specifies the binding orientation to be used for dynamic parameters.

To select column-wise binding for parameters, this field is set to SQL_BIND_BY_COLUMN (the default).

This field in the APD can also be set by calling **SQLSetStmtAttr** with the SQL_ATTR_PARAM_BIND_TYPE *Attribute*.

SQL_DESC_COUNT [All]

This SQLSMALLINT header field specifies the 1-based index of the highest-numbered record that contains data. When the driver sets the data structure for the descriptor, it must also set the SQL_DESC_COUNT field to show how many records are significant. When an application allocates an instance of this data structure, it does not have to specify how many records to reserve room for. As the application specifies the contents of the records, the driver takes any required action to ensure that the descriptor handle refers to a data structure of the adequate size.

SQL_DESC_COUNT is not a count of all data columns that are bound (if the field is in an ARD), or all parameters that are bound (if the field is in an APD), but the number of the highest-numbered record. If the highest-numbered column or parameter is unbound, then SQL_DESC_COUNT is changed to the number of the next highest-numbered column or parameter. If a column or a parameter with a number that is less than the number of the highest-numbered column is unbound (by calling **SQLBindCol** with the *TargetValuePtr* argument set to a null pointer, or **SQLBindParameter** with the *ParameterValuePtr* argument set to a null pointer), SQL_DESC_COUNT is not changed. If additional columns or parameters are bound with numbers greater than the highest-numbered record that contains data, the driver automatically increases the value in the SQL_DESC_COUNT field. If all columns are unbound by calling **SQLFreeStmt** with the SQL_UNBIND option, the SQL_DESC_COUNT fields in the ARD and IRD are set to 0. If **SQLFreeStmt** is called with the SQL_RESET_PARAMS option, the SQL_DESC_COUNT fields in the APD and IPD are set to 0.

The value in SQL_DESC_COUNT can be set explicitly by an application by calling **SQLSetDescField**. If the value in SQL_DESC_COUNT is explicitly decreased, all records with numbers greater than the new value in SQL_DESC_COUNT are effectively removed. If the value in SQL_DESC_COUNT is explicitly set to 0, and the field is in an ARD, all data buffers except a bound bookmark column are released.

The record count in this field of an ARD does not include a bound bookmark column. The only way to unbind a bookmark column is to set the SQL_DESC_DATA_PTR field to a null pointer.

SQL_DESC_ROWS_PROCESSED_PTR [Implementation descriptors]

In an IRD, this SQLUINTEGER * header field points to a buffer containing the number of rows fetched after a call to **SQLFetch** or **SQLFetchScroll**, or the number of rows affected in a bulk operation performed by a call to **SQLBulkOperations** or **SQLSetPos**, including error rows.

In an IPD, this SQLUINTEGER * header field points to a buffer containing the number of sets of parameters that have been processed, including error sets. No number will be returned if this is a null pointer.

SQL_DESC_ROWS_PROCESSED_PTR is valid only after SQL_SUCCESS or SQL_SUCCESS_WITH_INFO has been returned after a call to **SQLFetch** or **SQLFetchScroll** (for an IRD field) or **SQLExecute**, **SQLExecDirect**, or **SQLParamData** (for an IPD field). If the call that fills in the buffer pointed to by this field does not return SQL_SUCCESS or SQL_SUCCESS_WITH_INFO, the contents of the buffer are undefined, unless it returns SQL_NO_DATA, in which case the value in the buffer is set to 0.

This field in the ARD can also be set by calling **SQLSetStmtAttr** with the SQL_ATTR_ROWS_FETCHED_PTR attribute. This field in the APD can also be set by calling **SQLSetStmtAttr** with the SQL_ATTR_PARAMS_PROCESSED_PTR attribute.

The buffer pointed to by this field is allocated by the application. It is a deferred output buffer that is set by the driver. It is set to a null pointer by default.

Record Fields

Each descriptor contains one or more records consisting of fields that define either column data or dynamic parameters, depending on the type of descriptor. Each record is a complete definition of a single column or parameter.

SQL_DESC_AUTO_UNIQUE_VALUE [IRDs]

This read-only SQLINTEGER record field contains SQL_TRUE if the column is an auto-incrementing column, or SQL_FALSE if the column is not an auto-incrementing column. This field is read-only, but the underlying auto-incrementing column is not necessarily read-only.

SQL_DESC_BASE_COLUMN_NAME [IRDs]

This read-only SQLCHAR * record field contains the base column name for the result set column. If a base column name does not exist (as in the case of columns that are expressions), then this variable contains an empty string.

SQL_DESC_BASE_TABLE_NAME [IRDs]

This read-only SQLCHAR * record field contains the base table name for the result set column. If a base table name cannot be defined or is not applicable, then this variable contains an empty string.

SQL_DESC_CASE_SENSITIVE [Implementation descriptors]

This read-only SQLINTEGER record field contains SQL_TRUE if the column or parameter is treated as case-sensitive for collations and comparisons, or SQL_FALSE if the column is not treated as case-sensitive for collations and comparisons, or if it is a non-character column.

SQL_DESC_CATALOG_NAME [IRDs]

This read-only SQLCHAR * record field contains the catalog for the base table that contains the column. The return value is driver-dependent if the column is an expression or if the column is part of a view. If the data source does not support catalogs or the catalog cannot be determined, this variable contains an empty string.

SQL_DESC_CONCISE_TYPE [All]

This SQLSMALLINT header field specifies the concise data type for all data types, including the datetime and interval data types.

The values in the SQL_DESC_CONCISE_TYPE, SQL_DESC_TYPE, and SQL_DESC_DATETIME_INTERVAL_CODE fields are interdependent. Each time one of the fields is set, the other must also be set. SQL_DESC_CONCISE_TYPE can be set by a call to **SQLBindCol** or **SQLBindParameter**, or **SQLSetDescField**. SQL_DESC_TYPE can be set by a call to **SQLSetDescField** or **SQLSetDescRec**.

If SQL_DESC_CONCISE_TYPE is set to a concise data type other than an interval or datetime data type, the SQL_DESC_TYPE field is set to the same value, and the SQL_DESC_DATETIME_INTERVAL_CODE field is set to 0.

If SQL_DESC_CONCISE_TYPE is set to the concise datetime or interval data type, the SQL_DESC_TYPE field is set to the corresponding verbose type (SQL_DATETIME or SQL_INTERVAL), and the SQL_DESC_DATETIME_INTERVAL_CODE field is set to the appropriate subcode.

SQL_DESC_DATA_PTR [Application descriptors and IPDs]

This SQLPOINTER record field points to a variable that will contain the parameter value (for APDs) or the column value (for ARDs). This field is a *deferred field*: It is not used at the time it is set, but is used at a later time by the driver to retrieve data.

The column specified by the SQL_DESC_DATA_PTR field of the ARD is unbound if the *TargetValuePtr* argument in a call to **SQLBindCol** is a null pointer, or the SQL_DESC_DATA_PTR field in the ARD is set by a call to **SQLSetDescField** or **SQLSetDescRec** to a null pointer. Other fields are not affected if the SQL_DESC_DATA_PTR field is set to a null pointer.

If the call to **SQLFetch** or **SQLFetchScroll** that fills in the buffer pointed to by this field did not return SQL_SUCCESS or SQL_SUCCESS_WITH_INFO, the contents of the buffer are undefined.

Whenever the SQL_DESC_DATA_PTR field of an APD, ARD, or IPD is set, the driver checks that the value in the SQL_DESC_TYPE field contains one of the valid ODBC C data types or a driver-specific data type, and that all other fields affecting the data types are consistent. Prompting a consistency check is the only use of the SQL_DESC_DATA_PTR field of an IPD. Specifically, if an application sets the SQL_DESC_DATA_PTR field of an IPD and later calls **SQLGetDescField** on this field, it is not necessarily returned the value that it had set. For more information, see "Consistency Checks" in **SQLSetDescRec**.

SQL_DESC_DATETIME_INTERVAL_CODE [All]

This SQLSMALLINT record field contains the subcode for the specific datetime or interval data type when the SQL_DESC_TYPE field is SQL_DATETIME or SQL_INTERVAL. This is true for both SQL and C data types. The code consists of the data type name with "CODE" substituted for either "TYPE" or "C_TYPE" (for datetime types), or "CODE" substituted for "INTERVAL" or "C_INTERVAL" (for interval types).

If SQL_DESC_TYPE and SQL_DESC_CONCISE_TYPE in an application descriptor are set to SQL_C_DEFAULT and the descriptor is not associated with a statement handle, the contents of SQL_DESC_DATETIME_INTERVAL_CODE are undefined.

This field can be set to the following for datetime data types:

Datetime types	DATETIME_INTERVAL_CODE
SQL_TYPE_DATE/ SQL_C_TYPE_DATE	SQL_CODE_DATE
SQL_TYPE_TIME/ SQL_C_TYPE_TIME	SQL_CODE_TIME
SQL_TYPE_TIMESTAMP/ SQL_C_TYPE_TIMESTAMP	SQL_CODE_TIMESTAMP

This field can be set to the following for interval data types:

Interval type	DATETIME_INTERVAL_CODE
SQL_INTERVAL_DAY/ SQL_C_INTERVAL_DAY	SQL_CODE_DAY
SQL_INTERVAL_DAY_TO_HOUR/ SQL_C_INTERVAL_DAY_ TO_HOUR	SQL_CODE_DAY_TO_HOUR
SQL_INTERVAL_DAY_ TO_MINUTE/ SQL_C_INTERVAL_DAY_TO_ MINUTE	SQL_CODE_DAY_TO_MINUTE
SQL_INTERVAL_DAY_ TO_SECOND/ SQL_C_INTERVAL_DAY_TO_ SECOND	SQL_CODE_DAY_TO_SECOND
SQL_INTERVAL_HOUR/ SQL_C_INTERVAL_HOUR	SQL_CODE_HOUR
SQL_INTERVAL_HOUR_TO_ MINUTE/ SQL_C_INTERVAL_HOUR_TO_ MINUTE	SQL_CODE_HOUR_TO_MINUTE
SQL_INTERVAL_ HOUR_TO_SECOND/ SQL_C_INTERVAL_HOUR_TO_ SECOND	SQL_CODE_HOUR_TO_SECOND
SQL_INTERVAL_MINUTE/ SQL_C_INTERVAL_MINUTE	SQL_CODE_MINUTE
SQL_INTERVAL_MINUTE_TO_ SECOND/ SQL_C_INTERVAL_MINUTE_TO_ SECOND	SQL_CODE_MINUTE_TO_SECOND

Interval type	DATETIME_INTERVAL_CODE
SQL_INTERVAL_MONTH/ SQL_C_INTERVAL_MONTH	SQL_CODE_MONTH
SQL_INTERVAL_SECOND/ SQL_C_INTERVAL_SECOND	SQL_CODE_SECOND
SQL_INTERVAL_YEAR/ SQL_C_INTERVAL_YEAR	SQL_CODE_YEAR
SQL_INTERVAL_ YEAR_TO_MONTH/ SQL_C_INTERVAL_YEAR_TO_ MONTH	SQL_CODE_YEAR_TO_MONTH

For more information about the data intervals and this field, see "Data Type Identifiers and Descriptors" in Appendix D, "Data Types."

SQL_DESC_DATETIME_INTERVAL_PRECISION [All]
This SQLINTEGER record field contains the interval leading precision if the SQL_DESC_TYPE field is SQL_INTERVAL. When the SQL_DESC_DATETIME_INTERVAL_CODE field is set to an interval data type, this field is set to the default interval leading precision.

SQL_DESC_DISPLAY_SIZE [IRDs]
This read-only SQLINTEGER record field contains the maximum number of characters required to display the data from the column. The value in this field is not the same as the descriptor field SQL_DESC_LENGTH because the SQL_DESC_LENGTH field is undefined for all numeric types.

SQL_DESC_FIXED_PREC_SCALE [Implementation descriptors]
This read-only SQLSMALLINT record field is set to SQL_TRUE if the column is an exact numeric column and has a fixed precision and non-zero scale, or SQL_FALSE if the column is not an exact numeric column with a fixed precision and scale.

SQL_DESC_INDICATOR_PTR [Application descriptors]
In ARDs, this SQLINTEGER * record field points to the indicator variable. This variable contains SQL_NULL_DATA if the column value is a NULL. For APDs, the indicator variable is set to SQL_NULL_DATA to specify NULL dynamic arguments. Otherwise, the variable is zero (unless the values in SQL_DESC_INDICATOR_PTR and SQL_DESC_OCTET_LENGTH_PTR are the same pointer).

If the SQL_DESC_INDICATOR_PTR field in an ARD is a null pointer, the driver is prevented from returning information about whether the column is NULL or not. If the column is NULL and SQL_DESC_INDICATOR_PTR is a null pointer, SQLSTATE 22002 (Indicator variable required but not supplied) is returned when the driver attempts to populate the buffer after a call to **SQLFetch** or **SQLFetchScroll**. If the call to **SQLFetch** or **SQLFetchScroll** did not return SQL_SUCCESS or SQL_SUCCESS_WITH_INFO, the contents of the buffer are undefined.

The SQL_DESC_INDICATOR_PTR field determines whether the field pointed to by SQL_DESC_OCTET_LENGTH_PTR is set. If the data value for a column is NULL, the driver sets the indicator variable to SQL_NULL_DATA. The field pointed to by SQL_DESC_OCTET_LENGTH_PTR is then not set. If a NULL value is not encountered during the fetch, the buffer pointed to by SQL_DESC_INDICATOR_PTR is set to zero, and the buffer pointed to by SQL_DESC_OCTET_LENGTH_PTR is set to the length of the data.

If the SQL_DESC_INDICATOR_PTR field in an APD is a null pointer, the application cannot use this descriptor record to specify NULL arguments.

This field is a *deferred field*: It is not used at the time it is set, but is used at a later time by the driver to indicate nullability (for ARDs) or to determine nullability (for APDs).

SQL_DESC_LABEL [IRDs]

This read-only SQLCHAR * record field contains the column label or title. If the column does not have a label, this variable contains the column name. If the column is unnamed and unlabeled, this variable contains an empty string.

SQL_DESC_LENGTH [All]

This SQLUINTEGER record field is either the maximum or actual character length of a character string or a binary data type. It is the maximum character length for a fixed-length data type, or the actual character length for a variable-length data type. Its value always excludes the null-termination character that ends the character string. For values whose type is SQL_TYPE_DATE, SQL_TYPE_TIME, SQL_TYPE_TIMESTAMP, or one of the SQL interval data types, this field has the length in characters of the character string representation of the datetime or interval value. Note that this field is a count of characters, not a count of bytes.

The value in this field may be different from the value for "length" as defined in ODBC 2.*x*. For more information, see Appendix D, "Data Types."

SQL_DESC_LITERAL_PREFIX [IRDs]

This read-only SQLCHAR * record field contains the character or characters that the driver recognizes as a prefix for a literal of this data type. This variable contains an empty string for a data type for which a literal prefix is not applicable.

SQL_DESC_LITERAL_SUFFIX [IRDs]

This read-only SQLCHAR * record field contains the character or characters that the driver recognizes as a suffix for a literal of this data type. This variable contains an empty string for a data type for which a literal suffix is not applicable.

SQL_DESC_LOCAL_TYPE_NAME [Implementation descriptors]

This read-only SQLCHAR * record field contains any localized (native language) name for the data type that may be different from the regular name of the data type. If there is no localized name, then an empty string is returned. This field is for display purposes only.

SQL_DESC_NAME [Implementation descriptors]

This SQLCHAR * record field in a row descriptor contains the column alias, if it applies. If the column alias does not apply, the column name is returned. In either case, the driver sets the SQL_DESC_UNNAMED field is to SQL_NAMED when it sets the SQL_DESC_NAME field. If there is no column name or a column alias, the driver returns an empty string in the SQL_DESC_NAME field and sets the SQL_DESC_UNNAMED field to SQL_UNNAMED.

An application can set the SQL_DESC_NAME field of an IPD to a parameter name or alias to specify stored procedure parameters by name. (For more information, see "Binding Parameters by Name (Named Parameters)" in Chapter 9, "Executing Statements.") The SQL_DESC_NAME field of an IRD is a read-only field; SQLSTATE HY091 (Invalid descriptor field identifier) will be returned if an application attempts to set it.

In IPDs, this field is undefined if the driver does not support named parameters. If the driver supports named parameters and is capable of describing parameters, then the parameter name is returned in this field.

SQL_DESC_NULLABLE [Implementation descriptors]

In IRDs, this read-only SQLSMALLINT record field is SQL_NULLABLE if the column can have NULL values; SQL_NO_NULLS if the column does not have NULL values; or SQL_NULLABLE_UNKNOWN if it is not known whether the column accepts NULL values. This field pertains to the result set column, not the base column.

In IPDs, this field is always set to SQL_NULLABLE, since dynamic parameters are always nullable, and cannot be set by an application.

SQL_DESC_NUM_PREC_RADIX [All]

This SQLINTEGER field contains a value of 2 if the data type in the SQL_DESC_TYPE field is an approximate numeric data type, because the SQL_DESC_PRECISION field contains the number of bits. This field contains a value of 10 if the data type in the SQL_DESC_TYPE field is an exact numeric data type, because the SQL_DESC_PRECISION field contains the number of decimal digits. This field is set to 0 for all non-numeric data types.

SQL_DESC_OCTET_LENGTH [All]

This SQLINTEGER record field contains the length, in bytes, of a character string or binary data type. For fixed-length character or binary types, this is the actual length in bytes. For variable-length character or binary types, this is the maximum length in bytes. This value always excludes space for the null-termination character for implementation descriptors and always includes space for the null-termination character for application descriptors. For application data, this field contains the size of the buffer. For APDs, this field is defined only for output or input/output parameters.

SQL_DESC_OCTET_LENGTH_PTR [Application descriptors]

This SQLINTEGER * record field points to a variable that will contain the total length in bytes of a dynamic argument (for parameter descriptors) or of a bound column value (for row descriptors).

For an APD, this value is ignored for all arguments except character string and binary; if this field points to SQL_NTS, the dynamic argument must be null-terminated. To indicate that a bound parameter will be a data-at-execution parameter, an application sets this field in the appropriate record of the APD to a variable that, at execute time, will contain the value SQL_DATA_AT_EXEC or the result of the SQL_LEN_DATA_AT_EXEC macro. If there is more than one such field, SQL_DESC_DATA_PTR can be set to a value uniquely identifying the parameter to help the application determine which parameter is being requested.

If the OCTET_LENGTH_PTR field of an ARD is a null pointer, the driver does not return length information for the column. If the SQL_DESC_OCTET_LENGTH_PTR field of an APD is a null pointer, the driver assumes that character strings and binary values are null-terminated. (Binary values should not be null-terminated, but should be given a length to avoid truncation.)

If the call to **SQLFetch** or **SQLFetchScroll** that fills in the buffer pointed to by this field did not return SQL_SUCCESS or SQL_SUCCESS_WITH_INFO, the contents of the buffer are undefined. This field is a *deferred field*: It is not used at the time it is set, but is used at a later time by the driver to determine or indicate the octet length of the data.

SQL_DESC_PARAMETER_TYPE [IPDs]

This SQLSMALLINT record field is set to SQL_PARAM_INPUT for an input parameter, SQL_PARAM_INPUT_OUTPUT for an input/output parameter, or SQL_PARAM_OUTPUT for an output parameter. Set to SQL_PARAM_INPUT by default.

For an IPD, the field is set to SQL_PARAM_INPUT by default if the IPD is not automatically populated by the driver (the SQL_ATTR_ENABLE_AUTO_IPD statement attribute is SQL_FALSE). An application should set this field in the IPD for parameters that are not input parameters.

SQL_DESC_PRECISION [All]

This SQLSMALLINT record field contains the number of digits for an exact numeric type, the number of bits in the mantissa (binary precision) for an approximate numeric type, or the numbers of digits in the fractional seconds component for the SQL_TYPE_TIME, SQL_TYPE_TIMESTAMP, or SQL_INTERVAL_SECOND data type. This field is undefined for all other data types.

The value in this field may be different from the value for "precision" as defined in ODBC 2.*x*. For more information, see Appendix D, "Data Types."

SQL_DESC_SCALE [All]

This SQLSMALLINT record field contains the defined scale for decimal and numeric data types. The field is undefined for all other data types.

The value in this field may be different from the value for "scale" as defined in ODBC 2.*x*. For more information, see Appendix D, "Data Types."

SQL_DESC_SCHEMA_NAME [IRDs]

This read-only SQLCHAR * record field contains the schema name of the base table that contains the column. The return value is driver-dependent if the column is an expression or if the column is part of a view. If the data source does not support schemas or the schema name cannot be determined, this variable contains an empty string.

SQL_DESC_SEARCHABLE [IRDs]

This read-only SQLSMALLINT record field is set to one of the following values:

- SQL_PRED_NONE if the column cannot be used in a **WHERE** clause. (This is the same as the SQL_UNSEARCHABLE value in ODBC 2.*x*.)
- SQL_PRED_CHAR if the column can be used in a **WHERE** clause, but only with the **LIKE** predicate. (This is the same as the SQL_LIKE_ONLY value in ODBC 2.*x*.)
- SQL_PRED_BASIC if the column can be used in a **WHERE** clause with all the comparison operators except **LIKE**. (This is the same as the SQL_EXCEPT_LIKE value in ODBC 2.*x*.)
- SQL_PRED_SEARCHABLE if the column can be used in a **WHERE** clause with any comparison operator.

SQL_DESC_TABLE_NAME [IRDs]

This read-only SQLCHAR * record field contains the name of the base table that contains this column. The return value is driver-dependent if the column is an expression or if the column is part of a view.

SQL_DESC_TYPE [All]

This SQLSMALLINT record field specifies the concise SQL or C data type for all data types except datetime and interval data types. For the datetime and interval data types, this field specifies the verbose data type, which is SQL_DATETIME or SQL_INTERVAL.

Whenever this field contains SQL_DATETIME or SQL_INTERVAL, the SQL_DESC_DATETIME_INTERVAL_CODE field must contain the appropriate subcode for the concise type. For datetime data types, SQL_DESC_TYPE contains SQL_DATETIME, and the SQL_DESC_DATETIME_INTERVAL_CODE field contains a subcode for the specific datetime data type. For interval data types, SQL_DESC_TYPE contains SQL_INTERVAL, and the SQL_DESC_DATETIME_INTERVAL_CODE field contains a subcode for the specific interval data type.

The values in the SQL_DESC_TYPE and SQL_DESC_CONCISE_TYPE fields are interdependent. Each time one of the fields is set, the other must also be set. SQL_DESC_TYPE can be set by a call to **SQLSetDescField** or **SQLSetDescRec**. SQL_DESC_CONCISE_TYPE can be set by a call to **SQLBindCol** or **SQLBindParameter**, or **SQLSetDescField**.

If SQL_DESC_TYPE is set to a concise data type other than an interval or datetime data type, the SQL_DESC_CONCISE_TYPE field is set to the same value, and the SQL_DESC_DATETIME_INTERVAL_CODE field is set to 0.

If SQL_DESC_TYPE is set to the verbose datetime or interval data type (SQL_DATETIME or SQL_INTERVAL), and the SQL_DESC_DATETIME_INTERVAL_CODE field is set to the appropriate subcode, the SQL_DESC_CONCISE TYPE field is set to the corresponding concise type. Trying to set SQL_DESC_TYPE to one of the concise datetime or interval types will return SQLSTATE HY021 (Inconsistent descriptor information).

When the SQL_DESC_TYPE field is set by a call to **SQLBindCol**, **SQLBindParameter**, or **SQLSetDescField**, the following fields are set to the following default values. The values of the remaining fields of the same record are undefined.

Value of SQL_DESC_TYPE	Other fields implicitly set
SQL_CHAR, SQL_VARCHAR, SQL_C_CHAR, SQL_C_VARCHAR	SQL_DESC_LENGTH is set to 1. SQL_DESC_PRECISION is set to 0.
SQL_DATETIME	When SQL_DESC_DATETIME_INTERVAL_CODE is set to SQL_CODE_DATE or SQL_CODE_TIME, SQL_DESC_PRECISION is set to 0. When it is set to SQL_DESC_TIMESTAMP, SQL_DESC_PRECISION is set to 6.
SQL_DECIMAL, SQL_NUMERIC, SQL_C_NUMERIC	SQL_DESC_SCALE is set to 0. SQL_DESC_PRECISION is set to the implementation-defined precision for the respective data type.

Value of SQL_DESC_TYPE	Other fields implicitly set
SQL_FLOAT, SQL_C_FLOAT	SQL_DESC_PRECISION is set to the implementation-defined default precision for SQL_FLOAT.
SQL_INTERVAL	When SQL_DESC_DATETIME_INTERVAL_CODE is set to an interval data type, SQL_DESC_DATETIME_INTERVAL_PRECISION is set to 2 (the default interval leading precision). When the interval has a seconds component, SQL_DESC_PRECISION is set to 6 (the default interval seconds precision).

When an application calls **SQLSetDescField** to set fields of a descriptor, rather than calling **SQLSetDescRec**, the application must first declare the data type. When it does, the other fields indicated in the previous table are implicitly set. If any of the values implicitly set are unacceptable, the application can then call **SQLSetDescField** or **SQLSetDescRec** to set the unacceptable value explicitly.

SQL_DESC_TYPE_NAME [Implementation descriptors]

This read-only SQLCHAR * record field contains the data source–dependent type name (for example, "CHAR", "VARCHAR", and so on). If the data type name is unknown, this variable contains an empty string.

SQL_DESC_UNNAMED [Implementation descriptors]

This SQLSMALLINT record field in a row descriptor is set by the driver to either SQL_NAMED or SQL_UNNAMED when it sets the SQL_DESC_NAME field. If the SQL_DESC_NAME field contains a column alias, or if the column alias does not apply, the driver sets the SQL_DESC_UNNAMED field to SQL_NAMED. If an application sets the SQL_DESC_NAME field of an IPD to a parameter name or alias, the driver sets the SQL_DESC_UNNAMED field of the IPD to SQL_NAMED. If there is no column name or a column alias, the driver sets the SQL_DESC_UNNAMED field to SQL_UNNAMED.

An application can set the SQL_DESC_UNNAMED field of an IPD to SQL_UNNAMED. A driver returns SQLSTATE HY091 (Invalid descriptor field identifier) if an application attempts to set the SQL_DESC_UNNAMED field of an IPD to SQL_NAMED. The SQL_DESC_UNNAMED field of an IRD is read-only; SQLSTATE HY091 (Invalid descriptor field identifier) will be returned if an application attempts to set it.

SQL_DESC_UNSIGNED [Implementation descriptors]

This read-only SQLSMALLINT record field is set to SQL_TRUE if the column type is unsigned or non-numeric, or SQL_FALSE if the column type is signed.

SQL_DESC_UPDATABLE [IRDs]

This read-only SQLSMALLINT record field is set to one of the following values:

- SQL_ATTR_READ_ONLY if the result set column is read-only.
- SQL_ATTR_WRITE if the result set column is read-write.
- SQL_ATTR_READWRITE_UNKNOWN if it is not known whether the result set column is updatable or not.

SQL_DESC_UPDATABLE describes the updatability of the column in the result set, not the column in the base table. The updatability of the column in the base table on which this result set column is based may be different than the value in this field. Whether a column is updatable can be based on the data type, user privileges, and the definition of the result set itself. If it is unclear whether a column is updatable, SQL_ATTR_READWRITE_UNKNOWN should be returned.

Consistency Checks

A consistency check is performed by the driver automatically whenever an application passes in a value for the SQL_DESC_DATA_PTR field of the ARD, APD, or IPD. If any of the fields is inconsistent with other fields, **SQLSetDescField** will return SQLSTATE HY021 (Inconsistent descriptor information). For more information, see "Consistency Check" in **SQLSetDescRec**.

Related Functions

For information about	See
Binding a column	**SQLBindCol**
Binding a parameter	**SQLBindParameter**
Getting a descriptor field	**SQLGetDescField**
Getting multiple descriptor fields	**SQLGetDescRec**
Setting multiple descriptor fields	**SQLSetDescRec**

SQLSetDescRec

Conformance

Version Introduced: ODBC 3.0
Standards Compliance: ISO 92

Summary

The **SQLSetDescRec** function sets multiple descriptor fields that affect the data type and buffer bound to a column or parameter data.

Syntax

```
SQLRETURN SQLSetDescRec(
    SQLHDESC       DescriptorHandle,
    SQLSMALLINT    RecNumber,
    SQLSMALLINT    Type,
    SQLSMALLINT    SubType,
    SQLINTEGER     Length,
    SQLSMALLINT    Precision,
    SQLSMALLINT    Scale,
    SQLPOINTER     DataPtr,
    SQLINTEGER *   StringLengthPtr,
    SQLINTEGER *   IndicatorPtr);
```

Arguments

DescriptorHandle [Input]
Descriptor handle. This must not be an IRD handle.

RecNumber [Input]
Indicates the descriptor record that contains the fields to be set. Descriptor records are numbered from 0, with record number 0 being the bookmark record. This argument must be equal to or greater than 0. If *RecNumber* is greater than the value of SQL_DESC_COUNT, SQL_DESC_COUNT is changed to the value of *RecNumber*.

Type [Input]
The value to which to set the SQL_DESC_TYPE field for the descriptor record.

SubType [Input]
For records whose type is SQL_DATETIME or SQL_INTERVAL, this is the value to which to set the SQL_DESC_DATETIME_INTERVAL_CODE field.

Length [Input]
The value to which to set the SQL_DESC_OCTET_LENGTH field for the descriptor record.

Precision [Input]
The value to which to set the SQL_DESC_PRECISION field for the descriptor record.

Scale [Input]
The value to which to set the SQL_DESC_SCALE field for the descriptor record.

DataPtr [Deferred Input or Output]
The value to which to set the SQL_DESC_DATA_PTR field for the descriptor record. *DataPtr* can be set to a null pointer.

The *DataPtr* argument can be set to a null pointer to set the SQL_DESC_DATA_PTR field to a null pointer. If the handle in the *DescriptorHandle* argument is associated with an ARD, this unbinds the column.

StringLengthPtr [Deferred Input or Output]
The value to which to set the SQL_DESC_OCTET_LENGTH_PTR field for the descriptor record. *StringLengthPtr* can be set to a null pointer to set the SQL_DESC_OCTET_LENGTH_PTR field to a null pointer.

IndicatorPtr [Deferred Input or Output]
The value to which to set the SQL_DESC_INDICATOR_PTR field for the descriptor record. *IndicatorPtr* can be set to a null pointer to set the SQL_DESC_INDICATOR_PTR field to a null pointer.

Returns

SQL_SUCCESS, SQL_SUCCESS_WITH_INFO, SQL_ERROR, or SQL_INVALID_HANDLE.

Diagnostics

When **SQLSetDescRec** returns SQL_ERROR or SQL_SUCCESS_WITH_INFO, an associated SQLSTATE value can be obtained by calling **SQLGetDiagRec** with a *HandleType* of SQL_HANDLE_DESC and a *Handle* of *DescriptorHandle*. The following table lists the SQLSTATE values commonly returned by **SQLSetDescRec** and explains each one in the context of this function; the notation "(DM)" precedes the descriptions of SQLSTATEs returned by the Driver Manager. The return code associated with each SQLSTATE value is SQL_ERROR, unless noted otherwise.

SQLSTATE	Error	Description
01000	General warning	Driver-specific informational message. (Function returns SQL_SUCCESS_WITH_INFO.)
07009	Invalid descriptor index	The *RecNumber* argument was set to 0, and the *DescriptorHandle* referred to an IPD handle. The *RecNumber* argument was less than 0. The *RecNumber* argument was greater than the maximum number of columns or parameters that the data source can support, and the *DescriptorHandle* argument was an APD, IPD, or ARD. The *RecNumber* argument was equal to 0, and the *DescriptorHandle* argument referred to an implicitly allocated APD. (This error does not occur with an explicitly allocated application descriptor, because it is not known whether an explicitly allocated application descriptor is an APD or ARD until execute time.)
08S01	Communication link failure	The communication link between the driver and the data source to which the driver was connected failed before the function completed processing.
HY000	General error	An error occurred for which there was no specific SQLSTATE and for which no implementation-specific SQLSTATE was defined. The error message returned by **SQLGetDiagRec** in the **MessageText* buffer describes the error and its cause.
HY001	Memory allocation error	The driver was unable to allocate memory required to support execution or completion of the function.
HY010	Function sequence error	(DM) The *DescriptorHandle* was associated with a *StatementHandle* for which an asynchronously executing function (not this one) was called and was still executing when this function was called. (DM) **SQLExecute**, **SQLExecDirect**, **SQLBulkOperations**, or **SQLSetPos** was called for the *StatementHandle* with which the *DescriptorHandle* was associated and returned SQL_NEED_DATA. This function was called before data was sent for all data-at-execution parameters or columns.

SQLSTATE	Error	Description
HY013	Memory management error	The function call could not be processed because the underlying memory objects could not be accessed, possibly because of low memory conditions.
HY016	Cannot modify an implementation row descriptor	The *DescriptorHandle* argument was associated with an IRD.
HY021	Inconsistent descriptor information	The *Type* field, or any other field associated with the SQL_DESC_TYPE field in the descriptor, was not valid or consistent. Descriptor information checked during a consistency check was not consistent. (See "Consistency Checks" later in this section.)
HY090	Invalid string or buffer length	(DM) The driver was an ODBC 2.*x* driver, the descriptor was an ARD, the *ColumnNumber* argument was set to 0, and the value specified for the argument *BufferLength* was not equal to 4.
HYT01	Connection timeout expired	The connection timeout period expired before the data source responded to the request. The connection timeout period is set through **SQLSetConnectAttr**, SQL_ATTR_CONNECTION_TIMEOUT.
IM001	Driver does not support this function	(DM) The driver associated with the *DescriptorHandle* does not support the function.

Comments

An application can call **SQLSetDescRec** to set the following fields for a single column or parameter:

- SQL_DESC_TYPE
- SQL_DESC_DATETIME_INTERVAL_CODE (for records whose type is SQL_DATETIME or SQL_INTERVAL)
- SQL_DESC_OCTET_LENGTH
- SQL_DESC_PRECISION
- SQL_DESC_SCALE
- SQL_DESC_DATA_PTR
- SQL_DESC_OCTET_LENGTH_PTR
- SQL_DESC_INDICATOR_PTR

Note If a call to **SQLSetDescRec** fails, the contents of the descriptor record identified by the *RecNumber* argument are undefined.

When binding a column or parameter, **SQLSetDescRec** allows you to change multiple fields affecting the binding without calling **SQLBindCol** or **SQLBindParameter**, or making multiple calls to **SQLSetDescField**. **SQLSetDescRec** can set fields on a descriptor not currently associated with a statement. Note that **SQLBindParameter** sets more fields than **SQLSetDescRec**, can set fields on both an APD and an IPD in one call, and does not require a descriptor handle.

Note The statement attribute SQL_ATTR_USE_BOOKMARKS should always be set before calling **SQLSetDescRec** with a *RecNumber* argument of 0 to set bookmark fields. While this is not mandatory, it is strongly recommended.

Consistency Checks

A consistency check is performed by the driver automatically whenever an application sets the SQL_DESC_DATA_PTR field of an APD, ARD, or IPD. If any of the fields is inconsistent with other fields, **SQLSetDescRec** will return SQLSTATE HY021 (Inconsistent descriptor information).

Whenever an application sets the SQL_DESC_DATA_PTR field of an APD, ARD, or IPD, the driver checks that the value of the SQL_DESC_TYPE field and the values applicable to that SQL_DESC_TYPE field are valid and consistent. This check is always performed when **SQLBindParameter** or **SQLBindCol** is called, or when **SQLSetDescRec** is called for an APD, ARD, or IPD. This consistency check includes the following checks on descriptor fields:

- The SQL_DESC_TYPE field must be one of the valid ODBC C or SQL types or a driver-specific SQL type. The SQL_DESC_CONCISE_TYPE field must be one of the valid ODBC C or SQL types or a driver-specific C or SQL type, including the concise datetime and interval types.
- If the SQL_DESC_TYPE record field is SQL_DATETIME or SQL_INTERVAL, then the SQL_DESC_DATETIME_INTERVAL_CODE field must be one of the valid datetime or interval codes (see the description of the SQL_DESC_DATETIME_INTERVAL_CODE field in **SQLSetDescField**).
- If the SQL_DESC_TYPE field indicates a numeric type, the SQL_DESC_PRECISION and SQL_DESC_SCALE fields are verified to be valid.
- If the SQL_DESC_CONCISE_TYPE field is a time or timestamp data type or an interval type with a seconds component, or one of the interval data types with a time component, the SQL_DESC_PRECISION field is verified to be a valid seconds precision.
- If the SQL_DESC_CONCISE_TYPE is an interval data type, the SQL_DESC_DATETIME_INTERVAL_PRECISION field is verified to be a valid interval leading precision value.

The SQL_DESC_DATA_PTR field of an IPD is not normally set; however, an application can do so to force a consistency check of IPD fields. A consistency check cannot be performed on an IRD. The value that the SQL_DESC_DATA_PTR field of the IPD is set to is not actually stored, and cannot be retrieved by a call to **SQLGetDescField** or **SQLGetDescRec**; the setting is made only to force the consistency check.

Related Functions

For information about	See
Binding a column	**SQLBindCol**
Binding a parameter	**SQLBindParameter**
Getting a single descriptor field	**SQLGetDescField**
Getting multiple descriptor fields	**SQLGetDescRec**
Setting single descriptor fields	**SQLSetDescField**

SQLSetEnvAttr

Conformance

Version Introduced: ODBC 3.0
Standards Compliance: ISO 92

Summary

SQLSetEnvAttr sets attributes that govern aspects of environments.

Syntax

SQLRETURN **SQLSetEnvAttr**(
    SQLHENV *EnvironmentHandle*,
    SQLINTEGER *Attribute*,
    SQLPOINTER *ValuePtr*,
    SQLINTEGER *StringLength*);

Arguments

EnvironmentHandle [Input]
Environment handle.

Attribute [Input]
Attribute to set, listed in "Comments."

ValuePtr [Input]
Pointer to the value to be associated with *Attribute*. Depending on the value of *Attribute*, *ValuePtr* will be a 32-bit integer value or point to a null-terminated character string.

StringLength [Input] If *ValuePtr* points to a character string or a binary buffer, this argument should be the length of **ValuePtr*. If *ValuePtr* is an integer, *StringLength* is ignored.

Returns

SQL_SUCCESS, SQL_SUCCESS_WITH_INFO, SQL_ERROR, or SQL_INVALID_HANDLE.

Diagnostics

When **SQLSetEnvAttr** returns SQL_ERROR or SQL_SUCCESS_WITH_INFO, an associated SQLSTATE value can be obtained by calling **SQLGetDiagRec** with a *HandleType* of SQL_HANDLE_ENV and a *Handle* of *EnvironmentHandle*. The following table lists the SQLSTATE values commonly returned by **SQLSetEnvAttr** and explains each one in the context of this function; the notation "(DM)" precedes the descriptions of SQLSTATEs returned by the Driver Manager. The return code associated with each SQLSTATE value is SQL_ERROR, unless noted otherwise. If a driver does not support an environment attribute, the error can be returned only during connect time.

SQLSTATE	Error	Description
01000	General warning	Driver-specific informational message. (Function returns SQL_SUCCESS_WITH_INFO.)
01S02	Option value changed	The driver did not support the value specified in *ValuePtr* and substituted a similar value. (Function returns SQL_SUCCESS_WITH_INFO.)
HY000	General error	An error occurred for which there was no specific SQLSTATE and for which no implementation-specific SQLSTATE was defined. The error message returned by **SQLGetDiagRec** in the **MessageText* buffer describes the error and its cause.
HY001	Memory allocation error	The driver was unable to allocate memory required to support execution or completion of the function.
HY009	Invalid use of null pointer	The Attribute argument identified an environment attribute that required a string value, and the *ValuePtr* argument was a null pointer.
HY011	Attribute cannot be set now	A connection handle has been allocated on *EnvironmentHandle*. (DM) The *Attribute* argument was SQL_ATTR_OUTPUT_NTS, and the SQL_ATTR_ODBC_VERSION attribute had not been set.
HY013	Memory management error	The function call could not be processed because the underlying memory objects could not be accessed, possibly because of low memory conditions.
HY024	Invalid attribute value	Given the specified *Attribute* value, an invalid value was specified in *ValuePtr*.
HY090	Invalid string or buffer length	The *StringLength* argument was less than 0, but was not SQL_NTS.
HY092	Invalid attribute/option identifier	(DM) The value specified for the argument *Attribute* was not valid for the version of ODBC supported by the driver.
HYC00	Optional feature not implemented	The value specified for the argument *Attribute* was a valid ODBC environment attribute for the version of ODBC supported by the driver, but was not supported by the driver. (DM) The *Attribute* argument was SQL_ATTR_OUTPUT_NTS, and *ValuePtr* was SQL_FALSE.

Comments

An application can call **SQLSetEnvAttr** only if no connection handle is allocated on the environment. All environment attributes successfully set by the application for the environment persist until **SQLFreeHandle** is called on the environment. More than one environment handle can be allocated simultaneously in ODBC 3.0.

The format of information set through *ValuePtr* depends on the specified *Attribute*. **SQLSetEnvAttr** will accept attribute information in one of two different formats: a null-terminated character string or a 32-bit integer value. The format of each is noted in the attribute's description.

There are no driver-specific environment attributes.

Connections attribute cannot be set by a call to **SQLSetEnvAttr**. Attempting to do so will return SQLSTATE HY092 (Invalid attribute/option identifier).

Attribute	*ValuePtr* **contents**
SQL_ATTR_ CONNECTION_POOLING (ODBC 3.0)	A 32-bit SQLUINTEGER value that enables or disables connection pooling at the environment level. The following values are used: SQL_CP_OFF = Connection pooling is turned off. This is the default. SQL_CP_ONE_PER_DRIVER = A single connection pool is supported for each driver. Every connection in a pool is associated with one driver. SQL_CP_ONE_PER_HENV = A single connection pool is supported for each environment. Every connection in a pool is associated with one environment. Connection pooling is enabled by calling **SQLSetEnvAttr** to set the SQL_ATTR_CONNECTION_POOLING attribute to SQL_CP_ONE_PER_DRIVER or SQL_CP_ONE_PER_HENV. This call must be made before the application allocates the shared environment for which connection pooling is to be enabled. The environment handle in the call to **SQLSetEnvAttr** is set to null, which makes SQL_ATTR_CONNECTION_POOLING a process-level attribute. After connection pooling is enabled, the application then allocates an implicit shared environment by calling **SQLAllocHandle** with the *InputHandle* argument set to SQL_HANDLE_ENV. After connection pooling has been enabled and a shared environment has been selected for an application, SQL_ATTR_CONNECTION_POOLING cannot be reset for that environment, since **SQLSetEnvAttr** is called with a null environment handle when setting this attribute. If this attribute is set while connection pooling is already enabled on a shared environment, the attribute only affects shared environments that are allocated subsequently. For more information, see "Connection Pooling" in Chapter 6, "Connecting to a Data Source or Driver."

Attribute	*ValuePtr* contents
SQL_ATTR_CP_MATCH (ODBC 3.0)	A 32-bit SQLUINTEGER value that determines how a connection is chosen from a connection pool. When **SQLConnect** or **SQLDriverConnect** is called, the Driver Manager determines which connection is reused from the pool. The Driver Manager attempts to match the connection options in the call and the connection attributes set by the application to the keywords and connection attributes of the connections in the pool. The value of this attribute determines the level of precision of the matching criteria. The following values are used to set the value of this attribute: SQL_CP_STRICT_MATCH = Only connections that exactly match the connection options in the call and the connection attributes set by the application are reused. This is the default. SQL_CP_RELAXED_MATCH = Connections with matching connection string keywords can be used. Keywords must match, but not all connection attributes must match. For more information on how the Driver Manager performs the match in connecting to a pooled connection, see **SQLConnect**. For more information on connection pooling, see "Connection Pooling" in Chapter 6, "Connecting to a Data Source or Driver."
SQL_ATTR_ODBC_VERSION (ODBC 3.0)	A 32-bit integer that determines whether certain functionality exhibits ODBC 2.*x* behavior or ODBC 3.0 behavior. The following values are used to set the value of this attribute: SQL_OV_ODBC3 = The Driver Manager and driver exhibit the following ODBC 3.0 behavior: • The driver returns and expects ODBC 3.0 codes for date, time, and timestamp. • The driver returns ODBC 3.0 SQLSTATE codes when **SQLError**, **SQLGetDiagField**, or **SQLGetDiagRec** are called. • The *CatalogName* argument in a call to **SQLTables** accepts a search pattern.

Attribute	ValuePtr contents
SQL_ATTR_ODBC_VERSION (ODBC 3.0) (*continued*)	SQL_OV_ODBC2 = The Driver Manager and driver exhibit the following ODBC 2.*x* behavior. This is especially useful for an ODBC 2.*x* application working with an ODBC 3.0 driver. • The driver returns and expects ODBC 2.*x* codes for date, time, and timestamp. • The driver returns ODBC 2.*x* SQLSTATE codes when **SQLError**, **SQLGetDiagField**, or **SQLGetDiagRec** are called. • The *CatalogName* argument in a call to **SQLTables** does not accept a search pattern. An application must set this environment attribute before calling any function that has an SQLHENV argument, or the call will return SQLSTATE HY010 (Function sequence error). For more information, see "Declaring the Application's ODBC Version" in Chapter 6, "Connecting to a Data Source or Driver" and "Behavioral Changes" in Chapter 17, "Programming Considerations."
SQL_ATTR_OUTPUT_NTS (ODBC 3.0)	A 32-bit integer that determines how the driver returns string data. If SQL_TRUE, the driver returns string data null-terminated. If SQL_FALSE, the driver does not return string data null-terminated. This attribute defaults to SQL_TRUE. A call to **SQLSetEnvAttr** to set it to SQL_TRUE returns SQL_SUCCESS. A call to **SQLSetEnvAttr** to set it to SQL_FALSE returns SQL_ERROR and SQLSTATE HYC00 (Optional feature not implemented).

Related Functions

For information about	See
Allocating a handle	**SQLAllocHandle**
Returning the setting of an environment attribute	**SQLGetEnvAttr**

SQLSetParam

Conformance

Version Introduced: ODBC 1.0
Standards Compliance: Deprecated

Summary

In ODBC 2.0, the ODBC 1.0 function **SQLSetParam** has been replaced by **SQLBindParameter**. For more information, see **SQLBindParameter**.

Note For more information about what the Driver Manager maps this function to when an ODBC 2.*x* application is working with an ODBC 3.0 driver, see "Mapping Deprecated Functions" in Appendix G, "Driver Guidelines for Backward Compatibility."

SQLSetPos

Conformance

Version Introduced: ODBC 1.0
Standards Compliance: ODBC

Summary

SQLSetPos sets the cursor position in a rowset and allows an application to refresh data in the rowset, or update or delete data in the result set.

Syntax

SQLRETURN **SQLSetPos**(
    SQLHSTMT *StatementHandle*,
    SQLUSMALLINT *RowNumber*,
    SQLUSMALLINT *Operation*,
    SQLUSMALLINT *LockType*);

Arguments

StatementHandle [Input]
Statement handle.

RowNumber [Input]
Position of the row in the rowset on which to perform the operation specified with the *Operation* argument. If *RowNumber* is 0, the operation applies to every row in the rowset.

For additional information, see "Comments."

Operation [Input]
Operation to perform:

SQL_POSITION
SQL_REFRESH
SQL_UPDATE
SQL_DELETE

Note The SQL_ADD value for the *Operation* argument has been deprecated for ODBC 3.0. ODBC 3.0 drivers will need to support SQL_ADD for backward compatibility. This functionality has been replaced by a call to **SQLBulkOperations** with an *Operation* of SQL_ADD. When an ODBC 3.0 application works with an ODBC 2.*x* driver, the Driver Manager maps a call to **SQLBulkOperations** with an *Operation* of SQL_ADD to **SQLSetPos** with an *Operation* of SQL_ADD.

For more information, see "Comments."

LockType [Input]
Specifies how to lock the row after performing the operation specified in the *Operation* argument.

SQL_LOCK_NO_CHANGE
SQL_LOCK_EXCLUSIVE
SQL_LOCK_UNLOCK

For more information, see "Comments."

Returns

SQL_SUCCESS, SQL_SUCCESS_WITH_INFO, SQL_NEED_DATA, SQL_STILL_EXECUTING, SQL_ERROR, or SQL_INVALID_HANDLE.

Diagnostics

When **SQLSetPos** returns SQL_ERROR or SQL_SUCCESS_WITH_INFO, an associated SQLSTATE value may be obtained by calling **SQLGetDiagRec** with a *HandleType* of SQL_HANDLE_STMT and a *Handle* of *StatementHandle*. The following table lists the SQLSTATE values commonly returned by **SQLSetPos** and explains each one in the context of this function; the notation "(DM)" precedes the descriptions of SQLSTATEs returned by the Driver Manager. The return code associated with each SQLSTATE value is SQL_ERROR, unless noted otherwise.

For all those SQLSTATEs that can return SQL_SUCCESS_WITH_INFO or SQL_ERROR (except 01xxx SQLSTATEs), SQL_SUCCESS_WITH_INFO is returned if an error occurs on one or more, but not all, rows of a multirow operation, and SQL_ERROR is returned if an error occurs on a single-row operation.

SQLSTATE	Error	Description
01000	General warning	Driver-specific informational message. (Function returns SQL_SUCCESS_WITH_INFO.)
01001	Cursor operation conflict	The *Operation* argument was SQL_DELETE or SQL_UPDATE, and no rows or more than one row were deleted or updated. (For more information about updates to more than one row, see the description of the SQL_ATTR_SIMULATE_CURSOR *Attribute* in **SQLSetStmtAttr**.) (Function returns SQL_SUCCESS_WITH_INFO.) The *Operation* argument was SQL_DELETE or SQL_UPDATE, and the operation failed because of optimistic concurrency. (Function returns SQL_SUCCESS_WITH_INFO.)

SQLSTATE	Error	Description
01004	String data right truncation	The *Operation* argument was SQL_REFRESH, and string or binary data returned for a column or columns with a data type of SQL_C_CHAR or SQL_C_BINARY resulted in the truncation of non-blank character or non-NULL binary data.
01S01	Error in row	The *RowNumber* argument was 0 and an error occurred in one or more rows while performing the operation specified with the *Operation* argument. (SQL_SUCCESS_WITH_INFO is returned if an error occurs on one or more, but not all, rows of a multirow operation, and SQL_ERROR is returned if an error occurs on a single-row operation.) (This SQLSTATE is returned only when **SQLSetPos** is called after **SQLExtendedFetch**, if the driver is an ODBC 2.*x* driver and the cursor library is not used.)
01S07	Fractional truncation	The *Operation* argument was SQL_REFRESH, the data type of the application buffer was not SQL_C_CHAR or SQL_C_BINARY, and the data returned to application buffers for one or more columns was truncated. For numeric data types, the fractional part of the number was truncated. For time, timestamp, and interval data types containing a time component, the fractional portion of the time was truncated. (Function returns SQL_SUCCESS_WITH_INFO.)
07006	Restricted data type attribute violation	The data value of a column in the result set could not be converted to the data type specified by *TargetType* in the call to **SQLBindCol**.
07009	Invalid descriptor index	The argument *Operation* was SQL_REFRESH or SQL_UPDATE, and a column was bound with a column number greater than the number of columns in the result set.
21S02	Degree of derived table does not match column list	The argument *Operation* was SQL_UPDATE, and no columns were updatable because all columns were either unbound, read-only, or the value in the bound length/indicator buffer was SQL_COLUMN_IGNORE.

SQLSTATE	Error	Description
22001	String data, right truncation	The *Operation* argument was SQL_UPDATE, and the assignment of a character or binary value to a column resulted in the truncation of non-blank (for characters) or non-null (for binary) characters or bytes.
22003	Numeric value out of range	The argument *Operation* was SQL_UPDATE, and the assignment of a numeric value to a column in the result set caused the whole (as opposed to fractional) part of the number to be truncated. The argument *Operation* was SQL_REFRESH, and returning the numeric value for one or more bound columns would have caused a loss of significant digits.
22007	Invalid datetime format	The argument *Operation* was SQL_UPDATE, and the assignment of a date or timestamp value to a column in the result set caused the year, month, or day field to be out of range. The argument *Operation* was SQL_REFRESH, and returning the date or timestamp value for one or more bound columns would have caused the year, month, or day field to be out of range.
22008	Date/time field overflow	The *Operation* argument was SQL_UPDATE, and the performance of datetime arithmetic on data being sent to a column in the result set resulted in a datetime field (the year, month, day, hour, minute, or second field) of the result being outside the permissible range of values for the field, or being invalid based on the natural rules for datetimes based on the Gregorian calendar. The *Operation* argument was SQL_REFRESH, and the performance of datetime arithmetic on data being retrieved from the result set resulted in a datetime field (the year, month, day, hour, minute, or second field) of the result being outside the permissible range of values for the field, or being invalid based on the natural rules for datetimes based on the Gregorian calendar.

SQLSTATE	Error	Description
22015	Interval field overflow	The *Operation* argument was SQL_UPDATE, and the assignment of an exact numeric or interval C type to an interval SQL data type caused a loss of significant digits. The *Operation* argument was SQL_UPDATE; when assigning to an interval SQL type, there was no representation of the value of the C type in the interval SQL type. The *Operation* argument was SQL_REFRESH, and assigning from an exact numeric or interval SQL type to an interval C type caused a loss of significant digits in the leading field. The *Operation* argument was SQL_ REFRESH; when assigning to an interval C type, there was no representation of the value of the SQL type in the interval C type.
22018	Invalid character value for cast specification	The *Operation* argument was SQL_REFRESH; the C type was an exact or approximate numeric, a datetime, or an interval data type; the SQL type of the column was a character data type; and the value in the column was not a valid literal of the bound C type. The argument *Operation* was SQL_UPDATE; the SQL type was an exact or approximate numeric, a datetime, or an interval data type; the C type was SQL_C_CHAR; and the value in the column was not a valid literal of the bound SQL type.
23000	Integrity constraint violation	The argument *Operation* was SQL_DELETE or SQL_UPDATE, and an integrity constraint was violated.

24000	Invalid cursor state	The *StatementHandle* was in an executed state but no result set was associated with the *StatementHandle*. (DM) A cursor was open on the *StatementHandle* but **SQLFetch** or **SQLFetchScroll** had not been called. A cursor was open on the *StatementHandle* and **SQLFetch** or **SQLFetchScroll** had been called, but the cursor was positioned before the start of the result set or after the end of the result set. The argument *Operation* was SQL_DELETE, SQL_REFRESH, or SQL_UPDATE, and the cursor was positioned before the start of the result set or after the end of the result set.
40001	Serialization failure	The transaction was rolled back due to a resource deadlock with another transaction.
40003	Statement completion unknown	The associated connection failed during the execution of this function and the state of the transaction cannot be determined.
42000	Syntax error or access violation	The driver was unable to lock the row as needed to perform the operation requested in the argument *Operation*. The driver was unable to lock the row as requested in the argument *LockType*.
44000	WITH CHECK OPTION violation	The *Operation* argument was SQL_UPDATE, and the update was performed on a viewed table or a table derived from the viewed table which was created by specifying **WITH CHECK OPTION**, such that one or more rows affected by the update will no longer be present in the viewed table.
HY000	General error	An error occurred for which there was no specific SQLSTATE and for which no implementation-specific SQLSTATE was defined. The error message returned by **SQLGetDiagRec** in the **MessageText* buffer describes the error and its cause.
HY001	Memory allocation error	The driver was unable to allocate memory required to support execution or completion of the function.

SQLSTATE	Error	Description
HY008	Operation canceled	Asynchronous processing was enabled for the *StatementHandle*. The function was called and before it completed execution, **SQLCancel** was called on the *StatementHandle*, and then the function was called again on the *StatementHandle*. The function was called and, before it completed execution, **SQLCancel** was called on the *StatementHandle* from a different thread in a multithread application.
HY010	Function sequence error	(DM) The specified *StatementHandle* was not in an executed state. The function was called without first calling **SQLExecDirect**, **SQLExecute**, or a catalog function. (DM) An asynchronously executing function (not this one) was called for the *StatementHandle* and was still executing when this function was called. (DM) **SQLExecute**, **SQLExecDirect**, **SQLBulkOperations**, or **SQLSetPos** was called for the *StatementHandle* and returned SQL_NEED_DATA. This function was called before data was sent for all data-at-execution parameters or columns. **SQLSetPos** was called for a *StatementHandle* before **SQLFetchScroll** or **SQLFetch** was called. (DM) The driver was an ODBC 2.*x* driver, and **SQLSetPos** was called for a *StatementHandle* after **SQLFetch** was called.
HY011	Attribute cannot be set now	(DM) The driver was an ODBC 2.*x* driver; the SQL_ATTR_ROW_STATUS_PTR statement attribute was set; then **SQLSetPos** was called before **SQLFetch**, **SQLFetchScroll**, or **SQLExtendedFetch** was called.
HY013	Memory management error	The function call could not be processed because the underlying memory objects could not be accessed, possibly because of low memory conditions.

SQLSTATE	Error	Description
HY090	Invalid string or buffer length	The *Operation* argument was SQL_UPDATE, a data value was a null pointer, and the column length value was not 0, SQL_DATA_AT_EXEC, SQL_COLUMN_IGNORE, SQL_NULL_DATA, or less than or equal to SQL_LEN_DATA_AT_EXEC_OFFSET.
		The *Operation* argument was SQL_UPDATE, a data value was not a null pointer; the C data type was SQL_C_BINARY or SQL_C_CHAR; and the column length value was less than 0, but not equal to SQL_DATA_AT_EXEC, SQL_COLUMN_IGNORE, SQL_NTS, or SQL_NULL_DATA, or less than or equal to SQL_LEN_DATA_AT_EXEC_OFFSET.
		The value in a length/indicator buffer was SQL_DATA_AT_EXEC; the SQL type was either SQL_LONGVARCHAR, SQL_LONGVARBINARY, or a long, data source–specific data type; and the SQL_NEED_LONG_DATA_LEN information type in **SQLGetInfo** was "Y".
HY092	Invalid attribute identifier	(DM) The value specified for the *Operation* argument was invalid.
		(DM) The value specified for the *LockType* argument was invalid.
		The *Operation* argument was SQL_UPDATE or SQL_DELETE, and the SQL_ATTR_CONCURRENCY statement attribute was SQL_ATTR_CONCUR_READ_ONLY.
HY107	Row value out of range	The value specified for the argument *RowNumber* was greater than the number of rows in the rowset.

SQLSTATE	Error	Description
HY109	Invalid cursor position	The cursor associated with the *StatementHandle* was defined as forward-only, so the cursor could not be positioned within the rowset. See the description for the SQL_ATTR_CURSOR_TYPE attribute in **SQLSetStmtAttr**. The *Operation* argument was SQL_UPDATE, SQL_DELETE, or SQL_REFRESH, and the row identified by the *RowNumber* argument had been deleted or had not been fetched. (DM) The *RowNumber* argument was 0 and the *Operation* argument was SQL_POSITION. **SQLSetPos** was called after **SQLBulkOperations** was called, and before **SQLFetchScroll** or **SQLFetch** was called.
HYC00	Optional feature not implemented	The driver or data source does not support the operation requested in the *Operation* argument or the *LockType* argument.
HYT00	Timeout expired	The query timeout period expired before the data source returned the result set. The timeout period is set through **SQLSetStmtAttr** with an *Attribute* of SQL_ATTR_QUERY_TIMEOUT.
HYT01	Connection timeout expired	The connection timeout period expired before the data source responded to the request. The connection timeout period is set through **SQLSetConnectAttr**, SQL_ATTR_CONNECTION_TIMEOUT.
IM001	Driver does not support this function	(DM) The driver associated with the *StatementHandle* does not support the function.

Comments

Caution For information on which statement states **SQLSetPos** can be called in and what it needs to do for compatibility with ODBC 2.*x* applications, see the "Block Cursors, Scrollable Cursors, and Backward Compatibility" section in Appendix G, "Driver Guidelines for Backward Compatibility."

RowNumber Argument

The *RowNumber* argument specifies the number of the row in the rowset on which to perform the operation specified by the *Operation* argument. If *RowNumber* is 0, the operation applies to every row in the rowset. *RowNumber* must be a value from 0 to the number of rows in the rowset.

Note In the C language, arrays are 0-based, while the *RowNumber* argument is 1-based. For example, to update the fifth row of the rowset, an application modifies the rowset buffers at array index 4, but specifies a *RowNumber* of 5.

All operations position the cursor on the row specified by *RowNumber*. The following operations require a cursor position:

- Positioned update and delete statements.
- Calls to **SQLGetData**.
- Calls to **SQLSetPos** with the SQL_DELETE, SQL_REFRESH, and SQL_UPDATE options.

For example, if *RowNumber* is 2 for a call to **SQLSetPos** with an *Operation* of SQL_DELETE, the cursor is positioned on the second row of the rowset, and that row is deleted. The entry in the implementation row status array (pointed to by the SQL_ATTR_ROW_STATUS_PTR statement attribute) for the second row is changed to SQL_ROW_DELETED.

An application can specify a cursor position when it calls **SQLSetPos**. Generally, it calls **SQLSetPos** with the SQL_POSITION or SQL_REFRESH operation to position the cursor before executing a positioned update or delete statement or calling **SQLGetData**.

Operation Argument

The *Operation* argument supports the following operations. To determine which options are supported by a data source, an application calls **SQLGetInfo** with the SQL_DYNAMIC_CURSOR_ATTRIBUTES1, SQL_FORWARD_ONLY_CURSOR_ATTRIBUTES1, SQL_KEYSET_CURSOR_ATTRIBUTES1, or SQL_STATIC_CURSOR_ATTRIBUTES1 information type (depending on the type of the cursor).

Operation argument	Operation
SQL_POSITION	The driver positions the cursor on the row specified by *RowNumber*. The contents of the row status array pointed to by the SQL_ATTR_ROW_OPERATION_PTR statement attribute are ignored for the SQL_POSITION *Operation*.
SQL_REFRESH	The driver positions the cursor on the row specified by *RowNumber* and refreshes data in the rowset buffers for that row. For more information about how the driver returns data in the rowset buffers, see the descriptions of row-wise and column-wise binding in **SQLBindCol**. **SQLSetPos** with an *Operation* of SQL_REFRESH updates the status and content of the rows within the current fetched rowset. This includes refreshing the bookmarks. Because the data in the buffers is refreshed, but not refetched, the membership in the rowset is fixed. This is different from the refresh performed by a call to **SQLFetchScroll** with a *FetchOrientation* of SQL_FETCH_RELATIVE and an *RowNumber* equal to 0, which refetches the rowset from the result set, so it can show added data and remove deleted data if those operations are supported by the driver and the cursor. A successful refresh with **SQLSetPos** will not change a row status of SQL_ROW_DELETED. Deleted rows within the rowset will continue to be marked as deleted until the next fetch. The rows will disappear at the next fetch if the cursor supports packing (in which a subsequent **SQLFetch** or **SQLFetchScroll** does not return deleted rows). Added rows do not appear when a refresh with **SQLSetPos** is performed. Note that this behavior is different from **SQLFetchScroll** with a *FetchType* of SQL_FETCH_RELATIVE and a *RowNumber* equal to 0, which also refreshes the current rowset, but will show added records or pack deleted records if these operations are supported by the cursor. A successful refresh with **SQLSetPos** will change a row status of SQL_ROW_ADDED to SQL_ROW_SUCCESS (if the row status array exists). A successful refresh with **SQLSetPos** will change a row status of SQL_ROW_UPDATED to the row's new status (if the row status array exists). If an error occurs in a **SQLSetPos** operation on a row, the row status is set to SQL_ROW_ERROR (if the row status array exists).

***Operation* argument**	**Operation**
SQL_REFRESH (*continued*)	For a cursor opened with an SQL_ATTR_CONCURRENCY statement attribute of SQL_CONCUR_ROWVER or SQL_CONCUR_VALUES, a refresh with **SQLSetPos** might update the optimistic concurrency values used by the data source to detect that the row has changed. If this occurs, the row versions or values used to ensure cursor concurrency are updated whenever the rowset buffers are refreshed from the server. This occurs for each row that is refreshed. The contents of the row status array pointed to by the SQL_ATTR_ROW_OPERATION_PTR statement attribute are ignored for the SQL_REFRESH *Operation*.
SQL_UPDATE	The driver positions the cursor on the row specified by *RowNumber* and updates the underlying row of data with the values in the rowset buffers (the *TargetValuePtr* argument in **SQLBindCol**). It retrieves the lengths of the data from the length/indicator buffers (the *StrLen_or_IndPtr* argument in **SQLBindCol**). If the length of any column is SQL_COLUMN_IGNORE, the column is not updated. After updating the row, the driver changes the corresponding element of the row status array to SQL_ROW_UPDATED or SQL_ROW_SUCCESS_WITH_INFO (if the row status array exists). It is driver-defined what the behavior is if **SQLSetPos** with an *Operation* argument of SQL_UPDATE is called on a cursor that contains duplicate columns. The driver can return a driver-defined SQLSTATE, can update the first column that appears in the result set, or other driver-defined behavior. The row operation array pointed to by the SQL_ATTR_ROW_OPERATION_PTR statement attribute can be used to indicate that a row in the current rowset should be ignored during a bulk update. For more information, see "Status and Operation Arrays" later in this function reference.

Operation argument	Operation
SQL_DELETE	The driver positions the cursor on the row specified by *RowNumber* and deletes the underlying row of data. It changes the corresponding element of the row status array to SQL_ROW_DELETED. After the row has been deleted, the following are not valid for the row: positioned update and delete statements, calls to **SQLGetData**, and calls to **SQLSetPos** with *Operation* set to anything except SQL_POSITION. For drivers that support packing, the row is deleted from the cursor when new data is retrieved from the data source. Whether the row remains visible depends on the cursor type. For example, deleted rows are visible to static and keyset-driven cursors but invisible to dynamic cursors. The row operation array pointed to by the SQL_ATTR_ROW_OPERATION_PTR statement attribute can be used to indicate that a row in the current rowset should be ignored during a bulk delete. For more information, see "Status and Operation Arrays" later in this function reference.

LockType Argument

The *LockType* argument provides a way for applications to control concurrency. Generally, data sources that support concurrency levels and transactions will only support the SQL_LOCK_NO_CHANGE value of the *LockType* argument. The *LockType* argument is generally used only for file-based support.

The *LockType* argument specifies the lock state of the row after **SQLSetPos** has been executed. Note that if the driver is unable to lock the row either to perform the requested operation or to satisfy the *LockType* argument, it returns SQL_ERROR and SQLSTATE 42000 (Syntax error or access violation).

Although the *LockType* argument is specified for a single statement, the lock accords the same privileges to all statements on the connection. In particular, a lock that is acquired by one statement on a connection can be unlocked by a different statement on the same connection.

A row locked through **SQLSetPos** remains locked until the application calls **SQLSetPos** for the row with *LockType* set to SQL_LOCK_UNLOCK, or the application calls **SQLFreeHandle** for the statement or **SQLFreeStmt** with the SQL_CLOSE option. For a driver that supports transactions, a row locked through **SQLSetPos** is unlocked when the application calls **SQLEndTran** to commit or roll back a transaction on the connection (if a cursor is closed when a transaction is committed or rolled back, as indicated by the SQL_CURSOR_COMMIT_BEHAVIOR and SQL_CURSOR_ROLLBACK_BEHAVIOR information types returned by **SQLGetInfo**).

The *LockType* argument supports the following types of locks. To determine which locks are supported by a data source, an application calls **SQLGetInfo** with the SQL_DYNAMIC_CURSOR_ATTRIBUTES1, SQL_FORWARD_ONLY_CURSOR_ATTRIBUTES1, SQL_KEYSET_CURSOR_ATTRIBUTES1, or SQL_STATIC_CURSOR_ATTRIBUTES1 information type (depending on the type of the cursor).

LockType argument	Lock type
SQL_LOCK_NO_CHANGE	The driver or data source ensures that the row is in the same locked or unlocked state as it was before **SQLSetPos** was called. This value of *LockType* allows data sources that do not support explicit row-level locking to use whatever locking is required by the current concurrency and transaction isolation levels.
SQL_LOCK_EXCLUSIVE	The driver or data source locks the row exclusively. A statement on a different connection or in a different application cannot be used to acquire any locks on the row.
SQL_LOCK_UNLOCK	The driver or data source unlocks the row.

If a driver supports SQL_LOCK_EXCLUSIVE, but does not support SQL_LOCK_UNLOCK, a row that is locked will remain locked until one of the function calls described in the previous paragraph.

If a driver supports SQL_LOCK_EXCLUSIVE, but does not support SQL_LOCK_UNLOCK, a row that is locked will remain locked until the application calls **SQLFreeHandle** for the statement or **SQLFreeStmt** with the SQL_CLOSE option. If the driver supports transactions and closes the cursor upon committing or rolling back the transaction, the application calls **SQLEndTran**.

For the update and delete operations in **SQLSetPos**, the application uses the *LockType* argument as follows:

- To guarantee that a row does not change after it is retrieved, an application calls **SQLSetPos** with *Operation* set to SQL_REFRESH and *LockType* set to SQL_LOCK_EXCLUSIVE.
- If the application sets *LockType* to SQL_LOCK_NO_CHANGE, the driver guarantees that an update or delete operation will succeed only if the application specified SQL_CONCUR_LOCK for the SQL_ATTR_CONCURRENCY statement attribute.
- If the application specifies SQL_CONCUR_ROWVER or SQL_CONCUR_VALUES for the SQL_ATTR_CONCURRENCY statement attribute, the driver compares row versions or values and rejects the operation if the row has changed since the application fetched the row.
- If the application specifies SQL_CONCUR_READ_ONLY for the SQL_ATTR_CONCURRENCY statement attribute, the driver rejects any update or delete operation.

For more information about the SQL_ATTR_CONCURRENCY statement attribute, see **SQLSetStmtAttr**.

Status and Operation Arrays

The following status and operation arrays are used when calling **SQLSetPos**:

- The row status array (as pointed to by the SQL_DESC_ARRAY_STATUS_PTR field in the IRD and the SQL_ATTR_ROW_STATUS_ARRAY statement attribute) contains status values for each row of data in the rowset. The driver sets the status values in this array after a call to **SQLFetch**, **SQLFetchScroll**, **SQLBulkOperations**, or **SQLSetPos**. This array is pointed to by the SQL_ATTR_ROW_STATUS_PTR statement attribute.
- The row operation array (as pointed to by the SQL_DESC_ARRAY_STATUS_PTR field in the ARD and the SQL_ATTR_ROW_OPERATION_ARRAY statement attribute) contains a value for each row in the rowset that indicates whether a call to **SQLSetPos** for a bulk operation is ignored or performed. Each element in the array is set to either SQL_ROW_PROCEED (the default) or SQL_ROW_IGNORE. This array is pointed to by the SQL_ATTR_ROW_OPERATION_PTR statement attribute.

The number of elements in the status and operation arrays must equal the number of rows in the rowset (as defined by the SQL_ATTR_ROW_ARRAY_SIZE statement attribute).

For information about the row status array, see **SQLFetch**. For information about the row operation array, see "Ignoring a Row in a Bulk Operation" later in this section.

Using SQLSetPos

Before an application calls **SQLSetPos**, it must perform the following sequence of steps:

1. If the application will call **SQLSetPos** with *Operation* set to SQL_UPDATE, call **SQLBindCol** (or **SQLSetDescRec**) for each column to specify its data type and bind buffers for the column's data and length.
2. If the application will call **SQLSetPos** with *Operation* set to SQL_DELETE or SQL_UPDATE, call **SQLColAttribute** to make sure that the columns to be deleted or updated are updatable.
3. Call **SQLExecDirect**, **SQLExecute**, or a catalog function to create a result set.
4. Call **SQLFetch** or **SQLFetchScroll** to retrieve the data.

   Note In ODBC 3.0, **SQLSetPos** can be called before **SQLFetch** or **SQLFetchScroll**. For more information, see the "Block Cursors, Scrollable Cursors, and Backward Compatibility" section in Appendix G, "Driver Guidelines for Backward Compatibility."

For more information about using **SQLSetPos**, see "Updating Data with SQLSetPos" in Chapter 12, "Updating Data."

Deleting Data Using SQLSetPos

To delete data with **SQLSetPos**, an application:

- Calls **SQLSetPos** with *RowNumber* set to the number of the row to delete and *Operation* set to SQL_DELETE.

After the data has been deleted, the driver changes the value in the implementation row status array for the appropriate row to SQL_ROW_DELETED (or SQL_ROW_ERROR).

Updating Data Using SQLSetPos

An application can pass the value for a column either in the bound data buffer or with one or more calls to **SQLPutData**. Columns whose data is passed with **SQLPutData** are known as *data-at-execution columns*. These are commonly used to send data for SQL_LONGVARBINARY and SQL_LONGVARCHAR columns and can be mixed with other columns.

To update data with **SQLSetPos**, an application:

1. Places values in the data and length/indicator buffers bound with **SQLBindCol**:
   - For normal columns, the application places the new column value in the **TargetValuePtr* buffer and the length of that value in the **StrLen_or_IndPtr* buffer. If the row should not be updated, the application places SQL_ROW_IGNORE in that row's element of the row operation array.
   - For data-at-execution columns, the application places an application-defined value, such as the column number, in the **TargetValuePtr* buffer. The value can be used later to identify the column.

     The application places the result of the SQL_LEN_DATA_AT_EXEC(*length*) macro in the **StrLen_or_IndPtr* buffer. If the SQL data type of the column is SQL_LONGVARBINARY, SQL_LONGVARCHAR, or a long, data source–specific data type and the driver returns "Y" for the SQL_NEED_LONG_DATA_LEN information type in **SQLGetInfo**, *length* is the number of bytes of data to be sent for the parameter; otherwise, it must be a nonnegative value and is ignored.
2. Calls **SQLSetPos** with the *Operation* argument set to SQL_UPDATE to update the row of data.
   - If there are no data-at-execution columns, the process is complete.
   - If there are any data-at-execution columns, the function returns SQL_NEED_DATA, and proceeds to step 3.
3. Calls **SQLParamData** to retrieve the address of the **TargetValuePtr* buffer for the first data-at-execution column to be processed. **SQLParamData** returns SQL_NEED_DATA. The application retrieves the application-defined value from the **TargetValuePtr* buffer.

Note Although data-at-execution parameters are similar to data-at-execution columns, the value returned by **SQLParamData** is different for each.

Data-at-execution parameters are parameters in an SQL statement for which data will be sent with **SQLPutData** when the statement is executed with **SQLExecDirect** or **SQLExecute**. They are bound with **SQLBindParameter**, or by setting descriptors with **SQLSetDescRec**. The value returned by **SQLParamData** is a 32-bit value passed to **SQLBindParameter** in the *ParameterValuePtr* argument.

Data-at-execution columns are columns in a rowset for which data will be sent with **SQLPutData** when a row is updated with **SQLSetPos**. They are bound with **SQLBindCol**. The value returned by **SQLParamData** is the address of the row in the **TargetValuePtr* buffer that is being processed.

4. Calls **SQLPutData** one or more times to send data for the column. More than one call is needed if all the data value cannot be returned in the **TargetValuePtr* buffer specified in **SQLPutData**; note that multiple calls to **SQLPutData** for the same column are allowed only when sending character C data to a column with a character, binary, or data source–specific data type or when sending binary C data to a column with a character, binary, or data source–specific data type.
5. Calls **SQLParamData** again to signal that all data has been sent for the column.
   - If there are more data-at-execution columns, **SQLParamData** returns SQL_NEED_DATA and the address of the *TargetValuePtr* buffer for the next data-at-execution column to be processed. The application repeats steps 4 and 5.
   - If there are no more data-at-execution columns, the process is complete. If the statement was executed successfully, **SQLParamData** returns SQL_SUCCESS or SQL_SUCCESS_WITH_INFO; if the execution failed, it returns SQL_ERROR. At this point, **SQLParamData** can return any SQLSTATE that can be returned by **SQLSetPos**.

If data has been updated, the driver changes the value in the implementation row status array for the appropriate row to SQL_ROW_UPDATED.

If the operation is canceled, or an error occurs in **SQLParamData** or **SQLPutData**, after **SQLSetPos** returns SQL_NEED_DATA, and before data is sent for all data-at-execution columns, the application can only call **SQLCancel**, **SQLGetDiagField**, **SQLGetDiagRec**, **SQLGetFunctions**, **SQLParamData**, or **SQLPutData** for the statement or the connection associated with the statement. If it calls any other function for the statement or the connection associated with the statement, the function returns SQL_ERROR and SQLSTATE HY010 (Function sequence error).

If the application calls **SQLCancel** while the driver still needs data for data-at-execution columns, the driver cancels the operation. The application can then call **SQLSetPos** again; canceling does not affect the cursor state or the current cursor position.

When the SELECT-list of the query specification associated with the cursor contains more than one reference to the same column, it is driver-defined whether:

- An error is generated

  or

- The driver ignores the duplicated references and performs the requested operations.

Performing Bulk Operations

If the *RowNumber* argument is 0, the driver performs the operation specified in the *Operation* argument for every row in the rowset that has a value of SQL_ROW_PROCEED in its field in the row operation array pointed to by SQL_ATTR_ROW_OPERATION_PTR statement attribute. This is a valid value of the *RowNumber* argument for an *Operation* argument of SQL_DELETE, SQL_REFRESH, or SQL_UPDATE, but not SQL_POSITION. **SQLSetPos** with an *Operation* of SQL_POSITION and a *RowNumber* equal to 0 will return SQLSTATE HY109 (Invalid cursor position).

If an error occurs that pertains to the entire rowset, such as SQLSTATE HYT00 (Timeout expired), the driver returns SQL_ERROR and the appropriate SQLSTATE. The contents of the rowset buffers are undefined and the cursor position is unchanged.

If an error occurs that pertains to a single row, the driver:

- Sets the element for the row in the row status array pointed to by the SQL_ATTR_ROW_STATUS_PTR statement attribute to SQL_ROW_ERROR.
- Posts one or more additional SQLSTATEs for the error in the error queue, and sets the SQL_DIAG_ROW_NUMBER field in the diagnostic data structure.

After it has processed the error or warning, if the driver completes the operation for the remaining rows in the rowset, it returns SQL_SUCCESS_WITH_INFO. Thus, for each row that returned an error, the error queue contains zero or more additional SQLSTATEs. If the driver stops the operation after it has processed the error or warning, it returns SQL_ERROR.

If the driver returns any warnings, such as SQLSTATE 01004 (Data truncated), it returns warnings that apply to the entire rowset or to unknown rows in the rowset before it returns the error information that applies to specific rows. It returns warnings for specific rows along with any other error information about those rows.

If *RowNumber* is equal to 0 and *Operation* is SQL_UPDATE, SQL_REFRESH, or SQL_DELETE, then the number of rows that **SQLSetPos** operates on is pointed to by the SQL_ATTR_ROWS_FETCHED_PTR statement attribute.

If *RowNumber* is equal to 0 and *Operation* is SQL_DELETE, SQL_REFRESH, or SQL_UPDATE, the current row after the operation is the same as the current row before the operation.

Ignoring a Row in a Bulk Operation

The row operation array can be used to indicate that a row in the current rowset should be ignored during a bulk operation using **SQLSetPos**. To direct the driver to ignore one or more rows during a bulk operation, an application should perform the following steps:

1. Call **SQLSetStmtAttr** to set the SQL_ATTR_ROW_OPERATION_PTR statement attribute to point to an array of SQLUSMALLINTs. This field can also be set by calling **SQLSetDescField** to set the SQL_DESC_ARRAY_STATUS_PTR header field of the ARD, which requires that an application obtains the descriptor handle.
2. Set each element of the row operation array to one of two values:
   - SQL_ROW_IGNORE, to indicate that the row is excluded for the bulk operation.
   - SQL_ROW_PROCEED, to indicate that the row is included in the bulk operation. (This is the default value.)
3. Call **SQLSetPos** to perform the bulk operation.

The following rules apply to the row operation array:

- SQL_ROW_IGNORE and SQL_ROW_PROCEED only affect bulk operations using **SQLSetPos** with an *Operation* of SQL_DELETE or SQL_UPDATE. They do not affect calls to **SQLSetPos** with an *Operation* of SQL_REFRESH or SQL_POSITION.
- The pointer is set to null by default.
- If the pointer is null, then all rows are updated, as if all elements were set to SQL_ROW_PROCEED.
- Setting an element to SQL_ROW_PROCEED does not guarantee that the operation will occur on that particular row. For example, if a certain row in the rowset has the status SQL_ROW_ERROR, then the driver may not be able to update that row regardless of whether the application specified SQL_ROW_PROCEED or not. An application must always check the row status array to see whether the operation was successful.
- SQL_ROW_PROCEED is defined as 0 in the header file. An application can initialize the row operation array to 0 in order to process all rows.
- If element number "n" in the row operation array is set to SQL_ROW_IGNORE, and **SQLSetPos** is called to perform a bulk update or delete operation, then the nth row in the rowset remains unchanged after the call to **SQLSetPos**.
- An application should automatically set a read-only column to SQL_ROW_IGNORE.

Ignoring a Column in a Bulk Operation

To avoid unnecessary processing diagnostics generated by attempted updates to one or more read-only columns, an application can set the value in the bound length/indicator buffer to SQL_COLUMN_IGNORE. For more information, see **SQLBindCol**.

Code Example

In the following example, an application allows a user to browse the ORDERS table and update order status. The cursor is keyset-driven with a rowset size of 20 and uses optimistic concurrency control comparing row versions. After each rowset is fetched, the application prints them and allows the user to select and update the status of an order. The application uses **SQLSetPos** to position the cursor on the selected row and performs a positioned update of the row. (Error handling is omitted for clarity.)

```
#define ROWS 20
#define STATUS_LEN 6

SQLCHAR         szStatus[ROWS][STATUS_LEN], szReply[3];
SQLINTEGER      cbStatus[ROWS], cbOrderID;
SQLUSMALLINT    rgfRowStatus[ROWS];
SQLUINTEGER     sOrderID, crow = ROWS, irow;
SQLHSTMT        hstmtS, hstmtU;

SQLSetStmtAttr(hstmtS, SQL_ATTR_CONCURRENCY, (SQLPOINTER) SQL_CONCUR_ROWVER, 0);
SQLSetStmtAttr(hstmtS, SQL_ATTR_CURSOR_TYPE, (SQLPOINTER) SQL_CURSOR_KEYSET_DRIVEN, 0);
SQLSetStmtAttr(hstmtS, SQL_ATTR_ROW_ARRAY_SIZE, (SQLPOINTER) ROWS, 0);
SQLSetStmtAttr(hstmtS, SQL_ATTR_ROW_STATUS_PTR, (SQLPOINTER) rgfRowStatus, 0);
SQLSetCursorName(hstmtS, "C1", SQL_NTS);
SQLExecDirect(hstmtS, "SELECT ORDERID, STATUS FROM ORDERS ", SQL_NTS);

SQLBindCol(hstmtS, 1, SQL_C_ULONG, &sOrderID, 0, &cbOrderID);
SQLBindCol(hstmtS, 2, SQL_C_CHAR, szStatus, STATUS_LEN, &cbStatus);

while ((retcode == SQLFetchScroll(hstmtS, SQL_FETCH_NEXT, 0)) != SQL_ERROR) {
   if (retcode == SQL_NO_DATA_FOUND)
      break;
   for (irow = 0; irow < crow; irow++) {
      if (rgfRowStatus[irow] != SQL_ROW_DELETED)
         printf("%2d %5d %*s\n", irow+1, sOrderID, NAME_LEN-1, szStatus[irow]);
   }
   while (TRUE) {
      printf("\nRow number to update?");
      gets(szReply);
      irow = atoi(szReply);
      if (irow > 0 && irow <= crow) {
         printf("\nNew status?");
         gets(szStatus[irow-1]);
         SQLSetPos(hstmtS, irow, SQL_POSITION, SQL_LOCK_NO_CHANGE);
         SQLPrepare(hstmtU,
            "UPDATE ORDERS SET STATUS=? WHERE CURRENT OF C1", SQL_NTS);
         SQLBindParameter(hstmtU, 1, SQL_PARAM_INPUT,
                          SQL_C_CHAR, SQL_CHAR,
                          STATUS_LEN, 0, szStatus[irow], 0, NULL);
```

Column name	Column number	Data type	Comments
BUFFER_LENGTH (ODBC 1.0)	6	Integer	The length in bytes of data transferred on an **SQLGetData** or **SQLFetch** operation if SQL_C_DEFAULT is specified. For numeric data, this size may be different than the size of the data stored on the data source. This value is the same as the COLUMN_SIZE column for character or binary data. For more information, see "Column Size, Decimal Digits, Transfer Octet Length, and Display Size," in Appendix D, "Data Types."
DECIMAL_DIGITS (ODBC 1.0)	7	Smallint	The decimal digits of the column on the data source. NULL is returned for data types where decimal digits are not applicable. For more information concerning decimal digits, see "Column Size, Decimal Digits, Transfer Octet Length, and Display Size," in Appendix D, "Data Types."
PSEUDO_COLUMN (ODBC 2.0)	8	Smallint	Indicates whether the column is a pseudo-column, such as Oracle ROWID: SQL_PC_UNKNOWN SQL_PC_NOT_PSEUDO SQL_PC_PSEUDO **Note** For maximum interoperability, pseudo-columns should not be quoted with the identifier quote character returned by **SQLGetInfo**.

After the application retrieves values for SQL_BEST_ROWID, the application can use these values to reselect that row within the defined scope. The **SELECT** statement is guaranteed to return either no rows or one row.

If an application reselects a row based on the rowid column or columns and the row is not found, then the application can assume that the row was deleted or the rowid columns were modified. The opposite is not true: even if the rowid has not changed, the other columns in the row may have changed.

Columns returned for column type SQL_BEST_ROWID are useful for applications that need to scroll forward and back within a result set to retrieve the most recent data from a set of rows. The column or columns of the rowid are guaranteed not to change while positioned on that row.

The column or columns of the rowid may remain valid even when the cursor is not positioned on the row; the application can determine this by checking the SCOPE column in the result set.

Columns returned for column type SQL_ROWVER are useful for applications that need the ability to check whether any columns in a given row have been updated while the row was reselected using the rowid. For example, after reselecting a row using rowid, the application can compare the previous values in the SQL_ROWVER columns to the ones just fetched. If the value in a SQL_ROWVER column differs from the previous value, the application can alert the user that data on the display has changed.

Code Example

For a code example of a similar function, see **SQLColumns**.

Related Functions

For information about	See
Binding a buffer to a column in a result set	**SQLBindCol**
Canceling statement processing	**SQLCancel**
Returning the columns in a table or tables	**SQLColumns**
Fetching a single row or a block of data in a forward-only direction	**SQLFetch**
Fetching a block of data or scrolling through a result set	**SQLFetchScroll**
Returning the columns of a primary key	**SQLPrimaryKeys**

SQLStatistics

Conformance

Version Introduced: ODBC 1.0
Standards Compliance: ISO 92

Summary

SQLStatistics retrieves a list of statistics about a single table and the indexes associated with the table. The driver returns the information as a result set.

Syntax

```
SQLRETURN SQLStatistics(
      SQLHSTMT       StatementHandle,
      SQLCHAR *      CatalogName,
      SQLSMALLINT    NameLength1,
      SQLCHAR *      SchemaName,
      SQLSMALLINT    NameLength2,
      SQLCHAR *      TableName,
      SQLSMALLINT    NameLength3,
      SQLUSMALLINT   Unique,
      SQLUSMALLINT   Reserved);
```

Arguments

StatementHandle [Input]
Statement handle.

CatalogName [Input]
Catalog name. If a driver supports catalogs for some tables but not for others, such as when the driver retrieves data from different DBMSs, an empty string ("") denotes those tables that do not have catalogs. *CatalogName* cannot contain a string search pattern.

If the SQL_ATTR_METADATA_ID statement attribute is set to SQL_TRUE, *CatalogName* is treated as an identifier, and its case is not significant. If it is SQL_FALSE, *CatalogName* is an ordinary argument; it is treated literally, and its case is significant. For more information, see "Arguments in Catalog Functions" in Chapter 7, "Catalog Functions."

NameLength1 [Input]
Length of **CatalogName*.

SchemaName [Input]
Schema name. If a driver supports schemas for some tables but not for others, such as when the driver retrieves data from different DBMSs, an empty string ("") denotes those tables that do not have schemas. *SchemaName* cannot contain a string search pattern.

If the SQL_ATTR_METADATA_ID statement attribute is set to SQL_TRUE, *SchemaName* is treated as an identifier, and its case is not significant. If it is SQL_FALSE, *SchemaName* is an ordinary argument; it is treated literally, and its case is significant.

NameLength2 [Input]
Length of **SchemaName*.

TableName [Input]
Table name. This argument cannot be a null pointer. *SchemaName* cannot contain a string search pattern.

If the SQL_ATTR_METADATA_ID statement attribute is set to SQL_TRUE, *TableName* is treated as an identifier, and its case is not significant. If it is SQL_FALSE, *TableName* is an ordinary argument; it is treated literally, and its case is significant.

NameLength3 [Input]
Length of **TableName*.

Unique [Input]
Type of index: SQL_INDEX_UNIQUE or SQL_INDEX_ALL.

Reserved [Input]
Indicates the importance of the CARDINALITY and PAGES columns in the result set. The following options affect the return of the CARDINALITY and PAGES columns only; index information is returned even if CARDINALITY and PAGES are not returned.

SQL_ENSURE requests that the driver unconditionally retrieve the statistics. (Drivers that conform only to the X/Open standard and do not support ODBC extensions will not be able to support SQL_ENSURE.)

SQL_QUICK requests that the driver retrieve the CARDINALITY and PAGE only if they are readily available from the server. In this case, the driver does not ensure that the values are current. (Applications that are written to the X/Open standard will always get SQL_QUICK behavior from ODBC 3.0-compliant drivers.)

Returns

SQL_SUCCESS, SQL_SUCCESS_WITH_INFO, SQL_STILL_EXECUTING, SQL_ERROR, or SQL_INVALID_HANDLE.

Diagnostics

When **SQLStatistics** returns SQL_ERROR or SQL_SUCCESS_WITH_INFO, an associated SQLSTATE value may be obtained by calling **SQLGetDiagRec** with a *HandleType* of SQL_HANDLE_STMT and a *Handle* of *StatementHandle*. The following table lists the SQLSTATE values commonly returned by **SQLStatistics** and explains each one in the context of this function; the notation "(DM)" precedes the descriptions of SQLSTATEs returned by the Driver Manager. The return code associated with each SQLSTATE value is SQL_ERROR, unless noted otherwise.

SQLSTATE	Error	Description
01000	General warning	Driver-specific informational message. (Function returns SQL_SUCCESS_WITH_INFO.)
08S01	Communication link failure	The communication link between the driver and the data source to which the driver was connected failed before the function completed processing.
24000	Invalid cursor state	A cursor was open on the *StatementHandle* and **SQLFetch** or **SQLFetchScroll** had been called. This error is returned by the Driver Manager if **SQLFetch** or **SQLFetchScroll** has not returned SQL_NO_DATA, and is returned by the driver if **SQLFetch** or **SQLFetchScroll** has returned SQL_NO_DATA. A cursor was open on the *StatementHandle* but **SQLFetch** or **SQLFetchScroll** had not been called.
40001	Serialization failure	The transaction was rolled back due to a resource deadlock with another transaction.
40003	Statement completion unknown	The associated connection failed during the execution of this function and the state of the transaction cannot be determined.
HY000	General error	An error occurred for which there was no specific SQLSTATE and for which no implementation-specific SQLSTATE was defined. The error message returned by **SQLGetDiagRec** in the **MessageText* buffer describes the error and its cause.
HY001	Memory allocation error	The driver was unable to allocate memory required to support execution or completion of the function.

SQLSTATE	Error	Description
HY008	Operation canceled	Asynchronous processing was enabled for the *StatementHandle*. The function was called and before it completed execution, **SQLCancel** was called on the *StatementHandle*, and then the function was called again on the *StatementHandle*. The function was called and, before it completed execution, **SQLCancel** was called on the *StatementHandle* from a different thread in a multithread application.
HY009	Invalid use of null pointer	The *TableName* argument was a null pointer. (DM) The SQL_ATTR_METADATA_ID statement attribute was set to SQL_TRUE, the *CatalogName* argument was a null pointer, and the SQL_CATALOG_NAME *InfoType* returns that catalog names are supported. (DM) The SQL_ATTR_METADATA_ID statement attribute was set to SQL_TRUE, and the *SchemaName* argument was a null pointer.
HY010	Function sequence error	(DM) An asynchronously executing function (not this one) was called for the *StatementHandle* and was still executing when this function was called. (DM) **SQLExecute**, **SQLExecDirect**, **SQLBulkOperations**, or **SQLSetPos** was called for the *StatementHandle* and returned SQL_NEED_DATA. This function was called before data was sent for all data-at-execution parameters or columns.
HY013	Memory management error	The function call could not be processed because the underlying memory objects could not be accessed, possibly because of low memory conditions.
HY090	Invalid string or buffer length	(DM) The value of one of the name length arguments was less than 0, but not equal to SQL_NTS. The value of one of the name length arguments exceeded the maximum length value for the corresponding name.
HY100	Uniqueness option type out of range	(DM) An invalid *Unique* value was specified.
HY101	Accuracy option type out of range	(DM) An invalid *Reserved* value was specified.

SQLSTATE	Error	Description
HYC00	Optional feature not implemented	A catalog was specified and the driver or data source does not support catalogs. A schema was specified and the driver or data source does not support schemas. The combination of the current settings of the SQL_ATTR_CONCURRENCY and SQL_ATTR_CURSOR_TYPE statement attributes was not supported by the driver or data source. The SQL_ATTR_USE_BOOKMARKS statement attribute was set to SQL_UB_VARIABLE, and the SQL_ATTR_CURSOR_TYPE statement attribute was set to a cursor type for which the driver does not support bookmarks.
HYT00	Timeout expired	The query timeout period expired before the data source returned the requested result set. The timeout period is set through **SQLSetStmtAttr**, SQL_ATTR_QUERY_TIMEOUT.
HYT01	Connection timeout expired	The connection timeout period expired before the data source responded to the request. The connection timeout period is set through **SQLSetConnectAttr**, SQL_ATTR_CONNECTION_TIMEOUT.
IM001	Driver does not support this function	(DM) The driver associated with the *StatementHandle* does not support the function.

Comments

SQLStatistics returns information about a single table as a standard result set, ordered by NON_UNIQUE, TYPE, INDEX_QUALIFIER, INDEX_NAME, and ORDINAL_POSITION. The result set combines statistics information (in the CARDINALITY and PAGES columns of the result set) for the table with information about each index. For information about how this information might be used, see "Uses of Catalog Data" in Chapter 7, "Catalog Functions."

To determine the actual lengths of the TABLE_CAT, TABLE_SCHEM, TABLE_NAME, and COLUMN_NAME columns, an application can call **SQLGetInfo** with the SQL_MAX_CATALOG_NAME_LEN, SQL_MAX_SCHEMA_NAME_LEN, SQL_MAX_TABLE_NAME_LEN, and SQL_MAX_COLUMN_NAME_LEN options.

Note For more information about the general use, arguments, and returned data of ODBC catalog functions, see Chapter 7, "Catalog Functions."

The following columns have been renamed for ODBC 3.0. The column name changes do not affect backward compatibility because applications bind by column number.

ODBC 2.0 column	ODBC 3.0 column
TABLE_QUALIFIER	TABLE_CAT
TABLE_OWNER	TABLE_SCHEM
SEQ_IN_INDEX	ORDINAL_POSITION
COLLATION	ASC_OR_DESC

The following table lists the columns in the result set. Additional columns beyond column 13 (FILTER_CONDITION) can be defined by the driver. An application should gain access to driver-specific columns by counting down from the end of the result set rather than specifying an explicit ordinal position. For more information, see "Data Returned by Catalog Functions" in Chapter 7, "Catalog Functions."

Column name	Column number	Data type	Comments
TABLE_CAT (ODBC 1.0)	1	Varchar	Catalog name of the table to which the statistic or index applies; NULL if not applicable to the data source. If a driver supports catalogs for some tables but not for others, such as when the driver retrieves data from different DBMSs, it returns an empty string ("") for those tables that do not have catalogs.
TABLE_SCHEM (ODBC 1.0)	2	Varchar	Schema name of the table to which the statistic or index applies; NULL if not applicable to the data source. If a driver supports schemas for some tables but not for others, such as when the driver retrieves data from different DBMSs, it returns an empty string ("") for those tables that do not have schemas.
TABLE_NAME (ODBC 1.0)	3	Varchar not NULL	Table name of the table to which the statistic or index applies.
NON_UNIQUE (ODBC 1.0)	4	Smallint	Indicates whether the index prohibits duplicate values: SQL_TRUE if the index values can be nonunique. SQL_FALSE if the index values must be unique. NULL is returned if TYPE is SQL_TABLE_STAT.

Column name	Column number	Data type	Comments
INDEX_QUALIFIER (ODBC 1.0)	5	Varchar	The identifier that is used to qualify the index name doing a **DROP INDEX**; NULL is returned if an index qualifier is not supported by the data source or if TYPE is SQL_TABLE_STAT. If a non-null value is returned in this column, it must be used to qualify the index name on a **DROP INDEX** statement; otherwise the TABLE_SCHEM should be used to qualify the index name.
INDEX_NAME (ODBC 1.0)	6	Varchar	Index name; NULL is returned if TYPE is SQL_TABLE_STAT.
TYPE (ODBC 1.0)	7	Smallint not NULL	Type of information being returned: SQL_TABLE_STAT indicates a statistic for the table (in the CARDINALITY or PAGES column). SQL_INDEX_BTREE indicates a B-Tree index. SQL_INDEX_CLUSTERED indicates a clustered index. SQL_INDEX_CONTENT indicates a content index. SQL_INDEX_HASHED indicates a hashed index. SQL_INDEX_OTHER indicates another type of index.
ORDINAL_ POSITION (ODBC 1.0)	8	Smallint	Column sequence number in index (starting with 1); NULL is returned if TYPE is SQL_TABLE_STAT.
COLUMN_NAME (ODBC 1.0)	9	Varchar	Column name. If the column is based on an expression, such as SALARY + BENEFITS, the expression is returned; if the expression cannot be determined, an empty string is returned. NULL is returned if TYPE is SQL_TABLE_STAT.
ASC_OR_DESC (ODBC 1.0)	10	Char(1)	Sort sequence for the column; "A" for ascending; "D" for descending; NULL is returned if column sort sequence is not supported by the data source or if TYPE is SQL_TABLE_STAT.

Column name	Column number	Data type	Comments
CARDINALITY (ODBC 1.0)	11	Integer	Cardinality of table or index; number of rows in table if TYPE is SQL_TABLE_STAT; number of unique values in the index if TYPE is not SQL_TABLE_STAT; NULL is returned if the value is not available from the data source.
PAGES (ODBC 1.0)	12	Integer	Number of pages used to store the index or table; number of pages for the table if TYPE is SQL_TABLE_STAT; number of pages for the index if TYPE is not SQL_TABLE_STAT; NULL is returned if the value is not available from the data source, or if not applicable to the data source.
FILTER_ CONDITION (ODBC 2.0)	13	Varchar	If the index is a filtered index, this is the filter condition, such as SALARY > 30000; if the filter condition cannot be determined, this is an empty string. NULL if the index is not a filtered index, it cannot be determined whether the index is a filtered index, or TYPE is SQL_TABLE_STAT.

If the row in the result set corresponds to a table, the driver sets TYPE to SQL_TABLE_STAT and sets NON_UNIQUE, INDEX_QUALIFIER, INDEX_NAME, ORDINAL_POSITION, COLUMN_NAME, and ASC_OR_DESC to NULL. If CARDINALITY or PAGES are not available from the data source, the driver sets them to NULL.

Code Example

For a code example of a similar function, see **SQLColumns**.

Related Functions

For information about	See
Binding a buffer to a column in a result set	**SQLBindCol**
Canceling statement processing	**SQLCancel**
Fetching a single row or a block of data in a forward-only direction.	**SQLFetch**
Fetching a block of data or scrolling through a result set	**SQLFetchScroll**
Returning the columns of foreign keys	**SQLForeignKeys**
Returning the columns of a primary key	**SQLPrimaryKeys**

SQLTablePrivileges

Conformance

Version Introduced: ODBC 1.0
Standards Compliance: ODBC

Summary

SQLTablePrivileges returns a list of tables and the privileges associated with each table. The driver returns the information as a result set on the specified statement.

Syntax

```
SQLRETURN SQLTablePrivileges(
      SQLHSTMT      StatementHandle,
      SQLCHAR *     CatalogName,
      SQLSMALLINT   NameLength1,
      SQLCHAR *     SchemaName,
      SQLSMALLINT   NameLength2,
      SQLCHAR *     TableName,
      SQLSMALLINT   NameLength3);
```

Arguments

StatementHandle [Input]
Statement handle.

CatalogName [Input]
Table catalog. If a driver supports catalogs for some tables but not for others, such as when the driver retrieves data from different DBMSs, an empty string ("") denotes those tables that do not have catalogs. *CatalogName* cannot contain a string search pattern.

If the SQL_ATTR_METADATA_ID statement attribute is set to SQL_TRUE, *CatalogName* is treated as an identifier, and its case is not significant. If it is SQL_FALSE, *CatalogName* is an ordinary argument; it is treated literally, and its case is significant. For more information, see "Arguments in Catalog Functions" in Chapter 7, "Catalog Functions."

NameLength1 [Input]
Length of **CatalogName*.

SchemaName [Input]
String search pattern for schema names. If a driver supports schemas for some tables but not for others, such as when the driver retrieves data from different DBMSs, an empty string ("") denotes those tables that do not have schemas.

If the SQL_ATTR_METADATA_ID statement attribute is set to SQL_TRUE, *SchemaName* is treated as an identifier, and its case is not significant. If it is SQL_FALSE, *SchemaName* is a pattern value argument; it is treated literally, and its case is significant.

NameLength2 [Input]
Length of **SchemaName*.

TableName [Input]
String search pattern for table names.

If the SQL_ATTR_METADATA_ID statement attribute is set to SQL_TRUE, *TableName* is treated as an identifier, and its case is not significant. If it is SQL_FALSE, *TableName* is a pattern value argument; it is treated literally, and its case is significant.

NameLength3 [Input]
Length of **TableName*.

Returns

SQL_SUCCESS, SQL_SUCCESS_WITH_INFO, SQL_STILL_EXECUTING, SQL_ERROR, or SQL_INVALID_HANDLE.

Diagnostics

When **SQLTablePrivileges** returns SQL_ERROR or SQL_SUCCESS_WITH_INFO, an associated SQLSTATE value may be obtained by calling **SQLGetDiagRec** with a *HandleType* of SQL_HANDLE_STMT and a *Handle* of *StatementHandle*. The following table lists the SQLSTATE values commonly returned by **SQLTablePrivileges** and explains each one in the context of this function; the notation "(DM)" precedes the descriptions of SQLSTATEs returned by the Driver Manager. The return code associated with each SQLSTATE value is SQL_ERROR, unless noted otherwise.

SQLSTATE	Error	Description
01000	General warning	Driver-specific informational message. (Function returns SQL_SUCCESS_WITH_INFO.)
08S01	Communication link failure	The communication link between the driver and the data source to which the driver was connected failed before the function completed processing.
24000	Invalid cursor state	A cursor was open on the *StatementHandle* and **SQLFetch** or **SQLFetchScroll** had been called. This error is returned by the Driver Manager if **SQLFetch** or **SQLFetchScroll** has not returned SQL_NO_DATA, and is returned by the driver if **SQLFetch** or **SQLFetchScroll** has returned SQL_NO_DATA. A cursor was open on the *StatementHandle* but **SQLFetch** or **SQLFetchScroll** had not been called.
40001	Serialization failure	The transaction was rolled back due to a resource deadlock with another transaction.

SQLSTATE	Error	Description
40003	Statement completion unknown	The associated connection failed during the execution of this function and the state of the transaction cannot be determined.
HY000	General error	An error occurred for which there was no specific SQLSTATE and for which no implementation-specific SQLSTATE was defined. The error message returned by **SQLGetDiagRec** in the **MessageText* buffer describes the error and its cause.
HY001	Memory allocation error	The driver was unable to allocate memory required to support execution or completion of the function.
HY008	Operation canceled	Asynchronous processing was enabled for the *StatementHandle*. The function was called and before it completed execution, **SQLCancel** was called on the *StatementHandle*. Then the function was called again on the *StatementHandle*. The function was called and, before it completed execution, **SQLCancel** was called on the *StatementHandle* from a different thread in a multithread application.
HY009	Invalid use of null pointer	(DM) The SQL_ATTR_METADATA_ID statement attribute was set to SQL_TRUE, the *CatalogName* argument was a null pointer, and the SQL_CATALOG_NAME *InfoType* returns that catalog names are supported. (DM) The SQL_ATTR_METADATA_ID statement attribute was set to SQL_TRUE, and the *SchemaName* or *TableName* argument was a null pointer.
HY010	Function sequence error	(DM) An asynchronously executing function (not this one) was called for the *StatementHandle* and was still executing when this function was called. (DM) **SQLExecute**, **SQLExecDirect**, **SQLBulkOperations**, or **SQLSetPos** was called for the *StatementHandle* and returned SQL_NEED_DATA. This function was called before data was sent for all data-at-execution parameters or columns.
HY013	Memory management error	The function call could not be processed because the underlying memory objects could not be accessed, possibly because of low memory conditions.

SQLSTATE	Error	Description
HY090	Invalid string or buffer length	(DM) The value of one of the name length arguments was less than 0, but not equal to SQL_NTS. The value of one of the name length arguments exceeded the maximum length value for the corresponding qualifier or name.
HYC00	Optional feature not implemented	A catalog was specified and the driver or data source does not support catalogs. A schema was specified and the driver or data source does not support schemas. A string search pattern was specified for the table schema, table name, or column name and the data source does not support search patterns for one or more of those arguments. The combination of the current settings of the SQL_ATTR_CONCURRENCY and SQL_ATTR_CURSOR_TYPE statement attributes was not supported by the driver or data source. The SQL_ATTR_USE_BOOKMARKS statement attribute was set to SQL_UB_VARIABLE, and the SQL_ATTR_CURSOR_TYPE statement attribute was set to a cursor type for which the driver does not support bookmarks.
HYT00	Timeout expired	The query timeout period expired before the data source returned the result set. The timeout period is set through **SQLSetStmtAttr**, SQL_ATTR_QUERY_TIMEOUT.
HYT01	Connection timeout expired	The connection timeout period expired before the data source responded to the request. The connection timeout period is set through **SQLSetConnectAttr**, SQL_ATTR_CONNECTION_TIMEOUT.
IM001	Driver does not support this function	(DM) The driver associated with the *StatementHandle* does not support the function.

Comments

The *SchemaName* and *TableName* arguments accept search patterns. For more information about valid search patterns, see "Pattern Value Arguments" in Chapter 7, "Catalog Functions."

SQLTablePrivileges returns the results as a standard result set, ordered by TABLE_CAT, TABLE_SCHEM, TABLE_NAME, and PRIVILEGE.

To determine the actual lengths of the TABLE_CAT, TABLE_SCHEM, and TABLE_NAME columns, an application can call **SQLGetInfo** with the SQL_MAX_CATALOG_NAME_LEN, SQL_MAX_SCHEMA_NAME_LEN, and SQL_MAX_TABLE_NAME_LEN options.

Note For more information about the general use, arguments, and returned data of ODBC catalog functions, see Chapter 7, "Catalog Functions."

The following columns have been renamed for ODBC 3.0. The column name changes do not affect backward compatibility because applications bind by column number.

ODBC 2.0 column	ODBC 3.0 column
TABLE_QUALIFIER	TABLE_CAT
TABLE_OWNER	TABLE_SCHEM

The following table lists the columns in the result set. Additional columns beyond column 7 (IS_GRANTABLE) can be defined by the driver. An application should gain access to driver-specific columns by counting down from the end of the result set rather than specifying an explicit ordinal position. For more information, see "Data Returned by Catalog Functions" in Chapter 7, "Catalog Functions."

Column name	Column Number	Data type	Comments
TABLE_CAT (ODBC 1.0)	1	Varchar	Catalog name; NULL if not applicable to the data source. If a driver supports catalogs for some tables but not for others, such as when the driver retrieves data from different DBMSs, it returns an empty string ("") for those tables that do not have catalogs.
TABLE_SCHEM (ODBC 1.0)	2	Varchar	Schema name; NULL if not applicable to the data source. If a driver supports schemas for some tables but not for others, such as when the driver retrieves data from different DBMSs, it returns an empty string ("") for those tables that do not have schemas.
TABLE_NAME (ODBC 1.0)	3	Varchar not NULL	Table name.
GRANTOR (ODBC 1.0)	4	Varchar	Name of the user who granted the privilege; NULL if not applicable to the data source. For all rows in which the value in the GRANTEE column is the owner of the object, the GRANTOR column will be "_SYSTEM".

Column name	Column Number	Data type	Comments
GRANTEE (ODBC 1.0)	5	Varchar not NULL	Name of the user to whom the privilege was granted.
PRIVILEGE (ODBC 1.0)	6	Varchar not NULL	The table privilege. May be one of the following or a data source–specific privilege. SELECT: The grantee is permitted to retrieve data for one or more columns of the table. INSERT: The grantee is permitted to insert new rows containing data for one or more columns into the table. UPDATE: The grantee is permitted to update the data in one or more columns of the table. DELETE: The grantee is permitted to delete rows of data from the table. REFERENCES: The grantee is permitted to refer to one or more columns of the table within a constraint (for example, a unique, referential, or table check constraint). The scope of action permitted the grantee by a given table privilege is data source–dependent. For example, the UPDATE privilege might permit the grantee to update all columns in a table on one data source and only those columns for which the grantor has the UPDATE privilege on another data source.
IS_GRANTABLE (ODBC 1.0)	7	Varchar	Indicates whether the grantee is permitted to grant the privilege to other users; "YES", "NO", or NULL if unknown or not applicable to the data source. A privilege is either grantable or not grantable, but not both. The result set returned by **SQLColumnPrivileges** will never contain two rows for which all columns except the IS_GRANTABLE column contain the same value.

Code Example

For a code example of a similar function, see **SQLColumns**.

Related Functions

For information about	See
Binding a buffer to a column in a result set	**SQLBindCol**
Canceling statement processing	**SQLCancel**
Returning privileges for a column or columns	**SQLColumnPrivileges**
Returning the columns in a table or tables	**SQLColumns**
Fetching a single row or a block of data in a forward-only direction	**SQLFetch**
Fetching a block of data or scrolling through a result set	**SQLFetchScroll**
Returning table statistics and indexes	**SQLStatistics**
Returning a list of tables in a data source	**SQLTables**

SQLTables

Conformance

Version Introduced: ODBC 1.0
Standards Compliance: X/Open

Summary

SQLTables returns the list of table, catalog, or schema names, and table types, stored in a specific data source. The driver returns the information as a result set.

Syntax

SQLRETURN **SQLTables**(
    SQLHSTMT *StatementHandle*,
    SQLCHAR * *CatalogName*,
    SQLSMALLINT *NameLength1*,
    SQLCHAR * *SchemaName*,
    SQLSMALLINT *NameLength2*,
    SQLCHAR * *TableName*,
    SQLSMALLINT *NameLength3*,
    SQLCHAR * *TableType*,
    SQLSMALLINT *NameLength4*);

Arguments

StatementHandle [Input]
Statement handle for retrieved results.

CatalogName [Input]
Catalog name. The *CatalogName* argument accepts search patterns if the SQL_ODBC_VERSION environment attribute is SQL_OV_ODBC3; it does not accept search patterns if SQL_OV_ODBC2 is set. If a driver supports catalogs for some tables but not for others, such as when a driver retrieves data from different DBMSs, an empty string ("") denotes those tables that do not have catalogs.

If the SQL_ATTR_METADATA_ID statement attribute is set to SQL_TRUE, *CatalogName* is treated as an identifier, and its case is not significant. If it is SQL_FALSE, *CatalogName* is a pattern value argument; it is treated literally, and its case is significant. For more information, see "Arguments in Catalog Functions" in Chapter 7, "Catalog Functions."

NameLength1 [Input]
Length of **CatalogName*.

SchemaName [Input]
String search pattern for schema names. If a driver supports schemas for some tables but not for others, such as when the driver retrieves data from different DBMSs, an empty string ("") denotes those tables that do not have schemas.

If the SQL_ATTR_METADATA_ID statement attribute is set to SQL_TRUE, *SchemaName* is treated as an identifier, and its case is not significant. If it is SQL_FALSE, *SchemaName* is a pattern value argument; it is treated literally, and its case is significant.

NameLength2 [Input]
Length of **SchemaName*.

TableName [Input]
String search pattern for table names.

If the SQL_ATTR_METADATA_ID statement attribute is set to SQL_TRUE, *TableName* is treated as an identifier, and its case is not significant. If it is SQL_FALSE, *TableName* is a pattern value argument; it is treated literally, and its case is significant.

NameLength3 [Input]
Length of **TableName*.

TableType [Input]
List of table types to match.

Note that the SQL_ATTR_METADATA_ID statement attribute has not effect upon the *TableType* argument. *TableType* is a value list argument no matter what the setting of SQL_ATTR_METADATA_ID.

NameLength4 [Input]
Length of **TableType*.

Returns

SQL_SUCCESS, SQL_SUCCESS_WITH_INFO, SQL_STILL_EXECUTING, SQL_ERROR, or SQL_INVALID_HANDLE.

Diagnostics

When **SQLTables** returns SQL_ERROR or SQL_SUCCESS_WITH_INFO, an associated SQLSTATE value may be obtained by calling **SQLGetDiagRec** with a *HandleType* of SQL_HANDLE_STMT and a *Handle* of *StatementHandle*. The following table lists the SQLSTATE values commonly returned by **SQLTables** and explains each one in the context of this function; the notation "(DM)" precedes the descriptions of SQLSTATEs returned by the Driver Manager. The return code associated with each SQLSTATE value is SQL_ERROR, unless noted otherwise.

SQLSTATE	Error	Description
01000	General warning	Driver-specific informational message. (Function returns SQL_SUCCESS_WITH_INFO.)
08S01	Communication link failure	The communication link between the driver and the data source to which the driver was connected failed before the function completed processing.
24000	Invalid cursor state	A cursor was open on the *StatementHandle* and **SQLFetch** or **SQLFetchScroll** had been called. This error is returned by the Driver Manager if **SQLFetch** or **SQLFetchScroll** has not returned SQL_NO_DATA, and is returned by the driver if **SQLFetch** or **SQLFetchScroll** has returned SQL_NO_DATA. A cursor was open on the *StatementHandle* but **SQLFetch** or **SQLFetchScroll** had not been called.
40001	Serialization failure	The transaction was rolled back due to a resource deadlock with another transaction.
40003	Statement completion unknown	The associated connection failed during the execution of this function and the state of the transaction cannot be determined.
HY000	General error	An error occurred for which there was no specific SQLSTATE and for which no implementation-specific SQLSTATE was defined. The error message returned by **SQLGetDiagRec** in the **MessageText* buffer describes the error and its cause.
HY001	Memory allocation error	The driver was unable to allocate memory required to support execution or completion of the function.
HY008	Operation canceled	Asynchronous processing was enabled for the *StatementHandle*. The function was called and before it completed execution, **SQLCancel** was called on the *StatementHandle*. Then the function was called again on the *StatementHandle*. The function was called and, before it completed execution, **SQLCancel** was called on the *StatementHandle* from a different thread in a multithread application.

SQLSTATE	Error	Description
HY009	Invalid use of null pointer	(DM) The SQL_ATTR_METADATA_ID statement attribute was set to SQL_TRUE, the *CatalogName* argument was a null pointer, and the SQL_CATALOG_NAME *InfoType* returns that catalog names are supported. (DM) The SQL_ATTR_METADATA_ID statement attribute was set to SQL_TRUE, and the *SchemaName* or *TableName* argument was a null pointer.
HY010	Function sequence error	(DM) An asynchronously executing function (not this one) was called for the *StatementHandle* and was still executing when this function was called. (DM) **SQLExecute**, **SQLExecDirect**, **SQLBulkOperations**, or **SQLSetPos** was called for the *StatementHandle* and returned SQL_NEED_DATA. This function was called before data was sent for all data-at-execution parameters or columns.
HY013	Memory management error	The function call could not be processed because the underlying memory objects could not be accessed, possibly because of low memory conditions.
HY090	Invalid string or buffer length	(DM) The value of one of the length arguments was less than 0, but not equal to SQL_NTS. The value of one of the name length arguments exceeded the maximum length value for the corresponding name.

SQLSTATE	Error	Description
HYC00	Optional feature not implemented	A catalog was specified and the driver or data source does not support catalogs. A schema was specified and the driver or data source does not support schemas. A string search pattern was specified for the catalog name, table schema, or table name and the data source does not support search patterns for one or more of those arguments. The combination of the current settings of the SQL_ATTR_CONCURRENCY and SQL_ATTR_CURSOR_TYPE statement attributes was not supported by the driver or data source. The SQL_ATTR_USE_BOOKMARKS statement attribute was set to SQL_UB_VARIABLE, and the SQL_ATTR_CURSOR_TYPE statement attribute was set to a cursor type for which the driver does not support bookmarks.
HYT00	Timeout expired	The query timeout period expired before the data source returned the requested result set. The timeout period is set through **SQLSetStmtAttr**, SQL_ATTR_QUERY_TIMEOUT.
HYT01	Connection timeout expired	The connection timeout period expired before the data source responded to the request. The connection timeout period is set through **SQLSetConnectAttr**, SQL_ATTR_CONNECTION_TIMEOUT.
IM001	Driver does not support this function	(DM) The driver associated with the *StatementHandle* does not support the function.

Comments

SQLTables lists all tables in the requested range. A user may or may not have SELECT privileges to any of these tables. To check accessibility, an application can:

- Call **SQLGetInfo** and check the SQL_ACCESSIBLE_TABLES information type.
- Call **SQLTablePrivileges** to check the privileges for each table.

Otherwise, the application must be able to handle a situation where the user selects a table for which **SELECT** privileges are not granted.

The *SchemaName* and *TableName* arguments accept search patterns. The *CatalogName* argument accepts search patterns if the SQL_ODBC_VERSION environment attribute is SQL_OV_ODBC3; it does not accept search patterns if SQL_OV_ODBC2 is set. If SQL_OV_ODBC3 is set, an ODBC 3.0 driver will require that wildcard characters in the *CatalogName* argument be escaped to be treated literally. For more information about valid search patterns, see "Pattern Value Arguments" in Chapter 7, "Catalog Functions."

Note For more information about the general use, arguments, and returned data of ODBC catalog functions, see Chapter 7, "Catalog Functions."

To support enumeration of catalogs, schemas, and table types, the following special semantics are defined for the *CatalogName*, *SchemaName*, *TableName*, and *TableType* arguments of **SQLTables**:

- If *CatalogName* is SQL_ALL_CATALOGS and *SchemaName* and *TableName* are empty strings, then the result set contains a list of valid catalogs for the data source. (All columns except the TABLE_CAT column contain NULLs.)
- If *SchemaName* is SQL_ALL_SCHEMAS and *CatalogName* and *TableName* are empty strings, then the result set contains a list of valid schemas for the data source. (All columns except the TABLE_SCHEM column contain NULLs.)
- If *TableType* is SQL_ALL_TABLE_TYPES and *CatalogName*, *SchemaName*, and *TableName* are empty strings, then the result set contains a list of valid table types for the data source. (All columns except the TABLE_TYPE column contain NULLs.)

If *TableType* is not an empty string, it must contain a list of comma-separated values for the types of interest; each value may be enclosed in single quotation marks (') or unquoted. For example, "'TABLE','VIEW'" or "TABLE, VIEW". An application should always specify the table type in uppercase; the driver should convert the table type to whatever case is needed by the data source. If the data source does not support a specified table type, **SQLTables** does not return any results for that type.

SQLTables returns the results as a standard result set, ordered by TABLE_TYPE, TABLE_CAT, TABLE_SCHEM, and TABLE_NAME. For information about how this information might be used, see "Uses of Catalog Data" in Chapter 7, "Catalog Functions."

To determine the actual lengths of the TABLE_CAT, TABLE_SCHEM, and TABLE_NAME columns, an application can call **SQLGetInfo** with the SQL_MAX_CATALOG_NAME_LEN, SQL_MAX_SCHEMA_NAME_LEN, and SQL_MAX_TABLE_NAME_LEN information types.

The following columns have been renamed for ODBC 3.0. The column name changes do not affect backward compatibility because applications bind by column number.

ODBC 2.0 column	ODBC 3.0 column
TABLE_QUALIFIER	TABLE_CAT
TABLE_OWNER	TABLE_SCHEM

The following table lists the columns in the result set. Additional columns beyond column 5 (REMARKS) can be defined by the driver. An application should gain access to driver-specific columns by counting down from the end of the result set rather than specifying an explicit ordinal position. For more information, see "Data Returned by Catalog Functions" in Chapter 7, "Catalog Functions."

Column name	Column number	Data type	Comments
TABLE_CAT (ODBC 1.0)	1	Varchar	Catalog name; NULL if not applicable to the data source. If a driver supports catalogs for some tables but not for others, such as when the driver retrieves data from different DBMSs, it returns an empty string ("") for those tables that do not have catalogs.
TABLE_SCHEM (ODBC 1.0)	2	Varchar	Schema name; NULL if not applicable to the data source. If a driver supports schemas for some tables but not for others, such as when the driver retrieves data from different DBMSs, it returns an empty string ("") for those tables that do not have schemas.
TABLE_NAME (ODBC 1.0)	3	Varchar	Table name.
TABLE_TYPE (ODBC 1.0)	4	Varchar	Table type name; one of the following: "TABLE", "VIEW", "SYSTEM TABLE", "GLOBAL TEMPORARY", "LOCAL TEMPORARY", "ALIAS", "SYNONYM", or a data source–specific type name. The meanings of "ALIAS" and "SYNONYM" are driver-specific.
REMARKS (ODBC 1.0)	5	Varchar	A description of the table.

Code Example

For a code example of a similar function, see **SQLColumns**.

Related Functions

For information about	See
Binding a buffer to a column in a result set	**SQLBindCol**
Canceling statement processing	**SQLCancel**
Returning privileges for a column or columns	**SQLColumnPrivileges**
Returning the columns in a table or tables	**SQLColumns**
Fetching a single row or a block of data in a forward-only direction	**SQLFetch**
Fetching a block of data or scrolling through a result set	**SQLFetchScroll**
Returning table statistics and indexes	**SQLStatistics**
Returning privileges for a table or tables	**SQLTablePrivileges**

SQLTransact

Conformance

Version Introduced:	ODBC 1.0
Standards Compliance:	Deprecated

Summary

In ODBC 3.0, the ODBC 2.*x* function **SQLTransact** has been replaced by **SQLEndTran**. For more information, see **SQLEndTran**.

Note For more information about what the Driver Manager maps this function to when an ODBC 2.*x* application is working with an ODBC 3.0 driver, see "Mapping Deprecated Functions" in Appendix G, "Driver Guidelines for Backward Compatibility."

CHAPTER 22

Setup DLL API Reference

This chapter describes the syntax of the driver setup DLL API which consists of two functions (**ConfigDriver** and **ConfigDSN**). **ConfigDriver** and **ConfigDSN** may be either in the driver DLL or in a separate setup DLL.

In addition, this chapter also describes the syntax of the translator setup DLL API, which consists of a single function (**ConfigTranslator**). **ConfigTranslator** may be either in the translator DLL or in a separate setup DLL.

Each function is labeled with the version of ODBC in which it was introduced.

ConfigDriver

Conformance

Version Introduced: ODBC 2.5

Summary

ConfigDriver allows a setup program to perform install and uninstall functions without requiring the program to call **ConfigDSN**. This function will perform driver-specific functions such as creating driver-specific system information and performing DSN conversions during installation, and cleaning up system information modifications during uninstall. This function is exposed by the driver setup DLL or a separate setup DLL.

Syntax

```
BOOL ConfigDriver (
    HWND      hwndParent,
    WORD      fRequest,
    LPCSTR    lpszDriver,
    LPCSTR    lpszArgs,
    LPSTR     lpszMsg,
    WORD      cbMsgMax,
    WORD *    pcbMsgOut);
```

Arguments

hwndParent [Input]
Parent window handle. The function will not display any dialog boxes if the handle is null.

fRequest [Input]
Type of request. *fRequest* must contain one of the following values:

ODBC_INSTALL_DRIVER: Install a new driver.

ODBC_REMOVE_DRIVER: Remove a driver.

This option can also be driver-specific, in which case the *fRequest* for the first option must start from ODBC_CONFIG_DRIVER_MAX+1. The *fRequest* for any additional option must also start from a value greater than ODBC_CONFIG_DRIVER_MAX+1.

lpszDriver [Input]
The name of the driver as registered in the ODBCINST.INI key of the system information.

lpszArgs [Input]
A null-terminated string containing arguments for a driver-specific *fRequest*.

lpszMsg [Output]
A null-terminated string containing an output message from the driver setup.

cbMsgMax [Input]
Length of *lpszMsg*.

pcbMsgOut [Output]
Total number of bytes available to return in *lpszMsg*.

If the number of bytes available to return is greater than or equal to *cbMsgMax*, the output message in *lpszMsg* is truncated to *cbMsgMax* minus the null-termination character. The *pcbMsgOut* argument can be a null pointer.

Returns

The function returns TRUE if it is successful, FALSE if it fails.

Diagnostics

When **ConfigDriver** returns FALSE, an associated **pfErrorCode* value is posted to the installer error buffer by a call to **SQLPostInstallerError**, and may be obtained by calling **SQLInstallerError**. The following table lists the **pfErrorCode* values that can be returned by **SQLInstallerError** and explains each one in the context of this function.

**pfErrorCode*	Error	Description
ODBC_ERROR_ INVALID_HWND	Invalid window handle	The *hwndParent* argument was invalid.
ODBC_ERROR_ INVALID_ REQUEST_TYPE	Invalid type of request	The *fRequest* argument was not one of the following: ODBC_INSTALL_DRIVER. ODBC_REMOVE_DRIVER. The driver-specific option was less than or equal to ODBC_CONFIG_DRIVER_MAX.
ODBC_ERROR_ INVALID_NAME	Invalid driver or translator name	The *lpszDriver* argument was invalid. It could not be found in the registry.
ODBC_ERROR_ REQUEST_ FAILED	*Request* failed	Could not perform the operation requested by the *fRequest* argument.
ODBC_ERROR_ DRIVER_ SPECIFIC	Driver- or translator-specific error	A driver-specific error for which there is no defined ODBC installer error. The *SzError* argument in a call to the **SQLPostInstallerError** function should contain the driver-specific error message.

Comments

Driver-Specific Options

An application can request driver-specific features exposed by the driver by using the *fRequest* argument. The *fRequest* for the first option will be ODBC_CONFIG_DRIVER_MAX plus 1, and additional options will be incremented by 1 from that value. Any arguments required by the driver for that function should be provided in a null-terminated string passed in the *lpszArgs* argument. Drivers providing such functionality should maintain a table of driver-specific options. The options should be fully documented in driver documentation. Application writers who make use of driver-specific options should be aware that this use will make the application less interoperable.

Messages

A driver setup routine can send a text message to an application as a null-terminated string in the *lpszMsg* buffer. The message will be truncated to *cbMsgMax* minus the null-termination character by the **ConfigDriver** function if it is greater than or equal to *cbMsgMax* characters.

ConfigDSN

Conformance

Version Introduced: ODBC 1.0

Summary

ConfigDSN adds, modifies, or deletes data sources from the system information. It may prompt the user for connection information. It can be in the driver DLL or a separate setup DLL.

Syntax

BOOL **ConfigDSN**(
    HWND *hwndParent*,
    WORD *fRequest*,
    LPCSTR *lpszDriver*,
    LPCSTR *lpszAttributes*);

Arguments

hwndParent [Input]
Parent window handle. The function will not display any dialog boxes if the handle is null.

fRequest [Input]
Type of request. *fRequest* must contain one of the following values:

ODBC_ADD_DSN: Add a new data source.
ODBC_CONFIG_DSN: Configure (modify) an existing data source.
ODBC_REMOVE_DSN: Remove an existing data source.

lpszDriver [Input]
Driver description (usually the name of the associated DBMS) presented to users instead of the physical driver name.

lpszAttributes [Input]
List of attributes in the form of keyword-value pairs. For information about the list structure, see "Comments."

Returns

The function returns TRUE if it is successful, FALSE if it fails.

Diagnostics

When **ConfigDSN** returns FALSE, an associated **pfErrorCode* value is posted to the installer error buffer by a call to **SQLPostInstallerError**, and may be obtained by calling **SQLInstallerError**. The following table lists the **pfErrorCode* values that can be returned by **SQLInstallerError** and explains each one in the context of this function.

**pfErrorCode*	Error	Description
ODBC_ERROR_ INVALID_HWND	Invalid window handle	The *hwndParent* argument was invalid.
ODBC_ERROR_ INVALID_ KEYWORD_ VALUE	Invalid keyword-value pairs	The *lpszAttributes* argument contained a syntax error.
ODBC_ERROR_ INVALID_NAME	Invalid driver or translator name	The *lpszDriver* argument was invalid. It could not be found in the registry.
ODBC_ERROR_ INVALID_ REQUEST_TYPE	Invalid type of request	The *fRequest* argument was not one of the following: ODBC_ADD_DSN ODBC_CONFIG_DSN ODBC_REMOVE_DSN
ODBC_ERROR_ REQUEST_ FAILED	*Request* failed	Could not perform the operation requested by the *fRequest* argument.
ODBC_ERROR_ DRIVER_ SPECIFIC	Driver- or translator-specific error	A driver-specific error for which there is no defined ODBC installer error. The *SzError* argument in a call to the **SQLPostInstallerError** function should contain the driver-specific error message.

Comments

ConfigDSN receives connection information from the installer DLL as a list of attributes in the form of keyword-value pairs. Each pair is terminated with a null byte and the entire list is terminated with a null byte (that is, two null bytes mark the end of the list). Spaces are not allowed around the equal sign in the keyword-value pair. **ConfigDSN** can accept keywords that are not valid keywords for **SQLBrowseConnect** and **SQLDriverConnect**. **ConfigDSN** does not necessarily support all keywords that are valid keywords for **SQLBrowseConnect** and **SQLDriverConnect**. (**ConfigDSN** does not accept the **DRIVER** keyword.) The keywords used by the **ConfigDSN** function must support all the options required to re-create the data source using the AUTO setup feature of the installer. When the uses of the **ConfigDSN** values and the connection string values are the same, the same keywords should be used.

As in **SQLBrowseConnect** and **SQLDriverConnect**, the keywords and their values should not contain the []{}(),;?*=!@ characters, and the value of the **DSN** keyword cannot consist only of blanks. Because of the registry grammar, keywords and data source names cannot contain the backslash (\) character.

ConfigDSN should call **SQLValidDSN** to check the length of the data source name, and to verify that no invalid characters are included in the name. If the data source name is longer than SQL_MAX_DSN_LENGTH, or includes invalid characters, then **SQLValidDSN** returns an error, and **ConfigDSN** returns an error. The length of the data source name is also checked by **SQLWriteDSNToIni**.

For example, to configure a data source that requires a user ID, password, and database name, a setup application might pass the following keyword-value pairs:

```
DSN=Personnel Data\0UID=Smith\0PWD=Sesame\0DATABASE=Personnel\0\0
```

For more information about these keywords, see **SQLDriverConnect** and each driver's documentation.

To display a dialog box, *hwndParent* must not be null.

Adding a Data Source

If a data source name is passed to **ConfigDSN** in *lpszAttributes*, **ConfigDSN** checks that the name is valid. If the data source name matches an existing data source name and *hwndParent* is null, **ConfigDSN** overwrites the existing name. If it matches an existing name and *hwndParent* is not null, **ConfigDSN** prompts the user to overwrite the existing name.

If *lpszAttributes* contains enough information to connect to a data source, **ConfigDSN** can add the data source or display a dialog box with which the user can change the connection information. If *lpszAttributes* does not contain enough information to connect to a data source, **ConfigDSN** must determine the necessary information; if *hwndParent* is not null, it displays a dialog box to retrieve the information from the user.

If **ConfigDSN** displays a dialog box, it must display any connection information passed to it in *lpszAttributes*. In particular, if a data source name was passed to it, **ConfigDSN** displays that name but does not allow the user to change it. **ConfigDSN** can supply default values for connection information not passed to it in *lpszAttributes*.

If **ConfigDSN** cannot get complete connection information for a data source, it returns FALSE.

If **ConfigDSN** can get complete connection information for a data source, it calls **SQLWriteDSNToIni** in the installer DLL to add the new data source specification to the ODBC.INI file (or registry). **SQLWriteDSNToIni** adds the data source name to the [ODBC Data Sources] section, creates the data source specification section, and adds the **DRIVER** keyword with the driver description as its value. **ConfigDSN** calls **SQLWritePrivateProfileString** in the installer DLL to add any additional keywords and values used by the driver.

Modifying a Data Source

To modify a data source, a data source name must be passed to **ConfigDSN** in *lpszAttributes*. **ConfigDSN** checks that the data source name is in the ODBC.INI file (or registry).

If *hwndParent* is null, **ConfigDSN** uses the information in *lpszAttributes* to modify the information in the ODBC.INI file (or registry). If *hwndParent* is not null, **ConfigDSN** displays a dialog box using the information in *lpszAttributes*; for information not in *lpszAttributes*, it uses information from the system information. The user can modify the information before **ConfigDSN** stores it in the system information.

If the data source name was changed, **ConfigDSN** first calls **SQLRemoveDSNFromIni** in the installer DLL to remove the existing data source specification from the ODBC.INI file (or registry). It then follows the steps in the previous section to add the new data source specification. If the data source name was not changed, **ConfigDSN** calls **SQLWritePrivateProfileString** in the installer DLL to make any other changes. **ConfigDSN** may not delete or change the value of the **Driver** keyword.

Deleting a Data Source

To delete a data source, a data source name must be passed to **ConfigDSN** in *lpszAttributes*. **ConfigDSN** checks that the data source name is in the ODBC.INI file (or registry). It then calls **SQLRemoveDSNFromIni** in the installer DLL to remove the data source.

Related Functions

For information about	See
Adding, modifying, or removing a data source	**SQLConfigDataSource**
Getting a value from the ODBC.INI file or the registry	**SQLGetPrivateProfileString**
Removing the default data source	**SQLRemoveDefaultDataSource**
Removing a data source name from ODBC.INI (or registry)	**SQLRemoveDSNFromIni**
Adding a data source name to ODBC.INI (or registry)	**SQLWriteDSNToIni**
Writing a value to the ODBC.INI file or the registry	**SQLWritePrivateProfileString**

ConfigTranslator

Conformance

Version Introduced: ODBC 2.0

Summary

ConfigTranslator returns a default translation option for a translator. It can be in the translator DLL or a separate setup DLL.

Syntax

```
BOOL ConfigTranslator(
    HWND     hwndParent,
    DWORD *  pvOption);
```

Arguments

hwndParent [Input]
Parent window handle. The function will not display any dialog boxes if the handle is null.

pvOption [Output]
A 32-bit translation option.

Returns

The function returns TRUE if it is successful, FALSE if it fails.

Diagnostics

When **ConfigTranslator** returns FALSE, an associated **pfErrorCode* value is posted to the installer error buffer by a call to **SQLPostInstallerError**, and may be obtained by calling **SQLInstallerError**. The following table lists the **pfErrorCode* values that can be returned by **SQLInstallerError** and explains each one in the context of this function.

**pfErrorCode*	Error	Description
ODBC_ERROR_ INVALID_HWND	Invalid window handle	The *hwndParent* argument was invalid or NULL.
ODBC_ERROR_ DRIVER_ SPECIFIC	Driver- or translator-specific error	A driver-specific error for which there is no defined ODBC installer error. The *SzError* argument in a call to the **SQLPostInstallerError** function should contain the driver-specific error message.
ODBC_ERROR_ INVALID_OPTION	Invalid translation option	The *pvOption* argument contained an invalid value.

Comments

If the translator supports only a single translation option, **ConfigTranslator** returns TRUE and sets *pvOption* to the 32-bit option. Otherwise, it determines the default translation option to use. **ConfigTranslator** can display a dialog box with which a user selects a default translation option.

Related Functions

For information about	See
Getting a translation option	**SQLGetConnectAttr**
Selecting a translator	**SQLGetTranslator**
Setting a translation option	**SQLSetConnectAttr**

CHAPTER 23

Installer DLL API Reference

This chapter describes the syntax of the functions in the installer DLL API. The installer DLL API consists of twenty functions. Three of these functions, **SQLGetTranslator**, **SQLRemoveDSNFromIni**, and **SQLWriteDSNToIni**, are called only by setup DLLs. The other functions are called by the setup and administration programs.

Each function is labeled with the version of ODBC in which it was introduced.

SQLConfigDataSource

Conformance

Version Introduced: ODBC 1.0

Summary

SQLConfigDataSource adds, modifies, or deletes data sources.

Syntax

```
BOOL SQLConfigDataSource(
     HWND       hwndParent,
     WORD       fRequest,
     LPCSTR     lpszDriver,
     LPCSTR     lpszAttributes);
```

Arguments

hwndParent [Input]
Parent window handle. The function will not display any dialog boxes if the handle is null.

fRequest [Input]
Type of request. *fRequest* must contain one of the following values:

ODBC_ADD_DSN: Add a new user data source.

ODBC_CONFIG_DSN: Configure (modify) an existing user data source.

ODBC_REMOVE_DSN: Remove an existing user data source.

ODBC_ADD_SYS_DSN: Add a new system data source.

ODBC_CONFIG_SYS_DSN: Modify an existing system data source.

ODBC_REMOVE_SYS_DSN: Remove an existing system data source.

ODBC_REMOVE_DEFAULT_DSN: Remove the default data source specification section from the system information. It also removes the default driver specification section from the ODBCINST.INI entry in the system information. (This *fRequest* performs the same function as the deprecated **SQLRemoveDefaultDataSource** function.) When this option is specified, all of the other parameters in the call to **SQLConfigDataSource** should be NULLs; if they are not NULL, they will be ignored.

lpszDriver [Input]
Driver description (usually the name of the associated DBMS) presented to users instead of the physical driver name.

lpszAttributes [Input]
List of attributes in the form of keyword-value pairs. For more information, see **ConfigDSN** in Chapter 22, "Setup DLL Function Reference."

Returns

The function returns TRUE if it is successful, FALSE if it fails. If no entry exists in the system information when this function is called, the function returns FALSE.

Diagnostics

When **SQLConfigDataSource** returns FALSE, an associated **pfErrorCode* value may be obtained by calling **SQLInstallerError**. The following table lists the **pfErrorCode* values that can be returned by **SQLInstallerError** and explains each one in the context of this function.

**pfErrorCode*	Error	Description
ODBC_ERROR_GENERAL_ERR	General installer error	An error occurred for which there was no specific installer error.
ODBC_ERROR_INVALID_HWND	Invalid window handle	The *hwndParent* argument was invalid or NULL.
ODBC_ERROR_INVALID_REQUEST_TYPE	Invalid type of request	The *fRequest* argument was not one of the following: ODBC_ADD_DSN ODBC_CONFIG_DSN ODBC_REMOVE_DSN ODBC_ADD_SYS_DSN ODBC_CONFIG_SYS_DSN ODBC_REMOVE_SYS_DSN ODBC_REMOVE_DEFAULT_DSN
ODBC_ERROR_INVALID_NAME	Invalid driver or translator name	The *lpszDriver* argument was invalid. It could not be found in the registry.
ODBC_ERROR_INVALID_KEYWORD_VALUE	Invalid keyword-value pairs	The *lpszAttributes* argument contained a syntax error.
ODBC_ERROR_REQUEST_FAILED	*Request* failed	The installer could not perform the operation requested by the *fRequest* argument. The call to **ConfigDSN** failed.
ODBC_ERROR_LOAD_LIBRARY_FAILED	Could not load the driver or translator setup library	The driver setup library could not be loaded.
ODBC_ERROR_OUT_OF_MEM	Out of memory	The installer could not perform the function because of a lack of memory.

Comments

SQLConfigDataSource uses the value of *lpszDriver* to read the full path of the setup DLL for the driver from the system information. It loads the DLL and calls **ConfigDSN** with the same arguments that were passed to it.

SQLConfigDataSource returns FALSE if it is unable to find or load the setup DLL, or if the user cancels the dialog box. Otherwise, it returns the status it received from **ConfigDSN**.

SQLConfigDataSource maps the System DSN *fRequest*s to the User DSN *fRequest*s (ODBC_ADD_SYS_DSN to ODBC_ADD_DSN, ODBC_CONFIG_SYS_DSN to ODBC_CONFIG_DSN, and ODBC_REMOVE_SYS_DSN to ODBC_REMOVE_DSN). To distinguish user and System DSNs, **SQLConfigDataSource** sets the installer configuration mode according to the following table. Prior to returning, **SQLConfigDataSource** resets configuration mode to BOTHDSN.

fRequest	Configuration mode
ODBC_ADD_DSN	USERDSN_ONLY
ODBC_CONFIG_DSN	USERDSN_ONLY
ODBC_REMOVE_DSN	USERDSN_ONLY
ODBC_ADD_SYS_DSN	SYSTEMDSN_ONLY
ODBC_CONFIG_SYS_DSN	SYSTEMDSN_ONLY
ODBC_REMOVE_SYS_DSN	SYSTEMDSN_ONLY

Related Functions

For information about	See
Adding, modifying, or removing a data source	**ConfigDSN** (in the setup DLL)
Removing a data source name from the system information	**SQLRemoveDSNFromIni**
Adding a data source name to the system information	**SQLWriteDSNToIni**

SQLConfigDriver

Conformance

Version Introduced: ODBC 2.5

Summary

SQLConfigDriver loads the appropriate driver setup DLL and calls the **ConfigDriver** function.

Syntax

```
BOOL SQLConfigDriver (
    HWND       hwndParent,
    WORD       fRequest,
    LPCSTR     lpszDriver,
    LPCSTR     lpszArgs,
    LPSTR      lpszMsg,
    WORD       cbMsgMax,
    WORD *     pcbMsgOut);
```

Arguments

hwndParent [Input]
Parent window handle. The function will not display any dialog boxes if the handle is null.

fRequest [Input]
Type of request. *fRequest* must contain one of the following values:

ODBC_CONFIG_DRIVER: Changes the connection pooling timeout used by the driver.

ODBC_INSTALL_DRIVER: Installs a new driver.

ODBC_REMOVE_DRIVER: Removes an existing driver.

This option can also be driver-specific, in which case the *fRequest* for the first option must start from ODBC_CONFIG_DRIVER_MAX+1. The *fRequest* for any additional option must also start from a value greater than ODBC_CONFIG_DRIVER_MAX+1.

lpszDriver [Input]
The name of the driver as registered in the system information.

lpszArgs [Input]
A null-terminated string containing arguments for a driver-specific *fRequest*.

lpszMsg [Output]
A null-terminated string containing an output message from the driver setup.

cbMsgMax [Input]
Length of *lpszMsg*.

pcbMsgOut [Output]
Total number of bytes available to return in *lpszMsg*. If the number of bytes available to return is greater than or equal to *cbMsgMax*, the output message in *lpszMsg* is truncated to *cbMsgMax* minus the null-termination character. The *pcbMsgOut* argument can be a null pointer.

Returns

The function returns TRUE if it is successful, FALSE if it fails.

Diagnostics

When **SQLConfigDriver** returns FALSE, an associated **pfErrorCode* value may be obtained by calling **SQLInstallerError**. The following table lists the **pfErrorCode* values that can be returned by **SQLInstallerError** and explains each one in the context of this function.

**pfErrorCode*	Error	Description
ODBC_ERROR_GENERAL_ERR	General installer error	An error occurred for which there was no specific installer error.
ODBC_ERROR_INVALID_BUFF_LEN	Invalid buffer length	The *lpszMsg* argument was invalid.
ODBC_ERROR_INVALID_HWND	Invalid window handle	The *hwndParent* argument was invalid.
ODBC_ERROR_INVALID_REQUEST_TYPE	Invalid type of request	The *fRequest* argument was not one of the following: ODBC_INSTALL_DRIVER ODBC_REMOVE_DRIVER The *fRequest* argument was a driver-specific option that was less than or equal to ODBC_CONFIG_DRIVER_MAX.
ODBC_ERROR_INVALID_NAME	Invalid driver or translator name	The *lpszDriver* argument was invalid. It could not be found in the registry.
ODBC_ERROR_INVALID_KEYWORD_VALUE	Invalid keyword-value pairs	The *lpszAttributes* argument contained a syntax error.

**pfErrorCode*	Error	Description
ODBC_ERROR_ REQUEST_ FAILED	*Request* failed	The installer could not perform the operation requested by the *fRequest* argument. The call to **ConfigDriver** failed.
ODBC_ERROR_ LOAD_LIBRARY_ FAILED	Could not load the driver or translator setup library	The driver setup library could not be loaded.
ODBC_ERROR_ OUT_OF_MEM	Out of memory	The installer could not perform the function because of a lack of memory.

Comments

SQLConfigDriver allows an application to call a driver's **ConfigDriver** routine without having to know the name and load the driver-specific setup DLL. A setup program calls this function after the driver setup DLL has been installed. The calling program should be aware that this function may not be available for all drivers. In such a case, the calling program should continue without error.

Driver-Specific Options

An application can request driver-specific features exposed by the driver by using the *fRequest* argument. The *fRequest* for the first option will be ODBC_CONFIG_DRIVER_MAX+1, and additional options will be incremented by 1 from that value. Any arguments required by the driver for that function should be provided in a null-terminated string passed in the *lpszArgs* argument. Drivers providing such functionality should maintain a table of driver-specific options. The options should be fully documented in driver documentation. Application writers who make use of driver-specific options should be aware that this use will make the application less interoperable.

Setting Connection Pooling Timeout

Connection pool timeout properties can be set when setting the configuration of the driver. **SQLConfigDriver** is called with an *fRequest* of ODBC_CONFIG_DRIVER and *lpszArgs* set to **CPTimeout**. **CPTimeout** determines the amount of time that a connection can remain in the connection pool without being used. When the timeout expires, the connection is closed and removed from the pool. The default timeout is 60 seconds.

When **SQLConfigDriver** is called with *fRequest* set to ODBC_INSTALL_DRIVER or ODBC_REMOVE_DRIVER, the Driver Manager loads the appropriate driver setup DLL and calls the **ConfigDriver** function. When **SQLConfigDriver** is called with an *fRequest* of ODBC_CONFIG_DRIVER, all processing is performed in the ODBC installer, so the driver setup DLL does not need to be loaded.

Messages

A driver setup routine can send a text message to an application as null-terminated strings in the *lpszMsg* buffer. The message will be truncated to *cbMsgMax* minus the null-termination character by the **ConfigDriver** function if it is greater than or equal to *cbMsgMax* characters.

Related Functions

For information about	See
Adding, modifying, or removing a driver	**ConfigDriver** (in the setup DLL)
Removing the default data source	**SQLRemoveDefaultDataSource**

SQLCreateDataSource

Conformance

Version Introduced: ODBC 2.0

Summary

SQLCreateDataSource displays a dialog box with which the user can add a data source.

Syntax

```
BOOL SQLCreateDataSource(
      HWND      hwnd,
      LPSTR     lpszDS);
```

Arguments

hwnd [Input]
Parent window handle.

lpszDS [Input]
Data source name. *lpszDS* can be a null pointer or an empty string.

Returns

SQLCreateDataSource returns TRUE if the data source is created. Otherwise, it returns FALSE.

Diagnostics

When **SQLCreateDataSource** returns FALSE, an associated **pfErrorCode* value may be obtained by calling **SQLInstallerError**. The following table lists the **pfErrorCode* values that can be returned by **SQLInstallerError** and explains each one in the context of this function.

**pfErrorCode*	Error	Description
ODBC_ERROR_ GENERAL_ERR	General installer error	An error occurred for which there was no specific installer error.
ODBC_ERROR_ INVALID_HWND	Invalid window handle	The *hwnd* argument was invalid or NULL.
ODBC_ERROR_ INVALID_DSN	Invalid DSN	The *lpszDS* argument contained a string that was invalid for a DSN.
ODBC_ERROR_ REQUEST_ FAILED	*Request* failed	The call to **ConfigDSN** with the ODBC_ADD_DSN option failed.
ODBC_ERROR_ LOAD_LIBRARY_ FAILED	Could not load the driver or translator setup library	The driver setup library could not be loaded.
ODBC_ERROR_ USER_CANCELED	User canceled operation	User canceled creation of a new data source.

**pfErrorCode*	Error	Description
ODBC_ERROR_ CREATE_DSN_ FAILED	Could not create the requested DSN	Could not connect to the database; the call to **SQLDriverConnect** for a File DSN did not return a successful connection. Could not write to the file.
ODBC_ERROR_ OUT_OF_MEM	Out of memory	The installer could not perform the function because of a lack of memory.

Comments

If *hwnd* is null, **SQLCreateDataSource** returns FALSE. Otherwise, it displays the **Create New Data Source** dialog box with a wizard page for choosing the type of data source to be set up:

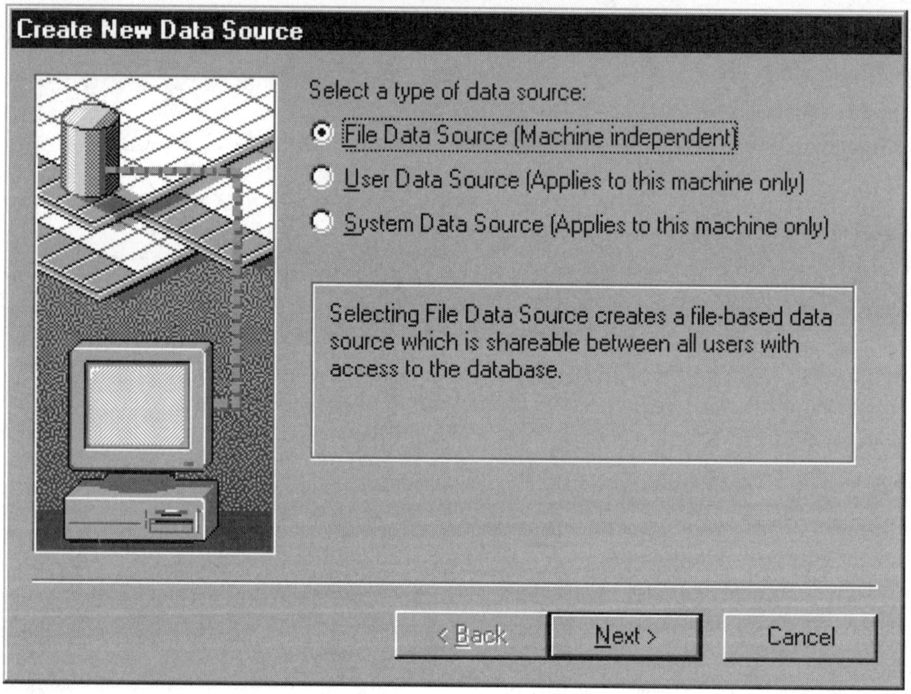

The default option is **File Data Source**. When a data source has been chosen, a wizard page containing a list of installed drivers is displayed:

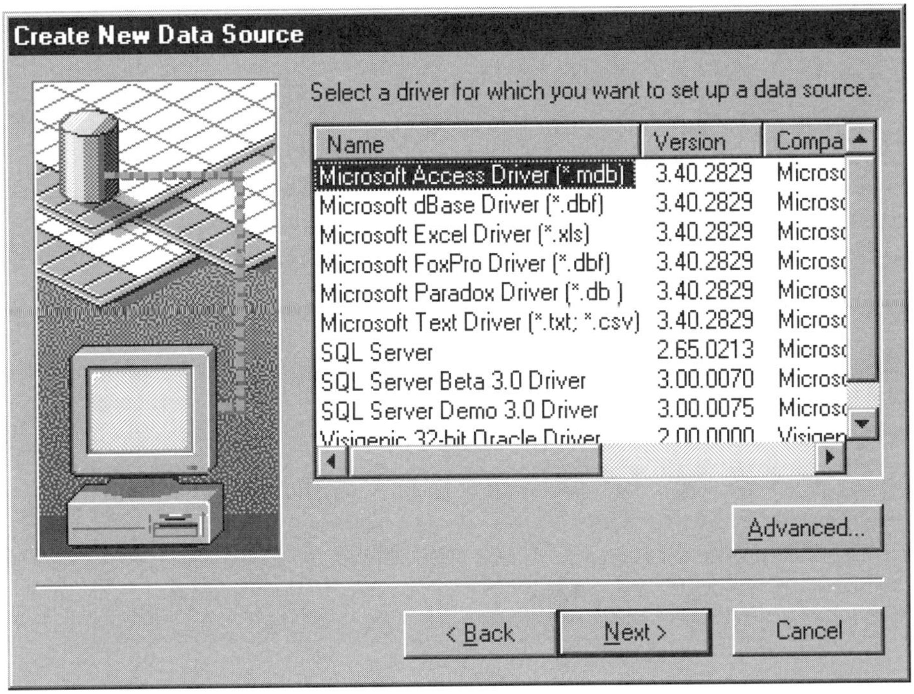

If the **Cancel** button is clicked, then the dialog box disappears and **SQLCreateDataSource** returns FALSE with the error code of ODBC_ERROR_USER_CANCELED. If either the **User Data Source** or **System Data Source** option was selected, then the **Advanced** button is unavailable.

When the **Next** button is clicked, then one of the following will occur, depending on which type of data source was selected:

- If **File Data Source** was selected, then a wizard page is displayed for the user to enter a file name.
- If either **User Data Source** or **System Data Source** was selected, then a wizard page displaying the type of data source and driver is displayed for review, and when the **Finish** button is chosen, the data source is set up.

If the **Advanced** button is clicked from the driver list wizard page, a wizard page is displayed for the user to enter driver-specific information. In the text box of this dialog box, type the driver and keywords separated by returns, as follows:

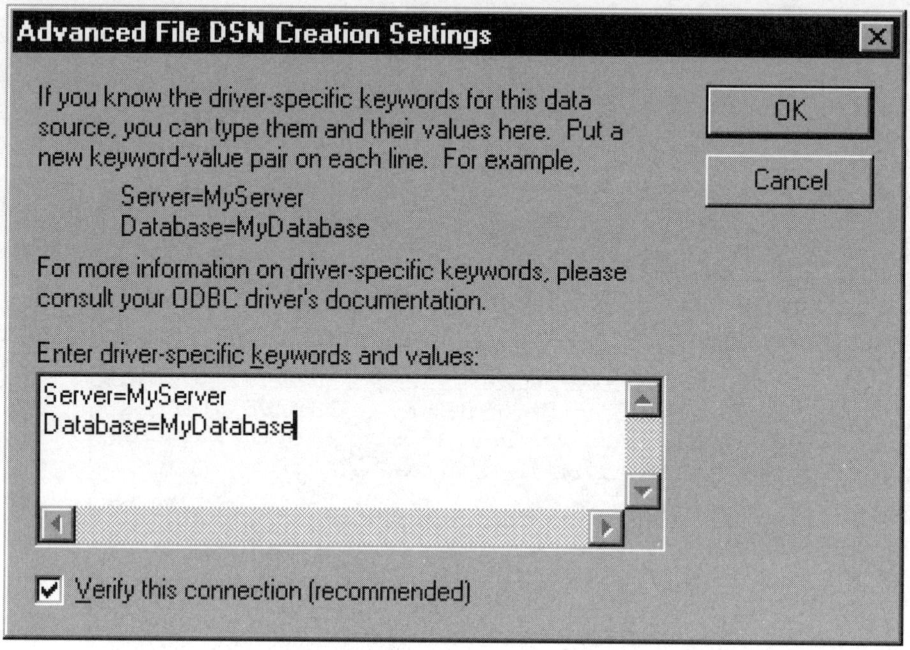

The default for the **Verify This Connection** option is TRUE. This default applies regardless of whether this wizard page is activated. If the **OK** button is selected, then the string specified in the text box and the **Verify This Connection** option value are cached. (If the **X** button or **Cancel** is selected, then newly entered driver-specific information is lost, because the string specified in the text box and the **Verify This Connection** option value are not cached.)

If **File Data Source** was selected in the first wizard page, then after a driver has been selected and the keyword values have been entered in the Advanced wizard page, the user is prompted to enter a file name. The **Browse** button can be used to search for a file name, in which case the default directory in the **Browse** box is specified by a combination of the path specified by CommonFileDir in HKEY_LOCAL_MACHINE\SOFTWARE\Microsoft\Windows\CurrentVersion and "ODBC\DataSources". (If CommonFileDir was "C:\Program Files\Common Files", the default directory would be "C:\Program Files\Common Files\ODBC\Data Sources".)

When a file name has been entered and the **Next** button clicked, then the file name entered is checked for validity against the standard file-naming rules of the operating system. If the file name is invalid, then an error message box notifies the user that an invalid file name was entered. After the user acknowledges the message box, the focus is returned to the wizard page in which the file name is entered. If the file name is valid, then a wizard page showing the selected keyword-value pairs is displayed for review.

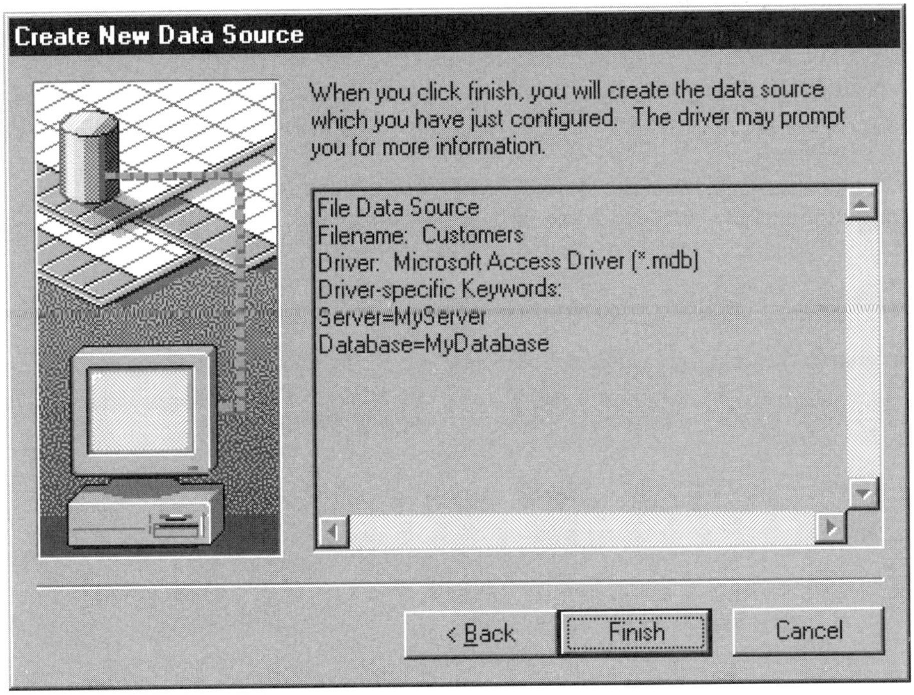

If the **Finished** button is clicked, and **File Data Source** was selected as the data source type, and the **Verify this connection** option is TRUE, then **SQLDriverConnect** is called with the **SAVEFILE** and **DRIVER** keywords. The *DriverCompletion* argument is set to SQL_DRIVER_COMPLETE. The file name for the **SAVEFILE** keyword is the name that was entered or chosen, and, and the driver name for the **DRIVER** keyword is the name that was chosen. If a driver-specific connection string was specified in the Advanced wizard page, then that string is appended after the **DRIVER** keyword.

If **SQLDriverConnect** returns SQL_SUCCESS, then the Driver Manager has created the File DSN. **SQLCreateDataSource** returns TRUE. If **SQLDriverConnect** does not return SQL_SUCCESS, then a warning message box indicates that a connection could not be made to the data source. A DSN with minimal connection information can still be created. This message box allows the user to either cancel or continue with the File DSN creation.

If the user chooses to continue creating the DSN, then this process continues as if the **Verify this connection** option were set to FALSE. If the user chooses to cancel, then FALSE is returned for **SQLCreateDataSource** with an error code of ODBC_ERROR_CREATE_DSN_FAILED.

If **File Data Source** was selected as the data source type, and the **Verify this connection** option is FALSE, then a File DSN is created with the **DRIVER** keyword and user-specified connect string (if any) from the Advanced wizard page. If the file creation was successful, TRUE is returned for **SQLCreateDataSource**. If the file creation was not successful, then an error message box notifies the user with whatever error was returned from the operating system. FALSE is returned for **SQLCreateDataSource** with an error code of ODBC_ERROR_CREATE_DSN_FAILED. For more information on file data sources, see "Connecting Using File Data Sources" in Chapter 6, "Connecting to a Data Source or Driver," or see **SQLDriverConnect**.

If **User** or **System Data Source** was selected as the data source type, then **ConfigDSN** in the driver setup library is called with the ODBC_ADD_DSN *fRequest*. For more information, see **ConfigDSN** in Chapter 22, "Setup DLL Function Reference."

Related Functions

For information about	See
Managing data sources	**SQLManageDataSources**

SQLGetConfigMode

Conformance

Version Introduced: ODBC 3.0

Summary

SQLGetConfigMode retrieves the configuration mode that indicates where the ODBC.INI entry listing DSN values is in the system information.

Syntax

BOOL **SQLGetConfigMode**(
    UWORD * *pwConfigMode*);

Arguments

pwConfigMode [Output]
Pointer to the buffer containing the configuration mode (see "Comments"). The value in **pwConfigMode* can be:

ODBC_USER_DSN
ODBC_SYSTEM_DSN
ODBC_BOTH_DSN

Returns

The function returns TRUE if it is successful, FALSE if it fails.

Diagnostics

When **SQLGetConfigMode** returns FALSE, an associated **pfErrorCode* value may be obtained by calling **SQLInstallerError**. The following table lists the **pfErrorCode* values that can be returned by **SQLInstallerError** and explains each one in the context of this function.

**pfErrorCode*	Error	Description
ODBC_ERROR_OUT_OF_MEM	Out of memory	The installer could not perform the function because of a lack of memory.

Comments

This function is used to determine where the ODBC.INI entry listing DSN values is in the system information. If **pwConfigMode* is ODBC_USER_DSN, the DSN is a User DSN and the function reads from the ODBC.INI entry in HKEY_CURRENT_USER. If it is ODBC_SYSTEM_DSN, the DSN is a System DSN and the function reads from the ODBC.INI entry in HKEY_LOCAL_MACHINE. If it is ODBC_BOTH_DSN, HKEY_CURRENT_USER is tried, and if it fails, then HKEY_LOCAL_MACHINE is used.

By default, **SQLGetConfigMode** returns ODBC_BOTH_DSN. When a User DSN or a System DSN is created by a call to **SQLConfigDataSource**, the function sets the configuration mode to ODBC_USER_DSN or ODBC_SYSTEM_DSN to distinguish user and System DSNs while modifying a DSN. Prior to returning, **SQLConfigDataSource** resets the configuration mode to ODBC_BOTH_DSN.

Related Functions

For information about	See
Setting the configuration mode	**SQLSetConfigMode**

SQLGetInstalledDrivers

Conformance

Version Introduced: ODBC 1.0

Summary

SQLGetInstalledDrivers reads the [ODBC Drivers] section of the system information and returns a list of descriptions of the installed drivers.

Syntax

BOOL **SQLGetInstalledDrivers**(
LPSTR *lpszBuf*,
WORD *cbBufMax*,
WORD * *pcbBufOut*);

Arguments

lpszBuf [Output]
List of descriptions of the installed drivers. For information about the list structure, see "Comments."

cbBufMax [Input]
Length of *lpszBuf*.

pcbBufOut [Output]
Total number of bytes (excluding the null-termination byte) returned in *lpszBuf*. If the number of bytes available to return is greater than or equal to *cbBufMax*, the list of driver descriptions in *lpszBuf* is truncated to *cbBufMax* minus the null-termination character. The *pcbBufOut* argument can be a null pointer.

Returns

The function returns TRUE if it is successful, FALSE if it fails.

Diagnostics

When **SQLGetInstalledDrivers** returns FALSE, an associated **pfErrorCode* value may be obtained by calling **SQLInstallerError**. The following table lists the **pfErrorCode* values that can be returned by **SQLInstallerError** and explains each one in the context of this function.

**pfErrorCode*	Error	Description
ODBC_ERROR_ GENERAL_ERR	General installer error	An error occurred for which there was no specific installer error.
ODBC_ERROR_ INVALID_BUFF_ LEN	Invalid buffer length	The *lpszBuf* argument was NULL or invalid, or the *cbBufMax* argument was less than or equal to 0.
ODBC_ERROR_ COMPONENT_ NOT_FOUND	Component not found in registry	The installer could not find the [ODBC Drivers] section in the registry.
ODBC_ERROR_ OUT_OF_MEM	Out of memory	The installer could not perform the function because of a lack of memory.

Comments

Each driver description is terminated with a null byte and the entire list is terminated with a null byte (that is, two null bytes mark the end of the list). If the allocated buffer is not large enough to hold the entire list, the list is truncated without error. An error is returned if a null pointer is passed in as *lpszBuf*.

Related Functions

For information about	See
Returning driver descriptions and attributes	**SQLDrivers**

SQLGetPrivateProfileString

Conformance

Version Introduced: ODBC 2.0

Summary

SQLGetPrivateProfileString gets a list of names of values or data corresponding to a value of the system information.

Syntax

int **SQLGetPrivateProfileString**(
    LPCSTR *lpszSection*,
    LPCSTR *lpszEntry*,
    LPCSTR *lpszDefault*,
    LPCSTR *RetBuffer*,
    INT *cbRetBuffer*,
    LPCSTR *lpszFilename*);

Arguments

lpszSection [Input]
Points to a null-terminated string that specifies the section containing the key name. If this argument is NULL, the function copies all section names in the file to the supplied buffer.

lpszEntry [Input]
Points to the null-terminated string containing the key name whose associated string is to be retrieved. If this argument is NULL, all key names in the section specified by the lpszSection argument are copied to the buffer specified by the RetBuffer argument.

lpszDefault [Input]
Points to a null-terminated string that specifies the default value for the given key if the key cannot be found in the initialization file. This argument cannot be NULL.

RetBuffer [Output]
Points to the buffer that receives the retrieved string.

cbRetBuffer [Input]
Specifies the size, in characters, of the buffer pointed to by the RetBuffer argument.

lpszFilename [Output]
Points to a null-terminated string that names the initialization file. If this argument does not contain a full path to the file, the default directory is searched.

Returns

SQLGetPrivateProfileString returns an integer value that indicates the number of characters read.

Diagnostics

When a call to **SQLGetPrivateProfileString** fails, an associated **pfErrorCode* value may be obtained by calling **SQLInstallerError**. The following table lists the **pfErrorCode* values that can be returned by **SQLInstallerError** and explains each one in the context of this function.

**pfErrorCode*	Error	Description
ODBC_ERROR_GENERAL_ERR	General installer error	An error occurred for which there was no specific installer error.
ODBC_ERROR_OUT_OF_MEM	Out of memory	The installer could not perform the function because of a lack of memory.

Comments

SQLGetPrivateProfileString is provided as a simple way to port drivers and driver setup DLLs from Windows to Windows NT. Calls to **GetPrivateProfileString** that retrieve a profile string from the ODBC.INI file should be replaced with calls to **SQLGetPrivateProfileString**. **SQLGetPrivateProfileString** calls functions in the Win32 API to retrieve the requested names of values or data corresponding to a value of the ODBC.INI subkey of the system information.

The configuration mode (as set by **SQLSetConfigMode**) indicates where the ODBC.INI entry listing DSN values is in the system information. If the DSN is a User DSN (the configuration mode is USERDSN_ONLY), the function reads from the ODBC.INI entry in HKEY_CURRENT_USER. If the DSN is a System DSN (SYSTEMDSN_ONLY), the function reads from the ODBC.INI entry in HKEY_LOCAL_MACHINE. If the configuration mode is BOTHDSN, HKEY_CURRENT_USER is tried, and if it fails, then HKEY_LOCAL_MACHINE is used.

Related Functions

For information about	See
Writing a value to the system information	**SQLWritePrivateProfileString**

SQLGetTranslator

Conformance

Version Introduced: ODBC 2.0

Summary

SQLGetTranslator displays a dialog box from which a user can select a translator.

Syntax

```
BOOL SQLGetTranslator(
    HWND        hwndParent,
    LPSTR       lpszName,
    WORD        cbNameMax,
    WORD *      pcbNameOut,
    LPSTR       lpszPath,
    WORD        cbPathMax,
    WORD *      pcbPathOut,
    DWORD *     pvOption);
```

Arguments

hwndParent [Input]
Parent window handle.

lpszName [Input/Output]
Name of the translator from the system information.

cbNameMax [Input]
Maximum length of the *lpszName* buffer.

pcbNameOut [Input/Output]
Total number of bytes (excluding the null-termination byte) passed or returned in *lpszName*. If the number of bytes available to return is greater than or equal to *cbNameMax*, the translator name in *lpszName* is truncated to *cbNameMax* minus the null-termination character. The *pcbNameOut* argument can be a null pointer.

lpszPath [Output]
Full path of the translation DLL.

cbPathMax [Input]
Maximum length of the *lpszPath* buffer.

pcbPathOut [Output]
Total number of bytes (excluding the null-termination byte) returned in *lpszPath*. If the number of bytes available to return is greater than or equal to *cbPathMax*, the translation DLL path in *lpszPath* is truncated to *cbPathMax* minus the null-termination character. The *pcbPathOut* argument can be a null pointer.

pvOption [Output]
32-bit translation option.

Returns

The function returns TRUE if it is successful, FALSE if it fails or the user cancels the dialog box.

Diagnostics

When **SQLGetTranslator** returns FALSE, an associated **pfErrorCode* value may be obtained by calling **SQLInstallerError**. The following table lists the **pfErrorCode* values that can be returned by **SQLInstallerError** and explains each one in the context of this function.

**pfErrorCode*	Error	Description
ODBC_ERROR_GENERAL_ERR	General installer error	An error occurred for which there was no specific installer error.
ODBC_ERROR_INVALID_BUFF_LEN	Invalid buffer length	The *cbNameMax* or *cbPathMax* argument was less than or equal to 0.
ODBC_ERROR_INVALID_HWND	Invalid window handle	The *hwndParent* argument was invalid or NULL.
ODBC_ERROR_INVALID_NAME	Invalid driver or translator name	The *lpszName* argument was invalid. It could not be found in the registry.
ODBC_ERROR_LOAD_LIBRARY_FAILED	Could not load the driver or translator setup library	The translator library could not be loaded.
ODBC_ERROR_INVALID_OPTION	Invalid transaction option	The *pvOption* argument contained an invalid value.
ODBC_ERROR_OUT_OF_MEM	Out of memory	The installer could not perform the function because of a lack of memory.

Comments

If *hwndParent* is null, or *lpszName*, *lpszPath*, or *pvOption* is a null pointer, **SQLGetTranslator** returns FALSE. Otherwise, it displays the list of installed translators in the following dialog box:

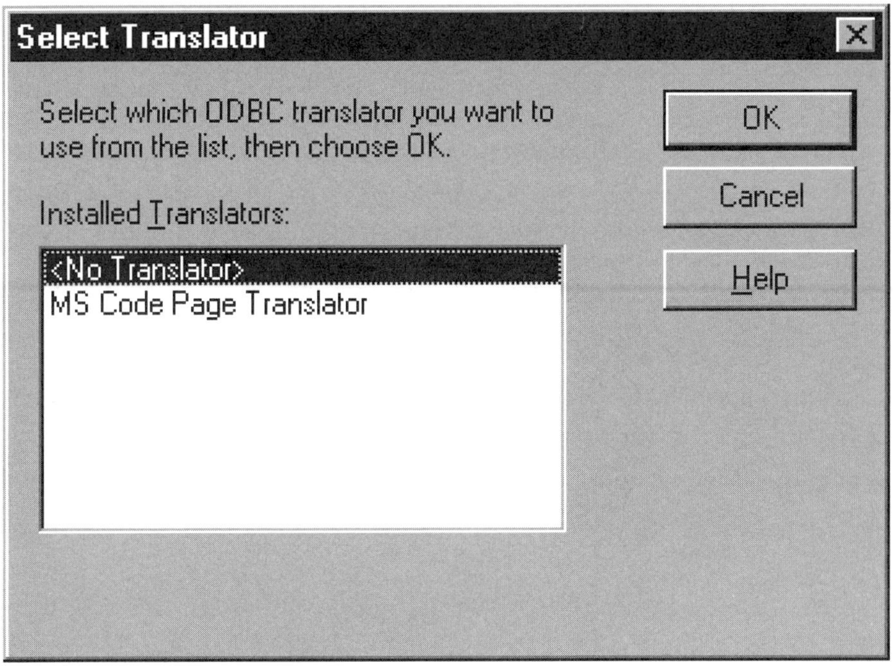

If *lpszName* contains a valid translator name, it is selected. Otherwise, <No Translator> is selected.

If the user chooses <No Translator>, the contents of *lpszName*, *lpszPath*, and *pvOption* are not touched. **SQLGetTranslator** sets *pcbNameOut* and *pcbPathOut* to 0 and returns TRUE.

If the user chooses a translator, **SQLGetTranslator** calls **ConfigTranslator** in the translator's setup DLL. If **ConfigTranslator** returns FALSE, **SQLGetTranslator** returns to its dialog box. If **ConfigTranslator** returns TRUE, **SQLGetTranslator** returns TRUE, along with the selected translator name, path, and translation option.

Related Functions

For information about	See
Configuring a translator	**ConfigTranslator**
Getting a translation attribute	**SQLGetConnectAttr**
Setting a translation attribute	**SQLSetConnectAttr**

SQLInstallDriverEx

Conformance

Version Introduced: ODBC 3.0

Summary

SQLInstallDriverEx adds information about the driver to the ODBCINST.INI entry in the system information and increments the driver's *UsageCount* by 1. However, if a version of the driver already exists, but the *UsageCount* value for the driver does not exist, the new *UsageCount* value is set to 2.

This function does not actually copy any files. It is the responsibility of the calling program to copy the driver's files to the target directory properly.

Syntax

BOOL **SQLInstallDriverEx**(
LPCSTR *lpszDriver*,
LPCSTR *lpszPathIn*,
LPSTR *lpszPathOut*,
WORD *cbPathOutMax*,
WORD * *pcbPathOut,*
WORD *fRequest,*
LPDWORD *lpdwUsageCount*);

Arguments

lpszDriver [Input]
The driver description (usually the name of the associated DBMS) presented to users instead of the physical driver name. The *lpszDriver* argument must contain a list of keyword-value pairs describing the driver.

For more information, see "Comments."

lpszPathIn [Input]
Full path of the target directory of the installation, or a null pointer. If *lpszPathIn* is a null pointer, the drivers will be installed in the System directory.

lpszPathOut [Output]
Path of the target directory where the driver should be installed. If the driver has not previously been installed, then *lpszPathOut* should be the same as *lpszPathIn*. If the driver was previously installed, then *lpszPathOut* is the path of the previous installation.

cbPathOutMax [Input]
Length of *lpszPathOut*.

pcbPathOut [Output]
Total number of bytes (excluding the null-termination character) available to return in *lpszPathOut*. If the number of bytes available to return is greater than or equal to *cbPathOutMax*, then the output path in *lpszPathOut* is truncated to *cbPathOutMax* minus the null-termination character. The *pcbPathOut* argument can be a null pointer.

fRequest [Input]
Type of request. The *fRequest* argument must contain one of the following values:

ODBC_INSTALL_INQUIRY: Inquire about where a driver can be installed.

ODBC_INSTALL_COMPLETE: Complete the installation request.

lpdwUsageCount [Output]
The usage count of the driver after this function has been called.

Returns

The function returns TRUE if it is successful, FALSE if it fails.

Diagnostics

When **SQLInstallDriverEx** returns FALSE, an associated **pfErrorCode* value may be obtained by calling **SQLInstallerError**. The following table lists the **pfErrorCode* values that can be returned by **SQLInstallerError** and explains each one in the context of this function.

**pfErrorCode*	Error	Description
ODBC_ERROR_ GENERAL_ERR	General installer error	An error occurred for which there was no specific installer error.
ODBC_ERROR_ INVALID_BUFF_ LEN	Invalid buffer length	The *lpszPathOut* argument was not large enough to contain the output path. The buffer contains the truncated path. The *cbPathOutMax* argument was 0 and *fRequest* was ODBC_INSTALL_COMPLETE.
ODBC_ERROR_ INVALID_ REQUEST_TYPE	Invalid type of request	The *fRequest* argument was not one of the following: ODBC_INSTALL_INQUIRY ODBC_INSTALL_COMPLETE
ODBC_ERROR_ INVALID_ KEYWORD_ VALUE	Invalid keyword-value pairs	The *lpszDriver* argument contained a syntax error.

**pfErrorCode*	Error	Description
ODBC_ERROR_ INVALID_PATH	Invalid install path	The *lpszPathIn* argument contained an invalid path.
ODBC_ERROR_ LOAD_LIBRARY_ FAILED	Could not load the driver or translator setup library	The driver setup library could not be loaded.
ODBC_ERROR_ INVALID_ PARAM_ SEQUENCE	Invalid parameter sequence	The *lpszDriver* argument did not contain a list of keyword-value pairs.
ODBC_ERROR_ USAGE_ UPDATE_FAILED	Could not increment or decrement the component usage count	The installer failed to increment the driver's usage count.

Comments

The *lpszDriver* argument is a list of attributes in the form of keyword-value pairs. Each pair is terminated with a null byte and the entire list is terminated with a null byte (that is, two null bytes mark the end of the list). The format of this list is:

driver-desc\0Driver=*driver-DLL-filename*\0[Setup=*setup-DLL-filename*\0]
➥ [*driver-attr-keyword1*=*value1*\0][*driver-attr-keyword2*=*value2*\0]...\0

where \0 is a null byte and *driver-attr-keywordn* is any driver attribute keyword described in "Driver Keyword Sections" in Chapter 18, "Installing ODBC Components." The keywords must appear in the specified order. For example, suppose a driver for formatted text files has separate driver and setup DLLs and can use files with the .txt and .csv extensions. The *lpszDriver* argument for this driver might be:

```
Text\0Driver=TEXT.DLL\0Setup=TXTSETUP.DLL\0FileUsage=1\0
➥ FileExtns=*.txt,*.csv\0\0
```

Suppose that a driver for SQL Server does not have a separate setup DLL and does not have any driver attribute keywords. The *lpszDriver* argument for this driver might be:

```
SQL Server\0Driver=SQLSRVR.DLL\0\0
```

After **SQLInstallDriverEx** retrieves information about the driver from the *lpszDriver* argument, it adds the driver description to the [ODBC Drivers] section of the ODBCINST.INI entry in the system information. It then creates a section titled with the driver's description and adds the full paths of the driver DLL and the setup DLL. Finally, it returns the path of the target directory of the installation but does not copy the driver files to it. The calling program must actually copy the driver files to the target directory.

SQLInstallDriverEx increments the component usage count for the installed driver by 1. If a version of the driver already exists, but the component usage count for the driver does not exist, the new component usage count value is set to 2.

The application setup program is responsible for physically copying the driver file, and maintaining the file usage count. If the driver file has not previously been installed, the application setup program must copy the file in the *lpszPathIn* path, and create the file usage count. If the file has previously been installed, the setup program merely increments the file usage count, and returns the path of the prior installation in the *lpszPathOut* argument.

Note For more information about component usage counts and file usage counts, see "Usage Counting" in Chapter 18, "Installing ODBC Components."

If an older version of the driver file was previously installed by the application, the driver should be uninstalled, then reinstalled, so that the driver component usage count is valid. **SQLConfigDriver** (with an *fRequest* of ODBC_REMOVE_DRIVER) should first be called, then **SQLRemoveDriver** should be called to decrement the component usage count. **SQLInstallDriverEx** should then be called to reinstall the driver, incrementing the component usage count. The application setup program must physically replace the old file with the new file. The file usage count will remain the same, and any other application that used the older version file will now use the newer version.

Note If the driver was previously installed, and **SQLInstallDriverEx** is called to install the driver in a different directory, the function will return TRUE, but *lpszPathOut* will include the directory where the driver was already installed. It will not include the directory entered in the *lpszDriver* argument.

The length of the path in *lpszPathOut* in **SQLInstallDriverEx** allows for a two-phase install process, so an application can determine what *cbPathOutMax* should be by calling **SQLInstallDriverEx** with an *fRequest* of ODBC_INSTALL_INQUIRY mode. This will return the total number of bytes available in the *pcbPathOut* buffer. **SQLInstallDriverEx** can then be called with an *fRequest* of ODBC_INSTALL_COMPLETE and the *cbPathOutMax* argument set to the value in the *pcbPathOut* buffer, plus the null-termination character.

If you choose not to use the two-phase model for **SQLInstallDriverEx**, then you must set *cbPathOutMax*, which defines the size of the storage for the path of the target directory, to the value _MAX_PATH, as defined in STDLIB.H, to prevent truncation.

When *fRequest* is ODBC_INSTALL_COMPLETE, **SQLInstallDriverEx** does not allow *lpszPathOut* to be NULL (or *cbPathOutMax* to be 0). If *fRequest* is ODBC_INSTALL_COMPLETE, FALSE is returned when the number of bytes available to return is greater than or equal to *cbPathOutMax*, with the result that truncation occurs.

After **SQLInstallDriverEx** has been called, and the application setup program has copied the driver file (if necessary), the driver setup DLL must call **SQLConfigDriver** to set the configuration for the driver.

Related Functions

For information about	See
Installing the Driver Manager	**SQLInstallDriverManager**

SQLInstallDriverManager

Conformance

Version Introduced: ODBC 1.0

Summary

SQLInstallDriverManager returns the path of the target directory for the installation of the ODBC core components. The calling program must actually copy the Driver Manager's files to the target directory.

Syntax

BOOL **SQLInstallDriverManager**(
    LPSTR *lpszPath*,
    WORD *cbPathMax*,
    WORD * *pcbPathOut*);

Arguments

lpszPath [Output]
Path of the target directory of the installation.

cbPathMax [Input]
Length of *lpszPath*. This must be at least _MAX_PATH bytes.

pcbPathOut [Output]
Total number of bytes (excluding the null-termination byte) returned in *lpszPath*. If the number of bytes available to return is greater than or equal to *cbPathMax*, the path in *lpszPath* is truncated to *cbPathMax* minus the null-termination character. The *pcbPathOut* argument can be a null pointer.

Returns

The function returns TRUE if it is successful, FALSE if it fails.

Diagnostics

When **SQLInstallDriverManager** returns FALSE, an associated **pfErrorCode* value may be obtained by calling **SQLInstallerError**. The following table lists the **pfErrorCode* values that can be returned by **SQLInstallerError** and explains each one in the context of this function.

**pfErrorCode*	Error	Description
ODBC_ERROR_ GENERAL_ERR	General installer error	An error occurred for which there was no specific installer error.
ODBC_ERROR_ INVALID_BUFF_ LEN	Invalid buffer length	The *lpszPath* argument was not large enough to contain the output path. The buffer contains the truncated path. The *cbPathMax* argument was less than _MAX_PATH.
ODBC_ERROR_ USAGE_ UPDATE_FAILED	Could not increment or decrement the component usage count	The installer failed to increment the ODBC core component usage count.
ODBC_ERROR_ OUT_OF_MEM	Out of memory	The installer could not perform the function because of a lack of memory.

Comments

SQLInstallDriverManager is called to return the path for ODBC core components and increment the component usage count in the system information. If a version of the Driver Manager already exists, but the component usage count for the driver does not exist, the new component usage count value is set to 2.

The application setup program is responsible for physically copying the core component files, and maintaining the file usage counts. If a core component file has not previously been installed, the application setup program must copy the file, and create the file usage count. If the file has previously been installed, the setup program merely increments the file usage count.

If an older version of the Driver Manager was previously installed by the application setup program, the core components should be uninstalled, then reinstalled, so that the core component usage count is valid. **SQLRemoveDriverManager** should first be called to decrement the component usage count. **SQLInstallDriverManager** should then be called to increment the component usage count. The application setup program must physically replace the old core component files with the new files. The file usage counts will remain the same, and other applications that used the older version core component files will now use the newer version files.

In a fresh install of the ODBC core components, drivers, and translators, the application setup program should call the following functions in sequence: **SQLInstallDriverManager**, **SQLInstallDriverEx**, **SQLConfigDriver** (with an *fRequest* of ODBC_INSTALL_DRIVER), then **SQLInstallTranslatorEx**. In an uninstall of the core components, drivers, and translators, the application setup program should call the following functions in sequence: **SQLRemoveTranslator**, **SQLRemoveDriver**, then **SQLRemoveDriverManager**. These functions must be called in this sequence. In an upgrade of all components, all the uninstall functions should be called in sequence, then all the install functions should be called in sequence.

Related Functions

For information about	See
Adding, modifying, or removing a driver	**SQLConfigDriver**
Installing a driver	**SQLInstallDriverEx**
Installing a translator	**SQLInstallTranslatorEx**
Removing a driver	**SQLRemoveDriver**
Removing the Driver Manager	**SQLRemoveDriverManager**
Removing a translator	**SQLRemoveTranslator**

SQLInstallerError

Conformance

Version Introduced: ODBC 3.0

Summary

SQLInstallerError returns error or status information for the ODBC installer functions.

Syntax

RETCODE **SQLInstallerError**(
WORD *iError*,
DWORD * *pfErrorCode*,
LPSTR *lpszErrorMsg*,
WORD *cbErrorMsgMax*,
WORD * *pcbErrorMsg*);

Arguments

iError [Input]
Error record number. Valid numbers are from 1 to 8.

pfErrorCode [Output]
Installer error code. (For more information, see "Comments.")

lpszErrorMsg [Output]
Pointer to storage for the error message text.

cbErrorMsgMax [Input]
Maximum length of the *szErrorMsg* buffer. This must be less than or equal to SQL_MAX_MESSAGE_LENGTH minus the null-termination character.

cbErrorMsgMax [Input]
Maximum length of the *szErrorMsg* buffer. This must be less than or equal to SQL_MAX_MESSAGE_LENGTH minus the null-termination character.

pcbErrorMsg [Output]
Pointer to the total number of bytes (excluding the null-termination character) available to return in *lpszErrorMsg*. If the number of bytes available to return is greater than or equal to *cbErrorMsgMax*, the error message text in *lpszErrorMsg* is truncated to *cbErrorMsgMax* minus the null-termination character bytes. The *pcbErrorMsg* argument can be a null pointer.

Returns

SQL_SUCCESS, SQL_SUCCESS_WITH_INFO, SQL_NO_DATA, or SQL_ERROR.

Diagnostics

SQLInstallerError does not post error values for itself. **SQLInstallerError** returns SQL_NO_DATA when it is unable to retrieve any error information (in which case *pfErrorCode* is undefined). If **SQLInstallerError** cannot access error values for any reason that would normally return SQL_ERROR, **SQLInstallerError** returns SQL_ERROR, but does not post any error values. If either the *lpszErrorMsg* argument is NULL, the *cbErrorMsgMax* is less than or equal to 0, then this function returns SQL_ERROR. If the buffer for the error message is too short, **SQLInstallerError** returns SQL_SUCCESS_WITH_INFO, and returns the correct *pfErrorCode* value for **SQLInstallerError**.

To determine whether a truncation occurred in the error message, an application can compare the value in the *cbErrorMsgMax* argument to the actual length of the message text written to the *pcbErrorMsg* argument. If truncation does occur, the correct buffer length should be allocated for *lpszErrorMsg* and **SQLInstallerError** should be called again with the corresponding *iError* record.

Comments

An application calls **SQLInstallerError** when a previous call to the ODBC installer function returns FALSE. ODBC installer and driver or translator setup functions post zero or more errors only when the function fails (returns FALSE); therefore, an application calls **SQLInstallerError** only after an ODBC installer function fails.

The ODBC installer error queue is flushed each time a new installer function is called. Therefore, an application cannot expect to retrieve errors for functions other than from the last installer function call.

To retrieve multiple errors for a function call, an application calls **SQLInstallerError** multiple times.

When there is no additional information, **SQLInstallerError** returns SQL_NO_DATA, the *pfErrorCode* argument is undefined, the *pcbErrorMsg* argument equals 0, and the *lpszErrorMsg* argument contains a single null-termination character (unless the *cbErrorMsgMax* argument is equal to 0).

SQLInstallTranslator

Conformance

Version Introduced: ODBC 2.5, Deprecated

Summary

In ODBC 3.0, **SQLInstallTranslator** has been replaced by **SQLInstallTranslatorEx**. Calls to **SQLInstallTranslator** will be mapped to **SQLInstallTranslatorEx**. For more information, see **SQLInstallTranslatorEx**.

SQLInstallTranslator will return FALSE if an application calls it in the ODBC 3.0 Driver Manager with the *lpszInfFile* argument set to a value other than NULL. The ODBC.INF file used in ODBC 2.*x* is no longer supported in ODBC 3.0, even for backward compatibility.

SQLInstallTranslatorEx

Conformance

Version Introduced: ODBC 3.0

Summary

SQLInstallTranslatorEx adds information about a translator to the ODBCINST.INI section of the system information.

Syntax

BOOL **SQLInstallTranslatorEx** (
    LPCSTR *lpszTranslator*,
    LPCSTR *lpszPathIn*,
    LPSTR *lpszPathOut*,
    WORD *cbPathOutMax*,
    WORD * *pcbPathOut*,
    WORD *fRequest*,
    LPDWORD *lpdwUsageCount*);

Arguments

lpszTranslator [Input]

This must contain a list of keyword-value pairs describing the translator. The **Translator** and **Setup** keywords have to be included in the *lpszTranslator* string. The translation DLL is listed with the **Translator** keyword, and the translator setup DLL is listed with the **Setup** keyword. Each pair is terminated with a NULL byte, and the entire list is terminated with a NULL byte (that is, two NULL bytes mark the end of the list). The format of *lpszTranslator* is:

translator-desc\0Translator=*translator-DLL-filename*\0[Setup=*setup-DLL-filename*\0]\0

lpszPathIn [Input]

Full path of where the translator is to be installed or a null pointer. If *lpszPath* is a null pointer, then the translators will be installed in the System directory.

lpszPathOut [Output]

The path of the target directory where the translator should be installed. If the translator has never been installed, then *lpszPathOut* is the same as *lpszPathIn*. If there exists a prior installation of the translator, then *lpszPathOut* is the path of the prior installation.

cbPathOutMax [Input]

Length of *lpszPathOut*.

pcbPathOut [Output]

Total number of bytes available to return in *lpszPathOut*. If the number of bytes available to return is greater than or equal to *cbPathOutMax*, the output path in *lpszPathOut* is truncated to *pcbPathOutMax* minus the null-termination character. The *pcbPathOut* argument can be a null pointer.

fRequest [Input]

Type of request. *fRequest* must contain one of the following values:

ODBC_INSTALL_INQUIRY: Inquire about where a translator can be installed.

ODBC_INSTALL_COMPLETE: Complete the installation request.

lpdwUsageCount [Output]

The usage count of the translator after this function has been called.

Returns

The function returns TRUE if it is successful, FALSE if it fails.

Diagnostics

When **SQLInstallTranslatorEx** returns FALSE, an associated **pfErrorCode* value may be obtained by calling **SQLInstallerError**. The following table lists the **pfErrorCode* values that can be returned by **SQLInstallerError** and explains each one in the context of this function.

**pfErrorCode*	Error	Description
ODBC_ERROR_GENERAL_ERR	General installer error	An error occurred for which there was no specific installer error.
ODBC_ERROR_INVALID_BUFF_LEN	Invalid buffer length	The *lpszPathOut* argument was not large enough to contain the output path. The buffer contains the truncated path. The *cbPathOutMax* argument was 0 and the *fRequest* argument was ODBC_INSTALL_COMPLETE.
ODBC_ERROR_INVALID_REQUEST_TYPE	Invalid type of request	The *fRequest* argument was not one of the following: ODBC_INSTALL_INQUIRY ODBC_INSTALL_COMPLETE
ODBC_ERROR_INVALID_KEYWORD_VALUE	Invalid keyword-value pairs	The *lpszTranslator* argument contained a syntax error.

pfErrorCode	Error	Description
ODBC_ERROR_INVALID_PATH	Invalid install path	The *lpszPathIn* argument contained an invalid path.
ODBC_ERROR_INVALID_PARAM_SEQUENCE	Invalid parameter sequence	The *lpszTranslator* argument did not contain a list of keyword-value pairs.
ODBC_ERROR_USAGE_UPDATE_FAILED	Could not increment or decrement the registry's component usage count	The installer failed to increment the translator's usage count.

Comments

SQLInstallTranslatorEx provides a mechanism to install just the translator. This function does not actually copy any files. The calling program is responsible for copying the translator files.

SQLInstallTranslatorEx increments the component usage count for the installed translator by 1. If a version of the translator already exists, but the component usage count for the translator does not exist, the new component usage count value is set to 2.

The application setup program is responsible for physically copying the translator file, and maintaining the file usage count. If the translator file has not previously been installed, the application setup program must copy the file or files, and create the file or files usage count. If the file has previously been installed, the setup program simply increments the file usage count.

If an older version of the translator was previously installed by the application, the translator should be uninstalled, then reinstalled, so that the translator component usage count is valid. **SQLRemoveTranslator** should be called to decrement the component usage count, and then **SQLInstallTranslatorEx** should then be called to increment the component usage count. The application setup program must physically replace the old file or files with the new file. The file usage count will remain the same, and other applications that used the older version file will now use the newer version.

The length of the path in *lpszPathOut* in **SQLInstallTranslatorEx** allows for a two-phase install process, so an application can determine what *cbPathOutMax* should be by calling **SQLInstallTranslatorEx** with an *fRequest* of ODBC_INSTALL_INQUIRY mode. This will return the total number of bytes available in the *pcbPathOut* buffer. **SQLInstallTranslatorEx** can then be called with an *fRequest* of ODBC_INSTALL_COMPLETE and the *cbPathOutMax* argument set to the value in the *pcbPathOut* buffer, plus the null-termination character.

If you choose not to use the two-phase model for **SQLInstallTranslatorEx**, then you must set *cbPathOutMax*, which defines the size of the storage for the path of the target directory, to the value _MAX_PATH, as defined in STDLIB.H, to prevent truncation.

When *fRequest* is ODBC_INSTALL_COMPLETE, **SQLInstallTranslatorEx** does not allow *lpszPathOut* to be NULL (or *cbPathOutMax* to be 0). If *fRequest* is ODBC_INSTALL_COMPLETE, FALSE is returned when the number of bytes available to return is greater than or equal to *cbPathOutMax*, with the result that truncation occurs.

Related Functions

For information about	See
Returning a default translation option	**ConfigTranslator**
Selecting translators	**SQLGetTranslator**
Removing translators	**SQLRemoveTranslator**

SQLManageDataSources

Conformance

Version Introduced: ODBC 2.0

Summary

SQLManageDataSources displays a dialog box with which users can set up, add, and delete data sources in the system information.

Syntax

```
BOOL SQLManageDataSources(
     HWND hwnd);
```

Arguments

hwnd [Input]
Parent window handle.

Returns

SQLManageDataSources returns FALSE if *hwnd* is not a valid window handle. Otherwise, it returns TRUE.

Diagnostics

When **SQLManageDataSources** returns FALSE, an associated **pfErrorCode* value may be obtained by calling **SQLInstallerError**. The following table lists the **pfErrorCode* values that can be returned by **SQLInstallerError** and explains each one in the context of this function.

**pfErrorCode*	Error	Description
ODBC_ERROR_GENERAL_ERR	General installer error	An error occurred for which there was no specific installer error.
ODBC_ERROR_REQUEST_FAILED	*Request* failed	The call to **ConfigDSN** failed.
ODBC_ERROR_INVALID__HWND	Invalid window handle	The *hwnd* argument was invalid or NULL.
ODBC_ERROR_OUT_OF_MEM	Out of memory	The installer could not perform the function because of a lack of memory.

Comments

Managing Data Sources

SQLManageDataSources initially displays the ODBC Data Source Administrator dialog box.

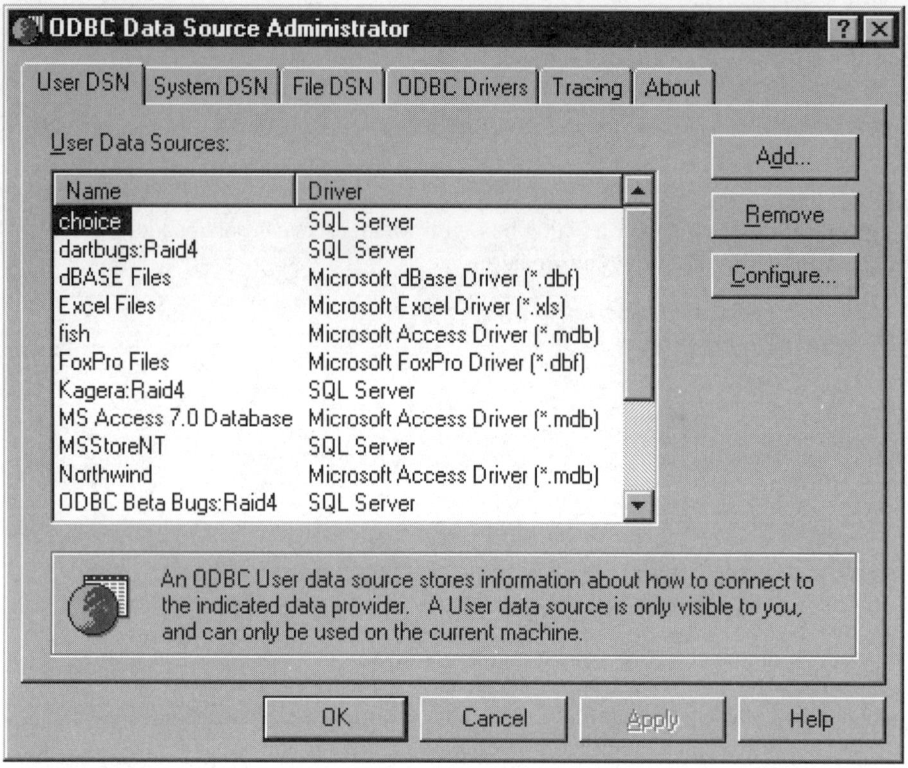

The dialog box displays the data sources listed in the system information under three tabs: **User DSN**, **System DSN**, and **File DSN**. If the user double-clicks a data source or selects a data source and clicks the **Configure** button, **SQLManageDataSources** calls **ConfigDSN** in the setup DLL with the ODBC_CONFIG_DSN option.

If the user clicks the **Add** button, **SQLManageDataSources** displays the **Create New Data Source** dialog box, shown in the following figure.

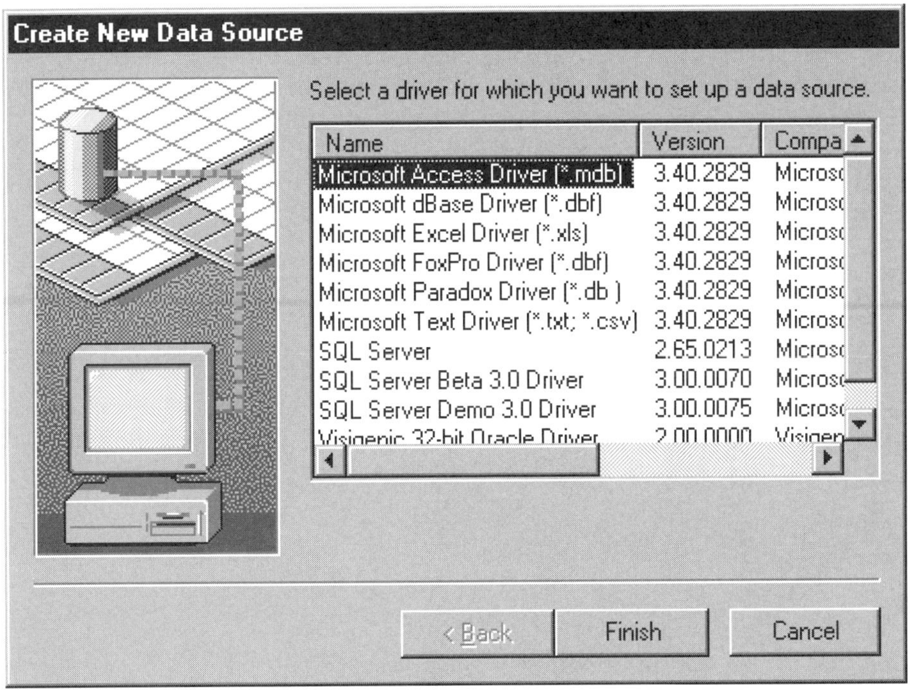

The dialog box displays a list of installed drivers. If the user double-clicks a driver or selects a driver and clicks the **OK** button, **SQLManageDataSources** calls **ConfigDSN** in the setup DLL and passes it the ODBC_ADD_DSN option.

If the user selects a data source and clicks the **Remove** button, **SQLManageDataSources** asks if the user wants to delete the data source. If the user clicks the **Yes** button, **SQLManageDataSources** calls **ConfigDSN** in the setup DLL with the ODBC_REMOVE_DSN option.

The **Add Data Source** dialog box is used to add or delete either a user data source, a system data source, or a file data source.

System DSNs

The **Create New Data Source** dialog box allows you to add a system data source to your local computer or delete one, or to set the configuration for a system data source.

A data source set up with a system data-source name (DSN) can be used by more than one user on the same machine. It can also be used by a system-wide service, which can then gain access to the data source even if no user is logged onto the machine.

A System DSN is registered in the HKEY_LOCAL_MACHINE entry in the system information, rather than the HKEY_CURRENT_USER entry. It is not tied to one user who logs on with his or her particular user name and password, but can be used by any user of that machine, or by an automatic system-wide service. The System DSN is, however, tied to one machine. It does not support the capability of using remote DSNs between machines. System DSNs are registered as follows in the system information:

```
HKEY_LOCAL_MACHINE
    SOFTWARE
        ODBC
            ODBC.INI
```

User DSNs

DSNs created for individual users will be called User DSNs, to distinguish them from System DSNs. User DSNs are registered as follows in the system information:

```
HKEY_CURRENT_USER
    SOFTWARE
        ODBC
            ODBC.INI
```

File DSNs

A file data source does not have a data source name, as does a machine data source, and is not registered to any one user or machine. The connection information for that data source is contained in a .dsn file that can be copied to any machine. A file data source can be shareable, in which case the .dsn file resides on a network and can be used simultaneously by multiple users on the network as long as the user has the appropriate driver installed. A file data source can also be unshareable, in which case it can only be used on a single machine.

For more information on file data sources, see "Connecting Using File Data Sources" in Chapter 6, "Connecting to a Data Source or Driver," or see **SQLDriverConnect**.

Managing Drivers

If the user clicks the **ODBC Drivers** tab in the **ODBC Data Source Administrator** dialog box, **SQLManageDataSources** displays a list of ODBC driver installed on the system, and information about the drivers. The date displayed is the creation date of the driver.

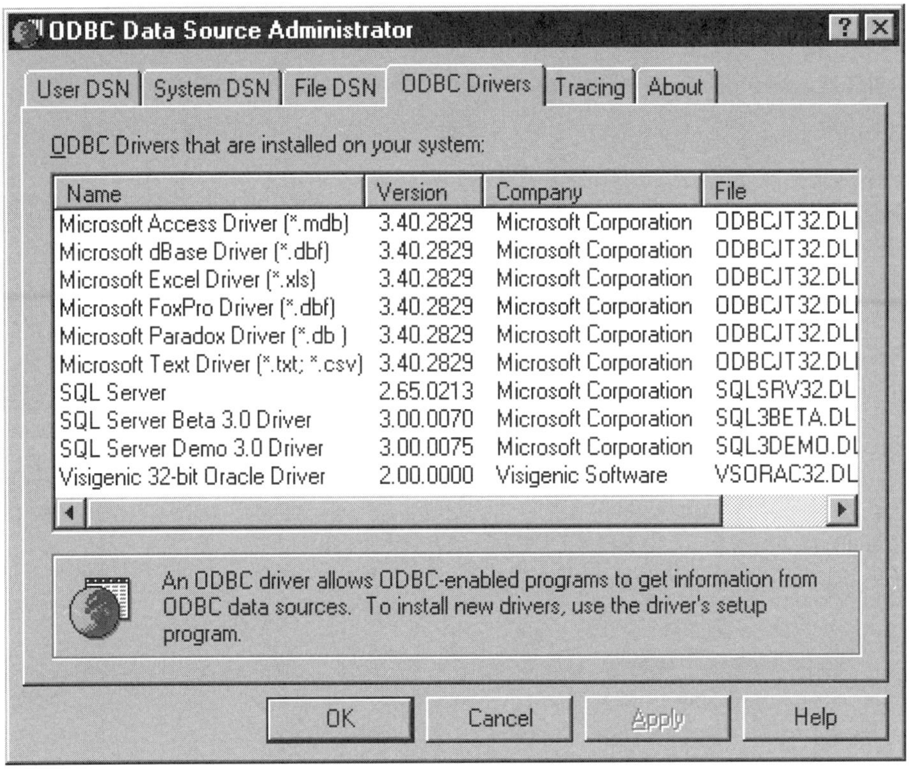

Tracing Options

If the user clicks the **Tracing** tab in the **ODBC Data Source Administrator** dialog box, **SQLManageDataSources** displays tracing options.

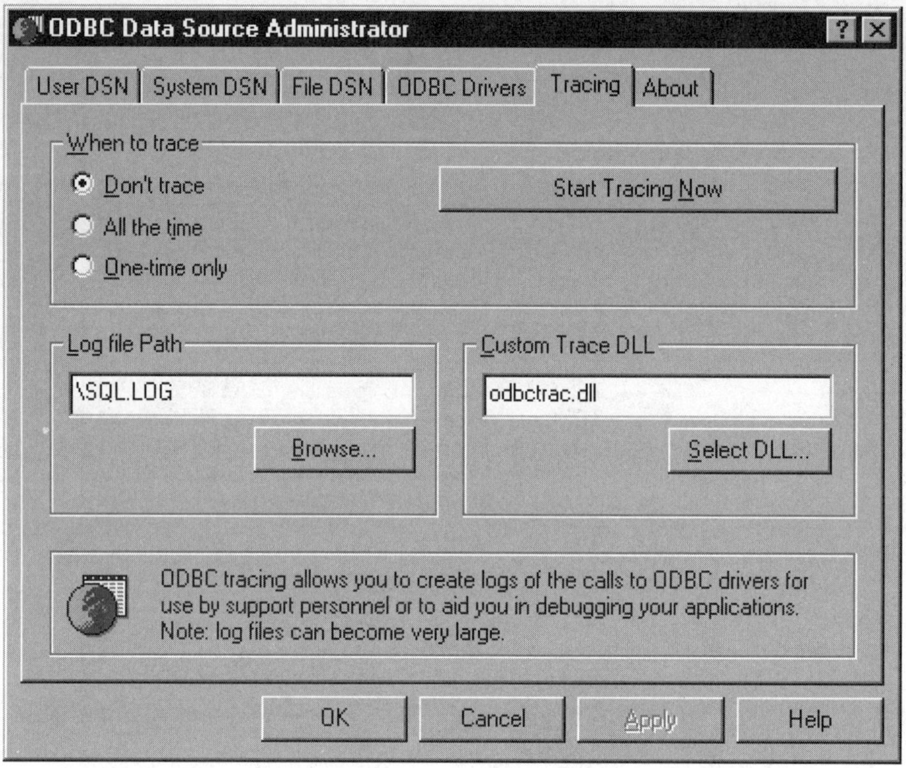

If the user selects or clears any of the check boxes in the **When to trace** section of the tab page, and clicks the **OK** button, **SQLManageDataSources** sets the **Trace** keyword in the [ODBC] section of the system information to 1 or 0 accordingly. If **All the time** is chosen, tracing is performed for each subsequent connection; if **One-time only** is chosen, tracing is performed for the duration of the connection only.

If the user clicks the **Start Tracing Now** button, and clicks the **OK** button, **SQLManageDataSources** enables tracing manually for all applications currently running on the machine.

If the user specifies the name of a trace file in the **Log file Path** text box, then clicks the **OK** button, **SQLManageDataSources** sets the **TraceFile** keyword in the [ODBC] section of the system information to the specified name.

For more information on tracing, see "Tracing" in Chapter 17, "Programming Considerations." For more information about the **Trace**, **TraceAutoStop**, and **TraceFile** keywords, see "ODBC Subkey" in Chapter 19, "Configuring Data Sources."

Related Functions

For information about	See
Creating data sources	**SQLCreateDataSource**

SQLPostInstallerError

Conformance

Version Introduced: ODBC 3.0

Summary

SQLPostInstallerError provides a mechanism for a driver or translator setup library to report errors for the **ConfigDriver**, **ConfigDSN**, and **ConfigTranslator** functions to the installer error queue. Applications do not use this API; they use **SQLInstallerError** to retrieve the error.

Syntax

```
RETCODE SQLPostInstallerError (
      DWORD      fErrorCode,
      LPSTR      szErrorMsg);
```

Arguments

fErrorCode [Input]
Installer error code.

szErrorMsg [Input]
Error message text.

Returns

SQL_SUCCESS or SQL_ERROR.

Diagnostics

SQLPostInstallerError does not post error values for itself. If the error was successfully posted to the installer error queue (retrievable using **SQLInstallerError**), SQL_SUCCESS is returned. SQL_ERROR will be returned if the value in the *dwErrorCode* argument is not one of the specified installer error codes.

Related Functions

For information about	See
Adding, modifying, or removing a driver	**ConfigDriver**
Adding, modifying, or removing data sources	**ConfigDSN**
Setting a translation option	**ConfigTranslator**

SQLReadFileDSN

Conformance

Version Introduced: ODBC 3.0

Summary

SQLReadFileDSN reads information from a File DSN.

Syntax

BOOL **SQLReadFileDSN**(
    LPCSTR *lpszFileName*,
    LPCSTR *lpszAppName*,
    LPCSTR *lpszKeyName*,
    LPSTR *lpszString*,
    WORD *cbString*,
    WORD * *pcbString*);

Arguments

lpszFileName [Input]

Pointer to the data buffer containing the name of the .dsn file. A .dsn extension is appended to all file names that do not already have a .dsn extension. The value in **lpszFileName* must be a null-terminated string.

lpszAppName [Input]

Pointer to the data buffer containing the name of the application. This is "ODBC" for the ODBC section. The value in **lpszAppName* must be a null-terminated string.

lpszKeyName [Input]

Pointer to the data buffer containing the name of the key to be read. See "Comments" for reserved keywords. The value in **lpszAppName* must be a null-terminated string.

lpszString [Output]

Pointer to the data buffer containing the string associated with the key to be read.

If **lpszFileName* is a valid .dsn file name, but the *lpszAppName* argument is a null pointer and the *lpszKeyName* argument is a null pointer, then **lpszString* contains a list of valid applications. If **lpszFileName* is a valid .dsn file name, and **lpszAppName* is a valid application name, but the *lpszKeyName* argument is a null pointer, then **lpszString* contains a list of valid reserved keywords in the appropriate section of the DSN file, delimited by semicolons. If **lpszFileName* is a valid .dsn file name, but **lpszAppName* is a null pointer, and the *lpszKeyName* argument is a null pointer, then **lpszString* contains a list of the sections in the DSN file, delimited by semicolons.

cbString [Input]
Length of the **lpszString* buffer.

pcbString [Output]
Total number of bytes available to return in **lpszString*. If the number of bytes available to return is greater than or equal to *cbString*, the output string in **lpszString* is truncated to *cbString* minus the null-termination character. The *pcbString* argument can be a null pointer.

Returns

The function returns TRUE if it is successful, FALSE if it fails.

Diagnostics

When **SQLReadFileDSN** returns FALSE, an associated **pfErrorCode* value may be obtained by calling **SQLInstallerError**. The following table lists the **pfErrorCode* values that can be returned by **SQLInstallerError** and explains each one in the context of this function.

**pfErrorCode*	Error	Description
ODBC_ERROR_GENERAL_ERR	General installer error	An error occurred for which there was no specific installer error.
ODBC_ERROR_INVALID_BUFF_LEN	Invalid buffer length	The *lpszString* argument was NULL. The *cbString* argument was less than or equal to 0.
ODBC_ERROR_INVALID_PATH	Invalid install path	The path of the file name specified in the *lpszFileName* argument was invalid.
ODBC_ERROR_INVALID_REQUEST_TYPE	Invalid type of request	The *lpszAppName* argument was NULL while the *lpszKeyName* argument was valid.
ODBC_ERROR_OUT_OF_MEM	Out of memory	The installer could not perform the function because of a lack of memory.
ODBC_ERROR_OUTPUT_STRING_TRUNCATED	Output string truncated	The string returned in **lpszString* was truncated because the value in *cbString* was less than or equal to the value in **pcbString*.
ODBC_ERROR REQUEST_FAILED	Request failed	The keyword did not exist in the file DSN.

Comments

ODBC reserves the section name [ODBC] in which to store the connection information. The reserved keywords for this section are the same as those reserved for a connect string in **SQLDriverConnect** (for more information, see the **SQLDriverConnect** function description).

Applications may use these reserved keywords to read the information in a File DSN. If an applications wants to find out the DSN-less connection string associated with a File DSN, it can call **SQLReadFileDSN** for any of the reserved connection string keywords in the [ODBC] section. The full connection string passed in a DSN-less connection is a combination of all of the keywords (reserved and driver-specific) in the [ODBC] section.

Related Functions

For information about	See
Writing information to a File DSN	**SQLWriteFileDSN**

SQLRemoveDefaultDataSource

Conformance

Version Introduced: ODBC 1.0, Deprecated

Summary

In ODBC 3.0, the **SQLRemoveDefaultDataSource** function has been replaced by a call to **SQLConfigDataSource** with an *fRequest* argument of ODBC_REMOVE_DEFAULT_DSN. If an ODBC 2.*x* installation program calls this function, the ODBC installer will map it to the following **SQLConfigDataSource** call:

```
SQLConfigDataSource (NULL, ODBC_REMOVE_DEFAULT_DSN, NULL, NULL)
```

SQLRemoveDriver

Conformance

Version Introduced: ODBC 3.0

Summary

SQLRemoveDriver changes or removes information about the driver from the ODBCINST.INI entry in the system information.

Syntax

```
BOOL SQLRemoveDriver (
     LPCSTR      lpszDriver,
     BOOL        fRemoveDSN,
     LPDWORD     lpdwUsageCount);
```

Arguments

lpszDriver [Input]

The name of the driver as registered in the ODBCINST.INI key of the system information.

fRemoveDSN [Input]

The valid values are:

TRUE:

Remove DSNs associated with the driver specified in *lpszDriver*.

FALSE:

Do not remove DSNs associated with the driver specified in *lpszDriver*.

lpdwUsageCount [Output]

The usage count of the driver after this function has been called.

Returns

The function returns TRUE if it is successful, FALSE if it fails. If no entry exists in the system information when this function is called, the function returns FALSE.

Diagnostics

When **SQLRemoveDriver** returns FALSE, an associated **pfErrorCode* value may be obtained by calling **SQLInstallerError**. The following table lists the **pfErrorCode* values that can be returned by **SQLInstallerError** and explains each one in the context of this function.

**pfErrorCode*	Error	Description
ODBC_ERROR_ GENERAL_ERR	General installer error	An error occurred for which there was no specific installer error.
ODBC_ERROR_ COMPONENT_ NOT_FOUND	Component not found in registry	The installer could not remove the driver information because it either did not exist in the registry or could not be found in the registry.

**pfErrorCode*	Error	Description
ODBC_ERROR_ INVALID_NAME	Invalid driver or translator name	The *lpszDriver* argument was invalid.
ODBC_ERROR_ USAGE_ UPDATE_ FAILED	Could not increment or decrement the component usage count	The installer failed to decrement the usage count of the driver.
ODBC_ERROR_ REQUEST_ FAILED	Request failed	The *fRemoveDSN* argument was TRUE; however, one or more DSNs could not be removed. The call to **SQLConfigDriver** with the ODBC_REMOVE_DRIVER request failed.
ODBC_ERROR_ OUT_OF_MEM	Out of memory	The installer could not perform the function because of a lack of memory.

Comments

SQLRemoveDriver complements the **SQLInstallDriverEx** function, and updates the component usage count in the system information. This function should only be called from a setup application.

SQLRemoveDriver will decrement the component usage count value by 1. If the component usage count goes to 0, then the following will occur:

1. **The SQLConfigDriver** function with the ODBC_REMOVE_DRIVER option will be called. If the *fRemoveDSN* option is set to TRUE, the **ConfigDSN** function calls **SQLRemoveDSNFromIni** to remove all the data sources associated with the driver specified in *lpszDriver*. If the *fRemoveDSN* option is set to FALSE, the data sources will not be deleted.
2. The driver entry in the system information will be removed. The driver entry is in the following system information location, under the driver name:

   HKEY_LOCAL_MACHINE
       SOFTWARE
           ODBC
               ODBCINST.INI

SQLRemoveDriver does not actually remove any files. The calling program is responsible for deleting files, and maintaining the file usage count. Only after both the component usage count and the file usage count have reached zero is a file physically deleted. Some files in a component can be deleted, and others not deleted, depending upon whether the files are used by other applications that have incremented the file usage count.

SQLRemoveDriver is also called as part of an upgrade process. If an application detects that it has to perform an upgrade, and it has previously installed the driver, then the driver should be removed, then reinstalled. **SQLRemoveDriver** should first be called to decrement the component usage count, then **SQLInstallDriverEx** should then be called to increment the component usage count. The application setup program must physically replace the old files with the new files. The file usage count will remain the same, and other applications that use the older version files will now use the newer version.

Related Functions

For information about	See
Adding, modifying, or removing a driver	**ConfigDriver** (in the Setup DLL)
Adding, modifying, or removing a driver	**SQLConfigDriver**
Installing a driver	**SQLInstallDriverEx**

SQLRemoveDriverManager

Conformance

Version Introduced: ODBC 3.0

Summary

SQLRemoveDriverManager changes or removes information about the ODBC core components from the ODBCINST.INI entry in the system information.

Syntax

BOOL **SQLRemoveDriverManager** (
    LPDWORD *pdwUsageCount*);

Arguments

pdwUsageCount [Output]
The usage count of the Driver Manager after this function has been called.

Returns

The function returns TRUE if it is successful, FALSE if it fails. If no entry exists in the system information when this function is called, the function returns FALSE.

Diagnostics

When **SQLRemoveDriverManager** returns FALSE, an associated **pfErrorCode* value may be obtained by calling **SQLInstallerError**. The following table lists the **pfErrorCode* values that can be returned by **SQLInstallerError** and explains each one in the context of this function.

**pfErrorCode*	Error	Description
ODBC_ERROR_GENERAL_ERR	General installer error	An error occurred for which there was no specific installer error.
ODBC_ERROR_COMPONENT_NOT_FOUND	Component not found in registry	The installer could not remove the Driver Manager information because it either did not exist in the registry or could not be found in the registry.
ODBC_ERROR_USAGE_UPDATE_FAILED	Could not increment or decrement the component usage count	The installer failed to decrement the usage count of the Driver Manager.
ODBC_ERROR_OUT_OF_MEM	Out of memory	The installer could not perform the function because of a lack of memory.

Comments

SQLRemoveDriverManager complements the **SQLInstallDriverManager** function, and updates the component usage count in the system information. This function should only be called from a setup application.

SQLRemoveDriverManager will decrement the core component usage count by 1. If the component usage count goes to 0, then the entry system information will be removed. The core component entry is in the following location in the system information, under the title "ODBC Core":

HKEY_LOCAL_MACHINE
    SOFTWARE
        ODBC
            ODBCINST.INI

Caution An application should not physically remove Driver Manager files when the component usage count and the file usage count reach zero.

SQLRemoveDriverManager does not actually remove any files. The calling program is responsible for deleting files and maintaining the file usage counts. Driver Manager files should not, however, be removed when both the component usage count and the file usage count have reached zero, because these files may be used by other applications that have not incremented the file usage count.

SQLRemoveDriverManager is called as part of the Uninstall process. ODBC core components (which include the Driver Manager, Cursor Library, Installer, Language Library, Administrator, thunking files, and so on) are uninstalled as a whole. The following files are not removed when **SQLRemoveDriverManager** is called as part of the Uninstall process:

ODBC32DLL	ODBCCP32.DLL
ODBCCR32.DLL	ODBC16GT.DLL
ODBCCU32.DLL	ODBC32GT.DLL
ODBCINT.DLL	DS16GT.DLL
ODBCTRAC.DLL	DS32GT.DLL
MSVCRT40.DLL	ODBCAD32.EXE
ODBCCP32.CPL	

SQLRemoveDriverManager is also called as part of an upgrade process. If an application detects that it has to perform an upgrade, and it has previously installed the driver, then the driver should be removed, and then reinstalled. **SQLRemoveDriverManager** should first be called to decrement the component usage count. **SQLInstallDriverEx** should then be called to increment the component usage count. The application setup program must physically replace the old core component files with the new files. The file usage counts will remain the same, and other applications that use the older version core component files will now use the newer version files.

Related Functions

For information about	See
Installing a Driver Manager	**SQLInstallDriverManager**

SQLRemoveDSNFromIni

Conformance

Version Introduced: ODBC 1.0

Summary

SQLRemoveDSNFromIni removes a data source from the system information.

Syntax

```
BOOL SQLRemoveDSNFromIni(
        LPCSTR        lpszDSN);
```

Arguments

lpszDSN [Input]
Name of the data source to remove.

Returns

The function returns TRUE if it removes the data source or the data source was not in the ODBC.INI file. It returns FALSE if it fails to remove the data source.

Diagnostics

When **SQLRemoveDSNFromIni** returns FALSE, an associated **pfErrorCode* value may be obtained by calling **SQLInstallerError**. The following table lists the **pfErrorCode* values that can be returned by **SQLInstallerError** and explains each one in the context of this function.

*pfErrorCode	Error	Description
ODBC_ERROR_GENERAL_ERR	General installer error	An error occurred for which there was no specific installer error.
ODBC_ERROR_INVALID_DSN	Invalid DSN	The *lpszDSN* argument was invalid.
ODBC_ERROR_REQUEST_FAILED	Request failed	The installer could not remove the DSN info from the registry.
ODBC_ERROR_OUT_OF_MEM	Out of memory	The installer could not perform the function because of a lack of memory.

Comments

SQLRemoveDSNFromIni removes the data source name from the [ODBC Data Sources] section of the system information. It also removes the data source specification section from the system information.

This function should only be called from a driver setup library.

Related Functions

For information about	See
Adding, modifying, or removing a data source	**ConfigDSN**
Adding, modifying, or removing a data source	**SQLConfigDataSource**
Removing the default data source	**SQLRemoveDefaultDataSource**
Adding a data source name to the system information	**SQLWriteDSNToIni**

SQLRemoveTranslator

Conformance

Version Introduced: ODBC 3.0

Summary

SQLRemoveTranslator removes information about a translator from the ODBCINST.INI section of the system information and decrements the translator's component usage count by 1.

Syntax

```
BOOL SQLRemoveTranslator (
      LPCSTR        lpszTranslator,
      LPDWORD       lpdwUsageCount);
```

Arguments

lpszTranslator [Input]
The name of the translator as registered in the ODBCINST.INI key of the system information.

lpdwUsageCount [Output]
The usage count of the translator after this function has been called.

Returns

The function returns TRUE if it is successful, FALSE if it fails. If no entry exists in the system information when this function is called, the function returns FALSE.

Diagnostics

When **SQLRemoveTranslator** returns FALSE, an associated **pfErrorCode* value may be obtained by calling **SQLInstallerError**. The following table lists the **pfErrorCode* values that can be returned by **SQLInstallerError** and explains each one in the context of this function.

**pfErrorCode*	Error	Description
ODBC_ERROR_GENERAL_ERR	General installer error	An error occurred for which there was no specific installer error.
ODBC_ERROR_COMPONENT_NOT_FOUND	Component not found in registry	The installer could not remove the translator information because it either did not exist in the registry or could not be found in the registry.
ODBC_ERROR_INVALID_NAME	Invalid driver or translator name	The *lpszTranslator* argument was invalid.

**pfErrorCode*	Error	Description
ODBC_ERROR_ USAGE_ UPDATE_ FAILED	Could not increment or decrement the component usage count	The installer failed to decrement the usage count of the driver.
ODBC_ERROR_ OUT_OF_MEM	Out of memory	The installer could not perform the function because of a lack of memory.

Comments

SQLRemoveTranslator complements the **SQLInstallTranslatorEx** function, and updates the component usage count in the system information. This function should only be called from a setup application.

SQLRemoveTranslator will decrement the component usage count by 1. If the component usage count goes to 0, then the translator entry in the system information will be removed. The translator entry is in the following location in the system information, under the translator name:

```
HKEY_LOCAL_MACHINE
    SOFTWARE
        ODBC
            ODBCINST.INI
```

SQLRemoveTranslator does not actually remove any files. The calling program is responsible for deleting files, and maintaining the file usage count. Only after both the component usage count and the file usage count have reached zero is a file physically deleted. Some files in a component can be deleted, and others not deleted, depending upon whether the files are used by other applications that have incremented the file usage count.

SQLRemoveTranslator is also called as part of an upgrade process. If an application detects that it has to perform an upgrade, and it has previously installed the driver, then the driver should be removed, then reinstalled. **SQLRemoveTranslator** should first be called to decrement the component usage count, then **SQLInstallTranslatorEx** should then be called to increment the component usage count. The application setup program must physically replace the old files with the new files. The file usage count will remain the same, and other applications that use the older version files will now use the newer version.

Related Functions

For information about	See
Installing a translator	**SQLInstallTranslatorEx**

SQLSetConfigMode

Conformance

Version Introduced: ODBC 3.0

Summary

SQLSetConfigMode sets the configuration mode that indicates where the ODBC.INI entry listing DSN values is in the system information.

Syntax

BOOL **SQLSetConfigMode**(
UWORD *wConfigMode*);

Arguments

wConfigMode [Input]
The installer configuration mode (see "Comments"). The value in *wConfigMode* can be:

ODBC_USER_DSN
ODBC_SYSTEM_DSN
ODBC_BOTH_DSN

Returns

The function returns TRUE if it is successful, FALSE if it fails.

Diagnostics

When **SQLSetConfigMode** returns FALSE, an associated **pfErrorCode* value may be obtained by calling **SQLInstallerError**. The following table lists the **pfErrorCode* values that can be returned by **SQLInstallerError** and explains each one in the context of this function.

**pfErrorCode*	Error	Description
ODBC_ERROR_INVALID_PARAM_SEQUENCE	Invalid parameter sequence	The *wConfigMode* argument did not contain ODBC_USER_DSN, ODBC_SYSTEM_DSN, or ODBC_BOTH_DSN.

Comments

This function is used to set where the ODBC.INI entry listing DSN values is in the system information. If *wConfigMode* is ODBC_USER_DSN, the DSN is a User DSN and the function reads from the ODBC.INI entry in HKEY_CURRENT_USER. If it is ODBC_SYSTEM_DSN, the DSN is a System DSN and the function reads from the ODBC.INI entry in HKEY_LOCAL_MACHINE. If it is ODBC_BOTH_DSN, HKEY_CURRENT_USER is tried, and if it fails, then HKEY_LOCAL_MACHINE is used.

This function does not affect **SQLCreateDataSource** and **SQLDriverConnect**. The configuration mode has to be set when a driver reads from the registry by calling **SQLGetPrivateProfileString** or writes to the registry by calling **SQLWritePrivateProfileString**. Calls to **SQLGetPrivateProfileString** and **SQLWritePrivateProfileString** use the configuration mode to know which part of the registry to operate on.

Caution **SQLSetConfigMode** should only be called when necessary; if the mode is improperly set, the ODBC Installer may fail to function properly.

SQLSetConfigMode makes a direct registry modification of the configuration mode. This is apart from the process of modifying the configuration mode by a call to **SQLConfigDataSource**. A call to **SQLConfigDataSource** sets the configuration mode to distinguish user and System DSNs when modifying a DSN. Prior to returning, **SQLConfigDataSource** resets the configuration mode to BOTHDSN.

Related Functions

For information about	See
Creating a data source	**SQLCreateDataSource**
Connecting to a data source using a connection string or dialog box	**SQLDriverConnect**
Retrieving the configuration mode	**SQLGetConfigMode**

SQLValidDSN

Conformance

Version Introduced: ODBC 2.0

Summary

SQLValidDSN checks the length and validity of the data source name before the name is added to the system information.

Syntax

```
BOOL SQLValidDSN(
     LPCSTR      lpszDSN);
```

Arguments

lpszDSN [Input]
Data source name to be checked.

Returns

The function returns TRUE if the data source name is valid. It returns FALSE if the data source name is invalid or the function call failed.

Diagnostics

When **SQLValidDSN** returns FALSE, an associated **pfErrorCode* value may be obtained by calling **SQLInstallerError**. A **pfErrorCode* is returned only if the function call failed, not if FALSE was returned because the data source name is invalid. The following table lists the **pfErrorCode* values that can be returned by **SQLInstallerError** and explains each one in the context of this function.

**pfErrorCode*	Error	Description
ODBC_ERROR_ GENERAL_ERR	General installer error	An error occurred for which there was no specific installer error.
ODBC_ERROR_ OUT_OF_MEM	Out of memory	The installer could not perform the function because of a lack of memory.

Comments

SQLValidDSN is called by a driver's **ConfigDSN** to check the length of the data source name, and the validity of the individual characters in the data source name. It checks whether the length of the name is greater than SQL_MAX_DSN_LENGTH, as defined in SQLEXT.H. (Note that the length of the data source name is also checked by **SQLWriteDSNToIni**.) **SQLValidDSN** checks whether any of the following invalid characters are included in the data source name:

[ ] { } ( ) , ; ? * = ! @ \

Related Functions

For information about	See
Adding, modifying, or removing a data source	**ConfigDSN** (in the Setup DLL)
Adding, modifying, or removing a data source	**SQLConfigDataSource**
Writing a data source name to the system information	**SQLWriteDSNToIni**

SQLWriteDSNToIni

Conformance

Version Introduced: ODBC 1.0

Summary

SQLWriteDSNToIni adds a data source to the system information.

Syntax

```
BOOL SQLWriteDSNToIni(
        LPCSTR      lpszDSN,
        LPCSTR      lpszDriver);
```

Arguments

lpszDSN [Input]
Name of the data source to add.

lpszDriver [Input]
Driver description (usually the name of the associated DBMS) presented to users instead of the physical driver name.

Returns

The function returns TRUE if it is successful, FALSE if it fails.

Diagnostics

When **SQLWriteDSNToIni** returns FALSE, an associated **pfErrorCode* value may be obtained by calling **SQLInstallerError**. The following table lists the **pfErrorCode* values that can be returned by **SQLInstallerError** and explains each one in the context of this function.

**pfErrorCode*	Error	Description
ODBC_ERROR_GENERAL_ERR	General installer error	An error occurred for which there was no specific installer error.
ODBC_ERROR_INVALID_DSN	Invalid DSN	The *lpszDSN* argument contained a string that was invalid for a DSN.
ODBC_ERROR_INVALID_NAME	Invalid driver or translator name	The *lpszDriver* argument was invalid.
ODBC_ERROR_REQUEST_FAILED	Request failed	The installer failed to create a DSN in the registry.
ODBC_ERROR_OUT_OF_MEM	Out of memory	The installer could not perform the function because of a lack of memory.

Comments

SQLWriteDSNToIni adds the data source to the [ODBC Data Sources] section of the system information. It then creates a specification section for the data source and adds a single keyword (**Driver**) with the name of the driver DLL as its value. If the data source specification section already exists, **SQLWriteDSNToIni** removes the old section before creating the new one.

The caller of this function must add any driver-specific keywords and values to the data source specification section of the system information.

If the name of the data source is Default, **SQLWriteDSNToIni** also creates the default driver specification section in the system information.

This function should only be called from a setup DLL.

Related Functions

For information about	See
Adding, modifying, or removing a data source	**ConfigDSN** (in the Setup DLL)
Adding, modifying, or removing a data source	**SQLConfigDataSource**
Removing a data source name from the system information	**SQLRemoveDSNFromIni**

SQLWriteFileDSN

Conformance

Version Introduced: ODBC 3.0

Summary

SQLWriteFileDSN writes information to a File DSN.

Syntax

```
BOOL SQLWriteFileDSN(
     LPCSTR     lpszFileName,
     LPCSTR     lpszAppName,
     LPCSTR     lpszKeyName,
     LPCSTR     lpszString);
```

Arguments

lpszFileName [Input]
Pointer to the name of the File DSN. A DSN extension is appended to all file names that do not already have a DSN extension.

lpszAppName [Input]
Pointer to the name of the application. This is "ODBC" for the ODBC section.

lpszKeyName [Input]
Pointer to the name of the key to be read. See "Comments" for reserved keywords.

lpszString [Output]
Pointed to the string associated with the key to be written. The maximum length of the string pointed to by this argument is 32,767 bytes.

Returns

The function returns TRUE if it is successful, FALSE if it fails.

Diagnostics

When **SQLWriteFileDSN** returns FALSE, an associated **pfErrorCode* value may be obtained by calling **SQLInstallerError**. The following table lists the **pfErrorCode* values that can be returned by **SQLInstallerError** and explains each one in the context of this function.

**pfErrorCode*	Error	Description
ODBC_ERROR_ GENERAL_ERR	General installer error	An error occurred for which there was no specific installer error.
ODBC_ERROR_ INVALID_ PATH	Invalid install path	The path of the file name specified in the *lpszFileName* argument was invalid.
ODBC_ERROR_ INVALID_ REQUEST_TYPE	Invalid type of request	The *lpszAppName*, *lpszKeyName*, or *lpszString* argument was NULL.

Comments

ODBC reserves the section name [ODBC] in which to store the connection information. The reserved keywords for this section are the same as those reserved for a connect string in **SQLDriverConnect** (for more information, see the **SQLDriverConnect** function description).

Applications may use these reserved keywords to write information directly to a File DSN. If an application wants to create or modify the DSN-less connection string associated with a File DSN, it can call **SQLWriteFileDSN** for any of the reserved connection string keywords in the [ODBC] section.

If the *lpszString* argument is a null pointer, the keyword pointed to by the *lpszKeyName* argument will be deleted from the .dsn file. If the *lpszString* and *lpszKeyName* arguments are both null pointers, the section pointed to by the *lpszAppName* argument will be deleted from the .dsn file.

Related Functions

For information about	See
Reading information from File DSNs	**SQLReadFileDSN**

SQLWritePrivateProfileString

Conformance

Version Introduced: ODBC 2.0

Summary

SQLWritePrivateProfileString writes a value name and data to the ODBC.INI subkey of the system information.

Syntax

BOOL **SQLWritePrivateProfileString**(
LPCSTR *lpszSection*,
LPCSTR *lpszEntry*,
LPCSTR *lpszString*,
LPCSTR *lpszFilename*);

Arguments

lpszSection [Input]
Points to a null-terminated string containing the name of the section to which the string will be copied. If the section does not exist, it is created. The name of the section is case-independent; the string can be any combination of uppercase and lowercase letters.

lpszEntry [Input]
Points to a null-terminated string containing the name of the key to be associated with a string. If the key does not exist in the specified section, it is created. If this *argument* is NULL, the entire section, including all entries within the section, is deleted.

lpszString [Input]
Points to a null-terminated string to be written to the file. If this argument is NULL, the key pointed to by the *lpszEntry* argument is deleted.

lpszFilename [Output]
Points to a null-terminated string that names the initialization file.

Returns

The function returns TRUE if it is successful, FALSE if it fails.

Diagnostics

When **SQLWritePrivateProfileString** returns FALSE, an associated **pfErrorCode* value may be obtained by calling **SQLInstallerError**. The following table lists the **pfErrorCode* values that can be returned by **SQLInstallerError** and explains each one in the context of this function.

**pfErrorCode*	Error	Description
ODBC_ERROR_ GENERAL_ERR	General installer error	An error occurred for which there was no specific installer error.
ODBC_ERROR_ REQUEST_FAILED	Request failed	The requested system information could not be written.
ODBC_ERROR_ OUT_OF_MEM	Out of memory	The installer could not perform the function because of a lack of memory.

Comments

SQLWritePrivateProfileString is provided as a simple way to port drivers and driver setup DLLs from Windows to Windows NT. Calls to **WritePrivateProfileString** that write a profile string to the ODBC.INI file should be replaced with calls to **SQLWritePrivateProfileString**. **SQLWritePrivateProfileString** calls functions in the Win32 API to add the specified value name and data to the ODBC.INI subkey of the system information.

A configuration mode indicates where the ODBC.INI entry listing DSN values is in the system information. If the DSN is a User DSN (the state variable is USERDSN_ONLY), the function writes to the ODBC.INI entry in HKEY_CURRENT_USER. If the DSN is a System DSN (SYSTEMDSN_ONLY), the function writes to the ODBC.INI entry in HKEY_LOCAL_MACHINE. If the state variable is BOTHDSN, HKEY_CURRENT_USER is tried, and if it fails, then HKEY_LOCAL_MACHINE is used.

Related Functions

For information about	See
Getting a value from the system information	**SQLGetPrivateProfileString**

CHAPTER 24

Translation DLL Function Reference

This chapter describes the syntax of the translation DLL API, which consists of two functions: **SQLDriverToDataSource** and **SQLDataSourceToDriver**. These functions must be included in the DLL that performs translation for the driver.

SQLDataSourceToDriver

SQLDataSourceToDriver supports translations for ODBC drivers. This function is not called by ODBC-enabled applications; applications request translation through **SQLSetConnectAttr**. The driver associated with the *ConnectionHandle* specified in **SQLSetConnectAttr** calls the specified DLL to perform translations of all data flowing from the data source to the driver. A default translation DLL can be specified in the ODBC initialization file.

Syntax

```
BOOL SQLDataSourceToDriver(
        UDWORD     fOption,
        SWORD      fSqlType,
        PTR        rgbValueIn,
        SDWORD     cbValueIn,
        PTR        rgbValueOut,
        SDWORD     cbValueOutMax,
        SDWORD *   pcbValueOut,
        UCHAR *    szErrorMsg,
        SWORD      cbErrorMsgMax,
        SWORD *    pcbErrorMsg);
```

Arguments

fOption [Input]
Option value.

fSqlType [Input]
The SQL data type. This argument tells the driver how to convert *rgbValueIn* into a form acceptable by the application. For a list of valid SQL data types, see the "SQL Data Types" section in Appendix D, "Data Types."

rgbValueIn [Input]
Value to translate.

cbValueIn [Input]
Length of *rgbValueIn*.

rgbValueOut [Output]
Result of the translation.

Note The translation DLL does not null-terminate this value.

cbValueOutMax [Input]
Length of *rgbValueOut*.

pcbValueOut [Output]
The total number of bytes (excluding the null-termination byte) available to return in *rgbValueOut*.

For character or binary data, if this is greater than or equal to *cbValueOutMax*, the data in *rgbValueOut* is truncated to *cbValueOutMax* bytes.

For all other data types, the value of *cbValueOutMax* is ignored and the translation DLL assumes the size of *rgbValueOut* is the size of the default C data type of the SQL data type specified with *fSqlType*.

The *pcbValueOut* argument can be a null pointer.

szErrorMsg [Output]
Pointer to storage for an error message. This is an empty string unless the translation failed.

cbErrorMsgMax [Input]
Length of *szErrorMsg*.

pcbErrorMsg [Output]
Pointer to the total number of bytes (excluding the null-termination byte) available to return in *szErrorMsg*. If this is greater than or equal to *cbErrorMsg*, the data in *szErrorMsg* is truncated to *cbErrorMsgMax* minus the null-termination character. The *pcbErrorMsg* argument can be a null pointer.

Returns

TRUE if the translation was successful.

FALSE if the translation failed.

Comments

The driver calls **SQLDataSourceToDriver** to translate *all* data (result set data, table names, row counts, error messages, and so on) passing from the data source to the driver. The translation DLL may not translate some data, depending on the data's type and the purpose of the translation DLL; for example, a DLL that translates character data from one code page to another ignores all numeric and binary data.

The value of *fOption* is set to the value of *vParam* specified by calling **SQLSetConnectAttr** with the SQL_ATTR_TRANSLATE_OPTION attribute. It is a 32-bit value which has a specific meaning for a given translation DLL. For example, it could specify a certain character set translation.

If the same buffer is specified for *rgbValueIn* and *rgbValueOut*, the translation of data in the buffer will be performed in place.

Note that, although *cbValueIn*, *cbValueOutMax*, and *pcbValueOut* are of the type SDWORD, **SQLDataSourceToDriver** does not necessarily support huge pointers.

If **SQLDataSourceToDriver** returns FALSE, data truncation may have occurred during translation. If *pcbValueOut*, the number of bytes available to return in the output buffer is greater than *cbValueOutMax*, the length of the output buffer, then truncation occurred. The driver must determine whether the truncation was acceptable. If truncation did not occur, the **SQLDataSourceToDriver** returned FALSE due to another error. In either case, a specific error message is returned in *szErrorMsg*.

For more information about translating data, see "Translation DLLs" in Chapter 17, "Programming Considerations."

Related Functions

For information about	See
Translating data being sent to the data source	**SQLDriverToDataSource**
Returning the setting of a connection attribute	**SQLGetConnectAttr**
Setting a connection attribute	**SQLSetConnectAttr**

SQLDriverToDataSource

SQLDriverToDataSource supports translations for ODBC drivers. This function is not called by ODBC-enabled applications; applications request translation through **SQLSetConnectAttr**. The driver associated with the *ConnectionHandle* specified in **SQLSetConnectAttr** calls the specified DLL to perform translations of all data flowing from the driver to the data source. A default translation DLL can be specified in the ODBC initialization file.

Syntax

```
BOOL SQLDriverToDataSource(
        UDWORD    fOption,
        SWORD     fSqlType,
        PTR       rgbValueIn,
        SDWORD    cbValueIn,
        PTR       rgbValueOut,
        SDWORD    cbValueOutMax,
        SDWORD *  pcbValueOut,
        UCHAR *   szErrorMsg,
        SWORD     cbErrorMsgMax,
        SWORD *   pcbErrorMsg);
```

Arguments

fOption [Input]
Option value.

fSqlType [Input]
The ODBC SQL data type. This argument tells the driver how to convert *rgbValueIn* into a form acceptable by the data source. For a list of valid SQL data types, see the "SQL Data Types" section in Appendix D, "Data Types."

rgbValueIn [Input]
Value to translate.

cbValueIn [Input]
Length of *rgbValueIn*.

rgbValueOut [Output]
Result of the translation.

Note The translation DLL does not null-terminate this value.

cbValueOutMax [Input]
Length of *rgbValueOut*.

pcbValueOut [Output]
The total number of bytes (excluding the null-termination byte) available to return in *rgbValueOut*.

For character or binary data, if this is greater than or equal to *cbValueOutMax*, the data in *rgbValueOut* is truncated to *cbValueOutMax* bytes.

For all other data types, the value of *cbValueOutMax* is ignored and the translation DLL assumes the size of *rgbValueOut* is the size of the default C data type of the SQL data type specified with *fSqlType*.

The *pcbValueOut* argument can be a null pointer.

szErrorMsg [Output]
Pointer to storage for an error message. This is an empty string unless the translation failed.

cbErrorMsgMax [Input]
Length of *szErrorMsg*.

pcbErrorMsg [Output]
Pointer to the total number of bytes (excluding the null-termination byte) available to return in *szErrorMsg*. If this is greater than or equal to *cbErrorMsg*, the data in *szErrorMsg* is truncated to *cbErrorMsgMax* minus the null-termination character. The *pcbErrorMsg* argument can be a null pointer.

Returns

TRUE if the translation was successful.

FALSE if the translation failed.

Comments

The driver calls **SQLDriverToDataSource** to translate *all* data (SQL statements, parameters, and so on) passing from the driver to the data source. The translation DLL may not translate some data, depending on the data's type and the purpose of the translation DLL. For example, a DLL that translates character data from one code page to another ignores all numeric and binary data.

The value of *fOption* is set to the value of *vParam* specified by calling **SQLSetConnectAttr** with the SQL_ATTR_TRANSLATE_OPTION attribute. It is a 32-bit value that has a specific meaning for a given translation DLL. For example, it could specify a certain character set translation.

If the same buffer is specified for *rgbValueIn* and *rgbValueOut*, the translation of data in the buffer will be performed in place.

Note that, although *cbValueIn*, *cbValueOutMax*, and *pcbValueOut* are of the type SDWORD, **SQLDriverToDataSource** does not necessarily support huge pointers.

If **SQLDriverToDataSource** returns FALSE, data truncation may have occurred during translation. If *pcbValueOut*, the number of bytes available to return in the output buffer is greater than *cbValueOutMax*, the length of the output buffer, then truncation occurred. The driver must determine whether or not the truncation was acceptable. If truncation did not occur, the **SQLDriverToDataSource** returned FALSE due to another error. In either case, a specific error message is returned in *szErrorMsg*.

For more information about translating data, see "Translation DLLs" in Chapter 17, "Programming Considerations."

Related Functions

For information about	See
Translating data returned from the data source	**SQLDataSourceToDriver**
Returning the setting of a connection attribute	**SQLGetConnectAttr**
Setting a connection attribute	**SQLSetConnectAttr**

Appendixes

APPENDIX A

ODBC Error Codes

SQLGetDiagRec or **SQLGetDiagField** returns SQLSTATE values as defined by X/Open Data Management: Structured Query Language (SQL), Version 2 (March 1995). SQLSTATE values are strings that contain five characters. The following table lists SQLSTATE values that a driver can return for **SQLGetDiagRec**.

The character string value returned for an SQLSTATE consists of a two-character class value followed by a three-character subclass value. A class value of "01" indicates a warning and is accompanied by a return code of SQL_SUCCESS_WITH_INFO. Class values other than "01," except for the class "IM," indicate an error and are accompanied by a return code of SQL_ERROR. The class "IM" is specific to warnings and errors that derive from the implementation of ODBC itself. The subclass value "000" in any class indicates that there is no subclass for that SQLSTATE. The assignment of class and subclass values is defined by SQL-92.

Note Although successful execution of a function is normally indicated by a return value of SQL_SUCCESS, the SQLSTATE 00000 also indicates success.

SQLSTATE	Error	Can be returned from
01000	General warning	All ODBC functions except: **SQLError** **SQLGetDiagField** **SQLGetDiagRec**
01001	Cursor operation conflict	**SQLExecDirect** **SQLExecute** **SQLParamData** **SQLSetPos**
01002	Disconnect error	**SQLDisconnect**

SQLSTATE	Error	Can be returned from
01003	NULL value eliminated in set function	**SQLExecDirect** **SQLExecute** **SQLParamData**
01004	String data, right truncated	**SQLBrowseConnect** **SQLBulkOperations** **SQLColAttribute** **SQLDataSources** **SQLDescribeCol** **SQLDriverConnect** **SQLDrivers** **SQLExecDirect** **SQLExecute** **SQLExtendedFetch** **SQLFetch** **SQLFetchScroll** **SQLGetConnectAttr** **SQLGetCursorName** **SQLGetData** **SQLGetDescField** **SQLGetDescRec** **SQLGetEnvAttr** **SQLGetInfo** **SQLGetStmtAttr** **SQLNativeSql** **SQLParamData** **SQLPutData** **SQLSetCursorName**
01006	Privilege not revoked	**SQLExecDirect** **SQLExecute** **SQLParamData**
01007	Privilege not granted	**SQLExecDirect** **SQLExecute** **SQLParamData**
01S00	Invalid connection string attribute	**SQLBrowseConnect** **SQLDriverConnect**
01S01	Error in row	**SQLBulkOperations** **SQLExtendedFetch** **SQLSetPos**

SQLSTATE	Error	Can be returned from
01S02	Option value changed	**SQLBrowseConnect** **SQLConnect** **SQLDriverConnect** **SQLExecDirect** **SQLExecute** **SQLParamData** **SQLPrepare** **SQLSetConnectAttr** **SQLSetDescField** **SQLSetEnvAttr** **SQLSetStmtAttr**
01S06	Attempt to fetch before the result set returned the first rowset	**SQLExtendedFetch** **SQLFetchScroll**
01S07	Fractional truncation	**SQLBulkOperations** **SQLExecDirect** **SQLExecute** **SQLExtendedFetch** **SQLFetch** **SQLFetchScroll** **SQLGetData** **SQLParamData** **SQLSetPos**
01S08	Error saving File DSN	**SQLDriverConnect**
01S09	Invalid keyword	**SQLDriverConnect**
07002	COUNT field incorrect	**SQLExecDirect** **SQLExecute** **SQLParamData**
07005	Prepared statement not a *cursor-specification*	**SQLColAttribute** **SQLDescribeCol**

SQLSTATE	Error	Can be returned from
07006	Restricted data type attribute violation	**SQLBindCol** **SQLBindParameter** **SQLBulkOperations** **SQLExecDirect** **SQLExecute** **SQLExtendedFetch** **SQLFetch** **SQLFetchScroll** **SQLGetData** **SQLParamData** **SQLPutData** **SQLSetPos**
07009	Invalid descriptor index	**SQLBindCol** **SQLBindParameter** **SQLBulkOperations** **SQLColAttribute** **SQLDescribeCol** **SQLFetch** **SQLFetchScroll** **SQLGetData** **SQLGetDescField** **SQLGetDescRec** **SQLParamData** **SQLSetDescField** **SQLSetDescRec** **SQLSetPos**
07S01	Invalid use of default parameter	**SQLExecDirect** **SQLExecute** **SQLParamData** **SQLPutData**
08001	Client unable to establish connection	**SQLBrowseConnect** **SQLConnect** **SQLDriverConnect**
08002	Connection name in use	**SQLBrowseConnect** **SQLConnect** **SQLDriverConnect** **SQLSetConnectAttr**

SQLSTATE	Error	Can be returned from
08003	Connection does not exist	**SQLAllocHandle** **SQLDisconnect** **SQLEndTran** **SQLGetConnectAttr** **SQLGetInfo** **SQLNativeSql** **SQLSetConnectAttr**
08004	Server rejected the connection	**SQLBrowseConnect** **SQLConnect** **SQLDriverConnect**
08007	Connection failure during transaction	**SQLEndTran**
08S01	Communication link failure	**SQLBrowseConnect** **SQLColumnPrivileges** **SQLColumns** **SQLConnect** **SQLCopyDesc** **SQLDescribeCol** **SQLDescribeParam** **SQLDriverConnect** **SQLExecDirect** **SQLExecute** **SQLExtendedFetch** **SQLFetch** **SQLFetchScroll** **SQLForeignKeys** **SQLGetConnectAttr** **SQLGetData** **SQLGetDescField** **SQLGetDescRec** **SQLGetFunctions** **SQLGetInfo** **SQLGetTypeInfo** **SQLMoreResults** **SQLNativeSql** **SQLNumParams** **SQLNumResultCols**

SQLSTATE	Error	Can be returned from
08S01 (*continued*)	Communication link failure	**SQLParamData** **SQLPrepare** **SQLPrimaryKeys** **SQLProcedureColumns** **SQLProcedures** **SQLPutData** **SQLSetConnectAttr** **SQLSetDescField** **SQLSetDescRec** **SQLSetEnvAttr** **SQLSetStmtAttr** **SQLSpecialColumns** **SQLStatistics** **SQLTablePrivileges** **SQLTables**
21S01	Insert value list does not match column list	**SQLExecDirect** **SQLPrepare**
21S02	Degree of derived table does not match column list	**SQLBulkOperations** **SQLExecDirect** **SQLExecute** **SQLParamData** **SQLPrepare** **SQLSetPos**
22001	String data, right truncated	**SQLBulkOperations** **SQLExecDirect** **SQLExecute** **SQLFetch** **SQLFetchScroll** **SQLParamData** **SQLPutData** **SQLSetDescField** **SQLSetPos**
22002	Indicator variable required but not supplied	**SQLExecDirect** **SQLExecute** **SQLExtendedFetch** **SQLFetch** **SQLFetchScroll** **SQLGetData** **SQLParamData**

SQLSTATE	Error	Can be returned from
22003	Numeric value out of range	**SQLBulkOperations** **SQLExecDirect** **SQLExecute** **SQLExtendedFetch** **SQLFetch** **SQLFetchScroll** **SQLGetData** **SQLGetInfo** **SQLParamData** **SQLPutData** **SQLSetPos**
22007	Invalid datetime format	**SQLBulkOperations** **SQLExecDirect** **SQLExecute** **SQLExtendedFetch** **SQLFetch** **SQLFetchScroll** **SQLGetData** **SQLParamData** **SQLPutData** **SQLSetPos**
22008	Datetime field overflow	**SQLBulkOperations** **SQLExecDirect** **SQLExecute** **SQLParamData** **SQLPutData**
22012	Division by zero	**SQLExecDirect** **SQLExecute** **SQLExtendedFetch** **SQLFetch** **SQLFetchScroll** **SQLGetData** **SQLParamData** **SQLPutData**

SQLSTATE	Error	Can be returned from
22015	Interval field overflow	**SQLBulkOperations** **SQLExecDirect** **SQLExecute** **SQLExtendedFetch** **SQLFetch** **SQLFetchScroll** **SQLGetData** **SQLParamData** **SQLPutData** **SQLSetPos**
22018	Invalid character value for cast specification	**SQLBulkOperations** **SQLExecDirect** **SQLExecute** **SQLExtendedFetch** **SQLFetch** **SQLFetchScroll** **SQLGetData** **SQLParamData** **SQLPutData** **SQLSetPos**
22019	Invalid escape character	**SQLExecDirect** **SQLExecute** **SQLPrepare**
22025	Invalid escape sequence	**SQLExecDirect** **SQLExecute** **SQLPrepare**
22026	String data, length mismatch	**SQLParamData**
23000	Integrity constraint violation	**SQLBulkOperations** **SQLExecDirect** **SQLExecute** **SQLParamData** **SQLSetPos**

SQLSTATE	Error	Can be returned from
24000	Invalid cursor state	**SQLBulkOperations** **SQLCloseCursor** **SQLColumnPrivileges** **SQLColumns** **SQLExecDirect** **SQLExecute** **SQLExtendedFetch** **SQLFetch** **SQLFetchScroll** **SQLForeignKeys** **SQLGetData** **SQLGetStmtAttr** **SQLGetTypeInfo** **SQLNativeSql** **SQLPrepare** **SQLPrimaryKeys** **SQLProcedureColumns** **SQLProcedures** **SQLSetConnectAttr** **SQLSetCursorName** **SQLSetPos** **SQLSetStmtAttr** **SQLSpecialColumns** **SQLStatistics** **SQLTablePrivileges** **SQLTables**
25000	Invalid transaction state	**SQLDisconnect**
25S01	Transaction state	**SQLEndTran**
25S02	Transaction is still active	**SQLEndTran**
25S03	Transaction is rolled back	**SQLEndTran**
28000	Invalid authorization specification	**SQLBrowseConnect** **SQLConnect** **SQLDriverConnect**
34000	Invalid cursor name	**SQLExecDirect** **SQLPrepare** **SQLSetCursorName**
3C000	Duplicate cursor name	**SQLSetCursorName**

SQLSTATE	Error	Can be returned from
3D000	Invalid catalog name	**SQLExecDirect** **SQLPrepare** **SQLSetConnectAttr**
3F000	Invalid schema name	**SQLExecDirect** **SQLPrepare**
40001	Serialization failure	**SQLBulkOperations** **SQLColumnPrivileges** **SQLColumns** **SQLEndTran** **SQLExecDirect** **SQLExecute** **SQLFetch** **SQLFetchScroll** **SQLForeignKeys** **SQLGetTypeInfo** **SQLMoreResults** **SQLParamData** **SQLPrimaryKeys** **SQLProcedureColumns** **SQLProcedures** **SQLSetPos** **SQLSpecialColumns** **SQLStatistics** **SQLTablePrivileges** **SQLTables**
40003	Statement completion unknown	**SQLBulkOperations** **SQLColumnPrivileges** **SQLColumns** **SQLExecDirect** **SQLExecute** **SQLFetch** **SQLFetchScroll** **SQLForeignKeys** **SQLGetTypeInfo** **SQLMoreResults** **SQLPrimaryKeys** **SQLProcedureColumns** **SQLProcedures** **SQLParamData** **SQLSetPos** **SQLSpecialColumns** **SQLStatistics** **SQLTablePrivileges** **SQLTables**

SQLSTATE	Error	Can be returned from
42000	Syntax error or access violation	**SQLBulkOperations** **SQLExecDirect** **SQLExecute** **SQLParamData** **SQLPrepare** **SQLSetPos**
42S01	Base table or view already exists	**SQLExecDirect** **SQLPrepare**
42S02	Base table or view not found	**SQLExecDirect** **SQLPrepare**
42S11	Index already exists	**SQLExecDirect** **SQLPrepare**
42S12	Index not found	**SQLExecDirect** **SQLPrepare**
42S21	Column already exists	**SQLExecDirect** **SQLPrepare**
42S22	Column not found	**SQLExecDirect** **SQLPrepare**
44000	WITH CHECK OPTION violation	**SQLBulkOperations** **SQLExecDirect** **SQLExecute** **SQLParamData** **SQLSetPos**
HY000	General error	All ODBC functions except: **SQLError** **SQLGetDiagField** **SQLGetDiagRec**
HY001	Memory allocation error	All ODBC functions except: **SQLError** **SQLGetDiagField** **SQLGetDiagRec**
HY003	Invalid application buffer type	**SQLBindCol** **SQLBindParameter** **SQLGetData**
HY004	Invalid SQL data type	**SQLBindParameter** **SQLGetTypeInfo**

SQLSTATE	Error	Can be returned from
HY007	Associated statement is not prepared	**SQLCopyDesc** **SQLGetDescField** **SQLGetDescRec**
HY008	Operation canceled	All ODBC functions that can be processed asynchronously: **SQLBulkOperations** **SQLColAttribute** **SQLColumnPrivileges** **SQLColumns** **SQLDescribeCol** **SQLDescribeParam** **SQLExecDirect** **SQLExecute** **SQLExtendedFetch** **SQLFetch** **SQLFetchScroll** **SQLForeignKeys** **SQLGetData** **SQLGetTypeInfo** **SQLMoreResults** **SQLNumParams** **SQLNumResultCols** **SQLParamData** **SQLPrepare** **SQLPrimaryKeys** **SQLProcedureColumns** **SQLProcedures** **SQLPutData** **SQLSetPos** **SQLSpecialColumns** **SQLStatistics** **SQLTablePrivileges** **SQLTables**
HY009	Invalid use of null pointer	**SQLAllocHandle** **SQLBindParameter** **SQLBulkOperations** **SQLColumnPrivileges** **SQLColumns** **SQLExecDirect** **SQLForeignKeys** **SQLGetCursorName**

SQLSTATE	Error	Can be returned from
HY009 (*continued*)	Invalid use of null pointer	**SQLGetData** **SQLGetFunctions** **SQLNativeSql** **SQLPrepare** **SQLPrimaryKeys** **SQLProcedureColumns** **SQLProcedures** **SQLPutData** **SQLSetConnectAttr** **SQLSetCursorName** **SQLSetEnvAttr** **SQLSetStmtAttr** **SQLSpecialColumns** **SQLStatistics** **SQLTablePrivileges** **SQLTables**
HY010	Function sequence error	**SQLAllocHandle** **SQLBindCol** **SQLBindParameter** **SQLBulkOperations** **SQLCloseCursor** **SQLColAttribute** **SQLColumnPrivileges** **SQLColumns** **SQLCopyDesc** **SQLDescribeCol** **SQLDescribeParam** **SQLDisconnect** **SQLEndTran** **SQLExecDirect** **SQLExecute** **SQLExtendedFetch** **SQLFetch** **SQLFetchScroll** **SQLForeignKeys** **SQLFreeHandle** **SQLFreeStmt** **SQLGetConnectAttr** **SQLGetCursorName** **SQLGetData** **SQLGetDescField** **SQLGetDescRec** **SQLGetFunctions**

SQLSTATE	Error	Can be returned from
HY010 (*continued*)	Function sequence error	**SQLGetStmtAttr** **SQLGetTypeInfo** **SQLMoreResults** **SQLNumParams** **SQLNumResultCols** **SQLParamData** **SQLPrepare** **SQLPrimaryKeys** **SQLProcedureColumns** **SQLProcedures** **SQLPutData** **SQLRowCount** **SQLSetConnectAttr** **SQLSetCursorName** **SQLSetDescField** **SQLSetDescRec** **SQLSetPos** **SQLSetStmtAttr** **SQLSpecialColumns** **SQLStatistics** **SQLTablePrivileges** **SQLTables**
HY011	Attribute cannot be set now	**SQLBulkOperations** **SQLParamData** **SQLSetConnectAttr** **SQLSetEnvAttr** **SQLSetPos** **SQLSetStmtAttr**
HY012	Invalid transaction operation code	**SQLEndTran**
HY013	Memory management error	All ODBC functions except: **SQLGetDiagField** **SQLGetDiagRec**
HY014	Limit on the number of handles exceeded	**SQLAllocHandle**
HY015	No cursor name available	**SQLGetCursorName**
HY016	Cannot modify an implementation row descriptor	**SQLCopyDesc** **SQLSetDescField** **SQLSetDescRec**

SQLSTATE	Error	Can be returned from
HY017	Invalid use of an automatically allocated descriptor handle	**SQLFreeHandle** **SQLSetStmtAttr**
HY018	Server declined cancel request	**SQLCancel**
HY019	Non-character and non-binary data sent in pieces	**SQLPutData**
HY020	Attempt to concatenate a null value	**SQLPutData**
HY021	Inconsistent descriptor information	**SQLBindParameter** **SQLCopyDesc** **SQLGetDescField** **SQLSetDescField** **SQLSetDescRec**
HY024	Invalid attribute value	**SQLSetConnectAttr** **SQLSetEnvAttr** **SQLSetStmtAttr**
HY090	Invalid string or buffer length	**SQLBindCol** **SQLBindParameter** **SQLBrowseConnect** **SQLBulkOperations** **SQLColAttribute** **SQLColumnPrivileges** **SQLColumns** **SQLConnect** **SQLDataSources** **SQLDescribeCol** **SQLDriverConnect** **SQLDrivers** **SQLExecDirect** **SQLExecute** **SQLFetch** **SQLFetchScroll** **SQLForeignKeys** **SQLGetConnectAttr**

SQLSTATE	Error	Can be returned from
HY090 (*continued*)	Invalid string or buffer length	**SQLGetCursorName** **SQLGetData** **SQLGetDescField** **SQLGetInfo** **SQLGetStmtAttr** **SQLNativeSql** **SQLParamData** **SQLPrepare** **SQLPrimaryKeys** **SQLProcedureColumns** **SQLProcedures** **SQLPutData** **SQLSetConnectAttr** **SQLSetCursorName** **SQLSetDescField** **SQLSetDescRec** **SQLSetEnvAttr** **SQLSetStmtAttr** **SQLSetPos** **SQLSpecialColumns** **SQLStatistics** **SQLTablePrivileges** **SQLTables**
HY091	Invalid descriptor field identifier	**SQLColAttribute** **SQLGetDescField** **SQLSetDescField**
HY092	Invalid attribute/option identifier	**SQLAllocHandle** **SQLBulkOperations** **SQLCopyDesc** **SQLDriverConnect** **SQLEndTran** **SQLFreeStmt** **SQLGetConnectAttr** **SQLGetEnvAttr** **SQLGetStmtAttr** **SQLParamData** **SQLSetConnectAttr** **SQLSetDescField** **SQLSetEnvAttr** **SQLSetPos** **SQLSetStmtAttr**
HY093	Invalid parameter number	**SQLDescribeParam**

SQLSTATE	Error	Can be returned from
HY095	Function type out of range	**SQLGetFunctions**
HY096	Invalid information type	**SQLGetInfo**
HY097	Column type out of range	**SQLSpecialColumns**
HY098	Scope type out of range	**SQLSpecialColumns**
HY099	Nullable type out of range	**SQLSpecialColumns**
HY100	Uniqueness option type out of range	**SQLStatistics**
HY101	Accuracy option type out of range	**SQLStatistics**
HY103	Invalid retrieval code	**SQLDataSources** **SQLDrivers**
HY104	Invalid precision or scale value	**SQLBindParameter**
HY105	Invalid parameter type	**SQLBindParameter** **SQLExecDirect** **SQLExecute** **SQLParamData** **SQLSetDescField**
HY106	Fetch type out of range	**SQLExtendedFetch** **SQLFetchScroll**
HY107	Row value out of range	**SQLExtendedFetch** **SQLFetch** **SQLFetchScroll** **SQLSetPos**
HY109	Invalid cursor position	**SQLExecDirect** **SQLExecute** **SQLGetData** **SQLGetStmtAttr** **SQLNativeSql** **SQLParamData** **SQLSetPos**

SQLSTATE	Error	Can be returned from
HY110	Invalid driver completion	**SQLDriverConnect**
HY111	Invalid bookmark value	**SQLExtendedFetch** **SQLFetchScroll**
HYC00	Optional feature not implemented	**SQLBindCol** **SQLBindParameter** **SQLBulkOperations** **SQLColAttribute** **SQLColumnPrivileges** **SQLColumns** **SQLDriverConnect** **SQLEndTran** **SQLExecDirect** **SQLExecute** **SQLExtendedFetch** **SQLFetch** **SQLFetchScroll** **SQLForeignKeys** **SQLGetConnectAttr** **SQLGetData** **SQLGetEnvAttr** **SQLGetInfo** **SQLGetStmtAttr** **SQLGetTypeInfo** **SQLParamData** **SQLPrepare** **SQLPrimaryKeys** **SQLProcedureColumns** **SQLProcedures** **SQLSetConnectAttr** **SQLSetEnvAttr** **SQLSetPos** **SQLSetStmtAttr** **SQLSpecialColumns** **SQLStatistics** **SQLTablePrivileges** **SQLTables**

SQLSTATE	Error	Can be returned from
HYT00	Timeout expired	**SQLBrowseConnect** **SQLBulkOperations** **SQLColumnPrivileges** **SQLColumns** **SQLConnect** **SQLDriverConnect** **SQLExecDirect** **SQLExecute** **SQLExtendedFetch** **SQLForeignKeys** **SQLGetTypeInfo** **SQLParamData** **SQLPrepare** **SQLPrimaryKeys** **SQLProcedureColumns** **SQLProcedures** **SQLSetPos** **SQLSpecialColumns** **SQLStatistics** **SQLTablePrivileges** **SQLTables**
HYT01	Connection timeout expired	All ODBC functions except: **SQLDrivers** **SQLDataSources** **SQLGetEnvAttr** **SQLSetEnvAttr**
IM001	Driver does not support this function	All ODBC functions except: **SQLAllocHandle** **SQLDataSources** **SQLDrivers** **SQLFreeHandle** **SQLGetFunctions**
IM002	Data source name not found and no default driver specified	**SQLBrowseConnect** **SQLConnect** **SQLDriverConnect**
IM003	Specified driver could not be loaded	**SQLBrowseConnect** **SQLConnect** **SQLDriverConnect**
IM004	Driver's SQLAllocHandle on SQL_HANDLE_ENV failed	**SQLBrowseConnect** **SQLConnect** **SQLDriverConnect**

SQLSTATE	Error	Can be returned from
IM005	Driver's SQLAllocHandle on SQL_HANDLE_DBC failed	**SQLBrowseConnect** **SQLConnect** **SQLDriverConnect**
IM006	Driver's SQLSetConnectAttr failed	**SQLBrowseConnect** **SQLConnect** **SQLDriverConnect**
IM007	No data source or driver specified; dialog prohibited	**SQLDriverConnect**
IM008	Dialog failed	**SQLDriverConnect**
IM009	Unable to load translation DLL	**SQLBrowseConnect** **SQLConnect** **SQLDriverConnect** **SQLSetConnectAttr**
IM010	Data source name too long	**SQLBrowseConnect** **SQLConnect** **SQLDriverConnect**
IM011	Driver name too long	**SQLBrowseConnect** **SQLDriverConnect**
IM012	DRIVER keyword syntax error	**SQLBrowseConnect** **SQLDriverConnect**
IM013	Trace file error	All ODBC functions
IM014	Invalid name of File DSN	**SQLDriverConnect**
IM015	Corrupt file data source	**SQLDriverConnect**

APPENDIX B

ODBC State Transition Tables

The tables in this appendix show how ODBC functions cause transitions of the environment, connection, statement, and descriptor states. Generally speaking, the state of the environment, connection, statement, or descriptor dictates when functions that use the corresponding type of handle (environment, connection, statement, or descriptor) can be called. The environment, connection, statement, and descriptor states overlap roughly as shown in the following figure. For example, the exact overlap of connection states C5 and C6 and statement states S1 through S12 is data source–dependent, since transactions begin at different times on different data sources, and descriptor state D1i (implicitly allocated descriptor) depends on the state of the statement with which the descriptor is associated, while state D1e (explicitly allocated descriptor) is independent of the state of any statement. For a description of each state, see "Environment Transitions," "Connection Transitions," "Statement Transitions," and "Descriptor Transitions," later in this appendix.

The environment and connection states overlap as follows:

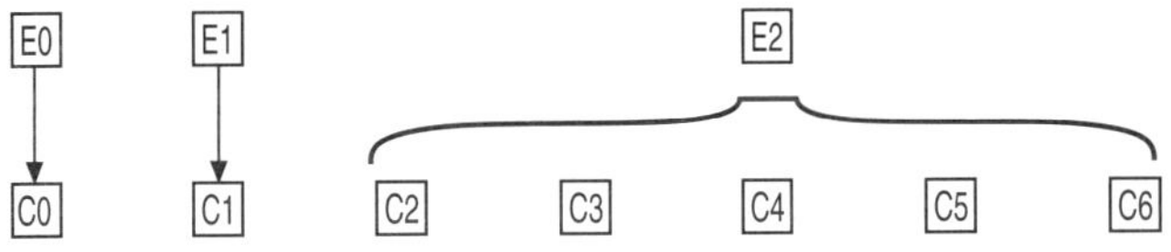

The connection and statement states overlap as follows:

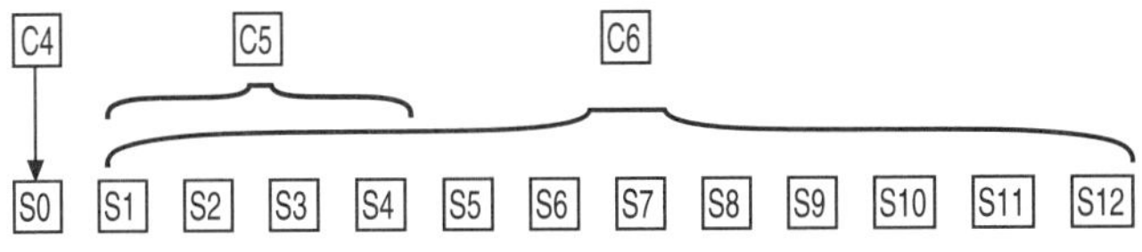

The statement and descriptor states overlap as follows:

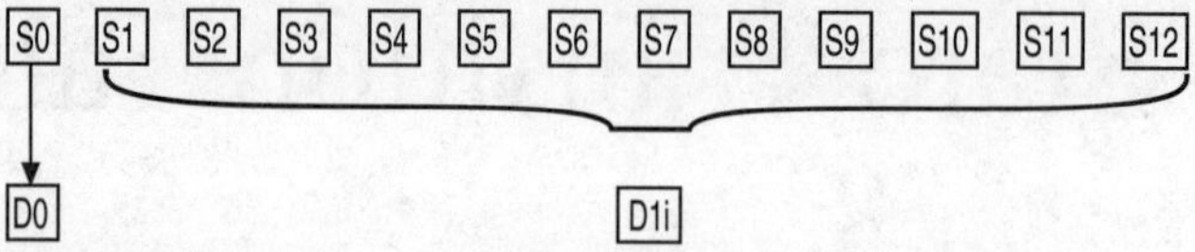

The connection and descriptor states overlap as follows:

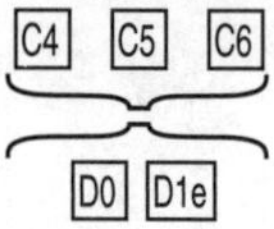

Each entry in a transition table can be one of the following values:

- **--** The state is unchanged after executing the function.
- **E*n***, **C*n***, **S*n***, or **D*n*** The environment, connection, statement, or descriptor state moves to the specified state.
- **(IH)** An invalid handle was passed to the function. If the handle was a null handle or was a valid handle of the wrong type—for example, a connection handle was passed when a statement handle was required—the function returns SQL_INVALID_HANDLE; otherwise the behavior is undefined and probably fatal. This error is shown only when it is the only possible outcome of calling the function in the specified state. This error does not change the state and is always detected by the Driver Manager, as indicated by the parentheses.
- **NS** Next State. The statement transition is the same as if the statement had not gone through the asynchronous states. For example, suppose a statement that creates a result set enters state S11 from state S1 because **SQLExecDirect** returned SQL_STILL_EXECUTING. The NS notation in state S11 means that the transitions for the statement are the same as those for a statement in state S1 that creates a result set: if **SQLExecDirect** returns an error; the statement remains in state S1; if it succeeds, the statement moves to state S5; if it needs data, the statement moves to state S8; and if it is still executing, it remains in state S11.
- ***XXXXX*** or (***XXXXX***) An SQLSTATE that is related to the transition table; SQLSTATEs detected by the Driver Manager are enclosed in parentheses. The function returned SQL_ERROR and the specified SQLSTATE, but the state does not change. For example, if **SQLExecute** is called before **SQLPrepare**, it returns SQLSTATE HY010 (Function sequence error).

Note The tables do not show errors unrelated to the transition tables that do not change the state. For example, when **SQLAllocHandle** is called in environment state E1 and returns SQLSTATE HY001 (Memory allocation error), the environment remains in state E1; this is not shown in the environment transition table for **SQLAllocHandle**.

If the environment, connection, statement, or descriptor can move to more than one state, each possible state is shown and one or more footnotes explain the conditions under which each transition takes place. The following footnotes may appear in any table.

Footnote	Meaning
b	Before or after. The cursor was positioned before the start of the result set or after the end of the result set.
c	Current function. The current function was executing asynchronously.
d	Need data. The function returned SQL_NEED_DATA.
e	Error. The function returned SQL_ERROR.
i	Invalid row. The cursor was positioned on a row in the result set and the row had either been deleted or an error had occurred in an operation on the row. If the row status array existed, the value in the row status array for the row was SQL_ROW_DELETED or SQL_ROW_ERROR. (The row status array is pointed to by the SQL_ATTR_ROW_STATUS_PTR statement attribute.)
nf	Not found. The function returned SQL_NO_DATA. This does not apply when **SQLExecDirect**, **SQLExecute**, or **SQLParamData** returns SQL_NO_DATA after executing a searched update or delete statement.
np	Not prepared. The statement was not prepared.
nr	No results. The statement will not or did not create a result set.
o	Other function. Another function was executing asynchronously.
p	Prepared. The statement was prepared.
r	Results. The statement will or did create a (possibly empty) result set.
s	Success. The function returned SQL_SUCCESS_WITH_INFO or SQL_SUCCESS.
v	Valid row. The cursor was positioned on a row in the result set and the row had either been successfully inserted, successfully updated, or another operation on the row had been successfully completed. If the row status array existed, the value in the row status array for the row was SQL_ROW_ADDED, SQL_ROW_SUCCESS, or SQL_ROW_UPDATED. (The row status array is pointed to by the SQL_ATTR_ROW_STATUS_PTR statement attribute.)
x	Executing. The function returned SQL_STILL_EXECUTING.

For example, the row in the environment state transition table for **SQLFreeHandle** when *HandleType* is SQL_HANDLE_ENV is as follows.

SQLFreeHandle

E0 Unallocated	E1 Allocated	E2 Connection
(IH)	E0	(HY010)

If **SQLFreeHandle** is called in environment state E0 with *HandleType* set to SQL_HANDLE_ENV, the Driver Manager returns SQL_INVALID_HANDLE. If it is called in state E1 with *HandleType* set to SQL_HANDLE_ENV, the environment moves to state E0 if the function succeeds and remains in state E1 if the function fails. If it is called in state E2 with *HandleType* set to SQL_HANDLE_ENV, the Driver Manager always returns SQL_ERROR and SQLSTATE HY010 (Function sequence error) and the environment remains in state E2.

To understand the state transition tables, it is necessary to understand which item (environment, connection, statement, or descriptor) they refer to. Suppose a function accepts the handle of an item of type X. The X state transition table for that function describes how calling the function—with the handle of an item of type X—affects that item. For example, **SQLDisconnect** accepts a connection handle. The connection state transition table for **SQLDisconnect** describes how **SQLDisconnect** affects the state of the connection for which it is called.

Suppose a function accepts the handle of an item of type Y, where Y is not equal to X. The X state transition table for that function describes how calling the function—with a handle of type X that is associated with the item of type Y—affects the item of type Y. For example, the statement state transition table for **SQLDisconnect** describes how **SQLDisconnect** affects the state of a statement when called with the handle of the connection with which the statement is associated.

Environment Transitions

ODBC environments have the following three states.

State	Description
E0	Unallocated environment
E1	Allocated environment, unallocated connection
E2	Allocated environment, allocated connection

The following tables show how each ODBC function affects the environment state.

SQLAllocHandle

E0 Unallocated	E1 Allocated	E2 Connection
E1 [1]	-- [4]	-- [4]
(IH) [2]	E2 [5] (HY010) [6]	-- [4]
(IH) [3]	(IH)	-- [4]

1 This row shows transitions when *HandleType* was SQL_HANDLE_ENV.

2 This row shows transitions when *HandleType* was SQL_HANDLE_DBC.

3 This row shows transitions when *HandleType* was SQL_HANDLE_STMT or SQL_HANDLE_DESC.

4 Calling **SQLAllocHandle** with *OutputHandlePtr* pointing to a valid handle overwrites that handle. This may be an application programming error.

5 The SQL_ATTR_ODBC_VERSION environment attribute had been set on the environment.

6 The SQL_ATTR_ODBC_VERSION environment attribute had not been set on the environment.

SQLDataSources and SQLDrivers

E0 Unallocated	E1 Allocated	E2 Connection
(IH)	-- [1] (HY010) [2]	-- [1] (HY010) [2]

1 The SQL_ATTR_ODBC_VERSION environment attribute had been set on the environment.

2 The SQL_ATTR_ODBC_VERSION environment attribute had not been set on the environment.

SQLEndTran

E0 Unallocated	E1 Allocated	E2 Connection
(IH) [1]	-- [3] (HY010) [4]	-- [3] (HY010) [4]
(IH) [2]	(IH)	--

1 This row shows transitions when *HandleType* was SQL_HANDLE_ENV.

2 This row shows transitions when *HandleType* was SQL_HANDLE_DBC.

3 The SQL_ATTR_ODBC_VERSION environment attribute had been set on the environment.

4 The SQL_ATTR_ODBC_VERSION environment attribute had not been set on the environment.

SQLFreeHandle

E0 Unallocated	E1 Allocated	E2 Connection
(IH) [1]	E0	(HY010)
(IH) [2]	(IH)	-- [4] E1 [5]
(IH) [3]	(IH)	--

1 This row shows transitions when *HandleType* was SQL_HANDLE_ENV.

2 This row shows transitions when *HandleType* was SQL_HANDLE_DBC.

3 This row shows transitions when *HandleType* was SQL_HANDLE_STMT or SQL_HANDLE_DESC.

4 There were other allocated connection handles.

5 The connection handle specified in *Handle* was the only allocated connection handle.

SQLGetDiagField and SQLGetDiagRec

E0 Unallocated	E1 Allocated	E2 Connection
(IH) [1]	--	--
(IH) [2]	(IH)	--

1 This row shows transitions when *HandleType* was SQL_HANDLE_ENV.

2 This row shows transitions when *HandleType* was SQL_HANDLE_DBC, SQL_HANDLE_STMT, or SQL_HANDLE_DESC.

SQLGetEnvAttr

E0 Unallocated	E1 Allocated	E2 Connection
(IH)	-- [1] (HY010) [2]	--

1 The SQL_ATTR_ODBC_VERSION environment attribute had been set on the environment.

2 The SQL_ATTR_ODBC_VERSION environment attribute had not been set on the environment.

SQLSetEnvAttr

E0 Unallocated	E1 Allocated	E2 Connection
(IH)	-- [1] (HY010) [2]	(HY011)

1 The SQL_ATTR_ODBC_VERSION environment attribute had been set on the environment.

2 The *Attribute* argument was not SQL_ATTR_ODBC_VERSION and the SQL_ATTR_ODBC_VERSION environment attribute had not been set on the environment.

All Other ODBC Functions

E0 Unallocated	E1 Allocated	E2 Connection
(IH)	(IH)	--

Connection Transitions

ODBC connections have the following states.

State	Description
C0	Unallocated environment, unallocated connection
C1	Allocated environment, unallocated connection
C2	Allocated environment, allocated connection
C3	Connection function needs data
C4	Connected connection
C5	Connected connection, allocated statement
C6	Connected connection, transaction in progress. It is possible for a connection to be in state C6 without having any statements allocated on the connection. For example, suppose the connection is in manual commit mode and is in state C4. If a statement is allocated, executed (starting a transaction), and then freed, the transaction remains active but there are no statements on the connection.

The following tables show how each ODBC function affects the connection state.

SQLAllocHandle

C0 No Env.	C1 Unallocated	C2 Allocated	C3 Need Data	C4 Connected	C5 Statement	C6 Transaction
C1 [1]	-- [5]	-- [5]	-- [5]	-- [5]	-- [5]	-- [5]
(IH) [2]	C2	-- [5]	-- [5]	-- [5]	-- [5]	-- [5]
(IH) [3]	(IH)	(08003)	(08003)	C5	-- [5]	-- [5]
(IH) [4]	(IH)	(08003)	(08003)	-- [5]	-- [5]	-- [5]

1 This row shows transitions when *HandleType* was SQL_HANDLE_ENV.

2 This row shows transitions when *HandleType* was SQL_HANDLE_DBC.

3 This row shows transitions when *HandleType* was SQL_HANDLE_STMT.

4 This row shows transitions when *HandleType* was SQL_HANDLE_DESC.

5 Calling **SQLAllocHandle** with *OutputHandlePtr* pointing to a valid handle overwrites that handle without any regard for the previous contents to that handle, and may cause problems for ODBC drivers. It is incorrect ODBC application programming to call **SQLAllocHandle** twice with the same application variable defined for **OutputHandlePtr* without calling **SQLFreeHandle** to free the handle before reallocating it. Overwriting ODBC handles in such a manner may lead to inconsistent behavior or errors on the part of ODBC drivers.

SQLBrowseConnect

C0 No Env.	C1 Unallocated	C2 Allocated	C3 Need Data	C4 Connected	C5 Statement	C6 Transaction
(IH)	(IH)	C3 [d] C4 [s]	-- [d] C2 [e] C4 [s]	(08002)	(08002)	(08002)

SQLCloseCursor

C0 No Env.	C1 Unallocated	C2 Allocated	C3 Need Data	C4 Connected	C5 Statement	C6 Transaction
(IH)	(IH)	(IH)	(IH)	(IH)	--	-- [1] C5 [2]

1 The connection was in manual-commit mode.

2 The connection was in auto-commit mode.

SQLColumnPrivileges, SQLColumns, SQLForeignKeys, SQLGetTypeInfo, SQLPrimaryKeys, SQLProcedureColumns, SQLProcedures, SQLSpecialColumns, SQLStatistics, SQLTablePrivileges, and SQLTables

C0 No Env.	C1 Unallocated	C2 Allocated	C3 Need Data	C4 Connected	C5 Statement	C6 Transaction
(IH)	(IH)	(IH)	(IH)	(IH)	-- [1] C6 [2]	--

1 The connection was in auto-commit mode or the data source did not begin a transaction.

2 The connection was in manual-commit mode and the data source began a transaction.

SQLColumns: see SQLColumnPrivileges

SQLConnect

C0 No Env.	C1 Unallocated	C2 Allocated	C3 Need Data	C4 Connected	C5 Statement	C6 Transaction
(IH)	(IH)	C4	(08002)	(08002)	(08002)	(08002)

SQLCopyDesc, SQLGetDescField, SQLGetDescRec, SQLSetDescField, and SQLSetDescRec

C0 No Env.	C1 Unallocated	C2 Allocated	C3 Need Data	C4 Connected	C5 Statement	C6 Transaction
(IH)	(IH)	(IH)	(IH)	-- [1]	--	--

1 In this state, the only descriptors available to the application are explicitly allocated descriptors.

SQLDataSources and SQLDrivers

C0 No Env.	C1 Unallocated	C2 Allocated	C3 Need Data	C4 Connected	C5 Statement	C6 Transaction
(IH)	--	--	--	--	--	--

SQLDisconnect

C0 No Env.	C1 Unallocated	C2 Allocated	C3 Need Data	C4 Connected	C5 Statement	C6 Transaction
(IH)	(IH)	(08003)	C2	C2	C2	25000

SQLDriverConnect

C0 No Env.	C1 Unallocated	C2 Allocated	C3 Need Data	C4 Connected	C5 Statement	C6 Transaction
(IH)	(IH)	C4 s -- nf	(08002)	(08002)	(08002)	(08002)

SQLDrivers: see SQLDataSources

SQLEndTran

C0 No Env.	C1 Unallocated	C2 Allocated	C3 Need Data	C4 Connected	C5 Statement	C6 Transaction
(IH) [1]	-- [3]	-- [3]	-- [3]	--	--	-- [4 or (5, 6, and 8)] C4 [5 and 7] C5 [5, 6, and 9]
(IH) [2]	(IH)	(08003)	(08003)	--	--	C5

1 This row shows transitions when *HandleType* was SQL_HANDLE_ENV.

2 This row shows transitions when *HandleType* was SQL_HANDLE_DBC.

3 Because the connection is not in a connected state, it is unaffected by the transaction.

4 The commit or rollback failed on the connection. The function returns SQL_ERROR in this case.

5 The commit or rollback succeeded on the connection. The function returns SQL_ERROR if the commit or rollback failed on another connection, or SQL_SUCCESS if the commit or rollback succeeded on all connections.

6 There was at least one statement allocated on the connection.

7 There were no statements allocated on the connection.

8 The connection had at least one statement for which there was an open cursor and the data source preserves cursors when transactions are committed or rolled back, whichever applies depending on whether *CompletionType* was SQL_COMMIT or SQL_ROLLBACK. For more information, see the SQL_CURSOR_COMMIT_BEHAVIOR and SQL_CURSOR_ROLLBACK_BEHAVIOR attributes in **SQLGetInfo**.

9 If the connection had any statements for which there were open cursors, the cursors were not preserved when the transaction was committed or rolled back.

SQLExecDirect and SQLExecute

C0 No Env.	C1 Unallocated	C2 Allocated	C3 Need Data	C4 Connected	C5 Statement	C6 Transaction
(IH)	(IH)	(IH)	(IH)	(IH)	-- [1] C6 [2] C6 [3]	--

1 The connection was in auto-commit mode and the statement executed was not a *cursor specification* (such as a SELECT statement); or the connection was in manual-commit mode and the statement executed did not begin a transaction.

2 The connection was in auto-commit mode and the statement executed was a *cursor specification* (such as a SELECT statement).

3 The connection was in manual-commit mode and data source began a transaction.

SQLExecute: see SQLExecDirect

SQLForeignKeys: see SQLColumnPrivileges

SQLFreeHandle

C0 No Env.	C1 Unallocated	C2 Allocated	C3 Need Data	C4 Connected	C5 Statement	C6 Transaction
(IH) [1]	C0	(HY010)	(HY010)	(HY010)	(HY010)	(HY010)
(IH) [2]	(IH)	(C1)	(HY010)	(HY010)	(HY010)	(HY010)
(IH) [3]	(IH)	(IH)	(IH)	(IH)	C4 [5] -- [6]	-- [7] C4 [5 and 8] C5 [6 and 8]
(IH) [4]	(IH)	(IH)	(IH)	--	--	--

1 This row shows transitions when *HandleType* was SQL_HANDLE_ENV.

2 This row shows transitions when *HandleType* was SQL_HANDLE_DBC.

3 This row shows transitions when *HandleType* was SQL_HANDLE_STMT.

4 This row shows transitions when *HandleType* was SQL_HANDLE_DESC.

5 There was only one statement allocated on the connection.

6 There were multiple statements allocated on the connection.

7 The connection was in manual commit mode.

8 The connection was in auto-commit mode.

SQLFreeStmt

C0 No Env.	C1 Unallocated	C2 Allocated	C3 Need Data	C4 Connected	C5 Statement	C6 Transaction
(IH) [1]	(IH)	(IH)	(IH)	(IH)	--	C5 [3] -- [4]
(IH) [2]	(IH)	(IH)	(IH)	(IH)	--	--

1 This row shows transactions when the *Option* argument is SQL_CLOSE.

2 This row shows transactions when the *Option* argument is SQL_UNBIND or SQL_RESET_PARAMS.

3 The connection was in auto-commit mode and no cursors were open on any statements except this one.

4 The connection was in manual-commit mode, or it was in auto-commit mode and a cursor was open on at least one other statement.

SQLGetConnectAttr

C0 No Env.	C1 Unallocated	C2 Allocated	C3 Need Data	C4 Connected	C5 Statement	C6 Transaction
(IH)	(IH)	-- [1] (08003) [2]	(HY010)	--	--	--

1 The *Attribute* argument was SQL_ATTR_ACCESS_MODE, SQL_ATTR_AUTOCOMMIT, SQL_ATTR_LOGIN_TIMEOUT, SQL_ATTR_ODBC_CURSORS, SQL_ATTR_TRACE, or SQL_ATTR_TRACEFILE, or a value had been set for the connection attribute.

2 The *Attribute* argument was not SQL_ATTR_ACCESS_MODE, SQL_ATTR_AUTOCOMMIT, SQL_ATTR_LOGIN_TIMEOUT, SQL_ATTR_ODBC_CURSORS, SQL_ATTR_TRACE, or SQL_ATTR_TRACEFILE, and a value had not been set for the connection attribute.

SQLGetDiagField and SQLGetDiagRec

C0 No Env.	C1 Unallocated	C2 Allocated	C3 Need Data	C4 Connected	C5 Statement	C6 Transaction
(IH) [1]	--	--	--	--	--	--
(IH) [2]	(IH)	--	--	--	--	--
(IH) [3]	(IH)	(IH)	(IH)	(IH)	--	--
(IH) [4]	(IH)	(IH)	(IH)	--	--	--

1 This row shows transitions when *HandleType* was SQL_HANDLE_ENV.

2 This row shows transitions when *HandleType* was SQL_HANDLE_DBC.

3 This row shows transitions when *HandleType* was SQL_HANDLE_STMT.

4 This row shows transitions when *HandleType* was SQL_HANDLE_DESC.

SQLGetEnvAttr

C0 No Env.	C1 Unallocated	C2 Allocated	C3 Need Data	C4 Connected	C5 Statement	C6 Transaction
(IH)	--	--	--	--	--	--

SQLGetFunctions

C0 No Env.	C1 Unallocated	C2 Allocated	C3 Need Data	C4 Connected	C5 Statement	C6 Transaction
(IH)	(IH)	(HY010)	(HY010)	--	--	--

SQLGetInfo

C0 No Env.	C1 Unallocated	C2 Allocated	C3 Need Data	C4 Connected	C5 Statement	C6 Transaction
(IH)	(IH)	-- [1] (08003) [2]	(08003)	--	--	--

1 The *InfoType* argument was SQL_ODBC_VER.

2 The *InfoType* argument was not SQL_ODBC_VER.

SQLGetTypeInfo: see SQLColumnPrivileges

SQLMoreResults

C0 No Env.	C1 Unallocated	C2 Allocated	C3 Need Data	C4 Connected	C5 Statement	C6 Transaction
(IH)	(IH)	(IH)	(IH)	(IH)	-- [1] C6 [2]	-- [3] C5 [1]

1 The connection was in auto-commit mode and the call to **SQLMoreResults** has not initialized the processing of a result set of a cursor specification.

2 The connection was in auto-commit mode and the call to **SQLMoreResults** has initialized the processing of a result set of a cursor specification.

3 The connection was in manual-commit mode.

SQLNativeSql

C0 No Env.	C1 Unallocated	C2 Allocated	C3 Need Data	C4 Connected	C5 Statement	C6 Transaction
(IH)	(IH)	(08003)	(08003)	--	--	--

SQLPrepare

C0 No Env.	C1 Unallocated	C2 Allocated	C3 Need Data	C4 Connected	C5 Statement	C6 Transaction
(IH)	(IH)	(IH)	(IH)	(IH)	-- [1] C6 [2]	--

1 The connection was in auto-commit mode or the data source did not begin a transaction.

2 The connection was in manual–commit mode and the data source began a transaction.

SQLPrimaryKeys: see SQLColumnPrivileges

SQLProcedureColumns: see SQLColumnPrivileges

SQLProcedures: see SQLColumnPrivileges

SQLSetConnectAttr

C0 No Env.	C1 Unallocated	C2 Allocated	C3 Need Data	C4 Connected	C5 Statement	C6 Transaction
(IH)	(IH)	--[1] (08003)[2]	(HY010)	--[3] (08002)[4] HY011[5]	--[3] (08002)[4] HY011[5]	--[3 and 6] C5[8] (08002)[4] HY011[5 or 7]

1 The *Attribute* argument was not SQL_ATTR_TRANSLATE_LIB or SQL_ATTR_TRANSLATE_OPTION.

2 The *Attribute* argument was SQL_ATTR_TRANSLATE_LIB or SQL_ATTR_TRANSLATE_OPTION.

3 The *Attribute* argument was not SQL_ATTR_ODBC_CURSORS or SQL_ATTR_PACKET_SIZE.

4 The *Attribute* argument was SQL_ATTR_ODBC_CURSORS.

5 The *Attribute* argument was SQL_ATTR_PACKET_SIZE.

6 The *Attribute* argument was not SQL_ATTR_AUTOCOMMIT, or the *Attribute* argument was SQL_ATTR_AUTOCOMMIT and setting this attribute did not commit the transaction.

7 The *Attribute* argument was SQL_ATTR_TXN_ISOLATION.

8 The *Attribute* argument was SQL_ATTR_AUTOCOMMIT and setting this attribute committed the transaction.

SQLSetEnvAttr

C0 No Env.	C1 Unallocated	C2 Allocated	C3 Need Data	C4 Connected	C5 Statement	C6 Transaction
(IH)	--	--	(HY010)	--	--	--

SQLSpecialColumns: see SQLColumnPrivileges

SQLStatistics: see SQLColumnPrivileges

SQLTablePrivileges: see SQLColumnPrivileges

SQLTables: see SQLColumnPrivileges

All Other ODBC Functions

C0 No Env.	C1 Unallocated	C2 Allocated	C3 Need Data	C4 Connected	C5 Statement	C6 Transaction
(IH)	(IH)	(IH)	(IH)	(IH)	--	--

Statement Transitions

ODBC statements have the following states.

State	Description
S0	Unallocated statement. (The connection state must be C4, C5, or C6. For more information, see "Connection Transitions," earlier in this appendix.)
S1	Allocated statement.
S2	Prepared statement. No result set will be created.
S3	Prepared statement. A (possibly empty) result set will be created.
S4	Statement executed and no result set was created.
S5	Statement executed and a (possibly empty) result set was created. The cursor is open and positioned before the first row of the result set.
S6	Cursor positioned with **SQLFetch** or **SQLFetchScroll**.
S7	Cursor positioned with **SQLExtendedFetch**.
S8	Function needs data. **SQLParamData** has not been called.
S9	Function needs data. **SQLPutData** has not been called.
S10	Function needs data. **SQLPutData** has been called.
S11	Still executing. A statement is left in this state after a function that is executed asynchronously returns SQL_STILL_EXECUTING. A statement is temporarily in this state while any function that accepts a statement handle is executing. Temporary residence in state S11 is not shown in any state tables except the state table for **SQLCancel**. While a statement is temporarily in state S11, the function can be canceled by calling **SQLCancel** from another thread.
S12	Asynchronous execution canceled. In S12, an application must call the canceled function until it returns a value other than SQL_STILL_EXECUTING. The function was canceled successfully only if the function returns SQL_ERROR and SQLSTATE HY008 (Operation canceled). If it returns any other value, such as SQL_SUCCESS, the cancel operation failed and the function executed normally.

States S2 and S3 are known as the prepared states, states S5 through S7 as the cursor states, states S8 through S10 as the need data states, and states S11 and S12 as the asynchronous states. In each of these groups, the transitions are shown separately only when they are different for each state in the group; generally, the transitions for each state in each a group are the same.

The following tables show how each ODBC function affects the statement state.

SQLAllocHandle

S0 Unallocated	S1 Allocated	S2 – S3 Prepared	S4 Executed	S5 – S7 Cursor	S8 – S10 Need Data	S11 – S12 Async
-- 1, 5, 6	-- 5	-- 5	-- 5	-- 5	-- 5	-- 5
-- 2, 5	-- 5	-- 5	-- 5	-- 5	-- 5	-- 5
S1 3	-- 5	-- 5	-- 5	-- 5	-- 5	-- 5
-- 4, 5	-- 5	-- 5	-- 5	-- 5	-- 5	-- 5

1 This row shows transitions when *HandleType* was SQL_HANDLE_ENV.

2 This row shows transitions when *HandleType* was SQL_HANDLE_DBC.

3 This row shows transitions when *HandleType* was SQL_HANDLE_STMT.

4 This row shows transitions when *HandleType* was SQL_HANDLE_DESC.

5 Calling **SQLAllocHandle** with *OutputHandlePtr* pointing to a valid handle overwrites that handle without any regard for the previous contents to that handle, and may cause problems for ODBC drivers. It is incorrect ODBC application programming to call **SQLAllocHandle** twice with the same application variable defined for **OutputHandlePtr* without calling **SQLFreeHandle** to free the handle before reallocating it. Overwriting ODBC handles in such a manner may lead to inconsistent behavior or errors on the part of ODBC drivers.

SQLBindCol

S0 Unallocated	S1 Allocated	S2 – S3 Prepared	S4 Executed	S5 – S7 Cursor	S8 – S10 Need Data	S11 – S12 Async
(IH)	--	--	--	--	(HY010)	(HY010)

SQLBindParameter

S0 Unallocated	S1 Allocated	S2 – S3 Prepared	S4 Executed	S5 – S7 Cursor	S8 – S10 Need Data	S11 – S12 Async
(IH)	--	--	--	--	(HY010)	(HY010)

SQLBrowseConnect, SQLConnect, and SQLDriverConnect

S0 Unallocated	S1 Allocated	S2 – S3 Prepared	S4 Executed	S5 – S7 Cursor	S8 – S10 Need Data	S11 – S12 Async
(08002)	(08002)	(08002)	(08002)	(08002)	(08002)	(08002)

SQLBulkOperations

S0 Unallocated	S1 Allocated	S2 – S3 Prepared	S4 Executed	S5 – S7 Cursor	S8 – S10 Need Data	S11 – S12 Async
(IH)	(HY010)	(HY010)	24000	see next table	(HY010)	NS c (HY010) o

SQLBulkOperations (Cursor states)

S5 Opened	S6 SQLFetch or SQLFetchScroll	S7 SQLExtendedFetch
-- [s] S8 [d] S11 [x]	-- [s] S8 [d] S11 [x]	(HY010)

SQLCancel

S0 Unallocated	S1 Allocated	S2 – S3 Prepared	S4 Executed	S5 – S7 Cursor	S8 – S10 Need Data	S11 – S12 Async
(IH)	--	--	--	--	S1 [1] S2 [nr and 2] S3 [r and 2] S5 [3 and 5] S6 [(3 or 4) and 6] S7 [4 and 7]	see next table

1 **SQLExecDirect** returned SQL_NEED_DATA.

2 **SQLExecute** returned SQL_NEED_DATA.

3 **SQLBulkOperations** returned SQL_NEED_DATA.

4 **SQLSetPos** returned SQL_NEED_DATA.

5 **SQLFetch**, **SQLFetchScroll**, or **SQLExtendedFetch** had not been called.

6 **SQLFetch** or **SQLFetchScroll** had been called.

7 **SQLExtendedFetch** had been called.

SQLCancel (Asynchronous states)

S11 Still executing	S12 Asynch canceled
NS [1] S12 [2]	S12

1 The statement was temporarily in state S11 while a function was executing. **SQLCancel** was called from a different thread.

2 The statement was in state S11 because a function called asynchronously returned SQL_STILL_EXECUTING.

SQLCloseCursor

S0 Unallocated	S1 Allocated	S2 – S3 Prepared	S4 Executed	S5 – S7 Cursor	S8 – S10 Need Data	S11 – S12 Async
(IH)	24000	24000	24000	S1 [np] S3 [p]	(HY010)	(HY010)

SQLColAttribute

S0 Unallocated	S1 Allocated	S2 – S3 Prepared	S4 Executed	S5 – S7 Cursor	S8 – S10 Need Data	S11 – S12 Async
(IH)	(HY010)	see next table	24000	-- [s] S11 [x]	(HY010)	NS [c] (HY010) [o]

SQLColAttribute (Prepared states)

S2 No Results	S3 Results
-- [1] 07005 [2]	-- [s] S11 [x]

1 *FieldIdentifier* was SQL_DESC_COUNT.

2 *FieldIdentifier* was not SQL_DESC_COUNT.

SQLColumnPrivileges, SQLColumns, SQLForeignKeys, SQLGetTypeInfo, SQLPrimaryKeys, SQLProcedureColumns, SQLProcedures, SQLSpecialColumns, SQLStatistics, SQLTablePrivileges, and SQLTables

S0 Unallocated	S1 Allocated	S2 – S3 Prepared	S4 Executed	S5 – S7 Cursor	S8 – S10 Need Data	S11 – S12 Async
(IH)	S5 [s] S11 [x]	S1 [e] S5 [s] S11 [x]	S1 [e and 1] S5 [s and 1] S11 [x and 1] 24000 [2]	see next table	(HY010)	NS [c] (HY010) [o]

1 The current result is the last or only result or there are no current results. For more information about multiple results, see "Multiple Results" in Chapter 11, "Retrieving Results (Advanced)."

2 The current result is not the last result.

SQLColumnPrivileges, SQLColumns, SQLForeignKeys, SQLGetTypeInfo, SQLPrimaryKeys, SQLProcedureColumns, SQLProcedures, SQLSpecialColumns, SQLStatistics, SQLTablePrivileges, and SQLTables (Cursor states)

S5 Opened	S6 SQLFetch or SQLFetchScroll	S7 SQLExtendedFetch
24000	(24000) [1]	(24000)

1 This error is returned by the Driver Manager if **SQLFetch** or **SQLFetchScroll** has not returned SQL_NO_DATA, and is returned by the driver if **SQLFetch** or **SQLFetchScroll** has returned SQL_NO_DATA.

SQLColumns: see **SQLColumnPrivileges**

SQLConnect: see **SQLBrowseConnect**

SQLCopyDesc

S0 Unallocated	S1 Allocated	S2 – S3 Prepared	S4 Executed	S5 – S7 Cursor	S8 – S10 Need Data	S11 – S12 Async
(IH) [1]	--	--	--	--	(HY010)	NS [c and 3] (HY010) [o or 4]
(IH) [2]	(HY010)	see next table	24000	-- [s] S11 [x]	(HY010)	NS [c and 3] (HY010) [o or 4]

1 This row shows transitions when the *SourceDescHandle* argument was an ARD, APD, or IPD.

2 This row shows transitions when the *SourceDescHandle* argument was an IRD.

3 Both the *SourceDescHandle* and *TargetDescHandle* arguments were the same as in the **SQLCopyDesc** function that is running asynchronously.

4 Either the *SourceDescHandle* argument or the *TargetDescHandle* argument (or both) were different than in the **SQLCopyDesc** function that is running asynchronously.

SQLCopyDesc (Prepared states)

S2 No Results	S3 Results
24000 [1]	-- [s] S11 [x]

1 This row shows transitions when the *SourceDescHandle* argument was an IRD.

SQLDataSources and **SQLDrivers**

S0 Unallocated	S1 Allocated	S2 – S3 Prepared	S4 Executed	S5 – S7 Cursor	S8 – S10 Need Data	S11 – S12 Async
--	--	--	--	--	--	--

SQLDescribeCol

S0 Unallocated	S1 Allocated	S2 – S3 Prepared	S4 Executed	S5 – S7 Cursor	S8 – S10 Need Data	S11 – S12 Async
(IH)	(HY010)	see next table	24000	-- [s] S11 [x]	(HY010)	NS [c] (HY010) [o]

SQLDescribeCol (Prepared states)

S2 No Results	S3 Results
07005	-- [s] S11 [x]

SQLDescribeParam

S0 Unallocated	S1 Allocated	S2 – S3 Prepared	S4 Executed	S5 – S7 Cursor	S8 – S10 Need Data	S11 – S12 Async
(IH)	(HY010)	-- [s] S11 [x]	(HY010)	(HY010)	(HY010)	NS [c] (HY010) [o]

SQLDisconnect

S0 Unallocated	S1 Allocated	S2 – S3 Prepared	S4 Executed	S5 – S7 Cursor	S8 – S10 Need Data	S11 – S12 Async
-- [1]	S0 [1]	S0 [1]	S0 [1]	S0 [1]	(HY010)	(HY010)

1 Calling **SQLDisconnect** frees all statements associated with the connection. Furthermore, this returns the connection state to C2; the connection state must be C4 before the statement state is S0.

SQLDriverConnect: see SQLBrowseConnect

SQLDrivers: see SQLDataSources

SQLEndTran

S0 Unallocated	S1 Allocated	S2 – S3 Prepared	S4 Executed	S5 – S7 Cursor	S8 – S10 Need Data	S11 – S12 Async
--	--	-- [2 or 3] S1 [1]	-- [3] S1 [np and (1 or 2)] S1 [p and 1] S2 [p and 2]	-- [3] S1 [np and (1 or 2)] S1 [p and 1] S3 [p and 2]	(HY010)	(HY010)

1 The *CompletionType* argument is SQL_COMMIT and **SQLGetInfo** returns SQL_CB_DELETE for the SQL_CURSOR_COMMIT_BEHAVIOR information type, or the *CompletionType* argument is SQL_ROLLBACK and **SQLGetInfo** returns SQL_CB_DELETE for the SQL_CURSOR_ROLLBACK_BEHAVIOR information type.

2 The *CompletionType* argument is SQL_COMMIT and **SQLGetInfo** returns SQL_CB_CLOSE for the SQL_CURSOR_COMMIT_BEHAVIOR information type, or the *CompletionType* argument is SQL_ROLLBACK and **SQLGetInfo** returns SQL_CB_CLOSE for the SQL_CURSOR_ROLLBACK_BEHAVIOR information type.

3 The *CompletionType* argument is SQL_COMMIT and **SQLGetInfo** returns SQL_CB_PRESERVE for the SQL_CURSOR_COMMIT_BEHAVIOR information type, or the *CompletionType* argument is SQL_ROLLBACK and **SQLGetInfo** returns SQL_CB_PRESERVE for the SQL_CURSOR_ROLLBACK_BEHAVIOR information type.

SQLExecDirect

S0 Unallocated	S1 Allocated	S2 – S3 Prepared	S4 Executed	S5 – S7 Cursor	S8 – S10 Need Data	S11 – S12 Async
(IH)	S4 s and nr S5 s and r S8 d S11 x	-- e and 1 S1 e and 2 S4 s and nr S5 s and r S8 d S11 x	-- e, 1, and 3 S1 e, 2, and 3 S4 s, nr, and 3 S5 s, r, and 3 S8 d and 3 S11 x and 3 24000 4	see next table	(HY010)	NS c (HY010) o

1 The error was returned by the Driver Manager.

2 The error was not returned by the Driver Manager.

3 The current result is the last or only result or there are no current results. For more information about multiple results, see "Multiple Results" in Chapter 11, "Retrieving Results (Advanced)."

4 The current result is not the last result.

SQLExecDirect (Cursor states)

S5 Opened	S6 SQLFetch or SQLFetchScroll	S7 SQLExtendedFetch
24000	(24000) 1	(24000)

1 This error is returned by the Driver Manager if **SQLFetch** or **SQLFetchScroll** has not returned SQL_NO_DATA, and is returned by the driver if **SQLFetch** or **SQLFetchScroll** has returned SQL_NO_DATA.

SQLExecute

S0 Unallocated	S1 Allocated	S2 – S3 Prepared	S4 Executed	S5 – S7 Cursor	S8 – S10 Need Data	S11 – S12 Async
(IH)	(HY010)	see next table	S2 e, p, and 1 S4 s, p, nr, and 1 S5 s, p, r, and 1 S8 d, p, and 1 S11 x, p, and 1 24000 p and 2 (HY010) np	see cursor states table	(HY010)	NS c (HY010) o

1 The current result is the last or only result or there are no current results. For more information about multiple results, see "Multiple Results" in Chapter 11, "Retrieving Results (Advanced)."

2 The current result is not the last result.

SQLExecute (Prepared states)

S2 No Results	S3 Results
S4 [s]	S5 [s]
S8 [d]	S8 [d]
S11 [x]	S11 [x]

SQLExecute (Cursor states)

S5 Opened	S6 SQLFetch or SQLFetchScroll	S7 SQLExtendedFetch
24000 [p]	(24000) [p, 1]	(24000) [p]
(HY010) [np]	(HY010) [np]	(HY010) [np]

1 This error is returned by the Driver Manager if **SQLFetch** or **SQLFetchScroll** has not returned SQL_NO_DATA, and is returned by the driver if **SQLFetch** or **SQLFetchScroll** has returned SQL_NO_DATA.

SQLExtendedFetch

S0 Unallocated	S1 Allocated	S2 – S3 Prepared	S4 Executed	S5 – S7 Cursor	S8 – S10 Need Data	S11 – S12 Async
(IH)	(S1010)	(S1010)	24000	see next table	(S1010)	NS [c] (S1010) [o]

SQLExtendedFetch (Cursor states)

S5 Opened	S6 SQLFetch or SQLFetchScroll	S7 SQLExtendedFetch
S7 [s or nf]	(S1010)	-- [s or nf]
S11 [x]		S11 [x]

SQLFetch and SQLFetchScroll

S0 Unallocated	S1 Allocated	S2 – S3 Prepared	S4 Executed	S5 – S7 Cursor	S8 – S10 Need Data	S11 – S12 Async
(IH)	(HY010)	(HY010)	24000	see next table	(HY010)	NS [c] (HY010) [o]

SQLFetch and SQLFetchScroll (Cursor states)

S5 Opened	S6 SQLFetch or SQLFetchScroll	S7 SQLExtendedFetch
S6 [s or nf]	-- [s or nf]	(HY010)
S11 [x]	S11 [x]	

SQLForeignKeys: see SQLColumnPrivileges

SQLFreeHandle

S0 Unallocated	S1 Allocated	S2 – S3 Prepared	S4 Executed	S5 – S7 Cursor	S8 – S10 Need Data	S11 – S12 Async
-- [1]	(HY010)	(HY010)	(HY010)	(HY010)	(HY010)	(HY010)
(IH) [2]	S0	S0	S0	S0	(HY010)	(HY010)
-- [3]	--	--	--	--	--	--

1 This row shows transitions when *HandleType* was SQL_HANDLE_ENV or SQL_HANDLE_DBC.

2 This row shows transitions when *HandleType* was SQL_HANDLE_STMT.

3 This row shows transitions when *HandleType* was SQL_HANDLE_DESC and the descriptor was explicitly allocated.

SQLFreeStmt

S0 Unallocated	S1 Allocated	S2 – S3 Prepared	S4 Executed	S5 – S7 Cursor	S8 – S10 Need Data	S11 – S12 Async
(IH) [1]	--	--	S1 [np] S2 [p]	S1 [np] S3 [p]	(HY010)	(HY010)
(IH) [2]	--	--	--	--	(HY010)	(HY010)

1 This row shows transitions when *Option* was SQL_CLOSE.

2 This row shows transitions when *Option* was SQL_UNBIND or SQL_RESET_PARAMS. If the *Option* argument was SQL_DROP and the underlying driver is an ODBC 3.0 driver, the Driver Manager maps this to a call to **SQLFreeHandle** with *HandleType* set to SQL_HANDLE_STMT. For more information, see the transition table for **SQLFreeHandle**.

SQLGetConnectAttr

S0 Unallocated	S1 Allocated	S2 – S3 Prepared	S4 Executed	S5 – S7 Cursor	S8 – S10 Need Data	S11 – S12 Async
--	--	--	--	--	--	--

SQLGetCursorName

S0 Unallocated	S1 Allocated	S2 – S3 Prepared	S4 Executed	S5 – S7 Cursor	S8 – S10 Need Data	S11 – S12 Async
(IH)	--	--	--	--	(HY010)	(HY010)

SQLGetData

S0 Unallocated	S1 Allocated	S2 – S3 Prepared	S4 Executed	S5 – S7 Cursor	S8 – S10 Need Data	S11 – S12 Async
(IH)	(HY010)	(HY010)	(24000)	see next table	(HY010)	NS [c] (HY010) [o]

SQLGetData (Cursor states)

S5 Opened	S6 SQLFetch or SQLFetchScroll	S7 SQLExtendedFetch
(24000)	-- s or nf S11 x 24000 b HY109 i	-- s or nf S11 x 24000 b HY109 i

SQLGetDescField and **SQLGetDescRec**

S0 Unallocated	S1 Allocated	S2 – S3 Prepared	S4 Executed	S5 – S7 Cursor	S8 – S10 Need Data	S11 – S12 Async
(IH)	-- 1 or 2 (HY010) 3	see next table	-- 1 or 2 24000 3	-- 1, 2, or 3 S11 3 and x	(HY010)	NS c or 4 (HY010) o and 5

1 The *DescriptorHandle* argument was an APD or ARD.

2 The *DescriptorHandle* argument was an IPD.

3 The *DescriptorHandle* argument was an IRD.

4 The *DescriptorHandle* argument was the same as the *DescriptorHandle* argument in the **SQLGetDescField** or **SQLGetDescRec** function that is running asynchronously.

5 The *DescriptorHandle* argument was different than the *DescriptorHandle* argument in the **SQLGetDescField** or **SQLGetDescRec** function that is running asynchronously.

SQLGetDescField and **SQLGetDescRec** (Prepared states)

S2 No Results	S3 Results
-- 1, 2, or 3	-- 1, 2, or 3
S11 2 and x	S11 x

1 The *DescriptorHandle* argument was an APD or ARD.

2 The *DescriptorHandle* argument was an IPD.

3 The *DescriptorHandle* argument was an IRD. Note that these functions always return SQL_NO_DATA in state S2 when *DescriptorHandle* was an IRD.

SQLGetDiagField and **SQLGetDiagRec**

S0 Unallocated	S1 Allocated	S2 – S3 Prepared	S4 Executed	S5 – S7 Cursor	S8 – S10 Need Data	S11 – S12 Async
-- [1]	--	--	--	--	--	--
(IH) [2]	-- [3]	-- [3]	--	--	-- [3]	-- [3]

1 This row shows transitions when *HandleType* was SQL_HANDLE_ENV, SQL_HANDLE_DBC, or SQL_HANDLE_DESC.

2 This row shows transitions when *HandleType* was SQL_HANDLE_STMT.

3 **SQLGetDiagField** always returns an error in this state when *DiagIdentifier* is SQL_DIAG_ROW_COUNT.

SQLGetEnvAttr

S0 Unallocated	S1 Allocated	S2 – S3 Prepared	S4 Executed	S5 – S7 Cursor	S8 – S10 Need Data	S11 – S12 Async
--	--	--	--	--	--	--

SQLGetFunctions

S0 Unallocated	S1 Allocated	S2 – S3 Prepared	S4 Executed	S5 – S7 Cursor	S8 – S10 Need Data	S11 – S12 Async
--	--	--	--	--	--	--

SQLGetInfo

S0 Unallocated	S1 Allocated	S2 – S3 Prepared	S4 Executed	S5 – S7 Cursor	S8 – S10 Need Data	S11 – S12 Async
--	--	--	--	--	--	--

SQLGetStmtAttr

S0 Unallocated	S1 Allocated	S2 – S3 Prepared	S4 Executed	S5 – S7 Cursor	S8 – S10 Need Data	S11 – S12 Async
(IH)	-- [1] (24000) [2]	-- [1] (24000) [2]	-- [1] (24000) [2]	see next table	(HY010)	(HY010)

1 The statement attribute was not SQL_ATTR_ROW_NUMBER.

2 The statement attribute was SQL_ATTR_ROW_NUMBER.

SQLGetStmtAttr (Cursor states)

S5 Opened	S6 SQLFetch or SQLFetchScroll	S7 SQLExtendedFetch
-- [1]	-- [1 or (v and 2)]	-- [i or (v and 2)]
(24000) [2]	24000 [b and 2] HY109 [i and 2]	24000 [b and 2] HY109 [1 and 2]

1 The *Attribute* argument was not SQL_ATTR_ROW_NUMBER.

2 The *Attribute* argument was SQL_ATTR_ROW_NUMBER.

SQLGetTypeInfo: see SQLColumnPrivileges

SQLMoreResults

S0 Unallocated	S1 Allocated	S2 – S3 Prepared	S4 Executed	S5 – S7 Cursor	S8 – S10 Need Data	S11 – S12 Async
(IH)	-- 1	-- 1	-- s and 2 S1 nf, np, and 4 S2 nf, p, and 4 S5 s and 3 S11 x	S1 nf, np, and 4 S3 nf, p and 4 S4 s and 2 S5 s and 3 S11 x	(HY010)	NS c (HY010) o

1 The function always returns SQL_NO_DATA in this state.

2 The next result is a row count.

3 The next result is a result set.

4 The current result is the last result.

SQLNativeSql

S0 Unallocated	S1 Allocated	S2 – S3 Prepared	S4 Executed	S5 – S7 Cursor	S8 – S10 Need Data	S11 – S12 Async
--	--	--	--	--	--	--

SQLNumParams

S0 Unallocated	S1 Allocated	S2 – S3 Prepared	S4 Executed	S5 – S7 Cursor	S8 – S10 Need Data	S11 – S12 Async
(IH)	(HY010)	-- s S11 x	-- s S11 x	-- s S11 x	(HY010)	NS c (HY010) o

SQLNumResultCols

S0 Unallocated	S1 Allocated	S2 – S3 Prepared	S4 Executed	S5 – S7 Cursor	S8 – S10 Need Data	S11 – S12 Async
(IH)	(HY010)	-- s S11 x	-- s S11 x	-- s S11 x	(HY010)	NS c (HY010) o

SQLParamData

S0 Unallocated	S1 Allocated	S2 – S3 Prepared	S4 Executed	S5 – S7 Cursor	S8 – S10 Need Data	S11 – S12 Async
(IH)	(HY010)	(HY010)	(HY010)	(HY010)	see next table	NS c (HY010) o

SQLParamData (Need Data states)

S8 Need Data	S9 Must Put	S10 Can Put
S1 e and 1 S2 e, nr, and 2 S3 e, r, and 2 S5 e and 4 S6 e and 5 S7 e and 3 S9 d S11 x	HY010	S1 e and 1 S2 e, nr, and 2 S3 e, r, and 2 S4 s, nr, and (1 or 2) S5 s, r, and (1 or 2) S5 (s or e) and 4 S6 (s or e) and 5 S7 (s or e) and 3 S9 d S11 x

1 **SQLExecDirect** returned SQL_NEED_DATA.

2 **SQLExecute** returned SQL_NEED_DATA.

3 **SQLSetPos** had been called from state S7 and returned SQL_NEED_DATA.

4 **SQLBulkOperations** had been called from state S5 and returned SQL_NEED_DATA.

5 **SQLSetPos** or **SQLBulkOperations** had been called from state S6 and returned SQL_NEED_DATA.

SQLPrepare

S0 Unallocated	S1 Allocated	S2 – S3 Prepared	S4 Executed	S5 – S7 Cursor	S8 – S10 Need Data	S11 – S12 Async
(IH)	S2 s and nr S3 s and r S11 x	-- s or (e and 1) S1 e and 2 S11 x	S1 e and 3 S2 s, nr, and 3 S3 s, r, and 3 S11 x and 3 24000 4	see next table	(HY010)	NS c (HY010) o

1 The preparation fails for a reason other than validating the statement (the SQLSTATE was HY009 (Invalid argument value) or HY090 (Invalid string or buffer length)).

2 The preparation fails while validating the statement (the SQLSTATE was not HY009 (Invalid argument value) or HY090 (Invalid string or buffer length)).

3 The current result is the last or only result, or there are no current results. For more information about multiple results, see "Multiple Results" in Chapter 11, "Retrieving Results (Advanced)."

4 The current result is not the last result.

SQLPrepare (Cursor states)

S5 Opened	S6 SQLFetch or SQLFetchScroll	S7 SQLExtendedFetch
24000	(24000)	(24000)

SQLPrimaryKeys: see SQLColumnPrivileges

SQLProcedureColumns: see SQLColumnPrivileges

SQLProcedures: see SQLColumnPrivileges

SQLPutData

S0 Unallocated	S1 Allocated	S2 – S3 Prepared	S4 Executed	S5 – S7 Cursor	S8 – S10 Need Data	S11 – S12 Async
(IH)	(HY010)	(HY010)	(HY010)	(HY010)	see next table	NS c (HY010) o

SQLPutData (Need Data states)

S8 Need Data	S9 Must Put	S10 Can Put
HY010	S1 e and 1 S2 e, nr, and 2 S3 e, r, and 2 S5 e and 4 S6 e and 5 S7 e and 3 S10 s S11 x	-- s S1 e and 1 S2 e, nr, and 2 S3 e, r, and 2 S5 e and 4 S6 e and 5 S7 e and 3 S11 x HY011 6

1 **SQLExecDirect** returned SQL_NEED_DATA.

2 **SQLExecute** returned SQL_NEED_DATA.

3 **SQLSetPos** had been called from state S7 and returned SQL_NEED_DATA.

4 **SQLBulkOperations** had been called from state S5 and returned SQL_NEED_DATA.

5 **SQLSetPos** or **SQLBulkOperations** had been called from state S6 and returned SQL_NEED_DATA.

6 One or more calls to **SQLPutData** for a single parameter returned SQL_SUCCESS, then a call to **SQLPutData** was made for the same parameter with *StrLen_or_Ind* set to SQL_NULL_DATA.

SQLRowCount

S0 Unallocated	S1 Allocated	S2 – S3 Prepared	S4 Executed	S5 – S7 Cursor	S8 – S10 Need Data	S11 – S12 Async
(IH)	(HY010)	(HY010)	--	--	(HY010)	(HY010)

SQLSetConnectAttr

S0 Unallocated	S1 Allocated	S2 – S3 Prepared	S4 Executed	S5 – S7 Cursor	S8 – S10 Need Data	S11 – S12 Async
-- [1]	--	--	--	--[2] 24000 [3]	(HY010)	(HY010)

1 This row shows transitions when *Attribute* was a connection attribute. For transitions when *Attribute* was a statement attribute, see the statement transition table for **SQLSetStmtAttr**.

2 The *Attribute* argument was not SQL_ATTR_CURRENT_CATALOG.

3 The *Attribute* argument was SQL_ATTR_CURRENT_CATALOG.

SQLSetCursorName

S0 Unallocated	S1 Allocated	S2 – S3 Prepared	S4 Executed	S5 – S7 Cursor	S8 – S10 Need Data	S11 – S12 Async
(IH)	--	--	(24000)	(24000)	(HY010)	(HY010)

SQLSetDescField and SQLSetDescRec

S0 Unallocated	S1 Allocated	S2 – S3 Prepared	S4 Executed	S5 – S7 Cursor	S8 – S10 Need Data	S11 – S12 Async
(IH) [1]	--	--	--	--	(HY010)	(HY010)

1 This row shows transitions where the *DescriptorHandle* argument is an ARD, APD, IPD, or (for **SQLSetDescField**) an IRD when the *FieldIdentifier* argument is SQL_DESC_ARRAY_STATUS_PTR or SQL_DESC_ROWS_PROCESSED_PTR. It is an error to call **SQLSetDescField** for an IRD when *FieldIdentifier* is any other value.

SQLSetEnvAttr

S0 Unallocated	S1 Allocated	S2 – S3 Prepared	S4 Executed	S5 – S7 Cursor	S8 – S10 Need Data	S11 – S12 Async
(HY011)	(HY011)	(HY011)	(HY011)	(HY011)	(HY011)	(HY011)

SQLSetPos

S0 Unallocated	S1 Allocated	S2 – S3 Prepared	S4 Executed	S5 – S7 Cursor	S8 – S10 Need Data	S11 – S12 Async
(IH)	(HY010)	(HY010)	(24000)	see next table	(HY010)	NS [c] (HY010) [o]

SQLSetPos (Cursor states)

S5 Opened	S6 SQLFetch or SQLFetchScroll	S7 SQLExtendedFetch
	-- [s]	-- [s]
(24000)	S8 [d]	S8 [d]
	S11 [x]	S11 [x]
	24000 [b]	24000 [b]
	HY109 [i]	HY109 [i]

SQLSetStmtAttr

S0 Unallocated	S1 Allocated	S2 – S3 Prepared	S4 Executed	S5 – S7 Cursor	S8 – S10 Need Data	S11 – S12 Async
(IH)	--	-- [1] (HY011) [2]	-- [1] (24000) [2]	-- [1] (24000) [2]	(HY010) [np or 1] (HY011) [p and 2]	(HY010) [np or 1] (HY011) [p and 2]

1 The *Attribute* argument was not SQL_ATTR_CONCURRENCY, SQL_ATTR_CURSOR_TYPE, SQL_ATTR_SIMULATE_CURSOR, SQL_ATTR_USE_BOOKMARKS, SQL_ATTR_CURSOR_SCROLLABLE, or SQL_ATTR_CURSOR_SENSITIVITY.

2 The *Attribute* argument was SQL_ATTR_CONCURRENCY, SQL_ATTR_CURSOR_TYPE, SQL_ATTR_SIMULATE_CURSOR, SQL_ATTR_USE_BOOKMARKS, SQL_ATTR_CURSOR_SCROLLABLE, or SQL_ATTR_CURSOR_SENSITIVITY.

SQLSpecialColumns: see **SQLColumnPrivileges**

SQLStatistics: see **SQLColumnPrivileges**

SQLTablePrivileges: see **SQLColumnPrivileges**

SQLTables: see **SQLColumnPrivileges**

Descriptor Transitions

ODBC descriptors have the following three states.

State	Description
D0	Unallocated descriptor
D1i	Implicitly allocated descriptor
D1e	Explicitly allocated descriptor

The following tables show how each ODBC function affects the descriptor state.

SQLAllocHandle

D0 Unallocated	D1i Implicit	D1e Explicit
D1i [1]	--	--
D1e [2]	--	--

1 This row shows transitions when *HandleType* was SQL_HANDLE_STMT.

2 This row shows transitions when *HandleType* was SQL_HANDLE_DESC.

SQLCopyDesc

D0 Unallocated	D1i Implicit	D1e Explicit
(IH)	--	--

SQLFreeHandle

D0 Unallocated	D1i Implicit	D1e Explicit
-- [1]	D0	--
(IH) [2]	(HY017)	D0

1 This row shows transitions when *HandleType* was SQL_HANDLE_STMT.

2 This row shows transitions when *HandleType* was SQL_HANDLE_DESC.

SQLGetDescField and SQLGetDescRec

D0 Unallocated	D1i Implicit	D1e Explicit
(IH)	--	--

SQLSetDescField and SQLSetDescRec

D0 Unallocated	D1i Implicit	D1e Explicit
(IH) [1]	--	--

1 This row shows transitions when *DescriptorHandle* was the handle of an ARD, APD, or IPD, or (for **SQLSetDescField**) when *DescriptorHandle* was the handle of an IRD and *FieldIdentifier* was SQL_DESC_ARRAY_STATUS_PTR or SQL_DESC_ROWS_PROCESSED_PTR.

All Other ODBC Functions

D0 Unallocated	D1i Implicit	D1e Explicit
--	--	--

APPENDIX C

SQL Grammar

This appendix describes the minimum SQL syntax that an ODBC driver must support. It also describes ODBC escape sequences, interval literals, numeric literals, and provides a list of reserved keywords.

SQL Minimum Grammar

This section describes the minimum SQL syntax that an ODBC driver must support. The syntax described in this section is a subset of the Entry level syntax of SQL-92.

An application can use any of the syntax in this section, and be assured that any ODBC-compliant driver will support that syntax. To determine if additional features of SQL-92 not in this section are supported, the application should call **SQLGetInfo** with the SQL_SQL_CONFORMANCE information type. Even if the driver does not conform to any SQL-92 conformance level, an application can still use the syntax described in this section. If a driver conforms to an SQL-92 level, on the other hand, it supports all syntax included in that level. This includes the syntax in this section because the minimum grammar described here is a pure subset of the lowest SQL-92 conformance level. Once the application knows the SQL-92 level supported, it can determine if a higher-level feature is supported (if any) by calling **SQLGetInfo** with the individual information type corresponding to that feature.

Drivers that work only with read-only data sources may not support those parts of the grammar included in this section that deal with changing data. An application can determine if a data source is read-only by calling **SQLGetInfo** with the SQL_DATA_SOURCE_READ_ONLY information type.

Statement

---

create-table-statement ::=
CREATE TABLE *base-table-name*
(*column-identifier data-type* [,*column-identifier data-type*]...)

Important As a *data-type* in a *create-table-statement*, applications must use a data type from the TYPE_NAME column of the result set returned by **SQLGetTypeInfo**.

---

delete-statement-searched ::=
DELETE FROM *table-name* [WHERE *search-condition*]

---

drop-table-statement ::=
DROP TABLE *base-table-name*

---

insert-statement ::=
INSERT INTO *table-name* [(*column-identifier* [, *column-identifier*]...)]
VALUES (*insert-value*[, *insert-value*]...)

---

select-statement ::=
SELECT [ALL | DISTINCT] *select-list*
FROM *table-reference-list*
[WHERE *search-condition*]
[*order-by-clause*]

---

statement ::= *create-table-statement*
| *delete-statement-searched*
| *drop-table-statement*
| *insert-statement*
| *select-statement*
| *update-statement-searched*

---

update-statement-searched
UPDATE *table-name*
SET *column-identifier* = {*expression* | NULL }
[, *column-identifier* = {*expression* | NULL}]...
[WHERE *search-condition*]

Elements Used in SQL Statements

The following elements are used in the SQL statements listed previously.

Element

base-table-identifier ::= *user-defined-name*

base-table-name ::= *base-table-identifier*

boolean-factor ::= [NOT] *boolean-primary*

boolean-primary ::= *comparison-predicate* | (*search-condition*)

boolean-term ::= *boolean-factor* [AND *boolean-term*]

character-string-literal ::= '{*character*}...'

(*character* is any character in the character set of the driver/data source. To include a single literal quote character (') in a character-string-literal, use two literal quote characters ('').)

column-identifier ::= *user-defined-name*

column-name ::= [*table-name*.]*column-identifier*

comparison-operator ::= < | > | ≤ | ≥ | = | ≠

comparison-predicate ::= *expression comparison-operator expression*

data-type ::= *character-string-type*

(*character-string-type* is any data type for which the "DATA_TYPE" column in the result set returned by **SQLGetTypeInfo** is either SQL_CHAR or SQL_VARCHAR.)

digit ::= 0 | 1 | 2 | 3 | 4 | 5 | 6 | 7 | 8 | 9

dynamic-parameter ::= ?

expression ::= *term* | *expression* {+|–} *term*

factor ::= [+|–]*primary*

insert-value ::=
  dynamic-parameter
  | *literal*
  | NULL
  | USER

letter ::= *lower-case-letter* | *upper-case-letter*

literal ::= *character-string-literal*

lower-case-letter ::= a | b | c | d | e | f | g | h | i | j | k | l | m | n | o | p | q | r | s | t | u | v | w | x | y | z

order-by-clause ::= ORDER BY *sort-specification* [, *sort-specification*]...

Element

primary ::= *column-name*
  | *dynamic-parameter*
  | *literal*
  | (*expression*)

search-condition ::= *boolean-term* [OR *search-condition*]
select-list ::= * | *select-sublist* [, *select-sublist*]... (*select-list* cannot contain parameters.)
select-sublist ::= *expression*
sort-specification ::= {*unsigned-integer* | *column-name*} [*ASC* | *DESC*]
table-identifier ::= *user-defined-name*
table-name ::= *table-identifier*
table-reference ::= *table-name*
table-reference-list ::= *table-reference* [,*table-reference*]...
term ::= *factor* | *term* {*|/} *factor*
unsigned-integer ::= {*digit*}
upper-case-letter ::= *A* | *B* | *C* | *D* | *E* | *F* | *G* | *H* | *I* | *J* | *K* | *L* | *M* | *N* | *O* | *P* | *Q* | *R* | *S* | *T* | *U* | *V* | *W* | *X* | *Y* | *Z*
user-defined-name ::= *letter*[*digit* | *letter* | _]...

Data Type Support

ODBC drivers must support at least one of SQL_CHAR and SQL_VARCHAR. Support for other data types is determined by the driver's or data source's SQL-92 conformance level. An application should call **SQLGetTypeInfo** to determine the data types supported by the driver.

For more information on data types, see Appendix D, "Data Types."

Parameter Data Types

Even though each parameter specified with **SQLBindParameter** is defined using an SQL data type, the parameters in an SQL statement have no intrinsic data type. Therefore, parameter markers can be included in an SQL statement only if their data types can be inferred from another operand in the statement. For example, in an arithmetic expression such as ? + COLUMN1, the data type of the parameter can be inferred from the data type of the named column represented by COLUMN1. An application cannot use a parameter marker if the data type cannot be determined.

The following table describes how a data type is determined for several types of parameters, in accordance with SQL-92. For a more comprehensive specification on inferring the parameter type when other SQL clauses are used, see the SQL-92 specification.

Location of parameter	Assumed data type
One operand of a binary arithmetic or comparison operator	Same as the other operand
The first operand in a **BETWEEN** clause	Same as the second operand
The second or third operand in a **BETWEEN** clause	Same as the first operand
An expression used with **IN**	Same as the first value or the result column of the subquery
A value used with **IN**	Same as the expression or the first value if there is a parameter marker in the expression.
A pattern value used with **LIKE**	VARCHAR
An update value used with **UPDATE**	Same as the update column

Parameter Markers

In accordance with the SQL-92 specification, an application cannot place parameter markers in the following locations. For a more comprehensive list, see the SQL-92 specification.

- In a **SELECT** list
- As both *expressions* in a *comparison-predicate*
- As both operands of a binary operator
- As both the first and second operands of a **BETWEEN** operation

- As both the first and third operands of a **BETWEEN** operation
- As both the expression and the first value of an **IN** operation
- As the operand of a unary + or – operation
- As the argument of a *set-function-reference*

For more information about parameter markers, see the SQL-92 specification. For more information about parameters, see "Statement Parameters" in Chapter 9, "Executing Statements."

ODBC Escape Sequences

The following escape sequences are used in ODBC. The grammar in this section uses some elements defined in the "Elements Used in SQL Statements" section.

Date, Time, and Timestamp Escape Sequences

ODBC defines escape sequences for date, time, and timestamp literals. The syntax of these escape sequences is as follows:

{*d* '*value*'}
{*t* '*value*'}
{*ts* '*value*'}

In BNF notation, the syntax is as follows:

ODBC-date-time-escape ::=
  ODBC-date-escape
  | *ODBC-time-escape*
  | *ODBC-timestamp-escape*

ODBC-date-escape ::=
  ODBC-esc-initiator d '*date-value*' *ODBC-esc-terminator*

ODBC-time-escape ::=
  ODBC-esc-initiator t '*time-value*' *ODBC-esc-terminator*

ODBC-timestamp-escape ::=
  ODBC-esc-initiator ts '*timestamp-value*' *ODBC-esc-terminator*

ODBC-esc-initiator ::= {

ODBC-esc-terminator ::= }

date-value ::=
  years-value date-separator months-value date-separator days-value

time-value ::=
  hours-value time-separator minutes-value time-separator seconds-value

timestamp-value ::= *date-value timestamp-separator time-value*

date-separator ::= -

time-separator ::= :

timestamp-separator ::=
(The blank character)

years-value ::= *digit digit digit digit*

months-value ::= *digit digit*

days-value ::= *digit digit*

hours-value ::= *digit digit*

minutes-value ::= *digit digit*

seconds-value ::= *digit digit*[.*digit*...]

The date, time, and timestamp literal escape sequences are supported if the date, time, and timestamp data types are supported by the data source. An application should call **SQLGetTypeInfo** to determine whether these data types are supported.

Interval Escape Sequences

ODBC uses escape sequences for interval literals. The syntax of this escape sequence is as follows:

{*interval-literal*}

For the BNF syntax of *interval-literal*, see the "Interval Literal Syntax" section later in this appendix.

The interval literal escape sequence is supported if the interval data types are supported by the data source. An application should call **SQLGetTypeInfo** to determine whether these data types are supported.

Like Escape Sequence

ODBC uses escape sequences for the like clause. The syntax of this escape sequence is as follows:

{**escape** '*escape-character*'}

In BNF notation, the syntax is as follows:

ODBC-like-escape ::=
  ODBC-esc-initiator escape '*escape-character*' *ODBC-esc-terminator*

escape-character ::= *character*

ODBC-esc-initiator ::= {

ODBC-esc-terminator ::= }

To determine if the driver supports the LIKE escape sequence, an application can call **SQLGetInfo** with the SQL_LIKE_ESCAPE_CLAUSE information type.

Outer Join Escape Sequence

ODBC uses escape sequences for outer joins. The syntax of this escape sequence is as follows:

{oj *outer-join***}**

In BNF notation, the syntax is as follows:

ODBC-outer-join-escape ::=
  ODBC-esc-initiator oj *outer-join ODBC-esc-terminator*

outer-join ::= *table-name* [*correlation-name*] {LEFT | RIGHT | FULL}
  OUTER JOIN{*table-name* [*correlation-name*] | *outer-join*} ON *search-condition*

correlation-name ::= *user-defined-name*

ODBC-esc-initiator ::= {

ODBC-esc-terminator ::= }

To determine which parts of this statement are supported, an application calls **SQLGetInfo** with the SQL_OJ_CAPABILITIES information type. For outer joins, *search-condition* must contain only the join condition between the specified *table-names*.

Procedure Call Escape Sequence

ODBC uses escape sequences for procedure calls. The syntax of this escape sequence is as follows:

{[?=]**call** *procedure-name*[([*parameter*][,[*parameter*]]...)]}

In BNF notation, the syntax is as follows:

ODBC-procedure-escape ::=
  | *ODBC-esc-initiator* [?=] call *procedure ODBC-esc-terminator*

procedure ::= *procedure-name* | *procedure-name* (*procedure-parameter-list*)

procedure-identifier ::= *user-defined-name*

procedure-name ::= *procedure-identifier*
| *owner-name.procedure-identifier*
| *catalog-name catalog-separator procedure-identifier*
| *catalog-name catalog-separator* [*owner-name*].*procedure-identifier*

(The third syntax is valid only if the data source does not support owners.)

owner-name ::= *user-defined-name*

catalog-name ::= *user-defined-name*

catalog-separator ::= {*implementation-defined*}
(The catalog separator is returned through **SQLGetInfo** with the SQL_CATALOG_NAME_SEPARATOR information option.)

procedure-parameter-list ::= *procedure-parameter*
| *procedure-parameter, procedure-parameter-list*

procedure-parameter ::= *dynamic-parameter* | *literal* | *empty-string*

empty-string ::=

ODBC-esc-initiator ::= {

ODBC-esc-terminator ::= }

(If a procedure parameter is an empty string, the procedure uses the default value for that parameter.)

To determine if the data source supports procedures and the driver supports the ODBC procedure invocation syntax, an application can call **SQLGetInfo** with the SQL_PROCEDURES information type.

Scalar Function Escape Sequence

ODBC uses escape sequences for scalar functions. The syntax of this escape sequence is as follows:

{fn *scalar-function***}**

In BNF notation, the syntax is as follows:

ODBC-scalar-function-escape ::=
ODBC-esc-initiator fn *scalar-function ODBC-esc-terminator*

scalar-function ::= *function-name* (*argument-list*)

(The definitions for the non-terminals *function-name* and *function-name* (*argument-list*) are derived from the list of scalar functions in Appendix E, "Scalar Functions.")

ODBC-esc-initiator ::= {

ODBC-esc-terminator ::= }

To determine if the data source supports procedures and the driver supports the ODBC procedure invocation syntax, an application can call **SQLGetInfo**. For more information, see Appendix E, "Scalar Functions."

Literals in ODBC

The syntax in the following sections is used for interval and numeric literals in ODBC. This syntax is provided here as an aid to driver writers when conversions are performed from a character string type to a numeric or interval type, or from a numeric or interval type to a character string type. For more information, see the "Interval Literals" and "Numeric Literals" sections in Appendix D, "Data Types."

Interval Literal Syntax

The following syntax is used for interval literals in ODBC.

interval-literal ::= INTERVAL [+|-] *interval-string interval-qualifier*

interval-string ::= *quote* { *year-month-literal* | *day-time-literal* } *quote*

year-month-literal ::= *years-value* | [*years-value* -] *months-value*

day-time-literal ::= *day-time-interval* | *time-interval*

day-time-interval ::= *days-value* [*hours-value* [:*minutes-value*[:*seconds-value*]]]

time-interval ::= *hours-value* [:*minutes-value* [:*seconds-value*]]
| *minutes-value* [:*seconds-value*]
| *seconds-value*

years-value ::= *datetime-value*

months-value ::= *datetime-value*

days-value ::= *datetime-value*

hours-value ::= *datetime-value*

minutes-value ::= *datetime-value*

seconds-value ::= *seconds-integer-value* [.[*seconds-fraction*]]

seconds-integer-value ::= *unsigned-integer*

seconds-fraction ::= *unsigned-integer*

datetime-value ::= *unsigned-integer*

interval-qualifier ::= *start-field* TO *end-field* | *single-datetime-field*

start-field ::= *non-second-datetime-field* [(*interval-leading-field-precision*)]

end-field ::= *non-second-datetime-field*
| SECOND[(*interval-fractional-seconds-precision*)]

single-datetime-field ::= *non-second-datetime-field* [(*interval-leading-field-precision*)]
| SECOND[(*interval-leading-field-precision* [, (*interval-fractional-seconds-precision*)]

datetime-field ::= *non-second-datetime-field* | SECOND

non-second-datetime-field ::= YEAR | MONTH | DAY | HOUR | MINUTE

interval-fractional-seconds-precision ::= *unsigned-integer*

interval-leading-field-precision ::= *unsigned-integer*

quote ::= '

unsigned-integer ::= *digit…*

Numeric Literal Syntax

The following syntax is used for numeric literals in ODBC.

numeric-literal ::= *signed-numeric-literal* | *unsigned-numeric-literal*

signed-numeric-literal ::= [*sign*] *unsigned-numeric-literal*

unsigned-numeric-literal ::= *exact-numeric-literal* | *approximate-numeric-literal*

exact-numeric-literal ::= *unsigned-integer* [*period*[*unsigned-integer*]] |
period unsigned-integer

sign ::= *plus-sign* | *minus-sign*

approximate-numeric-literal ::= *mantissa E exponent*

mantissa ::= *exact-numeric-literal*

exponent ::= *signed-integer*

signed-integer ::= [*sign*] *unsigned-integer*

unsigned-integer ::= *digit...*

plus-sign ::= +

minus-sign ::= -

digit ::= 1 | 2 | 3 | 4 | 5 | 6 | 7 | 8 | 9 | 0

period ::= .

List of Reserved Keywords

The following words are reserved for use in ODBC function calls. These words do not constrain the minimum SQL grammar; however, to ensure compatibility with drivers that support the core SQL grammar, applications should avoid using any of these keywords. The **#define** value SQL_ODBC_KEYWORDS contains a comma-separated list of these keywords.

ABSOLUTE
ACTION
ADA
ADD
ALL
ALLOCATE
ALTER
AND
ANY
ARE
AS
ASC
ASSERTION
AT
AUTHORIZATION
AVG
BEGIN
BETWEEN
BIT
BIT_LENGTH
BOTH
BY
CASCADE
CASCADED
CASE
CAST
CATALOG
CHAR
CHAR_LENGTH
IS
ISOLATION
JOIN
KEY
LANGUAGE
LAST
LEADING
LEFT
LEVEL
LIKE
LOCAL
LOWER
MATCH
MAX
MIN
MINUTE
MODULE
MONTH
NAMES
NATIONAL
NATURAL
NCHAR
NEXT
NO
NONE
NOT
NULL
NULLIF
NUMERIC

CHARACTER
CHARACTER_LENGTH
CHECK
CLOSE
COALESCE
COLLATE
COLLATION
COLUMN
COMMIT
CONNECT
CONNECTION
CONSTRAINT
CONSTRAINTS
CONTINUE
CONVERT
CORRESPONDING
COUNT
CREATE
CROSS
CURRENT
CURRENT_DATE
CURRENT_TIME
CURRENT_TIMESTAMP
CURRENT_USER
CURSOR
DATE
DAY
DEALLOCATE
DEC
DECIMAL
DECLARE
DEFAULT
DEFERRABLE
DEFERRED
DELETE
DESC

OCTET_LENGTH
OF
ON
ONLY
OPEN
OPTION
OR
ORDER
OUTER
OUTPUT
OVERLAPS
PAD
PARTIAL
PASCAL
POSITION
PRECISION
PREPARE
PRESERVE
PRIMARY
PRIOR
PRIVILEGES
PROCEDURE
PUBLIC
READ
REAL
REFERENCES
RELATIVE
RESTRICT
REVOKE
RIGHT
ROLLBACK
ROWS
SCHEMA
SCROLL
SECOND
SECTION

DESCRIBE
DESCRIPTOR
DIAGNOSTICS
DISCONNECT
DISTINCT
DOMAIN
DOUBLE
DROP
ELSE
END
END-EXEC
ESCAPE
EXCEPT
EXCEPTION
EXEC
EXECUTE
EXISTS
EXTERNAL
EXTRACT
FALSE
FETCH
FIRST
FLOAT
FOR
FOREIGN
FORTRAN
FOUND
FROM
FULL
GET
GLOBAL
GO
GOTO
GRANT
GROUP
HAVING

SELECT
SESSION
SESSION_USER
SET
SIZE
SMALLINT
SOME
SPACE
SQL
SQLCA
SQLCODE
SQLERROR
SQLSTATE
SQLWARNING
SUBSTRING
SUM
SYSTEM_USER
TABLE
TEMPORARY
THEN
TIME
TIMESTAMP
TIMEZONE_HOUR
TIMEZONE_MINUTE
TO
TRAILING
TRANSACTION
TRANSLATE
TRANSLATION
TRIM
TRUE
UNION
UNIQUE
UNKNOWN
UPDATE
UPPER

HOUR
IDENTITY
IMMEDIATE
IN
INCLUDE
INDEX
INDICATOR
INITIALLY
INNER
INPUT
INSENSITIVE
INSERT
INT
INTEGER
INTERSECT
INTERVAL
INTO
USAGE
USER
USING
VALUE
VALUES
VARCHAR
VARYING
VIEW
WHEN
WHENEVER
WHERE
WITH
WORK
WRITE
YEAR
ZONE

APPENDIX D

Data Types

ODBC defines two sets of data types: SQL data types and C data types. SQL data types indicate the data type of data stored at the data source. C data types indicate the data type of data stored in application buffers.

SQL data types are defined by each DBMS in accordance with the SQL-92 standard. For each SQL data type specified in the SQL-92 standard, ODBC defines a type identifier, which is a **#define** value that is passed as an argument in ODBC functions or returned in the metadata of a result set. The only SQL-92 data types not supported by ODBC are BIT (the ODBC SQL_BIT type has different characteristics), BIT_VARYING, TIME_WITH_TIMEZONE, TIMESTAMP_WITH_TIMEZONE, and NATIONAL_CHARACTER. Drivers are responsible for mapping data source–specific SQL data types to ODBC SQL data type identifiers and driver-specific SQL data type identifiers. The SQL data type is specified in the SQL_DESC_CONCISE_TYPE field of an implementation descriptor.

ODBC defines the C data types and their corresponding ODBC type identifiers. An application specifies the C data type of the buffer that will receive result set data by passing the appropriate C type identifier in the *TargetType* argument in a call to **SQLBindCol** or **SQLGetData**. It specifies the C type of the buffer containing a statement parameter by passing the appropriate C type identifier in the *ValueType* argument in a call to **SQLBindParameter**. The C data type is specified in the SQL_DESC_CONCISE_TYPE field of an application descriptor.

Note There are no driver-specific C data types.

Each SQL data type corresponds to an ODBC C data type. Before returning data from the data source, the driver converts it to the specified C data type. Before sending data to the data source, the driver converts it from the specified C data type.

This appendix discusses the following:

- ODBC SQL data types
- ODBC C data types
- Interval data types
- Numeric literals

- Data type identifiers, including pseudo type identifiers, transferring data in its binary form, and information on descriptors
- Column size, decimal digits, transfer octet length, and display size of SQL data types
- Converting data from SQL to C data types
- Converting data from C to SQL data types

For an explanation of ODBC data types, see "Data Types in ODBC" in Chapter 4, "ODBC Fundamentals." For information about driver-specific SQL data types, see the driver's documentation.

Using Data Type Identifiers

Applications use data type identifiers in two ways: to describe their buffers to the driver, and to retrieve metadata about the result set from the driver so they can determine what type of C buffers to use to store the data. Applications call the following functions to perform these tasks:

- **SQLBindParameter**, **SQLBindCol**, and **SQLGetData** to describe the C data type of application buffers.
- **SQLBindParameter** to describe the SQL data type of dynamic parameters.
- **SQLColAttribute** and **SQLDescribeCol** to retrieve the SQL data types of result set columns.
- **SQLDescribeParameter** to retrieve the SQL data types of parameters.
- **SQLColumns**, **SQLProcedureColumns**, and **SQLSpecialColumns** to retrieve the SQL data types of various schema information
- **SQLGetTypeInfo** to retrieve a list of supported data types.

Data type identifiers are stored in the SQL_DESC_CONCISE_TYPE field of a descriptor. The descriptor functions **SQLSetDescField** and **SQLSetDescRec** can be used with the appropriate types to perform the tasks listed in the previous list. For more information, see **SQLSetDescField**.

SQL Data Types

Each DBMS defines its own SQL types. Each ODBC driver exposes only those SQL data types that the associated DBMS defines. How a driver maps DBMS SQL types to the ODBC-defined SQL type identifiers, and how a driver maps DBMS SQL types to its own driver-specific SQL type identifiers, are returned through a call to **SQLGetTypeInfo**. A driver also returns the SQL data types when describing the data types of columns and parameters through calls to **SQLColAttribute**, **SQLColumns**, **SQLDescribeCol**, **SQLDescribeParam**, **SQLProcedureColumns**, and **SQLSpecialColumns**.

Note The SQL data types are contained in the SQL_DESC_ CONCISE_TYPE, SQL_DESC_TYPE, and SQL_DESC_DATETIME_INTERVAL_CODE fields of the implementation descriptors. Characteristics of the SQL data types are contained in the SQL_DESC_PRECISION, SQL_DESC_SCALE, SQL_DESC_LENGTH, and SQL_DESC_OCTET_LENGTH fields of the implementation descriptors. For more information, see "Data Type Identifiers and Descriptors" later in this appendix.

A given driver and data source do not necessarily support all of the SQL data types defined in this appendix. A driver's support for SQL data types depends upon the level of SQL-92 that the driver conforms to. To determine the level of SQL-92 grammar supported by the driver, an application calls **SQLGetInfo** with the SQL_SQL_CONFORMANCE information type. Furthermore, a given driver and data source may support additional, driver-specific SQL data types. To determine which data types a driver supports, an application calls **SQLGetTypeInfo**. For information about driver-specific SQL data types, see the driver's documentation. For information about the data types in a specific data source, see the documentation for that data source.

Important The tables throughout this appendix are only a guideline and show commonly used names, ranges, and limits of SQL data types. A given data source may support only some of the listed data types and the characteristics of the supported data types may differ from those listed.

The following table lists valid SQL type identifiers for all SQL data types. The table also lists the name and description of the corresponding data type from SQL-92 (if one exists).

SQL type identifier [1]	Typical SQL data type [2]	Typical type description
SQL_CHAR	CHAR(*n*)	Character string of fixed string length *n*.
SQL_VARCHAR	VARCHAR(*n*)	Variable-length character string with a maximum string length *n*.
SQL_LONGVARCHAR	LONG VARCHAR	Variable length character data. Maximum length is data source–dependent. [9]

SQL type identifier [1]	Typical SQL data type [2]	Typical type description
SQL_DECIMAL	DECIMAL(*p*,*s*)	Signed, exact, numeric value with a precision of at least *p* and scale *s. (The maximum precision is driver-defined.)* $(1 \leq p \leq 15; s \leq p)$. [4]
SQL_NUMERIC	NUMERIC(*p*,*s*)	Signed, exact, numeric value with a precision *p* and scale *s* $(1 \leq p \leq 15; s \leq p)$. [4]
SQL_SMALLINT	SMALLINT	Exact numeric value with precision 5 and scale 0 (signed: $-32,768 \leq n \leq 32,767$, unsigned: $0 \leq n \leq 65,535$) [3] .
SQL_INTEGER	INTEGER	Exact numeric value with precision 10 and scale 0 (signed: $-2[31] \leq n \leq 2[31] - 1$, unsigned: $0 \leq n \leq 2[32] - 1$) [3] .
SQL_REAL	REAL	Signed, approximate, numeric value with a binary precision 24 (zero or absolute value 10[–38] to 10[38]).
SQL_FLOAT	FLOAT(*p*)	Signed, approximate, numeric value with a binary precision of at least p. (The maximum precision is driver-defined.) [5]
SQL_DOUBLE	DOUBLE PRECISION	Signed, approximate, numeric value with a binary precision 53 (zero or absolute value 10[–308] to 10[308]).
SQL_BIT	BIT	Single bit binary data. [8]
SQL_TINYINT	TINYINT	Exact numeric value with precision 3 and scale 0 (signed: $-128 \leq n \leq 127$, unsigned: $0 \leq n \leq 255$) [3] .
SQL_BIGINT	BIGINT	Exact numeric value with precision 19 (if signed) or 20 (if unsigned) and scale 0 (signed: $-2[63] \leq n \leq 2[63] - 1$, unsigned: $0 \leq n \leq 2[64] - 1$) [3], [9].
SQL_BINARY	BINARY(*n*)	Binary data of fixed length *n*. [9]
SQL_VARBINARY	VARBINARY(*n*)	Variable length binary data of maximum length *n*. The maximum is set by the user. [9]
SQL_LONGVARBINARY	LONG VARBINARY	Variable length binary data. Maximum length is data source–dependent. [9]

SQL type identifier [1]	Typical SQL data type [2]	Typical type description
SQL_TYPE_DATE [6]	DATE	Year, month, and day fields, conforming to the rules of the Gregorian calendar (see "Constraints of the Gregorian Calendar" later in this appendix).
SQL_TYPE_TIME [6]	TIME(p)	Hour, minute, and second fields, with valid values for hours of 00 to 23, valid values for minutes of 00 to 59, and valid values for seconds of 00 to 61. Precision p indicates the seconds precision.
SQL_TYPE_TIMESTAMP [6]	TIMESTAMP(p)	Year, month, day, hour, minute, and second fields, with valid values as defined for the DATE and TIME data types.
SQL_INTERVAL_MONTH [7]	INTERVAL MONTH(p)	Number of months between two dates; p is the interval leading precision.
SQL_INTERVAL_YEAR [7]	INTERVAL YEAR(p)	Number of years between two dates; p is the interval leading precision.
SQL_INTERVAL_YEAR_TO_MONTH [7]	INTERVAL YEAR(p) TO MONTH	Number of years and months between two dates; p is the interval leading precision.
SQL_INTERVAL_DAY [7]	INTERVAL DAY(p)	Number of days between two dates; p is the interval leading precision.
SQL_INTERVAL_HOUR [7]	INTERVAL HOUR(p)	Number of hours between two date/times; p is the interval leading precision.
SQL_INTERVAL_MINUTE [7]	INTERVAL MINUTE(p)	Number of minutes between two date/times; p is the interval leading precision.
SQL_INTERVAL_SECOND [7]	INTERVAL SECOND(p,q)	Number of seconds between two date/times; p is the interval leading precision and q is the interval seconds precision.
SQL_INTERVAL_DAY_TO_HOUR [7]	INTERVAL DAY(p) TO HOUR	Number of days/hours between two date/times; p is the interval leading precision.
SQL_INTERVAL_DAY_TO_MINUTE [7]	INTERVAL DAY(p) TO MINUTE	Number of days/hours/minutes between two date/times; p is the interval leading precision.
SQL_INTERVAL_DAY_TO_SECOND [7]	INTERVAL DAY(p) TO SECOND(q)	Number of days/hours/minutes/seconds between two date/times; p is the interval leading precision and q is the interval seconds precision.

SQL type identifier [1]	Typical SQL data type [2]	Typical type description
SQL_INTERVAL_HOUR_ TO_MINUTE [7]	INTERVAL HOUR(p) TO MINUTE	Number of hours/minutes between two date/times; p is the interval leading precision.
SQL_INTERVAL_HOUR_ TO_SECOND [7]	INTERVAL HOUR(p) TO SECOND(q)	Number of hours/minutes/seconds between two date/times; p is the interval leading precision and q is the interval seconds precision.
SQL_INTERVAL_	INTERVAL MINUTE(p) TO SECOND(q)	Number of minutes/seconds between two date/times; p is the interval leading precision and q is the interval seconds precision.
MINUTE_TO_SECOND [7]	INTERVAL MINUTE(p) TO SECOND(q)	Number of minutes/seconds between two date/times; p is the interval leading precision and q is the interval seconds precision.

1 This is the value returned in the DATA_TYPE column by a call to **SQLGetTypeInfo**.

2 This is the value returned in the NAME and CREATE PARAMS column by a call to **SQLGetTypeInfo**. The NAME column returns the designation; for example, CHAR, while the CREATE PARAMS column returns a comma-separated list of creation parameters such as precision, scale, and length.

3 An application uses **SQLGetTypeInfo** or **SQLColAttribute** to determine if a particular data type or a particular column in a result set is unsigned.

4 SQL_DECIMAL and SQL_NUMERIC data types differ only in their precision. The precision of a DECIMAL(p,s) is an implementation-defined decimal precision that is no less than p, while the precision of a NUMERIC(p,s) is exactly equal to p.

5 Depending on the implementation, the precision of SQL_FLOAT can be either 24 or 53: if it is 24, the SQL_FLOAT data type is the same as SQL_REAL, if it is 53, the SQL_FLOAT data type is the same as SQL_DOUBLE.

6 In ODBC 3.0, the SQL date, time, and timestamp data types are SQL_TYPE_DATE, SQL_TYPE_TIME, and SQL_TYPE_TIMESTAMP, respectively; in ODBC 2.*x*, the data types are SQL_DATE, SQL_TIME, and SQL_TIMESTAMP.

7 For more information on the interval SQL data types, see the “Interval Data Types” section later in this appendix.

8 The SQL_BIT data type has different characteristics than the BIT type in SQL-92.

9 This data type has no corresponding data type in SQL-92.

Example SQLGetTypeInfo Result Set

An application calls **SQLGetTypeInfo** to determine which data types are supported by a data source and the characteristics of those data types. The following tables show a sample result set returned by **SQLGetTypeInfo** for a data source that supports SQL_CHAR, SQL_LONGVARCHAR, SQL_DECIMAL, SQL_REAL, SQL_DATETIME, SQL_INTERVAL_YEAR, and SQL_INTERVAL_DAY_MONTH.

TYPE_ NAME	DATA_ TYPE	COLUMN_ SIZE	LITERAL_ PREFIX	LITERAL_ SUFFIX	CREATE_ PARAMS	NULL- ABLE
"char"	SQL_CHAR	255	""	""	"length"	SQL_ TRUE
"text"	SQL_LONG VARCHAR	2147483647	""	""	<Null>	SQL_ TRUE
"decimal"	SQL_ DECIMAL	28	<Null>	<Null>	"precision, scale"	SQL_ TRUE
"real"	SQL_ REAL	7	<Null>	<Null>	<Null>	SQL_ TRUE
"datetime"	SQL_TYPE_ TIMESTAMP	23	""	""	<Null>	SQL_ TRUE
"INTER- VAL YEAR() TO YEAR"	SQL_ INTERVAL_ YEAR	9	""	""	"precision"	SQL_ TRUE
"INTER- VAL DAY() TO FRAC- TION(5)"	SQL_ INTERVAL_ DAY_TO_ SECOND	24	""	""	"precision"	SQL_ TRUE

	CASE_ SENSI- TIVE	SEARCH- ABLE	UNSIGNED_ ATTRIBUTE	FIXED_ PREC_ SCALE	AUTO_ UNIQUE_ VALUE	LOCAL_ TYPE_ NAME
SQL_CHAR	SQL_ FALSE	SQL_ SEARCH- ABLE	<Null>	SQL_ FALSE	<Null>	"char"
SQL_LONG VARCHAR	SQL_ FALSE	SQL_ PRED_ CHAR	<Null>	SQL_ FALSE	<Null>	"text"
SQL_ DECIMAL	SQL_ FALSE	SQL_ PRED_ BASIC	SQL_ FALSE	SQL_ FALSE	SQL_ FALSE	"decimal"
SQL_ REAL	SQL_ FALSE	SQL_ PRED_ BASIC	SQL_ FALSE	SQL_ FALSE	SQL_ FALSE	"real"
SQL_TYPE_ TIMESTAMP	SQL_ FALSE	SQL_ SEARCH- ABLE	<Null>	SQL_ FALSE	<Null>	"datetime"
SQL_ INTERVAL_ YEAR	SQL_ FALSE	SQL_ SEARCH- ABLE	<Null>	SQL_ FALSE	<Null>	"INTER- VAL YEAR() TO YEAR"
SQL_ INTERVAL_ DAY_TO_ SECOND	SQL_ FALSE	SQL_ PRED_ BASIC	<Null>	SQL_ FALSE	<Null>	"INTER- VAL DAY() TO FRAC- TION(5)"

	MINIMUM_SCALE	MAXIMUM_SCALE	SQL_DATA_TYPE	SQL_DATETIME_SUB	NUM_PREC_RADIX	INTERVAL_PRECISION
SQL_CHAR	<Null>	<Null>	SQL_CHAR	<Null>	<Null>	<Null>
SQL_LONG VARCHAR	<Null>	<Null>	SQL_LONG-VARCHAR	<Null>	<Null>	<Null>
SQL_DECIMAL	0	28	SQL_DECIMAL	<Null>	10	<Null>
SQL_REAL	<Null>	<Null>	SQL_REAL	<Null>	10	<Null>
SQL_TYPE_TIME-STAMP	3	3	SQL_DATE-TIME	SQL_CODE_TIME-STAMP	<Null>	12
SQL_INTERVAL_YEAR	0	0	SQL_INTERVAL	SQL_CODE_INTERVAL YEAR	<Null>	9
SQL_INTERVAL_DAY_TO_SECOND	5	5	SQL_INTERVAL	SQL_CODE_INTERVAL DAY_TO_SECOND	<Null>	9

C Data Types

ODBC C data types indicate the data type of C buffers used to store data in the application.

All drivers must support all C data types. This is required because all drivers must support all C types to which SQL types that they support can be converted, and all drivers support at least one character SQL type. Because the character SQL type can be converted to and from all C types, all drivers must support all C types.

The C data type is specified in the **SQLBindCol** and **SQLGetData** functions with the *TargetType* argument and in the **SQLBindParameter** function with the *ValueType* argument. It can also be specified by calling **SQLSetDescField** to set the SQL_DESC_CONCISE_TYPE field of an ARD or APD, or by calling **SQLSetDescRec** with the *Type* argument (and the *SubType* argument if needed) and the *DescriptorHandle* argument set to the handle of an ARD or APD.

The following table lists valid type identifiers for the C data types. The table also lists the ODBC C data type that corresponds to each identifier and the definition of this data type.

C type identifier	ODBC C typedef	C type
SQL_C_CHAR	SQLCHAR *	unsigned char *
SQL_C_SSHORT [j]	SQLSMALLINT	short int
SQL_C_USHORT [j]	SQLUSMALLINT	unsigned short int
SQL_C_SLONG [j]	SQLINTEGER	long int
SQL_C_ULONG [j]	SQLUINTEGER	unsigned long int
SQL_C_FLOAT	SQLREAL	float
SQL_C_DOUBLE	SQLDOUBLE, SQLFLOAT	double
SQL_C_BIT	SQLCHAR	unsigned char
SQL_C_STINYINT [j]	SQLSCHAR	signed char
SQL_C_UTINYINT [j]	SQLCHAR	unsigned char
SQL_C_SBIGINT	SQLBIGINT	_int64 [h]
SQL_C_UBIGINT	SQLUBIGINT	unsigned _int64 [h]
SQL_C_BINARY	SQLCHAR *	unsigned char *
SQL_C_BOOKMARK [i]	BOOKMARK	unsigned long int [d]
SQL_C_VAR-BOOKMARK	SQLCHAR *	unsigned char *
SQL_C_TYPE_DATE [c]	SQL_DATE_STRUCT	struct tagDATE_STRUCT { SQLSMALLINT year; SQLUSMALLINT month; SQLUSMALLINT day; } DATE_STRUCT; [a]
SQL_C_TYPE_TIME [c]	SQL_TIME_STRUCT	struct tagTIME_STRUCT { SQLUSMALLINT hour; SQLUSMALLINT minute; SQLUSMALLINT second; } TIME_STRUCT; [a]

C type identifier	ODBC C typedef	C type
SQL_C_TYPE_ TIMESTAMP[c]	SQL_TIMESTAMP_ STRUCT	struct tagTIMESTAMP_STRUCT { SQLSMALLINT year; SQLUSMALLINT month; SQLUSMALLINT day; SQLUSMALLINT hour; SQLUSMALLINT minute; SQLUSMALLINT second; SQLUINTEGER fraction;[b] } TIMESTAMP_STRUCT;[a]
SQL_C_NUMERIC	SQL_NUMERIC_ STRUCT	struct tag SQL_NUMERIC_STRUCT { SQLCHAR precision; SQLSCHAR scale; SQLCHAR sign[g]; SQLCHAR val[SQL_MAX_NUMERIC_LEN]; [e, f] } SQL_NUMERIC_STRUCT;
All C interval data types	SQL_INTERVAL_STRUCT	See the "C Interval Structure" section later in this appendix.

a The values of the year, month, day, hour, minute, and second fields in the datetime C data types must conform to the constraints of the Gregorian calendar (see "Constraints of the Gregorian Calendar" later in this appendix).

b The value of the fraction field is the number of billionths of a second and ranges from 0 to 999,999,999 (1 less than 1 billion). For example, the value of the fraction field for a half-second is 500,000,000, for a thousandth of a second (one millisecond) is 1,000,000, for a millionth of a second (one microsecond) is 1,000, and for a billionth of a second (one nanosecond) is 1.

c In ODBC 2.*x*, the C date, time, and timestamp data types are SQL_C_DATE, SQL_C_TIME, and SQL_C_TIMESTAMP.

d ODBC 3.0 applications should use SQL_C_VARBOOKMARK, not SQL_C_BOOKMARK. When an ODBC 3.0 application works with an ODBC 2.*x* driver, the ODBC 3.0 Driver Manager will map SQL_C_VARBOOKMARK to SQL_C_BOOKMARK.

e A number is stored in the *val* field of the SQL_NUMERIC_STRUCT structure as a scaled integer, in little endian mode (the leftmost byte being the least-significant byte). For example, the number 10.001 base 10, with a scale of 4, is scaled to an integer of 100010. Because this is 186AA in hexadecimal format, the value in SQL_NUMERIC_STRUCT would be "AA 86 01 00 00 … 00", with the number of bytes defined by the SQL_MAX_NUMERIC_LEN **#define**.

f The precision and scale fields of the SQL_C_NUMERIC data type are never used for input from an application, only for output from the driver to the application. When the driver writes a numeric value into the SQL_NUMERIC_STRUCT, it will use its own driver-specific default as the value for the *precision* field, and it will use the value in the SQL_DESC_SCALE field of the application descriptor (which defaults to 0) for the *scale* field. An application can provide its own values for precision and scale by setting the SQL_DESC_PRECISION and SQL_DESC_SCALE fields of the application descriptor.

g The sign field is 1 if positive, 2 if negative.

h _int64 may not be supplied by some compilers.

i _SQL_C_BOOKMARK has been deprecated in ODBC 3.0.

j _SQL_C_SHORT, SQL_C_LONG, and SQL_C_TINYINT have been replaced in ODBC by signed and unsigned types: SQL_C_SSHORT and SQL_C_USHORT, SQL_C_SLONG and SQL_C_ULONG, and SQL_C_STINYINT and SQL_C_UTINYINT. An ODBC 3.0 driver that should work with ODBC 2.*x* applications should support SQL_C_SHORT, SQL_C_LONG, and SQL_C_TINYINT, because when they are called, the Driver Manager passes them through to the driver.

64-Bit Integer Structures

The C type for the SQL_C_SBIGINT and SQL_C_UBIGINT data type identifiers on Microsoft C compilers is _int64. When a compiler other than a Microsoft C compiler is used, the C type might be different. If the compiler supports 64-bit integers natively, the driver or application should define ODBCINT64 to be the native 64-bit integer type. If the compiler does not support 64-bit integers natively, an application or driver can define the following structures to ensure that it has access to this data:

```
typedef struct{
SQLUINTEGER dwLowWord;
SQLUINTEGER dwHighWord;
} SQLUBIGINT
```

```
typedef struct{
SQLUINTEGER dwLowWord;
SQLINTEGER sdwHighWord;
} SQLBIGINT
```

These structures should be aligned to an 8-byte boundary because a 64-bit integer is aligned to the 8-byte boundary.

Data Type Identifiers and Descriptors

64-bit integersThe data types listed in the "SQL Data Types" and "C Data Types" sections earlier in this appendix are "concise" data types: Each identifier refers to a single data type. There is a one-to-one correspondence between the identifier and the data type. Descriptors, however, do not in all cases use a single value to identify data types. In some cases, they use a "verbose" data type, and a type subcode. For all data types except datetime and interval data types, the verbose type identifier is the same as the concise type identifier and the value in SQL_DESC_DATETIME_INTERVAL_CODE is equal to 0. For datetime and interval data types, however, a verbose type (SQL_DATETIME or SQL_INTERVAL) is stored in SQL_DESC_TYPE, a concise type is stored in SQL_DESC_CONCISE_TYPE, and a subcode for each concise type is stored in SQL_DESC_DATETIME_INTERVAL_CODE. Setting one of these fields affects the others. For more information on these fields, see the **SQLSetDescField** function description.

When the SQL_DESC_TYPE or SQL_DESC_CONCISE_TYPE field is set for some data types, the SQL_DESC_DATETIME_INTERVAL_PRECISION, SQL_DESC_LENGTH, SQL_DESC_PRECISION, and SQL_DESC_SCALE fields are automatically set to default values, as applicable for the data type. For more information, see the description of the SQL_DESC_TYPE field in **SQLSetDescField**. If any of the default values set is not appropriate, the application should explicitly set the descriptor field through a call to **SQLSetDescField**.

The following table shows the concise type identifier, verbose type identifier, and type subcode for each datetime and interval SQL and C type identifier. As this table indicates, for datetime and interval data types the SQL_DESC_TYPE and SQL_DESC_DATETIME_INTERVAL_CODE fields have the same manifest constants for both SQL data types (in implementation descriptors) and C data types (in application descriptors).

Concise SQL type	Concise C type	Verbose Type	DATETIME_INTERVAL_CODE
SQL_TYPE_DATE	SQL_C_TYPE_DATE	SQL_DATETIME	SQL_CODE_DATE
SQL_TYPE_TIME	SQL_C_TYPE_TIME	SQL_DATETIME	SQL_CODE_TIME
SQL_TYPE_TIMESTAMP	SQL_C_TYPE_TIMESTAMP	SQL_DATETIME	SQL_CODE_TIMESTAMP
SQL_INTERVAL_MONTH	SQL_C_INTERVAL_MONTH	SQL_INTERVAL	SQL_CODE_MONTH
SQL_INTERVAL_YEAR	SQL_C_INTERVAL_YEAR	SQL_INTERVAL	SQL_CODE_YEAR
SQL_INTERVAL_YEAR_TO_MONTH	SQL_C_INTERVAL_YEAR_TO_MONTH	SQL_INTERVAL	SQL_CODE_YEAR_TO_MONTH
SQL_INTERVAL_DAY	SQL_C_INTERVAL_DAY	SQL_INTERVAL	SQL_CODE_DAY
SQL_INTERVAL_HOUR	SQL_C_INTERVAL_HOUR	SQL_INTERVAL	SQL_CODE_HOUR
SQL_INTERVAL_MINUTE	SQL_C_INTERVAL_MINUTE	SQL_INTERVAL	SQL_CODE_MINUTE
SQL_INTERVAL_SECOND	SQL_C_INTERVAL_SECOND	SQL_INTERVAL	SQL_CODE_SECOND
SQL_INTERVAL_DAY_TO_HOUR	SQL_C_INTERVAL_DAY_TO_HOUR	SQL_INTERVAL	SQL_CODE_DAY_TO_HOUR
SQL_INTERVAL_DAY_TO_MINUTE	SQL_C_INTERVAL_DAY_TO_MINUTE	SQL_INTERVAL	SQL_CODE_DAY_TO_MINUTE
SQL_INTERVAL_DAY_TO_SECOND	SQL_C_INTERVAL_DAY_TO_SECOND	SQL_INTERVAL	SQL_CODE_DAY_TO_SECOND
SQL_INTERVAL_HOUR_TO_MINUTE	SQL_C_INTERVAL_HOUR_TO_MINUTE	SQL_INTERVAL	SQL_CODE_HOUR_TO_MINUTE

Concise SQL type	Concise C type	Verbose Type	DATETIME_INTERVAL_CODE
SQL_INTERVAL_ HOUR_TO_SECOND	SQL_C_INTERVAL_ HOUR_TO_SECOND	SQL_INTERVAL	SQL_CODE_HOUR_TO_ SECOND
SQL_INTERVAL_ MINUTE_TO_SECOND	SQL_C_INTERVAL_ MINUTE_TO_SECOND	SQL_INTERVAL	SQL_CODE_MINUTE_TO_ SECOND

Pseudo Type Identifiers

For application programming convenience, ODBC defined a number of pseudo type identifiers. These identifiers do not actually correspond to actual data types, but instead resolve to existing data types depending on the situation.

Default C Data Types

If an application specifies SQL_C_DEFAULT in **SQLBindCol**, **SQLGetData**, or **SQLBindParameter**, the driver assumes that the C data type of the output or input buffer corresponds to the SQL data type of the column or parameter to which the buffer is bound.

Important Interoperable applications should not use SQL_C_DEFAULT. Instead, they should always specify the C type of the buffer they are using. The reason for this is that drivers cannot always correctly determine the default C type for the following reasons:

- If the DBMS promotes an SQL data type of a column or parameter, the driver cannot determine the original SQL data type of a column or parameter. Therefore, it cannot determine the corresponding default C data type.
- If the driver cannot determine whether a particular column or parameter is signed, as is often the case when this is handled by the DBMS, the driver cannot determine whether the corresponding default C data type should be signed or unsigned.

Because SQL_C_DEFAULT is provided only as a programming convenience, the application does not lose any functionality when it specifies the actual C data type.

A table showing the default C data type for each SQL data type is included in "Converting Data from SQL to C Data Types" later in this appendix.

Bookmark C Data Type

The bookmark C data type allows an application to retrieve a bookmark. The bookmark C types are used only to retrieve bookmark values that can be variable in length; they should not be converted to other data types. An application retrieves a bookmark either from column 0 of the result set with **SQLBulkOperations** (with an operation of SQL_ADD), **SQLFetch**, **SQLFetchScroll**, or **SQLGetData**. For more information, see "Bookmarks" in Chapter 11, "Retrieving Results (Advanced)."

The following table lists the value of *CType* for the bookmark C data type, the ODBC C data type that implements the bookmark C data type, and the definition of this data type from SQL.H.

Note The SQL_C_BOOKMARK data type has been deprecated. ODBC 3.0 applications should not use SQL_C_BOOKMARK. ODBC 3.0 drivers need to support SQL_C_BOOKMARK only if they want to work with ODBC 2.*x* applications that use it. The Driver Manager maps SQL_C_VARBOOKMARK to SQL_C_BOOKMARK when an application works with an ODBC 2.*x* driver.

C type identifier	ODBC C typedef	C type
SQL_C_BOOKMARK (Deprecated)	BOOKMARK	unsigned long int
SQL_C_VARBOOKMARK	SQLCHAR *	unsigned char *

SQL_ARD_TYPE

The SQL_ARD_TYPE type identifier is used to indicate that the data in a buffer will be of the type specified in the SQL_DESC_CONCISE_TYPE field of the ARD. SQL_ARD_TYPE is entered in the *TargetType* argument of a call to **SQLGetData** instead of a specific data type, and enables an application to change the data type of the buffer by changing the descriptor field. This value ties the data type of the **TargetValuePtr* buffer to the descriptor field. (SQL_ARD_TYPE is not entered in a call to **SQLBindCol** or **SQLBindParameter** because the type of the bound buffer is already tied to the SQL_DESC_TYPE and SQL_DESC_CONCISE_TYPE fields, and can be changed at any time by changing either of those fields.)

The SQL_ARD_TYPE type identifier can be used to specify non-default values for leading precision and seconds precision of interval data types, and precision and scale values for the SQL_C_NUMERIC data type. For more information, see "Overriding Default Leading and Seconds Precision for Interval Data Types" and "Overriding Precision and Scale for Numeric Data Types" later in this appendix.

Transferring Data in its Binary Form

An application can safely transfer data in the internal form used by that DBMS between two data sources that use the same DBMS and hardware platform. For a given piece of data, the SQL data types must be the same in the source and target data sources. The C data type is SQL_C_BINARY.

When the application calls **SQLFetch**, **SQLFetchScroll**, or **SQLGetData** to retrieve the data from the source data source, the driver retrieves the data from the data source and transfers it, without conversion, to a storage location of type SQL_C_BINARY. When the application calls **SQLBulkOperations**, **SQLExecute**, **SQLExecDirect**, **SQLPutData**, or **SQLSetPos** to send the data to the target data source, the driver retrieves the data from the storage location and transfers it, without conversion, to the target data source.

Note Applications th0at transfer any data (except binary data) in this manner are not interoperable among DBMSs.

SQLCopyDesc can be used to copy row bindings from the source DBMS to parameter bindings in the target DBMS.

Guidelines for Interval and Numeric Data Types

The following sections address interval and numeric data types.

Interval Data Types

An interval is defined as the difference between two dates and times. Intervals are expressed in one of two different ways. One is a *year-month* interval that expresses intervals in terms of years and an integral number of months. The other is a *day-time* interval that expresses intervals in terms of days, minutes, and seconds. These two types of intervals are distinct and cannot be mixed, because months may have differing numbers of days.

An interval consists of a set of fields. There is an implied ordering among the fields. For example, in a year-to-month interval, the year comes first, followed by the month. Similarly, in a day-to-minute interval, the fields are in the order day, hour, and minute. The first field in an interval type is called the *leading* field, or the *high-order* field. The last field is called the *trailing* field.

In all intervals, the leading field is not constrained by rules of the Gregorian calendar. For example, in an hour-to-minute interval, the hour field is not constrained to be between 0 and 23 (inclusive), as it normally is. The trailing fields subsequent to the leading field follow the usual constraints of the Gregorian calendar. For more information, see "Constraints of the Gregorian Calendar," later in this appendix.

There are 13 interval SQL data types and 13 interval C data types. Each of the interval C data types uses the same structure, SQL_INTERVAL_STRUCT, to contain the interval data. (For more information, see the next section, "C Interval Structure.") For more information on the SQL data types, see "SQL Data Types" earlier in this appendix; for more information on the C data types, see "C Data Types."

Type identifier	Class	Description
MONTH	Year-Month	Number of months between two dates.
YEAR	Year-Month	Number of years between two dates.
YEAR_ TO_MONTH	Year-Month	Number of years and months between two dates.
DAY	Day-Time	Number of days between two dates.
HOUR	Day-Time	Number of hours between two date/times.
MINUTE	Day-Time	Number of minutes between two date/times.
SECOND	Day-Time	Number of seconds between two date/times.
DAY_TO_HOUR	Day-Time	Number of days/hours between two date/times.
DAY_TO_MINUTE	Day-Time	Number of days/hours/minutes between two date/times.
DAY_TO_SECOND	Day-Time	Number of days/hours/minutes/seconds between two date/times.
HOUR_TO_MINUTE	Day-Time	Number of hours/minutes between two date/times.
HOUR_TO_SECOND	Day-Time	Number of hours/minutes/seconds between two date/times.
MINUTE_TO_SECOND	Day-Time	Number of minutes/seconds between two date/times.

C Interval Structure

Each of the C interval data types listed in the "C Data Types" section uses the same structure to contain the interval data. When **SQLFetch**, **SQLFetchScroll**, or **SQLGetData** is called, the driver returns data into the SQL_INTERVAL_STRUCT structure, uses the value that was specified by the application for the C data types (in the call to **SQLBindCol**, **SQLGetData**, or **SQLBindParameter**) to interpret the contents of SQL_INTERVAL_STRUCT, and populates the *interval_type* field of the structure with the *enum* value corresponding to the C type. Note that drivers do not read the *interval_type* field to determine the type of the interval; they retrieve the value of the SQL_DESC_CONCISE_TYPE descriptor field. When the structure is used for parameter data, the driver uses the value specified by the application in the SQL_DESC_CONCISE_TYPE field of the APD to interpret the contents of SQL_INTERVAL_STRUCT even if the application sets the value of the *interval_type* field to a different value.

This structure is defined as follows:

```
typedef struct tagSQL_INTERVAL_STRUCT
{
   SQLINTERVAL interval_type;
   SQLSMALLINT interval_sign;
   union {
         SQL_YEAR_MONTH_STRUCT       year_month;
         SQL_DAY_SECOND_STRUCT              day_second;
         } intval;
} SQL_INTERVAL_STRUCT;
typedef enum
{
   SQL_IS_YEAR = 1,
   SQL_IS_MONTH = 2,
   SQL_IS_DAY = 3,
   SQL_IS_HOUR = 4,
   SQL_IS_MINUTE = 5,
   SQL_IS_SECOND = 6,
   SQL_IS_YEAR_TO_MONTH = 7,
   SQL_IS_DAY_TO_HOUR = 8,
   SQL_IS_DAY_TO_MINUTE = 9,
   SQL_IS_DAY_TO_SECOND = 10,
   SQL_IS_HOUR_TO_MINUTE = 11,
   SQL_IS_HOUR_TO_SECOND = 12,
   SQL_IS_MINUTE_TO_SECOND = 13
} SQLINTERVAL;

typedef struct tagSQL_YEAR_MONTH
{
   SQLUINTEGER year;
   SQLUINTEGER month;
} SQL_YEAR_MONTH_STRUCT;
```

```
typedef struct tagSQL_DAY_SECOND
{
   SQLUINTEGER day;
   SQLUINTEGER hour;
   SQLUINTEGER minute;
   SQLUINTEGER second;
   SQLUINTEGER fraction;
} SQL_DAY_SECOND_STRUCT;
```

The *interval_type* field of the SQL_INTERVAL_STRUCT indicates to the application what structure is held in the union and also what members of the structure are relevant. The *interval_sign* field has the value SQL_FALSE if the interval leading field is unsigned; if it is SQL_TRUE, then the leading field is negative. Note that the value in the leading field itself is always unsigned, regardless of the value of *interval_sign*. The *interval_sign* field acts as a sign bit.

Interval Data Type Precision

Precision for an interval data type includes interval leading precision, interval precision, and seconds precision.

The leading field of an interval is a signed numeric. The maximum number of digits for the leading field is determined by a quantity called *interval leading precision*, which is a part of the data type declaration. For example, the declaration: INTERVAL HOUR(5) TO MINUTE has an interval leading precision of 5; the HOUR field can take values from –99999 to 99999. The interval leading precision is contained in the SQL_DESC_DATETIME_INTERVAL_PRECISION field of the descriptor record.

The list of fields that an interval data type is made up of is called *interval precision*. It is not a numeric value, as the term "precision" might imply. For example, the interval precision of the type INTERVAL DAY TO SECOND is the list DAY, HOUR, MINUTE, SECOND. There is no descriptor field that holds this value; the interval precision can always be determined by the interval data type.

Any interval data type that has a SECOND field has a *seconds precision*. This is the number of decimal digits allowed in the fractional part of the seconds value. This is different than for other data types, where precision indicates the number of digits before the decimal point. The seconds precision of an interval data type is the number of digits after the decimal point. For other data types, this is referred to as scale. Interval seconds precision is contained in the SQL_DESC_PRECISION field of the descriptor. If the precision of the fractional seconds component of the SQL interval value is greater than what can be held in the C interval structure, it is driver-defined whether the fractional seconds value in the SQL interval is rounded or truncated when converted to the C interval structure.

When the SQL_DESC_CONCISE_TYPE field is set to an interval data type, the SQL_DESC_TYPE field is set to SQL_INTERVAL, and the SQL_DESC_DATETIME_INTERVAL_CODE is set to the code for the interval data type. The SQL_DESC_DATETIME_INTERVAL_PRECISION field is automatically set to the default interval leading precision of 2, and the SQL_DESC_PRECISION field is automatically set to the default interval seconds precision of 6. If either of these values is not appropriate, the application should explicitly set the descriptor field through a call to **SQLSetDescField**.

Interval Data Type Length

The following rules are used to determine the length of an interval data type in characters. Length is expressed in number of characters. The number of bytes depends upon the character set. The length includes the following values added together:

- Two characters for every field in the interval that is not the leading field.
- For the leading field, the number of characters that is the express or implicit leading precision. If the leading precision is not specified, the default value is 2.
- One character for the separator between the fields.
- One plus the express or implied seconds precision. If the seconds precision is not specified, the default value is 6.

Specific column length values for each interval data type are contained in "Column Size" later in this appendix.

Interval Literals

ODBC requires that all drivers support conversion of the SQL_CHAR or SQL_VARCHAR data type to all C interval data types. If the underlying data source does not support interval data types, however, the driver needs to know the correct format of the value in the SQL_CHAR field in order to support these conversions. Similarly, ODBC requires that any ODBC C type be convertible to SQL_CHAR or SQL_VARCHAR, so a driver needs to know what format an interval stored in the character field should have. This section describes the syntax of interval literals, which the driver writer needs to use to validate the SQL_CHAR fields during conversion either to or from C interval data types.

Note The complete BNF for interval literals is shown in Appendix C, "SQL Grammar."

To pass interval literals as part of an SQL statement, an escape clause syntax is defined for interval literals. For more information, see "Datetime Interval Literals" in Chapter 8, "SQL Statements."

An interval literal is of the form:

```
INTERVAL [<sign>] 'value' <interval qualifier>
```

where "INTERVAL" indicates that the character literal is an interval. The sign can be either plus or minus; it is outside the interval string and is optional.

The interval qualifier can either be a single datetime field or be composed of two datetime fields, in the form: <leading field> TO <trailing field>.

- When the interval is composed of a single field, the single field can be a non-second field that may be accompanied by an optional leading precision in parentheses. The single datetime field can also be a second field that may be accompanied by the optional leading precision, the optional fractional-seconds precision in parentheses, or both. If both a leading precision and a fractional-seconds precision are present for a seconds field, they are separated by commas. If the seconds field has a fractional-seconds precision, it must also have a leading precision.
- When the interval is composed of leading and trailing fields, the leading field is a non-second field that may be accompanied by the interval leading-field precision in parentheses. The trailing field can be either a non-second field, or a second field that may be accompanied by an interval fractional-seconds precision in parentheses.

The interval string in *value* is enclosed in single quotation marks. It can be either a year-month literal or a day-time literal. The format of the string in *value* is determined by the following rules:

- The string contains a decimal value for every field that is implied by the <interval qualifier>.
- If the interval precision includes the fields YEAR and MONTH, then the values of these fields are separated by a minus sign.
- If the interval precision includes the fields DAY and HOUR, then the values of these fields are separated by a space.
- If the interval precision includes the field HOUR and the lower order fields (MINUTE and SECOND), then the values of these fields are separated by a colon (:).

- If the interval precision includes a SECOND field and the expressed or implied seconds precision is non-zero, then the character immediately before the first digit of the fractional part of the second is a period (.).
- No field can be more than two digits long, except:
  - The value of the leading field can be as long as the expressed or implied interval leading precision.
  - The fractional part of the SECOND field can be as long as the expressed or implied seconds precision.
  - The trailing fields follow the usual constraints of the Gregorian calendar (see "Constraints of the Gregorian Calendar" later in this appendix).

The following table lists examples of valid interval literals as included in the ODBC escape clause for intervals. The syntax of the escape clause is as follows:

{INTERVAL sign interval-string interval-qualifier}

Literal escape clause	Interval specified
{INTERVAL '326' YEAR(4)}	Specifies an interval of 326 years. The interval leading precision is 4.
{INTERVAL '326' MONTH(3)}	Specifies an interval of 326 months. The interval leading precision is 3.
{INTERVAL '3261' DAY(4)}	Specifies an interval of 3261 days. The interval leading precision is 4.
{INTERVAL '163' HOUR(3)}	Specifies an interval of 163 days. The interval leading precision is 3.
{INTERVAL '163' MINUTE(3)}	Specifies an interval of 163 minutes. The interval leading precision is 3.
{INTERVAL '223.16' SECOND(3,2)}	Specifies an interval of 223.16 seconds. The interval leading precision is 3 and the seconds precision is 2.
{INTERVAL '163-11' YEAR(3) TO MONTH}	Specifies an interval of 163 years and 11 months. The interval leading precision is 3.
{INTERVAL '163 12' DAY(3) TO HOUR}	Specifies an interval of 163 days and 12 hours. The interval leading precision is 3.
{INTERVAL '163 12:39' DAY(3) TO MINUTE}	Specifies an interval of 163 days, 12 hours, and 39 minutes. The interval leading precision is 3.

Literal escape clause	Interval specified
{INTERVAL '163 12:39:59.163' DAY(3) TO SECOND(3)}	Specifies an interval of 163 days, 12 hours, 39 minutes, and 59.163 seconds. The interval leading precision is 3, and the seconds precision is 3.
{INTERVAL '163:39' HOUR(3) TO MINUTE}	Specifies an interval of 163 hours and 39 minutes. The interval leading precision is 3.
{INTERVAL '163:39:59.163' HOUR(3) TO SECOND(4)}	Specifies an interval of 163 hours, 39 minutes, and 59.163 seconds. The interval leading precision is 3, and the seconds precision is 4.
{INTERVAL '163:59.163' MINUTE(3) TO SECOND(5)}	Specifies an interval of 163 minutes and 59.163 seconds. The interval leading precision is 3, and the seconds precision is 5.
{INTERVAL -'16 23:39:56.23' DAY TO SECOND}	Specifies an interval of minus 16 days, 23 hours, 39 minutes, and 56.23 seconds. The implied leading precision is 2 and the implied seconds precision is 6.

The following table lists examples of invalid interval literals:

Literal escape clause	Reason why invalid
{INTERVAL '163' HOUR(2)}	The interval leading precision is 2, but the value of the leading field is 163.
{INTERVAL '223.16' SECOND(2,2)} {INTERVAL '223.16' SECOND(3,1)}	In the first example, the leading precision is too small, and in the second example, the seconds precision is too small.
{INTERVAL '223.16' SECOND} {INTERVAL '223' YEAR}	Since the leading precision is unspecified, it defaults to 2, which is too small to hold the specified literal.
{INTERVAL '22.1234567' SECOND}	The seconds precision is unspecified and so defaults to 6. The literal has seven digits after the decimal point.

Literal escape clause	Reason why invalid
{INTERVAL '163-13' YEAR(3) TO MONTH}	The trailing field does not follow the rules of the Gregorian Calendar.
{INTERVAL '163 65' DAY(3) TO HOUR}	
{INTERVAL '163 62:39' DAY(3) TO MINUTE}	
{INTERVAL '163 12:125:59.163' DAY(3) TO SECOND(3)}	
{INTERVAL '163:144' HOUR(3) TO MINUTE}	
{INTERVAL '163:567:234.163' HOUR(3) TO SECOND(4)}	
{INTERVAL '163:591.163' MINUTE(3) TO SECOND(5)}	

Overriding Default Leading and Seconds Precision for Interval Data Types

When the SQL_DESC_TYPE field of an ARD is set to a datetime or interval C type, either by calling **SQLBindCol** or **SQLSetDescField**, the SQL_DESC_PRECISION field (which contains the interval seconds precision) is set to the following defaults:

- 6 for timestamp and all interval data types with a second component.
- 0 for all other data types.

For all interval data types, the SQL_DESC_DATETIME_INTERVAL_PRECISION descriptor field, which contains the interval leading field precision, is set to a default value of 2.

When the SQL_DESC_TYPE field in an APD is set to a datetime or interval C type, either by calling **SQLBindParameter** or **SQLSetDescField**, the SQL_DESC_PRECISION and SQL_DESC_DATETIME_INTERVAL_PRECISION fields in the APD are set to the default given previously. This is true for input parameters, but not for input/output or output parameters.

A call to **SQLSetDescRec** sets the interval leading precision to the default, but sets the interval seconds precision (in the SQL_DESC_PRECISION field) to the value of its *Precision* argument.

If either of the defaults given previously is not acceptable to an application, the application should set the SQL_DESC_PRECISION or SQL_DESC_DATETIME_INTERVAL_PRECISION field by calling **SQLSetDescField**.

If the application calls **SQLGetData** to return data into a datetime or interval C type, the default interval leading precision and interval seconds precision are used. If either default is not acceptable, the application must call **SQLSetDescField** to set either descriptor field, or **SQLSetDescRec** to set SQL_DESC_PRECISION. The call to **SQLGetData** should have a *TargetType* of SQL_ARD_TYPE to use the values in the descriptor fields.

When **SQLPutData** is called, the interval leading precision and interval seconds precision are read from the fields of the descriptor record that correspond to the data-at-execution parameter or column, which are APD fields for calls to **SQLExecute** or **SQLExecDirect**, or ARD fields for calls to **SQLBulkOperations** or **SQLSetPos**.

Numeric Literals

Numeric literals are used when numeric data values are stored in character strings. For conversion of numeric SQL data to a SQL_C_CHAR string, or conversion of numeric C data to a SQL_CHAR or SQL_VARCHAR string, numeric literal syntax is used to specify what is stored in the target. For conversion of a numeric stored as a SQL_C_CHAR string to numeric SQL data, or a numeric stored as a SQL_CHAR string to numeric C data, this syntax is used to validate what is stored in the source.

Numeric literals should conform to the syntax defined in Appendix C, "SQL Grammar."

Rules for Conversions

The rules in this section apply for conversions involving numeric literals. For the purposes of these rules, the following terms are defined:

- Store assignment: When you are sending data into a table column in a database. This occurs during calls to **SQLExecute**, **SQLExecDirect**, and **SQLSetPos**. During store assignment, "target" refers to a database column, and "source" refers to data in application buffers.
- Retrieval assignment: When you are retrieving data from the database into application buffers. This occurs during calls to **SQLFetch**, **SQLGetData**, **SQLFetchScroll**, and **SQLSetPos**. During retrieval assignment, "target" refers to the application buffers, and "source" refers to the database column.
- CS: The value in the character source.
- NT: The value in the numeric target.
- NS: The value in the numeric source.
- CT: The value in the character target.

- Precision of an exact numeric literal: the number of digits it contains.
- The scale of an exact numeric literal: the number of digits to the right of the expressed or implied period.
- The precision of an approximate numeric literal: the precision of its mantissa.

Character Source to Numeric Target

The rules for converting from a character source (CS) to a numeric target (NT) are:

1. Replace CS with the value obtained by removing any leading or trailing spaces in CS. If CS is not a valid *numeric-literal*, SQLSTATE 22018 (Invalid character value for cast specification) is returned.
2. Replace CS with the value obtained by removing leading zeroes before the decimal point, trailing zeroes after the decimal point, or both.
3. Convert CS to NT. If the conversion results in a loss of significant digits, then SQLSTATE 22003 (Numeric value out of range) is returned. If the conversion results in the loss of non-significant digits, then SQLSTATE 01S07 (Fractional truncation) is returned.

Numeric Source to Character Target

The rules for converting from a numeric source (NS) to a character target (CT) are:

1. Let LT be the length in characters of CT. For retrieval assignment, LT is equal to the length of the buffer in characters minus the number of bytes in the null-termination character for this character set.
2. Cases:

- If NS is an exact numeric type, then let YP equal the shortest character string that conforms to the definition of *exact-numeric-literal* such that the scale of YP is the same as the scale of NS, and the interpreted value of YP is the absolute value of NS.
- If NS is an approximate numeric type, then let YP be a character string as follows:
- Case:
  - If NS is equal to 0, then YP is 0.
  - Let YSN be the shortest character string that conforms to the definition of exact-*numeric-literal* and whose interpreted value is the absolute value of NS. If the length of YSN is less than the (*precision* + 1) of the data type of NS, then let YP equal YSN.
  - Otherwise, YP is the shortest character string that conforms to the definition of *approximate-numeric-literal* whose interpreted value is the absolute value of NS and whose *mantissa* consists of a single *digit* that is not '0', followed by a *period* and an *unsigned-integer*.

3. Case:

- If NS is less than 0, then let Y be the result of:
- '-' || YP
- where '||' is the string concatenation operator.
- Otherwise, let Y equal YP.

4. Let LY be the length in characters of Y.
5. Case:

- If LY equals LT, then CT is set to Y.
- If LY is less than LT, then CT is set to Y extended on the right by appropriate number of spaces.
- Otherwise (LY > LT), copy the first LT characters of Y into CT. Case:
  - If this is a store assignment, return the error SQLSTATE 22001 (String data, right truncated).
  - If this is retrieval assignment, return the warning SQLSTATE 01004 (String data, right truncated). When the copy results in the loss of fractional digits (other than trailing zeros), then it is driver-defined whether one of the following occurs:

    (1) The driver truncates the string in Y to an appropriate scale (which can be zero also) and writes the result into CT.
    (2) The driver rounds the string in Y to an appropriate scale (which can be zero also) and writes the result into CT.
    (3) The driver neither truncates nor rounds, but just copies the first LT characters of Y into CT.

Overriding Default Precision and Scale for Numeric Data Types

When the SQL_DESC_TYPE field in an ARD is set to SQL_C_NUMERIC, either by calling **SQLBindCol** or **SQLSetDescField**, the SQL_DESC_SCALE field in the ARD is set to 0, and the SQL_DESC_PRECISION field is set to a driver-defined default precision. This is also true when the SQL_DESC_TYPE field in an APD is set to SQL_C_NUMERIC, either by calling **SQLBindParameter** or **SQLSetDescField**. This is true for input, input/output, or output parameters.

If either of the defaults described previously are not acceptable for an application, the application should set the SQL_DESC_SCALE or SQL_DESC_PRECISION field by calling **SQLSetDescField** or **SQLSetDescRec**.

If the application calls **SQLGetData** to return data into an SQL_C_NUMERIC structure, the default SQL_DESC_SCALE and SQL_DESC_PRECISION fields are used. If the defaults are not acceptable, the application must call **SQLSetDescRec** or **SQLSetDescField** to set the fields, and then call **SQLGetData** with a *TargetType* of SQL_ARD_TYPE to use the values in the descriptor fields.

When **SQLPutData** is called, the call uses the SQL_DESC_SCALE and SQL_DESC_PRECISION fields of the descriptor record that corresponds to the data-at-execution parameter or column, which are APD fields for calls to **SQLExecute** or **SQLExecDirect**, or ARD fields for calls to **SQLBulkOperations** or **SQLSetPos**.

Constraints of the Gregorian Calendar

Date and datetime data types, and the trailing fields of interval data types, must conform to the constraints of the Gregorian calendar. These constraints are as follows:

- The value of the month field must be between 1 and 11, inclusive.
- The value of the day field must be in the range from 1 to the number of days in the month. The number of days in the month is determined from the values of the year and months fields, and is 28, 29, 30, or 31. The number of days in the month can also depend upon whether it is a leap year.
- The value of the hour field must be between 0 and 23, inclusive.
- The value of the minute field must be between 0 and 59, inclusive.
- For the trailing seconds field of interval data types, the value of the seconds field must be between 0 and 59.9(*n*), inclusive, where *n* is the number of digits in the fractional seconds precision.
- For the trailing seconds field of datetime data types, the value of the seconds field must be between 0 and 61.9(*n*), inclusive, where *n* specifies the number of "9" digits and the value of *n* is the fractional seconds precision. (The range of seconds allows as many as two leap seconds to maintain synchronization of sidereal time.)

Column Size, Decimal Digits, Transfer Octet Length, and Display Size

Data types are characterized by their column (or parameter) size, decimal digits, length, and display size. The following ODBC functions return these attributes for a parameter in an SQL statement or an SQL data type on a data source. Each ODBC function returns a different set of these attributes, as follows:

- **SQLDescribeCol** returns the column size and decimal digits of the columns it describes.
- **SQLDescribeParam** returns the parameter size and decimal digits of the parameters it describes. Note that **SQLBindParameter** sets the parameter size and decimal digits for a parameter in an SQL statement.
- The catalog functions **SQLColumns**, **SQLProcedureColumns**, and **SQLGetTypeInfo** return attributes for a column in a table, result set, or a procedure parameter and the catalog attributes of the data types in the data source. **SQLColumns** returns the column size, decimal digits, and length of a column in specified tables (such as the base table, view, or a system table). **SQLProcedureColumns** returns the column size, decimal digits, and length of a column in a procedure. **SQLGetTypeInfo** returns the maximum column size and the minimum and maximum decimal digits of an SQL data type on a data source.

The values returned by these functions for the column or parameter size correspond to "precision" as defined in ODBC 2.*x*. However, the values do not necessarily correspond to the values returned in SQL_DESC_PRECISION, or any other one descriptor field. The same is true for decimal digits, which correspond to "scale" as defined in ODBC 2.*x*. It does not necessarily correspond to the values returned in SQL_DESC_SCALE, or any other one descriptor field, but comes from different descriptor fields depending on the data type. For further information, see the "Column Size" and "Decimal Digits" sections later in this appendix.

Similarly, the values for transfer octet length do not come from SQL_DESC_LENGTH. They come from the SQL_DESC_OCTET_LENGTH of a field of a descriptor for all character and binary types. There is no descriptor field that holds this information for other types.

The display size value for all data types corresponds to the value in a single descriptor field, SQL_DESC_DISPLAY_SIZE.

Descriptor fields describe the characteristics of a result set. Descriptor fields do not contain valid values about data before statement execution. The values for column size, decimal digits, and display size returned by **SQLColumns**, **SQLProcedureColumns**, and **SQLGetTypeInfo**, on the other hand, return characteristics of database objects, such as table columns and data types, that exist in the data source's catalog. Likewise, in its result set **SQLColAttribute** returns the column size, decimal digits, and transfer octet length of columns at the data source; these values are not necessarily the same as the values in the SQL_DESC_PRECISION, SQL_DESC_SCALE, and SQL_DESC_OCTET_LENGTH descriptor fields.

For more information about these descriptor fields, see **SQLSetDescField**.

Column Size

The column (or parameter) size of numeric data types is defined as the maximum number of digits used by the data type of the column or parameter, or the precision of the data. For character types, this is the length in characters of the data; for binary data types, column size is defined as the length in bytes of the data. For the time, timestamp, and all interval data types, this is the number of characters in the character representation of this data. The column size defined for each concise SQL data type is shown in the following table.

SQL type identifier	Column size
All character types [a], [b]	The defined or maximum column size in characters of the column or parameter (as contained in the SQL_DESC_LENGTH descriptor field). For example, the column size of a single-byte character column defined as CHAR(10) is 10.
SQL_DECIMAL SQL_NUMERIC	The defined number of digits. For example, the precision of a column defined as NUMERIC(10,3) is 10.
SQL_BIT [c]	1
SQL_TINYINT [c]	3
SQL_SMALLINT [c]	5
SQL_INTEGER [c]	10
SQL_BIGINT [c]	19 (if signed) or 20 (if unsigned)
SQL_REAL [c]	7
SQL_FLOAT [c]	15
SQL_DOUBLE [c]	15

SQL type identifier	Column size
All binary types [a, b]	The defined or maximum length in bytes of the column or parameter. For example, the length of a column defined as BINARY(10) is 10.
SQL_TYPE_DATE [c]	10 (the number of characters in the yyyy-mm-dd format).
SQL_TYPE_TIME [c]	8 (the number of characters in the hh-mm-ss format), or 9 + s (the number of characters in the hh:mm:ss[.fff…] format, where s is the seconds precision).
SQL_TYPE_TIMESTAMP	19 (the number of characters in the yyyy-mm-dd hh:mm:ss format) or 20 + s (the number of characters in the yyyy-mm-dd hh:mm:ss[.fff…] format, where s is the seconds precision).
SQL_INTERVAL_SECOND	Where p is the interval leading precision and s is the seconds precision, p (if s=0) or p+s+1 (if s>0). [d]
SQL_INTERVAL_DAY_ TO_SECOND	Where p is the interval leading precision and s is the seconds precision, 9+p (if s=0) or 10+p+s (if s>0). [d]
SQL_INTERVAL_HOUR_TO_ SECOND	Where p is the interval leading precision and s is the seconds precision, 6+p (if s=0) or 7+p+s (if s>0). [d]
SQL_INTERVAL_ MINUTE_TO_ SECOND	Where p is the interval leading precision and s is the seconds precision, 3+p (if s=0) or 4+p+s (if s>0). [d]
SQL_INTERVAL_YEAR SQL_INTERVAL_MONTH SQL_INTERVAL_DAY SQL_INTERVAL_HOUR SQL_INTERVAL_MINUTE	p, where p is the interval leading precision. [d]

SQL type identifier	Column size
SQL_INTERVAL_ YEAR_TO_MONTH SQL_INTERVAL_DAY_ TO_HOUR	3+p, where p is the interval leading precision. [d]
SQL_INTERVAL_ DAY_TO_MINUTE	6+p, where p is the interval leading precision. [d]
SQL_INTERVAL_HOUR_TO_ MINUTE	3+p, where p is the interval leading precision. [d]

[a] For an ODBC 1.0 application calling **SQLSetParam** in an ODBC 2.0 driver, and for an ODBC 2.0 application calling **SQLBindParameter** in an ODBC 1.0 driver, when **StrLen_or_IndPtr* is SQL_DATA_AT_EXEC for a SQL_LONGVARCHAR or SQL_LONGVARBINARY type, *ColumnSize* must be set to the total length of the data to be sent, not the precision as defined in this table.

[b] If the driver cannot determine the column or parameter length for a variable type, it returns SQL_NO_TOTAL.

[c] The *ColumnSize* argument of **SQLBindParameter** is ignored for this data type.

[d] For general rules about column length in interval data types, see "Interval Data Type Length" earlier in this appendix.

The values returned for the column (or parameter) size do not correspond to the values in any one descriptor field. The values can come from either the SQL_DESC_PRECISION or SQL_DESC_LENGTH field, depending on the type of data, as shown in the following table.

SQL type	Descriptor field corresponding to column or parameter size
All character and binary types	LENGTH
All numeric types	PRECISION
All datetime and interval types	LENGTH
SQL_BIT	LENGTH

Decimal Digits

The decimal digits of decimal and numeric data types is defined as the maximum number of digits to the right of the decimal point, or the scale of the data. For approximate floating point number columns or parameters, the scale is undefined, since the number of digits to the right of the decimal point is not fixed. For datetime or interval data that contains a seconds component, the decimal digits is defined as the number of digits to the right of the decimal point in the seconds component of the data.

For the SQL_DECIMAL and SQL_NUMERIC data types, the maximum scale is generally the same as the maximum precision. However, some data sources impose a separate limit on the maximum scale. To determine the minimum and maximum scales allowed for a data type, an application calls **SQLGetTypeInfo**.

The decimal digits defined for each concise SQL data type is shown in the following table.

SQL type	Decimal digits
All character and binary types [a]	n/a
SQL_DECIMAL SQL_NUMERIC	The defined number of digits to the right of the decimal point. For example, the scale of a column defined as NUMERIC(10,3) is 3. This can be a negative number to support storage of very large numbers without using exponential notation; for example, "12000" could be stored as "12" with a scale of –3.
All exact numeric types other than SQL_DECIMAL and SQL_NUMERIC [a]	0
All approximate data types [a]	n/a
SQL_TYPE_DATE, and all interval types with no seconds component [a]	n/a
All datetime types except SQL_TYPE_DATE, and all interval types with a seconds component	The number of digits to the right of the decimal point in the seconds part of the value (fractional seconds). This number cannot be negative.

[a] The *DecimalDigits* argument of **SQLBindParameter** is ignored for this data type.

The values returned for the decimal digits do not correspond to the values in any one descriptor field. The values can come from either the SQL_DESC_SCALE or SQL_DESC_PRECISION field, depending on the data type, as shown in the following table.

SQL type	Descriptor field corresponding to decimal digits
All character and binary types	n/a
All exact numeric types	SCALE
SQL_BIT	n/a
All approximate numeric types	n/a

SQL type	Descriptor field corresponding to decimal digits
All datetime types	PRECISION
All interval types with a seconds component	PRECISION
All interval types with no seconds component	n/a

Transfer Octet Length

The transfer octet length of a column is the maximum number of bytes returned to the application when data is transferred to its default C data type. For character data, the transfer octet length does not include space for the null-termination character. Note that the transfer octet length of a column may be different than the number of bytes required to store the data on the data source.

The transfer octet length defined for each ODBC SQL data type is shown in the following table.

SQL type identifier	Length
All character types [a]	The number of bytes required to hold the defined or maximum (for variable types) number of characters. This is the same value as the descriptor field SQL_DESC_OCTET_LENGTH.
SQL_DECIMAL SQL_NUMERIC	The number of bytes required to hold the character representation of this data. This is the maximum number of digits plus two, since the data is returned as a character string, and characters are needed for the digits, a sign, and a decimal point. For example, the transfer length of a column defined as NUMERIC(10,3) is 12.
SQL_TINYINT	1
SQL_SMALLINT	2
SQL_INTEGER	4
SQL_BIGINT	The number of bytes required to hold the character representation of this data, since this data type is returned as a character string by default. The character representation consists of 20 characters: 19 for digits and a sign, if signed, or 20 digits, if unsigned. Thus, the length is 20.
SQL_REAL	4
SQL_FLOAT	8

SQL type identifier	Length
SQL_DOUBLE	8
SQL_BIT	1
All binary types [a]	The number of bytes required to hold the defined (for fixed types) or maximum (for variable types) number of characters.
SQL_TYPE_DATE SQL_TYPE_TIME	6 (the size of the SQL_DATE_STRUCT or SQL_TIME_STRUCT structure).
SQL_TYPE_TIMESTAMP	16 (the size of the SQL_TIMESTAMP_STRUCT structure).
All interval data types	34 (the size of the interval structure).

[a] If the driver cannot determine the column or parameter length for variable types, it returns SQL_NO_TOTAL.

Display Size

The display size of a column is the maximum number of characters needed to display data in character form. The following table defines the display size for each ODBC SQL data type.

SQL type identifier	Display size
All character types [a]	The defined (for fixed types) or maximum (for variable types) number of characters needed to display the data in character form.
SQL_DECIMAL SQL_NUMERIC	The precision of the column plus 2 (a sign, *precision* digits, and a decimal point). For example, the display size of a column defined as NUMERIC(10,3) is 12.
SQL_BIT	1 (1 digit).
SQL_TINYINT	4 if signed (a sign and 3 digits) or 3 if unsigned (3 digits).
SQL_SMALLINT	6 if signed (a sign and 5 digits) or 5 if unsigned (5 digits).
SQL_INTEGER	11 if signed (a sign and 10 digits) or 10 if unsigned (10 digits).
SQL_BIGINT	20 (a sign and 19 digits if signed or 20 digits if unsigned).
SQL_REAL	13 (a sign, 7 digits, a decimal point, the letter E, a sign, and 2 digits).
SQL_FLOAT SQL_DOUBLE	22 (a sign, 15 digits, a decimal point, the letter E, a sign, and 3 digits).

SQL type identifier	Display size
All binary types [a]	The defined or maximum (for variable types) length of the column times 2 (each binary byte is represented by a 2-digit hexadecimal number).
SQL_TYPE_DATE	10 (a date in the format yyyy-mm-dd).
SQL_TYPE_TIME	8 (a time in the format hh:mm:ss) or 9 + s (a time in the format hh:mm:ss[.fff…], where s is the fractional seconds precision).
SQL_TYPE_TIMESTAMP	19 (for a timestamp in the yyyy-mm-dd hh:mm:ss format) or 20 + s (for a timestamp in the yyyy-mm-dd hh:mm:ss[.fff…] format, where s is the fractional seconds precision).
All interval data types	See the "Interval Data Type Length" section earlier in this appendix.

a If the driver cannot determine the column or parameter length of variable types, it returns SQL_NO_TOTAL.

Converting Data from SQL to C Data Types

When an application calls **SQLFetch**, **SQLFetchScroll**, or **SQLGetData**, the driver retrieves the data from the data source. If necessary, it converts the data from the data type in which the driver retrieved it to the data type specified by the *TargetType* argument in **SQLBindCol** or **SQLGetData**. Finally, it stores the data in the location pointed to by the *TargetValuePtr* argument in **SQLBindCol** or **SQLGetData** (and the SQL_DESC_DATA_PTR field of the ARD).

The following table shows the supported conversions from ODBC SQL data types to ODBC C data types. A filled circle indicates the default conversion for an SQL data type (the C data type to which the data will be converted when the value of *TargetType* is SQL_C_DEFAULT). A hollow circle indicates a supported conversion.

For an ODBC 3.0 application working with an ODBC 2.*x* driver, conversion from driver-specific data types may not be supported.

The format of the converted data is not affected by the Windows country setting.

SQL Data Type \ C Data Type	SQL_C_CHAR	SQL_C_BIT	SQL_C_NUMERIC	SQL_C_STINYINT	SQL_C_UTINYINT	SQL_C_TINYINT	SQL_C_SBIGINT	SQL_C_UBIGINT	SQL_C_SSHORT	SQL_C_USHORT	SQL_C_SHORT	SQL_C_SLONG	SQL_C_ULONG	SQL_C_LONG	SQL_C_FLOAT	SQL_C_DOUBLE	SQL_C_BINARY	SQL_C_TYPE_DATE	SQL_C_TYPE_TIME	SQL_C_TYPE_TIMESTAMP	INTERVAL C (DAY-TIME)	INTERVAL C (YEAR-MONTH)
SQL_CHAR	●	○	○	○	○	○	○	○	○	○	○	○	○	○	○	○	○	○	○	○	○	○
SQL_VARCHAR	●	○	○	○	○	○	○	○	○	○	○	○	○	○	○	○	○	○	○	○	○	○
SQL_LONGVARCHAR	●	○	○	○	○	○	○	○	○	○	○	○	○	○	○	○	○	○	○	○	○	○
SQL_DECIMAL	●	○	○	○	○	○	○	○	○	○	○	○	○	○	○	○	○				◉	◉
SQL_NUMERIC	●	○	○	○	○	○	○	○	○	○	○	○	○	○	○	○	○				◉	◉
SQL_BIT	○	●	○	○	○	○	○	○	○	○	○	○	○	○	○	○	○					
SQL_TINYINT (signed)	○	○	○	●	○	○	○	○	○	○	○	○	○	○	○	○	○				◉	◉
SQL_TINYINT (unsigned)	○	○	○	○	●	○	○	○	○	○	○	○	○	○	○	○	○				◉	◉
SQL_SMALLINT (signed)	○	○	○	○	○	○	○	○	●	○	○	○	○	○	○	○	○				◉	◉
SQL_SMALLINT (unsigned)	○	○	○	○	○	○	○	○	○	●	○	○	○	○	○	○	○				◉	◉
SQL_INTEGER (signed)	○	○	○	○	○	○	○	○	○	○	○	●	○	○	○	○	○				◉	◉
SQL_INTEGER (unsigned)	○	○	○	○	○	○	○	○	○	○	○	○	●	○	○	○	○				◉	◉
SQL_BIGINT(signed & unsigned)	●	○	○	○	○	○	○	○	○	○	○	○	○	○	○	○	○				◉	◉
SQL_REAL	○	○	○	○	○	○	○	○	○	○	○	○	○	○	●	○	○					
SQL_FLOAT	○	○	○	○	○	○	○	○	○	○	○	○	○	○	○	●	○					
SQL_DOUBLE	○	○	○	○	○	○	○	○	○	○	○	○	○	○	○	●	○					
SQL_BINARY	○																●					
SQL_VARBINARY	○																●					
SQL_LONGVARBINARY	○																●					
SQL_TYPE_DATE	○																○	●		○		
SQL_TYPE_TIME	○																○		●	○		
SQL_TYPE_TIMESTAMP	○																○	○	○	●		
INTERVAL SQL (DAY-TIME)	○	◉	◉	◉	◉	◉	◉	◉	◉	◉	◉	◉	◉	◉			○				●	
INTERVAL SQL (YEAR-MONTH)	○	◉	◉	◉	◉	◉	◉	◉	◉	◉	◉	◉	◉	◉			○					●

● Default Conversion

○ Supported Conversion

◉ Valid only for interval types with just a single field

The tables in the following sections describe how the driver or data source converts data retrieved from the data source; drivers are required to support conversions to all ODBC C data types from the ODBC SQL data types that they support. For a given ODBC SQL data type, the first column of the table lists the legal input values of the *TargetType* argument in **SQLBindCol** and **SQLGetData**. The second column lists the outcomes of a test, often using the *BufferLength* argument specified in **SQLBindCol** or **SQLGetData**, which the driver performs to determine if it can convert the data.

For each outcome, the third and fourth columns list the values placed in the buffers specified by the *TargetValuePtr* and *StrLen_or_IndPtr* arguments specified in **SQLBindCol** or **SQLGetData** after the driver has attempted to convert the data. (The *StrLen_or_IndPtr* argument corresponds to the SQL_DESC_OCTET_LENGTH_PTR field of the ARD.) The last column lists the SQLSTATE returned for each outcome by **SQLFetch**, **SQLFetchScroll**, or **SQLGetData**.

If the *TargetType* argument in **SQLBindCol** or **SQLGetData** contains an identifier for an ODBC C data type not shown in the table for a given ODBC SQL data type, **SQLFetch**, **SQLFetchScroll**, or **SQLGetData** returns SQLSTATE 07006 (Restricted data type attribute violation). If the *TargetType* argument contains an identifier that specifies a conversion from a driver-specific SQL data type to an ODBC C data type and this conversion is not supported by the driver, **SQLFetch**, **SQLFetchScroll**, or **SQLGetData** returns SQLSTATE HYC00 (Optional feature not implemented).

Though it is not shown in the tables, the driver returns SQL_NULL_DATA in the buffer specified by the *StrLen_or_IndPtr* argument when the SQL data value is NULL. For an explanation of the use of *StrLen_or_IndPtr* when multiple calls are made to retrieve data, see the **SQLGetData** function description. When SQL data is converted to character C data, the character count returned in **StrLen_or_IndPtr* does not include the null-termination byte. If *TargetValuePtr* is a null pointer, **SQLGetData** returns SQLSTATE HY009 (Invalid use of null pointer); in **SQLBindCol**, this unbinds the column.

The following terms and conventions are used in the tables:

- **Byte length of data** is the number of bytes of C data available to return in **TargetValuePtr*, regardless of whether the data will be truncated before it is returned to the application. For string data, this does not include the space for the null-termination character.
- **Character byte length** is the total number of bytes needed to display the data in character format. This is as defined for each C data type in the section "Display Size" earlier in this appendix, except character byte length is in bytes, while the display size is in characters.
- Words in *italics* represent function arguments or elements of the SQL grammar. For the syntax of grammar elements, see Appendix C, "SQL Grammar."

SQL to C: Character

The identifiers for the character ODBC SQL data types are:

SQL_CHAR
SQL_VARCHAR
SQL_LONGVARCHAR

The following table shows the ODBC C data types to which character SQL data may be converted. For an explanation of the columns and terms in the table, see "Converting Data from SQL to C Data Types" earlier in this appendix.

C type identifier	Test	**TargetValuePtr*	**StrLen_or_IndPtr*	SQL-STATE
SQL_C_CHAR	Byte length of data < *BufferLength.*	Data	Length of data in bytes	n/a
	Byte length of data ≥ *BufferLength.*	Truncated data	Length of data in bytes	01004
SQL_C_STINYINT SQL_C_UTINYINT SQL_C_TINYINT SQL_C_SBIGINT SQL_C_UBIGINT SQL_C_SSHORT SQL_C_USHORT SQL_C_SHORT SQL_C_SLONG SQL_C_ULONG SQL_C_LONG SQL_C_NUMERIC	Data converted without truncation. [b]	Data	Number of bytes of the C data type	n/a
	Data converted with truncation of fractional digits. [a]	Truncated data	Number of bytes of the C data type	01S07
	Conversion of data would result in loss of whole (as opposed to fractional) digits. [a]	Undefined	Undefined	22003
	Data is not a *numeric-literal.* [b]	Undefined	Undefined	22018
SQL_C_FLOAT SQL_C_DOUBLE	Data is within the range of the data type to which the number is being converted. [a]	Data	Size of the C data type	n/a
	Data is outside the range of the data type to which the number is being converted. [a]	Undefined	Undefined	22003
	Data is not a *numeric-literal.* [b]	Undefined	Undefined	22018

C type identifier	Test	*TargetValuePtr	*StrLen_or _IndPtr	SQL-STATE
SQL_C_BIT	Data is 0 or 1.	Data	1 [b]	n/a
	Data is greater than 0, less than 2, and not equal to 1.	Truncated data	1 [b]	01S07
	Data is less than 0 or greater than or equal to 2.	Undefined	Undefined	22003
	Data is not a *numeric-literal.*	Undefined	Undefined	22018
SQL_C_BINARY	Byte length of data ≤ *BufferLength.*	Data	Length of data in bytes	n/a
	Byte length of data > *BufferLength.*	Truncated data	Length of data	01004
SQL_C_TYPE_DATE	Data value is a valid *date-value.* [a]	Data	6 [b]	n/a
	Data value is a valid *timestamp-value*; time portion is zero. [a]	Data	6 [b]	n/a
	Data value is a valid *timestamp-value*; time portion is non-zero. [a, c]	Truncated data	6 [b]	01S07
	Data value is not a valid *date-value* or *timestamp-value.* [a]	Undefined	Undefined	22018
SQL_C_TYPE_TIME	Data value is a valid *time-value* and the fractional seconds value is 0. [a]	Data	6 [b]	n/a
	Data value is a valid *timestamp-value* or a valid *time-value*; fractional seconds portion is zero. [a, d]	Data	6 [b]	n/a
	Data value is a valid *timestamp-value*; fractional seconds portion is non-zero. [a, d, e]	Truncated data	6 [b]	01S07
	Data value is not a valid *time-value* or *timestamp-value.* [a]	Undefined	Undefined	22018

C type identifier	Test	*TargetValuePtr*	*StrLen_or_IndPtr*	SQL-STATE
SQL_C_TYPE_TIMESTAMP	Data value is a valid *timestamp-value or a valid time-value*; fractional seconds portion not truncated. [a]	Data	16 [b]	n/a
	Data value is a valid *timestamp-value or a valid time-value*; fractional seconds portion truncated. [a]	Truncated data	16 [b]	01S07
	Data value is a valid *date-value.* [a]	Data [f]	16 [b]	n/a
	Data value is a valid *time-value.* [a]	Data [g]	16 [b]	n/a
	Data value is not a valid *date-value*, *time-value*, or *timestamp-value.* [a]	Undefined	Undefined	22018
All C interval types	Data value is a valid *interval value*; no truncation.	Data	Length of data in bytes	n/a
	Data value is a valid *interval value*; truncation of one or more trailing fields.	Truncated data	Length of data in bytes	01S07
	Data is valid interval; leading field significant precision is lost.	Undefined	Undefined	22015
	The data value is not a valid interval value.	Undefined	Undefined	22018

a The value of *BufferLength* is ignored for this conversion. The driver assumes that the size of **TargetValuePtr* is the size of the C data type.

b This is the size of the corresponding C data type.

c The time portion of the *timestamp-value* is truncated.

d The date portion of the *timestamp-value* is ignored.

e The fractional seconds portion of the timestamp is truncated.

f The time fields of the timestamp structure are set to zero.

g The date fields of the timestamp structure are set to the current date.

When character SQL data is converted to numeric, date, time, timestamp, or interval C data, leading and trailing spaces are ignored.

SQL to C: Numeric

The identifiers for the numeric ODBC SQL data types are:

SQL_DECIMAL	SQL_BIGINT
SQL_NUMERIC	SQL_REAL
SQL_TINYINT	SQL_FLOAT
SQL_SMALLINT	SQL_DOUBLE
SQL_INTEGER	

The following table shows the ODBC C data types to which numeric SQL data may be converted. For an explanation of the columns and terms in the table, see "Converting Data from SQL to C Data Types."

C type identifier	Test	**TargetValuePtr*	**StrLen_or_IndPtr*	SQL-STATE
SQL_C_CHAR	Character byte length < *BufferLength*	Data	Length of data in bytes	n/a
	Number of whole (as opposed to fractional) digits < *BufferLength*	Truncated data	Length of data in bytes	01004
	Number of whole (as opposed to fractional) digits ≥ *BufferLength*	Undefined	Undefined	22003
SQL_C_STINYINT SQL_C_UTINYINT SQL_C_TINYINT SQL_C_SBIGINT SQL_C_UBIGINT SQL_C_SSHORT SQL_C_USHORT SQL_C_SHORT SQL_C_SLONG SQL_C_ULONG SQL_C_LONG SQL_C_NUMERIC	Data converted without truncation [a]	Data	Size of the C data type	n/a
	Data converted with truncation of fractional digits [a]	Truncated data	Size of the C data type	01S07
	Conversion of data would result in loss of whole (as opposed to fractional) digits [a]	Undefined	Undefined	22003
SQL_C_FLOAT SQL_C_DOUBLE	Data is within the range of the data type to which the number is being converted [a]	Data	Size of the C data type	n/a
	Data is outside the range of the data type to which the number is being converted [a]	Undefined	Undefined	22003

C type identifier	Test	**TargetValuePtr*	**StrLen_or_IndPtr*	SQL-STATE
SQL_C_BIT	Data is 0 or 1 [a]	Data	1 [b]	n/a
	Data is greater than 0, less than 2, and not equal to 1 [a]	Truncated data	1 [b]	01S07
	Data is less than 0 or greater than or equal to 2 [a]	Undefined	Undefined	22003
SQL_C_BINARY	Byte length of data ≤ *BufferLength*	Data	Length of data	n/a
	Byte length of data > *BufferLength*	Undefined	Undefined	22003
SQL_C_INTERVAL_MONTH [c] SQL_C_INTERVAL_YEAR [c] SQL_C_INTERVAL_DAY [c] SQL_C_INTERVAL_HOUR [c] SQL_C_INTERVAL_MINUTE [c] SQL_C_INTERVAL_SECOND [c]	Data not truncated	Data	Length of data in bytes	n/a
	Fractional seconds portion truncated	Truncated data	Length of data in bytes	01S07
	Whole part of number truncated	Undefined	Undefined	22015
SQL_C_INTERVAL_YEAR_TO_MONTH SQL_C_INTERVAL_DAY_TO_HOUR SQL_C_INTERVAL_DAY_TO_MINUTE SQL_C_INTERVAL_DAY_TO_SECOND SQL_C_INTERVAL_HOUR_TO_MINUTE SQL_C_INTERVAL_HOUR_TO_SECOND	Whole part of number truncated	Undefined	Undefined	22015

a The value of *BufferLength* is ignored for this conversion. The driver assumes that the size of **TargetValuePtr* is the size of the C data type.

b This is the size of the corresponding C data type.

c This conversion is supported only for the exact numeric data types (SQL_DECIMAL, SQL_NUMERIC, SQL_TINYINT, SQL_SMALLINT, SQL_INTEGER, and SQL_BIGINT). It is not supported for the approximate numeric data types (SQL_REAL, SQL_FLOAT, or SQL_DOUBLE).

SQL to C: Bit

The identifier for the bit ODBC SQL data type is:

SQL_BIT

The following table shows the ODBC C data types to which bit SQL data may be converted. For an explanation of the columns and terms in the table, see "Converting Data from SQL to C Data Types."

C type identifier	Test	**TargetValuePtr*	**StrLen_or_IndPtr*	SQL-STATE
SQL_C_CHAR	*BufferLength* > 1	Data	1	n/a
	BufferLength ≤ 1	Undefined	Undefined	22003
SQL_C_STINYINT SQL_C_UTINYINT SQL_C_TINYINT SQL_C_SBIGINT SQL_C_UBIGINT SQL_C_SSHORT SQL_C_USHORT SQL_C_SHORT SQL_C_SLONG SQL_C_ULONG SQL_C_LONG SQL_C_FLOAT SQL_C_DOUBLE SQL_C_NUMERIC	None [a]	Data	Size of the C data type	n/a
SQL_C_BIT	None [a]	Data	1 [b]	n/a
SQL_C_BINARY	*BufferLength* ≥ 1	Data	1	n/a
	BufferLength < 1	Undefined	Undefined	22003

a The value of *BufferLength* is ignored for this conversion. The driver assumes that the size of **TargetValuePtr* is the size of the C data type.

b This is the size of the corresponding C data type.

When bit SQL data is converted to character C data, the possible values are "0" and "1".

SQL to C: Binary

The identifiers for the binary ODBC SQL data types are:

SQL_BINARY
SQL_VARBINARY
SQL_LONGVARBINARY

The following table shows the ODBC C data types to which binary SQL data may be converted. For an explanation of the columns and terms in the table, see "Converting Data from SQL to C Data Types."

C type identifier	Test	**TargetValuePtr*	**StrLen_or_IndPtr*	SQL-STATE
SQL_C_CHAR	(Byte length of data) * 2 < *BufferLength*	Data	Length of data in bytes	n/a
	(Byte length of data) * 2 ≥ *BufferLength*	Truncated data	Length of data in bytes	01004
SQL_C_BINARY	Byte length of data ≤ *BufferLength*	Data	Length of data in bytes	n/a
	Byte length of data > *BufferLength*	Truncated data	Length of data in bytes	01004

When binary SQL data is converted to character C data, each byte (8 bits) of source data is represented as two ASCII characters. These characters are the ASCII character representation of the number in its hexadecimal form. For example, a binary 00000001 is converted to "01" and a binary 11111111 is converted to "FF".

The driver always converts individual bytes to pairs of hexadecimal digits and terminates the character string with a null byte. Because of this, if *BufferLength* is even and is less than the length of the converted data, the last byte of the **TargetValuePtr* buffer is not used. (The converted data requires an even number of bytes, the next-to-last byte is a null byte, and the last byte cannot be used.)

Note Application developers are discouraged from binding binary SQL data to a character C data type. This conversion is usually inefficient and slow.

SQL to C: Date

The identifier for the date ODBC SQL data type is:

SQL_TYPE_DATE

The following table shows the ODBC C data types to which date SQL data may be converted. For an explanation of the columns and terms in the table, see "Converting Data from SQL to C Data Types."

C type identifier	Test	**TargetValuePtr*	**StrLen_or_IndPtr*	SQL-STATE
SQL_C_CHAR	*BufferLength* > Character byte length	Data	10	n/a
	11 ≤ *BufferLength* ≤ Character byte length	Truncated data	Length of data in bytes	01004
	BufferLength < 11	Undefined	Undefined	22003
SQL_C_BINARY	Byte length of data ≤ *BufferLength*	Data	Length of data in bytes	n/a
	Byte length of data > *BufferLength*	Undefined	Undefined	22003
SQL_C_TYPE_DATE	None [a]	Data	6 [c]	n/a
SQL_C_TYPE_TIMESTAMP	None [a]	Data [b]	16 [c]	n/a

[a] The value of *BufferLength* is ignored for this conversion. The driver assumes that the size of **TargetValuePtr* is the size of the C data type.

[b] The time fields of the timestamp structure are set to zero.

[c] This is the size of the corresponding C data type.

When date SQL data is converted to character C data, the resulting string is in the "*yyyy-mm-dd*" format. This format is not affected by the Windows country setting.

SQL to C: Time

The identifier for the time ODBC SQL data type is:

SQL_TYPE_TIME

The following table shows the ODBC C data types to which time SQL data may be converted. For an explanation of the columns and terms in the table, see "Converting Data from SQL to C Data Types."

C type identifier	Test	*TargetValuePtr	*StrLen_or_IndPtr	SQL-STATE
SQL_C_CHAR	*BufferLength* > Character byte length	Data	Length of data in bytes	n/a
	9 ≤ *BufferLength* ≤ Character byte length	Truncated data [a]	Length of data in bytes	01004
	BufferLength < 9	Undefined	Undefined	22003
SQL_C_BINARY	Byte length of data ≤ *BufferLength*	Data	Length of data in bytes	n/a
	Byte ength of data > *BufferLength*	Undefined	Undefined	22003
SQL_C_TYPE_TIME	None [b]	Data	6 [d]	n/a
SQL_C_TYPE_TIMESTAMP	None [b]	Data [c]	16 [d]	n/a

[a] The fractional seconds of the time are truncated.

[b] The value of *BufferLength* is ignored for this conversion. The driver assumes that the size of **TargetValuePtr* is the size of the C data type.

[c] The date fields of the timestamp structure are set to the current date and the fractional seconds field of the timestamp structure is set to zero.

[d] This is the size of the corresponding C data type.

When time SQL data is converted to character C data, the resulting string is in the "*hh*:*mm*:*ss*" format. This format is not affected by the Windows country setting.

SQL to C: Timestamp

The identifier for the timestamp ODBC SQL data type is:

SQL_TYPE_TIMESTAMP

The following table shows the ODBC C data types to which timestamp SQL data may be converted. For an explanation of the columns and terms in the table, see "Converting Data from SQL to C Data Types."

C type identifier	Test	**TargetValuePtr*	**StrLen_or _IndPtr*	SQL-STATE
SQL_C_CHAR	*BufferLength* > Character byte length	Data	Length of data in bytes	n/a
	20 ≤ *BufferLength* ≤ Character byte length	Truncated data [b]	Length of data in bytes	01004
	BufferLength < 20	Undefined	Undefined	22003
SQL_C_BINARY	Byte length of data ≤ *BufferLength*	Data	Length of data in bytes	n/a
	Byte length of data > *BufferLength*	Undefined	Undefined	22003
SQL_C_TYPE_DATE	Time portion of timestamp is zero [a]	Data	6 [f]	n/a
	Time portion of timestamp is non-zero [a]	Truncated data [c]	6 [f]	01S07
SQL_C_TYPE_TIME	Fractional seconds portion of timestamp is zero [a]	Data [d]	6 [f]	n/a
	Fractional seconds portion of timestamp is non-zero [a]	Truncated data [d, e]	6 [f]	01S07
SQL_C_TYPE_ TIMESTAMP	Fractional seconds portion of timestamp is not truncated [a]	Data [e]	16 [f]	n/a
	Fractional seconds portion of timestamp is truncated [a]	Truncated data [e]	16 [f]	01S07

a The value of *BufferLength* is ignored for this conversion. The driver assumes that the size of **TargetValuePtr* is the size of the C data type.

b The fractional seconds of the timestamp are truncated.

c The time portion of the timestamp is truncated.

d The date portion of the timestamp is ignored.

e The fractional seconds portion of the timestamp is truncated.

f This is the size of the corresponding C data type.

When timestamp SQL data is converted to character C data, the resulting string is in the "*yyyy-mm-dd hh*:*mm*:*ss*[.*f*...]" format, where up to nine digits may be used for fractional seconds. This format is not affected by the Windows country setting. (Except for the decimal point and fractional seconds, the entire format must be used, regardless of the precision of the timestamp SQL data type.)

SQL to C: Year-Month Intervals

The identifiers for the year-month interval ODBC SQL data types are:

SQL_INTERVAL_YEAR
SQL_INTERVAL_YEAR_TO_MONTH
SQL_INTERVAL_MONTH

The following table shows the ODBC C data types to which year-month interval SQL data may be converted. For an explanation of the columns and terms in the table, see "Converting Data from SQL to C Data Types."

C type identifier	Test	**TargetValuePtr*	**StrLen_or_IndPtr*	SQL-STATE
SQL_C_INTERVAL_MONTH [a] SQL_C_INTERVAL_YEAR [a] SQL_C_INTERVAL_YEAR_TO_MONTH [a]	Trailing fields portion not truncated.	Data	Length of data in bytes	n/a
	Trailing fields portion truncated.	Truncated data	Length of data in bytes	01S07
	Leading precision of target is not big enough to hold data from source.	Undefined	Undefined	22015
SQL_C_STINYINT [b] SQL_C_UTINYINT [b] SQL_C_USHORT [b] SQL_C_SHORT [b] SQL_C_SLONG [b] SQL_C_ULONG [b] SQL_C_NUMERIC [b] SQL_C_BIGINT [b]	Interval precision was a single field and the data was converted without truncation.	Data	Size of the C data type	n/a
	Interval precision was a single field and truncated whole.	Truncated data	Length of data in bytes	22003
	Interval precision was not a single field.	Undefined	Size of the C data type	22015
SQL_C_BINARY	Byte length of data ≤ *BufferLength*	Data	Length of data in bytes	n/a
	Byte length of data > *BufferLength*	Undefined	Undefined	22003

C type identifier	Test	*TargetValuePtr	*StrLen_or _IndPtr	SQL-STATE
SQL_C_CHAR	Character byte length < *BufferLength*	Data	Size of the C data type	n/a
	Number of whole (as opposed to fractional) digits < *BufferLength*	Truncated data	Size of the C data type	01004
	Number of whole (as opposed to fractional) digits ≥ *BufferLength*	Undefined	Undefined	22003

a A year-month interval SQL type can be converted to any year-month interval C type.

b If the interval precision is a single field (one of YEAR or MONTH), then the interval SQL type can be converted to any exact numeric (SQL_C_STINYINT, SQL_C_UTINYINT, SQL_C_USHORT, SQL_C_SHORT, SQL_C_SLONG, SQL_C_ULONG, or SQL_C_NUMERIC).

The default conversion of an interval SQL type is to the corresponding C interval data type. The application then binds the column or parameter (or sets the SQL_DESC_DATA_PTR field in the appropriate record of the ARD) to point to the initialized SQL_INTERVAL_STRUCT structure (or passes a pointer to the SQL_INTERVAL_STRUCT structure as the *TargetValuePtr* argument in a call to **SQLGetData**).

SQL to C: Day-Time Intervals

The identifiers for the day-time interval ODBC SQL data types are:

SQL_INTERVAL_DAY
SQL_INTERVAL_HOUR
SQL_INTERVAL_MINUTE
SQL_INTERVAL_SECOND
SQL_INTERVAL_DAY_TO_HOUR
SQL_INTERVAL_DAY_TO_MINUTE
SQL_INTERVAL_DAY_TO_SECOND
SQL_INTERVAL_HOUR_TO_MINUTE
SQL_INTERVAL_HOUR_TO_SECOND
SQL_INTERVAL_MINUTE_TO_SECOND

The following table shows the ODBC C data types to which day-time interval SQL data may be converted. For an explanation of the columns and terms in the table, see "Converting Data from SQL to C Data Types."

C type identifier	Test	*TargetValuePtr	*StrLen_or_IndPtr	SQL-STATE
All day-time C interval types	Trailing fields portion not truncated	Data	Length of data	n/a
	Trailing fields portion truncated	Truncated data	Length of data	01S07
	Leading precision of target is not big enough to hold data from source	Undefined	Undefined	22015
SQL_C_STINYINT [b] SQL_C_UTINYINT [b] SQL_C_USHORT [b] SQL_C_SHORT [b] SQL_C_SLONG [b] SQL_C_ULONG [b] SQL_C_NUMERIC [b] SQL_C_BIGINT [b]	Interval precision was a single field and the data was converted without truncation.	Data	Size of the C data type	n/a
	Interval precision was a single field and truncated fractional.	Truncated data	Length of data	01S07
	Interval precision was a single field and truncated whole.	Truncated data	Length of data	22003
	Interval precision was not a single field.	Undefined	Size of the C data type	07006
SQL_C_BINARY	Byte length of data ≤ *BufferLength*	Data	Length of data	n/a
	Byte length of data > *BufferLength*	Undefined	Undefined	22003
SQL_C_CHAR	Character byte length < *BufferLength*	Data	Size of the C data type	n/a
	Number of whole (as opposed to fractional) digits < *BufferLength*	Truncated data	Size of the C data type	01004
	Number of whole (as opposed to fractional) digits ≥ *BufferLength*	Undefined	Undefined	22003

a A day-time interval SQL type can be converted to any day-time interval C type.

b If the interval precision is a single field (one of DAY, HOUR, MINUTE, or SECOND), then the interval SQL type can be converted to any exact numeric (SQL_C_STINYINT, SQL_C_UTINYINT, SQL_C_USHORT, SQL_C_SHORT, SQL_C_SLONG, SQL_C_ULONG, or SQL_C_NUMERIC).

The default conversion of an interval SQL type is to the corresponding C interval data type. The application then binds the column or parameter (or sets the SQL_DESC_DATA_PTR field in the appropriate record of the ARD) to point to the initialized SQL_INTERVAL_STRUCT structure (or passes a pointer to the SQL_INTERVAL_STRUCT structure as the *TargetValuePtr* argument in a call to **SQLGetData**).

The following example demonstrates how to transfer data from a column of type SQL_INTERVAL_DAY_TO_MINUTE into the SQL_INTERVAL_STRUCT structure such that it comes back as a DAY_TO_HOUR interval.

```
SQL_INTERVAL_STRUCT is;
SQLINTEGER          cbValue;
SQLUINTEGER         days, hours;

// Execute a select statement; "interval_column" is a column
// whose data type is SQL_INTERVAL_DAY_TO_MINUTE.
SQLExecDirect(hstmt, "SELECT interval_column FROM table", SQL_NTS);

// Bind
SQLBindCol(hstmt, 1, SQL_C_INTERVAL_DAY_TO_MINUTE, &is, sizeof(SQL_INTERVAL_STRUCT),
&cbValue);

// Fetch
SQLFetch(hstmt);

// Process data
days = is.intval.day_second.day;
hours = is.intval.day_second.hour;
```

SQL to C Data Conversion Examples

The examples shown in the following table illustrate how the driver converts SQL data to C data:

SQL type identifier	SQL data value	C type identifier	Buffer length	**TargetValuePtr*	SQL-STATE
SQL_CHAR	abcdef	SQL_C_CHAR	7	abcdef\0 [a]	n/a
SQL_CHAR	abcdef	SQL_C_CHAR	6	abcde\0 [a]	01004
SQL_DECIMAL	1234.56	SQL_C_CHAR	8	1234.56\0 [a]	n/a
SQL_DECIMAL	1234.56	SQL_C_CHAR	5	1234\0 [a]	01004
SQL_DECIMAL	1234.56	SQL_C_CHAR	4	----	22003
SQL_DECIMAL	1234.56	SQL_C_FLOAT	ignored	1234.56	n/a
SQL_DECIMAL	1234.56	SQL_C_SSHORT	ignored	1234	01S07

SQL type identifier	SQL data value	C type identifier	*Buffer length*	**TargetValuePtr*	SQL-STATE
SQL_DECIMAL	1234.56	SQL_C_STINYINT	ignored	----	22003
SQL_DOUBLE	1.2345678	SQL_C_DOUBLE	ignored	1.2345678	n/a
SQL_DOUBLE	1.2345678	SQL_C_FLOAT	ignored	1.234567	n/a
SQL_DOUBLE	1.2345678	SQL_C_STINYINT	ignored	1	n/a
SQL_TYPE_DATE	1992-12-31	SQL_C_CHAR	11	1992-12-31\0 [a]	n/a
SQL_TYPE_DATE	1992-12-31	SQL_C_CHAR	10	-----	22003
SQL_TYPE_DATE	1992-12-31	SQL_C_TIMESTAMP	ignored	1992,12,31, 0,0,0,0 [b]	n/a
SQL_TYPE_ TIMESTAMP	1992-12-31 23:45:55.12	SQL_C_CHAR	23	1992-12-31 23:45:55.12\0 [a]	n/a
SQL_TYPE_ TIMESTAMP	1992-12-31 23:45:55.12	SQL_C_CHAR	22	1992-12-31 23:45:55.1\0 [a]	01004
SQL_TYPE_ TIMESTAMP	1992-12-31 23:45:55.12	SQL_C_CHAR	18	----	22003

a "\0" represents a null-termination byte. The driver always null-terminates SQL_C_CHAR data.

b The numbers in this list are the numbers stored in the fields of the TIMESTAMP_STRUCT structure.

Converting Data from C to SQL Data Types

When an application calls **SQLExecute** or **SQLExecDirect**, the driver retrieves the data for any parameters bound with **SQLBindParameter** from storage locations in the application. When an application calls **SQLSetPos**, the driver retrieves the data for an update or add operation from columns bound with **SQLBindCol**. For data-at-execution parameters, the application sends the parameter data with **SQLPutData**. If necessary, the driver converts the data from the data type specified by the *ValueType* argument in **SQLBindParameter** to the data type specified by the *ParameterType* argument in **SQLBindParameter**, and then sends the data to the data source.

The following table shows the supported conversions from ODBC C data types to ODBC SQL data types. A filled circle indicates the default conversion for an SQL data type (the C data type from which the data will be converted when the value of *ValueType* or the SQL_DESC_CONCISE_TYPE descriptor field is SQL_C_DEFAULT). A hollow circle indicates a supported conversion.

The format of the converted data is not affected by the Windows country setting.

C Data Type \ SQL Data Type	SQL_CHAR	SQL_VARCHAR	SQL_LONGVARCHAR	SQL_DECIMAL	SQL_NUMERIC	SQL_BIT	SQL_TINYINT (signed)	SQL_TINYINT (unsigned)	SQL_SMALLINT (signed)	SQL_SMALLINT (unsigned)	SQL_INTEGER (signed)	SQL_INTEGER (unsigned)	SQL_BIGINT(signed & unsigned)	SQL_REAL	SQL_FLOAT	SQL_DOUBLE	SQL_BINARY	SQL_VARBINARY	SQL_LONGVARBINARY	SQL_TYPE_DATE	SQL_TYPE_TIME	SQL_TYPE_TIMESTAMP	INTERVAL SQL (DAY-TIME)	INTERVAL SQL (YEAR-MONTH)
SQL_C_CHAR	●	●	●	●	●	○	○	○	○	○	○	○	●	○	○	○	○	○	○	○	○	○	○	○
SQL_C_BIT	○	○	○	○	○	●	○	○	○	○	○	○	○	○	○	○							◍	◍
SQL_C_NUMERIC	○	○	○	○	●	○	○	○	○	○	○	○	○	○	○	○							◍	◍
SQL_C_STINYINT	○	○	○	○	○	○	●	○	○	○	○	○	○	○	○	○							◍	◍
SQL_C_UTINYINT	○	○	○	○	○	○	○	●	○	○	○	○	○	○	○	○							◍	◍
SQL_C_TINYINT	○	○	○	○	○	○	○	○	○	○	○	○	○	○	○	○							◍	◍
SQL_C_SBIGINT	○	○	○	○	○	○	○	○	○	○	○	○	●	○	○	○							◍	◍
SQL_C_UBIGINT	○	○	○	○	○	○	○	○	○	○	○	○	●	○	○	○							◍	◍
SQL_C_SSHORT	○	○	○	○	○	○	○	○	●	○	○	○	○	○	○	○							◍	◍
SQL_C_USHORT	○	○	○	○	○	○	○	○	○	●	○	○	○	○	○	○							◍	◍
SQL_C_SHORT	○	○	○	○	○	○	○	○	○	○	○	○	○	○	○	○							◍	◍
SQL_C_SLONG	○	○	○	○	○	○	○	○	○	○	●	○	○	○	○	○							◍	◍
SQL_C_ULONG	○	○	○	○	○	○	○	○	○	○	○	●	○	○	○	○							◍	◍
SQL_C_LONG	○	○	○	○	○	○	○	○	○	○	○	○	○	○	○	○							◍	◍
SQL_C_FLOAT	○	○	○	○	○	○	○	○	○	○	○	○	○	●	○	○								
SQL_C_DOUBLE	○	○	○	○	○	○	○	○	○	○	○	○	○	○	●	●								
SQL_C_BINARY	○	○	○	○	○	○	○	○	○	○	○	○	○	○	○	○	●	●	●	○	○	○	○	○
SQL_C_TYPE_DATE	○	○	○																	●		○		
SQL_C_TYPE_TIME	○	○	○																		●	○		
SQL_C_TYPE_TIMESTAMP	○	○	○																	○	○	●		
INTERVAL C (DAY-TIME)	○	○	○	◍	◍		◍	◍	◍	◍	◍	◍	◍										●	
INTERVAL C (YEAR-MONTH)	○	○	○	◍	◍		◍	◍	◍	◍	◍	◍	◍											●

● Default Conversion

○ Supported Conversion

◍ Valid only for interval types with just a single field

The tables in the following sections describe how the driver or data source converts data sent to the data source; drivers are required to support conversions from all ODBC C data types to the ODBC SQL data types that they support. For a given ODBC C data type, the first column of the table lists the legal input values of the *ParameterType* argument in **SQLBindParameter**. The second column lists the outcomes of a test that the driver performs to determine if it can convert the data. The third column lists the SQLSTATE returned for each outcome by **SQLExecDirect**, **SQLExecute**, **SQLBulkOperations**, **SQLSetPos**, or **SQLPutData**. Data is sent to the data source only if SQL_SUCCESS is returned.

If the *ParameterType* argument in **SQLBindParameter** contains the identifier of an ODBC SQL data type that is not shown in the table for a given C data type, **SQLBindParameter** returns SQLSTATE 07006 (Restricted data type attribute violation). If the *ParameterType* argument contains a driver-specific identifier and the driver does not support the conversion from the specific ODBC C data type to that driver-specific SQL data type, **SQLBindParameter** returns SQLSTATE HYC00 (Optional feature not implemented).

If the *ParameterValuePtr* and *StrLen_or_IndPtr* arguments specified in **SQLBindParameter** are both null pointers, that function returns SQLSTATE HY009 (Invalid use of null pointer). Though it is not shown in the tables, an application sets the value of the length/indicator buffer pointed to by the *StrLen_or_IndPtr* argument of **SQLBindParameter** or the value of the *StrLen_or_IndPtr* argument of **SQLPutData** to SQL_NULL_DATA to specify a NULL SQL data value. (The *StrLen_or_IndPtr* argument corresponds to the SQL_DESC_OCTET_LENGTH_PTR field of the APD.) The application sets these values to SQL_NTS to specify that the value in **ParameterValuePtr* in **SQLBindParameter** or **DataPtr* in **SQLPutData** (pointed to by the SQL_DESC_DATA_PTR field of the APD) is a null-terminated string.

The following terms are used in the tables:

- **Byte length of data** is the number of bytes of SQL data available to send to the data source, regardless of whether the data will be truncated before it is sent to the data source. For string data, this does not include space for the null-termination character.
- **Column byte length** is the number of bytes required to store the data at the data source.
- **Character byte length** is the maximum number of bytes needed to display data in character form. This is as defined for each SQL data type in the section "Display Size" earlier in this appendix, except character byte length is in bytes, while the display size is in characters.
- **Number of digits** is the number of characters used to represent a number, including the minus sign, decimal point, and exponent (if needed).
- Words in *italics* represent elements of the SQL grammar. For the syntax of grammar elements, see Appendix C, "SQL Grammar."

C to SQL: Character

The identifier for the character ODBC C data type is:

SQL_C_CHAR

The following table shows the ODBC SQL data types to which C character data may be converted. For an explanation of the columns and terms in the table, see "Converting Data from C to SQL Data Types."

SQL type identifier	Test	SQLSTATE
SQL_CHAR SQL_VARCHAR SQL_LONGVARCHAR	Byte length of data ≤ column length.	n/a
	Byte length of data > column length.	22001
SQL_DECIMAL SQL_NUMERIC SQL_TINYINT SQL_SMALLINT SQL_INTEGER SQL_BIGINT	Data converted without truncation.	n/a
	Data converted with truncation of fractional digits. [e]	22001
	Conversion of data would result in loss of whole (as opposed to fractional) digits. [e]	22001
	Data value is not a *numeric-literal.*	22018
SQL_REAL SQL_FLOAT SQL_DOUBLE	Data is within the range of the data type to which the number is being converted.	n/a
	Data is outside the range of the data type to which the number is being converted.	22003
	Data value is not a *numeric-literal.*	22018
SQL_BIT	Data is 0 or 1.	n/a
	Data is greater than 0, less than 2, and not equal to 1.	22001
	Data is less than 0 or greater than or equal to 2.	22003
	Data is not a *numeric-literal.*	22018
SQL_BINARY SQL_VARBINARY SQL_LONGVARBINARY	(Byte length of data) / 2 ≤ column byte length.	n/a
	(Byte length of data) / 2 > column byte length.	22001
	Data value is not a hexadecimal value.	22018

SQL type identifier	Test	SQLSTATE
SQL_TYPE_DATE	Data value is a valid *ODBC-date-literal.*	n/a
	Data value is a valid *ODBC-timestamp-literal*; time portion is zero.	n/a
	Data value is a valid *ODBC-timestamp-literal*; time portion is non-zero. [a]	22008
	Data value is not a valid *ODBC-date-literal* or *ODBC-timestamp-literal.*	22018
SQL_TYPE_TIME	Data value is a valid *ODBC-time-literal.*	n/a
	Data value is a valid *ODBC-timestamp-literal*; fractional seconds portion is zero. [b]	n/a
	Data value is a valid *ODBC-timestamp-literal*; fractional seconds portion is non-zero. [b]	22008
	Data value is not a valid *ODBC-time-literal* or *ODBC-timestamp-literal.*	22018
SQL_TYPE_TIMESTAMP	Data value is a valid *ODBC-timestamp-literal*; fractional seconds portion not truncated.	n/a
	Data value is a valid *ODBC-timestamp-literal*; fractional seconds portion truncated.	22008
	Data value is a valid *ODBC-date-literal.* [c]	n/a
	Data value is a valid *ODBC-time-literal.* [d]	n/a
	Data value is not a valid *ODBC-date-literal*, *ODBC-time-literal*, or *ODBC-timestamp-literal.*	22018

SQL type identifier	Test	SQLSTATE
All SQL interval types	Data value is a valid *interval value*; no truncation occurs.	n/a
	Data value is a valid *interval value*; the value in one of the fields is truncated.	22015
	The data value is not a valid interval literal.	22018

a The time portion of the timestamp is truncated.

b The date portion of the timestamp is ignored.

c The time portion of the timestamp is set to zero.

d The date portion of the timestamp is set to the current date.

e The driver/data source effectively waits until the entire string has been received (even if the character data is sent in pieces by calls to **SQLPutData**) before attempting to perform the conversion.

When character C data is converted to numeric, date, time, or timestamp SQL data, leading and trailing blanks are ignored.

When character C data is converted to binary SQL data, each two bytes of character data are converted to a single byte (8 bits) of binary data. Each two bytes of character data represent a number in hexadecimal form. For example, "01" is converted to a binary 00000001 and "FF" is converted to a binary 11111111.

The driver always converts pairs of hexadecimal digits to individual bytes and ignores the null-termination byte. Because of this, if the length of the character string is odd, the last byte of the string (excluding the null-termination byte, if any) is not converted.

Note Application developers are discouraged from binding character C data to a binary SQL data type. This conversion is usually inefficient and slow.

C to SQL: Numeric

The identifiers for the numeric ODBC C data types are:

SQL_C_STINYINT
SQL_C_UTINYINT
SQL_C_TINYINT
SQL_C_SSHORT
SQL_C_USHORT
SQL_C_SHORT
SQL_C_SBIGINT
SQL_C_SLONG
SQL_C_ULONG
SQL_C_LONG
SQL_C_FLOAT
SQL_C_DOUBLE
SQL_C_NUMERIC
SQL_C_UBIGINT

The following table shows the ODBC SQL data types to which numeric C data may be converted. For an explanation of the columns and terms in the table, see "Converting Data from C to SQL Data Types."

SQL type identifier	Test	SQL-STATE
SQL_CHAR SQL_VARCHAR SQL_LONGVARCHAR	Number of digits ≤ column byte length. Number of digits > column byte length.	n/a 22001
SQL_DECIMAL SQL_NUMERIC SQL_TINYINT SQL_SMALLINT SQL_INTEGER SQL_BIGINT	Data converted without truncation or with truncated of fractional digits. Data converted with truncation of whole digits.	n/a 22003
SQL_REAL SQL_FLOAT SQL_DOUBLE	Data is within the range of the data type to which the number is being converted. Data is outside the range of the data type to which the number is being converted.	n/a 22003
SQL_BIT	Data is 0 or 1. Data is greater than 0, less than 2, and not equal to 1. Data is less than 0 or greater than or equal to 2.	n/a 22001 22003
SQL_INTERVAL_YEAR [a] SQL_INTERVAL_MONTH [a] SQL_INTERVAL_DAY [a] SQL_INTERVAL_HOUR [a] SQL_INTERVAL_MINUTE [a] SQL_INTERVAL_SECOND [a]	Data not truncated. Data truncated.	n/a 22015

[a] These conversions are supported only for the exact numeric data types (SQL_C_STINYINT, SQL_C_UTINYINT, SQL_C_SSHORT, SQL_C_USHORT, SQL_C_SLONG, SQL_C_ULONG, or SQL_C_NUMERIC). They are not supported for the approximate numeric data types (SQL_C_FLOAT or SQL_C_DOUBLE). Exact numeric C data types cannot be converted to an interval SQL type whose interval precision is not a single field.

The driver ignores the length/indicator value when converting data from the numeric C data types and assumes that the size of the data buffer is the size of the numeric C data type. The length/indicator value is passed in the *StrLen_or_Ind* argument in **SQLPutData** and in the buffer specified with the *StrLen_or_IndPtr* argument in **SQLBindParameter**. The data buffer is specified with the *DataPtr* argument in **SQLPutData** and the *ParameterValuePtr* argument in **SQLBindParameter**.

C to SQL: Bit

The identifier for the bit ODBC C data type is:

SQL_C_BIT

The following table shows the ODBC SQL data types to which bit C data may be converted. For an explanation of the columns and terms in the table, see "Converting Data from C to SQL Data Types."

SQL type identifier	Test	SQL-STATE
SQL_CHAR SQL_VARCHAR SQL_LONGVARCHAR	None	n/a
SQL_DECIMAL SQL_NUMERIC SQL_TINYINT SQL_SMALLINT SQL_INTEGER SQL_BIGINT SQL_REAL SQL_FLOAT SQL_DOUBLE	None	n/a
SQL_BIT	None	n/a

The driver ignores the length/indicator value when converting data from the bit C data type and assumes that the size of the data buffer is the size of the bit C data type. The length/indicator value is passed in the *StrLen_or_Ind* argument in **SQLPutData** and in the buffer specified with the *StrLen_or_IndPtr* argument in **SQLBindParameter**. The data buffer is specified with the *DataPtr* argument in **SQLPutData** and the *ParameterValuePtr* argument in **SQLBindParameter**.

C to SQL: Binary

The identifier for the binary ODBC C data type is:

SQL_C_BINARY

The following table shows the ODBC SQL data types to which binary C data may be converted. For an explanation of the columns and terms in the table, see "Converting Data from C to SQL Data Types."

SQL type identifier	Test	SQL-STATE
SQL_CHAR SQL_VARCHAR SQL_LONGVARCHAR	Byte length of data ≤ column byte length Byte length of data > column byte length	n/a 22001
SQL_DECIMAL SQL_NUMERIC SQL_TINYINT SQL_SMALLINT SQL_INTEGER SQL_BIGINT SQL_REAL SQL_FLOAT SQL_DOUBLE SQL_BIT SQL_TYPE_DATE SQL_TYPE_TIME SQL_TYPE_TIMESTAMP	Byte length of data = SQL data length Byte length of data ≠ SQL data length	n/a 22003
SQL_BINARY SQL_VARBINARY SQL_LONGVARBINARY	Length of data ≤ column length Length of data > column length	n/a 22001

C to SQL: Date

The identifier for the date ODBC C data type is:

SQL_C_TYPE_DATE

The following table shows the ODBC SQL data types to which date C data may be converted. For an explanation of the columns and terms in the table, see "Converting Data from C to SQL Data Types."

SQL type identifier	Test	SQL-STATE
SQL_CHAR SQL_VARCHAR SQL_LONGVARCHAR	Column byte length ≥ 10. Column byte length < 10. Data value is not a valid date.	n/a 22001 22008
SQL_TYPE_DATE	Data value is a valid date. Data value is not a valid date.	n/a 22007
SQL_TYPE_TIMESTAMP	Data value is a valid date. [a] Data value is not a valid date.	n/a 22007

[a] The time portion of the timestamp is set to zero.

For information about what values are valid in a SQL_C_TYPE_DATE structure, see "C Data Types."

When date C data is converted to character SQL data, the resulting character data is in the "*yyyy-mm-dd*" format.

The driver ignores the length/indicator value when converting data from the date C data type and assumes that the size of the data buffer is the size of the date C data type. The length/indicator value is passed in the *StrLen_or_Ind* argument in **SQLPutData** and in the buffer specified with the *StrLen_or_IndPtr* argument in **SQLBindParameter**. The data buffer is specified with the *DataPtr* argument in **SQLPutData** and the *ParameterValuePtr* argument in **SQLBindParameter**.

C to SQL: Time

The identifier for the time ODBC C data type is:

SQL_C_TYPE_TIME

The following table shows the ODBC SQL data types to which time C data may be converted. For an explanation of the columns and terms in the table, see "Converting Data from C to SQL Data Types."

SQL type identifier	Test	SQL-STATE
SQL_CHAR SQL_VARCHAR SQL_LONGVARCHAR	Column byte length ≥ 8.	n/a
	Column byte length < 8.	22001
	Data value is not a valid time.	22008
SQL_TYPE_TIME	Data value is a valid time.	n/a
	Data value is not a valid time.	22007
SQL_TYPE_TIMESTAMP	Data value is a valid time. [a]	n/a
	Data value is not a valid time.	22007

[a] The date portion of the timestamp is set to the current date and the fractional seconds portion of the timestamp is set to zero.

For information about what values are valid in a SQL_C_TYPE_TIME structure, see "C Data Types" earlier in this appendix.

When time C data is converted to character SQL data, the resulting character data is in the "*hh:mm:ss*" format.

The driver ignores the length/indicator value when converting data from the time C data type and assumes that the size of the data buffer is the size of the time C data type. The length/indicator value is passed in the *StrLen_or_Ind* argument in **SQLPutData** and in the buffer specified with the *StrLen_or_IndPtr* argument in **SQLBindParameter**. The data buffer is specified with the *DataPtr* argument in **SQLPutData** and the *ParameterValuePtr* argument in **SQLBindParameter**.

C to SQL: Timestamp

The identifier for the timestamp ODBC C data type is:

SQL_C_TYPE_TIMESTAMP

The following table shows the ODBC SQL data types to which timestamp C data may be converted. For an explanation of the columns and terms in the table, see "Converting Data from C to SQL Data Types."

SQL type identifier	Test	SQL-STATE
SQL_CHAR SQL_VARCHAR SQL_LONGVARCHAR	Column byte length ≥ Character byte length.	n/a
	19 ≤ Column byte length < Character byte length.	22001
	Column byte length < 19.	22001
	Data value is not a valid timestamp.	22008
SQL_TYPE_DATE	Time fields are zero.	n/a
	Time fields are non-zero.	22008
	Data value does not contain a valid date.	22007
SQL_TYPE_TIME	Fractional seconds fields are zero. [a]	n/a
	Fractional seconds fields are non-zero. [a]	22008
	Data value does not contain a valid time.	22007
SQL_TYPE_TIMESTAMP	Fractional seconds fields are not truncated.	n/a
	Fractional seconds fields are truncated.	22008
	Data value is not a valid timestamp.	22007

[a] The date fields of the timestamp structure are ignored.

For information about what values are valid in a SQL_C_TIMESTAMP structure, see "C Data Types."

When timestamp C data is converted to character SQL data, the resulting character data is in the "*yyyy-mm-dd hh:mm:ss*[*.f...*]" format.

The driver ignores the length/indicator value when converting data from the timestamp C data type and assumes that the size of the data buffer is the size of the timestamp C data type. The length/indicator value is passed in the *StrLen_or_Ind* argument in **SQLPutData** and in the buffer specified with the *StrLen_or_IndPtr* argument in **SQLBindParameter**. The data buffer is specified with the *DataPtr* argument in **SQLPutData** and the *ParameterValuePtr* argument in **SQLBindParameter**.

C to SQL: Year-Month Intervals

The identifiers for the year-month interval ODBC C data types are:

SQL_C_INTERVAL_MONTH
SQL_C_INTERVAL_YEAR
SQL_C_INTERVAL_YEAR_TO_MONTH

The following table shows the ODBC SQL data types to which year-month interval C data may be converted. For an explanation of the columns and terms in the table, see "Converting Data from C to SQL Data Types."

SQL type identifier	Test	SQLSTATE
SQL_CHAR [a] SQL_VARCHAR [a] SQL_LONGVARCHAR [a]	Column byte length ≥ Character byte length.	n/a
	Column byte length < Character byte length. [a]	22001
	Data value is not a valid interval literal.	22015
SQL_TINYINT [b] SQL_SMALLINT [b] SQL_INTEGER [b] SQL_BIGINT [b] SQL_NUMERIC [b] SQL_DECIMAL [b]	Conversion of a single-field interval did not result in truncation of whole digits.	n/a
	Conversion resulted in truncation of whole digits.	22003
SQL_INTERVAL_MONTH SQL_INTERVAL_YEAR SQL_INTERVAL_YEAR_TO_MONTH	Data value was converted without truncation of any fields.	n/a
	One or more fields of data value were truncated during conversion.	22015

a All C interval data types can be converted to a character data type.

b If the type field in the interval structure is such that the interval is a single field, (SQL_YEAR or SQL_MONTH), then the interval C type can be converted to any exact numeric (SQL_TINYINT, SQL_SMALLINT, SQL_INTEGER, SQL_BIGINT, SQL_DECIMAL, or SQL_NUMERIC).

The default conversion of an interval C type is to the corresponding year-month interval SQL type.

The driver ignores the length/indicator value when converting data from the interval C data type and assumes that the size of the data buffer is the size of the interval C data type. The length/indicator value is passed in the *StrLen_or_Ind* argument in **SQLPutData** and in the buffer specified with the *StrLen_or_IndPtr* argument in **SQLBindParameter**. The data buffer is specified with the *DataPtr* argument in **SQLPutData** and the *ParameterValuePtr* argument in **SQLBindParameter**.

C to SQL: Day-Time Intervals

The identifiers for the day-time interval ODBC C data types are:

SQL_C_INTERVAL_DAY
SQL_C_INTERVAL_HOUR
SQL_C_INTERVAL_MINUTE
SQL_C_INTERVAL_SECOND
SQL_C_INTERVAL_DAY_TO_HOUR
SQL_C_INTERVAL_DAY_TO_MINUTE
SQL_C_INTERVAL_DAY_TO_SECOND
SQL_C_INTERVAL_HOUR_TO_MINUTE
SQL_C_INTERVAL_HOUR_TO_SECOND
SQL_C_INTERVAL_MINUTE_TO_SECOND

The following table shows the ODBC SQL data types to which interval C data may be converted. For an explanation of the columns and terms in the table, see "Converting Data from C to SQL Data Types."

SQL type identifier	Test	SQL-STATE
SQL_CHAR [a] SQL_VARCHAR [a] SQL_LONGVARCHAR [a]	Column byte length ≥ Character byte length.	n/a
	Column byte length < Character byte length. [a]	22001
	Data value is not a valid interval literal.	22015
SQL_TINYINT [b] SQL_SMALLINT [b] SQL_INTEGER [b] SQL_BIGINT [b] SQL_NUMERIC [b] SQL_DECIMAL [b]	Conversion of a single-field interval did not result in truncation of whole digits.	n/a
	Conversion resulted in truncation of whole digits.	22003

SQL type identifier	Test	SQL-STATE
SQL_INTERVAL_DAY SQL_INTERVAL_HOUR SQL_INTERVAL_MINUTE SQL_INTERVAL_SECOND SQL_INTERVAL_DAY_TO_HOUR SQL_INTERVAL_DAY_TO_MINUTE SQL_INTERVAL_DAY_TO_SECOND SQL_INTERVAL_HOUR_TO_MINUTE SQL_INTERVAL_HOUR_TO_SECOND SQL_INTERVAL_MINUTE_TO_SECOND	Data value was converted without truncation of any fields.	n/a
	One or more fields of data value were truncated during conversion.	22015

a All C interval data types can be converted to a character data type.

b If the type field in the interval structure is such that the interval is a single field, (SQL_DAY, SQL_HOUR, SQL_MINUTE, or SQL_SECOND), then the interval C type can be converted to any exact numeric (SQL_TINYINT, SQL_SMALLINT, SQL_INTEGER, SQL_BIGINT, SQL_DECIMAL, or SQL_NUMERIC).

The default conversion of an interval C type is to the corresponding day-time interval SQL type.

The driver ignores the length/indicator value when converting data from the interval C data type and assumes that the size of the data buffer is the size of the interval C data type. The length/indicator value is passed in the *StrLen_or_Ind* argument in **SQLPutData** and in the buffer specified with the *StrLen_or_IndPtr* argument in **SQLBindParameter**. The data buffer is specified with the *DataPtr* argument in **SQLPutData** and the *ParameterValuePtr* argument in **SQLBindParameter**.

The following example demonstrates how to send interval C data stored in the SQL_INTERVAL_STRUCT structure into a database column. The interval structure contains a DAY_TO_SECOND interval; it will be stored in a database column of type SQL_INTERVAL_DAY_TO_MINUTE.

```
SQL_INTERVAL_STRUCT is;
SQLINTEGER          cbValue;
```

```
// Initialize the interval struct to contain the DAY_TO_SECOND
// interval "154 days, 22 hours, 44 minutes, and 10 seconds"
is.intval.day_second.day    = 154;
is.intval.day_second.hour   = 22;
is.intval.day_second.minute = 44;
is.intval.day_second.second = 10;
is.interval_sign            = SQL_FALSE;

// Bind the dynamic parameter
SQLBindParameter(hstmt, 1, SQL_PARAM_INPUT, SQL_C_INTERVAL_DAY_TO_SECOND,
                 SQL_INTERVAL_DAY_TO_MINUTE, 0, 0, &is,
                 sizeof(SQL_INTERVAL_STRUCT), &cbValue);

// Execute an insert statement; "interval_column" is a column
// whose data type is SQL_INTERVAL_DAY_TO_MINUTE.
SQLExecDirect(hstmt,"INSERT INTO table(interval_column) VALUES (?)",SQL_NTS);
```

C to SQL Data Conversion Examples

The following examples illustrate how the driver converts C data to SQL data:

C type identifier	C data value	SQL type identifier	Column length	SQL data value	SQL-STATE
SQL_C_CHAR	abcdef\0 [a]	SQL_CHAR	6	abcdef	n/a
SQL_C_CHAR	abcdef\0 [a]	SQL_CHAR	5	abcde	22001
SQL_C_CHAR	1234.56\0 [a]	SQL_DECIMAL	8 [b]	1234.56	n/a
SQL_C_CHAR	1234.56\0 [a]	SQL_DECIMAL	7 [b]	1234.5	22001
SQL_C_CHAR	1234.56\0 [a]	SQL_DECIMAL	4	----	22003
SQL_C_FLOAT	1234.56	SQL_FLOAT	n/a	1234.56	n/a
SQL_C_FLOAT	1234.56	SQL_INTEGER	n/a	1234	22001
SQL_C_FLOAT	1234.56	SQL_TINYINT	n/a	----	22003
SQL_C_TYPE_DATE	1992,12,31 [c]	SQL_CHAR	10	1992-12-31	n/a
SQL_C_TYPE_DATE	1992,12,31 [c]	SQL_CHAR	9	----	22003
SQL_C_TYPE_DATE	1992,12,31 [c]	SQL_TIMESTAMP	n/a	1992-12-31 00:00:00.0	n/a
SQL_C_TYPE_TIMESTAMP	1992,12,31, 23,45,55, 120000000 [d]	SQL_CHAR	22	1992-12-31 23:45:55.12	n/a

C type identifier	C data value	SQL type identifier	Column length	SQL data value	SQL-STATE
SQL_C_TYPE_ TIMESTAMP	1992,12,31, 23,45,55, 120000000 [d]	SQL_CHAR	21	1992-12-31 23:45:55.1	22001
SQL_C_TYPE_ TIMESTAMP	1992,12,31, 23,45,55, 120000000 [d]	SQL_CHAR	18	----	22003

[a] "\0" represents a null-termination byte. The null-termination byte is required only if the length of the data is SQL_NTS.

[b] In addition to bytes for numbers, one byte is required for a sign and another byte is required for the decimal point.

[c] The numbers in this list are the numbers stored in the fields of the SQL_DATE_STRUCT structure.

[d] The numbers in this list are the numbers stored in the fields of the SQL_TIMESTAMP_STRUCT structure.

APPENDIX E

Scalar Functions

ODBC specifies five types of scalar functions:

- String functions
- Numeric functions
- Time and date functions
- System functions
- Data type conversion functions

The following sections list functions by function type. Descriptions include associated syntax.

ODBC does not mandate a data type for return values from scalar functions as the functions are often data source–specific. Applications should use the CONVERT scalar function whenever possible to force data type conversion.

ODBC and SQL-92 Scalar Functions

The tables in this appendix include functions that have been added in ODBC 3.0 to align with SQL-92. Those functions added for a particular type of scalar function, as defined in ODBC, are indicated in each section.

ODBC and SQL-92 classify their scalar functions differently. ODBC classifies scalar functions by argument type; SQL-92 classifies them by return value. For example, the EXTRACT function is classified as a timedate function by ODBC, because the extract-field argument is a datetime keyword and the extract-source argument is a datetime or interval expression. SQL-92, on the other hand, classifies EXTRACT as a numeric scalar function, because the return value is a numeric.

An application can determine which scalar functions a driver supports by calling **SQLGetInfo**. Information types are included for both ODBC and SQL-92 classifications of scalar functions. Because these classifications are different, the support for some scalar functions may be indicated in information types that do not correspond for ODBC and SQL-92. For example, support for EXTRACT in ODBC is indicated by the SQL_TIMEDATE_FUNCTIONS information type; support for EXTRACT in SQL-92, on the other hand, is indicated by the SQL_SQL92_NUMERIC_VALUE_FUNCTIONS information type.

String Functions

The following table lists string manipulation functions. An application can determine which string functions are supported by a driver by calling **SQLGetInfo** with an *information type* of SQL_STRING_FUNCTIONS.

Character string literals used as arguments to scalar functions must be bounded by single quotes.

Arguments denoted as *string_exp* can be the name of a column, a string literal, or the result of another scalar function, where the underlying data type can be represented as SQL_CHAR, SQL_VARCHAR, or SQL_LONGVARCHAR.

Arguments denoted as *character_exp* are a variable-length character string.

Arguments denoted as *start*, *length*, or *count* can be a numeric literal or the result of another scalar function, where the underlying data type can be represented as SQL_TINYINT, SQL_SMALLINT, or SQL_INTEGER.

The string functions listed here are 1-based, that is, the first character in the string is character 1.

The BIT_LENGTH, CHAR_LENGTH, CHARACTER_LENGTH, OCTET_LENGTH, and POSITION string scalar functions have been added in ODBC 3.0 to align with SQL-92.

Function	Description
ASCII(*string_exp*) (ODBC 1.0)	Returns the ASCII code value of the leftmost character of *string_exp* as an integer.
BIT_LENGTH(*string_exp*) (ODBC 3.0)	Returns the length in bits of the string expression.
CHAR(*code*) (ODBC 1.0)	Returns the character that has the ASCII code value specified by *code*. The value of *code* should be between 0 and 255; otherwise, the return value is data source–dependent.

Function	Description
CHAR_LENGTH(*string_exp*) (ODBC 3.0)	Returns the length in characters of the string expression, if the string expression is of a character data type; otherwise, returns the length in bytes of the string expression (the smallest integer not less than the number of bits divided by 8). (This function is the same as the CHARACTER_LENGTH function.)
CHARACTER_LENGTH (*string_exp*) (ODBC 3.0)	Returns the length in characters of the string expression, if the string expression is of a character data type; otherwise, returns the length in bytes of the string expression (the smallest integer not less than the number of bits divided by 8). (This function is the same as the CHAR_LENGTH function.)
CONCAT(*string_exp1*, *string_exp2*) (ODBC 1.0)	Returns a character string that is the result of concatenating *string_exp2* to *string_exp1*. The resulting string is DBMS-dependent. For example, if the column represented by *string_exp1* contained a NULL value, DB2 would return NULL, but SQL Server would return the non-NULL string.
DIFFERENCE(*string_exp1*, *string_exp2*) (ODBC 2.0)	Returns an integer value that indicates the difference between the values returned by the SOUNDEX function for *string_exp1* and *string_exp2*.
INSERT(*string_exp1*, *start,length*, *string_exp2*) (ODBC 1.0)	Returns a character string where *length* characters have been deleted from *string_exp1* beginning at *start* and where *string_exp2* has been inserted into *string_exp,* beginning at *start*.
LCASE(*string_exp*) (ODBC 1.0)	Returns a string equal to that in *string_exp* with all uppercase characters converted to lowercase.
LEFT(*string_exp*, *count*) (ODBC 1.0)	Returns the leftmost *count* characters of *string_exp*.
LENGTH(*string_exp*) (ODBC 1.0)	Returns the number of characters in *string_exp,* excluding trailing blanks.

Function	Description
LOCATE(*string_exp1***,** *string_exp2*[**,** *start*]**)** (ODBC 1.0)	Returns the starting position of the first occurrence of *string_exp1* within *string_exp2*. The search for the first occurrence of *string_exp1* begins with the first character position in *string_exp2* unless the optional argument, *start*, is specified. If *start* is specified, the search begins with the character position indicated by the value of *start*. The first character position in *string_exp2* is indicated by the value 1. If *string_exp1* is not found within *string_exp2,* the value 0 is returned. If an application can call the LOCATE scalar function with the *string_exp1*, *string_exp2*, and *start* arguments, then the driver returns SQL_FN_STR_LOCATE when **SQLGetInfo** is called with an *Option* of SQL_STRING_FUNCTIONS. If the application can call the LOCATE scalar function with only the *string_exp1* and *string_exp2* arguments, then the driver returns SQL_FN_STR_LOCATE_2 when **SQLGetInfo** is called with an *Option* of SQL_STRING_FUNCTIONS. Drivers that support calling the LOCATE function with either two or three arguments return both SQL_FN_STR_LOCATE and SQL_FN_STR_LOCATE_2.
LTRIM(*string_exp***)** (ODBC 1.0)	Returns the characters of *string_exp,* with leading blanks removed.
OCTET_LENGTH*(string_exp)* (ODBC 3.0)	Returns the length in bytes of the string expression. The result is the smallest integer not less than the number of bits divided by 8.
POSITION(*character_exp* **IN** *character_exp***)** (ODBC 3.0)	Returns the position of the first character expression in the second character expression. The result is an exact numeric with an implementation-defined precision and a scale of 0.
REPEAT(*string_exp***,** *count***)** (ODBC 1.0)	Returns a character string composed of *string_exp* repeated *count* times.
REPLACE(*string_exp1***,** *string_exp2***,** *string_exp3***)** (ODBC 1.0)	Search *string_exp1 for* occurrences of *string_exp2* and replace with *string_exp3*.

Function	Description
RIGHT(*string_exp*, *count***)** (ODBC 1.0)	Returns the rightmost *count* characters of *string_exp*.
RTRIM(*string_exp***)** (ODBC 1.0)	Returns the characters of *string_exp* with trailing blanks removed.
SOUNDEX(*string_exp***)** (ODBC 2.0)	Returns a data source–dependent character string representing the sound of the words in *string_exp*. For example, SQL Server returns a 4-digit SOUNDEX code; Oracle returns a phonetic representation of each word.
SPACE(*count***)** (ODBC 2.0)	Returns a character string consisting of *count* spaces.
SUBSTRING(*string_exp*, *start*, *length***)** (ODBC 1.0)	Returns a character string that is derived from *string_exp* beginning at the character position specified by *start* for *length* characters.
UCASE(*string_exp***)** (ODBC 1.0)	Returns a string equal to that in *string_exp* with all lowercase characters converted to uppercase.

Numeric Functions

The following table describes numeric functions that are included in the ODBC scalar function set. An application can determine which numeric functions are supported by a driver by calling **SQLGetInfo** with an *information type* of SQL_NUMERIC_FUNCTIONS.

Arguments denoted as *numeric_exp* can be the name of a column, the result of another scalar function, or a numeric literal, where the underlying data type could be represented as SQL_NUMERIC, SQL_DECIMAL, SQL_TINYINT, SQL_SMALLINT, SQL_INTEGER, SQL_BIGINT, SQL_FLOAT, SQL_REAL, or SQL_DOUBLE.

Arguments denoted as *float_exp* can be the name of a column, the result of another scalar function, or a numeric literal, where the underlying data type can be represented as SQL_FLOAT.

Arguments denoted as *integer_exp* can be the name of a column, the result of another scalar function, or a numeric literal, where the underlying data type can be represented as SQL_TINYINT, SQL_SMALLINT, SQL_INTEGER, or SQL_BIGINT.

The CURRENT_DATE, CURRENT_TIME, and CURRENT_TIMESTAMP scalar functions have been added in ODBC 3.0 to align with SQL-92.

Function	Description
ABS(*numeric_exp***)** (ODBC 1.0)	Returns the absolute value of *numeric_exp*.
ACOS(*float_exp***)** (ODBC 1.0)	Returns the arccosine of *float_exp* as an angle, expressed in radians.
ASIN(*float_exp***)** (ODBC 1.0)	Returns the arcsine of *float_exp* as an angle, expressed in radians.
ATAN(*float_exp***)** (ODBC 1.0)	Returns the arctangent of *float_exp* as an angle, expressed in radians.
ATAN2(*float_exp1***,** *float_exp2***)** (ODBC 2.0)	Returns the arctangent of the x and y coordinates, specified by *float_exp1* and *float_exp2*, respectively, as an angle, expressed in radians.
CEILING(*numeric_exp***)** (ODBC 1.0)	Returns the smallest integer greater than or equal to *numeric_exp*.
COS(*float_exp***)** (ODBC 1.0)	Returns the cosine of *float_exp,* where *float_exp* is an angle expressed in radians.
COT(*float_exp***)** (ODBC 1.0)	Returns the cotangent of *float_exp,* where *float_exp* is an angle expressed in radians.
DEGREES(*numeric_exp***)** (ODBC 2.0)	Returns the number of degrees converted from *numeric_exp* radians.
EXP(*float_exp***)** (ODBC 1.0)	Returns the exponential value of *float_exp*.
FLOOR(*numeric_exp***)** (ODBC 1.0)	Returns the largest integer less than or equal to *numeric_exp*.
LOG(*float_exp***)** (ODBC 1.0)	Returns the natural logarithm of *float_exp*.
LOG10(*float_exp***)** (ODBC 2.0)	Returns the base 10 logarithm of *float_exp*.
MOD(*integer_exp1***,** *integer_exp2***)** (ODBC 1.0)	Returns the remainder (modulus) of *integer_exp1* divided by *integer_exp2*.
PI( ) (ODBC 1.0)	Returns the constant value of pi as a floating point value.
POWER(*numeric_exp***,** *integer_exp***)** (ODBC 2.0)	Returns the value of *numeric_exp* to the power of *integer_exp*.
RADIANS(*numeric_exp***)** (ODBC 2.0)	Returns the number of radians converted from *numeric_exp* degrees.
RAND([*integer_exp*]**)** (ODBC 1.0)	Returns a random floating point value using *integer_exp* as the optional seed value.
ROUND(*numeric_exp***,** *integer_exp***)** (ODBC 2.0)	Returns *numeric_exp* rounded to *integer_exp* places right of the decimal point. If *integer_exp* is negative, *numeric_exp* is rounded to |*integer_exp*| places to the left of the decimal point.

Function	Description
SIGN(*numeric_exp***)** (ODBC 1.0)	Returns an indicator of the sign of *numeric_exp*. If *numeric_exp* is less than zero, –1 is returned. If *numeric_exp* equals zero, 0 is returned. If *numeric_exp* is greater than zero, 1 is returned.
SIN(*float_exp***)** (ODBC 1.0)	Returns the sine of *float_exp,* where *float_exp* is an angle expressed in radians.
SQRT(*float_exp***)** (ODBC 1.0)	Returns the square root of *float_exp*.
TAN(*float_exp***)** (ODBC 1.0)	Returns the tangent of *float_exp,* where *float_exp* is an angle expressed in radians.
TRUNCATE(*numeric_exp***,** *integer_exp***)** (ODBC 2.0)	Returns *numeric_exp* truncated to *integer_exp* places right of the decimal point. If *integer_exp* is negative, *numeric_exp* is truncated to |*integer_exp*| places to the left of the decimal point.

Time, Date, and Interval Functions

The following table lists time and date functions that are included in the ODBC scalar function set. An application can determine which time and date functions are supported by a driver by calling **SQLGetInfo** with an *information type* of SQL_TIMEDATE_FUNCTIONS.

Arguments denoted as *timestamp_exp* can be the name of a column, the result of another scalar function, or a time, date, or timestamp literal, where the underlying data type could be represented as SQL_CHAR, SQL_VARCHAR, SQL_TYPE_TIME, SQL_TYPE_DATE, or SQL_TYPE_TIMESTAMP.

Arguments denoted as *date_exp* can be the name of a column, the result of another scalar function, or a date or timestamp literal, where the underlying data type could be represented as SQL_CHAR, SQL_VARCHAR, SQL_TYPE_DATE, or SQL_TYPE_TIMESTAMP.

Arguments denoted as *time_exp* can be the name of a column, the result of another scalar function, or a time or timestamp literal, where the underlying data type could be represented as SQL_CHAR, SQL_VARCHAR, SQL_TYPE_TIME, or SQL_TYPE_TIMESTAMP.

The CURRENT_DATE, CURRENT_TIME, and CURRENT_TIMESTAMP timedate scalar functions have been added in ODBC 3.0 to align with SQL-92.

Function	Description
CURRENT_DATE( ) (ODBC 3.0)	Returns the current date.
CURRENT_TIME[(*time-precision***)]** (ODBC 3.0)	Returns the current local time. The *time-precision* argument determines the seconds precision of the returned value.
CURRENT_TIMESTAMP [(*timestamp-precision***)]** (ODBC 3.0)	Returns the current local date and local time as a timestamp value. The *timestamp-precision* argument determines the seconds precision of the returned timestamp.
CURDATE( ) (ODBC 1.0)	Returns the current date.
CURTIME( ) (ODBC 1.0)	Returns the current local time.
DAYNAME(*date_exp***)** (ODBC 2.0)	Returns a character string containing the data source–specific name of the day (for example, Sunday, through Saturday or Sun. through Sat. for a data source that uses English, or Sonntag through Samstag for a data source that uses German) for the day portion of *date_exp*.
DAYOFMONTH(*date_exp***)** (ODBC 1.0)	Returns the day of the month based on the month field in *date_exp* as an integer value in the range of 1–31.
DAYOFWEEK(*date_exp***)** (ODBC 1.0)	Returns the day of the week based on the week field in *date_exp* as an integer value in the range of 1–7, where 1 represents Sunday.
DAYOFYEAR(*date_exp***)** (ODBC 1.0)	Returns the day of the year based on the year field in *date_exp* as an integer value in the range of 1–366.
EXTRACT(*extract-field FROM extract-source***)** (ODBC 3.0)	Returns the *extract-field* portion of the *extract-source*. The *extract-source* argument is a datetime or interval expression. The *extract-field* argument can be one of the following keywords: YEAR MONTH DAY HOUR MINUTE SECOND The precision of the returned value is implementation-defined. The scale is 0 unless SECOND is specified, in which case the scale is not less than the fractional seconds precision of the *extract-source* field.
HOUR(*time_exp***)** (ODBC 1.0)	Returns the hour based on the hour field in *time_exp* as an integer value in the range of 0–23.
MINUTE(*time_exp***)** (ODBC 1.0)	Returns the minute based on the minute field in *time_exp* as an integer value in the range of 0–59.

Function	Description
MONTH(*date_exp***)** (ODBC 1.0)	Returns the month based on the month field in *date_exp* as an integer value in the range of 1–12.
MONTHNAME(*date_exp***)** (ODBC 2.0)	Returns a character string containing the data source–specific name of the month (for example, January through December or Jan. through Dec. for a data source that uses English, or Januar through Dezember for a data source that uses German) for the month portion of *date_exp*.
NOW( ) (ODBC 1.0)	Returns current date and time as a timestamp value.
QUARTER(*date_exp***)** (ODBC 1.0)	Returns the quarter in *date_exp* as an integer value in the range of 1–4, where 1 represents January 1 through March 31.
SECOND(*time_exp***)** (ODBC 1.0)	Returns the second based on the second field in *time_exp* as an integer value in the range of 0–59.
TIMESTAMPADD(*interval***,** *integer_exp***,** *timestamp_exp***)** (ODBC 2.0)	Returns the timestamp calculated by adding *integer_exp* intervals of type *interval* to *timestamp_exp*. Valid values of *interval* are the following keywords: SQL_TSI_FRAC_SECOND SQL_TSI_SECOND SQL_TSI_MINUTE SQL_TSI_HOUR SQL_TSI_DAY SQL_TSI_WEEK SQL_TSI_MONTH SQL_TSI_QUARTER SQL_TSI_YEAR where fractional seconds are expressed in billionths of a second. For example, the following SQL statement returns the name of each employee and his or her one-year anniversary date: SELECT NAME, {fn TIMESTAMPADD(SQL_TSI_YEAR, 1, HIRE_DATE)} FROM EMPLOYEES If *timestamp_exp* is a time value and *interval* specifies days, weeks, months, quarters, or years, the date portion of *timestamp_exp* is set to the current date before calculating the resulting timestamp.

Function	Description
TIMESTAMPADD(*interval***,** *integer_exp***,** *timestamp_exp***)** (ODBC 2.0) (*continued*)	If *timestamp_exp* is a date value and *interval* specifies fractional seconds, seconds, minutes, or hours, the time portion of *timestamp_exp* is set to 0 before calculating the resulting timestamp. An application determines which intervals a data source supports by calling **SQLGetInfo** with the SQL_TIMEDATE_ADD_INTERVALS option.
TIMESTAMPDIFF(*interval***,** *timestamp_exp1***,** *timestamp_exp2***)** (ODBC 2.0)	Returns the integer number of intervals of type *interval* by which *timestamp_exp2* is greater than *timestamp_exp1*. Valid values of *interval* are the following keywords: SQL_TSI_FRAC_SECOND SQL_TSI_SECOND SQL_TSI_MINUTE SQL_TSI_HOUR SQL_TSI_DAY SQL_TSI_WEEK SQL_TSI_MONTH SQL_TSI_QUARTER SQL_TSI_YEAR where fractional seconds are expressed in billionths of a second. For example, the following SQL statement returns the name of each employee and the number of years he or she has been employed. SELECT NAME, {fn TIMESTAMPDIFF(SQL_TSI_YEAR, {fn CURDATE()}, HIRE_DATE)} FROM EMPLOYEES If either timestamp expression is a time value and *interval* specifies days, weeks, months, quarters, or years, the date portion of that timestamp is set to the current date before calculating the difference between the timestamps. If either timestamp expression is a date value and *interval* specifies fractional seconds, seconds, minutes, or hours, the time portion of that timestamp is set to 0 before calculating the difference between the timestamps. An application determines which intervals a data source supports by calling **SQLGetInfo** with the SQL_TIMEDATE_DIFF_INTERVALS option.
WEEK(*date_exp***)** (ODBC 1.0)	Returns the week of the year based on the week field in *date_exp* as an integer value in the range of 1–53.
YEAR(*date_exp***)** (ODBC 1.0)	Returns the year based on the year field in *date_exp* as an integer value. The range is data source–dependent.

System Functions

The following table lists system functions that are included in the ODBC scalar function set. An application can determine which system functions are supported by a driver by calling **SQLGetInfo** with an *information type* of SQL_SYSTEM_FUNCTIONS.

Arguments denoted as *exp* can be the name of a column, the result of another scalar function, or a literal, where the underlying data type could be represented as SQL_NUMERIC, SQL_DECIMAL, SQL_TINYINT, SQL_SMALLINT, SQL_INTEGER, SQL_BIGINT, SQL_FLOAT, SQL_REAL, SQL_DOUBLE, SQL_TYPE_DATE, SQL_TYPE_TIME, or SQL_TYPE_TIMESTAMP.

Arguments denoted as *value* can be a literal constant, where the underlying data type can be represented as SQL_NUMERIC, SQL_DECIMAL, SQL_TINYINT, SQL_SMALLINT, SQL_INTEGER, SQL_BIGINT, SQL_FLOAT, SQL_REAL, SQL_DOUBLE, SQL_TYPE_DATE, SQL_TYPE_TIME, or SQL_TYPE_TIMESTAMP.

Values returned are represented as ODBC data types.

Function	Description
DATABASE( ) (ODBC 1.0)	Returns the name of the database corresponding to the connection handle. (The name of the database is also available by calling **SQLGetConnectOption** with the SQL_CURRENT_QUALIFIER connection option.)
IFNULL(*exp*, *value***)** (ODBC 1.0)	If *exp* is null, *value* is returned. If *exp* is not null, *exp* is returned. The possible data type or types of *value* must be compatible with the data type of *exp*.
USER( ) (ODBC 1.0)	Returns the user name in the DBMS. (The user name is also available by way of **SQLGetInfo** by specifying the information type: SQL_USER_NAME.) This may be different than the login name.

Explicit Data Type Conversion

Explicit data type conversion is specified in terms of SQL data type definitions.

The ODBC syntax for the explicit data type conversion function does not restrict conversions. The validity of specific conversions of one data type to another data type will be determined by each driver-specific implementation. The driver will, as it translates the ODBC syntax into the native syntax, reject those conversions that, although legal in the ODBC syntax, are not supported by the data source. The ODBC function **SQLGetInfo** with the conversion options (such as SQL_CONVERT_BIGINT, SQL_CONVERT_BINARY, SQL_CONVERT_INTERVAL_YEAR_MONTH, and so on) provides a way to inquire about conversions supported by the data source.

The format of the **CONVERT** function is:

CONVERT(*value_exp*, *data_type*)

The function returns the value specified by *value_exp* converted to the specified *data_type*, where *data_type* is one of the following keywords:

SQL_BIGINT
SQL_BINARY
SQL_BIT
SQL_CHAR
SQL_DECIMAL
SQL_DOUBLE
SQL_FLOAT
SQL_INTEGER
SQL_INTERVAL_MONTH
SQL_INTERVAL_YEAR
SQL_INTERVAL_YEAR_TO_MONTH
SQL_INTERVAL_DAY
SQL_INTERVAL_HOUR
SQL_INTERVAL_MINUTE
SQL_INTERVAL_SECOND
SQL_INTERVAL_DAY_TO_HOUR
SQL_INTERVAL_DAY_TO_MINUTE
SQL_INTERVAL_DAY_TO_SECOND
SQL_INTERVAL_HOUR_TO_MINUTE
SQL_INTERVAL_HOUR_TO_SECOND
SQL_INTERVAL_MINUTE_TO_SECOND
SQL_LONGVARBINARY
SQL_LONGVARCHAR
SQL_NUMERIC
SQL_REAL
SQL_SMALLINT
SQL_TYPE_DATE
SQL_TYPE_TIME
SQL_TYPE_TIMESTAMP
SQL_TINYINT
SQL_VARBINARY
SQL_VARCHAR
SQL_WCHAR
SQL_WLONGVARCHAR
SQL_WVARCHAR

The ODBC syntax for the explicit data type conversion function does not support specification of conversion format. If specification of explicit formats is supported by the underlying data source, a driver must specify a default value or implement format specification.

The argument *value_exp* can be a column name, the result of another scalar function, or a numeric or string literal. For example:

```
{ fn CONVERT( { fn CURDATE() }, SQL_CHAR) }
```

converts the output of the CURDATE scalar function to a character string.

Because ODBC does not mandate a data type for return values from scalar functions as the functions are often data source–specific, applications should use the CONVERT scalar function whenever possible to force data type conversion.

The following two examples illustrate the use of the **CONVERT** function. These examples assume the existence of a table called EMPLOYEES, with an EMPNO column of type SQL_SMALLINT and an EMPNAME column of type SQL_CHAR.

If an application specifies the following SQL statement:

```
SELECT EMPNO FROM EMPLOYEES WHERE {fn CONVERT(EMPNO,SQL_CHAR)} LIKE '1%'
```

- A driver for ORACLE translates the SQL statement to:

  ```
  SELECT EMPNO FROM EMPLOYEES WHERE to_char(EMPNO) LIKE '1%'
  ```

- A driver for SQL Server translates the SQL statement to:

  ```
  SELECT EMPNO FROM EMPLOYEES WHERE convert(char,EMPNO) LIKE '1%'
  ```

If an application specifies the following SQL statement:

```
SELECT {fn ABS(EMPNO)}, {fn CONVERT(EMPNAME,SQL_SMALLINT)}
   FROM EMPLOYEES WHERE EMPNO <> 0
```

- A driver for ORACLE translates the SQL statement to:

  ```
  SELECT abs(EMPNO), to_number(EMPNAME) FROM EMPLOYEES WHERE EMPNO <> 0
  ```

- A driver for SQL Server translates the SQL statement to:

  ```
  SELECT abs(EMPNO), convert(smallint, EMPNAME) FROM EMPLOYEES
     WHERE EMPNO <> 0
  ```

- A driver for Ingres translates the SQL statement to:

  ```
  SELECT abs(EMPNO), int2(EMPNAME) FROM EMPLOYEES WHERE EMPNO <> 0
  ```

SQL-92 Cast Function

The CAST function defined in SQL-92 is equivalent to the CONVERT function defined in ODBC. The syntax of the equivalent functions is as follows:

```
{ fn CONVERT (value-exp, data-type)} /* ODBC
CAST (value-exp AS data-type) /* SQL-92
```

The SQL-92 CAST function mandates which data types can be converted to which other data types. (For more information, see the SQL-92 specification.) The CAST function is supported at the FIPS Transitional level.

An application can determine support for the CAST function as follows:

1. Call **SQLGetInfo** with the SQL_SQL_CONFORMANCE information type. If the return value for the information type is SQL_SC_FIPS127_2_TRANSITIONAL, SQL_SC_SQL92_INTERMEDIATE, or SQL_SC_SQL92_FULL, then the CAST function is supported.
2. If the return value of the SQL_SQL_CONFORMANCE information type is SQL_SC_ENTRY_LEVEL or 0, then call **SQLGetInfo** with the SQL_SQL92_VALUE_EXPRESSIONS information type. If the SQL_SVE_CAST bit is set, then the CAST function is supported.

APPENDIX F

ODBC Cursor Library

The ODBC cursor library (ODBCCR32.DLL) supports block scrollable cursors for any driver that complies with the Level 1 API conformance level; it can be redistributed by developers with their applications or drivers. The cursor library also supports positioned update and delete statements for result sets generated by **SELECT** statements. Although it only supports static and forward-only cursors, the cursor library satisfies the needs of many applications. Furthermore, it can provide good performance, especially for small- to medium-sized result sets, and for applications that do not have good cursor support.

The cursor library is a dynamic-link library (DLL) that resides between the Driver Manager and the driver. When an application calls a function, the Driver Manager calls the function in the cursor library, which either executes the function or calls it in the specified driver. For a given connection, an application specifies whether the cursor library is always used, used if the driver does not support scrollable cursors, or never used.

The cursor library appears as a driver to the Driver Manager. If the cursor library resides between the Driver Manager and an ODBC 2.*x* driver, the cursor library appears as an ODBC 2.*x* driver. If the cursor library resides between the Driver Manager and an ODBC 3.0 driver, the cursor library appears as an ODBC 3.0 driver. The behavior exhibited by the cursor library depends upon the version of the driver it is working with, with the exception of binding offsets, which is supported for both ODBC 2.*x* and ODBC 3.0 drivers.

To implement block cursors in **SQLFetch** and **SQLFetchScroll**, the cursor library repeatedly calls **SQLFetch** in the driver. To implement scrolling, it caches the data it has retrieved in memory and in disk files. When an application requests a new rowset, the cursor library retrieves it as necessary from the driver or the cache.

To implement positioned update and delete statements, the cursor library constructs an **UPDATE** or **DELETE** statement with a **WHERE** clause that specifies the cached value of each bound column in the row. When it executes a positioned update statement, the cursor library updates its cache from the values in the rowset buffers.

Using the ODBC Cursor Library

To use the ODBC cursor library, an application:

1. Calls **SQLSetConnectAttr** with an *Attribute* of SQL_ATTR_ODBC_CURSORS to specify how the cursor library should be used with a particular connection. The cursor library can be always used (SQL_CUR_USE_ODBC), used only if driver does not support scrollable cursors (SQL_CUR_USE_IF_NEEDED), or never used (SQL_CUR_USE_DRIVER).
2. Calls **SQLConnect**, **SQLDriverConnect**, or **SQLBrowseConnect** to connect to the data source.
3. Calls **SQLSetStmtAttr** to specify the cursor type (SQL_ATTR_CURSOR_TYPE), concurrency (SQL_ATTR_CONCURRENCY), and rowset size (SQL_ATTR_ROW_ARRAY_SIZE). The cursor library supports forward-only and static cursors. Forward-only cursors must be read-only, while static cursors may be read-only or use optimistic concurrency control comparing values.
4. Allocates one or more rowset buffers and calls **SQLBindCol** one or more times to bind these buffers to result set columns.
5. Generates a result set by executing a **SELECT** statement or a procedure, or by calling a catalog function. If the application will execute positioned update statements, it should execute a **SELECT FOR UPDATE** statement to generate the result set.
6. Calls **SQLFetch** or **SQLFetchScroll** one or more times to scroll through the result set.

The application can change data values in the rowset buffers. To refresh the rowset buffers with data from the cursor library's cache, an application calls **SQLFetchScroll** with the *FetchOrientation* argument set to SQL_FETCH_RELATIVE and the *FetchOffset* argument set to 0.

To retrieve data from an unbound column, the application calls **SQLSetPos** to position the cursor on the desired row. It then calls **SQLGetData** to retrieve the data.

To determine the number of rows that have been retrieved from the data source, the application calls **SQLRowCount**.

Executing Positioned Update and Delete Statements

After an application has fetched a block of data with **SQLFetchScroll**, it can update or delete the data in the block. To execute a positioned update or delete, the application:

1. Calls **SQLSetPos** to position the cursor on the row to be updated or deleted.
2. Constructs a positioned update or delete statement with the following syntax:

   UPDATE *table-name*
       SET *column-identifier* = {*expression* | **NULL**}
         [, *column-identifier* = {*expression* | **NULL**}]
       WHERE CURRENT OF *cursor-name*
   DELETE FROM *table-name* **WHERE CURRENT OF** *cursor-name*

   The easiest way to construct the **SET** clause in a positioned update statement is to use parameter markers for each column to be updated and use **SQLBindParameter** to bind these to the rowset buffers for the row to be updated. In this case, the C data type of the parameter will be the same as the C data type of the rowset buffer.
3. Updates the rowset buffers for the current row if it will execute a positioned update statement. After successfully executing a positioned update statement, the cursor library copies the values from each column in the current row to its cache.

   Caution If the application does not correctly update the rowset buffers before executing a positioned update statement, the data in the cache will be incorrect after the statement is executed.

   ---
4. Executes the positioned update or delete statement using a different statement than the statement associated with the cursor.

Caution The **WHERE** clause constructed by the cursor library to identify the current row can fail to identify any rows, identify a different row, or identify more than one row. For more information, see "Constructing Searched Statements" later in this appendix.

All positioned update and delete statements require a cursor name. To specify the cursor name, an application calls **SQLSetCursorName** before the cursor is opened. To use the cursor name generated by the driver, an application calls **SQLGetCursorName** after the cursor is opened.

After the cursor library executes a positioned update or delete statement, the status array, rowset buffers, and cache maintained by the cursor library contain the values shown in the following table.

Statement used	Value in row status array	Values in rowset buffers	Values in cache buffers
Positioned update	SQL_ROW_UPDATED	New values [1]	New values [1]
Positioned delete	SQL_ROW_DELETED	Old values	Old values

1 The application must update the values in the rowset buffers before executing the positioned update statement; after executing the positioned update statement, the cursor library copies the values in the rowset buffers to its cache.

Cursor Library Code Example

The following example uses the cursor library to retrieve each order's ID, open date, and status from the ORDERS table. It then displays 20 rows of data. If the user updates this data, the code updates the rowset buffers and executes a positioned update statement. Finally, it prompts the user for the direction to scroll and repeats the process.

```
#define ROWS 20
#define STATUS_LEN 6
#define OPENDATE_LEN 11
#define DONE -1

SQLHENV         henv;
SQLHDBC         hdbc;
SQLHSTMT        hstmt1, hstmt2;
SQLRETURN       retcode;
SQLCHAR         szStatus[ROWS][STATUS_LEN], szOpenDate[ROWS][OPENDATE_LEN];
SQLCHAR         szNewStatus[STATUS_LEN], szNewOpenDate[OPENDATE_LEN];
SQLSMALLINT     sOrderID[ROWS], sNewOrderID[ROWS];
SQLINTEGER      cbStatus[ROWS], cbOrderID[ROWS], cbOpenDate[ROWS];
SQLUINTEGER     FetchOrientation, crow, FetchOffset, irowUpdt;
SQLUSMALLINT    RowStatusArray[ROWS];

SQLAllocHandle(SQL_HANDLE_ENV, SQL_NULL_HANDLE, &henv);
SQLSetEnvAttr(henv, SQL_ATTR_ODBC_VERSION, SQL_OV_ODBC3,0);
SQLAllocHandle(SQL_HANDLE_DBC, henv, &hdbc);

/* Specify that the ODBC Cursor Library is always used, then connect. */

SQLSetConnectAttr(hdbc, SQL_ATTR_ODBC_CURSORS, SQL_CUR_USE_ODBC);
SQLConnect(hdbc, "SalesOrder", SQL_NTS,
                 "JohnS", SQL_NTS,
                 "Sesame", SQL_NTS);
```

```
if (retcode == SQL_SUCCESS || retcode == SQL_SUCCESS_WITH_INFO) {

   /* Allocate a statement handle for the result set and a statement */
   /* handle for positioned update statements.                        */

   SQLAllocHandle(SQL_HANDLE_STMT, hdbc, &hstmt1);
   SQLAllocHandle(SQL_HANDLE_STMT, hdbc, &hstmt2);

   /* Specify an updatable static cursor with 20 rows of data. Set */
   /* the cursor name, execute the SELECT statement, and bind the   */
   /* rowset buffers to result set columns in column-wise fashion. */
   SQLSetStmtAttr(hstmt1, SQL_ATTR_CONCURRENCY, SQL_CONCUR_VALUES, 0);
   SQLSetStmtAttr(hstmt1, SQL_ATTR_CURSOR_TYPE, SQL_CURSOR_STATIC, 0);
   SQLSetStmtAttr(hstmt1, SQL_ATTR_ROW_ARRAY_SIZE, ROWS, 0);
   SQLSetStmtAttr(hstmt1, SQL_ATTR_ROW_STATUS_PTR, RowStatusArray, 0);
   SQLSetStmtAttr(hstmt1, SQL_ATTR_ROWS_FETCHED_PTR, &crow, 0);
   SQLSetCursorName(hstmt1, "ORDERCURSOR", SQL_NTS);
   SQLExecDirect(hstmt1,
               "SELECT ORDERID, OPENDATE, STATUS FROM ORDERS ",
                SQL_NTS);
   SQLBindCol(hstmt1, 1, SQL_C_SSHORT, sOrderID, 0, cbName);
   SQLBindCol(hstmt1, 2, SQL_C_CHAR, szOpenDate, OPENDATE_LEN, cbOpenDate);
   SQLBindCol(hstmt1, 3, SQL_C_CHAR, szStatus, STATUS_LEN, cbStatus);

   /* Fetch the first block of data and display it. Prompt the user  */
   /* for new data values. If the user supplies new values, update   */
   /* the rowset buffers, bind them to the parameters in the update  */
   /* statement, and execute a positioned update on another hstmt.   */
   /* Prompt the user for how to scroll. Fetch and redisplay data as */
   /* needed.                                                         */

   FetchOrientation = SQL_FETCH_FIRST;
   FetchOffset = 0;
   do {

      SQLFetchScroll(hstmt1, FetchOrientation, FetchOffset);
      DisplayRows(sOrderID, szOpenDate, szStatus, RowStatusArray);

      if (PromptUpdate(&irowUpdt,&sNewOrderID,szNewOpenDate,szNewStatus)==TRUE){
         sOrderID[irowUpdt] = sNewOrderID;
         cbOrderID[irowUpdt] = 0;
         strcpy(szOpenDate[irowUpdt], szNewOpenData);
         cbOpenDate[irowUpdt] = SQL_NTS;
         strcpy(szStatus[irowUpdt], szNewStatus);
         cbStatus[irowUpdt] = SQL_NTS;
         SQLBindParameter(hstmt2, 1, SQL_PARAM_INPUT,
                          SQL_C_SSHORT, SQL_INTEGER, 0, 0,
                          &sOrderID[irowUpdt], 0, &cbOrderID[irowUpdt]);
         SQLBindParameter(hstmt2, 2, SQL_PARAM_INPUT,
                          SQL_C_CHAR, SQL_TYPE_DATE, OPENDATE_LEN, 0,
                          szOpenDate[irowUpdt], OPENDATE_LEN, &cbOpenDate[irowUpdt]);
```

```
            SQLBindParameter(hstmt2, 3, SQL_PARAM_INPUT,
                             SQL_C_CHAR, SQL_CHAR, STATUS_LEN, 0,
                             szStatus[irowUpdt], STATUS_LEN, &cbStatus[irowUpdt]);
            SQLExecDirect(hstmt2,
                          "UPDATE EMPLOYEE SET ORDERID = ?, OPENDATE = ?, STATUS = ?"
                          "WHERE CURRENT OF EMPCURSOR",
                          SQL_NTS);
        }

    while (PromptScroll(&FetchOrientation, &FetchOffset) != DONE)
}
```

Implementation Notes

This section describes how the ODBC cursor library is implemented. It describes how the cursor library maintains its cache, executes SQL statements, and implements ODBC functions.

Cursor Library Cache

For each row of data in the result set, the cursor library caches the data for each bound column, the length of the data in each bound column, and the status of the row. The cursor library uses the values in the cache both to return through **SQLFetch** and **SQLFetchScroll** and to construct searched statements for positioned operations. For more information, see "Constructing Searched Statements" later in this appendix.

Column Data

The cursor library creates a buffer in the cache for each data buffer bound to the result set with **SQLBindCol**. It uses the values in these buffers to construct a **WHERE** clause when it emulates a positioned update or delete statement. It updates these buffers from the rowset buffers when it fetches data from the data source and when it executes positioned update statements.

When the cursor library updates its cache from the rowset buffers, it transfers the data according to the C data type specified in **SQLBindCol**. For example, if the C data type of a rowset buffer is SQL_C_SLONG, the cursor library transfers four bytes of data; if it is SQL_C_CHAR and *BufferLength* is 10, the cursor library transfers 10 bytes of data. The cursor library does not perform any type checking or conversions on the data it transfers.

Note The cursor library does not update its cache for a column if **StrLen_or_IndPtr* in the corresponding rowset buffer is SQL_DATA_AT_EXEC or the result of the SQL_LEN_DATA_AT_EXEC macro.

When it updates a column, a data source blank-pads fixed-length character data and zero-pads fixed-length binary data as necessary. For example, a data source stores "Smith" in a CHAR(10) column as "Smith   ". The cursor library does not blank- or zero-pad data in the rowset buffers when it copies this data to its cache after executing a positioned update statement. Therefore, if an application requires that the values in the cursor library's cache are blank- or zero-padded, it must blank- or zero-pad the values in the rowset buffers before executing a positioned update statement.

Length of Column Data

The cursor library creates a buffer in the cache for each length/indicator buffer bound to the result set with **SQLBindCol**. It uses the values in these buffers to construct a **WHERE** clause when it emulates positioned update or delete statements. It updates these buffers from the rowset buffers when it fetches data from the data source and when it executes positioned update statements.

If the C type of a data buffer is SQL_C_CHAR or SQL_C_BINARY, and the length/indicator value is SQL_NTS, the string length of the data is put into the length/indicator buffer.

Note The cursor library does not update its cache for a column if **StrLen_or_IndPtr* in the corresponding rowset buffer is SQL_DATA_AT_EXEC or the result of the SQL_LEN_DATA_AT_EXEC macro.

Row Status

The cursor library creates a buffer in the cache for the row status. The cursor library retrieves values for the row status array (specified with the SQL_ATTR_ROW_STATUS_PTR statement attribute) from this buffer. For each row, the cursor library sets this buffer to:

- SQL_ROW_DELETED when it executes a positioned delete statement on the row.
- SQL_ROW_ERROR when it encounters an error retrieving the row from the data source with **SQLFetch**.
- SQL_ROW_SUCCESS when it successfully fetches the row from the data source with **SQLFetch**.
- SQL_ROW_UPDATED when it executes a positioned update statement on the row.

Location of Cache

The cursor library caches data in memory and in Windows temporary files. This limits the size of the result set that the cursor library can handle only by available disk space. A temporary file is used when the data to be cached would cross the segment boundary if inserted at the end of the cursor library cache. Instead, the data to be cached is added in place of the last-saved block of data in the cache. The last-saved block of data is saved in a temporary file. If the cursor library terminates abnormally, such as when the power fails, it may leave Windows temporary files on the disk. These are named ~CTT*nnnn*.TMP and are created in the current directory.

Note If the cursor library in Windows NT attempts to cache data in a temporary file on the current directory while the application is running from a read-only share or a compact disk (such as a Microsoft Foundation Class Library sample), SQLSTATE HY000 (General Error- Unable to create a file buffer) will be returned.

Processing SQL Statements

The ODBC cursor library passes all SQL statements directly to the driver except the following:

- Positioned update and delete statements
- **SELECT FOR UPDATE** statements
- Batched SQL statements

To execute positioned update and delete statements and to position the cursor on a row to call **SQLGetData** for that row, the cursor library constructs a searched statement that identifies the row.

Processing Positioned Update and Delete Statements

The cursor library supports positioned update and delete statements by replacing the **WHERE CURRENT OF** clause in such statements with a **WHERE** clause that enumerates the values stored in its cache for each bound column. The cursor library passes the newly constructed **UPDATE** and **DELETE** statements to the driver for execution. For positioned update statements, it then updates its cache from the values in the rowset buffers and sets the corresponding value in the row status array to SQL_ROW_UPDATED. For positioned delete statements, it sets the corresponding value in the row status array to SQL_ROW_DELETED.

Caution The **WHERE** clause constructed by the cursor library to identify the current row can fail to identify any rows, identify a different row, or identify more than one row. For more information, see "Constructing Searched Statements" later in this appendix.

Positioned update and delete statements are subject to the following restrictions:

- Positioned update and delete statements can only be used when a **SELECT** statement generated the result set, the **SELECT** statement did not contain a join, a **UNION** clause, or a **GROUP BY** clause, and any columns that used an alias or expression in the select list were not bound with **SQLBindCol**.
- If an application prepares a positioned update or delete statement, it must do so after it has called **SQLFetch** or **SQLFetchScroll**. Although the cursor library submits the statement to the driver for preparation, it closes the statement and executes it directly when the application calls **SQLExecute**.
- If the driver only supports one active statement, the cursor library fetches the rest of the result set and then refetches the current rowset from its cache before it executes a positioned update or delete statement. If the application then calls a function that returns metadata in a result set (for example, **SQLNumResultCols** or **SQLDescribeCol**), the cursor library returns an error.
- If a positioned update or delete statement is performed on a column of a table that includes a timestamp column that is automatically updated every time an update is performed, all subsequent positioned update or delete statements will fail if the timestamp column is bound. This occurs because the searched update or delete statement that the Cursor Library creates will not accurately identify the row to update. The value in the searched statement for the timestamp column will not match the automatically updated value of the timestamp column.

Processing SELECT FOR UPDATE Statements

For maximum interoperability, applications should generate result sets that will be updated with a positioned update statement by executing a **SELECT FOR UPDATE** statement. Although the cursor library does not require this, it is required by most data sources that support positioned update statements.

The cursor library ignores the columns in the **FOR UPDATE** clause of a **SELECT FOR UPDATE** statement; it removes this clause before passing the statement to the driver. In the cursor library, the SQL_ATTR_CONCURRENCY statement attribute, along with the restrictions mentioned in the previous section, controls whether the columns in a result set can be updated.

Processing Batches of SQL Statements

The cursor library does not support batches of SQL statements, including SQL statements for which the SQL_ATTR_PARAMSET_SIZE statement attribute is greater than 1. If an application submits a batch of SQL statements to the cursor library, the results are undefined.

Constructing Searched Statements

To support positioned update and delete statements, the cursor library constructs a searched **UPDATE** or **DELETE** statement from the positioned statement. To support calls to **SQLGetData** in a block of data, the cursor library constructs a searched **SELECT** statement to create a result set containing the current row of data. In each of these statements, the **WHERE** clause enumerates the values stored in the cache for each bound column that returns SQL_PRED_SEARCHABLE or SQL_PRED_BASIC for the SQL_DESC_SEARCHABLE field identifier in **SQLColAttribute**.

Caution The **WHERE** clause constructed by the cursor library to identify the current row can fail to identify any rows, identify a different row, or identify more than one row.

If a positioned update or delete statement affects more than one row, the cursor library updates the row status array only for the row on which the cursor is positioned and returns SQL_SUCCESS_WITH_INFO and SQLSTATE 01001 (Cursor operation conflict). If the statement does not identify any rows, the cursor library does not update the row status array and returns SQL_SUCCESS_WITH_INFO and SQLSTATE 01001 (Cursor operation conflict). An application can call **SQLRowCount** to determine the number of rows that were updated or deleted.

If the **SELECT** clause used to position the cursor for a call to **SQLGetData** identifies more than one row, **SQLGetData** is not guaranteed to return the correct data. If it does not identify any rows, **SQLGetData** returns SQL_NO_DATA.

If an application conforms to the following guidelines, the **WHERE** clause constructed by the cursor library should uniquely identify the current row, except when this is impossible, such as when the data source contains duplicate rows.

- **Bind columns that uniquely identify the row.** If the bound columns do not uniquely identify the row, the **WHERE** clause constructed by the cursor library might identify more than one row. In a positioned update or delete statement, such a clause might cause more than one row to be updated or deleted. In a call to **SQLGetData**, such a clause might cause the driver to return data for the wrong row. Binding all the columns in a unique key guarantees that each row is uniquely identified.
- **Allocate data buffers large enough that no truncation occurs.** The cursor library's cache is a copy of the values in the rowset buffers bound to the result set with **SQLBindCol**. If data is truncated when it is placed in these buffers, it will also be truncated in the cache. A **WHERE** clause constructed from truncated values might not correctly identify the underlying row in the data source.

- **Specify non-null length buffers for binary C data.** The cursor library allocates length buffers in its cache only if the *StrLen_or_IndPtr* argument in **SQLBindCol** is non-null. When the *TargetType* argument is SQL_C_BINARY, the cursor library requires the length of the binary data to construct a **WHERE** clause from the data. If there is no length buffer for a SQL_C_BINARY column and the application calls **SQLGetData** or attempts to execute a positioned update or delete statement, the cursor library returns SQL_ERROR and SQLSTATE SL014 (A positioned request was issued and not all column count fields were buffered).
- **Specify non-null length buffers for nullable columns.** The cursor library allocates length buffers in its cache only if the *StrLen_or_IndPtr* argument in **SQLBindCol** is non-null. Because SQL_NULL_DATA is stored in the length buffer, the cursor library assumes that any column for which no length buffer is specified is non-nullable. If no length column is specified for a nullable column, the cursor library constructs a **WHERE** clause that uses the data value for the column. This clause will not correctly identify the row.

ODBC Functions

When the ODBC cursor library is enabled for a connection, the Driver Manager calls functions in the cursor library instead of in the driver. The cursor library either executes the function or calls it in the specified driver.

ODBC Functions Executed by the Cursor Library

The cursor library executes the following functions. When an application calls a function in this list, the Driver Manager invokes the cursor library, not the driver. Note that the cursor library may call the driver when executing the function.

SQLBindCol
SQLBindParam
SQLBindParameter
SQLCloseCursor
SQLEndTran
SQLExtendedFetch
SQLFetchScroll
SQLFreeHandle
SQLFreeStmt
SQLGetData
SQLGetDescField
SQLGetDescRec
SQLGetFunctions
SQLGetInfo
SQLGetStmtAttr
SQLGetStmtOption
SQLNativeSql
SQLNumParams
SQLParamOptions
SQLRowCount
SQLSetConnectAttr
SQLSetConnectOption
SQLSetDescField
SQLSetDescRec
SQLSetPos
SQLSetScrollOptions
SQLSetStmtAttr
SQLSetStmtOption
SQLTransact

ODBC Functions Not Executed by the Cursor Library

The cursor library does not execute the following functions. When an application calls one of these functions, the Driver Manager invokes the driver, not the cursor library.

SQLFetch

SQLGetConnectAttr

SQLGetDiagField

SQLGetDiagRec

SQLGetEnvAttr

SQLSetDescRec

SQLSetEnvAttr

SQLBindCol in the Cursor Library

An application allocates one or more buffers for the cursor library to return the current rowset in. It calls **SQLBindCol** one or more times to bind these buffers to the result set.

An application can call **SQLBindCol** to rebind result set columns after it has called **SQLExtendedFetch**, **SQLFetch**, or **SQLFetchScroll**, as long as the C data type, column size, and decimal digits of the bound column remain the same. The application need not close the cursor to rebind columns to different addresses.

The cursor library supports setting the SQL_ATTR_ROW_BIND_OFFSET_PTR statement attribute to use bind offsets. (**SQLBindCol** does not have to be called for this rebinding to occur.) If the cursor library is used with an ODBC 3.0 driver, the bind offset is not used when **SQLFetch** is called. The bind offset is used if **SQLFetch** is called when the cursor library is used with an ODBC 2.*x* driver, because **SQLFetch** is then mapped to **SQLExtendedFetch**.

The cursor library supports calling **SQLBindCol** to bind the bookmark column.

When working with an ODBC 2.*x* driver, the cursor library returns SQLSTATE HY090 (Invalid string or buffer length) when **SQLBindCol** is called to set the buffer length for a bookmark column to a value not equal to 4. When working with an ODBC 3.0 driver, the cursor library allows the buffer to be any size.

SQLBindParameter in the Cursor Library

An application can call **SQLBindParameter** to rebind parameters, as long as the C data type, column size, and decimal digits of the bound column remain the same.

The cursor library supports setting the SQL_ATTR_ROW_BIND_OFFSET_PTR statement attribute to use bind offsets. (**SQLBindParameter** does not have to be called for this rebinding to occur.)

The cursor library supports binding data-at-execution parameters.

SQLBulkOperations and the Cursor Library

The cursor library does not support calling **SQLBulkOperations**.

SQLCloseCursor in the Cursor Library

The cursor library does not support calling **SQLCloseCursor** without an open cursor. Attempting this will return SQLSTATE 24000 (Invalid cursor state). Calling **SQLFreeStmt** with an *Option* of SQL_CLOSE when no cursor is open is supported by the cursor library.

SQLEndTran in the Cursor Library

The cursor library does not support transactions and passes calls to **SQLEndTran** directly to the driver. However, the cursor library does support the cursor commit and rollback behaviors as returned by the data source with the SQL_CURSOR_ROLLBACK_BEHAVIOR and SQL_CURSOR_COMMIT_BEHAVIOR information types:

- For data sources that preserve cursors across transactions, changes that are rolled back in the data source are not rolled back in the cursor library's cache. To make the cache match the data in the data source, the application must close and reopen the cursor.
- For data sources that close cursors at transaction boundaries, the cursor library closes the cursors and deletes the caches for all statements on the connection.
- For data sources that delete prepared statements at transaction boundaries, the application must reprepare all prepared statements on the connection before reexecuting them.

SQLExtendedFetch in the Cursor Library

The cursor library implements **SQLExtendedFetch** by repeatedly calling **SQLFetch** in the driver.

The cursor library supports calling **SQLExtendedFetch** with a *FetchOrientation* of SQL_FETCH_BOOKMARK.

When the cursor library is used, calls to **SQLExtendedFetch** cannot be mixed with calls to either **SQLFetchScroll** or **SQLFetch**.

SQLFetch in the Cursor Library

When the cursor library is used, calls to **SQLFetch** cannot be mixed with calls to either **SQLFetchScroll** or **SQLExtendedFetch**.

If **SQLFetch** is called with SQL_ATTR_ROW_ARRAY_SIZE set to a value greater than 1, the cursor library will pass the call to the driver. If the driver is an ODBC 2.*x* driver, the rowset size will be ignored and the call to **SQLFetch** will return a single row of data.

If the cursor library is used with an ODBC 2.*x* driver, a bind offset (as defined by the SQL_ATTR_ROW_BIND_OFFSET_PTR statement attribute) is not used when **SQLFetch** is called.

When the cursor library is loaded, an application cannot call **SQLFetch** to fetch bookmark columns. The cursor library passes the call to **SQLFetch** through to the driver, but the function calls to enable bookmarks and bind the bookmark column are intercepted by the cursor library.

SQLFetchScroll in the Cursor Library

The cursor library implements **SQLFetchScroll** by repeatedly calling **SQLFetch** in the driver. It transfers the data it retrieves from the driver to the rowset buffers provided by the application. It also caches the data in memory and disk files. When an application requests a new rowset, the cursor library retrieves it as necessary from the driver (if it has not been previously fetched) or the cache (if it has been previously fetched). Finally, the cursor library maintains the status of the cached data and returns this information to the application in the row status array.

When the cursor library is used, calls to **SQLFetchScroll** cannot be mixed with calls to either **SQLFetch** or **SQLExtendedFetch**.

When the cursor library is used, calls to **SQLFetchScroll** are supported for both ODBC 2.*x* and ODBC 3.0 drivers.

Rowset Buffers

The cursor library optimizes the transfer of data from the driver to the rowset buffer provided by the application if:

- The application uses row-wise binding.
- There are no unused bytes between fields in the structure the application declares to hold a row of data.
- The fields in which **SQLFetch** or **SQLFetchScroll** returns the length/indicator for a column follows the buffer for that column and precedes the buffer for the next column. Note that these fields are optional.

When the application requests a new rowset, the cursor library retrieves data from its cache and from the driver as necessary. If the new and old rowsets overlap, the cursor library may optimize its performance by reusing the data from the overlapping sections of the rowset buffers. Thus, unsaved changes to the rowset buffers are lost unless the new and old rowsets overlap and the changes are in the overlapping sections of the rowset buffers. To save the changes, an application submits a positioned update statement.

Note that the cursor library always refreshes the rowset buffers with data from the cache when an application calls **SQLFetchScroll** with the *FetchOrientation* argument set to SQL_FETCH_RELATIVE and the *FetchOffset* argument set to 0.

The cursor library supports calling **SQLSetStmtAttr** with an *Attribute* of SQL_ATTR_ROW_ARRAY_SIZE to change the rowset size while a cursor is open. The new rowset size will take effect the next time **SQLFetchScroll** is called.

Result Set Membership

The cursor library retrieves data from the driver only as the application requests it. Depending on the data source and the setting of the SQL_CONCURRENCY statement attribute, this has the following consequences:

- The data retrieved by the cursor library may differ from the data that was available at the time the statement was executed. For example, after the cursor was opened, rows inserted at a point beyond the current cursor position can be retrieved by some drivers.
- The data in the result set may be locked by the data source for the cursor library and therefore be unavailable to other users.

After the cursor library has cached a row of data, it cannot detect changes to that row in the underlying data source (except for positioned updates and deletes operating on the same cursor's cache). This occurs because, for calls to **SQLFetchScroll**, the cursor library never refetches data from the data source. Instead it refetches data from its cache.

Scrolling

The cursor library supports the following fetch types in **SQLFetchScroll**:

Cursor type	Fetch types
Forward-only	SQL_FETCH_NEXT
Static	SQL_FETCH_NEXT SQL_FETCH_PRIOR SQL_FETCH_FIRST SQL_FETCH_LAST SQL_FETCH_RELATIVE SQL_FETCH_ABSOLUTE SQL_FETCH_BOOKMARK

Errors

When **SQLFetchScroll** is called, and one of the calls to **SQLFetch** returns SQL_ERROR, the cursor library proceeds as follows. After it completes these steps, the cursor library continues processing.

1. Calls **SQLGetDiagRec** to obtain error information from the driver, and posts this as a diagnostic record in the Driver Manager.
2. Sets the SQL_DIAG_ROW_NUMBER field in the diagnostic record to the appropriate value.
3. Sets the SQL_DIAG_COLUMN_NUMBER field in the diagnostic record to the appropriate value, if applicable; otherwise, it sets it to 0.
4. Sets the value for the row in error in the row status array to SQL_ROW_ERROR.

After the cursor library has called **SQLFetch** multiple times in its implementation of **SQLFetchScroll**, any error or warning returned by one of the calls to **SQLFetch** will be in a diagnostic record, and may be retrieved by a call to **SQLGetDiagRec**. If the data was truncated when it was fetched, the truncated data will now reside in the cursor library's cache. Subsequent calls to **SQLFetchScroll** to scroll to a row with truncated data will return the truncated data, and no warning will be raised because the data is fetched from the cursor library's cache. To keep track of the length of data returned, so it can determine if the data returned in a buffer has been truncated, an application should bind the length/indicator buffer.

Bookmark Operations

The cursor library supports calling **SQLFetchScroll** with a *FetchOrientation* of SQL_FETCH_BOOKMARK. It also supports specifying an offset in the *FetchOffset* argument to be used in the bookmark operation. This is the only bookmark operation the cursor library supports. The cursor library does not support calling **SQLBulkOperations**.

If the application has set the SQL_ATTR_USE_BOOKMARKS statement attribute, and has bound to the bookmark column, then the cursor library generates a fixed-length bookmark and returns it to the application. The cursor library creates and maintains the bookmarks that it uses; it does not use bookmarks maintained at the data source. When **SQLFetchScroll** is called to retrieve a block of data that has already been fetched from the data source, it retrieves the data from the cursor library cache. As a result, the bookmark used in a call to **SQLFetchScroll** with a *FetchOrientation* of SQL_FETCH_BOOKMARK must be created and maintained by the cursor library.

Interaction with Other Functions

An application must call **SQLFetch** or **SQLFetchScroll** before it prepares or executes any positioned update or delete statements.

SQLFreeStmt in the Cursor Library

If an application calls **SQLFreeStmt** with the SQL_UNBIND option after it calls **SQLExtendedFetch**, **SQLFetch**, or **SQLFetchScroll**, the cursor library returns an error. Before it can unbind result set columns, an application must call **SQLCloseCursor** or **SQLFreeStmt** with the SQL_CLOSE option.

SQLGetData in the Cursor Library

The cursor library implements **SQLGetData** by first constructing a **SELECT** statement with a **WHERE** clause that enumerates the values stored in its cache for each bound column in the current row. It then executes the **SELECT** statement to reselect the row and calls **SQLGetData** in the driver to retrieve the data from the data source (as opposed to the cache).

Caution The **WHERE** clause constructed by the cursor library to identify the current row can fail to identify any rows, identify a different row, or identify more than one row. For more information, see "Constructing Searched Statements" earlier in this appendix.

If the SQL_ATTR_USE_BOOKMARKS statement attribute is set to SQL_UB_VARIABLE, **SQLGetData** can be called on column 0 to return bookmark data.

Calls to **SQLGetData** are subject to the following restrictions:

- **SQLGetData** cannot be called for forward-only cursors.
- **SQLGetData** can only be called when a **SELECT** statement generated the result set, the **SELECT** statement did not contain a join, a **UNION** clause, or a **GROUP BY** clause, and any columns that used an alias or expression in the select list were not bound with **SQLBindCol**.
- If the driver supports only one active statement, the cursor library fetches the rest of the result set before executing the **SELECT** statement and calling **SQLGetData**.

SQLGetDescField and SQLGetDescRec in the Cursor Library

The cursor library executes **SQLGetDescRec** to return metadata for bookmark columns. The cursor library executes **SQLGetDescField** to return the same fields returned by **SQLGetDescRec**, which are SQL_DESC_NAME, SQL_DESC_TYPE, SQL_DESC_DATETIME_INTERVAL_CODE, SQL_DESC_OCTET_LENGTH, SQL_DESC_PRECISION, SQL_DESC_SCALE, and SQL_DESC_NULLABLE. For consistency, **SQLGetDescField** also returns SQL_DESC_UNNAMED.

The cursor library executes **SQLGetDescField** when it is called to return the value of the following fields that are set for binding bookmark columns: SQL_DESC_DATA_PTR, SQL_DESC_INDICATOR_PTR, SQL_DESC_OCTET_LENGTH_PTR, and SQL_DESC_LENGTH.

The cursor library executes **SQLGetDescField** when it is called to return the value of the SQL_DESC_BIND_OFFSET_PTR, SQL_DESC_BIND_TYPE, SQL_DESC_ROW_ARRAY_SIZE, or SQL_DESC_ROW_STATUS_PTR field. These fields can be returned for any row, not just the bookmark row.

If an application calls **SQLGetDescField** to return the value of any field other than those mentioned previously, the cursor library passes the call to the driver.

SQLGetFunctions in the Cursor Library

The cursor library returns that it supports **SQLExtendedFetch**, **SQLFetchScroll**, **SQLSetPos**, and **SQLSetScrollOptions** in addition to the functions supported by the driver.

SQLGetInfo in the Cursor Library

The cursor library returns values for the following values of *InfoType* (| represents a bitwise OR); for all other values of *InfoType*, it calls **SQLGetInfo** in the driver:

InfoType	Returned value
SQL_BOOKMARK_ PERSISTENCE	SQL_BP_SCROLL
SQL_DYNAMIC_CURSOR_ ATTRIBUTES1	0
SQL_DYNAMIC_CURSOR_ ATTRIBUTES2	0
SQL_FETCH_DIRECTION [1]	SQL_FD_FETCH_ABSOLUTE | SQL_FD_FETCH_FIRST | SQL_FD_FETCH_LAST | SQL_FD_FETCH_NEXT | SQL_FD_FETCH_PRIOR | SQL_FD_FETCH_RELATIVE | SQL_FD_FETCH_BOOKMARK
SQL_FORWARD_ONLY_CURSOR_ ATTRIBUTES1	SQL_CA1_NEXT | SQL_CA1_ABSOLUTE | SQL_CA1_RELATIVE | SQL_CA1_LOCK_NO_CHANGE | SQL_CA1_POS_POSITION | SQL_CA1_POSITIONED_DELETE | SQL_CA1_POSITIONED_UPDATE | SQL_CA1_SELECT_FOR_UPDATE
SQL_FORWARD_ONLY_CURSOR_ ATTRIBUTES2	SQL_CA2_READ_ONLY_CONCUR | SQL_CA2_OPT_VALUES_ CONCURRENCY | SQL_CA2_SENSITIVITY_UPDATES
SQL_GETDATA_EXTENSIONS	SQL_GD_BLOCK | any values returned by the driver **Note** When data is retrieved with **SQLFetchScroll**, **SQLGetData** supports the functionality specified with the SQL_GD_ANY_COLUMN, SQL_GD_BOUND, and SQL_GD_ANY_ORDER bitmasks.
SQL_KEYSET_DRIVEN_CURSOR_ ATTRIBUTES1	0
SQL_KEYSET_DRIVEN_CURSOR_ ATTRIBUTES2	0
SQL_LOCK_TYPES [1]	SQL_LCK_NO_CHANGE

InfoType	Returned value
SQL_STATIC_CURSOR_ATTRIBUTES1	SQL_CA1_NEXT | SQL_CA1_ABSOLUTE | SQL_CA1_RELATIVE | SQL_CA1_BOOKMARK | SQL_CA1_LOCK_NO_CHANGE | SQL_CA1_POS_POSITION | SQL_CA1_POSITIONED_DELETE | SQL_CA1_POSITIONED_UPDATE | SQL_CA1_SELECT_FOR_UPDATE
SQL_STATIC_CURSOR_ATTRIBUTES2	SQL_CA2_READ_ONLY_CONCUR | SQL_CA2_OPT_VALUES_CONCURRENCY | SQL_CA2_SENSITIVITY_UPDATES
SQL_POS_OPERATIONS [1]	SQL_POS_POSITION
SQL_POSITIONED_STATEMENTS [1]	SQL_PS_POSITIONED_DELETE | SQL_PS_POSITIONED_UPDATE | SQL_PS_SELECT_FOR_UPDATE
SQL_ROW_UPDATES	"Y"
SQL_SCROLL_CONCURRENCY [1]	SQL_SCCO_READ_ONLY | SQL_SCCO_OPT_VALUES
SQL_SCROLL_OPTIONS	SQL_SO_FORWARD_ONLY | SQL_SO_STATIC
SQL_STATIC_SENSITIVITY [1]	SQL_SS_UPDATES

[1] Used only when the cursor library is used with an ODBC 2.*x* driver.

Important The cursor library implements the same cursor behavior when transactions are committed or rolled back as the data source. That is, committing or rolling back a transaction, either by calling **SQLEndTran** or by using the SQL_ATTR_AUTOCOMMIT connection attribute, can cause the data source to delete the access plans and close the cursors for all statements on a connection. For more information, see the SQL_CURSOR_COMMIT_BEHAVIOR and SQL_CURSOR_ROLLBACK_BEHAVIOR information types in **SQLGetInfo**.

SQLGetStmtAttr in the Cursor Library

The cursor library supports the following statement attributes with **SQLGetStmtAttr**:

SQL_ATTR_CONCURRENCY	SQL_ATTR_ROW_BIND_OFFSET_PTR
SQL_ATTR_CURSOR_TYPE	SQL_ATTR_ROW_BIND_TYPE
SQL_ATTR_FETCH_BOOKMARK_PTR	SQL_ATTR_ROW_NUMBER
SQL_ATTR_PARAM_BIND_OFFSET_PTR	SQL_ATTR_ROW_ARRAY_SIZE
SQL_ATTR_PARAM_BIND_TYPE	SQL_ATTR_SIMULATE_CURSOR

SQLGetStmtOption in the Cursor Library

The cursor library supports the following statement options with **SQLGetStmtOption**:

SQL_BIND_TYPE
SQL_CONCURRENCY
SQL_CURSOR_TYPE
SQL_GET_BOOKMARK
SQL_ROW_NUMBER
SQL_ROWSET_SIZE
SQL_SIMULATE_CURSOR

SQLNativeSql in the Cursor Library

If the driver supports this function, the cursor library calls **SQLNativeSql** in the driver and passes it the SQL statement. For positioned update, positioned delete, and **SELECT FOR UPDATE** statements, the cursor library modifies the statement before passing it to the driver.

Note The cursor library incorrectly returns SQLSTATE 34000 (Invalid cursor name) if the cursor name is invalid in a positioned update or delete statement that is passed in the *InStatementText* argument of **SQLNativeSql. SQLNativeSql** is not intended to return syntax errors, which are only returned upon statement preparation or execution.

SQLRowCount in the Cursor Library

When an application calls **SQLRowCount** with the statement associated with the cursor, the cursor library returns the number of rows of data it has retrieved from the driver.

When an application calls **SQLRowCount** with the statement associated with a positioned update or delete statement, the cursor library returns the number of rows affected by the statement.

When an application calls **SQLRowCount** after a SELECT statement, the cursor library returns –1.

SQLSetConnectAttr in the Cursor Library

An application calls **SQLSetConnectAttr** with the SQL_ATTR_ODBC_CURSORS attribute to specify whether the cursor library is always used, used if the driver does not support scrollable cursors, or never used. The cursor library assumes that a driver supports scrollable cursors if it returns SQL_CA1_RELATIVE for the SQL_STATIC_CURSOR_ATTRIBUTES1 information type in **SQLGetInfo**.

The application must call **SQLSetConnectAttr** to specify the cursor library usage after it calls **SQLAllocHandle** with a *HandleType* of SQL_HANDLE_DBC to allocate the connection and before it connects to the data source. If an application calls **SQLSetConnectAttr** with the SQL_ATTR_ODBC_CURSORS attribute while the connection is still active, the cursor library returns an error.

To set a statement attribute supported by the cursor library for all statements associated with a connection, an application must call **SQLSetConnectAttr** for that statement attribute after it connects to the data source and before it opens the cursor. If an application calls **SQLSetConnectAttr** with a statement attribute and a cursor is open on a statement associated with the connection, the statement attribute will not be applied to that statement until the cursor is closed and reopened.

SQLSetDescField and SQLSetDescRec in the Cursor Library

The cursor library executes **SQLSetDescField** when it is called to return the value of the fields set for bookmark columns: SQL_DESC_DATA_PTR, SQL_DESC_INDICATOR_PTR, SQL_DESC_OCTET_LENGTH_PTR, SQL_DESC_LENGTH, SQL_DESC_OCTET_LENGTH, SQL_DESC_DATETIME_INTERVAL_CODE, SQL_DESC_SCALE, SQL_DESC_PRECISION, SQL_DESC_TYPE, SQL_DESC_NAME, SQL_DESC_UNNAMED, and SQL_DESC_NULLABLE. The cursor library executes calls to **SQLSetDescRec** for a bookmark column.

When working with an ODBC 2.*x* driver, the cursor library returns SQLSTATE HY090 (Invalid string or buffer length) when **SQLSetDescField** or **SQLSetDescRec** is called to set the SQL_DESC_OCTET_LENGTH field for the bookmark record of an ARD to a value not equal to 4. When working with an ODBC 3.0 driver, the cursor library allows the buffer to be any size.

The cursor library executes **SQLSetDescField** when it is called to return the value of the SQL_DESC_BIND_OFFSET_PTR, SQL_DESC_BIND_TYPE, SQL_DESC_ROW_ARRAY_SIZE, or SQL_DESC_ROW_STATUS_PTR field. These fields can be returned for any row, not just the bookmark row.

The cursor library does not execute **SQLSetDescField** to change any descriptor field other than the fields mentioned previously. If an application calls **SQLSetDescField** to set any other field while the cursor library is loaded, the call is passed through to the driver.

The cursor library supports changing the SQL_DESC_DATA_PTR, SQL_DESC_INDICATOR_PTR, and SQL_DESC_OCTET_LENGTH_PTR fields of any row of an application row descriptor dynamically (after a call to **SQLExtendedFetch**, **SQLFetch**, or **SQLFetchScroll**). The SQL_DESC_OCTET_LENGTH_PTR field can be changed to a null pointer only to unbind the length buffer for a column.

The cursor library does not support changing the SQL_DESC_BIND_TYPE field in an APD or ARD when a cursor is open. The SQL_DESC_BIND_TYPE field can be changed only after the cursor is closed and before a new cursor is opened. The only descriptor fields that the cursor library supports changing when a cursor is open are SQL_DESC_ARRAY_STATUS_PTR, SQL_DESC_BIND_OFFSET_PTR, SQL_DESC_DATA_PTR, SQL_DESC_INDICATOR_PTR, SQL_DESC_OCTET_LENGTH_PTR, and SQL_DESC_ROWS_PROCESSED_PTR.

The cursor library does not support modifying the SQL_DESC_COUNT field of the ARD after **SQLExtendedFetch** or **SQLFetchScroll** has been called and before the cursor has been closed.

SQLSetEnvAttr and the Cursor Library

The cursor library is unaffected by the setting of the SQL_ATTR_ODBC_VERSION environment attribute, regardless of the application version or driver version.

SQLSetPos in the Cursor Library

The cursor library only supports the SQL_POSITION operation for the *Operation* argument in **SQLSetPos**. It only supports the SQL_LOCK_NO_CHANGE value for the *LockType* argument.

If the driver does not support bulk operations, the cursor library returns SQLSTATE HYC00 (Driver not capable) when **SQLSetPos** is called with *RowNumber* equal to 0. Note that this driver behavior is not recommended. Support for bulk operations will be mandatory in the future.

The cursor library does not support the SQL_UPDATE and SQL_DELETE operations in a call to **SQLSetPos**. The cursor library implements a positioned update or delete SQL statement by creating a searched update or delete statement with a WHERE clause that enumerates the values stored in its cache for each bound column. For more information, see "Processing Positioned Update and Delete Statements" earlier in this appendix.

If the driver does not support static cursors, an application working with the cursor library should only call **SQLSetPos** on a rowset fetched by **SQLExtendedFetch** or **SQLFetchScroll**, not **SQLFetch**. The cursor library implements **SQLExtendedFetch** and **SQLFetchScroll** by making repeated calls of **SQLFetch** (with a rowset size of 1) in the driver. The cursor library passes calls to **SQLFetch**, on the other hand, through to the driver. If **SQLSetPos** is called on a multi-row rowset fetched by **SQLFetch** when the driver does not support static cursors, the call will fail because **SQLSetPos** does not work with forward-only cursors. This will occur even if an application has successfully called **SQLSetStmtAttr** to set SQL_ATTR_CURSOR_TYPE to SQL_CURSOR_STATIC, which the cursor library supports even if the driver does not support static cursors.

SQLSetScrollOptions in the Cursor Library

The cursor library supports **SQLSetScrollOptions** only for backward compatibility; applications should use the SQL_ATTR_CONCURRENCY, SQL_ATTR_CURSOR_TYPE, and SQL_ATTR_ROW_ARRAY_SIZE statement attributes instead.

SQLSetStmtAttr in the Cursor Library

The cursor library supports the following statement attributes with **SQLSetStmtAttr**:

SQL_ATTR_CONCURRENCY
SQL_ATTR_CURSOR_TYPE
SQL_ATTR_FETCH_BOOKMARK_PTR
SQL_ATTR_PARAM_BIND_OFFSET_PTR
SQL_ATTR_PARAM_BIND_TYPE
SQL_ATTR_ROW_BIND_OFFSET_PTR
SQL_ATTR_ROW_BIND_TYPE
SQL_ATTR_ROWSET_ARRAY_SIZE
SQL_ATTR_SIMULATE_CURSOR
SQL_ATTR_USE_BOOKMARKS

The cursor library supports only the SQL_CURSOR_FORWARD_ONLY and SQL_CURSOR_STATIC values of the SQL_ATTR_CURSOR_TYPE statement attribute.

For forward-only cursors, the cursor library supports the SQL_CONCUR_READ_ONLY value of the SQL_ATTR_CONCURRENCY statement attribute. For static cursors, the cursor library supports the SQL_CONCUR_READ_ONLY and SQL_CONCUR_VALUES values of the SQL_ATTR_CONCURRENCY statement attribute.

The cursor library supports only the SQL_SC_NON_UNIQUE value of the SQL_ATTR_SIMULATE_CURSOR statement attribute.

Although the ODBC specification supports calls to **SQLSetStmtAttr** with the SQL_ATTR_PARAM_BIND_TYPE or SQL_ATTR_ROW_BIND_TYPE attributes after **SQLFetch** or **SQLFetchScroll** has been called, the cursor library does not. Before it can change the binding type in the cursor library, the application must close the cursor. The cursor library supports changing the SQL_ATTR_ROW_BIND_OFFSET_PTR, SQL_ATTR_PARAM_BIND_OFFSET_PTR, SQL_ATTR_ROWS_FETCHED_PTR, and SQL_ATTR_PARAMS_PROCESSED_PTR statement attributes when a cursor is open.

An application can call **SQLSetStmtAttr** with an *Attribute* of SQL_ATTR_ROW_ARRAY_SIZE to change the rowset size while a cursor is open. The new rowset size will take effect the next time **SQLFetchScroll** or **SQLFetch** is called.

The cursor library supports setting the SQL_ATTR_PARAM_BIND_OFFSET_PTR or SQL_ATTR_ROW_BIND_OFFSET_PTR statement attribute to enable binding offsets. The binding offset will not be used for calls to **SQLFetch** when the cursor library is used with an ODBC 2.*x* driver.

The cursor library supports setting the SQL_ATTR_USE_BOOKMARKS statement attribute to SQL_UB_VARIABLE.

ODBC Cursor Library Error Codes

The ODBC cursor library returns the following SQLSTATEs in addition to those listed in Chapter 21, "ODBC Function Reference."

Note The cursor library does not order status records; the Driver Manager and ODBC 3.0 drivers are responsible for ordering status records.

SQLSTATE	Description	Can be returned from
01000	Cursor is not updatable.	**SQLFetch** **SQLFetchScroll**
01000	Cursor library not used. Load failed.	**SQLBrowseConnect** **SQLConnect** **SQLDriverConnect**
01000	Cursor library not used. Insufficient driver support.	**SQLBrowseConnect** **SQLConnect** **SQLDriverConnect**
01000	Cursor library not used. Version mismatch with Driver Manager.	**SQLBrowseConnect** **SQLConnect** **SQLDriverConnect**
01000	Driver returned SQL_SUCCESS_WITH_INFO. The warning message has been lost.	**SQLFetch** **SQLFetchScroll**
S1000	General error: Unable to create file buffer.	**SQLFetch** **SQLFetchScroll** **SQLGetData**
S1000	General error: Unable to read from file buffer.	**SQLFetch** **SQLFetchScroll** **SQLGetData**
S1000	General error: Unable to write to file buffer.	**SQLFetch** **SQLFetchScroll** **SQLGetData**
S1000	General error: Unable to close or remove file buffer.	**SQLFreeHandle** **SQLFreeStmt**
SL001	Positioned request cannot be performed because no searchable columns were bound.	**SQLExecDirect** **SQLGetData** **SQLPrepare**

SQLSTATE	Description	Can be returned from
SL002	Positioned request could not be performed because result set was created by a join condition.	**SQLExecute** **SQLExecDirect** **SQLGetData**
SL003	Bound buffer exceeds maximum segment size.	**SQLFetch** **SQLFetchScroll**
SL004	Result set was not generated by a SELECT statement.	**SQLGetData**
SL005	SELECT statement contains a GROUP BY clause.	**SQLGetData**
SL006	Parameter arrays are not supported with positioned requests.	**SQLPrepare** **SQLExecDirect**
SL008	SQLGetData is not allowed on a forward-only (non-buffered) cursor.	**SQLGetData**
SL009	No columns were bound prior to calling SQLFetch or SQLFetchScroll.	**SQLFetch** **SQLFetchScroll**
SL010	SQLBindCol returned SQL_ERROR during an attempt to bind to an internal buffer.	**SQLFetch** **SQLFetchScroll** **SQLGetData**
SL011	Statement option is only valid after calling SQLFetch or SQLFetchScroll.	**SQLGetStmtAttr**
SL012	Statement bindings may not be changed while a cursor is open.	**SQLBindCol** **SQLFreeHandle** **SQLFreeStmt** **SQLSetStmtAttr**
SL014	A positioned request was issued and not all column count fields were buffered.	**SQLExecDirect** **SQLExecute** **SQLPrepare**
SL015	SQLFetch and SQLFetchScroll cannot be mixed.	**SQLExtendedFetch** **SQLFetch** **SQLFetchScroll**

APPENDIX G

Driver Guidelines for Backward Compatibility

This appendix provides information for driver writers working on ODBC 3.0 drivers that need to support ODBC 2.*x* applications. Changes between ODBC 2.*x* and ODBC 3.0 fall into three categories; for more information about these categories, see "Backward Compatibility and Standards Compliance" in Chapter 17, "Programming Considerations."

- **New Features**. New features are features that exist in ODBC 3.0 and not in ODBC 2.*x*. ODBC 3.0 drivers generally do not have to worry about backward compatibility with new features because ODBC 2.*x* applications never use it. The sole exception to this is features related to **SQLFetch**, **SQLFetchScroll**, **SQLSetPos**, and **SQLExtendedFetch**; for more information, see "Block Cursors, Scrollable Cursors, and Backward Compatibility," later in this appendix.
- **Duplicated Features**. Duplicated features are features that are implemented differently in ODBC 3.0 and ODBC 2.*x*. ODBC 3.0 drivers do not have to worry about backward compatibility with duplicated features because the Driver Manager always maps ODBC 2.*x* features to ODBC 3.0 features when calling an ODBC 3.0 driver. Thus, an ODBC 3.0 driver sees only ODBC 3.0 features. For more information about these mappings, see "Mapping Deprecated Functions," later in this appendix.
- **Behavioral Changes**. Behavior changes are features that are handled differently in ODBC 3.0 and ODBC 2.*x*. ODBC 3.0 drivers have to worry about behavior changes and act in response to the SQL_ATTR_ODBC_VERSION environment attribute set by the application. For more information, see "Behavioral Changes and ODBC 3.0 Drivers," later in this appendix.

Block Cursors, Scrollable Cursors, and Backward Compatibility

The existence of both **SQLFetchScroll** and **SQLExtendedFetch** represents the first clear split in ODBC between the Application Programming Interface (API), which is the set of functions the application calls, and the Service Provider Interface (SPI), which is the set of functions the driver implements. This split is required to balance the requirement in ODBC 3.0 to align with the standards, which uses **SQLFetchScroll**, and be compatible with ODBC 2.*x*, which uses **SQLExtendedFetch**.

The ODBC 3.0 API, which is the set of functions the application calls, includes **SQLFetchScroll** and related statement attributes. The ODBC 3.0 SPI, which is the set of functions the driver implements, includes **SQLFetchScroll**, **SQLExtendedFetch**, and related statement attributes. Note that because ODBC does not formally enforce this split between the API and the SPI, it is possible for ODBC 3.0 applications to call **SQLExtendedFetch** and related statement attributes. However, there is no reason for ODBC 3.0 application to do this. For more information about APIs and SPIs, see the introduction to Chapter 3, "ODBC Architecture."

For information about what functions and statement attributes an ODBC 3.0 application should use with block and scrollable cursors, see "Block Cursors, Scrollable Cursors, and Backward Compatibility for ODBC 3.0 Applications" in Chapter 17, "Programming Considerations."

What the Driver Manager Does

The following table summarizes how the ODBC 3.0 Driver Manager maps calls to ODBC 2.*x* and ODBC 3.0 drivers.

Function or statement attribute	Comments
SQL_ATTR_FETCH_BOOKMARK_PTR	• Points to the bookmark to use with **SQLFetchScroll**. The following are implementation details: • When an application sets this in an ODBC 2.*x* driver, the ODBC 3.0 Driver Manager caches it. It dereferences the pointer and passes the value to the ODBC 2.*x* driver in the *FetchOffset* argument of **SQLExtendedFetch**, when **SQLFetchScroll** is later called by the application. • When an application sets this in an ODBC 3.0 driver, the ODBC 3.0 Driver Manager passes the call to the driver.

<table>
<tr><th>Function or statement attribute</th><th>Comments</th></tr>
<tr><td>SQL_ATTR_ROW_ STATUS_PTR</td><td>

- Points to the row status array filled by **SQLFetch**, **SQLFetchScroll**, **SQLBulkOperations**, and **SQLSetPos**. The following are implementation details:
- When an application sets this in an ODBC 2.*x* driver, the ODBC 3.0 Driver Manager caches its value. It passes this value to the ODBC 2.*x* driver in the *RowStatusArray* argument of **SQLExtendedFetch** when **SQLFetchScroll** or **SQLFetch** is called.
- When an application sets this in an ODBC 3.0 driver, the ODBC 3.0 Driver Manager passes the call to the driver.
- In state S6, if an application sets SQL_ATTR_ROW_STATUS_PTR, and then calls **SQLBulkOperations** (with an *Operation* of SQL_ADD) or **SQLSetPos** without first calling **SQLFetch** or **SQLFetchScroll**, SQLSTATE HY011(Attribute cannot be set now) is returned.

</td></tr>
<tr><td>SQL_ATTR_ROWS_ FETCHED_PTR</td><td>

Points to the buffer in which **SQLFetch** and **SQLFetchScroll** return the number of rows fetched. The following are implementation details:

- When an application sets this in an ODBC 2.*x* driver, the ODBC 3.0 Driver Manager caches its value. It passes this value to the ODBC 2.*x* driver in the *RowCountPtr* argument of **SQLExtendedFetch**, when **SQLFetch** or **SQLFetchScroll** is called by the application.
- When an application sets this in an ODBC 3.0 driver, the ODBC 3.0 Driver Manager passes the call to the driver.

</td></tr>
<tr><td>SQL_ATTR_ ROW_ARRAY_SIZE</td><td>

Sets the rowset size. The following are implementation details:

- When an application sets this in an ODBC 2.*x* driver, the ODBC 3.0 Driver Manager maps it to the SQL_ROWSET_SIZE statement attribute.
- When an application sets this in an ODBC 3.0 driver, the ODBC 3.0 Driver Manager passes the call to the driver.
- When an application working with an ODBC 3.0 driver calls **SQLSetScrollOptions**, SQL_ROWSET_SIZE is set to the value in the *RowsetSize* argument if the underlying driver does not support **SQLSetScrollOptions**.

</td></tr>
</table>

<table>
<tr><th>Function or statement attribute</th><th>Comments</th></tr>
<tr><td>SQL_ROWSET_SIZE</td><td>Sets the rowset size used by SQLExtendedFetch when SQLExtendedFetch is called by an ODBC 2.x application. The following are implementation details.<ul><li>When an application sets this, the ODBC 3.0 Driver Manager passes the call to the driver, regardless of driver version.</li><li>When an application working with an ODBC 2.x driver calls SQLSetScrollOptions, SQL_ROWSET_SIZE is set to the value in the RowsetSize argument.</li></ul></td></tr>
<tr><td>SQLBulkOperations</td><td>Performs an insert operation, or update, delete, or fetch by bookmark operations. The following are implementation details:<ul><li>When an application calls SQLBulkOperations with an Operation of SQL_ADD in an ODBC 2.x driver, the ODBC 3.0 Driver Manager maps it to SQLSetPos with an Operation of SQL_ADD.</li><li>When working with an ODBC 2.x driver that does not support SQLSetPos with an Operation of SQL_ADD, the ODBC 3.0 Driver Manager does not map SQLSetPos with an Operation of SQL_ADD to SQLBulkOperations with an Operation of SQL_ADD. This is because SQLBulkOperations cannot be called in state S7, which in ODBC 2.x was the only state in which SQLSetPos could be called.</li><li>If the application calls SQLBulkOperations with an Operation of SQL_ADD in an ODBC 2.x driver before calling SQLFetchScroll, the ODBC 3.0 Driver Manager returns an error.</li></ul></td></tr>
<tr><td>SQLExtendedFetch</td><td>Returns the specified rowset. The following are implementation details:<ul><li>Except for the restriction just noted, the ODBC 3.0 Driver Manager passes calls to SQLExtendedFetch to the driver, regardless of the driver version.</li></ul></td></tr>
</table>

Function or statement attribute	Comments
SQLFetch	Returns the next rowset. The following are implementation details: • When an application calls **SQLFetch** in an ODBC 2.*x* driver, the ODBC 3.0 Driver Manager maps it to **SQLExtendedFetch**. The *FetchOrientation* argument of **SQLExtendedFetch** is set to SQL_FETCH_NEXT. The Driver Manager uses the cached value of the SQL_ATTR_ROW_STATUS_PTR statement attribute for the *RowStatusArray* argument and the cached value of the SQL_ATTR_ROWS_FETCHED_PTR statement attribute for the *RowCountPtr* argument. • An ODBC 3.0 application can mix calls to **SQLFetch** and **SQLFetchScroll** in an ODBC 2.*x* driver, because the ODBC 3.0 Driver Manager maps **SQLFetch** to **SQLExtendedFetch** when an application calls it in an ODBC 2.*x* driver. • If an ODBC 2.*x* driver does not support **SQLExtendedFetch**, the ODBC 3.0 Driver Manager does not map **SQLFetch** or **SQLFetchScroll** to **SQLExtendedFetch** when an application calls it in that driver. If the application attempts to set SQL_ATTR_ROW_ARRAY_SIZE to a value greater than 1, SQLSTATE HYC00 (Optional feature not implemented) is returned. • Except for the restrictions just noted, the ODBC 3.0 Driver Manager passes calls to **SQLFetch** to the driver, regardless of the driver version.
SQLFetchScroll	Returns the specified rowset. The following are implementation details: • When an application calls **SQLFetchScroll** in an ODBC 2.*x* driver, the ODBC 3.0 Driver Manager maps it to **SQLExtendedFetch**. It uses the cached value of the SQL_ATTR_ROW_STATUS_PTR statement attribute for the *RowStatusArray* argument and the cached value of the SQL_ATTR_ROWS_FETCHED_PTR statement attribute for the *RowCountPtr* argument. If the *FetchOrientation* argument in **SQLFetchScroll** is SQL_FETCH_BOOKMARK, it uses the cached value of the SQL_ATTR_FETCH_BOOKMARK_PTR statement attribute for the *FetchOffset* argument and returns an error if the *FetchOffset* argument of **SQLFetchScroll** is not 0. • When an application calls this in an ODBC 3.0 driver, the ODBC 3.0 Driver Manager passes the call to the driver.
SQLSetPos	Performs various positioned operations. The ODBC 3.0 Driver Manager passes calls to **SQLSetPos** to the driver, regardless of the driver version.

Function or statement attribute	Comments
SQLSetScrollOptions	When the Driver Manager maps **SQLSetScrollOptions** for an application working with an ODBC 3.0 driver that does not support **SQLSetScrollOptions**, the Driver Manager sets the SQL_ROWSET_SIZE statement option, not the SQL_ATTR_ROW_ARRAY_SIZE statement attribute, to the *RowsetSize* argument in **SQLSetScrollOption**. As a result, **SQLSetScrollOptions** cannot be used by an application when fetching multiple rows by a call to **SQLFetch** or **SQLFetchScroll**. It can only be used when fetching multiple rows by a call to **SQLExtendedFetch**.

What the Driver Does

The following table summarizes what functions and statement attributes an ODBC 3.0 driver should implement for block and scrollable cursors.

Function or statement attribute	Comments
SQL_ATTR_ROW_ STATUS_PTR	Sets the address of the row status array filled by **SQLFetch** and **SQLFetchScroll**. This array is also filled by **SQLSetPos** if **SQLSetPos** is called in statement state S6. If **SQLSetPos** is called in state S7, this array is not filled, but the array pointed to by the *RowStatusArray* argument of **SQLExtendedFetch** is filled. For more information, see "Statement Transitions" in Appendix B, "ODBC State Transition Tables."
SQL_ATTR_ROWS_ FETCHED_PTR	Sets the address of the buffer in which **SQLFetch** and **SQLFetchScroll** return the number of rows fetched. If **SQLExtendedFetch** is called, this buffer is not filled, but the *RowCountPtr* argument points to the number of rows fetched.
SQL_ATTR_ ROW_ARRAY_SIZE	Sets the rowset size used by **SQLFetch** and **SQLFetchScroll**.
SQL_ROWSET_SIZE	Sets the rowset size used by **SQLExtendedFetch**. ODBC 3.0 drivers implement this if they want to work with ODBC 2.*x* applications that call **SQLExtendedFetch** or **SQLSetPos**.
SQLBulkOperations	If an ODBC 3.0 driver should work with ODBC 2.*x* applications that use **SQLSetPos** with an *Operation* of SQL_ADD, then the driver must support **SQLSetPos** with an *Operation* of SQL_ADD in addition to **SQLBulkOperations** with an *Operation* of SQL_ADD.

Function or statement attribute	Comments
SQLExtendedFetch	Returns the specified rowset. ODBC 3.0 drivers implement this if they want to work with ODBC 2.*x* applications that call **SQLExtendedFetch** or **SQLSetPos**. The following are implementation details: • The driver retrieves the rowset size from the value of the SQL_ROWSET_SIZE statement attribute. • The driver retrieves the address of the row status array from the *RowStatusArray* argument, not the SQL_ATTR_ROW_STATUS_PTR statement attribute. The *RowStatusArray* argument in a call to **SQLExtendedFetch** must not be a null pointer. (Note that in ODBC 3.0, the SQL_ATTR_ROW_STATUS_PTR statement attribute can be a null pointer.) • The driver retrieves the address of the rows fetched buffer from the *RowCountPtr* argument, not the SQL_ATTR_ROWS_FETCHED_PTR statement attribute. • The driver returns SQLSTATE 01S01 (Error in row) to indicate that an error has occurred while rows were fetched by a call to **SQLExtendedFetch**. An ODBC 3.0 driver should return SQLSTATE 01S01 (Error in row) only when **SQLExtendedFetch** is called, not when **SQLFetch** or **SQLFetchScroll** is called. When SQLSTATE 01S01 (Error in row) is returned by **SQLExtendedFetch**, the Driver Manager does not order status records in the error queue according to the rules stated in the "Sequence of Status Records" section of SQLGetDiagField, to preserve backward compatibility.
SQLFetch	Returns the next rowset. The following are implementation details: • The driver retrieves the rowset size from the value of the SQL_ATTR_ROW_ARRAY_SIZE statement attribute. • The driver retrieves the address of the row status array from the SQL_ATTR_ROW_STATUS_PTR statement attribute. • The driver retrieves the address of the rows fetched buffer from the SQL_ATTR_ROWS_FETCHED_PTR statement attribute. • The application can mix calls between **SQLFetchScroll** and **SQLFetch**. • **SQLFetch** returns bookmarks if column 0 is bound. • **SQLFetch** can be called to return more than one row. • The driver does not return SQLSTATE 01S01 (Error in row) to indicate that an error has occurred while rows were fetched by a call to **SQLFetch**.

Function or statement attribute	Comments
SQLFetchScroll	Returns the specified rowset. The following are implementation details: • The driver retrieves the rowset size from the SQL_ATTR_ROW_ARRAY_SIZE statement attribute. • The driver retrieves the address of the row status array from the SQL_ATTR_ROW_STATUS_PTR statement attribute. • The driver retrieves the address of the rows fetched buffer from the SQL_ATTR_ROWS_FETCHED_PTR statement attribute. • The application can mix calls between **SQLFetchScroll** and **SQLFetch**. • The driver does not return SQLSTATE 01S01 (Error in row) to indicate that an error has occurred while rows were fetched by a call to **SQLFetchScroll**.
SQLSetPos	Performs various positioned operations. The following are implementation details: • This can be called in statement states S6 or S7. For more details, see "Statement Transitions" in Appendix B, "ODBC State Transition Tables." • If this is called in statement state S5 or S6, the driver retrieves the rowset size from the SQL_ATTR_ROWS_FETCHED_PTR statement attribute and the address of the row status array from the SQL_ATTR_ROW_STATUS_PTR statement attribute. • If this is called in statement state S7, the driver retrieves the rowset size from the SQL_ROWSET_SIZE statement attribute and the address of the row status array from the *RowStatusArray* argument of **SQLExtendedFetch**. • The driver only returns SQLSTATE 01S01 (Error in row) to indicate that an error has occurred while rows were fetched by a call to **SQLSetPos** to perform a bulk operation when the function is called in state S7. If SQLSTATE 01S01 (Error in row) is returned by **SQLSetPos**, the Driver Manager does not order status records in the error queue according to the rules stated in the "Sequence of Status Records" section of **SQLGetDiagField**, to preserve backward compatibility. • If the driver should work with ODBC 2.*x* applications that call **SQLSetPos** with an *Operation* argument of SQL_ADD, the driver must support **SQLSetPos** with an *Operation* argument of SQL_ADD.

Mapping Deprecated Functions

This section describes how deprecated functions are mapped by the ODBC 3.0 Driver Manager to guarantee backward compatibility of ODBC 3.0 drivers that are used with ODBC 2.*x* applications. The Driver Manager performs this mapping regardless of the version of the application. Because each of the ODBC 2.*x* functions in the following list is mapped to the corresponding ODBC 3.0 function when called in an ODBC 3.0 driver, the ODBC 3.0 driver does not have to implement the ODBC 2.*x* functions.

The mapping in the list is triggered when the driver is an ODBC 3.0 driver, and the driver does not support the function that is being mapped.

The following is a list of all duplicated functionality that was introduced in ODBC 3.0:

ODBC 2.*x* function	ODBC 3.0 function
SQLAllocConnect	**SQLAllocHandle**
SQLAllocEnv	**SQLAllocHandle**
SQLAllocStmt	**SQLAllocHandle**
SQLBindParam [1]	**SQLBindParameter**
SQLColAttributes	**SQLColAttribute**
SQLError	**SQLGetDiagRec**
SQLFreeConnect	**SQLFreeHandle**
SQLFreeEnv	**SQLFreeHandle**
SQLFreeStmt with an *Option* of SQL_DROP	**SQLFreeHandle**
SQLGetConnectOption	**SQLGetConnectAttr**
SQLGetStmtOption	**SQLGetStmtAttr**
SQLParamOptions	**SQLSetStmtAttr**
SQLSetConnectOption	**SQLSetConnectAttr**
SQLSetParam [2]	**SQLBindParameter**
SQLSetScrollOption	**SQLSetStmtAttr**
SQLSetStmtOption	**SQLSetStmtAttr**
SQLTransact	**SQLEndTran**

1 Even though this function did not exist in ODBC 2.*x*, it is in the X/Open and ISO standards.

2 This is an ODBC 1.0 function.

SQLAllocConnect Mapping

When an application calls **SQLAllocConnect** through an ODBC 3.0 driver, the call to **SQLAllocConnect**(*henv*, *phdbc*) is mapped to **SQLAllocHandle** as follows:

1. The Driver Manager allocates a connection and returns it to the application.
2. When the application establishes a connection, the Driver Manager calls

   ```
   SQLAllocHandle(SQL_HANDLE_DBC, InputHandle, OutputHandlePtr)
   ```

   in the driver with *InputHandle* set to *henv*, and *OutputHandlePtr* set to *phdbc*.

SQLAllocEnv Mapping

When an application calls **SQLAllocEnv** through an ODBC 3.0 driver, the call to **SQLAllocEnv**(*phenv*) is mapped to **SQLAllocHandle** as follows:

1. The Driver Manager allocates an environment handle and returns it to the application. The Driver Manager calls **SQLSetEnvAttr** to set the SQL_ATTR_ODBC_VERSION environment attribute to SQL_OV_ODBC2.
2. When the application establishes the first connection to a driver, the Driver Manager calls

   ```
   SQLAllocHandle(SQL_HANDLE_ENV, SQL_NULL_HANDLE, OutputHandlePtr)
   ```

   in the driver with *OutputHandlePtr* set to *phenv*.

SQLAllocStmt Mapping

When an application calls **SQLAllocStmt** through an ODBC 3.0 driver, the call to:

```
SQLAllocStmt(hdbc, phstmt)
```

is mapped to **SQLAllocHandle** by the Driver Manager in the driver as follows:

```
SQLAllocHandle(SQL_HANDLE_STMT, InputHandle, OutputHandlePtr)
```

with *InputHandle* set to *hdbc* and *OutputHandlePtr* set to *phstmt*.

SQLBindParam Mapping

SQLBindParam cannot truly be called deprecated because it was never there in ODBC; however, it does still represent duplicated functionality, since the Driver Manager needs to export it because ISO and X/Open–compliant applications will be using it. Because **SQLBindParameter** contains all the functionality of **SQLBindParam**, **SQLBindParam** will be mapped on top of **SQLBindParameter** (when the underlying driver is an ODBC 3.0 driver). An ODBC 3.0 driver does not need to implement **SQLBindParam**.

When the following call to **SQLBindParam** is made:

```
SQLBindParam(StatementHandle, ParameterNumber, ValueType, ParameterType, ColumnSize,
             DecimalDigits, ParameterValuePtr, StrLen_or_IndPtr)
```

the Driver Manager calls **SQLBindParameter** in the driver as follows:

```
SQLBindParameter(StatementHandle, ParameterNumber, SQL_PARAM_INPUT, ValueType,
                 ParameterType, ColumnSize, DecimalDigits, ParameterValuePtr,
                 BufferLength, StrLen_or_IndPtr)
```

SQLColAttributes Mapping

When an application calls **SQLColAttributes** through an ODBC 3.0 driver, the call to **SQLColAttributes** is mapped to **SQLColAttribute** as follows:

Note The prefix used in *FieldIdentifier* values in ODBC 3.0 has been changed from that used in ODBC 2.*x*. The new prefix is "SQL_DESC"; the old prefix was "SQL_COLUMN".

1. If the application is an ODBC 2.*x* application, *fDescType* is SQL_COLUMN_TYPE, and the returned type is a concise DATETIME type, the Driver Manager maps the return values for date, time, and timestamp codes.
2. If *fDescType* is SQL_COLUMN_NAME, SQL_COLUMN_NULLABLE, or SQL_COLUMN_COUNT, the Driver Manager calls **SQLColAttribute** in the driver with the *FieldIdentifier* argument mapped to SQL_DESC_NAME, SQL_DESC_NULLABLE, or SQL_DESC_COUNT, as appropriate. All other values of *fDescType* are passed through to the driver.

An ODBC 3.0 driver must support all the ODBC 3.0 *FieldIdentifiers* listed for **SQLColAttribute**.

An ODBC 3.0 driver must support both SQL_COLUMN_PRECISION and SQL_DESC_PRECISION, SQL_COLUMN_SCALE and SQL_DESC_SCALE, and SQL_COLUMN_LENGTH and SQL_DESC_LENGTH. These values are different because precision, scale, and length are defined differently in ODBC 3.0 than they were in ODBC 2.*x*. For more information, see "Column Size, Decimal Digits, Transfer Octet Length, and Display Size" in Appendix D, "Data Types."

SQLError Mapping

When an application calls **SQLError** through an ODBC 3.0 driver, the call to:

```
SQLError(henv, hdbc, hstmt, szSqlState, pfNativeError, szErrorMsg, cbErrorMsgMax,
        pcbErrorMsg)
```

is mapped to:

```
SQLGetDiagRec(HandleType, Handle, RecNumber, szSqlstate, pfNativeErrorPtr, szErrorMsg,
             cbErrorMsgMax, pcbErrorMsg)
```

with the *HandleType* argument set to the value SQL_HANDLE_ENV, SQL_HANDLE_DBC, or SQL_HANDLE_STMT, as appropriate, and the *Handle* argument set to the value in *henv*, *hdbc*, or *hstmt*, as appropriate. The *RecNumber* argument is determined by the Driver Manager.

SQLFreeConnect Mapping

When an application calls **SQLFreeConnect** through an ODBC 3.0 driver, the call to:

```
SQLFreeConnect(hdbc)
```

is mapped to:

```
SQLFreeHandle(SQL_HANDLE_DBC,Handle)
```

with the *Handle* argument set to the value in *hdbc*.

SQLFreeEnv Mapping

When an application calls **SQLFreeEnv** through an ODBC 3.0 driver, the call to:

```
SQLFreeEnv(henv)
```

is mapped to:

```
SQLFreeHandle(SQL_HANDLE_ENV,Handle)
```

with the *Handle* argument set to the value in *henv*.

SQLFreeStmt Mapping

When an application calls **SQLFreeStmt** with an *Option* argument of SQL_DROP through an ODBC 3.0 driver, the call to:

```
SQLFreeStmt(hstmt, SQL_DROP)
```

is mapped to:

```
SQLFreeHandle(SQL_HANDLE_STMT,Handle)
```

with the *Handle* argument set to the value in *hstmt*.

SQLGetConnectOption Mapping

When an application calls **SQLGetConnectOption** through an ODBC 3.0 driver, the call to:

```
SQLGetConnectOption(hdbc, fOption, pvParam)
```

is mapped as follows:

- If *fOption* indicates an ODBC-defined connection option that returns a string, then the Driver Manager calls:
  ```
  SQLGetConnectAttr(ConnectionHandle, Attribute,
                    ValuePtr, BufferLength, NULL)
  ```
- If *fOption* indicates an ODBC-defined connection option that returns a 32-bit integer value, then the Driver Manager calls:
  ```
  SQLGetConnectAttr(ConnectionHandle, Attribute, ValuePtr, 0, NULL)
  ```
- If *fOption* indicates a driver-defined statement option, then the Driver Manager calls:
  ```
  SQLGetConnectAttr(ConnectionHandle, Attribute,
                    ValuePtr, BufferLength, NULL)
  ```

In these three cases, the *ConnectionHandle* argument is set to the value in *hdbc*, the *Attribute* argument set to the value in *fOption*, and the *ValuePtr* argument set to the same value as *pvParam*.

For ODBC-defined string connection options, the Driver Manager sets the *BufferLength* argument in the call to **SQLGetConnectAttr** to the predefined maximum length (SQL_MAX_OPTION_STRING_LENGTH); for a non-string connection option, *BufferLength* is set to 0.

For an ODBC 3.0 driver, the Driver Manager no longer checks to see if *Option* is in between SQL_CONN_OPT_MIN and SQL_CONN_OPT_MAX, or is greater than SQL_CONNECT_OPT_DRVR_START. The driver must check the validity of the option values.

SQLGetStmtOption Mapping

When an application calls **SQLGetStmtOption** to an ODBC 3.0 driver that does not support it, the call to:

```
SQLGetStmtOption(hstmt, fOption, pvParam)
```

will result in:

- If *fOption* indicates an ODBC-defined statement option that returns a string, then the Driver Manager calls:

  ```
  SQLGetStmtAttr(StatementHandle, Attribute,
                 ValuePtr, BufferLength, NULL)
  ```

- If *fOption* indicates an ODBC-defined statement option that returns a 32-bit integer value, then the Driver Manager calls:

  ```
  SQLGetStmtAttr(StatementHandle, Attribute, ValuePtr, 0, NULL)
  ```

- If *fOption* indicates a driver-defined statement option, then the Driver Manager calls:

  ```
  SQLGetStmtAttr(StatementHandle, Attribute,
                 ValuePtr, BufferLength, NULL)
  ```

In these three cases, the *StatementHandle* argument is set to the value in *hstmt*, the *Attribute* argument is set to the value in *fOption*, and the *ValuePtr* argument is set to the same value as *pvParam*.

For ODBC-defined string connection options, the Driver Manager sets the *BufferLength* argument in the call to **SQLGetConnectAttr** to the predefined maximum length (SQL_MAX_OPTION_STRING_LENGTH); for a non-string connection option, *BufferLength* is set to 0.

The SQL_GET_BOOKMARK statement option has been deprecated in ODBC 3.0. For an ODBC 3.0 driver to work with ODBC 2.*x* applications that use SQL_GET_BOOKMARK, it must support it. For an ODBC 3.0 driver to work with ODBC 2.*x* applications, it must support setting SQL_USE_BOOKMARKS to SQL_UB_ON, and should expose fixed-length bookmarks. If an ODBC 3.0 driver supports only variable-length bookmarks, not fixed-length bookmarks, then it must return SQLSTATE HYC00 (Optional feature not implemented) if an ODBC 2.*x* application attempts to set SQL_USE_BOOKMARKS to SQL_UB_ON.

For an ODBC 3.0 driver, the Driver Manager no longer checks to see whether *Option* is in between SQL_STMT_OPT_MIN and SQL_STMT_OPT_MAX, or is greater than SQL_CONNECT_OPT_DRVR_START. The driver must check this.

SQLInstallTranslator Mapping

When an ODBC 2.*x* application calls **SQLInstallTranslator** through an ODBC 3.0 driver, the Driver Manager maps the call to **SQLInstallTranslatorEx**. An application should not call **SQLInstallTranslator** in the ODBC 3.0 Driver Manager with the *lpszInfFile* argument set to a value other than NULL. The ODBC.INF file used in ODBC 2.*x* is no longer supported in ODBC 3.0, even for backward compatibility.

SQLParamOptions Mapping

When an application calls **SQLParamOptions** through an ODBC 3.0 driver, the call:

```
SQLParamOptions(hstmt, crow, piRow);
```

will be mapped to two calls of **SQLSetStmtAttr** as follows:

```
SQLSetStmtAttr(hstmt, SQL_ATTR_PARAMSET_SIZE, crow, 0);
SQLSetStmtAttr(hstmt, SQL_ATTR_PARAMS_PROCESSED_PTR, piRow, 0);
```

SQLSetConnectOption Mapping

When an ODBC 2.*x* application calls **SQLSetConnectOption** through an ODBC 3.0 driver, the call to:

```
SQLSetConnectOption(hdbc, fOption, vParam)
```

will result in:

- If *fOption* indicates an ODBC-defined connection attribute that requires a string, then the Driver Manager calls:

  ```
  SQLSetConnectAttr(ConnectionHandle, Attribute, ValuePtr, SQL_NTS)
  ```

- If *fOption* indicates an ODBC-defined connection attribute that returns a 32-bit integer value, then the Driver Manager calls:

  ```
  SQLSetConnectAttr(ConnectionHandle, Attribute, ValuePtr, 0)
  ```

- If *fOption* indicates a driver-defined connection attribute, then the Driver Manager calls:

  ```
  SQLSetConnectAttr(ConnectionHandle, Attribute, ValuePtr, BufferLength)
  ```

In these three cases, the *ConnectionHandle* argument is set to the value in *hdbc*, the *Attribute* argument is set to the value in *fOption*, and the *ValuePtr* argument is set to the same value as *vParam*.

Because the Driver Manager does not know whether the driver-defined connection attribute needs a string or 32-bit integer value, it has to pass in a valid value for the *BufferLength* argument of **SQLSetConnectAttr**. If the driver has defined special semantics for driver-defined connect attributes and needs to be called using **SQLSetConnectOption**, then it must support **SQLSetConnectOption**.

If an ODBC 2.*x* application calls **SQLSetConnectOption** to set a driver-specific statement option in an ODBC 3.0 driver, and the option was defined in an ODBC 2.*x* version of the driver, a new manifest constant should be defined for the option in the ODBC 3.0 driver. If the old manifest constant is used in the call to **SQLSetConnectOption**, the Driver Manager will call **SQLSetConnectAttr** with the *StringLength* argument set to 0.

For an ODBC 3.0 driver, the Driver Manager no longer checks to see if *fOption* is in between SQL_CONN_OPT_MIN and SQL_CONN_OPT_MAX, or is greater than SQL_CONNECT_OPT_DRVR_START.

Setting Statement Options on the Connection Level

In ODBC 2.*x*, an application could call **SQLSetConnectOption** to set a statement option. When that is done, the driver establishes the statement option as a default for any statements later allocated for that connection. It is driver-defined whether the driver sets the statement option for any existing statements associated with the specified connection.

This ability has been deprecated in ODBC 3.0. ODBC 3.0 drivers need only support setting ODBC 2.*x* statement attributes at the connection level if they want to work with ODBC 2.*x* applications that do this. ODBC 3.0 applications should never set statement attributes at the connection level. ODBC 3.0 statement attributes cannot be set at the connection level, with the exception of the SQL_ATTR_METADATA_ID and SQL_ATTR_ASYNC_ENABLE attributes, which are both connection attributes and statement attributes, and can be set either at the connection level or the statement level.

SQLSetParam Mapping

SQLSetParam continues to be mapped on top of **SQLBindParameter** as in ODBC 2.*x*. Even though it is conceptually similar to **SQLBindParam**, the Driver Manager does not map **SQLSetParam** to **SQLBindParam**. This is because certain existing ODBC 2.*x* drivers use the special value of *BufferLength* (SQL_SETPARAM_VALUE_MAX) that the Driver Manager generates when it maps **SQLSetParam** on top of **SQLBindParameter** to determine when it is called by a 1.*x* ODBC application.

A call to:

```
SQLSetParam(hstmt, ipar, fCType, fSqlType, cbColDef, ibScale, rgbValue, pcbValue)
```

will result in:

```
SQLBindParameter(StatementHandle, ParameterNumber, SQL_PARAM_INPUT_OUTPUT, ValueType,
                 ParameterType, ColumnSize, DecimalDigits, ParameterValuePtr,
                 SQL_SETPARAM_VALUE_MAX, StrLen_or_IndPtr)
```

SQLSetScrollOptions Mapping

When an application calls **SQLSetScrollOptions** through an ODBC 3.0 driver, and the driver does not support **SQLSetScrollOptions**, the call to:

```
SQLSetScrollOptions (StatementHandle, Concurrency, KeysetSize, RowsetSize)
```

will result in:

1. A call to:

   ```
   SQLGetInfo (ConnectionHandle, InfoType, InfoValuePtr, BufferLength,
               StringLengthPtr)
   ```

   with the *InfoType* argument set to one of the following values, depending on the value of the *KeysetSize* argument in **SQLSetScrollOptions**:

KeysetSize argument	*InfoType* argument
SQL_SCROLL_FORWARD_ONLY	SQL_FORWARD_ONLY_CURSOR_ ATTRIBUTES2
SQL_SCROLL_STATIC	SQL_STATIC_CURSOR_ ATTRIBUTES2
SQL_SCROLL_KEYSET_DRIVEN	SQL_KEYSET_CURSOR_ ATTRIBUTES2
SQL_SCROLL_DYNAMIC	SQL_DYNAMIC_CURSOR_ ATTRIBUTES2
A value greater than the *RowsetSize* argument	SQL_KEYSET_CURSOR_ ATTRIBUTES2

   If the value of the *KeysetSize* argument is not listed in the previous table, the call to **SQLSetScrollOptions** returns SQLSTATE S1107 (Row value out of range), and none of the following steps are performed.

   The Driver Manager then verifies whether the appropriate bit is set in the **InfoValuePtr* value returned by the call to **SQLGetInfo**, according to the value of the *Concurrency* argument in **SQLSetScrollOptions**:

Concurrency argument	*InfoType* setting
SQL_CONCUR_READ_ONLY	SQL_CA2_READ_ONLY_ CONCURRENCY
SQL_CONCUR_LOCK	SQL_CA2_LOCK_CONCURRENCY
SQL_CONCUR_ROWVER	SQL_CA2_ROWVER_ CONCURRENCY
SQL_CONCUR_VALUES	SQL_CA2_VALUES_CONCURRENCY

   If the *Concurrency* argument is not one of the values in the previous table, the call to **SQLSetScrollOptions** returns SQLSTATE S1108 (Concurrency option out of range), and none of the following steps are performed. If the appropriate bit (as indicated in the previous table) is not set in **InfoValuePtr* to one of the values corresponding to the *Concurrency* argument, the call to **SQLSetScrollOptions** returns SQLSTATE S1C00 (Driver not capable) and none of the following steps are performed.

2. A call to:

```
SQLSetStmtAttr (StatementHandle, SQL_ATTR_CURSOR_TYPE, ValuePtr, 0)
```

with **ValuePtr* set to one of the following values, according to the value of the *KeysetSize* argument in **SQLSetScrollOptions**:

***KeysetSize* argument**	***ValuePtr***
SQL_SCROLL_FORWARD_ONLY	SQL_CURSOR_FORWARD_ONLY
SQL_SCROLL_STATIC	SQL_CURSOR_STATIC
SQL_SCROLL_KEYSET_DRIVEN	SQL_CURSOR_KEYSET_DRIVEN
SQL_SCROLL_DYNAMIC	SQL_CURSOR_DYNAMIC
A value greater than the *RowsetSize* argument	SQL_CURSOR_KEYSET_DRIVEN

3. A call to:

```
SQLSetStmtAttr (StatementHandle, SQL_ATTR_CONCURRENCY, ValuePtr, 0)
```

with **ValuePtr* set to the *Concurrency* argument in **SQLSetScrollOptions**.

4. If the *KeysetSize* argument in the call to **SQLSetScrollOptions** is positive, a call to:

```
SQLSetStmtAttr (StatementHandle, SQL_ATTR_KEYSET_SIZE, ValuePtr, 0)
```

with **ValuePtr* set to the *KeysetSize* argument in **SQLSetScrollOptions**.

5. A call to:

```
SQLSetStmtAttr (StatementHandle, SQL_ROWSET_SIZE, ValuePtr, 0)
```

with **ValuePtr* set to the *RowsetSize* argument in **SQLSetScrollOptions**.

Note When the Driver Manager maps **SQLSetScrollOptions** for an application working with an ODBC 3.0 driver that does not support **SQLSetScrollOptions**, the Driver Manager sets the SQL_ROWSET_SIZE statement option, not the SQL_ATTR_ROW_ARRAY_SIZE statement attribute, to the *RowsetSize* argument in **SQLSetScrollOption**. As a result, **SQLSetScrollOptions** cannot be used by an application when fetching multiple rows by a call to **SQLFetch** or **SQLFetchScroll**. It can only be used when fetching multiple rows by a call to **SQLExtendedFetch**.

SQLSetStmtOption Mapping

When an application calls **SQLSetStmtOption** through an ODBC 3.0 driver, the call to:

```
SQLSetStmtOption (StatementHandle, fOption, vParam)
```

will result in:

If *fOption* indicates an ODBC-defined statement attribute that is a string, then the Driver Manager calls:

```
SQLSetStmtAttr (StatementHandle, fOption, ValuePtr, SQL_NTS)
```

If *fOption* indicates an ODBC-defined statement attribute that returns a 32-bit integer value:

```
SQLSetStmtAttr (StatementHandle, fOption, ValuePtr, 0)
```

If *fOption* indicates a driver-defined statement attribute, then the Driver Manager calls:

```
SQLSetStmtAttr (StatementHandle, fOption, ValuePtr, BufferLength)
```

In these three cases, the *StatementHandle* argument is set to the value in *hstmt*, the *Attribute* argument is set to the value in *fOption*, and the *ValuePtr* argument is set to the value as *vParam*.

Because the Driver Manager does not know whether the driver-defined statement attribute needs a string or 32-bit integer value, it has to pass in a valid value for the *StringLength* argument of **SQLSetStmtAttr**. If the driver has defined special semantics for driver-defined statement attributes and needs to be called using **SQLSetStmtOption**, then it must support **SQLSetStmtOption**.

If an application calls **SQLSetStmtOption** to set a driver-specific statement option in an ODBC 3.0 driver, and the option was defined in an ODBC 2.*x* version of the driver, a new manifest constant should be defined for the option in the ODBC 3.0 driver. If the old manifest constant is used in the call to **SQLSetStmtOption**, the Driver Manager will call **SQLSetStmtAttr** with the *StringLength* argument set to 0.

When an application calls **SQLSetStmtAttr** to set SQL_ATTR_USE_BOOKMARKS to SQL_UB_ON in an ODBC 3.0 driver, the SQL_ATTR_USE_BOOKMARKS statement attribute is set to SQL_UB_FIXED. SQL_UB_ON is the same constant as SQL_UB_FIXED. The Driver Manager passes SQL_UB_FIXED through to the driver. SQL_UB_FIXED has been deprecated in ODBC 3.0, but an ODBC 3.0 driver must implement it to work with ODBC 2.*x* applications that use fixed-length bookmarks.

For an ODBC 3.0 driver, the Driver Manager no longer checks to see if *Option* is in between SQL_STMT_OPT_MIN and SQL_STMT_OPT_MAX, or is greater than SQL_CONNECT_OPT_DRVR_START.

SQLTransact Mapping

SQLTransact is now replaced by **SQLEndTran**. The major difference between the two functions is that **SQLEndTran** contains an argument *HandleType*, which specifies the scope of the work to be done. The *HandleType* argument can specify the environment or the connection handle. The following call to **SQLTransact**:

```
SQLTransact (henv, hdbc, fType)
```

is mapped to:

```
SQLEndTran (SQL_HANDLE_DBC, ConnectionHandle, CompletionType);
```

if *ConnectionHandle* is not equal to SQL_NULL_HDBC. The *ConnectionHandle* argument is set to the value of *hdbc*.

It is mapped to:

```
SQLEndTran (SQL_HANDLE_ENV, EnvironmentHandle, CompletionType);
```

if *ConnectionHandle* is equal to SQL_NULL_HDBC. The *EnvironmentHandle* argument is set to the value of *henv*.

In both of these cases, the *CompletionType* argument is set to the same value as *fType*.

Behavioral Changes and ODBC 3.0 Drivers

The environment attribute SQL_ATTR_ODBC_VERSION indicates to the driver whether it needs to exhibit ODBC 2.*x* behavior or ODBC 3.0 behavior. How the SQL_ATTR_ODBC_VERSION environment attribute is set depends on the application. ODBC 3.0 applications must call **SQLSetEnvAttr** to set this attribute after they call **SQLAllocHandle** to allocate an environment handle and before they call **SQLAllocHandle** to allocate a connection handle; if they fail to do this, the Driver Manager returns SQLSTATE HY010 (Function sequence error) on the latter call to **SQLAllocHandle**.

Note For more information on behavioral changes and how an application acts, see "Behavioral Changes" in Chapter 17, "Programming Considerations."

ODBC 2.*x* applications and ODBC 2.*x* applications recompiled with the ODBC 3.0 header files do not call **SQLSetEnvAttr**. However, they call **SQLAllocEnv** instead of **SQLAllocHandle** to allocate an environment handle. Therefore, when the application calls **SQLAllocEnv** in the Driver Manager, the Driver Manager calls **SQLAllocHandle** and **SQLSetEnvAttr** in the driver. Thus, ODBC 3.0 drivers can always count on this attribute being set.

If a standards-compliant application compiled with the ODBC_STD compile flag calls **SQLAllocEnv** (which may occur because **SQLAllocEnv** is not deprecated in ISO), the call is mapped to **SQLAllocHandleStd** at compile time. At run time, the application calls **SQLAllocHandleStd**. The Driver Manager sets the SQL_ATTR_ODBC_VERSION environment attribute to SQL_OV_ODBC3. A call to **SQLAllocHandleStd** is equivalent to a call to **SQLAllocHandle** with a *HandleType* of SQL_HANDLE_ENV and a call to **SQLSetEnvAttr** to set SQL_ATTR_ODBC_VERSION to SQL_OV_ODBC3.

In certain driver architectures, there is a need for the driver to appear as either an ODBC 2.*x* driver or an ODBC 3.0 driver, depending on the connection. The driver in this case may not actually be a driver, but a layer that resides between the Driver Manager and another driver. For example, it may mimic a driver, like ODBC Spy. In another example, it may act as a gateway, like EDA/SQL. Such drivers must be able to export **SQLAllocHandle**, to appear as an ODBC 3.0 driver, and must be able to export **SQLAllocConnect**, **SQLAllocEnv**, and **SQLAllocStmt**, to appear as an ODBC 2.*x* driver. When an environment, connection, or statement is to be allocated, the Driver Manager checks to see if this driver exports **SQLAllocHandle**. Since the driver does, the Driver Manager calls **SQLAllocHandle** in the driver. If the driver is working with an ODBC 2.*x* driver, the driver must map the call to **SQLAllocHandle** to **SQLAllocConnect**, **SQLAllocEnv**, or **SQLAllocStmt**, as appropriate. It must also do nothing with the **SQLSetEnvAttr** call when behaving as an ODBC 2.*x* driver.

Datetime Data Types

In ODBC 3.0, the identifiers for date, time, and timestamp SQL data types have changed from SQL_DATE, SQL_TIME, and SQL_TIMESTAMP (with instances of **#define** in the header file of 9, 10, and 11) to SQL_TYPE_DATE, SQL_TYPE_TIME, and SQL_TYPE_TIMESTAMP (with instances of **#define** in the header file of 91, 92, and 93), respectively. The corresponding C type identifiers have changed from SQL_C_DATE, SQL_C_TIME, and SQL_C_TIMESTAMP to SQL_C_TYPE_DATE, SQL_C_TYPE_TIME, and SQL_C_TYPE_TIMESTAMP, respectively, and the instances of **#define** have changed accordingly.

The column size and decimal digits returned for the SQL datetime data types in ODBC 3.0 are the same as the precision and scale returned for them in ODBC 2.*x*. These values are different than the values in the SQL_DESC_PRECISION and SQL_DESC_SCALE descriptor fields. (For more information, see Appendix D, "Data Types.")

These changes affect **SQLDescribeCol**, **SQLDescribeParam**, and **SQLColAttributes**; **SQLBindCol**, **SQLBindParameter**, and **SQLGetData**; and **SQLColumns**, **SQLGetTypeInfo**, **SQLProcedureColumns**, **SQLStatistics**, and **SQLSpecialColumns**.

An ODBC 3.0 driver processes the function calls listed in the previous paragraph according to the setting of the SQL_ATTR_ODBC_VERSION environment attribute. For **SQLColumns**, **SQLGetTypeInfo**, **SQLProcedureColumns**, **SQLSpecialColumns**, and **SQLStatistics**, if SQL_ATTR_ODBC_VERSION is set to SQL_OV_ODBC3, the functions return SQL_TYPE_DATE, SQL_TYPE_TIME, and SQL_TYPE_TIMESTAMP in the DATA_TYPE field. The COLUMN_SIZE column (in the result set returned by **SQLColumns**, **SQLGetTypeInfo**, **SQLProcedureColumns**, and **SQLSpecialColumns**) contains the binary precision for the approximate numeric type. The NUM_PREC_RADIX column (in the result set returned by **SQLColumns**, **SQLGetTypeInfo**, and **SQLProcedureColumns**), contains a value of 2. If SQL_ATTR_ODBC_VERSION is set to SQL_OV_ODBC2, the functions return SQL_DATE, SQL_TIME, and SQL_TIMESTAMP in the DATA_TYPE field, the COLUMN_SIZE column contains the decimal precision for the approximate numeric type, and the NUM_PREC_RADIX column contains a value of 10.

When all data types are requested in a call to **SQLGetTypeInfo**, the result set returned by the function will contain both SQL_TYPE_DATE, SQL_TYPE_TIME, and SQL_TYPE_TIMESTAMP as defined in ODBC 3.0, and SQL_DATE, SQL_TIME, and SQL_TIMESTAMP as defined in ODBC 2.*x*.

Because of how the ODBC 3.0 Driver Manager performs mapping of the date, time, and timestamp data types, ODBC 3.0 drivers need only recognize **#defines** of 91, 92, and 93 for the date, time, and timestamp C data types entered in the *TargetType* arguments of **SQLBindCol** and **SQLGetData** or the *ValueType* argument of **SQLBindParameter**, and need only recognize **#defines** of 91, 92, and 93 for the date, time, and timestamp SQL data types entered in the *ParameterType* argument of **SQLBindParameter** or the *DataType* argument of **SQLGetTypeInfo**. For more information, see "Datetime Data Type Changes" in Chapter 17, "Programming Considerations."

Backward Compatibility of C Data Types

SQL_C_SHORT, SQL_C_LONG, and SQL_C_TINYINT have been replaced in ODBC by signed and unsigned types: SQL_C_SSHORT and SQL_C_USHORT, SQL_C_SLONG and SQL_C_ULONG, and SQL_C_STINYINT and SQL_C_UTINYINT. An ODBC 3.0 driver that should work with ODBC 2.*x* applications should support SQL_C_SHORT, SQL_C_LONG, and SQL_C_TINYINT, because when they are called, the Driver Manager passes them through to the driver.

Fixed-Length Bookmarks

If an ODBC 3.0 driver should work with an ODBC 2.*x* application that uses fixed-length bookmarks, the driver must support the following:

- SQL_UB_ON as a value for the SQL_USE_BOOKMARKS statement option. (SQL_UB_ON is deprecated in ODBC 3.0.)
- The SQL_GET_BOOKMARK statement option.

SQLGetInfo Support

When an ODBC 2.*x* application calls **SQLGetInfo** to an ODBC 3.0 driver, the following *InfoType* arguments must be supported.

InfoType	Returns
SQL_ALTER_TABLE (ODBC 2.0) (Note: This information type is not deprecated; the bitmasks in the column to the right are deprecated.)	An SQLINTEGER bitmask enumerating the clauses in the **ALTER TABLE** statement supported by the data source. The following bitmasks are used to determine which clauses are supported: SQL_AT_DROP_COLUMN = The ability to drop columns is supported. Whether this results in cascade or restrict behavior is driver-defined. (ODBC 2.0) SQL_AT_ADD_COLUMN = The ability to add multiple columns in a single ALTER TABLE statement is supported. Note that this bit does not combine with other SQL_AT_ADD_COLUMN_XXX bits or SQL_AT_CONSTRAINT_XXX bits. (ODBC 2.0)
SQL_FETCH_DIRECTION (ODBC 1.0) The information type was introduced in ODBC 1.0; each bitmask is labeled with the version in which it was introduced.	A SQLINTEGER bitmask enumerating the supported fetch direction options. The following bitmasks are used in conjunction with the flag to determine which options are supported: SQL_FD_FETCH_NEXT (ODBC 1.0) SQL_FD_FETCH_FIRST (ODBC 1.0) SQL_FD_FETCH_LAST (ODBC 1.0) SQL_FD_FETCH_PRIOR (ODBC 1.0) SQL_FD_FETCH_ABSOLUTE (ODBC 1.0) SQL_FD_FETCH_RELATIVE (ODBC 1.0) SQL_FD_FETCH_BOOKMARK (ODBC 2.0)
SQL_LOCK_TYPES (ODBC 2.0)	A SQLINTEGER bitmask enumerating the supported lock types for the *fLock* argument in **SQLSetPos**. The following bitmasks are used in conjunction with the flag to determine which lock types are supported: SQL_LCK_NO_CHANGE SQL_LCK_EXCLUSIVE SQL_LCK_UNLOCK

InfoType	**Returns**
SQL_ODBC_API_ CONFORMANCE (ODBC 1.0)	An SQLSMALLINT value indicating the level of ODBC conformance. SQL_OAC_NONE = None SQL_OAC_LEVEL1 = Level 1 supported SQL_OAC_LEVEL2 = Level 2 supported
SQL_ODBC_SQL_ CONFORMANCE (ODBC 1.0)	An SQLSMALLINT value indicating SQL grammar supported by the driver. See Appendix C, "SQL Grammar," for definition of SQL conformance levels. SQL_OSC_MINIMUM = Minimum grammar supported SQL_OSC_CORE = Core grammar supported SQL_OSC_EXTENDED = Extended grammar supported
SQL_POS_OPERATIONS (ODBC 2.0)	A SQLINTEGER bitmask enumerating the supported operations in **SQLSetPos**. The following bitmasks are used to in conjunction with the flag to determine which options are supported: SQL_POS_POSITION (ODBC 2.0) SQL_POS_REFRESH (ODBC 2.0) SQL_POS_UPDATE (ODBC 2.0) SQL_POS_DELETE (ODBC 2.0) SQL_POS_ADD (ODBC 2.0)
SQL_POSITIONED_ STATEMENTS (ODBC 2.0)	A SQLINTEGER bitmask enumerating the supported positioned SQL statements. The following bitmasks are used to determine which statements are supported: SQL_PS_POSITIONED_DELETE SQL_PS_POSITIONED_UPDATE SQL_PS_SELECT_FOR_UPDATE
SQL_SCROLL_CONCURRENCY (ODBC 1.0)	A SQLINTEGER bitmask enumerating the concurrency control options supported for the cursor. The following bitmasks are used to determine which options are supported: SQL_SCCO_READ_ONLY = Cursor is read-only. No updates are allowed. SQL_SCCO_LOCK = Cursor uses the lowest level of locking sufficient to ensure that the row can be updated. SQL_SCCO_OPT_ROWVER = Cursor uses optimistic concurrency control, comparing row versions, such as SQLBase ROWID or Sybase TIMESTAMP. SQL_SCCO_OPT_VALUES = Cursor uses optimistic concurrency control, comparing values.

InfoType	Returns
SQL_STATIC_SENSITIVITY (ODBC 2.0)	A SQLINTEGER bitmask enumerating whether changes made by an application to a static or keyset-driven cursor through **SQLSetPos** or positioned update or delete statements can be detected by that application: SQL_SS_ADDITIONS = Added rows are visible to the cursor; the cursor can scroll to these rows. Where these rows are added to the cursor is driver-dependent. SQL_SS_DELETIONS = Deleted rows are no longer available to the cursor and do not leave a "hole" in the result set; after the cursor scrolls from a deleted row, it cannot return to that row. SQL_SS_UPDATES = Updates to rows are visible to the cursor; if the cursor scrolls from and returns to an updated row, the data returned by the cursor is the updated data, not the original data. This option only applies to static cursors or updates on keyset-driven cursors that do not update the key. This option does not apply for a dynamic cursor or in the case in which a key is changed in a mixed cursor. Whether an application can detect changes made to the result set by other users, including other cursors in the same application, depends on the cursor type.

An ODBC 3.0 application working with an ODBC 3.0 driver should not call **SQLGetInfo** with the *InfoType* arguments described in the previous table, but should use the ODBC 3.0 *InfoType* arguments listed in the following paragraph. There is not a one-to-one correspondence between *InfoType* arguments used in ODBC 2.*x* and those used in ODBC 3.0. An ODBC 3.0 application working with an ODBC 2.*x* driver, on the other hand, should use the *InfoType* arguments described previously.

Some of the information types in the previous table are deprecated in favor of the cursor attributes information types. These deprecated information types are SQL_FETCH_DIRECTION, SQL_LOCK_TYPES, SQL_POS_OPERATIONS, SQL_POSITIONED_STATEMENTS, SQL_SCROLL_CONCURRENCY, and SQL_STATIC_SENSITIVITY. The new cursor attributes types are SQL_XXX_CURSOR_ATTRIBUTES1and SQL_XXX_CURSOR_ATTRIBUTES2 where XXX equals DYNAMIC, FORWARD_ONLY, KEYSET_DRIVEN, or STATIC. Each of the new types indicates the driver capabilities for a single cursor type. For more information about these options, see the **SQLGetInfo** function description.

Returning SQL_NO_DATA

When an ODBC 2.*x* application working with an ODBC 3.0 driver calls **SQLExecDirect**, **SQLExecute**, or **SQLParamData**, and a searched update or delete statement was executed but did not affect any rows at the data source, the ODBC 3.0 driver should return SQL_SUCCESS. When an ODBC 3.0 application working with an ODBC 3.0 driver calls **SQLExecDirect**, **SQLExecute**, or **SQLParamData** with the same result, the ODBC 3.0 driver should return SQL_NO_DATA.

If a searched update or delete statement in a batch of statements does not affect any rows at the data source, **SQLMoreResults** returns SQL_SUCCESS. It cannot return SQL_NO_DATA, because that would mean that there are no more results, not that there is a result from a searched update/delete that affected no rows.

Calling SQLSetPos to Insert Data

When an ODBC 2.*x* application working with an ODBC 3.0 driver calls **SQLSetPos** with an *Operation* argument of SQL_ADD, the Driver Manager does not map this call to **SQLBulkOperations**. If an ODBC 3.0 driver should work with an application that calls **SQLSetPos** with SQL_ADD, the driver should support that operation.

One major difference in behavior when **SQLSetPos** is called with SQL_ADD occurs when it is called in state S6. In ODBC 2.*x*, the driver returned S1010 when **SQLSetPos** was called with SQL_ADD in state S6 (after the cursor has been positioned with **SQLFetch**). In ODBC 3.0, **SQLBulkOperations** with an *Operation* of SQL_ADD can be called in state S6. A second major difference in behavior is that **SQLBulkOperations** with an *Operation* of SQL_ADD can be called in state S5, while **SQLSetPos** with an *Operation* of SQL_ADD cannot. For the statement transitions that can occur for the same call in ODBC 3.0, see Appendix B, "ODBC State Transition Tables."

Loading by Ordinal

In ODBC 2.*x*, loading by ordinal could be performed to improve the performance of the connection process. An ODBC 2.*x* driver exports a dummy function with the ordinal 199; when the Driver Manager detects it, it resolves the addresses of the ODBC functions by ordinal, not by name. This functionality is still supported for ODBC 2.*x* drivers, but is not supported for ODBC 3.0 drivers.

Index

Symbols

A

B

D

E

F

G

H

I

J

K

L

M

N

O

P

Q

R

S

T

U

V

W

X

Y